16th Annual Meeting of the Special Interest Group on Discourse and Dialogue (SIGDIAL 2015)

Prague, Czech Republic
2 – 4 September 2015

ISBN: 978-1-5108-1156-0

Printed from e-media with permission by:

Curran Associates, Inc.
57 Morehouse Lane
Red Hook, NY 12571

proceedings.com

Some format issues inherent in the e-media version may also appear in this print version.

Printed by Curran Associates, Inc. (2016)

For permission requests, please contact the Association for Computational Linguistics at the address below.

Association for Computational Linguistics
209 N. Eighth Street
Stroudsburg, Pennsylvania 18360

Phone: 1-570-476-8006
Fax: 1-570-476-0860

acl@aclweb.org

Additional copies of this publication are available from:

Curran Associates, Inc.
57 Morehouse Lane
Red Hook, NY 12571 USA
Phone: 845-758-0400
Fax: 845-758-2634
Email: curran@proceedings.com
Web: www.proceedings.com

SIGDIAL 2015

16th Annual Meeting of the Special Interest Group on Discourse and Dialogue

Proceedings of the Conference

2-4 September 2015
Prague, Czech Republic

In cooperation with: Association for Computational Linguistics (ACL)
International Speech Communication Association (ISCA)
Association for the Advancement of Artificial Intelligence (AAAI)

We thank our sponsors:

Educational Testing Service (ETS) Microsoft Resarch Honda Research Institute (HRI)
Interactions Mitsubishi Electric Research Laboratories Turnitin/LightSide

Introduction

We are excited to welcome you to this year's SIGDIAL Conference, the 16th Annual Meeting of the Special Interest Group on Discourse and Dialogue. We are pleased to hold the conference this year in Prague, Czech Republic, on September 2nd-4th, in close proximity to INTERSPEECH 2015.

The SIGDIAL conference remains positioned as the publication venue for research under the broad umbrella of discourse and dialogue. This year, the program includes oral presentations and poster sessions on Dialogue Management, Discourse Strategy, Perspective and Point of View, and New Directions. SIGDIAL 2015 also hosts a special session entitled MultiLing 2015: Multilingual Summarization of Multiple Documents, organized by George Giannakopoulos. The papers from this special session that appear in the proceedings were submitted and reviewed as regular SIGDIAL papers, and cleared the same high bar for quality. Papers not accepted through the regular review process are not included in the proceedings, but were still invited to be presented as posters in the special session. Due to the success of last year's special session, this is the second year SIGDIAL has issued a general call for special sessions.

We received a record breaking number of submissions this year, 136 complete submissions altogether, which included 79 long papers, 42 short papers and 15 demo descriptions—from a broad, international set of authors. Additionally, 2 papers were submitted and then withdrawn, and 1 was rejected without review due to being out of scope. All papers received 3 reviews. We carefully considered both the numeric ratings and the tenor of the comments, both as written in the reviews, and as submitted in the discussion period, in making our selection for the program. Overall, the members of the Program Committee did an excellent job in reviewing the submitted papers. We thank them for the important role their reviews have played in selecting the accepted papers and for helping to maintain the high quality of the program. In line with the SIGDIAL tradition, our aim has been to create a balanced program that accommodates as many favorably rated papers as possible.

This year's SIGDIAL conference runs 2.5 days as it did in 2014, with the special session being held on the second day. Of the 79 long paper submissions: 14 were accepted as long papers for oral presentation, 21 were accepted as long papers for poster presentation. Of the 42 short paper submissions, 17 were accepted for poster presentation, for a total of 38 posters. There were 7 demonstration papers that were accepted. 3 of the long papers and 4 of the short papers accepted for poster presentation were accepted for publication to appear in the MULTILING Special Session.

We enthusiastically thank the two keynote speakers, Dilek Hakkani-Tur (Microsoft Research, USA) and Frank Fischer (Ludwigs Maximilian Universität München) and for their contributions to research on discourse and dialogue systems, and we look forward to their keynote talks!

We offer our thanks to Svetlana Stoyanchev, Mentoring Chair for SIGDIAL 2015, for her dedicated work on coordinating the mentoring process, just as last year. The goal of mentoring is to assist authors of papers that contain important ideas but lack clarity. Mentors work with the authors to improve English language usage or paper organization. This year, 3 of the accepted papers were mentored. We thank the Program Committee members who served as mentors: Pamela Jordan, Jason Williams, and Heriberto Cuayahuitl.

We extend special thanks to our local arrangements chair, Filip Jurcicek, and his team Libuse Brdickova, Ondrej Dusek, Lukas Zilka, and Ahmad Agha Ebrahimian. We know SIGDIAL 2015 would not have been possible without Filip and his team, who invested so much effort in arranging the conference hotel venue and accommodations, handling registration, making banquet arrangements, and handling numerous other preparations for the conference. The student volunteers for on-site assistance also deserve our appreciation.

Kristy Boyer, Sponsorships Chair, has earned our appreciation for recruiting and liaising with our conference sponsors, many of whom continue to contribute year after year. The sponsorship program enables valuable aspects of the program, such as the invited speakers, conference reception and dinner. In recognition of this, we gratefully acknowledge the support of our sponsors: Educational Testing Service, Interactions, Microsoft Research, Honda Research Institute, Mitsubishi Electric Research Laboratories, and Turnitin/LightSide. At the same time, we thank Priscilla Rasmussen at the ACL for tirelessly handling the financial aspects of sponsorship for SIGDIAL 2015, and for securing our ISBN on a moment's notice!

We also thank the SIGdial board, especially officers, Jason Williams, Amanda Stent and Kristiina Jokinen for their advice and support from beginning to end. We especially appreciate Jason's substantial, prompt and patient replies to numerous questions along the way.

Finally, we thank all the authors of the papers in this volume, and all the conference participants for making this stimulating event a valuable opportunity for growth in research in the areas of dialogue and discourse.

Alexander Koller and Gabriel Skantze,
General Co-Chairs
Masahiro Araki and Carolyn Penstein Rosé,
Technical Program Co-Chairs

SIGDIAL 2014

General Co-Chairs:

Alexander Koller, University of Potsdam, Germany
Gabriel Skantze, KTH Royal Institute of Technology, Sweden

Technical Program Co-Chairs:

Masahiro Araki, Kyoto Institute of Technology, Japan
Carolym Penstein Rosé, Carnegie Mellon University, United States

Local Chair:

Filip Jurcicek, Charles Univeristy, Czech Republic

Mentoring Chair:

Svetlana Stoyanchev, Interactions Corporation, United States

Sponsorship Chair:

Kristy Boyer, University of Florida, United States

SIGdial Officers:

President: Amanda Stent, Yahoo! Labs, United States
Vice President: Jason D. Williams, Microsoft Research, United States
Secretary/Treasurer: Kristiina Jokinen, University of Helsinki, Finland

Program Committee:

Jan Alexandersson, DFKI GmbH, Germany
Masahiro Araki, Kyoto Institute of Technology, Japan
Yasuo Ariki, Kobe University, Japan
Ron Artstein, USC Institute for Creative Technologies, United States
Timo Baumann, Universität Hamburg, Germany
Frederic Bechet, Aix Marseille Universite - LIF/CNRS, France
Steve Beet, Aculab plc, United Kingdom
Jose Miguel Benedi, Universitàt Politècnica de València, Spain
Nicole Beringer, Germany
Nate Blaylock, Nuance Communications, Canada
Dan Bohus, Microsoft Research, United States
Johan Boye, KTH, Sweden
Kristy Boyer, University of Florida, United States
Christophe Cerisara, CNRS, France
Joyce Chai, Michigan State University, United States
Mark Core, University of Southern California, United States
Paul Crook, Microsoft Corporation, United States
Heriberto Cuayahuitl, Heriot-Watt University, United Kingdom
Xiaodong Cui, IBM T. J. Watson Research Center, United States
David DeVault, USC Institute for Creative Technologies, United States
Barbara Di Eugenio, University of Illinois at Chicago, United States
Giuseppe Di Fabbrizio, Amazon.com, United States

Dimitrios Dimitriadis, IBM Watson, United States
Myroslava Dzikovska, University of Edinburgh, United Kingdom
Jens Edlund, KTH Speech, Music and Hearing, Sweden
Arash Eshghi, Heriot-Watt University, United Kingdom
Keelan Evanini, Educational Testing Service, United States
Mauro Falcone, Fondazione Ugo Bordoni, Italy
Benoit Favre, Aix-Marseille University LIF/CNRS, France
Raquel Fernandez, ILLC, University of Amsterdam, Netherlands
Kotaro Funakoshi, Honda Research Institute Japan Co., Ltd., Japan
Claire Gardent, CNRS/LORIA, France
Kallirroi Georgila, USC Institute for Creative Technologies, United States
Agustin Gravano, Universidad de Buenos Aires, Argentina
Nancy Green, University of North Carolina Greensboro, United States
Curry Guinn, University of North Carolina Wilmington, United States
Joakim Gustafson, KTH, Sweden
Dilek Hakkani-Tur, Microsoft Research, United States
Mark Hasegawa-Johnson, University of Illinois, United States
Helen Hastie, Heriot-Watt University, United Kingdom
Peter Heeman, OHSU / CSLU, United States
Ryuichiro Higashinaka, NTT Media Intelligence Labs, Japan
Keikichi Hirose, University of Tokyo, Japan
Anna Hjalmarsson, Speech, Music and Hearing, KTH, Sweden
David Janiszek, Université Paris Descartes, France
Kristiina Jokinen, University of Helsinki, Finland
Arne Jonsson, Linköping University, Sweden
Pamela Jordan, University of Pittsburgh, United States
Tatsuya Kawahara, Kyoto University, Japan
Simon Keizer, Heriot-Watt University, United Kingdom
Norihide Kitaoka, Nagoya University, Japan
Kazunori Komatani, Osaka University, Japan
Stefan Kopp, Bielefeld University, Germany
Romain Laroche, Orange Labs, France
Alex Lascarides, University of Edinburgh, United Kingdom
Sungjin Lee, Yahoo Labs, United States
Fabrice Lefevre, Univ. Avignon, France
James Lester, North Carolina State University, United States
Eduardo Lleida Solano, University of Zaragoza, Spain
Ramon Lopez-Cozar, University of Granada, Spain
Annie Louis, University of Edinburgh, United Kingdom
Florian Metze, Carnegie Mellon University, United States
Teruhisa Misu, Honda Research Institute, United States
Helena Moniz, INESC-ID, FLUL, Portugal
Satoshi Nakamura, Nara Institute of Science and Technology, Japan
Yukiko Nakano, Seikei University, Japan
Mikio Nakano, Honda Research Institute Japan Co., Ltd., Japan
Ani Nenkova, University of Pennsylvania, United States
Vincent Ng, University of Texas at Dallas, United States
Douglas O'Shaughnessy, INRS-EMT (Univ. of Quebec), Canada
Aasish Pappu, Yahoo! Labs, United States
Olivier Pietquin, University Lille 1 - LIFL (CNRS/Lille 1), France
Paul Piwek, The Open University, United Kingdom

Andrei Popescu-Belis, Idiap Research Institute, Switzerland
Matthew Purver, Queen Mary University of London, United Kingdom
Antoine Raux, Lenovo Labs, United States
Norbert Reithinger, DFKI GmbH, Germany
Carolym Penstein Rosé, Carnegie Mellon University, United States
Alexander Rudnicky, Carnegie Mellon University, United States
David Schlangen, Bielefeld University, Germany
Manfred Stede, University of Potsdam, Germany
Georg Stemmer, Intel Corp., Germany
Matthew Stone, Rutgers University, United States
Svetlana Stoyanchev, Interactions Corporation, United States
Kristina Striegnitz, Union College
Marc Swerts, Tilburg University, the Netherlands
António Teixeira, DETI/IEETA, University of Aveiro, Portugal
Joel Tetreault, Yahoo Labs, United States
Takenobu Tokunaga, Tokyo Institute of Technology, Japan
David Traum, USC Institute for Creative Technologies, United States
Gokhan Tur, Microsoft Research, United States
Renata Vieira, PUCRS, Brazil
Marilyn Walker, University of California Santa Cruz, United States
Hsin-Min Wang, Academia Sinica, Taiwan
Nigel Ward, University of Texas at El Paso, United States
Jason D Williams, Microsoft Research, United States
Steve Young, Cambridge University, United Kingdom
Kai Yu, Shanghai Jiao Tong University, China
Jian ZHANG , Dongguan University of Technology, China

Additional Reviewers:

Pierre Albert, DFKI GmbH, Germany
Merwan Barlier, Orange Labs, France
Aude Genevay, Orange Labs, France
Casey Kennington
Hatim Khouzaimi, Orange Labs, France
Sören Klett
Yashar Mehdad, Yahoo Labs, United States
Christer Samuelsson, DFKI GmbH, Germany
Ramin Yaghoubzadeh

Invited Speakers:

Professor Frank Fischer, Ludwigs Maximilian Universität München, Germany
Dilek Hakkani-Tur, Microsoft Research, United States

Table of Contents

Conference Program

Wednesday, September 2, 2015

09:10–10:10 Keynote I

Keynote: The Interplay of Discussion, Cognition and Instruction in Computer-Supported Collaborative Learning Environments
Frank Fischer

10:35–11:50 Oral Session 1: Dialogue Management

Human-Machine Dialogue as a Stochastic Game
Merwan Barlier, Julien Perolat, Romain Laroche and Olivier Pietquin

Knowledge transfer between speakers for personalised dialogue management
Iñigo Casanueva, Thomas Hain, Heidi Christensen, Ricard Marxer and Phil Green

Miscommunication Recovery in Physically Situated Dialogue
Matthew Marge and Alexander Rudnicky

13:00–13:50 Oral Session 2: Discourse Strategy

Reinforcement Learning in Multi-Party Trading Dialog
Takuya Hiraoka, Kallirroi Georgila, Elnaz Nouri, David Traum and Satoshi Nakamura

An Incremental Turn-Taking Model with Active System Barge-in for Spoken Dialog Systems
Tiancheng Zhao, Alan W Black and Maxine Eskenazi

Wednesday, September 2, 2015 (continued)

13:50–14:10 Poster madness

14:10–16:30 Poster session 1

Wednesday, September 2, 2015 (continued)

Conversational Knowledge Teaching Agent that uses a Knowledge Base
Kyusong Lee, Paul Hongsuck Seo, Junhwi Choi, Sangjun Koo and Gary Geunbae Lee

Information Theoretical and Statistical Features for Intrinsic Plagiarism Detection
Rashedur Rahman

A SIP of CoFee : A Sample of Interesting Productions of Conversational Feedback
Laurent Prévot, Jan Gorisch, Roxane Bertrand, Emilien Gorene and Brigitte Bigi

Reinforcement Learning of Multi-Issue Negotiation Dialogue Policies
Alexandros Papangelis and Kallirroi Georgila

Fast and easy language understanding for dialog systems with Microsoft Language Understanding Intelligent Service (LUIS)
Jason D Williams, Eslam Kamal, Mokhtar Ashour, Hani Amr, Jessica Miller and Geoff Zweig

Multilingual WikiTalk: Wikipedia-based talking robots that switch languages.
Graham Wilcock and Kristiina Jokinen

Modelling situated human-robot interaction using IrisTK
Gabriel Skantze and Martin Johansson

16:30–17:45 Oral Session 3: Perspective and Point of View

I Couldn't Agree More: The Role of Conversational Structure in Agreement and Disagreement Detection in Online Discussions
Sara Rosenthal and Kathy McKeown

Memory-Based Acquisition of Argument Structures and its Application to Implicit Role Detection
Christian Chiarcos and Niko Schenk

Generating Sentence Planning Variations for Story Telling
Stephanie Lukin, Lena Reed and Marilyn Walker

Thursday, September 3, 2015

Friday, September 4, 2015 (continued)

10:40–12:40 **Poster session 2**

Friday, September 4, 2015 (continued)

Learning Domain-Independent Dialogue Policies via Ontology Parameterisation
Zhuoran Wang, Tsung-Hsien Wen, Pei-Hao Su and Yannis Stylianou

Reward Shaping with Recurrent Neural Networks for Speeding up On-Line Policy Learning in Spoken Dialogue Systems
Pei-Hao Su, David Vandyke, Milica Gasic, Nikola Mrksic, Tsung-Hsien Wen and Steve Young

Effects of Game on User Engagement with Spoken Dialogue System
Hayato Kobayashi, Kaori Tanio and Manabu Sassano

Evaluation of Crowdsourced User Input Data for Spoken Dialog Systems
Maria Schmidt, Markus Müller, Martin Wagner, Sebastian Stüker, Alex Waibel, Hansjörg Hofmann and Steffen Werner

A distributed cloud-based dialog system for conversational application development
Vikram Ramanarayanan, David Suendermann-Oeft, Alexei V. Ivanov and Keelan Evanini

A TV Program Discovery Dialog System using recommendations
Deepak Ramachandran, Mark Fanty, Ronald Provine, Peter Yeh, William Jarrold, Adwait Ratnaparkhi and Benjamin Douglas

Description of the PatientGenesys Dialogue System
Leonardo Campillos Llanos, Dhouha Bouamor, Éric Bilinski, Anne-Laure Ligozat, Pierre Zweigenbaum and Sophie Rosset

The Cohort and Speechify Libraries for Rapid Construction of Speech Enabled Applications for Android
Tejaswi Kasturi, Haojian Jin, Aasish Pappu, Sungjin Lee, Beverley Harrison, Ramana Murthy and Amanda Stent

12:40–13:00 Best paper award ceremony and closing

Keynote: The Interplay of Discussion, Cognition and Instruction in Computer-Supported Collaborative Learning Environments

Frank Fischer
University of Munich, Germany
frank.fischer@psy.lmu.de

Educational discourse is an important area for impact, which is especially timely given recent attention given to online education. In this talk I will first present a theoretical account of the complex interplay between written or oral discourse, individual cognitive processes, and external guidance in Computer-Supported Collaborative Learning (CSCL) environments. Based on the Script Theory of Guidance I will analyze how cognitive configurations shape discussions, and how participation in discussions may lead to re-configuration of the participating individual student's cognition. Second, I will give an overview of studies demonstrating the instructional value of specific types of discussion contributions, namely transactive contributions. I will finally elaborate on ways in which transactive contributions to discourse can be facilitated through external guidance, and how technologies may play an important role both in research and in instruction.

Proceedings of the SIGDIAL 2015 Conference, page 1,
Prague, Czech Republic, 2-4 September 2015.

Human-Machine Dialogue as a Stochastic Game

Merwan Barlier[1,2]
[1]NaDia Team
Orange Labs
merwan.barlier@orange.com

Julien Perolat[2]
[2]Univ. Lille - CRIStAL lab
SequeL team
julien.perolat@univ-lille1.fr

Romain Laroche
NaDia Team
Orange Labs
romain.laroche@orange.com

Olivier Pietquin[2,3]
[3]Institut Universitaire de France
IUF
olivier.pietquin@univ-lille1.fr

Abstract

In this paper, an original framework to model human-machine spoken dialogues is proposed to deal with co-adaptation between users and Spoken Dialogue Systems in non-cooperative tasks. The conversation is modeled as a Stochastic Game: both the user and the system have their own preferences but have to come up with an agreement to solve a non-cooperative task. They are jointly trained so the Dialogue Manager learns the optimal strategy against the best possible user. Results obtained by simulation show that non-trivial strategies are learned and that this framework is suitable for dialogue modeling.

1 Introduction

In a Spoken Dialogue System (SDS), the Dialogue Manager (DM) is designed in order to implement a decision-making process (called *strategy* or *policy*) aiming at choosing the system interaction moves. The decision is taken according to the current interaction context which can rely on bad transcriptions and misunderstandings due to Automatic Speech Recognition (ASR) and Spoken Language Understanding (SLU) errors. Machine learning methods, such as Reinforcement Learning (RL) (Sutton and Barto, 1998), are now very popular to learn optimal dialogue policies under noisy conditions and inter-user variability (Levin and Pieraccini, 1997; Lemon and Pietquin, 2007; Laroche et al., 2010; Young et al., 2013). In this framework, the dialogue task is modeled as a (Partially Observable) Markov Decision Process ((PO)MDP), and the DM is an RL-agent learning an optimal policy. Yet, despite some rare examples, RL-based DMs only consider task-oriented dialogues and stationary (non-adapting) users.

Unfortunately, (PO)MDP are restricted to model game-against-nature problems (Milnor, 1951). These are problems in which the learning agent evolves in an environment that doesn't change with time and acts in a totally disinterested manner. (PO)MDP-based dialogue modeling thus applies only if 1) the user doesn't modify his/her behavior along time (the strategy is learned for a stationary environment) and 2) the dialogue is task-oriented and requires the user and the machine to positively collaborate to achieve the user's goal.

The first assumption doesn't hold if the user adapts his/her behavior to the continuously improving performance of a learning DM. Some recent studies have tried to model this co-adaptation effect between a learning machine and a human (Chandramohan et al., 2012b) but this approach still considers the user and the machine as independent learning agents. Although there has already been some few attempts to model the "co-evolution" of human machine interfaces (Bourguin et al., 2001), this work doesn't extend to RL-based interfaces (automatically learning) and is not related to SDS.

More challenging situations do also arise when the common-goal assumption doesn't hold either, which is the case in many interesting applications such as negotiation (El Asri et al., 2014), serious games, e-learning, robotic co-workers *etc*. Especially, adapting the MDP paradigm to the case of negotiation dialogues has been the topic of recent works. In (Georgila et al., 2014), the authors model the problem of negotiation as a Multi-Agent Reinforcement Learning (MARL) problem. Yet, this approach relies on algorithms that are treat-

Proceedings of the SIGDIAL 2015 Conference, pages 2–11,
Prague, Czech Republic, 2-4 September 2015.

ing the multi-player issue as a non-stationnarity problem (*e.g.* WoLF-PHC (Bowling and Veloso, 2002)). Each agent is assumed to keep a stable interaction policy for a time sufficiently long so that the other agent can learn it's current policy. Otherwise, there is no convergence guarantees. Another major issue with these works is that noise in the ASR or NLU results is not taken into account although this is a major reason for using stochastic dialogue models. In (Efstathiou and Lemon, 2014), the authors follow the same direction by considering both agents as acting in a stationary MDP.

In this paper, we propose a paradigm shift from the now state-of-the-art (PO)MDP model to Stochastic Games (Patek and Bertsekas, 1999) to model dialogue. This model extends the MDP paradigm to multi-player interactions and allows learning jointly the strategies of both agents (the user and the DM), which leads to the best system strategy in the face of the optimal user/adversary (in terms of his/her goal). This paradigm models both co-adaptation and possible non-cooperativness. Unlike models based on standard game theory (Caelen and Xuereb, 2011), Stochastic Games allow to learn from data. Especially, departing from recent results (Perolat et al., 2015), we show that the optimal strategy can be learned from batch data as for MDPs (Pietquin et al., 2011). This means that optimal negotiation policies can be learnt from non-optimal logged interactions. This new paradigm is also very different from MARL methods proposed in previous work (Chandramohan et al., 2012b; Georgila et al., 2014; Efstathiou and Lemon, 2014) since optimization is jointly performed instead of alternatively optimizing each agent, considering the other can stay stationary for a while. Although experiments are only concerned with purely adversarial tasks (Zero-Sum games), we show that it could be naturally extended to collaborative tasks (general sum games) (Prasad et al., 2015). Experiments show that an efficient strategy can be learned even under noisy conditions which is suitable for modeling realistic human-machine spoken dialogues.

2 Markov Decision Processes and Reinforcement Learning

As said before, human-machine dialogue has been modeled as an (PO)MDP to make it suitable for automatic strategy learning (Levin and Pieraccini, 1997; Young et al., 2013). In this framework, the dialogue is seen as a turn-taking process in which two agents (a user and a DM) interact through a noisy channel (ASR, NLU) to exchange information. Each agent has to take a decision about what to say next according to the dialogue context (also called dialogue state). In this section, MDPs (Puterman, 1994) and RL (Sutton and Barto, 1998; Bertsekas and Tsitsiklis, 1996) are briefly reviewed and formally defined which will help switching the Stochastic Games in Section 3.

2.1 Markov Decision Processes

Definition 2.1. A Markov Decision Process (MDP) is a tuple $\langle \mathcal{S}, \mathcal{A}, \mathcal{T}, \mathcal{R}, \gamma \rangle$ where: $\mathcal{S}$ is the discrete set of environment states, $\mathcal{A}$ the discrete set of actions, $\mathcal{T} : \mathcal{S} \times \mathcal{A} \times \mathcal{S} \rightarrow [0, 1]$ the state transition probability function and $\mathcal{R} : \mathcal{S} \times \mathcal{A} \rightarrow \mathbb{R}$ the reward function. Finally, $\gamma \in [0, 1)$ is a discount factor.

At each time step, the RL-agent acts according to a policy π, which is either deterministic or stochastic. In the first case, π is a mapping from state space to action space : $\pi : \mathcal{S} \rightarrow \mathcal{A}$, while in the latter, π is a probability distribution on the state-action space $\pi : \mathcal{S} \times \mathcal{A} \rightarrow [0, 1]$. Policies are generally designed to maximize the value of each state, *i.e.* the expected discounted cumulative reward: $\forall s \in \mathcal{S}, V^{\pi}(s) = E[\sum_{t=0}^{\infty} \gamma^t r(s_t, \pi(s_t)) | s_0 = s]$. Let $\mathcal{V}$ be the space of all possible value functions. The optimal value function V^* is the only value function such that: $\forall V \in \mathcal{V}, \forall s \in \mathcal{S}, V^* \geq V$. The following result, proved in (Puterman, 1994), is fundamental in the study of MDPs:

Theorem 2.1. *Let M be an MDP. Its optimal value function V^* exists, is unique and verifies:*

$$\forall s \in \mathcal{S}, V^*(s) = \max_{a \in \mathcal{A}} \Big(r(s, a) + \sum_{s' \in \mathcal{S}} \mathcal{T}(s, a, s') V^*(s') \Big)$$

Furthermore, one can always find a deterministic policy π^* inducing V^*.

The function $Q_\pi : (s, a) \mapsto r(s, a) + \sum_{s' \in \mathcal{S}} \mathcal{T}(s, a, s') V_\pi(s')$ is called Q-function. We thus have: $\pi^*(s) = \operatorname{argmax}_a Q_{\pi^*}(s, a) = \operatorname{argmax}_a Q^*(s, a)$.

2.2 Reinforcement Learning

In many cases, transition and reward functions are unknown. It is thus not possible to compute values nor Q-Functions, the RL-agent learns an approximation by sampling through actual interactions with the environment. The set of techniques solving this problem is called *Reinforcement Learning*.

For instance the *Q-Learning algorithm* (Watkins and Dayan, 1992) approximates, at each time step, the optimal Q-Function and uses the following update rule:

$$Q_{t+1}(s_t, a_t) \leftarrow Q_t(s_t, a_t) + \alpha[r_{t+1}(s_t, a_t) + \gamma \max_a Q_t(s_{t+1}, a) - Q_t(s_t, a_t)]$$

It can been shown that, under the assumption that $\sum \alpha = \infty$ and $\sum \alpha^2 < \infty$ and that all states are visited infinitely often, Q-values converge towards the optimal ones. Thus, by taking at each state the action maximizing those values, one finds the optimal policy. There are batch algorithms solving the same problem among which Fitted-Q (Gordon, 1999; Ernst et al., 2005).

3 Stochastic Games

Stochastic Games (Filar and Vrieze, 1996; Neyman and Sorin, 2003), introduced in (Shapley, 1953), are a natural extension of MDPs to the Multi-Agent setting.

3.1 Definitions

Definition 3.1. A discounted Stochastic Game (SG) is a tuple $\langle \mathcal{D}, \mathcal{S}, \mathbf{A}, \mathcal{T}, \mathbf{R}, \gamma \rangle$ where: $\mathcal{D} = \{1, ..., n\}$ represents the set of agents, $\mathcal{S}$ the discrete set of environment states, $\mathbf{A} = \times_{i \in \mathcal{D}} \mathcal{A}_i$ the joint action set, where for all $i = 1, ..., n$, $\mathcal{A}_i$ is the discrete set of actions available to the ith agent, $\mathcal{T} : \mathcal{S} \times \mathbf{A} \times \mathcal{S} \rightarrow [0, 1]$ the state transition probability function, $\mathbf{R} = \times_{i \in \mathcal{D}} \mathcal{R}_i$ the joint reward function, where for all $i = 1, ..., n$, $\mathcal{R}_i : \mathcal{S} \times \mathbf{A} \rightarrow \mathbb{R}$ is the reward function of agent i. Finally, $\gamma \in [0, 1)$ is a discount factor.

An agent i chooses its actions according to some *strategy* σ_i, which is in the general case a probability distribution on i's state-action space. If the whole space of agents is considered, we speak about the *joint strategy* $\boldsymbol{\sigma}$. The notation σ_{-i} represents the joint strategy of all agents except i.

This definition is general, every 'MDP' in which multiple agents interact may be interpreted as a Stochastic Game. It is therefore useful to introduce a taxonomy. A game where there are only two players and where the rewards are opposite (*i.e.* $\mathcal{R}_1 = -\mathcal{R}_2$) is called *Zero-Sum Game*. Conversely, a *Purely Cooperative Game* is a game where all the agents have the same reward (*i.e.* $\forall i \in \mathcal{D}, \mathcal{R}_i = \mathcal{R}$). A game which is neither Zero-Sum nor Purely Cooperative is said to be *General-Sum*.

3.2 Best Response

In all environments, agents learn by acting according to what has previously been learned. In other words, agents adapt to an environment. This is also valid in a multi-agent scenario, if agent i wants to learn about agent j, it will act according to what has previously been learned about j. But conversely, if j wants to learn about agent i, it will act according to what it knows about i. We say that agents co-adapt. Co-adapation is, due to this feedback loop, an intrinsically non-stationary process. An algorithm converges if it converges to stationary strategies.

Each agent acts in order to maximize its expected discounted cumulative reward, also called the discounted value of the joint strategy $\boldsymbol{\sigma}$ in state s to player i : $V_i(s, \boldsymbol{\sigma}) = E[\sum_{t=0}^{\infty} \gamma^t r(s_t, \boldsymbol{\sigma})]$. The Q-function is then defined as (Filar and Vrieze, 1996):

$$Q(s, \boldsymbol{\sigma}, \mathbf{a}) = R(s, \mathbf{a}) + \gamma \sum_{s' \in \mathcal{S}} \mathcal{T}(s, \mathbf{a}, s') V(s', \boldsymbol{\sigma})$$

This value function depends on the opponents' strategies. It is therefore not possible to define in the general case a strategy *optimal* against every other strategy. A Best Response is an optimal strategy given the opponents ones.

Definition 3.2. Agent i plays a Best Response σ_i against the other players' joint strategy σ_{-i} if σ_i is optimal given σ_{-i}. We write $\sigma_i \in BR(\sigma_{-i})$.

Best Response induces naturally the following definition:

Definition 3.3. The strategy profile $\{\sigma_i\}_{i \in \mathcal{D}}$ is a Nash Equilibrium (NE) if for all $i \in \mathcal{D}$, we have $\sigma_i \in BR(\sigma_{-i})$.

It is interesting to notice that in a single-player game, Nash Equilibrium strategies match the optimal policies defined in the previous section.

The existence of Nash Equilibria in all discounted Stochastic Games is assured by the following theorem (Filar and Vrieze, 1996):

Theorem 3.1. *In a discounted Stochastic Game G, there exists a Nash Equilibrium in stationary strategies.*

Two remarks need to be introduced here. First, nothing was said about uniqueness since in the general case, there are many Nash Equilibria. Equilibrium selection and tracking may be a big deal while working with SGs. Second, contrarily to the MDP case, there may be no deterministic Nash Equilibrium strategies (but only stochastic).

3.3 The Zero-Sum Case

There are two ways to consider a Zero-Sum Stochastic Game: one can see two agents aiming at maximizing two opposite Q-functions or one can also see only one Q-function, with the first agent (called the *maximizer*) aiming at maximizing it and the second one (the *minimizer*) aiming at minimizing it. One can prove (Patek and Bertsekas, 1999), that if both players follow those maximizing and minimizing strategies, the game will converge towards a Nash Equilibrium, which is the only one of the game. In this case, thanks to the Minmax theorem (Osborne and Rubinstein, 1994), the value of the game is (with player 1 maximizing and player 2 minimizing):

$$\begin{aligned} V^* &= \max_{\sigma_1} \min_{\sigma_2} V(\sigma_1, \sigma_2) \\ &= \min_{\sigma_2} \max_{\sigma_1} V(\sigma_1, \sigma_2) \end{aligned}$$

As we will see later, the existence of this unique value function for both player is helpful for finding efficient algorithms solving zero-sum SGs.

4 Algorithms

Even if the field of Reinforcement Learning in Stochastic Games is still young and guaranteed Nash Equilibrium convergence with tractable algorithms is, according to our knowledge, still an open problem, many algorithms have however already been proposed (Buşoniu et al., 2008), all with strengths and weaknesses.

Reinforcement Learning techniques to solve Stochastic Games were first introduced in (Littman, 1994). In his paper, Littman presents minimax-Q, a variant of the Q-Learning algorithm for the zero-sum setting, which is guaranteed to converge to the Nash Equilibrium in self-play. He then extended his work in (Littman, 2001) with Friend-or-Foe Q-Learning (FFQ), an algorithm assured to converge, and converging to Nash Equilibria in purely cooperative or purely competitive settings. The authors of (Hu and Wellman, 2003) were the first to propose an algorithm for general-sum Stochastic Games. Their algorithm, Nash-Q, is also a variant of Q-Learning able to allow the agents to reach a Nash Equilibrium under some restrictive conditions on the rewards' distribution. In the general case, they empirically proved that convergence was not guaranteed any more. (Zinkevich et al., 2006) proved by giving a counter-example that the Q-function does not contain enough information to converge towards a Nash Equilibrium in the general setting.

For any known Stochastic Game, the Stochastic Tracing Procedure algorithm (Herings and Peeters, 2000) finds a Nash Equilibrium of it. The algorithm proposed in (Akchurina, 2009) was the first learning algorithm converging to an approximate Nash Equilibrium in all settings (even with an unknown game). Equilibrium tracking is made here by solving at each iteration a system of ordinary differential equations. The algorithm has no guaranty to converge toward a Nash Equilibrium even however, it seems empirically to work. Finally, (Prasad et al., 2015) presented two algorithms converging towards a Nash Equilibrium in the General-Sum setting: one batch algorithm assuming the complete knowledge of the game and an on-line algorithm working with simulated transitions of the Stochastic Game.

In this paper we will use two algorithms which are reviewed hereafter: WoLF-PHC (Bowling and Veloso, 2002) and AGPI-Q (Perolat et al., 2015).

4.1 WoLF-PHC

WoLF-PHC is an extension of the Q-learning algorithm allowing probabilistic strategies. It considers independent agents evolving in an environment made non-stationary by the presence of the others. In such a setting, the aim of the agents is not to find a Nash Equilibrium (it is therefore not an SG algorithm) but to do as good as possible in this environment (and as a consequence, it may lead to a Nash Equilibrium). The algorithm is based on the following idea: convergence shall be facilitated if agents learn quickly to adapt when they are sub-optimal and learn slowly when they are near-optimal (in order to let the other agents adapt to this strategy).

Q-values are updated as in Q-learning and the probability of selecting the best action is incrementally increased according to some (variable) learning rate δ, which is decomposed into two learning rates δ_L and δ_W, with $\delta_L > \delta_W$. The policy update is made according to δ_L while losing and to δ_W while winning.

To determine if an agent is losing or winning, the expected value of its actual strategy π, is compared to the expected value of the average policy $\overline{\pi}$. Formally, an agent is winning if $\sum_a \pi(s,a)Q(s,a) > \sum_a \overline{\pi}(s,a)Q(s,a)$ and losing otherwise.

In the general case, convergence is not proven and it is even shown on some toy-examples that sometimes, the algorithm does not converge (Bowling and Veloso, 2002).

4.2 AGPI-Q

Approximate Generalized Policy Iteration-Q, or AGPI-Q (Perolat et al., 2015), is an extension of the Fitted-Q (Gordon, 1999; Ernst et al., 2005) algorithm solving Zero-Sum Stochastic Games in a batch setting. At the initialization step, N samples (s, a_1, a_2, r, s') and a Q-function (for instance, the null function) are given. The algorithm consists then in K iterations, each of them composed of two parts : a *greedy part* and an *evaluation part*. The algorithm provides then at each iteration a better approximation of the Q-function.

Let $j = (s^j, a^j, b^j, r^j, s'^j)$ be N collected samples. At time step $k+1$, the *greedy part* consists of finding the maximizer's maxminimizing action $\overline{a}$ of the matrix game defined by $Q^j_k(s'^j, a^j, b^j)$. In our case, a turn-based setting, this involves finding a maximum. Then, during the *evaluation part*, since the second agent plays a minimizing strategy, the following value is computed: $Q^j = r + \gamma \min_b Q^j_k(s'^j, \overline{a}^j, b)$. At each iteration, the algorithm returns the Q-function Q_{k+1} fitting at best these values over some hypothesis space.

5 Dialogue as a Stochastic Game

Dialogue is a multi-agent interaction and therefore, it shall be considered as such during the optimization process. If each agent (*i.e.* the user and the DM) has its own goals and takes its decisions to achieve them, it sounds natural to model it as an MDP. In traditional dialogue system studies, this is only done for one conversant over two. Since (Levin and Pieraccini, 1997; Singh et al., 1999), only the DM is encoded as an RL agent, despite rare exceptions (Chandramohan et al., 2011; Chandramohan et al., 2012b; Chandramohan et al., 2012a)). The user is rather considered as a stationary agent modeled as a Bayesian network (Pietquin, 2006) or an agenda-based process (Schatzmann et al., 2007), leading to modeling errors (Schatztnann et al., 2005; Pietquin and Hastie, 2013).

At first sight, it seems reasonable to think that if two RL agents, previously trained to reach an optimal strategy, interact with each other, it would result in "optimal" dialogues. Yet, this assertion is wrong. Each agent would be optimal given the environment it's been trained on, but given another environment, nothing can be said about the learnt policy. Furthermore, if two DMs are trained together with traditional RL techniques, no convergence is guaranteed since, as seen above, non-stationarities emerge. Indeed, non-stationarity is not well managed by standard RL methods although some methods can deal with it (Geist et al., 2009; Daubigney et al., 2012) but adaptation might not be fast enough.

Jointly optimizing RL-agents in the framework of Stochastic Games finds a Nash Equilibrium. This guarantees both strategies to be optimal and this makes a fundamental difference with previous work (Chandramohan et al., 2012b; Georgila et al., 2014; Efstathiou and Lemon, 2014).

In the next section, we illustrate how dialogue may be modeled by a Stochastic Game, how transitions and reward functions depend on the policy of both agents. We propose now a Zero-Sum dialogue game where agents have to drive efficiently the dialogue to gather information quicker than their opponent. In this example, human user (Agent 1) and DM (Agent 2) are modeled with MDPs: each of them has a goal encoded into reward functions $\mathcal{R}_1$ and $\mathcal{R}_2$ (they may depend on the *joint action*).

5.1 A Zero-Sum Dialogue Game

The task involves two agents, each of them receives a random secret number and aims at guessing the other agent's number. They are adversaries: if one wins, the other one loses as much.

To find the secret number out, agents may perform one of the following actions: `ask`, `answer`, `guess`, `ok`, `confirm` and `listen`.

During a dialogue turn, the agent asking the question is called the guesser and the one answering is the opponent. To retrieve information about the opponent's hidden number, the guesser may `ask` if this number is smaller or greater than some other number. The opponent is forced to `answer` the truth. To show that it has understood the answer, the agent says `ok` and releases then the turn to its adversary, which endorses the guesser's role.

Agents are not perfect, they can misunderstand what has been said. This simulates ASR and NLU errors arising in real SDSs. They have an indicator giving a hint about the probability of having well understood (a confidence level). They are however never certain and they may answer a wrong question, *e.g.* in the following exchange :

- Is your secret number greater than x ?

- My number is greater than y.

When such an error arises, Agent 1 is allowed to ask another question instead of just saying `ok`. This punishment is harsh for the agent which misunderstood, it is almost as if it has to pass its turn. Another dialogue act is introduced to deal with such situations. If an agent is not sure, it may ask to `confirm`. In this case, Agent 1 may ask its question again. To avoid abuses, *i.e.* infinitely ask for a confirmation, this action induces a cost (and therefore a gain for the opponent).

If an agent thinks that it has found the number out, it can make a `guess`. If it was right, it wins (and therefore its opponent loses), otherwise, it loses (and its opponent wins).

Since we model dialogue as a turn-based interaction and we will need to consider joint actions, we introduce the action `listen` corresponding to the empty action.

6 Experimental Setting

Effects of the multi-agent setting are studied here through one special feature of the human-machine dialogue: the uncertainty management due to the dysfunctions of the ASR and the NLU. To promote simple algorithms, we ran our experiments on the zero-sum dialogue game presented above.

On this task, we compare three algorithms: Q-Learning, WoLF-PHC and AGPI-Q. Among those algorithms, only AGPI-Q is proved to converge towards a Nash Equilibrium in a Multi-Agent setting. Q-Learning and WoLF-PHC have however been used as Multi-Agent learning algorithm in a dialogue setting (English and Heeman, 2005; Georgila et al., 2014). Similarly to these papers, experiments will be done using simulation. We will show that, contrarily to AGPI-Q, they do not converge towards the Nash Equilibrium and therefore do not fit to the dialogue problem.

6.1 Modeling ASR and NLU Confidence Estimation

One difficulty while working with Spoken Dialogue Systems is how can a DM deal with uncertainty resulting from ASR and NLU errors and reflected by their Confidence Scores. Those scores are not always a probability. The only assumption made here is that with a score lower (resp. greater) than 0.5, the probability to misunderstand the last utterance is greater (resp. lower) than 0.5. Since dialogues are simulated, the ASR and NLU confidence levels will be modeled the following way.

Each agent owns some fixed Sentence Error Rate (SER_i). With probability $(1 - \text{SER}_i)$, agent i receives each utterance undisrupted, while with probability SER_i, this utterance is misunderstood and replaced by another one.

A $(-\infty, \infty)$ score is then sampled according to a normal distribution centered in -1 for incorrect understanding and +1 for correct understanding. The (0,1) score is obtained by applying the sigmoid function $f(x) = \frac{1}{1+\exp(-x)}$, to the $(-\infty, \infty)$ score.

Since Q-Learning and WoLF-PHC are used in their tabular form, it was necessary to discretize this score. To have states where the agent is almost sure of having understood (or sure of having misunderstood), we discretized by splitting the score around the cut points 0.1, 0.5 and 0.9. By equity concerns, the same discretization was applied for the AGPI-Q algorithm.

6.2 Task Modeling

6.2.1 State Space

Consider two agents i and j. Their secret numbers are respectively m and n. To gather information about m, agent i asks if the secret number m is smaller or greater than some given number k. If agent j answers that m is greater (resp. smaller) than k, it will provides i a lower bound b_i (resp. an upper bound b'_i) on m. Agent i's knowledge on m may be represented by the interval $I_i = [b_i, b'_i]$. The probability of wining by making a `guess` is then given by $p = \frac{1}{b'_i - b_i + 1}$. Progress of agent i in the game may therefore measured by only $c_i = b'_i - b_i + 1$, the cardinal of I_i. At the beginning of the game, one has: $I_i = I_j = [1, 5]$. Since agents have to know the progress of the whole game, they both track c_i and c_j.

To take an action, an agent needs to remember who pronounced the last utterance, what was the last utterance it heard and to what extent it believes that what it heard was what had been said.

To summarize, agents taking actions make their decision according to the following features: the last utterance, its trust in this utterance, who uttered it, its progress in the game and its opponent's progress. they do not need to track the whole range of possible secret numbers but only the cardinal of these sets. *Dialogue turn, last action, confidence score, cardinal of possible numbers for both agents* are thus the five state features. The state space thus contains $2 * 5 * 4 * 5 * 5 = 1000$ states.

6.2.2 Action Space

Agents are able to make one of the following actions: `ask`, `answer`, `guess`, `confirm` and `listen`. The actions `ask`, `answer` and `guess` need an argument: the number the agent wants to compare to. To learn quicker, we chose not to take a decision about this value. When an agent asks, it asks if the secret number is greater or smaller than the number in the middle of his range (this range is computed by the environment, it is not taken into account in the states). An agent answering says that her secret number is greater or smaller than the number it heard (which may be not the uttered number). An agent guessing proposes randomly a number in his range of possible values.

6.2.3 Reward function

To define the reward function, we consider the maximizing player. It is its turn to play. If it is guessing the right number, it earns $+1$. If it asks for a confirmation, it earns -0.2. Therefore, it is never in its interest to block the dialogue by always asking for a confirmation (in the worst case, *ie* if second agent immediately wins, it earns -1 while if it infinitely blocks the dialogue, it earns $-0.2 \sum_{k=0}^{\infty} (\gamma^2)^k \approx -1.05$ for $\gamma = 0.9$).

6.3 Training of the algorithms

To train Q-Learning and WoLF-PHC, we followed the setup proposed in (Georgila et al., 2014). Both algorithms are trained in self-play by following an ϵ-greedy policy. Training is split into five epochs of 100000 dialogues. The exploration rate is set to 0.95 in the first epoch, 0.8 in the second, 0.5 in the third, 0.3 in the fourth and 0.1 in the fifth.

The parameters δ_L and δ_W of WoLF-PHC are set to $\delta_W = 0.05$ and $\delta_L = 0.2$. The ratio $\delta_L/\delta_W = 4$ assures an aggressive learning when losing.

As a batch RL algorithm, AGPI-Q requires samples. To generate them, we followed the setup proposed in (Pietquin et al., 2011). An optimal (or at least near) policy is first handcrafted. This policy is the following: an agent always `asks` for more information except when it or its opponent have enough information to make the right `guess` with probability 1. When the agent has to answer, it asks to `confirm` if its confidence score is below 0.5.

An ϵ-random policy is then designed. Agents make their decisions according the hand-crafted policy with probability ϵ and pick randomly actions with probability $(1 - \epsilon)$. Tuples (s, a_1, a_2, r, s') are then gathered. We are then assured that the problem space is well-sampled and that there also exists samples giving the successful task completion reward. To ensure convergence, 75000 such dialogues are generated.

To keep the model as parameter-free as possible, CART trees are used as hypothesis space for the regression.

Each algorithm is trained with the following SER values: 0, 0.1, 0.2, 0.3 and 0.4.

6.4 Results

The decision in the game is made on only two points: when is the best moment to end the dialogue with the `guess` action and what is the best way to deal with uncertainty by the use of the `confirm` action. Average duration of dialogues and average number of `confirm` actions are therefore chosen as the feature characterizing the Nash Equilibrium. Both are calculated over 5000 dialogues. Figures 1 and 2 illustrate those results.

Q-Learning dialogues' length decreases gradually with respect to an increasing SER (Figure 1). Figure 2 brings an explanation: Q-Learning agents do not learn to use the `CONFIRM` action. More, dialogue length is even not regular, proving that the algorithm did not converge to a 'stable' policy. Q-Learning is a slow algorithm and therefore, agents do not have enough time to face the non-stationarities of the multi-agent environment. Convergence is thus not possible.

WoLF-PHC does not treat uncertainty too. Its number of `confirm` actions is by far the highest but stays constant. If the SDS asks for confirmation, even when there is no noise, it may be because being disadvantaged, it always loses, and while losing, its quick learning rate makes its strategy always changing. As previously said, convergence was not guaranteed.

AGPI-Q is then the only algorithm providing robustness against noise. The length of dialogues and the number of `confirm` actions increase both gradually with the SER of the SDS. We are also assured by the theory that in this setting, no improvement is possible.

It is also interesting to note the emergence of non-trivial strategies coming from the interaction between the AGPI-Q agents. For instance, when both agents are almost at the end of the dialogue ($c_i = 2$ for each agent), agents make `guess`. Even if they have very low chances of wining, agents make also `guess` when it is sure that the adversary will win at the next turn.

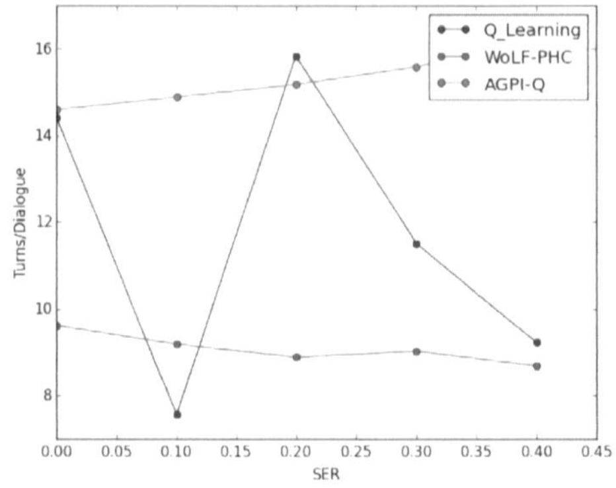

Figure 1: Length of dialogues

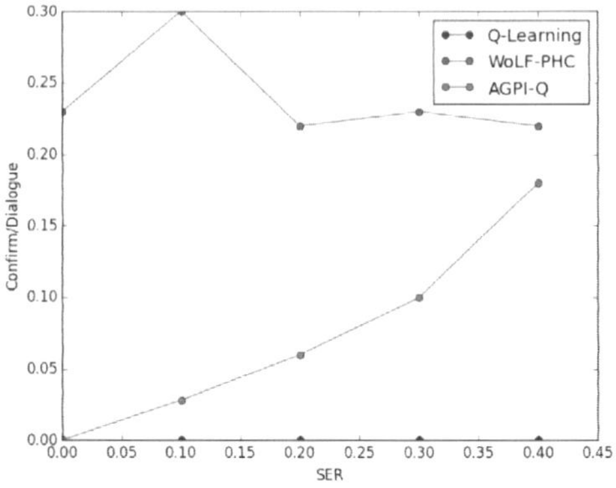

Figure 2: Frequency of the action `CONFIRM`

7 Conclusion: Beyond the Zero-Sum Setting

We provided a rigorous framework for co-learning in Dialogue Systems allowing optimization for both conversants. Its efficiency was shown on a purely adversarial setting under noisy conditions and an extension to situations more general than the purely adversarial setting is now proposed.

7.1 An appointment scheduling problem

The previous model considers only purely competitive scenarios. In this section, it is extended for the General-Sum case. We take as an example the task of scheduling the best appointment between two agents, where conversants have to interact to find an agreement.

Each agent i has its own preferences about a slot in their agenda, they are encoded into some reward function $\mathcal{R}_i$. At each turn, an agent `proposes` some slot k. Next turn, its interlocutor may `propose` another slot or `accept` this one. If it accepts, agent i earns $\mathcal{R}_i(k)$, it gets nothing otherwise. The conversation ends when an agent accepts an offered slot.

Agents, which are not always perfect, can misunderstand the last offer. An action `confirm` is therefore introduced. If an agent thinks that the last offer was on the slot k' instead of the slot k, the outcome may be disastrous. An agent has thus always to find a trade-off between the uncertainty management on the last offer and its impatience, (due to the discount factor γ which penalizes long dialogues).

Here, cooperation is implicit. Conversants are self-centered, they care only on their own value functions, but, since it depends on both actions, or more explicitly the opponent may refuse an offer, they have to take into account the opponent's behavior.

7.2 Future work

In future, using General-Sum algorithms (Prasad et al., 2015), our framework will be applied on those much more complicated dialogue situations where cooperative and competitive phenomenon get mixed up in addition to the noisy conditions encountered in dialogue.

The long-term goal of this work is to use the model on a real data set in order to provide model of real interactions and designing adaptive SDS freeing ourselves from user modeling.

Acknowledgement

This work has been partially funded by the French National Agency for Research (ANR) through the ContInt Project MaRDi (Man-Robot Dialogue) and by the French Ministry for Higher Education and Research (MESR).

References

Natalia Akchurina. 2009. Multiagent reinforcement learning: algorithm converging to nash equilibrium in general-sum discounted stochastic games. In *Proc. of AAMAS*.

Dimitri P. Bertsekas and John Tsitsiklis. 1996. *Neuro-Dynamic Programming*. Athena Scientific.

Grégory Bourguin, Alain Derycke, and Jean-Claude Tarby. 2001. Beyond the interface: Co-evolution inside interactive systems - a proposal founded on activity theory. In *People and Computers XV-Interaction without Frontiers*, pages 297–310. Springer.

Michael Bowling and Manuela Veloso. 2002. Multiagent learning using a variable learning rate. *Artificial Intelligence*, 136(2):215–250.

Lucian Buşoniu, Robert Babuska, and Bart De Schutter. 2008. A comprehensive survey of multiagent reinforcement learning. *Systems, Man, and Cybernetics, Part C: Applications and Reviews, IEEE Transactions on*, 38(2):156–172.

Jean Caelen and Anne Xuereb. 2011. Dialogue et théorie des jeux. In *Congrés international SPeD*.

Senthilkumar Chandramohan, Matthieu Geist, Fabrice Lefèvre, and Olivier Pietquin. 2011. User Simulation in Dialogue Systems using Inverse Reinforcement Learning. In *Proc. of Interspeech*.

Senthilkumar Chandramohan, Matthieu Geist, Fabrice Lefèvre, and Olivier Pietquin. 2012a. Behavior Specific User Simulation in Spoken Dialogue Systems. In *Proc. of ITG Conference on Speech Communication*.

Senthilkumar Chandramohan, Matthieu Geist, Fabrice Lefèvre, and Olivier Pietquin. 2012b. Co-adaptation in Spoken Dialogue Systems. In *Proc. of IWSDS*.

Lucie Daubigney, Matthieu Geist, Senthilkumar Chandramohan, and Olivier Pietquin. 2012. A comprehensive reinforcement learning framework for dialogue management optimization. *IEEE Journal of Selected Topics in Signal Processing*, 6(8):891–902.

Ioannis Efstathiou and Oliver Lemon. 2014. Learning non-cooperative dialogue behaviours. In *Proc. of SIGDIAL*.

Layla El Asri, Romain Laroche, and Olivier Pietquin. 2014. Dinasti : Dialogues with a negotiating appointment setting interface. In *Proc. of LREC*.

Michael S. English and Peter A. Heeman. 2005. Learning mixed initiative dialog strategies by using reinforcement learning on both conversants. In *Proc. of HLT/EMNLP*.

Damien Ernst, Pierre Geurts, and Louis Wehenkel. 2005. Tree-based batch mode reinforcement learning. pages 503–556.

Jerzy Filar and Koos Vrieze. 1996. *Competitive Markov decision processes*. Springer.

Matthieu Geist, Olivier Pietquin, and Gabriel Fricout. 2009. Tracking in reinforcement learning. In *Proc. of ICONIP*.

Kallirroi Georgila, Claire Nelson, and David Traum. 2014. Single-agent vs. multi-agent techniques for concurrent reinforcement learning of negotiation dialogue policies. In *Proc. of ACL*.

Geoffrey J. Gordon. 1999. *Approximate Solutions to Markov Decision Processes*. Ph.D. thesis, Carnegie Melon University.

P. Jean-Jacques Herings and Ronald Peeters. 2000. Stationary equilibria in stochastic games: structure, selection and computation.

Junling Hu and Michael P. Wellman. 2003. Nash q-learning for general-sum stochastic games. *Journal of Machine Learning Research*, 4:1039–1069.

Romain Laroche, Ghislain Putois, and Philippe Bretier. 2010. Optimising a handcrafted dialogue system design. In *Proc. of Interspeech*.

Oliver Lemon and Olivier Pietquin. 2007. Machine learning for spoken dialogue systems. In *Proc. of Interspeech*.

Esther Levin and Roberto Pieraccini. 1997. A stochastic model of computer-human interaction for learning dialogue strategies. In *Proc. of Eurospeech*.

Michael L. Littman. 1994. Markov games as a framework for multi-agent reinforcement learning. In *Proc. of ICML*.

Michael L. Littman. 2001. Friend-or-foe q-learning in general-sum games. In *Proc. of ICML*.

John Milnor. 1951. Games against nature. Technical report, RAND corporation.

Abraham Neyman and Sylvain Sorin. 2003. *Stochastic games and applications*, volume 570. Springer Science & Business Media.

Martin J. Osborne and Ariel Rubinstein. 1994. *A course in game theory*. MIT press.

Stephen D. Patek and Dimitri P. Bertsekas. 1999. Stochastic shortest path games. *SIAM Journal on Control and Optimization*, 37(3).

Julien Perolat, Bilal Piot, Bruno Scherrer, and Olivier Pietquin. 2015. Approximate dynamic programming for two-player zero-sum markov games. In *Proc. of ICML*.

Olivier Pietquin and Helen Hastie. 2013. A survey on metrics for the evaluation of user simulations. *The knowledge engineering review*, 28(01):59–73.

Olivier Pietquin, Matthieu Geist, Senthilkumar Chandramohan, and Hervé Frezza-Buet. 2011. Sample-efficient batch reinforcement learning for dialogue management optimization. *ACM Transactions on Speech and Language Processing (TSLP)*, 7(3).

Olivier Pietquin. 2006. Consistent goal-directed user model for realistic man-machine task-oriented spoken dialogue simulation. In *Proc of ICME*.

H.L. Prasad, L.A. Prashanth, and Shalabh Bhatnagar. 2015. Algorithms for nash equilibria in general-sum stochastic games. In *Proc. of AAMAS*.

Martin L. Puterman. 1994. *Markov decision processes: discrete stochastic dynamic programming*. John Wiley & Sons.

Jost Schatzmann, Blaise Thomson, Karl Weilhammer, Hui Ye, and Steve Young. 2007. Agenda-based user simulation for bootstrapping a pomdp dialogue system. In *Proc. of HLT*.

Jost. Schatztnann, Matthew Stuttle, Konrad Weilhammer, and Steve Young. 2005. Effects of the user model on simulation-based learning of dialogue strategies. In *Proc. of ASRU*.

Lloyd Shapley. 1953. Stochastic games. *Proc. of the National Academy of Sciences of the United States of America*, 39(10):1095–1100.

Satinder P. Singh, Michael J. Kearns, Diane J. Litman, and Marilyn A. Walker. 1999. Reinforcement learning for spoken dialogue systems. In *Proc. of NIPS*.

Richard S. Sutton and Andrew G. Barto. 1998. *Reinforcement learning: An introduction*. MIT press.

Christopher Watkins and Peter Dayan. 1992. Q-learning. *Machine learning*, 8(3-4):279–292.

Steve Young, Milica Gasic, Blaise Thomson, and Jason D. Williams. 2013. Pomdp-based statistical spoken dialog systems: A review. *Proceedings of the IEEE*, 101(5):1160–1179.

Martin Zinkevich, Amy Greenwald, and Michael L. Littman. 2006. Cyclic equilibria in markov games. In *Proc. of NIPS*.

Knowledge transfer between speakers for personalised dialogue management

Iñigo Casanueva, Thomas Hain, Heidi Christensen, Ricard Marxer and Phil Green
Department of Computer Science, University of Sheffield, United Kingdom
{i.casanueva, t.hain, h.christensen, r.marxer,
p.green}@sheffield.ac.uk

Abstract

Model-free reinforcement learning has been shown to be a promising data driven approach for automatic dialogue policy optimization, but a relatively large amount of dialogue interactions is needed before the system reaches reasonable performance. Recently, Gaussian process based reinforcement learning methods have been shown to reduce the number of dialogues needed to reach optimal performance, and pre-training the policy with data gathered from different dialogue systems has further reduced this amount. Following this idea, a dialogue system designed for a single speaker can be initialised with data from other speakers, but if the dynamics of the speakers are very different the model will have a poor performance. When data gathered from different speakers is available, selecting the data from the most similar ones might improve the performance. We propose a method which automatically selects the data to transfer by defining a similarity measure between speakers, and uses this measure to weight the influence of the data from each speaker in the policy model. The methods are tested by simulating users with different severities of dysarthria interacting with a voice enabled environmental control system.

1 Introduction

Partially observable Markov decision processes (POMDP) (Young et al., 2013) are a popular framework to model dialogue management as a reinforcement learning (RL) problem. In a POMDP, a state tracker (Thomson and Young, 2010)(Williams, 2014) maintains a distribution over possible user goals (states), called the belief state, and RL methods (Sutton and Barto, 1998) are used to optimize a metric called cumulative reward, a score that combines dialogue success rate and dialogue length. However, existing model-based RL approaches become intractable for real world sized dialogue systems (Williams and Young, 2007), and model-free approaches often need a large number of dialogues to converge to the optimal policy (Jurčíček et al., 2012).

Recently, Gaussian process (GP) based RL (Engel et al., 2005) has been proposed for dialogue policy optimization, reducing the number of interactions needed to converge to the optimal policy by an order of magnitude with respect to other POMDP models, allowing the policy to be learned directly from real users interactions (Gašić et al., 2013 a). In addition, using transfer learning methods (Taylor and Stone, 2009) to initialise the policy with data gathered from dialogue systems in different domains has increased the learning speed of the policy further (Gašić et al., 2013 b), and provided an acceptable system performance when there is no domain specific data available. In the case of dialogue managers personalised for a single speaker, data gathered from other "source" speakers can be used to pre-train the policy, but if the dynamics of the other speakers are very different, this data will have a different distribution than the data of the current "target" speaker, and therefore, using this data to train the policy model does not have any benefit. In the context of speaker specific acoustic models for users with dysarthria (a speech impairment), Christensen et al. (2014) demonstrated that using a speaker similarity metric to select the data to train the acoustic models improves ASR performance. Taking this idea into dialogue management, if a similarity metric is defined between different speakers, this metric can be used to select which data from the source speakers is used to train the model, and even to weight the influence of the data from each speaker in the model. As GP-RL is a non-parametric

Proceedings of the SIGDIAL 2015 Conference, pages 12–21,
Prague, Czech Republic, 2-4 September 2015.

method, a straightforward way to transfer knowledge is to directly initialise the GP model for the target speaker using data from source speakers, and update the GP with the data from the target speaker as this is gathered through interaction. But GP-RL soon becomes intractable as the data amount increases, limiting the amount of data that can be transferred. Gašić et al. (2013 a) proposes to transfer knowledge between domains by using the source data to train a prior GP, whose posterior is used as prior mean in the new GP. Another option is to use a GP approximation method (Quiñonero and Rasmussen, 2005) which permits data selection, use the speaker similarity metric to select the source data to initialise the policy, and then discard source data points as data points from the target speaker become available, keeping the number of data points up to a maximum.

This paper investigates knowledge transfer between speakers in the context of a spoken environmental control system personalised for speakers with dysarthria (Christensen et al., 2013), where the ASR is adapted as speaker specific data is gathered (Christensen et al., 2012), thus improving the ASR performance with usage. The paper is organised as follows: Section 2 gives the background of GP-RL and defines the methods to select and weight the transferred data. Section 3 presents the experimental setup of the environmental control system and the different dysarthric simulated users, as well as the different features used to define the speaker similarities. In Section 4 the results of the experiments are presented and explained and Section 5 concludes the paper.

2 GPs for reinforcement learning

The objective of a POMDP based dialogue manager is to find the policy $\pi(\mathbf{b}) = a$ that maximizes the expected cumulative reward c_i defined as the sum of immediate rewards from time step i until the dialogue is finished, where $a \in \mathcal{A}$ is the action taken by the manager, and the *belief state* $\mathbf{b}$ is a probability distribution over a discrete set of states $\mathcal{S}$. The *Q-function* defines the expected cumulative reward when the dialogue is in belief state $\mathbf{b}_i$ and action a_i is taken, following policy π:

$$Q(\mathbf{b}_i, a_i) = E_\pi[c_i] \text{ ; where } c_i = \sum_{n=i}^{N} \gamma^{n-i} r_n \quad (1)$$

where N is the time step at which the terminal action is taken (end of the dialogue), r_i is the immediate reward given by the reward function, and $0 \leq \gamma \leq 1$ is the discount factor, which weights future rewards. If c_i is considered to be a random variable, it can be modelled as a mean plus a residual, $c_i = Q(\mathbf{b}_i, a_i) + \Delta Q(\mathbf{b}_i, a_i)$. Then the immediate reward r_i can be written recursively as the temporal difference (TD) between Q at time i and $i+1$:

$$\begin{aligned} r_i &= Q(\mathbf{b}_i, a_i) + \Delta Q(\mathbf{b}_i, a_i) \\ &\quad -\gamma_i Q(\mathbf{b}_{i+1}, a_{i+1}) - \gamma_i \Delta Q(\mathbf{b}_{i+1}, a_{i+1}) \end{aligned} \quad (2)$$

where $\gamma_i = 0$ if a_i is a terminal action[1], and the discount factor γ otherwise. Given a set of observed *belief-action* points $(\mathbf{b}_i, a_i)$, with their respective r_i values, the set of linear equations can be represented in matrix form as:

$$\mathbf{r}_{t-1} = \mathbf{H}_t \mathbf{q}_t + \mathbf{H}_t \Delta \mathbf{q}_t \quad (3)$$

where $\mathbf{q}_t = [Q(\mathbf{b}_1, a_1), Q(\mathbf{b}_2, a_2), ..., Q(\mathbf{b}_t, a_t)]^\top$, $\Delta\mathbf{q}_t = [\Delta Q(\mathbf{b}_1, a_1), \Delta Q(\mathbf{b}_2, a_2), ..., \Delta Q(\mathbf{b}_t, a_t)]^\top$, $\mathbf{r}_{t-1} = [r_1, r_2, ..., r_{t-1}]^\top$ and

$$\mathbf{H}_t = \begin{bmatrix} 1 & -\gamma_1 & \dots & 0 & 0 \\ 0 & 1 & \dots & 0 & 0 \\ \vdots & \ddots & \ddots & \vdots & \vdots \\ 0 & 0 & \dots & 1 & -\gamma_{t-1} \end{bmatrix}$$

If the random variables $\mathbf{q}_t$ are assumed to have a joint Gaussian distribution with zero mean and $\Delta Q(\mathbf{b}_i, a_i) \sim \mathcal{N}(0, \sigma^2)$, the system can be modelled as a GP (Rasmussen and Williams, 2005), with the covariance matrix determined by a *kernel function* defined independently over the belief and the action space (Engel et al., 2005):

$$k_{i,j} = k((\mathbf{b}_i, a_i), (\mathbf{b}_j, a_j)) = k^b(\mathbf{b}_i, \mathbf{b}_j) k^a(a_i, a_j) \quad (4)$$

To simplify the notation, from now on $\mathbf{x}_i = (\mathbf{b}_i, a_i)$ will be defined as each belief-action point, and $\mathbf{K}_{Y,Y'}$ as the matrix of size $|\mathbf{Y}| \times |\mathbf{Y}'|$ whose elements are computed by the kernel function (eq. 4) between any set of points $\mathbf{Y}$ and $\mathbf{Y}'$. For a new belief-action point $\mathbf{x}_* = (\mathbf{b}_*, a_*)$, the posterior of the expected cumulative reward can be computed:

$$\begin{aligned} Q(\mathbf{x}_*)|\mathbf{X}_t, \mathbf{r}_{t-1} &\sim \mathcal{N}(\bar{Q}(\mathbf{x}_*), \hat{Q}(\mathbf{x}_*)) \\ \bar{Q}(\mathbf{x}_*) &= \mathbf{K}_{*,X} \mathbf{H}_t^\top (\mathbf{H}_t \mathbf{K}_{X,X} \mathbf{H}_t^\top + \mathbf{\Sigma}_t)^{-1} \mathbf{r}_{t-1} \\ \hat{Q}(\mathbf{x}_*) &= k(\mathbf{x}_*, \mathbf{x}_*) \\ &\quad - \mathbf{K}_{*,X} \mathbf{H}_t^\top (\mathbf{H}_t \mathbf{K}_{X,X} \mathbf{H}_t^\top + \mathbf{\Sigma}_t)^{-1} \mathbf{H}_t \mathbf{K}_{X,*} \end{aligned} \quad (5)$$

[1] As dialogue management is an episodic RL problem, the temporal difference relationship between 2 consecutive belief-action points only happens if the points belong to the same dialogue.

where $\mathbf{X}_t$ is the set of size t of all the previously visited $(\mathbf{b}_i, a_i)$ points, $*$ denotes the set of size 1 composed by the new belief-action point to be evaluated and $\mathbf{\Sigma}_t = \sigma^2 \mathbf{H}_t \mathbf{H}_t^\top$. $\bar{Q}$ and $\hat{Q}$ represent the mean and the variance of Q respectively.

To further simplify the notation it is possible to redefine eq. 5 by defining a kernel in the temporal difference space instead of in the belief-action space. If the set of belief-action points $\mathbf{X}_t$ is redefined[2] as $\mathbf{Z}_t$ where $\mathbf{z}_i = (\mathbf{b}_i, a_i, \mathbf{b}_{i+1}, a_{i+1})$, with $\mathbf{b}_{i+1}$ and a_{i+1} set to any default values if a_i is a terminal action, a kernel function between 2 temporal difference points can be defined as:

$$\begin{aligned} k_{i,j}^{td} &= k^{td}(\mathbf{z}_i, \mathbf{z}_j) \\ &= k^{td}((\mathbf{b}_i, a_i, \mathbf{b}_{i+1}, a_{i+1}), (\mathbf{b}_j, a_j, \mathbf{b}_{j+1}, a_{j+1})) \\ &= (k_{i,j} + \gamma_i \gamma_j k_{i+1,j+1} - \gamma_i k_{i+1,j} - \gamma_j k_{i,j+1}) \end{aligned} \tag{6}$$

where $k_{i,j}$ is the kernel function in the belief-action space (eq. 4) and $\gamma_i = 0$ and $\gamma_j = 0$ if a_i and a_j are terminal actions respectively, or the discount factor γ otherwise (as in eq. 2). When a_i is a terminal action, the value of a_{i+1} and $\mathbf{b}_{i+1}$ in $\mathbf{z}_i$ is irrelevant, as it will be multiplied by $\gamma_i = 0$. In the same way, when this kernel is used to compute the covariance vector between a new test point and the set $\mathbf{Z}_t$, as the new point $\mathbf{x}_* = (\mathbf{b}_*, a_*)$ lies in the belief-action space, it is redefined as $\mathbf{z}_* = (\mathbf{b}_*, a_*, \mathbf{b}_{*+1}, a_{*+1})$ with $\mathbf{b}_{*+1}$ and a_{*+1} set to default values. Then, a_* is considered a terminal action, so $\mathbf{b}_{*+1}$ and a_{*+1} won't affect the value of k_{i*}^{td} due to $\gamma_* = 0$. A more detailed derivation of the temporal difference kernel is given in appendix A. Using the temporal difference kernel defined in eq. 6, eq. 5 can be rewritten as:

$$\begin{aligned} &Q(\mathbf{z}_*)|\mathbf{Z}_t, \mathbf{r}_{t-1} \sim \mathcal{N}(\bar{Q}(\mathbf{z}_*), \hat{Q}(\mathbf{z}_*)) \\ &\bar{Q}(\mathbf{z}_*) = \mathbf{K}_{*,Z}^{td}(\mathbf{K}_{Z,Z}^{td} + \mathbf{\Sigma}_t)^{-1}\mathbf{r}_{t-1} \\ &\hat{Q}(\mathbf{z}_*) = k^{td}(\mathbf{z}_*, \mathbf{z}_*) - \mathbf{K}_{*,Z}^{td}(\mathbf{K}_{Z,Z}^{td} + \mathbf{\Sigma}_t)^{-1}\mathbf{K}_{Z,*}^{td} \end{aligned} \tag{7}$$

where $\mathbf{K}_{Y,Y'}^{td}$ is the covariance matrix computed with the temporal difference kernel between any set of TD points $\mathbf{Y}$ and $\mathbf{Y}'$. With this notation, the shape of the equation for the posterior of Q is equivalent to classic GP regression models. Thus, it is straightforward to apply a wide range of well studied GP techniques, such as sparse methods. Redefining the belief-action set of points $\mathbf{X}_t$ as the set of temporal difference points $\mathbf{Z}_t$ also simplifies the selection of data points (e.g. to select inducing points in sparse models), because the dependency between consecutive points is well defined.

The GP literature proposes various *sparse* methods which select a subset of *inducing points* $\mathbf{U}$ of size $m < t$ from the set of training points $\mathbf{Z}$ (Quiñonero and Rasmussen, 2005). In this paper the deterministic training conditional (DTC) method is used. Once the subset of points has been selected and assuming $\Delta Q(\mathbf{b}_i, a_i) - \gamma_i \Delta Q(\mathbf{b}_{i+1}, a_{i+1}) \sim \mathcal{N}(0, \sigma^2)$ as in (Engel et al., 2003), the GP posterior can be approximated in $\mathcal{O}(t \cdot m^2)$ with the DTC method as:

$$\begin{aligned} &Q^{dtc}(\mathbf{z}_*)|\mathbf{Z}_t, \mathbf{r}_{t-1} \sim \mathcal{N}(\bar{Q}^{dtc}(\mathbf{z}_*), \hat{Q}^{dtc}(\mathbf{z}_*)) \\ &\bar{Q}^{dtc}(\mathbf{z}_*) = \sigma^{-2}\mathbf{K}_{*,U}^{td}\mathbf{\Lambda}\mathbf{K}_{U,Z}^{td}\mathbf{r}_{t-1} \\ &\hat{Q}^{dtc}(\mathbf{z}_*) = k^{td}(\mathbf{z}_*, \mathbf{z}_*) - \mathbf{\Phi} + \mathbf{K}_{*,U}^{td}\mathbf{\Lambda}\mathbf{K}_{U,*}^{td} \end{aligned} \tag{8}$$

where $\mathbf{\Lambda} = (\sigma^{-2}\mathbf{K}_{U,Z}^{td}\mathbf{K}_{Z,U}^{td} + \mathbf{K}_{U,U}^{td})^{-1}$ and $\mathbf{\Phi} = \mathbf{K}_{*,U}^{td}(\mathbf{K}_{U,U}^{td})^{-1}\mathbf{K}_{U,*}^{td}$.

Once the posterior for any new belief-action point can be computed with eq. 7 or eq. 8, the policy $\pi(\mathbf{b}) = a$ can be computed as the action a that maximizes the Q-function from the current belief state $\mathbf{b}_*$, but in order to avoid getting stuck in a local optimum, an exploration-exploitation approach should be taken. One of the advantages of GPs is that they compute the uncertainty of the expected cumulative reward in form of a variance, which can be used as a metric for *active exploration* (Geist and Pietquin, 2011) to speed up the learning of the policy with an ϵ-greedy approach:

$$\pi(\mathbf{b}_*) = \begin{cases} \arg\max_{a \in \mathcal{A}} \bar{Q}(\mathbf{b}_*, a) \text{ with prob. } (1-\epsilon) \\ \arg\max_{a \in \mathcal{A}} \hat{Q}(\mathbf{b}_*, a) \text{ with prob. } \epsilon \end{cases} \tag{9}$$

where ϵ controls the exploration rate. The policy optimization loop is performed following the *Episodic GP-Sarsa* algorithm defined by (Gašić and Young, 2014).

2.1 Transfer learning with GP-RL

The scenario where a statistical model for a specific "target" task must be trained, but only data from different but related "source" tasks is available, is known as transfer learning (Pan and Yang, 2010). In the context of this paper the different tasks will be dialogues with different speakers, and three points of transfer learning will be addressed:

- *How to transfer the knowledge*
- In the case of multiple source speakers, *which data to transfer*, and

[2] Take into account that $|\mathbf{Z}_t| = |\mathbf{X}_t| - 1$

- *How to weight data from different sources.*

In the context of reinforcement learning (Taylor and Stone, 2009) and dialogue policy optimization (Gašić et al., 2013 a), transfer learning has been shown to increase the performance of the system in the initial stages of use and to speed up the policy learning, requiring a smaller amount of target data to reach the optimal policy.

2.1.1 Knowledge transfer

The most straightforward way to transfer the data in GP-RL is to initialise the set of temporal difference points $\mathbf{Z_t}$ of the GP with the source points and then continue updating it with target data points as they are gathered through interaction. However, this approach has a few shortcomings. First, as GP-RLs complexity increases with the number of data points, the model might quickly become intractable if it is initialised with too many source points. Also, when data points from the target speaker are gathered through interaction, the source points may not improve the performance of the system, while increasing the model complexity. Second, as the computation of the variance for a new point depends on the number of close points already visited, the variance of the new belief-action points will be reduced by the effect of the source points close in the belief-action space. If the distribution of the source data points is unbalanced, the effectiveness of the policy of eq. 9 will be affected. Gašić et al. (2013 a) proposes to use the source points to train a prior GP, and use its posterior as mean function for the GP trained with the target points. With this approach, the mean of the posterior in eq. 7 will be modified as:

$$\bar{Q}(\mathbf{z}_*) = m(\mathbf{z}_*) + \mathbf{K}^{td}_{*,Z}(\mathbf{K}^{td}_{Z,Z}+\Sigma)^{-1}(\mathbf{r}_{t-1}-\mathbf{m}_t) \tag{10}$$

where $m(\mathbf{z}_*)$ is the mean of the posterior of the Q-function given by the prior GP and $\mathbf{m}_t = [m(\mathbf{z}_0), ..., m(\mathbf{z}_t)]^\top$. If the DTC approach (eq. 8) is taken, the posterior Q-function mean becomes:

$$\bar{Q}^{dtc}(\mathbf{z}_*) = m(\mathbf{z}_*) + \sigma^{-2}\mathbf{K}^{td}_{*,U}\mathbf{\Lambda}\mathbf{K}^{td}_{U,Z}(\mathbf{r}_{t-1}-\mathbf{m}_t) \tag{11}$$

This approach has the advantage of being computationally cheaper than the former method while modelling the uncertainty for new target points more accurately, but at the cost of not taking into account the correlation between source and target points, which might reduce the performance when there is a small amount of target data.

A third approach combines the two previous methods, using a portion of the transfer points to train a GP for the prior mean function, while the rest is used to initialise the set $\mathbf{Z}_t$ of the GP that will be updated with target points. This method will be computationally cheaper than the first one while increasing the performance of the second method with a small amount of target data.

2.1.2 Transfer data selection

As non-parametric models, the complexity of GPs will increase with the number of data points, limiting the amount of source data that can be transferred. Additionally, if the points come from multiple sources, it is possible that the data distribution from some sources is more similar to the target speaker than others, hence transferring data from these sources will increase performance. We propose to extract a speaker feature vector $\mathbf{s}$ from each speaker and define a similarity function $f(\mathbf{s}, \mathbf{s}')$ between speakers (see sec. 3.4). The data can be selected by choosing the points from the source speakers more similar to the target.

With the DTC approach (eq. 8), a subset of inducing points $\mathbf{U}_m$ must be selected. The most straightforward way is to select the most similar points to the speaker from the transferred points. As the user interacts with the system and target data points are gathered, these points may be used as inducing points. This approach acts like another layer of data selection; the reduced complexity will allow for the transfer of more source points, while using the target points as inducing points will mean that only the source points that lie in the same part of the belief-action space as the target points have influence on the model.

2.1.3 Transfer data weighting

When transferring data from multiple sources, the similarity between each source and the target speaker might be different. Thus the data from a source more similar to the target should have more influence in the model than less similar ones. As a GP is defined by computing covariances between data points through a kernel function, one way to weight the data from different sources is to extend the belief-action vector used to compute the covariance with the speaker feature vector $\mathbf{s}$ explained in the previous section as $\mathbf{x}_i = (\mathbf{b}_i, a_i, \mathbf{s}_i)$, and then extend the kernel (eq. 4) by multiplying it by a new kernel in the speaker space k^s as:

$$k_{i,j}^{ext} = k((\mathbf{b}_i, a_i, \mathbf{s}_i), (\mathbf{b}_j, a_j, \mathbf{s}_j)) \\ = k^b(\mathbf{b}_i, \mathbf{b}_j) k^a(a_i, a_j) k^s(\mathbf{s}_i, \mathbf{s}_j) \quad (12)$$

By adding this extra space to the data points, the covariance between points will not only depend on the similarity between points in the belief-action space, but also in the speaker space, reducing the covariance between two points that lie in different parts of the speaker space. This approach will also help to partially deal with the variance computing problem of the first model in sec. 2.1.1, as the source points will lie on a different part of the speaker space than the new target points, thus having less influence in the variance computation.

3 Experimental setup

To test the system in a scenario with high variability between the dynamics of the speakers, the experiments are performed within the context of a voice-enabled control system designed to help speakers with dysarthria to interact with their home devices (TV, radio, lamps...), where the speakers have different severities of dysarthria (this is an instance of the homeService application (Christensen et al., 2013)). The system has a vocabulary of 36 commands and is organised in a tree setup where each node in the tree represents either a device (e.g. "TV"), a property of that device (e.g. "channel"), or actions that trigger some change in one of the devices (e.g. "one", child of "channel", will change the TV to channel one). When the system transitions to one of the terminal nodes that trigger an action, the action associated with this node is performed, and subsequently the system returns to the root node. In the following experiments a dialogue will be considered finished when one of the *terminal node actions* is carried out. In the non-terminal nodes, the user may either speak one of the commands available in that node (defined by its children nodes) to transition to them, or say the meta-command "back" to return to its parent node. The ASR is configured to recognise single words, so there is no need for a language understanding system, as the concepts are just a direct mapping from the ASR output. A more detailed explanation of the system is given in (Casanueva et al., 2014) and two example dialogues are presented in Appendix B.

3.1 Simulated dysarthric users

In the homeService application, each system is personalised for a single speaker by adapting the ASR system's acoustic model as more data is gathered through interaction, thus increasing the accuracy of the ASR over time. In the following experiments, the system is tested by interacting with a set of *simulated users* with dysarthria, where each user interacts with a set of different ASR simulators, arising from the different amounts of data used to adapt the ASR. To train the ASR simulator for these users, data from a dysarthric speech database (UASpeech database (Kim et al., 2008)) has been used. Table 1 shows the characteristics of the 15 speakers of the database, and the ASR accuracy for each speaker in the 36 word vocabulary of the system without adaptation and adapted with 500 words from that speaker. Additionally, an intelligibility measure assessment is presented for each speaker as the percentage of words spoken by each speaker which are understood by unfamiliar speakers; these are shown in the second column in table 1.

The system is tested with 6 different simulated users trained with data from low and medium intelligibility[3] speakers. Each user interacts with 4 different ASRs, adapted with 0, 150, 300 and 500 words respectively. For a more detailed explanation of the simulated users configuration, the reader may refer to (Casanueva et al., 2014).

3.2 POMDP setup

Each non-terminal node in the tree is modelled as an independent POMDP where the state set $\mathcal{S}$ is the set of possible goals of the node and the action set $\mathcal{A}$ is the set of actions associated with each goal plus an "ask" action, which requests the user to repeat his last command. The reward function for all the POMDPs is -1 for the "ask" action, and +10 for each other action if it corresponds to the user goal, or -10 otherwise, and $\gamma = 0.95$. The state tracker is a logistic regression classifier (Pedregosa et al., 2011), where classes are the set of states $\mathcal{S}$. The belief state $\mathbf{b}$ is computed as the posterior over the states given the last 5 observations (N-best lists with normalised confidence scores). For each speaker, the state tracker has been trained with data from the other 14 speakers.

[3]In (Casanueva et al., 2014) it was shown that, with a 36 command setup, statistical DM is most useful for low and medium intelligibility speakers. For high intelligibility speakers, the ASR accuracy is close to 100% so the improvement obtained from DM is small, and for very low intelligibility speakers, the absolute performance is not high enough to make the system useful.

Speaker intelligibility	Range of int. measures	Number of speakers	Speaker independent ASR accuracy range	Adapted ASR accuracy range
Very low	2% - 15%	4	12.04% - 46.80%	23.06% - 74.37%
Low	28% - 43%	3	27.04% - 55.99%	80.52% - 95.28%
Medium	58% - 62%	3	55.34% - 68.34%	85.93% - 89.61%
High	86% - 95%	5	68.14% - 97.76%	95.38% - 100.00%

Table 1: *Stats for the UASpeech database*

3.3 Policy models

The DTC approach (eq. 8) is used to compute the Q-function for the policy (eq. 9) with Gaussian noise variance $\sigma^2 = 5$. The kernel over the belief space is a radial basis function kernel (RBF):

$$k^b(\mathbf{b}_i, \mathbf{b}_j) = \sigma_k^2 \exp\left(-\frac{||\mathbf{b}_i - \mathbf{b}_j||^2}{2l_k^2}\right) \quad (13)$$

with variance $\sigma_k^2 = 25$ and lengthscale $l_k^2 = 0.5$. The delta kernel is used over the action space:

$$k^a(a_i, a_j) = \delta(a_i, a_j) = \begin{cases} 1 \text{ if } a_i = a_j \\ 0 \text{ otherwise} \end{cases} \quad (14)$$

and the kernels over the speaker space are defined in section 3.4. The size of the inducing set $\mathbf{U}_m$ is 500 and the maximum size of the TD points set $\mathbf{Z}_t$ is 2000. Whenever a new data point is observed from the target speaker, it is added to the set of inducing points $\mathbf{U}_m$, and the first point of the set $\mathbf{U}_m$ (which, due to the ordering done by data selection, corresponds to the least similar source point or to the oldest target point) is discarded from the inducing set. Whenever a new data point is observed and the size of the set of temporal difference points $|\mathbf{Z}_t| = 2000$, the first point of this set is discarded. Three variations of the DTC approach are used:

- *DTC*: Equation 8 is used to compute the Q posterior for the policy (eq. 9) and the set of temporal difference points $\mathbf{Z}_t$ is initialised with the source points.
- *Prior*: Equation 11 is used to compute the Q posterior for the policy (eq. 9) and the prior GP is trained with the source points.
- *Hybrid*: Equation 11 is used to compute the Q posterior for the policy (eq. 9), the prior GP is trained with half of the source points and the set of temporal difference points $\mathbf{Z}_t$ is initialised with the other half.

3.4 Speaker similarities

To compute the similarities between speakers a vector of speaker features $\mathbf{s}$ must be extracted. Different kinds of features may be extracted, such as meta-data based features, acoustic features, features related to the ASR performance, etc. In this paper, we explore 3 different methods to extract $\mathbf{s}$;

- *Intelligibility assessment*: The intelligibility assessment for each speaker in the UASpeech database (table 1) can be used as a single dimensional feature.
- *I-vectors*: Martínez et al. (2013) showed that *i-vectors* (Dehak et al., 2011) can be used to predict the intelligibility of a dysarthric speaker. For each speaker, $\mathbf{s}$ is defined as a 400 dimensional vector corresponding to the mean *i-vector* extracted from each utterance from that speaker. For more information on the *i-vector* extraction and characteristics, refer to (Martínez et al., 2014).
- *ASR accuracy*: The performance statistics of the ASR (e.g. accuracy) can be used as speaker features. In this paper we use the accuracy per word (command), defining $\mathbf{s}$ as a 36 dimensional vector where each element is the ASR accuracy for each of the 36 commands.

The kernel over the speaker space k^s (eq. 12), is defined as an RBF kernel (eq. 13). This kernel is used both to compute the similarity between speakers in order to select data (section 2.1.2), and to weight the data from each source speaker (section 2.1.3). k^s has variance $\sigma_k^2 = 1$ and the lengthscale l_k^2 varies depending on the features. For intelligibility features $l_k^2 = 0.5$, for *i-vectors* $l_k^2 = 8.0$ and for ASR accuracy features $l_k^2 = 4.0$

4 Results

In the following experiments the *reward* is computed as -1 for each dialogue turn, +20 if the dialogue was successful[4]. The system has been tested

[4]Because of the variable depth tree structure of the spoken dialogue system, the sum or average of cumulative rewards obtained in each sub-dialogue is not a good measure of the overall system performance. If the dialogue gets stuck in a loop going back and forth between two sub-dialogues, the extra amount of turns spent in this loop would not be reflected in the average of rewards

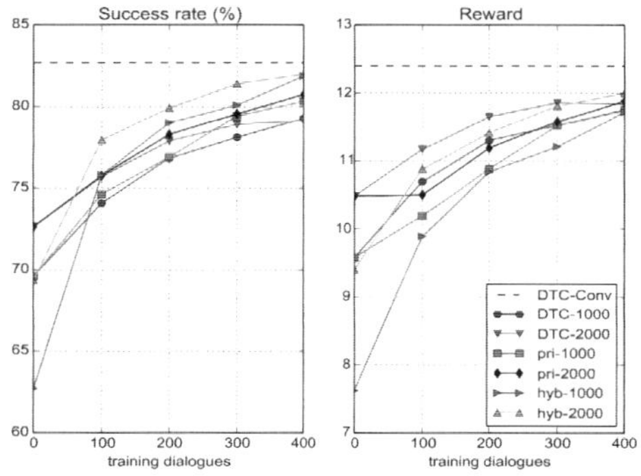

Figure 1: *different policy models compared*

with the 24 speaker-ASR pairs explained in section 3.1, and in the following figures, each plotted line is the average results for these 24 speaker-ASR pairs. As the behaviour of the simulated user and some data selection methods partially depend on random variables, each experiment has been initialised with four different seeds and all the results presented are the average of the four seeds tested over 500 dialogues. In all the experiments the data to initialise each POMDP is transferred from a pool of 4200 points corresponding to 300 points from each speaker in table 1 except the speaker being tested, where each data pool is different for each seed.

Figure 1 compares the different policy models presented in section 3.3 using the intelligibility measure based similarity to select and weight the data. The dotted line named *DTC-conv* shows the performance of the DTC policy when trained until convergence with the target speaker by simulating 1200 sub-dialogues in each node. *DTC-1000* and *DTC-2000* show the performance of the basic DTC approach when 1000 and 2000 source points are transferred respectively. It can be observed that, transferring more points boosts the performance, but at the cost of increasing the complexity. *pri-1000* and *pri-2000* show the performance of the prior policy with 1000 and 2000 transfer points respectively. The success rate is above the DTC policy but the learning rate for the reward is slower. This might be because the small amount of target data points make the predictions of the Q-function given by the GP unreliable. *Hyb-1000* and *hyb-2000* show the performance of the hybrid model, showing the best behaviour on success rate after 100 dialogues, and for *hyb-2000* even outperforming *DTC-2000* in reward after 400 dialogues.

In figure 2 the different approaches to compute the speaker similarities for data selection and weighting presented in section 3.4 are compared, using the DTC model with 1000 transfer points (named *DTC-1000* in the previous figure). *DTC-int* uses the intelligibility measure based features, *DTC-iv* the *i-vector* features and *DTC-acc* the ASR accuracy based features. *DTC-iv* outperforms the other two features, followed closely by *DTC-acc*. The performance of *DTC-int* is way below the other two metrics, suggesting that the information given by intelligibility assessments is a weak feature for source speaker selection (as it is done by humans, it might be very noisy). As *DTC-acc* uses information about the ASR statistics (which is the input for the dialogue manager), it might be expected that it will outperform the rest, but in this case a purely acoustic based measure such as the *DTC-iv* works better. The reason for this might be that these features are not correlated to the ASR performance, so hidden variables are used to better organise the data. To investigate the usefulness of similarity based data selection, two different data selection methods which do not weight the transferred data have been tried. *DTC-randspk* selects the ordering of the speakers from whom the data is transferred at random, and has a much worse performance than the similarity based method, but *DTC-allspk* selects the 1000 source points from all the speakers, selecting 1000 points at random from the pool of 4200 points and, as it can be seen, the reward obtained by this method is slightly better than with *DTC-iv*, even if the success rate is lower. This suggests that transferring points from more speakers rather than from just the closest ones is a better strategy, probably because points selected by this method are distributed more uniformly over the belief-action space. A method which does a trade-off between filling the belief-action space while selecting the most similar points could be a better option.

To further investigate the effect of selection and weighting of the data, figure 3 plots the results for the DTC policy model using the *i-vector* based similarity to weight the data but different data selection methods. *iv-clo* selects the closest speakers with respect to the *i-vector* metric, *iv-randspk* orders the speakers at random, and *iv-allspk* selects the 1000 transfer points from all the speakers but the tested one. As in the previous figure, selecting speakers by similarity works better than selecting speakers at random, but selecting the points from all the speakers and weighting them with the *i-vector* metric outperforms all the previous meth-

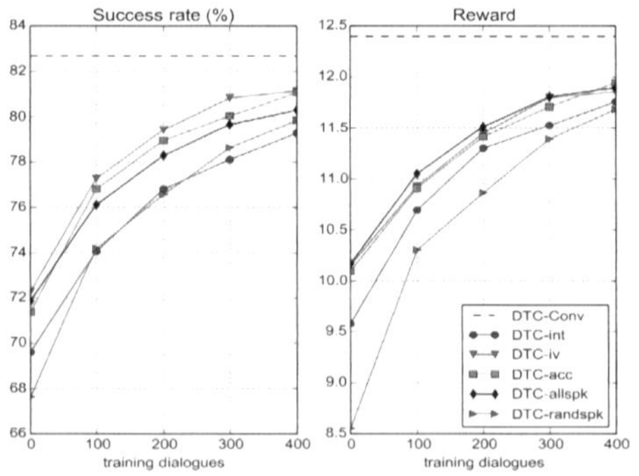

Figure 2: *different similarity metrics for data selection and weighting compared*

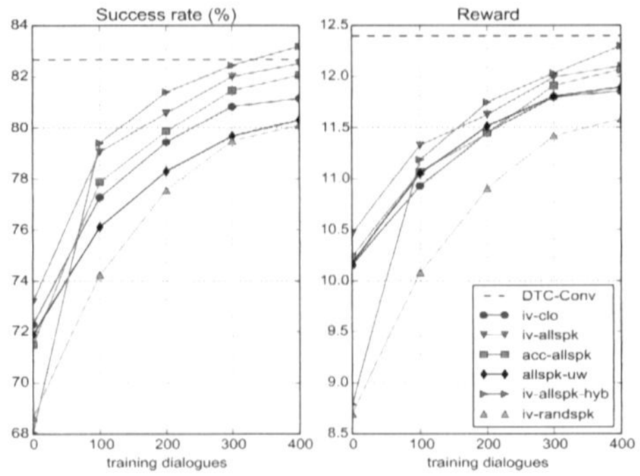

Figure 3: *different transfer data selection methods compared*

ods. This might be because weighting the data does a kind of data selection, as the data points from source speakers closer to the target will have more influence than the further ones, while transferring points from all the speakers covers a bigger part of the belief-action space. *acc-allspk* and *allspk-uw* show the results of weighting the data with the ASR accuracy metric and not weighting the data respectively, when selecting the data from all speakers. The accuracy metric performs worse than the *i-vector* metric once again, but it still outperforms not weighting the data, suggesting that data weighting works for different metrics. Finally *iv-allspk-hyb* plots the performance of the hybrid model when selecting the data from all the speakers and weighting it with the *i-vector* based similarity. Even if it is computationally cheaper, it outperforms *iv-allspk* after 100 dialogues, suggesting that with a good similarity metric and data selection method, the hybrid model in section 3.3 is the best option to take.

5 Conclusions

When transferring knowledge between speakers in a GP-RL based policy, weighting the data by using a similarity metric between speakers, and to a lesser extent, selecting the data using this similarity, improves the performance of the dialogue manager. By defining a kernel between temporal difference points and interpreting the Q-function as a GP regression problem where data points are in the TD space, sparse methods that allow the selection of the subset of inducing points such as DTC can be applied. In a transfer learning scenario, DTC permits a larger number of data points to be transferred and the selection of points collected from the target speaker as inducing points.

We showed that using part of the transferred data to train a prior GP for the mean function, and the rest to initialize the set of points of the GP, improves the performance of each of these approaches. Transferring data points from a larger number of speakers outperformed selecting the data points only from the more similar ones, probably because the belief-action space is covered better. This suggests that more complex data selection algorithms that trade-off between selecting the data points by similarity and covering more uniformly the belief-action space should be used. Also, increasing the amount of data transferred increased the performance, but the complexity increase of GP-RL limits the amount of data that can be transferred. More computationally efficient ways to transfer the data could be studied.

Of the three metrics based on speaker features tested (speaker intelligibility, *i-vectors* and ASR accuracy), *i-vectors* outperformed the rest. This suggest that *i-vectors* are a potentially good feature for speaker specific dialogue management and could be used in other tasks such as state tracking. ASR accuracy based metrics also outperformed the intelligibility based one, and as ASR accuracy and *i-vector* are uncorrelated features, a combination of them could give further improvement.

Finally, as the models were tested with simulated users in a hierarchically structured dialogue system (following the structure of the homeService application), future work directions include evaluating the policy models in a mixed initiative dialogue system and testing them with real users.

Acknowledgements

The research leading to these results was supported by the University of Sheffield studentship network PIPIN and EPSRC Programme Grant EP/I031022/1 (Natural Speech Technology). The authors would like to thank David Martínez for providing the *i-vectors* used in this paper.

References

I. Casanueva, H. Christensen, T. Hain, and P. Green. 2014. *Adaptive speech recognition and dialogue management for users with speech disorders*. Proceedings of Interspeech.

H. Christensen, S. Cunningham, C. Fox, P. Green, and T. Hain. 2012. *A comparative study of adaptive, automatic recognition of disordered speech*. Proceedings of Interspeech.

H. Christensen, I. Casanueva , S. Cunningham, P. Green, and T. Hain. 2013. *homeService: Voice-enabled assistive technology in the home using cloud-based automatic speech recognition*. Proceedings of SLPAT.

H. Christensen, I. Casanueva , S. Cunningham, P. Green, and T. Hain. 2014. *Automatic selection of speakers for improved acoustic modelling: recognition of disordered speech with sparse data*. Proceedings of SLT.

N. Dehak, P. Kenny, R. Dehak, P. Dumouchel, P. Ouellet. 2011. *Front-end factor analysis for speaker verification*. IEEE Transactions on Audio, Speech, and Language Processing.

Y. Engel, S. Mannor, R. Meir. 2003. *Bayes Meets Bellman: The Gaussian Process Approach to Temporal Difference Learning*. Proceedings of ICML.

Y. Engel, S. Mannor, R. Meir. 2005. *Reinforcement learning with Gaussian processes*. Proceedings of ICML.

M. Gašić, C. Breslin, M. Henderson, D. Kim, M. Szummer, B. Thomson, P. Tsiakoulis and S. Young. 2013. *On-line policy optimisation of Bayesian spoken dialogue systems via human interaction*. Proceedings of ICASSP.

M. Gašić, C. Breslin, M. Henderson, D. Kim, M. Szummer, B. Thomson, P. Tsiakoulis and S. Young. 2013. *POMDP-based dialogue manager adaptation to extended domains*. Proceedings of SIGDIAL.

M. Gašić and S. Young. 2014. *Gaussian Processes for POMDP-based dialogue manager opimisation*. IEEE Transactions on Audio, Speech and Language Processing.

M. Geist and O. Pietquin. 2011. *Managing uncertainty within the KTD framework*. Proceedings of JMLR.

F. Jurčíček, B. Thomson, and S. Young. 2012. *Reinforcement learning for parameter estimation in statistical spoken dialogue systems*. Computer Speech and Language.

H. Kim, M. Hasegawa-Johnson, A. Perlman, J. Gunderson, T. Huang, K. Watkin, and S. Frame. 2008. *Dysarthric speech database for universal access research*. Proceedings of Interspeech.

D. Martínez, P. Green and H. Christensen. 2013. *Dysarthria Intelligibility Assessment in a Factor Analysis Total Variability Space*. Proceedings of Interspeech.

D. Martínez, E. Lleida, P. Green, H. Christensen, A. Ortega and A. Miguel. 2015. *Intelligibility Assessment and Speech Recognizer Word Accuracy Rate Prediction for Dysarthric Speakers in a Factor Analysis Subspace*. ACM Transactions on Accessible Computing (TACCESS), Volume 6 Number 3. (Accepted)

S. Pan and Q. Yang. 2010. *A Survey on Transfer Learning*. IEEE Transactions on Knowledge and Data Engineering.

F. Pedregosa et al. 2011. *Scikit-learn: Machine Learning in Python*. Journal of Machine Learning Research.

J. Quiñonero and C. Rasmussen. 2005. *A Unifying View of Sparse Approximate Gaussian Process Regression*. Journal of Machine Learning Research.

C. Rasmussen and C. Williams. 2005. *Gaussian Processes for Machine Learning*,. MIT Press.

R. Sutton and G. Barto. 1998. *Introduction to Reinforcement Learning*. MIT Press.

M. Taylor, and P. Stone. 2009. *Transfer learning for reinforcement learning domains: A survey*. The Journal of Machine Learning Research.

B. Thomson, and S. Young. 2010. *Bayesian update of dialogue state: A POMDP framework for spoken dialogue systems*. Computer Speech and Language.

J. Williams and S. Young. 2007. *Partially observable Markov decision processes for spoken dialog systems*. Computer Speech and Language.

J. Williams. 2014. *Web-style Ranking and SLU Combination for Dialog State Tracking*. Proceedings of SIGDIAL.

S. Young, M. Gašić, B. Thomson and J. D. Williams. 2013. *POMDP-Based Statistical Spoken Dialog Systems: A Review*. Proceedings of the IEEE.

Appendix A. Temporal difference kernel

In equation 5, a linear transformation from the belief-action space to the temporal difference space is applied to the to the covariance vector $\mathbf{K}_{*,X}$ and to the covariance matrix $\mathbf{K}_{X,X}$ by multiplying them by the matrix $\mathbf{H}_t$. Deriving the term $\mathbf{H}_t\mathbf{K}_{X,X}\mathbf{H}_t^\top$ we obtain the matrix in eq. 15 (page bottom), where $k_{i,j}$ is the kernel function between two belief-action points $\mathbf{x}_i = (\mathbf{b}_i, a_i)$ and $\mathbf{x}_j = (\mathbf{b}_j, a_j)$, defined in eq. 4. The transformed matrix (eq. 15) has the form of a covariance matrix where each element is a sum of kernel functions $k_{i,j}$ between belief-action points on time i or $i+1$ weighted by the discount factors. So each element of this matrix can be defined as a function of 2 temporal differences between belief-action points (TD points), $\mathbf{z}_i = (\mathbf{b}_i, a_i, \mathbf{b}_{i+1}, a_{i+1})$ and $\mathbf{z}_j = (\mathbf{b}_j, a_j, \mathbf{b}_{j+1}, a_{j+1})$ in the form of (eq. 6):

$$k^{td}_{i,j} = (k_{i,j} + \gamma_i\gamma_j k_{i+1,j+1} - \gamma_i k_{i+1,j} - \gamma_j k_{i,j+1}) \quad (16)$$

where γ_i and γ_j will be 0 if a_i and a_j are terminal actions respectively. Deriving the term $\mathbf{K}_{*,X}\mathbf{H}_t^\top$ (and $\mathbf{H}_t\mathbf{K}_{X,*}$) we obtain:

$$\mathbf{K}_{*,X}\mathbf{H}_t^\top = \begin{bmatrix} (k_{1,*} & (k_{2,*} & \cdots & (k_{t-1,*} \\ -\gamma_1 k_{2,*}) & -\gamma_2 k_{3,*}) & & -\gamma_{t-1} k_{t,*}) \end{bmatrix} \quad (17)$$

which is a vector with $k^{td}_{i,*} = (k_{i,*} - \gamma_i k_{i+1,*})$ for each term. This is equivalent to equation 16 if the action of the new point a_* is considered a terminal action, thus $\gamma_* = 0$. Then, redefining the set of belief-action points $\mathbf{X}_t$ as the set of belief-action temporal difference points denoted as $\mathbf{Z}_t$, and defining $\mathbf{K}^{td}$ as the covariance matrix computed with the kernel function between two temporal difference points (eq. 6), eq. 7 can be derived from eq. 5 by doing the following substitutions: $\mathbf{K}_{*,X}\mathbf{H}_t^\top = \mathbf{K}^{td}_{*,Z}$, $\mathbf{H}_t\mathbf{K}_{X,*} = \mathbf{K}^{td}_{Z,*}$ and $\mathbf{H}_t\mathbf{K}_{X,X}\mathbf{H}_t^\top = \mathbf{K}^{td}_{Z,Z}$.

Appendix B. Example homeService dialogues

For a more detailed description of the hierarchical structure of the *homeService* environment, this appendix presents two example dialogues between an user and the system. The second column represents the actions taken either by the user (commands) or by the system (actions)

Dialogue 1: Goal = $\{$*TV, Channel, One*$\}$
Dialogue starts in node "Devices"

Sub-dialogue "Devices"

User	*TV* (Speaks the command "TV")
System	*Ask* (Requests to repeat last command)
User	*TV* (Repeats his last command)
System	*TV* (Dialogue transitions to node "TV")

Sub-dialogue "TV"

User	*Chan.* (Command "Channel")
System	*Chan.* (Transitions to node "Channel")

Sub-dialogue "Channel"

User	*One* (Command "One")
System	*One* (Performs action *TV-Channel-One*)

As an action has been taken in a terminal node, the dialogue ends.

Dialogue 2: Goal = $\{$*Hi-fi, On*$\}$
Dialogue starts in node "Devices"

Sub-dialogue "Devices"

User	*Hi-fi* (Command "Hi-fi")
System	*Light* (transitions to node Light)

Sub-dialogue "Light"

User	*Back* (Requests to go to previous node)
System	*Back* (transitions to node Devices)

Sub-dialogue "Devices"

User	*Hi-fi* (Command "Hi-fi")
System	*Hi-fi* (transitions to node Hi-fi)

Sub-dialogue "Hi-fi"

User	*On* (Command "On")
System	*Off* (Performs action *Hifi-Off*)

As the action taken in the terminal node does not match the goal, it is a failed dialogue.

$$\mathbf{H}_t\mathbf{K}_{X,X}\mathbf{H}_t^\top = \begin{bmatrix} (k_{1,1} + \gamma_1^2 k_{2,2} & (k_{1,2} + \gamma_1\gamma_2 k_{2,3} & \cdots & (k_{1,t_{-1}} + \gamma_1\gamma_{t-1} k_{2,t} \\ -2\gamma_1 k_{1,2}) & -\gamma_2 k_{2,2} - \gamma_1 k_{1,3}) & & -\gamma_{t-1} k_{2,t_{-1}} - \gamma_1 k_{1,t}) \\ (k_{1,2} + \gamma_1\gamma_2 k_{2,3} & (k_{2,2} + \gamma_2^2 k_{3,3} & \cdots & (k_{2,t_{-1}} + \gamma_2\gamma_{t-1} k_{3,t} \\ -\gamma_2 k_{2,2} - \gamma_1 k_{1,3}) & -2\gamma_2 k_{2,3}) & & -\gamma_{t-1} k_{3,t_{-1}} - \gamma_2 k_{2,t}) \\ \vdots & \vdots & \ddots & \vdots \\ (k_{1,t_{-1}} + \gamma_1\gamma_{t-1} k_{2,t} & (k_{2,t_{-1}} + \gamma_2\gamma_{t-1} k_{3,t} & \cdots & (k_{t_{-1},t_{-1}} + \gamma_{t-1}^2 k_{t,t} \\ -\gamma_{t-1} k_{2,t_{-1}} - \gamma_1 k_{1,t}) & -\gamma_{t-1} k_{3,t_{-1}} - \gamma_2 k_{2,t}) & & -2\gamma_{t-1} k_{t_{-1},t}) \end{bmatrix} \quad (15)$$

Miscommunication Recovery in Physically Situated Dialogue

Matthew Marge[*†]
[*]Army Research Laboratory
Adelphi, MD 20783
matthew.r.marge.civ@mail.mil

Alexander I. Rudnicky[†]
[†]Carnegie Mellon University
Pittsburgh, PA 15213
air@cs.cmu.edu

Abstract

We describe an empirical study that crowdsourced human-authored recovery strategies for various problems encountered in physically situated dialogue. The purpose was to investigate the strategies that people use in response to requests that are referentially ambiguous or impossible to execute. Results suggest a general preference for including specific kinds of visual information when disambiguating referents, and for volunteering alternative plans when the original instruction was not possible to carry out.

1 Introduction

Physically situated dialogue differs from traditional human-computer dialogue in that interactions will make use of reference to a dialogue agent's surroundings. Tasks may fail due to dependencies on specific environment configurations, such as when a robot's path to a goal is blocked. People will often help; in navigation dialogues they tend to ask proactive, task-related questions instead of simply signaling communication failure (Skantze, 2005). They supplement the agent's representation of the environment and allow it to complete tasks. The current study establishes an empirical basis for grounding in physically situated contexts. We had people provide recovery strategies for a robot in various situations.

The focus of this work is on recovery from *situated grounding problems*, a type of miscommunication that occurs when an agent fails to uniquely map a person's instructions to its surroundings (Marge and Rudnicky, 2013). A *referential ambiguity* is where an instruction resolves to more than one possibility (e.g., "Search the room on the left" when there are multiple rooms on the agent's left); an *impossible-to-execute* problem fails to resolve to any action (e.g., same instruction but there are no rooms on the agent's left). A common strategy evidenced in human-human corpora is for people to ask questions to recover from situated grounding problems (Tenbrink et al., 2010).

Dialogue divides into two levels: that of managing the actual dialogue—determining who has the floor, that an utterance was recognized, etc.—and the dialogue that serves the main *joint activities* that dialogue partners are carrying out, like a human-robot team exploring a new area (Bangerter and Clark, 2003). Most approaches to grounding in dialogue systems are managing the dialogue itself, making use of spoken language input as an indicator of understanding (e.g., (Bohus, 2007; Skantze, 2007)). Situated grounding problems are associated with the main joint activities; to resolve them we believe that the recovery model must be extended to include planning and environment information. Flexible recovery strategies make this possible by enabling dialogue partners to coordinate their joint activities and accomplish tasks.

We cast the problem space as one where the agent aims to select the most efficient recovery strategy that would resolve a user's intended referent. We expect that this efficiency is tied to the cognitive load it takes to produce clarifications. Viethen and Dale (2006) suggest a similar prediction in their study comparing human and automatically generated referring expressions of objects and their properties. We sought to answer the following questions in this work:

- How good are people at detecting situated grounding problems?
- How do people organize recovery strategies?
- When resolving ambiguity, which properties do people use to differentiate referents?
- When resolving impossible-to-execute instructions, do people use active or passive ways to get the conversation back on track?

Proceedings of the SIGDIAL 2015 Conference, pages 22–31,
Prague, Czech Republic, 2-4 September 2015.

We determined the most common recovery strategies for referential ambiguity and impossible-to-execute problems. Several patterns emerged that suggest ways that people expect agents to recover. Ultimately we intend for dialogue systems to use such strategies in physically situated contexts.

2 Related Work

Researchers have long observed miscommunication and recovery in human-human dialogue corpora. The HCRC MapTask had a direction giver-direction follower pair navigate two dimensional schematics with slightly different maps (Anderson et al., 1991). Carletta (1992) proposed several recovery strategies following an analysis of this corpus. The SCARE corpus collected human-human dialogues in a similar scenario where the direction follower was situated in a three-dimensional virtual environment (Stoia et al., 2008).

The current study follows up an initial proposal set of recovery strategies for physically situated domains (Marge and Rudnicky, 2011). Others have also developed recovery strategies for situated dialogue. Kruijff et al. (2006) developed a framework for a robot mapping an environment that employed conversational strategies as part of the grounding process. A similar study focused on resolving misunderstandings in the human-robot domain using the Wizard-of-Oz methodology (Koulouri and Lauria, 2009). A body of work on referring expression generation uses object attributes to generate descriptions of referents (e.g., (Guhe and Bard, 2008; Garoufi and Koller, 2014)). Viethen and Dale (2006) compared human-authored referring expressions of objects to existing natural language generation algorithms and found them to have very different content.

Crowdsourcing has been shown to provide useful dialogue data: Manuvinakurike and DeVault (2015) used the technique to collect game-playing conversations. Wang et al. (2012) and Mitchell et al. (2014) have used crowdsourced data for training, while others have used it in real time systems (Lasecki et al., 2013; Huang et al., 2014).

3 Method

In this study, participants came up with phrases that a search-and-rescue robot should say in response to an operator's command. The participant's task was to view scenes in a virtual environment then formulate the robot's response to an operator's request. Participants listened to an operator's verbal command then typed in a response.

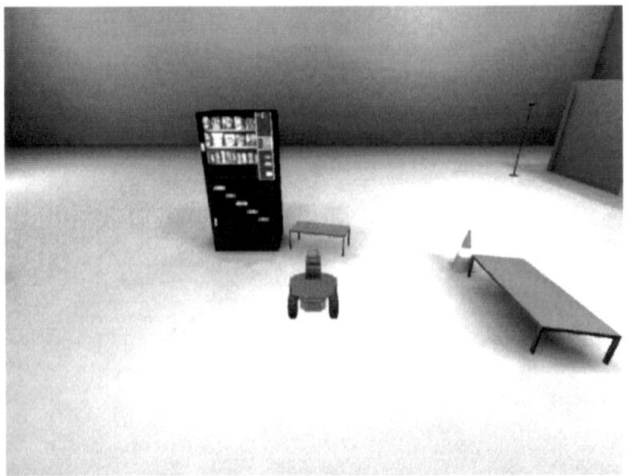

Figure 1: An example trial where the operator's command was "Move to the table". In red is the robot (*centered*) pointed toward the back wall. Participants would listen to the operator's command and enter a response into a text box.

Scenes displayed one of three situations: *referential ambiguity* (more than one possible action), *impossible-to-execute* (zero possible actions), and *executable* (one possible action). The instructions showed some example problems. All situations involved one operator and one robot.

3.1 Experiment Design

After instructions and a practice trial, participants viewed scenes in one of 10 different environments (see Figure 1). They would first watch a fly-over video of the robot's environment, then view a screen showing labels for all possible referable objects in the scene. The participant would then watch the robot enter the first scene. The practice trial and instructions did not provide any examples of questions.

The robot would stop and a spoken instruction from the operator would be heard. The participant was free to replay the instruction multiple times. They would then enter a response (say an acknowledgment or a question). Upon completion of the trial, the robot would move to a different scene, where the process was repeated.

Only self-contained questions that would allow the operator to answer without follow-up were allowed. Thus generic questions like "which one?" would not allow the operator to give the robot enough useful information to proceed. In the instructions, we suggested that participants include some detail about the environment in their ques-

Trial Group	#PARTIC	#AMB	#IMP	#EXE
1	15	9	9	7
2	15	16	6	3
Total	30	25	15	10

Table 1: Distribution of stimulus types across the two trial groups of participants (PARTIC). Trials either had referential ambiguity (AMB), were impossible-to-execute (IMP), or executable (EXE).

tions.

Participants used a web form[1] to view situations and provide responses. We recorded demographic information (gender, age, native language, native country) and time on task. The instructions had several attention checks (Paolacci et al., 2010) to ensure that participants were focusing on the task.

We created fifty trials across ten environments. Each environment had five trials that represented waypoints the robot was to reach. Participants viewed five different environments (totaling twenty-five trials). Each command from the remote operator to the robot was a route instruction in the robot navigation domain. Trials were assembled in two groups and participants were assigned randomly to one (see Table 1). Trial order was randomized according to a Latin Square.

3.1.1 Scenes and Environments

Scenes were of a 3D virtual environment at eye level, with the camera one to two meters behind the robot. Camera angle issues with environment objects caused this variation.

Participants understood that the fictional operator was not co-located with the robot. The USARSim robot simulation toolkit and the UnrealEd game map editor were used to create the environment. Cepstral's SwiftTalker was used for the operator voice.

Of the fifty scenes, twenty-five (50%) had referential ambiguities, fifteen (30%) were impossible-to-execute, and ten (20%) were executable controls. The selection was weighted to referential ambiguity, as these were expected to produce greater variety in recovery strategies. We randomly assigned each of fifty trials a stimulus type according to this distribution, then divided the list into ten environments. The environments featured objects and doorways appropriate to the trial type, as well as waypoints.

[1] See http://goo.gl/forms/ZGpK3L1nPh for an example.

Referential Ambiguity We arranged the sources of information participants could use to describe referents, to enable analysis of the relationship between context and recovery strategies. The sources of information (i.e., "situated dimensions") were: (1) *intrinsic properties* (either color or size), (2) *history* (objects that the robot already encountered), (3) *egocentric proximity* of the robot to candidate referents around it (the robot's perspective is always taken), and (4) *object proximity* (proximity of candidate referents to other objects). Table 2 provides additional details.

Scenes with referential ambiguity had up to four sources of information available. Information sources were evenly distributed across five trial types: one that included all four sources, and four that included all but one source of information (e.g., one division excluded using history information but did allow proximity, spatial, and object properties, one excluded proximity, etc.).

Impossible-to-Execute The impossible-to-execute trials divided into two broad types. Nine of the fifteen scenes were impossible because the operator's command did not match to any referent in the environment. The other six scenes were impossible because a path to get to the matching referent was not possible.

Executable Ten scenes were executable for the study and served as controls. The operator's command mentioned existing, unambiguous referents.

3.1.2 Robot Capabilities

Participants were aware of the robot's capabilities before the start of the experiment. The instructions said that the robot knew the locations of all objects in the environment and whether doors were closed or open. The robot also knew the color and size of objects in the environment (*intrinsic properties*), where objects were relative to the robot itself and to other objects (*proximity*), when objects were right, left, in front, and behind it (*spatial terms*), the room and hallway locations of objects (*location*), and the places it has been (*history*, the robot kept track of which objects it had visited). The robot could not pass through closed doors.

3.2 Hypotheses

We made five hypotheses about the organization and content of participant responses to situated grounding problems:

Dimension	Property	#Scenes
Intrinsic (aka "perceptual feature")	On no dimension does the target referent share an intrinsic property value with any other object of its type. The two intrinsic properties are color and size.	20
History (aka "conceptual feature")	The robot already visited the referent once.	14
Object Proximity (aka "functional relation")	The referent has a unique, nearby object that can serve as a "feature" for reference purposes.	21
Egocentric Proximity (aka "spatial relation")	The referent has a unique spatial relationship relative to the robot. The relation is prototypical, generally falling along a supposed axis with the robot.	20

Table 2: Ambiguous scene referent description space. Number of scenes was out of 25 total. We relate the current terms to general types defined by Carlson and Hill (2009).

- *Hypothesis 1:* Participants will have more difficulty detecting impossible-to-execute scenes than ambiguous ones. Determining a robot's tasks to be impossible requires good *situation awareness* (Nielsen et al., 2007) (i.e., an understanding of surroundings with respect to correctly completing tasks). Detecting referential ambiguity requires understanding the operator's command and visually inspecting the space (Spivey et al., 2002); detecting impossible commands also requires recalling the robot's capabilities and noticing obstacles. Previous research has noted that remote teleoperators have trouble establishing good situation awareness of a robot's surroundings (Casper and Murphy, 2003; Burke et al., 2004). Moreover, obstacles near a robot can be difficult to detect with a restricted view as in the current study (Alfano and Michel, 1990; Arthur, 2000).
- *Hypotheses 2a and 2b:* Responses will more commonly be single, self-contained questions instead of a scene description followed by a question (2a for scenes with referential ambiguity, 2b for scenes that were impossible-to-execute). This should reflect the principle of *least effort* (Clark, 1996), and follow from Carletta's (1992) observations in a similar dataset.
- *Hypothesis 3:* Responses will use the situated dimensions that require the least cognitive effort when disambiguating referents. Viethen and Dale (2006) suggest that minimizing cognitive load for the speaker or listener would produce more human-like referring expressions. We predict that responses will mention visually salient features of the scene, such as color or size of referents, more than history or object proximity. Desimone and Duncan (1995) found that color and shape draw more attention than other properties in visual search tasks when they are highly distinguishable.
- *Hypothesis 4:* In cases of referential ambiguity where two candidate referents are present, responses will confirm one referent in the form of a yes-no question more than presenting a list. Results from an analysis of task-oriented dialogue suggests that people are efficient when asking clarification questions (Rieser and Moore, 2005). Additionally, Clark's *least effort* principle (Clark, 1996) suggests that clarifying one referent using a yes-no confirmation would require less effort than presenting a list in two ways: producing a shorter question and constraining the range of responses to expect.
- *Hypothesis 5:* For impossible-to-execute instructions, responses will most commonly be ways for the robot to proactively work with the operator's instruction, in an effort to get the conversation back on track. The other possible technique, to simply declare that the problem is not possible, will be less common. This is because participants will believe such a strategy will not align with the task goal of having the robot say something that will allow it to proceed with the task. Skantze found that in human-human navigation dialogues, people would prefer to look for alternative ways to proceed rather than simply express non-understanding (Skantze, 2005).

3.3 Measures

The key independent variable in this study was the stimulus type that the participant viewed (i.e., referential ambiguity, impossible-to-execute, or executable). Dependent variables were observational measurements, presented below. We report Fleiss' kappa score for inter-annotator agreement between three native English speaking annotators on a subset of the data.

Correctness ($\kappa = 0.77$): Whether participants correctly determined the situation as ambiguous, impossible, or executable. Annotators labeled correctness based on the content of participant responses. This measure assessed participant accuracy for detecting situated grounding problems. Either *correct* or *incorrect*.

Sentence type ($\kappa = 0.82$): Either *declarative*, *interrogative*, *imperative*, or *exclamatory* (Cowan, 2008).

Question type ($\kappa = 0.92$): Sentences that needed an answer from the operator. The three types were *yes-no questions*, *alternative questions* (which presented a list of options and includes *wh-* questions that used sources from Table 2), and generic *wh- questions* (Cowan, 2008).

Situated dimensions in response ($\kappa = 0.75$): The capability (or capabilities) that the participant mentioned when providing a response. The types were *intrinsic* (color or size), *object proximity*, *egocentric proximity*, and *history*.

Projected belief (impossible-to-execute trials only, $\kappa = 0.80$): The participant's belief about the next task, given the current operator instruction (projected onto the robot). The types were *unknown* (response indicates participant is unsure what to do next), *ask for more* (ask for more details), *propose alternative* (propose alternative object), *ask for help* (ask operator to physically manipulate environment), and *off topic*.

3.4 Participation

We recruited 30 participants. All participants completed the web form through the Amazon Mechanical Turk (MTurk) web portal[2], all were located in the United States and had a task approval rate $\geq$95%. The group included 29 self-reported native English speakers born in the United States; 1 self-reported as a native Bangla speaker born in Bangladesh. The gender distribution was 15 male to 15 female. Participants ranged in age from 22 to 52 (*mean:* 33 years, *std. dev.:* 7.7). They were paid between \$1 and \$2 for their participation. We collected a total of 750 responses.

[2]https://www.mturk.com

Problem Type	Sample Crowdsourced Responses
Referential Ambiguity	▹ *Do you mean the table in front of me?* ▹ *Should I go to the small or big table?*
Impossible-to-Execute	▹ *There is not a lamp behind me. Would you like for me to go to the lamp in front of me?* ▹ *Do you mean the lamp in front of me?*

Table 3: Participants composed recovery strategies in response to operator commands that were referentially ambiguous or impossible-to-execute.

4 Results

We analyzed the measures by tabulating frequencies for each possible value. Table 3 presents some example responses.

4.1 Correctness

In general, participants were good at detecting situated grounding problems. Out of 750 responses, 667 (89%) implied the correct scene type. We analyzed correctness across actual stimulus types (ambiguous, impossible-to-execute, executable) using a mixed-effects analysis of variance model[3], with participant included as a random effect and trial group as a fixed effect.

Hypothesis 1 predicted that participants will do better detecting scenes with referential ambiguity than those that were impossible-to-execute; the results support this hypothesis. Actual stimulus type had a significant main effect on correctness ($F[2, 58] = 12.3$, $p < 0.001$); trial group did not ($F[1, 28] = 0.1$, $p = 0.72$). Participants had significantly worse performance detecting impossible-to-execute scenes compared to ambiguous ones ($p < 0.001$; Tukey HSD test). In fact, they were four times worse; of the impossible-to-execute scenes, participants failed to detect that 22% (50/225) of them were impossible, compared to 5% (17/375) of scenes with referential ambiguity. Of the 150 instructions that were executable, participants failed to detect 11% (16/150) of them as such.

4.2 Referential Ambiguity

We analyzed the 358 responses where participants correctly detected referential ambiguity.

[3]This approach computed standard least squares regression using reduced maximum likelihood (Harville, 1977).

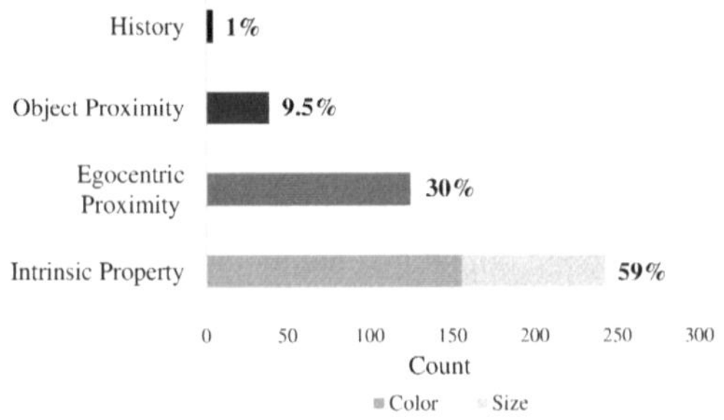

Figure 2: Counts of situated dimensions in recovery strategies for scenarios with referential ambiguity.

Hypothesis 2a predicted that participants would more commonly ask single, self-contained questions instead of describing the scene and asking a question. We assessed this by counting sentence types within a response. Responses that had both a declarative sentence and an interrogative would fit this case. The results confirmed this hypothesis. Only 4.5% (16/358) of possible responses had a declarative and an interrogative.

Hypothesis 3 predicted that participants would use the situated dimensions that require the least cognitive effort when disambiguating referents. More specifically, the most common mentions will be those that are visually apparent (intrinsic properties like color and size), while those that require more processing would have fewer mentions (history and to a lesser extent object proximity and egocentric proximity). We measured this by tabulating mentions of situated dimensions in all 358 correct participant responses, summarized in Figure 2. Multiple dimensions could occur in a single response. The results support this hypothesis. By far, across all ambiguous scenarios, the most mentioned dimension was an intrinsic property. More than half of all situated dimensions used were intrinsic (59%, 242/410 total mentions). This was followed by the dimensions that we hypothesize require more cognitive effort: egocentric proximity had 30% (125/410) of mentions, object proximity 9.5% (39/410), and history 1% (4/410). Of the intrinsic dimensions mentioned, most were only color (61%, 148/242), followed by size (33%, 81/242), and using both (5%, 13/242).

Hypothesis 4 predicted that participants would ask yes-no confirmation questions in favor of presenting lists when disambiguating a referent with exactly two candidates. The results suggest that the opposite is true; people strongly preferred to list options, even when a confirmation question about one would have been sufficient. Of the 285 responses that were correctly detected as ambiguous and were for scenes of exactly two possible referents, 74% (212/285) presented a list of options. Only 14% (39/285) asked yes-no confirmation questions. The remaining 34 questions (12%) were generic wh-questions. These results held in scenes where three options were present. Overall 72% (259/358) presented a list of options, while 16% (58/358) asked generic wh-questions and 11% (41/358) asked yes-no confirmations.

Projected Belief	Count	Percentage
Propose Alternative	72	41%
Unknown	56	32%
Ask for More	42	24%
Ask for Help	5	3%
Total	175	100%

Table 4: Projected belief annotations for the 175 correct detections of impossible-to-execute stimuli.

4.3 Impossible-to-Execute

We analyzed the 175 responses where participants correctly identified impossible-to-execute situations.

Hypothesis 2b predicted that participants would more often only ask a question than also describe the scene. Results confirmed this hypothesis. 42% (73/175) of responses simply asked a question, while 22% (39/175) used only a declarative. More than a third included a declarative as well (36%, 63/175). The general organization to these was to declare the problem then ask a question about it (89%, 56/63).

Hypothesis 5 predicted that responses for impossible-to-execute instructions will more commonly be proactive and make suggestions, instead of simply declaring that an action was not possible. Table 4 summarizes the results, which confirmed this hypothesis. The most common belief that participants had for the robot was to have it propose an alternative referent to the impossible one specified by the operator. The next-most common was to have the robot simply express uncertainty about what to do next. Though this belief occurred in about a third of responses, the remaining responses were all proactive ways for the robot to get the conversation back on track (i.e., propose alternative, ask for more, and ask for help).

5 Discussion

The results largely support the hypotheses, with the exception of Hypothesis 4. They also provide information about how people expect robots to recover from situated grounding problems.

Correctness Participants had the most trouble detecting impossible-to-execute scenes, supporting Hypothesis 1. An error analysis of the 50 responses for this condition had participants responding as if the impossible scenes were possible (62%, 31/50). The lack of good situation awareness was a factor, which agrees with previous findings in the human-robot interaction literature (Casper and Murphy, 2003; Burke et al., 2004). We found that participants had trouble with a specific scene where they confused the front and back of the robot (9 of the 31 impossible-executable responses were for this scene). Note that all scenes showed the robot entering the room with the same perspective, facing forward.

Referential Ambiguity Results for Hypothesis 2a showed that participants overwhelmingly asked only a single, self-contained question as opposed to first stating that there was an ambiguity. Participants also preferred to present a list of options, despite the number of possible candidates. This contradicted Hypothesis 4. Rieser and Moore (2005) found that in task-oriented human-human dialogues, clarification requests aim to be as efficient as possible; they are mostly partially formed. The results in our study were not of real-time dialogue; we isolated specific parts of what participants believed to be human-computer dialogue. Moreover, Rieser and Moore were observing clarifications at Bangerter and Clark's (2003) dialogue management level; we were observing them in service of the joint activity of navigating the robot. We believe that this difference resulted in participants using caution by disambiguating with lists.

These results suggest that dialogue systems should present detection of referential ambiguity implicitly, and as a list. Generic *wh-* questions (e.g., "which one?" without presenting a follow-on list) are less desirable because they don't constrain what the user can say, and don't provide any indication of what the dialogue system can understand. A list offers several benefits: it grounds awareness of surroundings, presents a fixed set of options to the user, and constrains the range of linguistic responses. This could also extend to general ambiguity, as in when there are a list of matches to a query, but that is outside the scope of this work. Lists may be less useful as they grow in size; in our study they could not grow beyond three candidates.

The data also supported Hypothesis 3. Participants generally preferred to use situated dimensions that required less effort to describe. Intrinsic dimensions (color and size) had the greatest count, followed by egocentric proximity, object proximity, and finally using history. We attribute these results to the salient nature of intrinsic properties compared to ones that must be computed (i.e., egocentric and object proximity require spatial processing, while history requires thinking about previous exchanges). This also speaks to a similar claim by Viethen and Dale (2006). Responses included color more than any other property, suggesting that an object's color draws more visual attention than its size. Bright colors and big shapes stand out most in visual search tasks; we had more of the former than the latter (Desimone and Duncan, 1995).

For an ambiguous scene, participants appear to traverse a *salience hierarchy* (Hirst et al., 1994) whereby they select the most visually salient feature that also uniquely teases apart candidates. While the salience hierarchy varies depending on the current context of a referent, we anticipate such a hierarchy can be defined computationally. Others have proposed similar processes for referring expression generation (Van Der Sluis, 2005; Guhe and Bard, 2008). One way to rank salience on the hierarchy could be predicted mental load; we speculate that this is a reason why history was barely mentioned to disambiguate. Another would be to model visual attention, which could explain why color was so dominant.

Note that only a few dimensions were "competing" at any given time, and their presence in the scenes was equal (save for history, which had slightly fewer due to task design constraints). Egocentric proximity, which uses spatial language to orient candidate referents relative to the robot, had a moderate presence. When intrinsic properties were unavailable in the scene, responses most often used this property. We found that sometimes participants would derive this property even if it wasn't made prototypical in the scene (e.g., referring to a table as "left" when it was in front and off to the left side of the robot). This suggests that using egocentric proximity to disambiguate makes a good fallback strategy when nothing else works. Another situated dimension emerged from the responses, disambiguation by location (e.g., "Do you mean the box in this room or the other one?"). Though not frequent, it provides another useful technique to disambiguate when visually salient properties are not available.

Our findings differ from those of Carlson and Hill (2009) who found that salience is not as prominent as spatial relationships between a target (in the current study, this would be the robot) and other objects. Our study did not direct participants to formulate spatial descriptions; they were free to compose responses. In addition, our work directly compares intrinsic properties for objects of the same broad type (e.g., disambiguation of a doors of different colors). Our findings suggest the opposite of Moratz et al. (2003), who found that when pointing out an object, describing its position may be better than describing its attributes in human-robot interactions. Their study only had one object type (cube) and did not vary color, size, or proximity to nearby objects. As a result, participants described objects using spatial terms. In our study, we explored variation of several attributes to determine participants' preferences.

Impossible-to-Execute Results supported Hypothesis 2b. Most responses had a single sentence type. Although unanticipated, a useful strategy emerged: describe the problem that makes the scene impossible, then propose an alternative referent. This type of strategy helped support Hypothesis 5. Responses for impossible scenes largely had the participant proactively presenting a way to move the task forward, similar to what Skantze (2005) observed in human-human dialogues. This suggests that participants believed the robot should ask directed questions to recover. These questions often took the form of posing alternative options.

5.1 Limitations

We used the Amazon Mechanical Turk web portal to gather responses in this study. As such we could not control the participant environment when taking the study, but we did include attention checks. Participants did not interact with a dialogue system. Instead we isolated parts of the interaction that were instances of where the robot would have to say something in response to an instruction. We asked participants to provide what they think the robot should say; there was no ongoing interaction. However, we maintained continuity by presenting videos of the robot navigating through the environment as participants completed the task. The robot was represented in a virtual environment, which prevents us from understanding if there are any influencing factors that may impact results if the robot were in physical form or co-present with the participant.

6 Conclusions

Recovery strategies allow situated agents like robots to recover from misunderstandings by using the human dialogue partner. We conducted a study that collected recovery strategies for physically situated dialogue with the goal of establishing an empirical basis for grounding in physically situated contexts. We crowdsourced 750 written strategies across 30 participants and analyzed their situated properties and how they were organized.

We found that participants' recovery strategies minimize cognitive effort and indicate a desire to successfully complete the task. For disambiguation, there was a preference for strategies that use visually salient properties over ones that require additional mental processing, like spatial reasoning or memory recall. For impossible-to-execute scenes, responses more often presented alternative referents than just noting non-understanding. We should note that some differences between our findings and those of others may in part rest on differences in task and environment, though intrinsic variables such as mental effort will likely persist over different situations.

In future work, we intend to use these data to model salience ranking in similar contexts. We will further assess the hypothesis that participants' preferences in this study will enhance performance in a spoken dialogue system that deploys similar strategies.

Acknowledgments

The authors thank Prasanna Kumar Muthukumar and Juneki Hong for helping to annotate recovery strategies. We also thank Taylor Cassidy, Arthur William Evans, and the anonymous reviewers for their valuable comments.

References

Patricia L. Alfano and George F. Michel. 1990. Restricting the field of view: Perceptual and performance effects. *Perceptual and Motor Skills*, 70(1):35–45.

Anne H. Anderson, Miles Bader, Ellen Gurman Bard, Elizabeth Boyle, Gwyneth Doherty, Simon Garrod, Stephen Isard, Jacqueline Kowtko, Jan McAllister, Jim Miller, Catherine Sotillo, Henry S. Thompson, and Regina Weinert. 1991. The HCRC Map Task Corpus. *Language and Speech*, 34(4):351–366.

Kevin Wayne Arthur. 2000. *Effects of field of view on performance with head-mounted displays*. Ph.D. thesis, University of North Carolina at Chapel Hill.

Adrian Bangerter and Herbert H. Clark. 2003. Navigating joint projects with dialogue. *Cognitive Science*, 27(2):195–225.

Dan Bohus. 2007. *Error Awareness and Recovery in Conversational Spoken Language Interfaces*. Ph.D. thesis, Carnegie Mellon University.

Jennifer L. Burke, Robin R. Murphy, Michael D. Coovert, and Dawn L. Riddle. 2004. Moonlight in Miami: Field study of human-robot interaction in the context of an urban search and rescue disaster response training exercise. *Human–Computer Interaction*, 19(1-2):85–116.

Jean Carletta. 1992. Planning to fail, not failing to plan: Risk-taking and recovery in task-oriented dialogue. In *Proc. of the 14th Conference on Computational Linguistics: Volume 3*, pages 896–900. Association for Computational Linguistics.

Laura A. Carlson and Patrick L. Hill. 2009. Formulating spatial descriptions across various dialogue contexts. In K. R. Coventry, T. Tenbrink, and J. Bateman, editors, *Spatial Language and Dialogue*. Oxford University Press.

Jennifer Casper and Robin R. Murphy. 2003. Human-robot interactions during the robot-assisted urban search and rescue response at the world trade center. *IEEE Transactions on Systems, Man, and Cybernetics, Part B: Cybernetics*, 33(3):367–385.

Herbert H. Clark. 1996. *Using Language*. Cambridge University Press.

Ron Cowan. 2008. *The Teacher's Grammar of English with Answers: A Course Book and Reference Guide*. Cambridge University Press.

Robert Desimone and John Duncan. 1995. Neural mechanisms of selective visual attention. *Annual Review of Neuroscience*, 18(1):193–222.

Konstantina Garoufi and Alexander Koller. 2014. Generation of effective referring expressions in situated context. *Language, Cognition and Neuroscience*, 29(8):986–1001.

Markus Guhe and Ellen Gurman Bard. 2008. Adapting referring expressions to the task environment. In *Proc. of the 30th Annual Conference of the Cognitive Science Society (CogSci)*, pages 2404–2409.

David A Harville. 1977. Maximum likelihood approaches to variance component estimation and to related problems. *Journal of the American Statistical Association*, 72(358):320–338.

Graeme Hirst, Susan McRoy, Peter Heeman, Philip Edmonds, and Diane Horton. 1994. Repairing conversational misunderstandings and non-understandings. *Speech Communication*, 15(3-4):213 – 229.

Ting-Hao K. Huang, Walter S. Lasecki, Alan L. Ritter, and Jeffrey P. Bigham. 2014. Combining non-expert and expert crowd work to convert web apis to dialog systems. In *Proc. of Second AAAI Conference on Human Computation and Crowdsourcing*.

Theodora Koulouri and Stanislao Lauria. 2009. Exploring miscommunication and collaborative behaviour in human-robot interaction. In *Proc. of SIGdial'09*, pages 111–119.

Geert-Jan Kruijff, Hendrik Zender, Patric Jensfelt, and Henrik I. Christensen. 2006. Situated dialogue and understanding spatial organization: Knowing what is where and what you can do there. In *Proc. of ROMAN'06*, pages 328–333.

Walter S. Lasecki, Rachel Wesley, Jeffrey Nichols, Anand Kulkarni, James F. Allen, and Jeffrey P. Bigham. 2013. Chorus: a crowd-powered conversational assistant. In *Proc. of the 26th Annual ACM Symposium on User Interface Software and Technology*, pages 151–162. ACM.

Ramesh Manuvinakurike and David DeVault. 2015. Pair me up: A web framework for crowd-sourced spoken dialogue collection. In *Proc. of IWSDS'15*.

Matthew Marge and Alexander I. Rudnicky. 2011. Towards overcoming miscommunication in situated dialogue by asking questions. In *Proc. of AAAI Fall Symposium Series - Building Representations of Common Ground with Intelligent Agents*, Washington, DC.

Matthew Marge and Alexander I. Rudnicky. 2013. Towards evaluating recovery strategies for situated grounding problems in human-robot dialogue. In *Proc. of ROMAN'13*, pages 340–341.

Margaret Mitchell, Dan Bohus, and Ece Kamar. 2014. Crowdsourcing language generation templates for dialogue systems. In *Proc. of INLG'14*.

Reinhard Moratz, Thora Tenbrink, John Bateman, and Kerstin Fischer. 2003. Spatial knowledge representation for human-robot interaction. In *Spatial Cognition III*, pages 263–286. Springer.

Curtis W Nielsen, Michael A Goodrich, and Robert W Ricks. 2007. Ecological interfaces for improving mobile robot teleoperation. *IEEE Transactions on Robotics*, 23(5):927–941.

Gabriele Paolacci, Jesse Chandler, and Panagiotis G. Ipeirotis. 2010. Running experiments on amazon mechanical turk. *Judgment and Decision Making*, 5(5):411–419.

Verena Rieser and Johanna D. Moore. 2005. Implications for generating clarification requests in task-oriented dialogues. In *Proc. of the ACL'05*, pages 239–246.

Gabriel Skantze. 2005. Exploring human error recovery strategies: Implications for spoken dialogue systems. *Speech Communication*, 45(3):325–341.

Gabriel Skantze. 2007. *Error Handling in Spoken Dialogue Systems: Managing Uncertainty, Grounding and Miscommunication*. Ph.D. thesis, KTH Royal Institute of Technology.

Michael J. Spivey, Michael K. Tanenhaus, Kathleen M. Eberhard, and Julie C. Sedivy. 2002. Eye movements and spoken language comprehension: Effects of visual context on syntactic ambiguity resolution. *Cognitive Psychology*, 45(4):447–481.

Laura Stoia, Darla M. Shockley, Donna K. Byron, and Eric Fosler-Lussier. 2008. Scare: A situated corpus with annotated referring expressions. In *Proc. of LREC'08*, Marrakesh, Morocco.

Thora Tenbrink, Robert J. Ross, Kavita E. Thomas, Nina Dethlefs, and Elena Andonova. 2010. Route instructions in map-based human-human and human-computer dialogue: A comparative analysis. *Journal of Visual Languages & Computing*, 21(5):292–309.

Ielka Francisca Van Der Sluis. 2005. *Multimodal Reference, Studies in Automatic Generation of Multimodal Referring Expressions*. Ph.D. thesis, University of Tilburg.

Jette Viethen and Robert Dale. 2006. Algorithms for generating referring expressions: Do they do what people do? In *Proc. of INLG'06*, pages 63–70.

William Yang Wang, Dan Bohus, Ece Kamar, and Eric Horvitz. 2012. Crowdsourcing the acquisition of natural language corpora: Methods and observations. In *Proc. of SLT'12*, pages 73–78.

Reinforcement Learning in Multi-Party Trading Dialog

Takuya Hiraoka
Nara Institute of Science and Technology
takuya-h@is.naist.jp

Kallirroi Georgila
USC Institute for Creative Technologies
kgeorgila@ict.usc.edu

Elnaz Nouri
USC Institute for Creative Technologies
nouri@ict.usc.edu

David Traum
USC Institute for Creative Technologies
traum@ict.usc.edu

Satoshi Nakamura
Nara Institute of Science and Technology
s-nakamura@is.naist.jp

Abstract

In this paper, we apply reinforcement learning (RL) to a multi-party trading scenario where the dialog system (learner) trades with one, two, or three other agents. We experiment with different RL algorithms and reward functions. The negotiation strategy of the learner is learned through simulated dialog with trader simulators. In our experiments, we evaluate how the performance of the learner varies depending on the RL algorithm used and the number of traders. Our results show that (1) even in simple multi-party trading dialog tasks, learning an effective negotiation policy is a very hard problem; and (2) the use of neural fitted Q iteration combined with an incremental reward function produces negotiation policies as effective or even better than the policies of two strong hand-crafted baselines.

1 Introduction

Trading dialogs are a kind of interaction in which an exchange of ownership of items is discussed, possibly resulting in an actual exchange. These kinds of dialogs are pervasive in many situations, such as marketplaces, business deals, school lunchrooms, and some kinds of games, like Monopoly or Settlers of Catan (Guhe and Lascarides, 2012). Most of these dialogs are non-cooperative (Traum, 2008; Asher and Lascarides, 2013), in the sense that mere recognition of the desire for one party to engage in a trade does not provide sufficient inducement for the other party to accept the trade. Usually a trade will only be accepted if it is in the perceived interest of each party. Trading dialogs can be considered as a kind of negotiation, in which participants use various tactics to try to reach an agreement. It is common to have dialogs that may involve multiple offers or even multiple trades. In this way, trading dialogs are different from other sorts of negotiation in which a single decision (possibly about multiple issues) is considered, for example partitioning a set of items (Nouri et al., 2013; Georgila et al., 2014). Another difference between trading dialogs and partitioning dialogs is what happens when a deal is not made. In partitioning dialogs, if an agreement is not reached, then participants get nothing, so there is a very strong incentive to reach a deal, which allows pressure and can result in a "chicken game", where people give up value in order to avoid a total loss. By contrast, in trading dialogs, if no deal is made, participants stick with the status quo. Competitive two-party trading dialogs may result in a kind of stasis, where the wealthier party will pass up mutually beneficial deals, in order to maintain primacy. On the other hand, multi-party trading dialogs involving more than two participants changes the dynamic again, because now a single participant cannot necessarily even block another from acquiring a missing resource, because it might be available through trades with a third party. A player who does not engage in deals may lose relative position, if the other participants make mutually beneficial deals.

In this paper, we present a first approach toward learning dialog policies for multi-party trading dialogs. We introduce a simple, but flexible game-like scenario, where items can have different values for different participants, and also where the value of an item can depend on the context of other items held. We examine a number of strategies for this game, including random, simple, and complex

Proceedings of the SIGDIAL 2015 Conference, pages 32–41,
Prague, Czech Republic, 2-4 September 2015.

hand-crafted strategies, as well as several reinforcement learning (RL) (Sutton and Barto, 1998) algorithms, and examine performance with different numbers and kinds of opponents.

In most of the previous work on statistical dialog management, RL was applied to cooperative slot-filling dialog domains. For example, RL was used to learn the policies of dialog systems for food ordering (Williams and Young, 2007a), tourist information (Williams and Young, 2007b), flight information (Levin et al., 2000), appointment scheduling (Georgila et al., 2010), and e-mail access (Walker, 2000). In these typical slot-filling dialog systems, the reward function depends on whether the user's goal has been accomplished or not. For example, in the food ordering system presented by Williams and Young (2007a), the dialog system earns higher rewards when it succeeds in taking the order from the user.

Recently, there has been an increasing amount of research on applying RL to negotiation dialog domains, which are generally more complex than slot-filling dialog because the system needs to consider its own goal as well as the user's goal, and may need to keep track of more information, e.g., what has been accepted or rejected so far, proposals and arguments on the table, etc. Georgila and Traum (2011) applied RL to the problem of learning negotiation dialog system policies for different cultural norms (individualists, collectivists, and altruists). The domain was negotiation between a florist and a grocer who had to agree on the temperature of a shared retail space. Georgila (2013) used RL to learn the dialog system policy in a two-issue negotiation domain where two participants (the user and the system) organize a party, and need to decide on both the day that the party will take place and the type of food that will be served. Also, Heeman (2009) modeled negotiation dialog for a furniture layout task, and Paruchuri et al. (2009) modeled negotiation dialog between a seller and buyer. More recently, Efstathiou and Lemon (2014) focused on non-cooperative aspects of trading dialog, and Georgila et al. (2014) used multi-agent RL to learn negotiation policies in a resource allocation scenario. Finally, Hiraoka et al. (2014) applied RL to the problem of learning cooperative persuasive policies using framing, and Nouri et al. (2012) learned models for cultural decision-making in a simple negotiation game (the Ultimatum Game). In contrast to typical slot-filling dialog systems, in these negotiation dialogs, the dialog system is rewarded based on the achievement of its own goals rather than those of its interlocutor. For example, in Georgila (2013), the dialog system gets a higher reward when its party plan is accepted by the other participant.

Note that in all of the previous work mentioned above, the focus was on negotiation dialog between two participants only, ignoring cases where negotiation takes place between more than two interlocutors. However, in the real world, multi-party negotiation is quite common. In this paper, as a first study on multi-party negotiation, we apply RL to a multi-party trading scenario where the dialog system (learner) trades with one, two, or three other agents. We experiment with different RL algorithms and reward functions. The negotiation strategy of the learner is learned through simulated dialog with trader simulators. In our experiments, we evaluate how the performance of the learner varies depending on the RL algorithm used and the number of traders. To the best of our knowledge this is the first study that applies RL to multi-party (more than two participants) negotiation dialog management. We are not aware of any previous research on dialog using RL to learn the system's policy in multi-party negotiation.[1]

Our paper is structured as follows. Section 2 provides an introduction to RL. Section 3 describes our multi-party trading domain. Section 4 describes the dialog state and set of actions for both the learner and the trader simulators, as well as the reward functions of the learner and the hand-crafted policies of the trader simulators. In Section 5, we present our evaluation methodology and results. Finally, Section 6 summarizes the paper and proposes future work.

2 Reinforcement Learning

Reinforcement learning (RL) is a machine learning technique for learning the policy of an agent

[1]Note that there is some previous work on using RL to learn negotiation policies among more than two participants. For example, Mayya et al. (2011) and Zou et al. (2014) used multi-agent RL to learn the negotiation policies of sellers and buyers in a marketplace. Moreover, Pfeiffer (2004) used RL to learn policies for board games where sometimes negotiation takes place among players. However, these works did not focus on negotiation dialog (i.e., exchange of dialog acts, such as offers and responses to offers), but only focused on specific problems of marketing or board games. For example, in Zou et al. (2014)'s work, RL was used to learn policies for setting selling/purchasing prices in order to achieve good payoffs.

that takes some action to maximize a reward (not only immediate but also long-term or delayed reward). In this section, we briefly describe RL in the context of dialog management. In dialog, the policy is a mapping function from a dialog state to a particular system action. In RL, the policy's goal is to maximize a reward function, which in traditional task-based dialog systems is user satisfaction or task completion (Walker et al., 1998). RL is applied to dialog modeling in the framework of Markov decision processes (MDPs) or partially observable Markov decision processes (POMDPs).

In this paper, we follow an MDP-based approach. An MDP is defined as a tuple $\langle S, A, P, R, \gamma \rangle$ where S is the set of states (representing different contexts) which the system may be in (the system's world), A is the set of actions of the system, $P : S \times A \rightarrow P(S, A)$ is the set of transition probabilities between states after taking an action, $R : S \times A \rightarrow \Re$ is the reward function, and $\gamma \in [0, 1]$ a discount factor weighting long-term rewards. At any given time step i the world is in some state $s_i \in S$. When the system performs an action $\alpha_i \in A$ following a policy $\pi : S \rightarrow A$, it receives a reward $r_i(s_i, \alpha_i) \in \Re$ and transitions to state s_{i+1} according to $P(s_{i+1}|s_i, \alpha_i) \in P$. The quality of the policy π followed by the agent is measured by the *expected future reward*, also called Q-function, $Q^\pi : S \times A \rightarrow \Re$.

We experiment with 3 different RL algorithms:

LinQ: This is the basic Q-learning algorithm with linear function approximation (Sutton and Barto, 1998). The Q-function is a weighted function of state-action features. It is updated whenever the system performs an action and gets a reward for that action (in contrast to batch RL mentioned below).

LSPI: In least-squares policy iteration (LSPI), the Q-function is also approximated by a linear function (similarly to LinQ). However, unlike LinQ, LSPI is a batch learning method. It samples the training data one or more times (batches) using a fixed system policy (the policy that has been learned so far), and the approximated Q-function is updated after each batch. We use LSPI because it has been shown to achieve higher performance than LinQ in some tasks (Lagoudakis and Parr, 2003).

NFQ: Neural fitted Q iteration (NFQ) uses a multi-layered perceptron as the Q-function approximator. Like LSPI, NFQ is a batch learning method. We introduce NFQ because it has been shown to perform well in some tasks (Riedmiller, 2005).

During training we use ϵ-greedy exploration, i.e., the system randomly selects an action with a probability of ϵ (we used a value of 0.1 for ϵ) otherwise it selects the action which maximizes the Q-function given the current state. During testing there is no exploration and the policy is dictated by the Q-values learned during training.

3 Multi-Party Trading Domain

Our domain is trading, where two or more traders have a number of items that they can keep or exchange with the other traders in order to achieve their goals. The value of each item for a trader is dictated by the trader's payoff matrix. So at the end of the interaction each trader earns a number of points based on the items that it holds and the value of each item. Note that each trader has its own payoff matrix. During the interaction, each trader can trade an item with the other traders (i.e., offer an item in exchange for another item). If the addressee of the offer accepts it, then the items of the traders involved in this exchange are updated. If the offer is not accepted, the dialog proceeds without any changes in the number of items that each trader possesses. To make the search space of possible optimal trading policies more tractable, we assume that each trader can only trade one item at a time, and also that each offer is addressed only to one other trader. Each trader can take the turn (decide to trade) in random order, unless there is a pending offer. That is, if a trader makes an offer to another trader, then the addressee of that offer has priority to take the next turn; the addressee can decide to accept the offer, or to do nothing, or to make a different offer. Note that the traders do not know each other's payoff matrices but they know the items that each trader owns. The dialog is completed after a fixed period of time passes or when all traders decide not to make any offers.

In our experiments, there are three types of items: apple, orange, and grape, and each trader may like, hate, or feel neutral about each type of fruit. At the end of the dialog the trader earns 100 points for each fruit that he likes, 0 points for each fruit that he is neutral to, and -100 points for each fruit that he hates. Payoff matrices are structured such that there is always one fruit that each trader likes, one fruit that he is neutral to, and one fruit that he hates. Furthermore, all traders can get a big payoff for having a fruit salad, i.e., the trader earns 500 additional points if he ends up with one fruit of each type. Thus even hated fruits may sometimes be beneficial, but only if they can be part of a fruit salad. Thus the outcome for a trader o_{tr} is calculated by Equation (1).

$$\begin{aligned} o_{tr} &= Pay(\text{apple}_{\text{tr}}) * Num(\text{apple}_{\text{tr}}) \\ &+ Pay(\text{orange}_{\text{tr}}) * Num(\text{orange}_{\text{tr}}) \\ &+ Pay(\text{grape}_{\text{tr}}) * Num(\text{grape}_{\text{tr}}) \\ &+ Pay(\text{salad}_{\text{tr}}) \end{aligned} \tag{1}$$

$$Pay(\text{salad}_{\text{tr}}) = \begin{cases} 500 & \text{if } Num(\text{apple}_{\text{tr}}) \geq 1 \\ & \text{and } Num(\text{orange}_{\text{tr}}) \geq 1 \\ & \text{and } Num(\text{grape}_{\text{tr}}) \geq 1 \\ 0 & \text{otherwise} \end{cases} \tag{2}$$

where Pay is a function which takes as argument a fruit type and returns the value of that fruit type for the trader, and Num shows the number of items of a particular fruit type that the trader possesses. At the beginning of each dialog, the initial conditions (i.e., number of items per fruit type and payoff matrix) of the traders (except for the learner) are randomly assigned. The learner always has the same payoff matrix for all dialogs, i.e., the learner always likes grape, always feels neutral about apple, and always hates orange. Also, the total number of fruits that the learner holds in the beginning of the dialog is always 3. However, the number of each fruit type that the learner holds is randomly initialized for each dialog, e.g., the learner could be initialized with (1 apple, 2 oranges, 0 grapes), or (1 apple, 1 orange, 1 grape), etc. The total number of fruits for each trader is determined based on his role (Rich: 4 items, Middle: 3 items, Poor: 2 items), which is also randomly assigned at the beginning of each dialog. Table 1 shows two example dialogs.

4 Methodology for Learning Multi-Party Negotiation Policies

In this section, we present our methodology for training the learner, including how we built our trader simulators. The trader simulators are used as negotiation partners of the learner for both training and evaluating the learner's policy (see Section 5).

4.1 Learner's Model

Below we define the reward function, sets of actions, and state of our MDP-based learner's model. Note that we use two kinds of rewards.

The first type of reward is based on Equation (3). In this case, the learner is rewarded based on its outcome only at the end of the dialog. In all other dialog turns i its reward is 0.

$$r_{end} = \begin{cases} o_{tr} & \text{if dialog ends} \\ 0 & \text{otherwise} \end{cases} \tag{3}$$

We also introduce an *incremental reward* for training, because rewarding a learning agent only at the end of the dialog makes the learning problem very difficult, thus sub-goals can be utilized to reward the learning agent incrementally (McGovern and Barto, 2001). The incremental reward at turn i is given by Equation (4), where $o_{tr}(i)$ is the outcome for a trader applied at time point i.

$$r_i' = \begin{cases} \gamma * o_{tr}(i) - o_{tr}(i-1) & \text{if } i > 0 \\ 0 & \text{if } i = 0 \end{cases} \tag{4}$$

This equation represents the improvement on the outcome of the learner at turn i compared to its outcome at the previous turn $i - 1$. Note that this implementation of the incremental reward function is basically the same as reward shaping, and has the following property (Ng et al., 1999; Asri et al., 2013): the policy learned by using Equation (4) maximizes the expectation of the cumulative reward given by Equation (3).

The learner's actions are presented below. By speaker we mean the trader who is performing the action. In this case, the speaker is the learner, but as we will see below this is also the set of actions that a trader simulator can perform.

Offer(A, I_s, I_a): offering addressee A to trade the speaker's item I_s for the addressee's item I_a.

Accept: accepting the most recent offer addressed to the speaker.

Keep: passing the turn without doing anything. If there is a pending offer addressed to the speaker, then this offer is rejected.

The dialog state consists of the *offered table* and the distribution of the items among the negotiators:

Offered table: The offered table consists of all possible tuples (Trading partner, Fruit requested, Fruit offered in return). If another

		Item			Outcome		
Speaker	Utterance	TR1	TR2	TR3	TR1	TR2	TR3
Dialog 1:							
1: TR1	TR2, could you give me an orange? I'll give you a grape. (Offer)	A: 0, O: 0, G: 3	A: 1, O: 1, G: 0	A: 0, O: 1, G: 2	0	-100	100
2: TR2	Okay. (Accept)	A: 0, O: 1, G: 2	A: 1, O: 0, G: 1	A: 0, O: 1, G: 2	100	0	100
Dialog 2:							
1: TR2	TR1, could you give me a grape? I'll give you a apple. (Offer)	A: 0, O: 0, G: 3	A: 1, O: 1, G: 0	A: 0, O: 1, G: 2	0	-100	100
2: TR1	I want to keep my fruits. (Keep)	A: 0, O: 0, G: 3	A: 1, O: 1, G: 0	A: 0, O: 1, G: 2	0	-100	100
3: TR3	TR2, could you give me an apple? I'll give you a grape. (Offer)	A: 0, O: 0, G: 3	A: 1, O: 1, G: 0	A: 0, O: 1, G: 2	0	-100	100
4: TR2	Okay. (Accept)	A: 0, O: 0, G: 3	A: 0, O: 1, G: 1	A: 1, O: 1, G: 1	0	100	500

Table 1: Examples of two trading dialogs among traders TR1, TR2, and TR3. In these examples, the payoff matrix of TR1 is (apple: -100, orange: 100, grape: 0), that of TR2 is (apple: -100, orange: 0, grape: 100), and that of TR3 is (apple: 0, orange: -100, grape: 100). Item and Outcome show the number of items per fruit type of each trader and the points that each trader has accumulated after an action. A stands for apple, O for orange, and G for grape.

agent makes an offer to the learner then the learner's offered table is updated. The dialog state is represented by binary variables (or features). In Example 1, we can see a dialog state in a 2-party dialog, after the learner receives an offer to give an orange and in return take an apple.

Number of items: The number of items for each fruit type that each negotiator possesses. Once a trade is performed, this part of the dialog state is updated in the dialog states of all agents involved in this trade.

4.2 Trader Simulator

In order to train the learner we need trader simulators to generate a variety of trading episodes, so that in the end the learner learns to follow actions that lead to high rewards and avoid actions that lead to penalties. The trader simulator has the same dialog state and actions as the learner. We have as many trader simulators as traders that the learner negotiates with. Thus in a 3-party negotiation we have 2 trader simulators. The policy of the trader simulator can be either hand-crafted, designed to maximize the reward function given by Equation (3); or random.

The hand-crafted policy is based on planning. More concretely, this policy selects an action based on the following steps:

1. Pre-compute all possible sets of items (called "hands", by analogy with card games, where

Example 1: Status of the learner's dialog state's features in a 2-party trading dialog (learner vs. Agent 1). Agent 1 has just offered the learner 1 apple for 1 of the learner's 2 oranges (but the learner has not accepted or rejected the offer yet). This is why the (Agent 1, orange, apple) tuple has value 1. Initially the learner has (O apples, 2 oranges, 1 grape) and Agent 1 has (1 apple, 0 oranges, 1 grape). Note that if we had more negotiators e.g., Agent 2, the dialog state would include features for offer tuples for Agent 2, and the number of items that Agent 2 possessed.

Trading partner	Item requested by partner	Item given by partner to learner	Occurrence binary value (used as feature)
Agent 1	apple	orange	0
	apple	grape	0
	orange	apple	1
	orange	grape	0
	grape	apple	0
	grape	orange	0

Agent who possesses fruits	Fruit type	Number of fruits (used as feature)
learner	apple	0
	orange	2
	grape	1
Agent 1	apple	1
	orange	0
	grape	1

each item is represented by a card), given the role of the trader (Rich, Middle, Poor) and how many items there can be in the hand.

2. Compute the valuation of each of the hands, according to the payoff matrix.
3. Based on the possible trades with the other agents, compute a set of achievable hands, and order them according to the valuations defined in step 2. A hand is "achievable" if there are enough of the right types of items in the deal. For example, if the hand is 4 apples, and there are only 3 apples in the deal, then this hand is not achievable.
4. Remove all hands that have a lower valuation than the current hand. The remaining set is the set of achievable goals.
5. Calculate a set of plans for each achievable goal. A plan is a sequence of trades (one item in hand for one item out of hand) that will lead to the goal. There are many possible plans for each goal. For simplicity, we ignore any plans that involve cycles, where the same hand appears more than once.
6. Calculate the expected utility (outcome) of each plan. Each plan will have a probability distribution of outcomes, based on the probability that each trade is successful. The outcome will be the hand that results from the end state, or the state before the trade that fails. For example, suppose the simulator's hand is (apple, apple, orange), and the simulator's plan is (apple→orange, orange→grape). The three possible outcomes are:

   (apple, orange, grape) (i.e., if the plan succeeds) the probability is calculated as $P(t1) * P(t2)$.

   (apple, orange, orange) (i.e., if the first trade succeeds and the second fails) the probability is calculated as $P(t1) * (1 - P(t2))$.

   (apple, apple, orange) (i.e., if the first trade fails) the probability is calculated as $1 - P(t1)$.

   Therefore, the simulator can calculate the expected utility of each plan, by multiplying the probability of each trade with the valuation of each hand from step 2. We set the probability of success of each trade to 0.5 (i.e., uninformative probability). This value of probability represents the fact that the simulator does not know a priori whether the trade will succeed or not.
7. Select the plan which has the highest expected utility as the plan that the policy will follow.
8. Select an action implementing the plan that was chosen in the previous step, as follows: if the plan is completed (i.e., the simulator reached the goal), the policy will select Keep as an action. If the plan is not completed and there is a pending offer which will allow the plan to move forward, the policy will select Accept as an action. Otherwise, the policy will select Offer as an action. The addressee of the offer is randomly selected from the traders holding the item which is required for moving the plan forward.

In addition to the above hand-crafted trader simulator's policy, we also use a random policy.

5 Evaluation

In this section, we evaluate the learner's policies learned with (1) different algorithms i.e., LinQ, LSPI, and NFQ (see Section 2), (2) different reward functions i.e., Equations 3 and 4 (see Section 4.1), and (3) different numbers of traders.

The evaluation is performed in trading dialogs with different numbers of participants (from 2 players to 4 players), and different trader simulator's policies (hand-crafted policy or random policy as presented in Section 4.2). More specifically, there are 9 different setups:

H: 2-party dialog, where the trader simulator follows a hand-crafted policy.

R: 2-party dialog, where the trader simulator follows a random policy.

HxH: 3-party dialog, where both trader simulators follow hand-crafted policies.

HxR: 3-party dialog, where one trader simulator follows a hand-crafted policy and the other one follows a random policy.

RxR: 3-party dialog, where both trader simulators follow random policies.

HxHxH: 4-party dialog, where all three trader simulators follow hand-crafted policies.

HxHxR: 4-party dialog, where two trader simulators follow hand-crafted policies and the other one follows a random policy.

HxRxR: 4-party dialog, where one trader simulator follows a hand-crafted policy and the other ones follow random policies.

RxRxR: 4-party dialog, where all three trader simulators follow random policies.

There are also 9 different learner policies:

AlwaysKeep: weak baseline which always passes the turn.

Random: weak baseline which randomly selects one action from all possible valid actions.

LinQ-End: learned policy using LinQ and reward given at the end of the dialog.

LSPI-End: learned policy using LSPI and reward given at the end of the dialog.

NFQ-End: learned policy using NFQ and reward given at the end of the dialog.

LinQ-Incr: learned policy using LinQ and an incremental reward.

LSPI-Incr: learned policy using LSPI and an incremental reward.

NFQ-Incr: learned policy using NFQ and an incremental reward.

Handcraft1: strong baseline following the hand-crafted policy presented in Section 4.2.

Handcraft2: strong baseline similar to Handcraft1 except the plan is randomly selected from the set of plans produced by step 6, rather than picking only the highest utility one (see Section 4.2).

We use the Pybrain library (Schaul et al., 2010) for the RL algorithms LinQ, LSPI, and NFQ. The learning parameters follow the default Pybrain settings except for the discount factor γ; we set the discount factor γ to 1. We consider 2000 dialogs as one epoch, and learning is finished when the number of epochs becomes 200 (400,000 dialogs). The policy at the epoch where the average reward reaches its highest value is used in the evaluation.

We evaluate the learner's policy against trader simulators. We calculate the average reward of the learner's policy in 20000 dialogs. Furthermore, we show how fast the learned policies converge as a function of the number of epochs in training.

In terms of comparing the average rewards of policies (see Figure 1), NFQ-Incr achieves the best performance in almost every situation. In 2-party trading, the performance of NFQ-Incr is almost the same as that of Handcraft2 which achieves the best score, and better than the performance of Handcraft1. In both 3-party and 4-party trading, the performance of NFQ-Incr is better than that of the two strong baselines, and achieves the best score. In contrast to NFQ-Incr, the performance of the other learned policies is much worse than that of the two strong baselines. As the number of trader simulators who follow a random policy increases, the difference in performance between NFQ-Incr and the other learned policies tends to also increase. One reason is that, as the number of trader simulators who follow a random policy increases, the variability of dialog flow also increases. Trader simulators that follow a hand-crafted policy behave more strictly than trader simulators that follow a random policy. For example, if the trader simulator following a hand-crafted policy reaches its goal, then there is nothing else to do except for Keep. In contrast, if a trader simulator following a random policy reaches its goal, there is still a chance that it will accept an offer which will be beneficial to the learner. As a result there are more chances for the learner to gain better outcomes, when the complexity of the dialog is higher. In summary, our results show that combining NFQ with an incremental reward produces the best results.

Moreover, the learning curve in 2-party trading (Figure 2 in the Appendix) indicates that, basically, only the NFQ-Incr achieves stable learning. NFQ-Incr reaches its best performance from epoch 140 to epoch 190. On the other hand, LSPI somehow converges fast, but its performance is not so high. Moreover, LinQ converges in the first epoch, but it performs the worst.

6 Conclusion

In this paper, we used RL to learn the dialog system's (learner's) policy in a multi-party trading scenario. We experimented with different RL algorithms and reward functions. The negotiation policies of the learner were learned and evaluated through simulated dialog with trader simulators. We presented results for different numbers of traders. Our results showed that (1) even in simple multi-party trading dialog tasks, learning an effective negotiation policy is a very hard problem; and (2) the use of neural fitted Q iteration combined with an incremental reward function produces as effective or even better negotiation policies than the policies of two strong hand-crafted baselines.

For future work we will expand the dialog model to augment the dialog state with information about the estimated payoff matrix of other traders. This means expanding from an MDP-

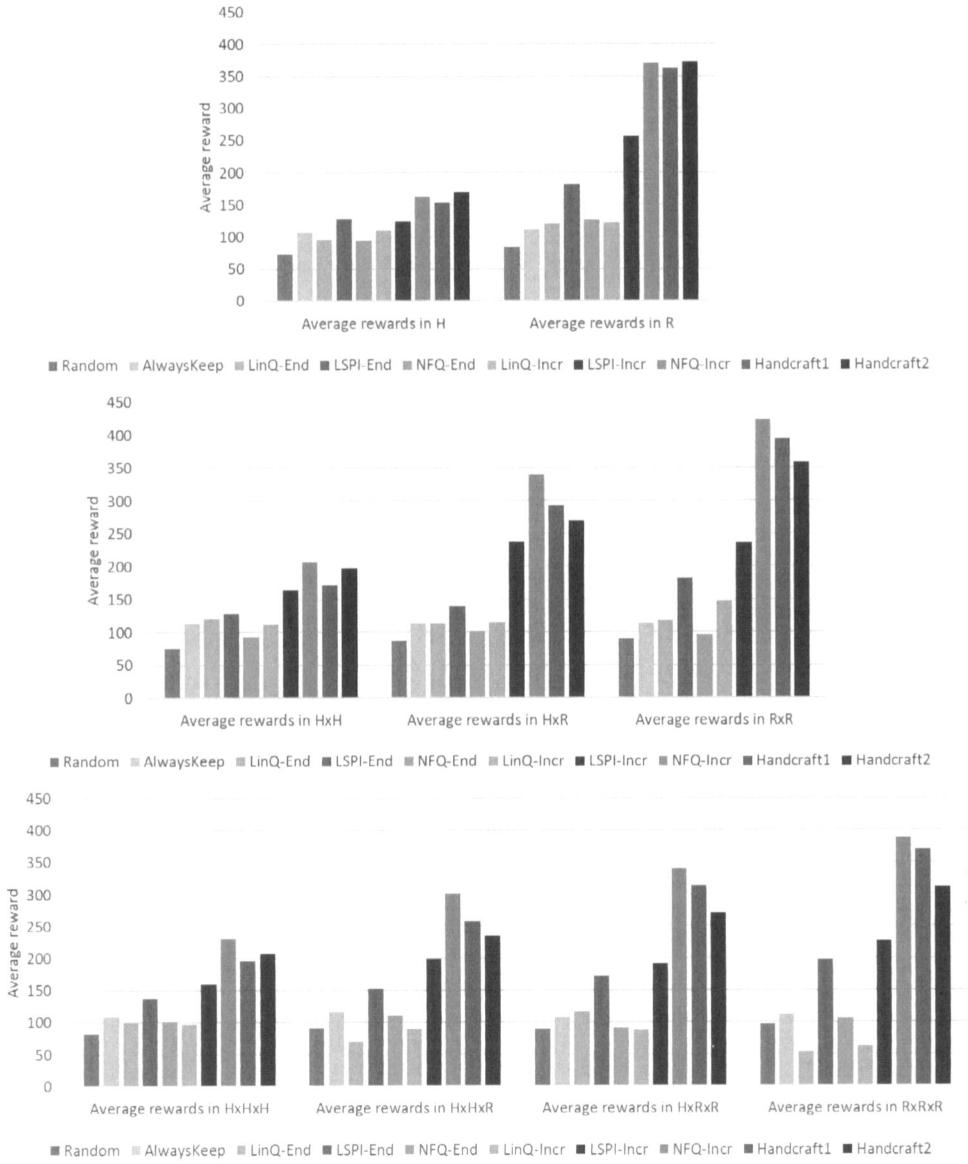

Figure 1: Comparison of RL algorithms and types of reward functions. The upper figure corresponds to 2-party dialog, the middle figure to 3-party dialog, and the lower figure to 4-party dialog. In these figures, the performances of the policies are evaluated by using the reward function given by Equation 3.

based dialog model to a POMDP-based model. We will also apply multi-agent RL (Georgila et al., 2014) to multi-party trading dialog. Furthermore, we will perform evaluation with human traders. Finally, we will collect and analyze data from human trading dialogs in order to improve our models and make them more realistic.

Acknowledgments

This research was partially supported by the 2014 Global Initiatives Program, JSPS KAKENHI Grant Number 24240032, and the Commissioned Research of the National Institute of Information and Communications Technology (NICT), Japan. This material was also based in part upon work supported by the National Science Foundation under Grant Number IIS-1450656, and the U.S. Army. Any opinions, findings, and conclusions or recommendations expressed in this material are those of the authors and do not necessarily reflect the views of the National Science Foundation or the United States Government, and no official endorsement should be inferred.

References

Nicholas Asher and Alex Lascarides. 2013. Strategic conversation. *Semantics and Pragmatics*, 6:2:1–62.

Layla El Asri, Romain Laroche, and Olivier Pietquin. 2013. Reward shaping for statistical optimisation of dialogue management. *In Proc. of SLSP.*

Ioannis Efstathiou and Oliver Lemon. 2014. Learning non-cooperative dialogue behaviours. In *Proc. of SIGDIAL.*

Kallirroi Georgila and David Traum. 2011. Reinforcement learning of argumentation dialogue policies in negotiation. In *Proc. of INTERSPEECH.*

Kallirroi Georgila, Maria K. Wolters, and Johanna D. Moore. 2010. Learning dialogue strategies from older and younger simulated users. In *Proc. of SIGDIAL.*

Kallirroi Georgila, Claire Nelson, and David Traum. 2014. Single-agent vs. multi-agent techniques for concurrent reinforcement learning of negotiation dialogue policies. In *Proc. of ACL.*

Kallirroi Georgila. 2013. Reinforcement learning of two-issue negotiation dialogue policies. In *Proc. of SIGDIAL.*

Markus Guhe and Alex Lascarides. 2012. Trading in a multiplayer board game: Towards an analysis of non-cooperative dialogue. In *Proc. of CogSci.*

Peter A. Heeman. 2009. Representing the reinforcement learning state in a negotiation dialogue. In *Proc. of ASRU.*

Takuya Hiraoka, Graham Neubig, Sakriani Sakti, Tomoki Toda, and Satoshi Nakamura. 2014. Reinforcement learning of cooperative persuasive dialogue policies using framing. In *Proc. of COLING.*

Michail G. Lagoudakis and Ronald Parr. 2003. Least-squares policy iteration. *The Journal of Machine Learning Research*, 4:1107–1149.

Esther Levin, Roberto Pieraccini, and Wieland Eckert. 2000. A stochastic model of human-machine interaction for learning dialog strategies. In *Proc. of ICASSP.*

Yun Mayya, Lee Tae Kyung, and Ko Il Seok. 2011. Negotiation and persuasion approach using reinforcement learning technique on broker's board agent system. In *Proc. of IJACT.*

Amy McGovern and Andrew G. Barto. 2001. Automatic discovery of subgoals in reinforcement learning using diverse density. In *Proc. of ICML.*

Andew Y. Ng, Daishi Harada, and Stuart Russell. 1999. Policy invariance under reward transformations: Theory and application to reward shaping. *In Proc. of ICML.*

Elnaz Nouri, Kallirroi Georgila, and David Traum. 2012. A cultural decision-making model for negotiation based on inverse reinforcement learning. In *Proc. of CogSci.*

Elnaz Nouri, Sunghyun Park, Stefan Scherer, Jonathan Gratch, Peter Carnevale, Louis-Philippe Morency, and David Traum. 2013. Prediction of strategy and outcome as negotiation unfolds by using basic verbal and behavioral features. In *Proc. of INTERSPEECH.*

Praveen Paruchuri, Nilanjan Chakraborty, Roie Zivan, Katia Sycara, Miroslav Dudik, and Geoff Gordon. 2009. POMDP based negotiation modeling. In *Proc. of MICON.*

Michael Pfeiffer. 2004. Reinforcement learning of strategies for Settlers of Catan. In *Proc. of the International Conference on Computer Games: Artificial Intelligence, Design and Education.*

Martin Riedmiller. 2005. Neural fitted Q iteration - first experiences with a data efficient neural reinforcement learning method. In *Proc. of ECML.*

Tom Schaul, Justin Bayer, Daan Wierstra, Yi Sun, Martin Felder, Frank Sehnke, Thomas Rückstieß, and Jürgen Schmidhuber. 2010. Pybrain. *The Journal of Machine Learning Research*, 11:743–746.

Richard S. Sutton and Andrew G. Barto. 1998. *Reinforcement learning: An introduction.* MIT Press.

David Traum. 2008. Extended abstract: Computational models of non-cooperative dialogue. *In Proc. of SEMDIAL-LONDIAL.*

Marilyn A. Walker, Diane J. Litman, Candace A. Kamm, and Alicia Abella. 1998. Evaluating spoken dialogue agents with PARADISE: Two case studies. *Computer Speech and Language*, 12(4):317–347.

Marilyn A. Walker. 2000. An application of reinforcement learning to dialogue strategy selection in a spoken dialogue system for email. *Journal of Artificial Intelligence Research*, 12:387–416.

Jason D. Williams and Steve Young. 2007a. Partially observable Markov decision processes for spoken dialog systems. *Computer Speech and Language*, 21(2):393–422.

Jason D. Williams and Steve Young. 2007b. Scaling POMDPs for spoken dialog management. *IEEE Trans. on Audio, Speech, and Language Processing*, 15(7):2116–2129.

Yi Zou, Wenjie Zhan, and Yuan Shao. 2014. Evolution with reinforcement learning in negotiation. *PLoS One*, 9(7).

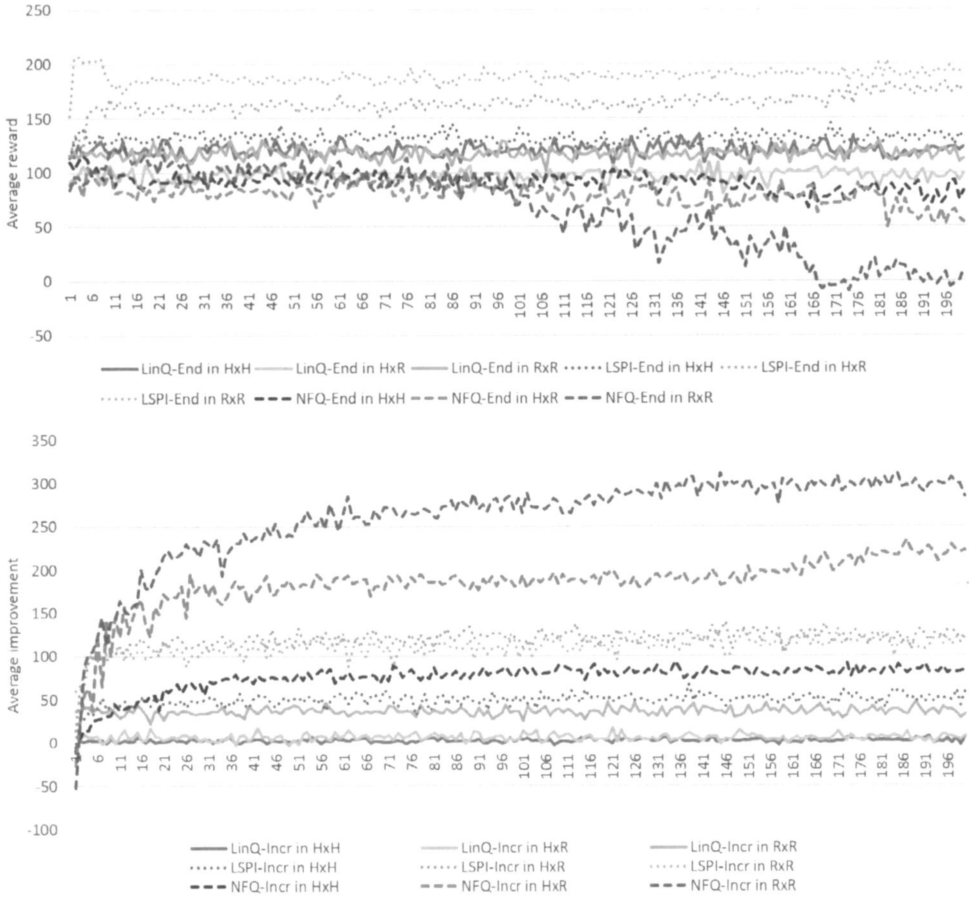

Figure 2: Number of epochs vs. performance of learned policies in 2-party trading. The upper figure shows the performance when the reward is given by Equation 3. The lower figure shows the performance when the reward is given by Equation 4.

An Incremental Turn-Taking Model with Active System Barge-in for Spoken Dialog Systems

Tiancheng Zhao, Alan W Black and Maxine Eskenazi
Language Technologies Institute
Carnegie Mellon University
Pittsburgh, Pennsylvania, USA
{tianchez,awb,max+}@cs.cmu.edu

Abstract

This paper deals with an incremental turn-taking model that provides a novel solution for end-of-turn detection. It includes a flexible framework that enables active *system barge-in*. In order to accomplish this, a systematic procedure of teaching a dialog system to produce meaningful *system barge-in* is presented. This procedure improves system robustness and success rate. It includes constructing cost models and learning optimal policy using reinforcement learning. Results show that our model reduces *false cut-in* rate by 37.1% and *response delay* by 32.5% compared to the baseline system. Also the learned *system barge-in* strategy yields a 27.7% increase in average reward from user responses.

1 Introduction

Human-human conversation has flexible turn-taking behavior: back channeling, overlapping speech and smooth turn transitions. Imitating human-like turn-taking in a spoken dialog system (SDS) is challenging due to the degradation in quality of the dialog when overlapping speech is produced in the wrong place. For this, a traditional SDS often uses a simplified turn-taking model with rigid turn taking. They only respond when users have finished speaking. Thus past research has mostly focused on end-of-turn detection, finding the end of the user utterance as quickly as possible while minimizing the chance of wrongly interrupting the users. We refer here to the interruption issue as *false cut-ins* (FCs).

Recent research in incremental dialog processing promises more flexible turn-taking behavior (Atterer et al., 2008; Breslin et al., 2013). Here, the automatic speech recognizer (ASR) and natural language understanding (NLU) incrementally produce partial decoding/understating messages for decision-making. This allows for *system barge-in* (SB), starting to respond before end-of-utterance. Although this framework has shown promising results in creating flexible SDSs, the following two fundamental issues remain:

1. We need a model that unifies incremental processing and traditional turn-taking behavior.
2. We also need a systematic procedure that trains a system to produce meaningful SBs.

This paper first proposes a finite state machine (FSM) that both shows superior performance in end-of-turn detection compared to previous methods and is compatible with incremental processing. Then we propose a systematic procedure to endow a system with meaningful SB by combining the theory of optimal stopping with reinforcement learning.

Section 2 of the paper discusses related work; Section 3 describes the finite state machine; Sections 4, 5, and 6 describe how to produce meaningful SB; Section 7 gives experimental results of an evaluation using the CMU Let's Go Live system and simulation results on the Dialog State Tracking Challenging (DTSC) Corpus and Section 8 concludes.

2 Related Work and Limitations

This work is closely related to end-of-turn detection and incremental processing (IP) dialog systems.

There are several methods for detecting the end-of-turn. Raux (2008) built a decision tree for final pause duration using ASR and NLU features. At runtime, the system first dynamically chooses the final pause duration threshold based on the dialog state and then predicts end-of-turn if final pause duration is longer than that threshold. Other work explored predicting end-of-turn within a user's speech. This showed substantial improvement in speed of response (Raux and Eske-

Proceedings of the SIGDIAL 2015 Conference, pages 42–50,
Prague, Czech Republic, 2-4 September 2015. ©2015 Association for Computational Linguistics

nazi, 2009). Another approach examined prosodic and semantic features such as pitch and speaking rate in human-human conversation for turn-yielding cues (Gravano, 2009).

The key limitation of those methods is that the decision made by the end-of-turn detector is treated as a "hard" decision, obliging developers to compromise in a tradeoff between response latency and FC rate (Raux and Eskenazi, 2008). Although adding more complex prosodic and semantic features can improve the performance of the detector, it also increases computation cost and requires significant knowledge of the SDS, which can limit the accessibility for non-expert developers.

For IP, Kim (2014) has demonstrated the possibility of learning turn-taking from human dialogs using inverse reinforcement learning. Other work has focused on incremental NLU (DeVault et al., 2009), showing that the correct interpretation of users' meaning can be predicted before end-of-turn. Another topic is modeling user and system barge-in. Selfridge (2013) has presented a FSM that predicts users' barge-ins. Also, Ghigi (2014) has shown that allowing SB when users produce lengthy speech increases robustness and task success.

Different from Kim's work that learns human-like turn-taking, our approach is more related to Ghigi's method, which tries to improve dialog efficiency from a system-centric perspective. We take one step further by optimizing the turn-taking using all available features based on a global objective function with machine learning methods.

3 A Finite State Turn-Taking Model

3.1 Model Description

Our model has two distinct modes: passive and active. The passive mode exhibits traditional rigid turn-taking behavior while the active mode has the system respond in the middle of a user turn. We first describe how these two modes operate, and then show how they are compatible with existing incremental dialog approaches.

The idea is to combine an aggressive speaker with a patient listener. The speaker consists of the Text-to-Speech (TTS) and Natural Language Generation (NLG) modules. The listener is composed of the ASR and Voice Activity Detection (VAD) modules. The system attempts to respond to a user every time it detects a short pause (e.g. 100ms). But before a long pause (e.g. 1000ms) is detected, the user's continued speech will stop the system from responding, as shown on Figure 1:

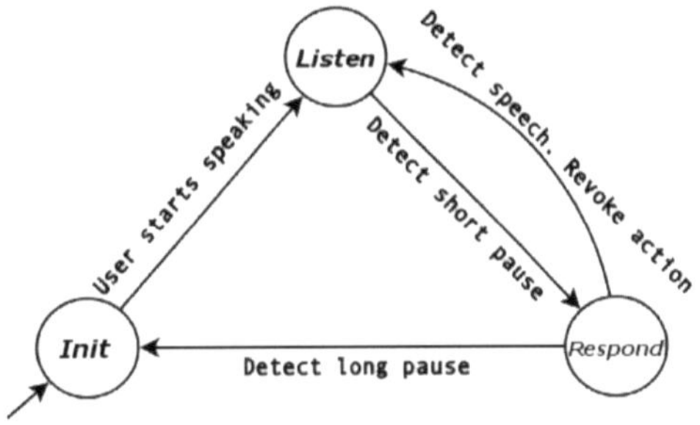

Figure 1: Turn-taking Model as a finite state machine

Most of the system's attempts to respond will thus be FCs. However, since the listener can stop the system from speaking, the FCs have no effect on the conversation (users may hear the false start of the system's prompt, but often the respond state is cancelled before the synthesized speech begins). If the attempt is correct, however, the system responds with almost 0-latency, as shown in Figure 2. Furthermore, because the dialog manager (DM) can receive partial ASR output whenever there is a short pause, this model produces relatively stable partial ASR output and supports incremental dialog processing.

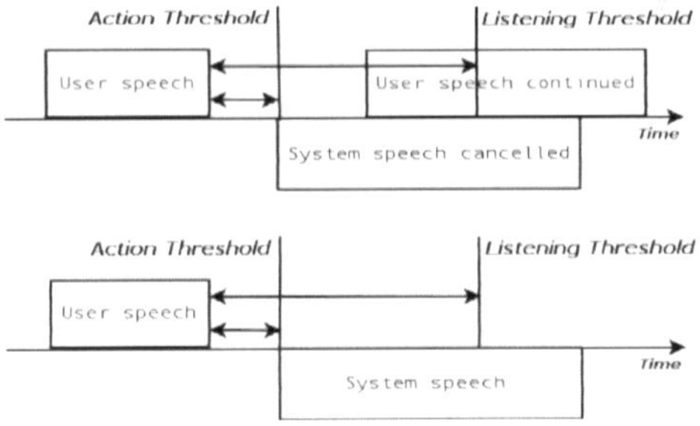

Figure 2: The first example illustrates the system canceling its response when it detects new speech before LT. The second example shows that users will not notice the waiting time between AT and LT.

We then define the short pause as the *action threshold* (AT) and the long pause as the *listening threshold* (LT), where $0 < AT \leq LT$, which can be interpreted respectively as the "aggression" and "patience" of the system. By changing the value of each of these thresholds we can modify the system's behavior from rigid turn taking to active SB.

1. Passive Agent: act fast and listen patiently (AT = small value, LT = large value)

2. Active Agent: act and listen impatiently. (AT = LT = small value)

This abstraction simplifies the challenge: "when the system should barge in" as the following transition: $Passive\,Agent \xrightarrow{\Phi(dialog\,state)} Active\,Agent$ where $\Phi(\cdot) : dialog\,State \rightarrow \{true, false\}$ is a function that outputs true whenever the agent should take the floor, regardless of the current state of the floor. For example, this function could output true when the current dialog states fulfill certain rules in a hand-crafted system, or could output true when the system has reached its maximal understanding of the user's intention (DeVault et al., 2009). A natural next step is to use statistical techniques to learn an optimized $\Phi(\cdot)$ based on all features related to the dialog states, in order to support more complex SB behavior.

3.2 Advantages over Past Methods

First our model solves end-of-turn detection by using a combination of VAD and TTS control, instead of trying to build a perfect classifier. This avoids the tradeoff between response latency and FC. Under the assumption that the TTS can operate at high speed, the proposed system can achieve almost 0-lag and 0-FC by setting AT to be small (e.g. 100ms). Second, the model does not require expensive prosodic and semantic turn-yielding cue detectors, thus simplifying the implementation.

4 Toward Active System Barge-in

In state-of-the-art SDS, the DM uses explicit/implicit confirmation to fill each slot and carries out an error recovery strategy for incorrectly recognized slots (Bohus and Rudnicky, 2009). The system should receive many correctly-recognized slots, thus avoiding lengthy error recovery. While a better ASR and NLU could help, Ghigh (2014) has shown that allowing the system to actively respond to users also leads to more correct slots.

Transcription	ASR Output
To Forbes, you know, at Squirrel Hill	To Forbes, **herron vee lyn road**
Leaving from Forbes, ⟨Noise⟩	Leaving from Forbes **from highland bus**
⟨Noise⟩, Leaving from Forbes	**PA 71C Pittsburgh, liberty** from Forbes

Table 1: Examples of wordy turns and noise presence. Bold text is the part of speech incorrectly recognized.

Table 1 demonstrates three cases where active SB can help. The first two rows show the first half of the user's speech being correctly recognized while the second half is not. In this scenario, if, in the middle of the utterance, the system can tell that the existing ASR hypothesis is sufficient and actively barges on the user, it can potentially avoid the poorly-recognized speech that follows. The third example has noise at the beginning of the user turn. The system could back channel in the middle of the utterance to ask the user to go to a quieter place or to repeat an answer. In these examples active SB can help improve robustness:

1. Barge in when the current hypothesis has high confidence and contains sufficient information to move the dialog along.
2. Barge in when the hypothesis confidence is low and the predicted future hypothesis will not get better. This can avoid recovering from a large number of incorrect slots.

A natural choice of objective function to train such a system is to maximize the expected quality of information in the users' utterances. The quality of the recognized information is positively correlated to number of correctly recognized slots (CS) and inversely correlated to the number of incorrectly recognized slots (ICS). In the next section, we describe how we transform CS and ICS into a real-value reward.

5 A Cost Model for System Barge-in

We first design a cost model that defines a reward function. This model is based on the assumption that the system will use explicit confirmation for every slot. We choose this because it is the most basic dialog strategy. A sample dialog for this strategy is as follows:

Sys: *Where do you want to leave from?*
User: *Leaving from X.*
Sys: *Do you mean leaving from Y?*
User: *No.*
Sys: *Where do you want to leave from?*
User: *<No Parse>*
Sys: *Where do you want to leave from?*
User: *I am leaving from X.*
Sys: *Do you mean X?*
User: *Yes.*

Given this dialog strategy the system spends one turn asking the question, and k turns confirming k slots in the user response. Also, for no-parse (0 slot) input, the system asks the same question again. Therefore, the minimum number of turns required to acquire n slots is $2n$. However, because user responses contain ICS and no-parses, the system takes more than $2n$ turns to obtain all the slot information (assume confirmation are never misrecognized).

We denote cs_i and ics_i as the number of correctly/incorrectly recognized slots in the user response. So the quality of the user response is captured by a tuple, (cs_i, ics_i). The goal is to obtain a reward function that maps from a given user response (cs_i, ics_i) to a reward value $r_i \in \Re$. This reward value should correlate with the overall efficiency of a dialog, which is inversely correlated with the number of turns needed for task completion.

Then for a dialog task that has n slots to fill, we can denote h_i as the number of turns already spent, f_i as the estimated number of future turns needed for task completion and $E[S]$ as the expected number of turns needed to fill 1 slot. Then for each new user response (cs_i, ics_i), we update the following recursive formulas:

Initialization: $h_0 = 0, f_0 = nE[s]$
Update Rules:

$$h_i = h_{i-1} + \underbrace{1}_{\text{question}} + \underbrace{cs_i + ics_i}_{\text{confirm}} \quad (1)$$

$$f_i = f_{i-1} - \underbrace{cs_i E[S]}_{\text{acquired slots}} \quad (2)$$

Based on the above setup, it is clear that $h_i + f_i$ equals the estimated total number of turns needed to fill n slots. Then the reward, r_i, associated with each user response can be expressed as the difference between the previous and current estimates:

$$r_i = (h_{i-1} + f_{i-1}) - (h_i + f_i) \quad (3)$$

$$= -1 + \underbrace{(E[S] - 1)}_{\text{weight to CS}} cs_i - ics_i \quad (4)$$

Therefore, a positive reward means the new user response reduces the estimated number of turns for task completion while a negative reward means the opposite. Another interpretation of this reward function is that for no-parse user response ($cs_i = 0, ics_i = 0$), the cost is to waste 1 turn asking the same question again. When there is a parse, each correct slot can save $E[S]$ turns in the future, while each slot, regardless of its correctness, needs a 1-turn confirmation. As a result, this rewards function is correlated with the global efficiency of a dialog because it assigns a corpus-dependent weight to cs_i, based on $E[S]$ estimated from historical dialogs.

6 Learning Active Turn-taking Policy

After modeling the cost of a user turn, we learn a turn-taking policy that can maximize the expected reward in user turns, namely the $\Phi(dialog\,state)$ that controls the switching between passive and active agent of our FSM in Section 3.1. Before going into detail, we first introduce the optimal stopping problem and reinforcement learning.

6.1 Optimal Stopping Problem and Reinforcement Learning

The theory of optimal stopping is an area of mathematics that addresses the decision of when to take a given action based on a set of sequentially observed random variables, in order to maximize an expected payoff (Ferguson, 2012).
A formal description is as follows:

1. A sequence of random variables $X_1, X_2...$
2. A sequence of real-valued reward functions, $y_0, y_1(x_1), y_2(x_1, x_2)...$

The decider may observe the sequence $x_1, x_2...$ and after observing $X_1 = x_1, ...X_n = x_n$, the decider may stop and receive the reward $y_n(x_1, ...x_n)$, or continue and observe X_{n+1}. The optimal stopping problem searches for an optimal stopping rule that maximizes the expected reward.

Reinforcement learning models are based on the *Markov decision process* (MDP). A (finite) MDP is a tuple $(S, A, \{P_{sa}\}, \gamma, R)$, where:

- S is a finite set of N states
- $A = a_1, ...a_k$ is a set of k actions
- $P_{sa}(\cdot)$ are the state transition probabilities on taking action a in state s.
- $\gamma \in [0, 1)$ is the discount factor
- $R : S \rightarrow \Re$ is the rewards function.

Then a policy, π , is a mapping from each state, $s \in S$ and action $a \in A$, to the probability $\pi(s, a)$ of taking action a when in state s (Sutton and Barto, 1998). Then, for MDPs, the Q-function, is the expected return starting from s taking action a and thereafter following policy π and has the Bellman equation:

$$Q^{\pi}(s, a) = R(s) + \gamma \sum_{s'} P(s'|s, a)V^{\pi}(s'). \quad (5)$$

The goal of reinforcement learning is to find the optimal policy π^*, such that $Q^{\pi}(s, a)$ can be maximized. Thus the optimal stopping problem can be formulated as an MDP, where the action space contains two actions $\{wait, stop\}$. Also, solving the optimal stopping rule is equivalent to finding the optimal policy, π^*.

6.2 Solving Active Turn-taking

Equipped with the above two frameworks, we first show that SB can be formulated as an optimal stopping problem. Then we propose a novel, non-iterative, model-free method for solving for the optimal policy.

An SDS dialog contains N user utterances. Each user utterance contains K partial hypotheses and each partial hypothesis, p_i, is associated with a tuple (cs_i, ics_i) and a feature vector, $x_i \in \Re^{f\times 1}$, where f is the dimension of the feature vector. We also assume that every user utterance is independent of every other utterance. We will call one user utterance an *episode*.

In an *episode*, the turn-taking decider will see each partial hypothesis sequentially over time, At each hypothesis it takes an action from $\{wait, stop\}$. $Wait$ means it continues to listen. $Stop$ means it takes the floor. The turn-taking decider receives 0 reward for taking the action $wait$ and receives the reward r_i from (cs_i, ics_i) according to our cost model for taking the action $stop$. This is an optimal stopping problem that can be formulated as an MDP:

- $S = \{x_1, ...\{x_1...x_K\}\}$
- $A = \{wait, stop\}$
- $R = -1 + (E[S] - 1)cs_i - ics_i$

Then the Bellman equations are:

$$Q^\pi(s, stop) = R(s) = r(s) \quad (6)$$

$$Q^\pi(s, wait) = \gamma \sum_{s'} P(s'|s,a)V^\pi(s') \quad (7)$$

The first equation shows that the Q-value for any state, s, with action, $stop$, is simply the immediate reward for s. The second equation shows that the Q-value for any state s, with action, $wait$, only depends on the future return by following policy π. This result is crucial because it means that $Q^\pi(s, stop)$ for any state, s, can be directly calculated based on the cost model, independent of the policy π. Also, given a policy π, $Q^\pi(s, wait)$can also be directly calculated as the discounted reward the first time that the policy chooses to stop.

Meanwhile, for a given *episode* with known reward r_i for each partial hypothesis p_i, optimal stopping means always to stop at the largest reward, meaning that we can obtain the oracle action for the training corpus. Given a sequence of reward $(r_i, ...r_K)$, the optimal policy, π, chooses to stop at partial p_m if $m = \arg\max_{j\in(i,K]} r_j$.

The Bellman equations become:

$$Q^\pi(s_i, stop) = r_i \quad (8)$$

$$Q^\pi(s_i, wait) = \gamma^{m-i} r_m \quad (9)$$

and the oracle action at any s can be obtained by :

$$a_i^* = wait \quad \text{if } Q^*(s_i, stop) < Q^*(s_i, wait)$$

$$a_i^* = stop \quad \text{if } Q^*(s_i, stop) \geq Q^*(s_i, wait)$$

This special property of optimal stopping problem allows us to use supervised learning methods directly modeling the optimal Q function, by finding a mapping from the input state space, s_i, into the Q-value for both actions: $Q(s_i, stop)^*$ and $Q(s_i, wait)^*$. Further, inspired by the work of reinforcement learning as classification (Lagoudakis and Parr, 2003), we decide to map directly from the input state space into the action space: $S \rightarrow A^*$, using a Support Vector Machine (SVM).

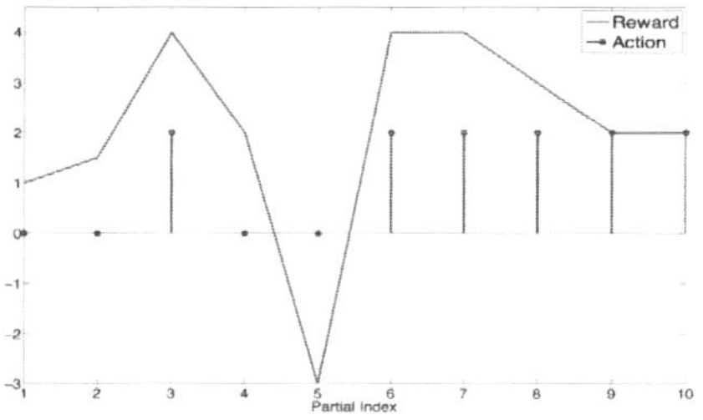

Figure 3: An example showing the oracle actions for one episode. $1 = stop$ and $0 = wait$.

Advantages of solving this problem as a classification rather than a regression include: 1) it explicitly models $sign(Q(s_i, stop)^* - Q(s_i, wait)^*)$, which sufficiently determines the behavior of the agent. 2) SVM is known as a state-of-the-art modeler for the binary classification task, due to its ability to find the separating hyperplane in nonlinear space.

6.3 Feature Construction

Since SVM requires a fixed input dimension size, while the available features will continue to increase as the turn-taking decider observes more partial hypotheses, we adopt the functional idea used by the openSMILE toolkit (Eyben et al., 2010). There are three categories of features: immediate feature, delta feature and long-term feature. Immediate features come from the ASR and the NLU in the latest partial hypothesis. Delta features are the first-order derivate of immediate features with respect to the previous observed feature. Long-term features are global statistics associated with all the observed features.

Immediate Features	
Final pause duration	Number of slots
Hypothesis stability	Transitions of (no)parse
Frame number	Number of words
Utterance duration	Number of unparsed gap
Language model score	Unparsed percentage
Word confidence	Max of pause duration
Number of noun	Mean of pause duration
Boundary LM score	Var of pause duration
First level matched	Hypothesis confidence
Long-term Functional Features	
Mean	Standard Deviation
Maximum	Position of maximum
Minimum	Position of miniumu

Table 2: List of immediate/long-term features

Table 2 shows that we have 18 immediate features, 18 delta features and $18 \times 7 = 126$ long-term features. Then we apply F-score feature selection as described in (Chen and Lin, 2006). The final feature set contains 138 features.

7 Experiments and Results

We conducted a live study and a simulation study. The live study evaluates the model's end-of-turn detection. The simulated study evaluates the active SB behavior.

7.1 Live Study

The finite state machine was implemented in the Interaction Manager of the CMU Lets Go system that provides bus information in Pittsburgh (Raux et al., 2005). We compared base system data from November 1-30, 2014 (773 dialogs), to data from our system from December 1-31, 2014 (565 dialogs).

The base system used the decision tree end-of-turn detector described in (Raux and Eskenazi, 2008) and the active SB algorithm described in (Ghigi et al., 2014). The *action threshold* (AT) in the new system was set at 60% of the decision tree output in the former system and the *listening threshold* (LT) was empirically set at $1200ms$.

7.2 Live Study Metrics

We observed that FCs result in several users' utterances having overlapping timestamps due to a built-in 500ms padding before an utterances in PocketSphinx. This means that we consider two consecutive utterances with a pause less than 500ms as one utterance. Figure 4 shows that when the end-of-turn detector produces an FC, the continued flow of user speech instantiates a new user utterance which overlaps with the previous one. In this example, utterances 0 and 1 have overlaps while utterance 2 does not. So users actually produce two utterances, while the system thinks there are three due to FC.

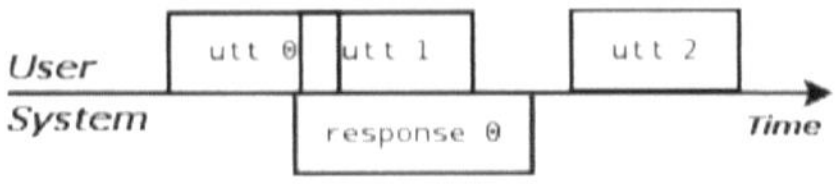

Figure 4: Utterance fragments caused by FCs. This example has $UFR = \frac{2}{3}$.

Thus, we can automatically calculate the FC rate of every dialog, by counting the number of user utterances with overlaps. We define an utterance fragment ratio (UFR) that measures the FC rate in a dialog.

$$UFR = \frac{\text{Number of user utterances with overlaps}}{\text{Total number of user utterances}}$$

We also manually label task success (TS) of all the dialogs. We define TS as: a dialog is successful if and only if the system conducted a back-end search for bus information with all required slots correctly recognized. In summary, we use the following metrics to evaluate the new system:

1. Task success rate
2. Utterance fragment ratio (UFR)
3. Average number of *system barge-in* (ANSB)
4. Proportion of long user utterances interrupted by *system barge-in* (PLUISB)
5. Average response delay (ARD)
6. Average user utterance duration over time

7.3 Live Study Results

Table 3 shows that the TS rate of the new system is 7.5% higher than the previous system (p-value $<$ 0.01). Table 4 shows that overall UFR decreased by 37.1%. UFR for successful and for failed dialogs indicates that the UFR decreases more in failed dialogs than in successful ones. One explanation is that failed dialogs usually have a noisier environment. The UFR reduction explains the increase in success rate since UFRs are positively correlated with TS rate, as reported in (Zhao and Eskenazi, 2015)

Table 5 shows that the SB algorithm was activated more often in the new system. This is because the SB algorithm described in (Ghigi et al., 2014) only activates for user utterances longer than 3 seconds. FCs will therefore hinder the ability of this algorithm to reliably measure user utterance dura-

	Success	Failed	TS Rate	P-value
New System	271	294	**48.0%**	**0.0096**
Old System	321	452	41.5%	

Table 3: Success rate between old and new systems. P-value is obtained via Wald Test

UFR	Overall	Successful dialog	Failed dialog
New System	12.2%	9.2%	15.0%
Old System	19.4%	12.5%	24.3%

Table 4: Breakdown into successful/failed dialogs

tion. This is an example of how reliable end-of-turn detection can benefit other SDS modules. Table 5 also shows that the new system is 32.5% more responsive than the old system. We purposely set the action threshold to 60% of the threshold in the old system, which demonstrates that the new model can have an response speed equals to action threshold that is independent of the FC rate.

Metric	Old System	New System
ANSB	1.04	1.50
PLUISB	53.9%	77.8%
ARD (ms)	853.49	576.09

Table 5: Comparison of barge-in activation rate and response delay

Figure 5 shows how average user utterance duration evolves in a dialog. Utterance duration is more stable in the new system than in the old one. Two possible explanations are: 1) since UFR is much higher in the old system, the system is more likely to cut in at the wrong time, possibly making users abandon their normal turn-taking behavior and talk over the system. 2) more frequent activation of the SB algorithm entrains the users to produce more concise utterances.

7.4 Simulation Study

This part of the experiment uses the DSTC corpus training2 (643 dialogs) (Black et al., 2013). The data was manually transcribed. The reported 1-best word error rate (WER) is 58.2% (Williams et al., 2013). This study focuses on all user responses to:"Where are you leaving from?" and "Where are you going?" which have 688 and 773 utterances respectively.

An automatic script, based on the manual transcription, labels the number of correct and incorrect

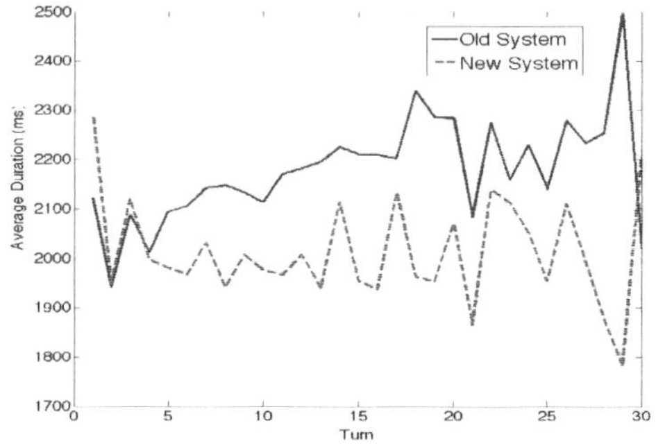

Figure 5: Average user utterance duration over the index of user turns in a dialog.

slots (cs_i, ics_i) for each partial hypothesis, p_i. Also from the training data, the expected number of turns needed to obtain 1 slot, $E[S]$, is 3.82. For simplicity, $E[S]$ is set to be 4. So the reward function discussed in Section 5 is: $r_i = -1 + 3cs_i - ics_i$.

After obtaining the reward value for each hypothesis, the oracle action at each partial hypothesis is calculated based on the procedure discussed in Section 6.3 with $\gamma = 1$.

We set the SVM kernel as RBF kernel and use a grid search to choose the best parameters for cost and kernel width using 5-fold cross validation on the training data (Hsu et al., 2003). The optimization criterion is the F-measure.

7.5 Simulation Study Metrics

The evaluation metrics have two parts: classification-related (precision and recall) and dialog-related. Dialog related metrics are:

1. Accuracy of system barge-in
2. Average decrease in utterance duration compared to no *system barge-in*
3. Percentage of no-parse utterance
4. Average CS per utterance
5. Average ICS per utterance
6. Average reward $= 1/T \sum_i r_i$, where T is the number of utterances in the test set.

The learned policy is compared to two reference systems: the oracle and the baseline system. The oracle directly follows optimal policy obtained from the ground-truth label. The baseline system always waits for the last partial (no SB).

Furthermore, a simple smoothing algorithm is applied to the SVM output for comparison. This algorithm confirms the stop action after two consecutive stop outputs from the classifier. This increases the classifier's precision.

7.6 Simulation Study Results

10-fold cross validation was conducted on the two datasets. Instead of using the SVM binary output, we apply a global threshold of 0.4 on the SVM decision function for output to achieve the best average reward. The threshold is determined based on cross-validation on training data.

Table 6 shows that the SVM classifier can achieve very high precision and high recall in predicting the correct action. The F-measure (after smoothing) is 84.46% for departure question responses and 85.99% for arrival questions.

	Precision	**Recall**	**Precision (smooth)**	**Recall (smooth)**
D	92.64%± 2.88	78.04%± 2.39	93.86%± 2.80	76.79%± 2.35
A	93.59%± 2.42	79.64%± 3.41	93.63%± 2.30	79.51%± 3.04

Table 6: Cross-validation precision and recall with standard error for SVM. D = responses to departure question, A = responses to arrival question.

Table 7 shows that learned policy increases the average reward by 27.7% and 14.9% compared to the baseline system for the departure and arrival responses respectively. We notice that the average reward of the baseline arrival responses is significantly higher. A possible reason is that by this second question the users are adapting to the system.

The decrease in average utterance duration shows some interesting results. For responses to both questions, the oracle system utterance duration is about 55% shorter than the baseline one. The learned policy is also 45% shorter, which means that at about the middle of a user utterance, the system can already predict that the user either has expressed enough information or that the ASR is so wrong that there is no point of continuing to listen.

	Depature		**Arrival**	
Policy	Average reward	Average duration decrease	Average reward	Average duration decrease
Baseline	0.795	0%	0.959	0%
Oracle	1.396	58.1%	1.430	55.7%
Learned	0.998	42.8%	1.089	47.6%
Learned (smooth)	**1.016**	45.6%	**1.102**	46.2%

Table 7: Average reward and duration decrease for baseline, oracle, SVM and smooth SVM system.

Table 8 expands our understanding of the oracle and learned policy behaviors. We see that the oracle produces a much higher percentage of no-parse utterances in order to maximize the average reward, which, at first, seems counter-intuitive. The reason is that some utterances contain a large number of incorrect slots at the end and the oracle chooses to barge in at the beginning of the utterance to avoid the large negative reward for waiting until the end. This is the expected behavior discussed in Section 4. The learned policy is more conservative in producing no-parse utterances because it cannot cheat like the oracle to access future information and know that all future hypotheses will contain only incorrect information. However, although the learned policy only has access to historical information, it manages to predict future return by increasing CS and reducing ICS compared to the baseline.

Policy	**No-parse percent**	**Average CS**	**Average ICS**
Baseline	6.86%	0.765	0.499
Oracle	14.71%	0.865	0.196
Learned	8.14%	**0.796**	0.389
Learned (smooth)	**8.71%**	0.789	**0.360**

Table 8: No parse percentages and average CS and ICS for responses to the departure question.

8 Conclusions and Future Directions

This paper describes a novel turn-taking model that unifies the traditional rigid turn-taking model with incremental dialog processing. It also illustrates a systematic procedure of constructing a cost model and teaching a dialog system to actively grab the conversation floor in order to improve system robustness. The turn-taking model was tested for end-of-turn detection and active SB. The proposed model has shown superior performance in reducing FC rate and *response delay*. Also, the proposed SB algorithm has shown promise in increasing the average reward in user responses.

Future studies will include constructing a more comprehensive cost model that not only takes into account of CS/ICS, but also includes other factors such as conversational behavior. Further, since $E[S]$ will decrease after applying the learned policy, it invalidates the previous reward function. Future work should investigate how the change in $E[S]$ impacts the optimality of the policy. Also, we will add more complex actions to the system such as back channeling, clarifications etc.

References

Michaela Atterer, Timo Baumann, and David Schlangen. 2008. Towards incremental end-of-utterance detection in dialogue systems. *Proceedings of the 22nd International Conference on Computational Linguistics*.

Alan Black, Maxine Eskenazi, Milica Gasic, Helen Hastie, KAIST Kee-Eung Kim, Korea Ian Lane, Sungjin Lee, NICT Teruhisa Misu, Japan Olivier Pietquin, France SUPELEC, et al. 2013. Dialog state tracking challenge. http://research.microsoft.com/en-us/events/dstc/.

Dan Bohus and Alexander I Rudnicky. 2009. The ravenclaw dialog management framework: Architecture and systems. *Computer Speech & Language*, 23(3):332–361.

Catherine Breslin, Milica Gasic, Matthew Henderson, Dongho Kim, Martin Szummer, Blaise Thomson, Pirros Tsiakoulis, and Steve Young. 2013. Continuous asr for flexible incremental dialogue. In *Acoustics, Speech and Signal Processing (ICASSP), 2013 IEEE International Conference on*, pages 8362–8366. IEEE.

Yi-Wei Chen and Chih-Jen Lin. 2006. Combining svms with various feature selection strategies. In *Feature extraction*, pages 315–324. Springer, Berlin Heidelberg.

David DeVault, Kenji Sagae, and David Traum. 2009. Can i finish?: learning when to respond to incremental interpretation results in interactive dialogue. In *Proceedings of the SIGDIAL 2009 Conference: The 10th Annual Meeting of the Special Interest Group on Discourse and Dialogue*, pages 11–20. Association for Computational Linguistics.

Florian Eyben, Martin Wöllmer, and Björn Schuller. 2010. Opensmile: the munich versatile and fast open-source audio feature extractor. In *Proceedings of the international conference on Multimedia*, pages 1459–1462. ACM.

Thomas S Ferguson. 2012. *Optimal stopping and applications*. University of California, Los Angeles.

Fabrizio Ghigi, Maxine Eskenazi, M Ines Torres, and Sungjin Lee. 2014. Incremental dialog processing in a task-oriented dialog. In *Fifteenth Annual Conference of the International Speech Communication Association*.

Agustin Gravano. 2009. *Turn-taking and affirmative cue words in task-oriented dialogue*. Ph.D. thesis.

Chih-Wei Hsu, Chih-Chung Chang, Chih-Jen Lin, et al. 2003. A practical guide to support vector classification. Technical report, Department of Computer Science and Information Engineering, National Taiwan University.

Dongho Kim, Catherine Breslin, Pirros Tsiakoulis, Milica Gašic, Matthew Henderson, and Steve Young. 2014. Inverse reinforcement learning for micro-turn management. In *Proceedings of the Annual Conference of the International Speech Communication Association, INTERSPEECH*, pages 328–332. International Speech and Communication Association.

Michail Lagoudakis and Ronald Parr. 2003. Reinforcement learning as classification: Leveraging modern classifiers. In *ICML*, volume 3, pages 424–431.

Antoine Raux and Maxine Eskenazi. 2008. Optimizing endpointing thresholds using dialogue features in a spoken dialogue system. In *Proceedings of the 9th SIGdial Workshop on Discourse and Dialogue*, pages 1–10. Association for Computational Linguistics.

Antoine Raux and Maxine Eskenazi. 2009. A finite-state turn-taking model for spoken dialog systems. In *Proceedings of Human Language Technologies: The 2009 Annual Conference of the North American Chapter of the Association for Computational Linguistics*, pages 629–637. Association for Computational Linguistics.

Antoine Raux, Brian Langner, Dan Bohus, Alan W Black, and Maxine Eskenazi. 2005. Lets go public! taking a spoken dialog system to the real world. In *in Proc. of Interspeech 2005*.

Ethan Selfridge, Iker Arizmendi, Peter Heeman, and Jason Williams. 2013. Continuously predicting and processing barge-in during a live spoken dialogue task. In *Proceedings of the SIGDIAL 2013 Conference*.

Richard S Sutton and Andrew G Barto. 1998. *Introduction to reinforcement learning*. MIT Press.

Jason Williams, Antoine Raux, Deepak Ramachandran, and Alan Black. 2013. The dialog state tracking challenge. In *Proceedings of the SIGDIAL 2013 Conference*, pages 404–413.

Tiancheng Zhao and Maxine Eskenazi. 2015. Human-system turn taking analysis for the let's go bus information system. Pittsburgh, May. The Meeting of the Acoustical Society of America.

Exploring the Effects of Redundancy within a Tutorial Dialogue System: Restating Students' Responses

Pamela Jordan **Patricia Albacete** **Sandra Katz**
Learning Research and Development Center
University of Pittsburgh
pjordan@pitt.edu

Abstract

Although restating part of a student's correct response correlates with learning and various types of restatements have been incorporated into tutorial dialogue systems, this tactic has not been tested in isolation to determine if it causally contributes to learning. When we explored the effect of tutor restatements that support inference on student learning, it did not benefit all students equally. We found that students with lower incoming knowledge tend to benefit more from an increased level of these types of restatement while students with higher incoming knowledge tend to benefit more from a decreased level of such restatements. This finding has implications for tutorial dialogue system design since an inappropriate use of restatements could dampen learning.

1 Introduction

A tutor restating part of a student's dialogue contribution can be motivated by a range of communicative intentions (e.g. a tutor intends to reformulate a response, so that it is correct) and at the surface level can range from exact repetitions, to using different words while keeping the content semantically equivalent, to semantic reformulations which are often prefaced by markers such as "in other words" and "this means that" (Hyland, 2007). Some of the intentions associated with reformulations in the context of classroom lectures (Murillo, 2008) that also appear in human tutorial dialogue (Jordan et al., 2012) include, among others, definition (reformulate a prior statement so terms are defined), correction (reformulate a prior statement so it is correct) and consequence (reformulate so implications of a prior statement are clear).

But restatements also have intentions unique to the context of interactive discourse. We observed that human tutors, like classroom teachers who encourage and support discussion, frequently implement two types of restatement moves: revoicing and marking. Revoicing is characterized by a reformulation of what the student said. Like classroom teachers who facilitate discussions using a technique called "Accountable Talk" (O'Connor and Michaels, 1993), tutors sometimes revoice in order to verify their understanding of what a student was trying to say and, in the case of a correct student contribution, perhaps to model a better way of saying it. Marking, on the other hand, emphasizes what the teacher or tutor considers most important in what the student said and attempts to direct the student to focus his/her continued discussion on that.

Several recent studies of human tutorial dialogue have looked at particular aspects of restatements, for example, (Chi and Roy, 2010; Becker et al., 2011; Dzikovska et al., 2008; Litman and Forbes-Riley, 2006). One study examines face-to-face naturalistic tutorial dialogue in which a tutor helps a student work through a physics problem (Chi and Roy, 2010). The authors suggest that when the tutor repeats part of what the student said, it is often done with the intention of providing positive feedback for correct answers. Another of these recent studies collected a corpus using trained human tutors who filled in for a conversational virtual tutor in a science education system (Becker et al., 2011) and noted that a restatement can help a student who is struggling with a particular concept by modeling a good answer and can mark an aspect of the student's response to focus on in the ongoing discussion. Below we show excerpts from our corpus of human-human typed dialogues that illustrate these uses of restatement.

T: How do we know if there is a net force on the bullet in this problem?

Proceedings of the SIGDIAL 2015 Conference, pages 51–59,
Prague, Czech Republic, 2-4 September 2015.

> S: *if m*a does not equal 0*
> T: Right, **if the bullet is accelerating it must have a net force on it** - [tutor restatement to mark and provide positive feedback]
> T: how do we know it is accelerating?

> T: What is speed?
> S: *it is velocity without direction*
> T: **Right, The (instantaneous) speed is the magnitude of the (instantenous) velocity.** [tutor restatement to model a good answer and provide positive feedback]

Because restatements of correct responses have been shown to correlate with learning (Dzikovska et al., 2008), this suggests the possibility that restatements could causally contribute to learning. While restatements of various types have been incorporated into a number of tutorial dialogue systems, restatement has not been tested in isolation from other tactics to determine whether it has any causal connection to learning. Examples of tutorial dialogue systems that have incorporated restatement include: AutoTutor (Person et al., 2003) where elaborations and summaries often include restatements, CIRCSIM-Tutor (Freedman, 2000), which restates students' answers that are nearly correct except for terminology, and Beetle II (Dzikovska et al., 2008), which restates the correct parts of students' nearly correct or partially correct answers.

Here, we explore the effects on student learning of a tutor's restatement of the student's correct response in the context of a consequence intention (Murillo, 2008)–that is, making an inference explicit as shown in the excerpt below from our corpus.

> T: How do we know that we have an acceleration in this problem?
> S: because velocity starts at zero, and since the stone is falling, it doesn't remain at zero, thus there is *a change in the velocity* of the stone
> T: Ok so because there is **a change in velocity** then there has to be an acc [sic] right? [tutor restatement of correct response while making its implications clear]

We test two alternative hypotheses about this type of restatement: 1) that it will benefit students and 2) that its effect varies according to students' incoming knowledge.

Our discussion of the study that we conducted to test our hypotheses will proceed as follows. First we discuss the motivation for our hypotheses and then we describe the existing tutorial dialogue system we used as a platform for conducting our experiments with three different populations of students. We characterize the degree of restatement supported by the unaltered system and the modifications we made to produce a high restatement and a low restatement version of the system. Next we describe the experimental design and discuss our results in relation to two earlier experiments using different populations and test materials. We conclude by summarizing our results and plans for future work.

2 Background

From the perspective of memory encoding, storage and retrieval (McLeod, 2007), simply repeating back a student's correct answer may have an effect similar to maintenance rehearsal which would just maintain it in the student's working memory but do little to aid transfer to long-term memory. However, connecting the correct answer to something else, which a consequence restatement would do, may have more of an elaborative rehearsal effect which is better for transfer to long-term memory (McLeod, 2007). But the effect may not be applicable for very low incoming knowledge students who are not correct often. Conversely, if the correct answer is already more strongly established in the student's long-term memory–as may be the case for high incoming knowledge students–then restating it could be detrimental, whether the tutor's restatement only acknowledges the student's correct answer or is in the context of a consequence. In this situation it may be better to focus on strengthening the connection between the correct knowledge and other knowledge by having the student recall the correct knowledge on his/her own when it is needed.

From the perspective of interactions between communication strategies and cognitive processing, simulations with artificial agents showed that task performance varied as communication strategies and cognitive processing limits varied (Walker, 1996; Jordan and Walker, 1996). For example, under certain conditions as attention became more limited, repetition of mutually known information displaced from attention other critical problem-solving knowledge for the "hearer" while, conversely, such redundancies could become beneficial when attention was less limited. Possibly a student should not have mutually known information repeated when they are deep in thought (i.e. the processing load is high), because it could displace critical knowledge. On the other hand, a student who may be having trouble getting started on a question (i.e. the processing load may be lower), may find the repetition beneficial because there is less chance of displacement. The former case may more often describe a high-knowledge student and the latter a low-knowledge student.

Two other strands of research in psychology that are related to our hypotheses examined the effect of text cohesiveness on comprehension for low-knowledge and high-knowledge readers. The first found that unpacking the inferences in text supports comprehension among low-knowledge readers, while less cohesive (higher inference-inducing) text is better suited for high-knowledge readers (McNamara et al., 1996). Forcing the student to figure out what led to a consequence when no premise is explicitly provided could make it similar to a higher inference-inducing text. Reduced cognitive load is a proposed alternative explanation for the "cohesion reversal effect", particularly for high-knowledge readers, who must reconcile their existing schema about the topic discussed in the text with the background material provided in a "highly coherent" text (Kalyuga and Ayres, 2003). High-knowledge students might benefit more from less frequent consequence restatements because these students can make more inferences on their own. Frequent consequence restatements might entail more frequent schema alignment, and therefore an increased cognitive load. However, both of these explanations of the cohesion reversal effect, with respect to high knowledge students (prompted inference-making, or increased cognitive load), may be less plausible for consequence restatement during tutorial dialogue than for reading, because the former involves a proposition that was recently explicitly covered in the dialogue.

3 Experimental Platform

We used an existing natural-language tutoring system, Rimac, to conduct our experiments. It is a web-based system that aims to improve students' conceptual understanding of physics through typed reflective dialogues (Katz and Albacete, 2013). Rimac was built using the TuTalk natural language (NL) tutorial dialogue toolkit (Jordan et al., 2007). Thus its dialogue can be represented as a finite state machine where each state represents a tutor turn. The arcs leaving a state correspond to all classifications of a student's response to the tutor's turn. When a student turn is received, the system determines which arc it best represents and this in turn indicates what tutor state to transition to next. In the context of restatements, because the arc that is the best classification of the student's response leads to a particular tutor state, the tutor state can include that arc in its representation and can easily restate that arc. Note that this simplified approach will produce more reformulations than exact repetitions of student responses but both are acceptable for our experiment.

For this experiment we used Rimac's dynamics content which covers three problems with two reflection questions per problem. These problems and their associated reflective dialogues (two dialogues per problem) were developed in consultation with high school physics teachers. The reflection question dialogues are tutor-initiative only. The tutor primarily asks short answer questions, to keep accuracy of automatic recognition of student responses high. However, the dialogues include some questions that prompt the student for explanations at key points and then presents a menu of responses to which students are directed to map their previously typed explanation. We expect there to be a comparable frequency of misclassification of student responses across the two versions of the system that we created for our experiments since we made no modifications to any student response arcs in the original system.

To create a high restatement system for this experiment, three dialogue content authors independently reviewed and cross-reviewed all of the tutor states in the dialogue specifications for the base system and added tutor restatements of student responses that occurred in two dialogue contexts. Those contexts were: 1) an explicit if-then statement or question that draws the "if" or "then" part from the student's immediately preceding response and 2) a statement or question at the end of a sub-dialogue that draws upon the student's responses during the sub-dialogue. An example for contexts 1 and 2 are shown below for the high restatement condition:

Context 1:

T: Now let's look at our case in which we have a flying arrow. While the arrow is flying is anything touching or in contact with it?
S: No [there is nothing touching the arrow during its flight]

T: I agree. Hence since **there is nothing touching the arrow during its flight** there is no contact force applied to it.

Context 2:

T: What is the initial velocity of the faster arrow in the vertical direction as it leaves the bow?
S: [the initial velocity is] 0
T: I agree. Now does the faster arrow have an acceleration in the vertical direction when it leaves the bow?
S: yes, [it has a vertical acceleration of] 9.8 m/s^2
T: Okay! Now that we know **the initial vertical velocity of the fast arrow is zero and that it has a vertical acceleration of 9.8 m/s^2**, what will the value of vertical velocity of the arrow be a second after it leaves the bow?

To create the low restatement system, the same dialogue content authors reviewed the dialogue specifications for all instances of consequence restatements and either deleted or replaced the restatement of the student's response with an anaphoric expression. But the content authors were further directed to not carry out any modification that would disturb the coherency of the dialogue. The low restatement version of the first example above would be identical, except for the second tutor turn, which would read: "I agree. Hence there is no contact force applied to it." The example for context 2 is shown below for the low restatement condition.

Context 2:

T: What is the initial velocity of the faster arrow in the vertical direction as it leaves the bow?
S: 0
T: I agree. Now does the faster arrow have an acceleration in the vertical direction when it leaves the bow?
S: yes, 9.8 m/s^2
T: Okay! Now given what we know about the fast arrow, what will the value of vertical velocity of the arrow be a second after it leaves the bow?

After the experiments (described below) were completed, one of the authors of this paper reviewed the tutor states in the base system and the high and low restatement systems to characterize the number of changes made to create the high and low restatement systems from the base system. These findings are shown in Table 1 in the columns "possible". The "other" restatements, as shown in column 3 of Table 1, include restating the correct part of a partially correct answer and restating a correct answer when it required deeper reasoning to produce. These remain because they were deemed essential to tutoring. Ideally the number of "other" restatements should be equal for "high" and "low". Content authors were instructed to remove repetitions of fully correct answers to simple short answer questions but some were missed for "high". In addition, some restatements that were added to increase consequence for "high" were instead simple repetitions. However, we do not expect simple repetitions to affect learning, especially when their frequency is low, as reflected in the "avg" columns.

Table 1: Modifications to create the high and low restatement systems from the base system (labeled "possible") and the average number of states students experienced (labeled "avg")

System	Number of Restatement States			
	Consequence		Other	
	possible	avg	possible	avg
Base	48	NA	18	NA
High	77	19.8	19	2.6
Low	4	.8	7	.375

4 Methods

Participants Our comparison of the high and low restatement versions of Rimac was conducted during high school physics classes at three schools in the Pittsburgh PA area. The study followed the course unit on dynamics with a total of 168 students participating. Students were randomly assigned to one of two conditions: high restatement (N= 88; 30 females, 58 males) and low restatement (N= 80; 27 females, 53 males).

Materials Students interacted with either a high or low restatement version of Rimac, as described in the previous section, to discuss the physics conceptual knowledge associated with three quantitative dynamics problems.

We developed a 21 item pretest and isomorphic post-test (that is, each question was equivalent to a pretest question, but with a different cover story) to measure learning differences from interactions with the system. The test included nine multiple choice problems and twelve open response problems and focused on testing students' conceptual understanding of physics instead of their ability to solve quantitative problems.

Procedure On the first day, the teacher gave the pretest in class and assigned the three dynamics problems for homework. During the next one to two class days (depending on whether classes

Table 2: Learning from interacting with the systems, for both conditions combined and separately for the high and low restatement conditions

Problems	**Condition**	**Pretest Mean (*SD*)**	**Posttest Mean (*SD*)**	***t(n), p***
All	Combined	7.90 (2.40) 0.376 (0.114)	8.97 (2.88) 0.427 (0.137)	$t(167)=5.60$, $p<0.01$
	High	7.71 (2.36) 0.367 (0.113)	8.73 (2.73) 0.416 (0.130)	$t(87)=3.56$, $p<0.01$
	Low	8.11 (2.44) 0.386 (0.116)	9.23 (3.02) 0.440 (0.144)	$t(79)=4.49$, $p<0.01$
Multiple-choice	Combined	4.73 (1.40) 0.525 (0.156)	5.20 (1.50) 0.578 (0.167)	$t(167)=3.63$, $p<0.01$
	High	4.67 (1.37) 0.519 (0.152)	5.16 (1.46) 0.573 (0.162)	$t(87)=2.73$, $p=0.01$
	Low	4.79 (1.44) 0.532 (0.160)	5.25 (1.55) 0.583 (0.173)	$t(79)=2.39$, $p=0.02$
Open-response	Combined	3.18 (1.48) 0.265 (0.124)	3.77 (1.78) 0.314 (0.148)	$t(167)=5.38$, $p<0.01$
	High	3.04 (1.47) 0.253 (0.123)	3.57 (1.68) 0.298 (0.140)	$t(87)=3.13$, $p<0.01$
	Low	3.32 (1.49) 0.277 (0.124)	3.98 (1.87) 0.332 (0.156)	$t(79)=4.8$, $p<0.01$

were approximately 45 min. or 80 min. long), students watched a video of a sample, worked-out solution to each homework problem in one of the two versions of Rimac and engaged in two "reflective dialogues" after each problem-solving video. The videos demonstrated how to solve the problem only and did not offer any conceptual explanations. Hence we do not believe that the videos contributed to learning gains. Finally, at the next class meeting, teachers gave the post-test.

5 Results

We evaluated the data to determine whether students who interacted with the tutoring system learned, as measured by gain from pretest to post-test, regardless of their treatment condition (i.e. which version of Rimac they were assigned to use), and if there was an aptitude-treatment interaction; in particular, an interaction between students' prior knowledge about physics (as measured by pretest score) and how much students learned in each condition (as measured by gain score).

The data was first analyzed considering all problems together and then multiple-choice and open-response problems were considered separately. The rationale for this further division of test items is that open-response problems, unlike multiple-choice problems, would allow us to determine whether students are able to verbalize coherent conceptual explanations of the physics phenomena tested in these problems. Moreover, open-response problems do not allow for guessing of the correct answer to the extent that multiple-choice test items do.

Learning Performance & Time on Task To determine whether interaction with the system, regardless of condition, promoted learning, we compared pretest scores with post-test scores. Towards this end, we performed paired samples t-tests. When all students were considered together, we found a statistically significant difference between pretest and post-test scores for all problems together, multiple-choice problems, and open-response problems as shown in Table 2. When students in each condition were considered separately, we again found a statistically significant difference between pretest and post-test for all problems together, multiple-choice problems, and open-response problems as shown in Table 2. These results suggest that students in both conditions learned from interacting with the system.

Prior to testing for differences between conditions, we tested for a difference in time on task between conditions. No statistically significant difference was found between conditions for the mean time on task.

High Restatement vs. Low Restatement First, we confirmed that there was significantly more consequence restatement in the high restatement condition than in the low restatement condition using independent samples t-tests: M(high)=20.4,

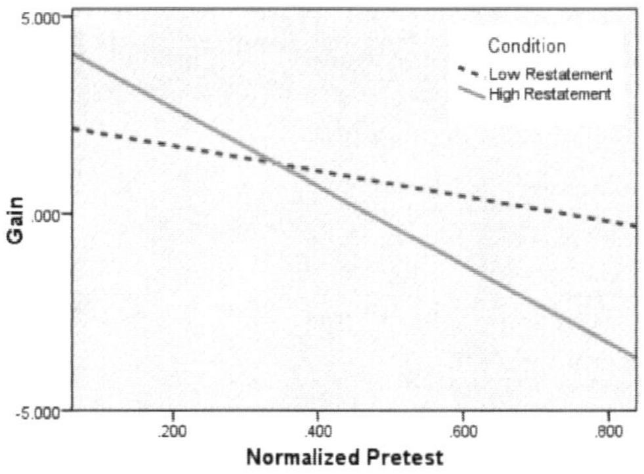

Figure 1: Prior knowledge-treatment interaction for All Problems

M(low)=.8; $t(91)=29.3, p<.0001$. Next, to test whether students who used the high restatement version of the system would perform differently from students who used the low restatement version, we compared students' gains from pretest to post-test between conditions using independent samples t-tests. Gains were defined as (post-test - pretest) and their normalized versions as (post-test/#problems) - (pretest/#problems).[1]

We found no significant differences in gains between conditions for any subset of problems. This suggests that the presence or absence of a consequence restatement has the same effect on learning when students of all knowledge levels are considered together.

Prior knowledge-treatment interaction To investigate whether there was a prior knowledge treatment interaction, we performed a multiple regression analysis using condition, prior-knowledge (as measured by pretest) and condition * prior-knowledge (interaction) as explanatory variables, and gain as the dependent variable. When all problems were considered together, we found a significant interaction between condition and prior knowledge in their effect on gains ($t=-2.126, p=0.04$). Likewise, we found a significant interaction when we considered only gains on open-response problems ($t=-2.689, p=0.01$). However, for multiple-choice problems we did not find a significant interaction.

The graph of gain vs. prior knowledge in Figure 1 shows the fitted lines for both conditions when considering all problems. It suggests that students with pretest scores that are 35% correct (7.5) or less benefit more from the high restatement version of the system than from the low restatement version. However students with pretest scores above 35% correct benefit more from the low restatement version of the system. The graph of gain vs. prior knowledge for open-response problems is shown in Figure 2. It suggests that students with pretest scores of 23% or less on open-response items benefit more from higher restatement and students with pretest scores greater than 23% benefit more from lower restatement. Both findings offer evidence to support the hypothesis that the effect of consequence restatements varies according to students' incoming knowledge. In particular, it suggests that lower knowledge students benefit more from high restatement in inferential contexts while higher knowledge students benefit more from low restatement.

[1] The reason for using both measures is that each measure relates the same information, but in a different way. The full test scores show means and standard deviations in terms of number of problems solved correctly (given that each test item has a score of 0-1) whereas the normalized values convey the same results in terms of percent of correct responses.

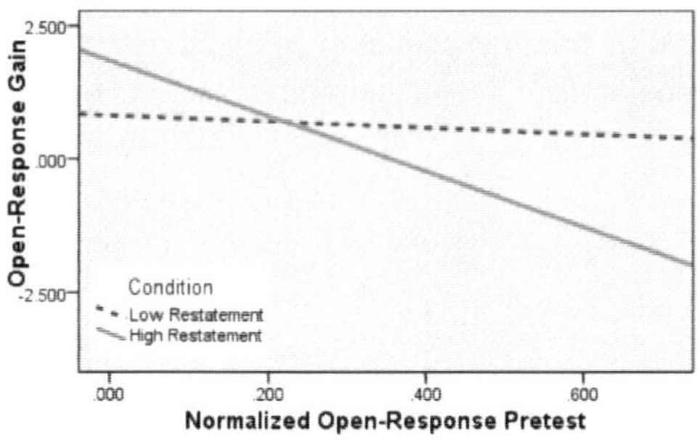

Figure 2: Prior knowledge-treatment interaction for Open-Response Problems

6 Additional Support for a Prior Knowledge-Treatment Interaction from Earlier Experiments

Prior to the study that we described in Section 5, which we will refer to now as experiment E3, we conducted two field trials, E1 and E2, which differed only by the versions of the tests that we administered and the populations recruited. We will refer to the test we previously described in Section 4 as T3, to distinguish it from the tests administered during the prior experiments (T1 and T2).

Field Trial E1 with test T1 The first field trial, E1, utilized undergraduate students only and test T1. We recruited undergraduates (N=62) who had taken only high school physics within the last two years. The goal was to sample students whose knowledge of physics was similar to that of our target high school population. Test T1 was used in previous experiments with high school students for the dynamics domain.

Just as with E3, we confirmed that there was significantly more consequence restatement in the high restatement condition than in the low restatement condition using independent samples t-tests: M(high)=24.2, M(low)=1.2; $t(36)=45.7, p<.0001$. Similarly, we found that for the undergraduate population there were no significant differences in gains between conditions. However, for this population there were no significant interactions between conditions and prior knowledge. Since we had found a prior knowledge treatment interaction in experiment E3, we re-examined the pretest scores of the undergraduates, to investigate whether students' incoming knowledge could have been a factor.

We found that the pretest mean for the undergraduates was 44% correct (SD=14%) while the pretest mean for the high school students who had taken test T1 was lower at 37% correct (SD=13%). Furthermore, the high school students who had taken T1 had a post-test mean of 40% correct (SD=16%) which was lower than the **pretest** mean of E1's undergraduates. The undergraduates' prior knowledge is clearly higher than that of the high school students. Given the higher prior knowledge of the undergraduates in E1 (compared with the high school students who had taken T1), we expected that the mean gain for the low restatement condition in E1 (M=2.71, SD=2.18; normalized M=.12, SD=.10) would tend to be higher than for the high restatement condition (M=1.99, SD=2.24; normalized M=.09, SD=.10) and that was the case.

Hence, this pattern is consistent with the second hypothesis that the effect of consequence restatements varies according to incoming knowledge. While there was no significant difference between conditions for the undergraduate population, undergraduates had higher prior knowledge than high school students and for undergraduates the mean gain for the low restatement condition was higher than for the high restatement condition which is in the same direction as the findings for E3.

Field Trial E2 with test T2 We decided to refine test T1, which was used in E1, to create test T2. We used test T2 in field trial E2 with high school students (N=88) who were from two different local high schools from those who participated in experiment E3.

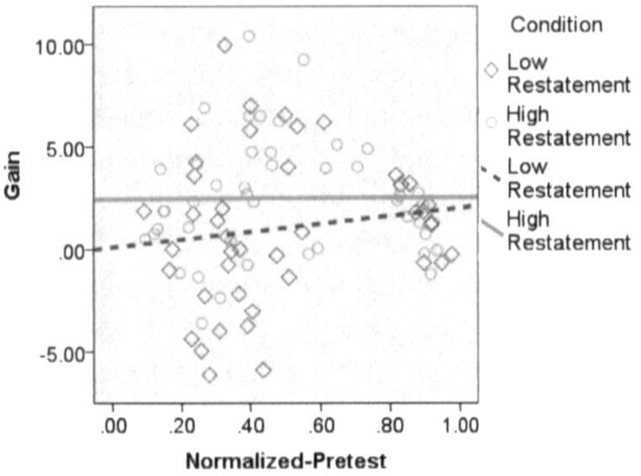

Figure 3: Prior knowledge-treatment interaction for All Problems for E2

As before with E3, we confirmed that there was significantly more consequence restatement in the high restatement condition than in the low restatement condition using independent samples t-tests: M(high)=20.3, M(low)=.64; $t(56)=21.8, p<.0001$. With this population, however, we found statistically significant differences in learning gains between conditions that favored the high restatement version of the system. Using independent samples t-tests, we found significant differences for all test problems together: M(high)=2.49 SD=2.90, M(low)=1.04 SD=3.68; $t(86)=2.07, p<.04$ and for multiple-choice problems: M(high)=.66 SD=1.27, M(low)=-.-6 SD=1.4; $t(86)=2.51, p<.01$ but not for open-response problems. However, there were no statistically significant interactions between condition and prior knowledge for any subset of test problems.

Given the results of experiment E3 and the pattern in E1, we re-examined the pretest scores of these high school students to consider whether their incoming knowledge could have been lower than the students in E3. The graph of the gain vs. pretest scores in Figure 3 shows that gains for students in the high restatement condition were better than for students in the low restatement condition. However, the difference was more pronounced for lower incoming knowledge students than for higher incoming knowledge students which agrees with the pattern in E3. Moreover, one of the schools in this sample had a significantly lower pretest mean than the other school (M=36%, SD=16% vs. M=86%, SD=8%;

t(86)=14.9,p=.000) and a larger sample size (N=65 vs. N=23). This suggests there were more lower incoming knowledge students in E2 than higher incoming knowledge students.

So there is a pattern that is consistent with the finding in E3 and the pattern in E1. The results suggested that the high restatement condition was significantly better than the low restatement one; however, more of the population seemed to have lower incoming knowledge which would favor the high restatement condition. However, more experimentation with populations similar to these two schools is needed. It is possible that the incoming knowledge in this one school is comparable to the ones in E3. This was the only high-school in which we had to move from the classroom to a computer lab. This added disruption to the usual classroom routine may have made it more difficult for students to "settle in" and concentrate. If the students had problems focusing, then the added repetitions may have been helpful.

Experiment E3 with test T3 After E2, we shortened the test to create T3, which was used in experiment E3, the focus of this paper. While the tests differed across all three experiments, so we cannot directly compare the populations, the patterns in each case seem consistent with the prior knowledge treatment interactions that we found in study E3, as reported in Section 5. However, experiments that use the same test would be necessary to verify these patterns.

7 Conclusions and Future Work

We found that students learned from the tutoring system, across conditions, as measured by differences in pre-test and post-test scores. In the main study reported here (E3), there was no difference in learning gains between conditions, which suggests that the presence or absence of consequence restatement in a system has a similar effect for all students considered together; that is, irrespective of their prior knowledge. However, we did find a prior knowledge treatment interaction which supported the hypothesis that the effect of consequence restatement varies according to students' prior knowledge. In particular, our results suggest that lower knowledge students would benefit more from a high restatement system while higher knowledge students would benefit more from a low restatement system.

Two earlier studies with different populations and tests also support this finding. While there was no significant difference in learning gains between conditions for the study with the undergraduate population (E1), undergraduates had higher prior knowledge than high school students and for undergraduates the low restatement condition had a higher mean gain than the high restatement condition. For the earlier study with a different set of high schools (E2), there was a significant difference in learning gains between the high and low restatement conditions that favored the high restatement condition but more of the population seemed to have lower incoming knowledge which would favor that condition. Moreover, the lower the student's incoming knowledge, the larger the benefit of high restatement. However, these results are preliminary and require further experimentation to better understand when and why consequence restatements can support learning.

The findings across the three experiments suggest that system designers may need to be careful in their use of restatement as it may dampen learning if there is a mismatch with students' prior knowledge levels. Further it suggests that when building tutorial dialogue systems, care must be taken in the tactics and strategies that may be applied to address system limitations. For example, spoken dialogue systems sometimes use an explicit confirmation strategy to address repeated speech recognition errors (Litman and Pan, 2000). Carrying such a strategy over to tutorial applications could have an unintended impact on some students' learning outcomes.

In future research, we plan to determine if the benefits of the high and low restatement versions of Rimac can be used advantageously in a system that adapts to students' knowledge levels and to formulate and test additional hypotheses for other types of restatement.

Acknowledgements.

We thank Stefani Allegretti, Michael Lipschultz, Diane Litman, Dennis Lusetich, Svetlana Romanova, and Scott Silliman for their contributions. This research was supported by the Institute of Education Sciences, U.S. Department of Education, through Grant R305A130441 to the University of Pittsburgh. The opinions expressed are those of the authors and do not necessarily represent the views of the Institute or the U.S. Department of Education.

References

L. Becker, W. Ward, S. Van Vuuren, and M. Palmer. 2011. Discuss: A dialogue move taxonomy layered over semantic representations. In *IWCS 2011: The 9th International Conference on Computational Semantics*, Oxford, England, January.

M. T. H. Chi and M. Roy. 2010. How adaptive is an expert human tutor? In *10th International Conference on Intelligent Tutoring Systems (ITS)*, pages 401–412.

M. Dzikovska, G. Campbell, C. Callaway, N. Steinhauser, E. Farrow, J. Moore, L. Butler, and C. Matheson. 2008. Diagnosing natural language answers to support adaptive tutoring. In *International FLAIRS Conference*.

R. Freedman. 2000. Using a reactive planner as the basis for a dialogue agent. In *International FLAIRS Conference*.

Ken Hyland. 2007. Applying a gloss: Exemplifying and reformulating in academic discourse. *Applied Linguistics*, 28(2):266–285.

P. Jordan and M. A. Walker. 1996. Deciding to remind during collaborative problem solving: Empirical evidence for agent strategies. In *AAAI-96*, pages 16–23, August.

P. Jordan, B. Hall, M. Ringenberg, Y. Cui, and C.P. Rosé. 2007. Tools for authoring a dialogue agent that participates in learning studies. In *AIED 2007*.

P. Jordan, S. Katz, P. Albacete, M. Ford, and C. Wilson. 2012. Reformulating student contributions in tutorial dialogue. In *7th International Natural Language Generation Conference*, pages 95–99.

S. Kalyuga and P. Ayres. 2003. The expertise reversal effect. *Educational Psychology*, 38:23–31.

S. Katz and P. Albacete. 2013. A tutoring system that simulates the highly interactive nature of human tutoring. *Educational Psychology (Special Issue on Advanced Learning Technologies)*, 105(4):1126–1141.

D. Litman and K. Forbes-Riley. 2006. Correlations between dialogue acts and learning in spoken tutoring dialogues. *Natural Language Engineering*, 12(2):161–176.

D. Litman and S. Pan. 2000. Predicting and adapting to poor speech recognition in a spoken dialogue system. In *AAAI/IAAI*, pages 722–728.

S. A. McLeod. 2007. Stages of memory - encoding storage and retrieval. Retrieved from http://www.simplypsychology.org/memory.html.

D.S. McNamara, E. Kintsch, N.B. Songer, and W. Kintsch. 1996. Are good texts always better? text coherence, background knowledge, and levels of understanding in learning from text. *Cognition and Instruction*, 14:1–43.

S. Murillo. 2008. The role of reformulation markers in academic lectures. In A.M. Hornero, M.J. Luzón, and S. Murillo, editors, *Corpus Linguistics: Applications for the Study of English*, pages 353–364. Peter Lang AG.

M.C. O'Connor and S. Michaels. 1993. Aligning academic task and participation status through revoicing: Analysis of a classroom discourse strategy. *Anthropology & Education Quarterly*, 24(4):318–335.

N. Person, A. Graesser, R. Kreuz, and V. Pomeroy. 2003. Simulating human tutor dialog moves in autotutor. *International Journal of Artificial Intelligence in Education*, 12(23-39).

M. A. Walker. 1996. The effect of resource limits and task complexity on collaborative planning in dialogue. *Artificial Intelligence Journal*, 85(1-2):181–243.

A Discursive Grid Approach to Model Local Coherence in Multi-document Summaries

Márcio S. Dias
Interinstitutional Center for Computational Linguistics (NILC)
University of São Paulo, São Carlos/SP, Brazil
marciosd@icmc.usp.br

Thiago A. S. Pardo
Interinstitutional Center for Computational Linguistics (NILC)
University of São Paulo, São Carlos/SP, Brazil
taspardo@icmc.usp.br

Abstract

Multi-document summarization is a very important area of Natural Language Processing (NLP) nowadays because of the huge amount of data in the web. People want more and more information and this information must be coherently organized and summarized. The main focus of this paper is to deal with the coherence of multi-document summaries. Therefore, a model that uses discursive information to automatically evaluate local coherence in multi-document summaries has been developed. This model obtains 92.69% of accuracy in distinguishing coherent from incoherent summaries, outperforming the state of the art in the area.

1 Introduction

In text generation systems (as summarizers, question-answering systems, etc.), coherence is an essential characteristic in order to produce comprehensible texts. As such, studies and theories on coherence ((Mann and Thompson, 1998), (Grosz et al., 1995)) have supported applications that involve text generation ((Seno, 2005), (Bosma, 2004), (Kibble and Power, 2004)).

According to Mani (2001), Multi-document Summarization (MDS) is the task of automatically producing a unique summary from a set of source texts on the same topic. In MDS, local coherence is as important as informativity. A summary must contain relevant information but also present it in a coherent, readable and understandable way.

Coherence is the possibility of establishing a meaning for the text (Koch and Travaglia, 2002). Coherence supposes that there are relationships among the elements of the text for it to make sense. It also involves aspects that are out of the text, for example, the shared knowledge between the producer (writer) and the receiver (reader/listener) of the text, inferences, intertextuality, intentionality and acceptability, among others (Koch and Travaglia, 2002).

Textual coherence occurs in local and global levels (Dijk and Kintsch, 1983). Local level coherence is presented by the local relationship among the parts of a text, for instance, sentences and shorter sequences. On the other hand, a text presents global coherence when this text links all its elements as a whole. Psycholinguistics consider that local coherence is essential in order to achieve global coherence (Mckoon, 1992).

The main phenomena that affect coherence in multi-document summaries are redundant, complementary and contradictory information (Jorge and Pardo, 2010). These phenomena may occur because the information contained in the summaries possibly come from different sources that narrate the same topic. Thus, a good multi-document summary should a) not contain redundant information, b) properly link and order complementary information, and c) avoid or treat contradictory information.

In this context, we present, in this paper, a discourse-based model for capturing the above properties and distinguishing coherent from incoherent (or less coherent) multi-document summaries. Cross-document Structure Theory (CST) (Radev, 2000) and Rhetorical Structure Theory (RST) (Mann and Thompson, 1998) relations are used to create the discursive model.

RST considers that each text presents an underlying rhetorical structure that allows the recovery of the writer's communicative intention. RST relations are structured in the form of a tree, where Elementary Discourse Units (EDUs) are located in the leaves of this tree. CST, in turn, organizes multiple texts on the same topic

Proceedings of the SIGDIAL 2015 Conference, pages 60–67,
Prague, Czech Republic, 2-4 September 2015.

and establishes relations among different textual segments.

In particular, this work is based on the following assumptions: (i) there are transition patterns of discursive relations (CST and RST) in locally coherent summaries; (ii) and coherent summaries show certain distinct intra- and inter-discursive relation organization (Lin et al., 2011), (Castro Jorge et al., 2014), (Feng et al., 2014). The model we propose aims at incorporating such issues, learning summary discourse organization preferences from corpus.

This paper is organized as follows: in Section 2, it is presented an overview of the most relevant researches related to local coherence; Section 3 details the proposed approach in this paper; Section 4 shows the experimental setup and the obtained results; finally, Section 5 presents some final remarks.

2 Related Work

Foltz et al. (1998) used Latent Semantic Analysis (LSA) (Landauer and Dumais, 1997) to compute a coherence value for texts. LSA produces a vector for each word or sentence, so that the similarity between two words or two sentences may be measured by their cosine (Salton, 1988). The coherence value of a text may be obtained by the cosine measures for all pairs of adjacent sentences. With this statistical approach, the authors obtained 81% and 87.3% of accuracy applied to the earthquakes and accidents corpus from North American News Corpus[1], respectively.

Barzilay and Lapata (2008) proposed to deal with local coherence with an Entity Grid Model. This model is based on Centering Theory (Grosz et al., 1995), whose assumption is that locally coherent texts present certain regularities concerning entity distribution. These regularities are calculated over an Entity Grid, i.e., a matrix in which the rows represent the sentences of the text and the columns the text entities. For example, Figure 2 shows part of the Entity Grid for the text in Figure 1. For instance, the "Depart." (Department) column in the grid (Figure 2) shows that the entity "Department" only happens in the first sentence in the Subject (S) position. Analogously, the marks O and X indicate the syntactical functions "Object" and "other syntactical functions" that are neither subject nor object, respectively. The hyphen ('-') indicates that the entity did not happen in the corresponding sentence.

Probabilities of entity transitions in texts may be computed from the entity grid and they compose a feature vector. For example, the probability of transition [O -] (i.e., the entity happened in the object position in one sentence and did not happen in the following sentence) in the grid in Figure 2 is 0.12, computed as the ratio between its occurrence in the grid (3 occurrences) and the total number of transitions (24).

1 (The Justice Department)$_S$ is conducting an (anti-trust trial)$_O$ against (Microsoft Corp.)$_X$ with (evidence)$_X$ that (the company)$_S$ is increasingly attempting to crush (competitors)$_O$.
2 (Microsoft)$_O$ is accused of trying to forcefully buy into (markets)$_X$ where (its own products)$_S$ are not competitive enough to unseat (established brands)$_O$.
3 (The case)$_S$ revolves around (evidence)$_O$ of (Microsoft)$_S$ aggressively pressuring (Netscape)$_O$ into merging (browser software)$_O$.
...

Figure 1. Text with syntactic tags (Barzilay and Lapata, 2008)

	Depart.	Trial	Microsoft	Evidence	Compet.	Markets	Products	Brands	Case	Netscape	Software	...	
1	S	O	S	X	O	-	-	-	-	-	-	-	1
2	-	-	O	-	-	X	S	O	-	-	-	-	2
3	-	-	S	O	-	-	-	-	S	O	O	-	3

Figure 2. Entity Grid (Barzilay and Lapata, 2008)

The authors evaluated the generated models in a text-ordering task (the one that interests us in this paper). In this task, each original text is considered "coherent", and a set of randomly sentence-permutated versions were produced and considered "incoherent" texts. Ranking values for coherent and incoherent texts were produced by a predictive model trained in the SVMlight (Joachims, 2002) package, using a set of text pairs (coherent text, incoherent text). It is supposed that the ranking values of coherent texts are higher than the ones for incoherent texts. Barzilay and Lapata obtained 87.2% and 90.4% of accuracy (fraction of correct pairwise rankings in the test set) applied respectively to the set of texts related to earthquakes and accidents, in English. Such results were achieved by a model considering three types of information, namely, coreference, syntactical and salience information.

[1] https://catalog.ldc.upenn.edu/LDC95T21

Using coreference, it is possible to recognize different terms that refer to the same entity in the texts (resulting, therefore, in only one column in the grid). Syntax provides the functions of the entities; if not used, the grid only indicates if an entity occurs or not in each sentence; if salience is used, different grids are produced for more frequent and less frequent entities. It is important to notice that any combination of these features may be used.

Lin et al. (2011) assumed that local coherence implicitly favors certain types of discursive relation transitions. Based on the Entity Model from Barzilay and Lapata (2008), the authors used terms instead of entities and discursive information instead of syntactic information. The terms are the stemmed forms of open class words: nouns, verbs, adjectives and adverbs. The discursive relations used in this work came from the Penn Discourse Treebank (PDTB) (Prasad et al., 2008). The authors developed the Discursive Grid, which is composed of sentences (rows) and terms (columns) with discursive relations used over their arguments. For example, part of the discursive grid (b) for a text (a) is shown in Figure 3.

(S1) Japan normally depends heavily on the Highland Valley and Cananea mines as well as the Bougainville mine in Papua New Guinea. (S2) Recently, Japan has been buying copper elsewhere.

(a)

	Terms			
	copper	cananea	depend	...
S_1	nil	Comp.Arg1	Comp.Arg1	
S_2	Comp.Arg2 Comp.Arg1	nil	nil	

(b)

Figure 3. A text (a) and part of its grid (b)

A cell contains the set of the discursive roles of a term that appears in a sentence Sj. For example, the term "depend" in S1 is part of the Comparison (Comp) relation as argument 1 (Arg1), so the cell Cdepend,S1 contains the Comp.Arg1 role. The authors obtained 89.25% and 91.64% of accuracy applied to the set of English texts related to earthquakes and accidents, respectively.

Guinaudeau and Strube (2013) created an approach based on graph to eliminate the process of machine learning of the Entity Grid Model from Barzilay and Lapata (2008). Due to this, the authors proposed to represent entities in a graph and then to model local coherence by applying centrality measures to the nodes in the graph. Their main assumption was that this bipartite graph contained the entity transition information needed for the computation of local coherence, thus feature vectors and a learning phase are unnecessary. Figure 4 shows part of the bipartite graph of the entity grid illustrated in Figure 2.

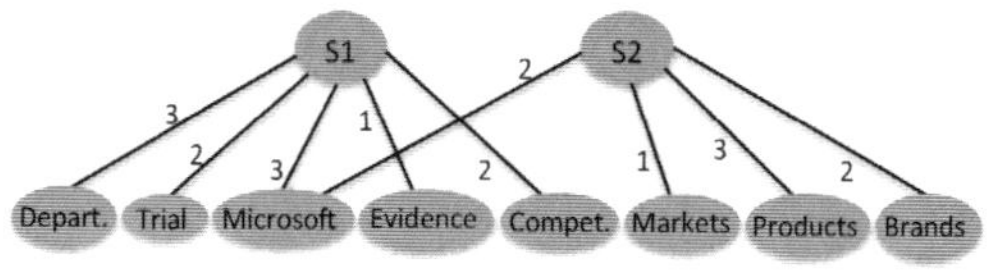

Figure 4. Bipartite graph

There is a group of nodes for the sentences and another group for the entities. Edges are stablished when the entities occur in the sentences, and their weights correspond to the syntactical function of the entities in the sentences (3 for subjects, 2 for objects and 1 for other functions).

Given the bipartite graph, the authors defined three kinds of projection graphs: *Unweighted One-mode Projection* (*PU*), *Weighted One-mode Projection* (*PW*) and *Syntactic Projection* (*PAcc*). In *PU*, weights are binary and equal to 1 when two sentences have at least one entity in common. In *PW*, edges are weighted according to the number of entities "shared" by two sentences. In *PAcc*, the syntactical weights are used. From *PU*, *PW* and *PAcc*, the local coherence of a text may be measured by computing the average outdegree of a projection graph. Distance information (*Dist*) between sentences may also be integrated in the weight of one-mode projections to decrease the importance of links that exist between non-adjacent sentences.

The approach was evaluated using the corpus from Barzilay and Lapata (2008). This model obtained 84.6% and 63.5% of accuracy in the Accidents and Earthquakes corpus, respectively.

Feng et al. (2014) is similar to Lin et al.'s (2011) work. Feng et al. (2014) created a discursive grid formed by sentences in rows and entities in columns. The cells of the grid are filled with RST relations together with nuclearity information. For example, Figure 5 shows a text fragment with 3 sentences and 7 EDUs. In Figure 6, a RST discourse tree representation of the text in Figure 5 is shown. Figure 7 shows a fragment of the RST-style discursive role grid of the text in Figure 5. This grid is based on the discursive tree representation in Figure 6. One may see in

Figure 7 that the entity "Yesterday" in sentence 1 occurs in the nuclei (N) of the Background and Temporal relations; the entity "session", in turn, is the satellite (S) of the Temporal relation.

S1: [The dollar finished lower yesterday,]e1 [after tracking another rollercoaster session on Wall Street.]e2
S2: [Concern about the volatile U.S. stock market had faded in recent sessions,]e3 [and traders appeared content to let the dollar languish in a narrow range until tomorrow,]e4 [when the preliminary report on third-quarter U.S. gross national product is released.]e5
S3: [But seesaw gyrations in the Dow Jones Industrial Average yesterday put Wall Street back in the spotlight]e6 [and inspired market participants to bid the U.S. unit lower.]e7

Figure 5. A text fragment (Feng et al., 2014)

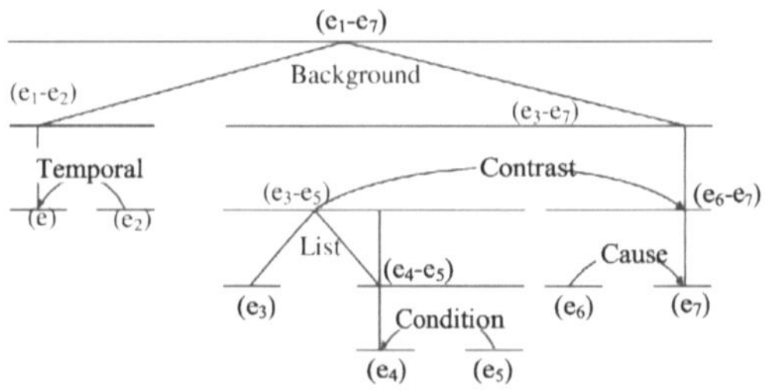

Figure 6. RST discursive tree representation (Feng et al., 2014)

	dollar	Yesterday	session	...
S1	Background.N Temporal.N	Background.N Temporal.N	Temporal.S	...
S2	List.N Condition.N Contrast.N	nil	nil	...
S3	Contrast.N Background.N Cause.N	Cause.S	nil	...

Figure 7. Part of the RST-style discursive role grid for the example text (Feng et al., 2014)

Feng et al. (2014) developed two models: the Full RST Model and the Shallow RST Model. The Full RST Model uses long-distance RST relations for the most relevant entities in the RST tree representation of the text. For example, considering the RST discursive tree representation in Figure 6, the Background relation was encoded for the entities "dollar" and "Yesterday" in S1, as well as the entity "dollar" in S3, but not for the remaining entities in the text, even though the Background relation covers the whole text. The corresponding full RST-style discursive role matrix for the example text is shown in Figure 7. The shallow RST Model only considers relations that hold between text spans of the same sentence, or between two adjacent sentences. The Full RST Model obtained an accuracy of 99.1% and the Shallow RST Model obtained 98.5% of accuracy in the text-ordering task.

Dias et al. (2014b) also implemented a coherence model that uses RST relations. The authors created a grid composed by sentences in rows and entities in columns. The cells were filled with RST relation. This model was applied to a corpus of news texts written in Brazilian Portuguese. This model had the accuracy of 79.4% with 10-fold cross validation in the text-ordering task. This model is similar to the Full RST Model. These models were created in parallel and used in corpora of different languages. Besides the corpus and the language, the Shallow RST Model only uses the RST relations of a sentence and/or adjacent sentences, while Dias et al. capture all the possible relations among sentences.

Regarding the model of Lin et al. (2011), the discursive information used by Lin et al. and Dias et al. is the main difference between these models, i.e., Dias et al. use RST relations and Lin et al. use PDTB-style discursive relations.

Castro Jorge et al. (2014) combined CST relations and syntactic information in order to evaluate the coherence of multi-document summaries. The authors created a CST relation grid represented by sentences in the rows and in the columns, and the cells were filled with 1 or 0 (presence/absence of CST relations – called Entity-based Model with CST bool). This model was applied to a corpus of news summaries written in Brazilian Portuguese and it obtained 81.39% of accuracy in the text-ordering task. Castro Jorge et al.'s model differs from the previous models since it uses CST information and a summarization corpus (instead of full texts).

3 The Discursive Model

The model proposed in this paper considers that all coherent multi-document summaries have patterns of discursive relation (RST and CST) that distinguish them from the incoherent (less coherent) multi-document summaries.

The model is based on a grid of RST and CST relations. Then, a predictive model that uses the probabilities of relations between two sentences as features was trained by the SVM^{light} package and evaluated in the text-ordering task.

As an illustration, Figure 8 shows a multi-document summary. The CST relation "Follow-up" relates the sentences S2 and S3. Between the sentences S1 and S3, there is the RST relation "elaboration". The RST relation "sequence" happens between S1 and S4. After the identification of the relations in the summary, a grid of discursive relations is created. Figure 9 shows the discursive grid for the summary in Figure 8. In this grid, the sentences of the summary are represented in the rows and in the columns. The cells are filled with RST and/or CST relations that happen in the transition between the sentences (the CST relations have their first letters capitalized, whereas RST relations do not).

(S1) Ended the rebellion of prisoners in the Justice Prisoners Custody Center (CCPJ) in São Luís, in the early afternoon of Wednesday (17).
(S2) After the prisoners handed the gun used to start the riot, the Military Police Shock troops entered the prison and freed 30 hostages - including 16 children.
(S3) The riot began during the Children's Day party, held on Tuesday (16).
(S4) According to the police, the leader of the rebellion was transferred to the prison of Pedrinhas, in the capital of Maranhão.

Figure 8. Summary with discursive information from the CSTNews corpus (Cardoso et al., 2011)

	S1	S2	S3	S4
S1		-	elaboration	Sequence
S2			Follow-up	-
S3				-
S4				

Figure 9. Discursive grid for Figure 8

Consider two sentences S_i and S_j (where i and j indicate the place of the sentence in the summary): if $i < j$, it is a valid transition and 1 is added to the total of possible relationships. Considering that the transitions are visualized from the left to the right in the discursive grid in Figure 9, the cells in gray do not characterize a valid transition (since only the superior diagonal of the grid is necessary in this model).

The probabilities of relations present in the transitions are calculated as the ratio between the frequency of a specific relation in the grid and the total number of valid transitions between two sentences. For instance, the probability of the RST relation "elaboration" (i.e., the relation "elaboration" to happen in a valid transition) in the grid in Figure 9 is 0.16, i.e., one occurrence of "*elaboration*" in 6 possible transitions.

The probabilities of all relations present in the summary (both RST and CST relations) form a feature vector. The feature vectors for all the summaries become training instances for a machine learning process. In Figure 10, part of the feature vector for the grid in Figure 9 is shown.

Follow-up	elaboration	sequence	...
0.16	0.16	0.16	...

Figure 10. Part of the feature vector for Figure 9

4 Experiments and Results

The text-ordering task from Barzilay and Lapata (2008) was used to evaluate the performance of the proposed model and to compare it with other methods in literature.

The corpus used was the CSTNews[2] from Cardoso et al. (2011). This corpus has been created for multi-document summarization. It is composed of 140 texts distributed in 50 sets of news texts written in Brazilian Portuguese from various domains. Each set has 2 or 3 texts from different sources that address the same topic. Besides the original texts, the corpus has several annotation layers: (i) CST and RST manual annotations; (ii) the identification of temporal expressions; (iii) automatic syntactical analyses; (iv) noun and verb senses; (v) text-summary alignments; and (vi) the semantic annotation of informative aspects in summaries; among others. For this work, the CST and RST annotations have been used.

Originally, the CSTNews corpus had one extractive multi-document summary for each set of texts. However, Dias et al (2014a) produced 5 more extractive multi-document summaries for each set of texts. Now, the corpus has 6 reference extractive multi-document summaries for each set of texts. In this work, 251 reference multi-document extracts (with average size of 6.5 sentences) and 20 permutations for each one (totalizing 5020 summaries) were used in the experiments.

Besides the proposed model, some other methods from the literature have also been re-implemented in order to compare our results to the current state of the art. The following methods were chosen based on their importance and on the techniques used to evaluate local coher-

[2] www.icmc.usp.br/~taspardo/sucinto/cstnews.html

ence: the *LSA* method of Foltz et al. (1998), the *Entity Grid Model* of Barzilay and Lapata (2008), the *Graph Model* of Guinaudeau and Strube (2013), the *Shallow RST Model* of Feng et al (2014), the *RST Model* of Dias et al. (2014b) and the *Entity-based Model with CST bool* of Castro Jorge et al. (2014). The *LSA* method, *Entity Grid*, *Graph* and *Shallow RST* Models were adapted to Brazilian Portuguese, using the appropriate available tools and resources for this language, as the PALAVRAS parser (Bick, 2000) that was used to identify the summary entities, which are all nouns and proper nouns. The implementation of these methods carefully followed each step of the original ones.

Barzilay and Lapata's method has been implemented without coreference information, since, to the best of our knowledge, there is no robust coreference resolution system available for Brazilian Portuguese, and the CSTNews corpus still does not have referential information in its annotation layers. Furthermore, the implementation of Barzilay and Lapata's approach produced 4 models: with syntax and salience information (referred by Syntactic+Salience+), with syntax but without salience information (Syntactic+Salience-), with salience information but without syntax (Syntactic-Salience+), and without syntax and salience information (Syntactic-Salience-), in which salience distinguishes entities with frequency higher or equal to 2.

The Full RST Approach is similar to Dias et al.'s model (2014b), and then it was not used in these experiments.

Lin et al.'s model (2011) was not used in the experiments, since the CSTNews corpus does not have the PDTB-style discursive relations annotated. However, according to Feng et al. (2014), the PDTB-style discursive relations encode only very shallow discursive structures, i.e., the relations are mostly local, e.g., within a single sentence or between two adjacent sentences. Due to this, the Shallow RST Model from Feng et al. (2014), which behaves as Lin et al.'s (2001), was used in these experiments.

Table 1 shows the accuracy of our approach compared to the other methods, ordered by accuracy.

Models	Acc. (%)
Our approach	**92.69**
Syntactic-Salience- of Barzilay and Lapata	68.40*
Syntactic+Salience+ of Barzilay and Lapata	64.78*
Syntactic-Salience+ of Barzilay and Lapata	61.99*
Syntactic+Salience- of Barzilay and Lapata	60.21*
Graph Model of Guinaudeau and Strube	57.69*
LSA of Foltz et al.	55.18*
RST Model of Dias et al.	51.32*
Shallow RST Model of Feng et al.	48.92*
Entity-based Model with CST bool of Castro Jorge et al.	32.53*

Table 1. Results of the evaluation, where diacritics * ($p < .01$) indicates whether there is a significant statistical difference in accuracy compared to our approach (using t-test)

The t-test has been used for pointing out whether differences in accuracy are statistically significant or not. Comparing our approach with the other methods, one may observe that the use of all the RST and CST relations obtained better results for evaluating the local coherence of multi-document summaries.

These results show that the combination of RST and CST relations with a machine learning process has a high discriminatory power. This is due to discursive relation patterns that are present in the transitions between two sentences in the reference summaries. The "elaboration" RST relation was the one that presented the highest frequency, 237 out of the 603 possible ones in the reference summaries. The transition between S1 and S2 in the reference summaries was the transition in which the "elaboration" relation more frequently occurred, 61 out of 237. After this one, the RST relation "list" had 115 occurrences, and the transition between S3 and S4 was the more frequent to happen with the "list" relation (17 times out of 115 occurrences).

The *Shallow RST Model* from Feng et al. (2014) and the *Entity-based Model with CST bool* from Castro Jorge et al. (2014), that also use discursive information, obtained the lowest accuracy in the experiments. The low accuracy may have been caused for the following reasons: (i) the discursive information used was not sufficient for capturing the discursive patterns of the reference summaries; (ii) the quantity of features used by these models negatively influenced in the learning process; and (iii) the type of text used in this work was not appropriate, because the *RST Model* of Dias et al. (2014b) and the *Shallow RST Model* of Feng et al. (2014) had better results with full/source texts. Besides this, the quantity of summaries may have influenced the performance of the *Entity-based Model with CST bool* of Castro Jorge et al. (2014), since their model was originally applied in 50 multi-document summaries, while 251 summaries were used in this work

The best result of the *Graph Model* of Guinaudeau and Strube (2013) (given in Table 1) used the *Syntactic Projection* (*PAcc*), without distance information (*Dist*).

Overall, our approach highly exceeded the results of the other methods, since we obtained a minimum gain of 35.5% in accuracy.

5 Final remarks

According to the results obtained in the text-ordering task, the use of RST and CST relations to evaluate local coherence in multi-document summaries obtained the best accuracy in relation to other tested models. We believe that such discourse information may be equally useful for dealing with full texts too, since it is known that discourse organization highly correlates with (global an local) coherence.

It is important to notice that the discursive information used in our model is considered as "subjective" knowledge and that automatically parsing texts to achieve it is an expensive task, with results still far from ideal. However, the obtained gain in comparison with the other approaches suggests that it is a challenge worthy of following.

Acknowledgements

The authors are grateful to CAPES, FAPESP, and the University of Goiás for supporting this work.

References

Aleixo, P. and Pardo, T.A.S. 2008. CSTNews: Um Córpus de Textos Jornalísticos Anotados Segundo a Teoria Discursiva Multidocumento CST (Cross-Document Structure Theory). Technical Report Interinstitutional Center for Computational Linguistics, University of São Paulo, n. 326. p.12. São Carlos-SP, Brazil.

Barzilay, R. and Lapata, M. 2008. Modeling local coherence: An entity-based approach. Computational Linguistics, v. 34, n. 1, p. 1-34, Cambridge, MA, USA.

Bosma, W. 2004. Query-Based Summarization using Rhetorical Structure Theory. In Proceedings of the15th Meetings of CLIN, LOT, Utrecht, pp. 29-44.

Bick, E. 2000. The Parsing System Palavras, Automatic Grammatical Analysis of Portuguese in a Constraint Grammar Framework, Aarhus University Press.

Cardoso, P., Maziero, E., Jorge, M., Seno, E., di Felippo, A., Rino, L., Nunes, M. and Pardo, T. 2011. CSTNews - a discourse-annotated corpus for single and multi-document summarization of news texts in brazilian portuguese. In Proceedings of the 3rd RST Brazilian Meeting. p. 88-105.

Castro Jorge, M.L.R., Dias, M.S. and Pardo, T.A.S. 2014. Building a Language Model for Local Coherence in Multi-document Summaries using a Discourse-enriched Entity-based Model. In the Proceedings of the Brazilian Conference on Intelligent Systems - BRACIS, p. 44-49. São Carlos-SP/Brazil.

Dias, M.S.; Bokan Garay, A.Y.; Chuman, C.; Barros, C.D.; Maziero, E.G.; Nobrega, F.A.A.; Souza, J.W.C.; Sobrevilla Cabezudo, M.A.; Delege, M.; Castro Jorge, M.L.R.; Silva, N.L.; Cardoso, P.C.F.; Balage Filho, P.P.; Lopez Condori, R.E.; Marcasso, V.; Di Felippo, A.; Nunes, M.G.V.; Pardo, T.A.S. 2014a. Enriquecendo o Corpus CSTNews - a Criação de Novos Sumários Multidocumento. In the (on-line) Proceedings of the I Workshop on Tools and Resources for Automatically Processing Portuguese and Spanish - ToRPorEsp, p. 1-8. São Carlos-SP/Brazil.

Dias, M.S.; Feltrim, V.D.; Pardo, T.A.S. 2014b. Using Rhetorical Structure Theory and Entity Grids to Automatically Evaluate Local Coherence in Texts. In the Proceedings of the 11st International Conference on Computational Processing of Portuguese - PROPOR (LNAI 8775), p. 232-243. October 6-9. São Carlos-SP/Brazil.

Dijk, T.V. and Kintsch, W. 1983. Strategics in discourse comprehension. Academic Press. New York.

Feng, V. W., Lin, Z. and Hirst G. 2014. The Impact of Deep Hierarchical Discourse Structures in the Evaluation of Text Coherence. In the Proceedings of the 25th International Conference on Computational Linguistics, p. 940-949, Dublin, Ireland.

Foltz, P. W., Foltz, P. W., Kintsch, W. and Landauer, T. K. 1998. The measurement of textual coherence with latent semantic analysis. Discourse Processes, v. 25, n. 2 & 3, p. 285-307.

Grosz, B., Aravind, K. J. and Scott, W. 1995. Centering: A framework for modeling the local coherence of discourse. Computational Linguistics, vol. 21, p. 203-225. MIT Press Cambridge, MA, USA.

Guinaudeau, C. and Strube, M. 2013. Graph-based Local Coherence Modeling. In the Proceedings of the 51st Annual Meeting of the Association for

Computational Linguistics. v. 1. p. 93-103, Sofia, Bulgaria.

Joachims T. 2002. Optimizing search engines using clickthrough data. In the Proceedings of the eighth ACM SIGKDD international conference on Knowledge discovery and data mining, p. 133–142. New York, NY, USA.

Jorge, M.L.C., Pardo, T.A.S. 2010. Experiments with CST-based Multidocument Summarization. In the Proceedings of the ACL Workshop TextGraphs-5: Graph-based Methods for Natural Language Processing, pp. 74-82, Uppsala/Sweden.

Kibble, R., Power, R. 2004. Optimising referential coherence in text generation. Computational Linguistic, vol. 30 n. 4, pp. 401-416.

Koch, I. G. V. and Travaglia, L. C. 2002. A coerência textual. 14rd edn. Editora Contexto.

Landauer, T. K., Dumais, S. T. 1997. A solution to Plato's problem: The latent semantic analysis theory of acquisition, induction and representation to coreference resolution. In Proceedings of the 40th Annual Meeting of the Association for Computational Linguistics, pp. 104 -111, Philadelphia, PA.

Lin, Z., Ng, H. T. and Kan, M.-Y. 2011. Automatically evaluating text coherence using discourse relations. In the Proceedings of the 49th Annual Meeting of the Association for Computational Linguistics: Human Language Technologies – v. 1, p. 997–1006, Stroudsburg, PA, USA.

Mani, I. (2001). Automatic Summarization. John Benjamins Publishing Co., Amsterdam.

Mann, W. C. and Thompson, S. A. 1987. Rhetorical Structure Theory: A theory of text organization. Technical Report, ISI/RS-87-190.

Mckoon, G. and Ratcliff, R. 1992. Inference during reading. Psychological Review, p. 440-446.

Prasad, R., Dinesh, N., Lee, A., Miltsakaki, E., Robaldo, L., Joshi, A. and Webber, B. 2008. The penn discourse treebank 2.0. In the Proceedings of the 6th Internacional Conference on Language Resources an Evaluation.

Radev, D.R. 2000. A common theory of information fusion from multiple text sources, step one: Cross-document structure. In the Proceedings of the 1st ACL SIGDIAL Workshop on Discourse and Dialogue, Hong Kong.

Salton, G. 1988. Term-Weighting Approaches in Automatic Text Retrieval. Information Processing and Management, p. 513-23.

Seno, E. R. M. 2005. Rhesumarst: Um sumarizador automático de estruturas RST. Master Thesis. University of São Carlos. São Carlos/SP.

Belief Tracking with Stacked Relational Trees

Deepak Ramachandran
Nuance Communications Inc.
1178 E Arques, Sunnyvale, CA
deepak.ramachandran@nuance.com

Adwait Ratnaparkhi
Nuance Communications Inc.
1178 E Arques, Sunnyvale, CA
adwait.ratnaparkhi@nuance.com

Abstract

We describe a new model for Dialog State Tracking called a Stacked Relational Tree, which naturally models complex relationships between entities across user utterances. It can represent multiple conversational intents and the change of focus between them. Updates to the model are made by a rule-based system in the language of tree regular expressions. We also introduce a probabilistic version that can handle ASR/NLU uncertainty. We show how the parameters can be trained from log data, showing gains on a variety of standard Belief Tracker metrics, and a measurable impact on the success rate of an end-to-end dialog system for TV program discovery.

1 Introduction

Significant advances have been made in recent years on the problem of Dialog State Tracking or Belief Tracking. Successive iterations of the Dialog State Tracking Challenge (Williams et al., 2013; Henderson et al., 2014b; Henderson et al., 2014a) have expanded the scope of the problem to more general settings such as changing goals and domain adaptation. It has been shown that improvements in Belief Tracking metrics lead to improvements in extrinsic measures of dialog success as well (Lee, 2014). However, the underlying representations of state have almost always been propositional i.e. defined by a collection of slot-value pairs, though the probability distribution used for tracking might be quite complex (Mehta et al., 2010). These representations are good for form-filling or information collection type dialogs that are most commonly deployed e.g. airline reservation systems that fill in all the constraints a user has (such as destination and source) before doing a database lookup. However, as dialog systems get more sophisticated, complex dialog phenomena present in human-human conversations such as common ground or conversational focus need to be supported as well.

This work is motivated by the need for a belief tracker capable of tracking conversations with the end-to-end conversational prototype for TV program discovery described in (Ramachandran et al., 2014). The prototype understands concepts at a deep relational level and and supports nested subdialogs with multiple intents of different types like searches, questions, and explanations. We introduce a representation called a *Stacked Relational Tree* to represent the state of a dialog between a user and system. It uses the notion of a *relational tree*, similar to a dependency graph but constructed between entities from a Named Entity Recognizer (NER), to represent each individual intent of the user. A stack (i.e. LIFO structure) of these trees is used to model the conversational focus and the structure of subdialogs. State updates are modeled by sequences of stack and tree-editing operations. Allowable operations are defined using the language of tree-regular expressions (Lai and Bird, 2004). The use of stacks to represent intentional structure is common in dialog modeling (Grosz and Sidner, 1986) and plan recognition (Carberry, 1990). Our novel contribution is to combine it with a semantic representation and update rules that are simple enough so that the entire model can be trained from dialog data.

A system using this belief tracker was deployed in a user study and made a dramatic difference in the task success rate. We also describe a probabilistic extension of this model for handling uncertainty in input and ambiguity in understanding. We show that training the weights of this model on log data can improve its performance.

2 Dialog State Representation

Most commercial and research dialog systems represent the state of a conversation as a collection

Proceedings of the SIGDIAL 2015 Conference, pages 68–76,
Prague, Czech Republic, 2-4 September 2015.

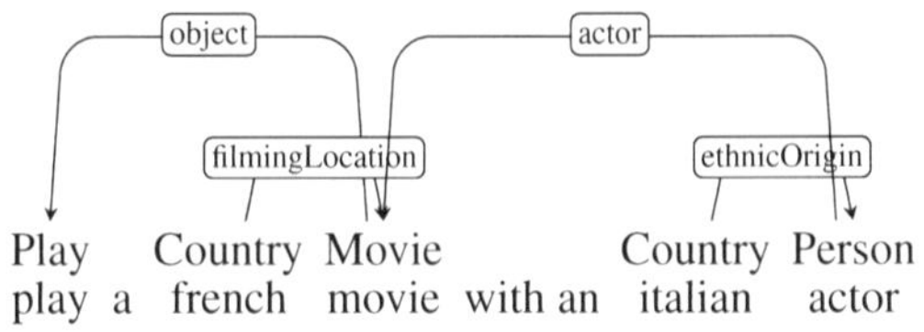

Figure 1: REL-Tree for the utterance "Play a French movie with an Italian actor."

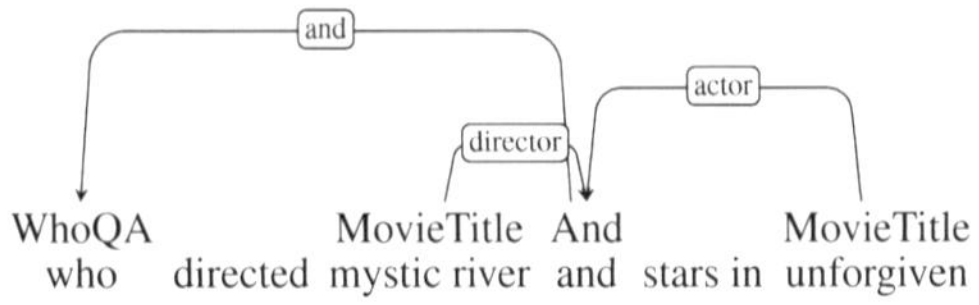

Figure 2: REL-Tree for the question "Who directed Mystic river and stars in Unforgiven?"

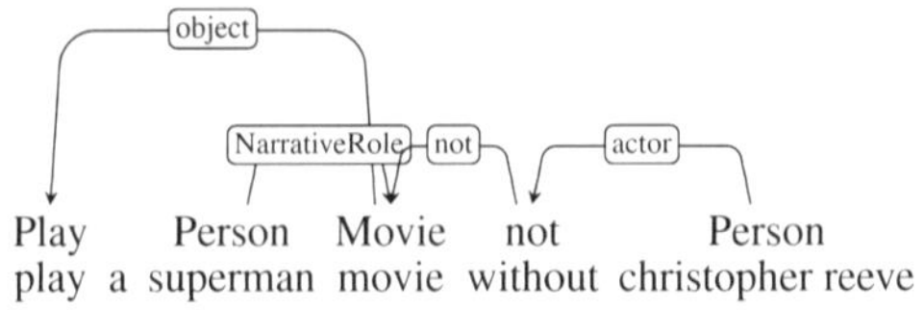

Figure 3: REL-Tree for the utterance "Play a Superman movie without Christopher Reeve."

of slot-value pairs that define the system's best understanding of the user's intent e.g. an airline reservation system might have slots for destination city, arrival city, and date. Shallow NLP techniques such as Named-Entity Recognition are used to extract the relevant slot-value pairs from each spoken utterance of the user. As successive utterances accumulate, a state tracking strategy is needed to update the state given the slot-value pairs provided at each turn. Traditionally, state tracking followed a simple replacement semantics. Modern systems maintain a probability distribution over possible states, reflecting all the uncertainty and ambiguity in ASR and NLU. Recent extensions have focused on adaptation to new domains (Henderson et al., 2014b) and changing user goals (Zhu et al., 2014). However, in most cases we are aware of, the base representation of the dialog state is propositional (i.e. a collection of slot-value pairs). This reflects the simple, goal-directed nature of the dialogs supported by such systems.

2.1 REL-Trees

Consider an utterance like "Play a French movie with an Italian actor." A slot-based system with a

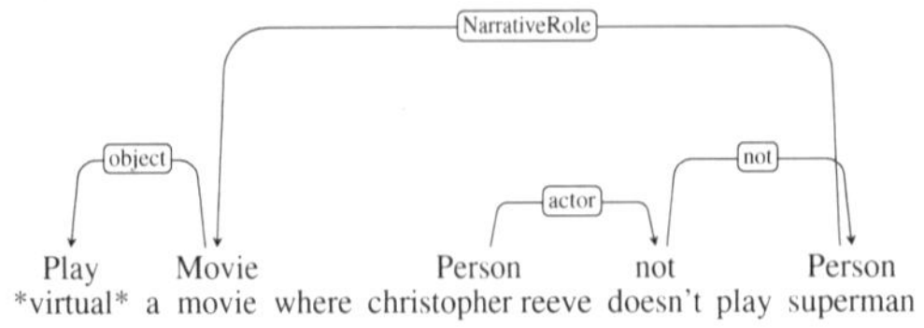

Figure 4: REL-Tree for the fragmentary utterance "A movie where Christopher Reeve doesn't play Superman."

slot called `Country` would not be able to distinguish between the filming location and the actor's country of origin. A possible solution is to introduce two separate slots called `actorEthnicity` and `filmingLocation`, but scaling this approach leads to a multiplicity of slots that becomes difficult to manage and extend. A more compact representation (called a *Relational Tree* or *REL-Tree*) is shown in Fig. 1. The only entity types are `Country`, `Movie`, and `Person`. To elaborate the meaning of the utterance, "French" is attached to the `Movie` entity by the relation `filmingLocation` and "italian" is attached to `Person` by the relation `ethnicOrigin`. A REL-Tree is a rooted tree with node labels corresponding to entities and edge labels corresponding to relations between them. In most cases, a relation link is analogous to a syntactic dependency link from a dependency parser – a link from child to parent signifies that the child is a modifier of the parent. The label at the root of the tree represents the intent of the utterance (e.g., "Play", "Who-QA", and "ExpressPreference") if one can be distinguished, see Fig. 2 for another example. Fragmentary utterances can have missing intents, in which case the root is simply labeled ROOT.

Comparing the REL-Trees in Figures 3 and 4 shows another example of the representational power of REL-Trees . The two utterances have different meanings and indeed yield different results (The 2013 movie "Man of Steel" had Christopher Reeve in a cameo role, but not as Superman). In our dialog system, REL-Trees are produced by a Relation Extraction component that operates after NER. Note that the NER is trained to label boolean connectors such as "and" and "without" as entities as well. In some cases, it adds "virtual" entities to fragmentary utterances when they are not explicit in the text (e.g. the `Play` entity in Fig. 4). For more details refer to (Ramachandran et al., 2014).

2.2 Stacks

The dialog example of Table 4 (see Appendix) illustrates another phenomenon not usually considered by belief trackers: multiple intents and the concept of a *conversational focus* (Grosz and Sidner, 1986). The user starts with the intention of finding a romantic movie to watch but is then led by the system response into asking a question about one of the search results (a query). He then modifies the argument of the query to ask about a different movie. Then, he gives a command to provide him with more suggestions. Finally, he goes back to the original search intent and modifies the genre. The second column of this table shows how we model multiple intents and the change in focus by a stack of REL-Trees (called a *Stacked REL-Tree* or a *Stack*). Each REL-Tree represents a separate intent of the user and the REL-Tree on top of the stack is the current focus of the conversation. Subsequent utterances are interpretated as refining or modifying this REL-Tree. If no such interpretation is possible, then either the focus is assumed to have shifted back to an earlier intent in the stack or we treat the utterance as a new intents. The allowable set of operations and the algorithm by which they are applied are fully specified in the next few sections. A REL-Tree that represents an utterance from the user will be called an *utterance REL-Tree* wherever it is necessary to make the distinction.

3 Update Rules

The Stacked REL-Tree representation of dialog state was introduced in the previous section and Table 4 shows how a dialog state progresses as each utterance comes in. A set of state update rules are used to specify how the REL-tree on the top of a stack is modified by the incoming utterance. To describe the update rules, we will need three definitions.

Tree Regular Expressions A *tree regular expression* (or tree regex) is a regular expression that matches against paths in a rooted tree from a node to one of its descendants, with node and edge labels serving as the tokens of the string (Lai and Bird, 2004). The basic elements of a tree regex are:

1. **Node and Edge labels**: These are represented by a string regular expression (i.e. a regular expression over strings) surrounded by "/ /" e.g. `/[actor|director]/` matches a node with an `actor` or `director` label. When labels are concantenated they represent a path from the root to a descendant node with each successive label alternatively matching node and edge labels on the path. For example, `/Movie/actor/Person/ethnicOrigin/Place` would match against the path from the "movie" node to the "italian" in Fig. 1. The empty label `//` matches any node or edge label.

2. **Node Values**: A node label followed by the expression `{V}` where `V` is a string regular expression, matches nodes where the surface text of the node equals `V`. e.g. `/Movie/narrativeRole/Person{superman}/` matches the path from the "movie" node to the "superman" node in Fig. 3.

3. **Operators**: The symbols $*$, ?, . have the usual meanings for regular expressions when placed after a tree regular expression. Note however, that $*$ and $+$ automatically match against alternating node and edge labels along a path. Thus, the expression `//*/Place/` matches against two paths from the root in Fig. 1. The operators $\wedge$ and `$` represent the root node and a leaf node respectively.

4. **Groups**: Groups are defined by enclosing a part of a tree regex inside parentheses. Let M be a successful match of a tree regex P to the tree T, the sub-path in M matching the ith group in P can be retrieved by $M.@i$. For example, for the tree in Fig. 2 and the pattern `/And/./(MovieTitle)`, there are two matches M_1 and M_2 with $M_1.@1$ having value "mystic river" and $M_2.@1$ having value "unforgiven."

Tree Constraints For tree regexes P_1 and P_2, a *Tree constraint* on P_1 and P_2 is an expression of the form $P_1.@i = P_2.@j$, $P_1.@i\{\} = P_2.@j\{\}$, or $P_1.@i\{\} < P_2.@j\{\}$. Here, $x < y$ means x is a substring of y. $\{\}$ retrieves the value of a node (the surface form).

Transformations A *transformation* τ on tree regexes P_1 and P_2, is a list of one or more of the following operations performed on paths that match against groups from P_1 and P_2 :

1. `Add`(g_1, g_2): Add the matched sub-path from group g_2 as a child of the head node of the matched sub-path from group g_1.

2. `Delete(`g`)`: Remove the head node and all descendants of the path matching group g.

3. `Unify(`g_1, g_2`)`: Replace the head node h_1, of g_1 with the head node, h_2 of g_2, and add all children of h_2 as children of h_1.

An *update rule* is defined as a tuple (P_1, P_2, E, τ) where P_1 and P_2 are tree regular expressions, E is a set of tree constraints on P_1 and P_2, and τ is a transformation on P_1 and P_2. An update rule U is *applicable* to a dialog state tree T and an input REL-tree L if:

1. P_1 has a match, M_1 on T
2. P_2 has a match, M_2 on L
3. E holds for the groups in M_1 and M_2.

In such case, the result of applying U on T and L are the trees S' and L' obtained by applying each operation in τ to $\{M_1, M_2\}$ in the order specified.

Here are some example update rules with explanations:

1. Head Variable Unification

```
P1:  /object/(Program/)
P2:  /object/([Movie|TvShow|Game]/)
E:   {}
τ:   {Unify(P1.@1,P2.@1)}
```

If the object of the current intent is `Program` and the current utterance from the user asks for either a movie, tv show, or game, then update the dialog state to reflect that we are searching for this kind of program (See Fig. 5 for an example).

2. Concept Replacement

```
P1:  ^///(///)$
P2:  ^///(///)$
E:   {P1.@1=P2.@1}
τ:   {Unify(P1.@1,P2.@1),Delete(P2.@1)})
```

This rule is applicable when the input utterance has a value for some attribute that is already present in the dialog state. In this case, the new value of the attribute replaces the old one. Note that the constraint in the utterance tree is also "consumed" by this rule (See Fig. 5 for an example).

3. Boolean fragment

```
P1:  (/[or|and]/[And|Or]/)*(/or/Or)(///)$
P2:  ^(/or/Or)(///)$
E:   {P1.@3=P2.@2}
τ:   {Add(P2.@2,P1.@3),Delete(P1.@3),
Add(P2.@2,P1.@2),Delete(P2.@2)})
```

This rule is applicable when the input utterance is a boolean fragment with an attribute already present in the dialog state. The subtrees are then unified as shown in Fig. 6.

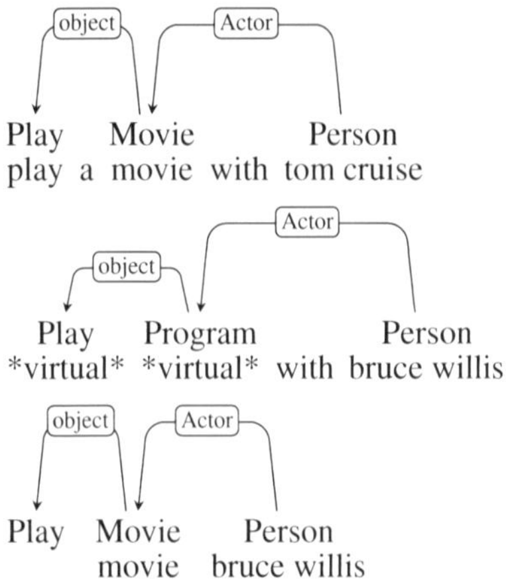

Figure 5: The tree at the bottom is the result of applying rules 1 and 2 to the trees at the top (current dialog state) and the middle (current utterance).

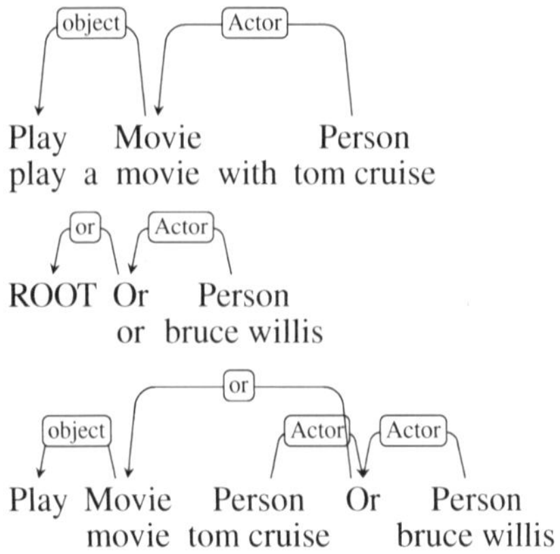

Figure 6: The tree at the bottom is the result of applying rules 1 and 3 to the trees at the top (current dialog state) and the middle (current utterance).

The definition of update rules and the allowable operations we have presented were tailored to our particular domain. In principle, it is possible to extend them to be more general, but care must be taken so that the operations and especially the regex matching algorithm can be efficiently implemented (Lai and Bird, 2004). For our implementation of tree regexes we adapted the TSurgeon package (Levy and Andrew, 2006) from the Stanford Parser.

```
Algorithm 1: UpdateDialogState
Data: Stacked REL-Tree S, utterance
      REL-Tree L, List of Update Rules R
Applied:=false, S_cur := S;
repeat
    T := S.pop();
    for each update rule R_i ∈ R in sequence
    do
        if R_i is applicable to (T, L) then
            Applied=true;
            Apply transformation τ_i (from R_i)
            to (T, L);
until S.empty() or Applied==true;
if not Applied then
    S:= S_cur;
    S.push(T);
return S;
```

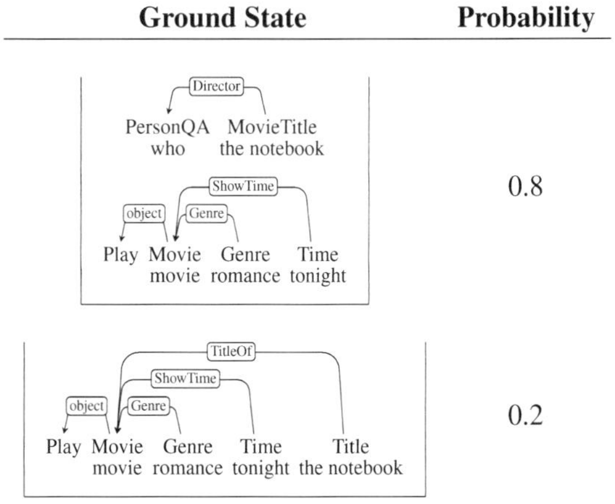

Figure 7: A sample belief state after turn 3 of the dialog in Table 4. The first ground state is the result of a merge of the utterance REL-Tree with the top of the stack. The second ground state is the result of a pop followed by a merge.

3.1 The Belief Tracking Algorithm

Recall that our state representation is a stack of REL-Trees as in Table 4. Algorithm 1 shows how we update the dialog state at each turn. It is parameterized by an ordered list of update rules as described in Section 3. We attempt to apply them in order to the REL-Tree at the top of the stack first. If no rule is applicable, this indicates that the conversational focus has shifted. We pop the top REL-Tree off the stack and try again with the REL-Tree below it. This process continues, until a rule is succesfully applied or the stack is empty. In the latter case, the utterance is regarded as being a new intent, and the utterance REL-Tree is pushed on top of the old dialog state.

4 A Probabilistic Extension

The State Tracker described above is able to model relational representations and shifting conversational focus. However, it is deterministic and thus unable to handle ambiguity caused by multiple applicable rules. Consider the third user turn in Table 4. We interpret "How about The Notebook?" as a modification to the question intent, but it is possible that the user intended it to be a refinement of his search intent i.e. he wants to watch "The Notebook". Furthermore, in most practical dialog systems the output of the ASR and NLU components will have multiple hypotheses with associated confidence scores or probabilities.

To represent this uncertainty in a compact way, we will expand our representation of dialog state to a *dialog belief state* that is a *probability distribution over Stacked REL-Trees*. An example belief state for the case above is shown in Fig. 7, having two ground dialog states (i.e. Stacked REL-Trees) with probability 0.8 and 0.2. The belief state, B_t, for a particular turn t, is constructed from the belief state of the previous turn B_{t-1}, by trying every combination of Stacked REL-Tree S_{t-1} in the support of B_{t-1}, utterance REL-Tree L, and sequence of applicable rule $\{R_i\}$ to yield a different Stacked REL-Tree S_t. The probability of S_t is given by:

$$Pr_{B_t}(S_t|S_{t-1}, L, \{R_i\}) = Pr_{B_{t-1}}(S_{t-1}) \cdot Pr_L(L) \cdot \prod_i Pr(R_i|S_{t-1}^{i-1}, L)$$

where S_t^i is obtained by applying R_i to S_t^{i-1}, and

$$Pr(R_i|S, L) \propto e^{-\mathbf{w}_i \cdot \mathbf{f}(S,L,R_i)} \quad (1)$$

Here, $\mathbf{f}(S, L, R_i)$ is a feature-generating function. It uses a combination of structural tree features such as number of children and depth from root and features from the surface text (e.g., functional words/phrases such as "and" or "instead of"). We also have special rules for *pushing* a REL-Tree on top of the stack, *popping* the top REL-Tree, and rules marked *terminal* indicating that no more rules are to be applied. The weights for all rules are trained by logistic regression.

Algorithm 2: UpdateBeliefState

Data: Belief State of previous turn $B_{t-1}(S)$, Distribution over utterance REL-Trees $P_L(L)$, List of Update Rules R

for *each stack* S *in the support of* B_{t-1} **do**
  for *each tree* L *in the support of* P_L **do**
    $W := B_{t-1}(S) \cdot P_L(L)$
    $B_t := B_t \cup$ UpdateI-State (S, L, W)

Prune B_t down to the top K elements;
Normalize the weights to 1.
return B_t

Algorithm 3: UpdateI-State

Data: Stacked REL-Tree S, Utterance REL-Tree L, List of Update Rules R, Prior Weight W

$\mathbf{S} = \{\}$
for *each update rule* $R_i \in R$ *applicable to* (S, L) **do**
  Apply transformation τ_i (from R_i) to (S, L) to get (S', L')
  $W_i := W \cdot Pr(R_i|S, L)$
  if R_i *is terminal* **then**
    $\mathbf{S} := \mathbf{S} + (S', W_i)$
  else
    $\mathbf{S} := \mathbf{S} \cup$ UpdateI-State(S', L', W_i)

return S;

The full probabilistic belief tracking algorithm is shown in Algorithm 2. It uses a recursive helper method (Algorithm 3) to apply rules successively to stacks in the input distribution. The intermediate states of this process are called *I-States*. To prevent a combinatorial explosion in the size of the belief state over successive turns, it is pruned down at the end to a distribution over at most K stacks ($K = 50$).

Training For training data, we use conversations with a full dialog-system. Each turn of the dialog is annotated with the sequence of update rules that are applied to the belief state of the previous turn to get the correct belief state for the current turn. From these, we can compute the sequence of I-States for that turn. Then, for each rule that is applicable to each of these I-States, a training instance is added to the classifier for that rule, along with a binary label indicating whether the rule was applied in that I-State or not. The classifier (using logistic regression) then learns to distinguish I-States where the rule should be used, from those where it should not. Note that this training protocol requires very strong labels from the annotator (a sequence of operations for every turn). This limits its scalability to larger training sets, but nevertheless we present it as a proof of concept that training this model is possible in principle. Exploring ways to ease this constraint is a topic we plan to explore in future work.

5 Evaluation

We present two evaluations of the tracking approaches described above. The first one measures the impact of using the deterministic algorithm as part of a larger conversational prototype for TV Program Discovery, in contrast to a system with no belief tracking (stateless). In the second, we show the additional value gained by the probabilistic version, trained on dialogs from developer logs. The framework for the second evaluation was made to be as close as possible to the methods in the DSTC competition.

5.1 User Study

An implementation of Algorithm 1 with 16 update rules and 4 kinds of user intents (search requests, questions, commands, and preference statements) was included as a component of a Spoken Dialog System for TV Program Discovery on an IPad. The system had an NER and a Relation Extractor as described in Section 2 as well as a dialog manager that operated on Stacked REL-Trees and a back-end for program search that used both structured database queries and graph inference on Freebase. For more details, see (Ramachandran et al., 2014). This system was evaluated in a user study with 14 subjects to determine how much the statefulness of the dialog model impacted success and usability. Subjects were presented with 7 scenarios to imagine themselves in and asked to find a suitable program to watch using the prototype, for example:

> You are at home and have young nieces and nephews coming over. Find a program to watch with them.

The subject was asked to continue speaking with the system until he/she either found a suitable program (in which case the scenario was recorded as a *success*) or gave up (in which case a *failure* was recorded). For this evaluation, the subject was

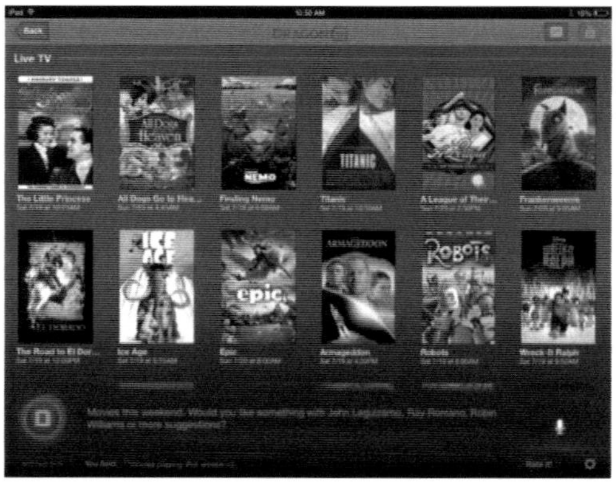

Figure 8: A Screenshot of our IPad Conversational Prototype after the query "Movies playing this weekend".

System	Succ. Rate	Avg. # of turns	SUS Score
Stateful	85.72 %	4.81	84.29 (15.7)
Stateless	63.27%	5.38	85.71 (15.5)

Table 1: Comparison of dialog system performance for 14 real users with and without the state tracker. SUS score is a industry-standard usability metric.

asked to do these tasks using both the complete stateful dialog system and a stateless *repeated one-shot* version where the belief tracker and dependent components were deactivated. Both systems were otherwise identical and the subjects were not told what the differences between them was. Table 1 summarizes the result of the comparsion. The use of belief tracking was found to make a 22% (absolute) difference to the objective success rate of the system. The stateful model allowed subjects to pose more complex requests that are difficult to formulate as a single utterance as a series of simpler ones; or allowed them to explore the space of options more efficiently. This was also reflected in a lower average number of turns per dialog. Interestingly, this did not lead to a significant difference in the perceived usability of the system, as measured by the industry standard SUS score (Brooke, 1996). Indeed, users barely noticed the stateful/stateless distinction between the systems. The overall usability was still pretty high, corresponding to an adjective rating of "Good" verging on "Excellent."

User	football games this weekend
Sys	Football games this weekend. Would you like College Football or Classic College Football?
User	or next weekend
Sys	Football games this weekend or next weekend. Would you like Classic College Football, College Football, or Rose Bowl?
User	romantic movies tomorrow
Sys	Ok starting a new search. Romantic movies tomorrow. Would you like something with Sandra Bullock, Nicole Kidman, Kristen Stewart, or more suggestions?
User	more suggestions
Sys	How about Robert Pattinson, Kate Winslet, Katherine Heigl or more suggestions?
User	Winslet
Sys	Romantic movies with Kate Winslet tomorrow. Would you like Titanic or Little Children?
User	the first one
Sys	You chose Titanic on Bravo at 10:30 AM on Saturday
User	movies about the gulf war
Sys	Movies set during the Gulf war. Would you like Courage Under Fire, Jarhead, or The Finest Hour?
User	explain the second one
Sys	This film is an adaptation of the book "Jarhead: a Marine's Chronicle of the Gulf War and Other Battles", whose subject is the Gulf War. Would you like Courage under Fire, Jarhead, or The Finest Hour?

Table 2: Example dialog with our system. System responses are accompanied by movie or TV thumbnail images on the iPad UI.

5.2 Probabilistic Belief Tracking

The Dialog State Track Competitions (Williams et al., 2013; Henderson et al., 2014b; Henderson et al., 2014a) introduced a shared evaluation task for belief tracking on a corpus of dialog data from various domains. Unfortunately, the data is purely slot-based so it cannot be used to evaluate our methods directly. However, the competitions also introduced a rubric for evaluation that we endevoured to follow as closely as possible in this section.

Algorithm 2 was implemented with 16 update rules similar to the deterministic tracker described above. The weight vectors for each rule were trained by logistic regression as described. The training data came from the developer logs of our system.[1] Each turn of dialog was labelled by us with the correct dialog-state (i.e. stacked REL-tree) and the sequence of updates rule that were applied to progress to the next state. The training protocol of Section 4 was then followed. Overall there were 673 dialogs with 1726 turns of speech and 3642 I-states. After training, the belief tracking algorithm (Algorithm 2) was evaluated on a held out test set of 50 dialogs with 142 turns.

The DSTC competitions identified 4 clusters of evaluation metrics that tended to rank various tracking algorithms equivalently. In Table 3 we show the performance of the trained tracker and the deter-

[1]Logs of conversations involving testing and bug fixing were removed.

System	Accuracy	L2	ROC.V2.CA20	ROC.V1.EER
Deterministic-Test Set	0.743	0.264	0.82	0.25
Trained-Test Set	0.788	0.237	0.73	0.22
Deterministic-User Study	0.661	0.348	0.75	0.35
Trained-User Study	0.680	0.335	0.72	0.33

Table 3: Comparsion of belief tracker performance with and without training using DSTC metrics.

mininstic baseline on one metric from each cluster: *Accuracy* measures the percent of turns where the top-ranked hypothesis is correct. *L2* measures the L^2 distance between the vector of scores for each hypothesis, and a vector of zeros with 1 in the position of the correct hypothesis. The other two measures relate to receiver-operating characteristic (ROC) curves, which measure the discrimination of the score for the highest-ranked state hypothesis. *ROC.V2.CA20* is the Correct acceptance-rate for the highest ranked hypothesis when the false-acceptance rate is set to 20%, for correctly classified utterances only. *ROC.V1.EER* is the Equal-error rate i.e. where false-acceptance rate equals false-reject rate, for all utterances. In addition to the test data-set, performance was also measured on all dialogs from the user study of Section 5.1. This gives a measure of generalization to dialogs from outside the training distribution. The results show that the trained belief tracker outperformed the handcrafted on all measures, though not by large amounts. As expected, performance was uniformly worse on the (out-of-sample) user study data but there was still some improvement.

6 Conclusions and Future Work

In this paper, we present the first (to our knowledge) Belief Tracking approach that represents the dialog state with a probabalistic relational and multi-intent model. We show that this model is effective when measured on standard metrics used for belief tracking, as well as making a marked difference in the task success rate of a complete dialog system.

The most serious shortcoming of this approach is the reliance on very strong labels for the training. To relax this requirement, we are exploring the possibility of training our model using weak labels (such as query results) in the manner of (Berant et al., 2013). Another direction to explore is the representation of distributions over Stacked REL-trees in compact forms.

References

J. Berant, A. Chou, R. Frostig, and P. Liang. 2013. Semantic parsing on Freebase from question-answer pairs. In *Empirical Methods in Natural Language Processing (EMNLP)*.

J. Brooke. 1996. SUS: A quick and dirty usability scale. In *Usability Evaluation in Industry*.

S. Carberry. 1990. *Plan recognition in natural language dialogue*. MIT press.

B. J. Grosz and C. L. Sidner. 1986. Attention, intentions, and the structure of discourse. *Computational linguistics*, 12(3):175–204.

M. Henderson, , B. Thomson, and J. Williams. 2014a. The third dialog state tracking challenge. *Proceedings of IEEE Spoken Language Technology*.

M. Henderson, B. Thomson, and J. Williams. 2014b. The second dialog state tracking challenge. In *Proceedings of the SIGDIAL 2014 Conference*, page 263.

C. Lai and S. Bird. 2004. Querying and updating treebanks: A critical survey and requirements analysis. In *Proceedings of the Australasian language technology workshop*, pages 139–146.

S. Lee. 2014. Extrinsic evaluation of dialog state tracking and predictive metrics for dialog policy optimization. In *15th Annual Meeting of the Special Interest Group on Discourse and Dialogue*, page 310.

R. Levy and G. Andrew. 2006. Tregex and tsurgeon: tools for querying and manipulating tree data structures. In *Proceedings of the fifth international conference on Language Resources and Evaluation*, pages 2231–2234. Citeseer.

N. Mehta, R. Gupta, A. Raux, D. Ramachandran, and S. Krawczyk. 2010. Probabilistic ontology trees for belief tracking in dialog systems. In *Proceedings of the SIGDIAL 2010 Conference*, pages 37–46. Association for Computational Linguistics.

D. Ramachandran, P. Yeh, W. Jarrold, B. Douglas, A. Ratnaparkhi, R. Provine, J. Mendel, and A. Emfield. 2014. An end-to-end dialog system for tv program discovery. In *SLT*.

J. Williams, A. Raux, D. Ramachandran, and A. Black. 2013. The dialog state tracking challenge. In *Proceedings of the SIGDIAL 2013 Conference*, pages 404–413.

S. Zhu, L. Chen, K. Sun, D. Zheng, and K. Yu. 2014. Semantic parser enhancement for dialogue domain extension with little data. In *Spoken Language Technology Workshop*.

A Dialog Example

In Table 4 we show the belief tracking process using a Stacked REL-Tree for a sample conversation.

<table>
<tr><th>Utterance</th><th>System state after utterance</th><th>Operation performed on stack</th></tr>
<tr><td>User: I want a romance movie tonight.</td><td>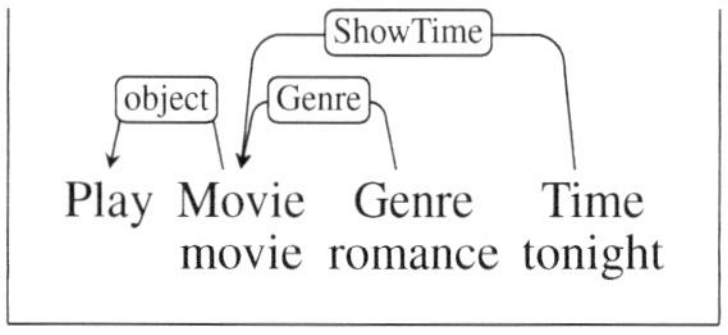
</td><td>Initial Search Intent</td></tr>
<tr><td>System: Ok how about The Notebook or Walk the Line?
User: Who directed walk the line?</td><td>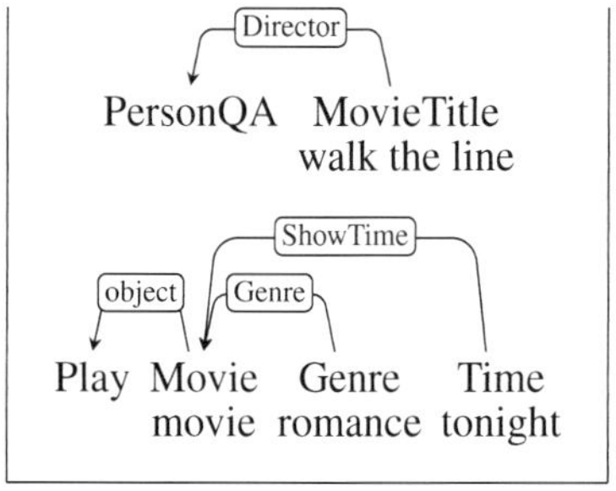
</td><td>New question intent put on top of stack</td></tr>
<tr><td>System: James Mangold
User: How about The Notebook?</td><td>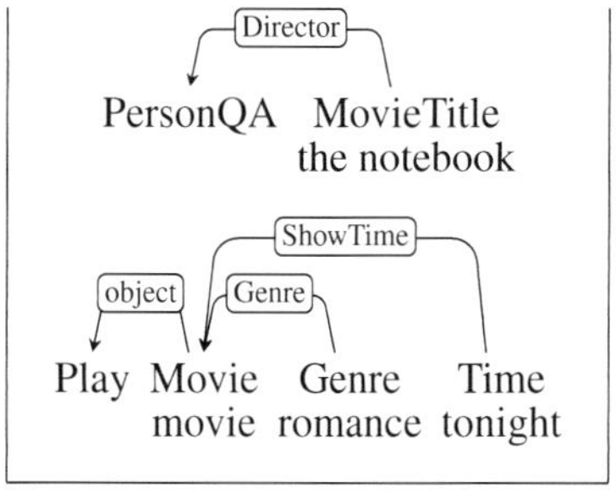
</td><td>Modification to question on top of stack.</td></tr>
<tr><td>System: Nick Cassavetes.
User: Give me more suggestions.</td><td>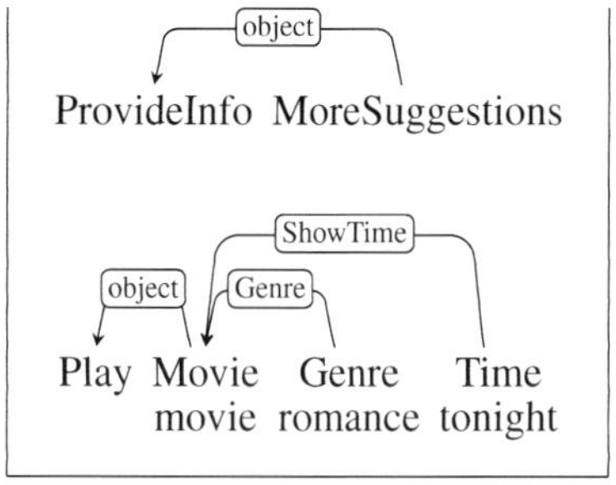
</td><td>Utterance is a command for more suggestions, gets placed on top of the stack replacing the question.</td></tr>
<tr><td>System: No more suggestions.
User: Ok well, let's try a comedy then.</td><td>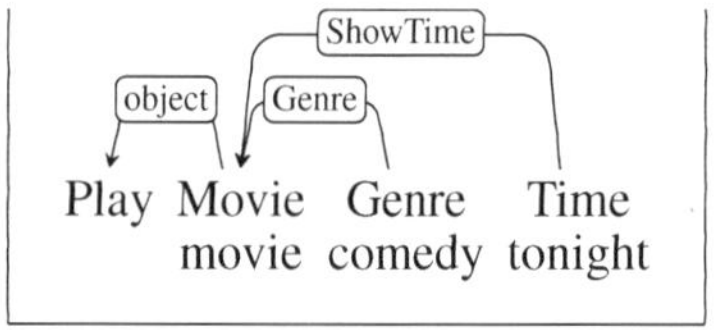
</td><td>Command is popped off, comedy replaces romance in the original search intent.</td></tr>
</table>

Table 4: Dialog State updates of the deterministic tracker (Algorithm 1) for each turn of a sample dialog.

"So, which one is it?" The effect of alternative incremental architectures in a high-performance game-playing agent

Maike Paetzel
University of Hamburg and
USC Institute for Creative Technologies
8paetzel@informatik.uni-hamburg.de

Ramesh Manuvinakurike and **David DeVault**
USC Institute for Creative Technologies
Playa Vista, CA, USA,
{manuvinakurike,devault}@ict.usc.edu

Abstract

This paper introduces Eve, a high-performance agent that plays a fast-paced image matching game in a spoken dialogue with a human partner. The agent can be optimized and operated in three different modes of incremental speech processing that optionally include incremental speech recognition, language understanding, and dialogue policies. We present our framework for training and evaluating the agent's dialogue policies. In a user study involving 125 human participants, we evaluate three incremental architectures against each other and also compare their performance to human-human gameplay. Our study reveals that the most fully incremental agent achieves game scores that are comparable to those achieved in human-human gameplay, are higher than those achieved by partially and non-incremental versions, and are accompanied by improved user perceptions of efficiency, understanding of speech, and naturalness of interaction.

1 Introduction

This paper presents and evaluates a game playing dialogue agent named Eve that relies on several forms of incremental language processing to achieve its best performance. In recent years, the development and adoption of incremental processing techniques in dialogue systems has continued to advance, and more-and-more research systems have included some form of incremental processing; see for example (Selfridge et al., 2013; Hastie et al., 2013; Baumann and Schlangen, 2013; Dethlefs et al., 2012; Selfridge et al., 2012; DeVault et al., 2011; Skantze and Schlangen, 2009; Schlangen et al., 2009). One compelling high-level motivation for systems builders to incorporate incremental processing into their systems is to reduce system response latency (Skantze and Schlangen, 2009). Recent studies have also demonstrated user preference of incremental systems over non-incremental counterparts (Skantze and Schlangen, 2009; Aist et al., 2007), shown positive effects of incrementality on user ratings of system efficiency and politeness (Skantze and Hjalmarsson, 2010), and even shown increases in the fluency of user speech when appropriate incremental feedback is provided (Gratch et al., 2006).

Despite this progress, there remain many open questions about the use of incremental processing in systems. One important research direction is to explore and clarify the implications and advantages of alternative incremental architectures. Using pervasive incremental processing in a dialogue system poses a fundamental challenge to traditional system architectures, which generally assume turn-level or dialogue act level units of processing rather than much smaller and higher frequency incremental units (Schlangen and Skantze, 2011). Rather than completely redesigning their architectures, system builders may be able to gain some of the advantages of incrementality, such as reduced response latencies, by incorporating incremental processing in select system modules such as automatic speech recognition or language understanding. The extent to which all modules of a dialogue system need to operate incrementally to achieve specific effects needs further exploration.

Another important research direction is to develop effective optimization techniques for dialogue policies in incremental systems. Incremental dialogue policies may need to make many fine-grained decisions per second, such as whether to initiate a backchannel or interruption of a user utterance in progress. Developing data-driven approaches to such decision-making may allow us to build more highly optimized, interactive, and ef-

Proceedings of the SIGDIAL 2015 Conference, pages 77–86,
Prague, Czech Republic, 2-4 September 2015.

fective systems than are currently possible (Ward and DeVault, 2015). Yet the computational techniques that can achieve this fine-grained optimization in practice are not yet clear. Approaches that use (Partially Observable) Markov Decision Processes and a reinforcement learning framework to optimize fine-grained turn-taking control may ultimately prove effective (see e.g. (Kim et al., 2014; Selfridge et al., 2012)), but optimizing live system interactions in this way remains a challenge.

In this paper, we present a case study of a high-performance incremental dialogue system that contributes to both of these research directions. First, our study investigates the effects of increasing levels of incremental processing on the performance and user perceptions of an agent that plays a fast-paced game where the value of rapid decision-making is emphasized. In a user study involving 125 human participants, we demonstrate a level of game performance that is broadly comparable to the performance of live human players. Only the version of our agent which makes maximal use of incremental processing achieves this level of performance, along with significantly higher user ratings of efficiency, understanding of speech, and naturalness of interaction.

Our study also provides a practical approach to the optimization of dialogue policies for incremental understanding of users' referential language in finite domains; see e.g. (Schlangen et al., 2009). Our optimization approach delivers a high level of performance for our agent, and offers insights into how the optimal decision-making policy can vary as the level of incrementality in system modules is changed. This supports a view of incremental policy optimization as a holistic process to be undertaken in conjunction with overall system design choices.

2 The RDG-Image Game

In the RDG-Image game (Paetzel et al., 2014; Manuvinakurike and DeVault, 2015), depicted in Figure 1, one person acts as a director and the other as a matcher. Players see a set of eight images on separate screens. The set of images is exactly the same for both players, but they are arranged in a different order on the screen. Image sets include pets (Figure 1), fruits, bicycles, road signs, and robots, among others.

One of the eight images is randomly selected as a target image (TI) and it is highlighted on the director's screen with a thick red border as shown in Figure 1. The goal of the director is to describe the TI so that the matcher is able to uniquely identify it from the distractors. The director and matcher are able to talk back-and-forth freely in order to identify the TI. When the matcher believes he has correctly identified the TI, he clicks on the image and communicates this to the director who has to press a button to continue with the next TI. The team scores a point for each correct guess, with a goal to complete as many images as possible.

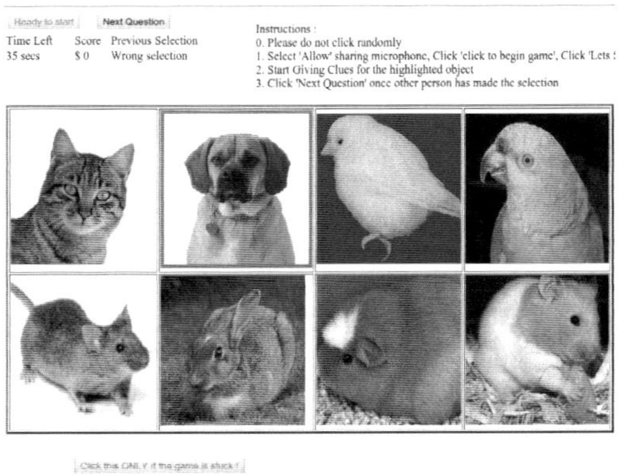

Figure 1: Browser interface for the director. The target image is highlighted by a red border. The *Next Question* button moves on to the next target.

Each team participates in 4 main game rounds. In this study, the roles remain the same for the players across all four rounds and our agent is always in the matcher role. The maximum number of TIs within each round is 12, and the rounds have a variable duration ranging from 45 to 60 seconds. The time limit for each round was chosen based on analysis of the subdialogues for that round's image sets in our earlier game corpora (Paetzel et al., 2014; Manuvinakurike and DeVault, 2015) and was set specifically to prevent participants in this study from exhausting the 12 images in a round before they run out of time. In this way, the speed and accuracy of communication are always the limiting factor to higher scores.

One game in this study consists of one training round, during which participants get comfortable with the interface and their partner, plus four main game rounds which are scored. The maximum game score is therefore 48 points (4*12). Following our approach in (Manuvinakurike and DeVault, 2015), participants are incentivized to score quickly with a bonus of $0.02 per point scored.

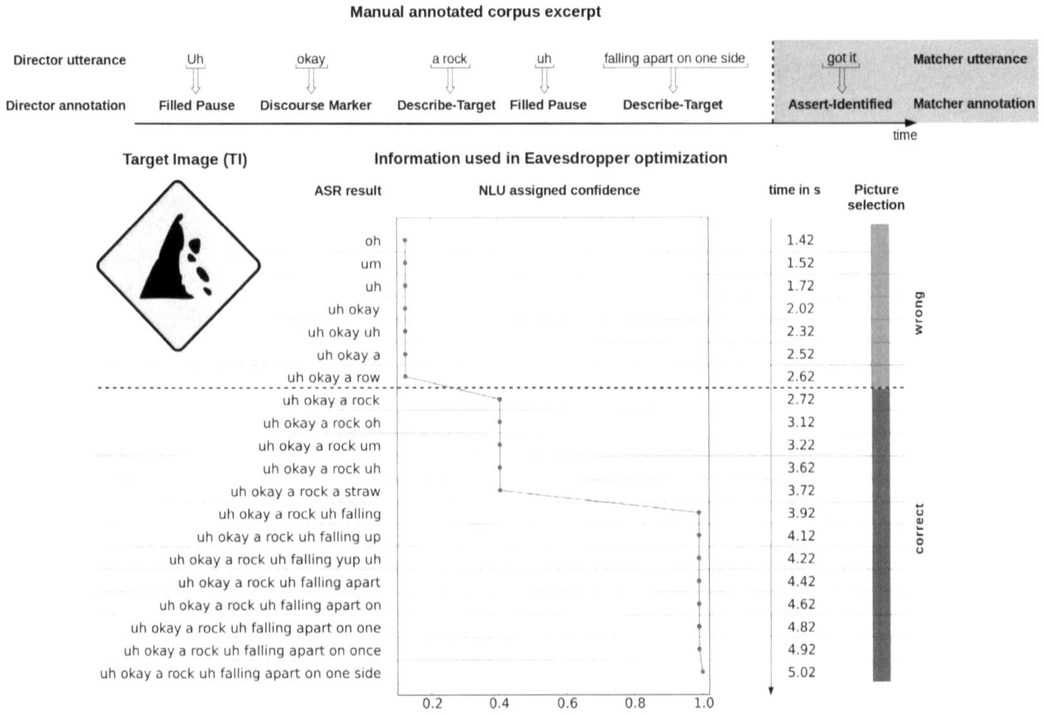

Figure 2: An image subdialogue from the RDG-Image lab corpus. The upper part shows the manual DA annotation. The lower part shows information used in the Eavesdropper policy optimization. For brevity, we include only partial ASR results that differ from the previous one. In the middle and at right are the NLU's evolving classification confidence, elapsed time, and correctness of the NLU's best guess image.

3 Observations of Human Matchers

Two corpora of human-human gameplay have previously been collected for the RDG-Image game, including the RDG-Image lab corpus (collected in our lab) (Paetzel et al., 2014) and the RDG-Image web corpus (collected on the web) (Manuvinakurike and DeVault, 2015). These corpora were used to design our automated agent.

A first step was to identify the most common types of matcher utterances and behaviour in our lab corpus. To support this analysis, 21 dialogue acts (DAs) were defined. The most important DAs for our automated matcher agents are *Assert-Identified*, used for utterances such as *Got it!* that assert the TI has been identified, and *Request-Skip*, used for utterances such as *Let's move on* that request the director to advance to the next TI.

34 human-human games were manually transcribed and annotated for dialogue acts (DAs) by a human annotator, resulting in 5415 annotated DAs. The inter-annotator agreement, measured by Krippendorf's alpha, is 0.83. 40.70% of all matcher DAs were *Assert-Identified*, and this is by far the most common DA by the matcher. For the matcher, this is followed by 15.83% of DAs which are annotated as *Out-of-domain* DAs such as laughter or meta-level discussion of the game. All other matcher DAs occur in less than 6.5% of DAs each.

Our analysis of these annotations revealed that, typically, the matcher simply listens to the director's continuing descriptions until they can perform an *Assert-Identified*, rather than taking the initiative to ask questions, for example. The top of Figure 2 shows a typical image subdialogue.

4 Design of the Agent Matcher

Based on our observations of human matchers, we focused our design of Eve on the *Assert-Identified* and *Request-Skip* acts. *Request-Skip* is a move not often used by matchers in human-human gameplay, where teams tend to take additional time as needed to agree on each image, and where teams eventually score a point for 92-98% of the TIs they encounter (depending on the image set). We anticipated that Eve might struggle with certain images

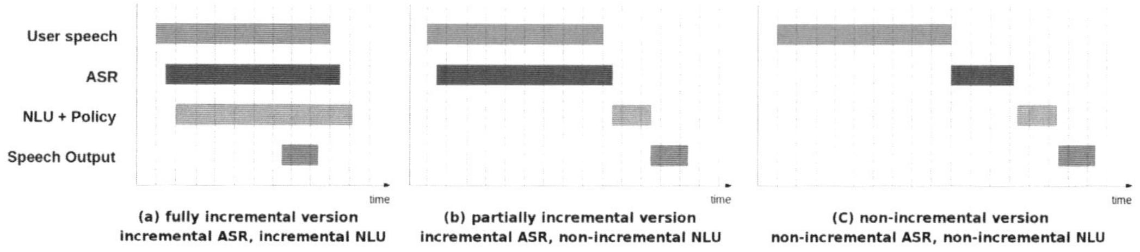

Figure 3: Timeline of the processing order of the modules in the three different versions of incrementality.

or image sets, because its NLU would be data-driven and its understanding limited to previously seen description types. Eve is therefore designed to use *Request-Skip* strategically if trying to score on the current TI appears not a good use of time.

To train our agent, the 16 image sets containing the most training examples per set were chosen from the RDG-Image lab and web corpora. Additionally, two sets of simple geometric shapes from the lab corpus were selected to serve as a training round in this study. The lab corpus includes 34 games with 68 unique participants and the web corpus includes 179 participants (some of them in multiple games). In our total training data, on average, there are 256.13 image subdialogues per image set.

4.1 Voice Activity Detection (VAD), Automatic Speech Recognition (ASR)

Audio is streamed from the user's browser to our voice activity detector, which uses the Adaptive Multi-Rate (AMR) codec (3rd Generation Partnership Project, 2008) to classify each incoming 20ms audio frame as containing voice activity or not. The VAD works incrementally in all versions of our agent. It emits voice activity events and delivers segments of detected speech (in units of 100ms) to the ASR.

Our ASR is based on Kaldi (Povey et al., 2011), and is specifically adapted from the work of (Plátek and Jurčíček, 2014), which provides support for online, incremental recognition using Kaldi. Discriminative acoustic models are trained using a combination of our in-domain audio data and out-of-domain audio using Boosted Maximum Mutual Information (BMMI) with LDA and MLLT feature transformations (Plátek and Jurčíček, 2014). Statistical language models are created using our transcribed data.

Incremental ASR. In versions of our agent with incremental ASR, detected user speech is streamed into the ASR every 100ms for online decoding, and incremental (partial) ASR results are immediately computed and sent to the NLU and policy modules. Incremental ASR is illustrated at the left of Figure 2. It is used in the fully incremental and partially incremental versions of our agent, which are illustrated in Figure 3(a) and (b).

Non-incremental ASR. In the non-incremental version of our agent (see Figure 3(c)), detected user speech is buffered until the VAD segment is concluded by the VAD. At that point, all speech is provided to the ASR and the final ASR result is computed and provided to the NLU and policy.

The non-incremental (NonInc) version serves as a performance baseline where none of ASR, NLU, or policy run incrementally. The partially incremental (PartInc) version helps quantify the benefits that come from reducing system latency through online decoding in the ASR. The fully incremental (FullInc) version explores the benefits of reacting more continuously during user speech.

4.2 Natural Language Understanding (NLU)

Our NLU operates on 1-best text outputs from the ASR. At each time t, all the 1-best texts for the current TI (i.e., spanning multiple VAD segments) are concatenated to form a combined text d_t which we call the image subdialogue text. For example, at time $t = 2.72$ in Figure 2, the NLU input is $d_t =$ *uh okay a rock*.

Prior to classification, stop-words are filtered out.[1] This process yields for example the filtered text $\mathrm{filtered}(\textit{uh okay a rock}) = \textit{rock}$. From the filtered text, unigrams and bigrams are calculated. To reduce overfitting, only those unigrams and bigrams which occur more than three times in our training corpus are kept. The remaining unigrams and bigrams are used as input for the classifiers.

[1]The stop-word list is based on http://jmlr.org/papers/volume5/lewis04a/a11-smart-stop-list/english.stop and extended by domain-specific stop words.

A separate classifier is trained for each image set. The approach is broadly similar to (DeVault et al., 2011), and each partial ASR result is probabilistically classified as one of the eight TIs. The training data maps all the image subdialogue texts in our corpora for that image set to the correct TI. To select the classifier type, Weka (Hall et al., 2009) was used on manually transcribed data from the RDG-Image lab corpus. Multiple classifiers were tested with 10-fold cross validation. The best performance was achieved using a Naive Bayes classifier, which classified 69.15% of test instances correctly. Maximum Entropy classification performed second best with 61.37% accuracy.

4.3 General Form of Eve's Dialogue Policies

Eve's dialogue policies take the following form. Let the image set at time t be $\mathcal{I}_t = \{i_1, ..., i_8\}$, with the correct target image $T \in \mathcal{I}_t$ unknown to the agent. The maximum probability assigned to any image at time t is $P_t^* = \max_j P(T = i_j | d_t)$. Let $\text{elapsed}(t)$ be the elapsed time spent on the current TI up to time t.

Eve's parameterized policy is to continue waiting for additional user speech until either her confidence P_t^* exceeds a threshold IT, or else the elapsed time on this TI exceeds a threshold GT. The *identification threshold (IT)* represents the minimal classifier confidence at which Eve performs an *Assert-Identified* (by saying *Got it!*). The *give-up threshold (GT)* is the time in seconds after which Eve performs a *Request-Skip*. Eve uses NeoSpeech[2] TTS to interact with the dialogue partner. All Eve utterances are pre-synthesized to minimize output latency.

Eve's policy is invoked by different trigger events depending on the incremental architecture. In the FullInc version (Figure 3(a)), the policy is invoked with each new partial and final ASR result (i.e. every 100ms during user speech). In the PartInc and NonInc versions (Figure 3(b) and (c)), the policy is invoked only after a new final ASR result becomes available.

Each time Eve's policy is invoked, Eve selects an action using Algorithm 1.[3] Eve's policy allows the agent to make trade-offs that incorporate both

Algorithm 1 Eve's dialogue policy

```
if P*_t > IT & |filtered(d_t)| ≥ 1 then
    Assert-Identified
else if elapsed(t) < GT then
    continue listening
else
    Request-Skip
end if
```

its confidence in its best guess and the opportunity cost of spending too much time on an image. In Section 5, we describe how we optimize the numeric parameters IT and GT in these policies.

Note that this policy learning problem could also be cast in a reinforcement learning (RL) framework. In theory, a RL model could learn when to Assert-Identified, continue listening, or Request-Skip based on the current dialogue state. One challenge in this approach would be encoding the state space in a compact way (while capturing aspects of history and temporal features relevant to action selection). A second challenge would be to use the modest amount of available data to build a user simulation that can generate incremental descriptions of objects by simulated users in a realistic way. It would be interesting to compare such an approach to our approach here in future work.

5 Policy Optimization

Optimization of the parameters IT and GT in Algorithm 1 is done using a metaphor of the agent as an *eavesdropper* on human-human gameplay. To train our agent, we start by imagining the agent as listening to the speech in human-human image subdialogues from our corpora. We imagine that as the human director describes an image to his partner, our eavesdropping agent simulates making its own independent decisions about when, if it were the matcher, it would commit to a specific TI (by saying "Got it!") or request an image skip.

For example, in Figure 2, we visualize the ASR results that would be arriving in the FullInc architecture, and the time at which they would be arriving, as this human director describes the TI as *uh okay a rock uh falling apart on one side*. In the middle and right, we visualize what the agent's NLU confidence would be in its best guess (P_t^*) as these ASR results arrive. At the right, we show that this best guess is incorrect until time 2.72.

In our optimizations in this study, we assume that the objective metric to be maximized is *points*

[2] http://www.neospeech.com/

[3] Requiring $|\text{filtered}(d_t)| \geq 1$ prevents Eve from ever saying *Got it!* before any content words (non-stop words) have been received from the ASR. This could otherwise happen if the learned IT happens to be less than Eve's prior at the start of a new image.

per second (points/s). The key idea in this optimization is that each value of parameters IT and GT in Algorithm 1 translates into a specific simulatable agent response and outcome for each director description of a TI in our corpus. For example, if IT=0.3 and GT=5, then in the figure's example the agent would commit to its best interpretation at time 2.72 by performing Assert-Identified ("Got it!"). The agent would turn out to be correct and score a point. The time taken to score this point would be 2.72 seconds, plus some additional time for the matcher to say "Got it!" and for the director to click the Next Question button in the UI (see Figure 1). Our agent needs 0.5 seconds to say "Got it!", and we add an additional 0.25 seconds equal to the mean additional director click latency in our corpora. The total simulated time for this image is therefore 2.72+0.5+0.25 = 3.47 seconds.[4]

If one simulates this decision-making across an entire corpus, then for each value of IT and GT, one can calculate the total number of points hypothetically scored, total time hypothetically elapsed, and thus an estimated performance in points/s for the policy. As the parameter space is tractable here, we perform grid search across possible values of IT (step .01) and GT (step 1) and select values that maximize total points/s. We carried out this optimization *for each combination of image set and incrementality type*. Our optimization accounts for when ASR results would become available in a given incremental architecture.

Perhaps the biggest concern with this approach is that it assumes that human directors, when interacting with the agent, would produce similar utterances to what they produced when interacting with a human matcher. We have two reasons for believing this is true enough. First, as discussed in Section 3, the matcher's utterances in human-human gameplay typically play a limited role in changing the director's descriptions. Second, our results in live human-agent interactions, reported in Section 7, confirm that high performance can be achieved under this assumption.

In Table 1, the learned values for IT and GT are compared over four sample image sets (from among the 18 that are trained) in various incrementality conditions. An interesting observation is that *the optimized dialogue policy changes as the incrementality type changes*. For example, the FullInc policy for pet images (depicted in Figure 1) will wait up to 8 seconds (GT) for the confidence to reach 0.7 or higher (IT). The NonInc policy, on the other hand, will give up if confidence does not reach 0.89 within 2 seconds. Intuitively, one reason these policies can vary is that an ability to understand and respond incrementally can reduce the risk associated with waiting for additional user speech and ASR results. In the PartInc and NonInc versions, once the user begins to speak, the agent must wait for the user to complete their (possibly long) utterance before it can assess the (possibly unhelpful) new information and respond. The decision to let the user speak is therefore relatively heavyweight. This leads for example to an immediate skip for the Bikes in the NonInc version. In the FullInc version, the agent always has the option to listen to a little more speech and reconsider.

	Fully Incremental		Partially Incremental		Non-incremental	
Image set	IT	GT	IT	GT	IT	GT
Pets	0.7	8	0.52	8	0.89	2
Zoo	0.61	8	0.58	3	0.23	4
Cocktails	0.88	8	0.48	1	0.44	10
Bikes	0.80	18	0.49	7	0.0	0

Table 1: *Identification threshold* and *give-up threshold* in optimized policies for 4 image sets.

5.1 Offline Policy Evaluation Results

Our eavesdropper framework allows policies to not only be trained, but also evaluated in offline simulation, both in terms of total points scored and total points/s (which is the direct optimization metric). An excerpt from our offline evaluation results, using hold-one-user-out cross-validation, is shown in Table 2. In these offline results, the agent is sometimes able to achieve higher points/s than our human matchers did in human-human gameplay. This is true for some image sets in all three incrementality types. In general, we also observe that simulated points/s decreases as the level of incrementality in the system decreases. Note that the total number of simulated points achieved by these policies is generally less than what human players scored; the agents optimized for points/s are less likely to score a point for each image, but make up for this in speed. These offline results led us to hypothesize that, in live interaction with users, the FullInc agent would score higher than the less incremental versions in a time-constrained game.

[4]Note that when our agent performs Request-Skip, it is still able to select its best guess image, and so it may still score a point for that image (as human players can).

	Fully Incremental		Partially Incremental		Non-Incremental		Human	
	Points/s	points	Points/s	points	Points/s	points	Points/s	points
Pets	0.185	182	0.151	188	0.151	154	0.069	227
Zoo	0.220	203	0.184	196	0.177	193	0.154	243
Cocktails	0.118	153	0.103	137	0.102	172	0.124	237
Bikes	0.077	126	0.073	147	0.071	100	0.072	223

Table 2: Offline policy evaluation results for all three incrementality types and four image sets. 14 additional image sets are omitted for space reasons.

6 Online Human-Agent Study

Our online data was captured with 125 remote participants, recruited on Amazon Mechanical Turk, who interacted entirely through their web browsers. They either conversed with each other or with one of our agents.

We captured the data using the Pair Me Up web framework (Manuvinakurike and DeVault, 2015), which enables spoken dialogues through a web browser using HTML5 libraries to stream audio between remote users and our server. In (Manuvinakurike and DeVault, 2015), we demonstrated the feasibility of collecting real-time, high quality human-human game data with this web framework. For this study, we adapted Pair Me Up to support human-agent interaction. See (Manuvinakurike et al., 2015) for a detailed discussion of our web architecture, study costs, and how we managed the Amazon HITs for this study, including steps to verify each participant's audio setup and network latency.

Of the 125 participants, 50 were paired with each other (forming 25 human-human pairs) and 25 were paired with each of the FullInc, PartInc, and NonInc agents. None participated in our study more than once. From self-disclosure of the directors, 50% were female, all were over 18 (mean age 31.01, std. 10.13), and all were native English speakers.

Excerpts of Eve's gameplay during the study are included in Figure 5 in the Appendix.

After each game, participants answered a questionnaire that included basic demographic questions and also asked for their judgments on various aspects of the interaction with their partner.

7 Human-Agent Evaluation Results

In this section, we summarize our user study results, many of which are visualized in Figure 4. We evaluate our FullInc, PartInc, and NonInc agents by game score and by user's perceptions as captured in post-game questionnaires. Users responded to a range of statements with answers on a five point Likert-scale ranging from *Totally disagree* (0) to *Totally agree* (4). We compare the responses of the director in human-human (HH) pairs to the responses of human directors playing with our agent as matcher. All significance tests in this section are Wilcoxon rank sum tests.

Score (Fig. 4a). We report scores in U.S. dollars paid to participants for correct TIs ($0.02/correct TI). The FullInc system achieved a mean score of $0.33 that is significantly better than the mean $0.25 for PartInc ($p = 0.013$) and the mean $0.23 for NonInc ($p = 0.002$). No significant difference in score was observed between the PartInc and NonInc versions. These results suggest that, beyond incorporating online decoding in the ASR to reduce ASR latency, also incorporating an incremental NLU+policy is important to score maximization.

Our FullInc agent's performance in terms of score is quite strong, and comparable to HH scores. Although the mean HH score of $0.36 was a little higher than that of our FullInc agent ($0.33), the difference is not significant. The best FullInc score of $0.50 achieved as part of the study is higher than 76% of HH teams, and its worst score of $0.14 is higher than 20% of HH teams. HH teams scored significantly higher than the PartInc ($p = 0.038$) and NonInc ($p = 0.008$) versions of the system, which underscores the importance of pervasive incremental processing to achieving human-like performance in some dialogue systems.

Satisfaction with score (Fig. 4d). Human participants were significantly more satisfied with their score when working with a human matcher than with any version of our agent (for the FullInc version, $p = 0.037$). Participants who played with the FullInc agent were significantly more satisfied with their score than those in the PartInc ($p = 0.002$) and NonInc ($p = 0.017$) conditions. These results generally mirror our findings

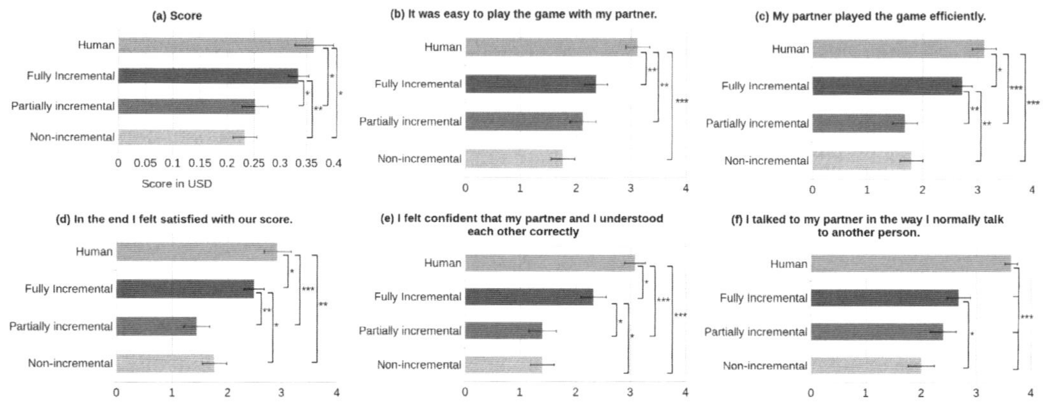

Figure 4: Scores and survey responses by condition (means and standard errors). Significant differences in Wilcoxon rank sum tests are indicated by * ($p < 0.05$), ** ($p < 0.005$), and *** ($p < 0.0005$).

for game score, and score and score satisfaction are clearly connected.

Perceived ease of gameplay (Fig. 4b). Human partners were perceived as significantly easier to play with than all agent versions. We observed a trend (not quite significant) for people to consider it easier to play with the FullInc version than with NonInc version ($p = 0.052$).

Perceived efficiency (Fig. 4c). Human partners were rated as significantly more efficient than the FullInc ($p = 0.038$), PartInc ($p < 0.0005$) and NonInc ($p < 0.0005$) agents. Among the agent versions, the FullInc agent was rated significantly more efficient than PartInc ($p = 0.001$) and NonInc ($p = 0.002$). This result echoes previous findings of increases in perceived efficiency for incremental systems, though here with a differing system architecture and task (Skantze and Hjalmarsson, 2010).

Perceived understanding of speech (Fig. 4e). Human partners elicited the most confidence that the two players were understanding each other. This perceived understanding of each other's speech was significantly higher in FullInc than in PartInc ($p = 0.010$) and NonInc ($p = 0.006$). It is interesting to consider that the NLU in these three versions is identical, and thus the level of actual understanding of user speech should be similar across conditions. We speculate that the greater responsiveness of the FullInc system increased confidence that users were being understood.

Perceived naturalness of user speech (Fig. 4f). One of our survey items investigated whether people felt they could speak naturally to their partner, "in the way I normally talk to another person". Human partners scored significantly higher than all agent versions here. The FullInc agent scored significantly higher than the NonInc agent ($p = 0.037$).

8 Conclusions

In this paper, we have presented the design, training, and evaluation of a high-performance agent that plays the RDG-Image game in the matcher role. Our policy training approach allows the system to be optimized based on its specific incremental processing architecture. In a live user evaluation, three agent versions utilizing different degrees of incremental processing were evaluated in terms of game performance and user perceptions. Our results showed that the most fully incremental agent achieves game scores that are comparable to those achieved in human-human gameplay, are higher than those achieved by partially and non-incremental versions, and are accompanied by improved user perceptions of efficiency, understanding of speech, and naturalness of interaction.

Acknowledgments

Thanks to Kallirroi Georgila and Cheng Qu. This work was supported by the National Science Foundation under Grant No. IIS-1219253 and by the U.S. Army. Any opinions, findings, and conclusions or recommendations expressed in this material are those of the author(s) and do not necessarily reflect the views, position, or policy of the National Science Foundation or the United States Government, and no official endorsement should be inferred.

References

3rd Generation Partnership Project. 2008. Technical specification group services and system aspects; ansi-c code for the adaptive multi rate (amr) speech codec (release 12).

Gregory Aist, James Allen, Ellen Campana, Carlos Gomez Gallo, Scott Stoness, Mary Swift, and Michael K. Tanenhaus. 2007. Incremental dialogue system faster than and preferred to its nonincremental counterpart. In *Proc. of the 29th Annual Conference of the Cognitive Science Society*.

Timo Baumann and David Schlangen. 2013. Open-ended, extensible system utterances are preferred, even if they require filled pauses. In *SigDial*, pages 280–283, August.

Nina Dethlefs, Helen Hastie, Verena Riser, and Oliver Lemon. 2012. Optimising incremental generation for spoken dialogue systems: Reducing the need for fillers. In *Seventh International Natural Language Generation Conference (INLG)*.

David DeVault, Kenji Sagae, and David Traum. 2011. Incremental interpretation and prediction of utterance meaning for interactive dialogue. *Dialogue & Discourse*, 2(1).

Jonathan Gratch, Anna Okhmatovskaia, Francois Lamothe, Stacy Marsella, Mathieu Morales, R. van der Werf, and Louis-Philippe Morency. 2006. Virtual Rapport. In Jonathan Gratch, Michael Young, Ruth Aylett, Daniel Ballin, and Patrick Olivier, editors, *Intelligent Virtual Agents*, volume 4133, chapter 2, pages 14–27. Springer Berlin Heidelberg, Berlin, Heidelberg.

Mark Hall, Eibe Frank, Geoffrey Holmes, Bernhard Pfahringer, Peter Reutemann, and Ian H. Witten. 2009. The weka data mining software: An update. *SIGKDD Explor. Newsl.*, 11(1):10–18, November.

Helen Hastie, Marie-Aude Aufaure, Panos Alexopoulos, Heriberto Cuayáhuitl, Nina Dethlefs, Milica Gasic, James Henderson, Oliver Lemon, Xingkun Liu, Peter Mika, et al. 2013. Demonstration of the parlance system: a data-driven, incremental, spoken dialogue system for interactive search. *Proc SIGDIAL*, pages 154–156.

Dongho Kim, Catherine Breslin, Pirros Tsiakoulis, Milica Gasic, Matthew Henderson, and Steve Young. 2014. Inverse reinforcement learning for micro-turn management. In *Interspeech*.

Ramesh Manuvinakurike and David DeVault. 2015. Pair Me Up: A Web Framework for Crowd-Sourced Spoken Dialogue Collection. In *The International Workshop on Spoken Dialog Systems (IWSDS)*.

Ramesh Manuvinakurike, Maike Paetzel, and David DeVault. 2015. Reducing the Cost of Dialogue System Training and Evaluation with Online, Crowd-Sourced Dialogue Data Collection. *Workshop on the Semantics and Pragmatics of Dialogue (SemDial)*.

Maike Paetzel, David Nicolas Racca, and David DeVault. 2014. A multimodal corpus of rapid dialogue games. In *Language Resources and Evaluation Conference (LREC)*, May.

Ondřej Plátek and Filip Jurčíček. 2014. Free on-line speech recogniser based on Kaldi ASR toolkit producing word posterior lattices. In *Proceedings of the 15th Annual Meeting of the Special Interest Group on Discourse and Dialogue (SIGDIAL)*, pages 108–112, Philadelphia, PA, U.S.A., June. Association for Computational Linguistics.

Daniel Povey, Arnab Ghoshal, Gilles Boulianne, Lukas Burget, Ondrej Glembek, Nagendra Goel, Mirko Hannemann, Petr Motlicek, Yanmin Qian, Petr Schwarz, Jan Silovsky, Georg Stemmer, and Karel Vesely. 2011. The kaldi speech recognition toolkit. In *IEEE 2011 Workshop on Automatic Speech Recognition and Understanding*. IEEE Signal Processing Society, December. IEEE Catalog No.: CFP11SRW-USB.

David Schlangen and Gabriel Skantze. 2011. A general, abstract model of incremental dialogue processing. *Dialogue and Discourse*, 2(1):83–111.

David Schlangen, Timo Baumann, and Michaela Atterer. 2009. Incremental reference resolution: The task, metrics for evaluation, and a Bayesian filtering model that is sensitive to disfluencies. In *The 10th Annual SIGDIAL Meeting on Discourse and Dialogue (SIGDIAL 2009)*.

Ethan O. Selfridge, Iker Arizmendi, Peter A. Heeman, and Jason D. Williams. 2012. Integrating incremental speech recognition and POMDP-based dialogue systems. In *Proceedings of the 13th Annual Meeting of the Special Interest Group on Discourse and Dialogue*, pages 275–279, Seoul, South Korea, July. Association for Computational Linguistics.

Ethan Selfridge, Iker Arizmendi, Peter Heeman, and Jason Williams. 2013. Continuously predicting and processing barge-in during a live spoken dialogue task. In *Proceedings of the SIGDIAL 2013 Conference*, pages 384–393, Metz, France, August. Association for Computational Linguistics.

Gabriel Skantze and Anna Hjalmarsson. 2010. Towards incremental speech generation in dialogue systems. In *Proceedings of the SIGDIAL 2010 Conference*, pages 1–8, Tokyo, Japan, September. Association for Computational Linguistics.

Gabriel Skantze and David Schlangen. 2009. Incremental dialogue processing in a micro-domain. In *Proceedings of the 12th Conference of the European Association for Computational Linguistics (EACL)*.

Nigel Ward and David DeVault. 2015. Ten challenges in highly-interactive dialog systems. In *AAAI Spring Symposium on Turn-taking and Coordination in Human-Machine Interaction*.

Appendix

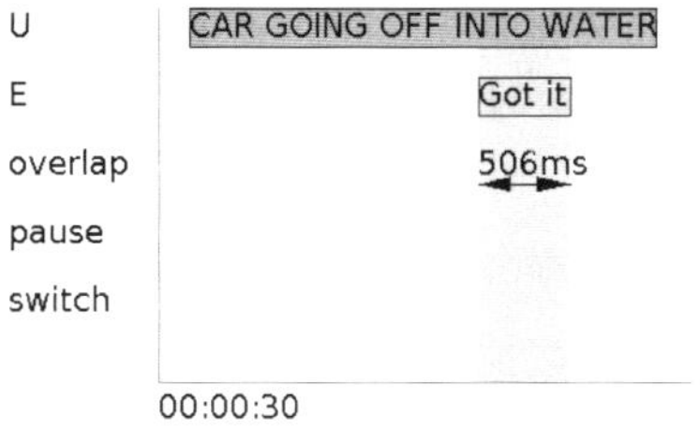

(a) Example of Eve in fully incremental mode

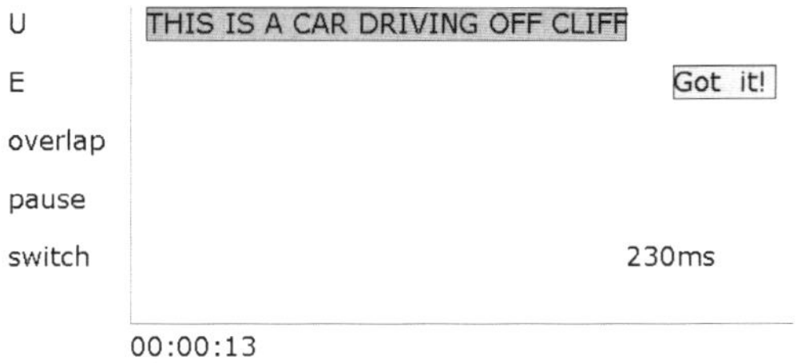

(b) Example of Eve in partially incremental mode

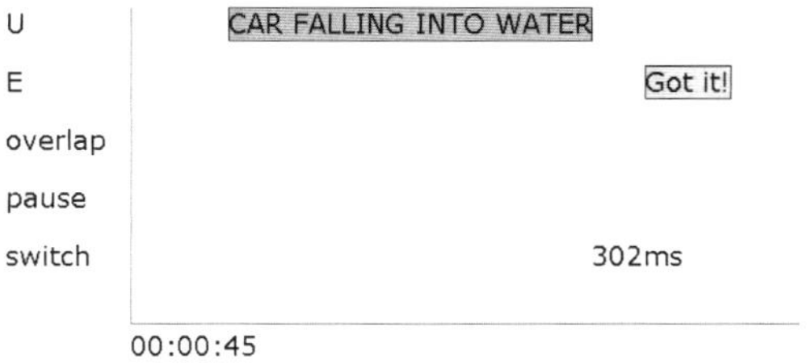

(c) Example of Eve in non-incremental mode

(d) The target image for these examples

Figure 5: Examples of Eve's behavior in this study as different users describe the target image in (d). Seven distractor signs are also present in the display (not shown). The timing of the user's ASR results (U) and Eve's utterances (E) are indicated.

Image sources

The images of pets used in Figure 1 and of the street signs used in Figure 2 and 5 are excerpted from pictures protected by copyright and released under different licenses by their original authors. In the following attributions, we will identify the 8 images shown in the director's screen capture in Figure 1 from left-right and top-down direction, with a number from 1 to 8. Thanks to Joaquim Alves Gaspar for image 1[5] and Magnus Colossus for image 3[6], both published under CC BY-SA 3.0. Thanks to Randy Pertiet for image 2[7], Brent Moore for image 7[8] and Domenique Godbout for image 8[9], all licensed under CC-BY 2.0 and to Opacha for image 4[10] and TomiTapio for image 6[11], both licenced under CC-BY 3.0. Additionally, we kindly acknowledge Ilmari Karonen for image 5[12] and the Irish Department of Transport for the street signs shown in Figure 2[13] and 5[14], all published under Public Domain.

[5] http://commons.wikimedia.org/wiki/File:Cat_March_2010-1a.jpg
[6] http://commons.wikimedia.org/wiki/File:Canario_canary_p%C3%A1jaro_bird.jpg
[7] http://www.flickr.com/photos/34652102N04/5428922582/
[8] http://commons.wikimedia.org/wiki/File:2006_TN_State_Fair-_Guinea_Pig.jpg
[9] https://www.flickr.com/photos/dominiquegodbout/5140544743/
[10] http://commons.wikimedia.org/wiki/File:Baby-_Yellow_Naped_Amazon_Parrot_Closeup.jpg
[11] http://tomitapio.deviantart.com/art/The-bunny-says-nothing-129138755
[12] https://commons.wikimedia.org/wiki/File:Mouse_white_background.jpg
[13] http://commons.wikimedia.org/wiki/File:Ireland_road_sign_W_164.svg
[14] http://commons.wikimedia.org/wiki/File:Ireland_road_sign_W_160.svg

Towards Taxonomy of Errors in Chat-oriented Dialogue Systems

Ryuichiro Higashinaka[1], **Kotaro Funakoshi**[2], **Masahiro Araki**[3],
Hiroshi Tsukahara[4], **Yuka Kobayashi**[5], **Masahiro Mizukami**[6]
[1]NTT Corporation, [2]Honda Research Institute Japan, [3]Kyoto Institute of Technology,
[4]Denso IT Laboratory, Inc., [5]Toshiba Corporation, [6]Nara Institute of Science and Technology

Abstract

This paper presents a taxonomy of errors in chat-oriented dialogue systems. Compared to human-human conversations and task-oriented dialogues, little is known about the errors made in chat-oriented dialogue systems. Through a data collection of chat dialogues and analyses of dialogue breakdowns, we classified errors and created a taxonomy. Although the proposed taxonomy may not be complete, this paper is the first to present a taxonomy of errors in chat-oriented dialogue systems. We also highlight the difficulty in pinpointing errors in such systems.

1 Introduction

The last decade has seen an emergence of systems that can engage in chat, small talk, or open-domain conversation. Such systems can be useful for cultivating trust between a system and users (Bickmore and Cassell, 2001), entertaining users (Wallace, 2004; Banchs and Li, 2012; Wilcock and Jokinen, 2013), and obtaining preferences from users for recommendations (Bang et al., 2015).

Error analysis is important to improve any system. However, little is known about the types of errors that can be made in chat-oriented dialogue systems. This is in contrast with many studies on task-oriented dialogue systems in which various taxonomies of errors have been proposed (Dybkjær et al., 1996; Möller et al., 2007; Ward et al., 2005; Green et al., 2006).

This paper presents a taxonomy of errors in chat-oriented dialogue systems. In our approach, we collect dialogues with a chat-oriented dialogue system and identify breakdowns (situations in which users cannot proceed with the conversation (Martinovsky and Traum, 2003)) as possible points of errors. Then, we classify the errors that led to such breakdowns to create a taxonomy. By having such a taxonomy, we hope to better grasp the main causes of breakdown in current chat-oriented dialogue systems; thereby, making it possible to make improvements. The contributions of this paper are that this is the first attempt to create a taxonomy of errors in chat-oriented dialogue systems and that we quantitatively show, by the distribution of error categories and inter-annotator agreement, the possibilities and difficulties in pinpointing errors in chat-oriented dialogue systems.

In Section 2, we cover related work on creating a taxonomy of errors in dialogue systems. In Section 3, we describe our data collection followed by the annotation of breakdowns in Section 4. In Section 5, we discuss the taxonomy we devised. In Section 6, we evaluate the taxonomy in terms of the distribution of errors and inter-annotator agreement. In Section 7, we summarize the paper and mention future work.

2 Related Work

In task-oriented dialogue systems, there is a good body of research related to the classification of errors. There are several ways to categorize errors.

One is to adopt the general taxonomy of miscommunication proposed by Clark (1996). According to Clark, there are four levels in communication; channel, signal, intention, and conversation, and by using these four levels, errors can be classified into four categories depending on which level the errors occurred. For example, if the system fails to take in audio input, it is regarded as a channel-level error. Bohus and Rudnicky (2005) applied this taxonomy to classify their non-understanding errors. A similar categorization was used by Möller et al. (2007) for their smart home and restaurant information systems. Paek (2003) discussed the generality of using the four levels for error analysis in dialogue systems, referring to the use cases across disciplines.

Proceedings of the SIGDIAL 2015 Conference, pages 87–95,
Prague, Czech Republic, 2-4 September 2015.

From the viewpoint of cooperativeness in dialogue, there is also a taxonomy based on Grice's maxims (Grice, 1975). Dybkjær et al. (1996) and Bernsen et al. (1996) had four categories of errors related to Grice's maxims; quantity, quality, relevance, and manner. They also added partner asymmetry, background knowledge, and metacommunication as error categories from their observation. Their evaluation indicated that the taxonomy can appropriately classify errors in their flight reservation system. The work by Möller (2005) also incorporated Grice's maxims into "cooperativity-related parameters" as important elements that affect interaction quality in telephone-based services.

There is also an approach to creating a task or system-specific taxonomy or errors. Aberdeen and Ferro (2003) analyzed misunderstandings by a DARPA communicator system and classified its errors into such categories as failure to obey command and repeated prompt. There is also a taxonomy for a service robot (Green et al., 2006), in which major errors are robot-specific, such as timing and reference (pointing) errors. Dzikovska et al. (2009) also classified errors in a tutorial dialogue system.

Dialogue systems are usually composed of various modules. Therefore, there is also an approach to attributing errors to modules. Ward et al. (2005) attributed causes of errors to modules, such as speech recognition, understanding, generation, and synthesis, and discussed their relative impact on usability. This approach is useful when the system has clear separation of modules.

Our approach is similar to that of (Dybkjær et al., 1996) in that we incorporate Grice's maxims into our error categories (See Section 5) and that we add other categories by our observation. The difference is that we deal with chat, which is very different from task-oriented dialogue. In this paper, we do not use their taxonomy to avoid preconception about possible errors. In this work, we did not use the four levels by Clark because we currently deal with text-based systems in which channel and signal level errors rarely occur. In addition, we do not categorize errors by modules as in (Ward et al., 2005) because chat-oriented dialogue systems usually do not have clear separation of modules.

3 Data Collection

Since there are no chat data available for analysis, we decided to create our own data set using a publicly available chat API. In this section, we describe our system based on the API, data collection procedure, and statistics of the collected dialogues.

3.1 System

We built a web-based dialogue data collection system using a chat API by NTT DOCOMO (Onishi and Yoshimura, 2014). The system is text-based, and users can chat with it in Japanese. Since the API is based on the system by Higashinaka et al. (2014a), which uses a number of natural language processing techniques (e.g., zero anaphora resolution, language generation from predicate-argument structures, and open-domain question answering), the system can be regarded as one of the most advanced (or at least complex) chat-oriented dialogue systems.

Users can chat with the system on a web browser to create 21-utterance-long dialogues; each dialogue consists of one system prompt followed by ten user-system utterance pairs. Figure 1 shows an excerpt of a dialogue collected with the system. As can be seen, the content of the conversation is open-domain. See (Higashinaka et al., 2014a) for more dialogue examples.

3.2 Procedure

We called for dialogue researchers (and their collaborators) in Japan to participate in our data collection. Since the system may not live up to their full expectations, we instructed them to follow a simple guideline that basically asked them to be as cooperative as possible. We also restricted the use of emoticons such as facial expressions. Other than that, the participants were free to chat about any topic.

3.3 Collected dialogues

One-hundred sixteen participants including the authors conversed using the system, resulting in the collection of 1,146 dialogues. Table 1 lists the statistics. This is a reasonably large data set for analyses with over 10,000 user utterances.

4 Annotation of dialogue breakdowns

Before analyzing errors, it is necessary to identify the areas of errors. To this end, we asked

S: Hello! I've been waiting for you.
U: Today, the temperature will hit 36 degrees Celsius. It's really hot.
S: Is the max temperature expected to be 17?
U: Not at all. It's a heat wave!
S: Are you prepared for a heat wave?
U: Yeah, with sunshades, water, and air-conditioners...
S: Air-conditioners make it comfortable.
U: Yeah, my company doesn't allow me to use air-conditioners in the morning, I'm gonna die.
S: In the company, air-conditioners really work.
U: Daytime, they work. They are necessary because we have many PCs here.
S: They don't work.
U: Really? Ours are fine here.
S: PCs are not user-friendly.

Figure 1: Excerpt of collected dialogue. S and U stand for system and user utterances, respectively. Dialogue was originally in Japanese and translated by authors.

# of Dialogues		1,146
# of Participants		116
	User	System
# of Utterances	11,460	12,606
# of Unique Utterances	10,452	7,777
# of Words	86,367	76,235
# of Unique Words	6,262	5,076

Table 1: Statistics of collected dialogues

annotators (researchers and their collaborators as in Section 3.2) to label system utterances indicating whether the utterances led to dialogue breakdowns. We used three labels depending on how easy/difficult it is to continue the conversation after each system utterance. The three labels are as follows:

(1) Not a breakdown: It is easy to continue the conversation.

(2) Possible breakdown: It is difficult to continue the conversation smoothly.

(3) Breakdown: It is difficult to continue the conversation.

We first divided the data into two sets: init100 (consisting of 100 randomly sampled dialogues)

	Breakdown label	Ratio	Freq.
(1)	Not a breakdown	59.3%	13,363
(2)	Possible breakdown	25.3%	5,805
(3)	Breakdown	16.4%	3,752

Table 2: Distributions of breakdown annotations for rest1046 data set

and rest1046 (the remaining 1046 dialogues). After some trial annotations with init100, we split rest1046 into eleven subsets (a–k) of 100 dialogues each (subset k contained only 46 dialogues) and allocated two annotators for each subset. For ten dialogues within each subset, we asked the annotators to provide reasons for their annotations as comments.

Table 2 shows the distribution of the three breakdown labels for the entire rest1046 data set. This shows that we have a good percentage (about 40%) of breakdowns for analysis. The inter-annotator agreement in Fleiss' κ was 0.28 (the macro-average over the subsets), showing the subjective nature of dialogue breakdown.

5 Creating taxonomy of errors

We manually examined the system utterances annotated with breakdowns and the comments provided by the annotators to create our taxonomy of errors. After several iterations of devising error categories and annotating system utterances with the categories, we reached our agreed-upon taxonomy. We explain the taxonomy in detail as follows.

5.1 Taxonomy

Since there were many comments related to the grammar and semantics of single utterances as well as the violation of adjacency pairs (Schegloff and Sacks, 1973) and pragmatic constraints, we thought it was better to have **main categories** that distinguish to which scope of the context the errors relate; namely, we distinguished utterance-level, response-level (adjacency pair), context-level (local context (Allen, 1995)), and environment-level (not within the local context) errors.

Within each main category, we created **sub-categories**. Since there were many comments mentioning the violation of principles of cooperativeness, we created sub-categories that correspond to Grice's maxims for response and context-level errors. We then added other error categories.

We describe each error category with examples as follows.

5.1.1 Utterance-level errors

Utterance-level errors are those that can be recognized as errors by looking at single utterances. They typically come from language-generation deficiencies of the system. Note that the system generates on the basis of automatically acquired resources from the web (Higashinaka et al., 2014a). In this level, we identified three sub-categories.

Syntactic error: The utterance is not grammatical or lacks important elements to be a valid sentence such as missing necessary arguments and particles.

(1) *Necchuusho ni ki wo tsuke ka
Heat stroke DAT care ACC take Q
'Do you take care against heat stroke?'

Here, 'tsuke' (take) should be 'tsukeru' or 'tsukemasu' for valid Japanese conjugation.

Semantic error: The utterance is semantically invalid such as when the combination of a predicate and its arguments cannot constitute any meaning.

(2) I am good at raining.
(one cannot be good at raining)

(3) The work is honest.
(work cannot be honest)

Uninterpretable: The utterance is not understandable. There are no recognizable words or it is just a fragment of an utterance.

(4) Chu-Chu
(seemingly expressing some noise)

5.1.2 Response-level errors

Response-level errors are those that can be recognized as errors by looking at adjacency pairs. In this level, we identified five sub-categories in which the first four relate to Grice's maxims.

Excess/lack of information: The utterance violates the maxim of quantity. The utterance misses some piece of information in response to the previous user utterance or contains unnecessary information.

(5) U: Good morning! It's nice and cool, recently.
S: I like. (missing object for a predicate)

(6) U: I think simple is best.
S: Oh, it's a serious problem.
(missing reason for a proposition)

Non-understanding: The utterance violates the maxim of quality. Because of the lack of understanding, the content of the utterance is false or inappropriate in terms of the previous user utterance such as when the system says something that contradicts what the user has said.

(7) U: I'm into video games lately.
S: Do you stay away from video games?

No-relevance: The utterance violates the maxim of relation. The utterance does not have a relation to the previous user utterance such as when the system ignores a user's question and continues with other topics.

(8) U: What is your hobby, then?
S: When was your last trip?

Unclear intention: The utterance violates the maxim of manner. The utterance relates to the previous user utterance in some way but the relation is not clear, leading to the difficulty in understanding the underlying intention of the utterance.

(9) U: What catches fire?
S: Fire goes into the oven.

Misunderstanding: The utterance displays the misunderstanding of the previous user utterance such as when the system mishandles the sense of a polysemic word.

(10) U: Good evening. I think watermelons are delicious.
S: Are you shopping using a SUICA?

Watermelon ("suika" in Japanese) was misunderstood for "SUICA", an IC-card used for mass-transit and shopping in Japan.

5.1.3 Context-level errors

Context-level errors are those that can be recognized as errors by looking at the local context, not just by adjacency pairs. In this level, we identified five sub-categories in which the first four relate to Grice's maxims. Compared to response-level errors, the errors here are more to do with propositions and topics in the current context.

Excess/lack of proposition: The utterance violates the maxim of quantity. The utterance does not provide any new proposition to the discourse context (e.g., repetition of already mentioned propositions) or provides excessive information than required.

(11) S: A typhoon is strong.
U: Because of it, I got soaked.
S: The force of the typhoon is strong.

Contradiction: The utterance violates the maxim of quality. The utterance contains propositions that contradict what has been said by the system or by the user. For example, the system changes its opinion or preferences within a dialogue.

(12) S: It's nice to go shopping alone.
U: I agree. That's nice.
S: Shopping takes time.
U: Window shopping is also fun.
S: It's fun to go shopping with somebody.

Non-relevant topic: The utterance violates the maxim of relation. The topic of the utterance is irrelevant to the current context such as when the system suddenly jumps to some other topic triggered by some particular word in the previous user utterance.

(13) S: I lose my SUICA.
U: Don't lose it!
S: I can get it reissued.
U: But, you can't get your deposit back.
S: I'll be careful.
U: Why don't you hang it from your neck.
S: You swing it, don't you?

'It' seems to refer to 'neck', which is a totally different topic from the previous topic "SUICA".

Unclear relation: The utterance violates the maxim of manner. Although the utterance relates to the previous user utterance, its relation to the current topic is unclear. Note that the utterance constitutes an appropriate adjacency pair but is contextually inappropriate.

(14) S: You are good at surfing.
U: I haven't tried yet.
S: The style is important.
U: Good style is cool.
S: Slender are stylish.

Although the system is talking about "style", its relation to surfing is unclear.

Topic switch error: The utterance displays the fact that the system missed the switch in topic by the user, continuing with the previous topic.

(15) S: I am going to the pool in the afternoon.
U: I envy you.
S: Oh!
U: It seems to continue to be hot in the afternoon.
S: The pool is dirty.

5.1.4 Environment-level errors

Environment-level errors are those that cannot be recognized as errors by the local context but by other issues outside the dialogue. In this level, we identified three sub-categories.

Lack of common ground: The utterance introduces, out of the blue, a proposition that has not been yet grounded.

(16) Tuna is stale, isn't it?
(Not all tuna is stale.)

Lack of common sense: The utterance displays a lack of common sense such as when the utterance has a proposition that is believed to be false in the real world.

(17) It's good to have a disease.

Lack of sociality: The utterance violates social common sense such as when the utterance breaks the social relationships with users such as insults and lack of politeness.

(18) U: I will look for a good pool for you.
S: Why don't you know it!

Main cat.	# of Ann	Ratio
UTT	220	0.126
RES	889	0.511
CON	521	0.299
ENV	110	0.063

Table 3: Number of annotations given to each main category. UTT, RES, CON, and ENV denote utterance, response, context, and environment levels, respectively.

6 Evaluation of the taxonomy

To test the validity of our taxonomy, we asked annotators to label system utterances in our data with our error categories.

One way to check the validity of a taxonomy is to observe the distribution of the annotations. When the annotations are biased towards certain categories, it is an indication that the taxonomy is not decomposing the phenomena appropriately. Another way for verifying the taxonomy is to check inter-annotator agreement. If the inter-annotator agreement is high, it is an indication that the categories are appropriately separated from each other.

We assigned three annotators for each subset of a–j (See Section 4; we did not use subset k because it had a small number of dialogues). Within each subset, we asked the annotators to annotate system utterances in the ten dialogues that had obligatory comments for breakdowns so that they could use the comments as hints to facilitate annotation. For each system utterance in question, a single error category label (i.e. sub-category label) was annotated. We instructed the annotators to check error categories from the utterance level to the environment level; that is, they first check whether the system utterance is an utterance-level error, if it is not, the check proceeds to the response level. For checking the response-level error, it was recommended that the annotators hide the context so that they can just focus on the adjacency pairs.

With this annotation process, 580 system utterances were annotated by 3 annotators with our error categories, resulting in 1740 (580 $\times$ 3) annotations. Note that we could not use the same annotators for all data because of the high burden of this annotation.

Main	Sub	# of Ann	Ratio
UTT	Syntactic error	48	0.028
	Semantic error	143	0.082
	Uninterpretable	29	0.017
RES	Excess/lack of information	185	0.106
	Non-understanding	292	0.168
	No relevance	168	0.097
	Unclear intention	186	0.107
	Misunderstanding	58	0.033
CON	Excess/lack of proposition	125	0.072
	Contradiction	132	0.076
	Non-relevant topic	71	0.041
	Unclear relation	95	0.055
	Topic switch error	98	0.056
ENV	Lack of common ground	41	0.024
	Lack of common sense	36	0.021
	Lack of sociality	33	0.019

Table 4: Number of annotations given to each sub-category. Ratio is calculated over all annotations.

6.1 Distribution of error categories

Table 3 shows the distribution of annotations summarized by the main categories. As can be seen from the table, the response-level error has the most annotations (more than 50%), followed by the context-level error. We also see quite a few utterance-level and environment-level errors.

Table 4 shows the distribution of annotations by sub-category. Within the utterance-level category, the semantic error is dominant. For the other levels, the errors seem to be equally distributed under each main category, although the number of RES-Non-understandings is larger and that of RES-Misunderstandings is less than the others. This is an indication that the taxonomy has a good categorization of errors since the distribution is not biased to only a small number of categories.

6.2 Inter-annotator agreement

Table 5 shows Fleiss' κ for main and sub-categories of errors. The kappa values were calculated within each subset because the annotators were different for each subset. The average value indicates the macro-average over the subsets.

For the main categories, the averaged Fleiss' κ was 0.4, which we consider as moderate agreement. It is quite surprising that there was some difficulty in distinguishing between such obvious levels of discourse scope. For a detailed analysis, we created a confusion matrix for the main cate-

Subset	# of Utts	Main cat.	Sub cat.
a	45	0.472	0.284
b	46	0.263	0.208
c	59	0.372	0.252
d	67	0.405	0.207
e	55	0.485	0.098
f	81	0.528	0.336
g	54	0.353	0.312
h	61	0.359	0.275
i	46	0.367	0.131
j	66	0.396	0.292
Avg		0.400	0.239

Table 5: Fleiss' κ for main and sub-categories of errors. # of Utts indicates number of annotated utterances in each subset.

	UTT	RES	CON	ENV
UTT	246	140	27	27
RES	140	1242	330	66
CON	27	330	654	31
ENV	27	66	31	96

Table 6: Confusion matrix for main categories

gories (See Table 6). There was most confusion with RES vs. CON. This may be understandable because responses are closely related to the context. It is also interesting that there was much confusion regarding UTT vs. RES. Some annotators seemed to be lenient on syntactic/semantic errors and considered such errors to be response-level. Another interesting point is regarding ENV because it was most confused with RES, not CON, which is in the next level. This may be attributable to the fact that ENV is concerned with something more than the discourse scope. Although we instructed annotators to proceed from utterance-level to environment-level errors, it might have been difficult for them to ignore easy-to-find errors related to sociality and common sense.

For the sub-categories, the averaged Fleiss' κ was 0.239, which is rather low. For subset e, the kappa value was as low as 0.098. To further investigate the cause of this low agreement, we created a confusion matrix for the sub-category annotations. Since there are 16 sub-categories and the number of possible confusing pairs is 120 (${}_{16}C_2$), for brevity, we only show the top-10 confusing sub-category pairs (See Table 7). From the table, the top six pairs are all between response-level errors. The top six confusing pairs comprise about 20% of all confusions. After that, the confused pairs are mostly between response and context levels.

The confusion between RES-Non-understanding and RES-No-relevance was probably because of the perception of "what the system really understood". Some annotators thought the system made an utterance that did not match the content of the previous user utterance because it did not "understand" the user; therefore, he/she used the RES-Non-understanding category, whereas others just used the RES-No-relevance category. In fact, other confusing pairs in the response level had similar problems. For example, the category RES-Excess/lack-of-information was confused with RES-Unclear-intention because some annotators thought the intention was unclear due to the lack of information. This lack of information also made an utterance seem irrelevant in some cases.

This analysis made it clear that it is difficult to distinguish between the categories related to Grice's maxims. This may be reasonable since Grice's maxims are not claimed to be mutually exclusive. However, considering that the maxims have been successfully used to classify errors in task-oriented dialogue (Bernsen et al., 1996; Dybkjær et al., 1996), this can be due to the nature of chat-oriented dialogue systems. Our hypothesis for this confusion is that system utterances in current chat-oriented dialogue systems are far from being cooperative; thus, are not placed within the understandable regions of conversational implicature, making the classification highly subjective. Another hypothesis is that there can be multiple cooperativeness errors for the same utterance. In this case, our single-label classification scheme may not be appropriate because it necessitates the subjective choice between the cooperativeness errors.

6.3 Discussions

Since errors were not biased to particular error categories in the annotation, the taxonomy seems to have a good decomposition of errors. The main categories, which roughly distinguish the errors by the scope of discourse context, also seem to be reasonable from moderate inter-annotator agreement. However, we encountered very low inter-annotator agreement for the sub-categories. According to our analysis, it was the difficulty in distinguish-

	Confusing sub-categories		Ratio	Accum
1	RES-Non-understanding	RES-No relevance	0.048	0.048
2	RES-Excess/lack of information	RES-Unclear intention	0.034	0.082
3	RES-Excess/lack of information	RES-Non-understanding	0.032	0.114
4	RES-Excess/lack of information	RES-No relevance	0.028	0.142
5	RES-No relevance	RES-Unclear intention	0.027	0.169
6	RES-Non-understanding	RES-Unclear intention	0.025	0.194
7	RES-Non-understanding	CON-Topic switch error	0.024	0.218
8	RES-Non-understanding	CON-Contradiction	0.017	0.235
9	CON-Non-relevant topic	CON-Unclear relation	0.017	0.252
10	RES-Unclear intention	CON-Unclear relation	0.017	0.270

Table 7: Top-10 confusing sub-category pairs

ing among the categories related to Grice's maxims that attributed to this low agreement, due to the possible reason of subjectivity.

While we improve the categories and the labeling scheme to cope with the subjectivity, our suggestion for the time being is to shrink Grice's maxim-related categories (in both RES and CON) to one "cooperativeness error" category. To support this idea, we shrank such categories and recalculated Fleiss' κ. As a result, we found that the inter-annotator agreement increased to 0.358 (macro-average over the subsets). Considering that this kappa value is bounded by that of the main categories (i.e., 0.4), the reliability of this classification is reasonable.

7 Summary and Future Work

We presented a taxonomy of errors in chat-oriented dialogue systems. Through a data collection of chat dialogues and analyses of dialogue breakdowns, we created a taxonomy of errors. We then evaluated the validity of our taxonomy from two view points: the distribution of error categories and inter-annotator agreement. We argued that our taxonomy is reasonable, although some amendments are necessary. Our contributions are that we presented the first taxonomy of errors in chat-oriented dialogue systems and quantitatively evaluated the taxonomy and highlighted the difficulties in mapping errors to Grice's maxims in such systems.

There are a number of limitations in this work. First, the kappa is still low. We need to refine the categories and their definitions to reduce subjectivity in our classification scheme. It may also be necessary to incorporate a multi-label scheme. Another limitation is that the research was conducted using a single system. Although the system we adopted had many advanced features in terms of natural language processing, for generality, we need to verify our taxonomy using data of other chat-oriented dialogue systems. Another limitation is the modality considered. We only dealt with text, whereas there are many systems based on other modalities. The research was conducted only in Japanese, which is another limitation. Although we believe our approach is language-independent, we need to verify this with systems using other languages.

Our ultimate goal is to reduce errors in chat-oriented dialogue systems. Although we strive to reduce errors ourselves, since the errors concern many aspects of conversation, we are planning to make dialogue-breakdown detection an open challenge. To this end, we have released the data[1] to the public so that researchers in the field can test their ideas for detecting breakdowns. Although there have been approaches to detecting errors in open-domain conversation, the reported accuracies are not that high (Xiang et al., 2014; Higashinaka et al., 2014b). We believe our taxonomy will be helpful for conceptualizing the errors, and the forthcoming challenge will encourage a more detailed analysis of errors in chat-oriented dialogue systems.

Acknowledgments

In Japan, there is an error analysis campaign called "Project Next NLP", and within this project, there is a dialogue task as a sub-group. This research was conducted with the collaboration of more than 32 researchers from 15 institutions in the dialogue

[1]The data are available at `https://sites.google.com/site/dialoguebreakdowndetection/`

task. Although the authors of this paper are those who participated in the final design of the taxonomy, we thank all members of the dialogue task for data collection, annotation, and fruitful discussions. We also thank NTT DOCOMO for letting us use their chat API for data collection.

References

John Aberdeen and Lisa Ferro. 2003. Dialogue patterns and misunderstandings. In *Proc. ISCA Workshop on Error Handling in Spoken Dialogue Systems*, pages 17–21.

James Allen. 1995. *Natural language understanding*. Benjamin/Cummings.

Rafael E Banchs and Haizhou Li. 2012. IRIS: a chat-oriented dialogue system based on the vector space model. In *Proc. the ACL 2012 System Demonstrations*, pages 37–42.

Jeesoo Bang, Hyungjong Noh, Yonghee Kim, and Gary Geunbae Lee. 2015. Example-based chat-oriented dialogue system with personalized long-term memory. In *Proc. BigComp*, pages 238–243.

Niels Ole Bernsen, Hans Dybkjaer, and Laila Dybkjaer. 1996. Principles for the design of cooperative spoken human-machine dialogue. In *Proc. ICSLP*, volume 2, pages 729–732.

Timothy W. Bickmore and Justine Cassell. 2001. Relational agents: a model and implementation of building user trust. In *Proc. CHI*, pages 396–403.

Dan Bohus and Alexander I Rudnicky. 2005. Sorry, i didn't catch that!–an investigation of non-understanding errors and recovery strategies. In *Proc. SIGDIAL*, pages 128–143.

Herbert H Clark. 1996. *Using language*. Cambridge university press.

Laila Dybkjær, Niels Ole Bernsen, and Hans Dybkjær. 1996. Grice incorporated: cooperativity in spoken dialogue. In *Proc. COLING*, volume 1, pages 328–333.

Myroslava O Dzikovska, Charles B Callaway, Elaine Farrow, Johanna D Moore, Natalie Steinhauser, and Gwendolyn Campbell. 2009. Dealing with interpretation errors in tutorial dialogue. In *Proc. SIGDIAL*, pages 38–45.

Anders Green, Kerstin Severinson Eklundh, Britta Wrede, and Shuyin Li. 2006. Integrating miscommunication analysis in natural language interface design for a service robot. In *Proc. IEEE/RSJ*, pages 4678–4683.

H. P. Grice. 1975. Logic and conversation. In P. Cole and J. Morgan, editors, *Syntax and Semantics 3: Speech Acts*, pages 41–58. New York: Academic Press.

Ryuichiro Higashinaka, Kenji Imamura, Toyomi Meguro, Chiaki Miyazaki, Nozomi Kobayashi, Hiroaki Sugiyama, Toru Hirano, Toshiro Makino, and Yoshihiro Matsuo. 2014a. Towards an open-domain conversational system fully based on natural language processing. In *Proc. COLING*, pages 928–939.

Ryuichiro Higashinaka, Toyomi Meguro, Kenji Imamura, Hiroaki Sugiyama, Toshiro Makino, and Yoshihiro Matsuo. 2014b. Evaluating coherence in open domain conversational systems. In *Proc. INTERSPEECH*, pages 130–133.

Bilyana Martinovsky and David Traum. 2003. The error is the clue: Breakdown in human-machine interaction. In *Proc. ISCA Workshop on Error Handling in Spoken Dialogue Systems*, pages 11–16.

Sebastian Möller, Klaus-Peter Engelbrecht, and Antti Oulasvirta. 2007. Analysis of communication failures for spoken dialogue systems. In *Proc. INTERSPEECH*, pages 134–137.

Sebastian Möller. 2005. Parameters for quantifying the interaction with spoken dialogue telephone services. In *Proc. SIGDIAL*, pages 166–177.

Kanako Onishi and Takeshi Yoshimura. 2014. Casual conversation technology achieving natural dialog with computers. *NTT DOCOMO Technical Jouranl*, 15(4):16–21.

Tim Paek. 2003. Toward a taxonomy of communication errors. In *Proc. ISCA Workshop on Error Handling in Spoken Dialogue Systems*, pages 53–58.

Emanuel A Schegloff and Harvey Sacks. 1973. Opening up closings. *Semiotica*, 8(4):289–327.

Richard S. Wallace. 2004. *The Anatomy of A.L.I.C.E.* A.L.I.C.E. Artificial Intelligence Foundation, Inc.

Nigel G Ward, Anais G Rivera, Karen Ward, and David G Novick. 2005. Root causes of lost time and user stress in a simple dialog system. In *Proc. INTERSPEECH*, pages 1565–1568.

Graham Wilcock and Kristiina Jokinen. 2013. Wikitalk human-robot interactions. In *Proc. ICMI*, pages 73–74.

Yang Xiang, Yaoyun Zhang, Xiaoqiang Zhou, Xiaolong Wang, and Yang Qin. 2014. Problematic situation analysis and automatic recognition for Chinese online conversational system. In *Proc. CLP*, pages 43–51.

PDTB Discourse Parsing as a Tagging Task: The Two Taggers Approach

Or Biran
Columbia University
orb@cs.columbia.edu

Kathleen McKeown
Columbia University
kathy@cs.columbia.edu

Abstract

Full discourse parsing in the PDTB framework is a task that has only recently been attempted. We present the Two Taggers approach, which reformulates the discourse parsing task as two simpler tagging tasks: identifying the relation within each sentence, and identifying the relation between each pair of adjacent sentences. We then describe a system that uses two CRFs to achieve an F1 score of 39.33, higher than the only previously existing system, at the full discourse parsing task. Our results show that sequential information is important for discourse relations, especially cross-sentence relations, and that a simple approach to argument span identification is enough to achieve state of the art results. We make our easy to use, easy to extend parser publicly available.

1 Introduction

Discourse structure is an important part of what makes a text coherent. Parts of the text are connected to one another by what is known as *discourse relations*, such as causality, contrast, and specification. Discourse parsing is the task of automatically determining the discourse structure of a text according to a particular theory of discourse. The ability to parse an entire document is crucial for understanding its linguistic structure and the intentions of its authors.

Discourse parsing is a difficult task. While some discourse relations have explicit lexical cues called discourse *connectives* or *markers*, such as "because" and "but", these are often ambiguous: they may apply to more than one relation category, or they may be used in a way that has nothing to do with discourse at all. In addition, many relations are not marked by connectives in text, and disambiguating these *implicit* relations is difficult even when it is known a relation exists. Adding to the difficulty is the fact that the arguments of the relation (there are usually two, although some frameworks allow more for certain relations) do not necessarily correspond to sentences or clauses, and may not even be contiguous under some theories.

Over the years, multiple theories of discourse have been proposed. Most recently, the Penn Discourse Treebank (PDTB) (Prasad et al., 2008) has been introduced, featuring hierarchical relation categories which generalize over other theories such as Rhetorical Structure Theory (RST) (Mann and Thompson, 1987) and SDRT (Asher and Lascarides, 2003), as well as a relatively large annotated corpus aligned with the WSJ section of the Penn Treebank (PTB) (Marcus et al., 1993). While the relation *categories* in PDTB are hierarchical, unlike RST and other frameworks, the discourse *structure* of a PDTB document is not fully hierarchical so that documents in general do not have a tree-like discourse structure. This is a crucial detail which allows our proposed method to work on PDTB documents.

While there has been much work recently on disambiguating discourse relations in the PDTB, most have not been full parsing systems. That is, they operate in an experimental environment where some information is given (for example, some systems disambiguate only implicit relations, where it is assumed that the arguments of the relation have been identified and that the relation is known to be implicit (Pitler and Nenkova, 2009; Park and Cardie, 2012)). Full systems, in contrast, operate on unannotated text documents producing the full discourse structure of the text, including both implicit and explicit relations, and so can be realistically used in NLP applications. Although not strictly parsing in the case of PTDB, such systems perform what has been called the *end-to-end*

Proceedings of the SIGDIAL 2015 Conference, pages 96–104,
Prague, Czech Republic, 2-4 September 2015.

discourse parsing task. Interest in full discourse parsing in the PDTB has been increasing, and it is this year's CoNLL shared task.

The only work, to our knowledge, which provides end-to-end PDTB discourse parsing is (Lin et al., 2014); they use a four-stage architecture where each stage carries out one subtask in identifying discourse relations (e.g., explicit or implicit). The parser is evaluated in terms of *exact match* and *partial match*. Unlike exact match results, which are considered correct only if both the relation type and the exact span of its arguments are identified correctly, partial match results are correct as long as the relation type is correctly identified and each proposed argument shares at least one noun and verb with the true argument. We believe that partial match results are best to focus on at this point in time, since current performance on exact match results is too low to be useful. Many current NLP applications (such as summarization and question answering) focus on sentences or clauses anyway and would find this formulation natural.

In this paper, we present a simple yet powerful sequential approach to PDTB discourse parsing, utilizing two CRFs and features that are designed to discriminate both explicit and implicit relations. We surpass state-of-the-art performance with a simpler structure, less hand-crafted rules for special scenarios and with an approach that makes adding new features extremely easy.

2 Related Work

Early data-driven work on discourse has focused on frameworks such as RST, using the small RST Discourse Treebank (Carlson et al., 2001). Marcu (1997) and later Soricut and Marcu (2003) developed methods for parsing documents into the RST discourse representation. There has also been more recent work on end-to-end RST-style parsing (LeThanh et al., 2004; duVerle and Prendinger, 2009).

Recently, there has been more focus on the PDTB (Prasad et al., 2008), the largest annotated discourse corpus currently in existence. Most work so far has focused on solving specific subtasks of the overall parsing task. Pitler and Nenkova (2009) focused on explicit relations and found that they are relatively easy to disambiguate using syntactic features. Wellner (2009) used both lexical and syntactic features to identify the arguments of a relation. Identifying and disambiguating implicit relations has been the hardest task to achieve good performance at, and is an active area of research. Pitler et al. (2009) were the first to identify implicit relations in the PDTB in a realistic setting, and later work has improved on their methods as well as introducing new ideas (Lin et al., 2009; Zhou et al., 2010; Park and Cardie, 2012; Biran and McKeown, 2013; Li and Nenkova, 2014a).

Most recently, Lin et al. (2014) have introduced and evaluated the first system which provides end-to-end discourse parsing over PDTB (the *Lin parser*). In their work, they have combined much of the earlier work on specific subtasks, utilizing a connective disambiguation component and an explicit relation disambiguation component inspired by Pitler and Nenkova (2009)'s method, as well as an implicit relation disambiguation component descending from their own previous work (Lin et al., 2009). Their approach is to decipher the document in a structured way, in four steps: first, identify explicit discourse connectives; second, identify the text spans of the arguments (in PDTB, there are always two arguments, arg1 and arg2) corresponding to the connective; third, identify the type of relation between the arguments (the third step completes the subtask of finding *explicit relations*); and fourth, for every adjacent pair of sentences, identify which type of *implicit relation* - relations where there is no connective - exists between them (or, if none does, identify the relation as EntRel - meaning the sentences share an entity but not a relation, or NoRel - meaning they share nothing at all). [1]

While the structured approach of the Lin parser has many advantages in that it attempts to solve the sub-tasks of discourse parsing in an organized, intuitive way, it has some disadvantages. One is that because of the pipeline structure, errors propagate from step to step. For example, if a (truly) implicit relation was incorrectly identified as an explicit relation because of a false connective, the features used by the implicit relation identifier that may correctly discriminate its type will not get a chance to be used.

Another disadvantage is the fact that in the

[1] There is also a fifth step, identifying spans that attribute a statement to a source, e.g. "B.P. explains that ...". Attribution span detection is a secondary task which is evaluated separately from the main discourse structure pipeline, and we are not concerned with it here.

structured approach, potential relations are considered individually, although adjacent relations can intuitively be indicators of the relation type.

Finally, building such a system requires significant design and engineering, and making changes that are not localized to a specific component can be difficult and time-consuming. At this point in time, when work on discourse parsing in PDTB is at its early stage, a more flexible and easily extensible approach would be beneficial to the community.

3 Method

PDTB discourse relations can be seen as a triple: relation type, argument 1 and argument 2. While in principle, the discourse structure theory of PDTB allows for the two arguments of a discourse relation to be located anywhere, in practice 92.9% of the relations annotated either a) are wholly contained in a single sentence, or b) span two adjacent sentences, with each argument contained in one of the sentences.[2]

Given this information, and the intuition that the structure of the document as a whole (in particular, the sequence of discourse relations) can be useful for determining the type of a relation, we reformulate the task of parsing the PDTB discourse relations as the combination of two tagging tasks. For each document, we separately tag the sequence of sentences for intra-sentence relations, and the sequence of adjacent sentence pairs for cross-sentence relations. While intra-sentence relations are always explicit, adjacent sentence relations may be explicit, implicit, or fall into the PDTB's AltLex or EntRel categories. Unlike previous work, we use a single method to disambiguate all adjacent sentence relations. We call this approach to discourse parsing the *Two Taggers* approach.

As a result, we have a sequence of sentences, each tagged with the relation that exists within it and each adjacent pair tagged with the relation that exists between them. In order to transform this structure to a full discourse parse, we must also identify the arguments and their spans. Since our goal is a simpler system and our focus is on partial match results, we avoid using a complicated syntactic rule system for each possible scenario in favor of a few simple rules. For adjacent sentence relations, we mark arg1 as being the entire first sentence and arg2 as being the entire second sentence (under partial match, this turns out to be correct in all but 0.002% of relations in the training set). For single-sentence relations, we distinguish among two cases: if the first word of the sentence is an intra-sentence initial connective[3] then we identify arg2 from the beginning of the sentence until the end of the first VP, and arg1 from there to the end of the sentence. Otherwise we identify arg1 from the beginning of the sentence to the middle connective (if there are more than one) and arg2 from there to the end of the sentence. While this approach ignores many complexities of the true argument structure of PDTB (for example, arguments may be nested, and a sentence may include text that is not inside an argument), it works well for partial match. In fact, as we show in our evaluation, it is also not too far behind the state of the art on a slightly more lenient version of exact match. We use Pitler and Nenkova (2009)'s high performing connective classifier (F1 above 95) to distinguish discourse connectives from their non-discourse counterparts.

The PDTB relation categories are hierarchical, and we are interested in finding the *type*, or second-level categories, of which there are 16 (plus EntRel and NoRel, for a total of 18). The first level (the *class*, of which there are 4) is too coarse to be useful for many applications, and the third level (the *subtype*, of which there are 25) is too fine-grained and difficult to disambiguate. Table 1 shows the hierarchy of 4 classes and 16 types. The Lin parser also deals with type-level categories, but almost all other previous work has focused on the significantly easier class-level categories.

Treating discourse parsing as a tagging problem has many advantages. Tagging tasks have been widely explored in NLP and there are many off-the-shelf tools and methods for tackling them. Many generic taggers that can be applied to this task with minimal effort are available to researchers, while generic parsers do no exist. Tagging is a simpler and often more tractable task than parsing, and it can be done using sequential classifiers, which are both fast and powerful.

There are also some limitations to the tagging

[2]It should be noted that by the definition given in the annotation manual, all implicit relations in PDTB exist between arguments contained within two adjacent sentences.

[3]*After, although, as, because, before, except, if, since, though, unless, until, when, whereas,* and *while* (as well as variations such as *if and when*).

approach. As mentioned earlier, some rare relations span more than two sentences, or sentences that are not adjacent. In addition, there are (also rare) situations where there are multiple relations in a single sentence, and with our approach we can at most tag one correctly. Because of these two limitations, we have an upper bound on F-measure performance of 89.4 in the PDTB corpus. Since current state-of-the-art performance is far below this level, we do not view this as an urgent problem. At any rate, additional specialized approaches can be added to correctly handle those rare cases.

In this paper, we use Conditional Random Fields (CRFs) for both taggers. CRFs were first introduced by Lafferty et al. (2001) and have been successfully used for many NLP tagging tasks such as named entity recognition (McCallum and Li, 2003) and shallow parsing (Sha and Pereira, 2003). We use simple linear-chain CRFs for both taggers. In the linear-chain CRF model, the posterior probabilities for an ordered sequence input $\mathbf{x} = \{x_1, \ldots, x_{|x|}\}$ of tag labels $\mathbf{y} = \{y_1, \ldots, y_{|x|}\}$ are defined as

$$P(\mathbf{y}|\mathbf{x}) \propto \prod_{i=1}^{|x|} exp\left(\sum_{k=1}^{K} \theta_k \Phi_k(y_{i-1}, \mathbf{x})\right)$$

where θ_k are weights corresponding to the features Φ_k. The feature values at index i of the sequence may be computed based on the previous tag in the sequence y_{i-1} and the entire sequence $\mathbf{x}$. The weights θ_k are estimated using gradient descent to maximize the likelihood of the input.

In our formulation, each $\mathbf{x}$ is a PDTB document, consisting of a sequence of sentences (for the intra-sentence relation tagger) or a sequence of sentence pairs (for the adjacent sentence relation tagger). $\mathbf{y}$ consists of all type-level discourse relation categories.

In our experiments, we used a maximum likelihood prior and limited the gradient descent to a maximum of 200 epochs instead of waiting for it to converge.

While CRFs have been used in the past for subtasks of RST discourse parsing (Feng and Hirst, 2014) and for finding the arguments of explicit relations in PDTB (Ghosh et al., 2011), no sequential approaches have ever been used in a way that models the sequential dependency between PDTB relations. Previous work (Pitler et al., 2009; Zhou et al., 2010) has utilized features that consider adjacent lexical information in relation type classification, but true sequential or joint classifications have not been attempted.

Class (Level 1)	Type (Level 2)
Comparison	Concession Contrast Pragmatic Concession Pragmatic Contrast
Contingency	Cause Condition Pragmatic Cause Pragmatic Condition
Expansion	Alternative Conjunction Exception Instantiation List Restatement
Temporal	Asynchronous Synchrony

Table 1: The PTDB relation category hierarchy, with level 1 classes and level 2 types. The level 3 subtypes are not shown

4 Features

4.1 Intra-sentence tagger

The intra-sentence tagger deals only with explicit relations, and as such focuses on features related to discourse connectives. We use Pitler and Nenkova (2009)'s connective classifier to identify discourse connectives within the sentence, and for each connective generate the following binary features:

- Connective
- Previous word + connective
- Connective + next word
- Connective's syntactic category
- Parent's category
- Left sibling's category
- Right sibling's category
- Path to root
- Compressed path to root

All of which are features used in explicit relation detection by Pitler and Nenkova (2009) or by Lin et al. (2014).

4.2 Adjacent sentence tagger

The adjacent sentence tagger utilizes a larger variety of features, designed to disambiguate relations across sentences that may be explicit, implicit, AltLex or EntRel.

We divide the features into four thematic types: lexical, connective-related, syntactic and structural features.

4.2.1 Lexical features

Lexical features are based on the surface lexical terms of the sentence pair.

In addition to **unigrams** and **bigrams**, we make use of **word pair similarity features**, the set of features described in Biran and McKeown (2013), which utilize sets of word pairs that were mined from unannotated corpora around each discourse connective. The word pair scores within the set are given by TF*IDF and treated as a vector. The feature value is the cosine similarity of the connective's vector to the vector of word pairs extracted from the pair of adjacent sentences, where each pair contains one word from each sentence. It models the similarity of the sentence pair to a sentence where the connective is used directly, and is intended to help in identifying implicit relations. We also add a variation on these features: the **word pair similarity average for connective pair**, where we get the similarities of the adjacent sentence pair to the word pair sets of a couple of connectives (we use every possible combination of two connectives) and use the average as the feature value. The idea is that if two connectives are related to the same relation type, a high average similarity to both may be a stronger indicator for that relation.

We also utilize a simplistic form of topic centrality. **Centrality in document** is the cosine similarity of the sentence pair to the document as a whole. The intuition is that certain relations (e.g., argumentative relations such as causality and concession) would tend to be more common around the main topic of the document.

Finally, we include features for words that are shared by both sentences called **expanded shared words** - expanded because we use WordNet (Fellbaum, 1998) to expand the usual list of words in each sentence with all synonyms and immediate hypernyms of each word's most frequent sense.

4.2.2 Connective features

For each sentence separately, we find all connectives (using Pitler and Nenkova (2009)'s connective classifier), and use the **connective** itself as a feature, as well as the **previous word and the connective**, which includes cases where the previous word is the implicit [START] (when the connective is the first word of the sentence). These features are mainly useful for disambiguating cross-sentence explicit relations.

4.2.3 Syntactic features

Syntactic features are derived from the parse tree of the sentence. We use the Stanford Parser (Klein and Manning, 2003) to derive the trees. Unlike much previous work, we do not use the gold parse trees of the PTB.

Lin et al. (2009) introduced the *production rule* features, which are some of the strongest for implicit relation disambiguation. Production rules are all parent-children relations in the constituent parse of a sentence, e.g. [VP $\rightarrow$ NP PP NP]. The binary feature formulation includes the existence of each rule in arg1, in arg2, and in both. Li and Nenkova (2014b) hypothesized that production rules are too sparse, and found that using their *production stick* features achieved higher performance. Unlike a production rule, which relates to all children of a parent, a production stick is a parent-single child relation. We experimented with both feature sets, and found that we achieve the best performance with a novel middle-ground formulation. **Production angles** are a family of features indicating the appearance of syntactic triples: a parent and two adjacent children. In cases where a parent has only one child, as in the lexical leaf nodes of the tree, we produce a stick-like feature (e.g. [NP $\rightarrow$ resources]. The triples are formed using the label of each node and the descendant directionality. We use features for angles in each sentence separately, as well as for angles that are shared by both.

4.2.4 Structural features

Structural features are related to the structure of the document. One intuitively important feature is the **paragraph split** feature which indicates whether the pair is split across two paragraphs or not. We also use a binary feature that specifies whether the sentence pair is in a **short document** (three sentences or less).

4.3 Sequential features

Sequential features are the *transitional* features that consider the previous tag in the sequence. The same sequential features are used in both taggers.

We use two basic pieces of information from the previous tag: the **previous tag type** is the type (second-level relation category) of the previous tag, while the **previous tag class** is the class (first-level relation category) of the previous tag.

5 Evaluation

Following Lin et al. (2014) and other previous work, we use sections 2-21 of the PDTB as the training set, section 22 as the development set, and section 23 as the test set. Since we use an automatic parser for our syntactic features, our results are equivalent to Lin et al.'s "Partial, Auto + EP" overall results for partial match, and to their "Exact, Auto + EP" results for exact match. We consider the results using gold standard parses to be less important for an end-to-end system, the main function of which is an out of the box document parsing tool. The evaluation metric in all experiments, following Lin et al., is the micro-averaged F1 score.

We show our final partial match results on the test set in Table 2, compared with the Lin Parser performance. We also compare our approach with the results achieved by using the exact same formulation and features (other than the sequential features, of course) in two Logistic Regression classifiers, to show that the sequential approach is in fact helpful. To illustrate the effect of our simplistic argument span identification rules, we also show results without span matching, where argument spans are presumed to always partially match if the sentence/sentences and relation type are correctly identified.

The results of each tagger individually are shown in Table 3. Note that the overall results are compared against all true relations in the document, including those that our method inherently cannot identify (hence the upper bound), while the individual tagger results are only in the context of the individual tagging task. This is why the recall of the end-to-end results is smaller than the recall of either of the individual taggers.

While we are focused on partial match results,

	Prec.	Recall	F1
Two classifiers	46.12	31.68	37.56
Lin Parser			38.18
Two Taggers	48.52	33.06	**39.33**
No span matching	48.72	33.32	39.57
Upper bound	100	80.82	89.40

Table 2: Partial match results on all relations in the PDTB. The Lin parser paper does not report precision and recall

	Prec.	Recall	F1
Intra-sent. tagger	66.36	49.82	**56.91**
Intra-sent. classifier	66.19	48.77	56.16
Adj. sent. tagger	40.31	36.53	**38.33**
Adj. sent. classifier	37.13	34.21	35.61

Table 3: Results for each of the two taggers separately

we also show exact match results in Table 4. In error analysis we noticed that many of our errors on exact match arise because we include in the span another discourse connective, or an initial word like "Eventually" or "Admittedly" in a non-discourse usage. We therefore include another set of results we call "almost-exact match" which allows a match if there is at most one word at the beginning or the end of the span that does not match. Using this less strict definition, we reach a performance that comes close to the Lin parser exact match results.

To emphasize how much harder it is to identify the level 2 relation types than it is to identify the level 1 classes, we also provide results on the class-level discourse parsing task in Table 5.

5.1 Discussion

As seen in Table 2, we achieve higher performance than the Lin parser on partial match results. This is despite the fact that we use fewer manually-crafted

	Prec.	Recall	F1
2T exact match	14.47	5.93	8.41
2T almost-exact match	29.61	14.75	19.69
Lin Parser			20.64

Table 4: Exact match results on all relations in the PDTB. The Lin parser paper does not report precision and recall

	Prec.	Recall	F1
Two Taggers	62.56	44.3	**51.87**
Upper bound	100	80.82	89.40

Table 5: Results for the same task when using the level 1 classes instead of the level 2 type relation categories

rules and do not rely on a complex argument span identification component. Moreover, the two taggers are clearly stronger than two classifiers with identical features, especially for the adjacent sentence task, which shows that there is value to the sequential approach.

It is clear from Table 3 that identifying relations in adjacent sentence pairs is a more difficult task than identifying them inside a single sentence. This makes sense because single sentence relations are always explicit in the PDTB while most adjacent sentence relations are implicit. It is well established that implicit relations are much harder to disambiguate than explicit ones. While we cannot provide an evaluation for implicit relations only - it is not clear how to fairly define false positives since we tag the entire document without differentiating between explicit and implicit relations - we can provide a lower bound for our performance by using only implicit relations to collect the true positives and false negatives, and all tagged relations to collect false positives. Our lower bound F-measure for implicit relations is 28.32.[4] In the Lin parser, the F-measure performance of the implicit relation classifier is 25.46, while the explicit relation classifier has an F-measure over 80. These numbers imply that our method is especially advantageous for implicit relations, while explicit relations may be harder to disambiguate without the specialized argument location/span identification step taken by the Lin parser. In addition, the relations that our approach inherently cannot handle are all explicit.

It is interesting to note that the difference between the taggers and the classifiers is much larger for the adjacent sentence pairs, meaning that the sequential features are very strong in the adjacent sentences tagger. This may indicate that intra-sentence relations are more "stand-alone" in nature while inter-sentence relations are more connected with the rest of the document. This result, and the fact that our performance on intra-sentence relations are not as high as previous results on explicit relations, suggest that one promising path for future work is the combination of a more structured intra-sentence explicit relation approach (one that would, among other advantages, allow finding multiple relations within the same sentence) with a sequential adjacent-sentence approach. Our performance suggests that this separation (intra-sentence and adjacent sentence) in methodology, which allows a sequential view, may in some cases be more useful than the traditional explicit vs. implicit separation.

Our approach beats state-of-the-art performance using partial match, which is the natural evaluation to use at this point in time given exact match performance (this view has been expressed by Lin et al. (2014) as well). While we do not achieve the same results on exact match, which is to be expected given our very simple approach to argument span identification, Table 4 shows that we come very close if a slightly less restrictive evaluation is used. This reaffirms the conclusion that exact match is a very difficult task: even with complex hand-crafted syntactic rules, correctly identified spans are relatively simple cases which can also be identified (if a single word error is allowed) by a much simpler method.

Table 5 illustrates how much harder the type-level parsing task is than the class-level parsing task. While it is possible that the class-level parsing can be useful for some downstream applications, we believe that the more granular type-level parsing is a better choice for properly understanding a document's discourse structure.

6 Conclusion and Future Work

We presented a reformulation of the PTDB discourse parsing task as two simple tagging tasks. This formulation makes it easier to approach the task and can be used as a convenient way to evaluate new ideas and features as they arise. Using chain-CRFs to implement this approach, we surpass state-of-the-art performance at the overall parsing task. While we used some of the strongest features that have shown up in the literature in this evaluation, there are many immediate candidate methods for improving the results, such as adding more specific features for the various grammatical classes of explicit connectives described in the PDTB.

[4]Precision is 28.02 and recall is 28.63.

Our results show that treating the task as sequential is useful. One interesting direction for continuing this research is to transform the two tagging tasks into two joint prediction tasks, and perhaps eventually into one joint prediction task.

While we build on previous work in defining our features, we also introduced some novel variations. We have defined the *production angles* family of features, which are related to the *production rules* of Lin et al. (2009) and the *production sticks* of Li and Nenkova (2014b). We also contribute to the *word pair features* line of research, which started with Marcu and Echihabi (2002) and has been part of most work on implicit relation disambiguation since, with our variations on the dense word pair similarity features introduced by Biran and McKeown (2013). Our *expanded shared words* features are also novel.

Our main aim in this paper was to show that experiments with discourse parsing can be done fairly easily using one of the many freely available sequential models. We hope that this method will make the task more accessible to researchers and help in moving towards a fully statistical and holistic approach to discourse parsing. The parser described in this paper is publicly available at `www.cs.columbia.edu/~orb`.

References

Nicholas Asher and Alex Lascarides. 2003. *Logics of Conversation*. Studies in Natural Language Processing Series. Cambridge University Press.

Or Biran and Kathleen McKeown. 2013. Aggregated word pair features for implicit discourse relation disambiguation. In *Proceedings of the 51st Annual Meeting of the Association for Computational Linguistics, ACL 2013, 4-9 August 2013, Sofia, Bulgaria, Volume 2: Short Papers*, pages 69–73. The Association for Computer Linguistics.

Lynn Carlson, Daniel Marcu, and Mary Ellen Okurowski. 2001. Building a discourse-tagged corpus in the framework of rhetorical structure theory. In *Proceedings of the Second SIGdial Workshop on Discourse and Dialogue - Volume 16*, SIGDIAL '01, pages 1–10, Stroudsburg, PA, USA. Association for Computational Linguistics.

David A. duVerle and Helmut Prendinger. 2009. A novel discourse parser based on support vector machine classification. In *Proceedings of the Joint Conference of the 47th Annual Meeting of the ACL and the 4th International Joint Conference on Natural Language Processing of the AFNLP: Volume 2 - Volume 2*, ACL '09, pages 665–673, Stroudsburg, PA, USA. Association for Computational Linguistics.

Christiane Fellbaum, editor. 1998. *WordNet An Electronic Lexical Database*. The MIT Press.

Vanessa Wei Feng and Graeme Hirst. 2014. A Linear-Time Bottom-Up Discourse Parser with Constraints and Post-Editing. In *Proceedings of the 52nd Annual Meeting of the Association for Computational Linguistics*, pages 511–521, Baltimore, Maryland, June. Association for Computational Linguistics.

Sucheta Ghosh, Richard Johansson, Giuseppe Riccardi, and Sara Tonelli. 2011. Shallow discourse parsing with conditional random fields. In *Proceedings of 5th International Joint Conference on Natural Language Processing*, pages 1071–1079.

Dan Klein and Christopher D. Manning. 2003. Accurate unlexicalized parsing. In *Proceedings of the 41st Annual Meeting on Association for Computational Linguistics - Volume 1*, ACL '03, pages 423–430, Stroudsburg, PA, USA. Association for Computational Linguistics.

John D. Lafferty, Andrew McCallum, and Fernando C. N. Pereira. 2001. Conditional random fields: Probabilistic models for segmenting and labeling sequence data. In *Proceedings of the Eighteenth International Conference on Machine Learning*, ICML '01, pages 282–289, San Francisco, CA, USA. Morgan Kaufmann Publishers Inc.

Huong LeThanh, Geetha Abeysinghe, and Christian Huyck. 2004. Generating discourse structures for written texts. In *Proceedings of the 20th International Conference on Computational Linguistics*, COLING '04, Stroudsburg, PA, USA. Association for Computational Linguistics.

Jessy Junyi Li and Ani Nenkova. 2014a. Addressing class imbalance for improved recognition of implicit discourse relations. In *Proceedings of the 15th Annual Meeting of the Special Interest Group on Discourse and Dialogue (SIGDIAL)*, pages 142–150. Association for Computational Linguistics.

Jessy Junyi Li and Ani Nenkova. 2014b. Reducing sparsity improves the recognition of implicit discourse relations. In *Proceedings of the 15th Annual Meeting of the Special Interest Group on Discourse and Dialogue (SIGDIAL)*, pages 199–207. Association for Computational Linguistics.

Ziheng Lin, Min-Yen Kan, and Hwee Tou Ng. 2009. Recognizing implicit discourse relations in the penn discourse treebank. In *Proceedings of the 2009 Conference on Empirical Methods in Natural Language Processing*, pages 343–351.

Ziheng Lin, Hwee Tou Ng, and Min-Yen Kan. 2014. A pdtb-styled end-to-end discourse parser. *Natural Language Engineering*, 20(2):151–184.

William C. Mann and Sandra A. Thompson. 1987. Rhetorical Structure Theory: A theory of text organization. Technical Report ISI/RS-87-190, ISI.

Daniel Marcu and Abdessamad Echihabi. 2002. An unsupervised approach to recognizing discourse relations. In *ACL*, pages 368–375. ACL.

Daniel Marcu. 1997. The rhetorical parsing, summarization, and generation of natural language texts. Technical report.

Mitchell P. Marcus, Mary Ann Marcinkiewicz, and Beatrice Santorini. 1993. Building a large annotated corpus of english: The penn treebank. *Comput. Linguist.*, 19(2):313–330, June.

Andrew McCallum and Wei Li. 2003. Early results for named entity recognition with conditional random fields, feature induction and web-enhanced lexicons. In *Proceedings of the Seventh Conference on Natural Language Learning at HLT-NAACL 2003 - Volume 4*, CONLL '03, pages 188–191, Stroudsburg, PA, USA. Association for Computational Linguistics.

Joonsuk Park and Claire Cardie. 2012. Improving implicit discourse relation recognition through feature set optimization. In *Proceedings of the 13th Annual Meeting of the Special Interest Group on Discourse and Dialogue*, pages 108–112.

Emily Pitler and Ani Nenkova. 2009. Using syntax to disambiguate explicit discourse connectives in text. In *ACL/IJCNLP (Short Papers)*, pages 13–16. The Association for Computer Linguistics.

Emily Pitler, Annie Louis, and Ani Nenkova. 2009. Automatic sense prediction for implicit discourse relations in text. In *ACL/IJCNLP*, pages 683–691. The Association for Computer Linguistics.

Rashmi Prasad, Nikhil Dinesh, Alan Lee, Eleni Miltsakaki, Livio Robaldo, Aravind Joshi, and Bonnie Webber. 2008. The penn discourse treebank 2.0. In *In Proceedings of LREC*.

Fei Sha and Fernando Pereira. 2003. Shallow parsing with conditional random fields. In *Proceedings of the 2003 Conference of the North American Chapter of the Association for Computational Linguistics on Human Language Technology - Volume 1*, NAACL '03, pages 134–141, Stroudsburg, PA, USA. Association for Computational Linguistics.

Radu Soricut and Daniel Marcu. 2003. Sentence level discourse parsing using syntactic and lexical information. In *Proceedings of the 2003 Conference of the North American Chapter of the Association for Computational Linguistics on Human Language Technology - Volume 1*, NAACL '03, pages 149–156, Stroudsburg, PA, USA. Association for Computational Linguistics.

Ben Wellner. 2009. *Sequence Models and Ranking Methods for Discourse Parsing*. Ph.D. thesis, Waltham, MA, USA. AAI3339383.

Zhi-Min Zhou, Yu Xu, Zheng-Yu Niu, Man Lan, Jian Su, and Chew Lim Tan. 2010. Predicting discourse connectives for implicit discourse relation recognition. In *Proceedings of the 23rd International Conference on Computational Linguistics*.

Which Synthetic Voice Should I Choose for an Evocative Task?

Eli Pincus, Kallirroi Georgila & David Traum
USC Institute for Creative Technologies
12015 Waterfront Dr
Playa Vista, CA 90094, USA
pincus,kgeorgila,traum@ict.usc.edu

Abstract

We explore different evaluation methods for 4 different synthetic voices and 1 human voice. We investigate whether intelligibility, naturalness, or likability of a voice is correlated to the voice's *evocative function potential*, a measure of the voice's ability to evoke an intended reaction from the listener. We also investigate the extent to which naturalness and likability ratings vary depending on whether or not exposure to a voice is extended and continuous vs. short-term and sporadic (interleaved with other voices). Finally, we show that an automatic test can replace the standard intelligibility tests for text-to-speech (TTS) systems, which eliminates the need to hire humans to perform transcription tasks saving both time and money.

1 Introduction

Currently there are a wealth of choices for which output voice to use for a spoken dialogue system. If the set of prompts is fixed and small, one can use a human voice actor. If a wider variety and/or dynamic utterances are needed, then text-to-speech synthesis (TTS) is a better solution. There are high quality commercial solutions as well as toolkits for building voices. While many of these are getting better, none are completely natural, especially when it comes to emotional and conversational speech. It can be difficult to decide which voice to choose for a specific system, given multiple criteria, and also since TTS evaluation is a labor-intensive process, without good automated understudies.

In this paper, we perform a comparative evaluation of several natural and synthetic voices using several different criteria, including subjective ratings and objective task measures. In particular, we compare the relationship of a voice's *evocative function potential*, a measure of the voice's ability to evoke an intended reaction from the listener, to the voice's intelligibility and to the listener's perception of the voice's naturalness and likability.

Our first hypothesis is that voice quality is a multi-dimensional construct, and that the best voice for some purposes may not be the best for all purposes. There may be different aspects that govern subjective perceptions of a voice and objective task performance, and different aspects may facilitate different tasks. For example, a neutral highly intelligible voice may be perfect for a system that provides information but very unpleasant for a story-telling system that is trying to express strong emotion.

Our second hypothesis is that naturalness and likability perceptions of a voice may depend on whether or not the user's exposure to a voice is extended and continuous vs. short-term and sporadic (interleaved with other voices). The current practice in speech synthesis evaluation is to ask human raters to rate isolated audio clips, usually in terms of naturalness and intelligibility (Fraser and King, 2007; Karaiskos et al., 2008), without extended exposure to a voice. This approach can certainly inform us about the general quality of a synthetic voice; but it cannot necessarily provide any insight about the appropriateness of this voice for a task that requires that the listener be exposed to that voice for a considerable amount of time. Furthermore, as the environments where these dialogue systems are deployed become increasingly immersive involving multiple agents, e.g., virtual and augmented reality environments, it becomes critical to determine how subjective perceptions of a voice change if voice exposure is sporadic and interleaved with other voices[1].

[1] From now on, we will assume that sporadic voice exposure implies that the user is exposed to multiple voices interleaved.

Proceedings of the SIGDIAL 2015 Conference, pages 105–113,
Prague, Czech Republic, 2-4 September 2015.

Noting that it is not always feasible to evaluate a voice in the context of a full dialogue task we seek to determine whether results from standard voice evaluation experiments can act as a valid proxy for results from experiments that feature voice evaluation in a manner that more closely approximates the full dialogue task. Taking this idea one step further, we explore whether or not standard TTS evaluation tests such as transcription tasks (designed to assess the intelligibility of a voice) can be fully automated by using automatic speech recognition (ASR) output rather than manual transcriptions.

To test our hypotheses we perform 5 experiments using 4 synthetic voices (covering a range of speech synthesis techniques) and 1 human voice. Each experiment is defined by a unique set of stimuli, subjects, and measures. In the first two experiments, we perform standard speech synthesis evaluation, i.e., human raters rate isolated audio clips with regard to naturalness in one experiment and likability in the other experiment (each rater has short-term sporadic exposure to the voices). Experiments 3 and 4 are intelligibility experiments; in one, participants transcribe the utterances that they hear; in the other, we send audio files through an ASR engine. The fifth experiment is conducted in the context of a guessing game with extended continuous naturalness and likability ratings collected from participants. The evocative intention of an utterance is the behavior of the addressee that a speaker intends to evoke (Allwood, 1976; Allwood, 1995). In the case of the guessing game, a clue is given to evoke the expression of a target word. We ascertain a voice's *evocative function potential* (EVP) by calculating the ratio of targets that a clue evokes from listeners. Each participant listens to many consecutive clues uttered with the same voice (extended continuous exposure). Our participants are recruited using the Amazon Mechanical Turk (AMT) service[2] in the same fashion as in (Wolters et al., 2010; Georgila et al., 2012). To the best of our knowledge, our work is the first to systematically attempt to validate or disprove the hypotheses mentioned above, and compare the results of human transcriptions to ASR results in order to determine whether or not the latter can be used as an automatic intelligibility test for TTS system evaluations. This is also a first important step towards speech synthesis evaluation in a full dialogue context. Finally, this is the first time that a systematic evaluation is conducted on a voice's EVP.

The rest of the paper is organized as follows. First, we discuss previous work in Section 2 on TTS system evaluations. In Section 3 we present the voices that we use as well as meta-data about the clues that the voices spoke. In Section 4 we delineate the experiment methodology, and in Section 5 we report the results of our experiments and some inferences we can draw from them. Finally, Section 6 concludes.

2 Previous Work

Our ultimate goal is to evaluate synthetic voices in the context of a full interaction with a dialogue system, and analysis of the effects of extended/continuous vs. short-term/sporadic exposure of a listener to a voice is a first important step towards this goal. There has been some work on comparing the effect of synthetic vs. human speech on the interaction with a dialogue system, e.g., a virtual patient dialogue system (Dickerson et al., 2006) and an intelligent tutoring dialogue system (Forbes-Riley et al., 2006), but none of these studies has compared a large variety of voices or conditions, e.g., length and content of utterances, etc.

Recently, Georgila et al. (2012) performed a systematic evaluation of human and synthetic voices with regard to naturalness, conversational aspect, and likability. They also varied the type (in- vs. out-of-domain), length, and content of utterances, and took into account the age and native language of raters as well as their familiarity with speech synthesis. However, this study was based on the standard speech synthesis evaluation.

3 Data

3.1 Materials

Our experiments use 4 different synthetic voices and 1 human voice, all male, with standard American accents.

- ***Human voice (HUM)***: The audio clips were recorded by the first author using a high-quality microphone with noise cancellation features. The resulting audio clips were very clear, almost studio-quality.
- ***Commercial voice 1 (US1)***: This is a high-quality commercial stylized voice based on

[2] https://www.mturk.com

Table 1: Example Clues

Clue	Type	Source	Target Word
"an explosive device fused to explode under specific conditions"	Definition	WordNet	Bomb
"a blank to talk too much"	Example Usage	Dictionary.com	Tendency
"taxi"	Word Relation	Human	Cab
"a mixture containing two or more blank elements or blank and nonblank elements usually fused together or dissolving into each other when molten"	Definition	WordNet	Metal
"elephants may look alike to you and me, but the shapes of their blank flaps and their tusks set them apart"	Example Usage	Dictionary.com	Ear
"um not video but"	Word Relation	Human	Audio

Unit-Selection (Hunt and Black, 1996; Black and Taylor, 1997).

- ***Commercial voice 2 (US2)***: This is a high-quality commercial customized Unit-Selection voice developed specifically for our institute.

- ***Hidden Markov model -based voice (HMM)***: This voice is based on **HMM** synthesis (Zen et al., 2009), in particular, speaker-adaptive HMM-based speech synthesis (Yamagishi et al., 2009). First an average voice was built using the CMU ARCTIC speech databases[3]. Then this average voice was adapted to the voice characteristics of a speaker using approx. 15 minutes of speech from that speaker (studio-quality recordings). We built this voice using the HTS toolkit with its standard vocoder (Zen et al., 2007).

- ***Lower quality voice (SAM)***: We used Microsoft **Sam**.

We measure a voice's EVP for the guessing task by providing clues for listeners to guess a specific target word. We used 54 clues from a corpus of automatically and human generated clues. The material for the automatically generated clues came from two sources: WordNet (Miller, 1995) and the Dictionary.com pages associated with the target word. We replaced any occurrence of the target word or inflected forms of the target word in the clues used with the word *"blank"*. The human clues were culled from the rapid dialogue game corpus which contains audio and video recordings of human pairs playing a word guessing game (Paetzel et al., 2014). We only used clues that were able to elicit at least one correct guess in a previous study designed to measure clue effectiveness (Pincus et al., 2014). Some example clues used in this experiment, their source, their type, and the target word they intend to evoke can be found in Table 1. Each of the 54 clues was synthesized in each of the voices.

We categorized the 54 clues into 3 main clue types: a *definition* type which provided a definition of the target word, an *example usage* type which is generally a commonly used sentence that contains the word, and a *word relation* type which refers to clue types such as synonyms, hyponyms, hypernyms, antonyms, etc. of the target word. Human clues were annotated according to this taxonomy (Pincus and Traum, 2014). For our analysis we looked at cumulative statistics for the full set of clues as well as statistics for two different partitions of the clue corpus; by type and by length ($> 5\ words$ and $\leq 5\ words$). The relative frequency for each type of clue can be found in Table 2; 24% or 13/54 of the clues are composed of 5 or fewer words while 76% (41/54) of the clues are composed of more than 5 words. The average clue length is 10.75 words and the standard deviation of clue lengths is 7.86 words.

3.2 Participants

We crowdsourced data collection for this experiment via Amazon Mechanical Turk. All Turkers who completed the task were required to have a 90% approval rating or higher and have at least 50

[3] `http://www.festvox.org/cmu_arctic/`

approved HITs. Note that no Turker participated in more than one of any of the experiments described in Section 4.

Table 2: Clue Type Frequency

Clue Type	Relative Frequency (absolute # / 54)
Definition	63% (34)
Example Usage	24% (13)
Word Relation	13% (7)

4 Method

A summary of the 5 experiments conducted in this study, introduced in section 1, and the measures obtained from each experiment can be found in Table 3. The standard naturalness, likability and intelligibility experiments featured short-term sporadic exposure to the 5 voices and were designed using the online survey software Qualtrics[4]. In these experiments all participating Turkers listened to 20 audio recordings (human or synthetic speech) of clues randomly selected from the 54 clues described previously. Each set of 20 audio recordings was balanced so that the participant would listen to 4 clips per voice. The order of clues and voices was randomized, i.e., there was constant switching from one voice to another (short-term sporadic exposure to a voice). Generally, each participant never heard a clue more than once. Turkers were instructed to listen to an audio file only once in these experiments in order to more accurately model a normal spoken language situation such as transcribing a lecture or simultaneous interpretation.

54 different Turkers participated in the standard naturalness experiment. After listening to an audio file a Turker answered the following question: "For the utterance you just heard, how did the voice sound?" (1=very unnatural, 2=somewhat unnatural, 3=neither natural nor unnatural, 4=somewhat natural, 5=very natural). We will call this a Turker's **short-term/sporadic (S/S) naturalness measure**.

54 different Turkers participated in the likability experiment. After listening to an audio file a Turker answered the following question: "Would you like to have a conversation with this speaker?" (1=definitely not, 2=maybe not, 3=cannot decide, 4=maybe yes, 5=definitely yes). We will call this a Turker's **short-term/sporadic (S/S) likability measure**.

[4]http://www.qualtrics.com/

Table 3: Experiments & Obtained Measures

Experiment	Obtained Measures
1. Standard Naturalness	1. Short-Term/Sporadic (S/S) Naturalness
2. Standard Likability	1. Short-Term/Sporadic (S/S) Likability
3. Standard Intelligibility	1. Human Wrd. Err. Rate 2. Human Miss. Word %
4. ASR Intelligibility	1. ASR Wrd. Err. Rate 2. ASR Miss. Word %
5. Guessability	1. Extended/Continuous (E/C) Naturalness 2. Extended/Continuous (E/C) Likability 3. Guessability

The standard intelligibility experiment was designed as a transcription task. 55 Turkers listened to audio recordings of the clues described previously and then wrote into a text box what they heard. 6 of the 55 Turkers' transcription results were discarded; 2 Turkers did not appear to make a best effort and 4 misread the instructions and provided guesses for the clues they heard rather than transcribing the audio. We compared the transcriptions with the actual text of the clue that was synthesized or recorded (reference). In order to compare the results of this intelligibility experiment with the results from an automatic test of intelligibility (ASR intelligibility experiment) we send the 54 audio recordings of each clue for each voice through the Google Chrome ASR[5]. For both standard and ASR intelligibility, we calculated **word error rate (WER)** (Equation 1), and the percentage of words contained in the reference but not in the target transcription (**missing word %**).

$$WER = \frac{Subs. + Delets. + Inserts.}{\# Of\ Words\ In\ Reference} \quad (1)$$

A web application was developed for the guessability experiment, and Turkers were redirected to this application from the AMT site to participate in the experiment. Each Turker in the guessing experiment had extended continuous exposure to 3 of the 5 voices, listening to 18 clues in each voice, for a total of 54 clues. We collected a full set of 54

[5]https://www.google.com/intl/en/chrome/demos/speech.html

recordings from 59 different Turkers and almost a full set (53/54) recordings from a 60th Turker (who failed to make a guess for the last clue). Note that many more Turkers attempted the experiment but failed to finish for unknown reasons. We do not consider this partially collected data except for the 60th Turker's data just mentioned. Turkers heard only one instance of each clue. The order of voices was balanced (there are 60 permutations of the voices possible with our experimental set up; so each Turker heard 3 voices in a unique order), but clues were presented in a fixed order. Each Turker, when listening to a clue, was instructed to make as many guesses as he could before a pop-up alert appeared (six seconds later), indicating that recording had ended and revealing the target word. After each clue the Turker was asked to rate the naturalness of the voice he had just heard on a Likert scale as in the previously described experiments except the word "clue" replaced the word "utterance" in the question. The average of these 18 naturalness scores for each Turker will be called a Turker's **extended/continuous (E/C) naturalness score**. After each set of 18 clues with the same voice, the Turker was asked whether or not he would like to have a conversation with the speaker the Turker had just been exposed to for the last 18 clues (same question as in the previously described likability experiment). We will call this a Turker's **extended/continuous (E/C) likability score**.

We annotated the 60 sets of audio recordings (3,239 audio files) of Turkers' guesses for whether or not the recording contained a correct guess. An audio recording was annotated as correct if it contained a guess composed of the target word or an inflected form of the target word for the previously spoken clue. We define a **guessability score** for a voice as the percentage of correctly guessed clues out of the total number of clues played to participants with that voice.

All the likability and naturalness measures we categorize as subjective measures while the intelligibility and guessability measures we categorize as objective measures.

5 Results

This section contains the results of our experiments including the S/S and E/C naturalness ratings in Table 4, and the S/S and E/C likability ratings in Table 5, and all the objective measures in Table 6. The general ranking of the voices across the various subjective and objective dimensions measured were (starting with the highest ranking voice and proceeding in decreasing order): human (HUM), commercial (US1), commercial (US2), hidden Markov model (HMM), lower quality voice (SAM). We will refer to this as the standard order. The existence of a standard order indicates that we did not find good evidence to support hypothesis 1. At first glance any measure is a good proxy for another measure; however there are some exceptions. If there is a statistically significant exception we will explicitly mention it. A marking of "***" by a measure in one of the three tables indicates that the difference between that measure with the measure for the next ranked voice is highly significant ($p<.001$)[6]. A marking of "**" by a measure in one of the three tables indicates that the difference between that measure with the measure for the next ranked voice is significant ($p<.01$). Finally, a marking of "#" by a measure in one of the three tables indicates that the difference between that measure and the voice ranked 2 below is significant ($p<.01$).

5.1 Subjective & Objective Measures

Table 4: S/S & E/C Naturalness Means

Voice	S/S Naturalness Avg.	E/C Naturalness Avg.
HUM	4.15***	4.59***
US1	3.93***	3.48***
US2	2.92***	2.04***
HMM	2.04***	1.83***
SAM	1.81	1.57

Table 5: S/S & E/C Likability Means

Voice	S/S Likability Avg.	E/C Likability Avg.
HUM	3.78#	4.17**
US1	3.63***	3.36***
US2	2.66***	1.69
HMM	1.81	1.53
SAM	1.72	1.35

The voices follow the standard order for both S/S and E/C mean naturalness, and all pair-wise

[6]Statistical tests conducted were paired or unpaired t-tests (based on the relationship of the data sets tested) with the use (if needed) of the Holm - Bonferroni method to counteract the issue of multiple comparisons.

Table 6: Objective Measure Means

Voice	Guessability	Human Word Err. Rate	Human Missing Word %	ASR Word Err. Rate	ASR Missing Word %
HUM	57.10%#	18.35% #	15.64%#	5.41%**	5.24%**
US1	59.72%**	23.31%***	20.53%***	6.11%#	4.54%#
US2	50.39%#	29.65%#	25.18%#	21.82%**	18.5%**
HMM	46.45%	29.32%***	25.44%***	13.26%#	10.3%#
SAM	42.44%	35.43%	32.36%	28.27%	24.78%

comparisons for both S/S and E/C show differences in means that were highly statistically significant. This indicates that synthetic voices, at least the ones tested, have still not reached human-level naturalness. There were no significant violations to this pattern in various subsets of clues tested. The S/S and E/C likability scores can be found in Table 5 for all clues. Again, both measures follow the standard order. It is interesting that the US1 and HUM voices do not have a significant difference in their S/S likability but do for their E/C likability ($p = 0.008$). In terms of naturalness and likability we believe the HMM scored low due to the fact that it was not trained on a large amount of data (only 15 minutes of speech was used for adaptation) and also the fact that it did not use a more advanced vocoder such as STRAIGHT (Speech Transformation and Representation using Adaptive Interpolation of weiGHTed spectrum) (Kawahara, 1997). Overall, this data suggests that synthetic voices are catching up faster in the likability dimension to HUM voices than in the naturalness dimension, although an experiment with more human voices is needed for more evidence of this trend.

For standard intelligibility results the standard order is followed for both WER and missing word %. The HUM voice performs best although its performance over US1 is not significant, demonstrating that synthetic voices are able to match human voices in intelligibility measures. We see from Table 6 that the overall intelligibility of US2 and HMM is comparable. However, the HMM voice outperformed US2 significantly ($WER : p = 0.002$, $missing\ word\ \% : p = 0.017$) on example usage clues. Noting that the HMM voice extended the pronunciation of the word "blank" (which appeared in almost all of the example usage clues) this could provide some support for a hypothesis that unnatural sounding words remained in the listeners' short-term memory more readily. However, further experiments are needed to verify whether or not this is just an aberration. For the ASR intelligibility results although the standard order was violated, HMM outperformed US2 for both WER and missing word % and US1 outperformed HUM for missing word %, these deviations were not significant. Overall, the intelligibility results indicate that Google Chrome ASR is much better than real-time Turkers at the transcription task (where Turkers have only a single opportunity to hear the audio).

In the guessability dimension the standard order is violated because US1 outperformed HUM there but we draw no conclusions from this as it is not a statistically significant difference. The performance of US1 for guessability is significantly ($p = 0.001$) better than US2 but has comparable performance to the HUM voice indicating that synthetic voices have reached an EVP approaching human level for the clue guessing task. One hypothesis on why US2 has significantly worse guessability than US1 and HUM is that although US2 is a high-quality voice, more effort has been put in making this voice expressive rather than making sure that all phonetic units are fully covered in all possible contexts. In terms of the guessability for the various sub-groups of clues it appears all voices are performing much better for long clues except for HUM which has similar performance for both long and short clues. SAM is particularly bad for short clues, with guessability 33.3% (compared to 45.3% for long clues).

These results indicate that if one is concerned with the subjective perception of the system carrying out the task or its intelligibility rather than only the task performance measure then HUM is the undeniable best voice. However, if one is only concerned with maximizing the EVP of a dialogue system then US1 might be the preferred choice; as it eliminates the need for human recordings.

5.2 Time/Continuity-Exposure

In order to determine if time/continuity of voice exposure is an important variable in determining people's subjective evaluations of a voice (note that hypothesis 2 was that this is an important variable) we consider the difference between 3 different pairs of statistics for each voice for all clues. The first pair of statistics we compare are the average S/S likability scores and the average E/C likability scores. These statistics are found in Table 5. We see that the likability scores decreased for all the synthetic voices (decrease in US2's likability scores highly statistically significant: $p = 3.6e^{-05}$) but increased for the human voice ($p = 0.04$) . The second pair of statistics we compare are the S/S naturalness scores and the E/C naturalness scores. These statistics are given in table 4. We see the same pattern with S/S and E/C naturalness scores that we saw with S/S and E/C likability scores for the 5 voices; increasing naturalness scores for the HUM voice and decreasing naturalness scores for the synthetic voices. Moreover, every difference is highly significant here ($HUM : p = 3.08e^{-16}$, $US1 : p = 1.01e^{-12}$, $US2 : p = 6.72e^{-33}$, $HMM : p = 0.06e^{-2}$, $SAM : p = 6.53e^{-05}$).

Table 7: First vs. Last Naturalness Scores

Voice	First Three Naturalness Avg.	Last Three Naturalness Avg.
HUM	4.25	4.81*
US1	3.42	3.52
US2	2.58	1.833*
HMM	1.69	1.78
SAM	1.67	1.31

An attempt to examine whether or not time exposure alone has an effect on subjective evaluation of a voice leads us to examine a third pair of statistics: comparing the average of the first three naturalness scores from a Turker in the guessability experiment to the average of the last three naturalness scores (of 18 total) of the same voice (first voice heard only). This comparison provides evidence that the pattern we are discussing is not simply due to the difference in the types of tasks participants were asked to perform. These scores can be found in Table 7. A "*" in the second column indicates that the corresponding increase or decrease is statistically significant ($HUM : p = 0.017, US2 : p = 0.013$). Although US1's and HMM's naturalness averages increase, these increases are not significant. One issue to point out here is that the order of clues was fixed so the synthetic voices might have had worse performance on the last clues vs. the first clues.

We now note that this study has results from two experiments where synthetic voices have a statistically significant decrease and where a human voice has a statistically significant increase in subjective evaluation ratings when comparing the ratings from people who had S/S vs. E/C exposure to the voices. These findings provide support for hypothesis 2 indicating that extended/continuous exposure to a synthetic voice negatively affects subjective perception of that voice. Furthermore, this study has shown results from one experiment which suggests that people's subjective perceptions of synthetic voices degrade over time while their subjective perceptions of human voices improve over time. Additional experiments with more human voices and a balanced order of clues could be conducted to provide further support for this phenomenon.

5.3 Correlation Analysis

Table 8 presents the results of a correlation analysis between guessability and the other dimensions previously discussed. The correlation results for guessability and the two naturalness scores do not lead us to any clear conclusions. The only statistically significant correlation is between E/C naturalness, which had ratings collected after a participant had received feedback on the correctness of their guess (which could affect the rating), and guessability.

Table 8: Guessability Correlations

Categories	r_s[7]	P-Value
Guessability & S/S Natural.	0.122	0.051
Guessability & E/C Natural.	0.31	$0.002e^{-4}$
Guessablity & S/S Likability	0.108	0.085
Guessability & Stand. Word Error Rate	-0.108	0.081
Guessability & % Stand. Missing Word %	-0.129	0.035

[7]Spearman's Rank-Order Correlation Coefficient

Table 9: Intelligibility Correlations

Voice	Word Error Rate Standard ASR Corr. $(\rho)^8$(p-val)	Missing Word % Standard ASR Corr. $(\rho)^8$ (p-val)
HUM	0.06 (0.37)	0.07 (0.29)
US1	0.27 ($1.66e^{-36}$)	0.26 ($3.97e^{-05}$)
US2	0.55 ($1.37e^{-05}$)	0.58 ($5.21e^{-23}$)
HMM	0.78 ($7.17e^{-52}$)	0.74 ($2.52e^{-43}$)
SAM	0.07 (0.29)	0.17 (0.007)

We find weak negative correlations between guessability and both of the measures from the standard intelligibility experiments. Note that only the correlation between missing word % and guessability is statistically significant. This indicates that while intelligibility measures of a voice could be useful information when evaluating a voice's EVP the correlation is not strong enough to suggest that they are valid proxy measures for a voice's EVP. Furthermore, performing voice evaluation in an experiment that features the full context of the system being evaluated might still be required for precise voice evaluation results of a dialogue system.

Table 9 shows the correlations for each voice between the ASR intelligibility experiment results and the standard intelligibility experiment results. For almost all of the synthetic voices there is a strong or somewhat strong positive correlation between the ASR intelligibility experiment results and the standard intelligibility results that has high statistical significance. The one exception to this is SAM's ASR WER which shows no significant relationship with the human transcriptions WER. It is also interesting that for the HUM voice the ASR intelligibility results show basically no correlation to the standard intelligibility results. Overall though, it appears that for synthetic voices intelligibility results can be obtained automatically by sending recordings of the voice to a well-trained ASR engine such as Google Chrome ASR; and these should be able to predict the results from a standard (human participant) intelligibility test.

6 Conclusion

We presented the results of an evaluation for 4 synthetic voices and 1 human voice that featured collection of data for subjective perception measures as well as for objective task measures of the voices. We demonstrated that synthetic voices do not always have significantly lower EVP than a human voice (US1 is similar); although they do significantly differ in subjective ratings assigned to them by listeners. For this reason, we would choose a human voice for a dialogue system designed to evoke an intended reaction from a listener only if subjective perceptions were important enough to the system designer to warrant the extra cost and time of making human audio recordings.

We showed via comparison of measures of the voice's EVP with measures of subjective perceptions and intelligibility that while you cannot always use standard measures of synthetic voice evaluation as a proxy for a new task, in determining the voice's effectiveness at that new task, the results from standard tests can provide useful information. Some of our data led us to suggest that synthetic voices' likability and naturalness perceptions degrade based on time/continuity of exposure while human voices' likability and naturalness perceptions improve with increasing time/continuity. Finally, we provided evidence that the automatic method of sending synthetic voice audio recordings through an ASR engine can serve as an adequate substitute for standard (human participant) intelligibility experimental results, and that the automatic method even outperforms Turkers' transcription ability (when Turkers hear the audio only once).

Future work includes additional experiments that will control for the order of the clues as well as cover a wider variety of tasks. Finally, we would like to evaluate EVP in the context of a full dialogue, where users can clarify and perform moves other than guesses, and multiple clues might contribute to a guess.

7 Acknowledgements

The effort described here is supported by the U.S. Army. Any opinion, content or information presented does not necessarily reflect the position or the policy of the United States Government, and no official endorsement should be inferred.

References

Jens Allwood. 1976. *Linguistic Communication as Action and Cooperation*. Ph.D. thesis, Göteborg University, Department of Linguistics.

[8] Pearson Product-Moment Correlation Coefficient

Jens Allwood. 1995. An activity based approach to pragmatics. Technical Report (GPTL) 75, Gothenburg Papers in Theoretical Linguistics, University of Göteborg.

Alan W. Black and Paul Taylor. 1997. Automatically clustering similar units for unit selection in speech synthesis. In *Proc. of the European Conference on Speech Communication and Technology (Eurospeech)*, Rhodes, Greece.

Robert Dickerson, Kyle Johnsen, Andrew Raij, Benjamin Lok, Amy Stevens, Thomas Bernard, and D. Scott Lind. 2006. Virtual patients: Assessment of synthesized versus recorded speech. In *Studies in Health Technology and Informatics*.

Kate Forbes-Riley, Diane Litman, Scott Silliman, and Joel Tetreault. 2006. Comparing synthesized versus pre-recorded tutor speech in an intelligent tutoring spoken dialogue system. In *Proc. of the International Florida Artificial Intelligence Research Society Conference*, Melbourne Beach, FL, USA.

Mark Fraser and Simon King. 2007. The Blizzard Challenge 2007. In *Proc. of the ISCA Workshop on Speech Synthesis*, Bonn, Germany.

Kallirroi Georgila, Alan W. Black, Kenji Sagae, and David Traum. 2012. Practical evaluation of human and synthesized speech for virtual human dialogue systems. In *Proc. of the International Conference on Language Resources and Evaluation (LREC)*, Istanbul, Turkey.

Andrew J. Hunt and Alan W. Black. 1996. Unit selection in a concatenative speech synthesis system using a large speech database. In *Proc. of the IEEE International Conference on Acoustics, Speech, and Signal Processing (ICASSP)*, Atlanta, GA, USA.

Vasilis Karaiskos, Simon King, Robert A. J. Clark, and Catherine Mayo. 2008. The Blizzard Challenge 2008. In *Proc. of the Blizzard Challenge*, Brisbane, Australia.

Hideki Kawahara. 1997. Speech representation and transformation using adaptive interpolation of weighted spectrum: vocoder revisited. In *IEEE International Conference On Acoustics, Speech, And Signal Processing*, Munich, Germany. Acoustics, Speech, and Signal Processing.

George A. Miller. 1995. WordNet: A lexical database for English. *Communications of the ACM*, 38(11):39–41.

Maike Paetzel, David Nicolas Racca, and David DeVault. 2014. A multimodal corpus of rapid dialogue games. In *Proc. of the International Conference on Language Resources and Evaluation (LREC)*, Reykjavik, Iceland.

Eli Pincus and David Traum. 2014. Towards a multimodal taxonomy of dialogue moves for word-guessing games. In *Proc. of the 10th Workshop on Multimodal Corpora (MMC)*, Reykjavik, Iceland.

Eli Pincus, David DeVault, and David Traum. 2014. Mr. Clue - A virtual agent that can play word-guessing games. In *Proc. of the 3rd Workshop on Games and NLP (GAMNLP)*, Raleigh, North Carolina, USA.

Maria K. Wolters, Karl B. Issac, and Steve Renals. 2010. Evaluating speech synthesis intelligibility using Amazon Mechanical Turk. In *Proc. of the ISCA Workshop on Speech Synthesis*, Kyoto, Japan.

Junichi Yamagishi, Takashi Nose, Heiga Zen, Zhen-Hua Ling, Tomoki Toda, Keiichi Tokuda, Simon King, and Steve Renals. 2009. Robust speaker-adaptive HMM-based text-to-speech synthesis. *IEEE Transactions on Audio, Speech, and Language Processing*, 17(6):1208–1230.

Heiga Zen, Takashi Nose, Junichi Yamagishi, Shinji Sako, Takashi Masuko, Alan W. Black, and Keiichi Tokuda. 2007. The HMM-based speech synthesis system (HTS) version 2.0. In *Proc. of the ISCA Workshop on Speech Synthesis*, Bonn, Germany.

Heiga Zen, Keiichi Tokuda, and Alan W. Black. 2009. Statistical parametric speech synthesis. *Speech Communication*, 51(11):1039–1064.

Dialog Act Annotation for Twitter Conversations

Elina Zarisheva
Hasso-Plattner-Institut
Potsdam, Germany
elina.zarisheva@student.hpi.uni-potsdam.de

Tatjana Scheffler
Department of Linguistics
University of Potsdam, Germany
tatjana.scheffler@uni-potsdam.de

Abstract

We present a dialog act annotation for German Twitter conversations. In this paper, we describe our annotation effort of a corpus of German Twitter conversations using a full schema of 57 dialog acts, with a moderate inter-annotator agreement of multi-π = 0.56 for three untrained annotators. This translates to an agreement of 0.76 for a minimal set of 10 broad dialog acts, comparable to previous work. Based on multiple annotations, we construct a merged gold standard, backing off to broader categories when needed. We draw conclusions wrt. the structure of Twitter conversations and the problems they pose for dialog act characterization.

1 Introduction

Social media and particularly Twitter have become a central data source for natural language processing methods and applications in recent years. One issue that has not received much attention yet, is the *social* or *interactive* nature of many posts. Often, only individual tweets are analyzed in isolation, ignoring the links between posts.[1] However, it is known that up to 40% of all Twitter messages are part of conversations—(Scheffler, 2014) report that 21.2% of all tweets in their German corpus are replies. In this paper, we view tweets in their original dialog context and apply a dialog annotation scheme to analyze the function of Twitter utterances. To our knowledge, this is the first attempt to apply a detailed dialog act annotation to Twitter dialogs[2].

We view our work as a first step in studying the make-up of Twitter conversations. So far, not much is known about the types of conversations that occur there, since the focus has been on analyzing single tweets. Our guiding question is in which way Twitter dialogs differ from the relatively well-studied genres of human-human and human-machine spoken dialogs. In this paper, we apply dialog act annotation because it captures the functional relevance of an utterance in context. This will enable us to answer questions about the nature of discourse on social media, such as whether individuals from different opinion "camps" talk with each other, whether Twitter dialogs are just exchanges of opinions and emotions, or whether true argumentation is taking place, etc. In addition, dialog act annotations are useful for further research on Twitter dialogs, as well as for applications dealing with this kind of data, e.g., automatic analyses of conversations on different types of topics, or simulated conversation participants (Twitter bots). We address both practical issues related to applying dialog act annotation to tweets as well as theoretical implications about the nature of (German) Twitter conversations that can be gleaned from our annotated data.

2 Related Work

In the following, we briefly summarize the relevant previous literature on dialog act annotation for other media, and existing research on Twitter dialogs in general.

Dialog act annotation One of the first steps towards analyzing the structure of dialogs is dialog act (DA) annotation. Dialog acts, a notion based on Austin's speech acts (Austin, 1975), characterize the dialog function of an utterance in broad terms, independent of its individual semantic content. There is a large number of DA schemata for conversational and task-based interactions (Core and Allen, 1997; Bunt et al., 2010; Traum, 2000, among many others), and these taxonomies have

[1] Usually, this is done by necessity, as Twitter data is most commonly accessed through an API stream that provides a random 1% of public statuses.

[2] really, multilogs, but we use the term broadly here

Proceedings of the SIGDIAL 2015 Conference, pages 114–123,
Prague, Czech Republic, 2-4 September 2015.

been applied to the construction of annotated corpora of human-human dialogs such as the MapTask corpus (Carletta et al., 1997), Verbmobil corpus (Jekat et al., 1995), or the AMI meeting corpus (McCowan et al., 2005). DA taxonomies and annotated resources have also been used in automatic DA recognition efforts (Stolcke et al., 2000, and many others). Dialog act annotation has also been carried out for some types of social media. (Forsyth and Martell, 2007) annotated chat messages with a custom-made schema of 15 dialog acts, and built a dialog act recognizer. They consider each turn to correspond to only one DA, even though they note that several acts can appear within one turn in their data. However, Twitter conversations have only recently become of interest to researchers.

Twitter conversations Twitter data is a mix of different genres and styles. But users are generally able to reply to existing messages, producing either personal discussions or interactions with strangers. Up to a quarter of tweets are replies to other messages (Scheffler, 2014; Honey and Herring, 2009), and due to the log-scale length distribution of conversations (most are just one tweet + its answer (Ritter et al., 2010)), around 40% of tweets thus are a part of conversations.

There are few studies that analyze Twitter dialogs, most likely because connected conversational data cannot easily be obtained through the Twitter API. Studies concentrate on samples based on individual, random users (Ritter et al., 2010) or based on frequently-updated snapshots over a short time-scale (Honey and Herring, 2009). We know of only two previous studies that address dialog acts in Twitter conversations. (Ritter et al., 2010) train an unsupervised model of dialog acts from Twitter data. Their system learns 8 dialog acts that were manually inspected and received labels such as STATUS, QUESTION, REACTION, COMMENT, etc. They also obtain an informative transition model between DAs from their data.

In contrast, (Zhang et al., 2011) build a supervised system that can classify between 5 broad speech acts (STATEMENT, QUESTION, SUGGESTION, COMMENT, MISC), using 8613 hand-annotated tweets to train their model. However, this work uses disconnected tweets in isolation (disregarding the underlying dialog structure). They do not report on inter-annotator agreement. Further, both this work and (Ritter et al., 2010) also assume that each tweet can be characterized by exactly one dialog act. We will show that this is not borne out in our data.

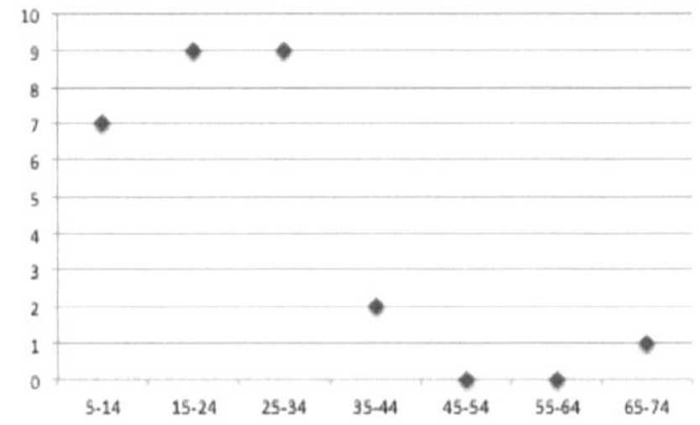

Figure 1: Distribution of depth in long conversations. X axis shows binned depth, values = number of conversations in the corpus.

3 Dialog Act Annotation

3.1 Corpus

For our work we use Twitter data that was collected within the BMBF project *Analysis of Discourses in Social Media*[3]. In the scope of this project, social media data concerning the topic *Energiewende* (energy turnaround) from Twitter and other sources was collected during the months of Aug-Nov, 2013. During November 11-30, Twitter conversations were automatically completed by re-crawling. Each conversation (= thread) can be represented as a tree with the first tweet as root node, and the edges between tweets drawn according to the `in_reply_to_status_id` field. The thread's *length* or size is the total number of tweets in the thread, its *depth* is the maximum level of embedding of a tweet (= the tree depth). Since we assume that the dialog structure of long Twitter discussions might differ from short interactions (which comprise the bulk of Twitter conversations), we extracted our corpus from the available data according to the two following criteria:

1. all *long* conversations of more than 20 tweets and minimum depth 5;

2. a random selection of *short* conversations of 4-5 tweets and arbitrary depth.

The total number of tweets is 1566, grouped in 172 dialogs. Figure 1 shows the depth distribution of long conversations.

[3]http://www.social-media-analytics.org/

For 18 tweets the text is missing: either they were deleted or they originate from a private account. To filter out non-German tweets we used the langid (Lui and Baldwin, 2012) and Compact Language Detection[4] libraries for Python 2.7, with some manual correction. 1271 tweets were recognized as German by both packages. Further problems with the raw and annotated data and our cleaning steps are described in Section 4.

3.2 Schema

We based our DA annotation schema on the general-purpose DIT++ taxonomy for dialog acts (Bunt et al., 2010)[5]. Twitter conversations are a type of human-human, non-task-oriented dialog. Many existing DA taxonomies are more suitable for task-oriented dialogs (even DIT++ has a very limited range of non-task-oriented acts) or for human-machine dialog. In order to reflect the type of interactions we expected in our data, and to reduce the difficulty of the annotation task, we changed the DIT++ schema according to our needs. Our adapted DA schema is shown in Figure 3 in the Appendix. In many places, the DA hierarchy was simplified by removing the finest distinctions, which are either hard to judge for novice annotators (e.g., subtypes of directives), or can be recovered from other properties of the data (e.g., types of check questions). We only included DAs from the dimensions Information Transfer, Action Discussion, and Social, as well as selected items from Discourse Structure Management and Communication Management. Even though the dimensions are in principle often independent of each other, we instructed the annotators to assign only the most relevant DA label to each segment.

3.3 Annotation task, annotators, tool

In recent years, crowdsourcing annotations has become ever more popular in linguistics. This approach is useful for quickly creating new resources based on newly available data (like the Twitter conversations we use). However, dialog act segmentation and labelling is a relatively complex task that is not easily done by untrained volunteers. For example, the taxonomy needs to be explained and internalized, and native knowledge of German is required. For this reason we used minimally trained undergraduate linguistics students as annotators for this study. The 36 students were participants of a Fall 2014 seminar on *Dialogs on Twitter* at the University of Potsdam, and received instruction on dialog acts as well as an overview of the DIT++ and other annotation schemes.

The students viewed entire conversations and were asked to segment each tweet (if necessary) into individual dialog acts and assign a DA label from the presented taxonomy. We used the WebAnno framework (Yimam et al., 2013), a free, web-based application that is especially easy to use for novice annotators. Although there were some technical problems with the tool (difficulty deleting annotations, the ability of annotators to add new labels), it was generally well-suited to the basic span-labelling annotation we required.

Each conversation in the corpus was assigned to three annotators, but no two annotators worked on the exact same set of conversations. For each annotator, WebAnno provides a token-based B-I label format as output, which is the basis of further analysis in this paper.

4 Annotation Validation

In this section we discuss initial steps to cleaning the raw annotation data and an evaluation of the quality of annotations.

4.1 Pre-processing

Before further analysis steps are possible, some cleaning steps were necessary. Although we designed the schema in a such way that tags are unambiguous, some tokens were assigned several tags by the same annotator. There are 122 tweets with ambiguous annotations. Unless one annotation was removed for another reason (see below), these additional annotations were retained during the construction of the gold standard.

In Section 3 we discussed that 1271 tweets of 1566 were classified as German. The other tweets were checked manually, so that only 106 tweets were deemed non-German and had to be excluded. We rebuilt the conversations by deleting non-German tweets, as well as all their replies (see Figure 2). After rebuilding, 1213 German tweets remain in the corpus.

As a second step, we standardized the annotations of @-tagged user names at the start of tweets, which mark the tweet as a reply to that user's tweet. Some annotators have included these @-tags in the following dialog act, others have not

[4]`https://code.google.com/p/cld2/`

[5]`http://dit.uvt.nl`

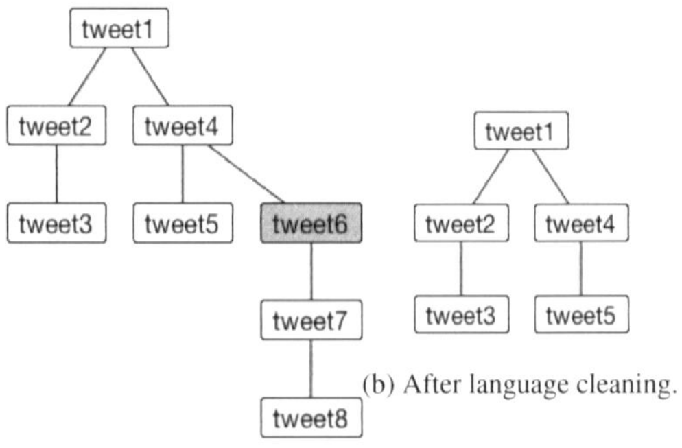

(b) After language cleaning.

(a) Before language cleaning.

Figure 2: Twitter conversation with non-German tweets (in gray) before and after cleaning.

tagged these at all. We decided to delete all tags for all user names at the start of the tweet. For this case we introduced a new label 0, indicating that there is no DA tag for this particular token.

The third step was to delete faulty annotations. In the annotations we found four "dialog act" labels that are not included in our DA schema and had been introduced by annotators: IRONIE (irony), NEIN (no), WURST (sausage) tags and the O- label (Table 1).

Tags and labels	Number of tweets
O-	51
IRONIE	72
NEIN	1
WURST	3

Table 1: Odd tags

We deleted these odd tags. In some cases (e.g., irony), an annotator also assigned a proper label to the token, which then remains as the sole annotation. In other cases, the token becomes untagged (marked with 0) for this annotator, resulting in missing annotations.

4.2 Segmentation

In order to evaluate the quality of the annotation and the chosen schema, we have separately determined the inter-annotator agreement for the segmentation and dialog act labelling steps.

Several of the proposed methods for determining the validity of annotations are based on comparing two annotations with each other (i.e., one candidate annotation with a gold standard). Even when more annotators can be included, it is often assumed that those annotators have worked on the same data, as for example with the popular Cohen's κ-statistic (Carletta, 1996). Instead, we chose *Fleiss' multi-*π, which measures how consistent the assigned labels are for each item, without regard to which annotator gave the label (Artstein and Poesio, 2008). In order to be able to use this metric, which nevertheless assumes a fixed number of annotations per item, we include in our validation only those tweets for which we have three annotations after the cleaning steps described above (1004 tweets). We exclude tweets with missing annotations and those where removal of spurious labels resulted in missing annotations for some tokens.

The overall observed agreement is the mean of the individual agreement values for each item:

$$agr_i = \frac{1}{\binom{c}{2}} \sum_{k \in K} \binom{n_{ik}}{2} \qquad (1)$$

$$A_o = \frac{1}{i} \sum_{i \in I} agr_i \qquad (2)$$

where agr_i is the relative frequency of agreeing judgment pairs among all pairs of judgments, I the number of taggable items in the corpus, k the number of tags in the schema, and $c = 3$ the number of annotators (Artstein and Poesio, 2008, p. 563).

The overall expected agreement is calculated as the random chance event that two annotators assign an item to the same category/DA k (4). Each annotator's chance of assigning an item to k is based on the overall proportion $\hat{P}(k)$ of items assigned to k, n_k, over all assignments.

$$\hat{P}(k) = \frac{n_k}{ic} \qquad (3)$$

$$A_e^{\pi} = \sum_{k \in K} (\hat{P}(k))^2 \qquad (4)$$

We calculate the amount of agreement beyond chance by the standard formula:

$$S_\pi = \frac{A_o - A_e}{1 - A_e} \qquad (5)$$

For the segmentation task, we used the simplest approach by taking each token to be a taggable item which can be labelled either a BOUNDARY or NON-BOUNDARY. As discussed in (Fournier and Inkpen, 2012), such measures are too strict by punishing even small disagreements over the exact location of a segment boundary (e.g., if annotators disagree by one token). In addition, since most judgments fall into the majority class (NON-BOUNDARY), the expected agreement will be high, making it harder to improve upon it. However, we show in Section 5.3 that the DA segments in our Twitter data are relatively short on average, possibly partially relieving this problem. Consequently, the agreement determined this way can be seen as a lower limit that underestimates the actual agreement between annotators.

We observe a segmentation agreement of 0.88 between three annotators, which indicates very good agreement. Disagreements are due to additional segments that some annotators posited (= Does an explanation after a question constitute its own speech act?) or were triggered by special Twitter vocabulary such as emoticons, to which some annotators assigned their own DA labels (see example (6) on page 8). Some of these disagreements can be solved by more comprehensive annotation guidelines.

	Segment.	**DA labelling**
A_o	0.966	0.658
A_e^π	0.716	0.224
Fleiss' multi-π	**0.883**	**0.559**

Table 2: Chance-corrected coefficient between three annotators for segmentation and DA labelling tasks.

4.3 DA labelling

We then computed the inter-annotator agreement for DA labels on the raw annotation data, using the same procedure. For this measure, we only included those tweets where all three annotators agreed on the segmentation. The results for the full DA schema of 57 dialog acts are shown in Table 2. As such, the agreement on DA labels is at most moderate, but the measure does not take the DA taxonomy into account. For example, disagreements on a subtype of QUESTION are counted as one error, just like a mix-up between top-level DA labels would be. Other annotation efforts report even worse IAA values with novice annotators, even using a weighted agreement score (Geertzen et al., 2008). In order to better compare our annotation effort to other work, we also computed agreement scores for two reduced DA schemas by merging similar DAs. With a reduced set of 14 DAs, three annotators achieve multi-$\pi = 0.65$, whereas a minimal DA set of 10 basic DAs yields multi-$\pi = 0.76$, a good agreement.

To better evaluate the chosen DA schema we built a confusion matrix, recording the DA labels that caused the most disagreements. The great majority of disagreements occurred within the different subtypes of INFORMATION PROVIDING functions. In addition, there were 36 cases of confusion between INFORM and the discourse structuring functions OPEN, TOPICINTRODUCTION and TOPICSHIFT. These errors indicate a limited applicability of the chosen schema to conversational Twitter data. The INFORM category is too broad for conversational statements, and annotators thus had two kinds of problems: First, clearly delineating plain INFORMs from other dialog moves that may be carried out simultaneously (like the discourse structuring moves or social moves), and second, deciding whether a statement can be classified as INFORM at all—in cases of doubt, annotators may have chosen the higher level label INFORMATION PROVIDING but not INFORM. We discuss this issue further in Section 6.

Another source of multiple disagreements is the distinction between different types of questions. These confusions are true errors than can be corrected with better training of annotators.

In contrast, there were no systematic cases of confusion between between the ACTION DISCUSSION, INFORMATION TRANSFER, and SOCIAL functions. Tables 8 and 9 in the Appendix show the frequencies of confusion between DA labels.

5 Analysis

The evaluation in the previous section has shown that (i) about two-thirds of judgment pairs on individual items are in agreement (i.e., on average, two out of the three annotators agree), and (ii) most disagreements between annotators exist in the lower tiers of the annotation schema, whereas the agreement on broader categories is better. Based on these observations, we devised an algorithm to automatically merge the annotations into a gold standard.

5.1 Merging annotations

As was mentioned in Section 3, each tweet should be annotated by three students, in principle providing a possibility to use majority voting (the most common decision tactic in crowdsourced lay annotations (Sabou et al., 2014)) to decide on the 'correct' annotation. However, since the annotators carry out two tasks simultaneously (segmenting and labelling), merging became less trivial. If we first merge the segmentations we would lose DA information. Instead we observe tag variations for a particular word token and determine the true tag based on the results.

In the raw data there were 1004 tweets annotated by three students, 180 tweets – by two, 29 – only by one. Moreover, some tokens have received more than one label even by the same annotator (contrary to the guidelines). Therefore we adapted our algorithm to differing numbers of annotations.

The merging process is composed of three steps. For this phase, we disregard segmentation boundaries because there are no tweets with several successive segments with the same tag. We can recognize segment boundaries by simply observing the tag change.

First step: Perfect agreement We find all tweets that have exactly the same segmentation for all their annotators (405 unique tweets). Among these, 82 tweets have the same annotation as well. Since there is already perfect agreement for these tweets, no further work is required.

Second step: Majority vote In this step we pick one tag from several for a particular token. For each occurrence of a tag we assign weight 1. Tags whose weight is higher than the sum of weights for other tags are deemed 'correct' and assigned to that token.

For example, the word *Erde* has been assigned INFORM once, tag DIRECTIVE once, QUESTION three times. Since $3 > 2$, we keep QUESTION and the other tags are deleted. After this step, another 421 tweets have no ambiguous tokens left and can be added to the 'done' tweets from the first step.

Third step: DA generalization Our DA taxonomy has a tree structure, viz., some DA labels have the same ancestor, or one tag is a child of another. In this phase we compare tags for a particular token based on their relationship in the DA hierarchy. In the DIT++ taxonomy, it is assumed that parent DAs subsume the function of all children (they indicate more general dialog functions). In case of inapplicability of all the leaf-level labels, or in case the annotator isn't sure, a higher-level DA label can be chosen from the hierarchy. In this step, we use this structure of the DA taxonomy in order to capture some of the information that annotators agreed upon when labelling tweets.

If DA tags for a token are in a direct inheritance (parent-child) relationship or siblings, we choose the parent tag for this token. The other tags that take part in this relationship are deleted (they are replaced by the higher-level option). Below is an example of the two scenarios.

Patent-child relationship:
Tag IT_IP_INFORM_AGREEMENT and parent tag IT_IP_INFORM. Parent tag IT_IP_INFORM is kept and child is deleted.

Siblings:
Tag IT_IP_INFORM_AGREEMENT and tag IT_IP_INFORM_DISAGREEMENT both have the parent tag IT_IP_INFORM. We assign tag IT_IP_INFORM and delete the siblings.

This step results in another 66 'done' tweets. To account for the changes in the voting pattern after the third step, we apply the second (majority vote) merging step once again. After each merge the segments are recalculated. As a result we have 816 'done' tweets and 397 tweets that still need to be reviewed because disagreements on at least one segment could not be resolved automatically. This happened particularly for tweets with only two annotators, where majority voting did not help to resolve problems. Two students among the annotators adjudicated the remaining problem tweets manually. Further analysis in this paper is based on this merged 'gold standard' dialog act annotation for German conversations, in part in comparison with the original raw annotations.

5.2 DA n-grams

First, we examine DA unigrams to see which kind of acts/functions are common in our data. Both the original and merged data lack the same two tags: PCM and INTRODUCE_RETURN. In the merged data the root tag of the annotation schema, DIT++ TAXONOMY appears additionally. This is the result of a merging error, unifying two top level dimension tags. These mistakes will be manually corrected in the future.

Table 3 shows the top 5 and bottom 5 tags that are used in the original and merged data. As we can observe, the top 5 tags stay the same after merging but some rare tags appear by merging (IS, the main question label), and some of the

Original annotation	Merged annotation
0	0
Inform	Inform
Answer	Answer
Agreement	Agreement
SetQuestion	SetQuestion
...	...
Apologize	OCM
Bye_Return	Bye_Return
Introduce	Introduce
OCM	IS
DSM	Introduce_ Initial

Table 3: Unigrams in the original and merged data.

rarest tags in the raw data move higher up after the merging process. We have also extracted the unigram frequencies for long and short conversations (see above) separately, but the frequency of certain DAs is generally very similar in these different types of conversations. By far the most frequent DA (26% or 22%, respectively) is Inform. This is in line with data from spoken human-human dialogs, where Statements are sometimes even more frequent, at 36% (Stolcke et al., 2000). However, about twice as many dialog acts (8.7%) are characterized as Social in the long conversations as in the short conversations (4.4%), showing that short conversations are more aligned with the task.

To get a first glimpse of the structure of Twitter conversations, we calculated DA label bigrams as well. Twitter dialogs differ from more conventional dialog types in their branching structure: one turn can have several replies, each of which can be the basis of additional answers (see Figure 2b). In Twitter, in contrast to spoken conversations, this does not necessarily indicate a split of the conversation (and participants) into two separate strands. Instead, speakers can monitor both parts of the conversation and potentially contribute. Still, since replies mostly refer to the linked previous tweet, we can observe DA bigrams either within one tweet or across a tweet and its reply. Thus the last tag from the previous tweet and the first tag of the reply tweet are registered as a bigram. To distinguish the conversation start, we add another additional tag <S> to mark the beginning of the conversation. We also skip 0-tags (marking primarily user names at the beginning of reply tweets). Tables 4 and 5 show the top 5 bigrams and the most common starts of conversations, respectively. Table 6 compares the frequent bigrams for short and long conversations.

Bigram	Occurrence
Inform, Inform	135
Answer, Inform	66
SetQuestion, Answer	64
Inform, Agreement	63
Agreement, Inform	59

Table 4: Top five bigrams in the merged data.

5.3 Structure within tweets

Our analysis shows that despite their brevity, most tweets exhibit some internal structure. In 1213 tweets, we annotated altogether 2936 dialog acts. Table 7 shows the distribution of segments in tweets. It demonstrates that even though tweets are generally short, many contain more than just one dialog act. Even disregarding 0-segments (user names), which cannot be seen as true dialog acts, almost 500 tweets (more than 1/3) carry out more than one dialog act.

A tweet consists of at most 140 symbols. Since German words are on average six letters long[6], one German tweet consists of up to 23 words. Thus, in a tweet with five or six segments, each segment should have four to five tokens. Below we show two examples that have more than five segments, together with their annotations. Whereas some segments are debatable (e.g. the split-off dash in (7)), these examples show that Twitter turns can be quite complex, combining social acts with statements, questions, and emotional comments.

[6]Values around 6 are reported for the large Duden corpus `http://www.duden.de/suchen/sprachwissen/Wortlänge`, as well as for the TIGER corpus

Bigram	Occurrence
<S>, Open	40
<S>, TopicInroduction	32
<S>, Inform	23
<S>, DSM	20
<S>, SetQuestion	9

Table 5: Most common starts of the conversation.

Long conversations	Short conversations
INFORM, INFORM	INFORM, INFORM
INFORM, AGREEMENT	<S >, OPEN
AGREEMENT, INFORM	SETQUESTION, ANSWER
ANSWER, INFORM	ANSWER, INFORM
SETQUESTION, ANSWER	<S >, TOPICINTRODUCTION

Table 6: Bigrams in merged long and short conversations.

Number of segments per tweet	Tweets
1 segment	89 times
2 segments	671 times
3 segments	320 times
4 segments	114 times
5 segments	17 times
6 segments	2 times

Table 7: Distribution of segments.

(6) | @Marsmaedschen | Hey Mella, | sage mal, kocht ihr auf einem Induktionsherd? | Wenn ja, von welcher Firma ist die Grillpfanne? | Sowas suche ich! | :-) |
| 0 | GREET | QUESTION | SETQUESTION | INFORM | 0 |

(7) |@TheBug0815 @Luegendetektor @McGeiz | Genau, wir brauchen gar keine Grundlast, ist nur ein kapitalistisches Konstrukt | - | Wind/PV reichen? | Lol |
| 0 | AGREEMENT| 0| PROPQUESTION| DISAGREEMENT|

6 Discussion

In this paper we presented our attempt to annotate Twitter conversations with a detailed dialog act schema. We achieved only moderate inter-annotator agreement of $\pi = 0.56$ between three annotators on the DA labelling task, in contrast with work in other domains that achieved good agreement ((Stolcke et al., 2000) report $\kappa = 0.8$ for DA labelling of spoken data using 42 categories). Partially, annotation accuracy can be improved by better annotator training, e.g. to distinguish the different question types (see Table 9).

On the other hand, our data shows that the DA schema exhibits some inherent problems when applied to Twitter dialogs. For example, even though opening a conversation is rarely the main function of a tweet, every dialog-initial tweet could be argued to fulfil both the conversation OPEN function as well as a TOPICINTRODUCTION function, in addition to its communicative function (QUESTION, INFORM, etc.). Annotators found it hard to decide which dimension is more important. In the future, annotation in multiple dimensions should probably be encouraged, just like it was done for spoken human-human dialogs (Core and Allen, 1997; Bunt et al., 2010).

Many annotation problems are due to the fuzzy nature of INFORM and its relatives. Some INFORMs are shown in translation in (8–11). Even though all have been annotated with the same DA, they constitute very different dialog functions. Some are factual statements (8), some meta-commentary or discourse management (9), some opinions (10) and some read like statements or opinions, but are extremely sarcastic/ironic and thus do not have a primary "Information Providing" function (11). In order to properly analyse Twitter discussions, it seems necessary to make a clearer distinction between these kinds of dialog moves.

(8) *Coal 300 kWh, nuclear power 100 kWh*

(9) *The link still doesn't work.*

(10) *I'm going to end it right away, it got boring anyway.*

(11) *And the solar panels and wind power plants in the Middle Ages were great*

One implication of our DA annotation was that assigning single DAs to entire tweets is not sufficient. Not only does one utterance in Twitter dialogs often express several dialog functions as argued above, our data also shows that many tweets are composed of several successive dialog acts. This can be due to two discussion strands being carried out in parallel (like in text messaging), but often results from a combination of dialog moves as in this example:

(12) *True, unfortunately. | But what about the realization of high solar activity in the 70s and 80s?*

Finally, the non-linear structure of Twitter dialogs has interesting implications for their structural analysis, e.g. for DA recognition approaches that take the context into account. In these cases, the initial tweet/DA will potentially be the first token of many DA bigrams. All answers taken together may provide context that helps determine what function the initial tweet was intended to fulfill. We leave these issues for further work.

Acknowledgements

The authors would like to thank the WebAnno development team for providing the annotation tool. We are extremely grateful to the participants in the Fall 2014 course *Dialogs on Twitter* at the University of Potsdam for their annotation effort. We are grateful to the anonymous reviewers for their detailed and helpful comments.

References

Ron Artstein and Massimo Poesio. 2008. Inter-Coder Agreement for Computational Linguistics. *Computational Linguistics*, 34(4):555–596.

John Langshaw Austin. 1975. *How to do things with words*, volume 367. Oxford university press.

Harry Bunt, Jan Alexandersson, Jean Carletta, Jae-Woong Choe, Alex Chengyu Fang, Koiti Hasida, Kiyong Lee, Volha Petukhova, Andrei Popescu-Belis, Laurent Romary, et al. 2010. Towards an ISO standard for dialogue act annotation. In *Proceedings of the Seventh conference on International Language Resources and Evaluation (LREC'10).*

Jean Carletta, Stephen Isard, Gwyneth Doherty-Sneddon, Amy Isard, Jacqueline C Kowtko, and Anne H Anderson. 1997. The reliability of a dialogue structure coding scheme. *Computational linguistics*, 23(1):13–31.

Jean Carletta. 1996. Assessing agreement on classification tasks: the kappa statistic. *Computational linguistics*, 22(2):249–254.

Mark Core and James Allen. 1997. Coding dialogs with the damsl annotation scheme. In *AAAI fall symposium on communicative action in humans and machines*, pages 28–35. Boston, MA.

Eric N. Forsyth and Craig H. Martell. 2007. Lexical and discourse analysis of online chat dialog. pages 19–26.

Chris Fournier and Diana Inkpen. 2012. Segmentation similarity and agreement. pages 152–161.

Jeroen Geertzen, Volha Petukhova, and Harry Bunt. 2008. Evaluating Dialogue Act Tagging with Naive and Expert Annotators. In *Proceedings of LREC*, pages 1076–1082.

Courtenay Honey and Susan C Herring. 2009. Beyond microblogging: Conversation and collaboration via twitter. In *System Sciences, 2009. HICSS'09. 42nd Hawaii International Conference on*, pages 1–10. IEEE.

Susanne Jekat, Alexandra Klein, Elisabeth Maier, Ilona Maleck, Marion Mast, and J. Joachim Quantz. 1995. Dialogue acts in Verbmobil. Technical report, Saarländische Universitäts- und Landesbibliothek.

Marco Lui and Timothy Baldwin. 2012. langid.py: An Off-the-shelf Language Identification Tool. *Proceedings of the 50th Annual Meeting of the Association for Computational Linguistics*, (July):25–30.

Iain McCowan, Jean Carletta, W Kraaij, S Ashby, S Bourban, M Flynn, M Guillemot, T Hain, J Kadlec, V Karaiskos, et al. 2005. The AMI meeting corpus. In *Proceedings of the 5th International Conference on Methods and Techniques in Behavioral Research.*

Alan Ritter, Colin Cherry, and Bill Dolan. 2010. Unsupervised modeling of Twitter conversations. In *Proceedings of NAACL.*

Marta Sabou, Kalina Bontcheva, Leon Derczynski, and Arno Scharl. 2014. Corpus annotation through crowdsourcing: Towards best practice guidelines. In *Proceedings of the Ninth International Conference on Language Resources and Evaluation*, number 2010, pages 859–866.

Tatjana Scheffler. 2014. A German Twitter snapshot. In N. Calzolari et al., editor, *Proceedings of the Ninth International Conference on Language Resources and Evaluation (LREC'14)*, Reykjavik, Iceland. European Language Resources Association (ELRA).

Andreas Stolcke, Klaus Ries, Noah Coccaro, Elizabeth Shriberg, Rebecca Bates, Daniel Jurafsky, Paul Taylor, Rachel Martin, Carol Van Ess-Dykema, and Marie Meteer. 2000. Dialogue act modeling for automatic tagging and recognition of conversational speech. *Computational linguistics*, 26(3):339–373.

David R Traum. 2000. 20 questions on dialogue act taxonomies. *Journal of semantics*, 17(1):7–30.

Seid Muhie Yimam, Iryna Gurevych, Richard Eckart de Castilho, and Chris Biemann. 2013. WebAnno: A flexible, web-based and visually supported system for distributed annotations. In *Proceedings of the 51st Annual Meeting of the Association for Computational Linguistics (System Demonstrations) (ACL 2013)*, pages 1–6, Stroudsburg, PA, USA, August. Association for Computational Linguistics.

Renxian Zhang, Dehong Gao, and Wenjie Li. 2011. What are tweeters doing: Recognizing speech acts in twitter. In *Workshops at the Twenty-Fifth AAAI Conference on Artificial Intelligence.*

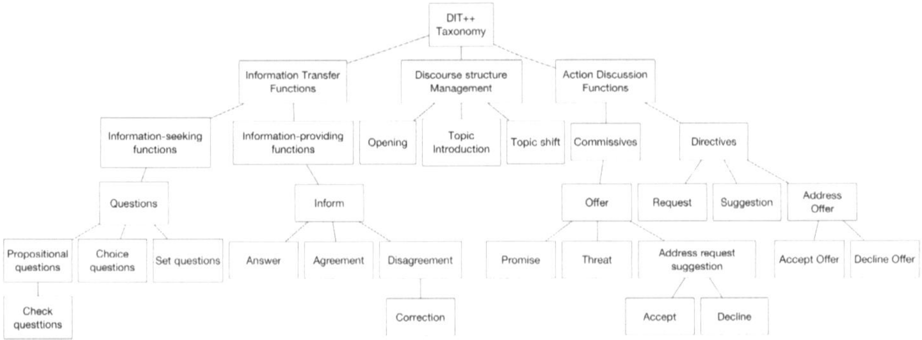

(a) Adapted DIT++ taxonomy (1).

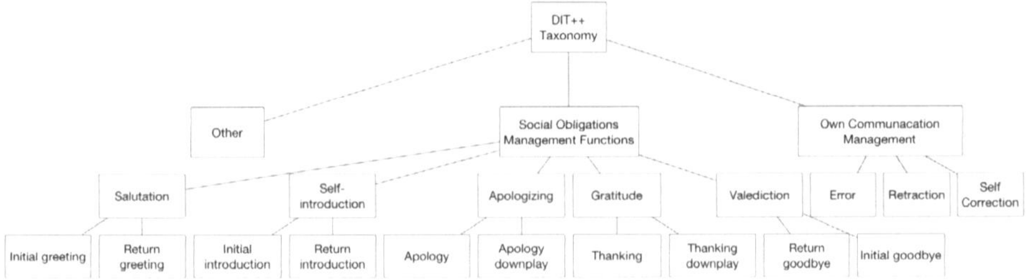

(b) Adapted DIT++ taxonomy (2).

Figure 3: Adapted DIT++ taxonomy.

		1	**2**	**3**	**4**	**5**	**6**	**7**	**8**	**9**
	DSM_OPEN	5	1	0	5	10	0	1	0	0
1	DSM_TOPICINTRODUCTION		0	0	0	9	1	1	0	0
2	DSM_TOPICSHIFT			0	3	17	3	8	1	5
3	IT				0	0	0	0	0	0
4	IT_IP					31	5	17	6	2
5	IT_IP_INFORM						26	45	31	15
6	IT_IP_INF_AGREEMENT							24	8	5
7	IT_IP_INF_ANSWER								14	8
8	IT_IP_INF_DISAGREEMENT									13
9	IT_IP_INF_DIS_CORRECTION									

Table 8: Annotation confusion matrix (1): Number of segments judged as both indicated dialog act labels by different annotators.

	PROPQUESTION_CHECKQ	SETQUESTION
PROPQUESTION	6	25
PROPQUESTION_CHECKQ		6

	PCM_COMPLETION	SOCIAL
INFORM	13	10
INFORM_AGREEMENT	2	15

Table 9: Annotation confusion matrix (2): Segments often confused within questions (top) or in other parts of the taxonomy (bottom).

Towards Improving Dialogue Topic Tracking Performances with Wikification of Concept Mentions

Seokhwan Kim, Rafael E. Banchs, Haizhou Li
Human Language Technology Department
Institute for Infocomm Research
Singapore 138632
{kims,rembanchs,hli}@i2r.a-star.edu.sg

Abstract

Dialogue topic tracking aims at analyzing and maintaining topic transitions in on-going dialogues. This paper proposes to utilize Wikification-based features for providing mention-level correspondences to Wikipedia concepts for dialogue topic tracking. The experimental results show that our proposed features can significantly improve the performances of the task in mixed-initiative human-human dialogues.

1 Introduction

Dialogue topic tracking aims at detecting topic transitions and predicting topic categories in on-going dialogues which address more than a single topic. Since human communications in real-world situations tend to consist of a series of multiple topics even for a single domain, tracking dialogue topics plays a key role in analyzing human-human dialogues as well as improving the naturalness of human-machine interactions by conducting multi-topic conversations.

Some researchers (Nakata et al., 2002; Lagus and Kuusisto, 2002; Adams and Martell, 2008) attempted to solve this problem with text categorization approaches for the utterances in a given turn. However, these approaches can only be effective for the cases when users mention the topic-related expressions explicitly in their utterances, because the models for text categorization assume that the proper category for each textual unit can be assigned based only on its own contents.

The other direction of dialogue topic tracking made use of external knowledge sources including domain models (Roy and Subramaniam, 2006), heuristics (Young et al., 2007), and agendas (Bohus and Rudnicky, 2003; Lee et al., 2008). While these knowledge-based methods have an advantage of dealing with system-initiative dialogues by controlling dialogue flows based on given resources, they have drawbacks in low flexibility to handle the user's responses and high costs for building the resources.

Recently, we have proposed to explore domain knowledge from Wikipedia for mixed-initiative dialogue topic tracking without significant costs for building resources (Kim et al., 2014a; Kim et al., 2014b). In these methods, a set of articles that have similar contents to a given dialogue segment are selected using vector space model. Then various types of information obtained from the articles are utilized to learn topic trackers based on kernel methods.

In this work, we focus on the following limitations of our former work in retrieving relevant concepts at a given turn with the term vector similarity between each pair of dialogue segment and Wikipedia article. Firstly, the contents of conversation could be expressed in totally different ways from the descriptions in the actual relevant articles in Wikipedia. This mismatch between spoken dialogues and written encyclopedia could bring about inaccuracy in selecting proper Wikipedia articles as sources for domain knowledge. Secondly, a set of articles that are selected by comparing with a whole dialogue segment can be limited to reflect the multiple relevances if more than one concept are actually mentioned in the segment. Lastly, lack of semantic or discourse aspects in concept retrieval could cause a limited capability of the tracker to deal with implicitly mentioned subjects.

To solve these issues, we propose to incorporate Wikification (Mihalcea and Csomai, 2007) features for building dialogue topic trackers. The goal of Wikification is resolving ambiguities and variabilities of every mention in natural language by linking the expression to its relevant Wikipedia concept. Since this task is performed using not

Proceedings of the SIGDIAL 2015 Conference, pages 124–128,
Prague, Czech Republic, 2-4 September 2015.

t	Speaker	Utterance	Topic Transition
0	Guide	How can I help you?	NONE→NONE
1	Tourist	Can you recommend some good places to visit in Singapore?	**NONE→ATTR**
	Guide	Well if you like to visit an icon of Singapore, Merlion park will be a nice place to visit.	
2	Tourist	That is a symbol for your country, right?	ATTR→ATTR
	Guide	Yes, we use that to symbolise Singapore.	
3	Tourist	Okay.	ATTR→ATTR
	Guide	The lion head symbolised the founding of the island and the fish body just symbolised the humble fishing village.	
4	Tourist	How can I get there from Orchard Road?	**ATTR→TRSP**
	Guide	You can take the red line train from Orchard and stop at Raffles Place.	
5	Tourist	Is this walking distance from the station to the destination?	TRSP→TRSP
	Guide	Yes, it'll take only ten minutes on foot.	
6	Tourist	Alright.	**TRSP→FOOD**
	Guide	Well, you can also enjoy some seafoods at the riverside near the place.	
7	Tourist	What food do you have any recommendations to try there?	FOOD→FOOD
	Guide	If you like spicy foods, you must try chilli crab which is one of our favourite dishes here.	
8	Tourist	Great! I'll try that.	FOOD→FOOD

Figure 1: Examples of dialogue topic tracking on Singapore tour guide dialogues

t	Speaker	Mention	Wikipedia Concept
1	Tourist	Singapore	Singapore
	Guide	Singapore	Singapore
		Merlion park	Merlion Park
2	Tourist	That	Merlion
		your country	Singapore
	Guide	that	Merlion
		Singapore	Singapore
4	Tourist	there	Merlion Park
		Orchard Road	Orchard Road
	Guide	red line train	North South MRT Line
		Orchard	Orchard MRT Station
		Raffles Place	Raffles Place MRT Station
5	Tourist	the station	Raffles Place MRT Station
		the destination	Merlion Park
6	Guide	seafoods	Seafood
		the riverside	Singapore River
		the place	Merlion Park
7	Tourist	there	Singapore River
	Guide	chilli crab	Chilli crab
		here	Singapore

Figure 2: Examples of Wikification on Singapore tour guide dialogues

only surface form features, but also various types of semantic and discourse aspects obtained from both given texts and Wikipedia collection, our proposed method utilizing the results from Wikification contributes to improve the tracking performances compared to the former approaches based on dialogue segment-level correspondences.

2 Dialogue Topic Tracking

Dialogue topic tracking can be defined as a classification problem to detect where topic transitions occur and what the topic category follows after each transition. The most probable pair of topics at just before and after each turn is predicted by the following classifier:

$$f(x_t) = (y_{t-1}, y_t),$$

where x_t contains the input features obtained at a turn t, $y_t \in C$, and C is a closed set of topic categories. If a topic transition occurs at t, y_t should be different from y_{t-1}. Otherwise, both y_t and y_{t-1} have the same value.

Figure 1 shows an example of dialogue topic tracking in a given dialogue fragment on Singapore tour guide domain between a tourist and a guide. This conversation is divided into four segments, since f detects three topic transitions at t_1, t_4 and t_6. The mixed-initiative aspects are also shown in this dialogue, because the first two transitions are initiated by the tourist, while the other one is driven by the guide without any explicit requirement from the tourist. From these results, we could obtain a topic sequence of 'Attraction', 'Transportation', and 'Food'.

3 Wikification of Concept Mentions in Spoken Dialogues

Wikification aims at linking mentions to the relevant entries in Wikipedia. As shown in the examples in Figure 2 for the dialogue in Figure 1, this task is performed by dealing with co-references, ambiguities, and variabilities of the mentions.

Following most previous work on Wikification (Bunescu and Pasca, 2006; Mihalcea and Csomai, 2007; Milne and Witten, 2008; Dredze et al., 2010; Han and Sun, 2011; Chen and Ji, 2011), this work also takes a supervised learning to rank algorithm for determining the most relevant concept for each mention in transcribed utterances.

In this work, every noun phrase in a given dialogue session is defined as a single mention. To capture more abstract concepts, we take not only named entities or base noun phrases, but also every complex or recursive noun phrase in a dialogue as the instance to be linked. For each mention, a set of candidates are retrieved from a Lucene [1] index on the whole Wikipedia collection divided by section-level. The ranking score $s(m, c)$ for a given pair of a mention m and its candidate concept c is assigned as follows:

$$s(m, c) = \begin{cases} 4 & \text{if } c \text{ is the exactly same as } g(m), \\ 3 & \text{if } c \text{ is the parent article of } g(m), \\ 2 & \text{if } c \text{ belongs to the same article} \\ & \text{but different section of } g(m), \\ 1 & \text{otherwise.} \end{cases},$$

where $g(m)$ is the manual annotation for the most relevant concept of m.

[1] http://lucene.apache.org/

Name	Description
SP	the speaker who spoke that mention
WM	word n-grams within the surface of m
WT	word n-grams within the title of c
EMT	whether the surface of m is same as the title of c
EMR	whether the surface of m is same as one of re-directions to c
MIT	whether the surface of m is a sub-string of the title of c
TIM	whether the title of c is a sub-string of the m's surface form
MIR	whether the surface of m is a sub-string of a re-directed title to c
RIM	whether a re-directed title to c is a sub-string of the m's surface form
PMT	similarity score based on edit distance between the surface of m and the title of c
PMR	maximum similarity score between the surface of m and the redirected titles to c
OC	whether c previously occurred in the full dialogue history
OC_w	whether c occurred within w previous turns with $w \in \{1, 3, 5, 10\}$

Table 1: List of features for training the ranking SVM model for Wikification

Then, a ranking SVM (Joachims, 2002) model, a pairwise ranking algorithm learned from the ranked lists, is trained based on the scores and the features in Table 1. In the execution time, the top-ranked item in the list of candidates scored by this model is considered as the result of Wikification for a given mention.

4 Wikification-based Features for Dialogue Topic Tracking

Following our previous work (Kim et al., 2014a; Kim et al., 2014b), the classifier f for dialogue topic tracking is trained on the labeled dataset using supervised machine learning techniques.

The simplest baseline is to learn the classifier based on the vector space model (Salton et al., 1975) considering bag-of-words for the terms within the given utterances. An instance for each turn is represented by a weighted term vector defined as follows:

$$\phi(x) = \left(\alpha_1, \alpha_2, \cdots, \alpha_{|W|}\right) \in R^{|W|},$$

where $\alpha_i = \sum_{j=0}^{h} \left(\lambda^j \cdot tfidf(w_i, u_{(t-j)})\right)$, u_t is the utterance mentioned in a turn t, $tfidf(w_i, u_t)$ is the product of term frequency of a word w_i in u_t and inverse document frequency of w_i, λ is a decay factor for giving more importance to more recent turns, $|W|$ is the size of word dictionary, and h is the number of previous turns considered as dialogue history features.

To overcome the limitations caused by lack of semantic or domain-specific aspects in the first baseline, we previosly proposed (Kim et al., 2014b) to leverage on Wikipedia as an external knowledge source with an extended feature space defined by concatenating the concept space with the previous term vector space as follows:

$$\phi'(x) = \left(\alpha_1, \alpha_2, \cdots, \alpha_{|W|}, \beta_1, \beta_2, \cdots, \beta_{|D|}\right),$$

where $\phi'(x) \in R^{|W|+|C|}$, β_i is the semantic relatedness between the input x and the concept in the i-th Wikipedia article and $|C|$ is the number of concepts in the Wikipedia collection. The value for β_i is computed with the cosine similarity between term vectors as follows:

$$\beta_i = \text{sim}(x, c_i) = \cos(\theta) = \frac{\phi(x) \cdot \phi(c_i)}{|\phi(x)||\phi(c_i)|},$$

where $\phi(c_i)$ is the term vector composed from the i-th Wikipedia concept in the collection.

In this work, the results of Wikification described in Section 3 are utilized to extend the feature space for training the topic tracker, instead of or in addition to the above mentioned feature values obtained from dialogue segment-level analyses. A value γ_i in the new feature space is defined as the weighted sum of the number of mentions linked to a given concept c_i within a dialogue segment as follows:

$$\gamma_i = \sum_{j=0}^{h} \left(\lambda^j \cdot \left|\{m_k \in u_{(t-j)} | g(m_k) = c_i\}\right|\right),$$

where m_k is the k-th mention in a given utterance u, $g(m)$ is the top-ranked result of Wikification for the mention m, λ is a decay factor, and h is the window size for considering dialogue history.

5 Evaluation

To demonstrate the effectiveness of our proposed approach for dialogue topic tracking using Wikification results, we performed experiments on the Singapore tour guide dialogues which consists of 35 sessions collected from human-human conversations between tour guides and tourists. All the recorded dialogues with the total length of 21 hours were manually transcribed, then these 31,034 utterances were manually annotated with the following nine topic categories: Opening, Closing, Itinerary, Accommodation, Attraction, Food, Transportation, Shopping, and Other.

	Schedule: All				Schedule: Tourist Turns				Schedule: Guide Turns			
	Transition			Turn	Transition			Turn	Transition			Turn
Features	P	R	F	ACC	P	R	F	ACC	P	R	F	ACC
α	42.08	53.48	47.10	67.97	41.88	52.59	46.63	67.15	41.96	52.11	46.49	67.13
α, β	42.12	53.38	47.08	67.98	41.84	52.75	46.67	67.08	41.91	52.03	46.42	67.13
α, γ	47.36	50.19	48.73	72.38	46.58	51.09	48.73	71.99	47.10	48.44	47.76	71.94
α, β, γ	47.35	50.24	48.75	72.43	46.57	51.09	48.72	71.99	47.02	48.21	47.61	71.93
α, γ'	50.77	49.36	50.06	79.12	50.51	49.58	50.04	81.10	50.94	49.10	50.00	78.92
α, β, γ'	50.82	49.41	50.10	79.15	50.43	49.58	50.00	81.10	50.98	49.02	49.98	78.92

Table 2: Comparisons of the topic tracking performances with different combinations of features

For topic tracking, an instance for both training and prediction of topic transition was created for every utterance in the dialogues. For each instance x, the term vector $\phi(x)$ was generated with the α values from utterances within the window sizes $h = 2$ for the current and previous turns and $h = 10$ for the history turns. The β values for representing the segment-level relevances were computed based on 3,155 Singapore-related articles which were used in our previous work (Kim et al., 2014b).

For Wikification, all the utterance were preprocessed by Stanford CoreNLP toolkit [2], firstly. Each noun phrase in the constituent trees provided by the parser was considered as an instance for Wikification and manually annotated with the corresponding concept in Wikipedia. For every mention, we retrieved top 100 candidates from the Lucene index based on the Wikipedia database dump as of January 2015 which has 4,797,927 articles and 25,577,464 sections in total and added one more special candidate for NIL detection. Then, a ranking function using SVM^{rank}[3] was trained on this dataset, which achieved 38.04, 31.97, and 34.74 in precision, recall, and F-measure, respectively, in the evaluation for Wikification for each mention-level based on five-fold cross validation. The γ values in our proposed approach were assigned based on the top-ranked results from this ranking fuction for the mentions in the dialogues.

In this evaluation, the following three different schedules were applied for both training the models and prediction the topic transitions: (a) taking every utterance regardless of the speaker into account; (b) considering only the turns taken by the tourists; and (c) by the guides. While the first schedule aims at learning the human behaviours in topic tracking from the third person point of view, the others could show the tracking capabilities of the models as a sub-component in the dialogue system which act as a guide and a tourist, respectively.

The SVM models were trained using SVM^{light} [4] (Joachims, 1999) with different combinations of the features. All the evaluations were done in five-fold cross validation to the manual annotations with two different metrics: one is accuracy of the predicted topic label for every turn, and the other is precision/recall/F-measure for each event of topic transition occurred either in the answer or the predicted result.

Table 2 compares the performances of the feature combinations for each schedule. While the dialogue segment-level β features failed to show significant improvement compared to the baseline only with term vectors, the models with our proposed Wikification-based features γ achieved better performances in both transition and turn-level evaluations for all the schedules. The further enhancement led by the oracle features with the manual annotations for Wikification represented by γ' indicates that the overall performances could be improved by refining the Wikification model.

6 Conclusions

This paper presented a dialogue topic tracking approach using Wikification-based features. This approach aimed to incorporate more detailed information regarding the correspondences between a given dialogue and Wikipedia concepts. Experimental results show that our proposed approach helped to improve the topic tracking performances compared to the baselines. For future work, we plan to apply the kernel methods proposed in our previous work also on the feature spaces based on Wikification as well as to improve the Wikification model itself for achieving better overall performances in dialogue topic tracking.

[2] http://nlp.stanford.edu/software/corenlp.shtml

[3] http://www.cs.cornell.edu/people/tj/svm_light/svm_rank.html

[4] http://svmlight.joachims.org/

References

P. H. Adams and C. H. Martell. 2008. Topic detection and extraction in chat. In *Proceedings of the 2008 IEEE International Conference on Semantic Computing*, pages 581–588.

D. Bohus and A. Rudnicky. 2003. Ravenclaw: dialog management using hierarchical task decomposition and an expectation agenda. In *Proceedings of the European Conference on Speech, Communication and Technology*, pages 597–600.

Razvan C. Bunescu and Marius Pasca. 2006. Using Encyclopedic Knowledge for Named entity Disambiguation. In *EACL*, volume 6, pages 9–16.

Zheng Chen and Heng Ji. 2011. Collaborative ranking: A case study on entity linking. In *Proceedings of the Conference on Empirical Methods in Natural Language Processing*, pages 771–781.

Mark Dredze, Paul McNamee, Delip Rao, Adam Gerber, and Tim Finin. 2010. Entity Disambiguation for Knowledge Base Population. In *Proceedings of the 23rd International Conference on Computational Linguistics*, COLING '10, pages 277–285, Stroudsburg, PA, USA.

Xianpei Han and Le Sun. 2011. A generative entity-mention model for linking entities with knowledge base. In *Proceedings of the 49th Annual Meeting of the Association for Computational Linguistics: Human Language Technologies-Volume 1*, pages 945–954. Association for Computational Linguistics.

T. Joachims. 1999. Making large-scale SVM learning practical. In B. Schölkopf, C. Burges, and A. Smola, editors, *Advances in Kernel Methods - Support Vector Learning*, chapter 11, pages 169–184. MIT Press, Cambridge, MA.

Thorsten Joachims. 2002. Optimizing search engines using clickthrough data. In *Proceedings of the eighth ACM SIGKDD international conference on Knowledge discovery and data mining*, pages 133–142.

S. Kim, R. E. Banchs, and H. Li. 2014a. A composite kernel approach for dialog topic tracking with structured domain knowledge from wikipedia. In *Proceedings of the 52nd Annual Meeting of the Association for Computational Linguistics (Volume 2: Short Papers)*, pages 19–23.

S. Kim, R. E. Banchs, and H. Li. 2014b. Wikipedia-based kernels for dialogue topic tracking. In *Acoustics, Speech and Signal Processing (ICASSP), 2014 IEEE International Conference on*, pages 131–135.

K. Lagus and J. Kuusisto. 2002. Topic identification in natural language dialogues using neural networks. In *Proceedings of the 3rd SIGdial workshop on Discourse and dialogue*, pages 95–102.

C. Lee, S. Jung, and G. G. Lee. 2008. Robust dialog management with n-best hypotheses using dialog examples and agenda. In *Proceedings of the 46th Annual Meeting of the Association for Computational Linguistics: Human Language Technologies*, pages 630–637.

Rada Mihalcea and Andras Csomai. 2007. Wikify!: linking documents to encyclopedic knowledge. In *Proceedings of the sixteenth ACM conference on Conference on information and knowledge management*, pages 233–242.

David Milne and Ian H. Witten. 2008. Learning to link with wikipedia. In *Proceedings of the 17th ACM conference on Information and knowledge management*, pages 509–518.

T. Nakata, S. Ando, and A. Okumura. 2002. Topic detection based on dialogue history. In *Proceedings of the 19th international conference on Computational linguistics (COLING)*, pages 1–7.

S. Roy and L. V. Subramaniam. 2006. Automatic generation of domain models for call centers from noisy transcriptions. In *Proceedings of COLING/ACL*, pages 737–744.

G. Salton, A. Wong, and C.S. Yang. 1975. A vector space model for automatic indexing. *Communications of the ACM*, 18(11):613–620.

S. Young, J. Schatzmann, K. Weilhammer, and H. Ye. 2007. The hidden information state approach to dialog management. In *Proceedings of the International Conference on Acoustics, Speech and Signal Processing (ICASSP)*, pages 149–152.

Exploiting knowledge base to generate responses for natural language dialog listening agents

Sangdo Han, Jeesoo Bang, Seonghan Ryu, Gary Geunbae Lee
Pohang University of Science and Technology (POSTECH), South Korea
hansd, jisus19, ryush, gblee@postech.ac.kr

Abstract

We developed a natural language dialog listening agent that uses a knowledge base (KB) to generate rich and relevant responses. Our system extracts an important named entity from a user utterance, then scans the KB to extract contents related to this entity. The system can generate diverse and relevant responses by assembling the related KB contents into appropriate sentences. Fifteen students tested our system; they gave it higher approval scores than they gave other systems. These results demonstrate that our system generated various responses and encouraged users to continue talking.

1 Introduction

Dialog systems can be separated into task-oriented dialog systems and nontask-oriented dialog systems. Task-oriented dialog systems have mainly been intended to communicate with devices like cellphones or televisions. Nontask-oriented dialog systems are intended for use as entertainment, or to provide casual dialog. In this paper, we studied the listening agent, which is one nontask-oriented dialog system.

The main objective of the listening agent is to analyze user's utterances and to generate appropriate response that satisfies user's desire to speak (Meguro et al., 2009). To satisfy this desire, the system should emulate actual 'listening' by responding appropriately to user utterances in ways that make the user feel that the system is responding specifically to the utterances.

Listening agents should generate various responses to encourage the user to continue the dialog. If responses are monotonous, a dialog can be boring, and a user may lose interest in talking to the system. In previous work, listening agents generated system responses to content extracted from user utterances (Weizenbaum, 1966; Han et al., 2013; Han et al., 2015). For example, when a user talk about the footballer Lionel Messi "I like Messi", the system responses are "Why do you like Messi?", or "You like Messi". However, by using only extracted contents from user utterances, system responses are too restricted to encourage the user to engage in conversation. To increase the user's motivation to interact with the system, the diversity and relevance of the external knowledge that it uses must be increased.

Our objective of this study is to increase the variety of system responses. For the previous example, our system could generate responses like: "What is Messi's position?", "Do you like David Beckham, too?", or "You like Messi, a football player". We also expected encouraging dialog by talking about related information, and increasing dialog satisfaction by pin-pointing the content that user want to talk about. The system extracts named entities from a user utterance, recognizes them, and extracts related information from a knowledge base (KB) to guide generation of responses.

2 Related Work

2.1 Listening Agent

Two main types of listening agents have been developed: non-verbal agents and verbal agents. Non-verbal listening agents generate multimodal responses from multimodal user input (Schroder et al., 2012). Verbal listening agents get text input from user and generate a text response (Weizenbaum, 1966; Han et al., 2013; Han et al., 2015). Our study focused on a verbal listening agent.

2.2 ELIZA & Counseling Dialog System

ELIZA (Weizenbaum, 1966) is a natural language conversation program that interacts with

Proceedings of the SIGDIAL 2015 Conference, pages 129–133,
Prague, Czech Republic, 2-4 September 2015.

a speaker as a psychoterapist would. The system models person-centered therapy, a counseling technique based on the reflective listening strategy (Rautalinko and Lisper, 2004), which aims to encourage a user to continue talking. It includes encouragement, recapitulation, questioning, and reflecting emotion. Because the system generates a response by matching keywords and replaces slot with the contents for user utterance, the variety of responses that it can generate is limited.

Han et al. (2015) developed a listening agent that uses a dialog strategy based on microskills (Ivey et al., 2013), which is a basic communication technique that includes attending, paraphrasing, questioning, and reflecting feeling. This is similar to the reflective listening strategy used in ELIZA. Han's system encourages users to continue talking. Because the system also generates a response based only on information extracted from user utterances, the variety of responses that it can generate is also limited.

ELIZA and Han's dialog strategies are both based on effective listening. In this study, we designed our dialog strategy, focusing on knowledge driven response generation while simultaneously communicating using microskills.

3 System Architecture

Our system (Figure 1) includes five modules: emotion detection, natural language understanding, related information extraction, dialog management, and natural language generation module. The natural language understanding module includes user intention detection, triple extraction, and named entity recognition module.

3.1 Emotion Detection

Our emotion detection module uses a keyword-based method (Guinn and Hubal, 2013). We assembled an emotional keyword lexicon, which includes 170 keywords with 7 basic emotions: sadness, anger, happiness, fear, disgust, contempt, and surprise. Emotional keywords were collected from Ivey's list of 'feeling words' (Ivey et al., 2013). We detect these basic emotion when a user utterance includes one or more of these keywords.

3.2 Natural Language Understanding

3.2.1 User Intention Detection

We detected user intention in collected listening agent training data. We collected dialogues with

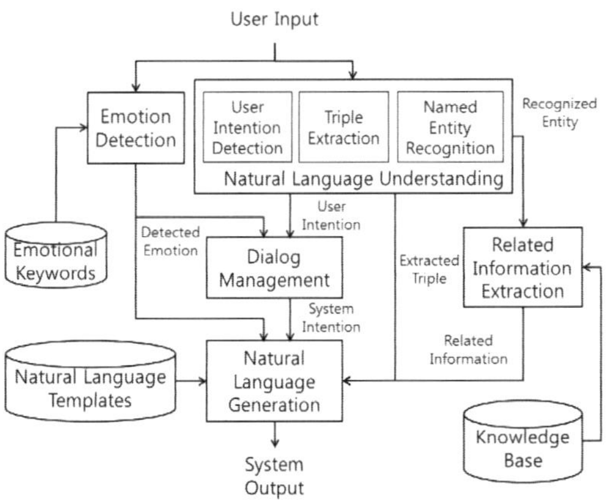

Figure 1: System Architecture. Components and processes are described in the text.

15 students who generated a total of 77 dialogues in English. Students worked in pairs to generate dialogues; one student had the role of speaker or the other had the role of listener. Listeners responded based on listening techniques of microskills. They communicated by text through the internet. The dialog topic was chosen freely by the speaker. Each conversation was restricted to 10 min. This corpus collection process was inspired by Meguro et al. (2009).

We defined five user intentions: 'greeting' (say 'hello' to user), 'self-disclosure' (express users preference and experience), 'informating' (providing information for the dialog), 'questioning' (asking questions to the listener), and 'else' (other utterances). Our definition of user intention also referenced Meguro et al. (2009). In total, 1281 utterances were collected from the speakers; 51.2% were self-disclosure, 32.7% were information, 7.6% were else, 5.7% were greetings, and 2.7% were questions.

We used the maximum entropy classifier (Ratnaparkhi, 1998) with word-n grams (uni-gram, bi-gram, and tri-gram) features to detect user intention.

3.2.2 Triple Extraction

We extracted arguments and their relation (triple) from user utterances. For example, a triple [I, like, Messi] is extracted from "I like Messi". These words are the subject, verb, and object of the sentence. We used ClausIE (Del Corro and Gemulla, 2013) to extract triples, then sent them to the natural language generation module.

3.2.3 Entity Recognition

To extract related information from the KB, the named entities in the user utterances were detected and recognized. Each entity was recognized by matching to an entity name in DBpedia, which is a structured database that contains data from Wikipedia. For example, when "I like Messi" is the input, the module detects "Messi" and matches it with "Lionel Messi", an entity of DBpedia (Auer et al., 2007). We used DBpedia Spotlight (Mendes et al., 2011) for entity detection and recognition. Recognized entities are sent to the related information extraction module.

3.3 Related Information Extraction

The related information extraction module takes a recognized entity as input, then extracts related information from the KB. We used Freebase (Bollacker et al., 2008) as our KB. Freebase is a database system which stores a public repository of the world's knowledge. Because Freebase includes DBpedia, we easily converted DBpedia entities to Freebase entities.

We should choose appropriate related information from Freebase. For example, when a user utterance includes the name of a football player, the topics of the system responses should also be about football players, or the player's position.

For the scenarios above, we extracted type, instances of the type, and properties of the type. For example, when the user talked about a football player, 'Lionel Messi', the system extracts type 'football player', instances of type 'David Beckham', 'Pélé', and other players, and properties such as 'position', 'matches played'.

We used 'notable type' of Freebase. Because an entity can have many types, we used a type that could be the best disambiguator. For example, 'Barack Obama' has multiple types: 'US President', 'Person', 'Politician', 'Author', 'Award Winner'. The 'notable type' that is the best disambiguator is 'US President'.

To generate a system response, we chose one instance and one property. The instance was chosen randomly from top-10 popular instances to find an instance that the user will find relevant interesting. We also chose one property randomly from properties whose object instance is in the top-10 popular instances. We used Freebase popularity score to get top-10 popular instances. Extracted information is sent to the language generation module.

3.4 Dialog Management

The dialog management module returns system intention based on interpretation of emotion and user intention. We generated a rule-based management strategy based on microskills (Algorithm 1) (Evans et al., 2010). Each system intention is given below:

Greeting: Say hello to user.

Attending: Encourage users to continue talking. For example, when a user enters "I watched Avatar", the system responses "Tell me more", "I see", or "Tell me about Avatar".

Paraphrasing: Reflect contents of user utterance. For example, "You watched Avatar", or "You watched Avatar, a movie".

Questioning: Ask questions from user utterance. For example, "Did you watch Titanic, too?", or "Do you know the genre of Avatar?" for same above input.

Reflect Feeling: Acknowledges the user's feeling. When user enters "I was so angry", or "I was annoyed", then the system response could "You were so mad".

Questioning Response: This is our additional strategy to deal with user questions. It changes topic or asks users to talk about themselves. For example, when user asks "Who is your mother?" to system, then questioning response could be "Let's just keep talking about Avatar", or "Why don't we talk about you?".

Algorithm 1 Dialog Management Strategy

```
if User Intention = Greeting then
  return Greeting
else if User Intention = Questioning then
  return Questioning Response
else if User Intention = Information then
  return Paraphrasing or Questioning
else if User Intention = Self Disclosure then
  if Emotion Detected then
    return Reflect Feeling
  else
    return Paraphrasing or Questioning
  end if
else
  return Attending
end if
```

3.5 Natural Language Generation

Our system response is generated using templates. A template is chosen by system intention, entity

System Intention	Entity Location	Related Information	Emotional Keyword	Response Template
Greeting	*	*	*	Nice to meet you.
Attending	*	type	*	Please tell me about the [type], [entity].
Paraphrase	*	*	*	[S] [V] [O].
Paraphrase	S	property	*	[entity], whose [property] is [object], [V] [O]
Questioning	O	instance, type	*	[S] [V] another [type], [instance], too?
Reflect Feeling	*	*	Sad	Oh, cheer up.
Questioning Response	*	*	*	Why don't we talk about you?

Table 1: System Utterance Template Examples. Slots: [S] subject of triple; [V] verb of triple; [O] object of triple; [object] object instance of Freebase triple ; * for don't care condition

Speaker	Utterance
User	Hello.
System	Hi. What do you want to talk about?
User	I want to talk about Messi.
System	Lionel Messi, a football player?
User	Yes. Messi is my favorite.
System	Is David Beckham your favorite, too?
User	No, I just like Messi.
System	What is Lionel Messi's position?
User	It's forward.

Table 2: Dialog Example

location, related information, and detected emotion (Table1). Entity location is the triple slot that includes entity. For example, when a user says, "I like Messi", then the entity location is the object; if the user says, "Messi is my favorite player", then the entity location is the subject. The system response is generated with filling slots with the extracted entity, an extracted triple, and related information. We changed words "I, my, myself, you" to "You, your, yourself, me" by applying simple rules. For example, when a user enters "I like Messi" and a system template "[S] [V] another [type], [instance], too?" is chosen, then system response generated is "You like another football player, David Beckham, too?".

3.6 Experiment and Results

We recruited another 15 students to evaluate our system, who did not join the dialogue generation task in Section 3.2.1. They chatted with three systems (ELIZA (Weizenbaum, 1966), Counseling Dialog System (Han et al., 2015), and our system) for 10 min, they rated each of them on three questions (Likert scale of 1 [low] to 10 [high]). The first question measured the variety of responses, the second question asked whether the system encouraged the user to continue talking, and the last question asked about overall satisfaction with the dialog. Our system got highest score for all questions (Figure 2).

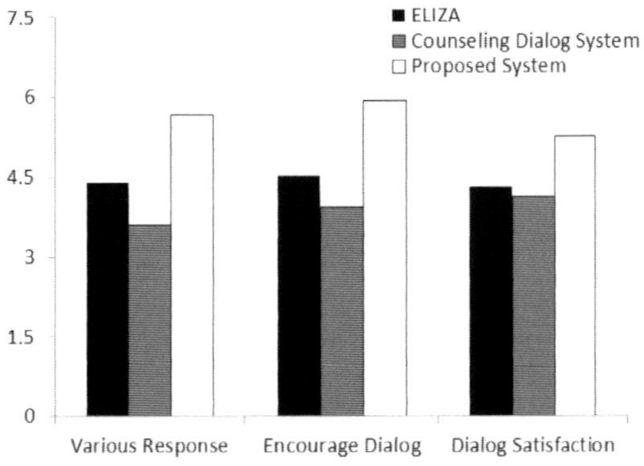

Figure 2: Averaged user experiment score.

3.7 Conclusion

We designed a natural language dialog listening agent that exploits the important and relevant information to the utterance from the KB. Results of our experiment indicated that our usage of a KB generated various responses and encouraged users to continue talking. Related information diversified the contents of system responses, and made users talk with the related information. Dialog satisfaction was increased by pin-pointing the content that user want to talk about.

Acknowledgments

This work was supported by the ICT R&D program of MSIP/IITP. [R0126-15-1117, Core technology development of the spontaneous speech dialogue processing for the language learning] and was partly supported by the ICT R&D progra of MSIP/IITP [14-824-09-014, Basic Software Research in Human-level Lifelong Machine Learning (Machine Learning Center)]

References

Sören Auer, Christian Bizer, Georgi Kobilarov, Jens Lehmann, Richard Cyganiak, and Zachary Ives. 2007. *Dbpedia: A nucleus for a web of open data*. Springer.

Kurt Bollacker, Colin Evans, Praveen Paritosh, Tim Sturge, and Jamie Taylor. 2008. Freebase: a collaboratively created graph database for structuring human knowledge. In *Proceedings of the 2008 ACM SIGMOD international conference on Management of data*, pages 1247–1250. ACM.

Luciano Del Corro and Rainer Gemulla. 2013. Clausie: clause-based open information extraction. In *Proceedings of the 22nd international conference on World Wide Web*, pages 355–366. International World Wide Web Conferences Steering Committee.

David Evans, Margaret Hearn, Max Uhlemann, and Allen Ivey. 2010. *Essential interviewing: A programmed approach to effective communication*. Cengage Learning.

Curry Guinn and Rob Hubal. 2013. Extracting emotional information from the text of spoken dialog. In *Proceedings of the 9th international conference on user modeling*. Citeseer.

Sangdo Han, Kyusong Lee, Donghyeon Lee, and Gary Geunbae Lee. 2013. Counseling dialog system with 5w1h extraction. In *Proceedings of the SIGDIAL2013 Conference*, pages 349–353.

Sangdo Han, Yonghee Kim, and Gary Geunbae Lee. 2015. Micro-counseling dialog system based on semantic content. In *Proceedings of the IWSDS2015 Conference*.

Allen Ivey, Mary Ivey, and Carlos Zalaquett. 2013. *Intentional interviewing and counseling: Facilitating client development in a multicultural society*. Cengage Learning.

Toyomi Meguro, Ryuichiro Higashinaka, Kohji Dohsaka, Yasuhiro Minami, and Hideki Isozaki. 2009. Analysis of listening-oriented dialogue for building listening agents. In *Proceedings of the SIGDIAL 2009 Conference: The 10th Annual Meeting of the Special Interest Group on Discourse and Dialogue*, pages 124–127. Association for Computational Linguistics.

Pablo N Mendes, Max Jakob, Andrés García-Silva, and Christian Bizer. 2011. Dbpedia spotlight: shedding light on the web of documents. In *Proceedings of the 7th International Conference on Semantic Systems*, pages 1–8. ACM.

Adwait Ratnaparkhi. 1998. *Maximum entropy models for natural language ambiguity resolution*. Ph.D. thesis, University of Pennsylvania.

Erik Rautalinko and Hans-Olof Lisper. 2004. Effects of training reflective listening in a corporate setting. *Journal of Business and Psychology*, 18(3):281–299.

Marc Schroder, Elisabetta Bevacqua, Roddy Cowie, Florian Eyben, Hatice Gunes, Dirk Heylen, Mark Ter Maat, Gary McKeown, Sathish Pammi, and Maja Pantic. 2012. Building autonomous sensitive artificial listeners. *Affective Computing, IEEE Transactions on*, 3(2):165–183.

Joseph Weizenbaum. 1966. Eliza: computer program for the study of natural language communication between man and machine. *Communications of the ACM*, 9(1):36–45.

Automated Speech Recognition Technology for Dialogue Interaction with Non-Native Interlocutors

Alexei V. Ivanov[†], **Vikram Ramanarayanan**[†], **David Suendermann-Oeft**[†], **Melissa Lopez**[‡], **Keelan Evanini**[‡] **and Jidong Tao**[‡]
Educational Testing Service R&D
[†] 90 New Montgomery St, # 1500, San Francisco, CA
[‡] 600 Rosedale Road, Princeton, NJ
{aivanou,vramanarayanan,suendermann-oeft,mlopez002,kevanini,jtao}@ets.org

Abstract

Dialogue interaction with remote interlocutors is a difficult application area for speech recognition technology because of the limited duration of acoustic context available for adaptation, the narrow-band and compressed signal encoding used in telecommunications, high variability of spontaneous speech and the processing time constraints. It is even more difficult in the case of interacting with non-native speakers because of the broader allophonic variation, less canonical prosodic patterns, a higher rate of false starts and incomplete words, unusual word choice and smaller probability to have a grammatically well formed sentence. We present a comparative study of various approaches to speech recognition in non-native context. Comparing systems in terms of their accuracy and real-time factor we find that a Kaldi-based Deep Neural Network Acoustic Model (DNN-AM) system with online speaker adaptation by far outperforms other available methods.

1 Introduction

Designing automatic speech recognition (ASR) and spoken language understanding (SLU) modules for spoken dialog systems (SDSs) poses more intricate challenges than standalone ASR systems, for many reasons. First, speech recognition latency is extremely important in a spoken dialog system for smooth operation and a good caller experience; one needs to ensure that recognition hypotheses are obtained in near real-time. Second, one needs to deal with the lack of (or minimal) context, since responses in dialogic situations can often be short and succinct. This also means that one might have to deal with minimal data for model adaptation. Third, these responses being typically spontaneous in nature, often exhibit pauses, hesitations and other disfluencies. Fourth, dialogic applications might have to deal with audio bandwidth limitations that will also have important implications for the recognizer design. For instance, in telephonic speech, the bandwidth (300-3200 Hz) is lesser than that of the hi-fidelity audio recorded at 44.1 kHz. All these issues can drive up the word error rate (WER) of the ASR component. In a recent study comparing several popular ASRs such as Kaldi (Povey et al., 2011), Pocketsphinx (Huggins-Daines et al., 2006) and cloud-based APIs from Apple[1], Google[2] and AT&T[3] in terms of their suitability for use in SDSs, In (Morbini et al., 2013) there was found no particular consensus on the best ASR, but observed that the open-source Kaldi ASR performed competently in comparison with the other closed-source industry-based APIs. Moreover, in a recent study, (Gaida et al., 2014) it was found that Kaldi significantly outperformed other open-source recognizers on recognition tasks on German Verbmobil and English Wall Street Journal corpora. The Kaldi online ASR was also shown to outperform the Google ASR API when integrated into the Czech-based ALEX spoken dialog framework (Plátek and Jurčíček, 2014).

The aforementioned issues with automatic speech recognition in SDSs are only exacerbated in the case of non-native speakers. Not only do non-native speakers pause, hesitate and make false starts more often than native speakers of a language, but their speech is also characterized by a broader allophonic variation, a less canonical prosodic pattern, a higher rate of incomplete words, unusual word choices and a lower probabil-

[1] Apple's Dictation is an OS level feature in both MacOSX and iOS.
[2] https://www.google.com/speech-api/v1/recognize
[3] https://service.research.att.com/smm

Proceedings of the SIGDIAL 2015 Conference, pages 134–138,
Prague, Czech Republic, 2-4 September 2015.

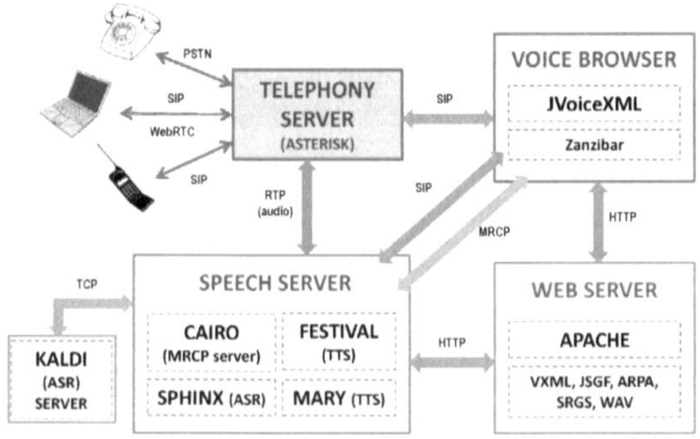

Figure 1: Architecture of the HALEF spoken dialog system.

ity of producing grammatically well-formed sentences. An important application scenario for non-native dialogic speech recognition is the case of conversation-based Computer-Assisted Language Learning (CALL) systems. For instance, *Subarashii* is an interactive dialog system for learning Japanese (Bernstein et al., 1999; Ehsani et al., 2000), where the ASR component of the system was built using the HTK speech recognizer (Young et al., 1993) with both native and non-native acoustic models. In general, the performance of the system after SLU was good for in-domain utterances, but not for out-of-domain utterances. As another example, in Robot Assisted Language Learning (Dong-Hoon and Chung, 2004) and CALL applications for Korean-speaking learners of English (Lee et al., 2010), whose authors showed that acoustic models trained on the Wall Street Journal corpus with an additional 17 hours of Korean children's transcribed English speech for adaptation produced as low as 22.8% WER across multiple domains tested. In the present work, we investigate the online and offline performance of a Kaldi Large Vocabulary Continuous Speech Recognition (LVCSR) system in conjunction with the open-source and distributed HALEF spoken dialog system (Mehrez et al., 2013; Suendermann-Oeft et al., 2015).

2 System description

Figure 1 schematically depicts the main components of the HALEF spoken dialog framework, of which the speech recognizer is a component. The various modules of HALEF include the Asterisk telephony server (van Meggelen et al., 2009), a voice browser based on JVoiceXML (Schnelle-Walka et al., 2013), a web server running Apache Tomcat, and a speech server, which consists of an MRCP server (Prylipko et al., 2011) in addition to text-to-speech (TTS) engines—Festival (Taylor et al., 1998) and Mary (Schröder and Trouvain, 2003)—as well as support for Sphinx-4 (Lamere et al., 2003) and Kaldi (Povey et al., 2011) ASRs. In contrast to Sphinx-4 which is tightly integrated into the speech server code base, Kaldi-based ASR is installed on an own server, which is communicating with the speech server via TCP socket. The advantages of this design decision are (a) the ease of management of the computational resources, required by Kaldi when operating in real-time mode (including the potential use of Graphical Processing Units (GPUs)), which could otherwise interfere with the other processes running on the speech server (audio streaming, TTS, Session Initiation Protocol (SIP) and Media Resource Control Protocol (MRCP) communication) and (b) the ease to test the very speech recognizer used in the live SDS also in the offline mode, for example for batch experiments. Often ASR configurations in live SDSs differ from batch systems that may result in different behaviour w.r.t. WER, latency, etc.

In this paper, we will be focusing specifically on evaluating the performance of the Kaldi ASR system within HALEF (we have already covered the Sphinx version in the papers cited above). We generally follow Kaldi's WSJ standard model generation recipe with a few modifications to accommodate our training data. The most sophisticated acoustic models are obtained with speaker adaptive training (SAT) on the feature Maximum Likelihood Linear Regression (fMLLR)-adapted data.

We use about 780 hours of non-native English speech to train the acoustic model. The speaker population covers a diversity of native languages, geographical locations and age groups. In order to match the audio quality standard of the Public Switched Telephone Network (PSTN), we reduce the sampling rate of our recordings down to 8 kHz. The language model was estimated on the manual transcriptions of the same training corpus consisting of ≈ 5.8 million tokens and finally was represented as a trigram language model with ≈ 525 thousand trigrams and ≈ 605 thousand bigrams over a lexicon of ≈ 23 thousand words which included entries for the most frequent partially produced words (e.g. ATTR-; ATTRA-; ATTRAC-

; ATTRACT; ATTRACT-; ATTRACTABLE). Ultimately, the final decoding graph was compiled having approximately 5.5 million states and 14 million arcs.

The default Kaldi speech recognizer use case is oriented towards optimal performance in transcription of large amounts of pre-recorded speech. In these circumstances there exists a possibility to perform several recognition passes and estimate the adaptation transformation from a substantial body of spoken material. The highest performing Deep Neural Network (DNN) acoustic model ("nnet2" in Kaldi notation) requires a prior processing pass with the highest performing Gaussian Mixture Model (GMM, "tri4b" in Kaldi notation), which in turn requires a prior processing pass with the same GMM in the speaker-independent mode.

However, in the dialogue environment, it is essential to be able to produce recognition results with the smallest possible latency and little adaptation material. That is the main reason for us to look for alternatives to the mentioned approach. One such possibility is to use the DNN acoustic model with un-adapted data and constrain its output via a speaker-dependent i-Vector (Dehak et al., 2011). This i-Vector contains information on centroids of the speaker-dependent GMM. The i-Vector can be continuously re-estimated based on the available up-to-the-moment acoustic evidence ("online" mode) or after presentation of the entire spoken content (the so called "offline" mode).

3 Experiments

The evaluation was performed using vocal productions obtained from language learners in the scope of large-scale internet-based language assessment. The production length is a major distinction of this data from the data one may expect to find in the spoken dialogue domain. The individual utterance is a quasi-spontaneous monologue elicited by a certain evaluation setup. The utterances were collected from six different test questions comprising two different speaking tasks: 1) providing an opinion based on personal experience and 2) summarizing or discussing material provided in a reading and/or listening passage. The longest utterances are expected to last up to a minute. The average speaking rate is about 2 words per second. Every speaker produces up to six such utterances. Speakers had a brief time to familiarize themselves with the task and prepare an approximate production plan. Although in strict terms, these productions are different from the true dialogue behavior, they are suitable for the purposes of the dialogic speech recognition system development.

The evaluation of the speech recognition system was performed using the data obtained in the same fashion as the training material. Two sets are used: the development set (dev), containing 593 utterances (68329 tokens, 3575 singletons, 0% OOV rate) coming from 100 speakers with the total amount of audio exceeding 9 hours; and the test set (test), that contains 599 utterances (68112 tokens, 3709 singletons, 0.18% OOV rate) coming from 100 speakers (also more than 9 hours of speech in total). We attempted to have a non-biased random speaker sampling, covering a broad range of native languages, English speaking proficiency levels, demographics, etc. However, no extensive effort has been spent to ensure that frequencies of the stratified sub-populations follow their natural distribution. Comparative results are presented in Table 1.

As it can be learned from Table 1, the "DNN i-Vector" method of speech recognition outperforms Kaldi's default "DNN fMLLR" setup. This can be explained by the higher variability of non-native speech. In this case the reduced complexity of the i-Vector speaker adaptation matches better the task that we attempt to solve. There is only a very minor degradation of the accuracy with the reduction of the i-Vector support data from the whole interaction to a single utterance. As expected, the "online" scenario loses some accuracy to the "offline" in the utterance beginning, as we could verify by analyzing multiple recognition results.

It is also important to notice that the accuracy of the "DNN i-Vector" system compares favorably with human performance in the same task. In fact, experts have the average WER of about 15% (Zechner, 2009), while Turkers in a crowdsourcing environment perform significantly worse, around 30% WER (Evanini et al., 2010). Our proposed system is therefore already approaching the level of broadly defined average human accuracy in the task of non-native speech transcription.

The "DNN i-Vector" ASR method vastly outperforms the baseline in terms of processing speed. Even with the large vocabulary model in a typical 10-second spoken turn we expect to have only 3 seconds of ASR-specific processing latency. Indeed, in order to obtain an expected de-

System	Adaptation	WER (dev)	WER (test)	xRT
GMM SI	Offline, whole interaction	37.58%	37.98%	0.46
GMM fMLLR	Offline, whole interaction	29.96%	31.73%	2.10
DNN fMLLR	Offline, whole interaction	22.58%	24.44%	3.44
DNN i-Vector	Online, whole interaction	21.87%	23.33%	1.11
DNN i-Vector	Offline, whole interaction	**21.81%**	23.29%	1.05
DNN i-Vector	Online, every utterance	22.01%	23.48%	**1.30**
DNN i-Vector	Offline, every utterance	21.90%	**23.22%**	1.13

Table 1: Accuracy and speed of the explored ASR configurations; WER – Word Error Rate; (dev) - as measured on the development set; (test) – as measured on the test set; xRT - Real Time factor, i.e. the ratio between processing time and audio duration; SI - Speaker Independent mode.

lay one shall subtract the duration of an utterance from the total processing time as the "online" recognizer commences speech processing at the moment that speech is started. That 3 seconds delay is very close to the natural inter-turn pause of 0.5 – 1.5 seconds. Better language modeling is expected to bring the xRT factor below one. The difference of the xRT factor between the "online" and "offline" modes can be explained with somewhat lower quality of acoustic normalization in the "online" case. Larger numbers of hypotheses fit within the decoder's search beam and, thus, increase the processing time.

4 Conclusions

The DNN i-Vector speech recognition method has proven to be sufficient in the task of supporting a dialogue interaction with non-native speakers. In respect to our baseline systems we observe improvements both in accuracy and processing speed. The "online" mode of operation appears particularly attractive because it allows to minimize the processing latency at the cost of a minor performance degradation. Indeed, the "online" recognizer is capable to start the processing simultaneously with the start of speech production. Thus, unlike the "offline" case, the total perceived latency in the case of "online" recognizer is xRT-1.

There are ways to improve our system by performing a more targeted language modeling and, possibly, language model adaptation to a specific dialogue turn. Our further efforts will be directed to reducing processing latency and increasing the system's robustness by incorporating interpretation feedback into the decoding process.

We plan to perform a comparative error analysis to have a better picture of how our automated system compares to the average human performance. It is important to separately evaluate WERs for the content vs functional word subgroups; determine the balance between insertions, deletions and substitutions in the optimal operating point; compare humans and machines in ability to recover back from the context of the mis-recognized word (e.g. a filler or false start).

We plan to collect actual spoken dialogue interactions to further refine our system through a crowdsourcing experiment in a language assessment task. Specifically, the ASR sub-sytem can benefit from sampling the elicited responses, measuring their apparent semantic uncertainty and tailoring system's lexicon and language model to better handle acoustic uncertainty of non-native speech.

References

Jared Bernstein, Amir Najmi, and Farzad Ehsani. 1999. Subarashii: Encounters in Japanese spoken language education. *CALICO Journal*, 16(3):361–384.

Najim Dehak, Patrick J. Kenny, Réda Dehak, Pierre Dumouchel, and Pierre Ouellet. 2011. Front–end factor analysis for speaker verication. In *IEEE Trans. on Audio, Speech and Language Processing*, volume 19, pages 788–798.

AHN Dong-Hoon and Minhwa Chung. 2004. One-pass semi-dynamic network decoding using a subnetwork caching model for large vocabulary continuous speech recongnition. *IEICE Trans. on Information and Systems*, 87(5):1164–1174.

Farzad Ehsani, Jared Bernstein, and Amir Najmi. 2000. An interactive dialog system for learning Japanese. *Speech Communication*, 30(2):167–177.

Keelan Evanini, Derrick Higgins, and Klaus Zechner. 2010. Using Amazon Mechanical Turk for transcription of non-native speech. In *Proc. of the NAACL HLT Conference, Los Angeles, CA*.

Christian Gaida, Patrick Lange, Rico Petrick, Patrick Proba, Ahmed Malatawy, and David Suendermann-Oeft. 2014. Comparing open-source speech recognition toolkits. In *Technical Report, http://suendermann.com/su/pdf/oasis2014.pdf*.

D. Huggins-Daines, M. Kumar, A. Chan, A. Black, M. Ravishankar, and A. Rudnicky. 2006. Pocketsphinx: a free, real-time continuous speech recognition system for hand-held devices. In *Proc. of the Int. Conf. on Acoustics, Speech and Signal Processing (ICASSP)*, Toulouse, France.

P. Lamere, P. Kwok, E. Gouvea, B. Raj, R. Singh, W. Walker, M. Warmuth, and P. Wolf. 2003. The CMU SPHINX-4 speech recognition system. In *Proc. of the Int. Conf. on Acoustics, Speech and Signal Processing (ICASSP)*, Hong Kong, China.

Sungjin Lee, Hyungjong Noh, Jonghoon Lee, Kyusong Lee, and G Lee. 2010. Postech approaches for dialog-based english conversation tutoring. *Proc. of Asia-Pacific Signal and Information Processing Association (APSIPA) Annual Summit and Conference, Singapore*, pages 794–803.

T. Mehrez, A. Abdelkawy, Y. Heikal, P. Lange, H. Nabil, and D. Suendermann-Oeft. 2013. Who discovered the electron neutrino? A telephony-based distributed open-source standard-compliant spoken dialog system for question answering. In *Proc. of the German Society for Computational Linguistics (GSCL), Int. Conf. of the*, Darmstadt, Germany.

Fabrizio Morbini, Kartik Audhkhasi, Kenji Sagae, Ron Artstein, Dogan Can, Panayiotis Georgiou, Shri Narayanan, Anton Leuski, and David Traum. 2013. Which asr should i choose for my dialogue system. In *Proc. of the 14th annual SIGdial Meeting on Discourse and Dialogue, Metz, France*, pages 394–403.

Ondřej Plátek and Filip Jurčíček. 2014. Integration of an on-line kaldi speech recogniser to the Alex dialogue systems framework. In *Text, Speech and Dialogue*, pages 603–610. Springer.

Daniel Povey, Arnab Ghoshal, Gilles Boulianne, Lukas Burget, Ondrej Glembek, Nagendra Goel, Mirko Hannemann, Petr Motlicek, Yanmin Qian, Petr Schwarz, Jan Silovsky, Georg Stemmer, and Karel Vesely. 2011. The Kaldi speech recognition toolkit. In *Proc. of the Automatic Speech Recognition and Understanding (ASRU), Int. Workshop on*, Hawaii, USA.

D. Prylipko, D. Schnelle-Walka, S. Lord, and A. Wendemuth. 2011. Zanzibar OpenIVR: an open-source framework for development of spoken dialog systems. In *Proc. of the Text, Speech and Dialogue (TSD), Int. Conf. on*, Pilsen, Czech Republic.

D. Schnelle-Walka, S. Radomski, and M. Mühlhäuser. 2013. JVoiceXML as a modality component in the W3C multimodal architecture. *Journal on Multimodal User Interfaces*, 7:183–194.

Marc Schröder and Jürgen Trouvain. 2003. The German text-to-speech synthesis system MARY: A tool for research, development and teaching. *International Journal of Speech Technology*, 6(4):365–377.

David Suendermann-Oeft, Vikram Ramanarayanan, Moritz Teckenbrock, Felix Neutatz, and Dennis Schmidt. 2015. Halef: an open-source standard-compliant telephony-based modular spoken dialog system–a review and an outlook. In *International Workshop on Spoken Dialog Systems (IWSDS) 2015, Busan, South Korea*.

P. Taylor, A. Black, and R. Caley. 1998. The architecture of the Festival speech synthesis system. In *Proc. of the ESCA Workshop on Speech Synthesis*, Jenolan Caves, Australia.

J. van Meggelen, J. Smith, and L. Madsen. 2009. *Asterisk: The Future of Telephony*. O'Reilly, Sebastopol, USA.

S. Young, P. Woodland, and W. Byrne. 1993. *The HTK Book, Version 1.5*. Cambridge University, Cambridge, UK.

Klaus Zechner. 2009. What did they actually say? Agreement and disagreement among transcribers of non-native spontaneous speech responses in an English proficiency test. In *Proc. of the ISCA SLaTE Workshop, Wroxall Abbey Estate, Warwickshire, England*.

Conversational Knowledge Teaching Agent that Uses a Knowledge Base

Kyusong LEE, Paul Hongsuck SEO, Junhwi CHOI, Sangjun KOO, Gary Geunbae LEE
Department of Computer Science and Engineering,
Pohang University of Science and Technology, South Korea
{Kyusonglee, hsseo, chasunee, giantpanda, gblee}@postech.ac.kr

Abstract

When implementing a conversational educational teaching agent, user-intent understanding and dialog management in a dialog system are not sufficient to give users educational information. In this paper, we propose a conversational educational teaching agent that gives users some educational information or triggers interests on educational contents. The proposed system not only converses with a user but also answer questions that the user asked or asks some educational questions by integrating a dialog system with a knowledge base. We used the Wikipedia corpus to learn the weights between two entities and embedding of properties to calculate similarities for the selection of system questions and answers.

1 Introduction

Dialog is the most natural interaction between a mentor and mentee in the real world. Therefore, dialog-based intelligent tutoring systems (ITSs) have been widely studied to teach science (Jordan et al., 2013; Litman and Silliman, 2004; Graesser et al., 2004; VanLehn et al., 2002; Vanlehn et al., 2005), foreign language (Kyusong et al., 2014;Lee et al., 2010; Lee et al., 2011;Johnson et al., 2007), and programming language (Fossati et al., 2008; Lane and VanLehn, 2015) usually without intervention from a human teacher. However, previous dialog-based language learning systems mostly only play the role of a conversational partner using chatting like spoken dialog technology, and providing feedback such as grammatical error correction and suggesting better expressions. However, in real situations, students usually ask many questions to indulge their curiosity and a tutor also asks questions to continue the conversation and maintain students' interest during the learning process. In science and programming language learning, mostly pre-designed scenarios and contents are necessary; these are usually handcrafted by human education experts. However, this process is expensive and time-consuming.

Our group is currently involved in a project called POSTECH Immersive English Study (POMY). The program allows users to exercise their visual, aural and tactile senses to receive a full immersion experience to develop into independent EFL learners and to increase their memory and concentration abilities to the greatest extent (Kyusong Lee et al., 2014). During field tests, we found that many advanced students asked questions that cannot be answered using only a dialog system[1]. Recently, knowledge base (KB) data such as freebase and DBpedia have become publicly available. Using the KB, knowledge base question answering (KB-QA) has been studied (Berant and Liang, 2014); it has advantages of very high precision because it exploits huge databases. Hence, we proposed a dialog-based intelligent tutoring system that uses a KB, as an extension of POMY, POMY Intelligent Tutoring System (POMY-ITS). The main advantage is that the human cost to manually construct educational contents is eliminated. Moreover, the system chooses its response after considering information importance, current discourse, relative weights between two entities, and property similarity. The additional functions of the POMY-ITS are that it:

1) Answers user's question such as factoid questions, word meaning;

[1] http://isoft.postech.ac.kr/research/language_learning/db-call/videos/e3-1.mp4

Proceedings of the SIGDIAL 2015 Conference, pages 139–143,
Prague, Czech Republic, 2-4 September 2015.

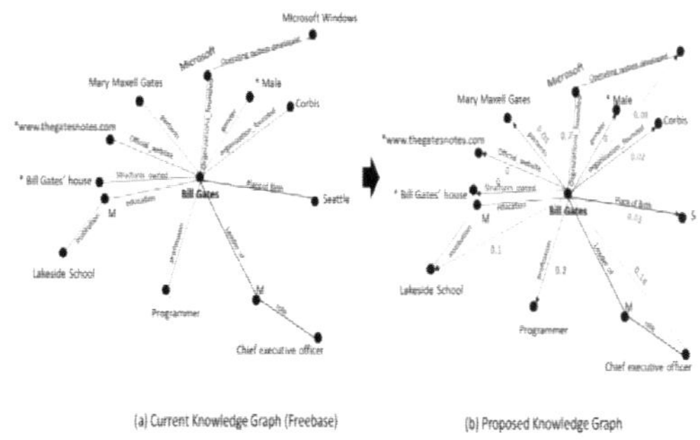

Figure 1: current knowledge graph is undirected graph and proposed knowledge graph is directed weighted graph. (* denote the weight is 0 which meant the tutor never asked about this question)

2) Generates questions to continue the conversation and to interest the user;
3) Uses entities and properties in freebase to generate useful information that might interest a user, and presents it in natural language.

To implement 1) the QA function, we used Parasempre (Berant and Liang, 2014) based KB-QA system as our QA system. However, in this paper, we focus only on 2) and 3) which are generating questions or informing by selecting appropriate entity and property in the KB; we do not present the detailed explanation or assess the accuracy of the QA system.

2 Intuition of the system

A user who asks about Bill Gates, may also be interested in Microsoft and Paul Allen, which are topics strongly related to Bill Gates. In the KB graph, the 'Bill Gates' entity is connected to many other entities. However, these connections present too much information, such as URLs of related websites, gender of Bill Gates, published books, music, and architecture. However, KB does not contain the entity importance or weighted relationship between entities and properties (Figure 1). This information can be useful to POMY-ITS to enable it to decide what to ask or talk about. When a system and a user are talking about Bill Gates' wife's name, the user may also want to know when they got married or who Bill Gates' other family members are. Manual construction of the entity relationship or order of scenarios would be very expensive. Our system considers entity and property to decide automatically what to ask or to inform. To deploy the system, we used the Wikipedia corpus to learn property similarity, and weight between two entity pairs.

Algorithm 1 : *RuleBasedDA* (U,S_{i-1})

Require: U: user utterance
Require: S_{i-1}: previous system action
1: ***if*** U contains WH questions **and** *IsEntity*(U)
2: ***then*** $DA = U{:}Question$
3: ***else* if** S_{i-1} is *S:Question*
4: ***then*** $DA = U{:}Answer$
5: ***else***
6: ***then*** $DA = U{:}others$

Algorithm 1: Generation Algorithm, *IsEntity* returns true is when entity is detected in user utterance

Table 1: Example dialog and user dialog act and system action (S:system, U:user)

Utterance	Dialog Act
U:Hi, nice to meet you.	U:others
S:Hello, good to see you.	Matched Example
U:Who is Bill Gates?	U:question
S:Bill Gates is organization learner and programmer.	S:Answer
S:Do you know what company Bill Gates founded?	S:Question
U:Microsoft	U:answer
S: That's right. S: Bill Gates founded Microsoft with Paul Allen	S:CheckAnswer S: Inform

3 Method

The main role of the POMY-ITS is to give information that a user wants to know. The KB-QA technology will give the answer if the utterance is a 'wh' question, but often, a user does not know what to ask. Thus, the conversation must include initiative dialog. When the dialog between a tutor and a user stalls, the tutor should ask a relevant question to or give useful information related to the current context.

3.1 The Role of Dialog Management

First, the system should know whether a user utterance is a question, an answer, or has some other function (Algorithm 1). If the user utterance is a question, KB-QA will answer. If the utterance is an answer, the system will check whether or not the user utterance is correct. Otherwise, we used the example based dialog system which uses a similarity measure to find an example sentence in the example DB (Nio et al., 2014), and utters the sentence (Table 1). The following are the system actions such as *Answer, Question (entity, property), Inform (entity, property, obj, CheckUserAnswer.* To generate the next system utterance, we should select arguments such as entity, property, and object. For example,

- *Question* (entity="*Bill Gates*", property="*organization.founded*") will generate "Do you

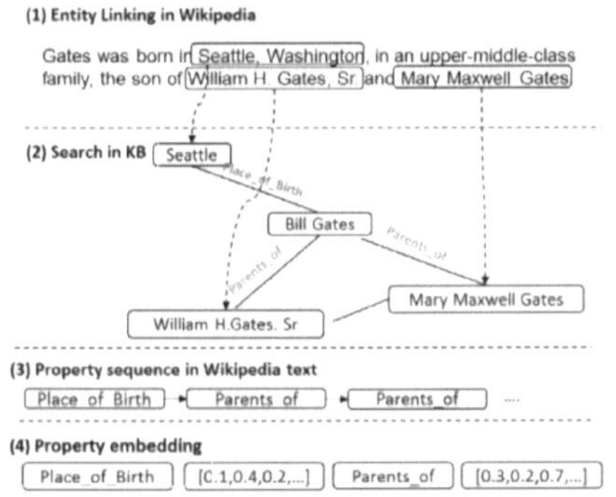

Figure 2: Procedure of property embedding

want to know the company Bill Gates founded?"

- *Inform(entity="Bill Gates", property=" organization.founded",obj="Microsoft")* will generate "Bill Gates founded Microsoft"

In this paper, we mainly explore how to select the most appropriate entity and property for generating system utterances.

3.2 Weight between two entities

Freebase is stored in a graph structure. The entity 'Bill Gates' is linked to many properties and entities in 'triple' format. However, the edges are not weighted. When the system provides useful information to a user about Bill Gates, then his profession, or books that he wrote will be more interesting to a user than Gates' gender or URL information. Moreover, the relationship between two entities can be represented as a directional graph. When we explain about Bill Gates, Basic programing language is important because he used it when he was programming. However, when we explain about Basic programing language, Bill Gates is not very important. Entities in Wikipedia are linked (Mendes et al., 2011) to obtain the weight information. Weight $w(v_t, v_j)$ is obtained as the follows when v_t is 'Bill Gates' and v_j is 'Microsoft'; First, we need the number of occurrence of "Microsoft" entity in the "Bill Gates" Wikipedia page to get $Freq(v_j)_{v_t}$. Second, we search the shortest path from "Bill Gates" to "Microsoft" in Freebase KB graph, then count the number of properties to get $n(v_t, v_j)$.

$$w(v_t, v_j) = \alpha \frac{Freq(v_j)_{v_t}}{\sum_{v_k \in \forall V_t} Freq(v_k)_{v_t}} + \beta \frac{1}{n(v_t, v_j)} \quad (1)$$

$Freq(v_j)_{v_t}$ denotes frequency of v_j in Wikipedia v_t page. $\forall V_t$ denotes all entities in the Wikipedia v_t page. $n(v_t, v_j)$ denotes # of hops between v_t and v_j (e.g., n(Billl Gates, Microsoft) = 1, n(Bill Gates, Microsoft Windows) = 2 in Figure 1-(a)) We eliminate edges that have $w(v_t, v_j) = 0$ and nodes where $n(v_t, v_j) > 2$ (a 'more than 3 hop' relationship). α and β are currently set to 1.

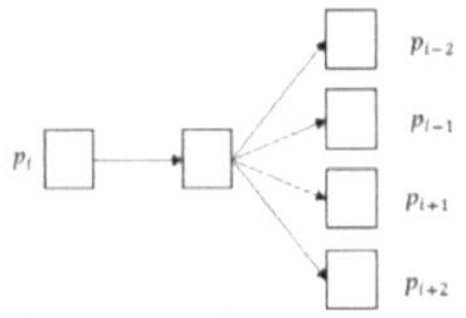

Figure 3 Skip-gram of property embedding

3.3 Property Embedding

The intuition of property-embedding similarity is as follows: when a user is talking about Bill Gates' professional achievement, POMY-ITS's best option would be to explain something related to professional achievement. However, designing all possible replies manually would be too expensive. When a user asks about Bill Gates' parents, POMY-ITS's best option would be to explain or ask the user about Gates' other family members. To determine that the "*people.person.parents*" property is more similar to "*people.person.children*" than "*people.person.employment_history*" (Figure 5), property-embedding vectors are generated to compute the similarity between two properties. We first obtain the sequence of the property from the Wikipedia corpus (Figure 2), then we use Skip-gram to train the vectors (Figure 3). The training objective of the Skip-gram model is to find word representations that are useful to predict the surrounding (Mikolov et al., 2013). We used skip-gram to predict the next property r given the current property as the following equation:

$$\frac{1}{T}\sum_{t=1}^{T} \sum_{-2<j<2, j\neq 0} log p(r_{t+j} | r_t) \quad (2)$$

where r_t denotes current property. The basic Skip-gram formulation uses the soft-max function to define $p(r_{t+j}|r_t)$:

$$p(r_O|r_I) = \frac{\exp(v'^{\top}_{r_O} v_{r_I})}{\sum_{r=1}^{R} exp(v'^{\top}_{r} v_{r_I})} \quad (3)$$

where v_r and v'_r are, respectively, the input and output vector representations of r, and R is the number of properties in Freebase.

3.4 System Utterance Generation

After choosing entity and property, we can generate either *question* or *inform* sentences. Template-based natural language generation uses rules (Table 2) to generate question utterances. Questions begin with a question word, are followed by the

Freebase description of the expected answer type d(t), the further followed by Freebase descriptions of entities d(e) and d(p). To fill in auxiliary verbs, determiners, and prepositions, we parse the description d(p) into one of NP, VP, PP, or NP VP. For *inform* system actions, we generate the sentences from triple <Bill Gates, organization.founded, Microsoft> to "Bill Gates founded Microsoft" as follows: extract the triple from the text, and disambiguate to KB entities. Then, align to existing triples in KB, fourth. Finally, collect matched phrase-property pairs from aligned triples.

Table 2: Template of questioning. WH represents "Do you know what".

Rule	Example
WH d(t) has d(e) as NP?	WH election contest has George Bush as winner?
WH d(t) (AUX) VP d(e)?	WH radio station serves area New-York?
WH PP d(e) ?	WH beer from region Argentina?
WH d(t) VP the NP d(e)?	WH mass transportation system served the area Berlin?

3.5 Experiment and Result

To compare the weight of two entities, 10 human experts ranked among the 60 entities that were most closely related to the target entity. We asked them to rank the entities as if they were teaching students about the target entities such as "Bill Gates", "Steve Jobs", "Seoul", etc. We considered the human labeled rankings to be the correct answers, and compared them to answers provided by the proposed method and word2vec[2] (Figure 4); as a similarity statistic we used the average score of Mean reciprocal rank (MRR). We obtained MRR scores 10 times, then got mean and standard deviation by repeating one human labels as the answer and another human labels as the test; this allows quantification of the correlation between human labels. The results show that human-to-human has the highest correlation. Next, the correlation between human and the proposed method is significantly better than between human and word2vec (Figure 4). We found that word2vec has high similarity when entities are of the same type; e.g., Melinda Gates, Steve Ballmer, and Jeff are all "person" in Table 3. However, humans and the proposed system selected entities of different types such as 'Microsoft' and "Windows". Thus, semantic similarity does not necessarily represent the most related entities for explanation about the target entity in the educational perspective. To show property similarity, we plot in the 2D space using t-SNE (Van der Maaten and Hinton, 2008).

Table 3: Ranked Results of the top 5 entities generated for Bill Gates

Rank	Human	Proposed	Word2Vec
1	Microsoft	Microsoft	Melinda Gates
2	MS Windows	Paul Allen	Steve Ballmer
3	MS-DOS	Harvard Unv.	Bill Melinda Gates Foundation
4	Harvard Univ.	Lakeside School	Feff_Raikes
5	OS/2	CEO	Ray Ozzie

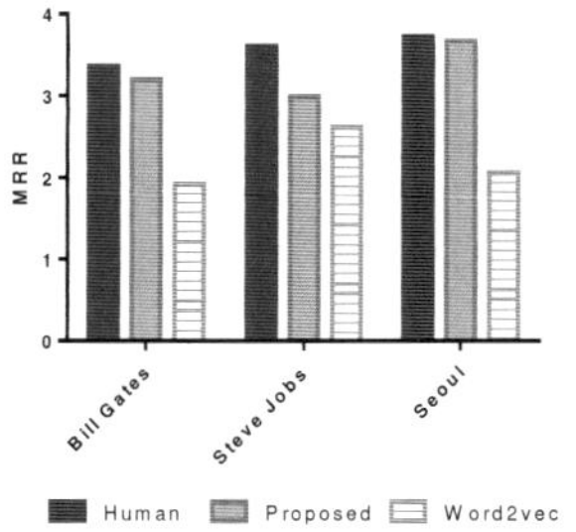

Figure 4: Mean and SD of MRR scores for 10 human labeled rankings

Figure 5: plotting property-embedding vectors

The graph shows that similar properties are closely plotted in 2D space, especially *people.person.children* and *people.person.parents* (Figure 5). This is exactly consistent with our purpose of property-embedding, and our property-embedding model is available[3] which includes 779 total properties and 100 dimension.

4 Conclusion

We developed a conversational knowledge-teaching agent using knowledge base for educational purposes. To generate proper system utterance, we obtained the weight between two entities and property similarity. The proposed method significantly improved upon baseline methods. In the future, we will improve our conversational agent for knowledge education more tightly integrated into QA systems and dialog systems.

[2] The model of freebase entity embedding is already available in https://code.google.com/p/word2vec/

[3] http://isoft.postech.ac.kr/~kyusonglee/sigdial/p.emb.vec

Acknowledgements

This research was supported by the Basic Science Research Program through the National Research Foundation of Korea (NRF) funded by the Ministry of Education, Science and Technology (2010-0019523) and was supported by ATC(Advanced Technology Center) Program-"Development of Conversational Q&A Search Framework Based On Linked Data: Project No. 10048448 and was partly supported by Institute for Information & communications Technology Promotion(IITP) grant funded by the Korea government(MSIP) (No. R0101-15-0176, Development of Core Technology for Human-like Self-taught Learning based on a Symbolic Approach)

References

Jonathan Berant and Percy Liang. 2014. Semantic parsing via paraphrasing. In Proceedings of ACL,volume 7, page 92.

Jenny Brusk, Preben Wik, and Anna Hjalmarsson. 2007. Deal a serious game for call practicing conversational skills in the trade domain. Proceedings of SLATE 2007.

Davide Fossati, Barbara Di Eugenio, Christopher Brown, and Stellan Ohlsson. 2008. Learning linked lists: Experiments with the ilist system. In Intelligent tutoring systems, pages 80–89. Springer.

Arthur C Graesser, Shulan Lu, George Tanner Jackson, Heather Hite Mitchell, Mathew Ventura, Andrew Olney, and Max M Louwerse. 2004. Autotutor: A tutor with dialogue in natural language. Behavior Research Methods, Instruments, & Computers, 36(2):180–192.

WLewis Johnson, NingWang, and ShuminWu. 2007. Experience with serious games for learning foreign languages and cultures. In Proceedings of the SimTecT Conference.

Pamela Jordan, Patricia Albacete, Michael J Ford, Sandra Katz, Michael Lipschultz, Diane Litman, Scott Silliman, and Christine Wilson. 2013. Interactive event: The rimac tutor-a simulation of the highly interactive nature of human tutorial dialogue. In Artificial Intelligence in Education, pages 928–929. Springer.

LEE Kyusong, Soo-Ok Kweon, LEE Sungjin, NOH Hyungjong, and Gary Geunbae Lee. 2014. Postech immersive english study (pomy): Dialog-based language learning game. IEICE TRANSACTIONS on Information and Systems, 97(7):1830–1841.

H Chad Lane and Kurt VanLehn. 2005. Teaching the tacit knowledge of programming to noviceswith natural language tutoring. Computer Science Education, 15(3):183–201.

Sungjin Lee, Hyungjong Noh, Jonghoon Lee, Kyusong Lee, and G Lee. 2010. Postech approaches for dialog-based english conversation tutoring. Proc. APSIPA ASC, pages 794–803.

Sungjin Lee, Hyungjong Noh, Jonghoon Lee, Kyusong Lee, Gary Geunbae Lee, Seongdae Sagong, and Munsang Kim. 2011. On the effectiveness of robotassisted language learning. ReCALL, 23(01):25–58.

Diane J Litman and Scott Silliman. 2004. Itspoke: An intelligent tutoring spoken dialogue system. In Demonstration papers at HLT-NAACL 2004, pages 5–8. Association for Computational Linguistics.

Pablo N Mendes, Max Jakob, Andr´es Garc´ıa-Silva, and Christian Bizer. 2011. Dbpedia spotlight: shedding light on the web of documents. In Proceedings of the 7th International Conference on Semantic Systems, pages 1–8. ACM.

Tomas Mikolov, Kai Chen, Greg Corrado, and Jeffrey Dean. 2013. Efficient estimation of word representations in vector space. arXiv preprint arXiv:1301.3781.

Hazel Morton and Mervyn A Jack. 2005. Scenariobased spoken interaction with virtual agents. Computer Assisted Language Learning, 18(3):171–191.

Lasguido Nio, Sakriani Sakti, Graham Neubig, Tomoki Toda, and Satoshi Nakamura. 2014. Improving the robustness of example-based dialog retrieval using recursive neural network paraphrase identification. SLT 2014.

Laurens Van der Maaten and Geoffrey Hinton. 2008. Visualizing data using t-sne. Journal of Machine Learning Research, 9(2579-2605):85.

Kurt VanLehn, PamelaWJordan, Carolyn P Ros´e, Dumisizwe Bhembe, Michael B¨ottner, Andy Gaydos, Maxim Makatchev, Umarani Pappuswamy, Michael

Ringenberg, Antonio Roque, et al. 2002. The architecture of why2-atlas: A coach for qualitative physics essay writing. In Intelligent tutoring systems, pages 158–167. Springer.

Kurt Vanlehn, Collin Lynch, Kay Schulze, Joel A Shapiro, Robert Shelby, Linwood Taylor, Don Treacy, Anders Weinstein, and Mary Wintersgill. 2005. The andes physics tutoring system: Lessons learned. International Journal of Artificial Intelligence in Education, 15(3):147–204.

Information Theoretical and Statistical Features for Intrinsic Plagiarism Detection

Rashedur Rahman
IRT-SystemX & LIMSI-CNRS
Paris-Sud University
rashedur.rahman@limsi.fr

Abstract

In this paper we present some information theoretical and statistical features including function word skip n-grams for detecting plagiarism intrinsically. We train a binary classifier with different feature sets and observe their performances. Basically, we propose a set of 36 features for classifying plagiarized and non-plagiarized texts in suspicious documents. Our experiment finds that entropy, relative entropy and correlation coefficient of function word skip n-gram frequency profiles are very effective features. The proposed feature set achieves F-Score of 85.10%.

1 Introduction

Extrinsic plagiarism detection attempts to detect whether a document is plagiarised relative to reference documents. IPD (intrinsic plagiarism detection), which is relatively new, detects the plagiarised section(s) in a suspicious document *without* using any reference document. The basic hypothesis behind IPD is different writers have their own styles and they maintain these in their writings consciously or subconsciously. Sometimes it is very difficult to define the reference set for the task of external plagiarism detection. Additionally, the source of the plagiarized text may not be available in digitized format. Therefore, researchers are trying to answer whether it is possible to detect plagiarism without using any reference.

In this paper, we investigate some information theoretical and statistical measurements for IPD as a binary classification task. A set of 36 features has been proposed for classifying plagiarized and non-plagiarized segments in the suspicious documents. We use the PAN-PC-11 (Potthast et al., 2010) corpus compiled for IPD task. The PAN corpus is artificially plagiarised and it provides a meta-file mentioning the offsets of plagiarised and non-plagiarized parts for each suspicious document. We consider that each suspicious document is written by single author and it is either partially plagiarised or not plagiarised and we try to identify the text-segments that differ in writing style compared to the whole document. We train an SMO (Platt, 1998) classifier in Weka3.6 (Hall et al., 2009) by using 10 fold cross-validation. Then the classification performances are observed with different feature sets according to the standard precision, recall and F-score.

The next sections are organized as follows: section 2 discusses related works and section 3 briefly describes information theoretical and statistical features. The text segmentation and windowing process is summarized in section 4 while the experimental framework and baseline feature sets are discussed in section 5. Section 6 compares the classification performances with different feature sets and finally, the paper concludes in section 7.

2 Related Work

A series of regular studies on plagiarism detection were started following the first international competition for plagiarism detection, the PAN[1] workshop in 2009. Potthast et al. (2009) provides an overview on PAN'09 including the corpus design for plagiarism detection, quality measurements and the methods of plagiarism detection developed by the participants.

Zu Eissen and Stein (2006) proposed the first method for IPD and presented a taxonomy of plagiarism with methods for analysis. They also proposed some features including *average sentence length*, *part-of-speech* features, *average stopword number* and *averaged word frequency class* for quantifying the writing style. Some researchers used character n-gram profiles for the task of IPD

[1] http://pan.webis.de/

Proceedings of the SIGDIAL 2015 Conference, pages 144–148,
Prague, Czech Republic, 2-4 September 2015.

(Stamatatos, 2009; Kestemont et al., 2011). Oberreuter et al. (2011) proposed word n-gram based method and they assumed that different writers use different sets of words that they repeat frequently. Tschuggnall and Specht (2012) proposed the *Plag-Inn* algorithm that finds plagiarized sentences in a suspicious document by comparing grammar trees of the sentences.
Stamatatos (2009) introduced sliding window and proposed a *distance function* for calculating the dissimilarity between two texts based on a character tri-gram profile. Stamatatos (2011) employed n-grams of function word sequence with different lengths and found significant impact to distinguish between plagiarised and non-plagiarized texts. We employ function words differently as skip n-gram profiles for measuring entropy, relative entropy and correlation coefficient as discussed in Section 5.2. Stein et al. (2011) employed unmasking technique and proposed a set of features of different types for example POS, function words etc for intrinsic plagiarism analysis.

Seaward and Matwin (2009) and Chudá and Uhlík (2011) proposed compression based methods for IPD. They measured the *Kolmogorov complexity* of the distributions of different *parts-of-speech* and word classes in the sentences. For calculating the complexity a binary string is generated for each distribution and later the string is compressed by a compression algorithm.

3 Information Theoretical and Statistical Features

Shannon Entropy (Shannon, 1948) has a great impact on communication theory or theory of information transmission, it measures the uncertainty of a random variable. Mathematically, entropy is defined as in equation (1).

$$H(X) = -\sum_{i=1}^{n} p(x_i)\, log_2(p(x_i)) \quad (1)$$

$$KLD_{(p||q)} = \sum_{x \in X} p(x)\, log_2\left(\frac{p(x)}{q(x)}\right) \quad (2)$$

$$r = \frac{1}{n-1}\sum_{i=1}^{n}\left(\frac{X_i - \bar{X}}{s_X}\right)\left(\frac{Y_i - \bar{Y}}{s_Y}\right) \quad (3)$$

We measure entropy of n-gram frequency profile generated from each text-window (X) for quantifying the writing style. Manning and Schütze (1999) measured the distance between two probability distributions by using *Relative entropy* or *Kullback-Leibler divergence* (KLD) which is calculated by using the equation (2). The *Pearson correlation coefficient* (Pearson, 1920) or simply *correlation coefficient* measures the linear correlation between two samples that is calculated by the equation (3). Since the task of IPD does not use any reference document we require a robust method for comparing small sections of the document relative to the whole document under question. Measuring the relative entropy and correlation coefficient between a small section and the rest of the document are possible methods. We use the frequency profiles of n-grams generated from the individual text-window (X) and the complete suspicious document (Y) separately for calculating relative entropy and correlation coefficient. The probability distributions of n-gram frequencies (P and Q) is calculated from n-gram frequency profiles (from X and Y) for measuring the relative entropy.

4 Text Segmentation and windowing

To define the small sections of text for comparison to the rest of the document, we experiment with window of different lengths (1000, 2000, 5000 characters). To prepare the corpus for training and testing to support this additional experimentation, we separate plagiarised and non-plagiarized sections of the documents in the corpus according to the offsets (as indicated in the meta-file). By doing this we can guarantee that the smaller texts we generate are still accurately annotated as to whether the content is plagiarised or not. The whole procedure is illustrated in figure 1.

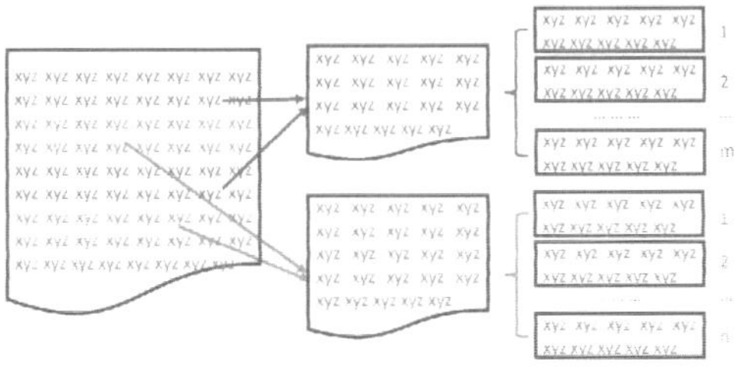

Figure 1: Text segmentation and windowing

5 Experimental Framework and Feature Sets

This section illustrates the experimental framework of IPD task by combining the preprocessing and classification tools, the framework is graphically described in figure 2. After extracting and windowing the corpus, we calculate different feature values for generating the feature vectors. Before calculating the features, several text preprocessing tasks, for example, tokenizing, sentence detection and POS-tagging are employed. We generate several feature vectors for different baseline feature sets and proposed feature set. Then a classifier model is trained with the feature sets, we train SMO classifier with 10 fold cross validation in *Weka 3.6* explorer interface. Equal number of plagiarized and non-plagiarized text samples are trained with the classifier. We train the classifier with 8,100 text segments from each class where each segment initially contains 5,000 characters. Finally, the classification performances are observed for different feature sets.

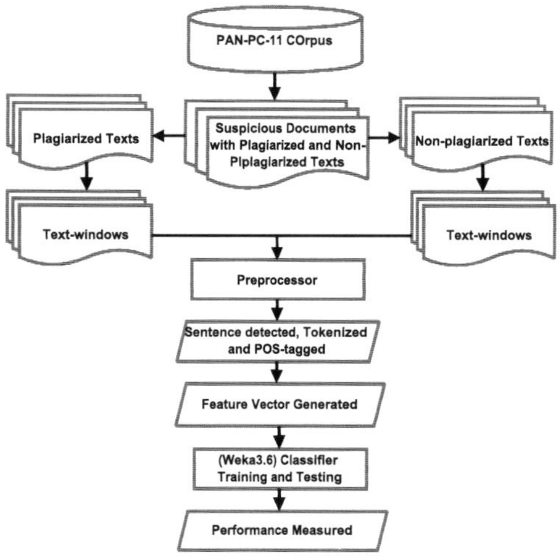

Figure 2: Experimental framework

5.1 Baseline feature sets

We used three different baseline feature sets for the experiment which are listed below:

- Baseline-1 (feature set used by Stein et al. (2011)): used 30 features that includes lexical and syntactical features, surface features, vocabulary richness and readability measurement-based features, n-gram-based features, POS-based features etc.
- Baseline-2 (feature set used by Seaward and Matwin (2009)): calculated the *Kolmogorov complexity* of function words and different parts-of-speech.
- Baseline-3 (*distance function* proposed by Stamatatos (2009)): measured *distance function* or *style-change score* of the text-windows with respect to the whole suspicious document by using their character tri-gram profiles.

5.2 Proposed feature set

We propose 36 features for IPD including entropy, relative entropy, correlation coefficient, skip n-grams of function words etc. Lavergne et al. (2008) and Zhao et al. (2006) used relative entropy for fake content detection and authorship attribution accordingly. Islam et al. (2012) classified readability levels of texts by using both entropy and relative entropy. Stamatatos (2011) used function word n-grams for exterinsic plagiarism detection but here we generate several skip n-grams of function words instead of simple n-grams. Guthrie et al. (2006) used 1 to 4 skip n-grams for modelling unseen sequences of words in the text. Here we summarize the proposed feature set:

- **Character *tri-gram* frequency profile**: we measure entropy for text windows and relative entropy and the correlation coefficient of the character tri-gram frequency profile for the text windows and documents. Additionally, we calculate *average n-gram frequency class* by using the equation of *average word frequency class* proposed by Zu Eissen and Stein (2006). Here we have 4 features: entropy, relative entropy, correlation coefficient and n-gram frequency class calculated from character tri-gram frequency profiles of text-windows and complete document.
- ***bi-gram* and *tri-gram* frequency profile with 1, 2, 3 and 4 skips** : we measure entropy, relative entropy, correlation coefficient of function-word bi-gram and tri-gram frequency profile with 1, 2, 3 and 4 skips. Additionally, we calculate the *style change scores* with these frequency profiles using the *distance function* proposed by Stamatatos (2009). For generating the skip n-gram profiles of function-words we extract the function words sequentially from each sentence.

We generate function-word skip n-gram profiles of the text segments by considering only the function words at sentence level instead of passage level as Stamatatos (2011) used. Here we have 32 features: entropy, relative entropy, correlation coefficient and style-change score calculated from 8 function-word skip n-gram frequency profiles.

6 Experimental Results

We observe that the proposed feature set achieves the highest F-Score compared to the baseline feature sets as illustrated in figure 3. All the feature sets together obtain a promising F-Score of 91% while the three baselines combined result in an F-Score around 89%. The proposed feature set achieves an 85% F-Score which is the highest compared to the three baseline feature sets. Baseline-1 and baseline-2 obtain F-Score around 68% and 62% while baseline-3 surprisingly results in an 84% F-Score as a single feature. We pair feature sets and observe their performances, figure 4 shows that the proposed feature set increases the F-Score with the combination of baseline feature sets.

Figure 5 depicts separate observations of entropy, relative entropy, correlation coefficient and distance function of function word skip n-gram frequency profiles. Here we notice that relative entropy achieves a very good F-Score of 72%, entropy and correlation coefficient also obtain better F-Scores than the distance function. Though distance function results in very good F-Score with the character tri-gram frequency profile it does not perform good enough with the function word skip n-gram frequency profile. Distance function with function word skip n-gram frequency profile obtains around a 35% F-Score which is the lowest compared to other functions with function word skip n-gram frequency profile. We also observe the effect of different window lengths (discussed in section 4) on classification performance, the classification performance increases for each feature set if the window length is increased. All the feature sets combined result in F-Score of 82% and 87% for window lengths of 1000 and 2000 characters accordingly while a 91% F-Score is achieved with the window length of 5000 characters.

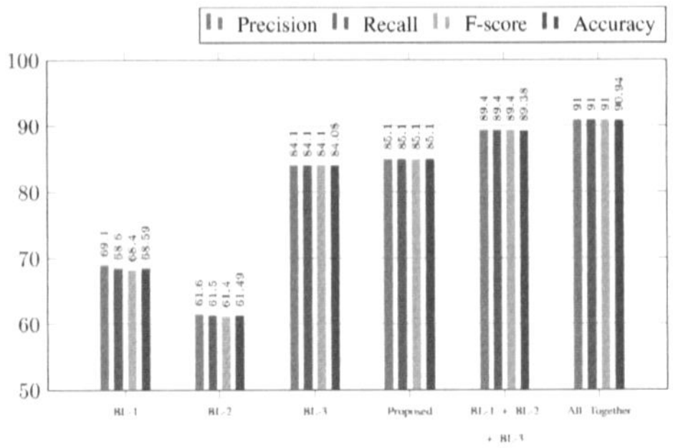

Figure 3: Performance observation of the baseline and proposed feature sets

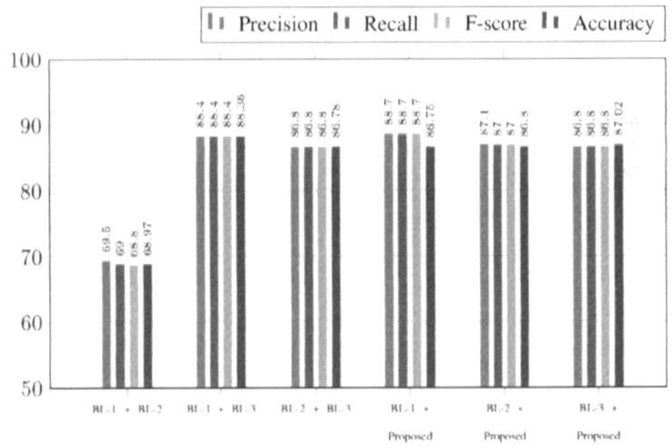

Figure 4: Performance observation of the coupled feature sets

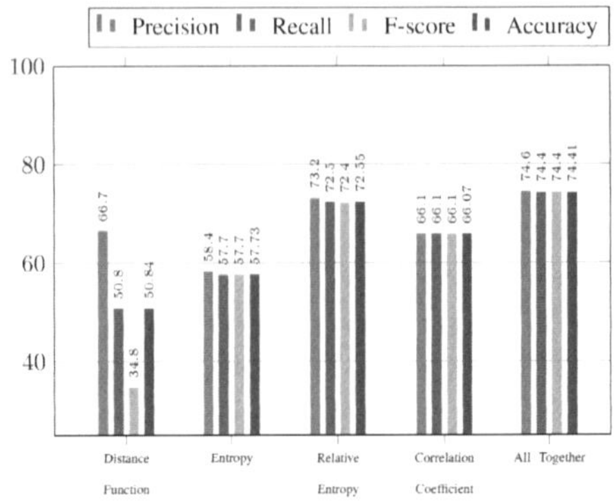

Figure 5: Performance observation of function word skip n-gram based features

7 Conclusion

In this paper we proposed a set of new features for intrinsic plagiarism detection that support arguments for continued research on IPD. In the future we would like to evaluate these features on human-plagiarised and different domain corpora. We are also interested in expanding the IPD task by considering the case that a suspicious document is written by multiple authors.

Acknowledgement

This paper is a part of my master thesis work while studied at Frankfurt University of Applied Sciences. I am very thankful to my thesis supervisor Dr. Alexander Mehler and my especial thanks to IRT-SystemX for ensuring me to attend at SIGdial conference. I also thank my SIGdial mentor and reviewers for their feedback and guidance.

References

Daniela Chudá and Martin Uhlík. The plagiarism detection by compression method. In *Proceedings of the 12th International Conference on Computer Systems and Technologies*, pages 429–434. ACM, 2011.

David Guthrie, Ben Allison, Wei Liu, Louise Guthrie, and Yorick Wilks. A closer look at skip-gram modelling. In *Proceedings of the 5th international Conference on Language Resources and Evaluation (LREC-2006)*, pages 1–4, 2006.

Mark Hall, Eibe Frank, Geoffrey Holmes, Bernhard Pfahringer, Peter Reutemann, and Ian H Witten. The weka data mining software: an update. *ACM SIGKDD Explorations Newsletter*, 11(1):10–18, 2009.

Zahurul Islam, Alexander Mehler, Rashedur Rahman, and AG Texttechnology. Text readability classification of textbooks of a low-resource language. In *Proceedings of the 26th Pacific Asia Conference on Language, Information, and Computation.(Accepted)*, 2012.

Mike Kestemont, Kim Luyckx, and Walter Daelemans. Intrinsic plagiarism detection using character trigram distance scores. *Proceedings of the PAN*, 2011.

Thomas Lavergne, Tanguy Urvoy, and François Yvon. Detecting fake content with relative entropy scoring. In *PAN*, 2008.

Christopher D Manning and Hinrich Schütze. *Foundations of statistical natural language processing*, volume 999. MIT Press, 1999.

Gabriel Oberreuter, Gaston LâĂŹHuillier, Sebastián A Ríos, and Juan D Velásquez. Approaches for intrinsic and external plagiarism detection. *Proceedings of the PAN*, 2011.

Karl Pearson. Notes on the history of correlation. *Biometrika*, 13(1):25–45, 1920.

John C. Platt. Sequential minimal optimization: A fast algorithm for training support vector machines. Technical report, ADVANCES IN KERNEL METHODS - SUPPORT VECTOR LEARNING, 1998.

Martin Potthast, Benno Stein, Andreas Eiselt, Alberto Barrón-Cedeno, and Paolo Rosso. Overview of the 1st international competition on plagiarism detection. In *3rd PAN WORKSHOP. UNCOVERING PLAGIARISM, AUTHORSHIP AND SOCIAL SOFTWARE MISUSE*, 2009.

Martin Potthast, Benno Stein, Alberto Barrón-Cedeño, and Paolo Rosso. An Evaluation Framework for Plagiarism Detection. In *Proceedings of the 23rd International Conference on Computational Linguistics (COLING 2010)*, Beijing, China, August 2010. Association for Computational Linguistics.

Leanne Seaward and Stan Matwin. Intrinsic plagiarism detection using complexity analysis. In *Proc. SEPLN*, pages 56–61, 2009.

Claude Elwood Shannon. A mathematical theory of communication. *ACM SIGMOBILE Mobile Computing and Communications Review*, 5(1): 3–55, 1948.

Efstathios Stamatatos. Intrinsic plagiarism detection using character n-gram profiles. *Proceedings of the PAN*, pages 38–46, 2009.

Efstathios Stamatatos. Plagiarism detection based on structural information. In *Proceedings of the 20th ACM international conference on Information and knowledge management*, pages 1221–1230. ACM, 2011.

Benno Stein, Nedim Lipka, and Peter Prettenhofer. Intrinsic plagiarism analysis. *Language Resources and Evaluation*, 45(1):63–82, 2011.

Michael Tschuggnall and Günther Specht. Plaginn: intrinsic plagiarism detection using grammar trees. In *Natural Language Processing and Information Systems*, pages 284–289. Springer, 2012.

Ying Zhao, Justin Zobel, and Phil Vines. Using relative entropy for authorship attribution. In *Information Retrieval Technology*, pages 92–105. Springer, 2006.

Sven Meyer Zu Eissen and Benno Stein. Intrinsic plagiarism detection. In *Advances in Information Retrieval*, pages 565–569. Springer, 2006.

A SIP of CoFee : A Sample of Interesting Productions of Conversational Feedback

Laurent Prévot[1] **Jan Gorisch**[1,2] **Roxane Bertrand**[1] **Emilien Gorène**[1] **Brigitte Bigi**[1]

[1] Aix-Marseille Université
CNRS, LPL UMR 7309
13100 Aix-en-Provence, France

[2]Nanyang Technological University
Division of Linguistics and Multilingual Studies
Singapore 637332

Abstract

Feedback utterances are among the most frequent in dialogue. Feedback is also a crucial aspect of linguistic theories that take social interaction, involving language, into account. This paper introduces the corpora and datasets of a project scrutinizing this kind of feedback utterances in French. We present the genesis of the corpora (for a total of about 16 hours of transcribed and phone force-aligned speech) involved in the project. We introduce the resulting datasets and discuss how they are being used in on-going work with focus on the form-function relationship of conversational feedback. All the corpora created and the datasets produced in the framework of this project will be made available for research purposes.

1 Introduction

Feedback utterances are the most frequent utterance type in dialogue (Stolcke et al., 2000; Misu et al., 2011). They also play a crucial role in managing the common ground of a conversation (Clark, 1996). However, perhaps due to their apparent simplicity, they have been ignored in many linguistic studies on dialogue. The main contribution to the understanding of the feedback utterance type comes from neighboring fields: (i) Conversational Analysis (CA) has shed light on turn-taking including a careful description of *response tokens*, such as "uh-huh" (Schegloff, 1982), formerly also termed *back-channels* by (ii) computational linguist Victor Yngve (Yngve, 1970)[1]; (iii) Dialogue engineers dealt with them because of their ubiquity in task-oriented dialogues (Traum, 1994); (iv) Cognitive psychologists gave them an important role in their theory of communication (Clark, 1996); (v) The most linguistic attempt to describe feedback is the work by Allwood et al. (1992) who suggest a semantic framework for it.

We take the apparent lack of sophistication of the lexical forms and structures involved in the majority of feedback utterances to be an interesting feature for a multimodal study. In our opinion, multimodal corpus studies are suffering form a combinatorial explosion that results from the simultaneous integration of complex phenomena and structures from all levels of analysis. Our aim is to use feedback as a filtering constraint on large multimodal corpora. In this way, all the dimensions will be analyzed but in a restricted way: on feedback utterances. Feedback production is known to be dependent on the discourse situation. Therefore, a second aim is to provide a model that is not domain-restricted: our objective is rather a model that is generalisable enough to be interesting from a linguistic viewpoint.

These parameters lead us to constitute a dataset that is built from four different corpora recorded in four different situations: almost free conversation (CID corpus), Map Task (MTR corpus), Face-to-Face Map Task (MTX corpus), and discussion / negotiation centered on DVD movies (DVD corpus). Since the overall goal of the project is a study of the form-function relationship of feedback utterances, the corpora are needed to create rich datasets that include extracted features from the audio, video, and their transcriptions, as well as annotated functions of the feedback utterances.

In this paper, after coming back to definitions, terminology and related work (Section 2), we present how the corpora were created (Section 3), including various stages of non-trivial post-processing, how they were pre-segmented in the gestural domain and annotated for communicative functions. We also present the different datasets (Section 4), including automatically enriched tran-

[1]See section 2 for details on the definitions and terminology.

Proceedings of the SIGDIAL 2015 Conference, pages 149–153,
Prague, Czech Republic, 2-4 September 2015.

scriptions and large feature files, how they were produced and how they can also be useful for other researchers and their studies.

2 Feedback items

Concerning the definition of the term *feedback utterance*, we follow Bunt (1994, p.27):

> "Feedback is the phenomenon that a dialogue participant provides information about his processing of the partner's previous utterances. This includes information about perceptual processing (hearing, reading), about interpretation (direct or indirect), about evaluation (agreement, disbelief, surprise,...) and about dispatch (fulfillment of a request, carrying out a command,...)."

As a working definition of our class *feedback*, we could have followed Gravano et al. (2012), who selected their tokens according to the individual word transcriptions. Alternatively, Neiberg et al. (2013) performed an acoustic automatic detection of potential feedback turns, followed by a manual check and selection. Given our objective, we preferred to use perhaps more complex units that are closer to *feedback utterances*. We consider that the feedback function is expressed overwhelmingly through short utterances or fragments (Ginzburg, 2012) or in the beginning of potentially longer contributions. We therefore automatically extracted candidate feedback utterances of these two kinds. Utterances are however already sophisticated objects that would require a specific segmentation campaign. We rely on a rougher unit: the Inter-Pausal Unit (IPU). IPUs are stretches of talk situated between silent pauses of a given duration, here 200 milliseconds. In addition to these *isolated feedback IPUs*, we added sequences of feedback-related lexical items situated at the very beginning of an IPU.

3 Corpora

Our collection is composed of four different corpora: an 8 hour conversational data corpus (Bertrand et al., 2008), a 2.5 hours MapTask corpus (Bard et al., 2013), a 2.5 hours face-to-face MapTask corpus (Gorisch et al., 2014) and a 4 hours DVD negotiation corpus. All these corpora are accessible as a collection of resources through the Ortolang platform (`http://sldr.org/ortolang-000911`).

3.1 Corpus creation: Protocols, Recordings and Transcriptions

All recordings include headset microphone channels that were transcribed on IPU level and automatically aligned on word and phone level. The recording setups are illustrated in Figure 1. The first two corpora (CID and MTR) already existed before our current project, while the other two (MTX and DVD) were specifically recorded and transcribed (using SPPAS (Bigi, 2012)) for this project and are therefore explained in more detail below. CID, MTX and DVD primary are directly accessible for research purposes; MTR requires agreement from its creators.

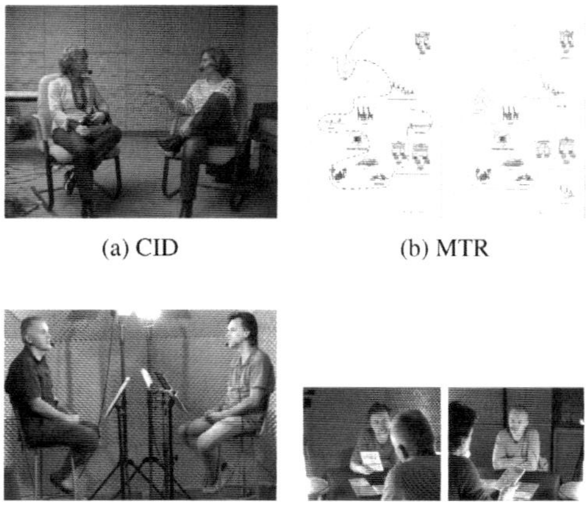

(a) CID (b) MTR (c) MTX (d) DVD

Figure 1: Recording setups of corpora.

CID Conversation Interaction Data (CID) includes participants having a chat about "strange things" (Bertrand et al., 2008). Each interaction took 60 minutes. Three of them were additionally recorded on video. Figure 1a illustrates the setup.

MTR The remote condition of the French MapTask corpus (MTR) (Bard et al., 2013) follows the original MapTask protocol (Anderson et al., 1991), where the role of map giver and follower change through the 8 maps per session. An example of a pair of maps is illustrated in Figure 1b. In this condition, the participants could not see each other and were therefore not recorded on video.

MTX The face-to-face condition of the French MapTask corpus (MTX) (Gorisch et al., 2014) includes additional video recordings for both participants individually as they could see each other during the dialogue (cf. Figure 1c). Similar to the remote condition, 4 maps were "given" by one participant and "followed" by the other and vice versa. Each map took ca. 5 minutes to complete.

DVD We recruited 16 participants to take part in the recording of this corpus. The aim was to involve them in a discussion on movies, DVDs, actors, and all other topics that they may come up with during a 30 minute conversation. A set of DVD boxes (with content) were placed on a table in front of them: 4 on each side (see Figure 1d). The instructions included that each participant can take 2 of the 8 boxes home if they are on their side once the recording session is finished (as compensation for participation). Several weeks prior to the recording session, the participants were asked to fill out a short questionnaire answering four questions: what are your preferred movie genres, what are your three most preferred movies, what are your dispreferred movie genres, and what are your three most dispreferred movies. According to the answers, we paired mis-matching participants, chose 8 DVDs and placed them on the two sides in a way that maximises negotiation (who takes which DVDs home). 2 dispreferred movies or genres were placed on the own side and two preferred ones were placed on the other side.

3.2 Post-processing

Due to clocking differences in the audio and video recording devices and random image loss in the video, both signals ran out of synchronisation over time. For multimodal analyses, such desynchronisation is not acceptable. The videos of the CID corpus have been corrected by hand in order to match the audio channels. A more precise and less time-consuming procedure was developed for the newer recordings of MTX and DVD, as it is described by Gorisch and Prévot (2015). First, the audio and video files were cut in a rough manner to the approximate start time of the task, e.g. maps in the MapTask. Second, a dynamic programming approach took the audio channel of the camera and aligned it to the headset microphone mix in order to estimate the missing images for each video. Third, scripts were used to extract all images, insert images at the appropriate places and recombine the images to a film that can run synchronously with the headset microphone channels. This procedure helped to repair the videos of 2h (out of 2.5h) of the MTX corpus and the entire DVD corpus.

3.3 Gesture pre-segmentation

As our project aims to describe conversational feedback in general, the visible part of that feedback should receive sufficient attention, too. Three of the four corpora include participants' visibility and video recordings. An entire labelling of all gestures of the corpus is however impossible. Therefore, we employed two students (working on gesture for their research) to perform a pre-segmentation task. Those sections of a video that involve feedback in the domain of gestures or facial expressions were segmented using the ELAN tool in its segmentation mode (Wittenburg et al., 2006). The focus on this pass was on recall rather than precision since all the marked units will be annotated later on for precise gestures and potentially discarded if it turns out that they are not feedback.

3.4 Quantitative presentation

The content of all corpora that are included in our SIP of CoFee database, sums up to almost 17 hours of actual speech duration, with a number of 268,581 tokens in 33,378 utterances (See Table 1). This relatively large collection is used in subsequent analyses in order to quantify the form-function relationship of conversational feedback. In Table 1, the column *# Feedback* includes all (13,036) candidate feedback units (isolated IPUs and initial of an IPU). How thay have been selected is explained in Section 4. The column *# Gestures* indicates the number of pre-segmented feedback gestures. In parenthesis is the number of those gestures that co-occur with verbal feedback items. The number of gestures however should not be taken as indicator of importance of gestures in different corpora: the CID corpus has only three hours out of eight that include video-recording, while MTX misses some video files due to technical issues (see Section 3.2).

4 Datasets

This section describes how the verbal units of feedback have been selected from the transcriptions, what basic features have been extracted and what communicative functions have been (and are currently) annotated in order to form the dataset for the form-function analysis.

Corpus	# Tokens	# IPUs	actual speech duration	# Feedback	# Gestures	
CID	125,619	13,134	7h 34min	4,795	802	(516)
MTR	42,016	6,425	2h 32min	2,622	-	-
MTX	36,923	5,830	2h 33min	2,484	652	(466)
DVD	64,023	7,989	4h 12min	3,135	1,386	(668)
CoFee (all)	268,581	33,378	16h 51min	13,036	2,840	(1,650)

Table 1: Basic figures of our SIP of CoFee

Extracting units of analysis We first identified the small set of most frequent items composing feedback utterances by building the token distribution for Inter-Pausal Units (IPUs) of length 3 or less. The 10 most frequent forms are: *ouais / yeah (2781), mh (2321), d'accord / agree-right (1082), laughter (920), oui / yes (888), euh / uh (669), ok (632), ah (433), voilà / that's it-right (360).* The next ones are *et / and (360), non / no (319), tu / you (287), alors / then (151), bon / well (150)* and then follows a series of other pronouns and determiners with frequency dropping quickly. After qualitative evaluation, we excluded *tu, et* and *alors* as they were unrelated to feedback in these short isolated IPUs. Table 2 shows the feedback tokens and the number of occurrences in each corpus. In order to count multiple sayings of a token in an IPU, such as *"oui oui"*, they appear in separate rows indicated by a plus sign (+). The category *complex* simply corresponds to any other transcription in the IPUs; it includes mainly various feedback item combinations (*ah ouais d'accord, euh ben ouais*) and repeated material from the left context. This yielded us a dataset of 13,036 utterances.

Feature extraction and function annotation In order to deepen our understanding of these feedback items, we extracted a set of form-related and contextual features. Concerning the form, aside the simplified transcription presented in Table 2, we included some features trying to describe the *complex* category (namely the presence of a given discourse marker in the unit or a repetition of the left context). Various acoustic features including duration, pitch, intensity and voice quality parameters were also extracted. Concerning contextual features, we extracted timing features within the speech environment (that provide us information about feedback timing and overlap), discourse lexical (initial and final n-grams) and acoustic (pitch, intensity, etc.) features defined in terms of properties of the previous IPU from speaker and interlocutor.

Token	CID	DVD	MTR	MTX	all
oui+	17	11	8	6	42
ouais+	141	63	26	22	252
voilà	47	41	133	105	326
ah	164	112	28	61	365
ok	5	47	132	213	397
non	109	112	103	91	415
oui	99	74	175	220	568
mh+	334	39	246	45	664
d'accord	35	83	199	366	683
mh	548	312	79	79	1,018
@	611	286	48	81	1,026
ouais	843	727	565	434	2,569
complex	1,842	1,228	880	761	4,711
Total	4,795	3,135	2,622	2,484	13,036

Table 2: Distribution of the 'simplified' transcription of IPUs.

We currently run campaigns to annotate the remaining data with feedback communicative functions (*acknowledgment, approval, answer,* etc.). Completely annotated subdatasets are used to run form-function classification experiments and correlation testing (Prévot and Gorisch, 2014).

5 Conclusion

The SIP of CoFee is ready for consumption. It is a composition of corpora of varying recording situations, including multimodality, and datasets that can be – and are currently – used for the study of one of the most basic practices in human communication, namely feedback.

Acknowledgements

This work is supported by *Agence Nationale de la Recherche* (ANR-12-JCJC-JSH2-006-01) and the *Erasmus Mundus Action 2* program *MULTI* (GA number 2010-5094-7). We would like to thank our transcribers and segmenters Aurélie Goujon, Charlotte Bouget and Léo Baiocchi.

References

J. Allwood, J. Nivre, and E. Ahlsen. 1992. On the semantics and pragmatics of linguistic feedback. *Journal of Semantics*, 9:1–26.

A. Anderson, M. Bader, E. Bard, E. Boyle, G. M. Doherty, S. Garrod, S. Isard, J. Kowtko, J. McAllister, J. Miller, C. Sotillo, H. S. Thompson, and R. Weinert. 1991. The HCRC map task corpus. *Language and Speech*, 34:351–366.

E. G. Bard, C. Astésano, M. D'Imperio, A. Turk, N. Nguyen, L. Prévot, and B. Bigi. 2013. Aix MapTask: A new French resource for prosodic and discourse studies. In *Proceedings of Tools and Resources for the Analysis of Speech Prosody (TRASP)*, Aix-en-Provence, France.

R. Bertrand, P. Blache, R. Espesser, G. Ferré, C. Meunier, B. Priego-Valverde, and S. Rauzy. 2008. Le CID-corpus of interactional data-annotation et exploitation multimodale de parole conversationnelle. *Traitement Automatique des Langues*, 49(3):1–30.

B. Bigi. 2012. SPPAS: a tool for the phonetic segmentation of speech. In *Proceedings of the Eighth International Conference on Language Resources and Evaluation (LREC'12)*, pages 1748–1755, ISBN 978–2–9517408–7–7, Istanbul, Turkey.

H. Bunt. 1994. Context and dialogue control. *Think Quarterly*, 3(1):19–31.

H.H. Clark. 1996. *Using Language*. Cambridge: Cambridge University Press.

J. Ginzburg. 2012. *The Interactive Stance: Meaning for Conversation*. Oxford University Press.

J. Gorisch and L. Prévot. 2015. Audio synchronisation with a tunnel matrix for time series and dynamic programming. In *Proceedings of ICASSP 2015 IEEE International Conference on Acoustics, Speech, and Signal Processing*, pages 3846–3850, Brisbane, Australia.

J. Gorisch, C. Astésano, E. Bard, B. Bigi, and L. Prévot. 2014. Aix Map Task corpus: The French multimodal corpus of task-oriented dialogue. In *Proceedings of The Ninth International Conference on Language Resources and Evaluation (LREC'14)*, Reykjavik, Iceland.

A. Gravano, J. Hirschberg, and Š. Beňuš. 2012. Affirmative cue words in task-oriented dialogue. *Computational Linguistics*, 38(1):1–39.

T. Misu, E. Mizukami, Y. Shiga, S. Kawamoto, H. Kawai, and S. Nakamura. 2011. Toward construction of spoken dialogue system that evokes users' spontaneous backchannels. In *Proceedings of the SIGDIAL 2011 Conference*, pages 259–265. Association for Computational Linguistics.

D. Neiberg, G. Salvi, and J. Gustafson. 2013. Semi-supervised methods for exploring the acoustics of simple productive feedback. *Speech Communication*, 55:451–469.

L. Prévot and J. Gorisch. 2014. Crossing empirical and formal approaches for studying french feedback items. In *Proceedings of Logic and Engineering of Natural Language Semantics 11*, Tokyo, Japan.

E. A. Schegloff. 1982. Discourse as an interactional achievement: Some use of 'uh-huh' and other things that come between sentences. *Georgetown University Round Table on Languages and Linguistics, Analyzing discourse: Text and talk*, pages 71–93.

A. Stolcke, K. Ries, N. Coccaro, E. Shriberg, R. Bates, D. Jurafsky, P. Taylor, R. Martin, C.V. Ess-Dykema, and M. Meteer. 2000. Dialogue act modeling for automatic tagging and recognition of conversational speech. *Computational linguistics*, 26(3):339–373.

D. Traum. 1994. *A computational theory of grounding in natural language conversation*. Ph.D. thesis, University of Rochester.

P. Wittenburg, H. Brugman, A. Russel, A. Klassmann, and H. Sloetjes. 2006. Elan: a professional framework for multimodality research. In *Proceedings of LREC 2006, Fifth International Conference on Language Resources and Evaluation*. Citeseer.

V. H. Yngve. 1970. On getting a word in edgewise. In *Papers from the Sixth Regional Meeting of the Chicago Linguistic Society*, pages 567–578.

Reinforcement Learning of Multi-Issue Negotiation Dialogue Policies

Alexandros Papangelis
Human-Computer Interaction Institute
Carnegie Mellon University
Pittsburgh, PA 15213, USA
apapa@cs.cmu.edu

Kallirroi Georgila
Institute for Creative Technologies
University of Southern California
Playa Vista, CA 90094, USA
kgeorgila@ict.usc.edu

Abstract

We use reinforcement learning (RL) to learn a multi-issue negotiation dialogue policy. For training and evaluation, we build a hand-crafted agenda-based policy, which serves as the negotiation partner of the RL policy. Both the agenda-based and the RL policies are designed to work for a large variety of negotiation settings, and perform well against negotiation partners whose behavior has not been observed before. We evaluate the two models by having them negotiate against each other under various settings. The learned model consistently outperforms the agenda-based model. We also ask human raters to rate negotiation transcripts between the RL policy and the agenda-based policy, regarding the rationality of the two negotiators. The RL policy is perceived as more rational than the agenda-based policy.

1 Introduction

Negotiation is a process in which two or more parties participate in order to reach a joint decision. Negotiators have goals and preferences, and follow a negotiation policy or strategy to accomplish their goals. There has been a lot of work on building automated agents for negotiation in the communities of autonomous agents and game theory. Lin and Kraus (2010) present a quite comprehensive survey on automated agents designed to negotiate with humans. Below we focus only on research that is directly related to our work.

English and Heeman (2005) and Heeman (2009) applied reinforcement learning (RL) to a furniture layout negotiation task. Georgila and Traum (2011) learned argumentation policies against users of different cultural norms in a one-issue negotiation scenario. Then Georgila (2013) learned argumentation policies in a two-issue negotiation scenario. These policies were trained for some initial conditions, and they could perform well only when they were tested under similar conditions. More recently, Efstathiou and Lemon (2014) learned negotiation behaviors for a non-cooperative trading game (the Settlers of Catan). Again, in Efstathiou and Lemon (2014)'s work, the initial settings were always the same. Georgila et al. (2014) used multi-agent RL to learn negotiation policies in a resource allocation scenario. They compared single-agent RL vs. multi-agent RL and they did not deal with argumentation, nor did they allow for a variety of initial conditions. Finally, Hiraoka et al. (2014) applied RL to the problem of learning cooperative persuasive policies using framing. Due to the complexity of negotiation tasks, none of the above works dealt with speech recognition or understanding errors.

In this paper, we focus on two-party negotiation, and use RL to learn a multi-issue negotiation policy for an agent aimed for negotiating with humans. We train our RL policy against a simulated user (SU), which plays the role of the other negotiator. Our SU is a hand-crafted negotiation dialogue policy inspired by the *agenda paradigm*, previously used for dialogue management (Rudnicky and Xu, 1999) and user modeling (Schatzmann and Young, 2009) in information providing tasks.

Both the agenda-based and the RL policies are designed to work for a variety of goals, preferences, and negotiation moves, even under conditions that are very different from the conditions that the agents have experienced before. We vary the goals of the agents, how easy it is for the agents to be persuaded, whether they have enough arguments to accomplish their goals (i.e., shift their partners' preferences), and the importance of each issue for each agent. We evaluate our two models by having them negotiate against each other under various settings. We also ask human raters to rate

Proceedings of the SIGDIAL 2015 Conference, pages 154–158,
Prague, Czech Republic, 2-4 September 2015. ©2015 Association for Computational Linguistics

negotiation transcripts between the RL policy and the agenda-based SU, regarding the rationality of the two negotiators.

In our negotiation task, both the agenda-based SU and the RL policy have human-like constraints of imperfect information about each other; they do not know each other's goals or preferences, number of available arguments, degree of persuadability, or degree of rationality. Furthermore, both agents are required to perform well for a variety of negotiation settings, and against opponents whose negotiation behavior has not been observed before and may vary from one interaction to another or even within the same interaction. Thus our negotiation task is very complex and it is not possible (or at least it is very difficult) to compute an analytical solution to the problem using game theory.

Our contributions are as follows. First, this is the first time in the literature that the agenda-based paradigm is applied to negotiation. Second, to our knowledge this is the first time that RL is used to learn so complex multi-issue negotiation and argumentation policies (how to employ arguments to persuade the other party) designed to work for a large variety of negotiation settings, including settings that did not appear during training.

2 Agenda-Based Negotiation Model

The original agenda-based SU factors the user state S into an agenda A and a goal G (Schatzmann and Young, 2009), and was used in a restaurant recommendation dialogue system. We replaced the constraints and requests (which refer to slot-value pairs) with *negotiation goals* and *negotiation profiles*, and designed new rules for populating the agenda.

The agenda can be thought of as a stack containing the SU's pending actions, also called speech acts (SAs), that are required for accomplishing the SU's goal. For example, the agenda could be initialized with offers for each issue (with the values preferred by the SU) and with requests for the opponent's preferences for each issue. Based on hand-crafted rules, new SAs are generated and pushed onto the agenda as a response to the opponent's actions. For example, if the opponent requests the SU's preference for an issue, a SA for providing this preference will be pushed onto the agenda and no longer relevant SAs will be removed from the agenda. When the SU is ready to respond, one or more SAs will be popped off the agenda based on a probability distribution. In our experiments, the maximum number of SAs that can be popped at the same time is 4 based on a probability distribution (popping 1 SA is more likely than popping 2 SAs, etc.).

The set of available SAs is: Offer(issue, value), TradeOff(issue$_1$, value$_1$, issue$_2$, value$_2$), ProvideArgument(issue, value, argument-strength), ProvidePreference(issue, value), RequestPreference(issue), Accept(issue$_1$, value$_1$, issue$_2$, value$_2$), Reject(issue, value), ReleaseTurn, and Null. TradeOff is a special action, where the agent commits to accept value$_1$ for issue$_1$, on the condition that the opponent accepts value$_2$ for issue$_2$. Accept refers to a TradeOff when all four arguments are present, or to an Offer when only two arguments are present. An agent is not allowed to partially accept a TradeOff. The agenda-based SU's internal state consists of the following features: "self standing offers", "self standing trade-offs", "agreed issues", "rejected offers", "self negotiation profile", "self goals", "opponent's standing offers", "opponent's standing trade-offs", "estimated opponent's goal", "estimated opponent's persuadability", "negotiation focus".

The *negotiation profile* models useful characteristics of the SU, such as persuadability, available arguments, and preferred/acceptable values (possible outcomes) for each issue. *Negotiation goals* represent the agent's best value (of highest preference) for each issue. *Negotiation focus* represents the current value on the table for each issue. Persuadability is defined as low, medium, or high, and reflects the number of arguments that the agent needs to receive to be convinced to change its mind. Arguments for an issue can be either strong or weak. We define strong arguments to count for 1 "persuasion point" and weak arguments to count for 0.25. Any combination of strong and weak arguments, whose cumulative points surpass the agent's persuadability (10 points for low, 5 points for medium, and 2 points for high persuadability), are enough to convince the agent and shift its negotiation goal for one issue. Also, the agent has a set number of arguments for each issue, not for each issue-value pair (this will be addressed in future work). Apart from persuadability, we model how important each issue is for the agent (a real number from 0 to 1). Rules, concerning whether a TradeOff or Offer should be accepted or not, take into account issue importance and number of available arguments for that issue (to see if there is any chance to convince the opponent).

There is a number of parameters used to configure the SU: number of issues under negotiation and possible values for each issue (in our setup 4 and 3 respectively); probability of number of SAs popped (this is based on a probability distribution as explained above); and minimum and maximum available arguments per issue (this applies separately to strong and weak arguments and in our setup is 0 and 4 respectively). The SU also keeps track of an estimate of the opponent's persuadability and the opponent's goal. These estimates are more accurate for longer dialogues. Table 3 (in the Appendix) shows an example interaction between the SU and another agent, including how the agenda is updated.

3 Negotiation Policy Learning

To deal with the very large state space, we experimented with different feature-based representations of the state and action spaces, and used Q-learning with function approximation (Szepesvári, 2010). We used 10 state-action features: "issue and value under negotiation", "are there enough arguments to convince the opponent?", "will my offer be accepted?", "opponent's offer quality", "opponent's trade-off quality", "are there pending issues?", "is there agreement for the current issue?", "is the agreed-upon value for the current issue good?", "importance of current issue", "current action".

We worked on a *summary state space*, rather than the *full state space*. The full state space keeps track of the interaction in detail, e.g., what offers have been made exactly, and the summary state space keeps track of more abstract representations, e.g., whether an offer was made, out of which we extract the 10 state-action features that the RL policy uses to make decisions. This is also similar to how our agenda-based SU works; rules, that decide on e.g., whether a trade-off should be proposed or accepted, take into account the opponent's estimated persuadability and context of the interaction, in essence allowing the agent to operate on a summary state space.

The learning algorithm was trained for 5 epochs (batches) of 20000 episodes each, with a limit to 35 iterations per episode, and was tuned with the following parameter values: α set to 0.95, decayed by $\frac{1}{1+N(s,a)}$ after each episode, where $N(s, a)$ is the number of times the state-action pair (s, a) has been explored so far, and γ set to 0.15. We varied the exploration rate ϵ. Initially it was set to 1, gradually decreasing until in the last epoch it was close to 0. To ensure that the policies did not converge by chance, we ran the training and test sessions 10 times each and we report averages. Thus all results presented below are averages of 10 runs.

In our reward function (regular reward), we penalized each turn if no agreement was reached or, in the opposite case, assigned a reward value inversely proportional to how far the agreed-upon values are from the agent's preferences.

During training we discovered that this reward function fails to capture the fact that depending on the initial conditions (agents' goals, number of arguments, etc.) it may not be possible to reach an agreement or to achieve one's goals. Therefore, we also calculated the best achievable score (BAS) of the policy, which is the best possible score that the agent can achieve given its resources (number of strong and weak arguments), the opponent's persuadability, and assuming the best possible circumstances (i.e., that the opponent is very cooperative and accepts everything).

To assess whether Q-learning has converged, we calculate a normalized score, reflecting how well the goals were achieved, similar to the regular reward function presented above. The difference is that we do not have a turn penalty and that the maximum penalty is set lower (in training the penalty for sub-optimal agreements was higher to ensure that the policy learns to avoid such cases).

Figure 1 shows the scores of the policy and the SU as a function of the training episodes, when we use the regular reward. We can also see the BAS for both the RL policy and the SU. The maximum possible value for each agent is 100 (the agent accomplishes its exact goals) and the minimum is 0 (there is no agreement for any issue at all). In the last training epoch the exploration rate ϵ is almost 0, and the RL policy consistently outperforms the SU. During training, in each episode, we randomly initialize the following settings for both agents: number of available strong and weak arguments, persuadability per issue, importance per issue, and preferences per issue.

4 Evaluation

For our evaluation, we have the RL policy interact with the agenda-based SU for 20000 episodes varying the initial settings for both agents in the same fashion as for training. Similarly to training, we have 10 runs and report averages (see Figure 1). The RL policy outperforms the agenda-based SU. The RL policy learned to exploit trade-offs that while not being optimal for the SU, they are good enough for the SU to accept (the SU is

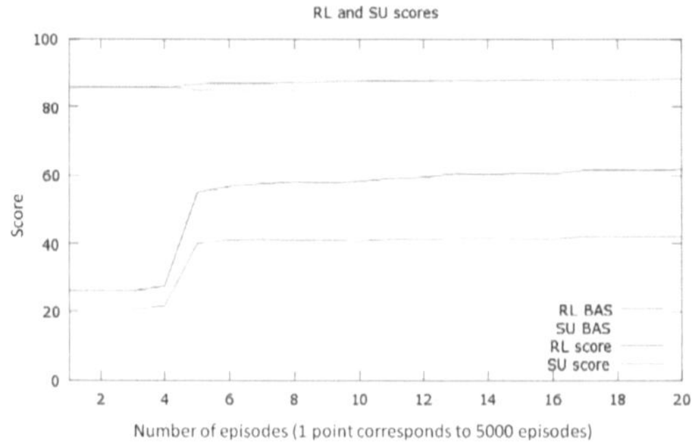

Figure 1: Average scores as a function of the number of episodes during training (10 runs). In the last 20000 episodes the exploration rate ϵ is almost 0 (similarly to testing).

designed to accept only trade-offs and offers that lead to reasonable agreements). Note that some decisions of the SU about what to accept are based on inaccurate estimates of its opponent's persuadability and goals.

Table 1 reports results about the success percentages of the RL policy and the agenda-based SU. We show on average how many times (10 runs) the agents fully succeeded in their goals (score equal to 100), how many times they achieved roughly at least their second best values for all issues (score > 65), and how many times they achieved roughly at least their third best values for all issues (score > 30). A higher than 65 score can also be achieved when an agent achieves the best possible outcome in some of the issues and the third possible outcome in the rest of the issues. Likewise for scores greater than 30.

In a second experiment we asked human raters to rate negotiation transcripts between the agenda-based SU and the RL policy. The domain was organizing a party. The negotiators had to agree on 4 issues (food type, drink, music, day of week) and there were 3 possible values per issue. We replaced the speech acts with full sentences but for arguments we used sentences such as "here is a strong argument supporting jazz for music". We randomly selected 20 negotiations between the RL policy and the agenda-based SU. In 10 of those the RL policy earned more points, and in the other 10 the agenda-based SU earned more points. This was to ensure that the transcripts were balanced and that we had not picked only transcripts where one of the agents was always better than the other. We did not tell raters that these were artificial dialogues. We deliberately included some questions with rather obvious answers (sanity checks) to check how committed the raters were. We recruited raters from MTurk (www.mturk.com). We asked raters to read 2 transcripts and for each transcript rate the negotiators in terms of how rationally they behaved, on a Likert scale from 1 to 5. We excluded ratings that were done in less than 3 minutes and that had failed in more than half of our sanity checks. In total there were 6 sanity checks (3 per negotiation transcript). Thus we ended up with 89 raters. Results are shown in Table 2. The RL policy was perceived as more rational, and both agents were rated as reasonably rational. Interestingly, rationality was perceived differently by different human raters, e.g., revisiting an agreed-upon issue was considered as rational by some and irrational by others.

	Full success (%)	At least second choice (%)	At least third choice (%)
Policy Score	10.3	30.7	53.5
SU Score	0	11.2	55.1
Policy BAS	20.2	73.3	100
SU BAS	18.1	75.8	100

Table 1: Average success percentages (10 runs).

Learned Policy Score	3.43
Agenda-based SU Score	3.02
p-value	0.027

Table 2: Human evaluation scores (the p-value is based on the Wilcoxon signed-rank test).

5 Conclusion

We built a hand-crafted agenda-based SU, which was then used together with RL to learn a multi-issue negotiation policy. Both the agenda-based SU and the RL policy were designed to work for a variety of goals, preferences, and negotiation moves. In both of our evaluation experiments, the learned model consistently outperformed the agenda-based SU, even though both models used similar features and heuristics, which shows the potential of using RL for complex negotiation domains. For future work, we plan to work on better estimates of the opponent's persuadability and goals, and employ multi-agent RL techniques (Bowling and Veloso, 2002; Georgila et al., 2014). Finally, we will have our policies directly negotiate with humans.

Acknowledgments

This work was funded by the NSF Grant #1117313.

References

Michael Bowling and Manuela Veloso. 2002. Multi-agent learning using a variable learning rate. *Artificial Intelligence*, 136(2):215–250.

Ioannis Efstathiou and Oliver Lemon. 2014. Learning non-cooperative dialogue behaviours. In *Proc. of the Annual SIGdial Meeting on Discourse and Dialogue*, Philadelphia, Pennsylvania, USA.

Michael S. English and Peter A. Heeman. 2005. Learning mixed initiative dialogue strategies by using reinforcement learning on both conversants. In *Proc. of the Conference on Empirical Methods in Natural Language Processing (EMNLP)*, Vancouver, Canada.

Kallirroi Georgila and David Traum. 2011. Reinforcement learning of argumentation dialogue policies in negotiation. In *Proc. of Interspeech*, Florence, Italy.

Kallirroi Georgila, Claire Nelson, and David Traum. 2014. Single-agent vs. multi-agent techniques for concurrent reinforcement learning of negotiation dialogue policies. In *Proc. of the Annual Meeting of the Association for Computational Linguistics (ACL)*, Baltimore, Maryland, USA.

Kallirroi Georgila. 2013. Reinforcement learning of two-issue negotiation dialogue policies. In *Proc. of the Annual SIGdial Meeting on Discourse and Dialogue*, Metz, France.

Peter A. Heeman. 2009. Representing the reinforcement learning state in a negotiation dialogue. In *Proc. of the IEEE Automatic Speech Recognition and Understanding Workshop (ASRU)*, Merano, Italy.

Takuya Hiraoka, Graham Neubig, Sakriani Sakti, Tomoki Toda, and Satoshi Nakamura. 2014. Reinforcement learning of cooperative persuasive dialogue policies using framing. In *Proc. of COLING*, Dublin, Ireland.

Raz Lin and Sarit Kraus. 2010. Can automated agents proficiently negotiate with humans? *Communications of the ACM*, 53(1):78–88.

A. Rudnicky and W. Xu. 1999. An agenda-based dialogue management architecture for spoken language systems. In *Proc. of the IEEE Automatic Speech Recognition and Understanding Workshop (ASRU)*, Keystone, Colorado, USA.

Jost Schatzmann and Steve Young. 2009. The hidden agenda user simulation model. *IEEE Transactions on Audio, Speech, and Language Processing*, 17(4):733–747.

Csaba Szepesvári. 2010. *Algorithms for Reinforcement Learning*. Morgan & Claypool Publishers.

Initial Conditions:
SU: args(strong: 3, weak: 1), persuadability: high prefs: A: a_1-a_2-a_3, B: b_3-b_1-b_2, C: c_1-c_3-c_2, D: d_1-d_3-d_2 importance: 0.2,0.2,0.7,0.9
Agent: args(strong: 2, weak: 2), persuadability: high prefs: A: a_2-a_1-a_3, B: b_2-b_1-b_3, C: c_1-c_2-c_3, D: d_3-d_2-d_1 importance: 0.7,0.3,0.3,0.9
Agenda: ReqB,ReqC,ReqD,OffA,OffB,OffC, OffD,ReqA (the agenda is randomly initialized) SA: RequestPreference(issueB) *SU: What do you prefer for issue B?* Agenda: ReqC,ReqD,OffA,OffB,OffC,OffD, ReqA
SA: ProvidePreference(issueB) *Agent: I prefer b_2 for issue B.*
Agenda: **ArgB**,ReqC,ReqD,OffA,OffB,OffC, OffD,ReqA SA: ProvideArgument(issueB,b_3,strong) *SU: Here's a strong argument, supporting b_3 for issue B.* Agenda: ReqC,ReqD,OffA,OffB,OffC,OffD, ReqA
SA: Trade-off(issueB,b_3,issueA,a_2), Offer(issueC,c_1) *Agent: I'll accept b_3 for issue B, if you accept a_2 for issue A.* *Agent: How about c_1, for issue C?*
Agenda: **ArgB,AccC**,ReqC,ReqD,OffA,OffB, OffC,OffD,ReqA SA: ProvideArgument(issueB,b_3,strong) *SU: Here's a strong argument, supporting b_3 for issue B.* Agenda: AccC,ReqC,ReqD,OffA,OffB,OffC, OffD,ReqA
SA: Offer(issueB,b_3) *Agent: How about b_3, for issue B?* (after 2 strong arguments the agent is convinced)
Agenda: **AccB**,AccC,ReqC,ReqD,OffA,OffB, OffC,OffD,ReqA SA: Accept(issueB,b_3) *SU: I accept b_3, for issue B.* SA: Accept(issueC,c_1) *SU: I accept c_1, for issue C.* Agenda: ReqD,OffA,OffD,ReqA

Table 3: Example interaction between our agenda-based SU and an agent. Actions that are pushed onto the SU agenda based on previous actions of the agent are shown in bold.

Fast and easy language understanding for dialog systems with Microsoft Language Understanding Intelligent Service (LUIS)

Jason D. Williams, Eslam Kamal, Mokhtar Ashour, Hani Amr, Jessica Miller, Geoff Zweig
Microsoft Research
One Microsoft Way
Redmond, WA 98052, USA
`jason.williams@microsoft.com`

Abstract

With Language Understanding Intelligent Service (LUIS), developers without machine learning expertise can quickly build and use language understanding models specific to their task. LUIS is entirely cloud-based: developers log into a website, enter a few example utterances and their labels, and then deploy a model to an HTTP endpoint. Utterances sent to the endpoint are logged and can be efficiently labeled using active learning. Visualizations help identify issues, which can be resolved by either adding more labels or by giving hints to the machine learner in the form of features. Altogether, a developer can create and deploy an initial language understanding model in minutes, and easily maintain it as usage of their application grows.

1 Introduction and Background

In a spoken dialog system, language understanding (LU) converts from the words in an utterance into a machine-readable meaning representation, typically indicating the *intent* of the utterance and any *entities* present in the utterance (Wang et al., 2005; Tur and Mori, 2011). For example, consider a physical fitness domain, with a dialog system embedded in a wearable device like a watch. This dialog system could recognize intents like `StartActivity` and `StopActivity`, and could recognize entities like `ActivityType`. In the user utterance "begin a jog", the goal of LU is to identify the utterance intent as `StartActivity`, and identify the entity `ActivityType=''jog''`.

Historically, there have been two options for implementing language understanding: machine-learning (ML) models and handcrafted rules. Handcrafted rules are accessible for general software developers, but they are difficult to scale up, and do not benefit from data. ML-based models are trained on real usage data, generalize well to new situations, and are superior in terms of robustness. However, they require rare and expensive expertise, and are therefore generally employed only by organizations with substantial resources.

Microsoft's Language Understanding Intelligent Service (LUIS) aims to enable software developers to create cloud-based machine-learning language understanding models specific to their application domain, *without ML expertise*. LUIS is built on prior work in Microsoft Research on interactive learning (Simard et al, 2014), and rapid development of language understanding models (Williams et al., 2015).

2 LUIS overview

Developers begin by creating a new LUIS "application", and specifying the intents and entities needed in their domain. They then enter a few utterances they would like their application to handle. For each, they choose the intent label by choosing from a drop-down, and specify any entities in the utterance by highlighting a contiguous subset of words in the utterance. As the developer enters labels, the model is automatically and asynchronously re-built (requring 1-2 seconds), and the current model is used to propose labels when new utterances are entered. These proposed labels serve two purposes: first, they act as a rotating test set and illustrate the performance of the current model on unseen data; second, when the proposed labels are correct, they act as an accelerator.

As labeling progresses, LUIS shows several visualizations which show performance, including overall accuracy and any confusions – for example, if an utterance is labeled with the intent `StartActivity` but is being classified as `StopActivity`, or if an utterance was la-

Proceedings of the SIGDIAL 2015 Conference, pages 159–161,
Prague, Czech Republic, 2-4 September 2015.

beled as containing an instance of the entity ActivityType, but that entity is not being detected. These visualizations are shown on all the data labeled so far; i.e., the visualizations show performance on the training set, which is important because developers want to ensure that their model will reproduce the labels they've entered.

When a classification error surfaces in a visualization, developers have a few options for fixing it: they can add more labels; they can change a label (for example, if an utterance was mis-labeled); or they can add a *feature*. A feature is a dictionary of words or phrases which will be used by the machine learning algorithm. Features are particularly useful for helping the models to generalize from very few examples – for example, to help a model generalize to many types of devices, the developer could add a feature called ActivityWords that contains 100 words like "run", "walk", "jog", "hike", and so on. This would help the learner generalize from a few examples like "begin a walk" and "start tracking a run", without needing to label utterances with every type of activity.

In addition to creating custom entities, developers can also add "pre-built" ready-to-use entities, including numbers, temperatures, locations, monetary amounts, ages, encyclopaedic concepts, dates, and times.

At any point, the developer can "publish" their models to an HTTP endpoint. This HTTP endpoint takes the utterance text as input, and returns an object in JavaScript Object Notation (JSON) form. An example of the return format is shown in Figure 1. This URL can then be called from within the developer's application. The endpoint is accessible by any internet-connected device, including mobile phones, tablets, wearables, robots, and embedded devices; and is optimized for real-time operation.

As utterances are received on the HTTP endpoint, they are logged, and are available for labeling in LUIS. However, successful applications will receive substantial usage, so labeling every utterance would be inefficient. LUIS provides two ways of managing large scale traffic efficiently. First, a conventional (text) search index is created which allows a developer to search for utterances that contain a word or phrase, like "switch on" or "air conditioning". This lets a developer explore the data to look for new intents or entirely new phrasings. Second, LUIS can *suggest* the most useful utterances to label by using active learning. Here, all logged utterances are scored with the current model, and utterances closest to the decision boundary are presented first. This ensures that the developer's labeling effort has maximal impact.


```
{
  "query": "start tracking a run",
  "entities": [
    {
      "entity": "run",
      "type": "ActivityType"
    }
  ],
  "intents": [
    {
      "intent": "StartActivity",
      "score": 0.993625045
    },
    {
      "intent": "None",
      "score": 0.03260582
    },
    {
      "intent": "StopActivity",
      "score": 0.0249939673
    },
    {
      "intent": "SetHRTarget",
      "score": 0.003474009
    }
  ]
}
```


Figure 1: Example JSON response for the utterance "start tracking a run".

3 Demonstration

This demonstration will largely follow the presentation of LUIS at the Microsoft //build developer event. A video of this presentation is available at www.luis.ai/home/video.

The demonstration begins by logging into www.luis.ai and inputting the intents and entities in the domain, including new domain-specific entities and pre-built entities. The developer then starts entering utterances in the domain and labeling them. After a label is entered, the model is re-built, and the visualizations are updated. When errors are observed, a feature is added to address them. The demonstration continues by publishing the model to an HTTP endpoint, and a few requests are made to the endpoint by using a second web browser window, or by running a Python script to simulate more usage. The demonstration then shows how these utterances are now available for labeling in LUIS, either through searching, or

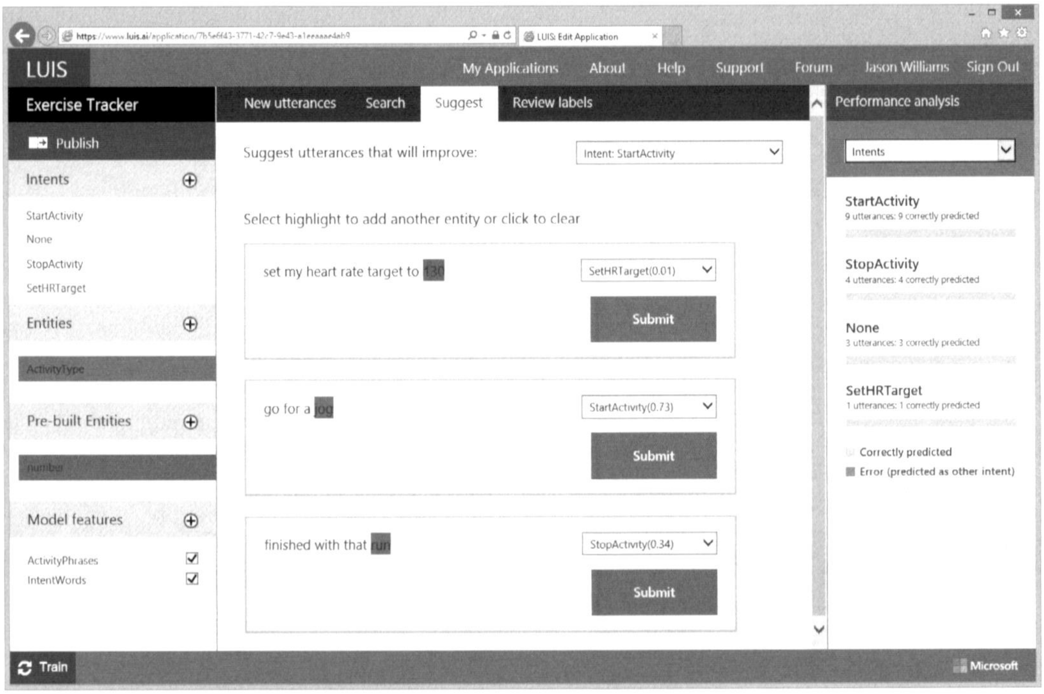

Figure 2: Microsoft Language Understanding Intelligent Service (LUIS). In the left pane, the developer can add or remove intents, entities, and features. By clicking on a feature, the developer can edit the words and phrases in that feature. The center pane provides different ways of labeling utterances: in the "New utterances" tab, the developer can type in new utterances; in the "Search" tab, the developer can run text searches for unlabeled utterances received on the HTTP endpoint; in the "Suggest" tab, LUIS scans utterances received on the HTTP endpoint and automatically suggests utterances to label using active learning; and in the "Review labels" tab, the developer can see utterances they've already labeled. The right pane, shows application performance – the drop-down box lets the developer drill down to see performance of individual intents or entities.

by using active learning. After labeling a few utterances using these methods, the demonstration concludes by showing how the updated application can be instantly re-published.

4 Access

LUIS is currently in use by hundreds of developers in an invitation-only beta – an invitation may be requested at `www.luis.ai`. We have begun in an invitation-only mode so that we can work closely with a group of developers of a manageable size, to understand their needs and refine the user interface. We expect to migrate to an open public beta in the coming months.

References

P Simard et al. 2014. ICE: Enabling non-experts to build models interactively for large-scale lopsided problems. `http://arxiv.org/ftp/arxiv/papers/1409/1409.4814.pdf`.

G Tur and R De Mori. 2011. *Spoken Language Understanding — Systems for Extracting Semantic Information from Speech*. John Wiley and Sons.

Y Wang, L Deng, and A Acero. 2005. Spoken language understanding. *Signal Processing Magazine, IEEE*, 22(5):16–31, Sept.

JD Williams, NB Niraula, P Dasigi, A Lakshmiratan, CGJ Suarez, M Reddy, and G Zweig. 2015. Rapidly scaling dialog systems with interactive learning. In *International Workshop on Spoken Dialog Systems, Busan, Korea*.

Multilingual WikiTalk: Wikipedia-based talking robots that switch languages

Graham Wilcock
CDM Interact and
University of Helsinki, Finland
graham.wilcock@cdminteract.com

Kristiina Jokinen
University of Tartu, Estonia and
University of Helsinki, Finland
kjokinen@ut.ee

Abstract

At SIGDIAL-2013 our talking robot demonstrated Wikipedia-based spoken information access in English. Our new demo shows a robot speaking different languages, getting content from different language Wikipedias, and switching languages to meet the linguistic capabilities of different dialogue partners.

1 Introduction

In the digital world, information services need to be multilingual. While there has been much progress in some areas such as on-line translation, it is less clear in other areas such as interactive applications. For many people, the most effective form of communication is face-to-face, and it is important to be able to use one's mother tongue when dealing with interactive services.

Our previous demo at SIGDIAL-2013 (Jokinen and Wilcock, 2013) showed spoken information access dialogues in English with a monolingual humanoid robot. Our new demo shows a robot speaking different languages, getting information from different language Wikipedias, and switching languages to meet the linguistic capabilities of different dialogue partners.

Section 2 gives a summary of our spoken information access system, which has been described in more detail in previous papers, and Section 3 outlines the development of multilingual versions of the system. A description of the language-switching demo is given in Section 4.

2 Outline of WikiTalk

WikiTalk (Wilcock, 2012) is a spoken dialogue system for Wikipedia-based information access. On humanoid robots WikiTalk uses face-tracking, nodding and gesturing to support interaction management and the presentation of new information (Jokinen and Wilcock, 2014).

The dialogue model uses a finite state machine but the states function at a dialogue management meta-level dealing primarily with topic initiation, topic continuation, and topic switching (Wilcock, 2012; Jokinen, 2015).

An important feature is the ability to make smooth topic shifts by following hyperlinks in Wikipedia when the user repeats the name of a link. For example if the robot is talking about Japan and mentions "kanji" when explaining the Japanese name for Japan, the user can say "kanji?" and the system will smoothly switch topics and start talking about kanji after getting information from Wikipedia about this new topic.

To jump to an unrelated topic, an awkward topic shift can be made by saying "Alphabet!" and spelling the first few letters of the new topic using a spelling alphabet (Alpha, Bravo, Charlie, etc.).

The user can interrupt the robot at any time by touching the top of the robot's head. The robot stops talking, says "Oh sorry!" and waits. The user can tell the robot to continue, go back, skip to another chunk, or switch to a new topic.

The robot can take the initiative by suggesting new topics, using the "Did you know ...?" sections from Wikipedia that are new every day.

The interaction history is stored by the dialogue manager. Using heuristics, the robot avoids giving the same instructions to the user in the same way. At first the robot gives simple instructions so the user can learn the basic functionalities. Later, it suggests new options that the user may not know.

3 Multilingual WikiTalk

The first version of WikiTalk was developed with the Pyro robotics simulator (Wilcock and Jokinen, 2011; Jokinen and Wilcock, 2012). This version was monolingual and used English Wikipedia and English speech components.

A humanoid robot version of WikiTalk was implemented at 8th International Summer Work-

Proceedings of the SIGDIAL 2015 Conference, pages 162–164,
Prague, Czech Republic, 2-4 September 2015.

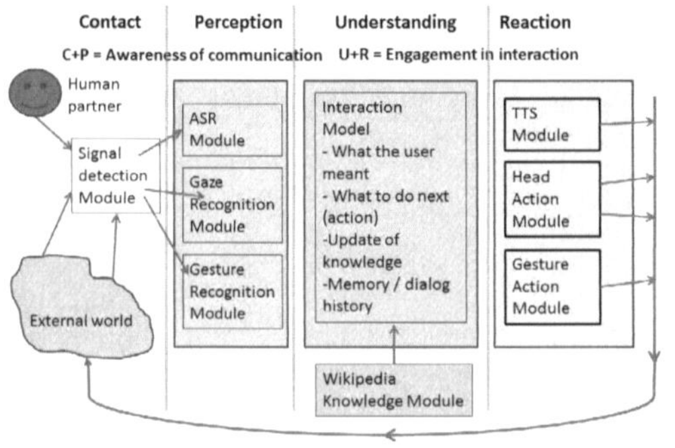

Figure 1: Architecture of WikiTalk for humanoid robots, from (Jokinen and Wilcock, 2014).

shop on Multimodal Interfaces (Csapo et al., 2012; Meena et al., 2012; Han et al., 2012). This version was also monolingual English. The system architecture is shown in Figure 1. An annotated video of the first demo can be seen at https://drive.google.com/open?id=0B-D1kVqPMlKdOEcyS25nMWpjUG8.

WikiTalk is very suitable for making multilingual versions. The essential requirements are the availablity of a Wikipedia in a given language and suitable speech components (recognition and synthesis) for the language. Advanced NLP tools such as syntactic parsers can also be useful but WikiTalk does not depend on them.

In order to prepare for making different language versions of WikiTalk for humanoid robots, an internationalized version of the software was developed (Laxström et al., 2014). The first two localizations were for English and Finnish. Each localized version is based on the internationalized system. Each version uses its own Wikipedia and its own speech components (i.e. English WikiTalk uses English Wikipedia and English speech components, Finnish WikiTalk uses Finnish Wikipedia and Finnish speech components).

Finnish WikiTalk was first demonstrated at EU Robotics Week 2014 in Helsinki. A video report by Iltalehti newspaper titled "This robot speaks Finnish and can tell you what is a robot" can be seen at www.iltalehti.fi/iltvdigi/201411290140927_v4.shtml.

A localized Japanese version of WikiTalk was developed in 2015 (Okonogi et al., 2015). This version uses Japanese Wikipedia and Japanese speech components.

We also intend to develop localized versions of WikiTalk for smaller languages such as Northern Sami which is spoken by a few thousand people in Lapland. For the revitalization of under-resourced languages in the digital world it is important for speakers of such languages to see that their language is part of the future as well as part of the past. This view may be strengthened by hearing robots speaking their language.

Currently the robot does not perform automatic language recognition, it switches language only when this is explicitly requested by the user. For example, the user says "Nihongo" to switch to Japanese, "Suomi" to switch to Finnish, "English" to switch to English. Robot-initiated language-switching raises interesting issues which will be addressed in future work.

4 The language-switching demo

The demo starts in English. The robot identifies a human face and makes eye-contact. It explains that it can talk about any topic in Wikipedia, and suggests some favourites such as Shakespeare and Manchester United. When the human moves, the robot does face-tracking to maintain eye contact.

The user selects a suggested topic, Shakespeare, so the robot downloads information about this topic directly from Wikipedia via a wifi network. The robot begins talking about Shakespeare and continues talking about this topic for a while as the human does not interrupt. After a paragraph, the robot stops and asks explicitly whether to continue or not.

After the user has listened to another paragraph about the same topic, the robot explains "You can change to other topics related to Shakespeare simply by saying them". The user then asks about Shakespeare's son Hamnet so the robot makes a smooth topic shift and talks about Hamnet Shakespeare.

The robot mentions Shakespeare's play Julius Caesar and the human says "Julius Caesar", so the robot starts talking about Julius Caesar (the play). While talking about the play, the robot mentions the historical person Julius Caesar and the human again says simply "Julius Caesar". This time the robot starts talking about the person Julius Caesar, not the play.

When the English-speaking user says "Enough" and moves away, a Japanese-speaking person approaches the robot and says "Nihongo". The robot makes eye-contact with the new person, and switches to Japanese speech. It explains in Japanese that it can talk about any topic in Wikipedia, suggesting some favourite topics. The Japanese user also selects Shakespeare, and the robot gets information about Shakespeare, but this time from Japanese Wikipedia.

While talking about Shakespeare in Japanese, the robot also explains the Japanese versions of some basic commands and interactions. After a while the Japanese-speaking user decides to stop. The English-speaker returns. He says "English" and the robot switches back to English speech.

An annotated video (Figure 2) of the English-Japanese language-switching demo can be seen at `https://drive.google.com/open?id=0B-D1kVqPMlKdRDlkVHh4Z2tUTG8`.

Figure 2: Annotated video of an English-Japanese language-switching robot.

Acknowledgements

The second author gratefully acknowledges the financial support of Estonian Science Foundation project IUT20-56 (Eesti keele arvutimudelid; computational models for Estonian)

We thank Niklas Laxström for his work on the internationalization of WikiTalk and the localized Finnish version. We also thank Kenichi Okonogi and Seiichi Yamamoto for their collaboration on the localized Japanese version.

References

Adam Csapo, Emer Gilmartin, Jonathan Grizou, JingGuang Han, Raveesh Meena, Dimitra Anastasiou, Kristiina Jokinen, and Graham Wilcock. 2012. Multimodal conversational interaction with a humanoid robot. In *Proceedings of 3rd IEEE International Conference on Cognitive Infocommunications (CogInfoCom 2012)*, pages 667–672, Kosice.

JingGuang Han, Nick Campbell, Kristiina Jokinen, and Graham Wilcock. 2012. Investigating the use of non-verbal cues in human-robot interaction with a Nao robot. In *Proceedings of 3rd IEEE International Conference on Cognitive Infocommunications (CogInfoCom 2012)*, pages 679–683, Kosice.

Kristiina Jokinen and Graham Wilcock. 2012. Constructive interaction for talking about interesting topics. In *Proceedings of Eighth International Conference on Language Resources and Evaluation (LREC 2012)*, Istanbul.

Kristiina Jokinen and Graham Wilcock. 2013. Open-domain information access with talking robots. In *14th Annual SIGdial Meeting on Discourse and Dialogue: Proceedings of the SIGDIAL 2013 Conference*, pages 360–362, Metz.

Kristiina Jokinen and Graham Wilcock. 2014. Multimodal open-domain conversations with the Nao robot. In Joseph Mariani, Sophie Rosset, Martine Garnier-Rizet, and Laurence Devillers, editors, *Natural Interaction with Robots, Knowbots and Smartphones: Putting Spoken Dialogue Systems into Practice)*, pages 213–224. Springer.

Kristiina Jokinen. 2015. Bridging gaps between planning and open-domain spoken dialogues. In Núria Gala, Reinhard Rapp, and Gemma Bel-Enguix, editors, *Language Production, Cognition, and the Lexicon*, pages 347–360. Springer.

Niklas Laxström, Kristiina Jokinen, and Graham Wilcock. 2014. Situated interaction in a multilingual spoken information access framework. In *Proceedings of the Fifth International Workshop on Spoken Dialog Systems (IWSDS 2014)*, Napa, California.

Raveesh Meena, Kristiina Jokinen, and Graham Wilcock. 2012. Integration of gestures and speech in human-robot interaction. In *Proceedings of 3rd IEEE International Conference on Cognitive Infocommunications (CogInfoCom 2012)*, pages 673–678, Kosice.

Kenichi Okonogi, Graham Wilcock, and Seiichi Yamamoto. 2015. Nihongo WikiTalk no kaihatsu (Development of Japanese WikiTalk). In *Forum on Information Technology (FIT 2015)*, Matsuyama, Japan. (in Japanese).

Graham Wilcock and Kristiina Jokinen. 2011. Adding speech to a robotics simulator. In *Proceedings of the Paralinguistic Information and its Integration in Spoken Dialogue Systems Workshop*, pages 371–376, Granada.

Graham Wilcock. 2012. WikiTalk: A spoken Wikipedia-based open-domain knowledge access system. In *Proceedings of the COLING 2012 Workshop on Question Answering for Complex Domains*, pages 57–69, Mumbai.

Modelling situated human-robot interaction using IrisTK

Gabriel Skantze and Martin Johansson
Department of Speech Music and Hearing, KTH
Stockholm, Sweden
{skantze,vhmj}@kth.se

Abstract

In this demonstration we show how situated multi-party human-robot interaction can be modelled using the open source framework IrisTK. We will demonstrate the capabilities of IrisTK by showing an application where two users are playing a collaborative card sorting game together with the robot head Furhat, where the cards are shown on a touch table between the players. The application is interesting from a research perspective, as it involves both multi-party interaction, as well as joint attention to the objects under discussion.

1 Introduction

Recently, there has been an increased interest in understanding and modelling multi-party, situated interaction between humans and robots (Bohus & Horvitz, 2011; Mutlu et al., 2012: Johansson et al., 2014; Al Moubayed et al., 2014). In situated interaction, the system is typically embodied and the space in which the interaction takes place is of importance. By modelling the physical situation, the system can track multiple users (and possibly system agents) that enter and leave the interaction. Also, the discussion can involve objects in the shared space. The possibility to model this kind of interaction is facilitated by the many affordable sensors that are becoming available, such as Microsoft Kinect. However, while there are many examples of research systems that can engage in situated interaction (Bohus & Horvitz, 2011; Mutlu et al., 2012), the combination of all these techniques together with spoken dialog technology is not trivial, and it might be hard for a novice to put such systems together. Face-to-face interaction involves a large amount of real-time events that need to be orchestrated in order to handle phenomena such as overlaps, interruptions, coordination of head pose and gaze in turn-taking, etc. Also, the knowledge to develop and put together the necessary modules is of a very interdisciplinary nature. This calls for a dialog system toolkit for multi-party face-to-face interaction, which provides necessary modules for multimodal input and output and allows the developer or researcher to author the dialog flow in a way that is simple to understand for the novice, yet powerful enough to model more sophisticated behaviours.

At KTH, we are developing the open source Java-based framework IrisTK (www.iristk.net), which has exactly this purpose (but can of course also be used for speech-only systems). Since we first presented it (Skantze & Al Moubayed, 2012), the framework has matured and has been applied in many different settings (Johansson et al., 2014; Al Moubayed et al., 2014; Skantze et al., 2014). In this demonstration, we will show a system that was implemented using IrisTK, and which was exhibited at the Swedish National Museum of Science and Technology, in November 15-23, 2014[1]. As can be seen in Figure 1, two visitors at a time can play a collaborative game together with the robot head Furhat (Al Moubayed et al., 2013). On the touch table between the players, a set of cards are shown. The two visitors and Furhat are given the task of sorting the cards according to some criterion. For example, the task could be to sort a set of inventions in the order they were invented, or a set of animals by how fast they can run. This is a collaborative game, which means that the visitors have to discuss the solution together with Furhat. However, Furhat does not have perfect knowledge about the solution. Instead, Furhat's behaviour is motivated by a randomized belief model. This means

[1] A video of the interaction can be seen at https://www.youtube.com/watch?v=5fhjuGu3d0I

Proceedings of the SIGDIAL 2015 Conference, pages 165–167,
Prague, Czech Republic, 2-4 September 2015. ©2015 Association for Computational Linguistics

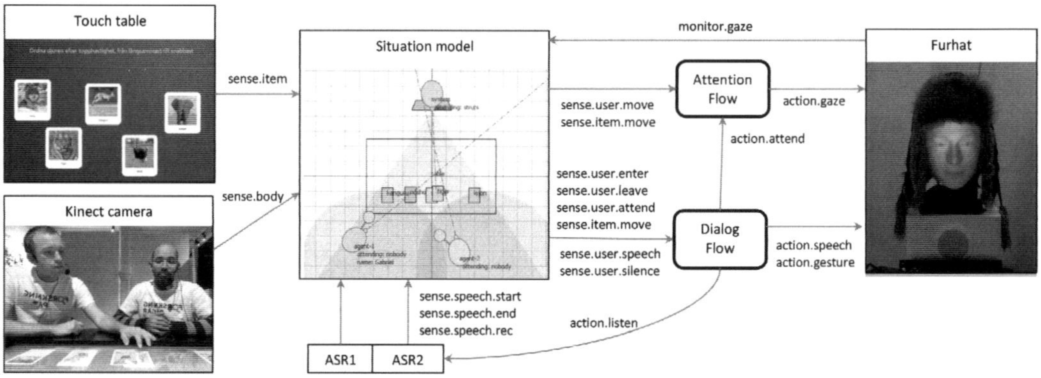

Figure 1. A schematic illustration of some of the modules and events used in the card sorting application.

that the visitors have to determine whether they should trust Furhat's belief or not, just like they have to do with each other. Thus, Furhat's role in the interaction is similar to that of the visitors, as opposed to for example a tutor role which is often given to robots in similar settings (cf. Al Moubayed et al., 2014).

2 Overview of IrisTK

The system architecture is schematically illustrated in Figure 1. IrisTK provides a large set of modules for processing multimodal input and output, and for dialogue management, that can be put together in different ways. The framework defines a set of standardized events (as can be seen in Figure 1), which makes it possible to easily switch different modules (such as system agents or speech recognizers), as well as implementing new ones.

2.1 Vision and Situation modelling

A Kinect camera (V1 or V2) can be used to track the location and rotation of the two users' heads, as well as their hands. The head pose of the users can for example be used to determine whether they are addressing Furhat or not. This data, together with the position of the five cards on the touch table are sent to a Situation model, which maintains a 3D representation of the situation (as seen in Figure 1). The task of the Situation model is to take all sensor data and merge them into a common coordinate system, assign speech events to the right users based on the spatial configuration, and produce higher-level events.

2.2 Speech processing

IrisTK supports different combinations of microphones and speech recognisers. In the museum setup, we used close talking microphones together with two parallel cloud-based large vocabulary speech recognizers, Nuance NDEV mobile[2], which allows Furhat to understand the users even when they are talking simultaneously. However, the modularity of the framework makes it very easy to use the array microphone in the Kinect sensor instead. It is also possible to use SRGS grammars for speech recognition and/or semantic parsing, as well as extending the audio processing chain to add for example prosodic analysis.

2.3 IrisFlow

IrisTK also provides an XML-based formalism (IrisFlow) for rapidly developing behaviour modules, based on the notion of Harel statecharts (Harel, 1987) and similar to SCXML[3]. As discussed in Skantze & Al Moubayed (2012), this formalism combines the intuitiveness of Finite State Machines with the flexibility and expressivity of the Information State Update approach to dialogue management. As can be seen in Figure 1, we use two such behaviour modules running in parallel for the museum application: one for dialogue management and one for maintaining Furhat's attention. Thus, IrisFlow can be used to script both higher-level and lower-level behaviours. The Dialogue Flow module orchestrates the spoken interaction, based on events from the Situation model, such as someone speaking, shifting attention, entering or leaving the interaction, or moving cards on the table. The Attention Flow keeps Furhat's attention to a specified target (a user or a card), even when the target is moving, by consulting the Situation model. The 3D position of the target is then transformed into neck and gaze movement of

[2] http://dragonmobile.nuancemobiledeveloper.com/
[3] http://www.w3.org/TR/scxml/

Furhat (again taking Furhat's position in the 3D space into account).

2.4 System output

For face-to-face interaction, IrisTK provides an animated agent that can be presented on a screen. While this solution suffice when only one person is interacting with the system, it does not work so well for multi-party interaction, due to the Mona Lisa effect (Al Moubayed et al., 2013), which means that it is impossible to achieve mutual gaze with only one of the users, or for users to infer the target of the agent's gaze in the shared space (such as the cards on the table). The preferable solution is to instead use a robot. IrisTK currently supports the Furhat robot head[4], but we are working on supporting other robot platforms. Furhat has an animated face back-projected on a translucent mask, as well as a mechanical neck, which allows Furhat to signal his focus of attention using a combination of head pose and eye-gaze. The animation solution makes it possible to express subtle and detailed facial gestures (such as raising the eye brows or smiling), as well as accurate lip sync. The facial manifestation is completely decoupled from the speech synthesis, so that different agents can be combined with different speech synthesizers.

3 Discussion

During the 9 days the system was exhibited at the Swedish National Museum of Science and Technology, we recorded data from 373 interactions with the system. To this end, IrisTK provides many tools for easily logging all events in the system, as well as the audio. Thus, we think that IrisTK is an excellent tool for doing research on situated interaction.

Apart from being used for research, IrisTK has also been used for education at KTH. In the course *Multimodal interaction and interfaces*, given to master students, it is used both for a three hour lab on conversational interfaces, as well as a platform for group projects. Only with two–three weeks of work and with little need for supervision, the students have used IrisTK to implement systems for travel booking, city exploration, cinema ticket booking, an interactive calendar and a virtual doctor[5].

We are still working on several ways to improve IrisTK. Currently it only runs on Windows (although it should be easy to port since it is Java based). We are also working on adding modules for face recognition, so that the system can maintain a long-term relationship with the users. Another improvement will be to add support for other robot platforms, such as NAO, which would also make it possible to explore body gestures. Another extension will be to combine the authoring of the flow with statistical models, such as reinforcement learning, so that some behaviours can be learned through interaction with users.

[4] http://www.furhatrobotics.com

[5] Videos of these system can be seen at http://www.iristk.net/examples.html

Acknowledgements

This work is supported by the Swedish research council (VR) project *Incremental processing in multimodal conversational systems* (2011-6237).

References

Al Moubayed, S., Beskow, J., Bollepalli, B., Hussen-Abdelaziz, A., Johansson, M., Koutsombogera, M., Lopes, J., Novikova, J., Oertel, C., Skantze, G., Stefanov, K., & Varol, G. (2014). Tutoring Robots: Multiparty multimodal social dialogue with an embodied tutor. In *Proceedings of eNTERFACE2013*. Springer.

Al Moubayed, S., Skantze, G., & Beskow, J. (2013). The Furhat Back-Projected Humanoid Head - Lip reading, Gaze and Multiparty Interaction. *International Journal of Humanoid Robotics, 10*(1).

Bohus, D., & Horvitz, E. (2011). Decisions about turns in multiparty conversation: from perception to action. In *ICMI '11 Proceedings of the 13th international conference on multimodal interfaces* (pp. 153-160).

Harel, D. (1987). Statecharts: A visual formalism for complex systems. *Science of Computer Programming, 8*, 231-274.

Johansson, M., Skantze, G., & Gustafson, J. (2014). Comparison of human-human and human-robot Turn-taking Behaviour in multi-party Situated interaction. In *International Workshop on Understanding and Modeling Multiparty, Multimodal Interactions, at ICMI 2014*. Istanbul, Turkey.

Mutlu, B., Kanda, T., Forlizzi, J., Hodgins, J., & Ishiguro, H. (2012). Conversational Gaze Mechanisms for Humanlike Robots. *ACM Trans. Interact. Intell. Syst., 1*(2), 12:1-12:33.

Skantze, G., & Al Moubayed, S. (2012). IrisTK: a statechart-based toolkit for multi-party face-to-face interaction. In *Proceedings of ICMI*. Santa Monica, CA.

Skantze, G., Hjalmarsson, A., & Oertel, C. (2014). Turn-taking, Feedback and Joint Attention in Situated Human-Robot Interaction. *Speech Communication, 65*, 50-66.

I Couldn't Agree More: The Role of Conversational Structure in Agreement and Disagreement Detection in Online Discussions

Sara Rosenthal
Columbia University
Computer Science Department
NY, NY, USA
sara@cs.columbia.edu

Kathleen McKeown
Columbia University
Computer Science Department
NY, NY, USA
kathy@cs.columbia.edu

Abstract

Determining when conversational participants agree or disagree is instrumental for broader conversational analysis; it is necessary, for example, in deciding when a group has reached consensus. In this paper, we describe three main contributions. We show how different aspects of conversational structure can be used to detect agreement and disagreement in discussion forums. In particular, we exploit information about meta-thread structure and accommodation between participants. Second, we demonstrate the impact of the features using 3-way classification, including sentences expressing disagreement, agreement or neither. Finally, we show how to use a naturally occurring data set with labels derived from the sides that participants choose in debates on createdebate.com. The resulting new agreement corpus, Agreement by Create Debaters (ABCD) is 25 times larger than any prior corpus. We demonstrate that using this data enables us to outperform the same system trained on prior existing in-domain smaller annotated datasets.

1 Introduction

Any time people have a discussion, whether it be to solve a problem, discuss politics, products, or more casually, gossip, they will express their opinions. As a conversation evolves, the participants of the discussion will agree or disagree with the views of others. The ability to automatically detect agreement and disagreement (henceforth referred to as (dis)agreement) in the discussion is useful for understanding how conflicts arise and are resolved, and the role of each person in the conversation. Furthermore, detecting (dis)agreement has been found to be useful for other tasks, such as detecting subgroups (Hassan et al. 2012), stance (Lin et al., 2006; Thomas et al., 2006), power (Danescu-Niculescu-Mizil et al., 2012; Biran et al., 2012), and interactions (Mukherjee and Liu, 2013).

In this paper, we explore a rich suite of features to detect (dis)agreement between two posts, the *quote* and the *response* (Q-R pairs (Walker et al., 2012)), in online discussions where the response post directly succeeds the quote post. We analyze the impact of features including meta-thread structure, lexical and stylistic features, Linguistic Inquiry Word Count categories, sentiment, sentence similarity and accommodation. Our research indicates that conversational structure, as indicated by meta-thread information as well as accommodation between participants, plays an important role. *Accommodation* (Giles et al., 1991), is a phenomenon where conversational participants adopt the conversational characteristics of the other participants as conversation progresses. Our approach represents accommodation as a complex interplay of semantic and syntactic shared information between the Q-R posts. Both meta-thread structure and accommodation use information drawn from both the quote and response; these features provide significant improvements over information from the response alone.

We detect (dis)agreement in a supervised machine learning setting using 3-way classification (agreement/disagreement/none) between Q-R posts in several datasets annotated for agreement, whereas most prior work uses 2-way classification. In many online discussions, none (i.e., the lack of (dis)agreement) is the majority category so leaving it out makes it impossible to accurately classify the majority of the sentences in an online discussion with a binary classification model.

We also present a new naturally occurring agreement corpus, Agreement by Create Debaters (ABCD), derived from a discussion forum web-

Proceedings of the SIGDIAL 2015 Conference, pages 168–177,
Prague, Czech Republic, 2-4 September 2015.

Example of disagreement in an ABCD discussion indicated by different sides (Against and For).
Abortion is WRONG! God created that person for a reason. If your not ready to raise a kid then put it up for adoption so it can be with a good family. Dont murder it! Its wrong. It has a life. If you can have sex then you should be ready for the consequences tht come with it! **Side:** ***Against***
Those who were raped through the multiple varieties of means, are expected to birth this child although it was coerced rape. I don't think so. Taking a woman's right to choice is wrong regardless what a church or the government suggests. **Side:** ***For***
Example of agreement in an ABCD discussion indicated by the same side (Against).
HELL NO! ... KILLING A INNOCENT BABY ISN'T GONNA JUST GO AWAY YOU WILL HAVE TO LIVE WITH THE GUILT FOREVER!!!!!!! **Side:** ***Against***
————————————> That is soo true living with the guilt forever know you murder you child it would have been even better if the murder hadn't been born. **Side:** ***Against***
Example of no (dis)agreement in an ABCD discussion between the original post and a response.
Coke or Pepsi?
They taste the same no big difference between them for me

Table 1: Examples of Agreement, Disagreement, and None in ABCD discussions

site, createdebate.com, where the participants are required to provide which side of the debate they are on. This enabled us to easily gather over 10,000 discussions in which there are over 200,000 posts containing (dis)agreement or the lack of, *25 times larger* than any pre-existing agreement dataset. We show that this large dataset can be used to successfully detect (dis)agreement in other forums (e.g. 4forums.com and Wikipedia Talk Pages) where the labels cannot be mined, thereby avoiding the time consuming and difficult annotation process.

In the following sections, we first discuss related work in spoken conversations and discussion forums. We then turn to describe our new dataset, ABCD, as well as two other manually annotated corpora, Internet Argument Corpus (IAC), and Agreement in Wikipedia Talk Pages (AWTP). We explain the features used in our system and describe our experiments and results. We conclude with a discussion containing an error analysis of the hard cases of (dis)agreement detection.

2 Related Work

Early prior work on detecting (dis)agreement has focused on spoken dialogue (Galley et al., 2004; Hillard et al., 2003; Hahn et al., 2006) using the ICSI meeting corpus (Janin et al., 2003). Germesin and Wilson (2009) detect (dis)agreement on dialog acts in the AMI meeting corpus (Mccowan et al., 2005) and Wang et al (2011a, 2011b) detect (dis)agreement in broadcast conversation in English and Arabic. Prior work in spoken dialog has motivated some of our features (e.g., lists of agreement and disagreement terms, sentiment and n-grams).

Recent work has turned to (dis)agreement detection in online discussions (Yin et al., 2012; Abbott et al., 2011; Misra and Walker, 2013; Mukherjee and Liu, 2012). The prior work performs 2-way classification between agreement and disagreement using features that are lexical (e.g. n-grams), basic meta-thread structure (e.g. post length), social media features (e.g. emoticons), and polarity using dictionaries (e.g. SentiWordNet). Yin et al (2012), detect local and global (dis)agreement in discussion forums where people debate topics. Their focus is global (dis)agreement, which occurs between a post and the root post of the discussion. They manually annotated posts from US Message Board (818 posts) and Political Forum (170 posts) for global agreement. This approach ignores off-topic posts in the discussion which can indicate incorrect labeling and the small size makes it difficult to determine how consistent their results would be in unseen datasets. Abbott et al (2011), look at (dis)agreement using 2,800 annotated posts from the Internet Argument Corpus (IAC) (Walker et al., 2012). Their work was extended to topic independent classification by Misra and Walker (2013). Since it is the largest previously used corpus, we use the IAC corpus in our experiments. Lastly, Mukherjee and Liu (2012) , developed an SVM+Joint Topic Model classifier to detect (dis)agreement using 2,000 posts. They studied accommodation across (dis)agreement by classifying over 300,000 posts and explore the difference in accommodation across LIWC categories. While they did not implement accommodation, they found that it is more common in agreement for most categories, except for a few style dimensions (e.g. negation) where it is reversed. This paper highly motivates our inclusion of accommodation for (dis)agreement detection.

In other work, Opitz and Zirn (2013) detect

(dis)agreement on sentences using the Authority and Alignments in Wikipedia Discussions corpus (Bender et al., 2011) which is different than the AWTP corpus used in this paper. In the future we would like to explore whether we could incorporate this corpus into ours. Wang and Cardie (2014) also detect (dis)agreement on the sentence and segment[1] level using this corpus and the IAC.

Our approach differs from prior work in that it explores (dis)agreement detection on a large, naturally occurring dataset where the annotations are derived from participant information. We explore new features representing aspects of conversational structure (e.g. sentence similarity) and the more difficult 3-way classification task of detecting agreement/disagreement/none.

3 Data

In this work we focus on direct (dis)agreement between quote-response (Q-R) posts in the three datasets described in the following subsections. Across all datasets we only include discussions of depth > 2 to ensure a response chain of at least three people and thus, a thread. We also excluded extremely large discussions to improve processing speed. We only consider entire posts in Q-R pairs.

3.1 Agreement by Create Debaters (ABCD)

Create Debate is a website where people can start a debate on a topic by asking a question. On this site, a debate can be:

- **open-ended**: there is no side
- **for-or-against**: two sided
- **multiple-sides**: three or more sides

In this paper, we only focus on debates of the for-or-against nature where there are two sides. For example, we use a debate discussing whether people are for or against abortion[2] in our examples throughout the paper. In this corpus, the participants in the debate choose what side they are on each time they participate in the discussion. Prior work (Abu-Jbara et al., 2012) has used the side label of this corpus to detect the subgroups in the discussion. We annotate the corpus as follows: the side label determines whether a post (the *Response*) is in agreement with the post prior to it (the *Quote*). If the two labels are the same, then they agree. If the two labels are different, they disagree. When the author is the same for both posts, there is no (dis)agreement as the second post is just a continuation of the first. Finally, the first post and its direct responses do not agree with anyone; the first post does not have a side as it is generally a question asking whether people are for, or against the topic of the debate. Examples of (dis)agreement and none are shown in Table 1. We call this corpus Agreement by Create Debaters or ABCD.

Dataset	Thread Count	Post Count	Agree	Disagree	None
ABCD	9981	185479	38195	60991	86293
IAC	1220	5940	428	1236	4276
AWTP	50	822	38	148	636

Table 2: Statistics for full datasets

Our dataset includes over 10,000 discussions which include 200,000 posts on a variety of topics. Additional statistics for ABCD are shown in Table 2. There are far more disagreements than agreements as people tend to be argumentative when they are debating a topic.

3.2 Internet Argument Corpus (IAC)

The second dataset we use is the IAC (Walker et al., 2012). The IAC consists of posts gathered from `4forums.com` discussions that were annotated on Mechanical Turk. The Turkers were provided with a Q-R pair and had to indicate the level of (dis)agreement using a scale of $[-5, 5]$ where -5 indicated high disagreement, 0 no (dis)agreement, and 5 high agreement. As in prior work with this corpus (Abbott et al., 2011; Misra and Walker, 2013), we converted the scalar values to (dis)agreement with $[-5, -2]$ as disagreement, $[-1, 1]$ as none, and $[2, 5]$ as agreement. In this dataset is it possible for multiple annotations to occur in a single post. We combine the annotation to the post level as follows. We ignored the none annotations unless there was no (dis)agreement. In all other cases, we use the average (dis)agreement score as the final score for the post. 10% of the posts had more than one annotation label. The number of annotations per class is shown in Table 2. Not all Q-R posts in a thread were annotated for agreement as is evident by the ratio of threads to post annotations.

3.3 Agreement in Wikipedia Talk Pages (AWTP)

Our last corpus is 50 Wikipedia talk pages (used to discuss edits) containing 822 posts (see full statistics in Table 2) that were manually annotated as the ATWP (Andreas et al., 2012). Although

[1] a segment is a portion of a post

[2] www.createdebate.com/debate/show/Abortion_9

smaller than the IAC, the advantage to this dataset is that each thread was annotated in its entirety. As in the create debate discussions, disagreement is more common than agreement due to the nature of the discussion. These annotations were on the sentence level where multiple sentences can be part of a single annotation. In 99% of the Q-R posts, there was just one pair of sentences that were annotated with a (dis)agreement label and we used that annotation for the post. When there was one more than one pair, we used the majority annotation. The post was labeled with none only when all sentences within the post had the none label. AWTP was annotated by three different people. Inter-Annotator Agreement (IAA) using the sentence pairs was very high because most annotations were none. Therefore, we computed IAA by randomly sampling an equivalent amount of sentences pairs per label from two of the annotators (A1 & A2) and had the third annotator (A3) annotate all of those sentence pairs. Cohen's κ for A1,A3 was .90 and for A2,A3 was .70 indicating high IAA.

4 Method

We model our data by posts. Each data point (the *Response*) is a single post and its label indicates whether it agrees, disagrees, or none, to the post it is responding to (the *Quote*). The following sections discuss the features used to train our model. Each feature is computed within the entire post. In addition, in all applicable features, we also indicate if the feature occurs in the first sentence of the post. Our analysis showed that (dis)agreement tends to occur in the first sentence of the response.

Meta-Thread Structure features include: 1) **The post is the root of the discussion**: This is useful because the root of the discussion tends to be a question (e.g., "Are you for or against abortion") and thus, does not express (dis)agreement. 2) **The reply was by the same author**: The second post is just a continuation of the first. 3) **The distance, or depth, of the post from the beginning of the discussion**: anyone that replied to the root (Depth of 1) has no (dis)agreement because the root is a question and therefore has no side. The average depth per thread is 4.9 in ABCD, 12.7 in IAC and 6.2 in ATWP, and 4) **The number of sentences in the response**: people who disagree tend to write more than those who agree.

Lexical Features are generated for each post. We use (1-3)gram features and also generate up to 4 possible Part of Speech (POS) tag features (Toutanova et al., 2003) for each word in the post. We include all unigram POS tags and perform Chi-Squared feature selection on everything else. In addition, we also generated small lists of negation terms (e.g. not, nothing; 11 terms in total), agreement terms (e.g. agree, concur; 16 terms in total), and disagreement terms (e.g. disagree, differ; 14 terms in total) and generate a binary feature for each list indicating that the post has one of the terms from the respective list of words. Finally, we also include a feature indicating whether there is a sentence that ends in a question as when someone asks a question, it may be followed by (dis)agreement, but it probably won't be in (dis)agreement with the post preceding it.

Lexical Stylistic Features that fall into two groups are included, **general**: ones that are common across online and traditional genres, and **social media**: ones that are far more common in online genres. Examples of general style features are exclamation points and ellipses. Examples of social media style features are emoticons and word lengthening (e.g. sweeeet).

Linguistic Inquiry Word Count The Linguistic Inquiry Word Count (LIWC) (Tausczik and Pennebaker, 2010) aims to capture the way people talk by categorizing words into a variety of categories such as negative emotion, past tense, and health and has been used previously in agreement (Abbott et al., 2011). The 2007 LIWC dictionary contains 4487 words with each word belonging in one or more categories. We use all the categories as features to indicate whether the response has a word in the category.

Sentiment By definition, (dis)agreement indicates whether someone has the same, or different, opinion than the original speaker. A sentence tagged with subjectivity can help differentiate between (dis)agreement and the lack thereof, while polarity can help differentiate between agreement and disagreement. We use a phrase-based sentiment detection system (Agarwal et al., 2009; Rosenthal et al., 2014) that has been optimized for lexical style to tag the sentences with opinion and polarity. For example, it produces the following tagged sentence "[That is soo true]/*Obj* [living with the guilt forever]/*neg* [know you murder you child]/*neg*..." We use the tagged sentence to generate several opinion-related features. We generate bag of words for all opinionated words in the opinion and polarity phrases, labeling each word as to which class it belongs to (opinion, positive, or negative). We also have binary features indicating the prominence of opinion and polarity (positive or negative).

Sentence Similarity A useful indicator for determining whether people are (dis)agreeing or not is if they are talking about the same topic. We use sentence similarity (Guo and Diab, 2012) to determine the similarity between the Q-R posts. For example the disagreement posts in Table 1 are similar because of the statements *"LIVE WITH THE GUILT FOREVER!!!!!!!"* and *"living with the guilt forever"*. We use the output of the system to indicate whether there are two similar sentences above some threshold and whether all the sentences are similar to one another.

Furthermore, we also look at similar Q-R phrases in conjunction with sentiment. We generate phrases using the Stanford parser (Socher et al., 2013) by adding reasonably sized branches of the parse tree as phrases. We then find the similarity (Guo and Diab, 2012) and opinion (Agarwal et al., 2009; Rosenthal et al., 2014) of the phrases and extract the unique words in the similar phrases as features. We hypothesize that this could help indicate disagreement, for example, if the word "not" was mentioned in one of the phrases, e.g. *"I do not see anything wrong with abortion =/"* vs *"I do see something wrong with abortion ..."*. We also include unique negation terms using the list described in the Lexical Feature section and features to indicate whether there is a similar phrase and if its opinion in the Q-R posts are of the same polarity (agree) or different polarity (disagree).

Accommodation When people speak to each other, they tend to take on the speaking habits and mannerisms of the person they are talking to (Giles et al., 1991). This phenomenon is known as *accommodation*. Mukherjee and Liu (2012) found that accommodation differs among people who (dis)agree. This strongly motivates using accommodation in (dis)agreement detection[3]. We partly capture this via sentence similarity which explores whether they share the same words. We also explore whether Q-R posts use the same syntax (POS, n-grams), copy lexical style, and use the same category of words (LIWC). We use the features as described in prior sections but only include ones that exist in the quote and response.

[3] Accommodation wasn't used to classify (dis)agreement.

5 Experiments

All of our experiments were run using Mallet (McCallum, 2002). We experimented with Naive Bayes, Maximum Entropy (i.e. Logistic Regression), and J48 Decision Trees and found that Maximum Entropy consistently outperformed or there was no statistically significant difference to the other classifiers; we only show the results for Maximum Entropy here. We show our results in terms of None, Agreement, and Disagreement F-Score as well as macro-average F-score for all three classes. The ABCD and IAC datasets were split into 80% train, 10% development, and 10% test. We use the entire AWTP dataset as a test set because of its small size. All results shown are using a balanced training set by downsampling and the full test set. It is important to use a balanced dataset for training because the ratio of agreement/disagreement/none differs in each dataset. We tuned the features using the development set and ran an exhaustive experiment to determine which features provided the best results and use that best group of features as an additional experiment in the test sets.

In order to show the impact of our large dataset, we experimented with increasing the size of the training set by starting with 25 posts from each class and increased the size until the full dataset is reached (e.g. 25, 50, 100, ...). We also show a more detailed analysis of the various features using the full datasets. In all datasets, the best experiment includes the features found to be most useful during development and differs per dataset.

We compare our experiments to two baselines. The first is the majority class, which is none. Although none is more common, it is important to note that we would prefer to achieve higher f-score in the other classes as our goal is to detect (dis)agreement. The second baseline is n-grams, the commonly used baseline in prior work. We compute statistical significance using the Approximate Randomization test (Noreen, 1989; Yeh, 2000), a suitable significance metric for F-score.

5.1 Agreement by Create Debaters (ABCD)

Our first experiments were performed on the large ABCD dataset of almost 10,000 discussions described in the Data Section. We experimented with balancing and unbalancing the training dataset and the balanced datasets consistently outperformed the unbalanced datasets. Therefore, we only used

Features	None	Agree	Disagree	Avg
majority	63.2	0.0	0.0	21.1
n-gram	45.7	35.6	41.3	40.9
n-grams+POS+lex.-style+ LIWC in R	58.7^{1}	42.2	51.6	50.8
Thread Structure	100	45.8	62.0	69.2
Accommodation	74.0	45.1	59.1	59.4
Thread+Accommodation	99.6	57.8	68.2	75.2
All	99.6	58.0	73.1	76.9
Best	100	58.5	73.0	77.6

Table 3: The effect, in F-score, of conversational structure in the ABCD corpus. Statistical significance is shown over majority$^{\alpha}$ and n-gram$^{\beta}$ baselines.

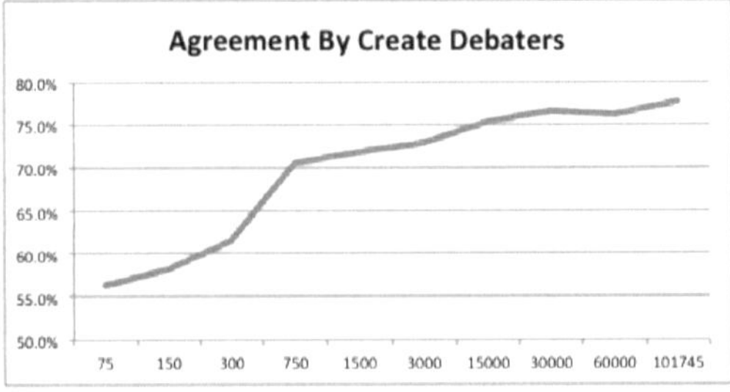

Figure 1: Average F-score as the ABCD training size increases when testing on the ABCD.

balanced datasets in the training set for the rest of the experiments. Table 3 shows how accommodation and meta-thread structure are very useful for detecting (dis)agreement. In fact, using n-grams, POS, LIWC, and lexical style features in just the response yields an average F-score of 50.8% whereas using POS, LIWC and lexical style in both the quote and response as well as sentence similarity yields a significant improvement of 8.6 points or 16.9% to an average F-score of 59.4%, indicating that conversational structure is very indicative of (dis)agreement. Using all features and the best features (computed using the development set) provide a statistically significant improvement at $\leq .05$ over both baselines. Our best results include all features except polarity with an average F-Score of 77.6%. Figure 1 shows that as the training size increases the results improve.

5.2 Internet Argument Corpus (IAC)

In contrast to prior work we detect (dis)agreement as a 3-way classification task: agreement, disagreement, none. Detecting (dis)agreement without including none pairs is unrealistic in a threaded discussion where the majority of posts will be neither agreement or disagreement. Additionally, we do not balance the test set as do Abbott et al (2011) and Walker et al (2013), but rather use all annotated posts to maintain a realistic agreement/disagreement/none ratio.

We experiment with using the small manually annotated in-domain IAC corpus and the large ABCD corpus. In contrast to the ABCD, we did not find accommodation to be significantly useful when training and testing using the IAC. We believe this is due to the large amount of none posts in the dataset (71.9%) where one does not expect accommodation to occur. However, in examining the average F-score for (dis)agreement, without none, we found that accommodation provides a 2.7 point or 11% improvement over only using features from the response. This improvement is masked by a 1.2 reduction in the none class where accommodation is not useful. The best IAC features differ depending on the training set and were computed using the IAC development set. Using the IAC training set, meta-thread structure, the LIWC, sentence similarity, and lexical style were most important. Using the ABCD corpus, the best features on the IAC development set were meta-thread structure, polarity, sentence similarity, the LIWC, and the negation/agreement/disagreement terms and question lexical features. We found it especially interesting that polarity and lexical features were useful on the ABCD while lexical style was useful for the IAC indicating clear variations in content across genres. Using the best features per corpus found from tuning towards the development sets (e.g. training and tuning on ABCD) provide a statistically significant improvement at $\leq .05$ over the n-gram baseline. The best and all (dis)agreement results provide a statistically significant improvement over the majority baseline. More detailed results are shown in Table 4. Finally, Figure 2a shows how increasing the size of the automatic ABCD training set improves the results compared to the manually annotated training set using the best feature set. Interestingly, there is little variation between the use of both datasets using the best features. We believe this is because thread structure is the most useful feature due to the large occurrence of none posts.

5.3 Agreement in Wikipedia Talk Pages (AWTP)

Our last set of experiments were performed on the AWTP which was annotated in-house. The advantage to the AWTP corpus is that the annotators were given the entire thread during annotation time, and annotated all (dis)agreement,

Features	IAC				ABCD			
	None	Agree	Disagree	Average	None	Agree	Disagree	Average
majority	85.1	0.0	0.0	28.4	85.1	0.0	0.0	28.4
n-gram	58.6	11.7	27.8	32.7	46.7	7.8	36.6	30.3
n-grams+POS+lexical-style+LIWC in R	54.1	12.0^{α}	29.7^{α}	31.9	43.9	13.6^{α}	30.1^{α}	29.2
Thread Structure	87.4^{β}	$25.3^{\alpha\beta}$	$50.0^{\alpha\beta}$	54.2^{β}	87.3^{β}	$26.4^{\alpha\beta}$	$53.8^{\alpha\beta}$	55.8^{β}
Accommodation	52.9	13.9^{α}	32.4^{α}	33.1	51.7	14.7^{α}	34.3^{α}	33.6
Thread+Accommodation	87.5^{β}	$26.5^{\alpha\beta}$	48.9^{β}	$54.3^{\alpha\beta}$	87.2^{β}	$28.0^{\alpha\beta}$	$55.5^{\alpha\beta}$	56.9^{β}
All	83.5^{β}	$28.8^{\alpha\beta}$	$50.4^{\alpha\beta}$	54.2^{β}	87.3^{β}	$27.0^{\alpha\beta}$	41.2^{α}	51.8
Best	87.4^{β}	$31.5^{\alpha\beta}$	$54.4^{\alpha\beta}$	57.8^{β}	87.3^{β}	$25.5^{\alpha\beta}$	$57.3^{\alpha\beta}$	56.7^{β}

Table 4: The effect, in F-score, of conversational structure in the IAC test set using the IAC and ABCD as training data. Results highlighted to indicate statistical significance over majority$^{\alpha}$ and n-gram$^{\beta}$ baselines.

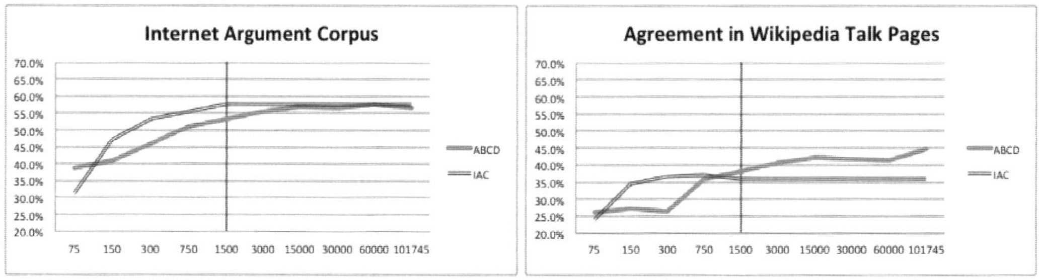

(a) (b)

Figure 2: Avg. F-score as the training size increases. The vertical line is the size of the IAC training set. The F-score succeeding the vertical line is the score at the peak size, included for contrast.

whether between Q-R pairs or not. In contrast, the IAC annotators were not provided with the entire thread. It was annotated only between Q-R pairs and even all Q-R pairs in a thread were not annotated. This means that each ATWP thread can be used for (dis)agreement detection in its entirety. Having fully annotated threads preserves the ratio of agreement/disagreement/none pairs better (the IAC has posts that are missing annotations).

We experiment with predicting (dis)agreement using the large naturally occurring ABCD dataset and the gold IAC dataset. Despite its advantage of gold labels, we found that using the ABCD as training consistently outperforms using the IAC as training on out-of-domain data, excluding when using just n-grams. In contrast to the other datasets, meta-thread structure and accommodation individually perform worse than using similar features found in the response alone. We believe this is because meta-thread structure is not strictly enforced in Wikipedia Talk Pages, providing an inaccurate representation of who is responding to who. Using all and the best features found during development (e.g. via training and tuning on ABCD) provide a statistically significant improvement at $\leq .05$ over the n-gram baseline for ABCD. The all and best (dis)agreement results provide a statistically significant improvement over the majority baseline for training on ABCD and IAC. More detailed results are shown in Table 3. We ran identical experiments to those performed on the IAC by increasing the training size of the ABCD corpus and IAC corpus to show their effects on the test set as shown in Figure 2b. The IAC dataset performs worse than using the ABCD dataset once the size of the ABCD training set exceeds the size of the IAC training set. This is further indication that automatic labeling is useful.

6 Discussion

We performed an error analysis to determine the kind of errors our system was making on 50 ABCD posts and 50 IAC posts from the development sets. In the ABCD posts we focused on agreement posts that were labeled incorrectly as our performance was worst in this class. Our analysis indicated that in most cases, 72.7% of the time, the error was due to the incorrect label; it should have been disagreement or none and not agreement as suggested by the side of the post. This is unsurprising as the label is determined using the side chosen by the post author. However, what is more surprising is that this was the common cause of error in the IAC

Features	IAC				ABCD			
	None	Agree	Disagree	Average	None	Agree	Disagree	Average
majority	87.2	0.0	0.0	29.1	87.2	0.0	0.0	29.1
n-gram	68.1	12.7	21.3	34.1	36.5	11.6	32	26.7
n-grams+POS+lexical-style+LIWC in R	64.1	12.1^{α}	22.7^{α}	33.0	54.0^{β}	$27.7^{\alpha\beta}$	$36.2^{\alpha\beta}$	39.3^{β}
Thread Structure	58.0	12.4^{α}	23.7^{α}	31.4	63.6^{β}	15.0^{α}	33.4^{α}	37.3
Accommodation	52.4	12.4^{α}	$30.7^{\alpha\beta}$	31.8	50.7^{β}	$17.5^{\alpha\beta}$	$40.1^{\alpha\beta}$	36.1^{β}
Thread+Accommodation	55.0	14.9^{α}	$37.2^{\alpha\beta}$	35.7	62.9^{β}	$21.3^{\alpha\beta}$	$52.2^{\alpha\beta}$	43.9^{β}
All	64.2	15.5^{α}	$36.4^{\alpha\beta}$	38.7	61.9^{β}	$25.8^{\alpha\beta}$	$43.5^{\alpha\beta}$	43.7^{β}
Best	59.3	14.4^{α}	$34.5^{\alpha\beta}$	36.1	63.6^{β}	$23.3^{\alpha\beta}$	$46.8^{\alpha\beta}$	44.4^{β}

Table 5: The effect, in F-score, of conversational structure in the AWTP test set using the IAC and ABCD as training data. Statistical significance is shown over majority$^{\alpha}$ and n-gram$^{\beta}$ baselines.

Dataset	Quote	Response	Description
ABCD	The same thing people use all words for; to convey information.	to convey information. Give me an example of when you are fully capable of saying this without offending someone.	The first sentence sounds like agreement but the second sentence is argumentative
IAC	Nowhere does it say, that she kept a gun in the bathroom emoticon_xkill	And nowhere does it say she went to her bedroom and retrieved a gun.	Agreement. It is an elaboration. Further context would help.

Table 6: Hard examples of (dis)agreement in ABCD and IAC

dataset as well, occurring 58.3% of the time. This is because the IAA using Cohen's κ among Amazon Turk workers for the IAC is low, averaging to .47 (Walker et al., 2012) across all topics. In addition, detecting agreement is hard as is evident in the incorrectly labeled examples in Table 6. Other errors were in posts where the agreement was a response, an elaboration, there was no (dis)agreement, and a conjunction indicating the post contained agreement and disagreement. To gain true insight into our model and gauge the impact of mislabeling, the labels of a small set of 60 threads (908 posts) were manually annotated to correct (dis)agreement errors resulting in 99 label changes. We allowed a post to be both agreement and disagreement and avoided changing labels to none as it is not a self-labeling option. This did not provide a significant change in F-score.

As is evident from our experiments, exploiting meta-thread structure and accommodation provide significant improvements. We also explored whether additional context would help by exploring the entire thread structure using general CRF. However, our experiments found that using CRF did not provide a significant improvement compared to using Maximum Entropy in the ABCD and AWTP corpora. This may be explained by our error analysis, which showed that in only 2/50 ABCD posts and 9/50 IAC posts further context beyond the Q-R posts would possibly help make it clearer whether it was agreement or disagreement.

7 Conclusion

We have shown that by exploiting conversational structure our system achieves significant improvements compared to using lexical features alone. In particular, our approach demonstrates the importance of meta-thread features, and accommodation between participants of an online discussion reflected in the semantic, syntactic and stylistic similarity between their posts. Furthermore, we use naturally occurring labels derived from Create Debate, to achieve improvements in detecting (dis)agreement compared to using smaller manually labeled datasets of the IAC and AWTP. The ABCD and AWTP datasets are available at `www.cs.columbia.edu/~sara/data.php`. This is promising for domains where no annotated data exists; the dataset can be used to avoid performing a time consuming and costly annotation effort. In the future we would like to take further advantage of existing manually annotated datasets by using domain adaptation to combine the datasets. In addition, our error analysis indicated that a significant amount of errors were due to mislabeling. We would like to explore improving results by using the system to automatically correct such errors in held-out training data and then using the corrected data to retrain the model.

Acknowledgments

This paper is based upon work supported by the DARPA DEFT Program. The views expressed are those of the authors and do not reflect the official policy or position of the Department of Defense or the U.S. Government. We thank several anonymous reviewers for their constructive feedback.

References

Rob Abbott, Marilyn Walker, Pranav Anand, Jean E. Fox Tree, Robeson Bowmani, and Joseph King. 2011. How can you say such things?!?: Recognizing disagreement in informal political argument. In *Proceedings of the Workshop on LSM*, LSM '11, pages 2–11, Portland, Oregon. ACL.

Amjad Abu-Jbara, Mona Diab, Pradeep Dasigi, and Dragomir Radev. 2012. Subgroup detection in ideological discussions. In *Proceedings of the 50th Annual Meeting of the ACL*, ACL '12, pages 399–409, Jeju Island, Korea. ACL.

Apoorv Agarwal, Fadi Biadsy, and Kathleen R. Mckeown. 2009. Contextual phrase-level polarity analysis using lexical affect scoring and syntactic n-grams. In *Proceedings of the 12th Conference of the European Chapter of the Association for Computational Linguistics*, EACL '09, pages 24–32, Stroudsburg, PA, USA. Association for Computational Linguistics.

Jacob Andreas, Sara Rosenthal, and Kathleen McKeown. 2012. Annotating agreement and disagreement in threaded discussion. In *Proceedings of the Eight International Conference on Language Resources and Evaluation (LREC'12)*, Istanbul, Turkey, may. European Language Resources Association (ELRA).

Emily M. Bender, Jonathan T. Morgan, Meghan Oxley, Mark Zachry, Brian Hutchinson, Alex Marin, Bin Zhang, and Mari Ostendorf. 2011. Annotating social acts: Authority claims and alignment moves in wikipedia talk pages. In *Proceedings of the Workshop on LSM*, LSM '11, pages 48–57, Portland, Oregon. ACL.

Or Biran, Sara Rosenthal, Jacob Andreas, Kathleen McKeown, and Owen Rambow. 2012. Detecting influencers in written online conversations. In *Proceedings of the 2nd Workshop on LSM*, LSM '12, pages 37–45, Montreal, Canada. ACL.

Cristian Danescu-Niculescu-Mizil, Lillian Lee, Bo Pang, and Jon Kleinberg. 2012. Echoes of power: Language effects and power differences in social interaction. In *Proceedings of the 21st International Conference on WWW*, WWW '12, pages 699–708, NYC, USA. ACM.

Michel Galley, Kathleen McKeown, Julia Hirschberg, and Elizabeth Shriberg. 2004. Identifying agreement and disagreement in conversational speech: use of bayesian networks to model pragmatic dependencies. In *Proceedings of the 43rd Annual Meeting of the ACL*, page 669, Barcelona, Spain. ACL.

Sebastian Germesin and Theresa Wilson. 2009. Agreement detection in multiparty conversation. In *ICMI*, pages 7–14. ACM.

Howard Giles, Nikolas Coupland, and Justine Coupland. 1991. Accommodation theory: Communication, context, and consequence. In *Contexts of Accommodation*, pages 1–68. Cambridge University Press. Cambridge Books Online.

Weiwei Guo and Mona Diab. 2012. Modeling sentences in the latent space. In *Proceedings of the 50th Annual Meeting of the ACL*, pages 864–872, Jeju Island, Korea, July. ACL.

Sangyun Hahn, Richard Ladner, and Mari Ostendorf. 2006. Agreement/disagreement classification: Exploiting unlabeled data using contrast classifiers. In *Proceedings of HLT-NAACL*, pages 53–56, NYC, USA, June. ACL.

Ahmed Hassan, Amjad Abu-Jbara, and Dragomir Radev. 2012. Detecting subgroups in online discussions by modeling positive and negative relations among participants. In *Proceedings of the Joint Conference on EMNLP and CoNLL*, EMNLP-CoNLL '12, pages 59–70, Jeju Island, Korea. ACL.

Dustin Hillard, Mari Ostendorf, and Elizabeth Shriberg. 2003. Detection of agreement vs. disagreement in meetings: Training with unlabeled data. In *Proceedings of HLT-NAACL*, Edmonton, Canada. ACL.

Adam Janin, Don Baron, Jane Edwards, Dan Ellis, David Gelbart, Nelson Morgan, Barbara Peskin, Thilo Pfau, Elizabeth Shriberg, Andreas Stolcke, and Chuck Wooters. 2003. The icsi meeting corpus. pages 364–367.

Wei-Hao Lin, Theresa Wilson, Janyce Wiebe, and Alexander Hauptmann. 2006. Which side are you on?: Identifying perspectives at the document and sentence levels. In *Proceedings of the 10th Conference on CoNLL*, CoNLL-X '06, pages 109–116, NYC, USA. ACL.

Andrew Kachites McCallum. 2002. Mallet: A machine learning for language toolkit. http://www.cs.umass.edu/ mccallum/mallet.

I. Mccowan, G. Lathoud, M. Lincoln, A. Lisowska, W. Post, D. Reidsma, and P. Wellner. 2005. The ami meeting corpus. In *Proceedings Measuring Behavior 2005, 5th International Conference on Methods and Techniques in Behavioral Research.*

Amita Misra and Marilyn Walker. 2013. Topic independent identification of agreement and disagreement in social media dialogue. In *Proceedings of the SIGDIAL 2013 Conference*, pages 41–50, Metz, France, August. ACL.

Arjun Mukherjee and Bing Liu. 2012. Analysis of linguistic style accommodation in online debates. In *Proceedings of COLING 2012*, pages 1831–1846, Mumbai, India, December. The COLING 2012 Organizing Committee.

Arjun Mukherjee and Bing Liu. 2013. Discovering user interactions in ideological discussions. In *Proceedings of the 51st Annual Meeting of the ACL*, pages 671–681, Sofia, Bulgaria, August. ACL.

Eric W. Noreen. 1989. *Computer-Intensive Methods for Testing Hypotheses : An Introduction*. Wiley-Interscience, April.

Bernd Opitz and Cecilia Zirn. 2013. Bootstrapping an unsupervised approach for classifying agreement and disagreement. volume 85. Linköping Univ. Electronic Press.

Sara Rosenthal, Apoorv Agarwal, and Kathy McKeown. 2014. Columbia nlp: Sentiment detection of sentences and subjective phrases in social media. In *Proceedings of the 8th International Workshop on Semantic Evaluation*, SemEval '14, Dublin, Ireland.

Richard Socher, John Bauer, Christopher D. Manning, and Ng Andrew Y. 2013. Parsing with compositional vector grammars. In *Proceedings of the 51st Annual Meeting of the ACL*, pages 455–465, Sofia, Bulgaria, August. ACL.

Yla R. Tausczik and James W. Pennebaker. 2010. The psychological meaning of words: Liwc and computerized text analysis methods.

Matt Thomas, Bo Pang, and Lillian Lee. 2006. Get out the vote: Determining support or opposition from Congressional floor-debate transcripts. In *Proceedings of the Conference on Empirical Methods in Natural Language Processing (EMNLP)*, pages 327–335.

Kristina Toutanova, Dan Klein, Christopher D. Manning, and Yoram Singer. 2003. Feature-rich part-of-speech tagging with a cyclic dependency network. In *Proceedings of HLT-NAACL*, NAACL '03, pages 173–180, Edmonton, Canada. ACL.

Marilyn Walker, Jean Fox Tree, Pranav Anand, Rob Abbott, and Joseph King. 2012. A corpus for research on deliberation and debate. In *Proceedings of the Eight International Conference on LREC (LREC'12)*, Istanbul, Turkey, may. European Language Resources Association (ELRA).

Lu Wang and Claire Cardie. 2014. Improving agreement and disagreement identification in online discussions with a socially-tuned sentiment lexicon. In *Proceedings of the 5th Workshop on Computational Approaches to Subjectivity, Sentiment and Social Media Analysis*, pages 97–106, Baltimore, Maryland, June. Association for Computational Linguistics.

Wen Wang, Kristin Precoda, Colleen Richey, and Geoffrey Raymond. 2011a. Identifying agreement/disagreement in conversational speech: A cross-lingual study. In *INTERSPEECH*, pages 3093–3096. ISCA.

Wen Wang, Sibel Yaman, Kristin Precoda, Colleen Richey, and Geoffrey Raymond. 2011b. Detection of agreement and disagreement in broadcast conversations. In *Proceedings of the 49th Annual Meeting of the ACL*, pages 374–378. ACL.

Alexander Yeh. 2000. More accurate tests for the statistical significance of result differences. In *Proceedings of the 18th Conference on Computational Linguistics - Volume 2*, COLING '00, pages 947–953, Stroudsburg, PA, USA. Association for Computational Linguistics.

Jie Yin, Paul Thomas, Nalin Narang, and Cecile Paris. 2012. Unifying local and global agreement and disagreement classification in online debates. In *Proceedings of the 3rd Workshop in WASSA*, WASSA '12, pages 61–69, Jeju Island, Korea. ACL.

Memory-Based Acquisition of Argument Structures and its Application to Implicit Role Detection

Christian Chiarcos and **Niko Schenk**
Applied Computational Linguistics Lab
Goethe University Frankfurt am Main, Germany
{chiarcos,n.schenk}@em.uni-frankfurt.de

Abstract

We propose a generic, memory-based approach for the detection of implicit semantic roles. While state-of-the-art methods for this task combine hand-crafted rules with specialized and costly lexical resources, our models use large corpora with automated annotations for *explicit* semantic roles only to capture the distribution of predicates and their associated roles. We show that memory-based learning can increase the recognition rate of implicit roles beyond the state-of-the-art.

1 Introduction

Automated implicit semantic role labeling (iSRL) has emerged as a novel area of interest in the recent years. In contrast to traditional SRL, which aims to detect events (e.g., verbal or nominal predicates) together with their associated semantic roles (*agent*, *theme*, *recipient*, etc.) as overtly realized in the current sentence, iSRL extends this analysis with locally *unexpressed* linguistic items. Hence, iSRL requires to broaden the scope beyond isolated sentences to the surrounding discourse. As an illustration, consider the following example from Roth and Frank (2013):

> El Salvador is now the only Latin American country which still has troops in [Iraq]. Nicaragua, Honduras and the Dominican Republic have withdrawn their troops [∅].

In the second sentence, a standard SRL parser would ideally identify *withdraw* as the main verbal predicate. In its thematic relation to the other words within the same sentence, all countries serve as the overtly expressed (explicit) agents, and are thus labeled as arguments A0.[1] Semantically, they are the action performers, whereas *troops* would carry the patient role A1 as the entity which undergoes the action of being withdrawn. However, given these explicit role annotations for A0 and A1 in the second sentence, the standard system would definitely fail to infer the underlying, linguistically unexpressed, i.e., non-overt realization of an *implicit* argument of *withdraw* (denoted by [∅]) about source information. Its corresponding realization is associated with *Iraq* in the preceding sentence, which is outside of the scope of any standard SRL parser. The resulting implicit role has the label A2.

Many role realizations are suppressed on the surface level. The automated detection of such implicit roles and their fillers, which are also called *null instantiations* (NIs) (Fillmore, 1986; Ruppenhofer, 2005), is a challenging task. Yet, if uncovered, NIs provide highly beneficial 'supplementary' information which in turn can be incorporated into practical, downstream NLU applications, like automated text summarization, recognizing textual entailment or question answering.

Current issues in iSRL Corpus data with manually annotated implicit roles is extremely sparse and hard to obtain, and annotation efforts have emerged only recently; cf. Ruppenhofer et al. (2010), Gerber and Chai (2012), and also Feizabadi and Padó (2015) for an attempt to enlarge the number of annotation instances by combination of scarce resources. As a result, most state-of-the-art iSRL systems cannot be trained in a supervised setting and thus integrate custom, rule-based components to detect NIs (we elaborate on related work in Section 2). To this end, a predicate's overt roles are matched against a predefined predicate-specific template. Informally, all roles found in the template but not in the text are regarded as null instantiations. Such pattern-based methods perform satisfactorily, yet there are drawbacks:
(1) They are inflexible and absolute according to

[1] For details on all PropBank labels used in our study, see Palmer et al. (2005).

Proceedings of the SIGDIAL 2015 Conference, pages 178–187,
Prague, Czech Republic, 2-4 September 2015.

their type, in that they assume that all candidate NIs are equally likely to be missing, which is unrealistic given the variety of different linguistic contexts in which predicates co-occur with their semantic roles.
(2) They are expensive in that they require handcrafted, idiosyncratic rules (Ruppenhofer et al., 2011) and rich background knowledge in the form of language-specific lexical resources, such as FrameNet (Baker et al., 1998), PropBank (Palmer et al., 2005) or NomBank (Meyers et al., 2004). Dictionaries providing information about each predicate and status of the individual roles (e.g., whether they can serve as implicit elements or not) are costly, and for most other languages not available to the same extent as for English.
(3) Most earlier studies heuristically restrict implicit arguments to *core* roles[2] only (Tonelli and Delmonte, 2010; Silberer and Frank, 2012), but this is problematic as it ignores the fact that implicit non-core roles also provide valid and valuable information. Our approach remains agnostic regarding the role inventory, and can address both core and non-core arguments. Yet, in accordance with the limited evaluation data and in line with earlier literature, we had to restrict ourselves to evaluate NI predictions for core arguments only.

Our contribution We propose a novel, generic approach to infer information about implicit roles which does not rely on the availability of manually annotated gold data. Our focus is exclusively on *NI role identification*, i.e., per-predicate detection of the missing implicit semantic role(s) given their overtly expressed explicit role(s) (without finding filler elements) as we believe that it serves as a crucial preprocessing step and still bears great potential for improvement. We treat NI identification *separately* from the resolution of their fillers, also because not all NIs are resolvable from the context. In order to facilitate a more flexible mechanism, we propose to condition on the presence of other roles, and primarily argue that NI detection should be **probabilistic instead of rule-based**. More specifically, we predict implicit arguments using large corpora from which we build a background knowledge base of predicates, co-occurring (explicit) roles and their probabilities. With such a **memory-based** approach, we generalize over large quantities of explicit roles to find evidence for implicit information in a mildly supervised manner. Our proposed models are largely domain independent, include a sense distinction for predicates, and are not bound to a specific release of a hand-maintained dictionary. Our approach is portable across languages in that training data can be created using projected SRL annotations. Unlike most earlier approaches, we employ a generic role set which is based on PropBank/NomBank rather than FrameNet: The PropBank format comprises a relatively small role inventory which is better suited to obtain statistical generalizations than the great variety of highly specific FrameNet roles. While FrameNet roles seem to be more fine-grained, their greater number arises mostly from predicate-specific semantic roles, whose specific semantics can be recovered from PropBank annotations by pairing semantic roles with the predicate.

Yet another motivation of our work is related to the recent development of AMR parsing (Banarescu et al., 2013, Abstract Meaning Representation) which aims at modeling the semantic representation of a sentence while abstracting from syntactic idiosyncrasies. This particular appraoch makes extensive use of the PropBank-style framesets, as well, and would greatly benefit from the integration of information on implicit roles.

The paper is structured as follows: Section 2 outlines related work in which we exclusively focus on how previous research has handled the sole identification of NIs. Sect. 3 describes our approach to probabilistic NI detection; Sect. 4 presents two experiments and their evaluation; Sect. 5 concludes our work.

2 Related Work

In the context of the 2010 SemEval Shared Task on *Linking Events and Their Participants in Discourse*[3] on implicit argument resolution, Ruppenhofer et al. (2010) have released a data set of fiction novels with manual NI role annotations for diverse predicates. The data has been referred to by various researchers in the community for direct or indirect evaluation of their results. The NIs in the data set are further subdivided into two categories: Definite NIs (DNIs) are locally unexpressed arguments which can be resolved to elements in the proceeding or following discourse;

[2] *Core* roles are obligatory arguments of a predicate. Informally, *non-core* roles are optional arguments often realized as adjuncts or modifiers.

[3] http://semeval2.fbk.eu/semeval2.php

Indefinite NIs (INIs) are elements for which no antecedent can be identified in the surrounding context.[4] Also, the evaluation data comes in two flavors: a base format which is compliant with the FrameNet paradigm and a CoNLL-based PropBank format. Previous research has exclusively focused on the former.

Chen et al. (2010) present an extension of an existing FrameNet-style parser (SEMAFOR) to handle implicit elements in text. The identification of NIs is guided by the assumption that, whenever the traditional SRL parser returns the default label involved in a non-saturated analysis for a sentence, an implicit role has to be found in the context instead. Additional FrameNet-specific heuristics are employed in which, e.g., the presence of one particular role in a frame makes the identification of another implicit role redundant.[5]

Tonelli and Delmonte (2010, VENSES++) present a deep semantic approach to NI resolution whose system-specific output is mapped to FrameNet valency patterns. For the detection of NIs, they assume that these are always core arguments, i.e., non-omissible roles in the interaction with a specific predicate. It is unclear how different predicate senses are handled by their approach. Moreover, not all types of NIs can be detected, resulting in a low overall recall of identified NIs, also having drawbacks for nouns. Again using FrameNet-specific modeling assumptions, their work has been significantly refined in Tonelli and Delmonte (2011).

Despite their good performance in the overall task, Silberer and Frank (2012, S&F) give a rather vague explanation regarding NI identification in text. Using a FrameNet API, the authors restrict their analysis only to the core roles by excluding "conceptually redundant" roles without further elaboration.

Laparra and Rigau (2013) propose a deterministic algorithm to detect NIs on grounds of discourse coherence: It predicts an NI for a predicate if the corresponding role has been explicitly realized for the same predicate in the preceding discourse but is currently unfilled. Their approach is promising but ignorant of INIs.

Earlier, Laparra and Rigau (2012, L&R) introduce a statistical approach to identifying NIs similar to ours in that they rely on frequencies from overt arguments to predict implicit arguments. For each predicate template (frame), their algorithm computes all Frame Element patterns, i.e., all co-occurring overt roles and their frequencies. For NI identification a given predicate and its overtly expressed roles are matched against the most frequent pattern not violated by the explicit arguments. Roles of the pattern which are not overtly expressed in the text are predicted as missing NIs. Even though their approach outperforms all previous results in terms of NI detection, Laparra and Rigau (2012) only estimate the *raw* frequencies from a very limited training corpus, raising the question whether all patterns are actually sufficiently robust. Also, the authors disregard all the valuable less frequent patterns and limit their analysis to only a subtype of NI instances which are resolvable from the context.

Finally, Gerber and Chai (2012) describe a supervised model for implicit argument resolution on the NomBank corpus which—unlike the previous literature—follows the PropBank annotation format. However, NI detection is still done by dictionary lookup, and the analysis is limited to only a small set of predicates with only one unambiguous sense. Again limiting NIs to only core roles, the authors empirically demonstrate that this simplification accounts for 8% of the overall error rate of their system.

3 Experimental Setup

3.1 Memory-Based Learning

Memory-based learning for NLP (Daelemans and van den Bosch, 2009) is a lazy learning technique which keeps a record of training instances in the form of a background knowledge base (BKB). Classification compares new items directly to the stored items in the BKB via a distance metric. In semantics, the method has been applied by, e.g., Peñas and Hovy (2010) for semantic enrichment, and Chiarcos (2012) to infer (implicit markers for) discourse relations. Here, we adopt its methodology to identify null-instantiated argument roles in text. More precisely, we setup a BKB of probablistic predicate-role co-occurrences and estimate thresholds which serve as a trigger for the prediction of an implicit role (a slight modification of the distance metric). We elaborate on this methodology in Section 4.

[4]The average F-score annotator agreement for frame assignments is about .75 (Ruppenhofer et al., 2010).

[5]Cf. *CoreSet* and *Exludes* relationship in FrameNet.

3.2 Data & Preprocessing

We train our model on a subset of the *WaCkypedia_EN*[6] corpus (Baroni et al., 2009). The data set provides a 2008 Wikipedia dump from which we extracted the tokens and sentences. We have further divided the dump into pieces of growing size (cumulatively by 100 sentences) and applied MATE[7] (Björkelund et al., 2009) for the automatic detection of semantic roles to the varying portions and annotated them with SRL information. For each sentence, MATE identifies the predicates and all of its associated core and non-core arguments.[8] MATE has been used in previous research on implicit elements in text (Roth and Frank, 2013) and provides semantic roles with a sense disambiguation for both verbal and nominal predicates. The resulting output is based on the PropBank format.

3.3 Model Generation

We build a probablistic model from annotated predicate-role co-occurrences as follows:

1. For every sentence, record all distinct predicate instances and their associated roles.
2. For every predicate instance, sort the role labels lexicographically (not the role fillers), disregarding their sequential order. (We thus obtain a normalized template of role co-occurrences for each frame instantiation.)
3. Compute the frequencies for all templates associated with the same predicate.
4. By relative frequency estimation, derive all conditional probabilities of the form:

$$P(r|R, \text{PREDICATE})$$

with $\mathcal{R}$ being the role inventory of the SRL parser, $R \subseteq \mathcal{R}$ a (sub)set of explicitly realized semantic roles, and $r \in \mathcal{R} \setminus R$ an arbitrary semantic role. When we try to gather information on null instantiated roles, r is typically an unrealized role label. The PREDICATE consists of the lemma of the corresponding verb or noun, optionally followed by sense number (if predicates are sense-disambiguated) and its part of speech (V/N), e.g., PLAY.01.N.

[6]http://wacky.sslmit.unibo.it/doku.php?id=corpora

[7]`http://code.google.com/p/mate-tools/`

[8]In order to minimize the noise in the data, we attempted to resplit unrealistically long sentences (> 90 tokens) by means of the Stanford Core NLP module (Manning et al., 2014). All resulting splits > 70 tokens were rejected.

Paradigm		#Roles			#Overt / #DNI+#INI
		Overt	DNI	INI	
Train	FrameNet	2,526	303	277	4.36
	PropBank	1,027	125	101	4.52
Test	FrameNet	3,141	349	361	4.42
	PropBank	1,332	167	85	5.28

Table 1: Label distribution of the SemEval 2010 data set for overt and null instantiated arguments for both the FrameNet (all roles and parts of speech) and the PropBank version (only core roles for nouns and verbs).

We build models from SRL data in PropBank format, both manually and automatically annotated. We experiment with models for two different styles of predicates: *Sense-ignorant* or ***SI model***s represent predicates by lemma and part of speech (PLAY.N), *sense-disambiguated* or ***SD model***s represent predicates by lemma, sense number and part of speech (PLAY.01.N, PLAY.02.N, etc.).

3.4 Annotated Data

In accordance with previous iSRL studies, we evaluate our model on the SemEval data set (Ruppenhofer et al., 2010). However, to the best of our knowledge, this is the first study to focus on the PropBank version of this data set. It has been derived semi-automatically from the FrameNet base format using hand-crafted mapping rules (as part of the data set) for both verbs and nouns. For example, a conversion for the predicate *fear* in FrameNet's EXPERIENCER_FOCUS frame is defined as *fear.01* (its first sense) with the roles EXPERIENCER and CONTENT mapped to PropBank labels A0 and A1, respectively. In accordance with the mapping patterns, the resulting distribution of NIs varies slightly from the base format. Table 1 shows the label distribution of overt roles, DNIs, INIs for both the FrameNet and PropBank versions, respectively. Some information is lost while the general proportions remain similar to the base format. This is also due to the fact that for some parts of speech (e.g., for adjectives) no mappings are defined, even though some of them are annotated with NI information in the FrameNet version. Moreover, mapping rules exist *only for core roles* A0-A4 (agent, patient, ...). As a consequence, we restrict our analysis to these five (unique) roles, even though our models described in this work incorporate probabilistic information for *all possible roles* in $\mathcal{R}$, i.e., A0-A4, but also for *non-core* (modifier) roles, such as AM-TEMP (temporal), AM-LOC (location), etc.

Role	Verbs		Nouns	
	Overt	NIs	Overt	NIs
A0	40	**45**	24	23
A1	83	39	29	**33**
A2	3	11	10	6
A3	-	7	-	1
A4	-	24	-	-
totals:	126	126	63	63

Table 2: Label distributions of all roles in both data sets from Experiment 1; majority NI classes in bold.

4 Experiments

4.1 Experiment 1

To evaluate the general usefulness of our memory-based approach to detect implicit roles, we set up a simplified framework for predicates with exactly *one overt argument and one NI* annotated in the SemEval data (for all verbs and all nouns and from both the train and test files to obtain a reasonably large sample; no differentiation of DNIs and INIs). This pattern accounts for 189 instances—roughly 9% of the data samples in the SemEval set. We divided the instances into two subsets based on the predicate's part of speech. The label distributions over overt and null instantiated roles for both verbal and nominal predicates are given in Table 2.

4.1.1 Task Description

Predict the role of the single missing NI (A0–A4) for each given predicate instance.

4.1.2 Predicting Null Instantiations

We trained one sense-disambiguated (*SD*) gold model for verbs (*PB*) and one for nouns (*NB*) according to Sect. 3.3 on the complete PropBank and the complete NomBank, respectively. This was compared with 30 separate *SD* and *SI* models on varying portions of the automatically annotated *WaCkypedia_EN* dump: These were trained on the first k sentences each, in order to make their prediction quality comparable, while k ranges from 50 sentences for the smallest model to $k = 10$ million for the largest model ($\approx \frac{1}{5}$ of the whole corpus). For NI role prediction, we return n_i, i.e., the maximally probable unrealized semantic role given the overt argument o_j plus the predicate:

$$n_i = \arg\max_{n \in \mathcal{R} \setminus R} P(n | o_j, \text{PREDICATE}),$$

where $R = \{o_j\}$, the predicate's single explicit role and $\mathcal{R} = \{A0..A4\} \supset R$, the role inventory.

4.1.3 Results & Evaluation

The prediction accuracies for verbal and nominal predicates are illustrated in Figure 1. Although the number of instances in the data sets is small, some general trends are clearly visible. Our major findings are:

By increasing the number of training sentences the performance of the *SD* and the *SI*-based classification models steadily increases as well. The trend is the same for both verbs and for nouns, even though training in the nominal domain requires more data to obtain similarly good results. More precisely, models trained on only 50k sentences already have an adequate performance on test data for verbs ($\approx$76% with the *SD* model). To reach a similar performance on nouns, we need to increase the training size roughly by a factor of 5.

Likewise, the performance of the *SD* models is better in general than the one of the *SI* models throughout all models analyzing verbal predicates, but only marginally better for nouns.

Both the *SD* and the *SI* models outperform the majority class baseline for both parts of speech.[9]

Also, with 800k sentences for nouns and only 50k sentences for verbs, both *SD* model types reach accuracies equal to or greater than the supervised *PB* and *NB* (gold) models which have been trained on the complete PropBank and NomBank corpus including sense distinctions, respectively.

The classification accuracies for the *SD* models reach their saturated maxima for verbs at around 91.27% (115/126) with 6 million training sentences and 85.71% (54/63) with 2.85 million sentences for nouns. For verbs, a χ^2 test confirms a significant ($p < .01$) improvement of our best model over the *PB* gold model. On the sparse evaluation data for nouns, the improvement over the *NB* gold model is, however, not significant.

Taken together, the improvements confirm that memory-based learning over mass data of automatically annotated (explicit) semantic roles can actually outperform gold models constructed from corpora with manual SRL annotations, even if the tools for automated mass annotation were trained on the very same corpora used to build the gold models (PropBank, NomBank). Also, the experiment demonstrated the feasibility of predicting implicit roles solely using information about the distribution of explicit roles. For the artificially

[9]35.71% with only 1k training sentences (verbs), 52.38% with 50k sentences (nouns).

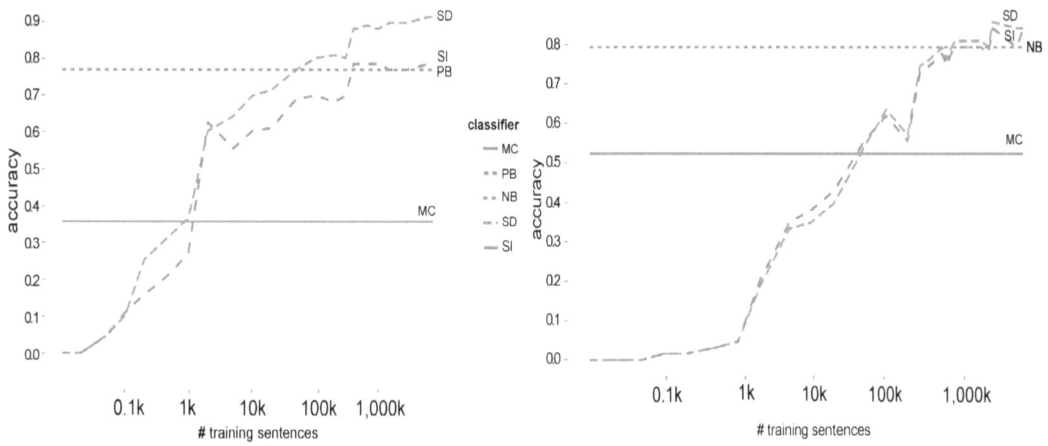

Figure 1: Prediction accuracies for verbal (left figure) and nominal predicates (right figure) from Experiment 1. Majority class (*MC*) baselines in red, PropBank (*PB*) and NomBank (*NB*) gold models in green. The log-scaled x-axis only refers to the *SD* and *SI* models and indicates first k sentences used for training.

simplified NI patterns in Experiment 1, already small portions of automatically annotated SRL data are sufficient to yield adequate results for both types (DNIs and INIs). Sense disambiguation of predicates generally increases the performance.[10]

4.2 Experiment 2

The setup from the previous experiment is by far too simplistic compared to a real linguistic scenario. Usually, a predicate can have an arbitrary number of overt arguments, and similarly the number of missing NIs varies. To tackle this problem, we take the original train and test split (744 vs. 929 unrestricted frame instances of the form: any combination of overt roles vs. any combination of NI roles per predicate). Again, we do not draw a distinction between DNIs and INIs, but treat them generally as NIs. Table 3 shows the distribution of the different NI role patterns in the test data.

4.2.1 Task Description

Given a predicate and its overtly expressed arguments (ranging from any combination of A0 to A4 or none), predict the correct set of null instantiations (which can also be empty or contain up to five different implicit elements).

[10]A simple error analysis of the misclassified noun instances revealed that classification on the test data suffers from sparsity issues: In the portions of the *WaCkypedia_EN* that we used for model building, three predicates were not attested (twice *murder.01* and once *murderer.01*). This has a considerable impact on test results.

NI Pattern	Freq	NI Pattern	Freq
-	706	A0 A2	7
A1	86	A1 A2	6
A0	51	A3	5
A2	35	A1 A4	3
A4	18	A0 A1 A2	1
A0 A1	11		

Table 3: The 929 NI role patterns from the test set sorted by their number of occurrence. Most of the predicates are saturated and do not seek an implicit argument. Only one predicate instance has three implicit roles.

4.2.2 Predicting Null Instantiations

We distinguish two main types of classifiers: *supervised classifiers* are directly obtained from NI annotations in the SemEval training data, *mildly supervised classifiers* instead use only information about (automatically obtained) explicitly realized semantic roles in a given corpus, *hybrid classifiers* combine both sources of information. We estimated all parameters optimizing F-measure on the train section of the SemEval data set. Their performance is evaluated on its test section. We aim to demonstrate that mildly supervised classifiers are capable of predicting implicit roles, and to study whether NI annotations can be used to improve their performance.

Baseline: Given the diversity of possible patterns, it is hard to decide how a suitable and competitive baseline should be defined: predicting the majority class means not to predict anything. So, instead, we predict implicit argument roles randomly, but in a way that emulates their frequency distribution in the SemEval data (cf. Tab. 3), i.e., predict

Classifier	A	B_1	B_2	C_0	C_1	C_2	C_3	C_4	$C_{4_{n,v}}$	$C_{4_{n,v,B1}}$	$C_{4_{n,v,B2}}$
Precision	*0.149*	0.848	**0.853**	*0.368*	*0.378*	0.398	0.400	0.400	0.423	0.561	0.582
Recall	*0.075*	*0.155*	*0.206*	**0.861**	0.851	0.837	0.837	0.837	0.782	0.615	0.814
F_1 Score	*0.100*	*0.262*	*0.332*	*0.516*	*0.523*	*0.540*	*0.541*	*0.541*	*0.549*	0.589	**0.679**

Table 4: Precision, recall and F_1 scores for all classifiers introduced in Experiment 2. Scores are compared row-wise to the best-performing classifier $C_{4_{n,v,B2}}$. A significant improvement over a cell entry with $p < .05$ is indicated in *italics*.

no NIs with a probability of 76.0% (706/929), A1 with 38.6% (86/929), etc. The baseline scores are averaged over 100 runs of this random 'classifier', further referred to as A.

Supervised classifier: Supervised classifiers, as understood here, are classifiers that use the information obtained from manual NI annotations. We set up *two* predictors B_1 and B_2 tuned on the SemEval training set: B_1 is obtained by counting for each predicate its *most frequent NI role pattern*. For instance, for *seem.02*—once annotated with implicit A1, but twice without implicit arguments—B_1 would predict an empty set of NIs. B_2 is similar to B_1 but conditions NI role patterns not only on the predicate, but also on its explicit arguments.[11] For prediction, these classifiers consult the most frequent NI pattern observed for a predicate (B_2: plus its overt arguments). If a test predicate is unknown (i.e., not present in the training data), we predict the majority class (empty set) for NI.

Mildly supervised classifier: Mildly supervised classifiers do not take any NI annotation into account. Instead, they rely on explicitly realized semantic roles observed in a corpus, but use explicit NI annotations only to estimate prediction thresholds. We describe an extension of our prediction method from Exp. 1 and present eight parameter-based classification algorithms for our best-performing *SD* model from Exp. 1, trained on 6 million sentences.

We define prediction for classifier $\mathbf{C}_0$ as follows: Given a predicate PREDICATE, the role inventory $\mathcal{R} = \{A0..A4\}$, its (possibly empty) set of overt roles $R \subseteq \mathcal{R}$ and a fixed, predicate-independent threshold t_0. We start by optimizing threshold t_0 on all predicate instances with *no* given overt argument. If there is *no* overt role and an unrealized role $n_i \in \mathcal{R}$ for which it is true that $P(n_i|\text{PREDICATE}) > t_0$, then predict n_i as an implicit role. If there is an overt role $o_j \in R$ and an unrealized role $n_i \in \mathcal{R} \setminus R$ for which it is true that $P(n_i|o_j,\text{PREDICATE}) > t_0$, then predict n_i as an implicit role. Note that C_0 requires that this condition to hold for *one* o_j, not all explicit arguments of the predicate instance (logical disjunction).

We refine this classifier by introducing an additional parameter that accounts for the group of overtly realized frames with exactly *one* overt argument, i.e., $\mathbf{C}_1$ predicts n_i if $P(n_i|o_j,\text{PREDICATE}) > t_1$; for all other configurations the procedure is the same as in C_0, i.e., the threshold t_0 is applied.

Classifiers $\mathbf{C}_2$, $\mathbf{C}_3$ and $\mathbf{C}_4$ extend C_1 accordingly and introduce additional thresholds t_2, t_3, t_4 for the respective number of overt arguments. For example, $\mathbf{C}_3$ predicts n_i if $P(n_i|o_{j_1}, o_{j_2}, o_{j_3},\text{PREDICATE}) > t_3$, for configurations with less arguments, it relies on C_2, etc. Our general intuition here is to see whether the increasing number of specialized parameters for increasingly marginal groups of frames is justified by the improvements we achieve in this way.

A final classifier $\mathbf{C}_{4_{n,v}}$ extends C_4 by distinguishing verbal and nominal predicates, yielding a total of ten parameters $t_{0_n}..t_{4_n}, t_{0_v}..t_{0_n}$.

Hybrid classifier: To explore to what extent explicit NI annotations improve the classification results, we combine the best-performing and most elaborate mildly supervised classifier $C_{4_{n,v}}$ with the supervised classifiers B_1 and B_2: For predicates encountered in the training data, $\mathbf{C}_{4_{n,v,B_1}}$ (resp., $\mathbf{C}_{4_{n,v,B_2}}$) uses B_1 (resp., B_2) to predict the most frequent pattern observed for the predicate; for unknown predicates, apply the threshold-based procedure of $C_{4_{n,v}}$.

4.2.3 Results & Evaluation

Table 4 contains the evaluation scores for the individual parameter-based classifiers. All classifiers demonstrate significant improvements over the random baseline. Also the mildly supervised

[11] Specifically, we extract finer-grained patterns, e.g., *evening.01*[A1] → {}=2, {A2}=3, where a predicate is associated with its overt role(s) (left side of the arrow). The corresponding implicit role patterns and their number of occurrence is shown to the right.

classifiers outperform the supervised algorithms in terms of F_1 score and recall. However, detecting NIs by the supervised classifiers is very accurate in terms of high precision. Classifier B_2 outperforms B_1 as a result of directly incorporating additional information about the overt arguments.

Concerning our parameter-based classifiers, the main observations are: First, the overall performance (F_1 score) increases from C_0 to C_4 (yet not significantly). Secondly, with more parameters, recall decreases while precision increases. We can observe, however, that improvements from C_2 to C_4 are marginal, at best, due to the sparsity of predicates with two or more overt arguments. Similar problems related to data sparsity have been reported in Chen et al. (2010). Results for C_3 and C_4 are identical, as no predicate with more than three overt arguments occurred in the test data. Encoding the distinction between verbal and nominal predicates into the classifier again slightly increases the performance.

A combination of the high-precision supervised classifiers and the best performing mildly supervised algorithm yields a significant boost in performance (Tab. 4, last two columns). The optimal parameter values for all classifiers $C_{4_{n,v}}$ estimated on the train section of the SemEval data set are given in Table 5.

Noun thresholds	$t_{C_{0_n}}$	$t_{C_{1_n}}$	$t_{C_{2_n}}$	$t_{C_{3_n}}$	$t_{C_{4_n}}$
Values	0.35	0.10	0.20	0.35	0.45
Verb thresholds	$t_{C_{0_v}}$	$t_{C_{1_v}}$	$t_{C_{2_v}}$	$t_{C_{3_v}}$	$t_{C_{4_v}}$
Values	0.05	0.25	0.25	0.30	0.20

Table 5: Optimal parameter values for the thresholds in all $C_{4_{n,v}}$ classifiers estimated on the train section of the SemEval data set.

In Table 6, we report the performance of our best classifier $C_{4_{n,v,B2}}$ with detailed label scores. Its overall NI recognition rate of 0.81 (recall) outperforms the state-of-the-art in implicit role identification: cf. L&P (0.66), SEMAFOR (0.63), S&F (0.58), T&D (0.54), VENSES++ (0.08).[12]

Summarizing our results, Exp. 2 has shown that combining supervised and mildly supervised strategies to NI detection achieves the best results on the SemEval test set. Concerning the mildly supervised, parameter-based classifiers, it

Roles	A0	A1	A2	A3	A4
# Labels	70	107	49	5	21
Precision	0.675	0.578	0.432	0.400	0.791
Recall	0.800	0.897	0.653	0.400	0.905
F_1 Score	0.732	0.703	0.520	0.400	0.844

Table 6: Evaluation of $C_{4_{n,v,B2}}$ for all 252 implicit roles.

has proven beneficial to incorporate a maximum of available information on overtly expressed arguments in order to determine implicit roles. Our best-performing classifier achieves NI recognition rate beyond state-of-the-art.

Interestingly, memory-based learning offers the capability to detect both DNIs (resolvable from context), as well as INIs (not resolvable from context), simply by learning patterns from local explicit role realizations. Subsequent experiments should extend this approach to distinguish between the two types, as well, which we have treated equivalently in our settings. First promising experiments in this direction are being conducted in Chiarcos and Schenk (2015).

5 Summary and Outlook

We have presented a novel, statistical method to infer evidence for implicit roles from their explicit realizations in large amounts of automatically annotated SRL data. We conclude that—especially when annotated training data is sparse—memory-based approaches to implicit role detection seem highly promising. With a much greater degree of flexibility, they offer an alternative solution to static rule-/template-based methods.

Despite its simplicity, we demonstrated the suitability of our approach: It is competitive with state-of-the-art systems in terms of the overall recognition rate, however, still suffers in precision of the respective null instantiated arguments. Thus, directions for future research should consider integrating additional contextual features, and would benefit from the *complete* role inventory of our models (including non-core roles). In this extended setting, we would like to experiment with other machine learning approaches to assess whether the accuracy of the detected NIs can be increased. Also, we plan to apply the memory-based strategy described in this paper to NI *resolution* (on top their detection), and in this context, examine more closely the characteristic (possibly contrastive) distributions of DNIs and INIs.

[12] Note that only an indirect comparison of these scores is possible due to the aforementioned difference between data formats and also because none of the other systems report precision scores for their pattern-based NI detection systems.

References

Collin F. Baker, Charles J. Fillmore, and John B. Lowe. 1998. The Berkeley FrameNet Project. In *Proceedings of the 36th Annual Meeting of the Association for Computational Linguistics and 17th International Conference on Computational Linguistics - Volume 1*, ACL '98, pages 86–90, Stroudsburg, PA, USA. Association for Computational Linguistics.

Laura Banarescu, Claire Bonial, Shu Cai, Madalina Georgescu, Kira Griffitt, Ulf Hermjakob, Kevin Knight, Philipp Koehn, Martha Palmer, and Nathan Schneider. 2013. Abstract Meaning Representation for Sembanking. Proc. Linguistic Annotation Workshop.

Marco Baroni, Silvia Bernardini, Adriano Ferraresi, and Eros Zanchetta. 2009. The WaCky Wide Web: A Collection of Very Large Linguistically Processed Web-Crawled Corpora. *Language Resources and Evaluation*, 43(3):209–226.

Anders Björkelund, Love Hafdell, and Pierre Nugues. 2009. Multilingual Semantic Role Labeling. In *Proceedings of the Thirteenth Conference on Computational Natural Language Learning (CoNLL 2009): Shared Task*, pages 43–48, Boulder, Colorado, June. Association for Computational Linguistics.

Desai Chen, Nathan Schneider, Dipanjan Das, and Noah A. Smith. 2010. SEMAFOR: Frame Argument Resolution with Log-linear Models. In *Proceedings of the 5th International Workshop on Semantic Evaluation*, SemEval '10, pages 264–267, Stroudsburg, PA, USA. Association for Computational Linguistics.

Christian Chiarcos and Niko Schenk. 2015. (accepted) Towards the Unsupervised Acquisition of Implicit Semantic Roles. In *Recent Advances in Natural Language Processing, RANLP 2015, September, 2015, Hissar, Bulgaria.*

Christian Chiarcos. 2012. Towards the Unsupervised Acquisition of Discourse Relations. In *Proceedings of the 50th Annual Meeting of the Association for Computational Linguistics: Short Papers - Volume 2*, ACL '12, pages 213–217, Stroudsburg, PA, USA. Association for Computational Linguistics.

Walter Daelemans and Antal van den Bosch. 2009. *Memory-Based Language Processing*. Cambridge University Press, New York, NY, USA, 1st edition.

Parvin Sadat Feizabadi and Sebastian Padó. 2015. Combining Seemingly Incompatible Corpora for Implicit Semantic Role Labeling. In *Proceedings of STARSEM*, pages 40–50, Denver, CO.

Charles J. Fillmore. 1986. Pragmatically Controlled Zero Anaphora. In *Proceedings of Berkeley Linguistics Society*, pages 95–107, Berkeley, CA.

Matthew Gerber and Joyce Chai. 2012. Semantic Role Labeling of Implicit Arguments for Nominal Predicates. *Comput. Linguist.*, 38(4):755–798, December.

Egoitz Laparra and German Rigau. 2012. Exploiting Explicit Annotations and Semantic Types for Implicit Argument Resolution. In *Sixth IEEE International Conference on Semantic Computing, ICSC 2012.*, Palermo, Italy. IEEE Computer Society.

Egoitz Laparra and German Rigau. 2013. ImpAr: A Deterministic Algorithm for Implicit Semantic Role Labelling. In *Proceedings of the 51st Annual Meeting of the Association for Computational Linguistics (Volume 1: Long Papers)*, pages 1180–1189. Association for Computational Linguistics.

Christopher D. Manning, Mihai Surdeanu, John Bauer, Jenny Finkel, Steven J. Bethard, and David McClosky. 2014. The Stanford CoreNLP natural language processing toolkit. In *Proceedings of 52nd Annual Meeting of the Association for Computational Linguistics: System Demonstrations*, pages 55–60.

Adam Meyers, Ruth Reeves, Catherine Macleod, Rachel Szekely, Veronika Zielinska, Brian Young, and Ralph Grishman. 2004. The NomBank Project: An Interim Report. In A. Meyers, editor, *HLT-NAACL 2004 Workshop: Frontiers in Corpus Annotation*, pages 24–31, Boston, Massachusetts, USA, May 2 - May 7. Association for Computational Linguistics.

Martha Palmer, Daniel Gildea, and Paul Kingsbury. 2005. The Proposition Bank: An Annotated Corpus of Semantic Roles. *Comput. Linguist.*, 31(1):71–106, March.

Anselmo Peñas and Eduard Hovy. 2010. Semantic Enrichment of Text with Background Knowledge. In *Proceedings of the NAACL HLT 2010 First International Workshop on Formalisms and Methodology for Learning by Reading*, FAM-LbR '10, pages 15–23, Stroudsburg, PA, USA. Association for Computational Linguistics.

Michael Roth and Anette Frank. 2013. Automatically Identifying Implicit Arguments to Improve Argument Linking and Coherence Modeling. In *Proceedings of the Second Joint Conference on Lexical and Computational Semantics (*SEM)*, pages 306–316, Atlanta, Georgia, USA, June. Association for Computational Linguistics.

Josef Ruppenhofer, Caroline Sporleder, Roser Morante, Collin Baker, and Martha Palmer. 2010. SemEval-2010 Task 10: Linking Events and Their Participants in Discourse. In *Proceedings of the 5th International Workshop on Semantic Evaluation*, SemEval '10, pages 45–50, Stroudsburg, PA, USA. Association for Computational Linguistics.

Josef Ruppenhofer, Philip Gorinski, and Caroline Sporleder. 2011. In Search of Missing Arguments: A Linguistic Approach. In Galia Angelova, Kalina Bontcheva, Ruslan Mitkov, and Nicolas Nicolov, editors, *RANLP*, pages 331–338. RANLP 2011 Organising Committee.

Josef Ruppenhofer. 2005. Regularities in Null Instantiation. Ms, University of Colorado.

Carina Silberer and Anette Frank. 2012. Casting Implicit Role Linking as an Anaphora Resolution Task. In *Proceedings of the First Joint Conference on Lexical and Computational Semantics - Volume 1: Proceedings of the Main Conference and the Shared Task, and Volume 2: Proceedings of the Sixth International Workshop on Semantic Evaluation*, SemEval '12, pages 1–10, Stroudsburg, PA, USA. Association for Computational Linguistics.

Sara Tonelli and Rodolfo Delmonte. 2010. VENSES++: Adapting a Deep Semantic Processing System to the Identification of Null Instantiations. In *Proceedings of the 5th International Workshop on Semantic Evaluation*, pages 296–299. Association for Computational Linguistics.

Sara Tonelli and Rodolfo Delmonte. 2011. Desperately Seeking Implicit Arguments in Text. In *Proceedings of the ACL 2011 Workshop on Relational Models of Semantics*, pages 54–62. Association for Computational Linguistics.

Generating Sentence Planning Variations for Story Telling

Stephanie M. Lukin, Lena I. Reed & Marilyn A. Walker
Natural Language and Dialogue Systems
University of California, Santa Cruz
Baskin School of Engineering
slukin,lireed,mawalker@ucsc.edu

Abstract

There has been a recent explosion in applications for dialogue interaction ranging from direction-giving and tourist information to interactive story systems. Yet the natural language generation (NLG) component for many of these systems remains largely handcrafted. This limitation greatly restricts the range of applications; it also means that it is impossible to take advantage of recent work in expressive and statistical language generation that can dynamically and automatically produce a large number of variations of given content. We propose that a solution to this problem lies in new methods for developing language generation resources. We describe the ES-TRANSLATOR, a computational language generator that has previously been applied only to fables, and quantitatively evaluate the domain independence of the EST by applying it to personal narratives from weblogs. We then take advantage of recent work on language generation to create a parameterized sentence planner for story generation that provides aggregation operations, variations in discourse and in point of view. Finally, we present a user evaluation of different personal narrative retellings.

1 Introduction

Recently there has been an explosion in applications for natural language and dialogue interaction ranging from direction-giving and tourist information to interactive story systems (Dethlefs et al., 2014; Walker et al., 2011; Hu et al., 2015). While this is due in part to progress in statistical natural language understanding, many applications require the system to actually respond in a meaningful way. Yet the natural language generation (NLG) component of many interactive dialogue systems remains largely handcrafted. This limitation greatly restricts the range of applications; it also means that it is impossible to take advantage of recent work in expressive and statistical language generation that can dynamically and automatically produce a large number of variations of given content (Rieser and Lemon, 2011; Paiva and Evans, 2004; Langkilde, 1998; Rowe et al., 2008; Mairesse and Walker, 2011). Such variations are important for expressive purposes, we well as for user adaptation and personalization (Zukerman and Litman, 2001; Wang et al., 2005; McQuiggan et al., 2008). We propose that a solution to this problem lies in new methods for developing language generation resources.

Original
This is one of those times I wish I had a digital camera. We keep a large stainless steel bowl of water outside on the back deck for Benjamin to drink out of when he's playing outside. His bowl has become a very popular site. Throughout the day, many birds drink out of it and bathe in it. The birds literally line up on the railing and wait their turn. Squirrels also come to drink out of it. The craziest squirrel just came by- he was literally jumping in fright at what I believe was his own reflection in the bowl. He was startled so much at one point that he leap in the air and fell off the deck. But not quite, I saw his one little paw hanging on! After a moment or two his paw slipped and he tumbled down a few feet. But oh, if you could have seen the look on his startled face and how he jumped back each time he caught his reflection in the bowl!

Table 1: The Startled Squirrel Weblog Story

First we describe the ES-TRANSLATOR (or EST), a computational language generator that has previously been applied only to fables, e.g. the fable in Table 3 (Rishes et al., 2013). We quantitatively evaluate the domain independence of the EST by applying it to social media narratives, such as the *Startled Squirrel* story in Table 1. We then present a parameterized general-purpose framework built on the EST pipeline, EST 2.0, that can generate many different tellings of the same story, by utilizing sentence planning and point of view parameters. Automatically generated story variations are shown in Table 2 and Table 4.

We hypothesize many potential uses for our ap-

Proceedings of the SIGDIAL 2015 Conference, pages 188–197,
Prague, Czech Republic, 2-4 September 2015.

EST 2.0
Benjamin wanted to drink the bowl's water, so I placed the bowl on the deck. The bowl was popular. The birds drank the bowl's water. The birds bathed themselves in the bowl. The birds organized themselves on the deck's railing because the birds wanted to wait. The squirrels drank the bowl's water. The squirrel approached the bowl. The squirrel was startled because the squirrel saw the squirrel's reflection. Because it was startled, the squirrel leapt. The squirrel fell over the deck's railing because the squirrel leaped because the squirrel was startled. The squirrel held the deck's railing with the squirrel's paw. The squirrel's paw slipped off the deck's railing. The squirrel fell.

Table 2: Retelling of the Startled Squirrel

Original
A Crow was sitting on a branch of a tree with a piece of cheese in her beak when a Fox observed her and set his wits to work to discover some way of getting the cheese. Coming and standing under the tree he looked up and said, "What a noble bird I see above me! Her beauty is without equal, the hue of her plumage exquisite. If only her voice is as sweet as her looks are fair, she ought without doubt to be Queen of the Birds." The Crow was hugely flattered by this, and just to show the Fox that she could sing she gave a loud caw. Down came the cheese,of course, and the Fox, snatching it up, said, "You have a voice, madam, I see: what you want is wits."

Table 3: "The Fox and the Crow"

proach to repurposing and retelling existing stories. First, such stories are created daily in the thousands and cover any topic imaginable. They are natural and personal, and may be funny, sad, heart-warming or serious. There are many potential applications: virtual companions, educational storytelling, or to share troubles in therapeutic settings (Bickmore, 2003; Pennebaker and Seagal, 1999; Gratch et al., 2012).

Previous research on NLG of linguistic style shows that dialogue systems are more effective if they can generate stylistic linguistic variations based on the user's emotional state, personality, style, confidence, or other factors (André et al., 2000; Piwek, 2003; McQuiggan et al., 2008; Porayska-Pomsta and Mellish, 2004; Forbes-Riley and Litman, 2011; Wang et al., 2005; Dethlefs et al., 2014). Other work focuses on variation in journalistic writing or instruction manuals, where stylistic variations as well as journalistic slant or connotations have been explored (Hovy, 1988; Green and DiMarco, 1993; Paris and Scott, 1994; Power et al., 2003; Inkpen and Hirst, 2004). Previous iterations of the EST simply presented a sequence of events (Rishes et al., 2013). This work implements parameterized variation of linguistic style in the context of weblogs in order to introduce discourse structure into our generated stories.

Our approach differs from previous work on NLG for narrative because we emphasize (1) domain-independent methods; and (2) generating a large range of variation, both narratological and stylistic. (Lukin and Walker, 2015)'s work on the EST is the first to generate dialogue within stories, to have the ability to vary direct vs. indirect speech, and to generate dialogue utterances using different stylistic models for character voices. Previous work can generate narratological variations, but is domain dependent (Callaway and Lester, 2002; Montfort, 2007).

Sec. 2 describes our corpus of stories and the architecture of our story generation framework, EST 2.0.[1] Sec. 3 describes experiments testing the coverage and correctness of EST 2.0. Sec. 4 describes experiments testing user perceptions of different linguistic variations in storytelling. Our contributions are:

- We produce SIG representations of 100 personal narratives from a weblog corpus, using the story annotation tool Scheherezade (Elson and McKeown, 2009; Elson, 2012);
- We compare EST 2.0 to EST and show how we have not only made improvements to the translation algorithm, but can extend and compare to personal narratives.
- We implement a parameterized variation of linguistic style in order to introduce discourse structure into our generated narratives.
- We carry out experiments to gather user perceptions of different sentence planning choices that can be made with complex sentences in stories.

We sum up and discuss future work in Sec. 5.

2 Story Generation Framework

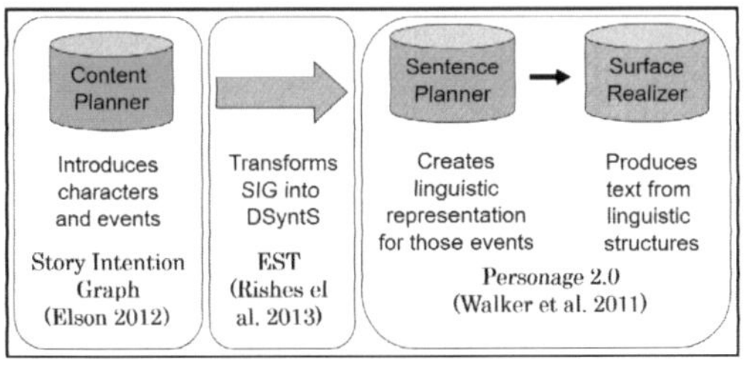

Figure 1: NLG pipeline method of the ES Translator.

Fig. 1 illustrates our overall architecture, which uses NLG modules to separate the process of planning *What to say* (content planning and selection,

[1]The corpus is available from `http:nlds.soe.ucsc.edu\story-database`.

fabula) from decisions about *How to say it* (sentence planning and realization, discourse). We build on three existing tools from previous work: the SCHEHEREZADE story annotation tool, the PERSONAGE generator, and the ES-TRANSLATOR (EST) (Elson, 2012; Mairesse and Walker, 2011; Rishes et al., 2013). The EST uses the STORY INTENTION GRAPH (SIG) representation produced by SCHEHEREZADE and its theoretical grounding as a basis for the content for generation. The EST bridges the narrative representation of the SIG to the representation required by PERSONAGE by generating the text plans and the deep syntactic structures that PERSONAGE requires. Thus any story or content represented as a SIG can be retold using PERSONAGE. See Fig. 1.

There are several advantages to using the SIG as the representation for a content pool:

- Elson's DRAMABANK provides stories encoded as SIGs including 36 Aesop's Fables, such as *The Fox and the Crow* in Table 3.
- The SIG framework includes an annotation tool called SCHEHERAZADE that supports representing any narrative as a SIG.
- SCHEHEREZADE comes with a realizer that regenerates stories from the SIG: this realizer provides alternative story realizations that we can compare to the EST 2.0 output.

We currently have 100 personal narratives annotated with the SIG representation on topics such as travel, storms, gardening, funerals, going to the doctor, camping, and snorkeling, selected from a corpus of a million stories (Gordon and Swanson, 2009). We use the stories in Tables 1 and 3 in this paper to explain our framework.

Fig. 2 shows the SIG for *The Startled Squirrel* story in Table 1. To create a SIG, SCHEHERAZADE annotators: (1) identify key entities; (2) model events and statives as propositions and arrange them in a timeline; and (3) model the annotator's understanding of the overarching goals, plans and beliefs of the story's agents. SCHEHERAZADE allows users to annotate a story along several dimensions, starting with the surface form of the story (first column in Table 2) and then proceeding to deeper representations. The first dimension (second column in Table 2) is called the "timeline layer", in which the story is encoded as predicate-argument structures (propositions) that are temporally ordered on a timeline. SCHEHERAZADE adapts information about predicate-argument structures from the VerbNet lexical database (Kipper et al., 2006) and uses

EST 2.0
The crow sat on the tree's branch. The cheese was in the crow's pecker. The crow thought "I will eat the cheese on the branch of the tree because the clarity of the sky is so-somewhat beautiful." The fox observed the crow. The fox thought "I will obtain the cheese from the crow's nib." The fox came. The fox stood under the tree. The fox looked toward the crow. The fox avered "I see you!" The fox alleged 'your's beauty is quite incomparable, okay?" The fox alleged 'your's feather's chromaticity is damn exquisite." The fox said "if your's voice's pleasantness is equal to your's visual aspect's loveliness you undoubtedly are every every birds's queen!" The crow thought "the fox was so-somewhat flattering." The crow thought "I will demonstrate my voice." The crow loudly cawed. The cheese fell. The fox snatched the cheese. The fox said "you are somewhat able to sing, alright?" The fox alleged "you need the wits!"

Table 4: Retelling of "The Fox and the Crow"

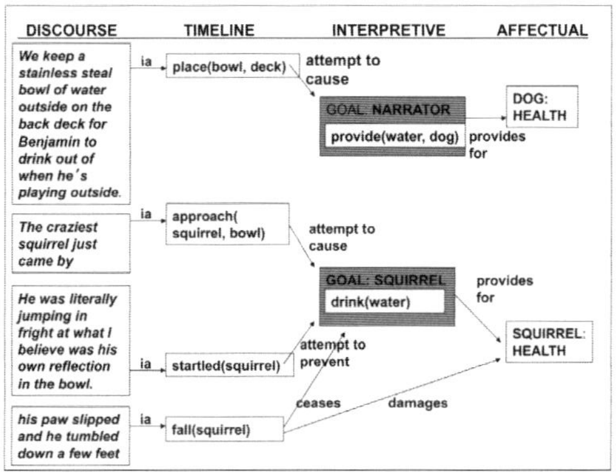

Figure 2: Part of the STORY INTENTION GRAPH (SIG) for *The Startled Squirrel.*

WordNet (Fellbaum, 1998) as its noun and adjectives taxonomy. The arcs of the story graph are labeled with discourse relations, such as *attempts to cause*, or *temporal order* (see Chapter 4 of (Elson, 2012).)

The EST applies a model of syntax to the SIG which translates from the semantic representation of the SIG to the syntactic formalism of Deep Syntactic Structures (DSYNTS) required by the PERSONAGE generator (Lavoie and Rambow, 1997; Melčuk, 1988; Mairesse and Walker, 2011). Fig. 1 provides a high level view of the architecture of EST. The full translation methodology is described in (Rishes et al., 2013).

DSYNTS are a flexible dependency tree representation of an utterance that gives us access to the underlying linguistic structure of a sentence that goes beyond surface string manipulation. The nodes of the DSYNTS syntactic trees are labeled with lexemes and the arcs of the tree are labeled with syntactic relations. The DSYNTS formalism distinguishes between arguments and modifiers and between different types of arguments

Variation	Blog Output	Fable Output
Original	We keep a large stainless steel bowl of water outside on the back deck for Benjamin to drink out of when he's playing outside.	The Crow was hugely flattered by this, and just to show the Fox that she could sing she gave a loud caw.
Sch	A narrator placed a steely and large bowl on a back deck in order for a dog to drink the water of the bowl.	The crow cawed loudly in order for she to show him that she was able to sing.
EST 1.0	I placed the bowl on the deck in order for Benjamin to drink the bowl's water.	The crow cawed loudly in order to show the fox the crow was able to sing.
becauseNS	I placed the bowl on the deck because Benjamin wanted to drink the bowl's water.	The crow cawed loudly because she wanted to show the fox the crow was able to sing.
becauseSN	Because Benjamin wanted to drink the bowl's water, I placed the bowl on the deck.	Because the crow wanted to show the fox the crow was able to sing, she cawed loudly.
NS	I placed the bowl on the deck. Benjamin wanted to drink the bowl's water.	The crow cawed loudly. She wanted to show the fox the crow was able to sing.
N	I placed the bowl on the deck.	The crow cawed loudly.
soSN	Benjamin wanted to drink the bowl's water, so I placed the bowl on the deck.	The crow wanted to show the fox the crow was able to sing, so she cawed loudly.

Table 5: Sentence Planning Variations added to EST 2.0 for Contingency relations, exemplified by *The Startled Squirrel* and *The Fox and the Crow*. Variation **N** is intended to test whether the content of the satellite can be recovered from context. **Sch** is the realization produced by Scheherezade.

(subject, direct and indirect object etc). Lexicalized nodes also contain a range of grammatical features used in generation. RealPro handles morphology, agreement and function words to produce an output string.

This paper utilizes the ability of the EST 2.0 and the flexibility of DSYNTS to produce direct speech that varies the character voice as illustrated in Table 4 (Lukin and Walker, 2015). By simply modifying the `person` parameter in the DSYNTS, we can change the sentence to be realized in the first person. For example, to produce the variations in Table 4, we use both first person, and direct speech, as well as linguistic styles from PERSONAGE: a neutral voice for the narrator, a shy voice for the crow, and a laid-back voice for the fox (Lukin and Walker, 2015). We fully utilize this variation when we retell personal narratives in EST 2.0.

This paper and introduces support for new discourse relations, such as aggregating clauses related by the contingency discourse relation (one of many listed in the Penn Discourse Tree Bank (PDTB) (Prasad et al., 2008)). In SIG encoding, contingency clauses are always expressed with the "in order to" relation (Table 6, 1). To support linguistic variation, we introduce "de-aggregation" onto these aggregating clauses in order to have the flexibility to rephrase, restructure, or ignore clauses as indicated by our parameterized sentence planner. We identify candidate story points in the SIG that contain a contingency relation (annotated in the Timeline layer) and deliberately break apart this hard relationship to create nucleus and satellite DSYNTS that represents the entire sentence (Table 6, 2) (Mann and Thompson, 1988). We create a text plan (Table 6, 3) to allow the sentence planner to reconstruct this content in various ways. Table 5 shows sentence planning variations for the contingency relation for both fables and personal narratives (**soSN**, **becauseNS**, **becauseSN**, **NS**, **N**), the output of EST 1.0, the original sentence (**original**), and the SCHEHERAZADE realization (**Sch**) which provides an additional baseline. The **Sch** variant is the original "in order to" contingency relationship produced by the SIG annotation. The **becauseNS** operation presents the *nucleus* first, followed by a *because*, and then the *satellite*. We can also treat the nucleus and satellite as two different sentences (**NS**) or completely leave off the satellite (**N**). We believe the **N** variant is useful if the satellite can be easily inferred from the prior context.

The richness of the discourse information present in the SIG and our ability to de-aggregate and aggregate will enable us to implement other discourse relations in future work.

3 Personal Narrative Evaluation

After annotating our 100 stories with the SCHEHERAZADE annotation tool, we ran them through the EST, and examined the output. We discovered several bugs arising from variation in the blogs that are not present in the Fables, and fixed them. In previous work on the EST, the machine translation metrics Levenshtein's distance and BLEU score were used to compare

Table 6: 1: original unbroken DSYNTS; 2) deaggregated DSYNTS; 3) contingency text plan

1: ORIGINAL

```
<dsynts id="5_6">
 <dsyntnode class="verb" lexeme="organize"
   mode="" mood="ind" rel="II" tense="past">
  <dsyntnode article="def" class="common_noun"
     lexeme="bird" number="pl" person="" rel="I"/>
  <dsyntnode article="def" class="common_noun"
     lexeme="bird" number="pl" person="" rel="II"/>
  <dsyntnode class="preposition" lexeme="on"
          rel="ATTR">
   <dsyntnode article="def" class="common_noun"
     lexeme="railing" number="sg" person="" rel="II">
     <dsyntnode article="no-art" class="common_noun"
     lexeme="deck" number="sg" person="" rel="I"/>
   </dsyntnode>
  </dsyntnode>
  <dsyntnode class="preposition" lexeme="in_order"
       rel="ATTR">
    <dsyntnode class="verb" extrapo="+" lexeme="wait"
       mode="inf-to" mood="inf-to"
       rel="II" tense="inf-to">
      <dsyntnode article="def" class="common_noun"
       lexeme="bird" number="pl" person="" rel="I"/>
    </dsyntnode>
  </dsyntnode>
</dsyntnode>
</dsynts>
```

2: DEAGGREGATION

```
<dsynts id="5">
  <dsyntnode class="verb" lexeme="organize"
     mood="ind" rel="II" tense="past">
    <dsyntnode article="def" class="common_noun"
     lexeme="bird" number="pl" person="" rel="I"/>
    <dsyntnode article="def" class="common_noun"
     lexeme="bird" number="pl" person="" rel="II"/>
    <dsyntnode class="preposition" lexeme="on"
              rel="ATTR">
     <dsyntnode article="def" class="common_noun" l
       lexeme="railing" number="sg"
       person="" rel="II">
      <dsyntnode article="no-art" class="common_noun"
       lexeme="deck" number="sg" person="" rel="I"/>
      </dsyntnode>
    </dsyntnode>
  </dsyntnode>
</dsynts>

<dsynts id="6">
  <dsyntnode class="verb" lexeme="want"
       mood="ind" rel="II" tense="past">
    <dsyntnode article="def" class="common_noun"
       lexeme="bird" number="pl" person="" r
    <dsyntnode class="verb" extrapo="+"
     lexeme="wait" mode="inf-to" mood="inf-to"
     rel="II" tense="inf-to"/>
  </dsyntnode>
</dsynts>
```

3: AGGREGATION TEXT PLAN

```
  <speechplan voice="Narrator">
  <rstplan>
    <relation name="contingency_cause">
      <proposition id="1" ns="nucleus"/>
      <proposition id="2" ns="satellite"/>
    </relation>
  </rstplan>
  <proposition dialogue_act="5" id="1"/>
  <proposition dialogue_act="6" id="2"/>
</speechplan>
```

the original Aesop's Fables to their generated EST and SCHEHERAZADE reproductions (denoted **EST** and **Sch**) (Rishes et al., 2013). These metrics are not ideal for evaluating story quality, especially when generating stylistic variations of the original story. However they allow us to automatically test some aspects of system coverage, so we repeat this evaluation on the blog dataset.

Table 7 presents BLEU and Levenshtein scores for the original 36 Fables and all 100 blog stories, compared to both **Sch** and EST 1.0. Levenshtein distance computes the minimum edit distance between two strings, so we compare the entire original story to a generated version. A lower score indicates a closer comparison. BLEU score computes the overlap between two strings taking word order into consideration: a higher BLEU score indicates a closer match between candidate strings. Thus Table 7 provides quantitative evidence that the style of the original blogs is very different from Aesop's Fables. Neither the EST output nor the **Sch** output comes close to representing the original textual style (Blogs Original-Sch and Original-EST).

Table 7: Mean for Levenshtein and BLEU on the Fables development set vs. the Blogs

		Lev	**BLEU**
FABLES	Sch-EST	72	.32
	Original-Sch	116	.06
	Original-EST	108	.03
BLOGS	Sch-EST	110	.66
	Original-Sch	736	.21
	Original-EST	33	.21

However we find that **EST** compares favorably to **Sch** on the blogs with a relatively low Levenshtein score, and higher BLEU score (Blogs Sch-EST) than the original Fables evaluation (Fables Sch-EST). This indicates that even though the blogs have a diversity of language and style, our translation comes close to the **Sch** baseline.

4 Experimental Design and Results

We conduct two experiments on Mechanical Turk to test variations generated with the deaggregation and point of view parameters. We compare the variations amongst themselves and to the original sentence in a story. We are also interested in identifying differences among individual stories.

In the first experiment, we show an excerpt from the original story telling and indicate to the participants that "any of the following sentences could come next in the story". We then list all variations of the following sentence with the "in order to" contingency relationship (examples from the *Startled Squirrel* labeled EST 2.0 in Table 5).

Our aim is to elicit rating of the variations in terms of correctness and goodness of fit within the story context (1 is best, 5 is worst), and to rank the sentences by personal preference (in experiment 1 we showed 7 variations where 1 is best, 7 is worst; in experiment 2 we showed 3 variations where 1 is best, 3 is worst). We also show the original blog sentence and the EST 1.0 output before de-aggregation and sentence planning. We emphasize that the readers should read each variation *in the context of the entire story* and encourage them to reread the story with each new sentence to understand this context.

In the second experiment, we compare the original sentence with our best realization, and the realization produced by SCHEHEREZADE (**Sch**). We expect that SCHEHEREZADE will score more poorly in this instance because it cannot change point of view from third person to first person, even though its output is more fluent than EST 2.0 for many cases.

4.1 Results Experiment 1

We had 7 participants analyze each of the 16 story segments. All participants were native English speakers. Table 8 shows the means and standard deviations for correctness and preference rankings in the first experiment. We find that averaged across all stories, there is a clear order for correctness and preference: original, soSN, becauseNS, becauseSN, NS, EST, N.

We performed an ANOVA on preference and found that story has no significant effect on the results ($F(1, 15) = 0.18, p = 1.00$), indicating that all stories are well-formed and there are no outliers in the story selection. On the other hand, realization does have a significant effect on preference ($F(1, 6) = 33.74, p = 0.00$). This supports our hypothesis that the realizations are distinct from each other and there are preferences amongst them.

Fig. 3 shows the average correctness and preference for all stories. Paired t-tests show that there is a significant difference in reported correctness between **orig** and **soSN** ($p < 0.05$), but no difference between **soSN** and **becauseNS** ($p = 0.133$), or **becauseSN** ($p = 0.08$). There is a difference between **soSN** and **NS** ($p < 0.005$), as well as between the two different **because** operations and **NS** ($p < 0.05$). There are no other significant differences.

The are larger differences on the preference metric. Paired t-tests show that there is a significant difference between **orig** and **soSN** ($p < 0.0001$) and **soSN** and **becauseNS** ($p < 0.05$). There is no difference in preference between **becauseNS** and **becauseSN** ($p = 0.31$). However there is a significant difference between **soSN** and **becauseSN** ($p < 0.005$) and **becauseNS** and **NS** ($p < 0.0001$). Finally, there is significant difference between **becauseSN** and **NS** ($p < 0.005$) and **NS** and **EST** ($p < 0.005$). There is no difference between **EST** and **N** ($p = 0.375$), but there is a difference between **NS** and **N** ($p < 0.05$).

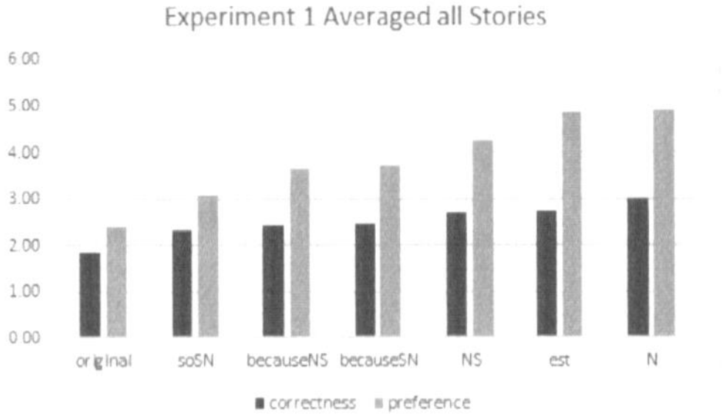

Figure 3: Histogram of Correctness and Preference for Experiment 1 averaged across story (lower is better)

These results indicate that the original sentence, as expected, is the most correct and preferred. Qualitative feedback on the original sentence included: "The one I ranked first makes a more interesting story. Most of the others would be sufficient, but boring."; "The sentence I ranked first makes more sense in the context of the story. The others tell you similar info, but do not really fit.". Some participants ranked **soSN** as their preferred variant (although the difference was never statistically significant): "The one I rated the best sounded really natural."

Although we observe an overall ranking trend, there are some differences by story for **NS** and **N**. Most of the time, these two are ranked the lowest. Some subjects observe: "#1 [**orig**] & #2 [**soSN**] had a lot of detail. #7 [**N**] did not explain what the person wanted to see" (a044 in Table 10); "The sentence I rated the worst [**N**] didn't explain why the person wanted to cook them, but it would have been an okay sentence." (a060 in Table 10); "I ranked the lower number [**N**] because they either did not contain the full thought of the subject or they added details that are to be assumed." (a044 in Table 10); "They were all fairly good sentences. The one I ranked worst [**N**] just left out why they decided to use facebook." (a042 in Table 10).

However, there is some support for **NS** and **N**. We also find that there is a significant interaction between story and realization ($F(2, 89) = 1.70$, $p = 0.00$), thus subjects' preference of the realization are based on the story they are reading. One subject commented: "#1 [**orig**] was the most descriptive about what family the person is looking for. I did like the way #3 [**NS**] was two sentences. It seemed to put a different emphasis on finding family" (a042 in Table 10). Another thought that the explanatory utterance altered the tone of the story: "The parent and the children in the story

		Orig	soSN	becauseNS	becauseSN	NS	EST	N
ALL	**C**	1.8	2.3	2.4	2.5	2.7	2.7	3.0
	P	2.4	3.1	3.7	3.8	4.2	4.9	4.9
Protest	**C**	4.9	2.7	2.4	3.9	2.1	2.7	2.7
	P	1.0	4.1	4.3	4.4	4.4	4.4	**2.8**
Story 042	**C**	4.2	4.2	4.3	3.8	3.7	4.2	2.7
	P	3.3	3.7	3.6	4.6	**3.1**	5	4

Table 8: Exp 1: Means for correctness **C** and preference **P** for original sentences and generated variations for **ALL** stories vs. the **Protest Story** and **a042** (stimuli in Table 10). Lower is better.

were having a good time. It doesn't make sense that parent would want to do something to annoy them [the satellite utterance]" (a060 in Table 10). This person preferred leaving off the satellite and ranked **N** as the highest preference.

We examined these interactions between story and preference ranking for **NS** and **N**. This may be depend on either context or on the SIG annotations. For example, in one story (protest in Table 10) our best realization **soSN**, produces: "The protesters wanted to block the street, so the person said for the protesters to protest in the street in order to block it." and **N** produces "The person said for the protesters to protest in the street in order to block it.". One subject, who ranked **N** second only to **original**, observed: "Since the police were coming there with tear gas, it appears the protesters had already shut things down. There is no need to tell them to block the street." Another subject who ranked **N** as second preference similarly observed "Frankly using the word protesters and protest too many times made it seem like a word puzzle or riddle. The meaning was lost in too many variations of the word 'protest.' If the wording was awkward, I tried to assign it toward the 'worst' end of the scale. If it seemed to flow more naturally, as a story would, I tried to assign it toward the 'best' end."

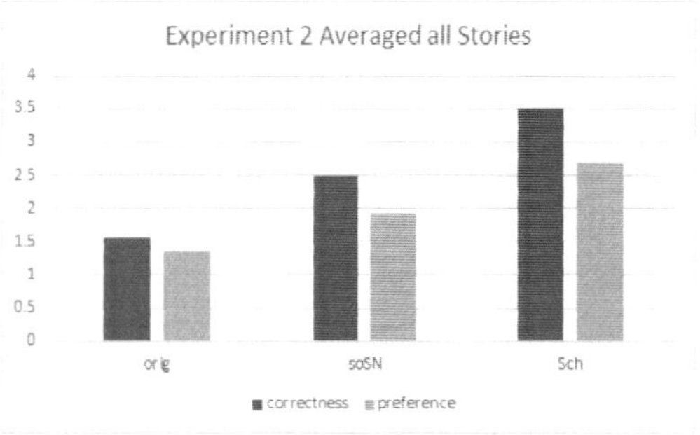

Figure 4: Histogram of Correctness and Preference for Experiment 1 averaged across story (lower is better)

Although the means in this story seem very distinct (Table 8), there is only a significant difference between **orig** and **N** ($p < 0.005$) and **N** and **EST** ($p < 0.05$). Table 8 also includes the means for story a042 (Table 10) where **NS** is ranked highest for preference. Despite this, the only significant difference between **NS** is with **EST 1.0** ($p < 0.05$).

4.2 Results Experiment 2

Experiment 2 compares our best realization to the SCHEHERAZADE realizer, exploiting the ability of EST 2.0 to change the point of view. Seven participants analyzed each of the 16 story segments. All participants were native English speakers.

	Original	soSN	Sch
Correctness	1.6	2.5	3.5
Preference	1.4	1.9	2.7

Table 9: Exp 2: Means for correctness and preference for original sentence, our best realization **soSN**, and Sch. Lower is better.

Table 9 shows the means for correctness and preference rankings. Figure 4 shows a histogram of average correctness and preference by realization for all stories. There is a clear order for correctness and preference: original, soSN, Sch, with significant differences between all pairs of realizations ($p < 0.0001$).

However, in six of the 19 stories, there is no significant difference between Sch and soSN. Three of them do not contain "I" or "the narrator" in the realization sentence. Many of the subjects comment that the realization with "the narrator" does not follow the style of the story: "The second [**Sch**] uses that awful 'narrator.'" (a001 in Table 10); "Forget the narrator sentence. From here on out it's always the worst!" (a001 in Table 10). We hypothesize that in the three sentences without "the narrator", **Sch** can be properly evaluated without the "narrator" bias. In fact, in these situations, **Sch** was rated higher than **soSN**: "I chose the sentences in order of best explanatory detail" (*Startled Squirrel* in Table 5).

Compare the **soSN** realization in the protest story in Table 10 "The leaders wanted to talk, so they met near the workplace." with **Sch** "The group of leaders was meeting in order to talk about running a group of countries and near a workplace." **Sch** has so much more detail than **soSN**. While the EST has massively improved and overall is preferred to **Sch**, some semantic components are lost in the translation process.

5 Discussion and Conclusions

To our knowledge, this is the first time that sentence planning variations for story telling have been implemented in a framework where the discourse (telling) is completely independent of the fabula (content) of the story (Lonneker, 2005). We also show for the first time that the SCHEHEREZADE annotation tool can be applied to informal narratives such as personal narratives from weblogs, and the resulting SIG representations work with existing tools for translating from the SIG to a retelling of a story.

We present a parameterized sentence planner for story generation, that provides aggregation operations and variations in point of view. The technical aspects of de-aggregation and aggregation builds on previous work in NLG and our earlier work on SPaRKy (Cahill et al., 2001; Scott and de Souza, 1990; Paris and Scott, 1994; Nakatsu and White, 2010; Howcroft et al., 2013; Walker et al., 2007; Stent and Molina, 2009). However we are not aware of previous NLG applications needing to first de-aggregate the content, before applying aggregation operations.

Our experiments show that, as expected, readers almost always prefer the original sentence over automatically produced variations, but that the **soSN** variant is preferred. We examine two specific stories where preferences vary from the overall trend: these stories suggest future possible experiments where we might vary more aspects of the story context and audience. We also compare our best variation to what SCHEHERAZADE produces. Despite the fact that the SCHEHERAZADE realizer was targeted at the SIG, our best variant is most often ranked as a preferred choice.

In future work, we aim to explore interactions between a number of our novel narratological parameters. We expect to do this both with a rule-based approach, as well as by building on recent work on statistical models for expressive generation (Rieser and Lemon, 2011; Paiva and Evans, 2004; Langkilde, 1998; Rowe et al., 2008; Mairesse and Walker, 2011). This should allow us to train a narrative generator to achieve particular narrative effects, such as engagement or empathy with particular characters. We will also expand the discourse relations that EST 2.0 can handle.

Acknowledgements. This research was supported by Nuance Foundation Grant SC-14-74, NSF Grants IIS-HCC-1115742 and IIS-1002921.

Appendix. Table 10 provides additional examples of the output of the EST 2.0 system, illustrating particular user preferences and system strengths and weaknesses.

References

E. André, T. Rist, S. van Mulken, M. Klesen, and S. Baldes. 2000. The automated design of believable dialogues for animated presentation teams. *Embodied conversational agents*, pp. 220–255.

T.W. Bickmore. 2003. *Relational agents: Effecting change through human-computer relationships*. Ph.D. thesis, MIT Media Lab.

L. Cahill, J. Carroll, R. Evans, D. Paiva, R. Power, D. Scott, and K. van Deemter. 2001. From rags to riches: exploiting the potential of a flexible generation architecture. In *ACL-01*

C.B. Callaway and J.C. Lester. 2002. Narrative prose generation* 1. *Artificial Intelligence*, 139(2):213–252.

N. Dethlefs, H. Cuayáhuitl, H. Hastie, V. Rieser, and O. Lemon. 2014. Cluster-based prediction of user ratings for stylistic surface realisation. *EACL 2014*, page 702.

D.K. Elson and K.R. McKeown. 2009. A tool for deep semantic encoding of narrative texts. In *Proc. of the ACL-IJCNLP 2009 Software Demonstrations*, pp. 9–12.

D.K. Elson. 2012. *Modeling Narrative Discourse*. Ph.D. thesis, Columbia University, New York City.

C. Fellbaum. 1998. *WordNet: An Electronic Lexical Database*. MIT Press, Cambridge, MA.

K. Forbes-Riley and D. Litman. 2011. Designing and evaluating a wizarded uncertainty-adaptive spoken dialogue tutoring system. *Computer Speech & Language*, 25(1):105–126.

A. Gordon and R. Swanson. 2009. Identifying personal stories in millions of weblog entries. In *Third Int. Conf. on Weblogs and Social Media, Data Challenge Workshop, San Jose, CA*.

J. Gratch, L.P. Morency, S. Scherer, G. Stratou, J. Boberg, S. Koenig, T. Adamson, A. Rizzo, et al. 2012. User-state sensing for virtual health agents and telehealth applications. *Studies in health technology and informatics*, 184:151–157.

a001	Bug out for blood the other night, I left the patio door open just long enough to let in a dozen bugs of various size. I didn't notice them until the middle of the night, when I saw them clinging to the ceiling. I grabbed the closest object within reach, and with a rolled-up comic book I smote mine enemies and smeared their greasy bug guts. All except for the biggest one. I only clipped that one, taking off one of its limbs. But it got away before I could finish the job. So now there's a five-limbed insect lurking in the apartment, no doubt looking for some vengeance against me.
orig	I'm looking around corners, checking the toilet before sitting down
Sch	The narrator began to check the toilet seat of the narrator for the leader of the group of bugs in order for she to sit down on the toilet seat of the narrator
EST	I wanted to sit down on my toilet seat, so I checked my toilet seat for the bugs's leader.
a042-1	This last week I was exploring the FamilySearch Learning Center area to see what was new. I randomly choose a video to check it out. In the middle of the video he was talking about using Facebook as a research tool. I listened as he talked about finding a family group on Facebook, on which he found pictures and information.
orig	I considered this and decided it was time to set up our Family Facebook to find those branches that have not yet been found.
Sch	The narrator decided to use the utility in order to find the family of the narrator.
soSN	I wanted to find my family, so I decided to use Facebook.
becauseNS	I decided to use Facebook because I wanted to find my family.
becauseSN	Because I wanted to find my family, I decided to use Facebook.
NS	I decided to use Facebook. I wanted to find my family.
EST	I decided to use Facebook in order for me to find my family.
N	I decided to use Facebook.
a044	I'm writing this from the Bogota airport, waiting for my flight back to Santiago. When I last posted, I was about to head off to northern Colombia to Cartagena. So, how was it?
orig	I split the 4 days between Cartagena and Santa Marta
Sch	
soSN	I wanted to see Cartagena, so I traveled to Colombia.
becauseNS	I traveled to Colombia because I wanted to see Cartagena.
becauseSN	Because I wanted to see Cartagena, I traveled to Colombia.
NS	I traveled to Colombia. I wanted to see Cartagena.
EST	I traveled to Colombia in order for me to see Cartagena and for me to see Santa Marta.
N	I traveled to Colombia.
a060-1	I hope everyone survived the snow! With the early school dismissal on Friday, it felt like a 3 day weekend. My kids are just not creatures of Winter. I did manage to take them and some of the neighborhood kids out sledding on Friday and Saturday. That was a blast. The kids had more fun, and I had a fire in the shelter with a bag of marshmallows and just enjoying myself. Followed up, of course, with hot chocolate at home. I even managed to cook cornbread from scratch, in an old (my grandmothers) cast-iron skillet, with chicken and gravy for dinner.
orig	If I had any collard greens, I think I would have cooked them too (just to annoy the kids).
Sch	The narrator wanted to cook a group of collards in order to annoy the group of children of the narrator.
soSN	I wanted to annoy my children, so I wanted to cook the collards.
becauseNS	I wanted to cook the collards because I wanted to annoy my children.
becauseSN	Because I wanted to annoy my children, I wanted to cook the collards.
NS	I wanted to cook the collards. I wanted to annoy my children.
EST	I wanted to cook the collards in order for me to annoy my child.
N	I wanted to cook the collards.
protest	The protesters apparently started their protest at the Capitol Building then moved to downtown. We happened to be standing at the corner of 16th and Stout when somebody said that the Police were getting ready to tear-gas a group of demonstrators. We looked around the corner and there were Police everywhere.
orig	They had blockaded the whole street, and shut down the light rail.
Sch	A person said that the group of protesters had protested in a street and in order to block the street.
soSN	The protesters wanted to block the street, so the person said for the protesters to protest in the street in order to block it.
becauseNS	The person said for the protesters to protest in the street in order to block it because the protesters wanted to block the street.
becauseSN	Because the protesters wanted to block the street, the person said for the protesters to protest in the street in order to block it.
NS	The person said for the protesters to protest in the street in order to block it. The protesters wanted to block the street.
EST	The person said for the protesters to protest in the street in order for the protesters to block the street.
N	The person said for the protesters to protest in the street in order to block it.

Table 10: Additional Examples of EST outputs

S.J. Green and C. DiMarco. 1993. Stylistic decision-making in natural language generation. In *Proc. of the 4th European Workshop on Natural Language Generation*.

E.H. Hovy. 1988. Planning coherent multisentential text. In *Proc. 26th Annual Meeting of the Association for Computational Linguistics*, pp. 163–169.

D. M. Howcroft, C. Nakatsu, and M. White. 2013. Enhancing the expression of contrast in the SPARKY restaurant corpus. *ENLG 2013*, page 30.

Z. Hu, M. Walker, M. Neff, and J.E. Fox Tree. 2015. Storytelling agents with personality and adaptivity. *Intelligent Virtual Agents*.

D.Z. Inkpen and G. Hirst. 2004. Near-synonym choice in natural language generation. In *Recent Advances in Natural Language Processing III*.

K. Kipper, A. Korhonen, N. Ryant, and M. Palmer. 2006. Extending verbnet with novel verb classes. In *Proc. of the 6th Int. Conf. on Language Resources and Evaluation (LREC 2006)*, Genoa, Italy.

I. Langkilde. 1998. Forest-based statistical sentence generation. In *In Proc. of the 1st Meeting of the North American Chapter of the ACL (ANLP-NAACL 2000)*, pp. 170–177.

B. Lavoie and O. Rambow. 1997. A fast and portable realizer for text generation systems. In *Proc. of the Third Conf. on Applied Natural Language Processing, ANLP97*, pp. 265–268.

B. Lonneker. 2005. Narratological knowledge for natural language generation. In *Proc. of the 10th European Workshop on Natural Language Generation (ENLG 2005)*, pp. 91–100, Aberdeen, Scotland.

S. Lukin and M. Walker. 2015. Narrative variations in a virtual storyteller. *Intelligent Virtual Agents*.

F. Mairesse and M.A. Walker. 2011. Controlling user perceptions of linguistic style: Trainable generation of personality traits. *Computational Linguistics*.

W.C. Mann and S.A. Thompson 1988. Rhetorical structure theory: Toward a functional theory of text organization. *Text-Interdisciplinary Journal for the Study of Discourse*.

S.W. McQuiggan, B.W. Mott, and J.C. Lester. 2008. Modeling self-efficacy in intelligent tutoring systems: An inductive approach. *User Modeling and User-Adapted Interaction*, 18-1:81123.

I.A. Melčuk. 1988. *Dependency Syntax: Theory and Practice*. SUNY, Albany, New York.

N. Montfort. 2007. *Generating narrative variation in interactive fiction*. Ph.D. thesis, University of Pennsylvania.

C. Nakatsu and M. White. 2010. Generating with Discourse Combinatory Categorial Grammar. In *Linguistic Issues in Language Technology*, 4(1). pp. 162.

D.S. Paiva and R. Evans. 2004. A framework for stylistically controlled generation. In *Natural Language Generation, Third Int. Conf., INLG 2004*, number 3123 in LNAI, pp 120–129.

C. Paris and D. Scott. 1994. Stylistic variation in multilingual instructions. In *The 7th Int. Conf. on Natural Language Generation*.

J.W. Pennebaker and J.D. Seagal. 1999. Forming a story: The health benefits of narrative. *Journal of clinical psychology*, 55(10):1243–1254.

P. Piwek. 2003. A flexible pragmatics-driven language generator for animated agents. In *Proc. of Annual Meeting of the European Chapter of the Association for Computational Linguistics (EACL)*.

K. Porayska-Pomsta and C. Mellish. 2004. Modelling politeness in natural language generation. In *Proc. of the 3rd Conf. on INLG*, pp. 141–150.

R. Power, D. Scott, and N. Bouayad-Agha. 2003. Generating texts with style. In *Proc. of the 4th Int. Conf. on Intelligent Text Processing and Computational Linguistics*.

R. Prasad, N. Dinesh, A. Lee, E. Miltsakaki, L. Robaldo, A. Joshi, K. Aravind B.L. Webber 2008. The Penn Discourse TreeBank 2.0. In *Language Resources and Evaluation Conference*.

V. Rieser and O. Lemon. 2011. *Reinforcement learning for adaptive dialogue systems: a data-driven methodology for dialogue management and natural language generation*. Springer.

E. Rishes, S.M. Lukin, D.K. Elson, and M.A. Walker. 2013. Generating different story tellings from semantic representations of narrative. In *Interactive Storytelling*, pp. 192–204. Springer.

J. Rowe, E. Ha, and J. Lester. 2008. Archetype-Driven Character Dialogue Generation for Interactive Narrative. In *Intelligent Virtual Agents*, pp. 45–58. Springer.

D. R. Scott and C. S. de Souza. 1990. Getting the message across in RST-based text generation. In Dale, Mellish, and Zock, ed, *Current Research in Natural Language Generation*.

A. Stent and M. Molina 2009 Evaluating automatic extraction of rules for sentence plan construction In *The 10th Annual Meeting of the Special Interest Group on Discourse and Dialogue*

M.A. Walker, A. Stent, F. Mairesse and R. Prasad 2007 Individual and Domain Adaptation in Sentence Planning for Dialogue Journal of Artificial Intelligence Research (JAIR). 30:413-456.

M.A. Walker, R. Grant, J. Sawyer, G.I. Lin, N. Wardrip-Fruin, and M. Buell. 2011. Perceived or not perceived: Film character models for expressive nlg. In *Int. Conf. on Interactive Digital Storytelling, ICIDS'11*.

N. Wang, W. Lewis Johnson, R.E. Mayer, P. Rizzo, E. Shaw, and H. Collins. 2005. The politeness effect: Pedagogical agents and learning gains. *Frontiers in Artificial Intelligence and Applications*, 125:686–693.

I. Zukerman and D. Litman. 2001. Natural language processing and user modeling: Synergies and limitations. *User Modeling and User-Adapted Interaction*, 11(1-2):129–158.

Keynote: Graph-based Approaches for Spoken Language Understanding

Dilek Hakkani-Tur
Microsoft Research, U.S.A.
dilek@ieee.org

Following an upsurge in mobile device usage and improvements in speech recognition performance, multiple virtual personal assistant systems have emerged, and have been widely adopted by users. While these assistants proved to be beneficial, their usage has been limited to certain scenarios and domains, with underlying language understanding models that have been finely tuned by their builders.

Simultaneously, there have been several recent advancements in semantic web knowledge graphs especially used for basic question answering, efforts for integrating statistical information on these graphs, graph-based generic semantic representations and parsers, all providing opportunities for open domain spoken language understanding.

In this talk, I plan to summarize recent work in these areas, focusing on their connection, as a promise for wide coverage spoken language understanding in conversational systems, while at the same time investigating what is still lacking for natural human-machine interactions and related challenges.

Proceedings of the SIGDIAL 2015 Conference, page 198,
Prague, Czech Republic, 2-4 September 2015.

Evaluating Spoken Dialogue Processing for Time-Offset Interaction

David Traum, Kallirroi Georgila, Ron Artstein, Anton Leuski
USC Institute for Creative Technologies
12015 Waterfront Drive, Playa Vista CA 90094-2536, USA
{traum|kgeorgila|artstein|leuski}@ict.usc.edu

Abstract

This paper presents the first evaluation of a full automated prototype system for time-offset interaction, that is, conversation between a live person and recordings of someone who is not temporally co-present. Speech recognition reaches word error rates as low as 5% with general-purpose language models and 19% with domain-specific models, and language understanding can identify appropriate direct responses to 60–66% of user utterances while keeping errors to 10–16% (the remainder being indirect, or off-topic responses). This is sufficient to enable a natural flow and relatively open-ended conversations, with a collection of under 2000 recorded statements.

1 Introduction

Time-offset interaction allows real-time synchronous conversational interaction with a person who is not only physically absent, but also not engaged in the conversation at the same time. The basic premise of time-offset interaction is that when the topic of conversation is known, the participants' utterances are predictable to a large extent (Gandhe and Traum, 2010). Knowing what an interlocutor is likely to say, a speaker can record statements in advance; during conversation, a computer program selects recorded statements that are appropriate reactions to the interlocutor's utterances. The selection of statements can be done in a similar fashion to existing interactive systems with synthetic characters (Leuski and Traum, 2011).

In Artstein et al. (2014) we presented a proof of concept of time-offset interaction, which showed that given sufficiently interesting content, a reasonable interactive conversation could be demonstrated. However that system had a very small amount of content, and would only really work if someone asked questions about a very limited set of topics. There is a big gap from this proof of concept to evidence that the technique can work more generally. One of the biggest questions is how much material needs to be recorded in order to support free-flowing conversation with naive interactors who don't know specifically what they can ask. This question was addressed, at least for one specific case, in Artstein et al. (2015). There we showed that an iterative development process involving two separated recording sessions, with Wizard of Oz testing in the middle, resulted in a body of material of around 2000 responses that could be used to answer over 95% of questions from the desired target audience. In contrast, the 1400 responses from the first recording session alone was sufficient to answer less than 70% of users' questions. Another question is whether current language processing technology is adequate to pick enough appropriate responses to carry on interesting and extended dialogues with a wide variety of interested interactors. The proof of concept worked extremely well, even when people phrased questions very differently from the training data. However, that system had very low perplexity, with fewer than 20 responses, rather than something two orders of magnitude bigger.

In this paper, we address the second question, of whether time-offset interaction can be automatically supported at a scale that can support interaction with people who know only the general topic of discussion, not what specific content is available. In the next section, we review related work that is similar in spirit to time-offset interaction. In Section 3 we review our materials, including the domain of interaction, the system architecture, dialogue policy, and collected training and test data. In Section 4, we describe our evaluation methodology, including evaluation of speech recognition and classifier. In Section 5, we present our results,

Proceedings of the SIGDIAL 2015 Conference, pages 199–208,
Prague, Czech Republic, 2-4 September 2015.

showing that over 70% of user utterances can be given a direct answer, and an even higher percentage can reach task success through a clarification process. We conclude with a discussion and future work in Section 6.

2 Related Work

The idea for time-offset interaction is not new. We see examples of this in science fiction and fantasy. For example, in the Hollywood movie "I, Robot", Detective Spooner (Will Smith) interviews a computer-driven hologram of a recently deceased Dr. Lanning (James Cromwell).

The first computer-based dialogue system that we are aware of, that enabled a form of time-offset interactions with real people was installed at the Nixon Presidential Library in late 1980s (Chabot, 1990). The visitors were able to select one of over 280 predefined questions on a computer screen and observe a video of Nixon answering that question, taken from television interviews or filmed specifically for the project. This system did not allow Natural language input.

In the late 1990s Marinelli and Stevens came up with the idea of a "Synthetic Interview", where users can interact with a historical persona that was composed using clips of an actor playing that historical character and answering questions from the user (Marinelli and Stevens, 1998). "Ben Franklin's Ghost" is a system built on those ideas and was deployed in Philadelphia from 2005–2007 (Sloss and Watzman, 2005). This system had a book in which users could select questions, but, again, did not use unrestricted natural language input.

What we believe is novel with our New Dimensions in Testimony prototype is the ability to interact with a real person, not an actor playing a historical person, and also the evaluation of its ability to interact naturally, face to face, using speech.

3 Materials

3.1 Domain

Our initial domain for time-offset interaction is the experiences of a Holocaust survivor. Currently, an important aspect of Holocaust education in museums and classrooms is the opportunity to meet a survivor, hear their story firsthand, and interact with them. This direct contact and ability to ask questions literally brings the topic to life and motivates many toward further historical study and appreciation and determination of tolerance for others. Unfortunately, due to the age of survivors, this opportunity will not be available far into the future. The New Dimensions in Testimony project (Maio et al., 2012) is an effort to preserve as much as possible of this kind of interaction.

The pilot subject is Pinchas Gutter, who has previously told his life story many times to diverse audiences. The most obvious topic of conversation is Pinchas' experiences during World War II, including the Nazi invasion of Poland, his time in the Warsaw Ghetto, his experiences in the concentration camps, and his liberation. But there are many other topics that people bring up with Pinchas, including his pre- and post-war life and family, his outlook on life, and his favorite songs and pastimes.

3.2 System architecture

The automatic system is built on top of the components from the USC ICT Virtual Human Toolkit, which is publicly available.[1] Specifically, we use the AcquireSpeech tool for capturing the user's speech, CMU PocketSphinx[2] and Google Chrome ASR[3] tools for converting the audio into text, NPCEditor (Leuski and Traum, 2011) for classifying the utterance text and selecting the appropriate response, and a video player to deliver the selected video response. The individual components run as separate applications on the user's machine and are linked together by ActiveMQ messaging[4]: An instance of ActiveMQ broker runs on the machine, each component connects to the server and sends and receives messages to other components via the broker. The system setup also includes the JLogger component for recording the messages, and the Launcher tool that controls starting and stopping of individual tools. For example, the user can select between PocketSphinx and Google ASR engines by checking the appropriate buttons in the Launcher interface. Figure 1 shows the overall system architecture. We show the data flow through the system as black lines. Gray arrows indicate the control messages from the Launcher interface. Solid arrows represent messages passed via ActiveMQ and dotted lines represent data going over TCP/IP.

While most of the system components already

[1] http://vhtoolkit.ict.usc.edu
[2] http://cmusphinx.sourceforge.net
[3] https://www.google.com/intl/en/chrome/demos/speech.html
[4] http://activemq.apache.org

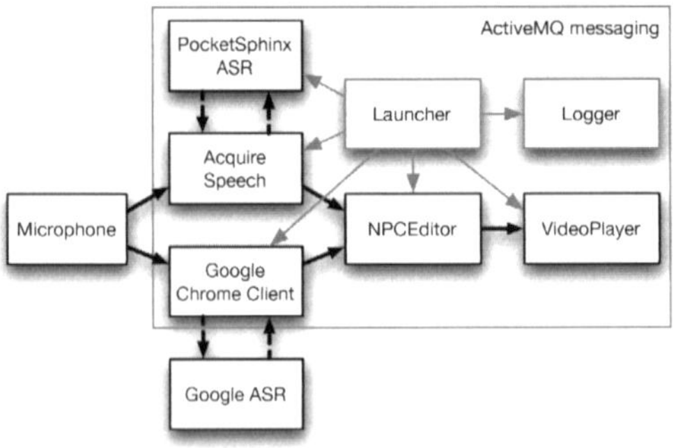

Figure 1: System architecture

existed before the start of this project, the Google Chrome ASR Client and VideoPlayer tools were developed in the course of this project. Google Chrome ASR client is a web application that takes advantage of the Google Speech API available in the Chrome browser. The tool provides push-to-talk interface control for acquiring user's speech; it uses the API to send audio to Google ASR servers, collect the recognition result, and broadcast it over the ActiveMQ messaging. We developed the VideoPlayer tool so that we can control the response playback via the same ActiveMQ messaging. VideoPlayer also implements custom transition between clips. It has video adjustment controls so that we can modify the scale and position of the video image, and it automatically displays a loop of idle video clips while the system is in resting or listening states.

While the system was developed to be cross-platform so that it can run both on OS X and Windows, we conducted all our testing and experiments on OS X. The system is packaged as a single OS X application that starts the Launcher interface and the rest of the system. This significantly simplifies distribution and installation of the system on different computers.

3.3 Speech recognition

Currently the system can work with two speech recognition engines, CMU PocketSphinx and Google Chrome ASR. But for our experiments we also considered Apple Dictation.[5]

One major decision when selecting a speech recognizer is whether it allows for training domain-specific language models (LMs) or not.[6] Purely domain-specific LMs cannot recognize out-of-domain words or utterances. On the other hand, general-purpose LMs do not perform well with domain-specific words or utterances. Unlike PocketSphinx, which supports trainable LMs, both Google Chrome ASR and Apple Dictation come with their own out-of-the-box LMs that cannot be modified.

Table 1 shows example outputs of all three recognizers (PocketSphinx examples were obtained with a preliminary LM). As we can see, Google Chrome ASR and Apple Dictation with their general-purpose LMs perform well for utterances that are not domain-specific. On the other hand, PocketSphinx clearly is much better at recognizing domain-specific words, e.g., "Pinchas", "Majdanek", etc. but fails to recognize general-purpose utterances if they are not included in its LM. For example, the user input "what's your favorite restaurant" is misrecognized as "what's your favorite rest shot" because the word "restaurant" or the sequence "favorite restaurant" was not part of the LM's training data. Similarly, the user input "did you serve in the army" is misrecognized as "did you certain the army" because the word "serve" or the sequence "serve in the army" was not included in the LM's training data.

For training LMs for PocketSphinx we used the CMU Statistical Language Modeling toolkit (Clarkson and Rosenfeld, 1997) with back-off 3-grams. The CMU pronouncing dictionary v0.7a (Weide, 2008) was used as the main dictionary with the addition of domain-dependent words, such as names. We used the standard US English acoustic models that are included in PocketSphinx.

3.4 Dialogue policy

As mentioned in section 3.2, NPCEditor combines the functions of Natural Language Understanding (NLU) and Dialogue Management – understanding the utterance text and selecting an appropriate response. The NLU functionality is a classifier trained on linked question-response pairs, which identifies the most appropriate response to new (unseen) user input. The dialogue management logic is designed to deal with instances where the classifier cannot identify a good direct response. During training, NPCEditor calculates a response

[5] https://support.apple.com/en-us/HT202584

[6] While the acoustic models of a speech recognizer recognize individual sounds, the LM provides information about what the recognizer should expect to listen to and recognize. If a word or a sequence of words is not included in the LM, they will never be recognized.

User Input	Google Chrome ASR Output	Apple Dictation Output	CMU Pocket Sphinx Output
hello pinchas	hello pinterest	hello princess	hello pinchas
where is lodz	where is lunch	where is lunch	where is lodz
were you in majdanek	were you in my dannic	were you in my donick	were you in majdanek
were you in kristallnacht	were you and krystal knox	where you went kristallnacht	where you when kristallnacht from
did you serve in the army	did you serve in the army	he served in the army	did you certain the army
have you ever lived in israel	have you ever lived in israel	that ever lived in israel	are you ever live in a israel
what's your favorite restaurant	what's your favorite restaurant	what's your favorite restaurant	what's your favorite rest shot

Table 1: Examples of speech recognition outputs

threshold based on the classifier's confidence in the appropriateness of selected responses: this threshold finds an optimal balance between false positives (inappropriate responses above threshold) and false negatives (appropriate responses below threshold) in the training data. At runtime, if the confidence for a selected response falls below the predetermined threshold, that response is replaced with an "off-topic" utterance that asks the user to repeat the question or takes initiative and changes the topic (Leuski et al., 2006); such failure to return a direct response, also called non-understanding (Bohus and Rudnicky, 2005), is usually preferred over returning an inappropriate one (misunderstanding).

The current system uses a five-stage off-topic selection algorithm which is an extension of that presented in Artstein et al. (2009). The first time Pinchas fails to understand an utterance, he will assume this is a speech recognition error and ask the user to repeat it. If the misunderstanding persists, Pinchas will say that he doesn't know (without asking for repetition), and the third time he will state that he cannot answer the user's utterance. In a severe misunderstanding that persists beyond three exchanges, Pinchas will suggest a new topic in the fourth turn, and if even this fails to bring the user to ask a question that Pinchas can understand, then in the fifth turn Pinchas will give a quick segue and launch into a story of his choice. If at any point Pinchas hears an utterance that he can understand (that is, if the classifier finds a response above threshold), Pinchas will answer this directly, and the off-topic state will reset to zero.

A separate component of the dialogue policy is designed to avoid repetition. Normally, Pinchas responds with the top-ranked response if it is above the threshold. However, if the top-ranked response has been recently used (within a 4-turn window) and a lower ranked response is also above the threshold, Pinchas will respond with the lower ranked response. If the only responses above threshold are among the recently used then Pinchas will choose one of them, since repetition is considered preferable to responding with an off-topic or inappropriate statement.

3.5 Data collection

The development process consisted of several stages: preliminary planning and question gathering, initial recording of survivor statements, Wizard of Oz studies using the recorded statements to identify gaps in the content, a second recording of survivor statements to address the gaps, assembly of an automated dialogue system, and continued testing with the automated system. The development process has been described in detail in Artstein et al. (2015); here we describe the data collected at the various stages of development, which constitute the training and test data for the automated system.

In the preliminary planning stages, potential user questions were collected from various sources, but these were not used directly as system training data. Instead, these questions formed the basis for an interview script that was used for eliciting the survivor statements during the recording sessions. The first training data include the actual utterances used during these elicitation interviews. The interviewer utterances were manually linked to the survivor responses; in the typical case, an utterance is linked to the response it elicited during the recording sessions, but the links were manually adjusted to remove instances when the response was not appropriate, and to add links to additional appropriate responses.

Additional training data were collected in the various stages of user testing – the Wizard of Oz testing between the first and second recording sessions, and fully automated system testing

Data source	Questions	Links
Elicitation	1546	2147
Wizard of Oz	1753	3329
System testing 2014	1825	1990
System testing 2015	1823	1959
Total	6947	9425

Table 2: Training data sets

Code	Interpretation
4	Directly addresses the user question.
3	Indirectly addresses the user question, or contains additional irrelevant material.
2	Does not address the user question, but is on a related topic.
1	Irrelevant to the user question.

Table 3: Coherence rating for system responses

following the second recording. Wizard of Oz testing took place in June and July 2014; participants sat in front of a screen that showed rough-cut video segments of Mr. Gutter's statements, selected by human operators in response to user utterances in real time. Since the Wizard of Oz testing took place prior to the second recording, wizards were only able to choose statements from the first recording. The user utterances were recorded, transcribed, and analyzed to form the basis for the elicitation script for the second recording. Subsequent to the second recording, these utterances were reannotated to identify appropriate responses from all of the recorded statements, and these reannotated question-response links form the Wizard of Oz portion of the training data.

Testing with the automated system was carried out starting in October 2014, following the second recording of survivor statements. Users spoke to the automated system, and their utterances were recorded, transcribed, and annotated with appropriate responses. These data are partitioned into two – the testing that took place in late 2014 was mostly internal, with team members, other institute staff, and visitors, while the testing from early 2015 was mostly external, conducted over 3 days at a local museum. We thus have 4 portions of training data, summarized in Table 2.

Test data for evaluating the classifier performance were taken from the system testing in late 2014. We picked a set of 400 user utterances, collected during the last day of testing, which was conducted off-site and therefore consisted primarily of external test participants (these utterances are not counted in Table 2 above). We only included in-domain utterances for which an appropriate on-topic response was available. The evaluation therefore measures the ability of the system to identify an appropriate response when one is available, not its ability to identify instances where an on-topic response is unavailable. There is some overlap in the test questions, so the 400 instances contain only 341 unique question types, with the most frequent question (*What is your name?*) occurring 5 times. We believe it is fair to include such overlap in the test set, since it gives higher weight to the more frequent questions. Also, while the text of overlapping questions is identical, each instance is associated with a unique audio file; these utterances may therefore yield different speech recognizer outputs, resulting in different outcomes.

The test set was specially annotated to serve as a test key. There is substantial overlap in content between the recorded survivor statements, so many user utterances can be addressed appropriately by more than one response. For training purposes it is sufficient to link each user utterance to some appropriate responses, but the test key must link each utterance to *all* appropriate responses. It is impractical to check each of the 400 test utterances against all 1726 possible responses, so instead we used the following procedure to identify responses that are likely to come up in response to specific test questions: we trained the system under different partitions of the training data and different training parameters, ran the test questions through each of the system versions, and from each system run we collected the responses that the system considered appropriate (that is, above threshold) for each question. This resulted in a set of 3737 utterance-response pairs, ranging from 3 to 19 responses per utterance, which represent likely system outputs for future training configurations. All the responses retrieved by the system were rated for coherence on a scale of 1–4 (Table 3). The responses rated 3 or 4 were deemed appropriate for inclusion in the test key, a total of 1838 utterance-response pairs, ranging from 1 to 10 responses per utterance.

4 Method

4.1 Speech recognition

As mentioned above, neither Google nor Apple ASRs allow for trainable LMs. But for PocketSphinx we experimented with different domain-specific LMs and below we report results on PocketSphinx performance with two different domain-specific LMs: one trained on Wizard of Oz and system testing data (approx. 5000 utterances) collected until December 2014 (LM-ds), and another one trained on additional data (approx. 6500 utterances) collected until January 2015 (LM-ds-add). The test set was the 400 utterances mentioned above. There was no overlap between the training and test data sets.

In order to evaluate the performance of the speech recognizers we use the standard word error rate (WER) metric:

$$\text{WER} = \frac{\text{Substitutions} + \text{Deletions} + \text{Insertions}}{\text{Length of transcription string}}$$

4.2 Classifier evaluation

Evaluation of the classifier is difficult, because it has to take into account the dialogue policy: the classifier typically returns the top-ranked response, but may return a lower-ranked response if it is above threshold and the higher-ranked responses were used recently. So while the classifier ranks all the available responses, anything below the top few will never be selected by the dialogue manager, rendering measures such as precision and recall quite irrelevant. An ideal evaluation should give highest weight to the correctness of the top-ranked response, with rapidly decreasing weight to the next several responses, but it is difficult to determine what weights are appropriate. We therefore focus on the top answer, since in most cases the top answer is what will get served to the user.

The top answer can be one of three outcomes: it can be appropriate (good), inappropriate (bad), or below threshold, in which case an off-topic response is served. A good response is better than an off-topic, which is in turn better than a bad response. This makes it difficult to compare systems with different off-topic rates: how do two systems compare if one gives more good and bad responses than the other, but fewer off-topics? We therefore compare systems using error return plots, which show the error rate across all possible return rates (Artstein, 2011): for each system we calculate the number of errors at each return rate, and then plot the number of errors against the number of off-topics.

We used 6 combinations of the training data described in section 3.5. The baseline is trained with only the elicitation questions, and represents the performance we might expect if we were to build a dialogue system based on the recording sessions alone, without collecting user question data (except to the extent that user questions influenced the second recording session). To this baseline we successively added training data from the Wizard of Oz testing, system testing 2014, and system testing 2015. Our final training sets include the elicitation questions and system testing 2014 (without Wizard of Oz data), and the same with the system testing 2015 added.

All of the classifiers were trained in NPCEditor using the same options: text unigrams for the question language models, text unigrams plus IDs for the response language models, and F-score as the classifier scoring function during training. We used 3 versions of the test utterances: the transcribed text, the output of Google ASR, and the output of PocketSphinx, and ran each version through each of the 6 classifiers – a total of 18 configurations. For each testing configuration, we retrieved the top-ranked response for each utterance, together with the classifier confidence and a true/false indication of whether the response matched the answer key. The responses were ranked by the classifier confidence, and for each possible cutoff point (from returning zero off-topic responses to returning off-topic responses for all 400 utterances), we calculated the number of errors among the on-topic responses and plotted that against the number of off-topics. Each plot represents the error-return tradeoff for a particular testing configuration (see section 5.2).

5 Results

5.1 Speech recognition evaluation

Table 4 shows the WERs for the three different speech recognizers and the two different LMs.

Note that we also experimented with interpolating domain-specific with background LMs available from `http://keithv.com/software`. Interpolation did not help but this is still an issue under investigation. Interpolation helped with speakers who had low WERs (smooth easy to recognize speech) but hurt in cases of speakers with high

Speech Recognizer	Language Model		
	General	LM-ds	LM-ds-add
Google	5.07%	—	—
Apple	7.76%	—	—
PocketSphinx	—	22.04%	19.39%

Table 4: Speech recognition results (WER). General LM stands for general-purpose LM, LM-ds stands for domain-specific LM trained with data collected until December 2014, and LM-ds-add stands for domain-specific LM trained with additional data collected until January 2015.

WERs. In the latter cases, having a background model meant that there were more choices for the speech recognizer to choose from, which instead of helping caused confusion.

We also noticed that PocketSphinx was less tolerant of environmental noises, which most of the time resulted in insertions and substitutions. For example, as we can see in Table 1, the user input "have you ever lived in israel" was misrecognized by PocketSphinx as "are you ever live in a israel". These misrecognitions do not necessarily confuse the classifier, but of course they often do.

5.2 Classifier evaluation

Classifier performance is best when training on all the data, and testing on transcriptions rather than speech recognizer output. Figure 2 shows the effect of the amount of training data on classifier performance when tested on transcribed text (a similar effect is observed when testing on speech recognizer output). Lower curves represent better performance. As expected, performance improves with additional training data – training on the full set of data cuts error rates by about a third compared to training on the elicitation questions alone. Additional training data (both new questions and question-response links) are likely to improve performance even further.

The effect of speech recognition on classifier performance is shown in Figure 3. Automatic speech recognition does impose a performance penalty compared to testing on transcriptions, but the penalty is not very large: classifier errors when testing with Google ASR are between 1 and 3 percentage points higher than with transcriptions, while PocketSphinx fares somewhat worse, with classifier errors about 5 to 8 percentage points higher than with transcriptions. At a 20% off-topic rate, the response error rates are 14% for transcriptions and 16% for Google ASR, meaning that almost two thirds of user utterances receive a direct appropriate response. At 30% off-topics, errors drop to 10–11%, and direct appropriate responses drop to just shy of 60%. Informal impressions from current testing at a museum (section 6) suggests that these numbers are sufficient to enable a reasonable conversation flow.

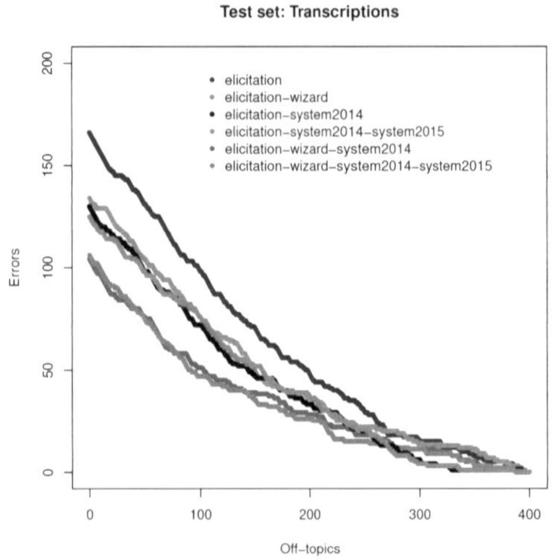

Figure 2: Tradeoff between errors and off-topics for various training sets (tested on transcribed text)

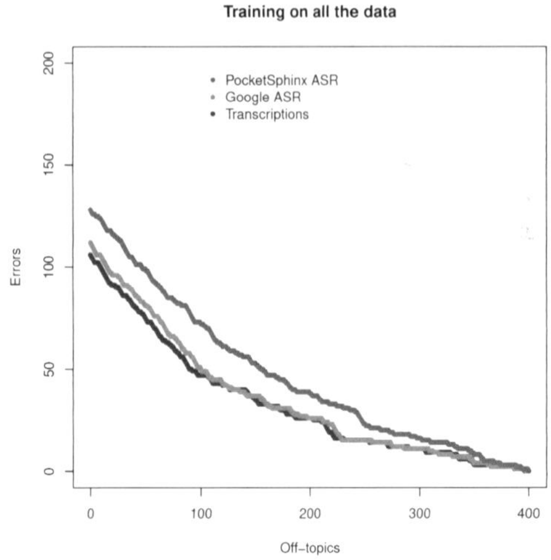

Figure 3: Tradeoff between errors and off-topics for different test sets (trained on the full data)

6 Discussion

This paper has demonstrated that time-offset interaction with a real person is achievable with present day spoken language processing technology. Not only are we able to collect a sufficiently large and varied set of statements to address user utterances (Artstein et al., 2015), we are also able to use speech recognition and language understanding technology to identify appropriate responses frequently enough to enable a natural interaction flow. Future work is needed in three areas: investigating the interaction quality of the dialogue system, improving the language processing, and generalizing the process to additional situations.

To investigate the interaction quality, we need to look at dialogues in context rather than as isolated utterances, and to collect user feedback. We are presently engaged in a joint testing, demonstration, and data collection effort that is intended to address these issues. The time-offset interaction system has been temporarily installed at the Illinois Holocaust Museum and Education Center in Skokie, Illinois, where visitors interact with the system as part of their museum experience (Isaacs, 2015). The system is set up in an auditorium and users talk to Pinchas in groups, in a setting that is similar to in-person encounters with Holocaust survivors which also take place at the museum. Due to physical limitations of the exhibit space, interaction is mediated by museum docents: each user question is relayed by the docent into the microphone, and Pinchas responds to the docent's speech. An excerpt of museum interaction is in the Appendix. Data and feedback from the museum installation will be used to evaluate the interaction quality, including user feedback as to the naturalness of the interaction and user satisfaction.

The ongoing testing also serves the purpose of data collection for improving system performance: Figure 2 shows that errors diminish with additional training data, and it appears that we have not yet reached the point of diminishing returns with about 7000 training utterances. We hope to collect an average of 10 training utterances per response, that is about 17000 user utterances. Annotation is also incomplete: the test key has an average of 4.6 links per utterance, as opposed to an average of around 1.4 links per utterance in the training data. While complete linking is not necessary for classifier operation, improving the links will probably improve performance.

In addition to improving performance through improved data, there are also algorithmic improvements that can be made to the language processing components. One goal is to leverage the relative strengths of the general purpose and domain-specific ASRs, e.g., through the classifier: past work has shown that language understanding can be improved by allowing NLU to select from among several hypotheses provided by a single speech recognizer (Morbini et al., 2012), and we propose to try a similar method to utilize the outputs of separate speech recognizers. Another idea is to combine/align the outputs of the speech recognizers (before they are forwarded to the classifier) taking into account information from the recognition confidence scores and lattices. This will potentially help in cases where different recognizers succeed in correctly recognizing different parts of the utterance.

Time-offset interaction has a large potential impact on preservation and education – people in the future will be able to not only see and listen to historical figures, but also to interact with them in conversation. Future research into time-offset interaction will need to generalize the development process, in order to enable efficient use of resources by identifying common user questions that are specific to the person, ones that are specific to the dialogue context or conversation topic, and ones that are of more general application.

Acknowledgments

This work was made possible by generous donations from private foundations and individuals. We are extremely grateful to The Pears Foundation, Louis F. Smith, and two anonymous donors for their support. The work was supported in part by the U.S. Army; statements and opinions expressed do not necessarily reflect the position or the policy of the United States Government, and no official endorsement should be inferred. Heather Maio and Alesia Gainer spent long hours on data collection and system testing. The Los Angeles Museum of the Holocaust, the Museum of Tolerance, and New Roads School in Santa Monica offered their facilities for data collection. The USC Shoah Foundation provided financial and administrative support, and facilities. Finally, we owe special thanks to Pinchas Gutter for sharing his story, and for his tireless efforts to educate the world about the Holocaust.

References

Ron Artstein, Sudeep Gandhe, Jillian Gerten, Anton Leuski, and David Traum. 2009. Semi-formal evaluation of conversational characters. In Orna Grumberg, Michael Kaminski, Shmuel Katz, and Shuly Wintner, editors, *Languages: From Formal to Natural. Essays Dedicated to Nissim Francez on the Occasion of His 65th Birthday*, volume 5533 of *Lecture Notes in Computer Science*, pages 22–35. Springer, Heidelberg, May.

Ron Artstein, David Traum, Oleg Alexander, Anton Leuski, Andrew Jones, Kallirroi Georgila, Paul Debevec, William Swartout, Heather Maio, and Stephen Smith. 2014. Time-offset interaction with a Holocaust survivor. In *Proceedings of IUI*, pages 163–168, Haifa, Israel, February.

Ron Artstein, Anton Leuski, Heather Maio, Tomer Mor-Barak, Carla Gordon, and David Traum. 2015. How many utterances are needed to support time-offset interaction? In *Proceedings of the Twenty-Eighth International Florida Artificial Intelligence Research Society Conference*, pages 144–149, Hollywood, Florida, May. AAAI Press.

Ron Artstein. 2011. Error return plots. In *Proceedings of SIGDIAL*, pages 319–324, Portland, Oregon, June.

Dan Bohus and Alexander I. Rudnicky. 2005. Sorry, I didn't catch that! – An investigation of non-understanding errors and recovery strategies. In *Proceedings of SIGDIAL*, pages 128–143, Lisbon, Portugal, September.

Lucy Chabot. 1990. Nixon library technology lets visitors 'interview' him. *Los Angeles Times*, July 21.

Philip Clarkson and Ronald Rosenfeld. 1997. Statistical language modeling using the CMU-Cambridge toolkit. In *Proc. of Eurospeech*, Rhodes, Greece, September.

Sudeep Gandhe and David Traum. 2010. I've said it before, and I'll say it again: An empirical investigation of the upper bound of the selection approach to dialogue. In *Proceedings of SIGDIAL*, pages 245–248, Tokyo, September.

Mike Isaacs. 2015. Holocaust Museum: Pilot program aims to preserve survivor voices for future generations. *Chicago Tribune*, May 19.

Anton Leuski and David Traum. 2011. NPCEditor: Creating virtual human dialogue using information retrieval techniques. *AI Magazine*, 32(2):42–56.

Anton Leuski, Ronakkumar Patel, David Traum, and Brandon Kennedy. 2006. Building effective question answering characters. In *Proceedings of SIGDIAL*, Sydney, Australia, July.

Heather Maio, David Traum, and Paul Debevec. 2012. New dimensions in testimony. *PastForward*, Summer:22–26.

Donald Marinelli and Scott Stevens. 1998. Synthetic interviews: The art of creating a 'dyad' between humans and machine-based characters. In *Proceedings of the Sixth ACM International Conference on Multimedia: Technologies for Interactive Movies (MULTIMEDIA)*, pages 11–16, New York, NY, USA. ACM.

Fabrizio Morbini, Kartik Audhkhasi, Ron Artstein, Maarten Van Segbroeck, Kenji Sagae, Panayiotis Georgiou, David R. Traum, and Shri Narayanan. 2012. A reranking approach for recognition and classification of speech input in conversational dialogue systems. In *Proceedings of the Fourth IEEE Workshop on Spoken Language Technology (SLT)*, pages 49–54, Miami Beach, Forida, December.

Eric Sloss and Anne Watzman. 2005. Carnegie Mellon's Entertainment Technology Center conjures up Benjamin Franklin's ghost. Press release, Carnegie Mellon Media Relations, June 28. `http://www.cmu.edu/PR/releases05/050628_etc.html`.

R.L. Weide. 2008. The CMU pronouncing dictionary.

A Dialogue sample

The following dialogue excerpt is taken from the beta testing in Illinois (see section 6). Speech recognition output is shown in italics when it departs substantially from the spoken text.

User Hello Pinchas, how are you?
Las Vegas how are you

Pinchas Can you just repeat that?

User Can you hear me OK?

Pinchas I can see you and I can hear you.

User Hello Pinchas, can you hear me?
how thick is can you hear me

Pinchas I can hear you, yeah.

User Pinchas, can you tell me how old you are?
Vegas can you tell me how old you are

Pinchas I was born in nineteen thirty two and we are now in two thousand and fourteen and you can make your own reckoning.

User Can you tell me a little bit about your childhood?

Pinchas My life before the war, I was born in Lodz in Poland, and I was eight years old when the war started. So the first eight years I lived in a home, a very religious one, a Hasidic home. I had a twin sister, my...

User Have you ever met Hitler?
mermaid Hitler

Pinchas Please repeat that.

User Did you ever meet Hitler?

Pinchas Did I ever meet Hitler? Well, Hitler was a Führer of Germany and I was born in Poland and I was a little Jewish boy, so the chances of somebody like me meeting Hitler was impossible, because Hitler was...

User What would you do if you met Hitler?

Pinchas Geyn drerd arein, that's Yiddish and what it means go and bury yourself.

THE REAL CHALLENGE 2014: PROGRESS AND PROSPECTS

Maxine Eskenazi, Alan W Black, Sungjin Lee
Language Technologies Institute
Carnegie Mellon University
5000 Forbes Ave
Pittsburgh PA 1521
{max,awb}@cs.cmu.edu, junion@yahoo-inc.com

David Traum
Institute for Creative Technologies
University of Southern California
12015 Waterfront Drive
Playa Vista, CA 90094
traum@ict.usc.edu

Abstract

The REAL Challenge took place for the first time in 2014, with a long term goal of creating streams of real data that the research community can use, by fostering the creation of systems that are capable of attracting real users. A novel approach is to have high school and undergraduate students devise the types of applications that would attract many real users and that need spoken interaction. The projects are presented to researchers from the spoken dialog research community and the researchers and students work together to refine and develop the ideas. Eleven projects were presented at the first workshop. Many of them have found mentors to help in the next stages of the projects. The students have also brought out issues in the use of speech for real applications. Those issues involve privacy and significant personalization of the applications. While long-term impact of the challenge remains to be seen, the challenge has already been a success at its immediate aims of bringing new ideas and new researchers into the community, and serves as a model for related outreach efforts.

1 Introduction

This paper describes the REAL Challenge (REAL), including the motivations for the challenge and preliminary results from the first year and prospects for the near future. The ultimate goal of REAL is to bring about a steady stream of data from real users talking to spoken dialogue systems, that can be used for academic research. The immediate goal of the first year of REAL is to bring together high school and undergraduate students, who have fresh ideas of how people will talk to things in the future and what the constraints may be, and seasoned researchers, who know how to create the systems and could work with the students to realize a Wizard of Oz (WOZ) study or a proof-of-concept prototype to try out the idea.

At SLT 2012, panelists stated that there was no publicly available, significant stream of spoken dialog data coming from real users other than the Lets Go data (Raux et al., 2006). Although Lets Go can be used to create statistical models for some information-giving systems, with the wide variety of community needs, it cannot satisfy applications that are not two-way and information giving. In answer to this, REAL was created to spark ideas for speech applications that are needed on a regular basis (fulfilling some real need) by real users. Observing present applications in the commercial and academic community and how little use that they are getting, it was apparent, at least to the authors of this paper, that new minds were needed to devise the right kind of applications. This led the REAL organizers to reach out to high school and undergraduate students.

From announcements in late summer 2013 to the REAL workshop on June 21, 2014, and beyond, this paper traces how REAL was managed, the proposals we received, what happened at the workshop, what follow up we have had and how we measure success.

2 Motivation

Speech and spoken dialog researchers often note that whereas industry has access to a wealth of ecologically valid speech data, the academic community lags far behind. The lag in quantity of data can impede research on system evaluation and in training the machine learning (ML) system components. This chasm can be filled by using recruited subjects. But studies (Ai et al., 2007) have found that the resulting data does not resemble real user data. Paid users follow the rules, but are usu-

Proceedings of the SIGDIAL 2015 Conference, pages 209–216,
Prague, Czech Republic, 2-4 September 2015.

ally just going through the motions. They do not create and follow their own personal goals. Without personal goals, they are not overly concerned about satisfying the problem they were asked to solve. For example, if they asked for a specific flight booking, they won't change their mind opportunistically when a better plan becomes available. Yet this ability to find alternative ways to accomplish a goal is present in real user behavior and poses interesting challenges to spoken dialog systems. Paid users are not bothered by system results that are not what they had requested. They often want to finish the task as rapidly as possible while real users will usually take a little more time to get what they want. And, they don't quit or curse the system at same rate if things are not going well. Thus, at evaluation time, the feedback from the paid user does not reflect the quality of system performance on real users.

Although simulated users can be another data-generating possibility, there are still several good reasons to pursue direct learning from human users. Usually conventional methods to build a user simulator follow a cycle of operations: data collection; annotation; model training and evaluation; and deployment for policy training. The whole development cycle takes quite a long time, and so user behavior can change by the time it is done. Moreover, it is highly likely that the new dialog policy, trained with the user simulator, will cause different user behavior patterns. Additionally, there are always discrepancies between real and simulated user behavior due to many simplifying assumptions in the user model. Thus, training on data from a simulated user can make dialog policies lag behind the ones that are optimal for real users.

While there are significant real user speech databases in industry, that data and the platforms that collected it are not available for release to researchers due to a variety of issues including intellectual property (IP), monetization, customer loyalty and information privacy concerns. So while industry can forge ahead (Halevy et al., 2009), academia is unable to show comparable performances, not due to poor research quality, but simply because of the lack of data.

Thus the community needs new streams of speech data that are available to academia. For this, we must find new applications that real users actually need and will use often. Although assistant applications like Siri, Cortana et al. have sparked the interest and imagination of the public, many people dont use them. The speech and spoken dialog communities must find something else, embracing novel interfaces and applications. And the research community may not be the place where these new ideas should come from. They might better originate with people who are: completely comfortable with the new technologies; not influenced by rigid ideas of what can and can't be done; and not limited by an agenda of what they need to do next. This leads us to believe that the community needs the input of young students who have always lived with the technology and know how they would use it in the future. Biased as the research community is by its knowledge of the science behind the systems, researchers also sometimes overlook some of the basic issues that must be dealt with, going forward. Younger students may also be able to identify the red flags that are keeping speech from being an interface of choice. An important side-benefit of this approach is that this challenge serves as an additional vehicle to bring new practitioners into the spoken dialogue community, by having early access to top researchers and training materials.

3 THE REAL CHALLENGE PROCESS

There is a significant leap from a young student's idea to a data-generating system. The process that REAL put in place breaks this leap into small, achievable steps. First, the organizers of REAL formed an international scientific committee, shown in Table 1. The scientific committee consisted of people who had espoused the spirit of REAL and were willing to work to make it a success.

A webpage (https://dialrc.org/realchallenge/) was created, including a timeline through the June 21st, 2014 workshop, a separate page with details of REAL for students and their teachers, contact information and an application form. Researchers around the world were contacted and asked to recruit students. Six countries began recruitment and four, China, Ireland, Korea and the US, had applicants for the 2014 challenge. One experienced researcher headed each country's efforts and was responsible for recruiting and organizing their students and for sending them to the workshop. The international Coordination Committee members are shown in Table 2.

Table 1: The REAL Scientific Committee

Alan W. Black	Carnegie Mellon University, USA
Maxine Eskenazi	Carnegie Mellon University, USA
Helen Hastie	Heriot-Watt University, Scotland
Gary Geunbae Lee	POSTECH South Korea
Sungjin Lee	Carnegie Mellon University, USA
Satoshi Nakamura	Nara Advanced Institute of Science and Technology, Japan
Elmar Noeth	Fredrich-Alexander University, Erlangen-Nuremberg, Germany
Antoine Raux	Lenovo, USA
David Traum	University of Southern California, USA
Jason Williams	Microsoft Research, USA

The students were encouraged to contact the organizers at any time for more information and/or for guidance in proposal writing. The proposals were submitted by April 1, 2014. They were sent to the scientific committee for review, with two reviewers per proposal. The reviewers, taking into account the age of the participants (from 13 to 23 years old), were asked to evaluate the proposals according the following criteria:

novelty: the proposal could not be exactly the same as an existing application. While existing applications could have the same subject, like cooking, the user interaction and/or function had to be novel.

speech is clearly necessary: the students needed to show that the application solves an issue thanks to its use of speech communication.

practical: this idea could be implemented either with current technology or with clearly definable extensions.

viable: this application is likely to attract real users — while it is not evident at present how best to measure viability, at this stage we could poll potential users. We also believe that the students are well aware of their peers habits and needs.

Table 2: International Coordination Committee

USA	Alan W. Black & Sungjin Lee	Carnegie Mellon University
China	Kai Yu	Shanghai Jiaotong University
Ireland	Emer Gilmartin	Trinity College Dublin
Korea	Gary Geunbae Lee	POSTECH
Scotland	Helen Hastie	Heriot-Watt University
Sweden	Samer Al Moubayed & Jose David Lopes	KTH

The reviews were edited to take into account the age of the students. They included feedback on shaping the ideas (focusing the application, getting rid of spurious activities) and requiring more details about the application (how would someone use it, under what conditions would someone use it. who would want to use it). After the students received their feedback, they were told what they would need to prepare for the workshop: a one-minute presentation of their idea, a poster and a presentation in front of the poster. Some students (China, Ireland) had exams at the time of the workshop and participated via Skype. These students were asked to record their in-front-of-poster presentations in case Skype was not working (in the end it worked very well!). Then the students were given some training:

- a class on speech and spoken dialog for the high school students (undergrads had had this in one of their regular classes);
- a video on how to make a poster – ensuring smooth communication between students and researchers on the day of the workshop: the poster included the goal, a comparison to what presently exists, why their idea was better, and an illustration of the use of their idea showing why it is needed, how someone would use it and how it solves the problem.

The workshop was held on June 21, 2014. After the one-minute presentations, the students stood in front of their posters for 90 minutes. In the following 30 minutes they could go around to see one another's posters. Then groups of researchers and students formed to discuss the ideas. All of the students found at least two researchers interested in having a discussion with them. Each group created a few slides summarizing their discussion and reported back to everyone. Most of the reports contained ways to focus ideas, to make them doable and most importantly, to define the next steps.

After the workshop, the organizers followed up with the researcher participants to find out their plans going forward. They were also asked whether they would be encouraging high school or undergraduates to join REAL in the next round.

Going forward, the organizers plan to have yearly REAL meetings. While the first workshop saw only proposals, the second and following ones should see both new proposals and results of WOZ studies and proof-of-concept demos from the proposals presented the previous year. This rolling participation enables new students and researchers to join at any time and puts less pressure on past participants – the successful projects will have something to show, but aren't expected to have a fully working system, within just one year. The intended cycle for successful proposals is the following:

1. find technical partners
2. for limitations that must be dealt with: work on why this is a limitation and what the possible fixes are
3. for applications or systems: work on the design then on the prototype or WOZ system
4. conduct a study (testing the prototype or WOZ system)
5. show study results (and possibly demo of system or propose a major design change for speech systems)
6. write a proposal for future funding to continue the work

4 Year One Winning Proposals

The first year of REAL enabled the organizers to assess how well its goals were fulfilled, what outcomes there were and what lessons were learned. The main outcome of REAL can first be shown in the quality of the proposals. Here are summaries of the 11 successful proposals from 2014 (note that all participants from outside the US are undergrads, the US participants are high school students):

Bocal (Jude Rosen, Joe Flot, US)
How can we protect the privacy of the user at the same time as offering a high quality of speech commanding and response? Bone-conducting devices can answer this question by capturing sounds emanating through skulls. The next step includes finding out a specific set of scenarios where the device will be useful and conducting Wizard of Oz experiments to collect data about how users would behave with the device on.

Daily Journaling (Keun Woo Park, Jungkook Park, Korea)
This system will help users record events in their everyday life. Lightweight and multimodal, it uses many sensors to determine what is going on around the user. To interpret what it captures, it asks the user questions. With the information gleaned from the questions, it updates its information about the user.

Fashion Advisor (Jung-eun Kim, Korea)
This advisor knows what clothing a person possesses and carries on a dialog in the morning to help the user choose what to wear. It would have a camera to capture the user and show them how they would look when wearing its suggestions (like a mirror). It also knows what the weather will be and will suggest appropriate clothing. It can also search sources such as Pinterest for clothes to purchase that would work with what the use has and their body type.

Gourmet (Jaichen Shi, China)
The Gourmet helps people choose a restaurant. Many people have dietary restrictions and the Gourmet would suggest restaurants where the user can be assured of finding something they can eat. It also tells the user what other diners have thought of a restaurant and can find specific feedback from diners who were at the restaurant on the present day. When a choice is made, it can call the restaurant for reservations.

Human Chatting System (Yunqi Guo, China)
This is a system that allows people to chat

with it. It is aimed at helping people rehearse discussions they would have with real people, either helping in how to deal with a difficult social situation (asking a girl for a date, for example), or speaking a new language (with a tutor that detects speaking errors and tells the student how to correct them).

Lecture Trainer (Qizhe Xie, China)
This application would listen to a user preparing a presentation and help them out. It could help with word choice, but also with grammar, intonation, and fluency. The user could choose a topic and also listen to recorded speeches from famous people so that the user could imitate the latter.

Mobile Cooking App (BongJin Sohn, Jong-Woo Choi, DongHyun Kim, Korea)
Modern-day appliances continue to evolve based on communication with users to identify and meet their needs. The cooking app will offer a cooking guide in the form of audio or video, voice control for oven and alarm setting, and provide a grocery list, etc. This app traces interaction history and each step of a recipe to make a dialog intelligent and efficient by being context-aware.

Neeloid (Neeloy Chakraborty, US)
The invention connects people with their surroundings. Camera and other sensors can also work together to create an accurate description of the audience's surroundings. It also understands gestures pointing at certain things for inquiry and looks into connected wiki to retrieve relevant information. This invention may give the visually impaired the confidence of knowing what is around them without the use of a white cane, hoople, guide, etc. Another application of this idea is as an educational tool that can be used by a wide variety of people, in particular, children full of curiosity.

Sam the Kitchen Assistant (Enno Hermann, Ireland)
Sam comes to the aid of the cook who has hands occupied and full of food and eyes also busy. Sam can tell a cook what to do next in a recipe, but also has information about how to adapt a recipe to any one of many dietary restrictions. Sam can suggest a recipe, on the way home, given what is in the house and list what needs to be bought.

SmartCID (Zachary McAlexander, David Donehue, US)
Millions of consumers today use smart technology in everyday life, including smartphones, tablets, and desktop computers. However, none of these technologies are truly easy-to-use. The user must always issue some command before the aid begins to operate. SmartCID solves this problem by automatically detecting external activity and instantaneously capturing content. For example, SmartCID can detect things like people posing for a picture, the word cheese said by a group, or a laugh from the user, to prompt the device to begin recording a video or audio file, allowing the user to review the funny moment at a later date.

Smart Watch (So Hyeon Jung, Korea)
This is a patient health care system. Elderly users (some with poor eyesight) can be told when to take their medication. They can also find out when their supply of medication is about to run out and get help ordering more. The system can also guide its users in healthy eating choices for the specific nutrients that the individual needs. And since it can suggest good foods, it can also help with calorie counts.

5 Outcomes from the First Year

The first outcome of the workshop was the proposals for new ideas, described in the previous section. All of them met the desired criteria of novelty, use of speech, with potential for practicality and viability. One of the ideas has already led to a peer-reviewed publication (Jung et al., 2015).

Another outcome of REAL is the set of issues in the ubiquitous use of speech that the students raised. First, the Bocal proposal raised the issue of privacy. Although we generally think that speech should be used in any setting, it is possible that privacy may restrict its frequent use in environments where there are other people in close proximity to the speaker. In this situation, it may indeed be necessary to either whisper or use a bone-conducting microphone. Second, several proposals, such as Mobile Cooking, Lecture Trainer, and Human Chatting System show that the most com-

Table 3: Next steps resulting from the Workshop

type - country	student	type of help	action
Academic -US	any	provide system components	Webinar on virtual human toolkit
Academic - US	KAIST	offer of mentorship	lectures to high school students, participation in next round
Academic - Germany	any present students	could mentor	students in next round
Academic/industry - Germany	-	-	students in next round
Academic - US	2 students from China	offer of internships	none
Industry - US	2 students from US	offer of internships	none
Academic - US	Three projects from US	mentorship	students in next round
Academic - Ireland	Student from Ireland	mentorship	Creating prototype of proposed system also young high school students in next round
Academic - Scotland	-	-	students in next round
Academic - Korea	One student from POSTECH	mentorship	Students will continue to participate next year
Academic - China	-	-	Students will continue to participate next year
Academic - Sweden			students in the next round

pelling applications for a user may not be for general use, but rather suites of applications that are important to individuals. Finally, we see that many of the proposals, without being prompted by organizers or teachers, were in a context of busy hands and eyes.

A third outcome of REAL is what took place the day of the workshop (described in Section 3). Students described their ideas to technologists/researchers. The participants met with students in the afternoon. The breakout reports from these meetings were given by both the researchers and the students. All had made slides and the one common element was the next steps points that all displayed. For many of the projects, the students got help in:

focus: concentrating on just one thing, deciding which thing was worth it, not trying to solve all of the worlds problems.

deciding what to do next: e.g., Is there hardware to concentrate on? Should a scenario be defined? What software is involved? What software modules exist and which ones must be built?

Finally, there is the promise of what is to come. Table 3 shows the post-meeting feedback from participants concerning their plans. For example, one academic participant is proposing internships to two of the students (from two different proposals).

6 Assessing REAL

The first year of REAL can be assessed using several metrics. But before the metrics are used, some perspective is needed. It is very difficult in one year to get a large part of the speech and spoken dialog community actively interested. It is hard to plan the venue of the workshop so that it coincides with a major meeting, while not taking place at the same time. It is also hard to organize students in many different countries, including the funding for the students. And finding support for REAL is also difficult. Industry is not yet sure what a company can get from this meeting. One measure is researcher participation. There were 21 researchers at the Workshop, 17 people were from academia, and the rest were from industry. Another metric is the depth and breadth of what is being proposed to the students to take their work forward. Yet another metric is whether colleagues plan to get more students involved in the coming year. This is also shown in Table 3. Three colleagues from three different countries proposed either to:

- increase the numbers of their participants next year
- bring in a new high school class
- bring in new undergraduate students

The use of Skype is considered to have been very helpful this year. If a student worked on a proposal during the year and could not, for some reason, attend the workshop (including exams, lack of travel funding, etc), then they were still able to make a presentation and get feedback. Another way to assess REAL is to observe the results of the interaction between the students and the researchers at the workshop breakout sessions. Some examples of the changes in the projects:

- Smart Watch project: there were four functions proposed: calorie-store, alarm, food recommendation, exercise recommendation. Issues that arose: hardware could become multiple devices; calorie store might be difficult for users; it should be multimodal, combining both spoken dialog and images for the users. Plan of action: break project into individual functions; examine existing apps to get a sense of range of interaction; do a WOZ data collection with diet expert function to observe dialogs and users reactions; use WOZ data to finalize design and train ASR/NLU. Subsequent to the workshop, this action plan was followed, and the food and exercise recommendation functions were implemented and tested, resulting in a peer review publication (Jung et al., 2015).
- Bocal project: focusing ideas into a platform for allowing system-user communication when privacy is important. Noting that the key technology will be transferring input from skull microphones to text, the main challenges were gaining an understanding of the differences between speech through skull and standard microphones and understanding how this technology will influence users' behavior. The action items were: choosing application domains that will necessitate privacy, like banking; collecting data with a WOZ setup; analyzing the data to find features for encoding the output of the skull microphone; developing models for transforming the output of the skull microphone to text; developing a spoken dialog system for exhibiting the feasibility of the approach.

Thus, the students got a considerable amount of help in focusing their ideas, in breaking down the steps that they need to take in the upcoming year to find out how feasible their projects are, and in understanding what the hardware and usage issues were. As seen on Table 3, several of the students have found mentors and they will be going forward with their projects.

7 CONCLUSIONS AND FUTURE DIRECTIONS

Although we have had a successful first year we are interested in the long term continued success of this challenge. As it grows in stability year to year it will be easier to get students to be aware of and take part in it. Even since out first year we have seen more standardized SDKs for developing speech based systems on more platforms. Microsoft's Cortana, and Amazon's Echo offer SDKs that we would like to utilize to aid student's proposals and eventual development.

The REAL Challenge is a bold step for researchers. Its stated goal was to find new applications that would create streams of spoken dialog data from real users. It has achieved this goal — students have proposed novel systems that have the potential to be very useful and thus to attract real users. Beyond the stated goals of the Challenge, the students have brought to the forefront issues that must be dealt with:

- The issue of privacy must be addressed. For example, real users would not dictate email or text messages if they feel that their messages are not secure.

- It is probable that the most successful speech applications will not be the general ones (like SIRI and Cortana), but may be the ones that are highly personalized to specific tasks.

Plans going forward concern both this year's projects and those to come in the future. REAL is seen as a regularly occurring event where there are multiple levels of presentation. There will be students who have proposed an idea (like all of the 2014 participants) who are looking for feedback and mentorship. There will be students who proposed their ideas the preceding year and are presenting either WOZ study results or a prototype. And ultimately there will be students (and researchers) who proposed one year, presented preliminary results the next year and are presenting a working system and real user data.

The REAL Challenge continues in its second year with renewed support from the National Science Foundation. Year two proposals for the REAL challenge are under development, with an intended participant workshop in Fall 2015. So far there are six proposals for 2015: three undergraduates and three high school students. The undergrad proposals are all new, while two of the ones from the high school students are updates of last years proposal and one is new. Table 4 shows this years proposals.

Table 4: REAL Challenge 2015 Entries

institution	**level**	**year**	**subject**
Heriot Watt	ugrad	Y1	Table talk - to order food at a restaurant
Heriot Watt	ugrad	Y1	BuddyBot - a companion for sick children in hospital
Pittsburgh Sci	high	Y2	next stage for Smart Content Interaction Device project
Pittsburgh Sci	high	Y1	multilinguistic conference meeting
Pittsburgh Sci	high	Y2	next stage, uses for bone conduction
Sogang U	ugrad	Y1	home chat system to dialog with home devices

Due to the differences in academic schedules around the world, to the success of virtual participation and to cost, the second year will see the students all participate remotely. Experts in the field will be brought in to the Workshop in person. Individual presentations will be given and group breakouts will be organized. Given that last year this Challenge not only proposed novel applications, but also unearthed interesting issues, part of the Workshop will address some of the issues (such as privacy) that are being brought to light.

ACKNOWLEDGEMENTS

The REAL Challenge has been sponsored by NSF grant no. CNS-1405644 and 1406000. The student participants in REAL were mentioned in the description of their projects. We would like to thank Ann Gollapudi, the teacher of the US high-school students. The persons who ran the Challenge in their own countries were:

- Gary Lee, Korea
- Kai Yu, China
- Emer Gilmartin, Ireland.

The authors would like to thank the researchers who took part in the Workshop, many of whom have made plans to follow up on projects and/or future versions of the Challenge.

References

Hua Ai, Antoine Raux, Dan Bohus, Maxine Eskenazi, and Diane Litman. 2007. Comparing spoken dialog corpora collected with recruited subjects versus real users. In *In Proceedings of the 8th SIGdial Workshop on Discourse and Dialogue*.

Alon Halevy, Peter Norvig, and Fernando Pereira. 2009. The unreasonable effectiveness of data. *IEEE Intelligent Systems*, 24(2):8–12, March.

Sohyeon Jung, SeonghanRyu, Sangdo Han, and Gary Geunbae Lee. 2015. Diettalk: Diet and health assistant based onspoken dialog system. In *Proceedings of Sixth International Workshop on Spoken Dialogue systems (IWSDS 2015)*, January.

Antoine Raux, Dan Bohus, Brian Langner, Alan W. Black, and Maxine Eskenazi. 2006. Doing research on a deployed spoken dialogue system: one year of let's go! experience. In *INTERSPEECH*. ISCA.

Argument Mining: Extracting Arguments from Online Dialogue

Reid Swanson & Brian Ecker & Marilyn Walker
Natural Language and Dialogue Systems
UC Santa Cruz
1156 High St.
Santa Cruz, CA, 95064
rwswanso,becker,mawalker@ucsc.edu

Abstract

Online forums are now one of the primary venues for public dialogue on current social and political issues. The related corpora are often huge, covering any topic imaginable. Our aim is to use these dialogue corpora to automatically discover the semantic aspects of arguments that conversants are making across multiple dialogues on a topic. We frame this goal as consisting of two tasks: argument extraction and argument facet similarity. We focus here on the argument extraction task, and show that we can train regressors to predict the quality of extracted arguments with RRSE values as low as .73 for some topics. A secondary goal is to develop regressors that are topic independent: we report results of cross-domain training and domain-adaptation with RRSE values for several topics as low as .72, when trained on topic independent features.

1 Introduction

Online forums are now one of the primary venues for public dialogue on current social and political issues. The related corpora are often huge, covering any topic imaginable, thus providing novel opportunities to address a number of open questions about the structure of dialogue. Our aim is to use these dialogue corpora to automatically discover the semantic aspects of arguments that conversants are making across multiple dialogues on a topic. We build a new dataset of 109,074 posts on the topics *gay marriage*, *gun control*, *death penalty* and *evolution*. We frame our problem as consisting of two separate tasks:

- **Argument Extraction**: How can we extract argument segments in dialogue that clearly express a particular argument facet?
- **Argument Facet Similarity**: How can we recognize that two argument segments are semantically similar, i.e. about the same facet of the argument?

Parent Post **P**, Response **R**
P1: A person should be executed for kicking a dog? Your neurologically imbalanced attitude is not only worrying, it is psychopathic. How would you prove guilt on somebody who 'kicked a dog'? And, in what way, is kicking a dog so morally abhorrant as to warrant a death sentence for the given act? ....   **R1**: Obviously you have issues. Any person who displays such a weakness of character cannot be allowed to contaminate the gene pool any further. Therefore, they must be put down. **If a dog bit a human, they would be put down, so why not do the same to a human?**
P2: So then **you will agree that evolution is useless in getting at possible answers on what really matters, how we got here?** If you concede that then I'm happy to end this discussion. I recall, however, visiting the Smithsonian and seeing a detailed description of how amino acids combined to form the building blocks of life. Evolutionary theory does address origins and its explanations are unsuppported by evidence.   **R2**: No, and no. **First, evolution provides the only scientific answers for how humans got here: we evolved from non-human ancestors.** That record is written in both the genes and the fossils. Science might even be able eventually to tell you what the forces of selection were that propelled this evolution.
P3: Do you have any idea how little violent crime involves guns? less than 10%. the US has violance problems, how about trying to controle the violance, not the tools.   **R3**: **But most murders are committed with guns.** So if you think it's important to reduce the murder rate, I don't think that guns can be ignored.
P4: Another lie used by people that want to ban guns. Guns as cars were invented to do what the owner uses them for! There is no difference in them. It takes a person to make them dangerous.   **R4**: **But guns were made specifically to kill people.** Cars were made to get a person from point A to B. When someone kills a person with a car, it's an accident. When someone kills a person with a gun, it's on purpose.

Figure 1: Sample Argument Segments for Gun Control, Death Penalty and Evolution.

Consider for example the sample posts and responses in Fig. 1. Argument segments that are good targets for argument extraction are indicated, in their dialogic context, in **bold**. Given extracted segments, the argument facet similarity module should recognize that **R3** and **R4** paraphrase the same argument facet, namely that there is a strong relationship between the availability of guns and the murder rate. This paper addresses only the argument extraction task, as an important first step towards producing argument summaries that reflect the range and type of arguments being made,

Proceedings of the SIGDIAL 2015 Conference, pages 217–226,
Prague, Czech Republic, 2-4 September 2015.

on a topic, over time, by citizens in public forums.

Our approach to the argument extraction task is driven by a novel hypothesis, the IMPLICIT MARKUP hypothesis. We posit that the arguments that are good candidates for extraction will be marked by cues (implicit markups) provided by the dialog conversants themselves, i.e. their choices about the surface realization of their arguments. We examine a number of theoretically motivated cues for extraction, that we expect to be domain-independent. We describe how we use these cues to sample from the corpus in a way that lets us test the impact of the hypothesized cues.

Both the argument extraction and facet similarity tasks have strong similarities to other work in natural language processing. Argument extraction resembles the sentence extraction phase of multi-document summarization. Facet similarity resembles semantic textual similarity and paraphrase recognition (Misra et al., 2015; Boltuzic and Šnajder, 2014; Conrad et al., 2012; Han et al., 2013; Agirre et al., 2012). Work on multi-document summarization also uses a similar module to merge redundant content from extracted candidate sentences (Barzilay, 2003; Gurevych and Strube, 2004; Misra et al., 2015).

Sec. 2 describes our corpus of arguments, and describes the hypothesized markers of high-quality argument segments. We sample from the corpus using these markers, and then annotate the extracted argument segments for ARGUMENT QUALITY. Sec. 3.2 describes experiments to test whether: (1) we can predict argument quality; (2) our hypothesized cues are good indicators of argument quality; and (3) an argument quality predictor trained on one topic or a set of topics can be used on unseen topics. The results in Sec. 4 show that we can predict argument quality with RRSE values as low as .73 for some topics. Cross-domain training combined with domain-adaptation yields RRSE values for several topics as low as .72, when trained on topic independent features, however some topics are much more difficult. We provide a comparison of our work to previous research and sum up in Sec. 5.

2 Corpus and Method

We created a large corpus consisting of 109,074 posts on the topics *gay marriage* (GM, 22425 posts), *gun control* (GC, 38102 posts), *death penalty* (DP, 5283 posts) and *evolution* (EV, 43624), by combining the Internet Argument Corpus (IAC) (Walker et al., 2012), with dialogues from `http://www.createdebate.com/`.

Our aim is to develop a method that can extract high quality arguments from a large corpus of argumentative dialogues, in a topic and domain-independent way. It is important to note that arbitrarily selected utterances are unlikely to be high quality arguments. Consider for example all the utterances in Fig. 1: many utterances are either not interpretable out of context, or fail to clearly frame an argument facet. Our IMPLICIT MARKUP hypothesis posits that arguments that are good candidates for extraction will be marked by cues from the surface realization of the arguments. We first describe different types of cues that we use to sample from the corpus in a way that lets us test their impact. We then describe the MT HIT, and how we use our initial HIT results to refine our sampling process. Table 2 presents the results of our sampling and annotation processes, which we will now explain in more detail.

2.1 Implicit Markup Hypothesis

The IMPLICIT MARKUP hypothesis is composed of several different sub-hypotheses as to how speakers in dialogue may mark argumentative structure.

The **Discourse Relation** hypothesis suggests that the Arg1 and Arg2 of explicit SPECIFICATION, CONTRAST, CONCESSION and CONTINGENCY markers are more likely to contain good argumentative segments (Prasad et al., 2008). In the case of *explicit* connectives, Arg2 is the argument to which the connective is syntactically bound, and Arg1 is the other argument. For example, a CONTINGENCY relation is frequently marked by the lexical anchor *If*, as in **R1** in Fig. 1. A CONTRAST relation may mark a challenge to an opponent's claim, what Ghosh et al. call *call-out-target* argument pairs (Ghosh et al., 2014b; Maynard, 1985). The CONTRAST relation is frequently marked by *But*, as in **R3** and **R4** in Fig. 1. A SPECIFICATION relation may indicate a focused detailed argument, as marked by *First* in **R2** in Fig. 1 (Li and Nenkova, 2015). We decided to extract only the Arg2, where the discourse argument is syntactically bound to the connective, since Arg1's are more difficult to locate, especially in dialogue. We began by extracting the Arg2's for the connectives most strongly associated with these discourse relations over the whole corpus, and then once we saw what the most frequent connectives were in our corpus, we refined this selection to include only *but*, *if*, *so*, and *first*. We sampled a roughly even distribution of sentences from each category as well as sentences without any discourse connectives, i.e. *None*. See Table. 2.

The **Syntactic Properties** hypothesis posits that syntactic properties of a clause may indicate good argument segments, such as being the main clause (Marcu, 1999), or the sentential complement of mental state or speech-act verbs, e.g. the SBAR

President Obama had tears in his eyes as he addressed the nation about the horrible tragedy.
This is of no relevance to the discussion.
President Obama has said before that he supports renewing the assault weapons ban.
Under Connecticut law the riffle that was used in the shooting was a prohibited firearm.
According to CNN, the killer used an AR-15 which I understand is a version of the M-16 assault riffle used in the military.
That is incorrect. The AR-15 and the M-16 share a similar appearance but they are not the same type of firearm in terms of function.

Table 1: An excerpt of a post that quotes its parent multiple times and the corresponding responses.

in *you agree that SBAR* as in **P2** in Fig. 1. Because these markers are not as frequent in our corpus, we do not test this with sampling: rather we test it as a feature as described in Sec. 3.2.

The **Dialogue Structure** hypothesis suggests that position in the post or the relation to a verbatim quote could influence argument quality, e.g. being turn-initial in a response as exemplified by **P2**, **R3** and **R4** in Fig. 1. We indicate sampling by position in post with **Starts: Yes/No** in Table. 2. Our corpora are drawn from websites that offer a "quoting affordance" in addition to a direct reply. An example of a post from the IAC corpus utilizing this mechanism is shown in Table 1, where the quoted text is highlighted in blue and the response is directly below it.

The **Semantic Density** hypothesis suggests that measures of rich content or SPECIFICITY will indicate good candidates for argument extraction (Louis and Nenkova, 2011). We initially posited that short sentences and sentences without any topic-specific words are less likely to be good. For the topics *gun control* and *gay marriage*, we filtered sentences less than 4 words long, which removed about 8-9% of the sentences. After collecting the argument quality annotations for these two topics and examining the distribution of scores (see Sec. 2.2 below), we developed an additional measure of semantic density that weights words in each candidate by its pointwise mutual information (PMI), and applied it to the *evolution* and *death penalty*. Using the 26 topic annotations in the IAC, we calculate the PMI between every word in the corpus appearing more than 5 times and each topic. We only keep those sentences that have at least one word whose PMI is above our threshold of 0.1. We determined this threshold by examining the values in *gun control* and *gay marriage*, such that at least 2/3 of the filtered sentences were in the bottom third of the argument quality score. The PMI filter eliminates 39% of the sentences from *death penalty* (40% combined with the length filter) and 85% of the sentences from *evolution* (87% combined with the length filter).

Table 2 summarizes the results of our sampling procedure. Overall our experiments are based on 5,374 sampled sentences, with roughly equal numbers over each topic, and equal numbers representing each of our hypotheses and their interactions.

2.2 Data Sampling, Annotation and Analysis

Table 8 in the Appendix provides example argument segments resulting from the sampling and annotation process. Sometimes arguments are completely self contained, e.g. **S1** to **S8** in Table 8. In other cases, e.g. **S9** to **S16** we can guess what the argument is based on using world knowledge of the domain, but it is not explicitly stated or requires several steps of inference. For example, we might be able to infer the argument in **S14** in Table 8, and the context in which it arose, even though it is not explicitly stated. Finally, there are cases where the user is not making an argument or the argument cannot be reconstructed without significantly more context, e.g. **S21** in Table 8.

We collect annotations for ARGUMENT QUALITY for all the sentences summarized in Table 2 on Amazon's Mechanical Turk (AMT) platform. Figure 3 in the Appendix illustrates the basic layout of the HIT. Each HIT consisted of 20 sentences on one topic which is indicated on the page. The annotator first checked a box if the sentence expressed an argument, and then rated the argument quality using a continuous slider ranging from hard (0.0) to easy to interpret (1.0).

We collected 7 annotations per sentence. All Turkers were required to pass our qualifier, have a HIT approval rating above 95%, and be located in the United States, Canada, Australia, or Great Britain. The results of the sampling and annotation on the final annotated corpus are in Table 2.

We measured the inter-annotator agreement (IAA) of the binary annotations using Krippendorff's α (Krippendorff, 2013) and the continuous values using the intraclass correlation coefficient (ICC) for each topic. We found that annotators could not distinguish between phrases that *did not express an argument* and *hard* sentences. See examples and definitions in Fig. 3. We therefore mapped unchecked sentences (i.e., non arguments) to zero argument quality. We then calculated the average pairwise ICC value for each rater between all Turkers with overlapping annotations, and removed the judgements of any Turker that did not have a positive ICC value. The ICC for each topic is shown in Table 2. The mean rating across the remaining annotators for each sentence was used as the gold standard for argument quality, with means in the **Argument Quality (AQ)** column of Table 2. The effect of the sampling on argument quality can be seen in Table 2. The differences between *gun control* and *gay marriage*, and the other two topics is due to effective use of the semantic density filter, which shifted the distribution of the annotated data towards higher quality arguments as we intended.

3 Experiments

3.1 Implicit Markup Hypothesis Validation

We can now briefly validate some of the IMPLICIT MARKUP hypothesis using an ANOVA testing the effect of a connective and its position in post on argument quality. Across all sentences in all topics, the presence of a connective is significant ($p = 0.00$). Three connectives, *if*, *but*, and *so*, show significant differences in AQ from no-connective phrases ($p = 0.00$, 0.02, 0.00, respectively). *First* does not show a significant effect. The mean AQ scores for sentences marked by *if*, *but*, and *so* differ from that of a no-connective sentence by 0.11, 0.04, and 0.04, respectively. These numbers support our hypothesis that there are certain discourse connectives or cue words which can help to signal the existence of arguments, and they seem to suggest that the CONTINGENCY category may be most useful, but more research using more cue words is necessary to validate this suggestion.

In addition to the presence of a connective, the dialogue structural position of being an initial sentence in a response post did not predict argument quality as we expected. Response-initial sentences provide significantly lower quality arguments ($p = 0.00$), with response-initial sentences having an average AQ score 0.03 lower (0.40 vs. 0.43).

3.2 Argument Quality Regression

We use 3 regression algorithms from the Java Statistical Analysis Toolkit[1]: Linear Least Squared Error (LLS), Ordinary Kriging (OK) and Support Vector Machines using a radial basis function kernel (SVM). A random 75% of the sentences of each domain were put into training/development and 25% into the held out test. Training involved a grid search over the hyper-parameters of each model[2] and a subset (2^3-2^9 and the complete set) of the top N features whose values correlate best with the argument quality dependent variable (using Pearson's). The combined set of parameters and features that achieved the best mean squared error over a 5-fold cross validation on the training data was used to train the complete model.

We also compare hand-curated feature sets that are motivated by our hypotheses to this simple feature selection method, and the performance of *in-domain*, *cross-domain*, and *domain-adaptation* training using "the frustratingly easy" approach (Daumé III, 2007).

We use our training and development data to develop a set of feature templates. The features are real-valued and normalized between 0 and 1, based on the min and max values in the training data for each domain. If not stated otherwise the presence of a feature was represented by 1.0 and its absence by 0.0. We describe all the hand-curated feature sets below.

Semantic Density Features: *Deictic Pronouns* **(DEI)**: The presence of anaphoric references are likely to inhibit the interpretation of an utterance. These features count the deictic pronouns in the sentence, such as *this*, *that* and *it*.

Sentence Length **(SLEN)**: Short sentences, particularly those under 5 words, are usually hard to interpret without context and complex linguistic processing, such as resolving long distance discourse anaphora. We thus include a single aggregate feature whose value is the number of words.

Word Length **(WLEN)**: Sentences that clearly articulate an argument should generally contain words with a high information content. Several studies show that word length is a surprisingly good indicator that outperforms more complex measures, such as rarity (Piantadosi et al., 2011). Thus we include features based on word length, including the min, max, mean and median. We also create a feature whose value is the count of words of lengths 1 to 20 (or longer).

Speciteller **(SPTL)**: We add a single aggregate feature from the result of Speciteller, a tool that assesses the specificity of a sentence in the range of 0 (least specific) to 1 (most specific) (Li and Nenkova, 2015; Louis and Nenkova, 2011). High specificity should correlate with argument quality.

Kullback-Leibler Divergence **(KLDiv)**: We expect that sentences on one topic domain will have different content than sentences outside the domain. We built two trigram language models using the Berkeley LM toolkit (Pauls and Klein, 2011). One (P) built from all the sentences in the IAC within the domain, excluding all sentences from the annotated dataset, and one (Q) built from all sentences in IAC outside the domain. The KL Divergence is then computed using the discrete n-gram probabilities in the sentence from each model as in equation (1).

$$D_{KL}(P||Q) = \sum_i P(i) \ln \frac{P(i)}{Q(i)} \quad (1)$$

Lexical N-Grams **(LNG)**: N-Grams are a standard feature that are often a difficult baseline to

[1] `https://github.com/EdwardRaff/JSAT`

[2] We used the default parameters for LLS and OK and only searched hyper-parameters for the SVM model.

Topic	Starts	Total	But	First	If	So	None	ICC	AQ
Gun Control	Yes	826	149	138	144	146	249		0.457
	No	764	149	145	147	149	174		0.500
	Total	1,590	298	283	291	295	423	0.45	0.478
Gay Marriage	Yes	779	137	120	149	148	225		0.472
	No	767	140	130	144	149	204		0.497
	Total	1,546	277	250	293	297	429	0.46	0.484
Death Penalty	Yes	399	60	17	101	100	121		0.643
	No	587	147	20	137	141	142		0.612
	Total	986	207	37	238	241	263	0.40	0.624
Evolution	Yes	609	143	49	147	138	132		0.571
	No	643	142	80	143	138	140		0.592
	Total	1,252	285	129	290	276	272	0.35	0.582

Table 2: Overview of the corpus and Argument Quality (AQ) annotation results.

beat. However they are not domain independent. We created a feature for every unigram and bigram in the sentence. The feature value was the inverse document frequency of that n-gram over all *posts* in the entire combined IAC plus `CreateDebate` corpus. Any n-gram seen less than 5 times was not included. In addition to the *specific lexical* features a set of *aggregate* features were also generated that only considered summary statistics of the lexical feature values, for example the min, max and mean IDF values in the sentence.

Discourse and Dialogue Features: We expect our features related to the discourse and dialogue hypotheses to be domain independent.

Discourse (**DIS**): We developed features based on discourse connectives found in the Penn Discourse Treebank as well as a set of additional connectives in our corpus that are related to dialogic discourse and not represented in the PDTB. We first determine if a discourse connective is present in the sentence. If not, we create a NO CONNECTIVE feature with a value of 1. Otherwise, we identify all connectives that are present. For each of them, we derive a set of *specific lexical* features and a set of generic *aggregate* features.

The *specific* features make use of the lexical (String) and PDTB categories (Category) of the found connectives. We start by identifying the connective and whether it started the sentence or not (Location). We then identify the connective's most likely PDTB category based on the frequencies stated in the PDTB manual and all of its parent categories, for example *but* → CONTRAST → COMPARISON. The *aggregate* features only consider how many discourse connectives and if any of them started the sentence. The templates are:

Specific:{Location}:{String}
Specific:{Location}:{Category}
Aggregate:{Location}:{Count}

For example, the first sentence in Table 8 would generate the following features:

Specific:Starts:but
Specific:Starts:Contrast
Specific:Starts:COMPARISON
Aggregate:Starts:1
Aggregate:Any:1

Because our hypothesis about dialogue structure was disconfirmed by the results described in section 3.1, we did not develop a feature to independently test position in post. Rather the Discourse features only encode whether the discourse cue starts the post or not.

Syntactic Property Features: We also expect syntactic property features to generalize across domains.

Part-Of-Speech N-Grams (**PNG**): Lexical features require large amounts of training data and are likely to be topic-dependent. Part-of-speech tags are less sparse and and less likely to be topic-specific. We created a feature for every unigram, bigram and trigram POS tag sequence in the sentence. Each feature's value was the relative frequency of the n-gram in the sentence.

Syntactic (**SYN**): Certain syntactic structures may be used more frequently for expressing argumentative content, such as complex sentences with verbs that take clausal complements. In `CreateDebate`, we found a number of phrases of the form **`I`** <**`VERB`**> **`that`** <**`X`**>, such as *I agree that*, *you said that*, *except that* and *I disagree because*. Thus we included two types of syntactic features: one for every internal node, excluding POS tags, of the parse tree (NODE) and another for each context free production rule (RULE) in the parse tree. The feature value is the relative frequency of the node or rule within the sentence.

Meta Features: The 3 meta feature sets are: (1) all features except lexical n-grams (**!LNG**); (2) all features that use specific lexical or categorical information (**SPFC**); and (3) aggregate statistics (**AGG**) obtained from our feature extraction process. The **AGG** set included features, such as sentence and word length, and summary statistics about the IDF values of lexical n-grams, but did not actually reference any lexical properties in the

GC	GM	DP	EV
SLEN	SLEN	LNG:penalty	LNG:⟨s⟩,**
NODE:ROOT	NODE:ROOT	LNG:death,penalty	PNG:⟨s⟩,SYM
PNG:NNS	PNG:IN	LNG:death	PNG:⟨s⟩,⟨s⟩,SYM
PNG:NN	Speciteller	LNG:the,death	LNG:**
PNG:IN	PNG:JJ	PNG:NN,NN	PNG:NNS
Speciteller	PNG:NN	NODE:NP	PNG:SYM
PNG:DT	PNG:NNS	PNG:DT,NN,NN	WLEN:Max
LNG:gun	LNG:marriage	KLDiv	WLEN:Mean
KLDiv	WLEN:Max	PNG:NN	NODE:X
PNG:JJ	PNG:DT	WLEN:7:Freq	PNG:IN

Table 3: The ten most correlated features with the quality value for each topic on the training data.

feature name. We expect both **!LNG** and **AGG** to generalize across domains.

4 Results

Sec. 4.1 presents the results of feature selection, which finds a large number of general features. The results for argument quality prediction are in Secs. 4.2 and 4.3.

4.1 Feature Selection

Our standard training procedure (**SEL**) incorporates all the feature templates described in Sec. 3.2, which generates a total of 23,345 features. It then performs a grid search over the model hyper-parameters and a subset of all the features using the simple feature selection technique described in section 3.2. Table 3 shows the 10 features most correlated with the annotated quality value in the training data for the topics *gun control* and *gay marriage*. A few domain specific lexical items appear, but in general the top features tend to be non-lexical and relatively domain independent, such as part-of-speech tags and sentence specificity, as measured by Speciteller (Li and Nenkova, 2015; Louis and Nenkova, 2011).

Sentence length has the highest correlation with the target value in both topics, as does the node:root feature, inversely correlated with length. Therefore, in order to shift the quality distribution of the sample that we put out on MTurk for the *death penalty* or *evolution* topics, we applied a filter that removed all sentences shorter than 4 words. For these topics, domain specific features such as lexical n-grams are better predictors of argument quality. As discussed above, the PMI filter that was applied only to these two topics during sampling removed some shorter low quality sentences, which probably altered the predictive value of this feature in these domains.

4.2 In-Domain Training

We first tested the performance of 3 regression algorithms using the training and testing data within each topic using 3 standard evaluation measures: R^2, Root Mean Squared Error (RMSE) and Root

Topic	Reg	# Feats	R^2	RMSE	RRSE
GC	LLS	64	0.375	0.181	0.791
GC	OK	ALL	0.452	0.169	0.740
GC	SVM	512	**0.466**	**0.167**	**0.731**
GM	LLS	64	0.401	0.182	0.774
GM	OK	ALL	**0.441**	**0.176**	**0.748**
GM	SVM	256	0.419	0.179	0.762
DP	LLS	16	**0.083**	0.220	0.957
DP	OK	ALL	0.075	**0.221**	0.962
DP	SVM	ALL	0.079	**0.221**	**0.960**
EV	LLS	ALL	0.016	0.236	0.992
EV	OK	ALL	0.114	0.224	0.941
EV	SVM	ALL	**0.127**	**0.223**	**0.935**

Table 4: The performance of in domain training for three regression algorithms.

Relative Squared Error (RRSE). R^2 estimates the amount of variability in the data that is explained by the model. Higher values indicate a better fit to the data. The RMSE measures the average squared difference between predicted values and true values, which penalizes wrong answers more as the difference increases. The RRSE is similar to RMSE, but is normalized by the squared error of a simple predictor that always guesses the mean target value in the test set. Anything below a 1.0 indicates an improvement over the baseline.

Table 4 shows that SVMs and OK perform the best, with better than baseline results for all topics. Performance for *gun control* and *gay marriage* are significantly better. See Fig. 2. Since SVM was nearly always the best model, we only report SVM results in what follows.

We also test the impact of our theoretically motivated features and domain specific features. The top half of Table 5 shows the RRSE for each feature set with darker cells indicating better performance. The feature acronyms are described in Sec 3.2. When training and testing on the same domain, using lexical features leads to the best performance for all topics (SEL, LEX, LNG and SPFC). However, we can obtain good performance on all of the topics without using any lexical information at all (!LNG, WLEN, PNG, and AGG), sometimes close to our best results. Despite the high correlation to the target value, sentence specificity as a single feature does not outperform any other feature sets. In general, we do better for *gun control* and *gay marriage* than for *death penalty* and *evolution*. Since the length and domain specific words are important features in the trained models, it seems likely that the filtering process made it harder to learn a good function.

The bottom half of Table 5 shows the results using training data from all other topics, when testing on one topic. The best results for GC are significantly better for several feature sets (**SEL,**

Topic	SEL	LEX	LNG	!LNG	SPTL	SLEN	WLEN	SYN	DIS	PNG	SPFC	AGG
GC	0.73	0.75	0.79	0.79	0.94	0.87	0.93	0.83	0.99	0.80	0.75	0.85
GM	0.76	0.75	0.79	0.81	0.95	0.89	0.91	0.87	0.99	0.83	0.77	0.82
DP	0.96	0.95	0.95	0.99	1.02	1.01	0.98	1.01	1.03	0.98	0.96	0.98
EV	0.94	0.92	0.93	0.96	1.00	0.99	0.99	1.00	1.00	0.96	0.94	0.96
GC^{ALL}	0.74	0.72	0.75	0.81	0.96	0.90	0.94	1.03	0.90	0.82	0.75	0.84
GM^{ALL}	0.72	0.74	0.78	0.79	0.96	0.91	0.92	1.03	0.91	1.02	0.74	0.83
DP^{ALL}	0.97	0.97	1.01	0.98	1.05	1.02	0.98	1.03	1.02	1.03	0.97	0.99
EV^{ALL}	0.93	0.94	0.96	0.97	1.02	1.04	0.98	1.01	1.04	1.01	0.93	0.96

Table 5: The RRSE for in-domain training on each of the feature sets. Darker values denote better scores. **SEL**=Feature Selection, **LEX**=Lexical, **LNG**=Lexical N-Grams, **!LNG**=Everything but LNG, **SPTL**=Speciteller, **SLEN**=Sentence Length, **WLEN**=Word Length, **SYN**=Syntactic, **DIS**=Discourse, **PNG**=Part-Of-Speech N-Grams, **SPFC**=Specific, **AGG**=Aggregate. XX^{ALL} indicates training on data from all topics and testing on the XX topic.

LEX, LNG), In general the performance remains similar to the in-domain training, with some minor improvements over the best performing models. These results suggest that having more data outweighs any negative consequences of domain specific properties.

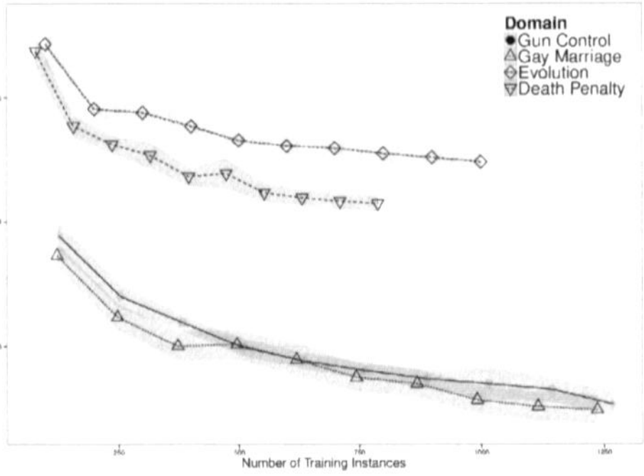

Figure 2: Learning curves for each of the 4 topics with 95% confidence intervals.

We also examine the effect of training set size on performance given the best performing feature sets. See Fig. 2. We randomly divided our entire dataset into an 80/20 training/testing split and trained incrementally larger models from the 80% using the default training procedure, which were then applied to the 20% testing data. The plotted points are the mean value of repeating this process 10 times, with the shaded region showing the 95% confidence interval. Although most gains are achieved within 500-750 training examples, all models are still trending downward, suggesting that more training data would be useful.

Finally, our results are actually even better than they appear. Our primary application requires extracting arguments at the *high* end of the scale (e.g., those above 0.8 or 0.9), but the bulk of our data is closer to the middle of the scale, so our regressors are conservative in assigning high or low values. To demonstrate this point we split the predicted values for each topic into 5 quantiles. The RMSE for each of the quantiles and domains in Table 6 demonstrates that the lowest RMSE is obtained in the top quantile.

%ile	GC	GM	DP	EV
0.2	**0.162**	**0.171**	0.237	**0.205**
0.4	0.184	0.201	0.238	0.242
0.6	0.198	0.181	0.225	0.211
0.8	0.166	0.176	**0.178**	0.208
1.0	**0.111**	**0.146**	**0.202**	**0.189**
ALL	0.167	0.176	0.217	0.220

Table 6: The RMSE for the best performing model in each domain given instances whose predicted quality value is in the given percentile.

4.3 Cross-Domain and Domain Adaptation

To investigate whether learned models generalize across domains we also evaluate the performance of training with data from one domain and testing on another. The columns labeled **CD** in Table 7 summarize these results. Although cross domain training does not perform as well as in-domain training, we are able to achieve much better than baseline results between *gun control* and *gay marriage* for many of the feature sets and some other minor transferability for the other domains. Although lexical features (e.g., lexical n-grams) perform best in-domain, the best performing features across domains are all non-lexical, i.e. **!LNG**, **PNG** and **AGG**.

We then applied Daume's "frustratingly easy domain adaptation" technique (**DA**), by transforming the original features into a new augmented feature space where, each feature, is transformed into a *general* feature and a domain specific feature, *source* or *target*, depending on the input domain (Daumé III, 2007). The training data from both the source and target domains are used to train

		SEL		LNG		!LNG		SPTL		DIS		PNG		AGG	
SRC	**TGT**	**CD**	**DA**	**CD**	**DA**	**CD**	**DA**	**CD**	**DA**	**CD**	**DA**	**CD**	**DA**	**CD**	**DA**
GC	GM	0.84	0.75	1.00	0.82	0.84	0.94	0.96	0.80	1.01	0.85	0.85	0.76	0.88	0.82
GC	DP	1.13	0.94	1.30	0.97	1.04	1.01	1.13	0.96	1.09	1.02	1.11	0.94	1.08	0.97
GC	EV	1.10	0.92	1.29	0.98	1.05	1.01	1.08	0.97	1.07	0.98	1.09	0.92	1.02	0.96
GM	GC	0.82	0.74	0.96	0.79	0.82	0.94	0.94	0.78	0.99	0.82	0.81	0.74	0.88	0.85
GM	DP	1.13	0.93	1.28	0.97	1.08	1.02	1.11	0.96	1.12	1.01	1.09	0.95	1.07	0.96
GM	EV	1.07	0.93	1.27	0.98	1.03	1.01	1.06	0.96	1.07	0.98	1.02	0.93	1.02	0.96
DP	GC	1.06	0.75	1.01	0.80	1.14	0.96	1.25	0.79	1.28	0.82	1.10	0.74	1.13	0.85
DP	GM	1.04	0.75	1.00	0.83	1.10	0.96	1.23	0.81	1.27	0.87	1.09	0.77	1.10	0.81
DP	EV	0.97	0.91	1.00	0.95	1.00	1.01	1.05	0.95	1.05	1.00	1.00	0.93	0.99	0.96
EV	GC	0.97	0.74	0.97	0.80	1.02	0.95	1.05	0.80	1.13	0.83	1.02	0.74	0.91	0.85
EV	GM	0.96	0.75	0.99	0.82	0.98	0.95	1.04	0.81	1.13	0.87	1.01	0.76	0.91	0.82
EV	DP	1.04	0.95	1.07	0.98	1.01	1.00	1.00	0.98	1.00	1.00	1.00	0.96	1.01	0.98

Table 7: The RRSE for cross-domain training (CD) and with domain adaptation (DA).

the model, unlike the cross-domain experiments where only the source data is used. These results are given in the columns labeled **DA** in Table 7, which are on par with the best in-domain training results, with minor performance degradation on some *gay marriage* and *gun control* pairs, and slight improvements on the difficult *death penalty* and *evolution* topics.

5 Discussion and Conclusions

This paper addresses the **Argument Extraction** task in a framework whose long-term aim is to first extract arguments from online dialogues, and then use them to produce a summary of the different facets of an issue. We have shown that we can find sentences that express clear arguments with RRSE values of .72 for gay marriage and gun control (Table 6) and .93 for death penalty and evolution (Table 8 cross domain with adaptation). These results show that sometimes the best quality predictors can be trained in a domain-independent way.

The two step method that we propose is different than much of the other work on argument mining, either for more formal texts or for social media, primarily because the bulk of previous work takes a supervised approach on a labelled topic-specific dataset (Conrad et al., 2012; Boltuzic and Šnajder, 2014; Ghosh et al., 2014b). Conrad & Wiebe developed a data set for supervised training of an argument mining system on weblogs and news about universal healthcare. They separate the task into two components: one component identifies ARGUING SEGMENTS and the second component labels the segments with the relevant ARGUMENT TAGS. Our argument extraction phase has the same goals as their first component. Boltuzic & Snajder also apply a supervised learning approach, producing arguments labelled with a concept similar to what we call FACETS. However they perform what we call argument extraction by hand, eliminating comments from comment streams that they call "spam" (Boltuzic and Šnajder, 2014). Ghosh et al. also take a supervised approach, developing techniques for argument mining on online forums about technical topics and applying a theory of argument structure that is based on identifying TARGETS and CALLOUTS, where the callout attacks a target proposition in another speaker's utterance (Ghosh et al., 2014b). However, their work does not attempt to discover high quality callouts and targets that can be understood out of context like we do. More recent work also attempts to do some aspects of argument mining in an unsupervised way (Boltuzic and Šnajder, 2015; Sobhani et al., 2015). However (Boltuzic and Šnajder, 2015) focus on the argument facet similarity task, using as input a corpus where the arguments have already been extracted. (Sobhani et al., 2015) present an architecture where arguments are first topic-labelled in a semi-supervised way, and then used for stance classification, however this approach treats the whole comment as the extracted argument, rather than attempting to pull out specific focused argument segments as we do here.

A potential criticism of our approach is that we have no way to measure the recall of our argument extraction system. However we do not think that this is a serious issue. Because we are only interested in determining the similarity between phrases that are high quality arguments and thus potential contributors to summaries of a specific facet for a specific topic, we believe that precision is more important than recall at this point in time. Also, given the redundancy of the arguments presented over thousands of posts on an issue it seems unlikely we would miss an important facet. Finally, a measure of recall applied to the facets of a topic may be irreconcilable with our notion that an argument does not have a limited, enumerable number of facets, and our belief that each facet is subject to judgements of granularity.

6 Appendix

Fig. 3 shows how the Mechanical Turk hit was defined and the examples that were used in the qualification task. Table 8 illustrates the argument quality scale annotations collected from Mechanical Turk.

We invite other researchers to improve upon our results. Our corpus and the relevant annotated data is available at `http://nldslab.soe.ucsc.edu/arg-extraction/sigdial2015/`.

7 Acknowledgements

This research is supported by National Science Foundation Grant CISE-IIS-RI #1302668.

References

E. Agirre, M.Diab, D. Cer, and A. Gonzalez-Agirre. 2012. Semeval-2012 task 6: A pilot on semantic textual similarity. In *Proc. of the Sixth Int. Workshop on Semantic Evaluation*, pp. 385–393. ACL.

R. Barzilay. 2003. *Information Fusion for Multidocument Summarization: Paraphrasing and Generation*. Ph.D. thesis, Columbia University.

F. Boltuzic and J. Šnajder. 2014. Back up your stance: Recognizing arguments in online discussions. In *Proc. of the First Workshop on Argumentation Mining*, pp. 49–58.

F. Boltuzic and J. Šnajder. 2015. Identifying prominent arguments in online debates using semantic textual similarity. In *Proc. of the Second Workshop on Argumentation Mining*.

A. Conrad, J. Wiebe, and R. Hwa. 2012. Recognizing arguing subjectivity and argument tags. In *Proc. of the Workshop on Extra-Propositional Aspects of Meaning in Computational Linguistics*, pp. 80–88. ACL.

H. Daumé III. 2007. Frustratingly Easy Domain Adaptation. In *Proc. of the 45th Annual Meeting of the Association of Computational Linguistics*, June.

D. Ghosh, S. Muresan, N. Wacholder, M. Aakhus, and M. Mitsui. 2014b. Analyzing argumentative discourse units in online interactions. *ACL 2014*, p. 39.

I. Gurevych and M. Strube. 2004. Semantic similarity applied to spoken dialogue summarization. In *Proc. of the 20th Int. conference on Computational Linguistics*, pp. 764–771. ACL.

L. Han, A. Kashyap, T. Finin, J. Mayfield, and J. Weese. 2013. Umbc ebiquity-core: Semantic textual similarity systems. *Atlanta, Georgia, USA*, p. 44.

K. Krippendorff. 2013. *Content analysis: an introduction to its methodology*. Sage, Los Angeles [etc.].

J. J Li and A.Nenkova. 2015. Fast and Accurate Prediction of Sentence Specificity. In *Proc. of the Twenty-Ninth Conf. on Artificial Intelligence (AAAI)*, January.

A. Louis and A. Nenkova. 2011. Automatic identification of general and specific sentences by leveraging discourse annotations. In *Proc. of 5th Int. Joint Conf. on Natural Language Processing*, pp. 605–613.

D. Marcu. 1999. Discourse trees are good indicators of importance in text. *Advances in automatic text summarization*, pp. 123–136.

D. W. Maynard. 1985. How Children Start Arguments. *Language in Society*, 14(1):1–29, March.

A. Misra, P. Anand, J. E. Fox Tree, and M.A. Walker. 2015. Using summarization to discover argument facets in dialog. In *Proc. of the 2015 Conf. of the North American Chapter of the ACL: Human Language Technologies*.

A. Pauls and D. Klein. 2011. Faster and Smaller N-gram Language Models. In *Proc. of the 49th Annual Meeting of the Association for Computational Linguistics: Human Language Technologies - Volume 1*, HLT '11, pp. 258–267, Stroudsburg, PA, USA. ACL.

S.T. Piantadosi, H. Tily, and E. Gibson. 2011. Word lengths are optimized for efficient communication. *Proc. of the National Academy of Sciences*, 108(9):3526–3529, March.

R. Prasad, N. Dinesh, A. Lee, E. Miltsakaki, L. Robaldo, A. Joshi, and B. Webber. 2008. The Penn Discourse Treebank 2.0. In *Proc. of the 6th Int. Conf. on Language Resources and Evaluation (LREC 2008)*, pp. 2961–2968.

P. Sobhani, D. Inkpen, and S. Matwin. 2015. From argumentation mining to stance classification. In *Proc. of the Second Workshop on Argumentation Mining*.

M.A. Walker, P. Anand, R. Abbott, and J. E. Fox Tree. 2012. A corpus for research on deliberation and debate. In *Language Resources and Evaluation Conf. , LREC2012*.

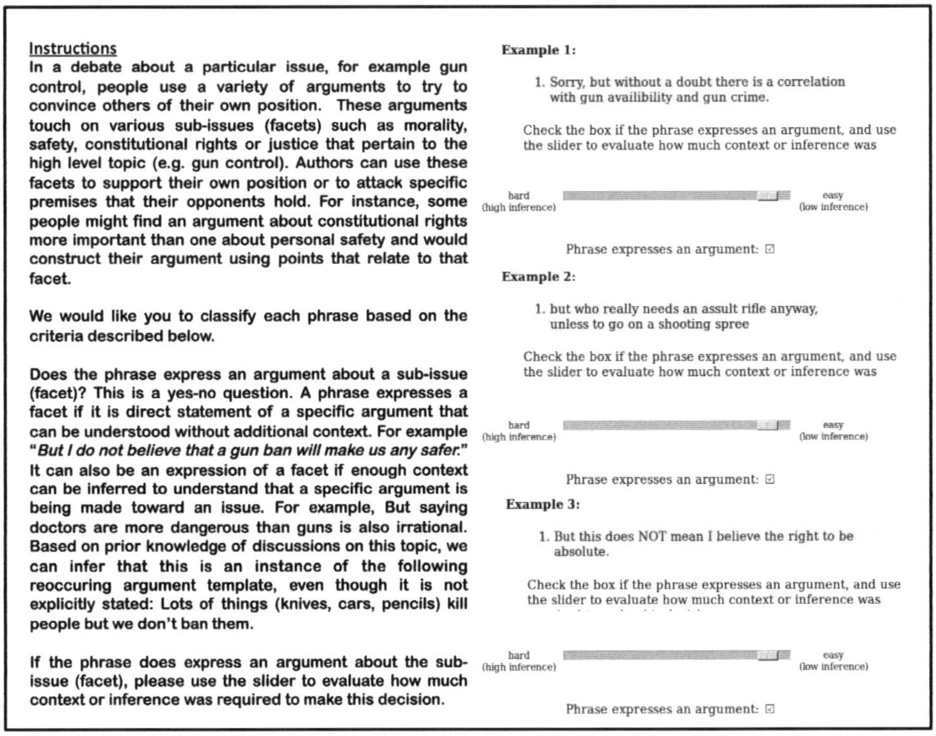

Figure 3: Argument Clarity Instructions and HIT Layout.

ID	Topic	Argument Quality	Sentence
S1	GC	0.94	But guns were made specifically to kill people.
S2	GC	0.93	If you ban guns crime rates will not decrease.
S3	GM	0.98	If you travel to a state that does not offer civil unions, then your union is not valid there.
S4	GM	0.92	Any one who has voted yes to place these amendments into state constitutions because they have a religious belief that excludes gay people from marriage has also imposed those religious beliefs upon gay people.
S5	DP	0.98	The main reasons I oppose the death penalty are: #1) It is permanent.
S6	DP	0.97	If a dog bit a human, they would be put down, so why no do the same to a human?
S7	EV	0.97	We didn't evolve from apes.
S8	EV	0.95	Creationists have to pretty much reject most of science.
S9	GC	0.57	IF they come from the Constitution, they're not natural... it is a statutory right.
S10	GC	0.52	This fear is doing more harm to the gun movement than anything else.
S11	GM	0.51	If it seems that bad to you, you are more than welcome to leave the institution alone.
S12	GM	0.50	Nobody is trying to not allow you to be you.
S13	DP	0.52	Why isn't the death penalty constructive?
S14	DP	0.50	But lets say the offender decides to poke out both eyes?
S15	EV	0.51	so no, you don't know the first thing about evolution.
S16	EV	0.50	But was the ark big enough to hold the number of animals required?
S17	GC	0.00	Sorry but you fail again.
S18	GC	0.00	Great job straight out of the leftard playbook.
S19	GM	0.00	First, I AIN'T your honey.
S20	GM	0.00	There's a huge difference.
S21	DP	0.03	But as that's not likely to occur, we fix what we can.
S22	DP	0.01	But you knew that, and you also know it was just your try to add more heat than light to the debate.
S23	EV	0.03	marc now resorts to insinuating either that I'm lying or can't back up my claims.
S24	EV	0.00	** That works for me.

Table 8: Example sentences in each topic domain from different sections of the quality distribution.

Multilingual Summarization with Polytope Model

Natalia Vanetik
Department of Software Engineering
Shamoon College of Engineering
Beer Sheva, Israel
natalyav@sce.ac.il

Marina Litvak
Department of Software Engineering
Shamoon College of Engineering
Beer Sheva, Israel
marinal@sce.ac.il

Abstract

The problem of extractive text summarization for a collection of documents is defined as the problem of selecting a small subset of sentences so that the contents and meaning of the original document set are preserved in the best possible way. In this paper we describe the linear programming-based global optimization model to rank and extract the most relevant sentences to a summary. We introduce three different objective functions being optimized. These functions define a relevance of a sentence that is being maximized, in different manners, such as: coverage of meaningful words of a document, coverage of its bigrams, or coverage of frequent sequences of words. We supply here an overview of our system's participation in the MultiLing contest of SIGDial 2015.

1 Introduction

Automated text summarization is an active field of research in various communities, including Information Retrieval, Natural Language Processing, and Text Mining.

Some authors reduce summarization to the maximum coverage problem (Takamura and Okumura, 2009; Gillick and Favre, 2009) which, despite positive results, is known as NP-hard (Khuller et al., 1999). Because linear programming (LP) helps to find an accurate approximated solution to this problem it has recently become very popular in the summarization field (Gillick and Favre, 2009; Woodsend and Lapata, 2010; Hitoshi Nishikawa and Kikui, 2010; Makino et al., 2011).

Trying to solve a trade-off between summary quality and time complexity, we propose a summarization model solving the approximated maximum coverage problem by linear programming in polynomial time. We measure information coverage by an objective function and strive to obtain a summary that preserves its optimal value as much as possible. Three objective functions considering different metrics of *information* are introduced and evaluated. The main achievement of our method is a text representation model expanding a classic vector space model (Salton et al., 1975) to hyperplane and half-spaces and making it possible to represent an exponential number of extracts without computing them explicitly. This model also enables us to find the optimal extract by simple optimizing an objective function in polynomial time, using linear programming over rationals. For the first time, the frequent sequence mining was integrated with the maximal coverage approach in order to obtain a summary that best describes the summarized document. One of the introduced objective functions implements this idea.

Our method ranks and extracts significant sentences into a summary, without any need in morphological text analysis. It was applied for both single-document (MSS) and multi-document (MMS) MultiLing 2015 summarization tasks, in three languages–English, Hebrew, and Arabic. In this paper we present experimental results in comparison with other systems that participated in the same tasks, using the same languages.

2 Preprocessing and definitions

We are given a document or a set of related documents in UTF-8 encoding. Documents are split into sentences $S_1, ..., S_n$. All sentences undergo tokenization, stop-word removal, and stemming. For some languages, stemming may be very basic or absent, and a list of stop-words may be unavailable. All these factors affect summarization quality.

Unique stemmed words are called *terms* and are denoted by $T_1, ..., T_m$. Every sentence is modeled as a sequence of terms from $T_1, ..., T_m$ where each

Proceedings of the SIGDIAL 2015 Conference, pages 227–231,
Prague, Czech Republic, 2-4 September 2015.

term may appear zero or more times in a sentence. We are also given the desired number of words for a summary, denoted by $MaxWords$.

The goal of extractive summarization is to find a subset of sentences $S_1, ..., S_n$ that has no more than $MaxWords$ words and conveys as much information as possible about the documents. Because it is difficult, or even impossible, to know what humans consider to be the best summary, we approximate the human decision process by optimizing certain *objective functions* over representation of input documents constructed according to our model. The number of words in a summary, sentences, and terms, are represented as *constraints* in our model.

3 Polytope model

3.1 Definitions

In the polytope model (Litvak and Vanetik, 2014) a document is viewed as an integer sentence-term matrix $A = (a_{ij})$, where a_{ij} denotes the number of appearances of term T_j in sentence S_i. A row i of matrix A is used to define a linear constraint for sentence S_i as follows:

$$\sum_{j=1}^{m} a_{ij}x_{ij} \leq \sum_{j=1}^{m} a_{ij} \tag{1}$$

Equation (1) also defines the lower half-space in $\mathbb{R}^{mn}$ corresponding to sentence S_i. Together with additional constraints, such as a bound $MaxWords$ on the number of words in the summary, we obtain a system of linear inequalities that describes the intersection of corresponding lower half-spaces of $\mathbb{R}^{mn}$, forming a closed convex polyhedron called a *polytope*:

$$\begin{cases} \sum_{j=1}^{m} a_{ij}x_{ij} \leq \sum_{j=1}^{m} a_{ij}, \ \forall i = 1..n \\ 0 \leq x_{ij} \leq 1, \ \forall i = 1..n, \ j = 1..m \\ \sum_{i=1}^{n} \sum_{j=1}^{m} a_{ij}x_{ij} \leq MaxWords \end{cases} \tag{2}$$

All possible extractive summaries are represented by vertices of the polytope defined in (2).

It remains only to define an *objective function* which optimum on the polytope boundary will define the summary we seek. Because such an optimum may be achieved not on a polytope vertex but rather on one of polytope faces (because we use linear programming over rationals), we need only to locate the vertex of a polytope closest to the point of optimum. This task is done by finding distances from the optimum to every one of the sentence hyperplanes and selecting those with minimal distance to the point of optimum. If there are too many candidate sentences, we give preference to those closest to the beginning of the document.

The main advantage of this model is the relatively low number of constraints (comparable with the number of terms and sentences in a document) and both the theoretical and practical polynomial running times of LP over rationals (Karmarkar, 1984).

3.2 Objective functions

In this section, we describe the objective functions we used in our system. Humans identify good summaries immediately, but specifying summary quality as a linear function of terms, sentences, and their parameters is highly nontrivial. In most cases, additional parameters, variables, and constraints must be added to the model.

3.3 Maximal sentence relevance

The first objective function maximizes relevance of sentences chosen for a summary, while minimizing pairwise redundancy between them.

We define relevance $cosrel_i$ of a sentence S_i as a *cosine similarity* between the sentence, viewed as a weighted vector of its terms, and the document. Relevance values are completely determined by the text and are not affected by choice of a summary. Every sentence S_i is represented by a sentence variable:

$$s_i = \sum_{j=1}^{m} a_{ij}x_{ij} / \sum_{j=1}^{m} a_{ij} \tag{3}$$

Formally, variable s_i represents the hyperplane bounding the lower half-space of $\mathbb{R}^{mn}$ related to sentence S_i and bounding the polytope. Clearly, s_i assumes values in range $[0, 1]$, where 0 means that the sentence is completely omitted from the summary and 1 means that the sentence is definitely chosen for the summary. Relevance of all sentences in the summary is described by the expression

$$\sum_{i=1}^{n} cosrel_i s_i \tag{4}$$

Redundancy needs to be modeled and computed for every pair of sentences separately. We use additional redundancy variables red_{ij} for every pair S_i, S_j of sentences where $i < j$. Every one of these variables is $0 - 1$ bounded and achieves a value of 1 only if both sentences are chosen for the summary with the help of these constraints:

$$\begin{cases} 0 \le red_{ij} \le 1,\ 0 \le i < j \le n \\ red_{ij} \le s_i,\ red_{ij} \le s_j \\ s_i + s_j - red_{ij} \le 1 \end{cases} \quad (5)$$

The numerical redundancy coefficient for sentences S_i and S_j is their cosine similarity as term vectors, which we compute directly from the text and denote by $cosred_{ij}$. The objective function we use to maximize relevance of the chosen sentences while minimizing redundancy is

$$\max \sum_{i=1}^{n} cosrel_i s_i - \sum_{i=1}^{n} \sum_{j=1}^{n} cosred_{ij} red_{ij} \quad (6)$$

3.4 Sum of bigrams

The second proposed objective function maximizes the weighted sum of bigrams (consecutive term pairs appearing in sentences), where the weight of a bigram denotes its importance.

The importance $count_{ij}$ of a bigram (T_i, T_j) is computed as the number of its appearances in the document. It is quite possible that this bigram appears twice in one sentence, and once in another, and $i = j$ is possible as well.

In order to represent bigrams, we introduce new bigram variables bg_{ij} for $i, j = 1..m$, covering all possible term pairs. An appearance of a bigram in sentence S_k is modeled by a $0-1$ bounded variable bg^k_{ij}, and c^k_{ij} denotes the number of times this bigram appears in sentence S_k. A bigram is represented by a *normalized sum of its appearances* in various sentences as follows:

$$\begin{cases} 0 \le bg^k_{ij} \le 1,\ \forall i, j, k \\ bg_{ij} = \sum_{k=1}^{n} c^k_{ij} bg^k_{ij} / \sum_{k=1}^{n} c^k_{ij} \end{cases} \quad (7)$$

Additionally, the appearance bg^k_{ij} of a bigram in sentence S_k is tied to terms T_i and T_j composing it, with the help of variables x_{ki} and x_{kj} denoting appearances of these terms in S_k:

$$\begin{cases} bg^k_{ij} \le x_{ki} \\ bg^k_{ij} \le x_{kj} \\ x_{ki} + x_{kj} - bg^k_{ij} \le 1 \end{cases} \quad (8)$$

The constraints in (8) express the fact that a bigram cannot appear without the terms composing it, and appearance of both terms causes, in turn, the appearance of a bigram. Our objective function is:

$$\max : \sum_{i=1}^{m} \sum_{j=1}^{m} count_{ij} bg_{ij} \quad (9)$$

3.5 Maximal relevance with frequent itemsets

The third proposed objective function modifies the model so that only the most important terms are taken into account.

Let us view each sentence S_i as a sequence $(T_{i1}, \dots, T_{in})$ of terms, and the order of terms preserves the original word order of a sentence. Source documents are viewed as a database of sentences. Database size is n. Let $s = (T_{i1}, \dots, T_{ik})$ be a sequence of terms of size k. *Support* of s in the database is the ratio of sentences containing this sequence, to the database size n.

Given a user-defined support bound $S \in [0, 1]$, a term sequence s is *frequent* if $support(s) \ge S$. Frequent term sequences can be computed by a multitude of existing algorithms, such as Apriori (Agrawal et al., 1994), FreeSpan (Han et al., 2000), GSP (Zaki, 2001), etc.

In order to modify the generic model described in (2), we first find all frequent sequences in the documents and store them in set F. Then we sort F first by decreasing sequence size and then by decreasing support, and finally we keep only top B sequences for a user-defined boundary B.

We modify the general model (2) by representing sentences as sums of their frequent sequences from F. Let $F = \{f_1, \dots, f_k\}$, sorted by decreasing size and then by decreasing support. A sentence S_i is said to *contain* f_j if it contains it as a term sequence and no part of f_j in S_i is covered by sequences $f_1, \dots, f_{j-1}$.

Let $count_{ij}$ denote the number of times sentence S_i contains frequent term sequence f_j. Variables f_{ij} denote the appearance of sequence f_j in sentence S_i. We replace the polytope (2) by:

$$\begin{cases} \sum_{j=1}^{k} count_{ij} f_{ij} \le \sum_{j=1}^{k} count_{ij},\ \forall i = 1..n \\ 0 \le f_{ij} \le 1,\ \forall i = 1..n,\ j = 1..k \end{cases} \quad (10)$$

We add variables describing the relevance of each sentence by introducing sentence variables:

$$s_i = \sum_{j=1}^{k} count_{ij} f_{ij} / \sum_{j=1}^{k} count_{ij} \quad (11)$$

Defining a boundary on the length of a summary now requires an additional constraint because frequent sequences do not contain all the terms in the sentences. Summary size is bounded as follows:

$$\sum_{i=1}^{n} length_i s_i \le MaxWords \quad (12)$$

Here, $length_i$ is the exact word count of sentence S_i.

Relevance $freqrel_i$ of a sentence S_i is defined as a *cosine similarity* between the vector of terms in S_i covered by members of F, and the entire document. The difference between this approach and the one described in Section 3.3 is that only frequent terms are taken into account when computing sentence-document similarity. The resulting objective function maximizes relevance of chosen sentences while minimizing redundancy defined in (5):

$$\max \sum_{i=1}^{n} freqrel_i s_i - \sum_{i=1}^{n} \sum_{j=1}^{n} cosred_{ij} red_{ij} \quad (13)$$

4 Experiments

Tables 4, 4, and 1 contain the summarized results of automated evaluations for MultiLing 2015, single-document summarization (MSS) task for English, Hebrew, and Arabic corpora, respectively. The quality of the summaries is measured by ROUGE-1 (Recall, Precision, and F-measure).(Lin, 2004) We also demonstrate the absolute ranks of each submission–P-Rank, R-Rank, and F-Rank–when their scores are sorted by Precision, Recall, and F-measure, respectively. Only the best submissions (in terms of F-measure) for each participated system are presented and sorted in descending order of their F-measure scores. Two systems–Oracles and Lead–were used as top-line and baseline summarizers, respectively. Oracles compute summaries for each article using the combinatorial covering algorithm in (Davis et al., 2012)–sentences were selected from a text to maximally cover the tokens in the human summary, using as few sentences as possible until its size exceeded the human summary, at which point it was truncated. Because Oracles can actually "see" the human summaries, it is considered as the optimal algorithm and its scores are the best scores that extractive approaches can achieve. Lead simply extracts the leading substring of the body text of the articles having the same length as the human summary of the article.

Below we summarize the comparative results for our summarizer (denoted in the following tables by **Poly**) in both tasks, in terms of Rouge-1, F-measure. For comparisons, we consider the best result out of 3 functions: coverage of frequent sequences for English and coverage of meaningful words for Hebrew and Arabic. **English**: 4th places out of 9 participants in both MSS and MMS tasks. **Hebrew**: 3rd place out of 7 and out of 9 participants in MSS and MMS tasks, respectively; and the highest recall score in MMS task. **Arabic**: 5th place out of 7 systems in MSS task, and 4th place out of 9 participants and the highest recall score in MMS task. As can be seen, the best performance for our summarizer has been achieved on the dataset of Hebrew documents. For example, only the top-line Oracles and the supervised MUSE summarizers outperformed our system in MSS task. Poly also outperformed Gillick (2009) model using ILP. The average running time for Poly is 500 ms per document.

system	P score	R score	F score	P-rank	R-rank	F-rank
Oracles	0.601	0.619	0.610	1	1	1
BGU-SCE-MUSE	0.488	0.500	0.494	3	2	2
CCS	0.477	0.495	0.485	6	3	4
Poly	**0.475**	**0.494**	**0.484**	**8**	**5**	**5**
EXB	0.467	0.495	0.480	13	4	9
NTNU	0.470	0.456	0.462	12	17	13
LCS-IESI	0.461	0.456	0.458	15	18	15
UA-DLSI	0.457	0.456	0.456	18	16	17
Lead	0.425	0.434	0.429	24	20	20
system	P score	R score	F score	P-rank	R-rank	F-rank
CCS	0.202	0.213	0.207	1	1	1
BGU-SCE-MUSE	0.196	0.210	0.203	2	2	2
Poly	**0.189**	**0.203**	**0.196**	**4**	**6**	**4**
EXB	0.186	0.205	0.195	5	4	5
Oracles	0.182	0.204	0.192	6	5	6
Lead	0.168	0.178	0.173	13	12	12
LCS-IESI	0.181	0.170	0.172	7	14	13
system	P score	R score	F score	P-rank	R-rank	F-rank
Oracles	0.630	0.658	0.644	1	1	1
BGU-SCE-MUSE	0.562	0.569	0.565	2	4	2
CCS	0.554	0.571	0.562	4	3	3
EXB	0.546	0.571	0.558	8	2	7
Poly	**0.545**	**0.560**	**0.552**	**10**	**9**	**9**
LCS-IESI	0.540	0.527	0.531	11	13	12
Lead	0.524	0.535	0.529	13	12	13

Table 1: MSS task. Rouge-1. **English**, **Hebrew**, and **Arabic**, top-down.

5 Conclusions and Future Work

In this paper we present an extractive summarization system based on a linear programming model. We represent the document as a set of intersecting hyperplanes. Every possible summary of a document is represented as the intersection of two or more hyperlanes. We consider the summary to be the best if the optimal value of the objective function is achieved during summarization. We introduce multiple objective functions describing the relevance of a sentence in terms of information coverage. The results obtained by automatic evaluation show that the introduced approach performs quite well for Hebrew and English. Only top-line and supervised summarizers outperform Poly on the Hebrew corpus. It is worth noting that our system is unsupervised and does not require annotated data, and it has polynomial running time.

References

Rakesh Agrawal, Ramakrishnan Srikant, et al. 1994. Fast algorithms for mining association rules. In *Proc. 20th int. conf. very large data bases, VLDB*, volume 1215, pages 487–499.

S.T. Davis, J.M. Conroy, and J.D. Schlesinger. 2012. OCCAMS – An Optimal Combinatorial Covering Algorithm for Multi-document Summarization. In *Proceedings of the IEEE 12th International Conference on Data Mining Workshops*, pages 454–463.

Dan Gillick and Benoit Favre. 2009. A Scalable Global Model for Summarization. In *Proceedings of the NAACL HLT Workshop on Integer Linear Programming for Natural Language Processing*, pages 10–18.

Jiawei Han, Jian Pei, Behzad Mortazavi-Asl, Qiming Chen, Umeshwar Dayal, and Mei-Chun Hsu. 2000. Freespan: frequent pattern-projected sequential pattern mining. In *Proceedings of the sixth ACM SIGKDD international conference on Knowledge discovery and data mining*, pages 355–359. ACM.

Yoshihiro Matsuo Hitoshi Nishikawa, Takaaki Hasegawa and Genichiro Kikui. 2010. Opinion Summarization with Integer Linear Programming Formulation for Sentence Extraction and Ordering. In *Coling 2010: Poster Volume*, pages 910–918.

N. Karmarkar. 1984. New polynomial-time algorithm for linear programming. *Combinatorica*, 4:373–395.

Samir Khuller, Anna Moss, and Joseph (Seffi) Naor. 1999. The budgeted maximum coverage problem. *Information Precessing Letters*, 70(1):39–45.

Chin-Yew Lin. 2004. Rouge: A package for automatic evaluation of summaries. In *Proceedings of the Workshop on Text Summarization Branches Out (WAS 2004)*, pages 25–26.

Marina Litvak and Natalia Vanetik. 2014. Efficient summarization with polytopes. *Innovative Document Summarization Techniques: Revolutionizing Knowledge Understanding: Revolutionizing Knowledge Understanding*, page 54.

Takuya Makino, Hiroya Takamura, and Manabu Okumura. 2011. Balanced coverage of aspects for text summarization. In *TAC '11: Proceedings of Text Analysis Conference*.

G. Salton, C. Yang, and A. Wong. 1975. A vector-space model for information retrieval. *Communications of the ACM*, 18.

Hiroya Takamura and Manabu Okumura. 2009. Text summarization model based on maximum coverage problem and its variant. In *EACL '09: Proceedings of the 12th Conference of the European Chapter of the Association for Computational Linguistics*, pages 781–789.

Kristian Woodsend and Mirella Lapata. 2010. Automatic Generation of Story Highlights. In *ACL '10: Proceedings of the 48th Annual Meeting of the Association for Computational Linguistics*, pages 565–574.

Mohammed J Zaki. 2001. Spade: An efficient algorithm for mining frequent sequences. *Machine learning*, 42(1-2):31–60.

Call Centre Conversation Summarization: A Pilot Task at Multiling 2015

Benoit Favre[1], **Evgeny Stepanov**[2], **Jérémy Trione**[1], **Frédéric Béchet**[1], **Giuseppe Riccardi**[2]
[1] Aix-Marseille University, CNRS, LIF UMR 7279, Marseille, France
[2] University of Trento, Via Sommarive 5, Trento, Italy
benoit.favre@lif.univ-mrs.fr

Abstract

This paper describes the results of the Call Centre Conversation Summarization task at Multiling'15. The CCCS task consists in generating abstractive synopses from call centre conversations between a caller and an agent. Synopses are summaries of the problem of the caller, and how it is solved by the agent. Generating them is a very challenging task given that deep analysis of the dialogs and text generation are necessary. Three languages were addressed: French, Italian and English translations of conversations from those two languages. The official evaluation metric was ROUGE-2. Two participants submitted a total of four systems which had trouble beating the extractive baselines. The datasets released for the task will allow more research on abstractive dialog summarization.

1 Introduction

Speech summarization has been of great interest to the community because speech is the principal modality of human communications, and it is not as easy to skim, search or browse speech transcripts as it is for textual messages. Speech recorded from call centres offers a great opportunity to study goal-oriented and focused conversations between an agent and a caller. The Call Centre Conversation Summarization (CCCS) task consists in automatically generating summaries of spoken conversations in the form of textual synopses that shall inform on the content of a conversation and might be used for browsing a large database of recordings. Compared to news summarization where extractive approaches have been very successful, the CCCS task's objective is to foster work on abstractive summarization in order to depict what happened in a conversation instead of what people actually said.

The track leverages conversations from the Decoda and Luna corpora of French and Italian call centre recordings, both with transcripts available in their original language as well as English translation (both manual and automatic). Recordings duration range from a few minutes to 15 minutes, involving two or sometimes more speakers. In the public transportation and help desk domains, the dialogs offer a rich range of situations (with emotions such as anger or frustration) while staying in a coherent and focused domain.

Given transcripts, participants to the task shall generate abstractive summaries informing a reader about the main events of the conversations, such as the objective of the caller, whether and how it was solved by the agent, and the attitude of both parties. Evaluation has been performed by comparing submissions to reference synopses written by quality assurance experts from call centres. Both conversations and reference summaries are kindly provided by the SENSEI project.

This paper reports on the results of the CCCS task in term ROUGE-2 evaluation metric. Two participants have submitted four systems to the task. In addition, we provide three baselines which frame the performance that would be obtained by extractive systems. The results are analysed according to language, human annotator coherence and the impact of automatic translation.

The remaining of the paper is organized as follows: Section 2 describes the synopsis generation task. Section 3 describes the CCCS corpus. Section 4 describes the results from the systems of the participants. Section 5 discusses future research avenues.

2 Task

The CCCS task consists in creating systems that can analyse call centre conversations and generate

Proceedings of the SIGDIAL 2015 Conference, pages 232–236,
Prague, Czech Republic, 2-4 September 2015.

written summaries reflecting why the customer is calling, how the agent answers that query, what are the steps to solve the problem and what is the resolution status of the problem.

Unlike news summarization which focuses on locating facts in text written by journalists and selecting the most relevant facts, conversation synopses require an extra level of analysis in order to achieve abstraction. Turn taking from the speakers has to be converted to generic expression of their needs, beliefs and actions. Even though extractive systems might give a glimpse of the dialogs, only abstraction can yield synopses that tell the story of what happens in the conversations.

Contrary to previous research on meeting summarization (Gillick et al., 2009; Erol et al., 2003; Lai and Renals, 2014; Wang and Cardie, 2012) (among others), we expect that the fact that conversations are focused and goal oriented will enable to foster research on more abstractive methods, such as (Murray, 2015; Mehdad et al., 2013) and deeper analysis of the conversations.

Participants to the CCCS task could submit system output in any of the supported languages, and could submit a maximum of three runs per language. For each conversation, they had to submit one synopsis of length 7% of the number of words of the transcript of that conversation.

3 Corpus description

The CCCS task draws from two call centre conversation corpora, the Decoda corpus in French and the Luna corpus in Italian. Subsets from both corpora have been translated to English.

Decoda corpus The French DECODA corpus consists in conversations between customers and one or more agent recorded in 2009 in a call centre of the public transport authority in Paris (Bechet et al., 2012). The topics of the conversations range from itinerary and schedule requests, to lost and found, to complaints (the calls were recorded during strikes). The dialogues, recorded in ecological conditions, are very spontaneous and focused on the objective of the caller. They are very challenging for Automatic Speech Recognition due to harsh acoustic conditions such as calling from mobile phones directly from the metro. For the CCCS task, manual transcripts were provided to the participants.

While the original language of the conversations is French, the SENSEI project provided manual translations in English by professional translators which were trained to keep the spontaneous aspects of the originals (a very challenging task according to them). 97 conversations were manually translated, on which an automatic translation system based on Moses was trained in order to produce automatic translations for the remaining of the corpus.

The original corpus consists of 1513 conversations (about 70h of speech). 1000 conversations have been distributed without synopses for unsupervised system training. 50 conversations were distributed with multiple synopses from up to five annotators. The test set consists of 47 manually translated conversations and corresponding synopses, and 53 automatically translated conversations and corresponding synopses. The data for training and testing is also provided in French.

Statistic	**FR**	**EN**
Conversations	100	100
Turns	7,905	7,909
Words	42,130	41,639
Average length	421.3	416.4
Lexicon size	2,995	2,940
Number of synopses	212	227
Average synopsis length	23.0	26.5

Table 1: Decoda test set statistics.

The human written synopses are very diverse and show a high degree of abstraction from the words of the conversation with third person writing, telegraphic style and analysis of the conversations. Examples:

- *A man is calling cause he got a fine. He is waiting for a new card so he used his wife's card. He must now write a letter asking for clemency.*
- *A user wants to go to the Ambroise Paré clinic but the employee misunderstands and gives her the wrong itinerary. Luckily the employee realises her mistake and gives the passenger the right information in the end.*
- *School bag lost on line 4, not found.*

Luna corpus The Italian human-human Luna corpus (Dinarelli et al., 2009) consists of 572 dialogs (≈ 26.5K turns & 30 hours of speech) in the hardware/software help desk domain, where a client and an agent are engaged in a problem solving task over the phone. The dialogs are organised in transcriptions and annotations created within the FP6 LUNA project. For the CCCS shared task, manual transcriptions were used.

Within the FP7 SENSEI project, 100 dialogs were translated from Italian to English using professional translation services according to the methodology described in (Stepanov et al., 2014). For more accurate translations, manual transcriptions were converted to an 'annotated' text format, which contained mark-up for overlapping turns, fillers, pauses, noise, partial words, etc.; and translators received detailed guidelines on how to handle each phenomenon in translation. Additionally, the translators were required to translate the speech phenomena such as disfluencies as closely as possible to the source language maintaining 'naturalness' in the target language.

Five native Italian speakers have annotated 200 Luna dialogs with synopses so that each dialog was processed by every annotator.[1] Synopses of the 100 translated dialogs were also manually translated to English.

The translated and annotated dialogs were equally split into training and test sets for the CCCS task. The training dialogs were used to automatically translate additional Luna dialogs and synopses for both training and testing. Similar to the DECODA corpus, for the unsupervised training of the systems a supplementary set of 261 dialogs was automatically translated and provided to the participants without synopses. Dialogs and their associated synopses were provided both in English and Italian. The statistics for Luna manual English test set are provided in Table 2.

Statistic	IT	EN
Conversations	100	100
Turns	4,723	4,721
Words	34,913	32,502
Average length	349.1	325.0
Lexicon size	3,393	2,451
Number of synopses	500	500
Average synopsis length	17.4	15.4

Table 2: Luna test set statistics.

[1]Few (2) synopses were found to address dialog dimensions other than the task and were removed.

4 Results

Metric Evaluation is performed with the ROUGE-2 metric (Lin, 2004). ROUGE-2 is the recall in term of word bigrams between a set of reference synopses and a system submission. The ROUGE 1.5.5 toolkit was adapted to deal with a conversation-dependent length limit of 7%, had lemmatization disabled and stop-words kept, to be as language independent as possible [2]. Jackknifing and resampling is used in order to compute confidence estimate intervals.

Participation Seven research groups had originally expressed their intention to participate to the CCCS task. Four groups downloaded the test data, and two groups actually submitted system output at the deadline. Those two groups generated four runs: `NTNU:1`, `NTNU:2`, `NTNU:3`, `LIA-RAG:1`. The technical details of these submissions are described in their own papers.

In addition to those four runs, we provide three baselines which serve to calibrate participant performance. The first baseline is Maximal Marginal Relevance (`Baseline-MMR`) (Carbonell and Goldstein, 1998) with $\lambda = 0.7$. The second baseline is the first words of the longest turn in the conversation, up to the length limit (`Baseline-L`). The third baseline is the words of the longest turn in the first 25% of the conversation, which usually corresponds to the description of the caller's problem (`Baseline-LB`). Those baselines are described in more details in (Trione, 2014).

In order to estimate the overlap between human synopses, we remove each of the human synopses in turn from the reference and compute their performance as if they were systems. Across languages, 11 annotators (denoted `human-1` to `human-5` for IT/EN, and `human-A` to `human-G` for FR/EN) produced from 5 to 100 synopses. Note that some annotators only worked on English conversations.

Performance Performance of the systems is reported in Table 3. It shows that in the source languages, the extractive baselines were difficult to beat while one of the systems significantly outperformed the baselines on English (the EN test set

[2]The options for running ROUGE 1.5.5 are `-a -l 10000 -n 4 -x -2 4 -u -c 95 -r 1000 -f A -p 0.5 -t 0`

corresponds to the union of manual and automatic translations).

System	EN	FR	IT
NTNU:1	0.023	0.035	0.013
NTNU:2	0.031	0.027	0.015
NTNU:3	0.024	0.034	0.012
LIA-RAG:1	-	0.037	-
Basline-MMR	0.029	0.045	0.020
Basline-L	0.023	0.040	0.015
Basline-LB	0.025	0.046	0.027

Table 3: ROUGE-2 performance of the submitted systems and baselines for each of the languages. Confidence intervals are not given but are very tight (± 0.005).

An analysis of the consistency of human synopsis writers is outlined in Table 4. Consistency is computed by considering in turn each of the human synopses as system output, and computing ROUGE-2 performance. Humans have much better scores than the systems, showing that they are consistent in producing the gold standard. However, human annotators suffer from a much higher performance variance than systems (for which confidence intervals are 4-5 times smaller). This partly comes from the low number of manual synopses which is greater impacted by resampling than if there were hundreds of references for each conversation. It also comes from local inconsistencies between humans on a given conversation, resulting in diverging choices in term of which information is important.

Annotator	FR	IT
human-1	-	0.121 ±0.023
human-2	-	0.213 ±0.023
human-3	-	0.175 ±0.022
human-4	-	0.073 ±0.014
human-5	-	0.125 ±0.018
human-A	0.194 ±0.029	-
human-B	0.207 ±0.036	-
human-D	0.077 ±0.048	-
human-F	0.057 ±0.039	-
human-G	0.113 ±0.054	-

Table 4: ROUGE-2 performance of the human annotators along with confidence intervals. Note that human-C and human-E only produced synopses in English.

Table 5 shows the impact of automatic translation on system performance for the English set. This experiment is hard to interpret as the set of conversations for automatic and manual translations is different. However, it seems that processing MT results leads to better ROUGE scores, probably due to the consistency with which the MT system translates words for both conversations and synopses (reference synopses are automatic translations of source language synopses for those conversations).

Annotator	EN-man	EN-auto
NTNU:1	0.018	0.023
NTNU:2	0.019	0.031
NTNU:3	0.015	0.024
Baseline-MMR	0.024	0.033
Baseline-L	0.015	0.030
Baseline-LB	0.023	0.027

Table 5: ROUGE-2 performance on English according to whether the conversations have been manually translated or automatically translated

5 Conclusion

The objective of the CCCS pilot task at Multiling'15 was to allow work on abstractive summarization of goal-oriented spoken conversations. This task involved generating synopses from French and Italian call centre recording transcripts, and English translations of those transcripts. Four systems were submitted by two participants, and obtained reasonable results but had trouble exceeding the performance of the extractive baselines.

Clearly, ROUGE evaluation is limited for abstractive summarization in that the wording of generated text might be very different from system to system, and from reference to reference, while conveying the same meaning. In addition, ROUGE does not assess fluency and readability of the summaries.

Future work will focus on proposing better evaluation metrics for the task, probably involving the community for manually evaluating the fluency and adequacy of the submitted system output. In addition, work will be conducted in evaluating and insuring the consistency of the human experts who create the gold standard for the task.

Acknowledgments

The research leading to these results has received funding from the European Union - Seventh Framework Programme (FP7/2007-2013) under grant agreement n.610916 - SENSEI.

References

Frederic Bechet, Benjamin Maza, Nicolas Bigouroux, Thierry Bazillon, Marc El-Beze, Renato De Mori, and Eric Arbillot. 2012. Decoda: a call-centre human-human spoken conversation corpus. In Nicoletta Calzolari (Conference Chair), Khalid Choukri, Thierry Declerck, Mehmet Uur Doan, Bente Maegaard, Joseph Mariani, Asuncion Moreno, Jan Odijk, and Stelios Piperidis, editors, *Proceedings of the Eight International Conference on Language Resources and Evaluation (LREC'12)*, Istanbul, Turkey, may. European Language Resources Association (ELRA).

Jaime Carbonell and Jade Goldstein. 1998. The use of mmr, diversity-based reranking for reordering documents and producing summaries. In *Proceedings of the 21st annual international ACM SIGIR conference on Research and development in information retrieval*, pages 335–336. ACM.

Marco Dinarelli, Silvia Quarteroni, Sara Tonelli, Alessandro Moschitti, and Giuseppe Riccardi. 2009. Annotating spoken dialogs: from speech segments to dialog acts and frame semantics. In *Proceedings of EACL Workshop on the Semantic Representation of Spoken Language*, Athens, Greece.

Berna Erol, D-S Lee, and Jonathan Hull. 2003. Multimodal summarization of meeting recordings. In *Multimedia and Expo, 2003. ICME'03. Proceedings. 2003 International Conference on*, volume 3, pages III–25. IEEE.

Daniel Gillick, Korbinian Riedhammer, Benoit Favre, and Dilek Hakkani-Tur. 2009. A global optimization framework for meeting summarization. In *Acoustics, Speech and Signal Processing, 2009. ICASSP 2009. IEEE International Conference on*, pages 4769–4772. IEEE.

Catherine Lai and Steve Renals. 2014. Incorporating lexical and prosodic information at different levels for meeting summarization. In *Fifteenth Annual Conference of the International Speech Communication Association*.

Chin-Yew Lin. 2004. Rouge: A package for automatic evaluation of summaries. In *Text Summarization Branches Out: Proceedings of the ACL-04 Workshop*, pages 74–81.

Yashar Mehdad, Giuseppe Carenini, Frank W Tompa, and Raymond T NG. 2013. Abstractive meeting summarization with entailment and fusion. In *Proceedings of the 14th European Workshop on Natural Language Generation*, pages 136–146.

Gabriel Murray. 2015. Abstractive meeting summarization as a markov decision process. In *Advances in Artificial Intelligence*, pages 212–219. Springer.

Evgeny A. Stepanov, Giuseppe Riccardi, and Ali Orkan Bayer. 2014. The development of the multilingual luna corpus for spoken language system porting. In *Proceedings of the Ninth International Conference on Language Resources and Evaluation (LREC'14)*, pages 2675–2678, Reykjavik, Iceland, May.

Jeremy Trione. 2014. Mthodes par extraction pour le rsum automatique de conversations parles provenant de centres dappel. In *RECITAL*.

Lu Wang and Claire Cardie. 2012. Focused meeting summarization via unsupervised relation extraction. In *Proceedings of the 13th Annual Meeting of the Special Interest Group on Discourse and Dialogue*, pages 304–313. Association for Computational Linguistics.

AllSummarizer system at MultiLing 2015: Multilingual single and multi-document summarization

Abdelkrime Aries **Djamel Eddine Zegour** **Khaled Walid Hidouci**
École Nationale Supérieure d'Informatique (ESI, ex. INI)
Oued-Smar, Algiers, Algeria
{ab_aries, d_zegour, w_hidouci}@esi.dz

Abstract

In this paper, we evaluate our automatic text summarization system in multilingual context. We participated in both single document and multi-document summarization tasks of MultiLing 2015 workshop.

Our method involves clustering the document sentences into topics using a fuzzy clustering algorithm. Then each sentence is scored according to how well it covers the various topics. This is done using statistical features such as TF, sentence length, etc. Finally, the summary is constructed from the highest scoring sentences, while avoiding overlap between the summary sentences. This makes it language-independent, but we have to afford preprocessed data first (tokenization, stemming, etc.).

1 Introduction

A document summary can be regarded as domain-specific or general-purpose, using the specificity as classification criterion (Hovy and Lin, 1998). We can, also, look at this criterion from language angle: language-specific or language-independent summarization. Language-independent systems can handle more than one language. They can be partially language-independent, which means they use language-related resources, and therefore you can't add a new language so easily. Inversely, they can be fully language-independent.

Recently, multilingual summarization has received the attention of the summarization community, such as Text Analysis Conference (TAC). The TAC 2011 workshop included a task called "MultiLing task", which aims to evaluate language-independent summarization algorithms on a variety of languages (Giannakopoulos et al., 2011). In the task's pilot, there were seven languages covering news texts: Arabic, Czech, English, French, Greek, Hebrew and Hindi, where each system has to participate for at least two languages. MultiLing 2013 workshop is a community-driven initiative for testing and promoting multilingual summarization methods. It aims to evaluate the application of (partially or fully) language-independent summarization algorithms on a variety of languages. There were three tasks: "Multi-document multilingual summarization"(Giannakopoulos, 2013), "Multilingual single document summarization" (Kubina et al., 2013) and "Multilingual summary evaluation". The multi-document task uses the 7 past languages along with three new languages: Chinese, Romanian and Spanish. The single document task introduces 40 languages.

This paper contains a description of our method (Aries et al., 2013) which uses sentences' clustering to define topics, and then trains on these topics to score each sentence. We will explain each task in the system (AllSummarizer), especially the preprocessing task which is language-dependent. Then, we will discuss how we fixed the summarization's hyper-parameters (threshold and features) for each language. The next section (Section 5) is reserved to discuss the experiments conducted in the MultiLing workshop. Finally, we will conclude by discussing possible improvements.

2 Related works

Clustering has been used for summarization in many systems, either using documents as units, sentences or words. The resulted clusters are used to extract the summary. Some systems use just the biggest cluster to score sentences and get the top ones. Others take from each cluster a representative sentence, in order to cover all topics. While there are systems, like ours, which score sentences according to all clusters.

Proceedings of the SIGDIAL 2015 Conference, pages 237–244,
Prague, Czech Republic, 2-4 September 2015.

"CIST" (Liu et al., 2011; Li et al., 2013) is a system which uses hierarchical Latent Dirichlet Allocation topic (hLDA) model to cluster sentences into sub-topics. A sub-topic containing more sentences is more important and therefore those containing just one or two sentences can be neglected. The sentences are scored using hLDA model combined with some traditional features. The system participated for multi-document summarization task, where all documents of the same topic are merged into a big text document.

Likewise, "UoEssex" (El-Haj et al., 2011) uses a clustering method (K-Means) to regroup similar sentences. The biggest cluster is used to extract the summary, while other clusters are ignored. Then, the sentences are scored using their cosine similarities to the cluster's centroid. The use of the biggest cluster is justified by the assumption that a single cluster will give a coherent summary.

The scoring functions of these two systems are based on statistical features like frequencies of words, cosine similarity, etc. In the contrary, systems like those of Conroy et al. (2011) ("CLASSY"), Varma et al. (2011) ("SIEL_IIITH"), El-Haj and Rayson (2013), etc. are corpus-based summarizers, which can make it hard to introduce new languages. "CLASSY" uses naïve Bayes to estimate the probability that a term may be included in the summary. The classifier was trained on DUC 2005-2007 data. As for backgrounds of each language, Wikinews are used to compute Dunning G-statistic. "SIEL_IIITH" uses a probabilistic Hyperspace Analogue to Language model. Given a word, it estimates the probability of observing another word with it in a window of size K, using a sufficiently large corpus. El-Haj and Rayson (2013) calculate the log-likelihood of each word using a corpus of words frequencies and the multiLing'13 dataset. The score of each sentence is the sum of its words' log-likelihoods.

In our method (Aries et al., 2013), we use a simple fuzzy clustering algorithm. We assume that a sentence can express many topics, and therefore it can belong to many clusters. Also, we believe that a summary must take in consideration other topics than the main one (the biggest cluster). To score sentences, we use a scoring function based on Naïve Bayes classification. It uses the clusters for training rather than a corpus, in order to avoid the problem of language dependency.

3 System overview

One of multilingual summarization's problem is the lack of resources such as labeled corpus used for learning. Learning algorithms were used either to select the sentences that should be in the summary, or to estimate the features' weights. Both cases need a training corpus given the language and the domain we want to adapt the summarizer to. To design a language-neutral summarization system, either we adapt a system for input languages (Partly language-neutral), or we design a system that can process any language (Fully language-neutral).

Our sentence extraction method can be applied to any language without any modifications, affording the pre-process step of the input language. To do this, we had to find a new method to train our system other than using a corpus (language and topic dependent). The idea was to find different topics in the input text using similarity between sentences. Then, we train the system using a scoring function based on Bayes classification algorithm and a set of features to find the probability of a feature given the topic. Finally, we calculate for each sentence a score that reflects how it can represent all the topics.

In our previous work (Aries et al., 2013), our system used only two features which have the same nature (TF: uni-grams and bi-grams). When we add new features, this can affect the final result (summary). Also, our clustering method lies on the clustering threshold which has to be estimated somehow. To handle multi-document summarization, we just fuse all documents in the same topic and consider them as one document. Figure 1 represents the general architecture of AllSummarizer[1].

3.1 Preprocessing

This is the language-dependent part, which can be found in many information retrieval (IR) works. In our system, we are interested in four preprocessing tasks:

- Normalizer: in this step, we can delete special characters. For Arabic, we can delete diacritics (Tashkiil) if we don't need them in the process (which is our case).
- Segmenter: The segmenter defines two func-

[1] https://github.com/kariminf/AllSummarizer

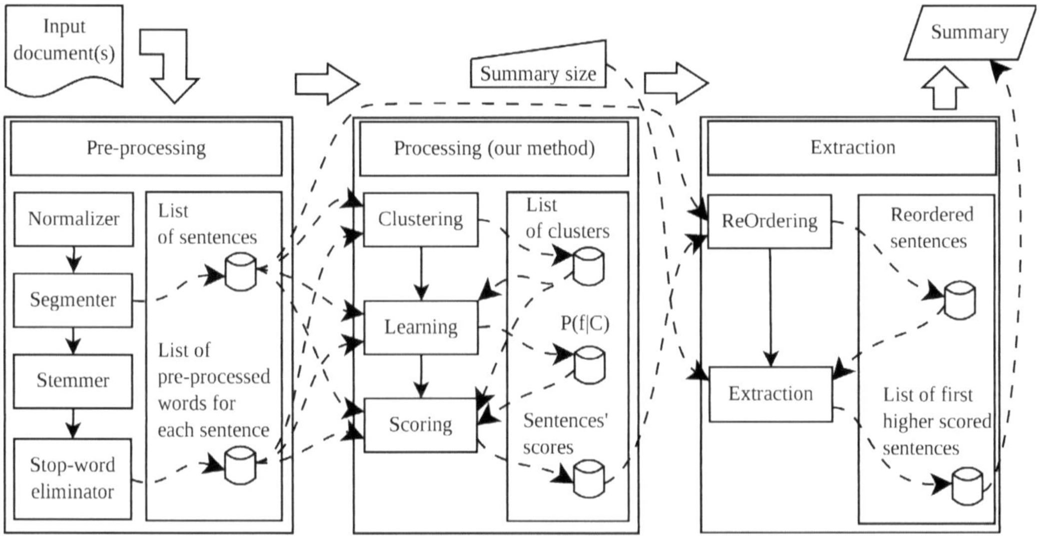

Figure 1: General architecture of AllSummarizer.

tions: sentence segmentation and word tokenization.

- Stemmer: The role of this task is to delete suffixes and prefixes so we can get the stem of a word.

- Stop-Words eliminator: It is used to remove the stop words, which are the words having no signification added to the text.

In this work, normalization is used just for Arabic and Persian to delete diacritics (Tashkiil). Concerning stop-word elimination, we use pre-compiled word-lists available on the web. Table 1 shows each language and the tools used in the remaining pre-processing tasks.

3.2 Topics clustering

Each text contains many topics, where a topic is a set of sentences having some sort of relationship between each other. In our case, this relationship is the cosine similarity between each two sentences. It means, the sentences that have many terms in common are considered in the same topic. Given two sentences X and Y, the cosine similar-

Table 1: Tools used to pre-process each language

Prerocess task	Tools	Languages
Sentence segmentation	openNLP[2]	Nl, En, De, It, Pt, Th
	JHazm[3]	Fa
	Regex	The remaining
Words tokenization	openNlp	Nl, En, De, It, Pt, Th
	Lucene[4]	Zh, Ja
	Regex	The remaining
Stemming	Shereen Khoja[5]	Ar
	JHazm	Fa
	HebMorph[6]	He
	Lucene	Bg, Cs, El, Hi, Id, Ja, No
	Snowball[7]	Eu, Ca, Nl, En (Porter), Fi, Fr, De, Hu, It, Pt, Ro, Ru, Es, Sv, Tr
	/	The remaining

[2] https://opennlp.apache.org/
[3] https://github.com/mojtaba-khallash/JHazm
[4] https://lucene.apache.org/
[5] http://zeus.cs.pacificu.edu/shereen/research.htm
[6] http://code972.com/hebmorph
[7] http://snowball.tartarus.org/

ity between them is expressed by equation 1.

$$cos(X, Y) = \frac{\sum_i x_i.y_i}{\sqrt{\sum_i (x_i)^2}.\sqrt{\sum_i (y_i)^2}} \quad (1)$$

Where x_i (y_i) denotes frequencies for each term in the sentence X (Y).

To generate topics, we use a simple algorithm (see algorithm 1) which uses cosine similarity and a clustering threshold th to cluster n sentences.

Algorithm 1: clustering method

```
Data: Pre-processed sentences
Result: clusters of sentences (C)
foreach sentence Si / i = 1 to n do
    Ci += Si ;
    // Ci:  ith cluster
    foreach sentence Sj / j = i + 1 to n do
        Sim = cosine similarity(Si, Sj) ;
        if sim > th then
            Ci += Sj ;
        end
    end
    C += Ci ;
end
foreach cluster Ci / i=n to 1 do
    foreach cluster Cj / j=i-1 to 1 do
        if Ci is included in Cj then
            C -= Ci ;
            break ;
        end
    end
end
```

3.3 Scoring function

A summary is a short text that is supposed to represent most information in the source text, and cover most of its topics. Therefore, we assume that a sentence s_i can be in the summary when it is most probable to represent all topics (clusters) $c_j \in C$ using a set of features $f_k \in F$. We used Naïve Bayes, assuming independence between different classes and different features (a sentence can have multiple classes). So, the score of a sentence s_i is the product over classes of the product over features of its score in a specific class and feature (see equation. 2).

$$Score(s_i, \bigcap_j c_j, F) = \prod_j \prod_k Score(s_i, c_j, f_k) \quad (2)$$

The score of a sentence s_i in a specific class c_j and feature f_k is the sum of probability of the feature's observations when $s_i \in c_j$ (see equation. 3). We add one to the sum, to avoid multiplying by a features' score of zero.

$$Score(s_i, c_j, f_k) = 1 + \sum_{\phi \in s_i} P(f_k = \phi | s_i \in c_j) \quad (3)$$

Where ϕ is an observation of the feature f_k in the sentence s_i. For example, assuming the feature f_1 is term frequency, and we have a sentence: "*I am studying at home.*". The sentence after pre-processing would be: s_1 = {"*studi*"(stem of "study"), "*home*"}. So, ϕ may be "*studi*" or "*home*", or any other term. If we take another feature f_2 which is sentence position, the observation ϕ may take 1st, 2nd, 3rd, etc. as values.

3.4 Statistical features

We use 5 statistical features to score the sentences: unigram term frequency (TFU), bigram term frequency (TFB), sentence position (Pos) and sentence length (Rleng, PLeng).

Each feature divides the sentences to several categories. For example, if we have a text written just with three characters: a, b and c, and the feature is the characters of the text, then we will have three categories. Each category has a probability to occur in a cluster, which is the number of its appearance in this cluster divided by all cluster's terms, as shown in equation 4.

$$P_f(f = \phi | c_j) = \frac{|\phi \in c_j|}{\sum_{c_l \in C} |\phi' \in c_l|} \quad (4)$$

Where f is a given feature. ϕ and ϕ' are observations (categories) of the feature f . C is the set of clusters.

3.4.1 Unigram term frequency

This feature is used to calculate the sentence pertinence depending on its terms. Each term is considered as a category.

3.4.2 Bigram term frequency

This feature is similar to unigram term frequency, but instead of one term we use two consecutive terms.

3.4.3 Sentence position

We want to use sentence positions in the original texts as a feature. The position feature used by Osborne (2002) divides the sentences into three sets: the ones in the 8 first paragraphs, those in last 3 paragraphs and the others in between. Following the assumption that the first sentences and last ones are more important than the others.

Three categories of sentence positions seem very small to express the diversity between the clusters. Instead of just three categories, we divided the position space into 10 categories. So, if we have 20 sentences, we will have 2 sentences per category.

3.4.4 Sentence length

One other feature applied in our system is the sentence length (number of words), which is used originally to penalize the short sentences. Following a sentence's length, we can put it in one of three categories: sentences with length less than 6 words, those with length more than 20 words, and those with length in between Osborne (2002).

Like sentence position, three categories is a small number. Therefore, we used each length as a category. Suppose we have 4 sentences which the lengths are: 5, 6, 5 and 7, then we will have 3 categories of lengths: 5, 6 and 7.

In our work, we use two types of sentence length:

- Real length (RLeng): which is the length of the sentence without removing stop-words.
- Pre-processed length (PLeng): which is the length of the sentence after pre-processing.

3.5 Summary extraction

To extract sentences, we reorder them decreasingly using their scores. Then we extract the first non similar sentences until we get the wanted size (see algorithm 2).

4 Summarization parameters

In this section, we describe how the summarization parameters have been chosen.

The first parameter is the clustering threshold, which will lead to few huge clusters if it is small, and inversely. The clustering threshold is used with sentences' similarities to decide if two sentences are similar or not. Our idea is to use statistic measures over those similarities to estimate the clustering threshold. Eight measures have been used:

- The median

Algorithm 2: extraction method

```
Data: input text
Result: a summary
add the first sentence to the summary;
foreach sentence in the text do
    calculate cosine similarity between this
    sentence and the last accepted one;
    if the simularity is under the threshold
    then
        add this sentence to the summary;
    end
    if the sum of the summary size and the
    current sentence's is above the maximum
    size then
        delete this sentence from the
        summary;
    end
end
```

- The mean
- The mode which can be divided to two: lower mode and higher mode, since we can have many modes.
- The variance
- $sDn = \frac{\sum |s|}{|D|*n}$
- $Dsn = \frac{|D|}{n*\sum |s|}$
- $Ds = \frac{|D|}{\sum |s|}$

Where, $|s|$ is the number of different terms in a sentence s. $|D|$ is the number of different terms in the document D. n is the number of sentences in this document.

The second parameter is the features' set, which is the combination of at least one of the five features described in section 3.4. We want to know which features are useful and which are not for a given language.

To fix the problem of the clustering threshold and the set of features, we used the training sets provided by the workshop organizers. For each document (or topic in multi-document), we generated summaries using the 8 measures of th, and different combinations of the scoring features. Then, we calculated the average ROUGE-2 score for each language. The threshold measure and the set of features that maximize this average will be used as parameters for the trained language.

Table 2 represents an example of the 10 languages and their parameters used for both tasks: MSS and MMS. We have to point out that the average is not always the best choice for the individual documents (or topic in multi-document). For example, in MSS, there is a document which gives a ROUGE-2 score of **0.28** when we use the parameters based on average scores. When we use the mean as threshold and just TFB as feature for the same document, we get a ROUGE-2 score of **0.31**.

5 Experiments

We participated in all workshop's languages, either in single document or multi-document tasks. To compare our system to others participated systems, we followed these steps (for every evaluation metric):

- For each system, calculate the average scores of all used languages.
- For our system, calculate the average scores of used languages by others. For example, BGU-SCE-M team uses Arabic, English and Hebrew; We calculate the average of scores of these languages for this system and ours.
- Then, we calculate the relative improvement using the averages $\frac{oursystem - othersystem}{othersystem}$.

5.1 Evaluation metrics

In "Single document summarization" task, ROUGE (Recall-Oriented Understudy for Gisting Evaluation) (Lin, 2004) is used to evaluate the participated systems. It allows us to evaluate automatic text summaries against human made abstracts. The principle of this method is to compare N-grams of two summaries based on the number of matches between these two based on the recall measure. Five metrics are used: ROUGE-1, ROUGE-2, ROUGE-3, ROUGE-4 and ROUGE-SU4.

In "Multi-document summarization" task, Three metrics are officially used: AutoSummENG, MeMoG (Giannakopoulos and Karkaletsis, 2011) and NPowER (Giannakopoulos and Karkaletsis, 2013).

5.2 Single document summarization

Besides our system (AllSummarizer), there are two more systems which participated in all 38 languages (EXB and CCS). Table 3 shows the comparison between our system and the other systems in single document task, using the relative improvement.

Looking at these results, our system took the fifth place out of seven participants. It outperforms the Lead baseline. It took the last place out of three participants in all 38 languages.

5.3 Multi-document summarization

Besides our system (AllSummarizer), there are 4 systems that participated with all the 10 languages. Table 4 shows a comparison between our system and the other systems in multi-document task, using the relative improvement. We used the parameters fixed for single document summarization to see if the same parameters are applicable for both single and multi-document summarizations.

Looking to the results, our system took the seventh place out of ten participants. When we use single document parameters, we can see that it doesn't outperform the results when using the parameters fixed for multi-document summarization. This shows that we can't use the same parameters for both single and multi-document summarization.

6 Conclusion

Our intension is to create a method which is language and domain independent. So, we consider the input text as a set of topics, where a sentence can belong to many topics. We calculated how much a sentence can represent all the topics. Then, the score is used to reorder the sentences and extract the first non redundant ones.

We tested our system using the average score of all languages, in single and multi-document summarization. Compared to other systems, it affords fair results, but more improvements have to be done in the future. We have to point out that our system participated in all languages. Also, it is easy to add new languages when you can afford tokenization and stemming.

We fixed the parameters (threshold and features) based on the average score of ROUGE-2 of all training documents. Further investigations must be done to estimate these parameters for each document based on statistical criteria. We want to investigate the effect of the preprocessing step and the clustering methods on the resulted summaries. Finally, readability remains a challenge for extractive methods, especially when we want to use a multilingual method.

Table 2: Example of the parameters used for MSS and MMS.

Lang	Single document (MSS)		Multidocument (MMS)	
	Th	Features	Th	Features
Ar	Ds	TFB, Pos, PLeng	Ds	TFB, Pos, RLeng, PLeng
Cs	HMode	TFU, TFB, Pos, PLeng	Ds	TFB, Pos, PLeng
El	Median	TFU, TFB, Pos, RLeng, PLeng	LMode	TFB, RLeng
En	Median	TFU, Pos, RLeng, PLeng	LMode	TFB, Pos, RLeng, PLeng
Es	sDn	TFB, PLeng	Ds	TFB, PLeng
Fr	Median	TFB, Pos, RLeng	Mean	TFU, TFB, Pos, PLeng
He	Ds	TFB, PLeng	Median	TFB, RLeng, PLeng
Hi	/	/	Ds	TFB, Pos, RLeng, PLeng
Ro	HMode	TFB, RLeng, PLeng	sDn	TFB, Pos, PLeng
Zh	HMode	TFB, RLeng, PLeng	sDn	TFU, Pos, RLeng, PLeng

Table 3: Relative improvement of our method against other methods on the MultiLing 2015 Single document testing dataset

Methods	Our method improvement %				
	ROUGE-1	ROUGE-2	ROUGE-3	ROUGE-4	ROUGE-SU4
BGU-SCE-M (ar, en, he)	-09.19	-14.02	-19.39	-25.12	-11.07
EXB (all 38)	-07.64	-10.55	-09.86	-07.92	-10.63
CCS (all 38)	-07.33	-13.24	-10.95	-03.04	-07.40
BGU-SCE-P (ar, en, he)	-04.33	-01.63	-02.69	-06.16	-01.89
UA-DLSI (en, de, es)	+02.12	+06.25	+13.86	+17.15	+05.62
NTNU (en, zh)	+06.44	+07.06	+11.50	+21.81	+05.74
Oracles (all 38) [TopLine]	-31.64	-49.00	-63.80	-72.91	-36.77
Lead (all 38) [BaseLine]	+02.39	+08.67	+08.20	+04.02	+05.82

Table 4: Relative improvement of our method against other methods on the MultiLing 2015 multi-document testing dataset. *The minus sign means that the system participated in all languages except those mentioned.*

SysID	Our method improvement %		
	AutoSummENG	MeMoG	NPowER
UJF-Grenoble (fr, en, el)	-08.87	-14.55	-03.62
UWB (all 10)	-22.56	-22.66	-07.54
ExB (all 10)	-09.44	-09.16	-02.80
IDA-OCCAMS (all 10)	-17.11	-17.68	-05.53
GiauUngVan (- zh, ro, es)	-16.43	-19.40	-05.68
SCE-Poly (ar, en, he)	-05.72	-03.35	-01.46
BUPT-CIST (all 10)	+10.67	+11.53	+02.85
BGU-MUSE (ar, en ,he)	+05.67	+06.92	+01.74
NCSR/SCIFY-NewSumRerank (- zh)	+01.53	-01.25	+00.13
our system (MSS parameters) (all 10)	+01.98	+02.35	+00.58

References

Abdelkrime Aries, Houda Oufaida, and Omar Nouali. 2013. Using clustering and a modified classification algorithm for automatic text summarization. volume 8658 of *Proc. SPIE*, pages 865811–865811–9.

John M. Conroy, Judith D. Schlesinger, and Jeff Kubina. 2011. Classy 2011 at TAC: Guided and multi-lingual summaries and evaluation metrics. In *Proceedings of the Fourth Text Analysis Conference (TAC 2011)–MultiLing Pilot Track.*, Gaithersburg, Maryland, USA.

Mahmoud El-Haj and Paul Rayson. 2013. Using a keyness metric for single and multi document summarisation. In *Proceedings of the MultiLing 2013 Workshop on Multilingual Multi-document Summarization*, pages 64–71, Sofia, Bulgaria, August. Association for Computational Linguistics.

Mahmoud El-Haj, Udo Kruschwitz, and Chris Fox. 2011. University of Essex at the TAC 2011 multilingual summarisation pilot. In *Proceedings of the Fourth Text Analysis Conference (TAC 2011)–MultiLing Pilot Track.*, Gaithersburg, Maryland, USA.

George Giannakopoulos and Vangelis Karkaletsis. 2011. Autosummeng and memog in evaluating guided summaries. In *TAC 2011 Workshop*, Gaithersburg, MD, USA. NIST.

George Giannakopoulos and Vangelis Karkaletsis. 2013. Together we stand npower-ed. In *Proceedings of CICLing 2013*, Karlovasi, Samos, Greece.

G. Giannakopoulos, M. El-Haj, B. Favre, M. Litvak, J. Steinberger, and V. Varma. 2011. Tac 2011 multiling pilot overview. In *Proceedings of the Fourth Text Analysis Conference (TAC 2011)–MultiLing Pilot Track.*, Gaithersburg, Maryland, USA.

George Giannakopoulos. 2013. Multi-document multilingual summarization and evaluation tracks in acl 2013 multiling workshop. In *Proceedings of the MultiLing 2013 Workshop on Multilingual Multi-document Summarization*, pages 20–28, Sofia, Bulgaria, August. Association for Computational Linguistics.

Eduard Hovy and Chin-Yew Lin. 1998. Automated text summarization and the SUMMARIST system. In *Proceedings of a workshop on held at Baltimore, Maryland: October 13-15, 1998*, pages 197–214. Association for Computational Linguistics.

Jeff Kubina, John Conroy, and Judith Schlesinger. 2013. Acl 2013 multiling pilot overview. In *Proceedings of the MultiLing 2013 Workshop on Multilingual Multi-document Summarization*, pages 29–38, Sofia, Bulgaria, August. Association for Computational Linguistics.

Lei Li, Corina Forascu, Mahmoud El-Haj, and George Giannakopoulos. 2013. Multi-document multilingual summarization corpus preparation, part 1: Arabic, english, greek, chinese, romanian. In *Proceedings of the MultiLing 2013 Workshop on Multilingual Multi-document Summarization*, pages 1–12, Sofia, Bulgaria, August. Association for Computational Linguistics.

Chin-Yew Lin. 2004. Rouge: A package for automatic evaluation of summaries. In *Proc. ACL workshop on Text Summarization Branches Out*, page 10.

Hongyan Liu, Pingan Liu, Wei Heng, and Lei Li. 2011. The cist summarization system at TAC 2011. In *Proceedings of the Fourth Text Analysis Conference (TAC 2011)–MultiLing Pilot Track.*, Gaithersburg, Maryland, USA.

Miles Osborne. 2002. Using maximum entropy for sentence extraction. In *Proceedings of the ACL-02 Workshop on Automatic Summarization - Volume 4*, AS '02, pages 1–8, Stroudsburg, PA, USA. Association for Computational Linguistics.

Vasudeva Varma, Sudheer Kovelamudi, Jayant Gupta, Nikhil Priyatam, Arpit Sood, Harshit Jain, Aditya Mogadala, and Srikanth Reddy Vaddepally. 2011. IIIT hyderabad in summarization and knowledge base population at TAC 2011. In *Proceedings of the Fourth Text Analysis Conference (TAC 2011)–MultiLing Pilot Track.*, Gaithersburg, Maryland, USA.

Comment-to-Article Linking in the Online News Domain

Ahmet Aker, Emina Kurtic, Mark Hepple, Rob Gaizauskas, Giuseppe Di Fabbrizio
University of Sheffield
ahmet.aker,e.kurtic,m.r.hepple,r.gaizauskas@sheffield.ac.uk,difabbrizio@gmail.com

Abstract

Online commenting to news articles provides a communication channel between media professionals and readers offering a crucial tool for opinion exchange and freedom of expression. Currently, comments are detached from the news article and thus removed from the context that they were written for. In this work, we propose a method to connect readers' comments to the news article segments they refer to. We use similarity features to link comments to relevant article segments and evaluate both word-based and term-based vector spaces. Our results are comparable to state-of-the-art topic modeling techniques when used for linking tasks. We demonstrate that article segments and comments representation are relevant to linking accuracy since we achieve better performances when similarity features are computed using similarity between terms rather than words.

1 Introduction

User comments on news articles and other online content provide a communication channel between journalists and their audience, which has previously replaced prevalent one-way reporting from journalists to their readers. Therefore, several user groups in media business now rely on online commenting to build and maintain their reputation and broaden their readers and customer base. To achieve this, however, it is essential to foster high quality discussions in online commenting forums because quality and tone of comments are shown to influence the readers' attitudes to online news content (Anderson et al., 2013; Diakopoulos and Naaman, 2011; Santana, 2014).

In the present set up of online forums, comments are difficult to organize, read and engage with, which affects the quality of discussion and the usefulness of comments for the interested parties. One problem with comments in their current form is their detachment from the original article. Placed at the end of the article without clear reference to the parts of the article that triggered them, comments are hard to put into the context from which they originated, and this makes them difficult to interpret and evaluate. Comment-article linking is also necessary in more complex systems for information extraction from comments such as comment summarization (Hu et al., 2008; Khabiri et al., 2011; Lu et al., 2009; Ma et al., 2012; Llewellyn et al., 2014). Such systems rely on identifying relevant comments and those that link to the articles are good candidates.

In this paper we report the results of our experiments in comment-article linking. Specifically, the task is to bring together readers' comments with online news article segments that comments refer to. We compare the performance of text similarity measures to that of more elaborate topic modeling methods such as the ones proposed by Sil et al. (2011) and Das et al. (2014) and demonstrate that comparable linking results can be achieved by simpler text similarity methods.

Given the weak lexical overlap between comments and source articles, we also investigate the effect of alternative representations of comments and news article texts on the results of comment-article linking with similarity metrics. We analyze the performance of the similarity method using terms, i.e., sequences of words which have all a meaning in a domain (de Bessé et al., 1997), and show that term based similarity linking outperforms similarity linking based on words.

The paper starts with defining the linking task and the pre-processing steps we perform on the article and comments (Section 2). Then we provide the description of our linking approach (Section 3). In Section 4 we report our experimental results. We summarize the paper in Section 5.

2 Task and Pre-processing

2.1 The task

For the linking task we assume a news article A is divided into n segments $S(A) = s_1, ..., s_n$. The article A is also associated with a set of comments $C(A) = c_1, ..., c_l$. The task is to link comments $c \in C(A)$ with article segments $s \in S(A)$. We express the strength of link between a comment c and an article segment s as their linking score ($Score$). A comment c and an article segment s are linked if and only if their $Score$ exceeds a threshold, which we experimentally optimized. $Score$ has the range $[0, 1]$, 0 indicating no linking and 1 defining a strong link.

2.2 Pre-processing

First, we split the news article into segments. To compare results with existing data sets and exist-

Proceedings of the SIGDIAL 2015 Conference, pages 245–249,
Prague, Czech Republic, 2-4 September 2015.

ing contributions, we comply with segmentation approaches used in previous work (Sil et al., 2011; Das et al., 2014). We treat each article sentence as a segment and group each comment into a single unit regardless of the number of sentences it contains. Then each sentence-comment pair is preprocessed before it is analyzed for linking. The example in Table 2.2 illustrates the outputs of the pre-processing pipeline.

The pre-processing includes tokenization[1] and lemmatization (step 2) in in Table 2.2, where an original article sentence is shown in step 1)). Next, we use either words with stop-word removal (step 3)) or terms (shown in 4) where each term is split by a semicolon) to represent the article sentence and also each comment. Terms are extracted using the freely available term extraction tool *Tilde's Wrapper System for CollTerm* (TWSC)[2] (Pinnis et al., 2012). We also record named entities (NEs) (shown in 5)) extracted from either article segments or comments.

3 Method

This work investigates a simple method for linking comments and news article sentences using a linear combination of similarity scores as computed through a number of different similarity metrics (features). However, some comments directly quote article segments verbatim, therefore explicitly linking comments to article segments. To account for this, we consider a comment and an article sentence linked if their quotation score ($quoteScore$) exceeds a threshold. Otherwise, a similarity score is computed and articles are linked if their similarity score is above a threshold. The following paragraphs describe how features and thresholds are computed.

Each metric is computed based on the comment $c \in C(A)$ and a segment $s \in S(A)$ as input. We pair every segment from $S(A)$ with every comment from $C(A)$. With this set up we are able to link one-to-many comments with one segment and also one-to-many segments with a particular comment, which implements an *n* to *m* comment-segment linking schema.

3.1 Quotation Based Linking

We link all comments including quotes to the article sentences they quote. To determine whether a segment is quoted in the comment, we compute $quoteScore = \text{len}(quote)/\text{len}(S)$ with *len* [3]. *len* returns the number of words of the given input and *quote* is a place holder for consecutive news article words found in the same order within the comment. If the $quoteScore$ exceeds an experimentally set threshold of 0.5 (50% of consecutive article segment words are found in the same order within the comment), then the segment is regarded as quoted in the comment, the comment-segment pair is linked, their linking $Score$ is set to $quoteScore$ and no further linking features are considered. However, qualitative observations on random data portions have shown that only sentences longer than 10 words render meaningful quote scores, so we add this as an additional constraint.

1	**Original article sentence:** *An Afghan policewoman walked into a high-security compound in Kabul Monday and killed an American contractor with a single bullet to the chest, the first such shooting by a woman in a spate of insider attacks by Afghans against their foreign allies.*
2	**After tokenization and lemmatization:** *an afghan policewoman walk into a high - security compound in kabul monday and kill an american contractor with a single bullet to the chest , the first such shooting by a woman in a spate of insider attack by afghan against their foreign allies .*
3	**When words are used:** *afghan, policewoman, walk, high, security, compound, kabul, monday, kill, american, contractor, single, bullet, chest, shooting, woman, spate, insider, attack, afghan, foreign, allies*
4	**When terms are used:** *shooting by a woman;woman in a spate; spate of insider; compound in kabul; kabul monday; insider attack; afghan policewoman; american contractor; single bullet; security compound; foreign allies; policewoman; security; compound; contractor; bullet; chest; shooting; woman; spate; insider; attack; allies; afghan; kabul; monday*
5	**Extracted NEs:** *Kabul*

Table 1: Text pre-processing pipeline example.

3.2 Similarity Linking

3.2.1 Similarity Feature Extraction

If a comment does not contain a quote as described above, we compute the following features to obtain the value of the similarity score without considering the quote feature:

- **Cosine:** The cosine similarity (Salton and Lesk, 1968) computes the cosine angle between two vectors. We fill the vectors with terms/word frequencies extracted from the article segment/comment.

[1]For shallow analysis we use the OpenNLP tools: https://opennlp.apache.org.

[2]TWSC uses POS-tag grammars to detect word collocations producing NP-like word sequences that we refer to as terms. Terms are extracted from the original version of the sentences, but words in the terms are replaced with their lemmas.

[3]For this feature the original version, i.e., without preprocessing, of article segment and comment are used.

- **Dice:**

$$dice = \frac{2 * \text{len}(I(S, C))}{\text{len}(S) + \text{len}(C)} \quad (1)$$

where $I(S, C)$ is the intersection set between the terms/words in the segment and in the comment. *len* returns the number of entries in the given set.

- **Jaccard:**

$$jaccard = \frac{\text{len}(I(S, C))}{\text{len}(U(S, C))} \quad (2)$$

where $U(S, C)$ is the union set between the terms/words in the segment and comment.

- **NE overlap:**

$$NE_{overlap} = \frac{\text{len}(I(S, C))}{\text{len}(U(S, C))} \quad (3)$$

where $I(S, C)$ is the intersection set between the named entities (NEs) in the segment and in the comment and $U(S, C)$ is the NEs union set.

- **DISCO 1 + DISCO 2:** *DISCO* (DIStributionally similar words using CO-occurrences) assumes words with similar meaning occur in similar context (Kolb, 2009). Using large text collections such as the BNC corpora or Wikipedia, distributional similarity between words is computed by using a simple context window of size ± 3 words for counting co-occurrences. DISCO computes two different similarities between words: *DISCO1* and *DISCO2*. In DISCO1 when two words are directly compared for exact similarity DISCO simply retrieves their word vectors from the large text collections and computes the similarity according to Lin's information theoretic measure (Lin, 1998). DISCO2 compares words based on their sets of distributional similar words.

3.2.2 Computing Similarity Linking Score

Using a linear function, we combine the scores of each of these features (*cosine* to *DISCO*) to produce a final similarity score for a comment-segment pair:

$$Score = \sum_{i=1}^{n} feature_i * weight_i \quad (4)$$

where $weight_i$ is the weight associated with the ith feature. The weights are trained based on linear regression using the Weka package and the training data described in the following section.

3.2.3 Training Data

Obtaining training data requires manual effort and human involvement and is thus very expensive, while resulting in relatively small training data sets. We therefore automatically assemble training data by using comments with article quotes as a training data set. As outlined above, in addition to original comment text, many comments include a brief quotation from the article, therefore directly indicating which article segments have triggered the comments. The set of comments with quotes linked to the article segments they quote are used as our training data.

To gather the training data, we downloaded 3,362 news articles along with their comments from The Guardian news paper web site[4] over a period of two months (June-July 2014). The Guardian provides for each topic (e.g., business, politics, art, etc.) a specific RSS feed URL. We manually collected RSS feeds for the topics: politics, health, education, business, society, media, science, the-northener, law, world-news, scotland-news, money and environment. Using an in-house tool, we visited the news published through the RSS feeds every 30 minutes, downloaded the article content and also recorded the news URL. Every recorded news URL was re-visited after a week (the time we found sufficient for an article to attract commenters) to obtain its comments. Articles contained between 1 and 6,223 comments, averaging 425.95 (median 231.5) comments per article.

Each article was split into sentences and for each of these sentences (containing at least 10 words) it was determined whether it is quoted in any of the comments as described above. In case the $quoteScore$ was above 0.5 for a sentence-comment pair, the pair was included in the training set. Using this process we have extracted 43,300 sentence-comment pairs to use for training. For each pair, the similarity features listed in Section 3.2.1 were extracted. The $quoteScore$ was used as the expected outcome. We also included 43,300 negative samples into the training data in order to present linear regression with the behavior of the features for wrong sentence-comment links. The negative samples were created by pairing every sentence containing at least 10 words of article X with every comment of article Y. In this way we pair comments with sentences of another article that have not originally triggered the comments. Similar to the positive samples, the quote score was taken as the expected outcome. However, unlike the positive samples, the $quoteScore$ threshold of 0.5 was not applied for the negative samples.

4 Evaluation

4.1 Test Data

In this study, we use the *AT* corpus (Das et al., 2014) to test the above linking method. The AT data set consists of articles with comments downloaded from the technology news website *Ars Technica* (AT). In this data set there are 501 articles. Each article contains between 8 and 132 sentences with an average of 38. Each article has between 2 and 59 linked comments with an average of 6.3. As reported in Das et al. (2014), two annotators mapped comments to article sentences; however, the agreement between annotators cannot be assessed from the available data set due to the lack of double annotations.

[4] `http://theguardian.com`

Method	Precision	Recall	F1
Metrics_{term}	**0.512**	0.292	0.372
Metrics_{word}	0.316	0.300	0.310
$\text{Metrics}_{termWord}$	0.414	0.310	0.356
SCTM	0.360	0.440	0.390
Corr-LDA	0.010	0.030	0.010

Table 2: Comparison of term/word based similarity metrics on article-comment linking to SCTM and Corr-LDA.

4.2 State-of-the art

The combined quotation and similarity-based linking investigated here is compared to the state-of-the-art SCTM method described in Das et al. (2014). SCTM (Specific Correspondence Topic Model that admits multiple topic vectors per article-comment pair) is an LDA-based topic modeling method that takes into account the multiplicity of topics in comments and articles. Their baseline is *Corr-LDA*, which Das et al. (2014) deem unsuitable since it is restricted to using only a single topic vector per article-comment pair. Evaluation on the same AT test data set allows for a direct comparison of our results to those of SCTM and Corr-LDA. Another recently proposed linking approach is reported in (Sil et al., 2011). However, it does not match the performance of its simple $tf * idf$ based baseline, so we do not consider this method in our evaluations.

4.3 Results

Table 4.3 shows the performance of the automated linking task using quotation and similarity metrics ($Metrics$) on the AT data.[5] The table shows the results for both term and word based representation of article segments (first two rows). Both results were obtained with the experimentally determined $Score >= 0.5$. The results in the table show that representation of article segments and comment texts as terms is superior to the bag-of-words representation for the comment-article linking task as it achieves substantially higher score in precision with a similar recall value. We also combined terms with words by merging the term list with the bag of words and used them to compute the metrics. The results are shown in the 3rd row. Compared to the word only variant, $Metrics_{word}$, we see a substantial improvement in the precision and a slight one in the recall score. However, compared to the term only variant, $Metrics_{term}$, the precision score is still low indicating that terms only are indeed the better choice for representing article segments and comments for the linking task.

The results in Table 4.3 show that the state-of-the-art baseline SCTM outperforms the $Metrics$ regarding the overall F1 score due to higher recall. However, this difference in F1 score is small. The precision of $Metrics_{term}$ based similarity is substantially higher than that of the SCTM method at the expense of recall. Higher precision may be preferable to higher recall for the linking task as including wrong links in order to have higher coverage is noisier and therefore more disturbing for both human and automatic processing of comment-article links than leaving relevant comments unlinked. These results suggest that term based similarity linking is performing almost as well as the SCTM method overall, and if increasing precision over recall is favored for the comment-article linking task, it even could be a preferred method for this task.

5 Conclusion

In this paper we report initial experiments on linking reader comments to the relevant segments in the articles – a task which has multiple applications in organization and retrievability of information from online commenting forums.

Linking between articles and comments implies capturing similarity between a comment and related article segments. In Das et al. (2014) the similarity is defined as similarity in topic. The claim is that multiple topics occurring in a comment and article need to be modeled in order to establish successful links. In this work our aim was to investigate how well known similarity metrics combined with a quotation heuristic perform on the linking task, and how their performance compares to refined topic similarity modeling proposed in previous work. The results showed that the overall performance of combined quote and similarity metrics is comparable to that of topic modeling method despite substantial domain difference between training and testing data sets. The bias of the quote and similarity method is towards precision and in topic modeling towards the recall. We also found that linking using similarity based on terms, i.e., specialized word sequences that have meaning in a domain, achieves better results than linking based on words. This is not surprising given a low lexical overlap between comments and article segments. The fact that terms achieved good results indicates that it is worth exploring further representations that abstract away from lexical items. This will be one of our immediate future studies. Furthermore, we plan to also address the recall problem by investigating clustering methods to group "similar" comments and link these groups instead of the single comments. Finally, we will investigate how the linking task can be used for summarizing news comments.

Acknowledgements

The research leading to these results has received funding from the European Union - Seventh Framework Program (FP7/2007-2013) under grant agreement n610916 SENSEI

[5] Note that the testing data does not contain any comment that quotes an article sentence as specified in our quote feature. This means all the results are achieved through the other features – cosine to Disco features.

Appendix – MultiLing Linking Task

We also participated in the linking task organized by MultiLing 2015. Similar to the task described in Section 2.1 the linking task within MultiLing was to link a comment to an article segment (sentence). However, unlike the task described above the comment was not treated as one unit, but split into sentences. This allowed to link parts of the comment (sentences) to article sentences and leave some out. Although the MultiLing linking task set-up defined this freedom within the comments we continued treating the entire comment as one unit. More precisely, when our linking approach found a link between a sentence in the comment and an article sentence it also linked all the remaining sentences within the comment to the article sentence. The evaluation was performed with English and Italian data.

Each participant was allowed to submit two runs. Our runs differed in how we set a threshold for linking similarity. The first run was set to a lower threshold (i.e. the $Score$ in equation 4 was set to 0.3). Anything below this threshold was not linked. In the second run the threshold was set to 0.5. For English both our runs were considered. However, for Italian there has been some problems in the submission, so that our second run with the threshold 0.5 was not considered.

Our results for English are that using our second run we obtained better results compared to all other 8 system submissions. With this set-up we achieved 89% precision. Our first run (run with the 0.3 threshold) achieved 82% precision. With this score it became the 5th system. For Italian our first run got the 6th position scoring 89% precision. Since our first run also did not perform well on the English data, it is likely that the performance on the Italian data would have been better could the second run be submitted.

References

Ashley A. Anderson, Dominique Brossard, Dietram A. Scheufele, Michael A. Xenos, and Peter Ladwig. 2013. The nasty effect: Online incivility and risk perceptions of emerging technologies. *Journal of Computer-Mediated Communication*.

Mrinal Kanti Das, Trapit Bansal, and Chiranjib Bhattacharyya. 2014. Going beyond Corr-LDA for detecting specific comments on news & blogs. In *Proceedings of the 7th ACM international conference on Web search and data mining*, pages 483–492. ACM.

Bruno de Bessé, Blaise Nkwenti-Azeh, and Juan C. Sager. 1997. Glossary of terms used in terminology. *Terminology. International Journal of Theoretical and Applied Issues in Specialized Communication*, 4:117–156(39).

Nicholas Diakopoulos and Mor Naaman. 2011. Towards quality discourse in online news comments. In *Proceedings of the ACM 2011 Conference on Computer Supported Cooperative Work*, CSCW '11, pages 133–142, New York, NY, USA. ACM.

Meishan Hu, Aixin Sun, and Ee-Peng Lim. 2008. Comments-oriented document summarization: understanding documents with readers' feedback. In *Proceedings of the 31st annual international ACM SIGIR conference on Research and development in information retrieval*, pages 291–298. ACM.

Elham Khabiri, James Caverlee, and Chiao-Fang Hsu. 2011. Summarizing user-contributed comments. In *ICWSM*.

Peter Kolb. 2009. Experiments on the difference between semantic similarity and relatedness. In *Proceedings of the 17th Nordic Conference on Computational Linguistics-NODALIDA09*.

Dekang Lin. 1998. Automatic retrieval and clustering of similar words. In *Proceedings of the 36th Annual Meeting of the Association for Computational Linguistics and 17th International Conference on Computational Linguistics-Volume 2*, pages 768–774. Association for Computational Linguistics.

Clare Llewellyn, Claire Grover, and Jon Oberlander. 2014. Summarizing newspaper comments. In *Eighth International AAAI Conference on Weblogs and Social Media*.

Yue Lu, ChengXiang Zhai, and Neel Sundaresan. 2009. Rated aspect summarization of short comments. In *Proceedings of the 18th international conference on World wide web*, pages 131–140. ACM.

Zongyang Ma, Aixin Sun, Quan Yuan, and Gao Cong. 2012. Topic-driven reader comments summarization. In *Proceedings of the 21st ACM international conference on Information and knowledge management*, pages 265–274. ACM.

Mārcis Pinnis, Nikola Ljubešić, Dan Ştefănescu, Inguna Skadiņa, Marko Tadić, and Tatiana Gornostay. 2012. Term extraction, tagging, and mapping tools for under-resourced languages. In *Proceedings of the 10th Conference on Terminology and Knowledge Engineering (TKE 2012), June*, pages 20–21.

G. Salton and M. Lesk, E. 1968. Computer evaluation of indexing and text processing. In *Journal of the ACM*, volume 15, pages 8–36, New York, NY, USA. ACM Press.

Arthur D. Santana. 2014. Virtuous or vitriolic. *Journalism Practice*, 8(1):18–33.

Dyut Kumar Sil, Srinivasan H Sengamedu, and Chiranjib Bhattacharyya. 2011. Supervised matching of comments with news article segments. In *Proceedings of the 20th ACM international conference on Information and knowledge management*, pages 2125–2128. ACM.

The University of Alicante at MultiLing 2015: approach, results and further insights

Marta Vicente
University of Alicante
Apdo. de correos 99
E-03080 Alicante, Spain
mvicente@dlsi.ua.es

Óscar Alcón
University of Alicante
Apdo. de correos 99
E-03080 Alicante, Spain
oalcon@dlsi.ua.es

Elena Lloret
University of Alicante
Apdo. de correos 99
E-03080 Alicante, Spain
elloret@dlsi.ua.es

Abstract

In this paper we present the approach and results of our participation in the 2015 MultiLing Single-document Summarization task. Our approach is based on the Principal Component Analysis (PCA) technique enhanced with lexical-semantic knowledge. For testing our approach, different configurations were set up, thus generating different types of summaries (i.e., generic and topic-focused), as well as testing some language-specific resources on top of the language-independent basic PCA approach, submitting a total of 6 runs for each selected language (English, German, and Spanish). Our participation in MultiLing has been very positive, ranking at intermediate positions when compared to the other participant systems, showing that PCA is a good technique for generating language-independent summaries, but the addition of lexical-semantic knowledge may heavily depend on the size and quality of the resources available for each language.

1 Introduction

Currently, the amount of on-line information generated per week reaches the same quantity of data that the one produced in the Internet between its inception and 2003, time of the Social Network emergency (Cambria and White, 2014). Moreover, the production of such volume of data is delivered in multiple languages, and accessing the relevant content of information or extracting the main features of documents in a competitive time is more and more challenging. Therefore, automatic tasks that can help processing all this information, such as multilingual text summarization techniques, are now becoming essential.

Back in 2011, the Text Analysis Conference MultiLing Pilot task[1] was first introduced as an effort of the community to promote and support the development of multilingual document summarization research. Considering the impact of this shared tasks in the progress of natural language processing technologies, a mutlilingual summarization workshop was also organized in 2013[2].

Nowadays, in 2015, we take part in the 3rd MultiLing event[3]. In this edition, new tasks have been added in order to adapt to social requirements. There were the traditional Multilingual Multi-document and Single-document Summarization (MMS and MSS), coming from previous events, but also new summarization tasks related to Online Fora (OnForumS) - on how to deal with reader comments- and Call Center Conversation (CCCS) - from spoken conversations to textual synopses.

Taking into consideration the interest that multilingual summarization approaches is gaining among the research community, and the positive impact and benefits it may have for the society, the objective of this paper is to present a multilingual summarization approach within the MultiLing 2015 competition, discussing its potentials and limitations, and providing some insights of the future of this type of summarization based on the average results obtained by us and other participants as well.

The remaining of the paper is organized as follows. In Section 2 we review the most relevant multilingual summarization approaches, some of them participating in previous MultiLing events. In Section 3, we explain our multilingual summarization approach and the required language-dependent knowledge. Section 4 describes the

[1] http://www.nist.gov/tac/2011/Summarization/

[2] http://multiling.iit.demokritos.gr/pages/view/662/multiling-2013

[3] http://multiling.iit.demokritos.gr/pages/view/1516/multiling-2015

Proceedings of the SIGDIAL 2015 Conference, pages 250–259,
Prague, Czech Republic, 2-4 September 2015.

task in which we participated, and the experiments performed. Furthermore, the results together with their discussion and comparison to other participants are provided in Section 5, followed by an analysis of the potentials and limitations of our approach in Section 6. Finally, the main conclusions are outlined in Section 7.

2 Related work

Eight teams participated in the Multilingual Pilot task in 2011, five of them testing their approaches for all the proposed languages (Arabic, Czech, English, French, Greek, Hebrew, and Hindi) (Giannakopoulos et al., 2011). Two systems are worth mentioning. On the one hand, the CLASSY system (Conroy et al., 2011) that ranked 2nd or 3rd in 5 out 7 languages. The main feature of this approach was that a model was first trained on a corpus of newswire taken from Wikinews, and then term scoring was limited to the naive Bayes term weighting. The final process of sentence selection was performed using non-negative matrix factorization and integer programming techniques. On the other hand, the best system on average was the one in (Steinberger et al., 2011), performing the 1st in five of the seven languages, and 4th in the two remaining ones. This approach did not used any language-dependent resources, apart from a stopword list for each language, and it relied on Latent Semantic Analysis and Singular Value Decomposition.

In the 2013 MultiLing edition, four teams participated submitting six systems to the task (Giannakopoulos, 2013). For their assessment in (Kubina et al., 2013), they were denoted as MUSE, MD, AIS and LAN. We briefly reviewed these approaches. MUSE (Litvak and Last, 2013), is a supervised learning approach that scores sets of sentences by means of a genetic algorithm. MD (Conroy et al., 2013) developed techniques both for MMS and MSS, examining the impact of dimensionality reduction and offering different weighting methods in the experiments: either considering the frequency of terms or applying a variant of TextRank, among others. Adapting their techniques to Arabic and English languages, the LAN team (El-Haj and Rayson, 2013) implements a system that recovers the most significant sentences for the summary using word frequency and keyness score, introducing a statistic approach that extracts those sentences with the maximum sum of log likelihood. Contrary to the previously described systems, mostly based in frequency of terms, AIS (Anechitei and Ignat, 2013) presented an approach based on the analysis of the discourse structure, exploiting, therefore, cohesion and coherence properties from the source articles. Although some of these participants performed well, achieving similar results as the ones obtained by human summaries, the WBU approach (Steinberger, 2013), was again the best performing summarization system in this MultiLing edition, reaching the first position in 5 of the 10 languages. Specifically, it was an improved version of the best-performing approach in MultiLing 2011 (Steinberger et al., 2011).

Outside the MultiLing competitions, other research works have been recently proposed, obtaining better results than existing commercial multilingual summarizers. An example of this can be found in (Lloret and Palomar, 2011) were three different approaches were analyzed and tested: i) one using language-independent techniques; ii) one with language-dependent resources; and iii) one using machine translation to monolingual summarization. The results obtained showed that having high-quality language specific resources often led to the best results; however, a simple language-independent approach based on term frequency was competitive enough, avoiding the effort needed to develop and/or obtain the particular resources for each language, when they were not available.

Having revised different multilingual summarization approaches, the main contribution of our paper is to propose a novel approach based on the Principal Component Analysis (PCA) technique, studying the influence of lexical-semantic knowledge to the base approach. To the best of our knowledge, although PCA has been already used for text summarization (for instance, in (Lee et al., 2003)), it has never been tested with the addition of semantic knowledge, nor in the context of multilingual summarization. Given that it bears some relation to LSA and SVD techniques, and it has been shown that such techniques are very competitive, MultiLing 2015 is the perfect context to test it.

3 The UA-DLSI Approach

In this Section, we present our proposed multilingual summarization approach (i.e., UA-DLSI approach).

As it was previously mentioned, the main technique that characterise the UA-DLSI approach is the Principal Component Analysis (PCA). PCA is a statistical technique focused on the synthesis of information to compress and interpret the data (Estellés Arolas et al., 2010).

As a method for developing summarization systems, PCA provides a way to determine the most relevant key terms of a document. It has been often employed in conjunction with other data mining techniques, such as Semantic Vector Space model (Vikas et al., 2008) or Singular Value Decomposition (Lee et al., 2005), using term-based frequency methods. Our main difference with respect to other summarization PCA-based approaches is the incorporation of lexical-semantic knowledge into the PCA technique, since it is necessary to go beyond the terms, and determine the meaningful sentences. Moreover, to finish the process, some strategies for selecting relevant information (in our case, choosing the most relevant sentences) needs to be defined as well.

For developing our UA-DLSI approach, we relied on the summary process stages outlined in (Sparck-Jones, 1999): 1) *interpretation*, 2) *transformation* and, finally, 3) the *summary generation*.

Interpretation. The first stage of our approach includes a linguistic and lexical-semantic processing (this latter part is optional). For the linguistic processing, sentence segmentation, tokenization and stopwords removal is applied. For the lexical-semantic processing, a named entity recognizer (*Standford Named Entity Recognizer*[4]) and semantic resources, such as *WordNet* (Miller, 1995) and *EuroWordNet* (Vossen, 2004) are employed. Whereas named entity recognizers mainly provide the identification of person, organization and place names in a document (Tjong et al., 2003), the semantic resources used comprises a set of synonyms grouped by means of the *synsets* that allow us to work with concept better than just with terms. In this manner, we group a set of synonyms under the same concept. For instance, *detonation* and *explosion* are different words but their share the same synset (*07323181*), so we would keep them as a single concept. For identifying concepts, we relied on the most frequent sense approach, and therefore, the process searches for the first synset of each word in the document, which corresponds to its most probable meaning. If two words have the same first synset, we will assume that they are synonyms and their occurrences will be added together.

The result of this stage is to build an initial lexical-semantic matrix, where for each sentence (rows in our matrix), we identify the units that will be later taken into account (i.e., terms, named entities, and/or concepts) which will correspond to the columns.

Transformation. It is in the transformation stage that we use the PCA method. In our approach, PCA is applied using the PCA_transform Java library[5] to process the covariance matrix that is computed from the lexical-semantic matrix obtained in the previous stage. Once PCA has been applied over the covariance matrix, the principal components (eigenvectors) and its corresponding weight (eigenvalue) are obtained. The eigenvectors are composed by the contribution of each variable, which determines the importance of the variable in the eigenvector. Moreover, the eigenvectors are derived in decreasing order of importance. In this manner, an eigenvector with high eigenvalue carries a great amount of information. Therefore, the first eigenvectors collect the major part of the information extracted from the covariance matrix, and they will be used for determining the most important sentences in the document, as it will be next shown.

Summary generation. In this final stage, the relevant sentences are selected and extracted, thus producing an extractive summary. Since from the previous stage, only the key elements (e.g., concepts) were determined, it is necessary to define some strategies for deciding which sentences containing these elements will be finally taking part in the summary.

Two strategies were proposed for selecting and ordering the most relevant sentences from the document, leading to two types of summaries: one generic and one topic-focused. In this manner, taking into account the element with the highest value for each eigenvector from the PCA matrix, we select and extract:

- one sentence (searching in order of appearance in the original text) in which

[4] `http://nlp.stanford.edu/software/CRF-NER.shtml`

[5] `https://github.com/mkobos/pca_transform`

such concept[6] appears. During this process, if a sentence had been already selected by a previous concept to take part in the summary, we would select and extract the following sentence in which the concept appears (generic summary).

- all the sentences (searched in order of appearance in the original text) in which such concept appears (topic-focused summary).

Regarding these strategies, it is worth mentioning that if we found different concepts with the same highest value for the same eigenvector, we would extract the corresponding sentences for all these concepts. In the same manner, if a synset is represented by several synonyms, we would extract the corresponding sentences for each of these synonyms.

4 Experimental Setup

This section describes the MultiLing 2015 task in which we participated, together with the dataset employed, and the explanation of the different variants of our approach submitted to the competition.

4.1 MSS - Multilingual Single-Document Summarization Task

The Multilingual Single Document Summarization task was initially proposed in MultiLing 2013, targeting the same goal in the current edition: to evaluate the performance of participant systems whose work is focused on generating a single document summary for all the given Wikipedia articles in some of the languages provided (at least the participants should select three languages). In the context of MultiLing 2015, two datasets were provided for the MSS task: a training dataset, containing 30 articles for each of the 38 available languages with their corresponding human-generated summaries; and a test dataset, which contains the same number of documents per language, but different from the training dataset, the human summaries were not provided. For both datasets, the character length that the target automatic summaries should aim was also provided (i.e., the *target length*), which coincided with the length of the human summaries that will be later used in the evaluation. Each automatic summary had to be as close to the target length provided as possible, and summaries exceeding the given target length were truncated to it.

In order to prove the adequacy of our approach to select the relevant sentences from a document, we decided to start testing it within small goals to be able to analyze and further improve the proposed approach. This was the main reason for participating in the MSS task rather than in the MMS, which had implied more complexity.

Concerning the language choice, since one of our main objectives was to evaluate the impact of lexical-semantic knowledge in the summary generation, some language-dependent resources were necessary (e.g. WordNet and EuroWordNet). The availability of these resources also conditioned the languages that were chosen for testing our apporach, in our case: English, German, and Spanish.

For each language considered, we computed the average length of the Wikipedia articles in the test corpus, both in characters and words. These figures are shown in Table 1. In addition, we also provide the target summary length (in characters) and the compression ratio for the summaries. As it can be seen, the length of the summaries compared to the original length of the Wikipedia articles (i.e., compression ratio) is very short, always below 10%. This means that generated summaries have to be very concise and precise in selecting the most relevant information.

	English	Spanish	German
Characters	25850	39202	38905
Words	4223	6271	5245
Target length	1858	2044	1071
Compression ratio	7.19%	5.21%	2.75%

Table 1: Average length (words and characters) of the test dataset, and target length and compression ratio for the summaries

4.2 Configuring the UA-DLSI approach to the MSS task

Having provided the information about the general multilingual summarization process in Section 3, and since each participant in the MSS task was allowed to submit up to six approaches, different versions of our approach were set to participate in MultiLing 2015.

Apart of the two types of summaries that could

[6] Concepts here refer to the possible elements that the matrix can have, e.g. named entities, synsets, or terms

be generated with our approach (*T1: generic summary; T3: topic-focused summary*), the incorporation of lexical-semantic knowledge was an optional substage, so we decided to test our approach also without any type of semantic knowledge, other than a list of stopwords for each language (*LI: language-independent; LEX: using lexical knowlege (named entity recognition); SEM: using semantic knowledge (i.e., WordNet and EuroWordNet)*). This way the performance of a fully language-independent summarization approach based on PCA could be also analyzed. Moreover, due to the nature of the test dataset (Wikipedia articles), all documents included headings for structuring different sections within them, so we opt for taking advantage of this information, considering only the words in these headings for the matrix construction (*OWFH*), instead of working with all words in the document, except stopwords (*AW*). Headings usually contain important concepts that reflect the main topic of the section that follows. Considering only this words, we also reduce the amount of information we have to process by 99% of the PCA matrix.

Therefore, given the impossibility to test all the variations taking into account these issues, our submitted approaches for MultiLing 2015, specifying also their priority, were the following:

- *T1_LI_AW* (UA-DLSI-*lang*-1): generic language-independent summarizer considering all words in the documents.
- *T1_LI_OWFH* (UA-DLSI-*lang*-3): generic language-independent summarizer considering only the words included in the headings of the documents.
- *T1_LEXSEM_AW* (UA-DLSI-*lang*-4): generic summarizer, including lexical-semantic knowledge into the interpretation stage, and considering all words in the documents.
- *T3_LI_OWFH* (UA-DLSI-*lang*-5): topic-focused language-independent summarizer considering only the words included in the headings of the documents.
- *T3_LEXSEM_AW* (UA-DLSI-*lang*-6): topic-focused summarizer, including lexical-semantic knowledge into the interpretation stage, and considering all words in the documents.
- *T3_LEXSEM_OWFH* (UA-DLSI-*lang*-2): topic-focused summarizer, including lexical-semantic knowledge into the interpretation stage, but considering only the words included in the headings of the documents.

5 Results and Analysis

After all participants submitted their runs to the MultiLing 2015 MSS task over the test dataset, the summaries were evaluated via automatic methods. ROUGE tool (Lin, 2004) was employed for automatic content evaluation, which allows the comparison between automatic and model summaries based on different types of n-grams. Specifically the ROUGE 1 (unigrams), 2 (bigrams), 3 (trigrams), and 4 (quadrigrams), ROUGE-SU4 (bigram similarity skipping unigrams) scores were computed. The files contain the overall and individual summary scores.

Moreover, two additional systems were proposed by the organizers. On the one hand, a system called *"Lead"*, which was the baseline summary used for the evaluation process. This approach selects the leading substring of the article's body text having the same length as the human summary of the article. On the other hand, a system called *"Oracles"* was also developed, where sentences were selected from the body text to maximally cover the tokens in the human summary using as few sentences as possible until its size exceeded the human summary, upon which it was truncated.

In this edition, five systems participated in the *MSS* task (details about their implementation have not made available yet). Three of them were applied to 38 languages, including English, Spanish and German. They are named as *CCS* - that implements five variations for each language- *LCS-IESI* and *EXB*. The fourth one, *BGU-SCE* has been proven for Arabic and Hebrew, besides English.

Table 2, Table 3, and Table 4 show the results obtained by all participants, and the two methods proposed by the organizers in the MultiLing 2015 competition for English, German, and Spanish. Due to size constraints, only the average results for the recall, precision and F-measure metrics of ROUGE 1 are shown, since this ROUGE metric takes into account the common vocabulary between the automatic and the human summaries, without taking into account stopwords.

Focusing only on the analysis of our six versions of our approach (UA-DLIS-*lang-priority*),

System	R1 recall	R1 precision	R1 F-measure
UA-DLSI-en-1	0.45488	0.45827	0.45605
UA-DLSI-en-2	0.42111	0.43774	0.42703
UA-DLSI-en-3	0.37175	0.49104	0.40551
UA-DLSI-en-4	0.45641	0.45673	0.45627
UA-DLSI-en-5	0.41994	0.43334	0.42419
UA-DLSI-en-6	0.42439	0.43093	0.42727
BGU-SCE-M-en-1	0.49195	0.48354	0.48744
BGU-SCE-M-en-2	0.47826	0.47953	0.47868
BGU-SCE-M-en-3	0.45955	0.46053	0.45974
BGU-SCE-M-en-4	0.46819	0.46651	0.46713
BGU-SCE-M-en-5	0.49982	0.48813	0.49361
BGU-SCE-P-en-1	0.46247	0.44367	0.45269
BGU-SCE-P-en-2	0.49420	0.47512	0.48425
BGU-SCE-P-en-3	0.46546	0.45039	0.45753
CCS-en-1	0.49507	0.47662	0.48539
CCS-en-2	0.49041	0.47299	0.48132
CCS-en-3	0.49130	0.47455	0.48255
CCS-en-4	0.48849	0.47211	0.47986
CCS-en-5	0.48689	0.47600	0.48117
EXB-en-1	0.49471	0.46692	0.48022
LCS-IESI-en-1	0.45556	0.46144	0.45811
NTNU-en-1	0.45585	0.46966	0.46213
Lead-en-1	0.43381	0.42495	0.42907
Oracles-en-1	0.61917	0.60114	0.60983

Table 2: Average results for English (recall, precision and F-measure ROUGE 1 (R1) values.

we observe that our approach with priority 3 is one of our best performing approaches considering the precision for the three tested languages. This version corresponds to *T1_LI_OWFH* approach - generic language-independent summarizer considering only the words included in the headings of the documents, and this means that the title headings of the Wikipedia articles do contain enough meaningful information of the documents. This is an interesting finding, because we are reducing the amount of information to be processed by almost 99%. Moreover, this also outlines the potential of the studied PCA technique for developing completely language-independent summarizers.

Other versions of our proposed approach, such as the ones submitted as priority 4, and priority 1 may obtained also competitive results for some languages. Again, the submission with priority 1 correspond to a generic language-independent summarizer considering all words in the documents (*T1_LI_AW*). It can be shown that when considering all words in the documents, instead of only the words in the headings, recall values improve, but for some languages, e.g. German, to take into account all the words does not have a positive influence in general. Regarding the submission with priority 4 (*T1_LEXSEM_AW*), the inclusion of lexical-semantic knowledge has been beneficial for the English results, but not for the other languages. This may be due to the type of semantic knowledge that is being used. WordNet for English is much bigger in size than for German and Spanish, and therefore, this could influence the results, not obtaining the expected improvements that were expected by using language-dependent resources. Generally speaking, from our approaches, apart from the previously mentioned findings, we can also observe that when summarizing Wikipedia articles, generic summarization has been shown to be more appropriate.

Analyzing all the results achieved by the other participants, we can observe that German is the language, among the three analyzed languages within our scope, that obtains poorer ROUGE results. This could occur since the summaries had a compression ratio lower than 3%, which is a

System	R1 recall	R1 precision	R1 F-measure
UA-DLSI-de-1	0.33993	0.34401	0.34110
UA-DLSI-de-2	0.33207	0.34331	0.33725
UA-DLSI-de-3	0.36126	0.36448	0.36236
UA-DLSI-de-4	0.33492	0.35565	0.34317
UA-DLSI-de-5	0.33023	0.33927	0.33437
UA-DLSI-de-6	0.34401	0.34807	0.34553
CCS-de-1	0.40140	0.36441	0.38163
CCS-de-2	0.40025	0.36601	0.38203
CCS-de-3	0.40257	0.37118	0.38575
CCS-de-4	0.40587	0.37234	0.38803
CCS-de-5	0.39356	0.38055	0.38665
EXB-de-1	0.37909	0.35621	0.36692
LCS-IESI-de-1	0.34844	0.36285	0.35504
Lead-de-1	0.33010	0.31562	0.32230
Oracles-de-1	0.54342	0.51331	0.52759

Table 3: Average results for German (recall, precision and F-measure ROUGE 1 (R1) values.

very low compression ratio for the summarization task. Moreover, it can be seen from the tables, that all systems overperformed the *"Lead"* baseline, but none of them surpassed the *"Oracles"* system. This was expected since the *"Oracles"* system was kind of upper boundary for the MSS task. Among the systems, the best performing ones taking into account the ROUGE 1 F-measure value were: the *BGU-SCE* team with their submission *BGU-SCE-M-en-5* for English; *CCS* team, with *CCS-de-4* for German; and again *CCS* team with *CCS-es-3* for Spanish. Taking into account the different submissions, our versions were not among the best performing approaches, despite obtaining results in line of the other participants. In general, there were not very big differences in results between the teams. In this sense, according to ROUGE 1 F-measure, we ranked[7] 15th out of 22nd for English with our *UA-DLSI-en-4* submission; 7th out of 13th for German with our *UA-DLSI-de-3* submission; and 8th out of 13th with our *UA-DLSI-es-1* submission. As it was previously discussed, for German and Spanish, the best submissions were the ones without using any type of lexical-semantic knowledge, whereas for English the use of a named entity recognizer, and a semantic knowledge base led to an improvement over the language-independent approach.

[7]The two systems provided by the organization has not been taken into account for the ranking.

6 Potentials and Limitations of the UA-DLSI Approach

From our participation in MultiLing 2015, we have tested our approach in a real competition and compared its performance with respect to state-of-the-art multilingual summarizers. Although in general terms, the best versions of our approach ranked at intermediate positions, the participation and evaluation process has been a positive issue for learning from errors, as well as gaining some insights into potentials and limitations that our approach and in general the multilingual summarization task may have.

After analyzing the performance of the different system configurations, it becomes clear that some of our assumptions need to be reviewed. Nevertheless, good positions were achieved when reducing the words to compute the PCA algorithm, which let us infer that article section headings contain enough information to produce accurate and precise summaries, while decreasing the amount of information to be processed by the system. Moreover, our results indicate that using PCA present advantages when language independent processing is required.

On the other hand, the limitations encountered are mostly related to inclusion of lexical-semantic knowledge. As it requires the use of external resources, the system performance becomes dependent of some aspects such as their quality, availability and size. The version of the system tak-

System	R1 recall	R1 precision	R1 F-measure
UA-DLSI-es-1	0.48273	0.49799	0.48977
UA-DLSI-es-2	0.46191	0.48250	0.47141
UA-DLSI-es-3	0.45203	0.50965	0.46979
UA-DLSI-es-4	0.47795	0.49211	0.48454
UA-DLSI-es-5	0.46748	0.48820	0.47691
UA-DLSI-es-6	0.46657	0.47827	0.47193
CCS-es-1	0.52817	0.50834	0.51783
CCS-es-2	0.53135	0.51065	0.52057
CCS-es-3	0.52430	0.50440	0.51388
CCS-es-4	0.53234	0.51121	0.52126
CCS-es-5	0.52410	0.51321	0.51835
EXB-es-1	0.53018	0.49760	0.51310
LCS-IESI-es-1	0.50057	0.50575	0.50213
Lead-es-1	0.46826	0.46419	0.46599
Oracles-es-1	0.62557	0.60875	0.61691

Table 4: Average results for Spanish (recall, precision and F-measure ROUGE 1 (R1) values.

ing into account this kind of background obtains better results in English language, for which resources as WordNet have reached a state of maturity higher than for other languages. In addition, and regarding the format of the source documents (Wikipedia articles), topic-focused summaries have been shown to be less adequate than generic summarization.

Concerning the multilingual summarization task from a broader perspective, it is worth stressing that this is a challenging task. On the one hand, language-independent methods exist, and they offer more capabilities to be employed for a wide range of languages; however, this type of techniques do not take into account any semantic analysis, so it is difficult that only with these techniques, abstractive summaries can be produced, thus limiting mostly to extractive summarization.

In the context of the MSS task, the summary compression ratio was extremely low, compared to the length of the original documents. This posed the task even more challenging, since the generated summaries had to be very concise as well as precise. Nevertheless, it is of great value to organize this type of events and have the possibility to participate in order to advance the state of the art, addressing difficult summarization challenges necessary in the current society.

7 Conclusions

In this paper we described our participation in MultiLing 2015 - Multilingual Single-document Summarization task, presenting our approach and comparing and discussing the results obtained with respect to the other participants in the task.

Our initial development was focused on the application of the PCA technique, given its suitability for developing language-independent approaches. Although some related work has been done on summarization, we contributed to the state of the art extending the PCA scope by the inclusion of lexical and semantic knowledge in its implementation and testing it in a multilingual scenario.

Our approach was tested in three languages, English, German, and Spanish, and six different configurations were submitted to the competition, obtaining average results when compared to other participants.

From our participation in MultiLing 2015, and the further analysis of our PCA based approach given the results obtained, three main conclusions can be drawn: i) PCA is a good technique for generating language-independent summaries; ii) generic summaries were more appropriate for the type of documents dealt with (i.e., Wikipedia documents); and iii) the title headings of Wikipedia articles were meaningful enough to build the PCA matrix in the summarization process, discarding the remaining words of the document. Although this version of our approach worked with very few content, it was shown to be one of our best performing approaches.

Acknowledgments

This research work has been partially funded by the University of Alicante, Generalitat Valenciana, Spanish Government and the European Commission through the projects, "Tratamiento inteligente de la información para la ayuda a la toma de decisiones" (GRE12-44), "Explotación y tratamiento de la información disponible en Internet para la anotación y generación de textos adaptados al usuario" (GRE13-15), DIIM2.0 (PROMETEOII/2014/001), ATTOS (TIN2012-38536-C03-03), LEGOLANG-UAGE (TIN2012-31224), and SAM(FP7-611312).

References

Daniel Anechitei and Eugen Ignat, 2013. *Proceedings of the MultiLing 2013 Workshop on Multilingual Multi-document Summarization*, chapter Multilingual summarization system based on analyzing the discourse structure at MultiLing 2013, pages 72–76. Association for Computational Linguistics.

Erik Cambria and Bebo White. 2014. Jumping nlp curves: A review of natural language processing research. *IEEE Computational Intelligence Magazine*, 9(2):48–57.

John M. Conroy, Judith D. Schlesinger, and Jeff Kubina. 2011. CLASSY 2011 at TAC: Guided and Multi-lingual Summaries and Evaluation Metrics. In *Proceedings of the Text Analysis Conference (TAC 2011)*.

John Conroy, T. Sashka Davis, Jeff Kubina, Yi-Kai Liu, P. Dianne O'Leary, and D. Judith Schlesinger, 2013. *Proceedings of the MultiLing 2013 Workshop on Multilingual Multi-document Summarization*, chapter Multilingual Summarization: Dimensionality Reduction and a Step Towards Optimal Term Coverage, pages 55–63. Association for Computational Linguistics.

Mahmoud El-Haj and Paul Rayson, 2013. *Proceedings of the MultiLing 2013 Workshop on Multilingual Multi-document Summarization*, chapter Using a Keyness Metric for Single and Multi Document Summarisation, pages 64–71. Association for Computational Linguistics.

Enrique Estellés Arolas, Fernando González Ladrón De Guevara, and Antonio Falcó Montesinos. 2010. Principal Component Analysis for Automatic Tag Suggestion. Technical report.

George Giannakopoulos, Mahmoud El-Haj, Benoit Favre, Litvak Marina, Josef Steinberger, and Vaduseva Varma. 2011. TAC2011 MultiLing Pilot Overview. In *Proceedings of the Text Analysis Conference (TAC 2011)*.

George Giannakopoulos. 2013. Multi-document multilingual summarization and evaluation tracks in acl 2013 multiling workshop. In *Proceedings of the MultiLing 2013 Workshop on Multilingual Multi-document Summarization*, pages 20–28, Sofia, Bulgaria, August. Association for Computational Linguistics.

Jeff Kubina, John M Conroy, and Judith D Schlesinger. 2013. Acl 2013 multiling pilot overview. *Proceedings of MultiLing 2013 Workshop on Multilingual Multi-document Summarization, Sofia, Bulgaria*, pages 29–38.

Chang Beom Lee, Min Soo Kim, and Hyuk Ro Park. 2003. Automatic Summarization Based on Principal Component Analysis. *Progress in Artificial Intelligence*, pages 409–413.

Chang B. Lee, Hyukro Park, and Cheolyoung Ock. 2005. Significant Sentence Extraction by Euclidean Distance Based on Singular Value Decomposition. In *Proceedings of the Natural Language Processing-IJCNLP 2005*, pages 636–645.

Chin-Yew Lin. 2004. Rouge: A package for automatic evaluation of summaries. In *Marie-Francine Moens, S. S., editor, Text Summarization Branches Out: Proceedings of the ACL-04 Workshop*, pages 74–81.

Marina Litvak and Mark Last. 2013. Multilingual single-document summarization with muse. *MultiLing 2013*, page 77.

Elena Lloret and Manuel Palomar. 2011. Finding the Best Approach for Multi-lingual Text Summarisation: A Comparative Analysis. In *International Conference Recent Advances in Natural Language Processing*, pages 194–201.

George A Miller. 1995. WordNet: A Lexical Database for English. *Communications of the ACM*, 38(11):39–41.

Karen Sparck-Jones. 1999. Automatic summarising : factors and directions. *Advances in automatic text summarisation*, pages 1–21.

Josef Steinberger, Mijail Kabadjov, Ralf Steinberger, Hristo Tanev, Marco Turchi, and Vanni Zaravella. 2011. JRC's Participation at TAC 2011: Guided and MultiLingual Summarization Tasks. In *Proceedings of the Text Analysis Conference (TAC 2011)*.

Josef Steinberger. 2013. The uwb summariser at multiling-2013. In *Proceedings of the MultiLing 2013 Workshop on Multilingual Multi-document Summarization*, pages 50–54, Sofia, Bulgaria, August. Association for Computational Linguistics.

Erik Tjong, Kim Sang, and Fien De Meulder. 2003. Introduction to the CoNLL-2003 Shared Task: Language-Independent Named Entity Recognition. In *7th conference on Natural language learning at HLT-NAACL 2003*, volume 4, pages 142–147.

Om Vikas, Akhil K Meshram, Girraj Meena, and Amit Gupta. 2008. Multiple Document Summarization Using Principal Component Analysis Incorporating Semantic Vector Space Model. *Computational Linguistics and Chinese Language Processing*, 13(2):141–156.

Piek Vossen. 2004. Eurowordnet: A multilingual database of autonomous and language-specific wordnets connected via an inter-lingual index. *International Journal of Lexicography Vol.17*, 2:161–173.

ExB Text Summarizer

Stefan Thomas, Christian Beutenmüller, Xose de la Puente
Robert Remus and **Stefan Bordag**
ExB Research & Development GmbH
Seeburgstr. 100
04103 Leipzig, Germany
{thomas, beutenmueller, puente, remus, bordag}@exb.de

Abstract

We present our state of the art multilingual text summarizer capable of single as well as multi-document text summarization. The algorithm is based on repeated application of TextRank on a sentence similarity graph, a bag of words model for sentence similarity and a number of linguistic pre- and post-processing steps using standard NLP tools. We submitted this algorithm for two different tasks of the MultiLing 2015 summarization challenge: *Multilingual Single-document Summarization* and *Multilingual Multi-document Summarization*.

1 Introduction

The amount of textual content that is produced and consumed each day all over the world, through news websites, social media, and other information sources, is constantly growing. This makes the process of selecting the right content to read and quickly recognizing basic facts and topics in texts a core task for making content accessible to the users. Automatic summarization strives to provide a means to this end. This paper describes our automatic summarization system, and its participation in the MultiLing 2015 summarization challenge.

Our focus has been on producing a largely language-independent solution for the MultiLing 2015 challenge that, in contrast to most attempts in this field, requires a strict minimum of language-specific components and uses no language-specific materials for the core innovative elements.

Our motivation comes in part from Hong et al. (2014), who compares a number of single language summarization systems on the same standardized data set and shows that many complex, language-specific, highly optimized and trained methods do not significantly out-perform simplistic algorithms that date back to the first summarization competitions in 2004.

Language-independent text summarization is generally based on sentence extractive methods: A subset of sentences in a text are identified and combined to form a summary, rather than performing more complex operations, and the primary task of summarization algorithms is to identify the set of sentences that form the best summary. In this case, algorithms differ mostly in how sentences are selected.

One textual feature that has proven useful in identifying good summary sentences is the relative prominence of specific words in texts when contrasted to a reference distribution (like frequency in a large general corpus). For example, the "keyness" metric in El-Haj and Rayson (2013), singular value decomposition on a term-vector matrix (Steinberger, 2013) and neural network-derived transformations of term vectors (Kågebäck et al., 2014) have all produced significant results. There are also a number of rule-based approaches like Anechitei and Ignat (2013). Hong et al. (2014) provides an overview of various current approaches, ranging from simple baseline algorithms to complex systems with many machine learning and rule-based components of various kinds.

One promising recent approach is graph theory-based schemes which construct sentence similarity graphs and use various graph techniques to determine the importance of specific sentences as a heuristic to identify good summary sentences (Barth, 2004; Li et al., 2013b; Mihalcea and Tarau, 2004).

In this paper, we describe ExB's graph-based summarization approach and its results in two MultiLing 2015 tasks: *Multilingual Single-document Summarization* and *Multilingual Multi-document Summarization*. ExB's submissions covered all languages in each task. Furthermore,

Proceedings of the SIGDIAL 2015 Conference, pages 260–269,
Prague, Czech Republic, 2-4 September 2015.

we summarize and discuss some unexpected negative experimental results, particularly in light of the problems posed by summarization tasks and their evaluation using ROUGE (Lin, 2004).

2 Process Overview

The procedures used in both tasks start from similar assumptions and use a generalized framework for language-independent sentence selection-based summarization.

We start from the same basic model as LDA approaches to text analysis: Every document contains a mixture of topics that are probabilistically indicative of the tokens present in it. We select sentences in order to generate summaries whose topic mixtures most closely match that of the document as a whole (Blei et al., 2003).

We construct a graph representation of the text in which each node corresponds to a sentence, and edges are weighted by a similarity metric for comparing them. We then extract key sentences for use in summaries by applying the PageRank/TextRank algorithm, a well-studied algorithm for measuring graph centrality. This technique has proven to be good model for similar extraction tasks in the past (Mihalcea and Tarau, 2004).

We deliberately chose not to optimize any parameters of our core algorithm for specific languages. Every parameter and design decision applied to all languages equally and was based on cross-linguistic performance. Typically it is possible to increase evaluation performance by 2%-4% through fine tuning, but this tends to produce overfitting and the gains are lost when applied to any broader set of languages or domains.

Our approach consists of three stages:

1. Preprocessing using common NLP tools. This includes steps like tokenization and sentence identification, and in the multilingual summarization case, an extractor for time references like dates and specific times of day. These tools are not entirely language-independent.

2. Sentence graph construction and sentence ranking as described in Sections 2.2 and 2.3 respectively.

3. Post-processing using simple and language-independent rules for selecting the highest ranking sentences up to the desired length of text.

2.1 Preprocessing

Our processing pipeline starts with tokenization and sentence boundary detection. For most languages we employ ExB's proprietary language-independent rule-based tokenizer. For Chinese, Japanese and Thai tokenization we use language-dependent approaches:

- Chinese is tokenized using a proprietary algorithm that relies on a small dictionary, the probability distribution of token lengths in Chinese, and a few handcrafted rules for special cases.

- For Thai, we use a dictionary containing data from NECTEC (2003) and Satayamas (2014) to calculate the optimal partition of Thai letter sequences based on a shortest path algorithm in a weighted, directed acyclic character graph using dictionary terms found in the text.

- For Japanese, we employ the CRF-based *MeCab* (Kudo et al., 2004; Kudo, 2013) morphological analyzer and tokenizer. *MeCab* is considered state-of-the-art and is currently being used in the construction of annotated reference corpora for Japanese by Maekawa et al. (2014).

Sentence boundary detection is rule-based and uses all sentence separators available in the Unicode range of the document's main language, along with an abbreviation list and a few rules to correctly identify expressions like "p.ex." or "..."

Finally, we use a proprietary SVM-based stemmer trained for a wide variety of languages on custom corpora.

2.2 Graph construction

Given a set of tokenized sentences S, we construct a weighted undirected graph $G = (V, E)$, where each vertex $V_i \in V$ corresponds to a sentence in S. The weighted edges (S_i, S_j, w) of the graph are defined as a subset of $S \times S$ where $i \neq j$ and $(w \leftarrow sim(S_i, S_j)) \geq t$ for a given similarity measure sim and a given threshold t. We always assume a normalized similarity measure with a scale between 0 and 1.

Sentence similarity is computed with the standard vector space model (Salton, 1989), where each sentence is defined by a vector of its tokens.

We compared these vectors using a number of techniques:

- An unweighted *bag-of-words* model with sentence similarity computed using the Jacquard index.
- Conventional cosine similarity of sentence vectors weighted by term frequency in the sentence.
- TF-IDF weighted cosine similarity, where term frequencies in sentences are normalized with respect to the document collection.
- Semantic similarity measured using the *ExB Themis* semantic approach described in Hänig et al. (2015).

We also evaluated different settings for the threshold t. We did not optimize t separately for different languages, instead setting a single value for all languages.

Surprisingly, when averaged over all 38 languages in the MSS training set, the simple bag-of-words model with a threshold $t = 0.3$ produced the best result using the ROUGE-2 measure.

2.3 Sentence ranking

We then apply to the sentence similarity graph an iterative extension of the *PageRank* algorithm (Brin and Page, 1998) that we have called *FairTextRank* (*FRank*) to rank the sentences in the graph. *PageRank* has been used as a ranker for an extractive summarizer before in Mihalcea and Tarau (2004), who named it *TextRank* when used for this purpose. *PageRank* constitutes a measure of graph centrality, so intuitively we would expect it to select the most central, topical, and summarizing sentences in the text.

Following our assumption that every document constitutes a mix of topics, we further assume that every topic corresponds to a cluster in the sentence graph. However, *PageRank* is not a cluster sensitive algorithm and does not, by itself, ensure coverage of the different clusters present in any graph. Therefore, our *FRank* algorithm invokes *PageRank* iteratively on the graph, at each step ranking all the sentences, then removing the top ranking sentence from the graph, and then running *PageRank* again to extract the next highest ranking sentence. Because the most central sentence in the entire graph is also, by definition, the most central sentence in some cluster, removing it weakens the centrality of the other sentences in that cluster and increases the likelihood that the next sentence selected will be the highest ranking sentence in another cluster.

A similar method of removing selected sentences is used in the *UWB Summarizer* by Steinberger (2013), which was one of the top performing systems at MultiLing 2013. However, the *UWB Summarizer* uses an LSA algorithm on a sentence-term matrix to identify representative sentences, where we have employed *PageRank*.

The complete algorithm is detailed in Algorithm 1. The function adj returns the weighted adjacency matrix of the sentence graph G. An inner for-loop transforms the weighted adjacency matrix into a column-stochastic matrix where for each column c, where $A[i, c]$ is the weight of the edge between sentence i and sentence c, the following expression holds: $\sum_{i \in |A|} A[i, c] = 1$. Informally, each column is normalized at each iteration so that its values sum to 1. pr is the *PageRank*-algorithm with the default parameters $\beta = 0.85$, a convergence threshold of 0.001 and allowed to run for at most 100 iterations as implemented in the JUNG API (O'Madadhain et al., 2010).

Algorithm 1 FairTextRank

function FRANK(G)
  $R \leftarrow []$
  while $|G| > 0$ **do**
    $A \leftarrow adj(G)$
    for $(r, c) \leftarrow |A|^2$ **do**
      $A_{norm}[r, c] \leftarrow \frac{A[r,c],}{\sum_{i \in |A|} A[i,c]}$
    $rank \leftarrow pr(A_{norm})$
    $v \leftarrow rank[0]$
    $R \leftarrow R + v$
    $G \leftarrow G \setminus v$
  return R

2.4 Post-processing

The final step in processing is the production of a plain text summary. Given a fixed maximum summary length, we selected the highest ranked sentences produced by the ranking algorithm until total text length was greater than the maximum allowed length, then truncated the last sentence to fit exactly the maximum allowed length. Although this reduces the human readability of the summary - the last sentence is interrupted without any consideration of the reader at all - it can only increase the score of an n-gram based evaluation metric like ROUGE.

3 Single Document Summarizer

The *Multilingual Single-document Summarization* (MSS) task consisted of producing summaries for Wikipedia articles in 38 languages. All articles were provided as UTF-8 encoded plain-text files and as XML documents that mark sections and other elements of the text structure. We took advantage of the availability of headers and section boundary information in performing this task.

There was no overlap between the training data and the evaluation data for the MSS task. The released training data consisted of the evaluation data set from MultiLing 2013 as described in Kubina et al. (2013). This training data contains 30 articles in each of 40 languages. The MSS task itself at MultiLing 2015 used 30 articles in each of 38 languages, dropping two languages because there were not enough new articles not included in the training data.

In addition to the preprocessing steps described in Section 2.1, for this task we applied a list of sentence filters developed specifically for Wikipedia texts:

- Skip all headers.
- Skip every sentence with with less than 2 tokens (mostly errors in sentence boundary detection).
- Skip every sentence that contains double quotes.

We then performed sentence graph construction and ranking as described in Sections 2.2 and 2.3

In the post-processing stage, we sorted the sentences selected to go into the summary in order of their position in the original article, before producing a plain text summary by concatenating them.

3.1 Results

The organizers of the MultiLing 2015 challenge measured the quality of our system's output using five different versions of the ROUGE score. We provide a summary of the results for all participants in Table 1. It shows the average ranking of each participating system over all the languages on which it was tested, as well as the number of languages on which each system was tested. The systems labelled **Lead** and **Oracles** are special systems. **Lead** just uses the beginning of the article as the summary and represents a very simple baseline. **Oracles**, on the other hand, is a cheating system that marks the upper bound for any extractive approach.

Only three submissions - highlighted in bold - participated in more than 3 languages. We submitted only one run of our system, defined as a fixed set of parameters that are the same over all languages. One of the other two systems that participated in all 38 languages submitted five runs. According to the frequently used ROUGE-1 and ROUGE-2 scores, our system achieved an average ranking of 3.2 and 3.3, respectively. This table shows that the CCS system performed better on average than our system, and the LCS-IESI system performed on average worse.

However, ROUGE-1 only measures matching single words, whereas ROUGE-2 measures matching bigrams. More complex combinations of words are more indicative of topic matches between gold standard data and system output. We believe that ROUGE-SU4, which measures bigrams of words with some gaps as well as unigrams, would be a better measure of output quality. When manually inspecting the summaries, we have the strong impression that system runs in which our system scored well by ROUGE-SU4 measures, but poorly by ROUGE-2, did produce better summaries with greater readability and topic coverage.

Our system achieves a significantly better overall ranking using ROUGE-SU4 instead of ROUGE-2, even though the system was optimized to produce the highest ROUGE-2 scores. Only two runs of the winning system CCS scored better than our system according to ROUGE-SU4. This underlines the robustness of our system's underlying principles, despite the known problems with ROUGE evaluations.

4 Multi Document Summarizer

The *Multilingual Multi-document Summarization* (MMS) task involves summarizing ten news articles on a single topic in a single language. For each language, the dataset consists of ten to fifteen topics, and ten languages were covered in all, including and expanding on the data used in the 2013 MMS task described by Li et al. (2013a).

The intuition guiding our approach to this task is the idea that if news articles on the same topic contain temporal references that are close together

Competitor system	Langs.	Rank R-1	Rank R-2	Rank R-3	Rank R-4	Rank R-4SU
BGU-SCE-M	3	2.0	3.3	3.7	4.3	3.0
BGU-SCE-P	3	5.0	4.7	5.0	4.3	4.3
CCS	38	2.1	2.1	2.2	2.3	2.5
ExB	38	3.2	3.3	3.7	3.8	2.8
LCS-IESI	38	4.1	4.1	4.0	4.0	4.1
NTNU	2	5.5	6.0	6.0	7.0	5.0
UA-DLSI	3	6.0	5.0	4.7	5.0	6.0
Lead	38	5.1	5.0	4.6	4.3	5.0
Oracles	38	1.1	1.2	1.2	1.2	1.2

Table 1: Number of covered languages and average rank for each system in MSS competition for ROUGE-(1,2,3,4,4-SU) measures. In bold, competitors in all available languages. *Lead* and *Oracles* are two reference systems created by the organizers.

or overlapping in time, then they are likely to describe the same event. We therefore cluster the documents in each collection by the points in time referenced in the text rather than attempting to summarize the concatenation of the documents directly. This approach has the natural advantage that we can present summary information in chronological order, thereby often improving readability. Unfortunately, this improvement is not measurable using ROUGE-style metrics as employed in evaluating this task.

An official training data set with model summaries was released, but too late to inform our submission, which was not trained with any new 2015 data. We did, however, use data from the 2011 MultiLing Pilot including gold standard summaries (Giannakopoulos et al., 2011), which forms a part of the 2015 dataset. We used only the 700 documents and summaries from the 2011 task as training data, and did not use any Chinese, Spanish or Romanian materials in preparing our submission.

Our submission follows broadly the same procedure as for the single document summarization task, as described in Section 2 and Section 3, except for the final step, which relies on section information not present in the news articles that form the dataset for this task. Instead, a manual examination of the dataset revealed that the news articles all have a fixed structure: the first line is the headline, the second is the date, and the remaining lines form the main text. We used this underlying structure in preprocessing to identify the dateline of the news article, and we use this date to disambiguate relative time expressions in the text like "yesterday" or "next week". Articles are also ordered in time with respect to each other on the basis of the article date.

Furthermore, we remove in preprocessing any sentence that contains only time reference tokens because they are uninformative for summarization.

We then extract temporal references from the text, using ExB's proprietary *TimeRec* framework described in Thomas (2012), which is available for all the languages used in this task. With the set of disambiguated time references in each document, we can provide a "timeframe" for each document that ranges from the earliest time referenced in the text to the latest. Note that this may not include the date of the document itself, if, for example, it is a retrospective article about an event that may have happened years in the past.

4.1 Time information processing

Ng et al. (2014) and Wan (2007) investigate using textural markers of time for multi-document summarization of news articles using very different algorithms. Our approach is more similar to Ng et al. in constructing a timeline for each document and for the collection as a whole based on references extracted from texts. Once document timeframes are ordered chronologically, we organize them into groups based on their positions on a time line. We explored two strategies to produce these groups:

- **Least Variance Clustering (LVC)**: Grouping the documents iteratively by adding a new document to the group if the overall variance of the group doesn't go over a threshold. We set the standard deviation limit of the group in 0.1. The algorithm is a divisive clustering algorithm based on the central time of the documents and the standard deviation. At first the minimal central time of a document collection is subtracted from all other central times, then we compute mean, variance and standard deviation based on days as a unit and normalized by the mean. Afterwards we recursively split the groups with the goal to minimize the variance of both splits until either a group consists only of one document or the recomputed standard deviation of a group is less than 0.1.

- **Overlapping Time Clustering (OTC)**: Grouping documents together if their timeframes overlap more than a certain amount, which we empirically set to 0.9 after experimenting with various values. This means that if two texts A and B are grouped together, then either A's timeframe includes at least 90% of B's timeframe, or B's timeframe includes 90% of A's. This approach proceeds iteratively, with each new addition to a group updating the timeframe of the group as a whole, and any text which overlaps more than 90% with this new interval is then grouped with it in the next iteration.

In addition, we provide two baseline clusterings:

- **One document per cluster (1PC)**: Each document is in a cluster by itself.

- **All in one cluster (AIO)**: All documents from one topic are clustered together.

In the LVC and OTC cases, clustering is iterative and starts with the earliest document as determined by a fixed "central" date for each document. We explored different ways of determining that "central" date: One was using the dateline found in preprocessing on the second line of each document, another was the median of the time references in the document. Our best result used the dateline from each article and, as can be seen in Table 2, was produced by the OTC strategy. This is a surprising result, as we expected LVC to perform better since variance is generally a better measure of clustering. However, we found that LVC generally produced more clusters than OTC and we believe that to account for its poor performance. We experimented with a number of other ordering and clustering approaches, although they do not figure into our submission to the MMS task, but in all cases they failed to out-perform the OTC approach according to the ROUGE-2 recall measure.

For all conditions, identical preprocessing was performed using ExB's proprietary language-specific tokenizer and sentence identifier. ROUGE scores, because they are based on token n-grams, are very sensitive to discrepancies between tokenizers and stemmers. In English, because most tokenizers perform very similarly, this causes fewer problems in scoring than for Arabic or other languages where tokenizers vary dramatically. We used the results in Table 2 to decide which conditions to use in the competition, but we cannot be sure to what degree our results have been influenced by these kinds of ROUGE-related problems.

After clustering, we perform graph-based sentence ranking as described in Sections 2.2 and 2.3 separately for each cluster. We then select sentences from each cluster, ensuring that they are all represented in the final summary, so that the entire time span of the articles is covered. We also order the selected sentences in the summary based on the temporal ordering of the clusters, so that summary presentation is in event order.

4.2 Experimental results

When experimenting with the challenge data we made several observations:

1. Since the dataset of MMS is composed of news articles, just selecting the headlines and first sentences will produce a strong baseline with very high ROUGE scores. It is difficult to beat this baseline using sentence extraction techniques.

2. The quality of the summaries varies a great deal between languages. Instead of producing fine-tuned configurations for each lan-

Clustering Algorithm	English	Arabic
1PC	18.08	26.06
AIO	18.94	24.5
LVC	15.54	24.25
OTC	**19.81**	25.34
1PC-Reorder	17.69	**33.63**

Table 2: ROUGE-2 recall results for different grouping algorithms in MMS-2011 dataset.

Language	AutoSummENG	MeMoG	NPowER	Rank/Total
Arabic	0.135	0.164	1.717	7/9
Chinese	0.118	0.141	1.654	1/5
Czech	0.188	0.2	1.874	4/7
English	0.167	0.191	1.817	6/10
French	0.2	0.195	1.892	5/8
Greek	0.147	0.17	1.75	5/8
Hebrew	0.115	0.147	1.655	8/9
Hindi	0.123	0.139	1.662	3/7
Romanian	0.168	0.183	1.809	4/6
Spanish	0.193	0.202	1.886	3/6

Table 3: Average per-language Score ranked against the best run of each system in MMS competition for MeMoG measure.

guage that optimize ROUGE scores, we focused on increasing the performance in English - a language we can read and in which we can qualitatively evaluate the produced summaries.

3. All the results here of the time information processing are at document-level. We also tried to apply the time grouping algorithms per sentence, but we noticed a drop of about 3% ROUGE-2 score on average.

The most important finding is that using temporal expressions and chronological information does improve the performance of the summary system, and that the iterative FairTextRank algorithm shows a solid performance even for multiple documents.

As can be seen in Table 3, our system gets ranked in middle position in the official scores of the challenge using the *NPowER*, *MeMoG* and *AutoSummENG* measures as described in Giannakopoulos and Karkaletsis (2013) and Giannakopoulos and Karkaletsis (2011). We also note that our system out-performs all other participants in Chinese, a language for which we had no training data.

5 Negative results

We feel that it is important not only to publish positive results, but also negative ones, to counter the strong publication bias identified in many areas in the natural and social sciences (Dickersin et al., 1987; Ioannidis, 2005). Since we conducted a large number of experiments in creating this system, we inevitably also came across a number of ideas that seemed good, but turned out to not improve our algorithm, at least as measured using ROUGE-2.

In another challenge participation we developed a very powerful "semantic text similarity" (STS) toolkit. In *SemEval 2015* Task 2 (Agirre et al., 2015), it achieved by far the highest scores for Spanish texts and the second best scores for English. Since our text summarization methodology is based on a sentence similarity graph, our intuitive hypothesis was that when using this module as opposed to simple matching-words strategies, performance should increase significantly. Matching-words strategies are used as the baseline in SemEval tasks, and it is easily out-performed by more sophisticated approaches.

Therefore, we tried out our STS module as a replacement for Jacquard and cosine similarity measures when constructing the sentence graph, while keeping all other parameters fixed. Surprisingly, it did not improve performance, and lowered ROUGE-2 scores by 2%. We also attempted to use *word2vec* embeddings precomputed on very large corpora (Mikolov et al., 2013) to represent words and hence compute a much finer-grained sentence similarity, but those results were 4% worse. It is possible that those systems were, in fact, better, but because ROUGE scoring focuses on word matches, any other improvement cannot be measured directly. We also attempted to include other factors such as sentence length, position, number of named entities, temporal expressions, and physical measurements into the sentence similarity score, all without seeing any increase in ROUGE scores.

Since identifying temporal expressions increases ROUGE scores, as this paper shows, we surmised that name recognition might also improve summarization. We applied our named entity recognition system, which is available in a number of different languages and won the Germeval 2014 (Benikova et al., 2014) NER challenge, and weighted more heavily sentences with detected names before extracting summary sentences. Interestingly, no matter how the weighting scheme was set up, the performance of the system always dropped by a few percent. Often, the system would select useless sentences that contain long lists of participating authors, or enumerations of entities participating in some reported event. Even when these kinds of sentences are explicitly removed, it still selects sentences that simply contain many names with little relevance to the topics of the news article. We conclude that sentences describing central topics in documents are not strongly correlated with named entity usage.

Another very intuitive assumption is that filtering stop words, or down-weighting very frequent words, or using a TF-IDF based scheme with a similar effect, would improve the results. However, we did not observe any improvement by using these techniques. Nonetheless, there are strong indications that this is due to the limitations of ROUGE-2 scoring and we cannot conclude that these kinds of techniques are useless for summarization. It is easy to achieve very competitive ROUGE-2 scores by just filling the summary with very frequent stop word combinations. A human would immediately recognize the uselessness of such a "summary", but ROUGE-2 would count many bigram matches with a gold standard summary.

Finally, we considered the hypothesis that the summary system could be helped by explicitly removing very similar sentences presenting redundant information. Surprisingly, explicitly removing such sentences did not improve the performance of the system. Manually inspecting a number of summaries, we notice that very similar sentences recurring often in texts are rarely selected by the *FRank* algorithm. We believe this is because our approach is sufficiently robust to discount these sentences on its own.

6 Conclusions

In this paper we outline ExB's largely language-independent system for text summarization based on sentence selection, and show that it supports at least the 38 languages used in this completion without any language-specific fine-tuning. Sentences are selected using an iterative extension of *PageRank calculation* on a sentence similarity graph. Our results in the MultiLing 2015 challenge have validated this approach by achieving the best scores for several languages and competitive scores for most of them, generally surpassed by only one other participating system.

We also show that one basic summarization system can apply to different domains, different languages, and different tasks without special configuration, while retaining state-of-the-art performance. Furthermore, for multi-document news summarization, we show that extracting temporal expressions is a useful feature for combining articles on the same topic.

Our most relevant conclusion is that both the current evaluation methodology (based on various forms of ROUGE) as well as the current principal approach to language-independent text summarization (context-free, sentence selection based) are highly inadequate to model the vague requirements users associate with a text summarization product.

Participants in MultiLing 2015 did not receive the scripts and parameters used in producing evaluations. This made it difficult to optimize parameters and algorithms and has a significant impact on results using ROUGE measures and probably the other measures as well. Hong et al. (2014), for example, notes values between 30.8% and 39.1% using ROUGE-1 for one well-known algorithm on one data set by different authors. It is not clear how the vastly different scores obtained for identical summaries using different ROUGE parameters correlate with the objective quality of a given summary. We have no clear indication that ROUGE scores really capture the quality of a given summary at all.

While it is possible to formulate summarization solutions based on sentence selection and even iteratively improve them using ROUGE scores, the actual achievable performance measured using ROUGE is very low. We have noticed that stemming, stopword filtering and various tokenization strategies can have a very large influence on ROUGE scores, especially in morphologically richer languages than English. More modern evaluation measures like *MeMog* or *NPoweR* might solve the problems inherent to ROUGE, however they currently lack widespread adoption in the research community.

Nonetheless, even if these issues in evaluation can be addressed, we do not believe that summaries based on sentence selection will ever reach a quality where they could be accepted as comparable to a human written summary.

References

Eneko Agirre, Carmen Banea, Claire Cardie, Daniel Cer, Mona Diab, Aitor Gonzalez-Agirre, Weiwei Guo, Iigo Lopez-Gazpio, Montse Maritxalar, Rada Mihalcea, German Rigau, Larraitz Uria, and Janyce Wiebe. 2015. SemEval-2015 Task 2: Semantic Textual Similarity, English, Spanish and Pilot on Interpretability. In *Proceedings of the 9th International Workshop on Semantic Evaluation (SemEval 2015)*, Denver, CO, June. ACL.

Daniel Alexandru Anechitei and Eugen Ignat. 2013. Multilingual summarization system based on analyzing the discourse structure at MultiLing 2013. *Proceedings of the Multiling 2013 Workshop on Multilingual Multi-document Summarization*, pages 72–76.

Michael Barth. 2004. Extraktion von Textelementen mittels "spreading activation" für indikative Textzusammenfassungen. Master's thesis, Universität Leipzig. Fakultät für Mathematik und Informatik. Institut für Informatik.

Darina Benikova, Chris Biemann, Max Kisselew, and Sebastian Pad. 2014. GermEval 2014 Named Entity Recognition Shared Task: Companion Paper. In *Proceedings of the KONVENS GermEval Shared Task on Named Entity Recognition*, pages 104–112, Hildesheim, Germany.

David M. Blei, Andrew Y. Ng, and Michael I. Jordan. 2003. Latent Dirichlet Allocation. *J. Mach. Learn. Res.*, 3:993–1022, March.

Sergey Brin and Lawrence Page. 1998. The Anatomy of a Large-scale Hypertextual Web Search Engine. *Comput. Netw. ISDN Syst.*, 30(1-7):107–117, April.

K. Dickersin, S. Chan, T. C. Chalmers, H. S. Sacks, and Smith. 1987. Publication bias and clinical trials. *Controlled Clinical Trials*, 8(4):343–353.

Mahmoud El-Haj and Paul Rayson. 2013. Using a Keyness Metric for Single and Multi Document Summarisation. *Proceedings of the Multiling 2013 Workshop on Multilingual Multi-document Summarization*, pages 64–71.

George Giannakopoulos and Vangelis Karkaletsis. 2011. AutoSummENG and MeMoG in Evaluating Guided Summaries. In *TAC 2011 Workshop NIST Gaithersburg, MD, USA*.

George Giannakopoulos and Vangelis Karkaletsis. 2013. Summary Evaluation: Together We Stand NPowER-ed. In Alexander Gelbukh, editor, *Computational Linguistics and Intelligent Text Processing*, volume 7817 of *Lecture Notes in Computer Science*, pages 436–450. Springer Berlin Heidelberg.

George Giannakopoulos, Mahmoud El-Haj, Benoit Favre, Marina Litvak, Josef Steinberger, and Vasudeva Varma. 2011. TAC2011 MultiLing Pilot Overview. In *TAC 2011 Workshop*, Gaithersburg, MD, USA. NIST.

Christian Hänig, Robert Remus, and Xose de la Puente. 2015. ExB Themis: Extensive Feature Extraction from Word Alignments for Semantic Textual Similarity. In *Proceedings of the 9th International Workshop on Semantic Evaluations*, Denver, USA. ACL - to appear.

Kai Hong, John Conroy, Benoit Favre, Alex Kulesza, Hui Lin, and Ani Nenkova. 2014. A Repository of State of the Art and Competitive Baseline Summaries for Generic News Summarization. In *Proceedings of the Ninth International Conference on Language Resources and Evaluation (LREC'14)*, pages 1608–1616, Reykjavik, Iceland, May. European Language Resources Association (ELRA).

John P. A. Ioannidis. 2005. Why Most Published Research Findings Are False. *PLoS Med*, 2(8):e124, 08.

Mikael Kågebäck, Olof Mogren, Nina Tahmasebi, and Devdatt Dubhashi. 2014. Extractive Summarization using Continuous Vector Space Models. In *Proceedings of the 2nd Workshop on Continuous Vector Space Models and their Compositionality (CVSC)*, pages 31–39. ACL.

Jeff Kubina, John Conroy, and Judith Schlesinger. 2013. ACL 2013 MultiLing Pilot Overview. In *Proceedings of the MultiLing 2013 Workshop on Multilingual Multi-document Summarization*, pages 29–38, Sofia, Bulgaria, August. ACL.

Taku Kudo, Kaoru Yamamoto, and Yuji Matsumoto. 2004. Applying Conditional Random Fields to Japanese Morphological Analysis. In *Proceedings of EMNLP 2004*, pages 230–237. ACL.

Taku Kudo. 2013. MeCab: Yet Another Part-of-Speech and Morphological Analyzer. `http://mecab.googlecode.com/svn/trunk/mecab/doc/index.html`. Accessed: 2015-04-24.

Lei Li, Corina Forascu, Mahmoud El-Haj, and George Giannakopoulos. 2013a. Multi-document multilingual summarization corpus preparation, Part 1: Arabic, English, Greek, Chinese, Romanian. In *Proceedings of the MultiLing 2013 Workshop on Multilingual Multi-document Summarization*, pages 1–12, Sofia, Bulgaria, August. ACL.

Lei Li, Lei Heng, Jia Yu, and Yu Li. 2013b. CIST System Report for ACL MultiLing 2013. *Proceedings of the Multiling 2013 Workshop on Multilingual Multi-document Summarization*, pages 39–44.

Chin-Yew Lin. 2004. ROUGE: A Package for Automatic Evaluation of Summaries. In Stan Szpakowicz Marie-Francine Moens, editor, *Text Summarization Branches Out: Proceedings of the ACL-04 Workshop*, pages 74–81, Barcelona, Spain, July. ACL.

Kikuo Maekawa, Makoto Yamazaki, Toshinobu Ogiso, Takehiko Maruyama, Hideki Ogura, Wakako Kashino, Hanae Koiso, Masaya Yamaguchi, Makiro Tanaka, and Yasuharu Den. 2014. Balanced corpus of contemporary written Japanese. *Language Resources and Evaluation*, 48(2):345–371.

Rada Mihalcea and Paul Tarau. 2004. TextRank: Bringing order into texts. *Proceedings of EMNLP 2004*, pages 404–411.

Tomas Mikolov, Kai Chen, Greg Corrado, and Jeffrey Dean. 2013. Efficient Estimation of Word Representations in Vector Space. In *Proceedings of the Workshops at ICLR 2013*, volume abs/1301.3781.

NECTEC. 2003. LEXiTRON. `http://www.nectec.or.th/`. An adapted version of LEXiTRON developed by NECTEC.

Jun-Ping Ng, Yan Chen, Min-Yen Kan, and Zhoujun Li. 2014. Exploiting Timelines to Enhance Multi-document Summarization. In *Proceedings of the 52nd Annual Meeting of the Association for Computational Linguistics, ACL*, pages 923–933.

Joshua O'Madadhain, Danyel Fisher, and Tom Nelson. 2010. JUNG: Java Universal Network/Graph Framework. `http://jung.sourceforge.net/`.

Gerard Salton. 1989. *Automatic Text Processing: The Transformation, Analysis, and Retrieval of Information by Computer*. Addison-Wesley Longman Publishing Co., Inc., Boston, MA, USA.

Vee Satayamas. 2014. thailang4r. `https://github.com/veer66/thailang4r`. Accessed: 2015-04-24.

Josef Steinberger. 2013. The UWB Summariser at Multiling-2013. *Proceedings of the MultiLing 2013 Workshop on Multilingual Multi-document Summarization*, pages 50–54.

Stefan Thomas. 2012. Verbesserung einer Erkennungs- und Normalisierungsmaschine für natürlichsprachige Zeitausdrücke. Master thesis, Universität Leipzig. Fakultät für Mathematik und Informatik. Institut für Informatik.

Xiaojun Wan. 2007. TimedTextRank: adding the temporal dimension to multi-document summarization. In *SIGIR 2007: Proceedings of the 30th Annual International ACM SIGIR Conference on Research and Development in Information Retrieval*, pages 867–868.

MultiLing 2015: Multilingual Summarization of Single and Multi-Documents, On-line Fora, and Call-center Conversations

George Giannakopoulos
NCSR Demokritos
Athens, Greece
ggianna@iit.demokritos.gr

Jeff Kubina
U.S. Dep. of Defense
Ft. Meade, MD
jmkubin@tycho.ncsc.mil

John M. Conroy
IDA/Center for Comp. Sciences
Bowie, MD
conroy@super.org

Josef Steinberger
University of West Bohemia
Pilsen, Czech Republic
jstein@kiv.zcu.cz

Benoit Favre
University of Marseille
Marseille, France
benoit.favre@lif.univ-mrs.fr

Mijail Kabadjov, Udo Kruschwitz, Massimo Poesio
University of Essex
Colchester, UK
{malexa,udo,poesio}@essex.ac.uk

Abstract

In this paper we present an overview of MultiLing 2015, a special session at SIGdial 2015. MultiLing is a community-driven initiative that pushes the state-of-the-art in Automatic Summarization by providing data sets and fostering further research and development of summarization systems. There were in total 23 participants this year submitting their system outputs to one or more of the four tasks of MultiLing: MSS, MMS, OnForumS and CCCS. We provide a brief overview of each task and its participation and evaluation.

1 Introduction

Initially text-summarization research was fostered by the evaluation exercises, or tasks, at the Document Understanding and Text Analysis Conferences that started in 2001. But within the past five years a community of researchers have formed that push forward the development of text-summarization methods by creating evaluation tasks, dubbed MultiLing, that involve many languages (not just English) and/or many topical domains (not just news). The MultiLing 2011 and 2013 tasks evolved into a community-driven initiative that pushes the state-of-the-art in Automatic Summarization by providing data sets and fostering further research and development of summarization systems. The aim of MultiLing (Giannakopoulos et al., 2015) at SIGdial 2015 is the same: provide tasks for single and multi-document multilingual summarization and introduce pilot tasks to promote research in summarizing human dialog in online fora and customer call centers. This report provides an outline of the four tasks MultiLing supported at SIGdial; specifically the objective of each task, the data sets used by each task, and the level of participation and success by the research community within the task.

The remainder of the paper is organised as follows: section §2 briefly presents the Multilingual Single-document Summarization task, section §3 the Multilingual Multi-document summarization task, section §4 the Online Forum Summarization task, section §5 the Call-center Conversation summarization task, and finally we draw conclusions on the overall endeavour in section §6.

2 Multilingual Single Document Summarization Task

2.1 Task Description

The multilingual single-document summarization (MSS) task (Kubina and Conroy, 2015a) was created to foster the research and development of single document summarization methods that perform well on documents covering many languages and topics. Historically such tasks have predominantly focused on English news documents, see for example Nenkova (2005). The specific objective for this task was to generate a single document summary for each of the provided Wikipedia featured articles within at least one of the 38 languages provided. Wikipedia featured articles are selected by the consensus of their editors to be examples of some of the best written articles of a Wikipedia that fulfil all the required criteria with respect to accuracy, neutrality, completeness, and

Proceedings of the SIGDIAL 2015 Conference, pages 270–274,
Prague, Czech Republic, 2-4 September 2015.

style. Such articles make an excellent source of test data for single document summarization methods since they each have a well written summary (one of the style criterion), cover many languages, and have a diverse range of topics.

2.2 Participation, Evaluation, and Results

Participation in the 2015 MSS task was excellent, 23 summarization systems were submitted by seven teams. Four of the teams submitted summaries for all 38 languages and the remaining three submitted summaries covering four languages. English was the only language for which all participating systems submitted summaries.

For the evaluation a simple baseline summary was created from each article using the initial text of the article's body truncated to the size of the articles human summary. Its purpose, since it is so easy to compute, is to provide a summary score that participating systems should be able to exceed. An oracle summary was computed for each article using a covering algorithm (Davis et al., 2012) that selected sentences from the body text that covers the words in the summary using a minimal number of sentences until their aggregate size exceeds the summary. The oracle summary scores provide an approximate upper bound on the achievable summary scores and were, as expected, much higher than any submitted systems score.

The baseline, oracle, and submitted summaries were scored against the human summaries using ROUGE-2, -3, -4 (Lin, 2004) and MeMoG (Giannakopoulos et al., 2008). Details of the preprocessing applied to the text and the performance of each submitted system are in (Kubina and Conroy, 2015b), but overall 14 of the 23 systems did better than the baseline summary for at least half of the languages they partook in.

The ROUGE and MeMog scoring methods provide an automatic measure of summaries, which are good predictors of human judgements. A human evaluation of the summaries, that is currently underway, will measure the responsiveness and readability of each teams best performing system.

3 Multilingual Multi-Document Summarization Task

3.1 Task Description

This multilingual multi-document summarization (MMS) (Giannakopoulos, 2015) task aims to evaluate the application of partially or fully language-independent summarization algorithms. Each system participating in the task was called upon to provide summaries for a range of different languages, based on corresponding language-specific corpora. Systems were to summarize texts in at least two of the ten different languages: Arabic, Chinese, Czech, English, French, Greek, Hebrew, Hindi, Romanian, Spanish.

The task aims at the real problem of summarizing news topics, parts of which may be described or may happen in different moments in time. We consider, similarly to previous MultiLing efforts (Giannakopoulos et al., 2011; Li et al., 2013) that news topics can be seen as *event sequences*:

Definition 1. *An event sequence is a set of atomic (self-sufficient) event descriptions, sequenced in time, that share main actors, location of occurrence or some other important factor. Event sequences may refer to topics such as a natural disaster, a crime investigation, a set of negotiations focused on a single political issue, a sports event.*

The multi-document summarization task required participants to generate a fluent and representative summary from the set of documents describing an event sequence. The language of each document set belonged to one of the aforementioned set of languages and all the documents in a set were of the same language. The output summary was expected to be in the same language and between 240 and 250 words, with the exception of Chinese, where the output summary size was expected to be 333 characters (i.e., 1000 bytes in UTF-8 encoding).

The task corpus is based on a set of WikiNews English news articles comprising 15 topics, each containing ten documents. Each English document was translated into the other nine languages to create sentence-parallel translations. (Li et al., 2013; Elhadad et al., 2013).

3.2 Participation, Evaluation, and Results

Ten teams submitted 18 systems to the MMS task. Three randomly chosen topics (namely topics M001, M002, M003) out of the 15 topics, were provided as training sets to the participants for the task and were excluded when ranking of the systems.

The ranking was based on automatic evaluations methods using human model summaries provided by fluent speakers of each corresponding language (native speakers in the general case).

ROUGE variations (ROUGE-1, ROUGE-2) (Lin, 2004) and the AutoSummENG-MeMoG (Giannakopoulos et al., 2008) and NPowER (Giannakopoulos and Karkaletsis, 2013) methods were applied to automatically evaluate the summarization systems. There was a clear indication that ROUGE measures were extremely sensitive to different preprocessing types and that different implementations (taking into account multilinguality or not during tokenization) may offer significantly different results (even different order of magnitude in the score). Thus, the evaluation was based on the language-independent MeMoG method.

On average 12 system runs were executed per language, with the least popular language being Chinese, and the most popular being English. On average across all languages, except for Chinese, 13 of the 18 systems surpassed the baseline, according to the automatic evaluation. The systems employed a variety of approaches to tackle the multi-document summarization challenge as described in the following paragraphs.

The approaches contained various types of preprocessing, from POS tagging and extraction of POS patterns, to the representation of documents to language-independent latent spaces before the summarization or reduced vector spaces (e.g. through PCA (Jolliffe, 2002)). It is also interesting to note that more than 10 different tools were used in various preprocessing steps, such as stemming, tokenization, sentence splitting, due to the language dependence limitations of many such tools. Overall, in comparison to the previous MultiLing MMS challenge, this time it appears that reuse of existing tools for such preprocessing was increased (as detailed in individual system reports).

Subtopics were identified in some cases through various methods, such as the use of bag-of-word vector space representation of sentences and cosine-similarity-based clustering, or probabilistic clustering methods (e.g. hLDA (Blei et al., 2004)).

For the sentence scoring, cosine similarity was also used as a means for sentence selection, where the topic(s) of a document group was projected in a vector space (either bag-of-words or latent topic space). Some of the MMS participants' systems used supervised optimization methods (e.g. polytope model optimization, genetic algorithms) on rich feature spaces to either maximize coverage of the output summaries, or train models for sentence scoring. The feature spaces went beyond words to linguistic features, position features, etc. Other systems used graph methods, relying on the "importance" of sentences as indicated by methods such as PageRank (Page et al., 1999).

Finally, redundancy was tackled through cosine similarity between sentences, or in the sentence selection process itself as penalty to optimization cost functions.

Overall, once again the multi-document, multilingual task showed that multilinguality implies a need for many linguistic resources, but is significantly helped by the application of machine learning methods. It appears that these latter approaches transfer the burden to the annotation of good training corpora.

4 OnForumS Task

4.1 Task description

The Online Forum Summarization (OnForumS) pilot task (Kabadjov and Steinberger, 2015) investigated how the mass of comments found on news providers web sites (e.g., The Guardian) can be summarized. We posited that a crucial initial step towards that goal is to determine what comments link to either specific news snippets or comments of other users. Furthermore, a set of labels for a given link is articulated to capture phenomena such as agreement and sentiment with respect to the comment target. Solving this labelled-linking problem can enable recognition of salience (e.g., snippets/comments with most links) and relations between comments (e.g., agreement). For instance, comment sentences linked to the same article sentence can be seen as forming a "cluster" of sentences on a specific point/topic. Moreover, having labels capturing argument structure and sentiment enables computing statistics within such topic clusters on how many readers are in favour or against the point raised by the article sentence and what is the general 'feeling' about it.

The task included data in two languages, English and Italian, provided by the FP7 SENSEI project.[1]

4.2 Participation, Evaluation and Results

Four research groups participated in the OnForumS, each submitting two runs. In addition, two baseline system runs were included making a total of ten different system runs.

[1] http://www.sensei-conversation.eu/

Submissions were evaluated via crowdsourcing on Crowd Flowerwhich is a commonly used method for evaluating HLT systems (Snow et al., 2008; Callison-Burch, 2009). The crowdsourcing HIT was designed as a validation task (as opposed to annotation), where each system proposed link and labels are presented to a contributor for their validation.

The approach used for the OnForumS evaluation is IR-inspired and based on the concept of *pooling* used in TREC (Soboroff, 2010), where the assumption is that possible links that were not proposed by any system are deemed irrelevant. Then from those links proposed by systems, four categories are formed as follows:

(a) links proposed in 4 or more system runs
(b) links proposed in 3 system runs
(c) links proposed in 2 system runs
(d) links proposed only once

Due to the volume of links proposed by systems, a stratified sample was extracted for evaluation based on the following strategy: all of the **a** and **b** links[2] and a third of each **c** and **d** links selected at random.

Once the crowdsourcing exercise was completed, correct and incorrect links were counted.[3] From those links validated as correct, the correct and incorrect argument and sentiment labels were counted. Using these counts precision scores were computed. System runs were then ranked based on these precision scores. For the linking task no system surpassed the baseline algorithm based on overlap and scores were substantially higher for English than for Italian.

A recall-based evaluation was also carried out on a smaller gold standard set created from the validated data by taking all 'yes' validations of links as gold links and then all labels for argument and sentiment with 'yes' validations as the gold labels for those links.

5 CCCS Task

5.1 Task description

The call-center conversation summarization pilot task consists in automatically generating abstractive summaries of spoken conversations between a customer and an agent solving a problem over the phone. This task is different from news summarization in that dialogues need to be analysed in a deeper manner in order to recover the problem being addressed and how it is solved, and convert spontaneous utterances to reported speech. Generating such summaries, called conversation synopses, in this framework, is challenging for extractive approaches, and therefore should make participants focus on abstractive summarization. The task leverages a corpus of French and Italian conversations as well as English translations of those dialogues. The data is provided by the FP7 SENSEI project. For more details on the CCCS task see (Favre et al., 2015).

5.2 Participation, evaluation and results

Four systems have been submitted to this first edition of the CCCS task, by two research groups. In addition, three extractive baselines were evaluated for comparison purposes. The official metric was ROUGE-2. Evaluation on each of the languages shows that the submitted systems had difficulties beating the extractive baselines, and that human annotators are consistent in their synopsis production (for more details see (Favre et al., 2015)). We will focus on extending the evaluation in order to overcome the limitations of ROUGE, and assess the abstractiveness of the generated synopses.

6 Conclusion

MultiLing has been running for a few years now and has proved a successful evaluation campaign for automatic summarization. MultiLing 2015 is the third chapter of the campaign and participation was excellent with 23 participants submitting two or more system runs across the four tasks that the campaign comprises.

The next steps for the classical tasks MSS and MMS is to continue expanding the corpora in size and across languages, whereas for the pilot tasks is to further precise the boundaries of the new tasks and bridge the gaps in the evaluation methodologies by overcoming the limitations of ROUGE in order to assess abstractiveness and minimizing the effect of 'cheating' workers in crowdsourcing (e.g., by incorporating a probabilistic model of annotation, such as the one put forward by (Passonneau and Carpenter, 2013) to filter better noisy crowdsourcing data).

The next MultiLing is planned for 2017.

[2] The popular links (**a** and **b**) were not that many, hence, we chose to include all.

[3] Based on CrowdFlower's aggregated judgements.

Acknowledgements

The research leading to these results has received funding from the European Union - 7th Framework Programme (FP7/2007-2013) under grant agreement 610916 SENSEI. The research leading to these results has received funding from the European Regional Development Fund of the European Union and from national funds in the context of the research project 'SentIMAGi - Brand monitoring and reputation management via multimodal sentiment analysis' (ISR_2935) under the Regional Operational Programme Attica (Priority Axis 3 Improving competitiveness, innovation and digital convergence) of the 'Bilateral R&D Cooperation between Greece and Israel 2013-2015' of the Action of national scope 'Bilateral , Multilateral and Regional R&D Cooperation'.

References

D. M. Blei, T. L. Griffiths, M. I. Jordan, and J. B. Tenenbaum. 2004. Hierarchical topic models and the nested chinese restaurant process. *NIPS*, 16:17.

C. Callison-Burch. 2009. Fast, cheap, and creative: Evaluating translation quality using amazons mechanical turk. In *Proceedings of EMNLP*, volume 1, pages 286–295.

S. T. Davis, J. M. Conroy, and J. D. Schlesinger. 2012. Occams - an optimal combinatorial covering algorithm for multi-document summarization. In *ICDM Workshops*, pages 454–463. IEEE Computer Society.

M. Elhadad, S. Miranda-Jiménez, J. Steinberger, and G. Giannakopoulos. 2013. Multi-document multilingual summarization corpus preparation, Part 2: Czech, Hebrew and Spanish. In *MultiLing 2013 Workshop in ACL 2013*, Sofia.

B. Favre, E. Stepanov, J. Trione, F. Béchet, and G. Riccardi. 2015. Call Centre Conversation Summarization: A Pilot Task at Multiling 2015. In *SIGDIAL*.

G. Giannakopoulos and V. Karkaletsis. 2013. Summary evaluation: Together we stand NPowER-ed. In *Computational Linguistics and Intelligent Text Processing*, pages 436–450. Springer.

G. Giannakopoulos, V. Karkaletsis, G. Vouros, and P. Stamatopoulos. 2008. Summarization system evaluation revisited: N-gram graphs. *ACM Trans. Speech Lang. Process.*, 5(3):5:1–5:39, October.

G. Giannakopoulos, M. El-Haj, B. Favre, M. Litvak, J. Steinberger, and V. Varma. 2011. TAC2011 MultiLing Pilot Overview. In *TAC 2011 Workshop*.

G. Giannakopoulos, J. Kubina, J. Conroy, J. Steinberger, B. Favre, M. Kabadjov, U. Kruschwitz, and M. Poesio. 2015. MultiLing 2015. `http://multiling.iit.demokritos.gr/pages/view/1516/multiling-2015`. [Online; accessed 19-July-2015].

G. Giannakopoulos. 2015. MMS MultiLing 2015 Task. `http://multiling.iit.demokritos.gr/pages/view/1540/task-mms-multi-document-summarization-data-and-information`. [Online; accessed 19-July-2015].

I. Jolliffe. 2002. *Principal component analysis*. Wiley Online Library.

M. A. Kabadjov and J. Steinberger. 2015. OnForumS MultiLing 2015 Task. `http://multiling.iit.demokritos.gr/pages/view/1531/task-onforums-data-and-information`. [Online; accessed 19-July-2015].

J. Kubina and J. Conroy. 2015a. MSS MultiLing 2015 Task. `http://multiling.iit.demokritos.gr/pages/view/1532/task-mss-single-document-summarization-data-and-information`. [Online; accessed 19-July-2015].

J. Kubina and J. Conroy. 2015b. SIGDIAL 2015 Multilingual Single-Document Summarization Task Overview. In *MultiLing 2015 Addendum*.

L. Li, C. Forascu, M. El-Haj, and G. Giannakopoulos. 2013. Multi-document multilingual summarization corpus preparation, part 1: Arabic, english, greek, chinese, romanian. In *MultiLing 2013 Workshop in ACL 2013*, Sofia.

C.-Y. Lin. 2004. Rouge: A package for automatic evaluation of summaries. In *Text Summarization Branches Out: Proceedings of the ACL-04 Workshop*, pages 74–81.

A. Nenkova. 2005. Automatic text summarization of newswire: lessons learned from the document understanding conference. In *Proceedings of AAAI*, pages 1436–1441. AAAI Press.

L. Page, S. Brin, R. Motwani, and T. Winograd. 1999. The PageRank citation ranking: bringing order to the Web. Technical report, Stanford InfoLab.

R. J. Passonneau and B. Carpenter. 2013. The Benefits of a Model of Annotation. In *Proceedings of the 7th LAW at ACL*, pages 187–195, Sofia.

R. Snow, B. O'Connor, D. Jurafsky, and A. Y. Ng. 2008. Cheap and fast – but is it good?: Evaluating nonexpert annotations for natural language tasks. In *Proceedings of EMNLP*, pages 254–263.

I. Soboroff. 2010. Test Collection Diagnosis and Treatment. In *Proceedings of the Third International Workshop on Evaluating Information Access (EVIA)*, pages 34–41, Tokyo.

Stochastic Language Generation in Dialogue using Recurrent Neural Networks with Convolutional Sentence Reranking

Tsung-Hsien Wen, Milica Gašić, Dongho Kim, Nikola Mrkšić,
Pei-Hao Su, David Vandyke and **Steve Young**
Cambridge University Engineering Department,
Trumpington Street, Cambridge, CB2 1PZ, UK
{thw28,mg436,dk449,nm480,phs26,djv27,sjy}@cam.ac.uk

Abstract

The natural language generation (NLG) component of a spoken dialogue system (SDS) usually needs a substantial amount of handcrafting or a well-labeled dataset to be trained on. These limitations add significantly to development costs and make cross-domain, multi-lingual dialogue systems intractable. Moreover, human languages are context-aware. The most natural response should be directly learned from data rather than depending on predefined syntaxes or rules. This paper presents a statistical language generator based on a joint recurrent and convolutional neural network structure which can be trained on dialogue act-utterance pairs without any semantic alignments or predefined grammar trees. Objective metrics suggest that this new model outperforms previous methods under the same experimental conditions. Results of an evaluation by human judges indicate that it produces not only high quality but linguistically varied utterances which are preferred compared to n-gram and rule-based systems.

1 Introduction

Conventional spoken dialogue systems (SDS) are expensive to build because many of the processing components require a substantial amount of handcrafting (Ward and Issar, 1994; Bohus and Rudnicky, 2009). In the past decade, significant progress has been made in applying statistical methods to automate the speech understanding and dialogue management components of an SDS, including making them more easily extensible to other application domains (Young et al., 2013; Gašić et al., 2014; Henderson et al., 2014). However, due to the difficulty of collecting semantically-annotated corpora, the use of data-driven NLG for SDS remains relatively unexplored and rule-based generation remains the norm for most systems (Cheyer and Guzzoni, 2007; Mirkovic and Cavedon, 2011).

The goal of the NLG component of an SDS is to map an abstract dialogue act consisting of an act type and a set of attribute-value pairs[1] into an appropriate surface text (see Table 1 below for some examples). An early example of a statistical NLG system is HALOGEN by Langkilde and Knight (1998) which uses an n-gram language model (LM) to rerank a set of candidates generated by a handcrafted generator. In order to reduce the amount of handcrafting and make the approach more useful in SDS, Oh and Rudnicky (2000) replaced the handcrafted generator with a set of word-based n-gram LM-based generators, one for each dialogue type and then reranked the generator outputs using a set of rules to produce the final response. Although Oh and Rudnicky (2000)'s approach limits the amount of handcrafting to a small set of post-processing rules, their system incurs a large computational cost in the over-generation phase and it is difficult to ensure that all of the required semantics are covered by the selected output. More recently, a phrase-based NLG system called BAGEL trained from utterances aligned with coarse-grained semantic concepts has been described (Mairesse et al., 2010; Mairesse and Young, 2014). By implicitly modelling paraphrases, Bagel can generate linguistically varied utterances. However, collecting semantically-aligned corpora is expensive and time consuming, which limits Bagel's scalability to new domains.

This paper presents a neural network based NLG system that can be fully trained from dia-

[1] Here and elsewhere, attributes are frequently referred to as *slots*.

Proceedings of the SIGDIAL 2015 Conference, pages 275–284,
Prague, Czech Republic, 2-4 September 2015.

log act-utterance pairs without any semantic alignments between the two. We start in Section 3 by presenting a generator based on a recurrent neural network language model (RNNLM) (Mikolov et al., 2010; Mikolov et al., 2011a) which is trained on a *delexicalised* corpus (Henderson et al., 2014) whereby each value has been replaced by a symbol representing its corresponding slot. In a final post-processing phase, these slot symbols are converted back to the corresponding slot values.

While generating, the RNN generator is conditioned on an auxiliary dialogue act feature and a controlling gate to over-generate candidate utterances for subsequent reranking. In order to account for arbitrary slot-value pairs that cannot be routinely delexicalized in our corpus, Section 3.1 describes a convolutional neural network (CNN) (Collobert and Weston, 2008; Kalchbrenner et al., 2014) sentence model which is used to validate the semantic consistency of candidate utterances during reranking. Finally, by adding a backward RNNLM reranker into the model in Section 3.2, output fluency is further improved. Training and decoding details of the proposed system are described in Section 3.3 and 3.4.

Section 4 presents an evaluation of the proposed system in the context of an application providing information about restaurants in the San Francisco area. In Section 4.2, we first show that new generator outperforms Oh and Rudnicky (2000)'s utterance class LM approach using objective metrics, whilst at the same time being more computationally efficient. In order to assess the subjective performance of our system, pairwise preference tests are presented in Section 4.3. The results show that our approach can produce high quality utterances that are considered to be more natural than a rule-based generator. Moreover, by sampling utterances from the top reranked output, our system can also generate linguistically varied utterances. Section 4.4 provides a more detailed analysis of the contribution of each component of the system to the final performance. We conclude with a brief summary and future work in Section 5.

2 Related Work

Conventional approaches to NLG typically divide the task into sentence planning, and surface realisation. Sentence planning maps input semantic symbols into an intermediary tree-like or template structure representing the utterance, then surface realisation converts the intermediate structure into the final text (Walker et al., 2002; Stent et al., 2004; Dethlefs et al., 2013). As noted above, one of the first statistical NLG methods that requires almost no handcrafting or semantic alignments was an n-gram based approach by Oh and Rudnicky (2000). Ratnaparkhi (2002) later addressed the limitations of n-gram LMs in the over-generation phase by using a more sophisticated generator based on a syntactic dependency tree.

Statistical approaches have also been studied for sentence planning, for example, generating the most likely context-free derivations given a corpus (Belz, 2008) or maximising the expected reward using reinforcement learning (Rieser and Lemon, 2010). Angeli et al. (2010) train a set of log-linear models to predict individual generation decisions given the previous ones, using only domain-independent features. Along similar lines, by casting NLG as a template extraction and reranking problem, Kondadadi et al. (2013) show that outputs produced by an SVM reranker are comparable to human-authored texts.

The use of neural network-based approaches to NLG is relatively unexplored. The stock reporter system ANA by Kukich (1987) is a network based NLG system, in which the generation task is divided into a sememe-to-morpheme network followed by a morpheme-to-phrase network. Recent advances in recurrent neural network-based language models (RNNLM) (Mikolov et al., 2010; Mikolov et al., 2011a) have demonstrated the value of distributed representations and the ability to model arbitrarily long dependencies for both speech recognition and machine translation tasks. Sutskever et al. (2011) describes a simple variant of the RNN that can generate meaningful sentences by learning from a character-level corpus. More recently, Karpathy and Fei-Fei (2014) have demonstrated that an RNNLM is capable of generating image descriptions by conditioning the network model on a pre-trained convolutional image feature representation. This work provides a key inspiration for the system described here. Zhang and Lapata (2014) describes interesting work using RNNs to generate Chinese poetry.

A specific requirement of NLG for dialogue systems is that the concepts encoded in the abstract system dialogue act must be conveyed accurately by the generated surface utterance, and simple unconstrained RNNLMs which rely on embedding at the word level (Mikolov et al., 2013; Pennington et al., 2014) are rather poor at this. As a consequence, new methods have been investigated to learn distributed representations for phrases and even sentences by training models using different structures (Collobert and Weston, 2008; Socher et al., 2013). Convolutional Neural Networks (CNNs) were first studied in computer vision for object recognition (Lecun et al., 1998). By stacking several convolutional-pooling layers followed by a fully connected feed-forward network, CNNs are claimed to be able to extract several levels of translational-invariant features that are useful in classification tasks. The convolutional sentence model (Kalchbrenner et al., 2014; Kim, 2014) adopts the same methodology but collapses the two dimensional convolution and pooling process into a single dimension. The resulting model is claimed to represent the state-of-the-art for many speech and NLP related tasks (Kalchbrenner et al., 2014; Sainath et al., 2013).

3 Recurrent Generation Model

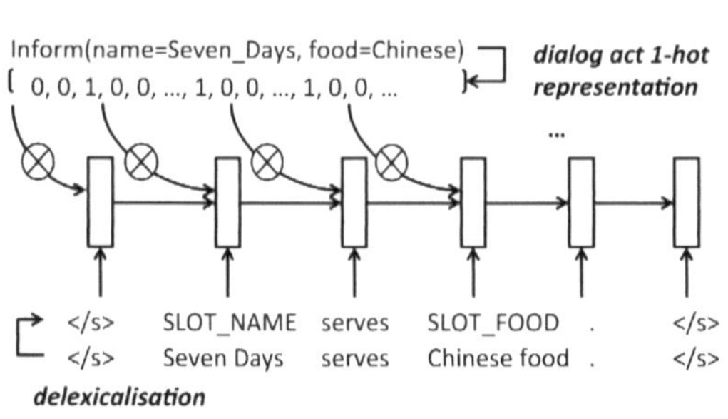

Figure 1: An unrolled view of the RNN-based generation model. It operates on a delexicalised utterance and a 1-hot encoded feature vector specified by a dialogue act type and a set of slot-value pairs. $\otimes$ indicates the gate used for controlling the on/off states of certain feature values. The output connection layer is omitted here for simplicity.

The generation model proposed in this paper is based on an RNNLM architecture (Mikolov et al., 2010) in which a 1-hot encoding $\mathbf{w}_t$ of a token[2] w_t is input at each time step t conditioned on a recurrent hidden layer $\mathbf{h}_t$ and outputs the probability distribution of the next token w_{t+1}. Therefore, by sampling input tokens one by one from the output distribution of the RNN until a stop sign is generated (Karpathy and Fei-Fei, 2014) or some required constraint is satisfied (Zhang and Lapata, 2014), the network can produce a sequence of tokens which can be lexicalised to form the required utterance.

In order to ensure that the generated utterance represents the intended meaning, the input vectors $\mathbf{w}_t$ are augmented by a control vector $\mathbf{f}$ constructed from the concatenation of 1-hot encodings of the required dialogue act and its associated slot-value pairs. The auxiliary information provided by this control vector tends to decay over time because of the *vanishing gradient problem* (Mikolov and Zweig, 2012; Bengio et al., 1994). Hence, $\mathbf{f}$ is reapplied to the RNN at every time step as in Karpathy and Fei-Fei (2014).

In detail, the recurrent generator shown in Figure 1 is defined as follows:

$$\mathbf{h}_t = sigmoid(\mathbf{W}_{hh}\mathbf{h}_{t-1} + \mathbf{W}_{wh}\mathbf{w}_t + \mathbf{W}_{fh}\mathbf{f}_t) \quad (1)$$

$$P(w_{t+1}|w_t, w_{t-1}, ...w_0, \mathbf{f}_t) = softmax(\mathbf{W}_{ho}\mathbf{h}_t) \quad (2)$$

$$w_{t+1} \sim P(w_{t+1}|w_t, w_{t-1}, ...w_0, \mathbf{f}_t) \quad (3)$$

where $\mathbf{W}_{hh}$, $\mathbf{W}_{wh}$, $\mathbf{W}_{fh}$, and $\mathbf{W}_{ho}$ are the learned network weight matrices. $\mathbf{f}_t$ is a gated version of $\mathbf{f}$ designed to discourage duplication of information in the generated output in which each segment $\mathbf{f}_s$ of the control vector $\mathbf{f}$ corresponding to slot s is replaced by

$$\mathbf{f}_{s,t} = \mathbf{f}_s \odot \delta^{t-t_s} \quad (4)$$

where t_s is the time at which slot s first appears in the output, $\delta \leq 1$ is a decay factor, and $\odot$ denotes element-wise multiplication. The effect of this gating is to decrease the probability of regenerating slot symbols that have already been generated, and to increase the probability of rendering all of the information encoded in $\mathbf{f}$.

The tokenisation resulting from delexicalising slots and values does not work for all cases. For example, some slot-value pairs such as *food=dont_care* or *kids_allowed=false* cannot be directly modelled using this technique because there is no explicit value to delexicalise in the training corpus. As a consequence, the model is prone to errors when these slot-value pairs are required. A further problem is that the RNNLM generator selects words based only on the preceding history, whereas some sentence forms depend on the backward context.

[2]We use *token* instead of *word* because our model operates on text for which slot names and values have been delexicalised.

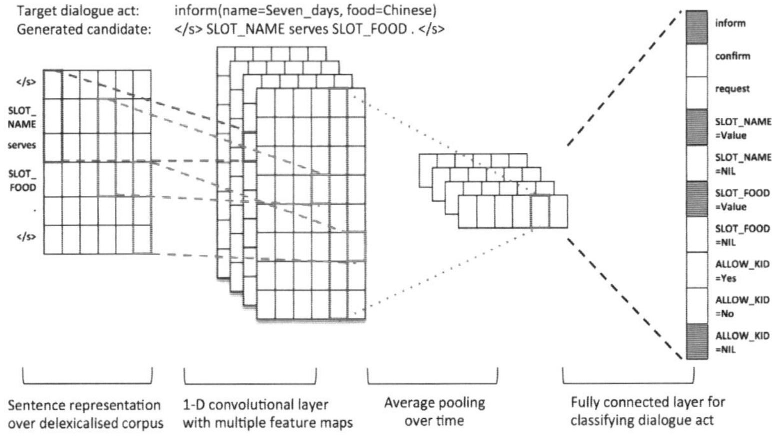

Figure 2: Our simple variant of CNN sentence model as described in Kalchbrenner et al. (2014).

To deal with these issues, candidates generated by the RNNLM are reranked using two models. Firstly, a convolutional neural network (CNN) sentence model (Kalchbrenner et al., 2014; Kim, 2014) is used to ensure that the required dialogue act and slot-value pairs are represented in the generated utterance, including the non-standard cases. Secondly, a *backward* RNNLM is used to rerank utterances presented in reverse order.

3.1 Convolutional Sentence Model

The CNN sentence model is shown in Figure 2. Given a candidate utterance of length n, an utterance matrix $\mathbf{U}$ is constructed by stacking embeddings $\mathrm{w_t}$ of each token in the utterance:

$$\mathbf{U} = \begin{bmatrix} \text{——} & \mathrm{w_0} & \text{——} \\ \text{——} & \mathrm{w_1} & \text{——} \\ & \ldots & \\ \text{——} & \mathrm{w_{n-1}} & \text{——} \end{bmatrix}. \quad (5)$$

A set of K convolutional mappings are then applied to the utterance to form a set of feature detectors. The outputs of these detectors are combined and fed into a fully-connected feed-forward network to classify the action type and whether each required slot is mentioned or not.

Each mapping k consists of a one-dimensional convolution between a filter $\mathbf{m}_\mathrm{k} \in \mathbb{R}^m$ and the utterance matrix $\mathbf{U}$ to produce another matrix $\mathbf{C}^\mathrm{k}$:

$$\mathbf{C}^\mathrm{k}{}_{i,j} = \mathbf{m}_\mathrm{k}{}^\intercal \mathbf{U}_{i-m+1:i,j} \quad (6)$$

where m is the filter size, and i,j is the row and column index respectively. The outputs of each column of $\mathbf{C}^\mathrm{k}$ are then pooled by averaging[3] over time:

$$\mathbf{h}_\mathrm{k} = \left[\bar{\mathbf{C}}^k_{:,0}, \bar{\mathbf{C}}^k_{:,1}, ..., \bar{\mathbf{C}}^k_{:,h-1}\right] \quad (7)$$

where h is the size of embedding and $k = 1 \ldots K$. Last, the K pooled feature vectors $\mathbf{h}_k$ are passed through a nonlinearity function to obtain the final feature map.

3.2 Backward RNN reranking

As noted earlier, the quality of an RNN language model may be improved if both forward and backward contexts are considered. Previously, bidirectional RNNs (Schuster and Paliwal, 1997) have been shown to be effective for handwriting recognition (Graves et al., 2008), speech recognition (Graves et al., 2013), and machine translation (Sundermeyer et al., 2014). However, applying a bidirectional RNN directly in our generator is not straightforward since the generation process is sequential in time. Hence instead of integrating the bidirectional information into a single unified network, the forward and backward contexts are utilised separately by firstly generating candidates using the forward RNN generator, then using the log-likelihood computed by a backward RNNLM to rerank the candidates.

3.3 Training

Overall the proposed generation architecture requires three models to be trained: a forward RNN generator, a CNN reranker, and a backward RNN reranker. The objective functions for training the

[3]Max pooling was also tested but was found to be inferior to average pooling

two RNN models are the cross entropy errors between the predicted word distribution and the actual word distribution in the training corpus, whilst the objective for the CNN model is the cross entropy error between the predicted dialogue act and the actual dialogue act, summed over the act type and each slot. An l_2 regularisation term is added to the objective function for every 10 training examples as suggested in Mikolov et al. (2011b). The three networks share the same set of word embeddings, initialised with pre-trained word vectors provided by Pennington et al. (2014). All costs and gradients are computed and stochastic gradient descent is used to optimise the parameters. Both RNNs were trained with back propagation through time (Werbos, 1990). In order to prevent overfitting, early stopping was implemented using a held-out validation set.

3.4 Decoding

The decoding procedure is split into two phases: (a) over-generation, and (b) reranking. In the over-generation phase, the forward RNN generator conditioned on the given dialogue act, is used to sequentially generate utterances by random sampling of the predicted next word distributions. In the reranking phase, the hamming loss $cost_{CNN}$ of each candidate is computed using the CNN sentence model and the log-likelihood $cost_{bRNN}$ is computed using the backward RNN. Together with the log-likelihood $cost_{fRNN}$ from the forward RNN, the reranking score R is computed as:

$$R = -(cost_{fRNN} + cost_{bRNN} + cost_{CNN}). \quad (8)$$

This is the reranking criterion used to analyse each individual model in Section 4.4.

Generation quality can be further improved by introducing a slot error criterion ERR, which is the *number of slots generated that is either redundant or missing*. This is also used in Oh and Rudnicky (2000). Adding this to equation (8) yields the final reranking score R^*:

$$\begin{aligned} R^* = -(&cost_{fRNN} + cost_{bRNN} + \\ &cost_{CNN} + \lambda \mathrm{ERR}) \end{aligned} \quad (9)$$

In order to severely penalise nonsensical utterances, λ is set to 100 for both the proposed RNN system and our implementation of Oh and Rudnicky (2000)'s n-gram based system. This reranking criterion is used for both the automatic evaluation in Section 4.2 and the human evaluation in Section 4.3.

4 Experiments

4.1 Experimental Setup

The target application area for our generation system is a spoken dialogue system providing information about restaurants in San Francisco. There are 8 system dialogue act types such as *inform* to present information about restaurants, *confirm* to check that a slot value has been recognised correctly, and *reject* to advise that the user's constraints cannot be met (Table 1 gives the full list with examples); and there are 12 attributes (slots): *name, count, food, near, price, pricerange, postcode, phone, address, area, goodformeal, and kidsallowed*, in which all slots are categorical except *kidsallowed* which is binary.

To form a training corpus, dialogues from a set of 3577 dialogues collected in a user trial of a statistical dialogue manager proposed by Young et al. (2013) were randomly sampled and shown to workers recruited via the Amazon Mechanical Turk service. Workers were shown each dialogue turn by turn and asked to enter an appropriate system response in natural English corresponding to each system dialogue act. The resulting corpus contains 5193 hand-crafted system utterances from 1006 randomly sampled dialogues. Each categorical value was replaced by a token representing its slot, and slots that appeared multiple times in a dialogue act were merged into one. This resulted in 228 distinct dialogue acts.

The system was implemented using the Theano library (Bergstra et al., 2010; Bastien et al., 2012). The system was trained by partitioning the 5193 utterances into a training set, validation set, and testing set in the ratio 3:1:1, respectively. The frequency of each action type and slot-value pair differs quite markedly across the corpus, hence up-sampling was used to make the corpus more uniform. Since our generator works stochastically and the trained networks can differ depending on the initialisation, all the results shown below[4] were averaged over 10 randomly initialised networks. The BLEU-4 metric was used for the objective evaluation (Papineni et al., 2002). Multiple references for each test dialogue act were obtained by mapping them back to the 228 distinct dialogue acts, merging those delexicalised templates that have the same dialogue act specification, and then lexicalising those templates back to

[4]Except human evaluation, in which only one set of network was used.

Table 1: The 8 system dialogue acts with example realisations

#	Dialogue act and example realisations of our system, by sampling from top-5 candidates
1	inform(name="stroganoff restaurant",pricerange=cheap,near="fishermans wharf") *stroganoff restaurant is a cheap restaurant near fishermans wharf .* *stroganoff restaurant is in the cheap price range near fishermans wharf .*
2	reject(kidsallowed=yes,food="basque") *unfortunately there are 0 restaurants that allow kids and serve basque .*
3	informonly(name="bund shanghai restaurant", food="shanghainese") *i apologize , no other restaurant except bund shanghai restaurant that serves shanghainese .* *sorry but there is no place other than the restaurant bund shanghai restaurant for shanghainese .*
4	confirm(goodformeal=dontcare) *i am sorry . just to confirm . you are looking for a restaurant good for any meal ?* *can i confirm that you do not care about what meal they offer ?*
5	request(near) *would you like to dine near a particular location ?*
6	reqmore() *is there anything else i can do for you ?*
7	select(kidsallowed=yes, kidsallowed=no) *are you looking for a restaurant that allows kids , or does not allow kids ?*
8	goodbye() *thank you for calling . good bye .*

Table 2: Comparison of top-1 utterance between the RNN-based system and three baselines. A two-tailed Wilcoxon rank sum test was applied to compare the RNN model with the best O&R system (the 3-slot, 5g configuration) over 10 random seeds. (*=p<.005)

Method	beam	BLEU	ERR
handcrafted	n/a	0.440	0
kNN	n/a	0.591	17.2
O&R,0-slot,5g	1/20	0.527	635.2
O&R,1-slot,5g	1/20	0.610	460.8
O&R,2-slot,5g	1/20	0.719	142.0
O&R,3-slot,3g	1/20	0.760	74.4
O&R,3-slot,4g	1/20	0.758	53.2
O&R,3-slot,5g	1/20	0.757	47.8
Our Model	1/20	**0.777***	**0***

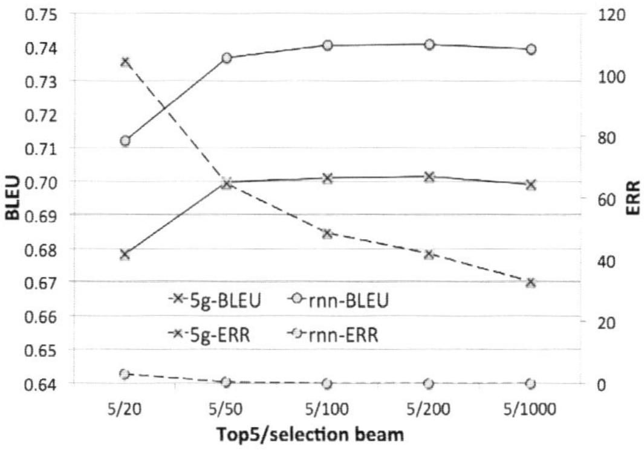

Figure 3: Comparison of our method (rnn) with O&R's approach (5g) in terms of optimising top-5 results over different selection beams.

form utterances. In addition, the slot error (ERR) as described in Section 3.4, out of 1848 slots in 1039 testing examples, was computed alongside the BLEU score.

4.2 Empirical Comparison

As can be seen in Table 2, we compare our proposed RNN-based method with three baselines: a handcrafted generator, a k-nearest neighbour method (kNN), and Oh and Rudnicky (2000)'s n-gram based approach (O&R). The handcrafted generator was tuned over a long period of time and has been used frequently to interact with real users. We found its performance is reliable and robust. The kNN was performed by computing the similarity of the testing dialogue act 1-hot vector against all training examples. The most similar template in the training set was then selected and lexicalised as the testing realisation. We found our RNN generator significantly outperforms these two approaches. While comparing with the O&R system, we found that by partitioning the corpus into more and more utterance classes, the O&R system can also reach a BLEU score of 0.76. However, the slot error cannot be efficiently reduced to zero even when using the error itself as a reranking criterion. This problem is also noted in Mairesse and Young (2014). In contrast, the RNN system produces utterances without slot errors when reranking using the same number of candidates, and it achieves the highest BLEU score. Figure 3 compares the RNN system with O&R's system when randomly select-

Table 3: Pairwise comparison between four systems. Two quality evaluations (rating out of 5) and one preference test were performed in each case. Statistical significance was computed using a two-tailed Wilcoxon rank sum test and a two-tailed binomial test (*=p<.05, **=p<.005).

Metrics	handcrafted	RNN_1	handcrafted	RNN_5	RNN_1	RNN_5	$O\&R_5$	RNN_5
	148 dialogs, 829 utt.		148 dialogs, 814 utt.		144 dialogs, 799 utt.		145 dialogs, 841 utt.	
Info.	3.75	3.81	3.85	3.93*	3.75	3.72	4.02	4.15*
Nat.	3.58	3.74**	3.57	3.94**	3.67	3.58	3.91	4.02
Pref.	44.8%	55.2%*	37.2%	62.8%**	47.5%	52.5%	47.1%	52.9%

ing from the top-5 ranked results in order to introduce linguistic diversity. Results suggest that although O&R's approach improves as the selection beam increases, the RNN-based system is still better in both metrics. Furthermore, the slot error of the RNN system drops to zero when the selection beam is around 50. This indicates that the RNN system is capable of generating paraphrases by simply increasing the number of candidates during the over-generation phase.

4.3 Human Evaluation

Whilst automated metrics provide useful information for comparing different systems, human testing is needed to assess subjective quality. To do this, about 60 judges were recruited using Amazon Mechanical Turk and system responses were generated for the remaining 2571 unseen dialogues mentioned in Section 4.1. Each judge was then shown a randomly selected dialogue, turn by turn. At each turn, two utterances were generated from two different systems and presented to the judge who was asked to score each utterance in terms of informativeness and naturalness (rating out of 5), and also asked to state a preference between the two taking account of the given dialogue act and the dialogue context. Here *informativeness* is defined as whether the utterance contains all the information specified in the dialogue act, and *naturalness* is defined as whether the utterance could have been produced by a human. The trial was run pairwise across four systems: the RNN system using 1-best utterance RNN_1, the RNN system sampling from the top 5 utterances RNN_5, the O&R approach sampling from top 5 utterances $O\&R_5$, and a handcrafted baseline.

The result is shown in Table 3. As can be seen, the human judges preferred both RNN_1 and RNN_5 compared to the rule-based generator and the preference is statistically significant. Furthermore, the RNN systems scored higher in both informativeness and naturalness metrics, though the difference for informativeness is not statistically significant. When comparing RNN_1 with RNN_5, RNN_1 was judged to produce higher quality utterances but overall the diversity of output offered by RNN_5 made it the preferred system. Even though the preference is not statistically significant, it echoes previous findings (Pon-Barry et al., 2006; Mairesse and Young, 2014) that showed that language variability by paraphrasing in dialogue systems is generally beneficial. Lastly, RNN_5 was thought to be significantly better than O&R in terms of informativeness. This result verified our findings in Section 4.2 that O&R suffers from high slot error rates compared to the RNN system.

4.4 Analysis

In order to better understand the relative contribution of each component in the RNN-based generation process, a system was built in stages training first only the forward RNN generator, then adding the CNN reranker, and finally the whole model including the backward RNN reranker. Utterance candidates were reranked using Equation (8) rather than (9) to minimise manual intervention. As previously, the BLEU score and slot error (ERR) were measured.

Gate The forward RNN generator was trained first with different feature gating factors δ. Using a selection beam of 20 and selecting the top 5 utterances, the result is shown in Figure 4 for δ=1 is (equivalent to not using the gate), δ=0.7, and δ=0 (equivalent to turning off the feature immediately its corresponding slot has been generated). As can be seen, use of the feature gating substantially improves both BLEU score and slot error, and the best performance is achieved by setting δ=0.

CNN The feature-gated forward RNN generator was then extended by adding a single convolutional-pooling layer CNN reranker. As shown in Figure 5, evaluation was performed on both the original dataset (*all*) and the dataset containing only binary slots and don't care values (*hard*). We found that the CNN reranker can better handle slots and values that cannot be explicitly

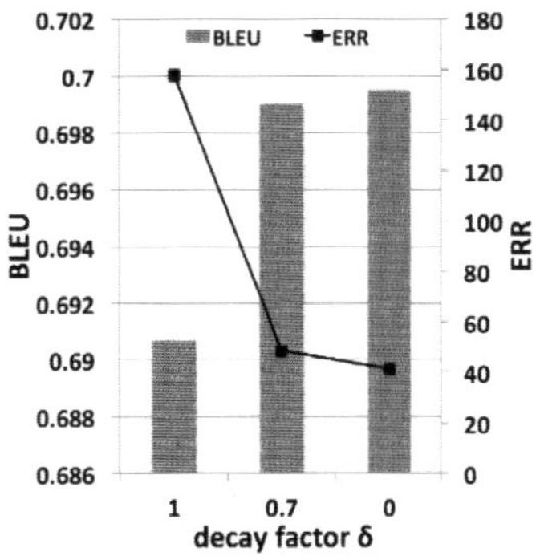

Figure 4: Feature gating effect

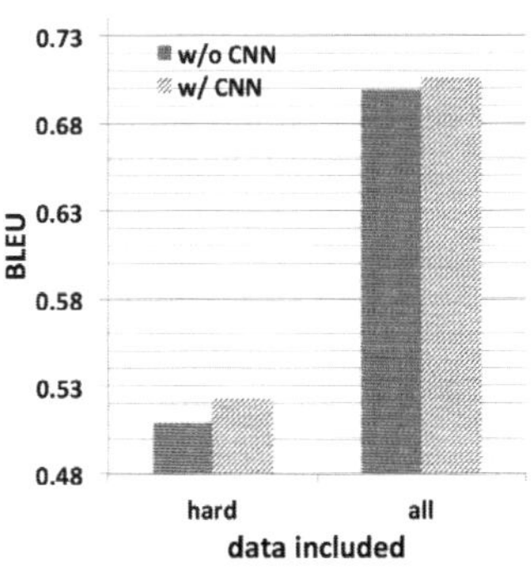

Figure 5: CNN effect

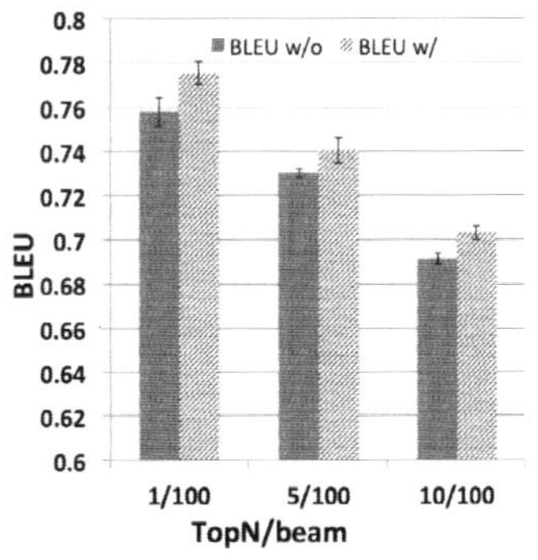

Figure 6: Backward RNN effect

delexicalised (1.5% improvement on *hard* comparing to 1% less on *all*).

Backward RNN Lastly, the backward RNN reranker was added and trained to give the full generation model. The selection beam was fixed at 100 and the n-best top results from which to select the output utterance was varied as $n = 1$, 5 and 10, trading accuracy for linguistic diversity. In each case, the BLEU score was computed with and without the backward RNN reranker. The results shown in Figure 6 are consistent with Section 4.2, in which BLEU score degraded as more n-best utterances were chosen. As can be seen, the backward RNN reranker provides a stable improvement no matter which value n is.

Training corpus size Finally, Figure 7 shows the effect of varying the size of the training corpus. As can be seen, if only the 1-best utterance is offered to the user, then around 50% of the data (2000 utterances) is sufficient. However, if the linguistic variability provided by sampling from the top-5 utterances is required, then the figure suggest that more than 4156 utterances in the current training set are required.

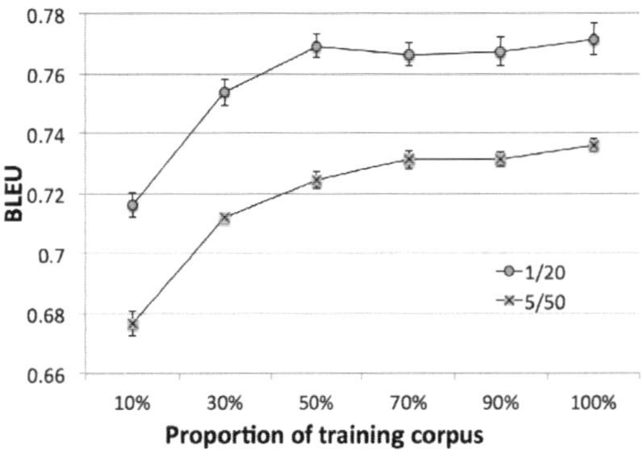

Figure 7: Networks trained with different proportion of data evaluated on two selection schemes.

5 Conclusion and Future Work

In this paper a neural network-based natural language generator has been presented in which a forward RNN generator, a CNN reranker, and backward RNN reranker are jointly optimised to generate utterances conditioned by the required dialogue act. The model can be trained on any corpus of dialogue act-utterance pairs without any semantic alignment and heavy feature engineering or handcrafting. The RNN-based generator is compared with an n-gram based generator which uses similar information. The n-gram generator can achieve similar BLEU scores but it is less efficient and prone to making errors in rendering all of the information contained in the input dialogue act.

An evaluation by human judges indicated that our system can produce not only high quality but linguistically varied utterances. The latter is particularly important in spoken dialogue systems where frequent repetition of identical output forms can rapidly become tedious.

The work reported in this paper is part of a larger programme to develop techniques for implementing open domain spoken dialogue. A key potential advantage of neural network based language processing is the implicit use of distributed representations for words and a single compact parameter encoding of a wide range of syntactic/semantic forms. This suggests that it should be possible to transfer a well-trained generator of the form proposed here to a new domain using a much smaller set of adaptation data. This will be the focus of our future work in this area.

6 Acknowledgements

Tsung-Hsien Wen and David Vandyke are supported by Toshiba Research Europe Ltd, Cambridge Research Laboratory.

References

Gabor Angeli, Percy Liang, and Dan Klein. 2010. A simple domain-independent probabilistic approach to generation. In *Proceedings of the 2010 Conference on Empirical Methods in Natural Language Processing*, EMNLP '10, pages 502–512. Association for Computational Linguistics.

Frédéric Bastien, Pascal Lamblin, Razvan Pascanu, James Bergstra, Ian J. Goodfellow, Arnaud Bergeron, Nicolas Bouchard, and Yoshua Bengio. 2012. Theano: new features and speed improvements. Deep Learning and Unsupervised Feature Learning NIPS 2012 Workshop.

Anja Belz. 2008. Automatic generation of weather forecast texts using comprehensive probabilistic generation-space models. *Natural Language Engineering*, 14(4):431–455, October.

Yoshua Bengio, Patrice Simard, and Paolo Frasconi. 1994. Learning long-term dependencies with gradient descent is difficult. *Neural Networks, IEEE Transactions on*, 5(2):157–166.

James Bergstra, Olivier Breuleux, Frédéric Bastien, Pascal Lamblin, Razvan Pascanu, Guillaume Desjardins, Joseph Turian, David Warde-Farley, and Yoshua Bengio. 2010. Theano: a CPU and GPU math expression compiler. In *Proceedings of the Python for Scientific Computing Conference*.

Dan Bohus and Alexander I. Rudnicky. 2009. The ravenclaw dialog management framework: Architecture and systems. *Computer Speech and Language*, 23(3):332–361, July.

Adam Cheyer and Didier Guzzoni. 2007. Method and apparatus for building an intelligent automated assistant. US Patent App. 11/518,292.

Ronan Collobert and Jason Weston. 2008. A unified architecture for natural language processing: Deep neural networks with multitask learning. In *Proceedings of the 25th International Conference on Machine Learning*, ICML '08, pages 160–167.

Nina Dethlefs, Helen Hastie, Heriberto Cuayhuitl, and Oliver Lemon. 2013. Conditional random fields for responsive surface realisation using global features. In *In Proceedings of ACL*.

Milica Gašić, Dongho Kim, Pirros Tsiakoulis, Catherine Breslin, Matthew Henderson, Martin Szummer, Blaise Thomson, and Steve Young. 2014. Incremental on-line adaptation of pomdp-based dialogue managers to extended domains. In *In Proceedings on InterSpeech*.

Alex Graves, Marcus Liwicki, Horst Bunke, Jürgen Schmidhuber, and Santiago Fernández. 2008. Unconstrained on-line handwriting recognition with recurrent neural networks. In *Advances in Neural Information Processing Systems*, pages 577–584.

Alex Graves, A-R Mohamed, and Geoffrey Hinton. 2013. Speech recognition with deep recurrent neural networks. In *Acoustics, Speech and Signal Processing (ICASSP), 2013 IEEE International Conference on*, pages 6645–6649. IEEE.

Matthew Henderson, Blaise Thomson, and Steve Young. 2014. Robust dialog state tracking using delexicalised recurrent neural networks and unsupervised adaptation. In *Proceedings of IEEE Spoken Language Technology*.

Nal Kalchbrenner, Edward Grefenstette, and Phil Blunsom. 2014. A convolutional neural network for modelling sentences. *CoRR*, abs/1404.2188.

Andrej Karpathy and Li Fei-Fei. 2014. Deep visual-semantic alignments for generating image descriptions. *CoRR*, abs/1412.2306.

Yoon Kim. 2014. Convolutional neural networks for sentence classification. In *Proceedings of the 2014 Conference on Empirical Methods in Natural Language Processing (EMNLP)*, pages 1746–1751, Doha, Qatar, October. Association for Computational Linguistics.

Ravi Kondadadi, Blake Howald, and Frank Schilder. 2013. A statistical nlg framework for aggregated planning and realization. In *Proceedings of the 51st Annual Meeting of the Association for Computational Linguistics (Volume 1: Long Papers)*, pages 1406–1415, Sofia, Bulgaria, August. Association for Computational Linguistics.

Karen Kukich. 1987. Where do phrases come from: Some preliminary experiments in connectionist phrase generation. In *Natural Language Generation*, volume 135 of *NATO ASI Series*, pages 405–421. Springer Netherlands.

Irene Langkilde and Kevin Knight. 1998. Generation that exploits corpus-based statistical knowledge. In *Proceedings of the 36th Annual Meeting of the Association for Computational Linguistics*, ACL '98, pages 704–710.

Yann Lecun, León Bottou, Yoshua Bengio, and Patrick Haffner. 1998. Gradient-based learning applied to document recognition. *Proceedings of the IEEE*, 86(11):2278–2324, Nov.

François Mairesse and Steve Young. 2014. Stochastic language generation in dialogue using factored language models. *Computer Linguistics*, 40(4):763–799.

François Mairesse, Milica Gašić, Filip Jurčíček, Simon Keizer, Blaise Thomson, Kai Yu, and Steve Young. 2010. Phrase-based statistical language generation using graphical models and active learning. In *Proceedings of the 48th Annual Meeting of the Association for Computational Linguistics*, ACL '10, pages 1552–1561.

Tomáš Mikolov and Geoffrey Zweig. 2012. Context dependent recurrent neural network language model. In *In Proceedings on IEEE SLT workshop*.

Tomáš Mikolov, Martin Karafit, Lukáš Burget, Jan Černocký, and Sanjeev Khudanpur. 2010. Recurrent neural network based language model. In *In Proceedings on InterSpeech*.

Tomáš Mikolov, Stefan Kombrink, Lukáš Burget, Jan H. Černocký, and Sanjeev Khudanpur. 2011a. Extensions of recurrent neural network language model. In *Acoustics, Speech and Signal Processing (ICASSP), 2011 IEEE International Conference on*.

Tomáš Mikolov, Stefan Kombrink, Anoop Deoras, Lukáš Burget, and Jan Černocký. 2011b. Rnnlm - recurrent neural network language modeling toolkit. In *In Proceedings on ASRU*.

Tomáš Mikolov, Ilya Sutskever, Kai Chen, Greg S. Corrado, and Jeff Dean. 2013. Distributed representations of words and phrases and their compositionality. In *Advances in Neural Information Processing Systems 26*, pages 3111–3119.

Danilo Mirkovic and Lawrence Cavedon. 2011. Dialogue management using scripts, February 16. EP Patent 1,891,625.

Alice H. Oh and Alexander I. Rudnicky. 2000. Stochastic language generation for spoken dialogue systems. In *Proceedings of the 2000 ANLP/NAACL Workshop on Conversational Systems - Volume 3*, ANLP/NAACL-ConvSyst '00, pages 27–32.

Kishore Papineni, Salim Roukos, Todd Ward, and Wei-Jing Zhu. 2002. Bleu: a method for automatic evaluation of machine translation. In *Proceedings of the 40th annual meeting on association for computational linguistics*, pages 311–318. Association for Computational Linguistics.

Jeffrey Pennington, Richard Socher, and Christopher Manning. 2014. Glove: Global vectors for word representation. In *Proceedings of the 2014 Conference on Empirical Methods in Natural Language Processing (EMNLP)*, pages 1532–1543. Association for Computational Linguistics, October.

Heather Pon-Barry, Karl Schultz, Elizabeth Owen Bratt, Brady Clark, and Stanley Peters. 2006. Responding to student uncertainty in spoken tutorial dialogue systems. *International Journal of Artificial Intelligence in Education*.

Adwait Ratnaparkhi. 2002. Trainable approaches to surface natural language generation and their application to conversational dialog systems. *Computer Speech and Language*. Spoken Language Generation.

Verena Rieser and Oliver Lemon. 2010. Natural language generation as planning under uncertainty for spoken dialogue systems. In *Empirical Methods in Natural Language Generation*, pages 105–120.

Tara N Sainath, A-r Mohamed, Brian Kingsbury, and Bhuvana Ramabhadran. 2013. Deep convolutional neural networks for lvcsr. In *Acoustics, Speech and Signal Processing (ICASSP), 2013 IEEE International Conference on*, pages 8614–8618. IEEE.

Mike Schuster and Kuldip K Paliwal. 1997. Bidirectional recurrent neural networks. *Signal Processing, IEEE Transactions on*, 45(11):2673–2681.

Richard Socher, Alex Perelygin, Jean Y. Wu, Jason Chuang, Christopher D. Manning, Andrew Y. Ng, and Christopher Potts. 2013. Recursive deep models for semantic compositionality over a sentiment treebank. In *Proceedings of the 2014 Conference on Empirical Methods in Natural Language Processing (EMNLP)*.

Amanda Stent, Rashmi Prasad, and Marilyn Walker. 2004. Trainable sentence planning for complex information presentation in spoken dialog systems. In *In Proceedings of the Annual Meeting of the Association for Computational Linguistics*, pages 79–86.

Martin Sundermeyer, Tamer Alkhouli, Joern Wuebker, and Hermann Ney. 2014. Translation modeling with bidirectional recurrent neural networks. In *Proceedings of the 2014 Conference on Empirical Methods in Natural Language Processing (EMNLP)*, pages 14–25. Association for Computational Linguistics.

Ilya Sutskever, James Martens, and Geoffrey E. Hinton. 2011. Generating text with recurrent neural networks. In *Proceedings of the 28th International Conference on Machine Learning (ICML-11)*, pages 1017–1024, New York, NY, USA. ACM.

Marilyn A Walker, Owen C Rambow, and Monica Rogati. 2002. Training a sentence planner for spoken dialogue using boosting. *Computer Speech and Language*, 16(3):409–433.

Wayne Ward and Sunil Issar. 1994. Recent improvements in the cmu spoken language understanding system. In *Proceedings of the Workshop on Human Language Technology*, HLT '94, pages 213–216. Association for Computational Linguistics.

Paul J Werbos. 1990. Backpropagation through time: what it does and how to do it. *Proceedings of the IEEE*, 78(10):1550–1560.

Steve Young, Milica Gašić, Blaise Thomson, and Jason D. Williams. 2013. Pomdp-based statistical spoken dialog systems: A review. *Proceedings of the IEEE*, 101(5):1160–1179, May.

Xingxing Zhang and Mirella Lapata. 2014. Chinese poetry generation with recurrent neural networks. In *Proceedings of the 2014 Conference on Empirical Methods in Natural Language Processing (EMNLP)*, pages 670–680. Association for Computational Linguistics, October.

The Ubuntu Dialogue Corpus: A Large Dataset for Research in Unstructured Multi-Turn Dialogue Systems

Ryan Lowe *[*], Nissan Pow[*], Iulian V. Serban[†] and Joelle Pineau[*]

[*]School of Computer Science, McGill University, Montreal, Canada
[†]Dept Computer Science and Operations Research, Université de Montréal, Montreal, Canada
{ryan.lowe, nissan.pow}@mail.mcgill.ca, julianserban@gmail.com, jpineau@cs.mcgill.ca

Abstract

This paper introduces the Ubuntu Dialogue Corpus, a dataset containing almost 1 million multi-turn dialogues, with a total of over 7 million utterances and 100 million words. This provides a unique resource for research into building dialogue managers based on neural language models that can make use of large amounts of unlabeled data. The dataset has both the multi-turn property of conversations in the Dialog State Tracking Challenge datasets, and the unstructured nature of interactions from microblog services such as Twitter. We also describe two neural learning architectures suitable for analyzing this dataset, and provide benchmark performance on the task of selecting the best next response.

1 Introduction

The ability for a computer to converse in a natural and coherent manner with a human has long been held as one of the primary objectives of artificial intelligence (AI). In this paper we consider the problem of building dialogue agents that have the ability to interact in one-on-one multi-turn conversations on a diverse set of topics. We primarily target *unstructured* dialogues, where there is no *a priori* logical representation for the information exchanged during the conversation. This is in contrast to recent systems which focus on structured dialogue tasks, using a slot-filling representation [10, 27, 32].

We observe that in several subfields of AI—computer vision, speech recognition, machine translation—fundamental break-throughs were achieved in recent years using machine learning methods, more specifically with neural architectures [1]; however, it is worth noting that many of the most successful approaches, in particular convolutional and recurrent neural networks, were known for many years prior. It is therefore reasonable to attribute this progress to three major factors: 1) the public distribution of very large rich datasets [5], 2) the availability of substantial computing power, and 3) the development of new training methods for neural architectures, in particular leveraging unlabeled data. Similar progress has not yet been observed in the development of dialogue systems. We hypothesize that this is due to the lack of sufficiently large datasets, and aim to overcome this barrier by providing a new large corpus for research in multi-turn conversation.

The new Ubuntu Dialogue Corpus consists of almost one million two-person conversations extracted from the Ubuntu chat logs[1], used to receive technical support for various Ubuntu-related problems. The conversations have an average of 8 turns each, with a minimum of 3 turns. All conversations are carried out in text form (not audio). The dataset is orders of magnitude larger than structured corpuses such as those of the Dialogue State Tracking Challenge [32]. It is on the same scale as recent datasets for solving problems such as question answering and analysis of microblog services, such as Twitter [22, 25, 28, 33], but each conversation in our dataset includes several more turns, as well as longer utterances. Furthermore, because it targets a specific domain, namely technical support, it can be used as a case study for the development of AI agents in targeted applications, in contrast to chatbox agents that often lack a well-defined goal [26].

In addition to the corpus, we present learning architectures suitable for analyzing this dataset, ranging from the simple frequency-inverse docu-

The first two authors contributed equally.

[1]These logs are available from 2004 to 2015 at `http://irclogs.ubuntu.com/`

Proceedings of the SIGDIAL 2015 Conference, pages 285–294,
Prague, Czech Republic, 2-4 September 2015.

ment frequency (TF-IDF) approach, to more sophisticated neural models including a Recurrent Neural Network (RNN) and a Long Short-Term Memory (LSTM) architecture. We provide benchmark performance of these algorithms, trained with our new corpus, on the task of selecting the best next response, which can be achieved without requiring any human labeling. The dataset is ready for public release[2]. The code developed for the empirical results is also available[3].

2 Related Work

We briefly review existing dialogue datasets, and some of the more recent learning architectures used for both structured and unstructured dialogues. This is by no means an exhaustive list (due to space constraints), but surveys resources most related to our contribution. A list of datasets discussed is provided in Table 1.

2.1 Dialogue Datasets

The Switchboard dataset [8], and the Dialogue State Tracking Challenge (DSTC) datasets [32] have been used to train and validate dialogue management systems for interactive information retrieval. The problem is typically formalized as a slot filling task, where agents attempt to predict the goal of a user during the conversation. These datasets have been significant resources for structured dialogues, and have allowed major progress in this field, though they are quite small compared to datasets currently used for training neural architectures.

Recently, a few datasets have been used containing unstructured dialogues extracted from Twitter[4]. Ritter et al. [21] collected 1.3 million conversations; this was extended in [28] to take advantage of longer contexts by using A-B-A triples. Shang et al. [25] used data from a similar Chinese website called Weibo[5]. However to our knowledge, these datasets have not been made public, and furthermore, the post-reply format of such microblogging services is perhaps not as representative of natural dialogue between humans as the continuous stream of messages in a chat room. In fact, Ritter et al. estimate that only 37% of posts on Twitter are 'conversational in nature', and 69% of their collected data contained exchanges of only length 2 [21]. We hypothesize that chat-room style messaging is more closely correlated to human-to-human dialogue than micro-blogging websites, or forum-based sites such as Reddit.

Part of the Ubuntu chat logs have previously been aggregated into a dataset, called the Ubuntu Chat Corpus [30]. However that resource preserves the multi-participant structure and thus is less amenable to the investigation of more traditional two-party conversations.

Also weakly related to our contribution is the problem of question-answer systems. Several datasets of question-answer pairs are available [3], however these interactions are much shorter than what we seek to study.

2.2 Learning Architectures

Most dialogue research has historically focused on structured slot-filling tasks [24]. Various approaches were proposed, yet few attempts leverage more recent developments in neural learning architectures. A notable exception is the work of Henderson et al. [11], which proposes an RNN structure, initialized with a denoising autoencoder, to tackle the DSTC 3 domain.

Work on unstructured dialogues, recently pioneered by Ritter et al. [22], proposed a response generation model for Twitter data based on ideas from Statistical Machine Translation. This is shown to give superior performance to previous information retrieval (e.g. nearest neighbour) approaches [14]. This idea was further developed by Sordoni et al. [28] to exploit information from a longer context, using a structure similar to the Recurrent Neural Network Encoder-Decoder model [4]. This achieves rather poor performance on A-B-A Twitter triples when measured by the BLEU score (a standard for machine translation), yet performs comparatively better than the model of Ritter et al. [22]. Their results are also verified with a human-subject study. A similar encoder-decoder framework is presented in [25]. This model uses one RNN to transform the input to some vector representation, and another RNN to 'decode' this representation to a response by generating one word at a time. This model is also evaluated in a human-subject study, although much smaller in size than in [28]. Overall, these models highlight the potential of neural learning architectures for interactive systems, yet so far they have

[2]http://www.cs.mcgill.ca/~jpineau/datasets/ubuntu-corpus-1.0

[3]http://github.com/npow/ubottu

[4]https://twitter.com/

[5]http://www.weibo.com/

Dataset	Type	Task	# Dialogues	# Utterances	# Words	Description
Switchboard [8]	Human-human spoken	Various	2,400	—	3,000,000	Telephone conversations on pre-specified topics
DSTC1 [32]	Human-computer spoken	State tracking	15,000	210,000		Bus ride information system
DSTC2 [10]	Human-computer spoken	State tracking	3,000	24,000	—	Restaurant booking system
DSTC3 [9]	Human-computer spoken	State tracking	2,265	15,000	—	Tourist information system
DSTC4[13]	Human-human spoken	State tracking	35	—	—	21 hours of tourist info exchange over Skype
Twitter Corpus [21]	Human-human micro-blog	Next utterance generation	1,300,000	3,000,000	—	Post/ replies extracted from Twitter
Twitter Triple Corpus [28]	Human-human micro-blog	Next utterance generation	29,000,000	87,000,000	—	A-B-A triples from Twitter replies
Sina Weibo [25]	Human-human micro-blog	Next utterance generation	4,435,959	8,871,918	—	Post/ reply pairs extracted from Weibo
Ubuntu Dialogue Corpus	**Human-human chat**	**Next utterance classification**	**930,000**	**7,100,000**	**100,000,000**	**Extracted from Ubuntu Chat Logs**

Table 1: A selection of structured and unstructured large-scale datasets applicable to dialogue systems. Faded datasets are not publicly available. The last entry is our contribution.

been limited to very short conversations.

3 The Ubuntu Dialogue Corpus

We seek a large dataset for research in dialogue systems with the following properties:

- Two-way (or *dyadic*) conversation, as opposed to multi-participant chat, preferably human-human.
- Large number of conversations; $10^5 - 10^6$ is typical of datasets used for neural-network learning in other areas of AI.
- Many conversations with several turns (more than 3).
- Task-specific domain, as opposed to chatbot systems.

All of these requirements are satisfied by the Ubuntu Dialogue Corpus presented in this paper.

3.1 Ubuntu Chat Logs

The Ubuntu Chat Logs refer to a collection of logs from Ubuntu-related chat rooms on the Freenode Internet Relay Chat (IRC) network. This protocol allows for real-time chat between a large number of participants. Each chat room, or channel, has a particular topic, and every channel participant can see all the messages posted in a given channel. Many of these channels are used for obtaining technical support with various Ubuntu issues.

As the contents of each channel are moderated, most interactions follow a similar pattern. A new user joins the channel, and asks a general question about a problem they are having with Ubuntu. Then, another more experienced user replies with a potential solution, after first addressing the 'username' of the first user. This is called a name mention [29], and is done to avoid confusion in the channel — at any given time during the day, there can be between 1 and 20 simultaneous conversations happening in some channels. In the most popular channels, there is almost never a time when only one conversation is occurring; this renders it particularly problematic to extract dyadic dialogues. A conversation between a pair of users generally stops when the problem has been solved, though some users occasionally continue to discuss a topic not related to Ubuntu.

Despite the nature of the chat room being a constant stream of messages from multiple users, it is through the fairly rigid structure in the messages that we can extract the dialogues between users. Figure 4 shows an example chat room conversation from the #ubuntu channel as well as the extracted dialogues, which illustrates how users usually state the username of the intended message recipient before writing their reply (we refer to all replies and initial questions as 'utterances'). For example, it is clear that users 'Taru' and 'kuja' are engaged in a dialogue, as are users 'Old' and 'bur[n]er', while user '_pm' is asking an initial question, and 'LiveCD' is perhaps elaborating on a previous comment.

3.2 Dataset Creation

In order to create the Ubuntu Dialogue Corpus, first a method had to be devised to extract dyadic dialogues from the chat room multi-party conversations. The first step was to separate every message into 4-tuples of (time, sender, recipient, utterance). Given these 4-tuples, it is straightforward to group all tuples where there is a matching sender and recipient. Although it is easy to separate the time and the sender from the rest, finding the intended recipient of the message is not always trivial.

3.2.1 Recipient Identification

While in most cases the recipient is the first word of the utterance, it is sometimes located at the end, or not at all in the case of initial questions. Furthermore, some users choose names corresponding to common English words, such as 'the' or 'stop', which could lead to many false positives. In order to solve this issue, we create a dictionary of usernames from the current and previous days, and compare the first word of each utterance to its entries. If a match is found, and the word does not correspond to a very common English word[6], it is assumed that this user was the intended recipient of the message. If no matches are found, it is assumed that the message was an initial question, and the recipient value is left empty.

3.2.2 Utterance Creation

The dialogue extraction algorithm works backwards from the first response to find the initial question that was replied to, within a time frame of 3 minutes. A first response is identified by the presence of a recipient name (someone from the recent conversation history). The initial question is identified to be the most recent utterance by the recipient identified in the first response.

All utterances that do not qualify as a first response or an initial question are discarded; initial questions that do not generate any response are also discarded. We additionally discard conversations longer than five utterances where one user says more than 80% of the utterances, as these are typically not representative of real chat dialogues. Finally, we consider only extracted dialogues that consist of 3 turns or more to encourage the modeling of longer-term dependencies.

To alleviate the problem of 'holes' in the dialogue, where one user does not address the other explicitly, as in Figure 5, we check whether each user talks to someone else for the duration of their conversation. If not, all non-addressed utterances are added to the dialogue. An example conversation along with the extracted dialogues is shown in Figure 5. Note that we also concatenate all consecutive utterances from a given user.

We do not apply any further pre-processing (e.g. tokenization, stemming) to the data as released in the Ubuntu Dialogue Corpus. However the use of pre-processing is standard for most NLP systems, and was also used in our analysis (see Section 4.)

[6]We use the GNU Aspell spell checking dictionary.

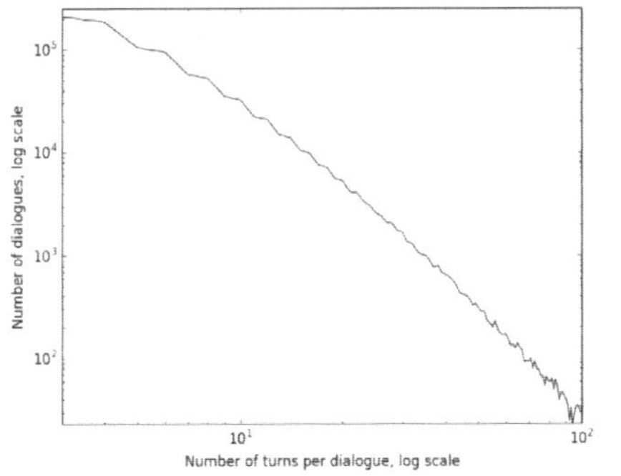

Figure 1: Plot of number of conversations with a given number of turns. Both axes use a log scale.

# dialogues (human-human)	930,000
# utterances (in total)	7,100,000
# words (in total)	100,000,000
Min. # turns per dialogue	3
Avg. # turns per dialogue	7.71
Avg. # words per utterance	10.34
Median conversation length (min)	6

Table 2: Properties of Ubuntu Dialogue Corpus.

3.2.3 Special Cases and Limitations

It is often the case that a user will post an initial question, and multiple people will respond to it with different answers. In this instance, each conversation between the first user and the user who replied is treated as a separate dialogue. This has the unfortunate side-effect of having the initial question appear multiple times in several dialogues. However the number of such cases is sufficiently small compared to the size of the dataset.

Another issue to note is that the utterance posting time is not considered for segmenting conversations between two users. Even if two users have a conversation that spans multiple hours, or even days, this is treated as a single dialogue. However, such dialogues are rare. We include the posting time in the corpus so that other researchers may filter as desired.

3.3 Dataset Statistics

Table 2 summarizes properties of the Ubuntu Dialogue Corpus. One of the most important features of the Ubuntu chat logs is its size. This is crucial for research into building dialogue managers based on neural architectures. Another important characteristic is the number of turns in these dialogues. The distribution of the number of turns is shown in Figure 1. It can be seen that the number of dialogues and turns per dialogue follow an approximate power law relationship.

3.4 Test Set Generation

We set aside 2% of the Ubuntu Dialogue Corpus conversations (randomly selected) to form a test set that can be used for evaluation of response selection algorithms. Compared to the rest of the corpus, this test set has been further processed to extract a pair of *(context, response, flag)* triples from each dialogue. The *flag* is a Boolean variable indicating whether or not the response was the actual next utterance after the given context. The *response* is a target (output) utterance which we aim to correctly identify. The *context* consists of the sequence of utterances appearing in dialogue prior to the response. We create a pair of triples, where one triple contains the correct response (i.e. the actual next utterance in the dialogue), and the other triple contains a false response, sampled randomly from elsewhere within the test set. The flag is set to 1 in the first case and to 0 in the second case. An example pair is shown in Table 3. To make the task harder, we can move from pairs of responses (one correct, one incorrect) to a larger set of wrong responses (all with flag=0). In our experiments below, we consider both the case of 1 wrong response and 10 wrong responses.

Context	Response	Flag
well, can I move the drives? __EOS__ ah not like that	I guess I could just get an enclosure and copy via USB	1
well, can I move the drives? __EOS__ ah not like that	you can use "ps ax" and "kill (PID #)"	0

Table 3: Test set example with (context, reply, flag) format. The '__EOS__' tag is used to denote the end of an utterance within the context.

Since we want to learn to predict all parts of a conversation, as opposed to only the closing statement, we consider various portions of context for the conversations in the test set. The context size is determined stochastically using a simple formula:

$$c = \min(t - 1, n - 1),$$

$$\text{where } n = \frac{10C}{\eta} + 2, \eta \sim Unif(C/2, 10C)$$

Here, C denotes the maximum desired context size, which we set to $C = 20$. The last term is the desired minimum context size, which we set to be 2. Parameter t is the actual length of that dialogue (thus the constraint that $c \leq t - 1$), and n is a random number corresponding to the randomly sampled context length, that is selected to be inversely proportional to C.

In practice, this leads to short test dialogues having short contexts, while longer dialogues are often broken into short or medium-length segments, with the occasional long context of 10 or more turns.

3.5 Evaluation Metric

We consider the task of best response selection. This can be achieved by processing the data as described in Section 3.4, without requiring any human labels. This classification task is an adaptation of the recall and precision metrics previously applied to dialogue datasets [24].

A family of metrics often used in language tasks is Recall@k (denoted R@1 R@2, R@5 below). Here the agent is asked to select the k most likely responses, and it is correct if the true response is among these k candidates. Only the R@1 metric is relevant in the case of binary classification (as in the Table 3 example).

Although a language model that performs well on response classification is not a gauge of good performance on next utterance generation, we hypothesize that improvements on a model with regards to the classification task will eventually lead to improvements for the generation task. See Section 6 for further discussion of this point.

4 Learning Architectures for Unstructured Dialogues

To provide further evidence of the value of our dataset for research into neural architectures for dialogue managers, we provide performance benchmarks for two neural learning algorithms, as well as one naive baseline. The approaches considered are: TF-IDF, Recurrent Neural networks (RNN), and Long Short-Term Memory (LSTM). Prior to applying each method, we perform standard pre-processing of the data using the NLTK[7] library and Twitter tokenizer[8] to parse each utterance. We use generic tags for various word categories, such as names, locations, organizations, URLs, and system paths.

[7] `www.nltk.org/`

[8] `http://www.ark.cs.cmu.edu/TweetNLP/`

To train the RNN and LSTM architectures, we process the full training Ubuntu Dialogue Corpus into the same format as the test set described in Section 3.4, extracting *(context, response, flag)* triples from dialogues. For the training set, we do not sample the context length, but instead consider each utterance (starting at the 3rd one) as a potential response, with the previous utterances as its context. So a dialogue of length 10 yields 8 training examples. Since these are overlapping, they are clearly not independent, but we consider this a minor issue given the size of the dataset (we further alleviate the issue by shuffling the training examples). Negative responses are selected at random from the rest of the training data.

4.1 TF-IDF

Term frequency-inverse document frequency is a statistic that intends to capture how important a given word is to some document, which in our case is the context [20]. It is a technique often used in document classification and information retrieval. The 'term-frequency' term is simply a count of the number of times a word appears in a given context, while the 'inverse document frequency' term puts a penalty on how often the word appears elsewhere in the corpus. The final score is calculated as the product of these two terms, and has the form:

$$\text{tfidf}(w, d, D) = f(w, d) \times \log \frac{N}{|\{d \in D : w \in d\}|},$$

where $f(w, d)$ indicates the number of times word w appeared in context d, N is the total number of dialogues, and the denominator represents the number of dialogues in which the word w appears.

For classification, the TF-IDF vectors are first calculated for the context and each of the candidate responses. Given a set of candidate response vectors, the one with the highest cosine similarity to the context vector is selected as the output. For Recall@k, the top k responses are returned.

4.2 RNN

Recurrent neural networks are a variant of neural networks that allows for time-delayed directed cycles between units [17]. This leads to the formation of an internal state of the network, h_t, which allows it to model time-dependent data. The internal state is updated at each time step as some function of the observed variables x_t, and the hidden state at the previous time step h_{t-1}. W_x and

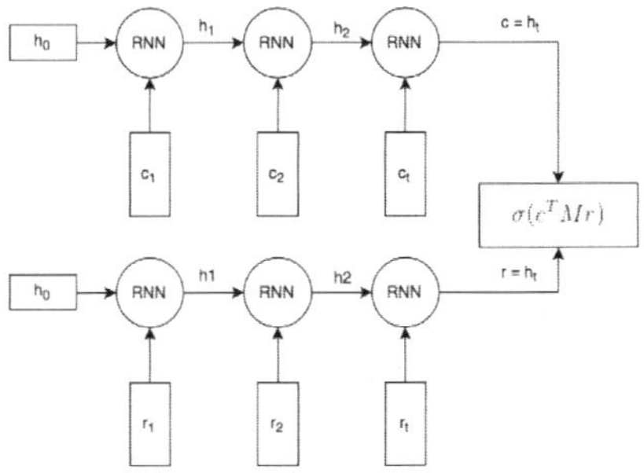

Figure 2: Diagram of our model. The RNNs have tied weights. c, r are the last hidden states from the RNNs. c_i, r_i are word vectors for the context and response, $i < t$. We consider contexts up to a maximum of $t = 160$.

W_h are matrices associated with the input and hidden state.

$$h_t = f(W_h h_{t-1} + W_x x_t).$$

A diagram of an RNN can be seen in Figure 2. RNNs have been the primary building block of many current neural language models [22, 28], which use RNNs for an encoder and decoder. The first RNN is used to encode the given context, and the second RNN generates a response by using beam-search, where its initial hidden state is biased using the final hidden state from the first RNN. In our work, we are concerned with classification of responses, instead of generation. We build upon the approach in [2], which has also been recently applied to the problem of question answering [33].

We utilize a siamese network consisting of two RNNs with tied weights to produce the embeddings for the context and response. Given some input context and response, we compute their embeddings — $c, r \in \mathbb{R}^d$, respectively — by feeding the word embeddings one at a time into its respective RNN. Word embeddings are initialized using the pre-trained vectors (Common Crawl, 840B tokens from [19]), and fine-tuned during training. The hidden state of the RNN is updated at each step, and the final hidden state represents a *summary* of the input utterance. Using the final hidden states from both RNNs, we then calculate the probability that this is a valid pair:

$$p(\text{flag} = 1|c, r) = \sigma(c^T M r + b),$$

where the bias b and the matrix $M \in \mathbb{R}^{d \times d}$ are learned model parameters. This can be thought of as a generative approach; given some input response, we generate a context with the product $c' = Mr$, and measure the similarity to the actual context using the dot product. This is converted to a probability with the sigmoid function. The model is trained by minimizing the cross entropy of all labeled (context, response) pairs [33]:

$$\mathcal{L} = -\log \prod_n p(\text{flag}_n | c_n, r_n) + \frac{\lambda}{2} ||\theta||_2^F$$

where $||\theta||_2^F$ is the Frobenius norm of $\theta = \{M, b\}$. In our experiments, we use $\lambda = 0$ for computational simplicity.

For training, we used a 1:1 ratio between true responses (flag = 1), and negative responses (flag=0) drawn randomly from elsewhere in the training set. The RNN architecture is set to 1 hidden layer with 50 neurons. The W_h matrix is initialized using orthogonal weights [23], while W_x is initialized using a uniform distribution with values between -0.01 and 0.01. We use Adam as our optimizer [15], with gradients clipped to 10. We found that weight initialization as well as the choice of optimizer were critical for training the RNNs.

4.3 LSTM

In addition to the RNN model, we consider the same architecture but changed the hidden units to long-short term memory (LSTM) units [12]. LSTMs were introduced in order to model longer-term dependencies. This is accomplished using a series of gates that determine whether a new input should be remembered, forgotten (and the old value retained), or used as output. The error signal can now be fed back indefinitely into the gates of the LSTM unit. This helps overcome the vanishing and exploding gradient problems in standard RNNs, where the error gradients would otherwise decrease or increase at an exponential rate. In training, we used 1 hidden layer with 200 neurons. The hyper-parameter configuration (including number of neurons) was optimized independently for RNNs and LSTMs using a validation set extracted from the training data.

5 Empirical Results

The results for the TF-IDF, RNN, and LSTM models are shown in Table 4. The models were evaluated using both 1 (1 in 2) and 9 (1 in 10) false examples. Of course, the Recall@2 and Recall@5 are not relevant in the binary classification case.

Method	TF-IDF	RNN	LSTM
1 in 2 R@1	65.9%	76.8%	87.8%
1 in 10 R@1	41.0%	40.3%	60.4%
1 in 10 R@2	54.5%	54.7%	74.5%
1 in 10 R@5	70.8%	81.9%	92.6%

Table 4: Results for the three algorithms using various recall measures for binary (1 in 2) and 1 in 10 (1 in 10) next utterance classification %.

We observe that the LSTM outperforms both the RNN and TF-IDF on all evaluation metrics. It is interesting to note that TF-IDF actually outperforms the RNN on the Recall@1 case for the 1 in 10 classification. This is most likely due to the limited ability of the RNN to take into account long contexts, which can be overcome by using the LSTM. An example output of the LSTM where the response is correctly classified is shown in Table 5.

We also show, in Figure 3, the increase in performance of the LSTM as the amount of data used for training increases. This confirms the importance of having a large training set.

Context
""any apache hax around ? i just deleted all of __path__ - which package provides it ?", "reconfiguring apache do n't solve it ?"

Ranked Responses	Flag
1. "does n't seem to, no"	1
2. "you can log in but not transfer files ?"	0

Table 5: Example showing the ranked responses from the LSTM. Each utterance is shown after preprocessing steps.

6 Discussion

This paper presents the Ubuntu Dialogue Corpus, a large dataset for research in unstructured multi-turn dialogue systems. We describe the construction of the dataset and its properties. The availability of a dataset of this size opens up several interesting possibilities for research into dialogue systems based on rich neural-network architectures. We present preliminary results demonstrating use of this dataset to train an RNN and an LSTM for the task of selecting the next best response in a conversation; we obtain significantly better results with the LSTM architecture. There are several interesting directions for future work.

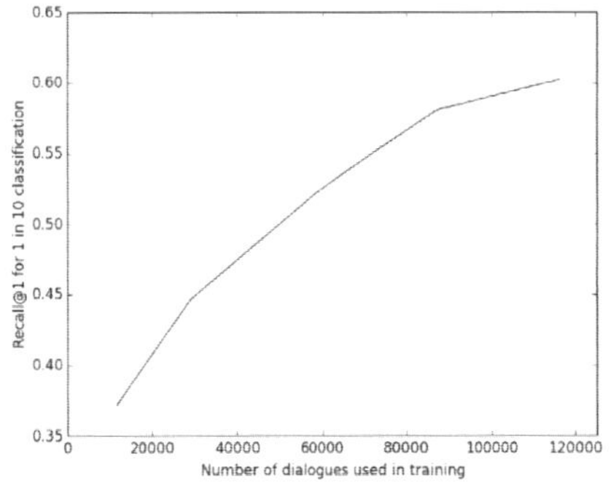

Figure 3: The LSTM (with 200 hidden units), showing Recall@1 for the 1 in 10 classification, with increasing dataset sizes.

6.1 Conversation Disentanglement

Our approach to conversation disentanglement consists of a small set of rules. More sophisticated techniques have been proposed, such as training a maximum-entropy classifier to cluster utterances into separate dialogues [6]. However, since we are not trying to replicate the *exact* conversation between two users, but only to retrieve *plausible* natural dialogues, the heuristic method presented in this paper may be sufficient. This seems supported through qualitative examination of the data, but could be the subject of more formal evaluation.

6.2 Altering Test Set Difficulty

One of the interesting properties of the response selection task is the ability to alter the task difficulty in a controlled manner. We demonstrated this by moving from 1 to 9 false responses, and by varying the Recall@k parameter. In the future, instead of choosing false responses randomly, we will consider selecting false responses that are similar to the actual response (e.g. as measured by cosine similarity). A dialogue model that performs well on this more difficult task should also manage to capture a more fine-grained semantic meaning of sentences, as compared to a model that naively picks replies with the most words in common with the context such as TF-IDF.

6.3 State Tracking and Utterance Generation

The work described here focuses on the task of response selection. This can be seen as an intermediate step between slot filling and utterance generation. In slot filling, the set of candidate outputs (*states*) is identified *a priori* through knowledge engineering, and is typically smaller than the set of responses considered in our work. When the set of candidate responses is close to the size of the dataset (e.g. all utterances ever recorded), then we are quite close to the response generation case.

There are several reasons not to proceed directly to response generation. First, it is likely that current algorithms are not yet able to generate good results for this task, and it is preferable to tackle metrics for which we can make progress. Second, we do not yet have a suitable metric for evaluating performance in the response generation case. One option is to use the BLEU [18] or METEOR [16] scores from machine translation. However, using BLEU to evaluate dialogue systems has been shown to give extremely low scores [28], due to the large space of potential sensible responses [7]. Further, since the BLEU score is calculated using N-grams [18], it would provide a very low score for reasonable responses that do not have any words in common with the ground-truth next utterance.

Alternatively, one could measure the difference between the generated utterance and the actual sentence by comparing their representations in some embedding (or *semantic*) space. However, different models inevitably use different embeddings, necessitating a standardized embedding for evaluation purposes. Such a standardized embeddings has yet to be created.

Another possibility is to use human subjects to score automatically generated responses, but time and expense make this a highly impractical option.

In summary, while it is possible that current language models have outgrown the use of slot filling as a metric, we are currently unable to measure their ability in next utterance generation in a standardized, meaningful and inexpensive way. This motivates our choice of response selection as a useful metric for the time being.

Acknowledgments

The authors gratefully acknowledge financial support for this work by the Samsung Advanced Institute of Technology (SAIT) and the Natural Sciences and Engineering Research Council of Canada (NSERC). We would like to thank Laurent Charlin for his input into this paper, as well as Gabriel Forgues and Eric Crawford for interesting discussions.

References

[1] Y. Bengio, A. Courville, and P. Vincent. Representation learning: A review and new perspectives. *Pattern Analysis and Machine Intelligence, IEEE Transactions on*, 35(8):1798–1828, 2013.

[2] A. Bordes, J. Weston, and N. Usunier. Open question answering with weakly supervised embedding models. In *MLKDD*, pages 165–180. Springer, 2014.

[3] J. Boyd-Graber, B. Satinoff, H. He, and H. Daume. Besting the quiz master: Crowdsourcing incremental classification games. In *EMNLP*, 2012.

[4] K. Cho, B. van Merrienboer, C. Gulcehre, F. Bougares, H. Schwenk, and Y. Bengio. Learning phrase representations using rnn encoder-decoder for statistical machine translation. *arXiv preprint arXiv:1406.1078*, 2014.

[5] J. Deng, W. Dong, R. Socher, L.J. Li, K. Li, and L. Fei-Fei. Imagenet: A large-scale hierarchical image database. In *CVPR*, 2009.

[6] M. Elsner and E. Charniak. You talking to me? a corpus and algorithm for conversation disentanglement. In *ACL*, pages 834–842, 2008.

[7] M. Galley, C. Brockett, A. Sordoni, Y. Ji, M. Auli, C. Quirk, M. Mitchell, J. Gao, and B. Dolan. deltableu: A discriminative metric for generation tasks with intrinsically diverse targets. *arXiv preprint arXiv:1506.06863*, 2015.

[8] J.J. Godfrey, E.C. Holliman, and J. McDaniel. Switchboard: Telephone speech corpus for research and development. In *ICASSP*, 1992.

[9] M. Henderson, B. Thomson, and J. Williams. Dialog state tracking challenge 2 & 3, 2014.

[10] M. Henderson, B. Thomson, and J. Williams. The second dialog state tracking challenge. In *SIGDIAL*, page 263, 2014.

[11] M. Henderson, B. Thomson, and S. Young. Word-based dialog state tracking with recurrent neural networks. In *SIGDIAL*, page 292, 2014.

[12] S. Hochreiter and J. Schmidhuber. Long short-term memory. *Neural computation*, 9(8):1735–1780, 1997.

[13] Dialog state tracking challenge 4.

[14] S. Jafarpour, C. Burges, and A. Ritter. Filter, rank, and transfer the knowledge: Learning to chat. *Advances in Ranking*, 10, 2010.

[15] D.P. Kingma and J. Ba. Adam: A method for stochastic optimization. *CoRR*, abs/1412.6980, 2014.

[16] A. Lavie and M.J. Denkowski. The METEOR metric for automatic evaluation of Machine Translation. *Machine Translation*, 23(2-3):105–115, 2009.

[17] L.R. Medsker and L.C. Jain. Recurrent neural networks. *Design and Applications*, 2001.

[18] K. Papineni, S. Roukos, T. Ward, and W.J. Zhu. Bleu: a method for automatic evaluation of machine translation. In *ACL*, 2002.

[19] J. Pennington, R. Socher, and C.D. Manning. GloVe: Global Vectors for Word Representation. In *EMNLP*, 2014.

[20] J. Ramos. Using tf-idf to determine word relevance in document queries. In *ICML*, 2003.

[21] A. Ritter, C. Cherry, and W. Dolan. Unsupervised modeling of twitter conversations. 2010.

[22] A. Ritter, C. Cherry, and W. Dolan. Data-driven response generation in social media. In *EMNLP*, pages 583–593, 2011.

[23] A.M. Saxe, J.L. McClelland, and S. Ganguli. Exact solutions to the nonlinear dynamics of learning in deep linear neural networks. *arXiv preprint arXiv:1312.6120*, 2013.

[24] J. Schatzmann, K. Georgila, and S. Young. Quantitative evaluation of user simulation techniques for spoken dialogue systems. In *SIGDIAL*, 2005.

[25] L. Shang, Z. Lu, and H. Li. Neural responding machine for short-text conversation. *arXiv preprint arXiv:1503.02364*, 2015.

[26] B. A. Shawar and E. Atwell. Chatbots: are they really useful? In *LDV Forum*, volume 22, pages 29–49, 2007.

[27] S. Singh, D. Litman, M. Kearns, and M. Walker. Optimizing dialogue management with reinforcement learning: Experiments with the NJFun system. *Journal of Artificial Intelligence Research*, 16:105–133, 2002.

[28] A. Sordoni, M. Galley, M. Auli, C. Brockett, Y. Ji, M. Mitchell, J.Y. Nie, J. Gao, and W. Dolan. A neural network approach

to context-sensitive generation of conversational responses. 2015.

[29] D.C. Uthus and D.W. Aha. Extending word highlighting in multiparticipant chat. Technical report, DTIC Document, 2013.

[30] D.C. Uthus and D.W Aha. The ubuntu chat corpus for multiparticipant chat analysis. In *AAAI Spring Symposium on Analyzing Microtext*, pages 99–102, 2013.

[31] H. Wang, Z. Lu, H. Li, and E. Chen. A dataset for research on short-text conversations. In *EMNLP*, 2013.

[32] J. Williams, A. Raux, D. Ramachandran, and A. Black. The dialog state tracking challenge. In *SIGDIAL*, pages 404–413, 2013.

[33] L. Yu, K. M. Hermann, P. Blunsom, and S. Pulman. Deep learning for answer sentence selection. *arXiv preprint arXiv:1412.1632*, 2014.

[34] M.D. Zeiler. Adadelta: an adaptive learning rate method. *arXiv preprint arXiv:1212.5701*, 2012.

Appendix A: Dialogue excerpts

Time	User	Utterance
03:44	Old	I dont run graphical ubuntu, I run ubuntu server.
03:45	kuja	Taru: Haha sucker.
03:45	Taru	Kuja: ?
03:45	bur[n]er	Old: you can use "ps ax" and "kill (PID#)"
03:45	kuja	Taru: Anyways, you made the changes right?
03:45	Taru	Kuja: Yes.
03:45	LiveCD	or killall speedlink
03:45	kuja	Taru: Then from the terminal type: sudo apt-get update
03:46	_pm	if i install the beta version, how can i update it when the final version comes out?
03:46	Taru	Kuja: I did.

Sender	Recipient	Utterance
Old		I dont run graphical ubuntu, I run ubuntu server.
bur[n]er	Old	you can use "ps ax" and "kill (PID#)"

Sender	Recipient	Utterance
kuja	Taru	Haha sucker.
Taru	Kuja	?
kuja	Taru	Anyways, you made the changes right?
Taru	Kuja	Yes.
kuja	Taru	Then from the terminal type: sudo apt-get update
Taru	Kuja	I did.

Figure 4: Example chat room conversation from the #ubuntu channel of the Ubuntu Chat Logs (top), with the disentangled conversations for the Ubuntu Dialogue Corpus (bottom).

Time	User	Utterance
[12:21]	dell	well, can I move the drives?
[12:21]	cucho	dell: ah not like that
[12:21]	RC	dell: you can't move the drives
[12:21]	RC	dell: definitely not
[12:21]	dell	ok
[12:21]	dell	lol
[12:21]	RC	this is the problem with RAID:)
[12:21]	dell	RC haha yeah
[12:22]	dell	cucho, I guess I could just get an enclosure and copy via USB...
[12:22]	cucho	dell: i would advise you to get the disk

Sender	Recipient	Utterance
dell		well, can I move the drives?
cucho	dell	ah not like that
dell	cucho	I guess I could just get an enclosure and copy via USB
cucho	dell	i would advise you to get the disk

Sender	Recipient	Utterance
dell		well, can I move the drives?
RC	dell	you can't move the drives. definitely not. this is the problem with RAID :)
dell	RC	haha yeah

Figure 5: Example of before (top box) and after (bottom box) the algorithm adds and concatenates utterances in dialogue extraction. Since `RC` only addresses `dell`, all of his utterances are added, however this is not done for `dell` as he addresses both `RC` and `cucho`.

Recurrent Polynomial Network for Dialogue State Tracking with Mismatched Semantic Parsers

Qizhe Xie, Kai Sun, Su Zhu, Lu Chen and Kai Yu
Key Lab. of Shanghai Education Commission for Intelligent Interaction and Cognitive Eng.
SpeechLab, Department of Computer Science and Engineering
Shanghai Jiao Tong University, Shanghai, China
{cheezer,accreator,paul2204,chenlusz,kai.yu}@sjtu.edu.cn

Abstract

Recently, constrained Markov Bayesian polynomial (CMBP) has been proposed as a data-driven rule-based model for dialog state tracking (DST). CMBP is an approach to bridge rule-based models and statistical models. Recurrent Polynomial Network (RPN) is a recent statistical framework taking advantages of rule-based models and can achieve state-of-the-art performance on the data corpora of DSTC-3, outperforming all submitted trackers in DSTC-3 including RNN. It is widely acknowledged that SLU's reliability influences tracker's performance greatly, especially in cases where the training SLU is poorly matched to the testing SLU. In this paper, this effect is analyzed in detail for RPN. Experiments show that RPN's tracking result is consistently the best compared to rule-based and statistical models investigated on different SLUs including mismatched ones and demonstrate RPN's is very robust to mismatched semantic parsers.

1 Introduction

Dialogue management is the core of a spoken dialogue system. As a dialogue progresses, dialogue management usually accomplishes two missions. One mission is called dialogue state tracking (DST), which is a process to estimate the distribution of the dialogue states. Another mission is to choose semantics-level machine dialogue acts to direct the dialogue given the information of the dialogue state, referred to as dialogue decision making. Due to unpredictable user behaviours, inevitable automatic speech recognition (ASR) and spoken language understanding (SLU) errors, dialogue state tracking and decision making are difficult (Williams and Young, 2007). Consequently, much research has been devoted to statistical dialogue management. In previous studies, dialogue state tracking and decision making are usually investigated together. In recent years, to advance the research of statistical dialogue management, the DST problem is raised out of the statistical dialogue management framework so that a bunch of models can be investigated for DST. Moreover, shared research tasks like the Dialog State Tracking Challenge (DSTC) (Williams et al., 2013; Henderson et al., 2014a; Henderson et al., 2014b) have provided a common testbed and evaluation suite to facilitate direct comparisons among DST models.

Two DST model categories are broadly known, i.e, rule-based models and statistical models. Recent studies on constrained Markov Bayesian polynomial (CMBP) framework took the first step towards bridging the gap between rule-based and statistical approaches for DST (Sun et al., 2014a; Yu et al., 2015). CMBP formulates rule-based DST in a general way and allows data-driven rules to be generated, so the performance can be improved when training data is available. This enables CMBP to achieve competitive performance to the state-of-the-art statistical approaches, while at the same time keeping most of the advantages of rule-based models. Nevertheless, adding features to CMBP is not as easy as in most other statistical approaches because additional prior knowledge is needed to be added to keep the search space tractable (Sun et al., 2014a; Yu et al., 2015). For the same reason, increasing the model complexity is difficult. To tackle the weakness of CMBP, recurrent polynomial network (RPN) (Sun et al., 2015) is proposed to further bridge the gap between rule-based and statistical approaches for DST (Sun et al., 2015). RPN's unique structure enables the framework to have all the advantages of CMBP. Additionally, RPN achieves more properties of statistical approaches than CMBP. RPN

Proceedings of the SIGDIAL 2015 Conference, pages 295–304,
Prague, Czech Republic, 2-4 September 2015.

uses gradient descent where CMBP uses Hill-climbing. Hence RPN can train its parameters faster and the parameter space are not limited to grid where parameters only takes values which are a multiple of a constant.

SLU is usually the input module of tracker. Hence its performance affect state tracking's performance greatly. However, it is hard to design a reliable parser because of ASR errors and the difficulty of obtaining in-domain data. Further, it is a common case that SLU on a tracker's training data is very different from SLU on a tracker's testing data in real world end-to-end dialogue system. Thus, RPN is evaluated on SLUs with great variance and especially in the case where SLU for training mismatches SLU for testing. RPN shows consistently best results among trackers investigated on all SLUs.

The contribution of this paper is to investigate more complex RPN structures with deeper layers, multiple activation nodes and more features and to evaluate RPN's performance in mismatched SLU condition.

The rest of the paper is organized as follows. Section 2 introduces rule-based models and statistical models used in DST. Section 3 introduces two frameworks – CMBP and RPN bridging rule-based models and statistical models. Complex RPN structures are also introduced in this section. Section 4 discusses the influence of SLU on tracking and the SLU mismatch condition. Section 5 evaluates RPN with different structures and features and these results are compared with state-of-the-art trackers in DSTC-3. Rule-based models, statistical models and mixed models' performance in cases where testing parser mismatches training parser are also compared. Finally, section 6 concludes the paper.

2 Rule-based and Statistical Models for DST

The results of the DSTCs demonstrated the power of statistical approaches, such as Maximum Entropy (MaxEnt) (Lee and Eskenazi, 2013), Conditional Random Field (Lee, 2013), Deep Neural Network (DNN) (Sun et al., 2014b), and Recurrent Neural Network (RNN) (Henderson et al., 2014d). However, statistical approaches have some disadvantages. For example, statistical approaches sometimes show large variation in performance and poor generalisation ability because of lack of data (Williams, 2012). Moreover, statistical models usually have a complex model structure and complex features, and thus can hardly achieve portability and interpretability.

In addition to statistical approaches, rule-based approaches have also been investigated in DSTC due to their efficiency, portability and interpretability and some of them showed good performance and generalisation ability in DSTC (Zilka et al., 2013; Wang and Lemon, 2013).

However, the performance of rule-based models is usually not competitive to the best statistical approaches. Furthermore, a general way is lacking to design rule-based models with prior knowledge and their performance can hardly be improved when training data is available.

3 Bridging Rule-based models and statistical models

There are two ways of bridging rule-based approaches and statistical approaches. One starts from rule-based models and uses data-driven approaches to find a good rule, while the other one is a statistical model taking advantage of prior knowledge and constraints.

3.1 Constrained Markov Bayesian Polynomial

Constrained Markov Bayesian Polynomial (CMBP) (Sun et al., 2014a; Yu et al., 2015) takes the first way of bridging rule-based models and statistical models.

Several probability features extracted from SLU results shown below are used in CMBP for each slot (Sun et al., 2014a; Yu et al., 2015):

- $P_t^+(v)$: sum of scores of SLU hypotheses informing or affirming value v at turn t
- $P_t^-(v)$: sum of scores of SLU hypotheses denying or negating value v at turn t
- $\tilde{P}_t^+(v) = \sum_{v' \notin \{v, \texttt{None}\}} P_t^+(v')$
- $\tilde{P}_t^-(v) = \sum_{v' \notin \{v, \texttt{None}\}} P_t^-(v')$
- $b_t(v)$: belief of "the value being v at turn t"
- b_t^r: probability of the value being $None$ (the value not mentioned) at turn t.

Because slots and values are assumed independent in CMBP. To simplify the notation, these features are denoted as $P_t^+, P_t^-, \tilde{P}_t^+, \tilde{P}_t^-, b_t^r, b_t$ in the rest of this paper.

With these probability features , a CMBP model is defined by

$$b_t = \mathcal{P}\left(P_t^+, P_t^-, \tilde{P}_t^+, \tilde{P}_t^-, b_{t-1}^r, b_{t-1}\right) \quad \text{s.t. constraints} \tag{1}$$

where the $\mathcal{P}$ is a multivariate polynomial function defined as

$$\mathcal{P}(x_1, \cdots, x_D) = \sum_{0 \le k_1 \le \cdots \le k_n \le D} g_{k_1, \cdots, k_n} \prod_{1 \le i \le n} x_{k_i} \tag{2}$$

where k_i is an index into input variables. n called order of the CMBP is the order of the polynomial, D denotes the number of inputs with $x_0 = 1$ and g is the parameter of CMBP.

In CMBP, prior knowledge or intuition is encoded by *constraints* in equation (1). For example, intuition that goal belief should be unchanged or positively correlated with the positive scores from SLU can be written to a constraint:

$$\frac{\partial \mathcal{P}(P_{t+1}^+, P_{t+1}^-, \tilde{P}_{t+1}^+, \tilde{P}_{t+1}^-, b_t^r, b_t)}{\partial P_{t+1}^+} \ge 0 \tag{3}$$

Further, these constraints are approximated to linear forms (Sun et al., 2014a; Yu et al., 2015).

With a set of linear constraints, integer linear programming can be used to get the integer parameters which satisfy the relaxed constraints. Then the tracking accuracy of each parameters can be evaluated and the best one is picked out. Hill-climbing can further be used to extend the best integer-coefficient CMBP to real-coefficient CMBP (Yu et al., 2015).

Note that in practice order 3 (n=3) is used to balance the performance and the complexity (Sun et al., 2014a; Yu et al., 2015). 3-order CMBP has achieved state-of-the art-performance on DSTC-2/3.

3.2 Recurrent Polynomial Network

Recurrent Polynomial network (Sun et al., 2015) takes the second way to bridge rule-based and statistical models. It is a computational network and a statistical framework, which takes advantage of prior knowledge by using CMBP to do initialization.

RPN contains two types of nodes, *input node* or *computational node*. Every node x has a value at every time t, denoted by $u_x^{(t)}$. The values of computational nodes at time t are evaluated using the nodes' values at time t and the nodes' values at time $t-1$ as inputs just like Recurrent Neural Networks (RNNs).

Two types of edges are introduced to denote the time relation between linked nodes. A node at time t takes the value of a node at time $t-1$ as input when they are connected by *type-1* edges, while *type-2* edges indicate that a node at time t takes the value of a node at time t.

Let I_x denote the set of nodes which are connected to node x by *type-1* edges. Similarly, let $\hat{I}_x$ denote the set of nodes which are connected to node x by *type-2* edges.

Generally, three types of computational node are used in RPN, which are *sum node*, *product node* and *activation node*.

- Sum node: For sum node x at time t, its value $u_x^{(t)}$ is the weighted sum of its inputs:

$$u_x^{(t)} = \sum_{y \in I_x} w_{x,y} u_y^{(t-1)} + \sum_{y \in \hat{I}_x} \hat{w}_{x,y} u_y^{(t)} \tag{4}$$

  where $w_{x,y}, \hat{w}_{x,y} \in \mathbb{R}$ are the weights of edges.

- Product node: For product node x at time t, its value $u_x^{(t)}$ is the product of its inputs. Note that there may be multiple edges connecting from node y to node x. Then node y's value should be multiplied to $u_x^{(t)}$ multiple times. Formally, let $M_{x,y}$ and $\hat{M}_{x,y}$ be the multiplicity of the *type-1* edge $\overrightarrow{yx}$ and the multiplicity of the *type-2* edge $\overrightarrow{yx}$ respectively. Node x's value $u_x^{(t)}$ is evaluated by

$$u_x^{(t)} = \prod_{y \in I_x} u_y^{(t-1)^{M_{x,y}}} \prod_{y \in \hat{I}_x} u_y^{(t)^{\hat{M}_{x,y}}} \tag{5}$$

- Activation node: As the value of product nodes and sum nodes are not bounded by certain range while the output belief should lie in $[0, 1]$, activation functions are needed to map values from $\mathbb{R}$ to some interval such as $[0, 1]$. An activation function is a univariate function. If node x is an activation node, there is only one *type-2* edge linked to it.

  Sun et al. (2015) investigated several activation functions and proposed an ascending, continuous function $softclip$ mapping from $\mathbb{R}$ to $[0, 1]$ which is linear on $[\epsilon, 1-\epsilon]$ with ϵ being a small value.

Note that $w, \hat{w}$ are the only parameters in RPN while $M_{x,y}$ and $\hat{M}_{x,y}$ are constant given the structure of RPN and each node can be used as output node in RPN.

3.2.1 Basic Structure

A basic 3-layer RPN shown in figure 1 is introduced here to help understand the correlation between 3-order CMBP and RPN.

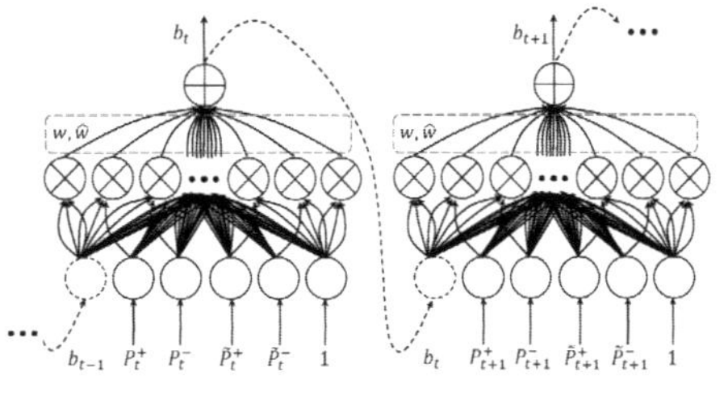

Figure 1: RPN for DST. (Here "+" nodes are sum nodes, "×" nodes are product nodes)

For simplicity, (l, i) is used to denote the index of the i-th node in the l-th layer. Then each layer is defined as follows:

- First layer / Input layer: In this layer, input nodes correspond to the variables in equation (1), i.e. the value of 6 input nodes $u^{(t)}_{(0,0)} \sim u^{(t)}_{(0,5)}$ are the same as variables b_{t-1}, P^+_t, P^-_t, $\tilde{P}^+_t$, $\tilde{P}^-_t$, 1 in equation (1).

  Feature b^r_{t-1} which is belief of the value at time $t-1$ being $None$ is not used here to make the RPN structure clear and compact. Experiments show that performance of CMBP without feature b^r_{t-1} would not degrade. It is not used by CMBP mentioned in the rest of paper either.

- Second layer: Every product node x in the second layer corresponds to a monomial in equation (2). To express different monomials, each triple of input nodes $(1, k_1)$, $(1, k_2)$, $(1, k_3)(0 \leq k_1 \leq k_2 \leq k_3 \leq 5)$ is enumerated to link to a product node $x = (2, i)$ in the second layer and $u^{(t)}_x = u^{(t)}_{(1,k_1)} u^{(t)}_{(1,k_2)} u^{(t)}_{(1,k_3)}$.

- Third layer: There is only one sum node $(3, 0)$ in the third layer corresponding to the belief value calculated by a polynomial. With the parameters set according to g_{k_1,k_2,k_3} in equation (2), the value $u^{(t)}_{(3,0)}$ is equal to b_t outputted by equation (1). It is the only output node in this structure.

From the explanation of basic structure in this section, it can be easily observed that a CMBP can be used to initialize RPN and thus RPN can achieve at least the same results with CMBP. So prior knowledge and constraints are used to find a suboptimum point in RPN parameter space and RPN as a statistical approach, can further optimize its parameters. Hence, RPN is a way of bridging rule-based models and statistical models.

3.2.2 Complete Structure

It is easy to add features to RPN as a statistical model. In the work of Sun et al. (2015), 4 more features about user dialogue acts and machine acts are introduced.

A new sum node $x = (3, 1)$ in the third layer is introduced to capture some property across turns just like belief b_t. Like the node $(3, 0)$ that outputs belief in the same layer, node $(3, 1)$ takes input from every product node in the second layer and is used as input features at next time.

Further, to map the output belief to $[0, 1]$, activation nodes with $softclip(\cdot)$ as their activation function are introduced.

The complete structure with the activation function, 4 more features and the new recurrent connection is shown in figure 2.

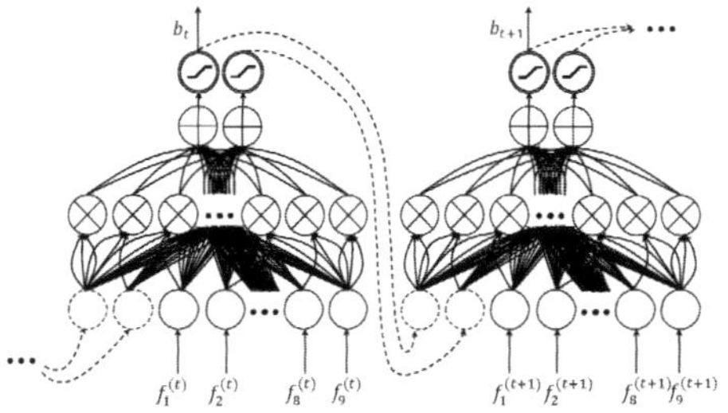

Figure 2: RPN with new features and more complex structure for DST (Sigmoid nodes mean activation)

The relation between a 3-order CMBP and the basic structure is shown in section 3.2.1. Similarly, the complete structure can also be initialized using CMBP by setting the weights of edges that do not appear in the basic structure to 0.

3.3 Complex RPN Structure

We next exam RPN's power of utilizing more features, multiple activation functions and a deeper structure with two interesting explorations on RPN structure are shown in this section. Although these extensions do not yield better results, this section covers these extensions to show the flexibility of the RPN approach.

3.3.1 Complex Structure

Firstly, to express a 4-order polynomial, simply using the structure shown in figure 2 with in-degree of nodes in the second layer increased to 4 would be sufficient. However, it can be expressed by a more compact RPN structure. To simplify the explanation, the example RPN expressing $1-(1-(b_{t-1})^2)(1-(P_t^+)^2)$ is shown in figure 3.

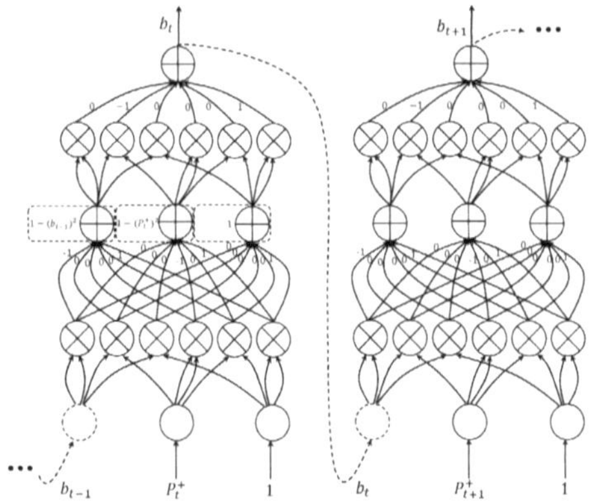

Figure 3: RPN for polynomial $1-(1-(b_{t-1})^2)(1-(P_t^+)^2)$

In figure 3, the first layer is used for input, and the values of the product nodes in the second layer are equal to the products of two features such as $(b_{t-1})^2$, $b_{t-1}P_t^+$, $(P_t^+)^2$ and so on. Every sum node in the third layer can express all the possible 2-order polynomial of features with weights set accordingly. In figure 3, the values of the three sum nodes are $1-(b_{t-1})^2$, $1-(P_t^+)^2$ and 1 respectively. Then similarly, with another product nodes layer and sum nodes layer, the value of the output node in the last layer equals the value of the 4-order polynomial $(1-(b_{t-1})^2)(1-(P_t^+)^2)$.

The complete RPN structure with same features shown in figure 2, the new recurrent connection and activation nodes that expresses 4-order CMBPs can be obtained similarly.

With limited sum nodes in the third layer, the complexity of the model is much smaller than using a structure shown in figure 2 with product node's in-degree increased to 4 and increasing the number of product nodes accordingly.

3.3.2 Complex Features

Secondly, RNN proposed by Henderson et al. (2014c) uses n-gram of ASR results and machine acts. Similar to that, features of n-gram of ASR results and machine acts are also investigated in RPN. Since RPN used in this paper is a binary classification model and assumes slots independent of each other, the n-gram features proposed by Henderson et al. (2014c) are modified in this paper by removing/merging some features to make the features independent of slots and values. When tracking slot s and value v, the sum of confidence scores of ASR hypothesises of the following cases are extracted:

- V: confidence score of ASR hypothesises where value v appears
- $\tilde{V}$: confidence score of ASR hypothesises where values other than v appear
- V^r: confidence score of ASR hypothesises where no value appear

Similar features for slots can be extracted. Then by looking at both slot and value features for ASR results, we can get the combination of conditions of slots and values.

n-gram features of machine acts about the tracking slot and value are also used as features. For example, given machine acts `hello() | inform(area=center) | inform(food=Chinese) | request(name)`, for slot *food* and value *Chinese*, the n-gram machine act features are `hello`, `inform`, `request`, `inform+slot`, `inform+value`, `inform+slot+value`, `slot`, `value`, `slot+value`. Features such as `request(name)` are about slot *name* and hence `request+slot` are not in the feature list.

To combine RPN with RNN proposed by Henderson et al. (2014c), input nodes of these n-gram features are not linked to product nodes in the second layer. Instead, a layer of sum nodes followed by a layer of activation nodes with sigmoid activation function, which are equivalent to a layer of neurons are introduced. These activation nodes are linked to sum nodes in the third layer just like product nodes in the second layer. The structure is illustrated by figure 4 clearly.

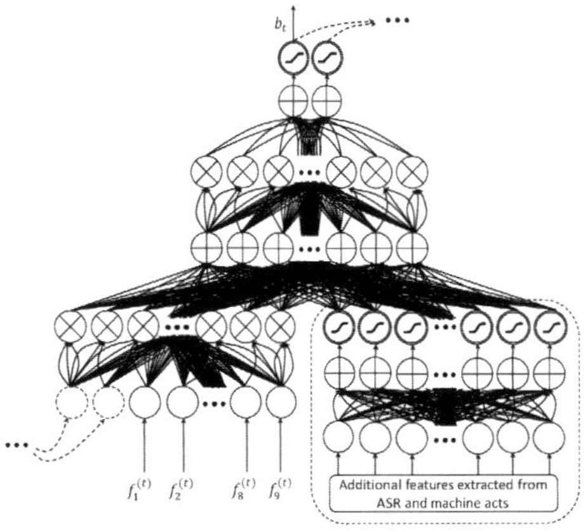

Figure 4: RPN structure combined with RNN features and structures

Experiments in section 5 show that these two structures do not yield better results when initialized randomly or initialized using 3-order CMBPs, although the model complexity increases a lot. This indicates the briefness and effectiveness of the simple structure shown in figure 2.

4 Uncertainty in SLU

In an end-to-end dialogue system, there are two challenges in spoken language understanding: ASR errors and insufficient in-domain dialogue data.

ASR errors make information contained in the user's utterance distorted or even missed. Thankfully, statistical approaches to SLU, trained on labeled in-domain examples, have been shown to be relatively robust to ASR errors. (Mairesse et al., 2009).

Even with an effective way to get SLU robust to ASR errors, it is hard to implement these SLUs for a new domain due to insufficient labelled data. In DSTC-3, only little data of new dialogue domain is provided.

Following the work of Zhu et al. (2014), the following steps are used to handle the two challenges stated above:

- Data generation: with sufficient data in restaurants domain in DSTC-2, data on tourists domain using ontology of DSTC-3 can be generated. Utterance patterns of data in the original domain are used to generate data for the new domain of DSTC-3. After preparing both the original data in DSTC-2 and the generated data of DSTC-3, a more general parser for these two domains can be built.
- ASR error simulation: after data generation, ASR error simulation (Zhu et al., 2014) is needed to make the prepared data resemble ASR output with speech recognition errors to train a parser robust to ASR errors. With a simple mapping from the pattern of transcription to the corresponding patterns of ASR n-best hypotheses learned from existing data and phone-based confusion for slot-values, pseudo ASR n-best hypotheses can be obtained. Note that methods proposed by Zhu et al. (2014) only do ASR error simulation for generated data in domain of DSTC-3 and leave the original data in DSTC-2 as its original ASR form,which may introduce the difference in the distribution between training data and testing data on two different domains for the tracker. So ASR error is simulated in data on both domains instead.
- Training: Using the data got from the previous steps, a statistical parser can be trained (Henderson et al., 2012). By varying the fraction of simulated vs. real data, and the simulated error rate, prior expectations about operating conditions can be expressed.

Although a semantic parser with state-of-the-art techniques can achieve good performance in some degree, parsing without any error is impossible because it is typical that a semantic parser gets high performance in speech patterns existing in the training dataset, while it fails to predict the correct semantics for some utterances unseen in training dataset. So it is common for SLU performance to differ significantly between training and test conditions in real world end-to-end systems.

It has been widely observed that SLU influences state tracking greatly because the confidence scores of SLU hypotheses are usually the key inputs for dialogue state tracking. When these confidence scores become unreliable, the performance of tracker is sure to degrade. Studies have shown that it is possible to improve SLU accuracy as compared to the live SLU in the DSTC data (Zhu et al., 2014; Sun et al., 2014b). Hence, most of the state-of-the-art results from DSTC-2 and DSTC-3 used refined SLU (either explicitly rebuild a SLU component or take the ASR hypotheses into the trackers (Williams, 2014; Sun et al., 2014b;

Henderson et al., 2014d; Henderson et al., 2014c; Kadlec et al., 2014; Sun et al., 2014a)). Kadlec et al.(2014) gets a tracking accuracy improvement of 7.6% when they use SLU refined by themselves instead of organiser-provided live SLU.

In semantic parser mismatch condition, the accuracy of state tracking can degrade badly. Mismatched SLU problem is a main challenge in DST. Trackers under mismatched SLU conditions are investigated in this paper.

5 Experiments

5.1 RPN with Different Structures

In this section, the performance of three structures shown in this paper is compared and RPN with the simple structure is evaluated on DSTC-3 and compared with the best submitted trackers. Only joint goal accuracy which is the most difficult task of DSTC-3 is of interest. Note that the integer-coefficient CMBP with the best performance on DSTC-2 is used to initialize RPN. As it is stated in section 4, SLU designed in this paper focuses on domain extension, so trackers are only evaluated on DSTC-3.

Order	n-gram features	Acc	L2
3	No	0.652	0.540
4	No	0.648	0.541
4	Yes	0.648	0.541

Table 1: Performance comparison among RPNs with three structures on `dstc3eval`

The RPN structures that express 3-order CMBP, 4-order CMBP without n-gram features and 4-order CMBP with n-gram features are evaluated. *Acc* is the accuracy of tracker's 1-best joint goal hypothesis, the larger the better. *L2* is the L2 norm between correct joint goal distribution and distribution tracker outputs, the smaller the better.

It can be seen from table 1 that the simple structure yields the best result. Note that parser used here is explained in work (Zhu et al., 2014). Experiments of the mismatched SLU case also use this SLU for training.

For DSTC-3, it can be seen from table 2, RPN trained on DSTC-2 can achieve state-of-the-art performance on DSTC-3 without modifying tracking method, outperforming all the submitted trackers in DSTC-3 including the RNN system.

Note that the simple structure is used here with SLU refined described in section 4. We picked the best practical one on dstc2-test among SLUs introduced in the following section as the training SLU and testing SLU.

System	Approach	Rank	Acc	L2
Baseline*	Rule	6	0.575	0.691
Henderson et al. (2014c)	RNN	1	0.646	0.538
Kadlec et al. (2014)	Rule	2	0.630	0.627
Sun et al. (2014a)	Int CMBP	3	0.610	0.556
RPN	RPN	0.5	0.660	0.518

Table 2: Performance comparison among RPN, real-coefficient CMBP and best trackers of DSTC-3 on `dstc3eval`. Baseline* is the best results from the 4 baselines in DSTC3.

5.2 RPN with Mismatched Semantic Parsers

As section 4 stated, SLU is the input module for dialogue state tracking whose confidence score is usually directly used as probability features and hence has tremendous effect on trackers. Handling mismatched semantic parsers is a main challenge to DST.

In this section, different tracking methods are evaluated when there is a mismatch between training data and testing data. More specifically, different tracking models are trained with the same fixed SLU and tested with different SLUs.

Three main categories of tracking models are investigated: rule-based models, statistical models and mixed models.

MaxEnt (Sun et al., 2014b) is a statistical model. HWU baseline (Wang, 2013) is selected as a competitive rule-based model. CMBP and RPN are mixed models.

Four type of SLUs with different levels of performance are used:

1 *Original*: SLU results provided by DSTC-3 organizer.

2 *Train*: SLU introduced in section 4 with $k(k = 25, 50)$ percent training data adding ASR error simulation and parsed on ASR-hypotheses.

3 *Combined*: SLU combining the *Original* type SLU and *Train* type SLU using averaging.

4 *Transcript*: SLU introduced in section 4 with k percent training data adding ASR error simulation and parsed on transcription. This setup assumes an oracle speech recognizer: it is not practical, and is included only for comparison.

It has been shown that the organiser-provided live SLU can be improved upon and so it is used as the worst SLU in the following comparison. Past work has shown that trained parser gets a performance improvement when combined with the one the organiser provided (Zhu et al., 2014). Using transcription for parsing gives a much more reliable SLU results than using ASR hypotheses. So generally speaking, performance of SLUs of different types is quite distinguished to each other. Six different SLUs whose performance score shown in table 3 are investigated.

SLU type	ASR error	ICE	Fscore	Precision	Recall
Original	-	1.719	0.824	0.852	0.797
Train	25%	1.441	0.836	0.863	0.811
	50%	1.425	0.837	0.862	0.813
Combined	25%	1.241	0.834	0.870	0.801
	50%	1.235	0.835	0.869	0.803
Transcript	50%	0.893	0.915	0.956	0.877

Table 3: Performance of six different SLUs

Note that ASR error here is the percent of training data with ASR error simulation when training SLU. The Item Cross Entropy (ICE) (Thomson et al., 2008) between the N-best SLU hypotheses and the semantic label assesses the overall quality of the semantic items distribution, and is shown to give a consistent performance ranking for both the confidence scores and the overall correctness of the semantic parser (Zhu et al., 2014). SLU with the lower ICE has better performance.

Precision and recall are evaluated using only SLU's 1-best hypothesis where ICE takes all hypothesises and their confidence score into consideration.

In results shown in figure 5, the training dataset for tracker is fixed, while testing dataset is outputted by different SLUs. The X-axis gives the SLU ICE and Y-axis gives the tracking accuracy on DSTC3-test. It can be observed that RPN achieves highest accuracy on every SLU among rule-based models, statistical models and mixed models. Thus, RPN shows its robustness on mismatched semantic parsers, which demonstrates the power of using both prior knowledge and being a statistical approach.

After evaluating the mismatched case, the matched case is also tested. When training dataset and testing dataset are outputted by the same SLU, RPN also outperforms all other models, shown in figure 6.

It can be observed that RPN achieves the highest accuracy among RPN, CMBP, MaxEnt, and HWU baseline whether there is a mismatch between training SLU and testing SLU or not.

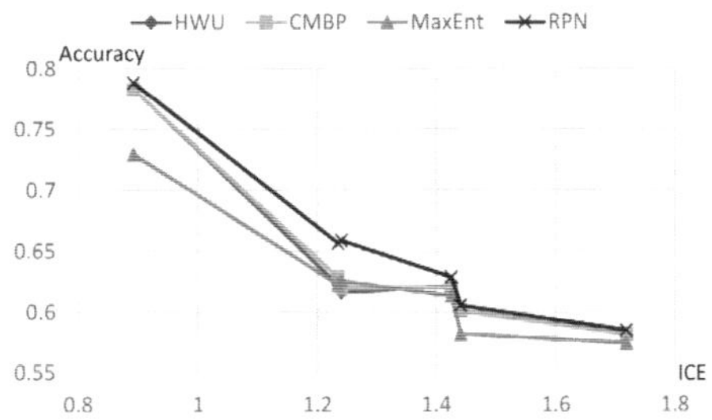

Figure 5: Trackers' performances with mismatched semantic parsers

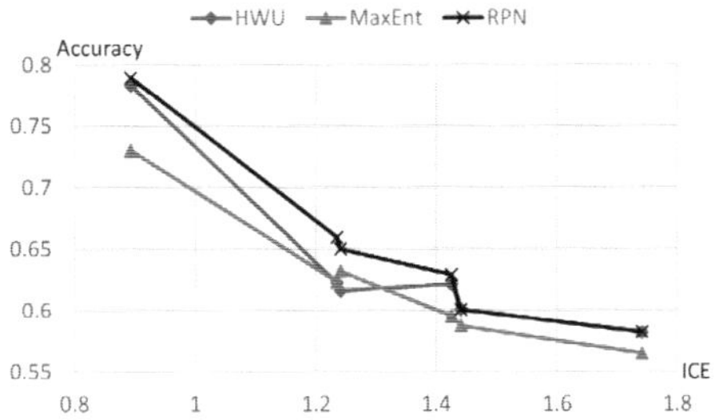

Figure 6: Trackers' performances with matched semantic parser

6 Conclusion

Recurrent Polynomial Network demonstrated in this paper is a recent framework to bridge rule-based and statistical models. Several networks are explored and the simple structure's performance outperforms others. Experiments show that RPN outperforms many state-of-the-art trackers on DSTC-3 and RPN performs best on all SLUs with mismatched SLU.

Acknowledgments

This work was supported by the Program for Professor of Special Appointment (Eastern Scholar) at Shanghai Institutions of Higher Learning, the China NSFC project No. 61222208 and the Chun-Tsung Program of SJTU. We thank Jason Williams for reviewing and providing suggestions to this paper.

Appendix

Activation function

An activation function $softclip(\cdot)$ is a combination of logistic function and clip function. Let ϵ denote a small value such as 0.01, δ denote the offset of sigmoid function such that $sigmoid\,(\epsilon - 0.5 + \delta) = \epsilon$. $sigmoid$ function here is defined as

$$sigmoid(x) = \frac{1}{1+e^{-x}} \tag{6}$$

The softclip function is defined as

$$softclip(x) \triangleq \begin{cases} sigmoid\,(x - 0.5 + \delta) \\ \quad \text{if } x \leq \epsilon \\ x \\ \quad \text{if } \epsilon < x < 1 - \epsilon \\ sigmoid\,(x - 0.5 - \delta) \\ \quad \text{if } x \geq 1 - \epsilon \end{cases} \tag{7}$$

It is a non-decreasing, continuous function, which is linear on $[\epsilon, 1-\epsilon]$. Its derivative is defined as follows:

$$\frac{\partial softclip(x)}{\partial x} \triangleq \begin{cases} \frac{\partial sigmoid(x-0.5+\delta)}{\partial x} \\ \quad \text{if } x \leq \epsilon \\ 1 \\ \quad \text{if } \epsilon < x < 1 - \epsilon \\ \frac{\partial sigmoid(x-0.5-\delta)}{\partial x} \\ \quad \text{if } x \geq 1 - \epsilon \end{cases} \tag{8}$$

Training

Backpropagation through time (BPTT) using mini-batch is used to train the network with batch size 50. Gradients of weights are calculated and accumulated within each batch. Gradients computed for each timestep are propagated to the first timestep. Mean squared error (MSE) is used as the criterion to measure the distance of the output belief to the correct belief distribution.

Derivative calculation

Let $\delta_x^{(t)}$ be the partial derivative of the cost function over value of node x, i.e., $\delta_x^{(t)} = \frac{\partial \mathcal{L}}{\partial u_x}$. Suppose node $x = (d, i)$ is a sum node, then when node x passes its error, the error of child node $y \in \hat{I}_x$ is updated as

$$\begin{aligned} \delta_y^{(t)} &= \delta_y^{(t)} + \frac{\partial \mathcal{L}}{\partial u_x^{(t)}} \frac{\partial u_x^{(t)}}{\partial u_y^{(t)}} \\ &= \delta_y^{(t)} + \delta_x^{(t)} \hat{w}_{x,y} \end{aligned} \tag{9}$$

Similarly, error of node $y \in I_x$ is updated as

$$\begin{aligned} \delta_y^{(t)} &= \delta_y^{(t)} + \frac{\partial \mathcal{L}}{\partial u_x^{(t)}} \frac{\partial u_x^{(t)}}{\partial u_y^{(t-1)}} \\ &= \delta_y^{(t)} + \delta_x^{(t)} w_{x,y} \end{aligned} \tag{10}$$

Suppose node $x = (d, i)$ is a product node, then when node x passes its error, error of node $y \in \hat{I}_x$ is updated as

$$\begin{aligned} \delta_y^{(t)} &= \delta_y^{(t)} + \frac{\partial \mathcal{L}}{\partial u_x^{(t)}} \frac{\partial u_x^{(t)}}{\partial u_y^{(t)}} \\ &= \delta_y^{(t)} + \\ &\quad \delta_x^{(t)} \hat{M}_{x,y} {u_y^{(t)}}^{\hat{M}_{x,y}-1} \\ &\quad \prod_{z \in \hat{I}_x - \{y\}} {u_z^{(t)}}^{\hat{M}_{x,z}} \prod_{z \in I_x} {u_z^{(t-1)}}^{M_{x,z}} \end{aligned} \tag{11}$$

Similarly, error of node $y \in I_x$ is updated as

$$\begin{aligned} \delta_y^{(t)} &= \delta_y^{(t)} + \frac{\partial \mathcal{L}}{\partial u_x^{(t)}} \frac{\partial u_x^{(t)}}{\partial u_y^{(t-1)}} \\ &= \delta_y^{(t)} + \\ &\quad \delta_x^{(t)} M_{x,y} {u_y^{(t-1)}}^{M_{x,y}-1} \\ &\quad \prod_{z \in \hat{I}_x} {u_z^{(t)}}^{\hat{M}_{x,z}} \prod_{z \in I_x - \{y\}} {u_z^{(t-1)}}^{M_{x,z}} \end{aligned} \tag{12}$$

References

Matthew Henderson, Milica Gasic, Blaise Thomson, Pirros Tsiakoulis, Kai Yu, and Steve Young. 2012. Discriminative spoken language understanding using word confusion networks. In *SLT*, pages 176–181.

Matthew Henderson, Blaise Thomson, and Jason D. Williams. 2014a. The second dialog state tracking challenge. In *Proceedings of the 15th Annual Meeting of the Special Interest Group on Discourse and Dialogue (SIGDIAL)*, pages 263–272, Philadelphia, PA, U.S.A., June. Association for Computational Linguistics.

Matthew. Henderson, Blaise. Thomson, and Jason D. Williams. 2014b. The third dialog state tracking challenge. In *Proceedings of IEEE Spoken Language Technology Workshop (SLT)*, December.

Matthew. Henderson, Blaise. Thomson, and Steve. Young. 2014c. Robust dialog state tracking using delexicalised recurrent neural networks and unsupervised adaptation. In *Proceedings of IEEE Spoken Language Technology Workshop (SLT)*, December.

Matthew Henderson, Blaise Thomson, and Steve Young. 2014d. Word-based dialog state tracking with recurrent neural networks. In *Proceedings of the 15th Annual Meeting of the Special Interest Group on Discourse and Dialogue (SIGDIAL)*, pages 292–299, Philadelphia, PA, U.S.A., June. Association for Computational Linguistics.

Rudolf Kadlec, Miroslav Vodoln, Jindrich Libovick, Jan Macek, and Jan Kleindienst. 2014. Knowledge-based dialog state tracking. In *Proceedings 2014 IEEE Spoken Language Technology Workshop*, South Lake Tahoe, USA, December.

Sungjin Lee and Maxine Eskenazi. 2013. Recipe for building robust spoken dialog state trackers: Dialog state tracking challenge system description. In *Proceedings of the SIGDIAL 2013 Conference*, pages 414–422, Metz, France, August. Association for Computational Linguistics.

Sungjin Lee. 2013. Structured discriminative model for dialog state tracking. In *Proceedings of the SIGDIAL 2013 Conference*, pages 442–451, Metz, France, August. Association for Computational Linguistics.

François Mairesse, Milica Gasic, Filip Jurcícek, Simon Keizer, Blaise Thomson, Kai Yu, and Steve Young. 2009. Spoken language understanding from unaligned data using discriminative classification models. In *Proceedings of ICASSP*.

Kai. Sun, Lu. Chen, Su. Zhu, and Kai. Yu. 2014a. A generalized rule based tracker for dialogue state tracking. In *Proceedings of IEEE Spoken Language Technology Workshop (SLT)*, December.

Kai Sun, Lu Chen, Su Zhu, and Kai Yu. 2014b. The SJTU system for dialog state tracking challenge 2. In *Proceedings of the 15th Annual Meeting of the Special Interest Group on Discourse and Dialogue (SIGDIAL)*, pages 318–326, Philadelphia, PA, U.S.A., June. Association for Computational Linguistics.

Kai Sun, Qizhe Xie, and Kai Yu. 2015. Recurrent polynomial network for dialogue state tracking. *submitted to Dialogue and Discourse*.

Blaise Thomson, Kai Yu, Milica Gasic, Simon Keizer, Francois Mairesse, Jost Schatzmann, and Steve Young. 2008. Evaluating semantic-level confidence scores with multiple hypotheses. In *INTERSPEECH*, pages 1153–1156.

Zhuoran Wang and Oliver Lemon. 2013. A simple and generic belief tracking mechanism for the dialog state tracking challenge: On the believability of observed information. In *Proceedings of the SIGDIAL 2013 Conference*, pages 423–432, Metz, France, August. Association for Computational Linguistics.

Zhuoran Wang. 2013. HWU baseline belief tracker for dstc 2 & 3. Technical report, October.

Jason D. Williams and Steve Young. 2007. Partially observable markov decision processes for spoken dialog systems. *Computer Speech & Language*, 21(2):393–422.

Jason Williams, Antoine Raux, Deepak Ramachandran, and Alan Black. 2013. The dialog state tracking challenge. In *Proceedings of the SIGDIAL 2013 Conference*, pages 404–413, Metz, France, August. Association for Computational Linguistics.

Jason D. Williams. 2012. Challenges and opportunities for state tracking in statistical spoken dialog systems: Results from two public deployments. *Selected Topics in Signal Processing, IEEE Journal of*, 6(8):959–970.

Jason D. Williams. 2014. Web-style ranking and SLU combination for dialog state tracking. In *Proceedings of the 15th Annual Meeting of the Special Interest Group on Discourse and Dialogue (SIGDIAL)*, pages 282–291, Philadelphia, PA, U.S.A., June. Association for Computational Linguistics.

Kai Yu, Kai Sun, Lu Chen, and Su Zhu. 2015. Constrained markov bayesian polynomial for efficient dialogue state tracking. *submitted to IEEE Transactions on Audio, Speech and Language Processing*.

Su Zhu, Lu Chen, Kai Sun, Da Zheng, and Kai Yu. 2014. Semantic parser enhancement for dialogue domain extension with little data. In *Proceedings of IEEE Spoken Language Technology Workshop (SLT)*, December.

Lukas Zilka, David Marek, Matej Korvas, and Filip Jurcicek. 2013. Comparison of bayesian discriminative and generative models for dialogue state tracking. In *Proceedings of the SIGDIAL 2013 Conference*, pages 452–456, Metz, France, August. Association for Computational Linguistics.

Opportunities and Obligations to Take Turns in Collaborative Multi-Party Human-Robot Interaction

Martin Johansson and Gabriel Skantze
Department of Speech Music and Hearing, KTH
Stockholm, Sweden
{vhmj,skantze}@kth.se

Abstract

In this paper we present a data-driven model for detecting opportunities and obligations for a robot to take turns in multi-party discussions about objects. The data used for the model was collected in a public setting, where the robot head Furhat played a collaborative card sorting game together with two users. The model makes a combined detection of addressee and turn-yielding cues, using multi-modal data from voice activity, syntax, prosody, head pose, movement of cards, and dialogue context. The best result for a binary decision is achieved when several modalities are combined, giving a weighted F_1 score of 0.876 on data from a previously unseen interaction, using only automatically extractable features.

1 Introduction

Robots of the future are envisioned to help people perform tasks, not only as mere tools, but as autonomous agents interacting and solving problems together with humans. Such interaction will be characterised by two important features that need to be taken into account when modelling the spoken interaction. Firstly, the robot should be able to solve problems together with several humans (and possibly other robots) at the same time, which means that we need to model *multi-party* interaction. Secondly, joint problem solving is in many cases *situated*, which means that the spoken discourse will involve references to, and manipulation of, objects in the shared physical space. When speaking about objects, humans typically pay attention to these objects and gaze at them. Also, placing or moving an object can be regarded as a communicative act in itself (Clark, 2005). To solve the task efficiently, interlocutors need to coordinate their attention, resulting in so-called joint attention (Clark & Marshall, 1981).

These characteristics of human-robot interaction pose many challenges for spoken dialogue systems. In this paper, we address the problem of turn-taking, which is a central problem for all spoken dialogue systems, but which is especially challenging when several interlocutors are involved. In multi-party interaction, the system does not only have to determine when a speaker yields the turn, but also whether it is yielded to the system or to someone else. This becomes even more problematic when the discussion involves objects in a shared physical space. For example, an obvious signal that humans use for yielding the turn in a face-to-face setting is to gaze at the next speaker (Vertegaal et al., 2001). However, in situated interaction, where the gaze is also used to pay attention to the objects which are under discussion, it is not obvious how this shared resource is used. While modelling all these aspects of the interaction is indeed challenging, the multi-modal nature of human-robot interaction also has the promise of offering redundant information that the system can utilize, thereby possibly increasing the robustness of the system (Vinyals et al., 2012).

The aim of this study is to develop a data-driven model that can be used by the system to decide when to take the turn and not. While there are many previous studies that have built such models based on human-human (Koiso et al., 1998; Morency et al., 2008) or human-machine interaction (Raux & Eskenazi, 2008; Skantze & Schlangen, 2009; Bohus & Horvitz, 2011; Meena et al., 2014), we are not aware of any previous studies that investigate multi-party human-robot discussions about objects.

The system that we build the model for, and use data from, is a collaborative game that was exhibited at the Swedish National Museum of

Proceedings of the SIGDIAL 2015 Conference, pages 305–314,
Prague, Czech Republic, 2-4 September 2015.

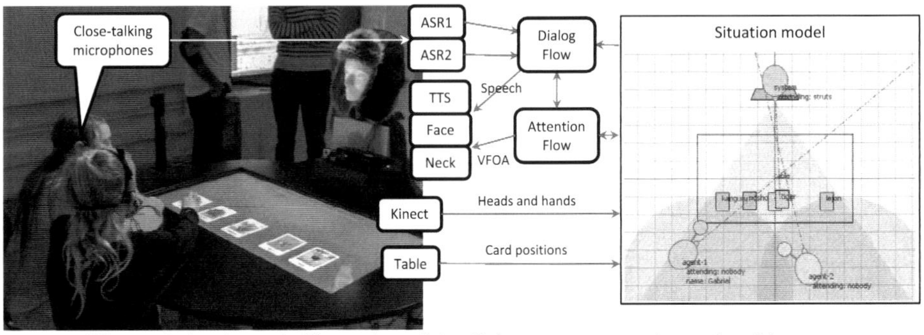

Figure 1: A schematic illustration of the dialogue system setting and architecture

Science and Technology in November 15-23, 2014. As can be seen in Figure 1, two visitors at a time could play a collaborative game together with the robot head Furhat (Al Moubayed et al., 2013). On the touch table between the players, a set of cards are shown. The two visitors and Furhat are given the task of sorting the cards according to some criterion. For example, the task could be to sort a set of inventions in the order they were invented, or a set of animals based on how fast they can run. This is a collaborative game, which means that the visitors have to discuss the solution together with Furhat. As we have discussed in previous work (Johansson et al., 2013), we think that the symmetry of the interaction is especially interesting from a turn-taking perspective. The setting also provides a wide range of multi-modal features that can be exploited: voice activity, syntax, prosody, head pose, movement of cards, and dialogue context[1].

The paper is organized as follows: In Section 2 we present and discuss related work, in Section 3 we describe the system and data annotation in more detail, in Section 4 we present the performance of the different machine learning algorithms and features sets, and in Section 5 we end with conclusions and a discussion of the results.

2 Background

2.1 Turn-taking in dialogue systems

Numerous studies have investigated how humans synchronize turn-taking in dialogue. In a seminal study, Duncan (1972) showed how speakers use prosody, syntax and gestures to signal whether the speaker wants to hold the turn or yield it to the interlocutor. For example, flat final pitch, syntactic incompleteness and filled pauses are strong cues to turn hold. In his analysis, Duncan found that as more turn yielding cues are presented together, the likelihood that the listener will try to take the turn increases. Later studies on human-human interaction have presented more thorough statistical analyses of turn-yielding and turn-holding cues (Koiso et al., 1998; Gravano & Hirschberg, 2011). Typically, for speech-only interaction, syntactic and semantic completeness is found to be the strongest cue, but prosody can also be informative, especially if other cues are not available. In face-to-face interaction, gaze has been found to be a strong turn-taking cue. Kendon (1967) found that the speaker gazes away from the listener during longer utterances, and then gazes at the listener as a turn-yielding cue near the end of the utterance.

Contrary to this sophisticated combination of cues for managing turn-taking, dialogue systems have traditionally only used a fixed silence threshold after which the system responds. While this model simplifies processing, it fails to account for many aspects of human-human interaction such as hesitations, turn-taking with very short gaps or brief overlaps and backchannels in the middle of utterances (Heldner & Edlund, 2010). More advanced models for turn-taking have been presented, where the system interprets syntactic and prosodic cues to make continuous decisions on when to take the turn or give feedback, resulting in both faster response time and less interruptions (Raux & Eskenazi, 2008; Skantze & Schlangen, 2009; Meena et al., 2014).

2.2 Turn-taking in multi-party interaction

Multi-party interaction differs from dyadic interaction in several ways (Traum & Rickel, 2001). First, in a dyadic interaction there are only two different roles that the speakers can have: speaker and listener. In multi-party interaction, humans may take on many different roles, such as side participant, overhearer and bystander (Mutlu et al., 2012). Second, in dyadic interaction, it is

[1] A video of the interaction can be seen at https://www.youtube.com/watch?v=5fhjuGu3d0I

always clear who is to speak next at turn shifts. In multi-party interaction, this has to be coordinated somehow. The most obvious signal is to use gaze to select the next speaker (Vertegaal et al., 2001). Thus, for multi-party interaction between a robot and several users, gaze is a valuable feature for detecting the addressee. Gaze tracking is however not trivial to utilize in many practical settings, since they typically have a limited in field-of-view, or (if head worn) are too invasive. In addition, they are not very robust to blinking or occlusion, and typically need calibration. Many systems therefore rely on head pose tracking, which is a simpler and more robust approach, but which cannot capture quick glances or track more precise gaze targets. However, previous studies have found head pose to be a fairly reliable indicator for gaze in multi-party interaction, given that the targets are clearly separated (Katzenmaier et al., 2004; Stiefelhagen & Zhu, 2002; Ba & Odobez, 2009). In addition to head pose, there are also studies which show that the addressee detection in human-machine interaction can be improved by also considering the speech signal, as humans typically talk differently to the machine compared to other humans (Shriberg et al., 2013). Vinyals et al. (2012) present an approach where the addressee detection is done using a large set of multi-modal features.

In situated interaction, speakers also naturally look at the objects which are under discussion. The speaker's gaze can therefore be used by the listener as a cue to the speaker's current focus of attention. This has been shown to clearly affect the extent to which humans otherwise gaze at each other to yield the turn. Argyle & Graham (1976) studied dyadic interactions involving additional targets for visual attention. Objects relevant to the task at hand were found to attract visual attention at the expense of the other subject. In a study on modelling turn-taking in three-party poster conversations, Kawahara et al. (2012) found that the participants almost always looked at the shared poster. Also, in most studies on human-robot interaction, the robot has a clear "function", and it is therefore obvious that the user is either addressing the machine or another human. However, in a previous study on multi-party human-robot discussion about objects (Johansson et al., 2013), which had a task that is very similar to the one used here, we found that the addressee of utterances is not so easy to determine. Sometimes, a question might be posed directly to the robot, which then results in an *obligation* to take the turn. But many times, utterances in multi-party discussions are not targeted towards a specific person, but rather to both interlocutors, resulting in an *opportunity* to take the turn.

The approach taken in this study is therefore to combine the turn taking and addressee detection into one decision: *Should the system take the turn or not?*, and then allow a gradual answer from a clear "no" (0) to a clear "yes" (1). If the answer is 0, it could be because a speaker is holding the turn, or that a question was clearly posed to someone else. If the answer is 1, the system is obliged to respond, most likely because one of the users has asked a question directly to the robot. But in many cases, the answer could be somewhere in between, indicating an opportunity to respond. In future work, we plan to use such a score together with a utility function in a decision-theoretic framework (Bohus & Horvitz, 2011). Thus, if the system has something urgent to say, it could do so even in a non-optimal location, whereas if what it has to say is not so important, this would require an obligation in order to respond

3 Data collection and annotation

3.1 System description

As described in the introduction, we use data from a multi-party human-robot interaction game that was exhibited in a public setting. The system was implemented using the open source dialogue system framework IrisTK (Skantze & Al Moubayed, 2012) and is schematically illustrated in Figure 1. The visitors are interacting with the Furhat robot head (Al Moubayed et al., 2013), which has an animated face back-projected on a translucent mask, as well as a mechanical neck, which allows Furhat to signal his focus of attention using a combination of head pose and eye-gaze. A Kinect camera (V2) is used to track the location and rotation of the two users' heads, as well as their hands. This data, together with the position of the five cards on the touch table are sent to a Situation model, which maintains a 3D representation of the situation. Two behaviour controllers based on the Harel statechart mechanism offered by IrisTK run in parallel: The Dialog Flow and the Attention Flow. The Attention Flow keeps Furhat's attention to a specified target (a user or a card), even when the target is moving, by consulting the Situation model. The 3D position of the target is then transformed into neck and gaze movement of Furhat (again taking Furhat's position in the 3D space into account).

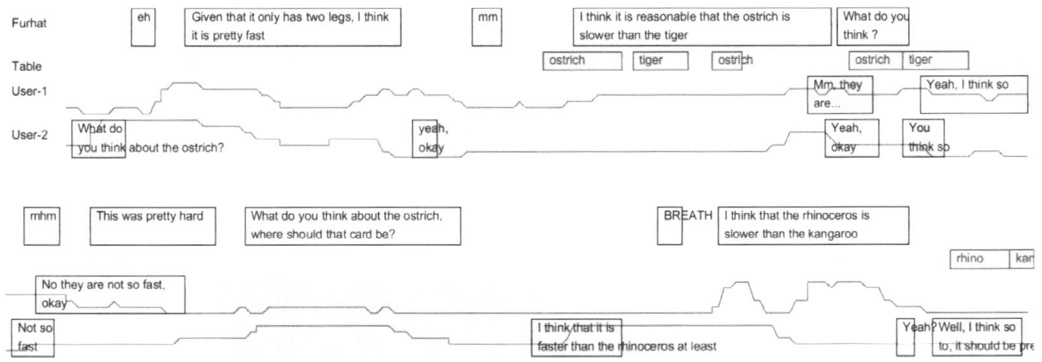

Figure 2: Dialogue fragment from an interaction (translated from Swedish). The shaded (green) track shows where Furhat's attention is directed. Card movements are illustrated in blue. Users' head poses are illustrated with red plots, where a high y-value means the angular distance towards Furhat is small.

This, together with the 3D design of Furhat, makes it possible to maintain exclusive mutual gaze with the users, and to let them infer the target of Furhat's gaze when directed towards the cards, in order to maintain joint attention (Skantze et al., 2014). Although the system can be configured to use the array microphone in the Kinect camera, we used close talking microphones in the museum. The main motivation for this is that the Kinect array microphone cannot separate the sound sources from the two users and we wanted to be able to run parallel speech recognizers for both users in order to capture overlapping speech (for both online and offline analysis). The speech recognition is done with two parallel cloud-based large vocabulary speech recognizers, Nuance NDEV mobile[2], which allows Furhat to understand the users even when they are talking simultaneously.

The Dialogue Flow module orchestrates the spoken interaction, based on input from the speech recognizers, together with events from the Situation model (such as cards being moved, or someone leaving or entering the interaction). The head pose of the users is used to make a simple decision of whether Furhat is being addressed. The game is collaborative, which means that the visitors have to discuss the solution together with Furhat. However, Furhat does not have perfect knowledge about the solution. Instead, Furhat's behaviour is motivated by a randomized belief model. This means that visitors have to determine whether they should trust Furhat's belief or not, just like they have to do with each other. Thus, Furhat's role in the interaction is similar to that of the visitors, as opposed to for example a tutor role which is often given to robots in similar settings. An excerpt from an interaction is shown in Figure 2, illustrating both clear turn changes and turns with overlapping speech.

3.2 Collected Data

The dialog system was exhibited at the Swedish National Museum of Science and Technology, in November 15-23, 2014. During the 9 days the system was exhibited, we recorded data from 373 interactions with the system, with an average length of 4.5 minutes. The dataset contains mixed ages: both adults playing with each other (40%), children playing with adults (27%), and children playing with each other (33%). For the present study, 9 dialogues were selected for training and tuning the turn-taking model, and one dialogue was selected for final evaluation and for verification of the annotation scheme.

3.3 Data Annotation

In order to build a supervised machine learning model for detecting turn-taking cues, we need some kind of ground truth. There have been different approaches to deriving the ground truth in previous studies. In studies of human-human interaction, the behaviour of the other interlocutor is typically used as a ground truth (Koiso et al., 1998; Morency et al., 2008). The problem with this approach is that much turn-taking behaviour is optional, and these studies typically report a relatively poor accuracy (albeit better than baseline). Also, it is not clear to what extent they can be applied to human-machine interaction.

In this paper we follow the approach taken in Meena et al. (2014) – to manually annotate appropriate places to take the turn. Although this is quite labour intensive, we think that this is the best method to obtain a consistent ground truth

[2] http://dragonmobile.nuancemobiledeveloper.com/

about potential turn-taking locations. To this end we used turn-taking decisions from one annotator (one of the authors), thus building models of one specific human's behaviour rather than an average of multiple humans' behaviour. However, as described further down, we have also evaluated the amount of agreement between this annotator with another annotator on the evaluation set.

Similarly to most previous studies on turn-taking reported above, we treat the end of Inter-Pausal Units (IPUs) as potential turn-taking locations. Each channel of the recorded audio was first echo-cancelled and then automatically segmented into IPUs, using an energy-based Voice Activity Detector (VAD), with a maximum of 200ms internal silence. The logged utterances from the dialogue system were then added as a third track of IPUs. A decision point was defined after every segmented user IPU where the system had not been speaking in the last three seconds. Figure 3 presents an example of sequences of subject IPUs with the location of decision points overlaid. Note that we also include locations where the other speaker is still speaking (1 in the figure), since the other speaker might for example be talking to herself while the first speaker asks Furhat something.

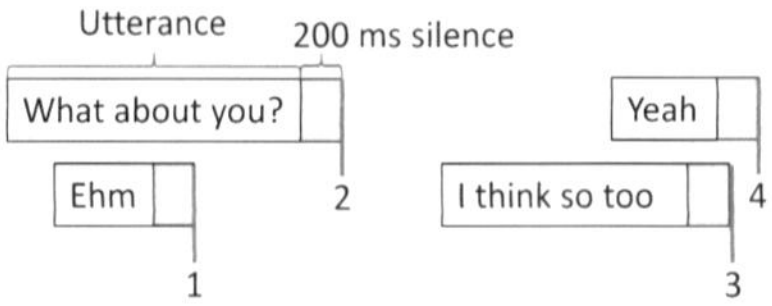

Figure 3: Four numbered decision points

A set of 688 decision points from the 9 selected dialogues were annotated for turn-taking decisions. The annotator was presented with five seconds of audio and video taken from the robot's point of view. A turn-taking decision was then annotated on a continuous scale ranging from "Absolutely don't take the turn" to "Must take the turn". The scale was visually divided into four equally wide classes to guide the annotator. The first section "**Don't**" (35% of annotated instances) represents instances where it would be inappropriate to take the turn, for example because the other interlocutor was either the addressee or currently speaking. The next section, "**If needed**" (19%), covers cases where it is not really appropriate, but possible if the system has a clear reason for saying something, while "**Good**" (21%) covers instances where it would not be inappropriate to take the turn. The final section, "**Obliged**" (25%), represents instances where it would be inappropriate not to take the turn, for example when the system clearly was the sole addressee.

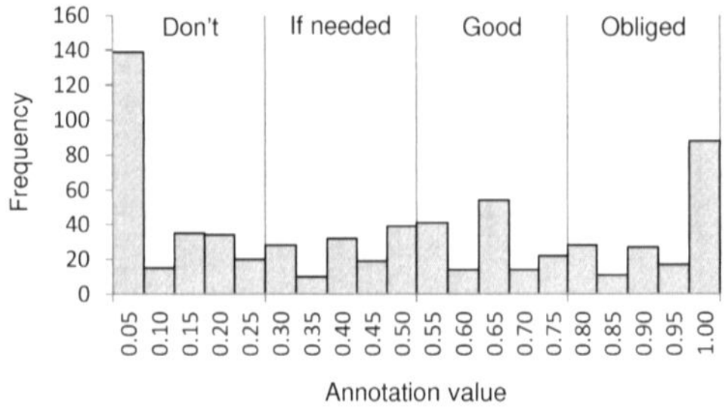

Figure 4: Histogram of annotated decisions on a scale from 0 (must not take turn) to 1 (must take turn)

The distribution of the decisions, illustrated in Figure 4, indicates a fairly even distribution across the x-axis, but with higher frequencies of annotations at the extremes of the scale.

For verification of the annotation scheme and final evaluation, we annotated a second set of 43 decision points from a tenth dialogue using both the original annotator and a second annotator. The inter-annotator agreement for the four classes was good, K_w=0.772 (Cohen's Kappa, equal weights), and neither annotator classified any decision point as "Don't" when the other had classified it as "Obliged".

4 Results

For this analysis we will first focus on the classes "Don't" and "Obliged" to make a binary turn-taking decision in section 4.1. We will then switch focus to the full range of annotations and predict turn-taking decisions numerically on a scale in section 4.2. Finally we evaluate the resulting models in 4.3 using annotations from a second annotator.

4.1 Binary Decision – Don't vs. Obliged

For every turn-taking decision the outcome will eventually be either to take the turn or to not. For the annotated classes "Don't" and "Obliged", there is a one-to-one mapping between the class and the correct turn-taking decisions. The classes "If needed" and "Good" on the other hand encode optional behaviour; both the decision to take the turn and to not take the turn can be considered correct at the same time, an opportunity to take the turn and not an obligation.

In this section we therefore build a model to distinguish between "Don't" and "Obliged". For this we explore the RIPPER (JRIP), Support Vector Machine (SVM) with linear kernel function and Multilayer Perceptron (MLP) classifiers in the WEKA toolkit (Hall et al., 2009), using the default parameters. All results in this section are based on 10-fold cross-validation. For statistical analysis, we have used two-tailed tests and chosen an alpha level of 0.05.

Features	JRIP	SVM	MLP
VAD *	0.727	0.734	0.723
Head pose *	0.690	0.724	0.709
Cards *	0.717	0.526	0.671
Prosody *	0.648	0.574	0.649
POS *	0.602	0.630	0.634
System DA	0.506	0.506	0.500

Table 1: Weighted F_1 score of the feature categories used in isolation. Results significantly better than baseline are marked with *.

Baseline

The majority-class baseline, always providing the classification "Don't", yields a weighted F_1 score of 0.432.

Voice Activity Features

A very basic feature to consult before taking the turn is to listen if **anyone is speaking**. Using only this feature the weighted F_1 score reaches 0.734, significantly better than the baseline. In addition, we also use features to add context: The amount of time each of the system and the other interlocutor has been **quiet**, and the **length of the last turn,** defined as a sequence of IPUs without IPUs from other speakers in-between, as well as **length of the last IPU** for the system and each of the two interlocutors. Thus, the total of VAD features is 9. The "anyone speaking" feature is the single feature yielding the highest weighted F_1 score, performing on par with the combination of all VAD features (Table 1).

Prosodic Features

As prosodic features, we used final pitch and energy. A pitch tracker based on the Yin algorithm (de Cheveigné & Kawahara, 2002) was used to estimate the F_0 at a rate of 100 frames per second. The F_0 values were then transformed to log scale and z-normalized for each user. For each IPU, the last voiced frame was identified and then regions of **200ms** and **500ms** ending in this frame were selected. For these different regions, we calculated the **mean**, **maximum**, **standard deviation** and **slope** of the normalized F_0 values. To calculate the slope, we took the average pitch of the second half of the region minus the average of the first half. Additionally, we calculated the maximum and standard deviation of the normalized F_0 values over the full IPU. We also Z-normalized the energy of the voiced frames and then calculated the **maximum energy** for the 200ms and 500ms regions and the full IPU. Thus, we used 13 prosodic features in total. Using MLP on the combination of all features yielded the highest weighted F_1 score (0.649, see Table 1). The features based on pitch were more useful than the ones based on energy.

Syntactic Features

Syntax has been shown to be a strong turn-yielding cue in previous studies (Koiso et al., 1998; Meena et al., 2014). For example, hesitations can occur in the middle of syntactic constructions, whereas turn ends are typically syntactically complete. In previous studies, the **part-of-speech** (POS) of the last two words has been shown to be a useful feature. Thus, we use the POS of the last two words in an IPU as a bigram. The POS tags were automatically extracted using Stagger (Östling, 2013) based on results from cloud-based large vocabulary speech recognizers, Nuance NDEV mobile ASR, as an automated system would need to rely on ASR. Despite a word error rate (WER) of 63.1% (*SD*=39.0) for the recognized IPUs, the generated POS feature performed significantly better than the baseline (Table 1). However, the increase is not very high compared to previous studies. This could both be due to the relatively high WER, but also due to the fact that syntax in itself does not indicate the addressee of the utterance.

Head Pose Features

Unlike the other feature categories, head pose can be used to both yield the turn and to select the next speaker, and is therefore expected to be a strong feature for the current task. We represent the interlocutors' head poses in terms of **angular distance** between the direction of the interlocutor's head and the robot's head. The angular distance is made available as **absolute angular distance** as well as signed **vertical and horizontal** angular distance separately. The sign of the horizontal distance is adjusted to account for the mirrored position of the two interlocutors. This representation allows the system to infer if someone is looking at the system (low absolute distance), towards the table (negative vertical distance) or towards the other interlocutor (high horizontal distance).

The head pose features are generated separately for the speaker ending the IPU and the other interlocutor as well as in two composite versions representing the joint (maximum) and disjoint (minimum) distance. The features are generated both at the end of the speech in the IPU and at the time of the decision point. Thus, there are a total of 24 features available for estimating visual focus of attention. Sorting the individual features from highest weighted F_1 score to lowest, we get the following top four groups in order: Last speaker (end of speech), last speaker (decision), disjoint (decision) and then joint (end of speech). As expected, the use of head pose gives a significantly better result than the baseline (Table 1).

Card Movement

The activity of the game table is represented in terms of card movement activity via 3 feature types. Note that we only know if a card is being moved, but not by whom. The first feature type is the **duration** of ongoing card movement. If no card is being moved at the moment, the value is set to 0. The second feature type is the duration of the most recently completed card movement. The final feature type is the **time passed** since the last movement of any card. These features are generated for two points in time; the end of the IPU relating to the decision point and the time when the decision is to be made. Thus, there are 6 card movement features in total. As can be seen in Table 1, this feature category alone performs significantly better than baseline, which is a bit surprising, given that the card movements are not necessarily linked to speech production and turn-taking.

The System's Previous Dialogue Act

To represent the dialogue context, we used the last system dialogue act as a feature. Whereas this feature gave a significant improvement in the data-driven models for dyadic turn-taking presented in Meena et al. (2014), it is the only feature category here that does not perform significantly better than the baseline (Table 1). The overall low performance of this feature could be due to the nature of multi-party dialogue, where the system doesn't necessarily have every second turn.

Combined Feature Categories

Until now we have only explored features where every category comprised one single modality. All feature categories, summarized in Table 1, have performed significantly better than the baseline with the exception of the system's last dialogue act.

Features	JRIP	SVM	MLP
Head pose (HP)	0.690	0.724	0.709
HP+VAD	0.742	0.786	0.764
HP+Cards (C)	0.780	0.753	0.772
HP+Prosody (P)	0.700	0.698	0.789
HP+POS	0.754	0.731	0.772
HP+System DA (SDA)	0.725	0.739	0.728
Best combination			
HP+POS+C+P+SDA	0.745	0.796	**0.851**

Table 2: Weighted F_1 score for different feature set combinations using RIPPER (JRIP), Support Vector Machine (SVM) and Multilayer Perceptron (MLP) classifiers

Features	GP	LR
System DA	0.090	0.129
Prosody	0.146	0.135
POS	0.193	0.188
Cards	0.351	0.226
VAD	0.416	0.368
Head Pose (HP)	0.447	0.376
HP+System DA	0.482	0.373
HP+Prosody	0.500	0.377
HP+POS	0.471	0.393
HP+Cards	0.572	0.431
HP+VAD	0.611	0.523
Best combination		
HP+VAD+Cards	**0.677**	0.580

Table 3: Correlation coefficient for different feature set combinations using Gaussian Processes (GP) and Linear Regression (LR) classifiers

In this section we explore the combinations of features from different modalities, summarized in Table 2. Combinations including head pose typically performed best. The maximum performance using automatically generated features is 0.851 using 5 feature categories: head pose, POS, card movements, prosody and the system's dialog act.

4.2 Regression Model

While the end result of a turn-taking decision has a binary outcome, the distribution of annotations on a scale (Figure 4) suggests that there are stronger and weaker decisions, reflecting opportunities and obligations to take turns. As discussed above, such a score could be used together with a utility to take turns in a decision-theoretic framework. Thus, we also want to see whether it is possible to reproduce decisions on the scale. For this we explore the Gaussian Processes (GP) and Linear Regression (LR) classifiers in the WEKA toolkit. All results in this section are based on 10-fold cross-validation.

The individual feature categories have positive but low correlation coefficients (Table 3). Combining the feature categories with highest correlation coefficients improve performance. The head pose in combination with VAD and card movements, using Gaussian Processes yields the highest correlation coefficient, 0.677.

4.3 Evaluation

We finally evaluated the best performing models built from the initial 9 dialogues on a separate test set of 43 decision points from a tenth dialogue, annotated both by the original annotator and a second annotator.

For the binary decision, we selected the MLP classifier with features from head pose, POS, card movements, prosody and the system's dialogue act. When evaluated on the test set annotated by the original annotator and the new annotator, the weighted F_1 score was 0.876 and 0.814 for 29 and 32 instances respectively. These are promising results, given the classifier's performance of 0.851 in the training set cross-validation (Table 2) and that the test set was from a previously unseen interaction.

The regression model was evaluated using the Gaussian Processes classifier with features from head pose, VAD and card movement. The correlation coefficients for the original annotator and the new annotator were 0.5959 and 0.5647 over 43 instances each, compared to 0.677 in the training set cross-validation (Table 3). The lower values could be due to a different distribution of annotations in the test set and the relatively small data set.

5 Discussion and Conclusions

In this study we have developed data-driven models that can be used by a robot to decide when to take the turn and not in multi-party situated interaction. In the case of a simple binary decision on whether to take the turn or not, the weighted F_1 score of 0.876 on data from previously unseen interactions, using several modalities in combination, is indeed promising, given a relatively small training material of 9 interactions and 688 instances. The decision process for the annotator is also simplified by not making separate decisions for turn ending and addressee detection. It should also be pointed out that we have only relied on automatically extractable features that can be derived in an online system. We have also achieved promising results for a regression model that could be used to identify both opportunities and obligations to take turns.

We have observed that combining features from different modalities yield performance improvements, and different combinations of features from diverse modalities can provide similar performance. This suggests that the multimodal redundancy indeed can be used to improve the robustness of the dialogue system. This is very relevant to the specific dialogue system in this study as head pose data sometimes is unavailable. Two possible remedies would be to only use classifiers that are robust against missing features, or to use multiple classifiers to step in when features are unavailable.

The results support that head pose, despite sometimes missing, is very useful for turn-taking decisions. This was expected, as head pose is the only of our available features that can be used to both select addressee and act as a turn-yielding cue. The results also indicate that POS provide useful information, even when based on ASR results with high WER. Provided that higher ASR performance becomes available, we could also benefit from other more sophisticated features, such as semantic completion (Gravano & Hirschberg, 2011), to predict turn-transition relevant places.

It is also interesting to see that the card movement is an important feature, as it suggests that moving of objects can be a dialogue act in itself, as discussed in Clark (2005). This makes situated dialogue systems – where the discussion involves actions and manipulation of objects – different from traditional dialogue systems, and should be taken into account when timing responses in such systems. This also suggests that it might be necessary to not just make turn-taking decisions at the end of IPUs, but rather continuous decisions. It is not obvious, however, how this would be annotated.

With the promising results of this study, we plan to expand on this work and integrate the turn-taking models into the live dialogue system, and see to what extent this improves the actual interaction. Of particular interest for future work is the regression model that could predict turn-taking on a continuous scale, which could be integrated into a decision-theoretic framework, so that the system could also take into account to what extent it has something important to say.

Acknowledgements

This work is supported by the Swedish research council (VR) project *Coordination of Attention and Turn-taking in Situated Interaction* (2013-1403, PI: Gabriel Skantze).

References

Al Moubayed, S., Skantze, G., & Beskow, J. (2013). The Furhat Back-Projected Humanoid Head - Lip reading, Gaze and Multiparty Interaction. *International Journal of Humanoid Robotics, 10*(1).

Argyle, M., & Graham, J. A. (1976). The central Europe experiment: Looking at persons and looking at objects. *Environmental Psychology and Nonverbal Behavior, 1*(1), 6-16.

Ba, S. O., & Odobez, J-M. (2009). Recognizing visual focus of attention from head pose in natural meetings. *IEEE Transactions on Systems, Man, and Cybernetics, Part B: Cybernetics, 39*(1), 16-33.

Bohus, D., & Horvitz, E. (2011). Decisions about turns in multiparty conversation: from perception to action. In *ICMI '11 Proceedings of the 13th international conference on multimodal interfaces* (pp. 153-160).

Clark, H. H., & Marshall, C. R. (1981). Definite reference and mutual knowledge. In Joshi, A. K., Webber, B. L., & Sag, I. A. (Eds.), *Elements of discourse understanding* (pp. 10–63). Cambridge, England: Cambridge University Press.

Clark, H. H. (2005). Coordinating with each other in a material world. *Discourse studies, 7*(4-5), 507-525.

Duncan, S. (1972). Some Signals and Rules for Taking Speaking Turns in Conversations. *J. of Personality and Social Psychology, 23*(2), 283-292.

Gravano, A., & Hirschberg, J. (2011). Turn-taking cues in task-oriented dialogue.. *Computer Speech & Language, 25*(3), 601-634.

Hall, M., Frank, E., Holmes, G., Pfahringer, B., Reutemann, P., & Witten, I. H. (2009). The WEKA Data Mining Software: An Update. *SIGKDD Explorations, 11*(1).

Heldner, M., & Edlund, J. (2010). Pauses, gaps and overlaps in conversations. *Journal of Phonetics, 38*, 555-568.

Johansson, M., Skantze, G., & Gustafson, J. (2013). Head Pose Patterns in Multiparty Human-Robot Team-Building Interactions. In *International Conference on Social Robotics - ICSR 2013*. Bristol, UK.

Katzenmaier, M., Stiefelhagen, R., Schultz, T., Rogina, I., & Waibel, A. (2004). Identifying the Addressee in Human-Human-Robot Interactions based on Head Pose and Speech. In *Proceedings of International Conference on Multimodal Interfaces ICMI 2004*. PA, USA: State College.

Kawahara, T., Iwatate, T., & Takanashi, K. (2012). Prediction of Turn-Taking by Combining Prosodic and Eye-Gaze Information in Poster Conversations.. In *Interspeech 2012*.

Kendon, A. (1967). Some functions of gaze direction in social interaction. *Acta Psychologica, 26*, 22-63.

Koiso, H., Horiuchi, Y., Tutiya, S., Ichikawa, A., & Den, Y. (1998). An analysis of turn-taking and backchannels based on prosodic and syntactic features in Japanese Map Task dialogs. *Language and Speech, 41*, 295-321.

Meena, R., Skantze, G., & Gustafson, J. (2014). Data-driven Models for timing feedback responses in a Map Task dialogue system. *Computer Speech and Language, 28*(4), 903-922.

Morency, L. P., de Kok, I., & Gratch, J. (2008). Predicting listener backchannels: A probabilistic multimodal approach. In *Proceedings of IVA* (pp. 176-190). Tokyo, Japan.

Mutlu, B., Kanda, T., Forlizzi, J., Hodgins, J., & Ishiguro, H. (2012). Conversational Gaze Mechanisms for Humanlike Robots. *ACM Trans. Interact. Intell. Syst., 1*(2), 12:1-12:33.

Raux, A., & Eskenazi, M. (2008). Optimizing endpointing thresholds using dialogue features in a spoken dialogue system. In *Proceedings of SIGdial 2008*. Columbus, OH, USA.

Shriberg, E., Stolcke, A., & Ravuri, S. (2013). Addressee detection for dialog systems using temporal and spectral dimensions of speaking style. In *Interspeech 2013* (pp. 2559-2563).

Skantze, G., & Al Moubayed, S. (2012). IrisTK: a statechart-based toolkit for multi-party face-to-face interaction. In *Proceedings of ICMI*. Santa Monica, CA.

Skantze, G., & Schlangen, D. (2009). Incremental dialogue processing in a micro-domain. In *Proceedings of the 12th Conference of the European Chapter of the Association for Computational Linguistics (EACL-09)*. Athens, Greece.

Skantze, G., Hjalmarsson, A., & Oertel, C. (2014). Turn-taking, Feedback and Joint Attention in Situated Human-Robot Interaction. *Speech Communication, 65*, 50-66.

Stiefelhagen, R., & Zhu, J. (2002). Head orientation and gaze direction in meetings. In *CHI '02 Extended Abstracts on Human Factors in Computing Systems* (pp. 858-859).

Traum, D., & Rickel, J. (2001). Embodied Agents for Multi-party Dialogue in Immersive Virtual Worlds. In *Proc. of IJCAI Workshop on Knowledge and Reasoning in Practical Dialogue Systems* (pp. 766-773). Seattle, WA, US.

Vertegaal, R., Slagter, R., van der Veer, G., & Nijholt, A. (2001). Eye gaze patterns in conversations: there is more to conversational agents than meets the eyes. In *Proceedings of ACM Conf. on Human Factors in Computing Systems*.

Vinyals, O., Bohus, D., & Caruana, R. (2012). Learning speaker, addressee and overlap detection models from multimodal streams. In *Proceedings of the 14th ACM international conference on Multimodal interaction* (pp. 417-424).

de Cheveigné, A., & Kawahara, H. (2002). YIN, a fundamental frequency estimator for speech and music. *The Journal of the Acoustical Society of America, 111*(4), 1917-1930.

Östling, R. (2013). Stagger: An open-source part of speech tagger for Swedish. *Northern European Journal of Language Technology (NEJLT), 3*, 1-18.

Appendix A. Gameplay Interaction – One Complete Round

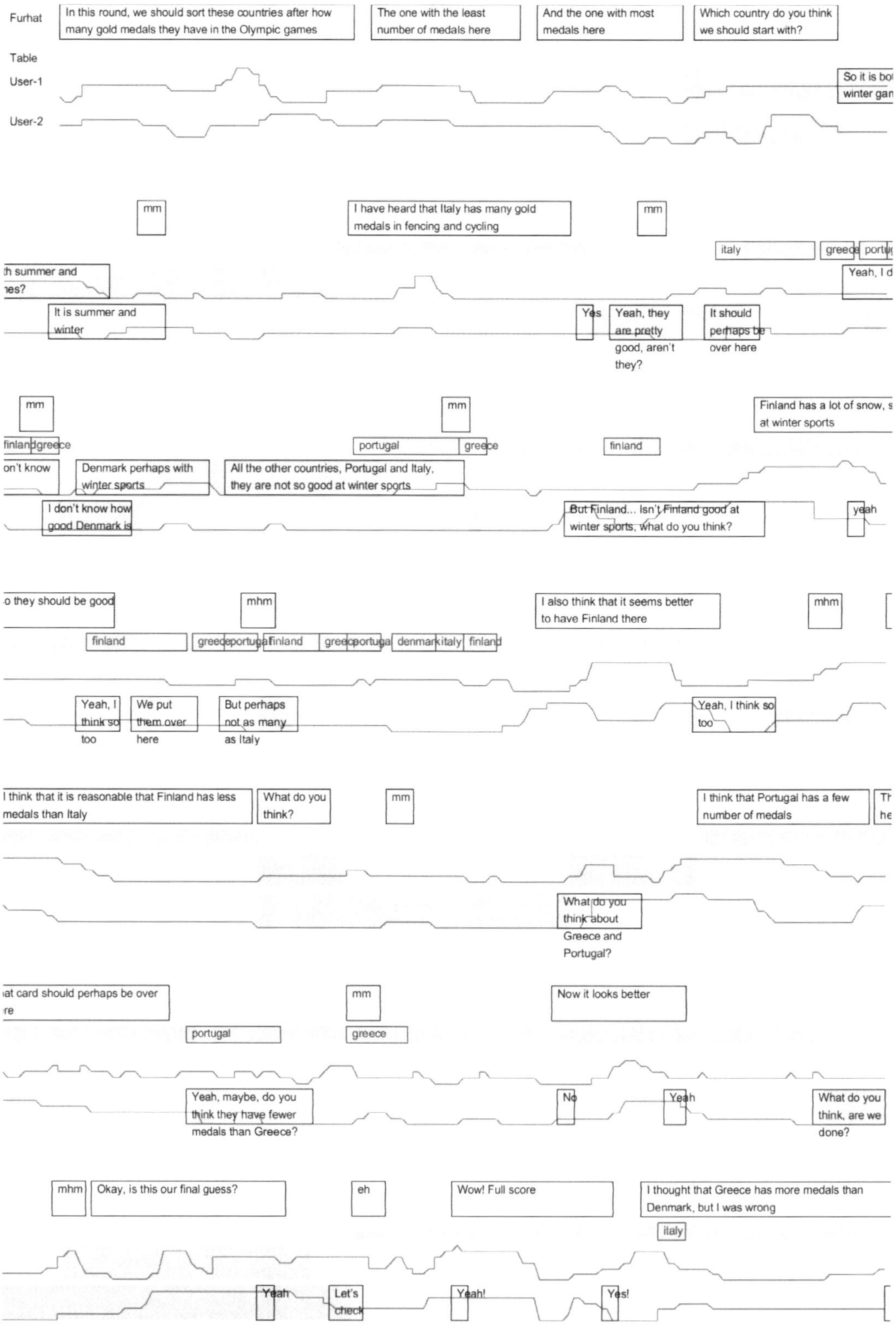

Optimising Turn-Taking Strategies With Reinforcement Learning

Hatim Khouzaimi
Orange Labs
LIA-CERI
France
hatim.khouzaimi@orange.com

Romain Laroche
Orange Labs,
Issy-les-Moulineaux,
France
romain.laroche@orange.com

Fabrice Lefèvre
LIA-CERI,
Univ. Avignon,
France
fabrice.lefevre@univ-avignon.fr

Abstract

In this paper, reinforcement learning (RL) is used to learn an efficient turn-taking management model in a simulated slot-filling task with the objective of minimising the dialogue duration and maximising the completion task ratio. Turn-taking decisions are handled in a separate new module, the Scheduler. Unlike most dialogue systems, a dialogue turn is split into micro-turns and the Scheduler makes a decision for each one of them. A Fitted Value Iteration algorithm, Fitted-Q, with a linear state representation is used for learning the state to action policy. Comparison between a non-incremental and an incremental handcrafted strategies, taken as baselines, and an incremental RL-based strategy, shows the latter to be significantly more efficient, especially in noisy environments.

1 Introduction

Most dialogue systems use a simple turn-taking model: the user speaks and when she finishes her utterance, the system detects a long enough silence and speaks afterwards. Quite often the latter cannot be interrupted neither. On the contrary, incremental dialogue systems are able to understand the user's utterance on the fly thus enabling a richer set of turn-taking behaviours. They can interrupt the user and quickly report a problem. They can be interrupted as well. In this paper, we explore the extent to which such capacity can improve the overall dialogue efficiency. Reinforcement learning (Sutton and Barto, 1998) is used to find optimal strategies.

Human beings use a rich set of incremental behaviours which help them recover from errors efficiently. As soon as a conversation participant detects a problem, she is able to interrupt the speaker so that he can correct his utterance or repeat a part of it for example. In this work, we implement in an expert handcrafted way 3 turn-taking phenomena amongst those classified in the taxonomy proposed in (Khouzaimi et al., 2015a). The resulting strategy is shown to achieve better performance than a non-incremental handcrafted strategy. Then, it is compared to an automatically learned incremental strategy and the latter is shown to achieve even better results.

Machine learning algorithms often need important sets of data in order to converge. In the field of dialogue systems, gathering data is expensive and as a consequence, researchers use simulated users for learning (Eckert et al., 1997; Chandramohan et al., 2011; Pietquin and Hastie, 2013). To run the experiments in this work, a simulated user interacts with a service that manages a personal agenda (Khouzaimi et al., 2015a).

In our work, the turn-taking task is separated from the common dialogue management one and it is handled by a separated module called the *Scheduler* (Khouzaimi et al., 2014). A considerable asset of this architecture is that it can just be added to the agenda service in order to make it incremental. Two versions of this module have been developed: the first one embeds the handcrafted strategy and the second one uses reinforcement learning to optimise turn-taking decisions with respect to objective criteria. Our goal is to improve the dialogue efficiency, therefore, as evaluation criteria and in order to design a reward function, dialogue duration and task completion are used. Fitted-Q (a Fitted Value Iteration algorithm) was used and we show that the optimal policy is quickly learned and that it outperforms both the non-incremental and the handcrafted strategies. These three strategies are then compared under different noise conditions and the automatically learned strategy is proven to be the most robust to high levels of noise.

Section 2 presents some related work and Sec-

Proceedings of the SIGDIAL 2015 Conference, pages 315–324,
Prague, Czech Republic, 2-4 September 2015.

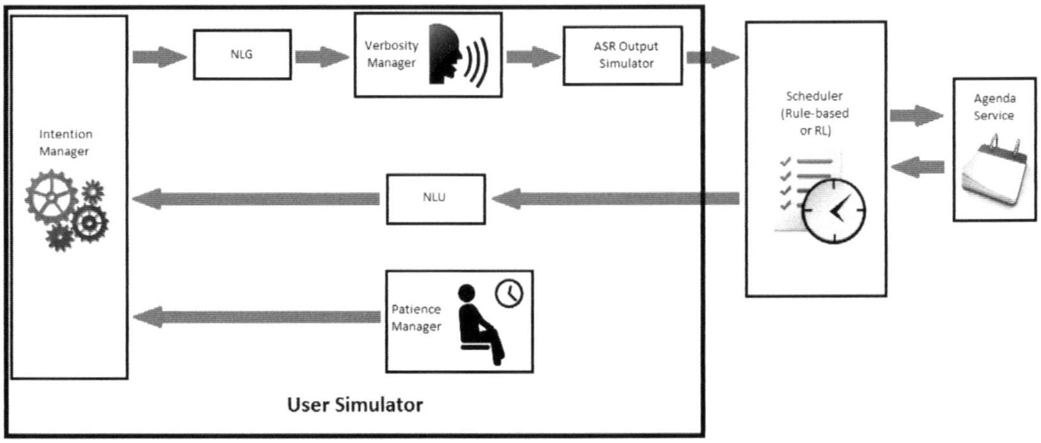

Figure 1: Simulated environment architecture

tion 3 describes the simulated environment used for the experiments. Then Section 4 describes the handcrafted turn-taking model as well as the RL one. Section 5 presents the experimentation and the results and finally, Section 6 gives some concluding remarks.

2 Related work

The idea of interrupting the user in order to improve the dialogue efficiency in terms of dialogue duration and task completion is tackled in (Ghigi et al., 2014). A corpus study shows that the users' utterances often go off-domain or contain the same piece of information several times. By detecting this kind of sentences and interrupting the user to report the problem promptly, the dialogue is more efficient and users tend to conform to the words and expressions that are known by the system. Only handcrafted settings are explored.

An approach based on Hierarchical Reinforcement Learning is presented in (Dethlefs et al., 2012; Hastie et al., 2013). An efficiency reward is used to optimise the Information Presentation strategy (common dialogue management task) whereas another reward based on Information Density is used for the barge-in and backchannel tasks. In our work, the efficiency reward is directly applied to turn-taking management.

A research branch in incremental dialogue focuses on the following principle laid in (Sacks et al., 1974): *Participants in a conversation attempt to minimize gaps and overlaps*.(Jonsdottir et al., 2008) uses a reinforcement learning approach based on this principle in order to achieve smooth turn-taking (only prosodic features are considered) whereas (Raux and Eskenazi, 2008; Raux and Eskenazi, 2012) proposes a classification method where the costs for silences and overlaps are handcrafted. Like the majority of contributions in the field of incremental dialogue, the main focus here is smooth turn-taking rather than improving the general dialogue efficiency.

In order to mimic human turn-taking capabilities, in (Kim et al., 2014) Inverse Reinforcement Learning has been applied to a system that can perform three turn taking actions: *speak*, *silent* and *overlap*. The main focus here is also end of utterance detection and smooth turn-taking.

In (DeVault et al., 2011), the ability of incremental dialogue systems to guess the remaining part of a user's utterance before its end is explored. (Lu et al., 2011) applies reinforcement learning to explore the tradeoff between the risk of error relative to a barge-in due to an early guess and the lack of reactivity in the case of late system responses.

Finally, reinforcement learning is also applied in (Selfridge and Heeman, 2010) in the case of mixed initiative dialogue systems. However the paper does not tackle the problem of barge-in management but initial turn-taking (who takes the floor first): the dialogue participant that has the most important thing to say to make progress in the dialogue takes the floor first.

3 Simulated environment

To learn the turn-taking policy, a simulated environment has been developed. Figure 1 gives an overview of its architecture. The six modules on the left constitute the user simulator: the Intention Manager, the Natural Language Generator (NLG), the Verbosity Manager, the ASR Output Simulator, the Patience Manager and the Natural Language Understanding module (NLU). The ASR Output Simulator communicates the N-Best corresponding to the current partial hypothesis to the Scheduler whose responses are conveyed to the NLU module.

3.1 Service task

The service used in our experiments is a personal agenda manager. The user can add events to the agenda, modify their attributes or delete them. To complicate a bit the task and justify the need for interactions a constraint has been introduced: all events must have separate time slots. If the user tries to overload a busy time slot, a warning is generated and the user is required to modify her request.

The simulated dialogue scenarios are defined by two event lists. The first one (*InitList*) is the list of events that already exist in the agenda before the dialogue and the second one (*ToAddList*) is the list of events, with priorities and alternative times, to add during the dialogue. The simulated user tries to make the maximum number of events with the highest priority values fit into the agenda. For example, if *InitList* contains the event {**title:** *house cleaning*, **date:** *January* 6th, **slot:** *from 18 to 20*, **priority:** *3*, **alternative 1:** *January* 7th, *from 18 to 20*, **alternative 2:** *January* 9th, *from 10 to 12*} and *ToAddList* contains the event {**title:** *birthday party*, **date:** *January* 6th, **slot:** *from 18 to 23*, **priority:** *2*} then the user simulator will first try to schedule his birthday party on January 6th from 18 to 23 but as a consequence, it will get a warning from the system because this slot is already booked for the house cleaning event. Therefore, the user simulator will reschedule the latter to January 7th from 18 to 20. If the house cleaning event was given with no alternative, it will be deleted as it has a lower priority compared to the birthday party.

3.2 Service implementation

The service is designed to process slot-filling requests in order to manage the user's personal agenda. The required slots are the *action type*, the event *description*, its *date* and its *time slot*. A keyword-based NLU module is configured to parse natural language requests.

A mixed initiative strategy is used for the interaction. First, the user takes the lead and utters a request in natural language. The system picks as many information slots as it can and if it still needs more information, it asks the user to complete her request slot by slot. In the following, a *dialogue task* refers to the portion of dialogue corresponding to a particular add, modify or remove action. In the best case, it consists of two dialogue turns only (request and confirmation) but if there is important noise, it might take several turns to complete (given that the user is patient enough not to hang up before the end of the dialogue task).

The following dialogue example is composed of two dialogue tasks. In the first one, the system manages to catch all the information needed to answer whereas in the second one, it missed the time slot and has to ask for it again. Moreover, the first dialogue task led to a conflict declaration whereas the second one could be accomplished:

- **System:** Hi! Welcome to your personal agenda service. How may I help you?
- **User:** Can you please add the event football game on November 9th from 18 to 20 if possible?
- **System:** Sorry. The time slot from 18 to 19 on November 9th is already booked for the event guitar course.
- **User:** Ok well, then move the event guitar course to November 10th from 18 to 19.
- **System:** Please specify a time slot.
- **User:** From 18 to 19.
- **System:** Great. So you want to move the event guitar course to November 10th from 18 to 19. Is that right?
- **User:** Yes.
- **System:** Good. Do you want to add another modification to your agenda?
- **User:** No.
- **System:** Bye.

3.3 ASR N-Best generation

Given *ToAddList* and the system responses, the Intent Manager is able to compute the user's immediate goal. Afterwards, the NLG transforms it into a sentence like *add the event birthday party on January* 6th *from 18 to 23*. Moreover, if the simulated user takes the lead and starts asking for a specific slot, it is also able to give the information directly.

In (Ghigi et al., 2014), a corpus study shows that the user is likely to use off-domain expression, to add unnecessary information and to repeat the same piece of information several times in the same sentence (especially after a misunderstanding). To simulate this phenomenon, the user's request in natural language is given to a Verbosity Manager module that adds prefixes like *I would like to* and suffixes like *if possible*, that repeats the same information after a misunderstanding (with a given probability, e.g. 0.3) and that replaces the request with an off-domain sentence (with a given probability, e.g. 0.1).

To our knowledge, apart from the simulator described in (Selfridge et al., 2012), existent user simulators are turn-based and therefore, only the user intent is communicated at each turn (in a concept format) so there is no need to take care of the utterance formulations. This is not the case when incremental dialogue and turn-taking are the object of interest. In this case, the user's sentence is processed chunk by chunk. The update step is called a *micro-turn* and in this paper, the unit chosen is the word. Suppose that the current user utterance contains N words $w_1, w_2, ...w_N$ then at micro-turn t, the Verbosity Manager sends w_t to the ASR Output simulator. The latter stores an N-Best list from the previous micro-turn $\{(s_1^{(t-1)}, hyp_1^{(t-1)}), \ldots, (s_N^{(t-1)}, hyp_N^{(t-1)})\}$ that is updated according to w_t and WER (hyp_i is the ith hypothesis in the N-Best and s_i is the corresponding confidence score). w_t can be replaced by a new word from a dictionary, deleted or a new word can be added to simulate the ASR noise, before it is added to the N-Best list.

The confidence score associated with the new word is computed as follows: if the word has not been modified, X is sampled from a Gaussian with mean 1 and variance 1 otherwise the mean is -1. We then compute the $sigmoid(X) = (1 + exp(-X))^{-1}$ as a word score (Figure 2 represents these two symmetric distributions). This

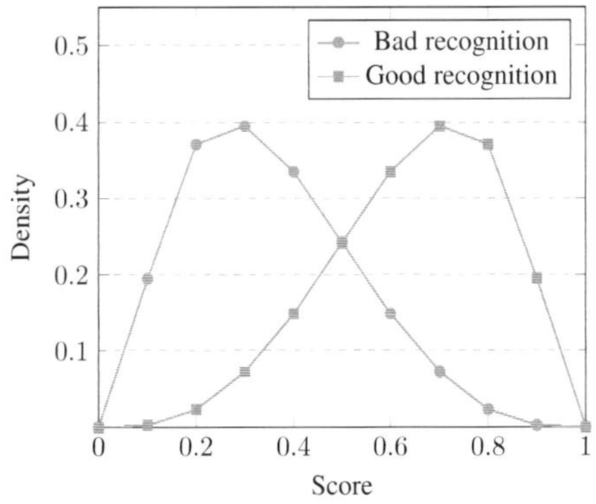

Figure 2: ASR score sampling distribution

is an adaptation of the simple ASR model introduced in (Pietquin and Beaufort, 2005). The score of the current partial utterance is the product of its words.

Another important aspect of incremental ASR is instability. A new ASR input does not necessarily translate into adding elements on top of the current output as it can change an important part if not the totality of it. For instance, in (Schlangen and Skantze, 2011), when the user says *forty*, it is first understood as *four* then *forty*. This is due to the fact that, given the language model, the new received chunk of information is more likely to complete a hypothesis that has a lower score in the N-Best list than the best hypothesis. In this work, as no language model is used, we use the NLU knowledge instead. If a new input leads to a new NLU key concept, then its score is boosted like in the following

$$s_i \leftarrow s_i + BF.(1 - s_i) \tag{1}$$

where the BF parameter (Boost Factor) is set to 0.2 in this work.

3.4 Time management and patience

In order to evaluate the time spent during the current dialogue, a speech rate of 200 words per minute is used (Yuan et al., 2006). Moreover, when the user hands the floor to the system, a silence of 2 seconds is added to this duration and 1 second the other way around. Finally, a Patience Manager module simulates the user patience: the maximum duration per dialogue task that the user can bear before hanging up. At each dialogue task, this value is computed as

$$d_{pat} = 2\mu_{pat}.sigmoid(X) \quad (2)$$

where μ_{pat} is the mean value (μ_{pat} = 180s).

3.5 Scheduler Module

A non-incremental dialogue system can be transformed into an incremental one by adding an extra module: the Scheduler (Khouzaimi et al., 2014). Its objective is to make turn-taking decisions (whether to take the floor or not). When the user speaks, its partial utterance grows over time. At each new change, it is sent to the Scheduler that immediately asks the service for a corresponding response and then rollbacks the system's context as long as it decides not to take the floor. If, on the other hand, it decides to commit to the last received partial utterance by taking the floor, then no rollback is performed and the dialogue context is effectively updated.

In this work, the Scheduler can perform two types of actions: WAIT and SPEAK, that is to say that it can wait for the next micro-turn without uttering anything or it can start retrieving the last response it got from the service.

Two versions of the Scheduler have been implemented: handcrafted rules were implemented in the first one whereas the second one embeds a reinforcement learning algorithm that learns to make turn-taking decisions by itself.

4 Turn-taking model

4.1 Turn-taking phenomena

Several turn-taking phenomena can be observed when analysing human conversations. A taxonomy of these phenomena is introduced in (Khouzaimi et al., 2015b), three of which are replicated here through the SPEAK action:

FAIL_RAW: The listener sometimes does not understand the speaker's message because of noise or unknown vocabulary. Therefore, she can barge-in and report the problem without waiting for the speaker to finish her sentence.

INCOHERENCE_INTERP: Unlike the previous phenomenon, in this case the listener fully understands the speaker's partial utterance. However, its content is considered problematic given the dialogue context and this can be reported immediately without waiting for the end of the utterance (system barge-in).

- Hi, I would like to book a room tonight and I...
- Sorry but there are no rooms available at the moment.

BARGE_IN_RESP: If the listener thinks she has all the information she needs to formulate a response, she can barge-in immediately which is frequent in human-human conversations.

4.2 Rule-based model

The three phenomena described above are replicated as handcrafted rules that have been implemented in the Scheduler:

FAIL_RAW: Depending on the last requested information by the system, it sets a threshold on the number of words. Whenever reached if the system still does not get any interesting information, it barges-in to warn the user about the problem:

1. Open question: this phenomenon is triggered if no action concept is detected (add, modify or delete) after 6 words (taking into account that the user can utter a prefix and leaving a margin because of the ASR instability).
2. Yes/no question: the threshold is set to 3.
3. Date question: it is set to 4.
4. Time slot question: it is set to 6.

INCOHERENCE_INTERP: An incoherence is detected in the user's utterance in the two following cases:

1. The user tries to fill a time slot that is already occupied.
2. The user tries to modify or delete a non-existing event.

Because of the ASR instability, as a security margin, the SPEAK decision will be taken two words after the incoherence is detected if it is maintained.

BARGE_IN_RESP: As soon as the service gives a full response to a partial utterance, the Scheduler considers that all the information needed has been given by the user. Like in the previous case, the decision is taken two words after.

4.3 Reinforcement learning

Despite late 20th century initial proposition (Levin and Pieraccini, 1997), reinforcement learning as the machine learning framework in the field of spoken dialogue systems is still largely explored in the current days (Lemon and Pietquin, 2007; Laroche et al., 2010; Pinault and Lefèvre, 2011; Ferreira and Lefevre, 2013; Young et al., 2013). In non-incremental systems, at each dialogue turn, the system has to make a decision (action) hence moving to a new state. In this paper, as we study dialogue from a turn-taking point of view, the decision unit is the micro-turn.

4.3.1 Background

The turn-taking problem is here cast as a Markovian Decision Process (MDP) (Sutton and Barto, 1998), that is to say a quintuple $(\mathcal{S}, \mathcal{A}, \mathcal{T}, \mathcal{R}, \gamma)$ where $\mathcal{S}$ is the set of states where the system can be during a dialogue and $\mathcal{A}$ is the set of actions that can be performed at each time step. $\mathcal{T}$ is the transition model, in other words, the set of probabilities $\mathbb{P}(s_{t+1} = s'|s_t = s, a_t = a)$ of getting to state s' at time $t + 1$ if the system was at state s at time t and performed action a. Such a decision makes the system get an immediate reward $r_t = R(s_t, a_t, s_{t+1})$ modeled by $\mathcal{R}$. The action to choose at each state is given by a policy π ($\pi(s_t) = a_t$) and the cumulative (discounted) reward is defined as $R_t = \sum_{t' \geq t} \gamma^{t'-t} r_{t'}$ (γ is called the discount factor). Finally, each couple (s, a) is associated with a value $Q^\pi(s, a) = \mathbb{E}[R_t|s_t = s, a_t = a]$ which is the expected cumulative reward for being at the state s, taking action a and following the policy π afterwards.

The goal of reinforcement learning is to find an optimal policy π^* such that, for every other policy π, and for every state-action couple (s, a), $Q^*(s, a) = Q^{\pi^*}(s, a) \geq Q^\pi(s, a)$.

4.3.2 State representation

The system state is characterised by the following features:

- **SYSTEM_REQ:** The current information that is asked for by the system. It can be a slot value, a confirmation or the system can ask an open question to make the user fill all the slots in one dialogue turn (6 alternatives).
- **LAST_INCR_RESP:** The Scheduler incrementally gets responses from the service. This feature corresponds to the last response obtained (11 alternatives).
- **NB_USER_WORDS:** The number of words added by the user after the last change in the value of LAST_INCR_RESP (after the last input that made the service catch a new piece of information and change its mind about the response to deliver).
- **NORMALISED_SCORE:** The ASR Output simulator estimates the score of a partial utterance as the product of its components. Therefore, the longer the sentence the worse the confidence score, even if all the components have a decent score. To neutralise this effect we normalise the score by taking its geometric mean given the number of words. Suppose there are n words in the current partial utterance and s its score, then NORMALISED_SCORE = $s^{\frac{1}{n}}$.
- **TIME:** The duration in seconds reached so far in the current task. This value is normalised so that it is around zero at the beginning of the task and around 1 for 6 minutes (maximum user patience).

In order to represent the function $Q(s, a)$, we maintain one linear model per action. There are 21 combinations between SYSTEM_REQ and LAST_INCR_RESP values that are the most likely to occur. They have been associated to the features δ_1 to δ_{21}. δ_i equals 1 when the ith combination happens in the current micro-turn and 0 otherwise. Less frequent combinations have been removed from this initial model: first they make the model more complex with in all likelihood no significant improvement in the performance (making the learning process slower to converge and more data demanding) and second, the Fitted-Q algorithm involves the inversion of a feature covariance matrix which could be ill-conditioned with these rare combinations.

NB_USER_WORDS is represented by three Radial Basis Function (RBF) features (Sutton and Barto, 1998) ϕ_1^{nw}, ϕ_2^{nw} and ϕ_3^{nw}. Their means are set to 0, 5 and 10 and the corresponding standard deviations are 2, 3 and 3. The same representation with 2 features is used for NORMALISED_SCORE: ϕ_1^{ns} and ϕ_2^{ns} centered at 0.25 and 0.75 and with a standard deviation of 0.3 for both.

Finally, TIME is represented as a single feature $T = sigmoid((TIME - 180)/60)$ so that it is almost 0 for TIME=0 and almost 1 after 6 minutes. As this variable increases, the user is more and more likely to hangup, therefore the Q function is supposed to be monotonous with respect to that feature so it is taken directly in the model without the use of RBFs.

As a consequence, 28 parameters are involved for each action (56 in total). Let $\Theta(a)$ be the parameter vector ($\Theta(a) = [\theta_0, \theta_1, ..., \theta_{27}]^T$) corresponding to action a and $\Phi(s, a)$ the feature vector corresponding to state s and action a, therefore:

$$\begin{aligned}\Phi(s,a) &= [1, \delta_1, ..., \delta_{21}, \phi_1^{nw}, \phi_2^{nw}, \phi_3^{nw}, \\ &\quad \phi_1^{ns}, \phi_2^{ns}, T]^T \quad (3)\\ Q(s,a) &= \Theta(a)^T \Phi(s,a) \quad (4)\end{aligned}$$

4.3.3 Learning

RL learning of the turn-taking policy is operated with Fitted-Q, a Fitted Value Iteration algorithm (Lagoudakis and Parr, 2003; Chandramohan et al., 2010). Fitted-Q is a batch learning algorithm for reinforcement learning. Standard Q-learning (Watkins, 1989) has also been tested as an online algorithm but unsuccessfully, which is compliant with previous works (e.g. (Daubigney et al., 2012)).

The optimal Q-function Q^* is known to be the solution of the Bellman optimality equation (Sutton and Barto, 1998):

$$\begin{aligned}Q^*(s,a) = \mathbb{E}_{s'|s,a}[R(s,a,s') \\ +\gamma \max_{a' \in \mathcal{A}} Q(s', a')] \quad (5)\end{aligned}$$

Therefore, the Fitted-Q algorithm is fed with a set of N MDP transitions (s_j, a_j, r_j, s'_j) and aims to approximate the representation parameters vector of the Q-function by performing a linear regression at each iteration step. In our case, for each action and at the iteration i, the parameter vector is updated as follows (for commodity, $\phi(s_j, a_j)$ is noted ϕ_j):

$$\Theta^{(i)}(a) = \arg\min_{\Theta(a)} \sum_{j=1}^{N} (R_j^{(i-1)} - \Theta(a)^T \phi_j)^2 \quad (6)$$

$$R_j^{(i-1)} = r_j + \gamma \max_{a \in \mathcal{A}} (\Theta_{i-1}^T \phi(s'_j, a)) \quad (7)$$

This is a classical linear regression problem and we use the closed formula for each iteration:

$$\Theta^{(i)} = (\sum_{j=1}^{N} \phi_j \phi_j^T)^{-1} \sum_{j=1}^{N} \phi_j R_j^{(i-1)} \quad (8)$$

The iteration stop criterion is

$$\sum_{a \in \mathcal{A}} ||\Theta^{(i)}(a) - \Theta^{(i-1)}(a)||_1 \leq \xi \quad (9)$$

In our experiments, the convergence threshold is set to $\xi = 0.01$.

5 Experiment

5.1 Experimental setup

Three dialogue scenario types involving diverse adding, modifying and deleting tasks were used for the experiments. For the training of the RL strategy, the simulated speech recognition WER was fixed at 0.15. We trained the system 50 times and each training session is made of 3000 episodes. The Fitted-Q algorithm was run every 500 episodes on the total batch from the beginning. During the first 500 episodes, a pure-exploration policy is used: it performs a WAIT action with a probability of 0.9 (hence a SPEAK action 10% of the times). An ϵ-greedy ($\epsilon = 0.1$) policy is then used until episode 2500. After that, a greedy policy is used (pure-exploitation).

Thus, 50 learning models are collected. As a linear model is used for the Q-function representation, we simply average the parameters to get an average model. The latter is then tested against the basic non-incremental strategy and our handcrafted baseline under different noise conditions by varying the WER parameter between 0 and 0.3 with a step of 0.03.

5.2 Results

The average learning curve is depicted in Figure 3. The reward levels corresponding to the non-incremental case and the handcrafted incremental strategy are indicated by the red and the blue lines. Each green triangle corresponds to the moving average reward over 100 episode of the RL strategy. The first 500 episodes are exclusively exploratory, therefore the system performance during that early stage of learning is pointless. Between episode 500 and episode 2500, we observe no improvement even though the policy is still partially exploring. This shows that the 500

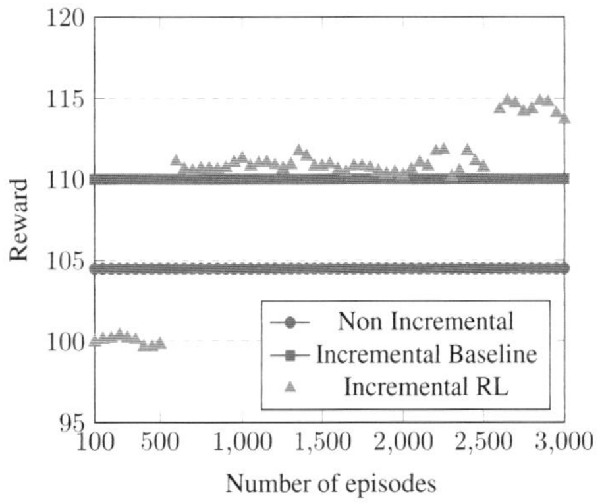

Figure 3: Learning curve (0-500: pure exploration, 500-2500: exploration/exploitation, 2500-3000: pure exploitation)

first episodes are enough to learn the optimal policy given our model. The 500 last episodes show that the learned strategy significantly outperforms the handcrafted baseline.

Incremental dialogue systems have the ability to report an error to the user in a more reactive way and to prevent it from speaking for a long time without being understood by the system. In noisy environments, these problems are even more likely to happen. Figures 4 and 5 show the effect of noise over dialogue duration and task completion. They represent the average performance over the 3 dialogue scenarios used in this experiment. Incremental dialogue, and the automatically learned strategy in particular, significantly increase the noise robustness. In the non-incremental case, the mean dialogue duration reaches 3 minutes and the task completion drops below 70%. Our learned strategy makes the dialogues finish 30 seconds earlier on average (17% gain) and the task completion is about 80%.

6 Conclusion and future work

In this paper, a simulated environment for a slot-filling task has been used to compare different expert and learned turn-taking strategies. A first one is non-incremental meaning that the user and the system cannot interrupt each other. As ASR noise increases, the dialogues tend to last longer leading to lower task completion. A second strategy is incremental, starting from three turn-taking phenomena present in the human-human interaction we translated them into a set of handcrafted rules for human-machine dialogue. This rule-

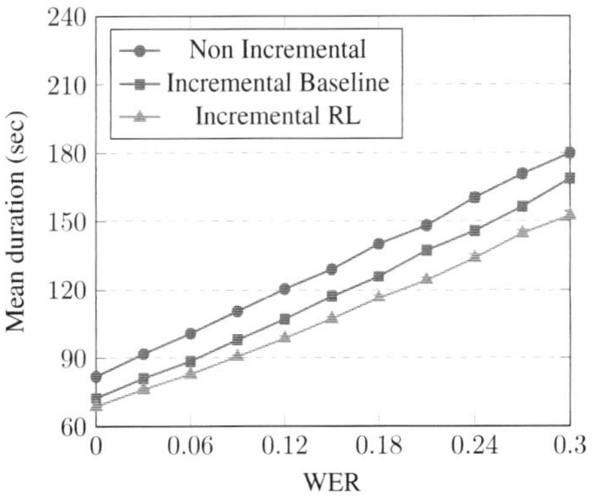

Figure 4: Simulated dialogue duration for different noise levels

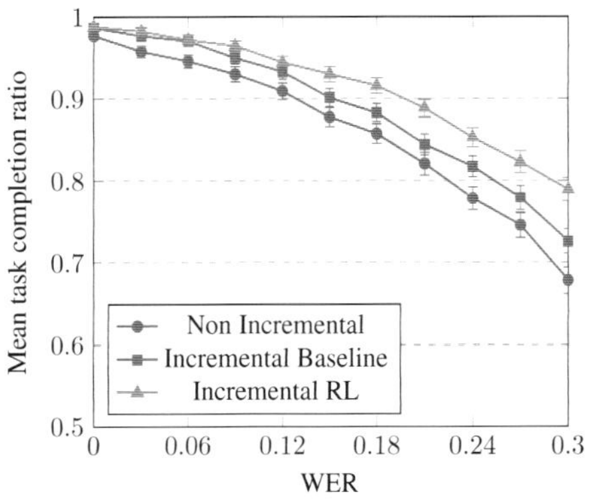

Figure 5: Simulated dialogue task completion for different noise levels

based strategy is then shown to have better performance than the non-incremental case in terms of dialogue duration and task completion ratio when the noise is increasing. Eventually the Fitted-Q algorithm has been retained to automatically learn a third turn-taking strategy, still with the same objective (minimising the dialogue duration and maximising the task completion). This third strategy significantly improves noise robustness of the simulated dialogue system. We are now planning to evaluate this approach with real users and by taking subjective scores into account for learning optimal turn-taking strategies with respect to enlarged view of the system performance, such as comfort of use, friendliness etc.

References

Senthilkumar Chandramohan, Matthieu Geist, and Olivier Pietquin. 2010. Optimizing spoken dialogue management with fitted value iteration. In *INTERSPEECH 11th Annual Conference of the International Speech*.

S. Chandramohan, M. Geist, F. Lefèvre, and O. Pietquin. 2011. User Simulation in Dialogue Systems using Inverse Reinforcement Learning. In *Interspeech*.

L. Daubigney, M. Geist, S. Chandramohan, and O. Pietquin. 2012. A comprehensive reinforcement learning framework for dialogue management optimization. *Selected Topics in Signal Processing, IEEE Journal of*.

Nina Dethlefs, Helen Wright Hastie, Verena Rieser, and Oliver Lemon. 2012. Optimising incremental dialogue decisions using information density for interactive systems. In *EMNLP-CoNLL*.

David DeVault, Kenji Sagae, and David Traum. 2011. Incremental interpretation and prediction of utterance meaning for interactive dialogue. *Dialogue and Discourse*, 2:143–170.

W. Eckert, E. Levin, and R. Pieraccini. 1997. User modeling for spoken dialogue system evaluation. In *Automatic Speech Recognition and Understanding, 1997. Proceedings., 1997 IEEE Workshop on*.

Emmanuel Ferreira and Fabrice Lefevre. 2013. Expert-based reward shaping and exploration scheme for boosting policy learning of dialogue management. In *Automatic Speech Recognition and Understanding (ASRU), 2013 IEEE Workshop on*, pages 108–113. IEEE.

Fabrizio Ghigi, Maxine Eskenazi, M Ines Torres, and Sungjin Lee. 2014. Incremental dialog processing in a task-oriented dialog. In *Fifteenth Annual Conference of the International Speech Communication Association*.

Helen Hastie, Marie-Aude Aufaure, Panos Alexopoulos, Heriberto Cuayáhuitl, Nina Dethlefs, Milica Gasic, James Henderson, Oliver Lemon, Xingkun Liu, Peter Mika, Nesrine Ben Mustapha, Verena Rieser, Blaise Thomson, Pirros Tsiakoulis, and Yves Vanrompay. 2013. Demonstration of the parlance system: a data-driven incremental, spoken dialogue system for interactive search. In *Proceedings of the SIGDIAL 2013 Conference*.

Gudny Ragna Jonsdottir, Kristinn R. Thorisson, and Eric Nivel. 2008. Learning smooth, human-like turntaking in realtime dialogue. In *In Proceedings of Intelligent Virtual Agents (IVA 08*, pages 162–175. Springer.

Hatim Khouzaimi, Romain Laroche, and Fabrice Lefèvre. 2014. An easy method to make dialogue systems incremental. In *Proceedings of the 15th Annual Meeting of the Special Interest Group on Discourse and Dialogue (SIGDIAL)*.

Hatim Khouzaimi, Romain Laroche, and Fabrice Lefèvre. 2015a. Dialogue efficiency evaluation of turn-taking phenomena in a multi-layer incremental simulated environment. In *Proceedings of the HCI International 2015 Conference (accepted)*.

Hatim Khouzaimi, Romain Laroche, and Fabrice Lefèvre. 2015b. Turn-taking phenomena in incremental dialogue systems. In *Proceedings of the EMNLP 2015 Conference (submitted)*.

Dongho Kim, Catherine Breslin, Pirros Tsiakoulis, Milica Gasic, Matthew Henderson, and Steve Young. 2014. Inverse reinforcement learning for micro-turn management. In *INTERSPEECH Proceedings*.

Michail G. Lagoudakis and Ronald Parr. 2003. Least-squares policy iteration. *JOURNAL OF MACHINE LEARNING RESEARCH*.

Romain Laroche, Ghislain Putois, and Philippe Bretier. 2010. Optimising a handcrafted dialogue system design. In *INTERSPEECH*.

Oliver Lemon and Olivier Pietquin. 2007. Machine learning for spoken dialogue systems. In *Proceedings of the European Conference on Speech Communication and Technologies (Interspeech'07)*.

Esther Levin and Roberto Pieraccini. 1997. A stochastic model of computer-human interaction for learning dialogue strategies. In *In EUROSPEECH 97*.

Di Lu, Takuya Nishimoto, and Nobuaki Minematsu. 2011. Decision of response timing for incremental speech recognition with reinforcement learning. In *ASRU*.

Olivier Pietquin and Richard Beaufort. 2005. Comparing asr modeling methods for spoken dialogue simulation and optimal strategy learning. In *INTERSPEECH*.

Olivier Pietquin and Helen Hastie. 2013. A survey on metrics for the evaluation of user simulations. *Knowledge Engineering Review*.

F. Pinault and F. Lefèvre. 2011. Unsupervised clustering of probability distributions of semantic graphs for pomdp based spoken dialogue systems with summary space. In *IJCAI 7th KRPDS Workshop*.

Antoine Raux and Maxine Eskenazi. 2008. Optimizing endpointing thresholds using dialogue features in a spoken dialogue system. In *SIGDIAL*.

Antoine Raux and Maxine Eskenazi. 2012. Optimizing the turn-taking behavior of task-oriented spoken dialog systems. *ACM Trans. Speech Lang. Process.*

Harvey Sacks, Emanuel A. Schegloff, and Gail Jefferson. 1974. A simplest systematics for the organization of turn-taking for conversation. *Language*, 50:696–735.

David Schlangen and Gabriel Skantze. 2011. A general, abstract model of incremental dialogue processing. *Dialogue and Discourse*, 2:83–111.

Ethan Selfridge and Peter A. Heeman. 2010. Importance-driven turn-bidding for spoken dialogue systems. In *ACL*, pages 177–185.

Ethan O. Selfridge, Iker Arizmendi, Peter A. Heeman, and Jason D. Williams. 2012. Integrating incremental speech recognition and pomdp-based dialogue systems. In *Proceedings of the 13th Annual Meeting of the Special Interest Group on Discourse and Dialogue*, July.

Richard S. Sutton and Andrew G. Barto. 1998. *Reinforcement Learning, An Introduction.* The MIT Press, Cambridge, Massachusetts, London, England.

Christopher John Cornish Hellaby Watkins. 1989. *Learning from Delayed Rewards.* Ph.D. thesis, King's College.

S. Young, M. Gasic, B. Thomson, and J.D. Williams. 2013. Pomdp-based statistical spoken dialog systems: A review. *Proceedings of the IEEE.*

Jiahong Yuan, Mark Liberman, and Christopher Cieri. 2006. Towards an integrated understanding of speaking rate in conversation. In *INTERSPEECH Proceedings*.

Acoustic-prosodic entrainment in Slovak, Spanish, English and Chinese: A cross-linguistic comparison

Rivka Levitan [1,2], **Štefan Beňuš** [3], **Agustín Gravano** [4,5], **Julia Hirschberg** [2]

[1] Department of Computer and Information Science, Brooklyn College CUNY, USA

[2] Department of Computer Science, Columbia University, USA

[3] Constantine the Philosopher University in Nitra & Institute of Informatics, Slovak Academy of Sciences, Slovakia

[4] National Scientific and Technical Research Council (CONICET), Buenos Aires, Argentina

[5] Departamento de Computación, FCEyN, Universidad de Buenos Aires, Argentina

levitan@sci.brooklyn.cuny.edu, sbenus@ukf.sk,
gravano@dc.uba.ar, julia@cs.columbia.edu

Abstract

It is well established that speakers of Standard American English entrain, or become more similar to each other as they speak, in acoustic-prosodic features of their speech as well as other behaviors. Entrainment in other languages is less well understood. This work uses a variety of metrics to measure acoustic-prosodic entrainment in four comparable corpora of task-oriented conversational speech in Slovak, Spanish, English and Chinese. We report the results of these experiments and describe trends and patterns that can be observed from comparing acoustic-prosodic entrainment in these four languages. We find evidence of a variety of forms of entrainment across all the languages studied, with some evidence of individual differences as well within the languages.

1 Introduction

In general, entrainment is a ubiquitous tendency observed in human-human dialogues in which interlocutors adapt their communicative behavior to the behavior of their conversational partners in several modalities. Empirical evidence of entrainment in human-human conversations has been documented for numerous acoustic-prosodic features, including intensity (Natale, 1975; Gregory et al., 1993; Ward and Litman, 2007), speaking rate (Street, 1984), and pitch (Gregory et al., 1993; Ward and Litman, 2007). Humans have been shown to entrain to their interlocutor's *language* as well, at the lexical level (Brennan, 1996), syntactic level (Branigan et al., 2000; Reitter et al., 2010), and on what (Niederhoffer and Pennebaker, 2002) called linguistic style, which includes, among other features, the use of pronouns and verb tenses (Niederhoffer and Pennebaker, 2002; Danescu-Niculescu-Mizil et al., 2011; Michael and Otterbacher, 2014). Motivated by Communication Accommodation Theory (CAT) (Giles et al., 1991), which holds that speakers converge to or diverge from their interlocutors in order to attenuate or accentuate social differences, numerous studies have looked for links between entrainment and positive social behavior. Entrainment on various features and at all levels of communication has been linked, respectively, to liking (Chartrand and Bargh, 1999; Street, 1984), positive affect in conversations between "seriously and chronically distressed" married couples discussing a problem in their relationship (Lee et al., 2010), mutual romantic interest in speed dating transcripts (Ireland et al., 2011), cooperation in a prisoner's dilemma (Manson et al., 2013), task success (Nenkova et al., 2008; Reitter and Moore, 2007; Friedberg et al., 2012; Thomason et al., 2013), and approval-seeking (Natale, 1975; Danescu-Niculescu-Mizil et al., 2012). Given that these social aspects are assumed to be culture-specific, and the fact that research on entrainment has been done mainly on English and other Germanic languages, the types and degree of entrainment in other languages and cultures should be explored. Although there are numerous studies documenting entrainment in different aspects of spoken dialogue in particular languages collected in particular circumstances, it has been difficult to compare entrainment across languages due to differences in the corpora examined and and analytical approaches employed. Recently, this gap has been addressed in (Xia et al., 2014; Beňuš et al., 2014) who report on commonalities observed across languages as well as systematic differences in *global* measures of acoustic-prosodic entrainment (i.e. over entire dialogues)

Proceedings of the SIGDIAL 2015 Conference, pages 325–334,
Prague, Czech Republic, 2-4 September 2015.

in comparable corpora of conversational speech in Chinese, English and Slovak.

In this study we expand on these findings by focusing on *local* acoustic-prosodic entrainment (i.e. dynamic adjustments at turn exchanges) on a session-by-session basis and present results from a comparative study of four very different languages, English, Chinese, Slovak, and Spanish, collected from subjects engaged in deliberately similar conversational tasks for the purpose of comparison: the Columbia Games Corpus (English), the SK-Games Corpus (Slovak), the Porteño Spanish Games Corpus, and the Tongji Games Corpus (Chinese), and employ identical tools and methods for their analysis. We present the results of analyses of these corpora for positive and negative (complementary) entrainment using a variety of metrics (proximity, synchrony and convergence), and a variety of acoustic and prosodic features (pitch, intensity, speaking rate, and several measures of voice quality).

Section 2 describes the four corpora used in our analysis, the features we examined in the study and the units of analysis over which they were calculated. Section 3 discusses three methods of measuring entrainment at the local level, *proximity*, *synchrony*, and *convergence*, and reports the results of applying each of these measures to the four corpora. Section 4 summarizes our results and discusses patterns that emerge from our analysis.

2 Data and features

This section describes the comparable task-oriented corpora that are analyzed in this study.

2.1 Columbia Games Corpus

The Columbia Games Corpus is a collection of 12 spontaneous dyadic conversations between native speakers of Standard American English (SAE). Thirteen subjects participated in the collection of the corpus. Eleven returned on another day for another session with a different partner. Their ages ranged from 20 to 50 years ($M = 30.0$, $SD = 10.9$). Six subjects were female, and seven were male; of the twelve dialogues in the corpus, three are between female-female pairs, three are between male-male pairs, and six are between mixed-gender pairs. All interlocutors were strangers to each other.

In order to elicit spontaneous, task-oriented speech, subjects were asked to play a series of four computer games of two kinds: Cards games and Objects games. The games were designed to require cooperation and communication in order to achieve a high score. Participants were motivated to do well by a monetary bonus that depended on the number of points they achieved in each game. All games were played on separate laptops whose screens were not visible to the other player; the players were separated by a curtain so that all communication would be vocal. During game play, keystrokes were captured and were later synchronized with the speech recordings and game events.

There are approximately 9 hours and 13 minutes of speech in the Games Corpus, of which approximately 70 minutes come from the first part of the Cards game, 207 minutes from the second part of the cards Game, and 258 minutes from the Objects game. On average, each session is approximately 46 minutes long, comprised of three Cards games of approximately 8 minutes each and one Objects game, which is approximately 22 minutes long.

The corpus has been orthographically transcribed and manually word-aligned by trained annotators. In addition, disfluencies and other paralinguistic events such as laughs, coughs and breaths were marked by the annotators. The corpus has also been annotated prosodically according to the ToBI framework (Silverman et al., 1992); all turns have been labeled by type; affirmative cue words have been labeled according to their pragmatic functions; and all questions have been categorized by form and function. The annotation of the Games Corpus is described in detail in (Gravano, 2009).

2.2 Sk-Games Corpus

SK-games is a corpus of native Slovak (SK) conversational speech that is identical to the Objects games of the Columbia Games Corpus for SAE barring adjustments to some of the screen images and their positioning. Subjects were seated in a quiet room facing computer screens without visual contact with each other. The corpus currently includes 9 dyadic sessions with a total of 11 speakers (5F, 6M). Seven of the speakers (4F, 3M) participated in two sessions and thus we can compare their behavior in identical communicative situations when they are paired with a different interlocutor. Of the nine sessions, two are between female-female pairs, two between male-

male pairs, and five between mixed-gender pairs. The analyzed material makes roughly six hours of speech, and consists of 35,758 words and 3,189 unique words. The audio signal was manually transcribed, and the transcripts were automatically aligned to the signal using the SPHINX toolkit adjusted for Slovak (Darjaa et al., 2011), which forces the alignment of both words and individual phonemes. This forced alignment was then manually corrected.

2.3 Porteño Spanish Games Corpus

The Spanish data were taken from a larger corpus of Porteño Spanish (Sp) that is currently under construction. Porteño is a variant of the Spanish language spoken by roughly 20-25 million people in East-Central Argentina and Uruguay. It is characterized by substantial differences with other variants of Spanish at the lexical, phonological and prosodic levels (e.g. (Colantoni and Gurlekian, 2004)). The portion of the corpus used in this study is also similar to the Objects games of the Columbia Games Corpus, and currently includes 7 dyadic sessions with a total of 12 native speakers of Porteño Spanish (7F, 5M); only two female speakers participated in two sessions, with different partners in each session. Of the seven sessions, three are between female-female pairs, one between male-male pairs, and three between mixed-gender pairs. The analyzed material makes roughly two hours of speech, and consists of 17,571 words and 1,139 unique words. The audio signal was manually transcribed, and the transcripts were manually aligned to the signal by trained annotators.

2.4 Tongji Games Corpus

The Tongji Games Corpus (Xia et al., 2014) is a corpus of spontaneous, task-oriented conversations in Mandarin Chinese (MC). The corpus contains approximately 12 hours of speech, comprising 99 conversations between 84 unique native speakers (57 female, 27 male), some of whom participated in more than one conversation with a different partner. Conversations average 6 minutes in length. Participants in the corpus were randomly selected from university students who had a National Mandarin Test Certificate level 2 with a grade of A or above. This restriction enforced that the elicited speech would be standard Mandarin, with minimal effect of regional dialect. As in the collection of the Columbia Games Corpus, recordings were made in a sound-proof booth on laptops with a curtain between participants so that neither could see the other's screen and so that all communication would be verbal.

Two games were used to elicit spontaneous speech in the collection of the corpus. In the **Picture Ordering** game, one subject, the information *giver*, gave the other, the *follower*, instructions for ordering a set of 18 cards. When the task was completed, the same pair switched roles and repeated the task. In the **Picture Classifying** game, each pair worked together to classify 18 pictures into appropriate categories by discussing each picture. Seventeen pairs played the Picture Ordering game, 39 pairs played the Picture Classification game, and 14 pairs played both games (each time with the same partner).

The corpus was segmented automatically using SPPAS (SPeech Phonetization Alignment and Syllabification) (Bigi and Hirst, 2012), a tool for automatic prosody analysis. The automatic segments were manually checked and orthographically transcribed. Turns were identified by two PhD students specializing in Conversation Analysis.

For our analysis, we include one randomly chosen conversation from each of ten female-female pairs, ten male-male pairs, and ten female-male pairs, for a total of 30 conversations.

2.5 Features

In each corpus, we look for evidence of entrainment on eight acoustic-prosodic features: intensity mean and max, pitch mean and max, jitter, shimmer, noise-to-harmonics ratio (NHR), and speaking rate. Speaking rate for English was determined from the orthographic transcriptions of the data using an online syllable dictionary. For Slovak, the syllable count for each word was determined algorithmically utilizing the availability of phonemes (from grapheme-to-phoneme conversion required for alignment) and a known set of phonemes forming syllable nuclei. For Spanish, syllable counts were computed automatically using the toolkit developed by Hernández-Figueroa et al. (2013). All other features were extracted using the open-source audio analysis tool Praat (Boersma and Weenink, 2012).

To allow for meaningful comparisons between female and male pitch values, female pitch values in the English, Spanish and Slovak corpora were linearly scaled to lie within the male pitch range. This gender normalization was not done for the Chinese data. However, a linear scaling of a given speaker's feature values does not affect the analysis, since all comparisons are relative to the speaker's own speech.

The analysis of the Chinese data did not consider the voice quality features (jitter, shimmer, or NHR).

The details of the feature extraction and audio analysis of the Columbia Games Corpus can be found in (Gravano, 2009); the same methods were used for the other three corpora, without any corpus-specific refinements.

2.6 Units of analysis

We compute and compare features from the following units of analysis:

An **inter-pausal unit (IPU)** is a pause-free chunk of speech from a single speaker. The threshold for pause length for three of the corpora was derived empirically from the average length of stop gaps in each corpus (50ms for English and Spanish, 80ms for Chinese); for the Slovak data, pauses were detected with a minimum threshold of 100ms and then manually adjusted.

A **turn** is a consecutive series of IPUs from a single speaker. We include in our definition of "turns" utterances that are not turns in the discourse sense of the term, such as backchannels or failed attempts to take the floor.

A **session** is a complete interaction between a pair of interlocutors.

3 Local entrainment

Local entrainment is defined as similarity between interlocutors at well-defined points in a conversation. Two speakers may be *globally* similar—for example, having similar feature means—while diverging widely at most given points in a conversation, as in Figure 1.

Local entrainment can be thought of as dynamic entrainment: a continuous reaction to one's interlocutor and updating of one's own output in response to what has just been heard. Such entrainment can be **convergent**, adjusting toward greater similarity to the interlocutor, or **complementary**, adjusting away from the interlocutor. Complementary entrainment is often called **disentrainment** or **divergence** (Healey et al., 2014), with the connotation that this behavior reflects a speaker's desire to distance herself from her interlocutor, but

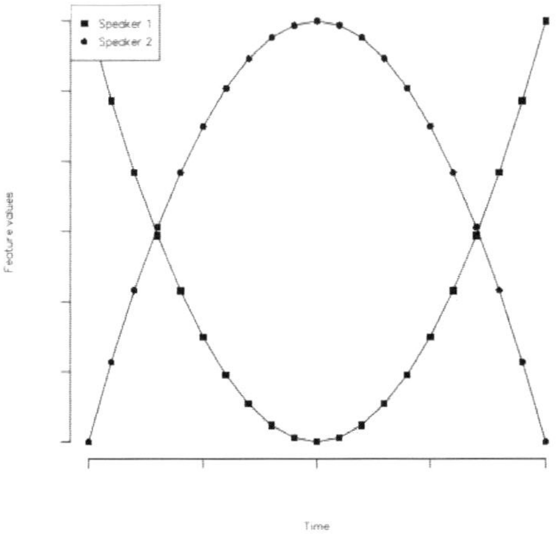

Figure 1: *Global vs. local entrainment*

it can also be viewed as a cooperative behavior in which a speaker completes or resolves the prosody of her interlocutor's previous turn. Independently of either interpretation, local entrainment denotes dynamic responsiveness to an interlocutor's behavior.

Following (Levitan and Hirschberg, 2011), and using the measures described there, we look for evidence of three aspects of local entrainment:*proximity*, *synchrony*, and *convergence*. (Xia et al., 2014) analyzed local entrainment in English and Chinese, and found similar patterns over entire corpora. Here, for a more nuanced view of the prevalence of local entrainment, we apply our analysis separately to each session.

Multiple statistical tests are conducted in the course of this analysis. All significance tests correct for family-wise Type I error by controlling the false discovery rate (FDR) at $\alpha = 0.05$. The kth smallest p value is considered significant if it is less than $\frac{k \times \alpha}{n}$ (where n is the number of p values).

3.1 Proximity

Proximity describes entrainment by value. A session that displays proximity on a given feature will have turns which are more similar to their preceding turns than they are to others of the interlocutor's turns in the session. To measure proximity, we look at the differences in feature values between adjacent IPUs at turn exchanges. For each turn t, and for each feature f, we calculate an *adjacent* difference—the absolute value of the difference between the value of f in the first IPU of t and the value of f in the last IPU of $t-1$—and a *non-adjacent* difference—the averaged absolute values of the differences between the value of f in the first IPU of t and the values of f in the last IPUs of 50 other turns chosen randomly from the turns of the other speaker.[1]

These non-adjacent differences serve as a baseline for the degree of similarity we might expect to see at turn exchanges if there is no effect of local entrainment. For each session and each feature, if adjacent differences are smaller than non-adjacent differences, we conclude that the speakers in that session are locally entraining to each other.

Table 1 shows the results of paired t-tests between adjacent and non-adjacent differences for each of the nine Slovak sessions we analyze. We see little evidence of local proximity in our Slovak data. Only two sessions show evidence of local proximity on intensity mean, and only one shows negative proximity for intensity max. No other feature shows evidence of local proximity, positive or negative.

Table 2 shows the results of the test for proximity in the seven Spanish sessions. Spanish shows even less evidence of local proximity: Only one session shows evidence of negative proximity of intensity max; there is no evidence of convergent proximity.

Feature	Session								
	1	2	3	4	5	6	7	8	9
IntMean			+	+					
IntMax						-			
PchMean									
PchMax									
Jitter									
Shimmer									
NHR									
Spkrt									

Table 1: *Local proximity by session in Slovak (+: significant positive proximity; -: significant negative proximity; ' ': no significant proximity)*

English, in contrast, shows significant positive local proximity on intensity mean and max in four out of 12 sessions. There is no evidence of positive local proximity on any other feature in English, and no evidence of negative local proximity at all.

The Chinese data also shows evidence of positive local proximity on intensity mean and max in several sessions (three out of 30 for intensity mean), but there is also evidence of negative proximity on those features in multiple sessions. In addition, nearly all sessions show strong negative proximity on the pitch features. Finally, one session (out of 30) shows negative proximity on speaking rate.

Feature	Session						
	1	2	3	4	5	6	7
IntMean							
IntMax			-				
PchMean							
PchMax							
Jitter							
Shimmer							
NHR							
Spkrt							

Table 2: *Local proximity by session in Spanish (+: significant positive proximity; -: significant negative proximity; ' ': no significant proximity)*

3.2 Synchrony

Synchrony describes entrainment by *direction* rather than value, measuring how the dynamics of an individual speaker's prosody relate to those of his or her interlocutor. We take the Pearson's correlation between feature values from adjacent IPUs at turn exchanges to see whether speakers' values at turn exchanges vary together, in synchrony, even if they are not similar in absolute values.

As Table 3 shows, synchrony is a much more significant factor in entrainment in Slovak than proximity is. Nearly every feature shows evidence of synchrony in multiple sessions. Strikingly, nearly every feature in fact shows *negative* synchrony, or *complementary* synchronous entrainment. Only intensity mean shows positive synchrony in three sessions (and negative synchrony in a fourth); synchrony on the other seven features is consistently negative.

Table 3 also makes it clear that this aspect of entrainment is highly individualized. Session 1, for example, shows no evidence of synchrony at all; Session 5 shows significant negative synchrony in

[1] Since some of the Spanish sessions did not have as many as 50 turns from the other speaker, the non-adjacent differences in the Spanish analysis were averaged over 20 turns from the other speaker.

Feature	Session								
	1	2	3	4	5	6	7	8	9
IntMean			+	+		+			-
IntMax					-	-			-
PchMean		-	-		-		-		-
PchMax		-	-				-		-
Jitter					-	-			
Shimmer					-				
NHR		-			-		-	-	
Spkrt					-				

Table 3: *Local synchrony in Slovak by session (+: significant positive synchrony; -: significant negative synchrony; ' ': no significant synchrony)*

Feature	Session						
	1	2	3	4	5	6	7
IntMean							
IntMax				-			
PchMean					-		
PchMax							
Jitter							
Shimmer		-			-		
NHR		-		-	-		
Spkrt			-				

Table 4: *Local synchrony in Spanish by session (+: significant positive synchrony; -: significant negative synchrony; ' ': no significant synchrony)*

everything except intensity mean and pitch max; Session 4 shows only positive synchrony in intensity mean; and Session 9 shows negative synchrony in intensity and pitch mean and max. Further research will be needed to explore the relationships between entrainment on different aspects of prosody.

Table 4 reveals similar trends in the Spanish data. Synchrony is evident for a plurality of features and sessions, and all observed synchrony is negative. One notable difference is in synchrony on pitch features, which is present in five of nine Slovak dialogues, and only one of seven Spanish dialogues. Intensity mean, which shows positive synchrony in three Slovak dialogues and negative synchrony in one, shows no evidence of synchrony in any Spanish dialogue.

In the English data, positive synchrony is evident for intensity mean in six of the 12 dialogues. Intensity max shows positive synchrony in three sessions and negative synchrony in another three. There is also some evidence of positive synchrony on pitch mean, pitch max, and shimmer (one session each), and negative synchrony on pitch mean (three sessions); pitch max, jitter, shimmer, and NHR (two sessions each); and speaking rate (one session).

The most notable aspect of entrainment by synchrony in the Chinese data is the strong negative synchrony on pitch that is present in many of the sessions (19 out of 30 for pitch mean, 15 for pitch max). One session shows positive synchrony on pitch max; none show positive synchrony on pitch mean. The results on intensity are more evenly split: for intensity mean, six sessions show positive synchrony and five show negative, while the count is 3-4 for intensity max. Three sessions show negative synchrony on speaking rate.

3.3 Convergence

We add another dimension to our analysis of local entrainment by looking at *convergence*: whether interlocutors become increasingly similar over the course of a conversation. Where previously we looked at the degree to which interlocutors react and adapt to each other at each turn exchange, now we look at how that degree of adaptation changes with time. This is measured by the Pearson's correlation between adjacent differences (absolute differences in feature values in adjacent IPUs at turn exchanges) and time. A significant negative correlation over a session (differences become *smaller* with time) is evidence of convergence.

Feature	**Session**								
	1	2	3	4	5	6	7	8	9
IntMean	-						+		
IntMax							+		
PchMean									
PchMax		-							
Jitter				+					
Shimmer									
NHR					-				
Spkrt									

Table 5: *Local convergence in Slovak by session (+: significant convergence; -: significant divergence; ' ': no significant convergence)*

Table 5 shows little evidence of local convergence in Slovak. Only two sessions show evidence of convergence: one on intensity mean and max, and one on jitter. Three others show evidence of *divergence*, differences that *increase* with

Feature	Session						
	1	2	3	4	5	6	7
IntMean	+		+				
IntMax							
PchMean							
PchMax							
Jitter							
Shimmer							
NHR				+			
Spkrt							

Table 6: *Local convergence in Spanish by session (+: significant convergence; -: significant divergence; ' ': no significant convergence)*

time: one on intensity mean, one on pitch max, and one on NHR. The diversity of these results, with individual interlocutor pairs converging or diverging on specific features, suggests a strong speaker-dependent component to this aspect of entrainment. The same is true for the Spanish data (Table 6) — two sessions show convergence on intensity mean, and one on NHR — and the Chinese data: one session shows convergence on intensity mean and one on pitch max. English is the outlier here, with evidence of local convergence on intensity mean (two sessions), intensity max (five sessions), pitch mean (six sessions), pitch max (three sessions), and NHR (three sessions).

The significant correlation strengths (for all languages) are not high, ranging in absolute value between 0.13 and 0.32. The effect of convergence, even when significant, is only one of numerous factors affecting speakers' prosodic expression.

4 Discussion

This analysis explored three kinds of local entrainment on eight features over a total of 58 sessions in four languages. Table 7 summarizes our findings. Out of all this data certain patterns emerge:

Negative (complementary) synchrony is more prevalent than positive (convergent) synchrony. In each of the four languages under analysis, negative synchrony is present in a greater number of dialogues and for a greater number of features than is positive synchrony. This seems to indicate that at a local level, and to some extent independently of the specific prosodic characteristics of the language being spoken, human interlocutors adjust the prosodic features of their speech in the *opposite* direction from the dynamics of their partner's speech. That is, if speaker A produces a turn ending in the low part of her range for turn endings, speaker B will produce a turn beginning in the high part of his range for turn beginnings. (This is, of course, simplistic; the correlation strengths are mainly low to moderate, and entrainment is only one of many factors influencing the prosody of a given production.) It should be noted that this relationship cannot be attributed to the prosodic differences inherent in turn beginnings and turn endings, since the Pearson's correlation compares fluctuations within a series rather than the actual values. These results do not show that a low IPU tends to be followed by a high IPU, but that an IPU that is low for a turn ending tends to be followed by one that is high for a turn beginning.

This finding is in line with recent research questioning the ubiquity of entrainment in the syntactic and semantic domains and calling for more refined analyses of entrainment behavior (Healey et al., 2014). As discussed above, negative synchrony may be termed "disentrainment" and interpreted as a distancing behavior. However, its prevalence in cooperative dialogues is an argument for a more neutral interpretation. This can be explored in future work by determining whether negative synchrony is associated with objective and subjective measures of partner engagement and liking, as in (Levitan et al., 2012).

Another consistency found across languages is that mean intensity is the only feature to show significant *positive* synchrony in a plurality of sessions. In English, in fact, it *only* shows positive synchrony, the only feature to do so; in the other three languages it is more evenly split between instances of positive and negative synchrony.

Synchrony is more prevalent than proximity. In measuring local entrainment, we have distinguished between *proximity*, the similarity of a pair of feature values, and *synchrony*, the similarity of the dynamics of two sets of feature values. Our results show that synchrony is a more useful measure for characterizing the way in which human interlocutors adjust to each other at the local level. This is especially true for Slovak and Spanish, which show almost no evidence of proximity, but show evidence of synchrony in multiple sessions for almost every feature. Comparing proximity and synchrony, however, should be taken with caution since their prevalence has been assessed with different statistical tests.

Feature	Proximity (% sessions)								Synchrony (% sessions)								Convergence (% sessions)							
	SAE		MC		Sk		Sp		SAE		MC		Sk		Sp		SAE		MC		Sk		Sp	
	+	-	+	-	+	-	+	-	+	-	+	-	+	-	+	-	+	-	+	-	+	-	+	-
IntMean	33		10	20	22				50		20	17	33	11			17		3		11	11	29	
IntMax	25		7	17		11		14	25	25	10	13		33		14	42				11			
PchMean				67					8	25		63		56		14	50							
PchMax				63					8	17	3	50		44			25		3			11		
Jitter			-	-						17	-	-		22					-	-	11			
Shimmer			-	-					8	17	-	-		11		28			-	-				
NHR			-	-						17	-	-		44		43	25		-	-		11	14	
Spkrt				3						8		10		11		14								

Table 7: *Cross-linguistic summary of results on local acoustic-prosodic entrainment as percentages of sessions with significant positive (+) and negative (-) entrainment type (proximity, synchrony, convergence) A '-' indicates that the corresponding statistical test was not done for that language.*

Chinese shows the strongest evidence of pitch synchrony. While all four languages show evidence of negative synchrony on pitch, Chinese has the strongest and most prevalent negative pitch synchrony: it is present in a majority of the sessions, with correlation strengths of about 0.90. The reason for this is unknown, but it is reasonable to hypothesize that it is linked to the importance of pitch in Chinese, a tonal language.

Pitch is also the feature displaying the strongest and most prevalent negative synchrony in Slovak: negative pitch synchrony is present in a majority of sessions, as in Chinese, with correlation strengths of about 0.50.

English shows the strongest evidence of local convergence. In English, we observe positive local convergence in a plurality of sessions, on all features except jitter, shimmer, and speaking rate. There is no evidence of negative convergence. The only other language with significant evidence of local convergence is Spanish, which displays local convergence on intensity mean in two sessions and on NHR in one (out of seven). Chinese and Slovak have scattered instances of convergence; Slovak is the only language to show negative convergence, though the evidence is sparse (one session each for intensity mean, jitter, and NHR).

Individual behavior varies. While the patterns we have identified are apparent when looking at the data in the aggregate, none can be said to apply to all the sessions they describe, or even almost all. Clearly, a session's entrainment behavior is significantly influenced by the particular dynamics of its speaker pair. Gender, power, liking, personality, and similar factors have all been shown to influence the degree of entrainment to some extent (Levitan et al., 2012; Š. Beňuš et al., 2014; Gravano et al., 2014). Exploring how these factors correlate with entrainment in different languages and cultures is an interesting area for future work.

5 Conclusion

We have presented the results of applying an identical analysis of acoustic-prosodic entrainment to comparable corpora in four different languages. This approach allows us to identify trends that are characteristic of human behavior independently of language and culture, and behaviors that seem to be characteristic of a given language.

This study can be considered an exploratory contribution to what is currently a very small body of work concerning language differences in entrainment. Since three of the corpora we analyze have a relatively small number of participants, it is possible that the differences we identify may be the products of individual behavior rather than the characteristics of the given language. In future work, these results will be confirmed or refined by further research on a larger scale.

Acknowledgments

This material is based upon work supported by the Air Force Office of Scientific Research, Air Force Material Command, USAF under Award No. FA9550-15-1-0055 and by UBACYT 20020120200025BA.

References

Š. Beňuš, R. Levitan, J. Hirschberg, A. Gravano, and S. Darjaa. 2014. Entrainment in Slovak collaborative dialogues. In *Proceedings of the 5th IEEE Conference on Cognitive Infocommunications*, pages 309–313.

Brigitte Bigi and Daniel Hirst. 2012. SPeech phonetization alignment and syllabification (SPPAS): a tool for the automatic analysis of speech prosody. In *Speech Prosody*, pages 19–22. Tongji University Press.

Paul Boersma and David Weenink. 2012. Praat: doing phonetics by computer [computer program].

Version 5.3.23, retrieved 21 August 2012 from http://www.praat.org.

Holly P. Branigan, Martin J. Pickering, and Alexandra A. Cleland. 2000. Syntactic co-ordination in dialogue. *Cognition*, 75(2):B13–B25.

Susan E Brennan. 1996. Lexical entrainment in spontaneous dialog. *Proceedings of ISSD*, pages 41–44.

T. L. Chartrand and J. A. Bargh. 1999. The chameleon effect: The perception-behavior link and social interaction. *Journal of Personality and Social Psychology*, 76(6):893–910.

L. Colantoni and J.A. Gurlekian. 2004. Convergence and intonation: Historical evidence from Buenos Aires Spanish. *Bilingualism: Language and Cognition*, 7(2):107–119.

Cristian Danescu-Niculescu-Mizil, Michael Gamon, and Susan Dumais. 2011. Mark my words! linguistic style accommodation in social media. In *Proceedings of WWW*.

Cristian Danescu-Niculescu-Mizil, Lillian Lee, Bo Pang, and Jon Kleinberg. 2012. Echoes of power: language effects and power differences in social interaction. In *Proceedings of WWW*.

S. Darjaa, M. Cerňak, M. Trnka, M. Rusko, and R. Sabo. 2011. Effective triphone mapping for acoustic modeling in speech recognition. In *Proceedings of Interspeech*.

Heather Friedberg, Diane Litman, and Susannah BF Paletz. 2012. Lexical entrainment and success in student engineering groups. In *Spoken Language Technology Workshop (SLT), 2012 IEEE*, pages 404–409. IEEE.

Howard Giles, Nikolas Coupland, and Justine Coupland. 1991. Accommodation theory: Communication, context, and consequence. *Contexts of accommodation: Developments in applied sociolinguistics*, 1.

A. Gravano, S. Benus, R. Levitan, and J. Hirschberg. 2014. Three tobi-based measures of prosodic entrainment and their correlations with speaker engagement. In *IEEE Spoken Language Technology Workshop (SLT)*.

Agustín Gravano. 2009. *Turn-taking and affirmative cue words in task-oriented dialogue*. Ph.D. thesis, Columbia University.

Stanford Gregory, Stephen Webster, and Gang Huang. 1993. Voice pitch and amplitude convergence as a metric of quality in dyadic interviews. *Language & Communication*, 13(3):195–217.

Patrick GT Healey, Matthew Purver, and Christine Howes. 2014. Divergence in dialogue. *PloS one*, 9(6):e98598.

Z. Hernández-Figueroa, F.J. Carreras-Riudavets, and G. Rodríguez-Rodríguez. 2013. Automatic syllabification for Spanish using lemmatization and derivation to solve the prefix's prominence issue. *Expert Systems with Applications*, 40(17):7122–7131.

Molly E Ireland, Richard B Slatcher, Paul W Eastwick, Lauren E Scissors, Eli J Finkel, and James W Pennebaker. 2011. Language style matching predicts relationship initiation and stability. *Psychological Science*, 22(1):39–44.

Chi-Chun Lee, Matthew Black, Athanasios Katsamanis, Adam Lammert, Brian Baucom, Andrew Christensen, Panayiotis G. Georgiou, and Shrikanth Narayanan. 2010. Quantification of prosodic entrainment in affective spontaneous spoken interactions of married couples. In *Proceedings of Interspeech*.

Rivka Levitan and Julia Hirschberg. 2011. Measuring acoustic-prosodic entrainment with respect to multiple levels and dimensions. In *Proceedings of Interspeech*.

Rivka Levitan, Agustín Gravano, Laura Willson, Stefan Benus, Julia Hirschberg, and Ani Nenkova. 2012. Acoustic-prosodic entrainment and social behavior. In *Proceedings of the 2012 Conference of the North American Chapter of the Association for Computational Linguistics: Human Language Technologies*, pages 11–19, Montréal, Canada, June. Association for Computational Linguistics.

Joseph H Manson, Gregory A Bryant, Matthew M Gervais, and Michelle A Kline. 2013. Convergence of speech rate in conversation predicts cooperation. *Evolution and Human Behavior*, 34(6):419–426.

Loizos Michael and Jahna Otterbacher. 2014. Write like i write: Herding in the language of online reviews. In *Proceedings of the Eigth International AAAI Conference on Weblogs and Social Media*.

Michael Natale. 1975. Convergence of mean vocal intensity in dyadic communication as a function of social desirability. *Journal of Personality and Social Psychology*, 32(5):790–804.

Ani Nenkova, Agustín Gravano, and Julia Hirschberg. 2008. High frequency word entrainment in spoken dialogue. In *Proceedings of the 46th Annual Meeting of the Association for Computational Linguistics on Human Language Technologies: Short Papers*, pages 169–172. Association for Computational Linguistics.

Kate G. Niederhoffer and James W. Pennebaker. 2002. Linguistic style matching in social interaction. *Journal of Language and Social Psychology*, 21(4):337–360.

David Reitter and Johanna D. Moore. 2007. Predicting success in dialogue. In *Proceedings of the 45th Annual Meeting of the Association of Computational Linguistics*, pages 808–815.

David Reitter, Johanna D. Moore, and Frank Keller. 2010. Priming of syntactic rules in task-oriented dialogue and spontaneous conversation.

K. Silverman, M. Beckman, J. Pitrelli, M. Ostendorf, C. Wightman, P. Price, J. Pierrehumbert, and J. Hirschberg. 1992. ToBI: A standard for labeling English prosody. In *International Conf. on Spoken Language Processing*, volume 2, pages 867–870.

Richard L Street. 1984. Speech convergence and speech evaluation in fact-finding interviews. *Human Communication Research*, 11(2):139–169.

Jesse Thomason, Huy V Nguyen, and Diane Litman. 2013. Prosodic entrainment and tutoring dialogue success. In *Artificial Intelligence in Education*, pages 750–753. Springer.

Š. Beňuš, A. Gravano, R. Levitan, S.I. Levitan, L. Willson, and J. Hirschberg. 2014. Entrainment, dominance and alliance in Supreme Court hearings. *Knowledge-Based Systems*, 71:3–14.

Arthur Ward and Diane Litman. 2007. Measuring convergence and priming in tutorial dialog. Technical report, University of Pittsburgh.

Zhihua Xia, Rivka Levitan, and Julia Hirschberg. 2014. Prosodic entrainment in Mandarin and English: A cross-linguistic comparison. In *Speech Prosody*.

A Statistical Approach for Non-Sentential Utterance Resolution for Interactive QA System

Dinesh Raghu *
IBM Watson
diraghu1@in.ibm.com

Sathish Indurthi *
IBM Watson
saindurt@in.ibm.com

Jitendra Ajmera
IBM Watson
jajmera1@in.ibm.com

Sachindra Joshi
IBM Watson
jsachind@in.ibm.com

Abstract

Non-Sentential Utterances (NSUs) are short utterances that do not have the form of a full sentence but nevertheless convey a complete sentential meaning in the context of a conversation. NSUs are frequently used to ask follow up questions during interactions with question answer (QA) systems resulting into in-correct answers being presented to their users. Most of the current methods for resolving such NSUs have adopted rule or grammar based approach and have limited applicability.

In this paper, we present a data driven statistical method for resolving such NSUs. Our method is based on the observation that humans identify keyword appearing in an NSU and place them in the context of conversation to construct a meaningful sentence. We adapt the keyword to question (K2Q) framework to generate natural language questions using keywords appearing in an NSU and its context. The resulting questions are ranked using different scoring methods in a statistical framework. Our evaluation on a data-set collected using mTurk shows that the proposed method perform significantly better than the previous work that has largely been rule based.

1 Introduction

Recently Question Answering (QA) systems have been built with high accuracies [Ferrucci, 2012]. The obvious next step for them is to assist people by improving their experience in seeking day to day information needs like product support and troubleshooting. For QA systems to be effective and usable they need to evolve into conversational systems. One extra challenge that conversational systems throw is that users tend to form successive queries that allude to the entities and concepts made in the past utterances. Therefore, among other things, such systems need to be equipped with the ability to understand what are called Non-Sentential Utterances (NSUs) [Fernández et al., 2005, Fernández, 2006].

NSUs are utterances that do not have the form of a full sentence, according to the most traditional grammars, but nevertheless convey a complete sentential meaning. Consider for example, the conversation between a sales staff of a mobile store (S) and one of their customers (C), where C:2 and C:3 are examples of NSUs.

S:1 Hi, How may I help you

C:1 How much does an Apple iPhone 6 cost ?

S:2 $ . . .

C:2 What about 6S ?

S:3 $ . . .

C:3 with 64 GB ?

S:4 $ . . .

Humans have the ability to understand these NSUs in a conversation based on the context derived so far. The conversation context could include topic(s) under discussion, the past history between the participants or even their geographical location.

In the example above, the sales staff, based on her domain knowledge, knows that iPhone 6 and iPhone 6S are different models of iPhone and all phones have a cost feature associated with them. Therefore an utterance *What about 6S*, in the context of utterance *How much does an Apple iPhone 6 cost*, would mean *How much does an Apple iPhone 6S cost*. Similarly, 64 GB is an attribute of iPhone 6S and therefore the utterance *with 64*

*D. Raghu and S. Indurthi contributed equally to this work

Proceedings of the SIGDIAL 2015 Conference, pages 335–343,
Prague, Czech Republic, 2-4 September 2015. ©2015 Association for Computational Linguistics

GB in the context of utterance *How much does an Apple iPhone 6S cost* would mean *How much does an Apple iPhone 6s with 64 GB cost.*

In fact, studies have suggested that users of interactive systems prefer on being as terse as possible and thus give rise to NSUs frequently. Cognizant of this limitation, some systems explicitly ask the users to avoid usage of pronouns and incomplete sentences [Carbonell, 1983]. The current state of the QA systems would not be able to handle such NSUs and would result into inappropriate answers.

In this paper we propose a novel approach for handling such NSUs arising when users are trying to seek information using QA systems. Resolving NSUs is the process of recovering a full clausal meaningful question for an NSU utterance, by utilizing the context of previous utterances.

The occurrence and resolution of NSUs in a conversation have been studied in the literature and is an active area of research. However, most of the proposed approaches in the past have adopted a rule or grammar based approach [Carbonell, 1983, Fernández et al., 2005, Giuliani et al., 2014]. The design of the rules or grammars in these works were motivated by the frequent patterns observed empirically which may not scale well for unseen or domain specific scenarios.

Also, note that while the NSU resolution task can be quite broad in scope and cover many aspects including ellipsis [Giuliani et al., 2014], we limit the investigation in this paper to only the *Question* aspect of NSU, i.e. resolving C:2 and C:3 in the example above. More specifically, we would not be trying to resolve the system (S:2, S:3, S:4) and other non-question utterances (e.g. *OK, Ohh! I see*). This focus and choice is primarily driven by our motivation of facilitating a QA system.

We propose a statistical approach to NSU resolution which is not restricted by limited number of patterns. Our approach is motivated by the observation that humans try to identify the keywords appearing in the NSU and place them in the context to construct a complete sentential form. For constructing a meaningful and relevant sentence from keywords, we adapt the techniques proposed for generating questions from keywords, also known as keyword-to-question (K2Q).

The K2Q [Zhao et al., 2011, Zheng et al., 2011, Liu et al., 2012] is a recently investigated problem with the motivation to convert succinct web queries to natural language (NL) questions to direct users to cQA (community QA) websites. As an example, the query *ticket Broadway New York* could be converted to a NL question *Where do I buy tickets for the Broadway show in New York ?*. We leverage the core idea for the question generation module from these approaches.

The main contributions of this paper are as follows:

1. We propose a statistical approach for NSU resolution which is not limited by a set of predefined patterns. To the best of our knowledge, statistical approaches have not been investigated for the purpose of NSU resolution.

2. We also propose a formulation that uses syntactic, semantic and lexical evidences to identify the most likely clausal meaningful question from a given NSU.

In Section 2 we present the related work. We describe the a simple rule based approach in section 3. In section 4 we present the details of the proposed NSU resolution system. In Section 5, we report experimental results on dataset collected through mTurk and finally conclude our work and discuss future work in section 6.

2 Related Work

A taxonomy of different types of NSUs used in conversations was proposed by [Fernández et al., 2005]. According to their taxonomy the replies from the sales staff (S:2, S:3 and S:4) are NSUs of type *Short Answers*. However, the utterances C:2 and C:3 which are the focus of this paper and referred to as *Question NSU*, are not a good fit in any of the proposed types. One possible reason why the authors in [Fernández et al., 2005] did not consider them, may be because of the type of dialog transcripts used in the study. The taxonomy was constructed by performing a corpus study on the dialogue transcripts of the British National Corpus (BNC) [Burnard, 2000]. Most of the used transcripts were from meetings, seminars and interviews.

Some authors have also referred to this phenomenon as *Ellipsis* because of the elliptical form of the NSU [Carbonell, 1983, Fernández et al., 2004, Dalrymple et al., 1991, Nielsen, 2004, Giuliani et al., 2014]. While the statistical approaches have been investigated for the purpose of ellipsis detection [Fernández et al., 2004, Nielsen, 2004, Giuliani et al., 2014], it has been a common practice to use rules – syntactic or semantic – for the purpose of Ellipsis resolution [Carbonell, 1983, Dalrymple et al., 1991, Giuliani et al., 2014].

A special class of ellipsis, verb phrase ellipsis (VPE) was investigated in [Nielsen, 2004] in a domain independent manner. The authors have taken the approach of first finding the modal verb which can be then used as a substitute for the verb phrase. For example, in the utterance *"Bill loves his wife. John does too"*, the modal verb *does* can be replaced by the verb phrase *loves his wife* to result in the resolved utterance *"John loves his wife too"*. Authors used a number of syntactical features such as part-of-speech (POS) tags and auxiliary verbs, derived from the automatic parsed text to detect the ellipsis.

Another important class of NSUs referred to as *Sluice* was investigated in [Fernández et al., 2004]. Sluices are those situations where a follow-up bare *wh*-phrase exhibits a sentential meaning. For example:

Sue You were getting a real panic then.

Angela When?

Authors in [Fernández et al., 2004] extract a set of heuristic principles from a corpus-based sample and formulate them as probabilistic Horn clauses. The predicates of such clauses are used to create a set of domain independent features to annotate an input dataset, and run machine learning algorithms. Authors achieved a success rate of 90% in identifying sluices.

Most of the previous work, as discussed here, have used statistical approaches for detection of ellipsis. However, the task of resolving these incomplete utterances – NSU resolution – has been largely based on rules. For example, a semantic space was defined based on "CaseFrames" in [Carbonell, 1983]. The notion of these frames is similar to a SQL query where conditions or rules can be defined for different attributes and their values. In contrast to this, we present a statistical approach for NSU resolution in this paper with the motivation of scaling the coverage of the overall solution.

3 Rule Based Approach

As a baseline, we built a rule based approach similar to the one proposed in [Carbonell, 1983]. The rules capture frequent discourse patterns in which NSUs are used by users of a question answering system.

As a first step, let us consider the following conversation involving an NSU:

- **Utt1:** Who is the president of USA?
- **Ans1:** Barack Obama
- **Utt2:** and India?

We use the following two rules for NSU resolution.

Rule 1: if $\exists s | s \in phrase(Utt1) \wedge s.type = P_{Utt2}.type$ then create an utterance by substituting s with P_{Utt2} in the utterance $Utt1$.

Rule 2: if wh_{Utt2} is the only $wh-$word in $Utt2$ and $wh_{Utt2} \neq wh_{Utt1}$ then create an utterance by substituting wh_{Utt1} by wh_{Utt2} in $Utt1$.

Here $phrase(Utt1)$ denotes the set of all the phrases in $Utt1$ and P_{Utt2} denotes the key phrase that occurs in utterance $Utt2$. $s.type$ denotes the named entity type associated with the phrase s wh_{S1} and wh_{S2} denote the *wh* word used in the $Utt1$ and $Utt2$ respectively.

This rule based approach suffers from two main problems. One, it is only as good as the named entity recognizer (NER). For example, if *antonym ?* occurs in context of *What is the synonym of nebulous ?*, it is not likely for the NER to detect synonym and antonym are of the same type. Two, the approach has a very limited scope. For example, if *with 64 GB ?* occurs in context of *What is the cost of iPhone 6?*, the approach will fail as the resolution cannot be modeled with a simple substitution.

4 Proposed NSU Resolution Approach

In this section, we explain the proposed approach used to resolve NSUs. In the context of the running example above, the proposed approach should result in a resolved utterance *"Who is the president of India?"*. As mentioned above, intuitively the resolved utterance should contain all the keywords from *Utt2*, and these keywords should be placed in an appropriate structure created by the context of *Utt1*. One possible approach towards this would be to identify all the keywords from *Utt1* and *Utt2* and then forming a meaningful question using an appropriate subset of these keywords. Accordingly, the proposed approach consists of the following three steps as shown in Figure 1.

- Candidate Keyword Set Generation
- Keyword to Question Generation (*K2Q*)
- Learning to Rank Generated Questions

These three steps are explained in the following subsections.

4.1 Candidate Keyword Set Generation

Given *Utt1*, *Ans1* and *Utt2* as outlined in the previous section, the first step is to remove all the non-essential words (stop words) from these and generate different combinations of the essential words (keywords).

Let $U_2 = \{U_{2i}, i \in 1 \ldots N\}$ be the set of keywords in *Utt2* and $U_1 = \{U_{1i}, i \in 1 \ldots M\}$ be the set of keywords in *Utt1*. For the example above, U_2 would be $\{India\}$ and U_1 would be $\{president, USA\}$. Let Φ_{U_1,U_2} represent the power set resulting from the union of U_1 and U_2. Now, we use the following constraints to further rule out some invalid combinations:

- Filter out all the sets that do not contain all the keywords in U_2.
- Filter out all the sets that do not contain at least one keyword from U_1.

The basis for these constraints is coming from the observation that the NSU resolution is about interpreting the current utterance in the context of the conversation so far. Therefore it should contain all the keywords from the current utterance and at least one keyword from the context.

The valid keyword sets that satisfy these constraint are now used to form a meaningful question as explained in the following section.

4.2 Keyword to Question Generation

Keyword-to-question (K2Q) generation is the process of generating a meaningful and relevant question from a given set of keywords. For each keyword set $K \in \Phi_{U_1,U_2}$ resulting from the previous step, we use the following template based approach to generate a set of candidate questions.

4.2.1 Template Based Approach for K2Q

In this section, we summarize the template based approach proposed by [Zhao et al., 2011] that was adopted for this work. It consists of the following three steps:

- *Template Generation:* This step takes as input a corpus of reference questions. This corpus should contain a large number of example meaningful questions, relevant for the task or domain at hand. The keyword terms (all non-stop words) in each question are replaced by variable slots to induce templates. For example, questions *"what is the price of laptop?"* and *"what is the capital of India"* would induce a template *"what is the T_1 of T_2?"*. In the following discussion, we would denote these associated questions as Q_{ref}. Subsequently, the rare templates that occur less than a pre-defined threshold are filtered out.

  This step is performed once in an offline manner. The result of this step is a database of templates associated with a set of questions $\{Q_{ref}\}$ that induced them.

- *Template Selection:* Given a set of keywords K, this step selects templates that meet the following criteria:
  - The template has the same number of slots as the number of query keywords.
  - At least one question Q_{ref} associated with the template has one user keyword in exact same position.

  For example, given a query *"price phone"*, the template *"what is the T1 of T2"* would be selected, if there is a question *"what is the price of laptop"* associated with this template that has *price* keyword at the first position.

- *Question Generation:* For each of the templates selected in the previous step, a question Q is hypothesized by substituting the slot variables by the keywords in K. For example, if the keywords are *president, India* and the template is *"who is the T1 of T2"*, then the resulting question would be *" who is the president of India"*.

4.3 Learning to Rank Generated Questions

The previous step of question generation results in a set of questions $\{Q\}$ given a set of keywords $\{K\}$. To rank these questions, we transform each question's candidate into a feature vector. These features capture various semantic and syntactic aspects of the candidate question as well as the context. In this section we explain the different fea-

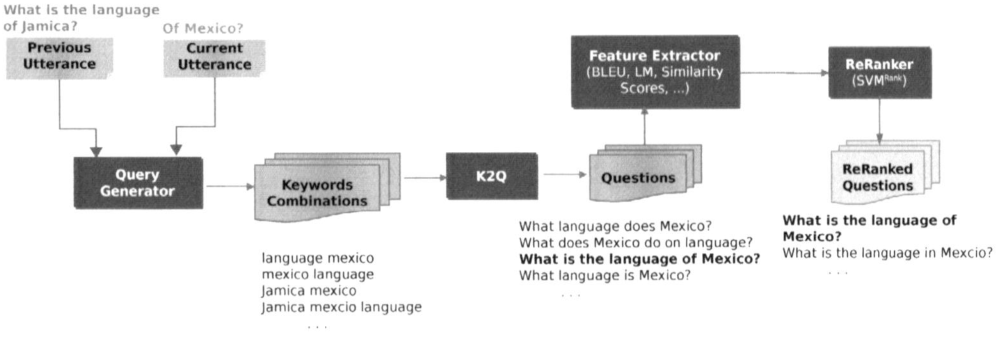

Figure 1: Architecture of NSU Resolution System

tures and ranking algorithm used to rank the generated questions.

- **Semantic Similarity Score:** A semantic similarity score is computed between the keyword set K and each example question Q_{ref} associated with the template from which Q was generated. The computation is based on the semantic similarity of the keywords involved in Q and Q_{ref}.

$$Sim(Q, Q_{ref}) = \Pi_i^N Sim(K_i, Q_{ref,i})^{\frac{1}{N}} \quad (1)$$

  where the similarity between the keywords involved $Sim(K_., Q_{ref,.})$ is computed as the cosine similarity of their word2vec representations [Mikolov et al., 2013].

- **Language Model Score:** To evaluate the syntactic correctness of the generated candidate question Q, we compute the language model score $LM(Q)$. A statistical language model assigns a probability to a sequence of n words (n-gram) by means of a probability distribution. The LM score represents how well a given sequence of n words is likely to be generated by this probability distribution. The distribution for the work presented in this paper is learned from the question corpus used in the template generation step above.

- **BLEU Score:** Intuitively, the intended sentential form of the resolved NSU should be similar to the preceding sentential form (*Utt1* in the example above). A similar requirement arises in evaluation of machine translation (MT) systems and BLEU score is the most commonly used metric for MT evaluation [Papineni et al., 2002]. We compute it as the amount of n-gram overlap between the generated question Q and the preceding utterance *Utt1*.

- **Rule Based Score:** Intuitively, the candidate question from K2Q should be similar to the resolved question generated by the rule based system (iff rules apply). As discussed in Section 3, we assign 1 to this feature when a rule fires, otherwise assign 0.

We use a learning to rank model for scoring each question $Q \in \{Q\}$, in the candidate pool for a given keyword set K: $w.\Psi(Q)$, where w is a model weight vector and $\Psi(Q)$ is the feature vector of question Q. The weights are trained using SVM^{rank} [Joachims, 2006] algorithm. To train it, for a given K, we assign higher rank to the correct candidate questions and all other candidates are ranked below.

5 Experiments

In this section, we present the datasets, evaluation approaches and results. We also present the comparative analysis of the performance obtained when we employ a rule-based baseline approach (Section 3) for this task.

5.1 Data

We organize the discussion around the data used for our evaluation in two parts. In the first part, we explain the dataset used for the purpose of setting up the template based K2Q approach described in Section 4.2. In the second part, we explain the dataset used for evaluating the performance of the NSU resolution.

Question	Answer	Q_{2e}	Q_{2r}
What does the golden marmoset eat?	flowers	and tiger?	What do tigers eat?
What is the average life span of Indian men?	65	And women	Average life span of women in India, is?
Who is the highest paid athlete today?	Tiger Woods	And in the 1990?	Who was the highest paid athlete in 1990?
Does a solid or liquid absorb more heat?	Liquid	What about gas or liquid?	Does a gas or a liquid absorb more heat?

Table 1: Examples of collected data entries from Amazon Mechanical Turk

5.1.1 Dataset for the K2Q Step

In section 4.2 we noted that the template generation step involves a large corpus of reference questions. One such large collection of open-domain questions is provided by the `WikiAnswers`* dataset.

The WikiAnswers corpus contains clusters of questions tagged by WikiAnswers users as paraphrases. Each cluster optionally contains an answer provided by WikiAnswers users. Since the scope of this work was limited to forming templates for the K2Q system, we use only the questions from this corpus. The corpus is split into 40 gzip-compressed files. The total compressed file size is 8GB. We use only the first two parts (out of 40) for the purpose of our experiments. After replacing the keywords by slot variables as required for template induction, this results into a total of $\approx 8M$ unique question-keyword-template tuples. Further, we filter out those templates which have less than five associated reference questions and this results into a total of $\approx 74K$ templates and corresponding $\approx 3.7M$ associated reference questions.

5.1.2 Dataset for NSU Resolution

In this section, we describe the data that we use for evaluating the performance of the proposed method for NSU resolution.

We used a subset of the data that was collected using Amazon Mechanical Turk. For collecting this data a question answer pair (Q,A) was presented to an mTurk worker and who was then asked to conceive another question Q_2 related to the pair (Q, A). The Q_2 was to be given in two different versions, an elliptical version Q_{2e} and a fully resolved version Q_{2r}. The original data contains 7400 such entries and contains examples for NSUs as well as anaphora in Q_2. We selected a subset of 500 entries from this dataset for our evaluation. Table 1 presents some examples entries from this data.

*Available at `http://knowitall.cs.washington.edu/oqa/data/wikianswers/`

5.2 Evaluations

We present our evaluations based on the following three different configurations to investigate the importance of various scoring and ranking modules. The configurations used are,

1. **Rule Based:** This configuration is used as a baseline system, as described in section 3. As rule based methodologies are dominant in the field of NSU resolutions, we compare to clearly illustrate the limitations of just using rules.

2. **Semantic Similarity:** We investigate how well the semantic similarity score as described in Section 4.3 works when we sort the candidate questions generated based on this feature alone.

3. **SVM Rank:** In this configuration, we use all the scores as described in Section 4.3 in an SVM Rank formulation.

5.2.1 Evaluation Methodology

Given the input conversation $\{Utt1, Ans1, Utt2\}$, system generated resolved utterance Q (corresponding to NSU $Utt2$) and the intended utterance Q_r, the goal of the evaluation metric is to judge how similar Q is to Q_r. We use BLEU score and human judgments for the purpose of this evaluation.

BLEU score is often used for evaluation of machine translation systems to judge the goodness of the translated text with the reference text. Please note that we also used the BLEU score as one of the features as mentioned in Section 4.3. There, it was computed between the generated question Q and the preceding utterance $Utt1$. Whereas, for evaluation purposes, this score is computed between the generated question Q and the intended question provided by the ground truth Q_r.

To account for the paraphrasing errors, as the same utterance can be said in several different ways, we also use human judgment for the evaluation.

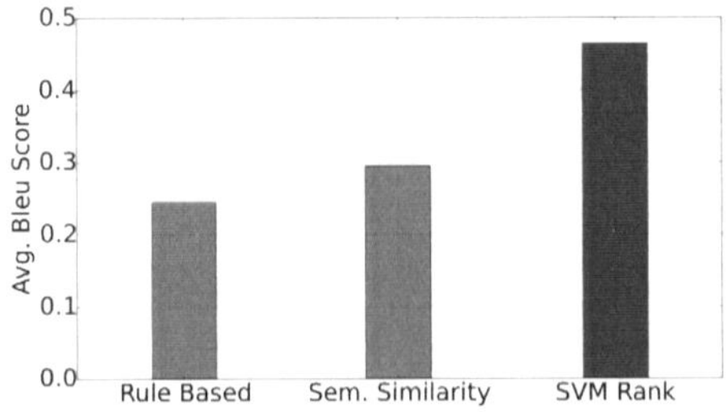

Figure 2: Average BLEU score for different configurations

Method	Recall@1
Rule Based	0.17
SVM Rank	**0.21**

Table 2: Comparing Recall@1 using Human Judgments

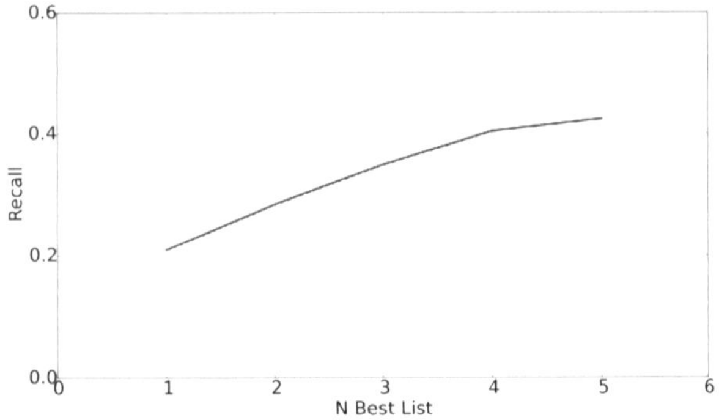

Figure 3: Recall@N obtained using human judgments

We use Recall@N to present the evaluation results when human judgments are used. Our test set comprises only of those utterances ($\{Utt2\}$) which require a resolution and therefore Recall@N captures how many of these NSUs were correctly resolved if candidates only up to top N are to be considered.

5.2.2 BLEU Score Evaluation

We compute the BLEU score between the candidate resolution Q and the ground truth utterance Q_r and compare it across the three configurations. Figure 2 shows the comparison of the average BLEU score at position 1. A low score for the rule based approach is expected as it resolves only those cases in which rules fire. The semantic similarity configuration gains over the rule based approach as it is able to utilize the template database generated using the WikiAnswers corpus. Finally, the SVM Rank uses various other scores (LM, BLEU score) on top of rule-based and semantic similarity score and therefore achieves higher BLEU Score.

5.2.3 Human Judgments Evaluation

Finally, to account for the paraphrasing artifacts manifested in human language, we use human judgments to make a true comparison between the rule based approach and the SVM Rank configuration.

For human judgments, we presented just the resolved Q and the ground truth Q_r. For all the 200 data points in the test set, top 5 candidates were presented to human annotators who were asked to decide if it was a correct resolution or not. We choose just the top 5 just to analyze the quality of the candidates generated at various positions by the system.

Table 2 shows the Recall@1 for the the two configurations. A better recall for the proposed

SVM configuration signifies the better coverage of the proposed approach beyond a pre-defined set of rules. The Recall@1 was used for this comparison since the rule-based approach can only yield a single candidate. To further see the behavior of the proposed approach as more candidates are considered, Recall@N is presented in Figure 3. The figure shows that a recall of 42.5% can be achieved when results up to top 5 are considered. The objective of this experiment is to study the quality of top (1-5) ranked generated questions. This experiment helps us conclude that improving the ranking module has the potential to improve the overall performance of the system.

5.3 Discussion

We discuss two types of scenarios where our SVM rank based approach works better than the baseline rule based approach. One of the rules to generate resolved utterance is to replace a phrase in *Utt1* with a phrase of the same semantic type in *Utt2*. Such an approach is limited by the availability of an exhaustive list of semantic types which is in general difficult to capture. In the following example, the phrases *antidote* and *symptoms* belong to the entity type *disease attribute*. However it may not be obvious to include *disease attribute* as a semantic type unless the context is specified. Our approach aims at capturing such semantic types automatically using the semantic similarity score.

Utt1 What is the antidote of streptokinase?

Utt2 What are the symptoms?

Resolved what are the symptoms of streptokinase

The baseline approach fails to handle cases where the resolved utterance cannot be generated by merely replacing a phrase in *Utt1* with a phrase in *Utt2*. While our approach can handle cases which requires sentence transformations such as the one shown below.

Utt1 Is cat scratch disease a viral or bacterial disease?

Utt2 What's the difference?

Resolved what's the difference between a viral and bacterial disease

One of the scenarios where our approach fails is when there are no keywords in *Utt2*. This is because the K2Q module tries to generate questions without any keywords (information) from *Utt2*. A few examples are given below.

Utt1 (a) Kansas sport teams?

Utt2 (a) What others?

Utt1 (b) Cell that forms in fertilization?

Utt2 (b) And ones that don't are called what?

6 Conclusion and Future Work

In this paper we presented a statistical approach for resolving questions appearing as non-sentential utterances (NSU) in an interactive question answering session. We adapted a keyword-to-question approach to generate a set of candidate questions and used various scoring methods to generate scores for the generated questions. We then used a learning to rank framework to select the best generated question. Our results show that the proposed approach has significantly better performance than a rule based method. The results also show that for many of the cases where the correct resolved question does not appear at the top, a correct candidate exists in the top 5 candidates. Thus it is possible that by employing more features and better ranking methods we can get further performance boost. We plan to explore this further and extend this method to cover other types of NSUs in our future work.

Acknowledgments

We thank Martin Schmid, IBM Watson Prague and Adam J Sporka, Pavel Slavik, Czech Techincal University Prague for providing us with the corpus of dialog ellipsis (dataset for NSU resolution) without which training and evaluation of our system would not have been possible.

References

Lou Burnard. Reference guide for the british national corpus. *Oxford University Computing Services*, 2000.

Jaime G. Carbonell. Discourse pragmatics and ellipsis resolution in task-oriented natural language interfaces. In *Proceedings of the 21st Annual Meeting on Association for Computational Linguistics*, pages 164–168, 1983.

Mary Dalrymple, Stuart M. Shieber, and Fernando C. N. Pereira. Ellipsis and higher-order unification. *Linguistics and Philosophy*, 14:399–452, 1991.

Fernández, Raquel, Jonathan Ginzburg, and Shalom Lappin. Classifying ellipsis in dialogue: A machine learning approach. In *Proceedings of the 20th International Conference on Computational Linguistics*, 2004.

Raquel Fernández. *Non-sentential utterances in dialogue: classification, resolution and use.* PhD thesis, University of London, 2006.

Raquel Fernández, Jonathan Ginzburg, and Shalom Lappin. Using machine learning for non-sentential utterance classification. pages 77–86, 2005.

David A Ferrucci. Introduction to this is watson. *IBM Journal of Research and Development*, 56 (3.4), 2012.

Manuel Giuliani, Thomas Marschall, and Amy Isard. Using ellipsis detection and word similarity for transformation of spoken language into grammatically valid sentences. In *Proceedings of the 15th Annual Meeting of the Special Interest Group on Discourse and Dialogue*, pages 243–250, 2014.

Thorsten Joachims. Training linear svms in linear time. In *Proceedings of the 12th ACM SIGKDD International Conference on Knowledge Discovery and Data Mining*, pages 217–226, 2006.

Qiaoling Liu, Eugene Agichtein, Gideon Dror, Yoelle Maarek, and Idan Szpektor. When web search fails, searchers become askers: Understanding the transition. In *Proceedings of the 35th International ACM SIGIR Conference on Research and Development in Information Retrieval*, pages 801–810, 2012.

Tomas Mikolov, Kai Chen, Greg Corrado, and Jeffrey Dean. Efficient estimation of word representations in vector space. In *Proceedings of Workshop at International Conference on Learning Representations*, 2013.

Leif Arda Nielsen. Robust vpe detection using automatically parsed text. In *Proceedings of the ACL Workshop on Student Research*, 2004.

Kishore Papineni, Salim Roukos, Todd Ward, and Wei-Jing Zhu. Bleu: a method for automatic evaluation of machine translation. In *Proceedings of the 40th Annual Meeting on Association for Computational Linguistics*, pages 311–318. Association for Computational Linguistics, 2002.

Shiqi Zhao, Haifeng Wang, Chao Li, Ting Liu, and Yi Guan. Automatically generating questions from queries for communitybased question answering. In *Proceedings of 5th International Joint Conference on Natural Language Processing*, pages 929–937, 2011.

Zhicheng Zheng, Xiance Si, Edward Y. Chang, and Xiaoyan Zhu. K2q: Generating natural language questions from keywords with user refinements. In *Proceedings of the 5th International Joint Conference on Natural Language Processing*, pages 947–955, 2011.

The Interplay of User-Centered Dialog Systems and AI Planning

Florian Nothdurft*, Gregor Behnke†, Pascal Bercher†, Susanne Biundo† and Wolfgang Minker*
*Institute of Communications Engineering, †Institute of Artificial Intelligence
Ulm University, Ulm, Germany
florian.nothdurft,gregor.behnke,pascal.bercher,
susanne.biundo,wolfgang.minker@uni-ulm.de

Abstract

Technical systems evolve from simple dedicated task solvers to cooperative and competent assistants, helping the user with increasingly complex and demanding tasks. For this, they may proactively take over some of the users responsibilities and help to find or reach a solution for the user's task at hand, using e.g., Artificial Intelligence (AI) Planning techniques. However, this intertwining of user-centered dialog and AI planning systems, often called mixed-initiative planning (MIP), does not only facilitate more intelligent and competent systems, but does also raise new questions related to the alignment of AI and human problem solving. In this paper, we describe our approach on integrating AI Planning techniques into a dialog system, explain reasons and effects of arising problems, and provide at the same time our solutions resulting in a coherent, user-friendly and efficient mixed-initiative system. Finally, we evaluate our MIP system and provide remarks on the use of explanations in MIP-related phenomena.

1 Introduction

Future intelligent assistance systems need to integrate cognitive capabilities to adequately support a user in a task at hand. Adding cognitive capabilities to a dialog system (DS) enables the user to solve increasingly complex and demanding tasks, as solving complex combinatorial problems can be delegated to the machine. Further, the user may be assisted in finding a solution in a more structured way. In this work we focus on the cognitive capability of problem solving via help of AI Planning technology in the form of Hierarchical Task Network (HTN) planning (Erol et al., 1994; Geier and Bercher, 2011). It resembles the human top-down way to solve problems. Such planners can help users to find courses of action, i.e., a sequence of actions, which achieve a given goal. In HTN planning the user states the goal in terms of a set of *abstract* actions, e.g., $train(abs)$, which are repeatedly refined into more concrete courses of action – using so-called methods – during the planning process. For example, $train(abs)$ could be refined into a $crunches(20)$ and a $sit\text{-}up(50)$ action. A solution is found if the the plan only contains *primitive* actions, i.e., actions which cannot be refined further, and the plan itself is executable.

In Section 2, we explain in more detail the advantages of integrating AI planning capabilities into a DS. Such an integration poses significant challenges, however. Most importantly, the way planners search for solution plans is very different from the way humans do, as their concern is mainly efficiency. In Section 3 we hence show how a planner can be adapted to better suit human needs. Further, we describe which kinds of planning-specific phenomena can not be avoided and thus the dialog manager must be able to handle. In Section 4 we describe the architecture of our intertwined system, followed by some remarks on the implementation in Section 5. Within this section we also discuss why a common source of knowledge for both the planner and the dialog manager is needed and how it can be created. Section 6 contains an evaluation of the implemented system in a fitness-training scenario.

2 Why Integrating a Planner?

In classical use-case scenarios for HTN planners (Nau et al., 2005; Biundo et al., 2011) a plan is generated without any user involvement, besides the specification of the goal, and afterwards presented to him. Hence, the planner is a black-box to the user, which is often not adequate. If executing the plan involves grave risks, e.g., in military

Proceedings of the SIGDIAL 2015 Conference, pages 344–353,
Prague, Czech Republic, 2-4 September 2015.

settings (Myers et al., 2002) or spaceflight (Ai-Chang et al., 2004), humans must have the final decision on which actions are to be contained in the plan. Planning systems can also be utilized to create plans for personal tasks like fitness training, cooking, or preparing a party. Here, it is expected that created plans are highly individualized, i.e., that they not only achieve given goals but also respect the user's wishes about the final plan. One might argue that such individualization could be achieved by integrating preferences or action costs into planning (Sohrabi et al., 2009). However, this approach requires that the user can specify his preferences completely and a priori and that they must be expressible, e.g., in terms of action or method costs or LTL formulae. Even if the user's preferences were expressible, it would be required to question the user extensively prior to the actual interaction, which is very likely to result in the user aborting the interaction.

Instead the dialog manager and especially the planner should learn about the user's preferences during interaction, fostering an understanding of the user's preferences. This requires the integration of the user into the planning process, resulting in a so-called mixed-initiative planning (MIP) system. A few approaches to creating such systems have already been investigated (Myers et al., 2003; Ai-Chang et al., 2004; Fernández-Olivares et al., 2006). Unfortunately, they cannot support a complete dialog with the user, as they mostly react on inquiries and demands from the user and only present the user with completed plans, i.e., plans that have already been refined into a solution. We deem such schemes impractical, as they require the user to comprehend a (potentially complicated) solution at once, making it hard to express opinions or wishes about it. For us, it would be more natural to iteratively integrate the user during the plan generation, making it on the one hand easier for the user to comprehend the plan and options to refine it, and on the other hand reducing the cognitive load, as the user does not have to understand the complete plan at once.

MIP can be interpreted as the system-initiated integration of the user in the planning process, but from a user's perspective it is the attempt to solve problems by using promised competencies of a technical system. For the user dedicating planning and decision-making to a technical system is done with the intent of finding a solution the user is not able to find at all or only with great effort. It aims at relieving the user's cognitive load and simplifying the problem at hand. Hence, the iterative integration of the user seems to be not only more natural, but also more practical for the user.

3 Challenges of MIP

In this section, we describe arising challenges of MIP. We discuss the differences between state-of-the-art AI Planning and the way humans solve problems, as they raise issues for a successful integration of a planner into a DS. To achieve it nevertheless, we show how a planner can be modified to accommodate them and which issues must be addressed by an advanced dialog management (DM).

How to Integrate the Planner. The integration of AI Planning begins with the statement of a planner objective in a dialog. This requires on the one hand a user-friendly and efficient objective-selection dialog, and on the other hand the creation of a valid *planning problem*. Thus, the semantics of the dialog has to be coherent to the *planning domain*, resulting in a valid *planning problem*.

User-friendly Search Strategies. Almost all AI Planning systems use efficient search strategies, like A^* or *greedy*, to find a solution for a given planning problem. The order with which plans are visited is based upon a heuristic estimating the number of modifications needed to refine the given plan into a solution. Plans with smaller heuristic value are hence regarded more promising and visited earlier. In A* search, as well as in any other heuristic-based search approach, it may happen that after one plan was explored, the next one explored will be *any* plan within the search space – not just one that is a direct successor of the plan explored last. As such, these strategies may result in the perception that the user's decisions only arbitrarily influence the planning process, which in turn may result in an experience of lack of control and transparency.

In contrast, humans tend to search for a plan by repeatedly refining the last one. A search strategy that resembles that strategy is *depth-first search* (DFS). Here, always the plan explored last is refined until a solution is found or the current plan is proved unsolvable, i.e., it cannot possibly be refined to a solution. In that case, the last refinement is reverted and another possible refinement option is chosen. If none exists the process is repeated recursively. A major drawback of DFS is that it does not consider a heuristic to select plans which are more promising, i.e., closer to a solution. DFS is blind, leading to a non-efficient search and non-optimal plans, i.e., the final plan may contain unnecessary actions. This problem can be addressed if the planner prefers refinements of plans with lower heuristic value if the user is indifferent about them. This scheme enables the interplay of user decisions and the planner's ability to solve complex combinatorial problems. The user controls the search until such a problem arises by selecting preferred refinements. Then he may signal the DS that he does not care about the remaining refinement, resulting in the planner using its heuristic to find a valid solution.

Handling of Failures During Planning. A major difference between human problem solving and DFS is the way failures are handled. In planning, a failure occurs if the current plan is proved unsolvable (e.g., by using well-informed heuristics). As mentioned earlier, DFS uses *backtracking* to systematically explore all remaining options for decisions that lead to a failure, until a successful option has been found. Practical heuristics are necessarily imperfect, i.e., they cannot determine for every plan whether it is unsolvable or it may be refined into a solution. Hence, even when using a well-informed heuristic, the planner will present the user with options for refining a plan that will inevitably cause *backtracking*. DFS *backtracking* is a very tedious and frustrating process, especially if the faulty decision was made early on but is found much later. Large parts of the search space, i.e., all plans that can be refined based on the faulty decision have to be explored manually until the actually faulty decision is reverted. This may result in the user deeming the system's strategy naive and the system itself incompetent. This is important, since the use of automation correlates highly to a user's trust into an automated system, which in turn depends mainly on the perception of its competence (Muir and Moray, 1996). To prevent the user, at least partially, from perceiving the system as incompetent, we can utilize the computing power of the planner to determine whether an option for refinement only leads to faulty plans. We call such refinements *dead-ends*. If options are presented to the user, the planner starts exploring the search space induced by each refinement using an efficient search procedure. If he determines that such a search space cannot contain a solution, the respective refinement is a *dead-end*. It is the objective of the dialog manager to appropriately convey this information to the user, especially if computing this information took noticeable time, i.e., the user has already considered the presented options and one has to be removed.

How to Integrate the User. Another important factor for a successful human-computer interaction is the question when a user should be involved into the planning process and if, how to do it. Clearly, the planner should not be responsible for this kind of decisions as it lacks necessary capabilities, but may contribute information for it, e.g., by determining how critical the current decision is with respect to the overall plan. From the planner's view every choice is delegated to the user via the DM, achieving maximal flexibility for the manager. The dialog manager on the other hand can either perform an interaction with the user, or determine by itself that the choice should be made by the planner, which is equivalent with the user signaling "Don't care". It should be considered whether interaction is critical and required to successfully continue the dialog or to achieve short-term goals, but risks the user's cooperativeness for interaction in the long run, e.g., by overstraining his cognitive capabilities or boring him. If the user is to be involved, the question arises how this should be rendered, i.e., what kind of integration is the most beneficial. Additionally, if he is not, the dialog manager must decide whether and if how he may be informed of the decisions the planner has made for him.

4 Concept and Design

The integration of AI Planning and user-centered dialog begins with the statement of an objective. This first dialog between user and machine has the goal of defining the task in a way understandable for the planner. Once the problem is passed to the planner the interactive planning itself may start. Using the described *depth-first search* the plan is refined by selecting appropriate modifications for open decisions. In order to decide whether to involve the user or not during this process, an elaborate decision model, integrating various information sources, is required. Relevant information sources are, e.g., the *dialog history* (e.g., was the user's decision the same for all past similar episodes?), the kind of *plan flaw* (e.g., is this flaw relevant for the user?), the *user profile* (e.g., does the user have the competencies for this decision?), or the current *situation* (e.g., is the current cognitive load of the user low enough for interaction?). Those examples of relevant information sources illustrate that a decision model can not be located *either* in the DM *or* the planner, but in a superordinate component, the so-called *Decision Model*.

In case of user involvement the information on the current *plan decision* has to be communicated to the user. This means that the open decision and the corresponding choice between available *modifications* have to be represented in a dialog suitable for the user. Hence, the corresponding plan information needs to be mapped to human-understandable dialog information. As this mapping is potentially required for every plan information and vice versa for every dialog information, coherent models between planner and DS become crucial for MIP systems. The thorough matching of both models would be an intricate and strenuous process, requiring constant maintenance, especially when models need to be updated. Thus, a more appropriate approach seems to be the automatic generation of the respective models using one mutual model as source, the *Mutual Knowledge Model*. This way, once the transformation functions work correctly, coherence is not an issue any more, even for updating the domain. How these essential constituents of a conceptual MIP system architecture (depicted in Figure 1) were implemented in our system, will be explained in the next Section.

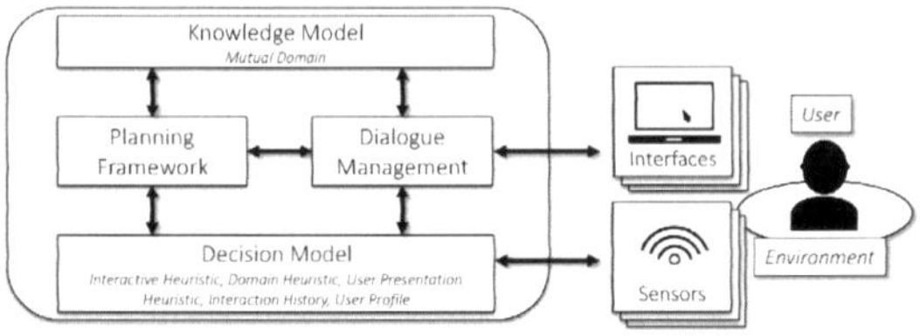

Figure 1: Essential components of a MIP system.

5 Implementation

We implemented and tested a multimodal MIP system using a knowledge-based cognitive architecture (Bercher et al., 2014). The multimodal interface uses speech and graphical user input as well as output. The *Dialog Management* uses a modality-independent representation, communicating with the user via the *Fission* (Honold et al., 2012), *User Interface* (Honold et al., 2013) , and *Fusion* (Schüssel et al., 2013) modules. Here, we will describe in more detail the two components, which are of particular interest for MIP systems: The *Mutual Knowledge Model* and the *Decision Model*.

5.1 Mutual Knowledge Model

This model, from which the planning and dialog domain models are automatically generated using automated reasoning, is crucial for a coherent MIP system. It is implemented in the form of an OWL ontology (W3C OWL Working Group, 2009). By generating the HTN planning domains from the ontology, a common vocabulary is ensured – for every planning task a corresponding concept exists in the ontology. Hierarchical structures (i.e., decomposition methods) inherent of HTN planning are derived using declarative background knowledge modeled in the ontology. For the delicacies of modeling planning domains in an ontology (e.g., how to model ordering or preconditions), including proofs for the transformation and remarks on the complexity of this problem, see Behnke et al. (2015) for further details.

The model is also utilized to infer a basic dialog structure, which is needed for the user to specify the objective for the planner. Using a mutual model addresses one of the challenges of MIP, since translation problems between dialog and planner semantics can be prevented. For the dialog domain generation a mapping between ontology concepts and dialogs is used. The dialog hierarchy can be derived using ontology knowledge. A dialog $\widetilde{A}$ can be decomposed into a sequence of sub dialogs containing the dialogs $\widetilde{B}_1, \ldots, \widetilde{B}_n$ by an axiom `Class:` A `EquivalentTo: includes onlysome` $[B_1, \ldots, B_n]$, which is interpreted by the dialog as a corresponding decomposition method. For example, a strength training can be conducted using a set of workouts $\widetilde{A}_1, \ldots, \widetilde{A}_n$, each of which consists of a set of exercises $\widetilde{B}_1, \ldots, \widetilde{B}_n$. This way a dialog hierarchy can be created, using the topmost elements as entry points for the dialog between user and machine. Nevertheless, this results only in a *valid* dialog structure, but not in a *most suitable* one for the individual user. For this, concepts of the ontology can be excluded from the domain generation or conjugated to other elements in a XML configuration file. This way unimportant elements can be hidden or rearranged for the user. The dialogs are also relevant during the MIP process. When selecting between several *Plan Modifications*, these have to be translated to a format understandable by the user. Hence, in addition to the knowledge used to generate plan steps, resources are required for communicating these steps to the user. Therefore, texts, pictures, or videos are needed, which can be easily referenced from an ontology. Using this information, dialogs suitable for a well-understandable human-computer interaction can be created and presented to the user.

One key aspect of state-of-the-art DS is the ability to individualize the ongoing dialog according to the user's needs, requirements, preferences, or history of interaction. Coupling the generation of the dialog domain to the ontology enables us to accomplish these requirements using ontological reasoning and explanation in various ways. The dialogs can be pruned using ontological reasoning according to the user's needs (e.g., "show only exercises which do not require gym access"), to the user's requirements (e.g., "show only beginner exercises") or adapted to the user's dialog history (e.g., "preselect exercises which were used the last time") and preferences (e.g., "present only exercises with dumbbells"). Additionally, integrating pro-active as well as requested explanations into the interaction is an important part of imparting used domain knowledge and clarifying system behavior. Using a coherent knowledge source to create dialog and planning domains enables us to use predefined declarative explanations (Nothdurft et al., 2014) together with dynamically generated plan explanation (Seegebarth et al., 2012) and explanations for ontological inferences (Schiller and Glimm, 2013) without dealing with inconsistency issues. This way *Plan Steps* (e.g., exercises) can be explained in detail, dependencies between plan steps can be explained to exemplify the necessity of tasks (i.e., plan explanation), and ontology explanations can justify decompositions from which the planning model and the dialog domain where generated. All of which increase the user's perceived system transparency.

5.2 Decision Model

This model is in charge of deciding when and how to involve the user in the planning process. It is the interface to the planner and decides, upon planner requests, whether a user involvement is useful. For this it includes a list of essential domain decisions that are interesting and relevant for the user (e.g., for a training domain: day, workout, and exercises) - the rest is left for the fallback-heuristic, and thus decided by the planner. Hence, the user is only involved in the decision making if a user-relevant planning decision is pending (e.g., "which leg exercise do you prefer?"). If it is in favor of user involvement the open decision and its modifications have to be passed to the user. Hence, the decision on the form of user integration has to be made. The dialog may either consist of the complete set of modifications, a pruned or sorted list, implicit or explicit confirmations of system-made preselections, or only of a user information. This decision depends not only on the interaction history, but also on additional information (e.g., affective user states like overextension, interest, or engagement) stored in the user state.

The *Decision Model* also records the dialog- and planning history. There are several reasons for that: The dialog history may enable a prediction of future user behavior (e.g., in selections), and additionally this knowledge is mandatory for *backtracking* processes, when the current plan does not lead to a solution. The history saves which decisions were made by the user. In case of *backtracking* the decisions are undone step-by-step, with the goal of finding a solution by applying alternative modifications. Whenever a user-made decision is undone, the user is notified, because this system behavior would otherwise appear irritating.

Since *backtracking* as well as *dead-ends* are peculiar phenomena in a MIP system, the communication of these might be a critical influence on the user experience. Together with the *DM*, the *Decision Model* orchestrates the corresponding system behavior. The main difference between *backtracking* and *dead-ends* is the temporal ordering of the awareness of the unsolvable plan and made decision. For *backtracking* the awareness is achieved after the decision, and for *dead-ends* during the decision. As we assumed that *backtracking* will impair the user experience significantly, a parallel search for *dead-ends*, as described in Section 3, was implemented. The process itself is, of course, inherently different from *backtracking*, but may prevent it. Removing dead-ends from the search space, when the relevant modification is not part of the current selection, is a rather easy task. Otherwise, the current selection has to be modified to prevent the user from selecting a *dead-end*. However, removing it without any notification from the list seems like a confusing behavior. As we had only hypotheses on the effects of these peculiar events as well as on the effects of the different forms of integrating the user into the planning process, we conducted a matching user study.

6 Evaluation

MIP may lead to the user experiencing planning-related phenomena, such as *backtracking* or *dead-ends*. These phenomena revoke decisions made by the user or alter the present decision-making and therefore may influence the user's experience of the system. As mentioned before, this may impair the perceived competency of the system, leading to a loss of trust, which correlates highly to a reduced use of automation (Muir and Moray, 1996). As our MIP system aims at assisting the user in complex and demanding tasks, maintaining the user's trust into the system and thereby the willingness to let the system decide autonomously is crucial. Furthermore, previous research has shown that the use of explanations can help to address trust issues related to intelligent adaptive systems (Glass et al., 2008) and that it may reduce negative effects in incomprehensible situations (Nothdurft et al., 2014). Therefore, we have assessed the effects of MIP phenomena like *backtracking* and *dead-ends* on the user-experience and tested different strategies, and especially explanations, to communicate these events to the user.

6.1 Methodology

For the subjective measurement through self-ratings by the user, questionnaires have been used. The most fundamental user data is personal information, assessing age, gender and education. We asked for the participants experience in the general use of technical systems and the user's foreknowledge in the corresponding domain of the experiment. Apart from the persona, we included a number of standardized and validated questionnaires: *Human-Computer Trust* (HCT) describes the trust relationship between human and machine and was assessed using the questionnaire by Madsen and Gregor (2000) measuring five dimensions (Perceived Understandability, Perceived Reliability, Perceived Technical Competence, Personal Attachment, Faith). The *AttrakDiff* questionnaire extends the assessment of a DS or software in general from the limited view of usability, which represents mostly pragmatic quality, to the integration of scales measuring hedonic qualities. This questionnaire was developed by Hassenzahl et al. (2003) and measures the perceived pragmatic quality, the hedonic qualities of stimulation and identity, and the attractiveness in general. In total 104 participants took part in the experiment. In average the subjects were 23.9 years old with the youngest being 18 and the oldest 41. Gender-wise the participants were almost equally distributed with 52.9% males and 47.1% females.

In this scenario the user's task was to create individual strength training workouts. In each strength training workout at least three different muscle groups had to be trained and exercises chosen accordingly. The user was guided through the process by the system, which provided a selection of exercises for training each specific muscle group necessary for the workout. For example, when planning a strength training for the upper body, the user had to select exercises to train the *chest* (see Figure 2). This selection corresponds to the integration of the user into the MIP process. The decision how to refine the task of training the chest is not made by the system, but left to the user.

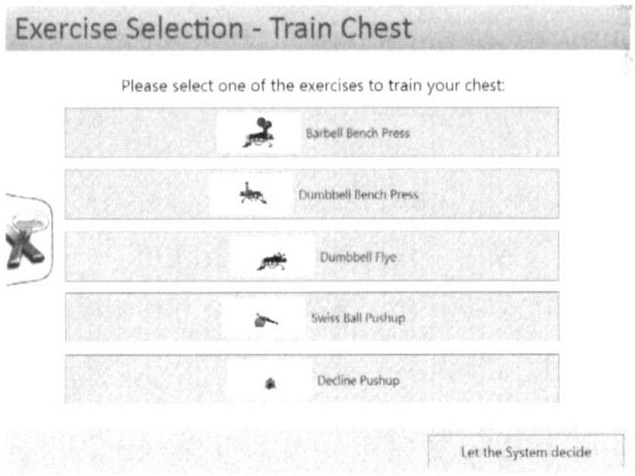

Figure 2: Screenshot of the UI. Here, the user has to select one chest exercise. If he doesn't want to decide, "Let the System decide" can be clicked or said, starting the planner for this decision.

6.2 MIP Phenomena

For the MIP phenomena we implemented 4 variants: The variants used in the evaluation were the following: *Backtracking with Notification* (BT-N) where the system informs the user that previously user-made decisions will not lead to a solution and have to be undone. *Dead-End Notification before (DE-B)*, where the user was presented the notification, beforehand on an extra slide, that some refinements had to be deactivated in the upcoming selections, because they would not lead to a solution. *Dead-End Notification during (DE-D)*, where the selection provided, on each selection slide, the notification that some of the options below had to be deactivated, because they would not lead to a solution. The fourth variant tested the effect of the content of the notification. This means, that the *Backtracking with Explanation (BT-E)* variation additionally explained to the user why the already made decisions had to be rolled back. The participants were distributed by a random-function to the variants, resulting in 25 participants for BT-N, 18 for BT-E, 18 for DE-B, and 21 for DE-D (without unusable subjects).

6.2.1 Temporal Contiguity

Our first hypothesis was that in general the temporal contiguity of the system-provided notification does affect the user-experience. We assumed that providing the notification before the upcoming selection will perform better than on the selection itself, and way better than providing the notification after the decision, because the amount of consequences for the user is directly influenced by the temporal contiguity of the notification. In terms of HCT we expected that especially the bases of perceived reliability and understandability will be defected stronger by a larger temporal contiguity.

Results. There was a statistically significant difference between groups with notifications (i.e., without BT-E) in HCT-bases (see fig. 3) as determined by one-way ANOVA for *perceived reliability* ($F(2, 70) = 3.548, p = .034$), *perceived understandability* ($F(2, 70) = 4.391, p = .016$), and significant for *personal attachment* ($F(2, 44) = 3.401, p = .042$). While analyzing the AttrakDiff questionnaire data we found a statistically significant difference for the dimension of *hedonic qualities - stimulation* between groups as determined by one-way ANOVA ($F(2, 44) = 3.266, p = .048$). The Fisher LSD post hoc test revealed statistical difference at the .05 level between BT-N ($M = 4.04, SD = 1.03$) and DE-D ($M = 3.26, SD = .72$). Also DE-D was significantly different at the .05 level from DE-B ($M = 4.12, SD = 1.03$).

Discussion. The results support our hypothesis that the temporal contiguity of the notification does indeed influence the user-experience. A technical system will be perceived to be most reliable, when the notification is presented before the decision-making (DE-B), because no unexpected events occur, and the least when user decisions have to be undone (BT-N). For perceived understandability presenting the notification during the decision performed best, maybe because the deactivation of selection options could be allocated more directly to the notification itself and therefore foster the user's understanding of the situation. The personal attachment was mostly defected when using notifications during decision making. The results in general support that a positive temporal contiguity (i.e., DE-B) seems to be the best option for a technical system. While the understandability performs only second best, the perceived reliability, personal attachment, overall cognitive load, difficulty, fun, extraneous load and pragmatic as well as hedonic qualities, and overall attractiveness perform either best or as good as the other conditions using only notifications. This notification, which only represents some sort of shallow justification for the experienced system behavior, also seems to be important for the perceived user-experience. Hence, we evaluated how a real explanation would perform opposed to shallow justifications (i.e., the notification condition).

6.2.2 The Effects of Explaining MIP

For testing the effects of an extensive explanation, we exchanged the *backtracking* notification with an explanation. The notification that the made decision will not lead to a solution was exchanged with "the system has detected that the gym is closed today due to a severe water damage. Therefore, you have to decide again and select exercises suitable for training at home". This condition (BT-E) was then compared to the notification condition (BT-N). Thus, a pairwise t-test was used.

Results. Examining the HCT-bases we found significant differences between BT-N ($M = 2.8, SD = 1.05$) and BT-E ($M = 3.56, SD = .82$) for *perceived reliability* ($t(3.0) = 57, p = .004$). For *perceived understandability* the mean differed significant ($t(3.99) = 57, p = .000$) with BT-N ($M = 2.40, SD = 1.05$) and BT-E ($M = 3.44, SD = .87$). Observing the *perceived technical competence* BT-N ($M = 2.75, SD = 1.03$) and BT-E ($M = 3.28, SD = .66$) also performed significantly different ($t(2.06) = 41, p = .045$).

In the AttrakDiff we observed a significant difference ($t(2.37) = 41, p = .022$) for the dimension of experienced *pragmatic qual-*

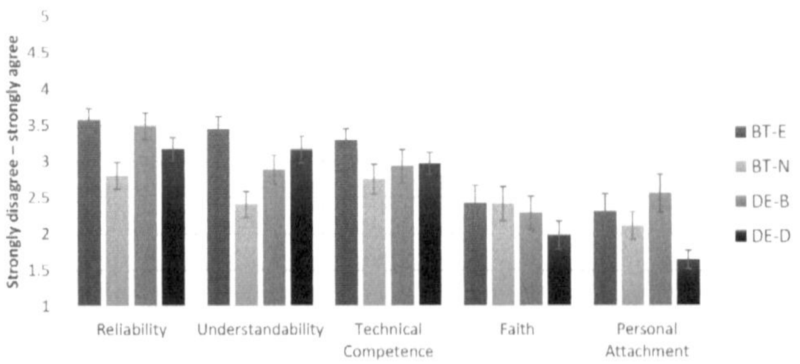

Figure 3: This shows the average mean of the bases of human-computer trust for each variant on a 5-point Likert scale. The whiskers represent the standard errors of the mean.

ities comparing BT-E ($M = 4.86, SD = 1.16$) and BT-N ($M = 4.01, SD = 1.15$). Taking a closer look at the word pairs significant differences below the .05 level were found for *complicated-simple*, *unpredictable-predictable*, *confusing-clearly structured*, *unruly-manageable*, as well as for *unpleasant-pleasant*.

Discussion. Providing detailed explanations of the system behavior, in this case of backtracking, does indeed help to perceive the system as more reliable, more understandable, and more technically competent. As only the *backtracking* notification was modified, we can only infer that for the other variants (i.e., DE-D and DE-B) the effect would be similar. However, this seems logical because the goal of increasing the system's transparency to the user can be achieved using similar explanations as well. Taking a look at the AttrakDiff and its single word pairs it becomes obvious that explaining system behavior helps to improve the pragmatic qualities of a system compared to providing none to minimal notifications. Systems with explanation capabilities seem to be perceived as not so complicated, more predictable, manageable, more clearly structured and in general as more pleasant.

Experiment Conclusion. Combing the results of both evaluated factors (i.e., temporal contiguity and explanations) we argue that the best option for MIP system behavior would be explaining the user why e.g., several options have been pruned from a selection beforehand. This strengthens the need for, on the one hand, intelligent and understandable explanation capabilities of such systems and on the other hand that the user is only integrated into the decision making when the system is sure that the presented options do in fact, or at least most probably, lead to a solution. Otherwise, the negative effects of occurring *backtracking* and similar planning peculiarities will impair the relationship between human and machine.

7 Conclusion

In this paper we pointed out the importance for future intelligent systems of intertwining dialog systems and AI Planning into a MIP system. First, we elucidated the potentials, but also the risks and arising problems of these mixed-initiative systems. On the one hand, humans can profit from planning techniques like parallel exploration, excluding non-valid planning paths from the search space. On the other hand, planning-related events like *backtracking* or *dead-ends* may impair the user experience. Second, we described our approach of a coherent and user-friendly mixed-initiative system. This included the use of a mutual knowledge model, in form of an ontology, to generate coherent domain models for dialog and planning as well as the development of a subordinate decision model, controlling who is in charge of the decision-making process. Furthermore, we evaluated our implementation on the effects of MIP events and tested different strategies to handle those. Concluding, we remark that the potentials of the integration of AI planning into a DS have to be weighed against the drawbacks like *backtracking* or *dead-ends* and their effects on the user experience. However, increasing the user's perceived system transparency by including valid explanations on these behaviors may mitigate the negative effects, thus increasing the potential areas of application for this kind of mixed-initiative systems.

Acknowledgment

This work was supported by the Transregional Collaborative Research Centre SFB/TRR 62 "Companion-Technology for Cognitive Technical Systems" which is funded by the German Research Foundation (DFG).

References

Mitchell Ai-Chang, John Bresina, Len Charest, Adam Chase, JC-J Hsu, Ari Jonsson, Bob Kanefsky, Paul Morris, Kanna Rajan, Jeffrey Yglesias, et al. 2004. Mapgen: mixed-initiative planning and scheduling for the mars exploration rover mission. *Intelligent Systems, IEEE*, 19(1):8–12.

Gregor Behnke, Denis Ponomaryov, Marvin Schiller, Pascal Bercher, Florian Nothdurft, Birte Glimm, and Susanne Biundo. 2015. Coherence across components in cognitive systems – one ontology to rule them all. In *Proc. of the 25th Int. Joint Conf. on Artificial Intelligence (IJCAI 2015)*. AAAI Press.

Pascal Bercher, Susanne Biundo, Thomas Geier, Thilo Hoernle, Florian Nothdurft, Felix Richter, and Bernd Schattenberg. 2014. Plan, repair, execute, explain - How planning helps to assemble your home theater. In *Proc. of the 24th Int. Conf. on Automated Planning and Scheduling (ICAPS 2014)*, pages 386–394. AAAI Press.

Susanne Biundo, Pascal Bercher, Thomas Geier, Felix Müller, and Bernd Schattenberg. 2011. Advanced user assistance based on AI planning. *Cognitive Systems Research*, 12(3-4):219–236. Special Issue on Complex Cognition.

Kutluhan Erol, James A. Hendler, and Dana S. Nau. 1994. UMCP: A sound and complete procedure for hierarchical task-network planning. In *Proc. of the 2nd Int. Conf. on Artificial Intelligence Planning Systems (AIPS 1994)*, pages 249–254. AAAI Press.

Juan Fernández-Olivares, Luis A. Castillo, Óscar García-Pérez, and Francisco Palao. 2006. Bringing users and planning technology together. experiences in SIADEX. In *Proc. of the 16th Int. Conf. on Automated Planning and Scheduling (ICAPS 2006)*, pages 11–20. AAAI Press.

Thomas Geier and Pascal Bercher. 2011. On the decidability of htn planning with task insertion. In *Proc. of the 22nd Int. Joint Conf. on Artificial Intelligence (IJCAI 2011)*, pages 1955–1961. AAAI Press.

Alyssa Glass, Deborah L. McGuinness, and Michael Wolverton. 2008. Toward establishing trust in adaptive agents. In *Proc. of the 13th Int. Conf. on Intelligent User Interfaces (IUI 2008)*, pages 227–236. ACM.

Marc Hassenzahl, Michael Burmester, and Franz Koller. 2003. Attrakdiff: Ein fragebogen zur messung wahrgenommener hedonischer und pragmatischer qualitt. In Gerd Szwillus and Jürgen Ziegler, editors, *Mensch & Computer 2003: Interaktion in Bewegung*, pages 187–196, Stuttgart. B. G. Teubner.

Frank Honold, Felix Schüssel, and Michael Weber. 2012. Adaptive probabilistic fission for multimodal systems. In *Proc. of the 24th Australian Computer-Human Interaction Conf.*, OzCHI '12, pages 222–231, New York, NY, USA, November, 26–30. ACM.

Frank Honold, Felix Schussel, Michael Weber, Florian Nothdurft, Gregor Bertrand, and Wolfgang Minker. 2013. Context models for adaptive dialogs and multimodal interaction. In *9th Int. Conf. on Intelligent Environments (IE 2013)*, pages 57–64. IEEE.

Maria Madsen and Shirley Gregor. 2000. Measuring human-computer trust. In *Proc. of the 11 th Australasian Conf. on Information Systems*, pages 6–8. ISMRC, QUT.

Bonnie M Muir and Neville Moray. 1996. Trust in automation. part ii. experimental studies of trust and human intervention in a process control simulation. *Ergonomics*, 39(3):429–460.

Karen L. Myers, W. Mabry Tyson, Michael J. Wolverton, Peter A. Jarvis, Thomas J. Lee, and Marie desJardins. 2002. PASSAT: A user-centric planning framework. In *Proc. of the 3rd Int. NASA Workshop on Planning and Scheduling for Space*, pages 1–10.

Karen L. Myers, Peter A. Jarvis, W. Mabry Tyson, and Michael J. Wolverton. 2003. A mixed-initiative framework for robust plan sketching. In *Proc. of the 13th Int. Conf. on Automated Planning and Scheduling (ICAPS 2003)*, pages 256–266. AAAI Press.

D. Nau, T.-C. Au, O. Ilghami, U. Kuter, D. Wu, F. Yaman, H. Munoz-Avila, and J.W. Murdock. 2005. Applications of shop and shop2. *Intelligent Systems, IEEE*, 20(2):34–41, March.

Florian Nothdurft, Felix Richter, and Wolfgang Minker. 2014. Probabilistic human-computer trust handling. In *Proc. of the Annual Meeting of the Special Interest Group on Discourse and Dialogue*, pages 51–59. ACL.

Marvin Schiller and Birte Glimm. 2013. Towards explicative inference for OWL. In *Proc. of the Int. Description Logic Workshop*, volume 1014, pages 930–941. CEUR.

Felix Schüssel, Frank Honold, and Michael Weber. 2013. Using the transferable belief model for multimodal input fusion in companion systems. In *Multimodal Pattern Recognition of Social Signals in HCI*, volume 7742 of *LNCS*, pages 100–115. Springer.

Bastian Seegebarth, Felix Müller, Bernd Schattenberg, and Susanne Biundo. 2012. Making hybrid plans more clear to human users – a formal approach for generating sound explanations. In *Proc. of the 22nd Int. Conf. on Automated Planning and Scheduling (ICAPS 2012)*, pages 225–233. AAAI Press.

Shirin Sohrabi, Jorge Baier, and Sheila A. McIlraith. 2009. HTN planning with preferences. In *21st Int. Joint Conf. on Artificial Intelligence (IJCAI 2009)*, pages 1790–1797. AAAI Press.

W3C OWL Working Group. 2009. *OWL 2 Web Ontology Language: Document Overview*. Available at `http://www.w3.org/TR/owl2-overview/`.

8 Appendix A: Example Planning and Dialog Snippet

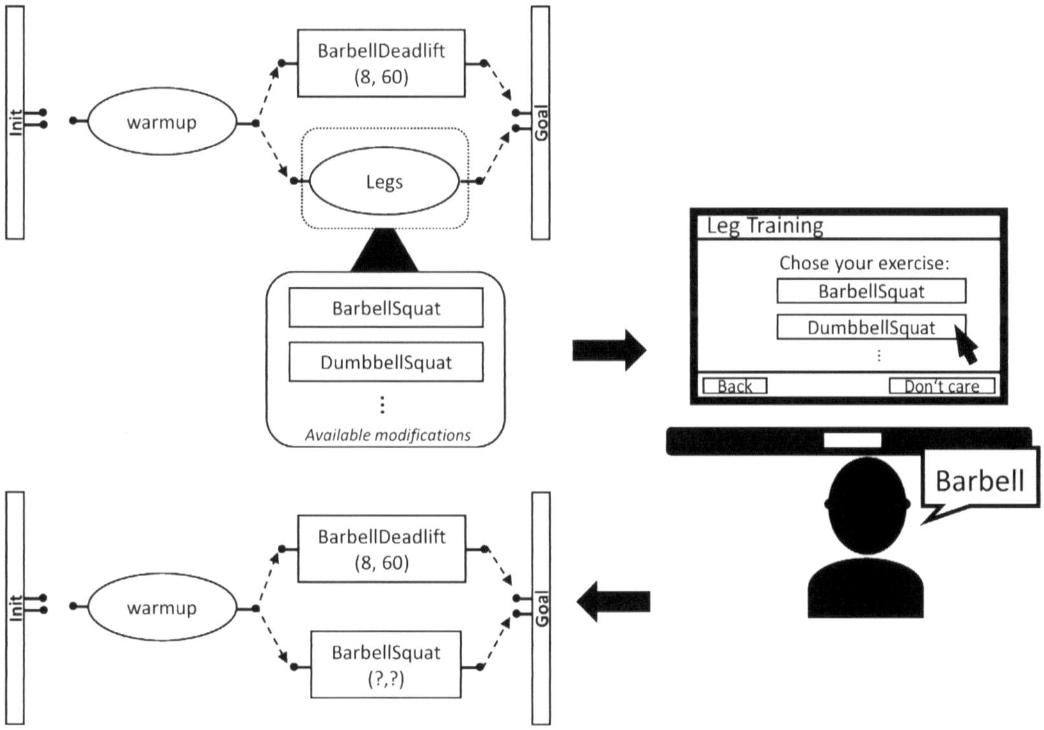

Figure 4: This figure shows an example planning and dialog snippet. The abstract planning task "Legs" has to be decomposed into a primitive task. In this case the decision that of the modifications is to be included in the plan is done by the user. A screenshot of an exemplary decision-making by the user was presented in Figure 2. Afterwards, the abstract task is refined using the selected modification and integrated with the plan.

Automatic Detection of Miscommunication in Spoken Dialogue Systems

Raveesh Meena **José Lopes** **Gabriel Skantze** **Joakim Gustafson**
KTH Royal Institute of Technology
School of Computer Science and Communication
Stockholm, Sweden
{raveesh,jdlopes,skantze,jkgu}@kth.se

Abstract

In this paper, we present a data-driven approach for detecting instances of miscommunication in dialogue system interactions. A range of generic features that are both automatically extractable and manually annotated were used to train two models for online detection and one for offline analysis. Online detection could be used to raise the error awareness of the system, whereas offline detection could be used by a system designer to identify potential flaws in the dialogue design. In experimental evaluations on system logs from three different dialogue systems that vary in their dialogue strategy, the proposed models performed substantially better than the majority class baseline models.

1 Introduction

Miscommunication is a frequent phenomenon in both human–human and human–machine interactions. However, while human conversational partners are skilled at detecting and resolving problems, state-of-the-art dialogue systems often have problems with this. Various works have been reported on detection of errors in human–machine dialogues. While the common theme among these works is to use error detection for making online adaption of dialogue strategies (e.g., implicit vs. explicit confirmations), they differ in what they model as error. For example, Walker et al. (2000) model dialogue success or failure as error, Bohus & Rudnicky (2002) refers to lack of confidence in understanding user intentions as error, Schmitt et al. (2011) use the notion of interaction quality in a dialogue as an estimate of errors at arbitrary point in a dialogue, Krahmer et al. (2001) and Swerts et al. (2000) model misunderstandings on the system's part as errors.

Awareness about errors in dialogues, however, has relevance not only for making online decisions, but also for dialogue system designers. Access to information about in which states the dialogue fails or runs into trouble could enable system designers to identify potential flaws in the dialogue design. Unfortunately, this type of error analysis is typically done manually, which is laborious and time consuming. Automation of this task has high relevance for dialogue system developers, particularly for interactive voice response (IVR) systems.

In this paper, we present a data-driven approach for detection of miscommunication in dialogue system interactions through automatic analysis of system logs. This analysis is based on the assumption that the onus of miscommunication is on the system. Thus, instances of non-understandings, implicit and explicit confirmations based on false assumptions, and confusing prompts are treated as problematic system actions that we want to detect in order to avoid them. Since our main goal is to integrate the approach in a toolkit for offline analysis of interaction logs we focus here largely on models for offline detection. For this analysis, we have the full dialogue context (backward and forward) at our disposal, and use features that are both automatically extractable from the system logs and manually annotated. However, we also report the performances of these models using only online features and limited dialogue context, and demonstrate our models' suitability for online use in detection of potential problems in system actions.

Proceedings of the SIGDIAL 2015 Conference, pages 354–363,
Prague, Czech Republic, 2-4 September 2015.

We evaluate our approach on datasets from three different dialogue systems that vary in their dialogue modeling, dialogue strategy, language, user types. We also report findings from an experimental work on cross-corpus analysis: using a model trained on logs from one system for analysis of interaction logs from another system. Thus the novelty of work reported here lies in our models' relevance for offline as well as online detection of miscommunications, and the applicability and generalizability of features across dialogue systems and domains.

The paper is structured as follows: we report the relevant literature in Section 2 and establish the ground for our work. In Section 3 we describe the three datasets used. The annotation scheme is discussed in Section 4. The complete set of features explored in this work is presented in Section 5. The experimental method is described in Section 6 and results are reported in Section 7. We conclude and outline our future work in Section 8.

2 Background

One way to analyze miscommunication is to make a distinction between *non-understanding* and *misunderstanding* (Hirst et al., 1994). While non-understandings are noticed immediately by the listeners, the information about misunderstandings may surface only at a later stage in the dialogue. This can be illustrated with the following human–machine interaction:

1	S:	*How may I help you?*
2	U:	Can you recommend a Turkish restaurant in downtown area?
3	S:	*Could you please rephrase that?*
4	U:	A Turkish restaurant in downtown.
5	S:	*Clowns, which serves Italian food, is a great restaurant in downtown area.*
6	U:	I am looking for a Turkish restaurant

Table 1: An illustration of miscommunication in human-machine interaction. S and U denote system and user turns respectively. User turns are transcriptions.

The system, in turn 3, expresses that a non-understanding of user intentions (in turn 2) has occurred. In contrast, in turn 5 – following the best assessment of user turn 4 – the system makes a restaurant recommendation, but misunderstands the user's choice of cuisine. However, this problem does not become evident until turn 6. The various approaches to detection of errors presented in the literature can be broadly classified in two categories – *early error detection* and *late error detection* – based on at what turns in the dialogue the assessments about errors are made (Skantze, 2007). In early error detection approaches the system makes an assessment of its current hypothesis of what the user just said. Approaches for detection of non-understanding, such as confidence annotation (Bohus & Rudnicky, 2002), fall in this category. In contrast, late error detection aims at finding out whether the system has made false assumptions about user's intentions in previous turns. These distinctions are vital from our viewpoint as they point out the turns in dialogue that are to be assessed and the scope of dialogue context that could be exploited to make such an assessment.

We now present some of the related works and highlight what has been modeled as error, stage in dialogue the assessment about errors are made, and type of features and span of dialogue context used. Following this we discuss the motivations and distinct contributions of our work.

Walker et al. (2000) presented a corpus based approach that used information from initial system-user turn exchanges alone to forecast whether the ongoing dialogue will fail. If the dialogue is likely to fail the call could be transferred to a human operator right away. A rule learner, RIPPER (Cohen, 1995), was trained to make a forecast about dialogue failure after every user turn. The model was trained on automatically extracted features from automatic speech recognizer (ASR), natural language understanding (NLU) and dialogue management (DM) modules.

Bohus & Rudnicky (2002) presented an approach to utterance level *confidence annotation* which aims at making an estimate of the system's understanding of the user's utterance. The model returns a confidence score which is then used by the system to select appropriate dialogue strategy, e.g. express non-understanding of user intention. The approach combines features from ASR, NLU and DM for determining the confidence score using logistic regression.

Schmitt et al. (2011) proposed a scheme to model and predict the quality of interaction at arbitrary points during an interaction. The task for the trained model was to predict a score, from 5 to 1 indicating very high to very poor quality of interaction, on having seen a system-user turn exchange. A Support Vector Machine model was trained on automatically extractable features from ASR, NLU and DM modules. They observed that additional information such as user's affect state (manually annotated) did not help the learning task.

In their investigations of a Dutch Train timetable corpus, Krahmer et al., 2001) observed that dialogue system users provide positive and negative cues about misunderstandings on the system's part. These cues include user feedback, such as corrections, confirmations, and marked disconfirmations, and can be exploited for late error detection.

Swerts et al. (2000) trained models for automatic prediction of user corrections. They observed that user repetition (or re-phrasing) is a cue to a prior error made by the system. They used prosodic features and details from the ASR and the DM modules to train a RIPPER learner. Their work highlights that user repetitions are useful cue for late error detection.

For our task, we have defined the problem as detecting miscommunication on the system's part. This could be misunderstandings, implicit and explicit confirmations based on false assumptions, or confusing system prompts. Since instances of non-understandings are self-evident cases of miscommunication we exclude them from the learning task. Detecting the other cases of miscommunications is non-trivial as it requires assessment of user feedback. The proposed scheme can be illustrated in the following example interaction:

1	S:	*How may I help you?*
2	U:	Sixty One D
3	S:	*The 61C.What's the departure station?*
4	U:	No

Table 2: An implicit confirmation based on false assumption is an instance of problematic system action. User turns are manual transcriptions

In the context of these four turns our task is to detect whether system turn 3 is problematic. If we want to use the model online for early error detection, the system should be able to detect the problem using only automatically extractable features from turn 1-3. Unlike *confidence annotation* (Bohus & Rudnicky, 2002), we also include what the system is about to say in turn 3 and make an anticipation (or forecast) of whether this turn would lead to a problem. Thus, it is possible for a system that has access to such a model to assess different alternative responses before choosing one of them. Besides using details from ASR and SLU components (exploited in the reported literature) the proposed *early model* is able to use details from Dialogue Manager and Natural Language Generation modules.

Next, we train another model that extends the anticipation model by also considering the user feedback in turn 4, similar to Krahmer et al., 2001) and Swerts et al. (2000). Such a model can also be used online in a dialogue system in order to detect errors after-the-fact, and engage in late error recovery (Skantze, 2007). The end result is a model that combines both anticipation and user feedback to make an assessment of whether system turns were problematic. We refer to this model as the *late model.*

Since both the early and late models are to be used online, they only have access to automatically extractable features. However, we also train an *offline model* that can be used by a dialogue designer to find potential flaws in the system. This model extends the late model in that it also has access to features that are derived from manual annotations in the logs.

In this work we also investigated whether models trained on logs of one system can be used for error detection in interaction logs from a different dialogue system. Towards this we trained our models on generic features and evaluated our approach on system logs from three dialogue systems that differ in their dialogue strategy.

3 Corpora

Dialogue system logs from two publicly available corpora and one from a commercially deployed system were used for building and evaluating the three models. The first dataset is from the CamInfo Evaluation Dialogues corpus. The corpus comprises of spoken interactions between the Cambridge Spoken Dialogue System and users, where the system provides restaurant recommendations for Cambridge. The dialogue system is a research system that uses dialogue-state tracking for dialogue management (Jurcicek et al., 2012). As the system is a research prototype, users of these systems are not real users in real need of information but workers recruited via the Amazon Mechanical Turk (AMT). Nevertheless, the dialogue system is state-of-the-art in statistical models for dialogue management. From this corpus 179 dialogues were used as the dataset, which we will refer to as the **CamInfo** set.

The second corpus comes from the **Let's Go** dialogue system. Let's Go (Raux et al., 2005) is developed and maintained by the Dialogue Research Center (DialRC) at Carnegie Mellon University that provides bus schedule information for Pittsburgh's Port Authority buses during off-peak hours. The users of Let's Go system are real users, which are in real need of the information. This makes the dataset interesting for us. The dataset used here consists of 41 dialogues selected from the data released for the 2010 Spoken Dialogue Challenge (Black et al., 2010).

The third dataset, **SweCC** – Swedish Call Center Corpus, is taken from a corpus of call logs from a commercial customer service provider in Sweden providing services in various domains. The system tries to extract some details from customers before routing the call to a human operator in the concerned department. Compared to CamInfo and Let's Go datasets, the SweCC corpus is from a commercially deployed system, with real users, and the interactions are in Swedish. From this corpus 219 dialogues were selected. Table 3 provides a comparative summary of the three datasets.

CamInfo	Let's Go	SweCC
Research	Research	Commercial
Hired users	Real users	Real users
Mostly implicit confirmation	Mostly explicit confirmation	Only explicit confirmation
Stochastic	Rule based	Rule based
English	English	Swedish
179 dialogues	41 dialogues	219 dialogues
5.2 exchanges on average per dialogue	19 exchanges on average per dialogue	6.6 exchanges on average per dialogue

Table 3: A comparative summary of the three datasets

4 Annotations

We take a supervised approach for detection of problematic system turns in the system logs. This requires each system turn in the training datasets to be labeled as to whether they are PROBLEMATIC (if the system turn reveals a miscommunication) or NOT-PROBLEMATIC. There are different schemes for labeling data. One approach is to ask one or two experts (having knowledge of the task) to label data and use inter-annotator agreement to set an acceptable goal for the trained model. Another approach is to use a few non-experts but use a set of guidelines so that the annotators are consistent (and to achieve a higher Kappa score, (Schmitt et al., 2011)). We take the crowdsourcing approach for annotating the CamInfo data and use the AMT platform. Thus, we avoid using both experts and guidelines. The key however is to make the task simple for the AMT-workers. Based on our earlier discussion on the role of dialogue context and type of errors assessed in early and late error detection, we set up the annotation tasks such that AMT workers saw two dialogue exchanges (4 turns in total), as shown in Table 2:. The workers were asked to label system turn 3 as PROBLEMATIC or NOT-PROBLEMATIC, depending on whether it was appropriate or not, or PARTIALLY-PROBLEMATIC when it is not straightforward to choose between the former two labels.

In the Let's Go dataset we observed that whenever the system engaged in consecutive confirmation requests the automatically extracted sub-dialogue (any four consecutive turns) did not always result in a meaningful sub-dialogue. Therefore the Let's Go data was annotated by one of the co-authors of the paper. The SweCC data could not be used on AMT platform due to the agreement with the data provider, and was annotated by the same co-author. See Appendix A for sample of annotated interactions.

Since we had access to the user feedback to the questionnaire for the CamInfo Evaluation Dialogues corpus, we investigated whether the problematic turns identified by the AMT-workers reflect the overall interaction quality, as experienced by the users. We observed a visibly strong correlation between the user feedback and the fractions of system turn per dialogue labeled as PROBLEMATIC by the AMT-workers. Figure 1 illustrates the correlation for one of the four questions in the questionnaire. This shows that the detection and avoidance of problematic turns (as defined here), will have bearing on the users' experience of the interaction.

Each system turn in the CamInfo dataset was initially labeled by two AMT-workers. In case of a tie, one more worker was asked to label that instance. In total 753 instances were labeled in the first step. We observed an inter-annotators agreement of 0.80 (Fleiss Kappa) among the annotators and only 113 instances had a tie and were annotated by a third worker. The label with the majority vote was chosen as the final class label for instances with ties in the dataset. Table 4 shows the distributions for the three annotation categories seen in the three datasets. Due to the imbalance of the PARTIALLY-PROBLEMATIC class in the three datasets we excluded this class from the learning task and focus only on classifying system turns as either PROBLEMATIC or NOT-PROBLEMATIC. System turns expressing non-understanding were also excluded from the learning task. The final datasets had the following representation for the PROBLEMATIC class: CamInfo (615) 86.0%, Let's Go (744) 57.5, and for SweCC (871) 65.7%. To mitigate the high class imbalance in CamInfo another 51 problematic dialogues (selected following the correlations of user feedback from Figure 1) were annotated by a second co-author. The resulting CamInfo dataset had 859 instances of which 75.3% are from PROBLEMATIC class.

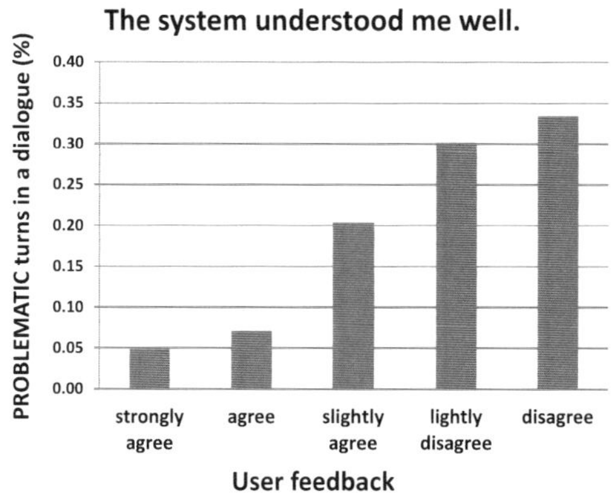

Figure 1: Correlation of system turns annotated as problematic with user feedback

Dataset (#instances)	CamInfo (753)	Let's Go (760)	SweCC (968)
PROBLEMATIC	16 %	42%	31%
NOT-PROBLEMATIC	73 %	57%	61%
PARTIALLY-PROBLEMATIC	11 %	1%	8%

Table 4: Distribution of the three annotation categories across the three datasets

5 Features

We wanted to train models that are generic and can be used to analyze system logs from different dialogue systems. Therefore we trained our models on only those features that were available in all the three datasets. Below we describe the complete feature set, which include features and manual annotations that were readily available in system logs. A range of higher-level features were also derived from the available features. Since the task of the three dialogue system is to perform slot-filling we use the term *concept* to refer to slot-types and slot-values.

***ASR*:** the best hypothesis, the recognition confidence score and the number of words. ***NLU*:** user dialogue act (the best parse hypothesis – **nlu_asr**), the best parse hypothesis obtained on manual transcription (**nlu_trn**), number of concepts in nlu_asr and nlu_trn, concept error rate: the Levenshtein distance between nlu_asr and nlu_trn, correctly transferred concepts: the fraction of concepts in nlu_trn observed in nlu_asr. ***NLG*:** system dialogue act, number of concepts in system act, system prompt, and number of words in the prompt.

***Manual annotations*:** manual transcriptions of the best ASR hypothesis, number of words in the transcription, word error rate: the Levenshtein distance between the recognized hypothesis and transcribed string, correctly transferred words: fraction of words in the transcription observed in the ASR hypothesis.

Discourse features*:** *position in dialogue*: fraction of turns completed up to the decision point. ***New information: fraction of new words (and concepts) in the successive prompts of a speaker. ***Repetition***: Two measures to estimate repetition in successive speaker turns were used: (i) cosine similarity, the cosine angle between vector representation of the two turns and (ii) the number of common concepts. ***Marked disconfirmation***: whether the user response to a system request for confirmation has a marked disconfirmation (e.g., "no", "not"). ***Corrections***: the number of slots-values in previous speaker turn that were given a new value in the following turn – by either the dialogue partner or the same speaker – were used as an estimate of user corrections, false assumptions and rectifications by the system, and change in user intentions.

6 Models and Method

As mentioned earlier, the *early* and *late* models are aimed at online use in dialogue systems, whereas the *offline model* is for offline analysis of interaction logs. A window of 4 turns, as discussed in Section 2, is used to limit the dialogue context for extraction of features. Accordingly, the *early model* uses features from turns 1-3; the *late model* uses features from the complete window, turns 1-4. The *offline model* like the *late model* uses the complete window, but additionally uses the manual transcription features or features derived from them, e.g. word error rate.

For the purpose of brevity, we report four sets of feature combinations: (i) Bag of words representation of system and user turns (BoW), (ii) DrW: a set containing all the features derived from the words in the user and system turns, e.g., turn length (measured in number of words), cosine similarity in speaker turns as an estimate of speaker repetition, (iii) Bag of concept representation of system and user dialogue acts (BoC), and (iv) DrC: a set with all the features derived from dialogue acts, e.g., turn length (measured in number of concepts).

Given the skew in distribution of the two classes in the three datasets (cf. Section 4) accuracy alone is not a good evaluation metric. A model can achieve high classification accuracy by simply predicting the value of the majority class (i.e. NOT-PROBLEMATIC) for all predictions. However, since we are equally interested in the recall for both PROBLEMATIC and NOT-PROBLEMATIC classes, we use the un-weighted average recall (UAR) to assess the model performance, similar to Higashinaka et al., 2010).

We explored various machine learning algorithms available in the Weka toolkit (Hall et al., 2009), but report here models trained using two different algorithms: JRIP, a Weka implementation of the RIPPER rule learning algorithm, and Support Vector Machine (SVM) with linear kernel. The rules learned by JRIP offer a simple insight into what features contribute in decision making. The SVM algorithm is capable of transforming the feature space into higher dimensions and learns sophisticated decision boundaries. The figures reported here are from a 10-fold cross-validation scheme for evaluation.

7 Results

7.1 Baseline

To assess the improvements made by the trained models we need a baseline model to draw comparisons. We can use the simple majority class baseline model that will predict the value of majority class for all predictions. The UAR for such a model is shown in Table 5 (row 1). The UAR for all the three datasets is 0.50.

All the three dialogue systems employ confirmation strategies, which are simple built-in mechanisms for detecting miscommunication online. Therefore, a model trained using the *marked disconfirmation* feature alone could be a more reasonable baseline model for comparison. Row 2 in Table 5 (feature category *MDisCnf)* shows the performances for such a baseline. The figures from *late* and *offline* models suggest that while this feature is not at all useful for CamInfo dataset (UAR = 0.50 for both JRIP and SVM) it makes substantial contributions to models for Let's Go and SweCC datasets. The *late model*, using the online features for marked disconfirmation and the JRIP algorithm obtained a UAR of 0.68 for Let's Go and 0.87 for SweCC. The corresponding *offline* models, which use the manual feature in addition, achieve even better results for the two datasets: UAR of 0.74 and 0.89 respectively. These figures clearly illustrate two things: First, while Let's Go and SweCC systems often employ explicit confirmation strategy, CamInfo hardly uses it. Second, the majority of problems in the Let's Go and SweCC are due to explicit confirmations based on false assumptions.

7.2 Word-related features

Using the bag of word (BoW) feature set alone, we observe that for CamInfo dataset the SVM achieved a UAR of 0.75 for the *early* model, 0.79 for the *late* model, and 0.80 for the *offline* model. These are comprehensive gains over the baseline of 0.50. The figures for the *early* model suggest that by looking only at (i) the most recent user prompt, (ii) the system prompt preceding it, and (ii) the current system prompt which is to be executed, the model can anticipate, well over chance whether the chosen system prompt would lead to a problem.

For the Let's Go and SweCC datasets, using the BoW feature set the *late model* achieved modest gains in performance over the corresponding MDisCnf baseline model. For example, using the SVM algorithm the late model for Let's Go achieved a UAR of 0.81. This is an absolute gain of 0.13 points over the UAR of 0.68 achieved using the marked disconfirmation feature set alone. This large gain can be attributed partly to the *early* model (a UAR of 0.74) and the late error detection features which add another 0.07 absolute points raising the UAR to 0.81. For the SweCC dataset, although the gains made by the JRIP learner models over the MDisCnf baseline are marginal, the fact that the *late* model gains in UAR scores over *early* model points to the contributions of words that indicate user disconfirmations, e.g. *no* or *not*.

Next, on using BoW feature set in combination with the DrW feature set that contains features derived from words, such as prompt length (number of words), speaker repetitions, ASR confidence score, etc., we achieved both minor gains and losses for the CamInfo and Let's Go dataset. The *offline* models for Let's Go (both JRIP as well as SVM) made a gain of approx. 0.04 over the *late* models. A closer look at the rules learned by the JRIP model indicates that features such as word error rate, cosine similarity measure of user repetition, number of words in user turns, contributed to rule learning.

In the SweCC dataset we observe that for all the *early* and *late* models the combination of BoW and DrW feature sets offered improved

SNr.			**CamInfo**		**Let's Go**		**SweCC**	
			UAR		*UAR*		*UAR*	
1.	*Majority class baseline*		0.50			0.50	0.50	
	Feature Set	***Model***	***JRip***	***SVM***	***JRip***	***SVM***	***JRip***	***SVM***
2.	*MDisCnf*	***Late***	0.50	0.50	0.68	0.68	0.87	0.83
		Offline	0.50	0.50	0.74	0.73	0.89	0.84
3.	*BoW*	***Early***	0.72	0.75	0.72	0.74	0.78	0.80
		Late	0.73	0.79	0.80	0.81	0.88	0.88
		Offline	0.78	0.80	0.84	0.82	0.90	0.89
4.	*BoW+DrW*	***Early***	0.75	0.77	0.71	0.75	0.84	0.82
		Late	0.71	0.82	0.82	0.80	0.92	0.91
		Offline	0.77	0.79	0.85	0.84	0.92	0.90
5.	*BoC*	***Early***	0.80	0.81	0.76	0.76	0.81	0.81
		Late	0.81	0.82	0.86	0.84	0.89	0.88
		Offline	0.81	0.82	**0.88**	0.85	-	-
6.	*BoC+DrC+DrW*	***Early***	0.80	0.83	0.70	0.80	0.84	0.82
		Late	0.78	0.82	0.84	0.85	**0.93**	0.89
		Offline	0.82	**0.84**	0.87	0.86	0.92	0.89

Table 5 : Performance of the various *early*, *late* and *offline* models for error detection on the three datasets

performances over using BoW alone. The rules learned by the JRIP indicate that in addition to the marked disconfirmation features the model is able to make use of features that indicate whether the system takes the dialogue forward, the ASR confidence score for user turns, the position in dialogue, and the user turn lengths.

7.3 Concept-related features

Next, we analyzed the model performances using the bag of concept (BoC) feature set alone. A cursory look at the performances in row 5 in Table 5 suggest that for both CamInfo and Let's Go the BoC feature set offers modest and robust improvement over using BoW feature set alone. In comparison, for the SweCC dataset the gains made by the models over using BoW alone are marginal. This is not surprising given the high UARs achieved for SweCC corresponding to the MDisCnf feature set (row 2), suggesting that most problems in SweCC dataset are inappropriate confirmation requests, and detection of user disconfirmations is a good enough measure.

We also observed that the contribution of the *late* model is much clearly seen in Let's Go and SweCC datasets while this is not true for CamInfo. In view of the earlier observation that explicit confirmations are seldom seen in CamInfo we can say that users are left to use strategies such as repetitions to correct false assumptions by the system. These cues of corrections are much harder to assess than the marked disconfirmations. The best performances were in general obtained by the *offline* models: UAR of 0.82 on CamInfo dataset using SVM algorithm and 0.88 for Let's Go using JRIP. Some of the features used by the JRIP rule learner include: number of concepts in parse hypothesis being zero, the system dialogue act indicating open prompts "How may I help you?" during the dialogue (suggesting a dialogue restart), and slot types which the system often had difficulty understanding. These were user requests for price range and postal codes in the CamInfo dataset, and time of travel and place of arrival in the Let's Go dataset. As the NLU for manual transcription is not available for the SweCC dataset the corresponding row for the *offline* model in Table 5 is empty.

Next, we trained the models on the combined feature set, i.e. BoC, DrC and DrW sets. We observed that while majority of models achieved marginal gains over using BoC set alone, the ones that did lose did not exhibit a major drop in performance. The best performance for the CamInfo is obtained by the *offline* model (using the SVM algorithm): a UAR of 0.84. For Let's Go the JRIP model achieved the best UAR, 0.87 for the *offline* model. For the SweCC the *late* model performed better than the *offline* model and achieved a UAR of 0.93 using the JRIP learner. These are comprehensive gains over the two baseline models. Appendix A shows two examples of offline error detection.

7.4 Impact of data on model performances

We also analyzed the impact of amount of training data used on model performances. A hold-out validation scheme was followed. A dataset was first randomized and then split into 5 sets, each containing equal number of dialogues. Each of the set was used as a hold-out test set for models trained on the remaining 4 sets. Starting with only one of the 4 sets as the training set, four rounds of training and testing were conducted. At each stage one whole set of dialogue was added to the existing training set. The whole exercise was conducted 5 times, resulting in a total of 5x5=25 observations per evaluation. Each point in Figure 2 illustrates the UAR averaged over these 25 observations by the *offline* model (JRIP learner using feature set 6, cf. row 6 in Table 5). The performance curves and their gradients suggest that all the models for the three datasets are likely to benefit from more training data, particularly the CamInfo dataset.

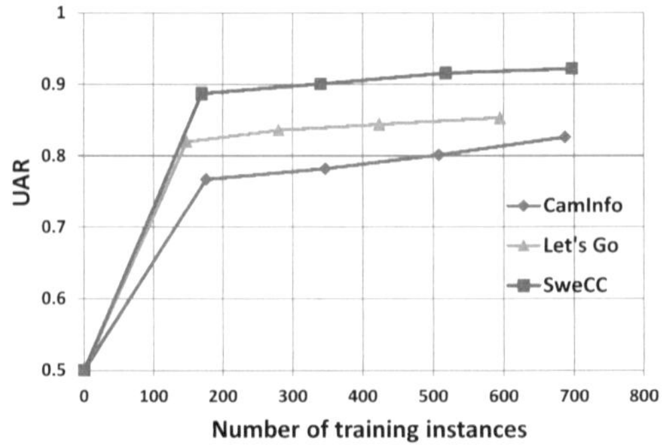

Figure 2: Gains in UAR made by the *offline* model (JRIP learner and feature set BoC+ DrW+DrC)

Training set →	CamInfo	Let's Go	SweCC
Test set	*UAR*	*UAR*	*UAR*
CamInfo	-	0.72	0.54
Let's Go	0.62	-	0.73
SweCC	0.53	0.89	-

Table 6: Cross-corpus performances of *offline* model (JRIP learner and feature set BoC+ DrW+DrC)

7.5 A model for cross-corpus analysis

We also investigated whether a model trained on annotated data from one dialogue system can be used for automatic detection of problematic system turns in interaction logs from another dialogue system. Table 6 illustrates the performances of the *offline* model (JRIP learner using feature set 6, cf. row 6 in Table 5). This experiment mostly used numeric features such as turn length, word error rate, and dialogue act features that are generic across domains, e.g., request for information, confirmations, and disconfirmations.

We observed that using the Let's Go dataset as the training set we can achieve a UAR of 0.89 for SweCC and 0.72 for CamInfo. Although both SweCC and Let's Go use explicit clarifications, since SweCC dataset exhibits limited error patterns a UAR of only 0.73 is obtained for Let's Go when using a model trained on SweCC. Models trained on CamInfo seem more appropriate for Let's Go than for SweCC.

8 Conclusions and Future work

We have presented a data-driven approach to detection of problematic system turns by automatic analysis of dialogue system interaction logs. Features that are generic across dialogue systems were automatically extracted from the system logs (of ASR, NLU and NLG modules) and the manual transcriptions. We also created abstract features to estimate discourse phenomena such as user repetitions and corrections, and discourse progression. The proposed scheme has been evaluated on interaction logs of three dialogue systems that differ in their domain of application, dialogue modeling, dialogue strategy and language. The trained models achieved substantially better recall on the three datasets. We have also shown that it is possible to achieve reasonable performance using models trained on one system to detect errors in another system.

We think that the models described here can be used in many different ways. A simple application of the online models could be to build an "error awareness" module in a dialogue system. For offline analysis, the late error detection model could be trained on a subset of data collected from a system, and then applied to the whole corpus in order to find problematic turns. Then only these turns would need to be transcribed and analyzed further, reducing a lot of manual work. However, we also plan in a next step to not only find instances of miscommunication automatically, but also summarize the main root causes of the problems, in order to help the dialogue designer to mitigate them. This could include extensions of grammars and vocabularies, prompts that need rephrasing, or lack of proper error handling strategies.

Acknowledgement

We would like to thank our colleagues Giampiero Salvi and Kalin Stefanov for their valuable discussions on machine learning. We also want to thank the CMU and Cambridge research groups for making the respective corpus publicly available. This research is supported by the EU project SpeDial – Spoken Dialogue Analytics, EU grant # 611396.

Reference

Black, A. W., Burger, S., Langner, B., Parent, G., & Eskenazi, M. (2010). Spoken Dialog Challenge 2010.. In Hakkani-Tür, D., & Ostendorf, M. (Eds.), *SLT* (pp. 448-453). IEEE.

Bohus, D., & Rudnicky, A. (2002). *Integrating multiple knowledge sources for utterance-level confidence annotation in the CMU Communicator spoken dialog system.* Technical Report CS-190, Carnegie Mellon University, Pittsburgh, PA.

Cohen, W. (1995). Fast effective rule induction. In *Proceedings of the Twelfth International Conference on Machine Learning.*

Hall, M., Frank, E., Holmes, G., Pfahringer, B., Reutemann, P., & Witten, I. H. (2009). The WEKA Data Mining Software: An Update. *SIGKDD Explorations, 11*(1).

Higashinaka, R., Minami, Y., Dohsaka, K., & Meguro, T. (2010). Modeling User Satisfaction Transitions in Dialogues from Overall Ratings. In *Proceedings of the SIGDIAL 2010 Conference* (pp. 18-27). Tokyo, Japan: Association for Computational Linguistics.

Hirst, G., McRoy, S., Heeman, P., Edmonds, P., & Horton, D. (1994). Repairing conversational misunderstandings and non-understandings. *Speech Communication, 15*, 213-230.

Jurcicek, F., Thomson, B., & Young, S. (2012). Reinforcement learning for parameter estimation in statistical spoken dialogue systems. *Computer Speech & Language, 26*(3), 168-192.

Krahmer, E., Swerts, M., Theune, M., & Weegels, M. (2001). Error detection in spoken human-machine interaction. *International Journal of Speech Technology, 4*(1), 19-29.

Raux, A., Langner, B., Bohus, D., Black, A. W., & Eskenazi, M. (2005). Let's go public! Taking a spoken dialog system to the real world.. In *INTERSPEECH* (pp. 885-888). ISCA.

Schmitt, A., Schatz, B., & Minker, W. (2011). Modeling and Predicting Quality in Spoken Human-computer Interaction. In *Proceedings of the SIGDIAL 2011 Conference* (pp. 173-184). Stroudsburg, PA, USA: Association for Computational Linguistics.

Skantze, G. (2007). *Error Handling in Spoken Dialogue Systems.* Doctoral dissertation, KTH.

Swerts, M., Hirschberg, J., & Litman, D. (2000). Corrections in spoken dialogue systems. In *Proceedings of the International Conference on Spoken Language Processing.* Beijng, China.

Walker, M. A., Langkilde, I., Wright, J., Gorin, A., & Litman, D. J. (2000). Learning to predict problematic situations in a spoken dialogue system: experiments with How may I help you?. In *Proceedings of North American Meeting of the Association of Computational Linguistics.*

Appendix A: Table 7 and Table 8 illustrate the predictions made by the *offline* model using JRIP rule learner and the combined features: BoC+DrW+DrC (cf. row 6, Table 5). Colum headings T and P contain the training and predicted labels, respectively. ☒ is PROBLEMATIC, ☑ is NOT-PROBLEMATIC, and ⊘ is an instance of non-understanding therefore excluded from the learning task. Table 9 illustrates the top rules learned by the JRIP learner, for each of the two datasets.

			T	P
1	S:	*Welcome to Cambridge system. How may I help you?*		
2	U:	I want to find a [I want to find a pub]		
3	S:	*The Avery is a great pub.*	☑	☑
4	U:	What is the phone number [what is the phone number]		
5	S:	*The phone number of The Avery is 01223 323405.*	☑	☑
6	U:	Does it have internet [Uh uh have in there]		
7	S:	*Can I help you with anything else?*	☒	⊘
8	U:	Does that pub have internet [Where is that er have in]		
9	S:	*The Avery is on 69-73 Regent Street.*	☒	☒
10	U:	Thank you bye.		

Table 7: Offline error detection on a CamInfo interaction. Text within [] is the top ASR hypothesis.

7	S:	*What can I do for you?*		
8	U:	Next bus [65e]		
9	S:	*The 65E. Did I get that right?*	☒	☒
10	U	No [no]		
11	S:	*What can I do for you?*	☑	☑
12	U:	61A [61A]		
13	S:	*The 61A. Did I get that right?*	☑	☑
14	U:	Yes [yes]		
15	S:	*Alright Where would you like to leave from?*	☑	☑
16	U:	Atwood [Duquensne]		
17	S:	*For example, you can say, NORTH BRADDOCK, FORBES AND MURRAY, or DOWNTOWN.*	☒	☒
18	U:	Forbes and Atwood [Forbes big at Atwood in wall]		
19	S:	*ATWOOD IN WALL. Did I get that right?*	☒	☒
20	U:	No [no]		

Table 8: Offline error detection on a Let's Go interaction. Text within [] is the top ASR hypothesis

The top rule learned by JRIP on CamInfo dataset	*The top 2 rules learned by JRIP on Let's Go dataset*
1. (ctc-svp-usr-2 <= 0.5) and (frc-new-slt-asr-usr-2 <= 0.5) =>class=problematic (83.0/9.0) **Rule 1:** If the correctly transferred concept rate for user turn 2 is <= 0.5 and the number of new slots mentioned are <= 0.5 then *anticipate* the system turn 3 as PROBLEMATIC. A total of 83 instances were labeled problematic by this rule, 9 of which were false predictions. ***Summary***: The user repeats (rephrases) to correct the system's mistake in grounding. However, the system does not have a good model to detect this and therefore the system response is most likely to be perceived in appropriate by the user.	1. (wer-tr-usr-2 >= 20) and (4-dact-tr_no >= 1) => class=problematic (121.0/3.0) 2. (ctc-svp-usr-2 <= 0.5) and (4-dact-tr_yes <= 0) => class=problematic (115.0/23.0) **Rule 1:** If WER for user turn 2 is more than 20 and the user d-act in turn 4 is "no" then the system response in turn 3 was PROBLEMATIC. **Rule 2:** Similar to the Rule 1 but uses different features. If correctly transferred concept rate for user turn 2 is <= 0.5 and in turn 4 the user act was not "yes" then the system action in turn 3 was PROBLEMATIC. ***Summary:*** Model uses late error detection cues such as marked disconfirmations to assess system actions.

Table 9: The top rules learned by the JRIP model for *offline* error detection on the CamInfo and Let's Go datasets (cf. row 6, Table 5).

Dialogue Management based on Multi-domain Corpus

Wendong Ge
Institute of Automation
Chinese Academy of Sciences
Beijing, China
wendong.ge@ia.ac.cn

Bo Xu
Institute of Automation
Chinese Academy of Sciences
Beijing, China
xubo@ia.ac.cn

Abstract

Dialogue Management (DM) is a key issue in Spoken Dialogue System. Most of the existing data-driven DM schemes train the dialogue policy for some specific domain (or vertical domain), only using the dialogue corpus in this domain, which might suffer from the scarcity of dialogue corpus in some domains. In this paper, we divide Dialogue Act (DA), as semantic representation of utterance, into DA type and slot parameter, where the former one is domain-independent and the latter one is domain-specific. Firstly, based on multiple-domain dialogue corpus, the DA type prediction model is trained via Recurrent Neutral Networks (RNN). Moreover, DA type decision problem is modeled as a multi-order POMDP, and transformed to be a one-order MDP with continuous states, which is solved by Natural Actor Critic (NAC) algorithm and applicable for every domain. Furthermore, a slot parameter selection scheme is designed to generate a complete machine DA according to the features of specific domain, which yields the Multi-domain Corpus based Dialogue Management (MCDM) scheme. Finally, extensive experimental results illustrate the performance improvement of the MCDM scheme, compared with the existing schemes.

1 Introduction

With the fast development of Automatic Speech Recognition (ASR) and Natural Language Processing (NLP), a lot of Spoken Dialogue Systems (SDS) appear in our lives as information assistants. In SDS, Dialogue Management (DM), as one of the most important modules, not only determines the current machine reaction, but also controls the process of future dialogue. Thus, it is important to study DM in the establishment of SDS.(Michael, 2002)

A lot of studies have been done on DM. (Thomson, 2010) introduces a new POMDP-based framework for building spoken dialogue systems by using Bayesian updates of the dialogue state. (Olivier, 2011) explores the possibility of using a set of approximate dynamic programming algorithms for policy optimization in SDS, which are combined to a method for learning a sparse representation of the value function. (Annemiek, 2012) analyzes current dialogue management in operating unmanned systems and develops a more advanced way of dialogue management and accompanying dialogue manager. (Yuan, 2012) proposes a task ontology model for domain independent dialogue management, where the knowledge of a specific task is modeled in its task ontology which is independent from dialogue control. (Daubigney, 2012) proposes to apply the Kalman Temporal Differences (KTD) framework to the problem of dialogue strategy optimization so as to address all these issues in a comprehensive manner with a single framework. (Emmanuel, 2013) proposes a scheme to utilize a socially-based reward function for Reinforcement Learning and uses it to fit the user adaptation issue for dialogue management. (Daniele, 2013) describes an architecture for a dialogue management system to be employed in serious games for natural language interaction with non-player characters. (Young et al., 2013) provides an overview of the current state of the art in the development of POMDP-based spoken dialog systems. (Hao, 2014) presents a dialogue manager based on a log-linear probabilistic model and uses context-free grammars to impart hierarchical structure to variables and features. (Kallirroi, 2014) uses single-agent Reinforcement Learning and multi-agent Reinforcement Learning for

Proceedings of the SIGDIAL 2015 Conference, pages 364–373,
Prague, Czech Republic, 2-4 September 2015.

learning dialogue policies in a resource allocation negotiation scenario. To sum up, most of these previous studies establish a specific-domain DM model, only using the dialogue corpus in this domain, which might suffer from scarcity of dialogue corpus in some vertical domains.

In this paper, we mainly consider the domains about slot-filling tasks such as hotel reservation, flight ticket booking, and shopping guidance. We utilize dialogue act (DA) as semantic representation of utterance, and divide it into DA type and slot parameter, where the former one is domain-independent and the latter one is domain-specific. Based on the dialogue corpus in multiple domains, we train the current machine DA type prediction model and the next user DA type prediction model via Recurrent Neutral Networks (RNN). With these two prediction models, the current machine DA type decision problem is modeled as a multi-order POMDP, and transformed to be a one-order MDP with continuous states, which could be solved by Natural Actor Critic (NAC) algorithm. This general DA type decision model could be applied to multiple domains. After calculating the machine DA type, we design a slot parameter selection scheme to generate a complete machine DA according to the features of vertical domain, which yields the Multi-domain Corpus based Dialogue Management (MCDM) scheme. The advantages of this scheme are as follows.

- The MCDM scheme separates DA into DA type and slot parameter, where DA type is domain-independent. It utilizes multi-domain corpus to train a general DA type decision model that is applicable to every domain. Namely, it extracts general dialogue knowledge from all the domains and put it into vertical domain DM model. Even for some vertical domain with insufficient dialogue corpus, it could work well.

- The MCDM scheme encodes the dialogue historical information into history vector via RNN, and utilizes this history vector to estimate the distribution over possible current machine DA type and the distribution over possible next user DA. Theoretically, the history vector contains the whole dialogue history, even the information of utterances in the first turn.

- The MCDM scheme models the machine DA type decision problem as a POMDP, which makes a decision in the limitation of unreliable ASR and NLP, and achieves a tradeoff between dialogue popularity (frequency of dialogue pattern) and slot-filling efficiency.

- The MCDM scheme designs a slot parameter selection method for generated machine DA type, according to the features of vertical domain.

The rest of this paper is organized as follows. In Section 2, system model is introduced. Section 3 establishes the current machine DA type prediction model and the next user DA type prediction model via RNN, and Section 4 models the DA type decision problem as a POMDP. Section 5 describes slot selection scheme for the given DA type and slot filling process. Extensive experimental results are provided in Section 6 to illustrate the performance comparison, and Section 7 concludes this study.

2 System Model

Generally, the SDS operates as follows. Receiving user voice input, Natural Language Understanding (NLU) module transforms it into semantic representation such as DA. There are two steps in NLU: the first is Automatic Speech Recognition (ASR) that turns voice into text (Willie, 2004) (Vinyals, 2012); the second is Semantic Decoder (SD) that extracts DA from text (Hea, 2006) (Mairesse, 2009). NLU is hardly able to analyze the exact DA of user input due to inevitable ambiguity, uncertainty and errors in ASR and SD. Thus, the distribution of possible DAs is utilized to represent the result of NLU. According to this distribution and dialogue history, Dialogue Management (DM) module calculates the optimal output DA. Finally, Natural Language Generation (NLG) module transforms output DA into voice, including sentence generation that generates sentence based on DA (Mairesse, 2007) and Text To Speech (TTS) that turns sentence text into output voice (Clark, 2004) (Zen, 2007).

In this paper, we focus on DM in SDS for the slot-filling task. Firstly, we collect the dialogue corpus in multiple domains such as hotel reservation, flight ticket booking and shopping guidance. We label the dialogue corpus with DA set introduced in (Stolcke, 2000). This set includes 42 DA labels, which is wildly used and cited over 600

Hotel Reservation

U1: Do you have a room tonight?
U1_DA: YES-NO-QUESTION(room_quantity=1, checkin_time=tonight)

M1: Yes, we have. What kind of room type you prefer?
M1_DA: YES-ANSWERS() + WH-QUESTION(room_type)

U2: A double room.
U2_DA: STATEMENT(room_type=double room, room_quantity=1)

M2: OK. What is your checkout time?
M2_DA: ACKNOWLEDGE() + WH-QUESTION(checkout_time)

U3: ···
M3_DA: ···

Figure 1: an example of labeled dialogue

times in Google Scholar. Fig.1 is an example of labeled dialogue. Additionally, DA is divided into two parts: DA type and slot parameters. For example, for the DA "WH-QUESTION (room_type)", the DA type is "WH-QUESTION", and the slot parameter is "room_type". It is observed that DA type is domain-independent while slot parameter is domain-specific.

Based on these labeled dialogues, we design the multi-domain DM scheme, which could be divided into two steps:

- DA type decision: The dialogue historical information is encoded into history vector via RNN. Based on this vector, we estimate the possible current machine DA types and possible next user DA types, which will be introduced in section 3. With these DA type estimations, the DA type decision process is modeled as a POMDP, which will be introduced in section 4. This DA type decision model is applicable to every vertical domain.

- Slot parameter selection: After determining the DA type, the slot parameter selection scheme is designed according to the features of vertical domain, in order to generate a complete machine output DA.

3 RNN based Prediction Model

In this section, we introduce current machine DA type prediction model and next user DA type prediction model. (Nagata, 1994) utilizes N-gram Language Model to predict DA type. As quantity of DA type combination in historical epoches grows exponentially with the increment of N, the parameter N could not be too big, namely Bigram and Tri-gram are usually used. Thus, N-gram based DA type prediction model could not consider the dialogue historical information efficiently. In order to solve this problem, we utilize RNN to predict the DA type. The details of prediction model are as follows.

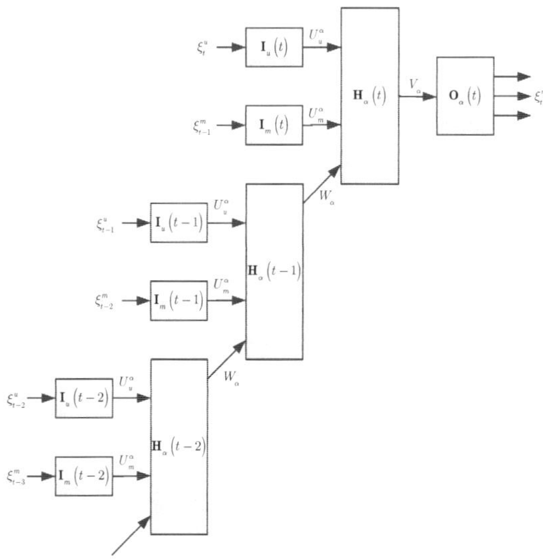

Figure 2: RNN for the current machine DA prediction

Firstly, the sentences in dialogue corpus are divided into two sets: sentence set spoken by machine (or service provider such as customer service representative in hotel reservation) and sentence set spoken by user (customer). We count the DA type combination in these two sets respectively, where the machine DA type combination set is denoted as $\mathscr{C}_m$ and the user DA type combination set is denoted as $\mathscr{C}_u$.

Secondly, we predict the probability distribution over current machine DA types. We denote the combination of DA type corresponding to user and machine sentences in t-th turn as ξ_t^m and ξ_t^u, where $\xi_t^m \in \mathscr{C}_m$ and $\xi_t^u \in \mathscr{C}_u$. The probability distribution over current machine DA types is determined by the current user DA type, the last machine DA type and the previous dialogue historical information, which is denoted as

$$\Pr\left\{\xi_t^m \left| \xi_t^u, \xi_{t-1}^m, \xi_{t-1}^u, \cdots, \xi_1^m, \xi_1^u \right.\right\} \quad (1)$$

We utilize RNN to estimate the conditional probability in equation (1). The architecture of this RNN is illustrated in Fig. 2. The inputs of RNN in the t-th turn are ξ_t^u and ξ_{t-1}^m. The input layers in this turn are one-hot representations (Turian, 2010) of ξ_t^u and ξ_{t-1}^m, denoted as $\mathbf{I}_u(t)$ and $\mathbf{I}_m(t)$. (The size of $\mathbf{I}_u(t)$ or $\mathbf{I}_m(t)$ is equivalent to $|\mathscr{C}_u|$

or $|\mathscr{C}_m|$. There is only one 1 in $\mathbf{I}_u(t)$ or $\mathbf{I}_m(t)$ corresponding to the ξ_t^u or ξ_{t-1}^m position, and other elements are zeros.) We denote hidden layer as $\mathbf{H}_\alpha(t)$ and output layer as $\mathbf{O}_\alpha(t)$. Thus, $\mathbf{O}_\alpha(t)$ is the probability distribution of current machine DA type combination, which could be calculated as (Mikolov, 2010)

$$\begin{aligned}\mathbf{H}_\alpha(t) = f\,(\mathbf{U}_u^\alpha \mathbf{I}_u(t) + \mathbf{U}_m^\alpha \mathbf{I}_m(t) \\ +\mathbf{W}_\alpha \mathbf{H}_\alpha(t-1))\end{aligned} \tag{2}$$

and

$$\mathbf{O}_\alpha(t) = g\,(\mathbf{V}_\alpha \mathbf{H}_\alpha(t)) \tag{3}$$

where $f(\cdot)$ is a sigmoid function, namely $f(x) = 1/(1+e^{-x})$ and $g(\cdot)$ is a soft-max function, namely $g(x_i) = e^{x_i} \Big/ \sum_{i=1}^{N_g} e^{x_i}$. The parameters of this RNN could be trained by the Back Propagation Through Time (BPTT) algorithm (Mikolov, 2012).

Thirdly, we predict the probability distribution over next user DA types based on the current machine DA type, the current user DA type and the previous dialogue historical information, which is denoted as

$$\Pr\left\{\xi_{t+1}^u \left| \xi_t^m, \xi_t^u, \xi_{t-1}^m, \xi_{t-1}^u, \cdots, \xi_1^m, \xi_1^u \right.\right\} \tag{4}$$

We also utilize the RNN with the same architecture mentioned above to predict this conditional probability, but inputs and outputs are different. The inputs in the t-th turn are ξ_t^m and ξ_t^u, and the output is the probability distribution of ξ_{t+1}^u, which is illustrated in Fig 3. The parameters of this RNN could be also trained by BPTT.

Besides, in different vertical domains, the pattern of DA type evolution might be different. For example, there might be a lot of question-answer exchanges in hotel reservation domain, because machine needs to collect a lot of information about reservation such as room type, check-in time and client name, and user also needs to inquire a lot of information about room and hotel such as room price and hotel address. While in other domains such as restaurant catering, the slots requested by machine are more than slots requested by user, which might lead to less question-answer exchanges. Thus, in order to solve this problem, when training some specific domain (target domain), we copy the dialogue corpus in the target domain repeatedly and control the size of target-domain corpus to be K_d times than the size of corpus in other domains, which increases the size of the corpus in the target domain and makes DA type prediction model fit for the features of the target domain.

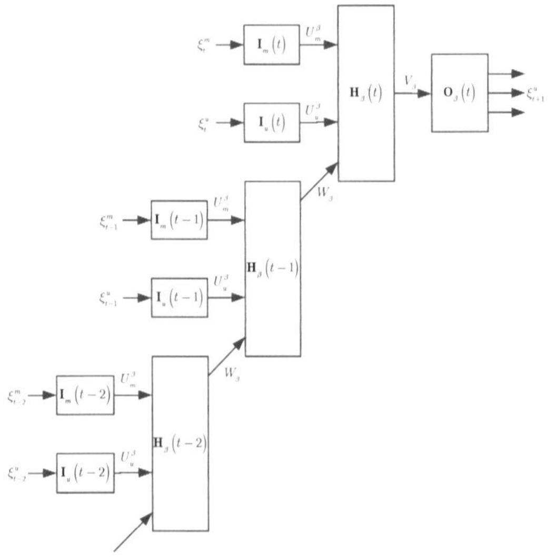

Figure 3: RNN for the next user DA prediction

4 Model DM as POMDP

In this section, we use POMDP (Littman, 2009) to model DM problem, illustrated in Fig.4. State is defined as the combination of user DA types in each turn, namely $s_t = \xi_t^u \in \mathscr{C}_u$. Action is defined as the combination of machine DA types in each turn, namely $a_t = \xi_t^m \in \mathscr{C}_m$. As the user DAs in $(t+1)$-th turn are not only determined by the user and machine DAs in t-th turn, but also related to the previous DAs, we define τ as a window size for this kind of relevance. Thus, the state transition probability could be represented as

$$\begin{aligned}&\Pr\{s_{t+1} | a_t, s_t, \cdots, a_1, s_1\} \\ &= \Pr\{s_{t+1} | a_t, s_t, \cdots, a_{t-\tau+1}, s_{t-\tau+1}\} \\ &= \Pr\left\{\xi_{t+1}^u \left| \xi_t^m, \xi_t^u, \cdots, \xi_{t-\tau+1}^m, \xi_{t-\tau+1}^u \right.\right\}\end{aligned} \tag{5}$$

This conditional probability could be estimated by RNN in section 3, which is denoted as π_{t+1}^u. Observation is defined as user input voice in each turn, denoted as $o_t \in \mathscr{O}$. As s_t could not be observed directly, o_t is utilized to estimate s_t, namely $\Pr\{s_t | o_t\}$, which could be obtained from ASR and SD and denoted as p_t^o. The reward function includes two parts: slot-filling efficiency and dialogue popularity, which is denoted as

$$\begin{aligned}r_t(s_t, a_t, s_{t+1}) = \lambda_1 F(s_t, a_t, s_{t+1}) \\ + \lambda_2 G(s_t, a_t, s_{t+1})\end{aligned} \tag{6}$$

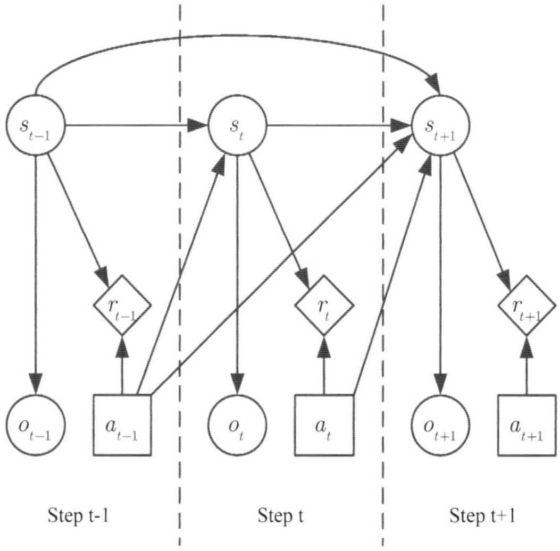

Figure 4: POMDP

where $F(\cdot)$ is a function mapping from the current user DA type, the current machine DA type and the next user DA type to the normalized quantity of filled slots that will be introduced in section 5, $G(\cdot)$ is the normalized quantity of sequence (s_t, a_t, s_{t+1}) that could be counted from dialogue corpus and represent dialogue popularity, λ_1 and λ_2 are the weights of slot filling reward and popularity reward, and $\lambda_1 + \lambda_2 = 1$. The policy is defined as a mapping from observation to action, which is denoted as $\zeta \in \mathscr{Z} : \mathscr{O} \to \mathscr{A}$. Thus, the DM problem is to find out the optimal policy to maximize the total expected discount reward, which is shown as

$$\begin{aligned} &\max_{\zeta \in \mathscr{Z}} E_\zeta \left[\sum_{t=1}^{T} \beta r_t(s_t, a_t, s_{t+1}) \right] \\ &s.t. \\ &\Pr\{s_{t+1} | a_t, s_t, \cdots, a_{t-\tau+1}, s_{t-\tau+1}\} = \pi^u_{t+1} \\ &\Pr\{s_t | o_t\} = p^o_t \end{aligned} \tag{7}$$

where β is a time discount factor. This problem is a τ order POMDP, which is difficult to slove directly. In the following, it will be transformed to be a MDP with continuous states.

We define belief state as $b_t \in \mathscr{B}$ to represent the distribution over possible states in the t-th turn, not only based on the current voice input, but also based on the dialogue history. The belief state updating process is the process of calculating b_{t+1} according to $\{b_t, b_{t-1}, \cdots, b_{t-\tau+1}\}$, which could be represented as

$$\begin{aligned} b_{t+1} = \kappa \cdot \Pr\{o_{t+1} | s_{t+1}\} \sum_{s_t} \cdots \sum_{s_{t-\tau+1}} \Pr\{s_{t+1} \\ | s_t, a_t, \cdots, s_{t-\tau+1}, a_{t-\tau+1}\} \prod_{i=t-\tau+1}^{t} b_i \end{aligned} \tag{8}$$

where κ is normalization constant. The deduction of this updating processing will be found in Appendix A. As user input voice is a continuous signal and different people have different habits of pronunciation and semantic representation, it is hard to estimate $\Pr\{o_{t+1} | s_{t+1}\}$ directly. Thus, according to Bayes Rules, $\Pr\{o_{t+1} | s_{t+1}\}$ could be shown as

$$\Pr\{o_{t+1} | s_{t+1}\} = \frac{\Pr\{s_{t+1} | o_{t+1}\} \Pr\{o_{t+1}\}}{\Pr\{s_{t+1}\}} \tag{9}$$

where $\Pr\{s_{t+1} | o_{t+1}\}$ could be estimated by ASR and SD, $\Pr\{s_{t+1}\}$ is prior distribution that could be counted in corpus, denoted as p^s_{t+1}, and $\Pr\{o_{t+1}\}$ is the same for different s_{t+1} that could be deleted. For belief state, the reward function could be redefined as

$$\begin{aligned} &r_t(b_t, a_t, \cdots, b_{t-\tau+1}, a_{t-\tau+1}) = \\ &\sum_{s_t} \cdots \sum_{s_{t-\tau+1}} \Big(r_t(s_t, a_t, s_{t+1}) \cdot \Pr\{s_{t+1} \\ &| s_t, a_t, \cdots, s_{t-\tau+1}, a_{t-\tau+1}\} \prod_{i=t-\tau+1}^{t} b_i + \\ &\Pr\{a_t | s_t, a_{t-1}, \cdots, s_{t-\tau+1}, a_{t-\tau}\} \prod_{i=t-\tau+1}^{t} b_i \Big) \end{aligned} \tag{10}$$

where the first part is the belief form of state reward and the second part is the expectation of the current machine DA type probability estimated by RNN in the section 3. We redefine the policy as a mapping from belief state to action, which is denoted as $\zeta' \in \mathscr{Z}' : \mathscr{B} \to \mathscr{A}$. Thus, the problem (7) could be reformulated as

$$\begin{aligned} &\max_{\zeta' \in \mathscr{Z}'} E_{\zeta'} \left[\sum_{t=1}^{T} \beta r_t(b_t, a_t, \cdots, b_{t-\tau+1}, a_{t-\tau+1}) \right] \\ &s.t. \\ &b_{t+1} = \kappa \cdot \frac{p^o_t}{p^s_{t+1}} \sum_{s_t} \cdots \sum_{s_{t-\tau+1}} \Pr\{s_{t+1} | s_t, a_t, \\ &\cdots, s_{t-\tau+1}, a_{t-\tau+1}\} \prod_{i=t-\tau+1}^{t} b_i, \\ &b_0 = p^o_0. \end{aligned} \tag{11}$$

This problem is a τ order MDP with continuous states, which will be transformed to be one order MDP.

We redefine new state as the sequence of belief state and action from the $(t-\tau+1)$-th turn to the t-th turn, which is denoted as $\bar{s}_t = \{b_t, a_{t-1}, b_{t-1}, \cdots, a_{t-\tau+1}, b_{t-\tau+1}\}$ and $\bar{s}_t \in \bar{\mathscr{S}}$. Thus, the state transition probability could be shown as

$$\begin{aligned}
&\Pr\{\bar{s}_{t+1} | \bar{s}_t, a_t\} \\
&= \Pr\{b_{t+1}, a_t, b_t, \cdots, a_{t-\tau+2}, b_{t-\tau+2} \\
&\quad | b_t, a_{t-1}, b_{t-1}, \cdots, a_{t-\tau+1}, b_{t-\tau+1}, a_t\} \\
&= \Pr\{b_{t+1}, | b_t, a_t, \cdots, b_{t-\tau+1}, a_{t-\tau+1}\}
\end{aligned} \tag{12}$$

which could be obtained from equation (8) and denoted as $\bar{\pi}_{\bar{s}_t, a_t}^{\bar{s}_{t+1}}$. The reward function could be rewritten as

$$\bar{r}_t(\bar{s}_t, a_t) = r_t(b_t, a_t, \cdots, b_{t-\tau+1}, a_{t-\tau+1}) \tag{13}$$

We redefine the policy as a mapping from new state to action, which is denoted as $\bar{\zeta} \in \bar{\mathscr{Z}} : \bar{\mathscr{S}} \to \mathscr{A}$. Thus, the problem (11) could be reformulated as

$$\begin{aligned}
&\max_{\bar{\zeta} \in \bar{\mathscr{Z}}} E_{\bar{\zeta}} \left[\sum_{t=1}^{T} \beta \bar{r}_t(\bar{s}_t, a_t) \right] \\
&s.t. \\
&\Pr\{\bar{s}_{t+1} | \bar{s}_t, a_t\} = \bar{\pi}_{\bar{s}_t, a_t}^{\bar{s}_{t+1}}
\end{aligned} \tag{14}$$

This problem is a one order MDP with continuous states, which could be solved by Natural Actor Critic algorithm (Peters, 2008) (Bhatnagar, 2009).

5 Slot Selection and Slot-filling

After determining the DA type of machine, the next step is selecting slot parameter for it to yield a complete output DA. Firstly, the parameters for DAs could be classified as follows.

- $\emptyset$: some DAs have no parameters, such as YES-ANSWERS ()
- $slot$: parameter of some DA is a slot, such as WH-QUESTION (room_type)
- $slot = value$: parameter of some DA is a slot value pair , such as STATEMENT (double_room_price= $100)

Additionally, The slots in human-machine dialogue could be divided into two categories, illustrated in Fig.5:

- Slots requested from machine to users, such as room_type, checkin_time, which is denote as $\mathscr{Q}_m$. The values of these slots are unknown for machine before the dialogue. In dialogue processing, we denote unfilled slots as $\mathscr{Q}_m^1$ and filled slots as $\mathscr{Q}_m^2$.
- Slots requested from users to machine, such as double_room_price, hotel_address, which is denote as $\mathscr{Q}_u$. The values of theses slot are known for machine before the dialogue.

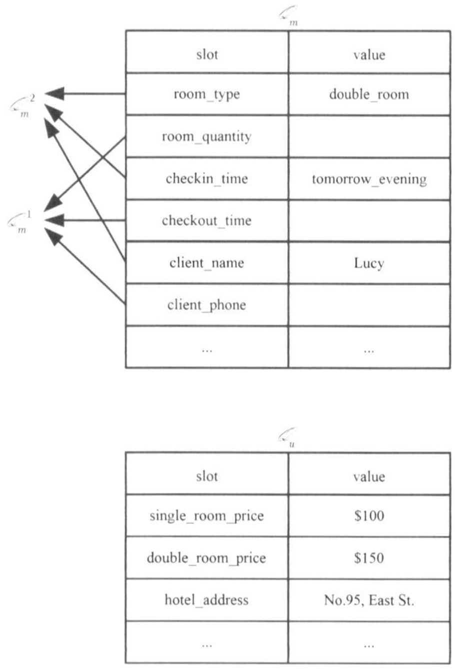

Figure 5: slot classification

The purpose of human-machine dialogue is to exchange these slot information. For example, in hotel reservation, machine is to request values of slots in $\mathscr{Q}_m$, while user is to request values of slots in $\mathscr{Q}_u$ in order to determine the values of slots in $\mathscr{Q}_m$ that user will inform to machine. Besides, it is obvious that $\mathscr{Q}_m^1$ is a set of slots, $\mathscr{Q}_m^2$ and $\mathscr{Q}_u$ are sets of slot value pairs.

Thus, there are three situations in the slot selection for a machine DA type

- If the parameter classification corresponding to the machine DA type is $\emptyset$, it is no need to select slot.
- If the parameter classification corresponding to the machine DA type is a slot, it is selected from $\mathscr{Q}_m^1$.
- If the parameter classification corresponding to the machine DA type is a slot value

pair, it is selected from $\mathscr{Q}_m^2$ and $\mathscr{Q}_u$. For example, for "STATEMENT", it is selected from $\mathscr{Q}_u$; for "DECLARATIVE YES-NO-QUESTION", it is selected from $\mathscr{Q}_m^2$.

In slot selection process, the orders of slots in $\mathscr{Q}_m^1$, $\mathscr{Q}_m^2$ and $\mathscr{Q}_u$ ought to be learned based on the dialogue corpus in vertical domain such as slot sequence in the task, slot dependency, slots that user request, domain expertise knowledge and so forth.

After obtaining a complete the machine, the last task is filling the slots according to the current DA and historical DA sequence. In this paper, we use handcrafted rules to fill the slots. For example, according to the DA sequence

user: STATEMENT (room_type = double room)
machine: DECLARATIVE YES-NO
-QUESTION (room_type = double room)
user: YES ANSWER ()
machine: ACKNOWLEDGE ()

The slot "room_type" is filled by the value "double room". This knowledge could be represented by the first order logic (Smullyan, 1995) as follow.

STATEMENT $(X = A) \wedge$ DECLARATIVE YES-NO-QUESTION $(X = A) \wedge$ YES ANSWER () $\wedge$ ACKNOWLEDGE () $\Rightarrow fill\,(X, A)$

6 Experimental Results

In this section, we compare the performance of the proposed DM schemes and the existing DM scheme. The DM scheme proposed in this paper is named as the RNN-MCDM scheme. In the N-Gram-MCDM scheme, the DA type is estimated by N-gram model, and other parts are the same as the RNN-MCDM scheme. In the existing scheme, the DM model in each domain is designed according to (Young et al., 2013), using the dialogue corpus in its own domain. Namely, for a given domain, the existing scheme does not utilize dialogue corpus in other domains.

The dialogue corpus for experiments covers five vertical domains, including hotel reservation (171 dialogues), shopping guidance (71 dialogues), banking service (64 dialogues), restaurant catering (46 dialogues), and taxi service (33 dialogues). Several slots are defined for each vertical domain. For example, in hotel reservation, the slots requested from machine to users include "room type", "room quantity", "client quantity", "checkin time", "checkout time", "breakfast demand"(yes or no), "breakfast type", "client name" and "client phone", while the slots requested from users to machine include "hotel address = No.95 East St.", "room type set = single room, double room, and deluxe room", "single room price = \$80", "double room price = \$100", "deluxe room price = \$150", "breakfast type set = Chinese breakfast, American breakfast, and Japanese breakfast", "Chinese breakfast price = \$12", "American breakfast price = \$15" and "Japanese breakfast price = \$10". Besides, we also define 8 slots for shopping guidance, 9 slots for banking service, 6 slots for restaurant catering and 4 slots for taxi service. The details of these slots are not described due to the limitation of pages. Besides, K_d is set to be 10.

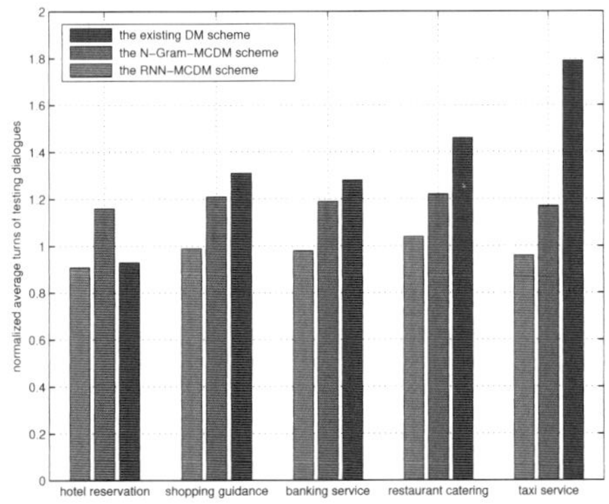

Figure 6: comparison of normalized average turn in different domains

The dialogues in corpus are divided into two parts: 70% corpus for training the DM model and 30% corpus for user simulation to test the systems. The simulated users are built via Bayesian Networks according to (Pietquin, 2005). There are two performance indices for SDS evaluation: average turn and success rate. Average turn is defined as the average dialogue turn cost for task completion. Generally, in different vertical domains, the dialogue turns are directly proportional to the quantities of slots. Thus, we define the normalized average turn as the ratio of average dialogue turn to slot number. In addition, success rate is defined as the ratio of the dialogues that complete the task in the threshold turns to all the dialogues. Here, we define the threshold as double of slot number.

Fig. 6 illustrates the normalized average turn in the RNN-MCDM scheme, the N-Gram-MCDM scheme and the existing DM scheme. The ver-

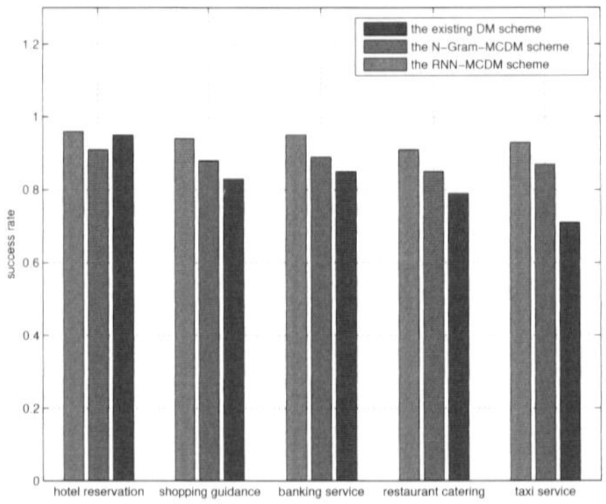

Figure 7: comparison of success rate in different domains

tical domains for comparison are hotel reservation, shopping guidance, banking service, restaurant catering and taxi service. From this picture, we have the following conclusions. For the existing DM scheme, in the vertical domain with more dialogue corpus it has lower normalized average turn, while it has higher normalized average turn in the vertical domain with less dialogue corpus. The reasons are as follows. The existing scheme only uses the dialogue corpus in one domain. Its trained DM model might not contain the abundant states if the size of dialogue corpus is small. Thus, when being in a unknown state, it could not calculate the optimal action, which might be detrimental to the efficiency of slot filling. However, the MCDM schemes have stable and better performance of normalized average turn, which should be ascribed to the fact that the proposed schemes train the general DM model based on the dialogue corpus in all the domains, and leaning general dialogue knowledge to guide the dialogue evolution. In addition, the N-Gram-MCDM scheme has lower normalized average turn than the existing scheme. Especially in the vertical domain with less dialogue corpus, performance improvement is more obvious. The reason is that the N-Gram-MCDM scheme could learn the general dialogue knowledge from all the domains, especially in the domain with less corpus it could use a part of other domain knowledge to train its optimal dialogue policy. Furthermore, the RNN-MCDM scheme has the lowest normalized average turn in every domain, because the RNN-MCDM scheme use RNN to learning history vector for DA prediction that takes the whole dialogue history into account. Namely, the RNN-MCDM scheme utilizes dialogue historical information more efficiently than the N-Gram-MCDM scheme, and RNN-based prediction model is smoother than N-Gram-based prediction model.

Fig. 7 compares the success rate among the RNN-MCDM scheme, the N-Gram-MCDM scheme and the existing DM scheme. From this picture, we can find out that the RNN-MCDM scheme has the highest success rate, and the success rate in the existing scheme is lower than the N-Gram-MCDM scheme, the gap become huge in the vertical domain with less dialogue corpus, which should be ascribed to the same reasons in Fig. 6.

7 Conclusion

In this paper, we proposed the DM scheme based on Multi-domain Corpus. In this scheme, DA is divided into DA type and slot parameter, where the former one is domain-independent and the latter one is domain-specific. We used RNN to estimate the probability distributions of next user DA type and current machine DA type with dialogue corpus in all the domains, and established a POMDP-based current machine DA type decision model that is applicable to all the vertical domains. Additionally, we designed a slot parameter selection scheme to generate a complete machine DA according to the features of vertical domain, which yields the MCDM scheme. Finally, extensive experimental results indicated that the proposed DM scheme is superior to the existing scheme.

Acknowledgments

This work is supported by the National Program on Key Basic Research Project (973 Program), basic theories and methods of Chinese Language Processing and Deep Computing in Internet environment, multi-lingual Automatic Speech Recognition for complex environments. (No. 2013CB329302)

Appendix A

In this section, we deduce the belief state updating process in equation (8). The belief state in the $(t+1)$-th turn could be represented as

$$b_{t+1} = \Pr\{s_{t+1} | o_{t+1}, b_t, a_t, \cdots, b_{t-\tau+1}, a_{t-\tau+1}\} \quad (15)$$

If we denote $b_t, a_t, \cdots, b_{t-\tau+1}, a_{t-\tau+1}$ as φ, b_{t+1} could be written as

$$b_{t+1} = \frac{\Pr\{s_{t+1}, o_{t+1}, \varphi\}}{\Pr\{o_{t+1}, \varphi\}}$$

$$= \frac{\Pr\{o_{t+1}|s_{t+1}, \varphi\}\Pr\{s_{t+1}|\varphi\}\Pr\{\varphi\}}{\Pr\{o_{t+1}|\varphi\}\Pr\{\varphi\}}$$

$$= \frac{\Pr\{o_{t+1}|s_{t+1}, \varphi\}\Pr\{s_{t+1}|\varphi\}}{\Pr\{o_{t+1}|\varphi\}} \quad (16)$$

According to (Thomson, 2009), $\Pr\{o_{t+1}|s_{t+1}, \varphi\} = \Pr\{o_{t+1}|s_{t+1}\}$. In addition, $\Pr\{s_{t+1}|\varphi\}$ could be shown as

$$\Pr\{s_{t+1}|\varphi\} = \sum_{s_t}\cdots\sum_{s_{t-\tau+1}}\Pr\{s_{t+1}|s_t, a_t, \cdots, s_{t-\tau+1}, a_{t-\tau+1}\}\Pr\{s_t, \cdots, s_{t-\tau+1}|\varphi\} \quad (17)$$

where

$$\Pr\{s_t, \cdots, s_{t-\tau+1}|\varphi\} = \prod_{i=t-\tau+1}^{t} b_i \quad (18)$$

Besides, $\Pr\{o_{t+1}|\varphi\}$ could be shown as

$$\Pr\{o_{t+1}|\varphi\} = \sum_{s_{t+1}}\Pr\{o_{t+1}|s_{t+1}\}\Pr\{s_{t+1}|\varphi\} \quad (19)$$

Accordingly,

$$b_{t+1} = \frac{\Pr\{o_{t+1}|s_{t+1}\}\Pr\{s_{t+1}|\varphi\}}{\sum_{s_{t+1}}\Pr\{o_{t+1}|s_{t+1}\}\Pr\{s_{t+1}|\varphi\}}$$

$$= \kappa \cdot \Pr\{o_{t+1}|s_{t+1}\}\sum_{s_t}\cdots\sum_{s_{t-\tau+1}}\Pr\{s_{t+1}|s_t, a_t, \cdots, s_{t-\tau+1}, a_{t-\tau+1}\}\prod_{i=t-\tau+1}^{t} b_i \quad (20)$$

where

$$\kappa = \frac{1}{\sum_{s_{t+1}}\Pr\{o_{t+1}|s_{t+1}\}\Pr\{s_{t+1}|\varphi\}} \quad (21)$$

is a normalization factor.

References

S. Bhatnagar, R. S. Sutton, M. Ghavamzadeh, M. Lee. 2009 Natural actorCcritic algorithms. *Automatica*, 45(11), 2471-2482, 2009.

R. A. Clark, K. Richmond, S. King. 2004 Festival 2-Build Your Own General Purpose Unit Selection Speech Synthesiser. *In Fifth ISCA Workshop on Speech Synthesis*, 2004.

L. Daubigney, M. Geist, S. Chandramohan, O. Pietquin. 2012. A Comprehensive Reinforcement Learning Framework for Dialogue Management Optimization. *IEEE Journal of Selected Topics in Signal Processing*, Vol. 6 No.8, pp: 891-902, 2012.

Annemiek van Drunen. 2012. Dialogue management and automation in interaction with unmanned systems. *Proceedings of the 2nd International Conference on Application and Theory of Automation in Command and Control System*, May 2012.

Emmanuel Ferreira, Fabrice Lefvre. 2013. Social signal and user adaptation in reinforcement learning-based dialogue management. *MLIS '13*, August 2013.

Kallirroi Georgila, Claire Nelson, David Traum. 2014. Single-Agent vs. Multi-Agent Techniques for Concurrent Reinforcement Learning of Negotiation Dialogue Policies. *The 52nd Annual Meeting of the Association for Computational Linguistics*, Jun, 2014.

Yulan Hea, Steve Young. 2006. Spoken language understanding using the Hidden Vector State Model. *Speech Communication*, Volume 48, Issues 3C4, Pages 262C275, 2006

M. L. Littman. 2009 A tutorial on partially observable Markov decision processes. *Journal of Mathematical Psychology*, 53(3), 119-125, 2009.

F. Mairesse, M. Gasic, F. Jurcicek, S. Keizer, B. Thomson, K. Yu, S. Young. 2009. Spoken language understanding from unaligned data using discriminative classificati.on models. *IEEE International Conference on Acoustics, Speech and Signal Processing*, 2009.

F. Mairesse, M. Walker. 2007 PERSONAGE: Personality generation for dialogue. *IEEE International Conference on Acoustics, Speech and Signal Processing*, 2007.

Michael F. Mctear. 2002. Spoken dialogue technology: enabling the conversational user interface. *ACM computing Survey*, volume 34, No. 1, pages: 90-169, 2002.

T. Mikolov. 2012 Statistical language models based on neural networks. *Presentation at Google, Mountain View*, 2012.

T. Mikolov, M. Karafit, L. Burget, J. Cernocky, S. Khudanpur. 2010 Recurrent neural network based language model. *11th Annual Conference of the International Speech Communication Association*, Sep, 2010.

Daniele Mori, Riccardo Berta, Alessandro De Gloria, Valentina Fiore, Lauto Magnani. 2013. An easy to author dialogue management system for serious games. *Journal on Computing and Cultural Heritage*, Vol.6 no.2 May 2013.

M. Nagata, T. Morimoto. 1994 First steps towards statistical modeling of dialogue to predict the speech act type of the next utterance. *Speech Communication*, 15(3), 193-203.

Reithinger Norbert, Elisabeth Maier. 1995 Utilizing statistical dialogue act processing in verbmobil. *Proceedings of ACL*, Jun, 1995.

J. Peters, S. Schaal. 2008 Natural actor-critic. *Neurocomputinge*, 71(7), 1180-1190, 2008.

O. Pietquin and T. Dutoit. 2005 A probabilistic framework for dialog simulation and optimal strategy learning. *IEEE Transactions on Speech and Audio Processing*, Special Issue on Data Mining of Speech, Audio and Dialog, 2005.

Olivier Pietquin, Matthieu Geist, Senthilkumar Chandramohan, Herv Frezza-Buet. 2011. Sample-efficient batch reinforcement learning for dialogue management optimization. *ACM Transactions on Speech and Language Processing*, Vol. 7 No. 3, May 2011.

R. M. Smullyan. 1995 First-order logic. *Courier Corporation*, 1995

A. Stolcke, K. Ries, N. Coccaro, E. Shriberg, R. Bates, D. Jurafsky. 2000 Dialogue act modeling for automatic tagging and recognition of conversational speech. *Computational linguistics*, 26(3), 339-373.

Hao Tang, S. Watanabe, T.K. Marks, J.R. Hershey. 2014. Log-linear dialog manager. *2014 IEEE International Conference on Acoustics, Speech and Signal Processing (ICASSP)*, pp: 4092 C 4096, May 2014.

B. Thomson. 2009 Statistical methods for spoken dialogue management. *Ph.D. dissertation, Cambridge*, 2009.

B. Thomson and S. Young. 2010. Bayesian update of dialogue state: A POMDP framework for spoken dialogue systems. *Comput. Speech Lang*, vol. 24, no. 4, pp. 562C588, 2010.

J. Turian, L. Ratinov, Y. Bengio. 2010 Word representations: a simple and general method for semi-supervised learning. *In Proceedings of the 48th annual meeting of the association for computational linguistics*, Jul, 2010.

O. Vinyals, S.V. Ravuri, D. Povey. 2012. Revisiting Recurrent Neural Networks for robust ASR. *2012 IEEE International Conference on Acoustics, Speech and Signal Processing (ICASSP)*, 2012.

Willie Walker, Paul Lamere, Philip Kwok. 2004. Sphinx-4: a flexible open source framework for speech recognition. *Technical Report, Sun Microsystems*

S. Young, M. Gasic, B. Thomson, J. D. Williams. (2013). 2013. Pomdp-based statistical spoken dialog systems: A review. *Proceedings of the IEEE*, 101(5), pages: 1160-1179, 2013.

Xiaobu Yuan, Guoying Liu. 2012. A task ontology model for domain independent dialogue management. *IEEE International Conference on Virtual Environments Human-Computer Interfaces and Measurement Systems*, 2012.

H. Zen, T. Nose, J. Yamagishi, S. Sako, T. Masuko, A. W. Black, K. Tokuda. 2007 The HMM-based speech synthesis system version 2.0. *In Proc. 6th ISCA Workshop on Speech Synthesis*, Aug, 2007.

Quality-adaptive Spoken Dialogue Initiative Selection And Implications On Reward Modelling

Stefan Ultes, Matthias Kraus, Alexander Schmitt, and Wolfgang Minker
Ulm University
Albert-Einstein-Allee 43
89081 Ulm, Germany
{fistname.lastname}@uni-ulm.de

Abstract

Adapting Spoken Dialogue Systems to the user is supposed to result in more efficient and successful dialogues. In this work, we present an evaluation of a quality-adaptive strategy with a user simulator adapting the dialogue initiative dynamically during the ongoing interaction and show that it outperforms conventional non-adaptive strategies and a random strategy. Furthermore, we indicate a correlation between Interaction Quality and dialogue completion rate, task success rate, and average dialogue length. Finally, we analyze the correlation between task success and interaction quality in more detail identifying the usefulness of interaction quality for modelling the reward of reinforcement learning strategy optimization.

1 Introduction

Maximizing task success in task-oriented dialogue systems has always been a central claim of Spoken Dialogue (SDS) research. Today, commercial systems are still inflexible and do not adapt to users or the dialogue flow. This usually results in bad performance and in frequently unsuccessful dialogues. In recent years, adaptation strategies have been investigated for rendering SDS more flexible and robust. The aim of those strategies is to adapt the dialogue flow based on observations that are made during an ongoing dialogue.

One approach to observe and score the interaction between the system and the user is the Interaction Quality (IQ) (Schmitt and Ultes, 2015) originally presented by Schmitt et al. (2011). Their Interaction Quality paradigm is one of the first metrics which can be used for this purpose. A pilot user study on adapting the dialogue to the Interaction Quality by Ultes et al. (2014b) in a limited domain has already shown encouraging results. There, similar dialogue performance was achieved for both the strategy adapting the grounding mechanism to Interaction Quality and the strategy of always applying implicit confirmation prompts previously known to achieve best user feedback.

While the previous experiment showed encouraging results for adapting the grounding strategy, it is unclear if other aspects of a dialogue strategy may also be positively affected. Hence, in this contribution, we investigate if applying rules for adapting the dialogue initiative to IQ may also result in an increase in IQ and if other metrics like task success rate or dialogue completion rate may correlate[1].

To investigate this, we have designed a basic experiment having an IQ-adaptive dialogue strategy adapting the dialogue initiative. Depending on the IQ score, the system chooses between user-initiative, system-initiative and mixed-initiative. Moreover, the performance of four additional strategies is analyzed regarding a correlation between IQ and other performance measures.

Besides the interest in the general performance of the quality-adaptive strategy, we are specifically interested whether implications may be drawn from the experiments about the usage of IQ in a reinforcement learning setting for modelling the reward function.

The outline of the paper is as follows: in Section 2, we present significant related work on adaptive dialogue and quality metrics including the Interaction Quality (IQ) paradigm, a more abstract form of user satisfaction. All five dialogue strategies are described in detail in Section 3. The experimental setup including the test system in the the "Let's Go" domain is presented in Section 4

[1] Automatic optimization aims at maximizing a reward function. If IQ was contributing positively to this reward function, optimisation would naturally result in an increase in IQ. As we do not perform optimization, this correlation does not automatically exist

Proceedings of the SIGDIAL 2015 Conference, pages 374–383,
Prague, Czech Republic, 2-4 September 2015.

followed by a thorough presentation of the experimental results based on dialogues with the user simulator. Based on the experiments' results, inferences are drawn on using IQ for reward modelling. Finally, we conclude and outline future work in Section 6.

2 Significant Related Work

The field of adaptive dialogue spans over many different types of adaptation. While some systems adapt to their environment (e.g., (Heinroth et al., 2010)), the focus of this work lies on systems that adapt to the user and the characteristics of the interaction. More specifically, an emphasis is placed on dynamic adaptation to the user during the ongoing dialogue.

2.1 User-Adaptive Dialogue

A very prominent work closely related to the topic of this contribution has been presented by Litman and Pan (2002). They identify problematic situations in dialogues by analyzing the performance of the speech recognizer (ASR) and use this information to adapt the dialogue strategy. Each dialogue starts off with a user initiated strategy without confirmations. Depending on the ASR performance, a system-directed strategy with explicit confirmations may eventually be employed. Applied to TOOT, a system for getting information about train schedules, the authors achieved significant improvement in task success compared to a non-adaptive system. While Litman and Pan adapt to the ASR performance as indicator for problematic dialogues (being a system property representing an objective adaptation criterion), the user is put into the focus of adaptation in this work by using an abstract form of user satisfaction hence applying a subjective criterion.

Further work on user-adaptive dialogue has been presented by Gnjatović and Rösner (2008) adapting to the user's emotional state and by Nothdurft et al. (2012) adapting to the user knowledge. For both, only simulated or predefined user states are used while this work uses a real estimation module deriving the user satisfaction.

Using user ratings to improve the dialogue performance in a reinforcement learning (RL) approach has been presented by Walker (2000), Rieser and Lemon (2008), Janarthanam and Lemon (2008), and Gašić et al. (2013). Walker applied RL to a MDP-based dialogue system ELVIS for accessing emails over the phone. They modeled the reward function using the PARADISE framework (Walker et al., 1997) showing that the resulting policy improved the system performance in terms of user satisfaction significantly. The resulting best policy showed, among other aspects, that the system-initiative strategy was found to work best. The group of Lemon also employed PARADISE for modelling the reward function. Using reinforcement learning, they found an optimal dialogue strategy for result presentation (Rieser and Lemon, 2008) or referring expressions (Janarthanam and Lemon, 2008) for natural language generation.

For a POMDP-based dialogue manager, Gašić et al. use a reward function based on user ratings to train the optimized policy. The user ratings are acquired using Amazon Mechanical Turk. They show that their approach converges much faster than conventional approaches using a user simulator. However, their approach does not allow for adapting the course of the dialogue online but relies on a pre-optimized dialogue strategy.

Finally, not directly providing user adaptivity but allowing for reacting to specific dialogue situations in a rule-based manner is VoiceXML (Oshry et al., 2007). By counting the number of "reprompts" or "nomatches", a suitable strategy may be selected. While these parameters are also part of the Interaction Quality used for adaptation within this work, the Interaction Quality captures more complex effects than the simple rules of VoiceXML. These effects may not be modeled easily using rules (Ultes and Minker, 2013).

2.2 Interaction Quality

While there is numerous work on investigating turn-wise quality ratings for SDSs, e.g., Engelbrecht et al. (2009), Higashinaka et al. (2010) and Hara et al. (2010), the Interaction Quality paradigm by Schmitt et al. (2011) seems to be the only metric fulfilling the requirements for adapting the dialogue online (Ultes et al., 2012).

For rendering an SDS adaptive to the user's satisfaction level, a module is needed to automatically derive the satisfaction from the ongoing interaction. For creating this module, usually, dialogues have to be annotated with ratings describing the user's satisfaction level. Schmitt et al. (2015) proposed a measure called "Interaction Quality" (IQ) which fulfills the requirements of a

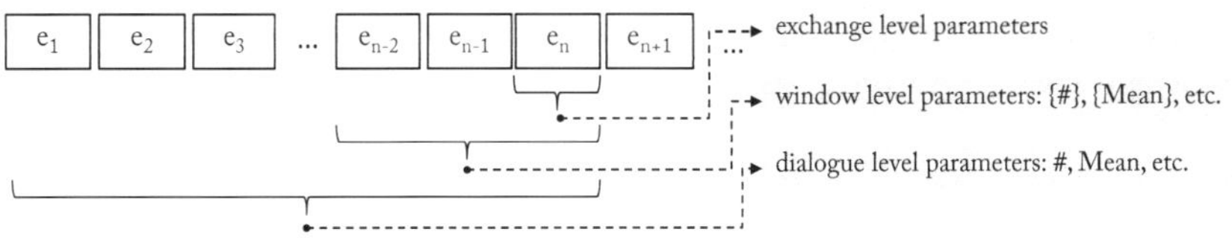

Figure 1: The three different modeling levels representing the interaction at exchange e_n: The most detailed exchange level, comprising parameters of the current exchange; the window level, capturing important parameters from the previous n dialogue steps (here $n = 3$); the dialogue level, measuring overall performance values from the entire previous interaction.

quality metric for adaptive dialogue identified by Ultes et al. (2012). For Schmitt et al., the main aspect of user satisfaction is that it is assigned by real users. However, this seems to be impractical in many real world scenarios. Hence, the usage of expert raters is proposed. Further studies have also shown a high correlation between quality ratings applied by experts and users (Ultes et al., 2013).

The IQ paradigm is based on automatically deriving interaction parameters from the SDS and feed these parameters into a statistical classification module which predicts the IQ level of the ongoing interaction at the current system-user-exchange [2]. The interaction parameters are rendered on three levels (see Figure 1): the exchange level, the window level, and the dialogue level. The exchange level comprises parameters derived from SDS modules Automatic Speech Recognizer, Spoken Language Understanding, and Dialogue Management directly. Parameters on the window and the dialogue level are sums, means, frequencies or counts of exchange level parameters. While dialogue level parameters are computed out of all exchanges up to the current exchange, window level parameters are only computed out of the last three exchanges.

These interaction parameters are used as input variables to a statistical classification module. The statistical model is trained based on annotated dialogues of the Lets Go Bus Information System in Pittsburgh, USA (Raux et al., 2006). Each of the 4,885 exchanges (200 calls) has been annotated by three different raters resulting in a rating agreement of $\kappa = 0.54$. The final IQ value of the three raters is derived using the median. Furthermore, the raters had to follow labeling guidelines to enable a consistent labeling process (Schmitt et al., 2012). Schmitt et al. (2011) estimated IQ with a Support Vector Machine using only automatically derivable parameters achieving an unweighted average recall of 0.59.

[2]A system turn followed by an user turn

3 Quality-Adaptive Dialogue

Within this section, we describe one part of the main contribution of rendering the dialogue initiative adaptive to Interaction Quality and compare the resulting strategy to several non-adaptive strategies. Conventional dialogue initiative categories are *user initiative*, *system initiative*, and *mixed initiative* (McTear, 2004). As there are different interpretations of what these initiative categories mean, we stick to the understanding of initiative as used by Litman and Pan (2002): the initiative influences the openness of the system question and the set of allowed user responses. The latter is realized by defining which slot values provided by the user are processed by the system and which are discarded. Hence, for *user initiative*, the system asks an open question allowing the user to respond with information for any slot. For *mixed initiative*, the system poses a question directly addressing a slot. However, the user may still provide information for any slot. This is in contrast to the *system initiative*, where the user may only respond with the slot addressed by the system. For instance, if the system asks for the arrival place and the user responds with a destination place, this information may either be used (*mixed initiative*) or discarded (*system initiative*).

In this work, five different strategies are created. Three basic non-adaptive strategies are compared against one adaptive and one random adaptive strategy. All of these strategies can be generated from the flow diagram in Figure 2 by varying the IQ value. The non-adaptive *user*, *system*, and *mixed initiative strategy* are well known concepts and will not further be described. In order to keep the strategies comparable, all have a similar structure: in each strategy, the system starts with

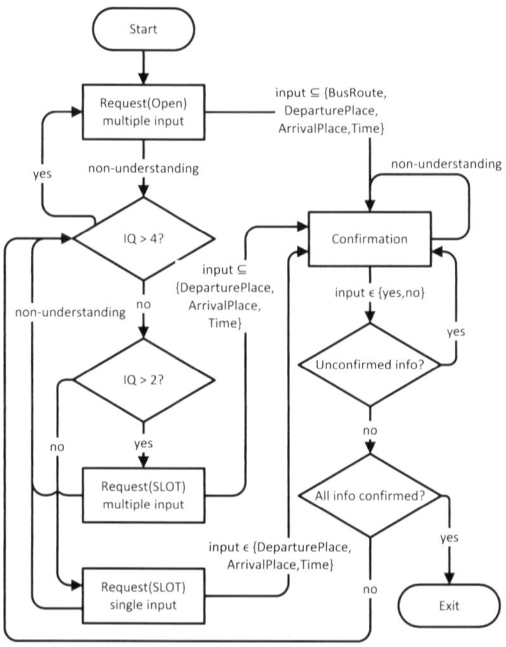

Figure 2: The flow chart describing the adaptive and non-adaptive strategies. For the adaptive strategy, the course of the dialogue as well as the allowed user input are influenced by the IQ value. For the random strategy, the IQ values are generated randomly. The non-adaptive strategies are realized by fixed IQ values: $IQ = 5$ for the user initiative strategy always posing open requests, $IQ = 3$ and $IQ = 1$ for mixed and system initiative explicitly requesting slot information. Provision of the bus route was not mandatory.

an open request allowing the user to respond with information for all slots. The system first continues with confirming provided information before continuing strategy-specific.

For adapting the initiative based on IQ, the *adaptive strategy* utilizes the basic concepts of the non-adaptive strategies, i.e., the pairs of system question and its restriction on the user input. Hence, the way missing information is requested depends on the Interaction Quality. For an IQ value of five, an open request is placed. For an IQ value greater than two, information for all missing slots is allowed as user input (same behavior as in the mixed initiative strategy) while only the requested information is allowed otherwise. If unconfirmed slot information is present, the strategy decides to first initialize grounding before other missing information is requested. If the user provides information for an already confirmed slot, this information is discarded. The same behavior is implemented into the *user* and *mixed* initiative strategies. Note that the thresholds between the different adaptation levels have been defined arbitrarily based on human judgement. An example dialogue is depicted in Figure 3.

System:	*Request(Open)*	
User:	Non-understanding	$IQ = 5$
System:	*Request(Open)*	
User:	Inform(Travel Time: 8pm)	$IQ = 5$
System:	*Confirm(Travel Time: 8pm)*	
User:	Deny	$IQ = 3$
System:	*Request(Departure place)*	
User:	Inform(Travel Time: now)	$IQ = 3$
System:	*Confirm(Travel Time: now)*	
User:	...	

Figure 3: Example dialogue of the adaptive strategy. As the IQ value is 5 in the beginning, the system requests openly for information. After the IQ value has dropped to 3, the mixed initiative is active. Hence, the system asks for specific information directly still allowing input for other slots.

The *random strategy* uses the same dialogue definition as the adaptive strategy. However, the initiative is selected randomly.

The dialogues of all strategies continue until all mandatory slots contain a confirmed value or the user terminates the interaction. If the user responds with information about a slot which is not in the set of allowed slot information, these values are discarded. This may lead to a 'Non-Understanding' (or 'out-of-grammar' user input) even though the user has provided information.

4 Experiments and Results

Evaluation of the dialogue strategies presented in Section 3 is performed using an adaptive dialogue system interacting with a user simulator. A user simulator offers an easy and cost-effective way for getting a basic impression about the performance of the designed dialogue strategies. Furthermore, we describe the setup of the experiments followed by a discussion of the results.

4.1 Let's Go Domain

For evaluating the adaptive strategies, we use the Let's Go Domain as it represents a domain of suitable complexity. The Let's Go Bus Information System (Raux et al., 2006) is a live system in Pittsburgh, USA providing bus schedule information to the user. The Let's Go User Simulator (LGUS) by Lee and Eskenazi (2012) is used for evaluation to replace the need for human evaluators.

The dialogue goal of Let's Go consists of four slots: bus number, departure place, arrival place, and travel time. However, the bus number is not mandatory. The original system contains more than 300,000 arrival or departure places, respectively. To acquire information about the specific goal of the user, the system may use one out of nine system actions to which the user responds with a subset of six user actions. In LGUS, the user actions are accompanied with a confidence score simulating automatic speech recognition performance. The system action is either requesting for information or explicitly confirming previously shared information. Hence, the user may either provide information about a certain slot or affirm or deny a slot value.

Any combination of the user actions is possible—even having contradicting information present, e.g., informing about two different values of the same slot or affirming and denying a value at the same time. As problems with the speech recognition and language understanding modules are also modeled by LGUS, these effects are reflected by the user action 'Non-Understanding'.

4.2 Experimental Setup

In order to evaluate the dialogue strategies, we use the adaptive dialogue manager OwlSpeak (Ultes and Minker, 2014), originally created by Heinroth et al. (2010), extended for including quality-adaptivity (Ultes et al., 2014a). OwlSpeak is based on the Model-View-Presenter paradigm separating the dialogue description and dialogue state in the model from the dialogue control logic in the presenter. Originally, the interface to a voice browser using VoiceXML (Oshry et al., 2007) is embedded in the view. For this work, the view has been replaced in order to provide an interface to LGUS which is instantiated as a server application communicating to other modules using JSON (Crockford, 2006). Furthermore, the system has been extended to handle multi-slot user input.

For rendering the system adaptive, Ultes et al. (2014a) included an interaction estimation module into the system. It is based on the Support Vector Machine (SVM (Vapnik, 1995)) implementation LibSVM (Chang and Lin, 2011) using a linear kernel. Interaction with real users requires a more complex system than an interaction with a simulated user. Thus, some SDS modules are missing and not all parameters of the IQ paradigm are available. This results in a feature set of only 16 parameters[3]. The trained model achieves an unweighted average recall[4] of 0.56[5] on the training data using 10-fold cross-validation which is a considerably good performance. All exchanges of the LEGO corpus (Schmitt et al., 2012) have been used for training.

Evaluation of the dialogue strategies is performed by creating 5,000 simulated dialogues for each strategy. Like Raux et al. (2006), short dialogues ($\leq$ 5 exchanges[6]) which are considered "not [to] be genuine attempts at using the system" are excluded from all statistics in this paper.

Three objective metrics are used to evaluate the dialogue performance: the average dialogue length (ADL), the dialogue completion rate (DCR) and task success rate (TSR). The ADL is modeled by the average number of exchanges per completed dialogue. A dialogue is regarded as being completed if the system provides a result—whether correct or not—to the user. Hence, DCR represents the ratio of dialogues for which the system was able to provide a result, i.e., provide schedule information:

$$DCR = \frac{\#completed}{\#all} .$$

TSR is the ratio of completed dialogues where the user goal matches the information the system acquired during the interaction:

$$TSR = \frac{\#correctResult}{\#completed} .$$

Here, only destination place, arrival place, and travel time are considered as the bus number is not a mandatory slot and hence not necessary for providing information to the user.

As a correlation between objective measures and IQ is investigated, the average IQ value (AIQ) is calculated for each strategy based on the IQ

[3]The parameters applied are ASRRecognitionStatus, ASRConfidence, RePrompt?, #Exchanges, ActivityType, Confirmation?, MeanASRConfidence, #ASRSuccess, %ASRSuccess, #ASRRejections, %ASRRejections, {Mean}ASRConfidence, {#}ASRSuccess, {#}ASRRejections, {#}RePrompts, {#}SystemQuestions.

[4]The arithemtic average over all class-wise recalls.

[5]Comparable to the best-know approaches.

[6]The minimum number of exchanges to successfully complete the dialogue is 5.

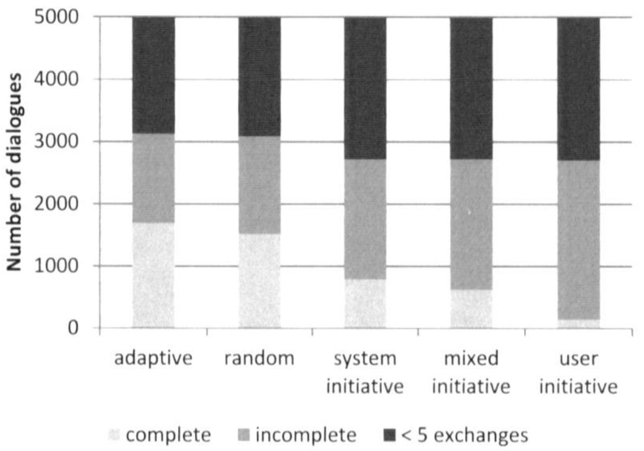

Figure 4: The ratio of omitted dialogues due to their length (< 5 exchanges), the completed dialogues (complete), and the dialogues which have been aborted by the user (incomplete) with respect to the dialogue strategy. While the amount of short dialogues is similar for each strategy, the number of completed dialogues varies strongly.

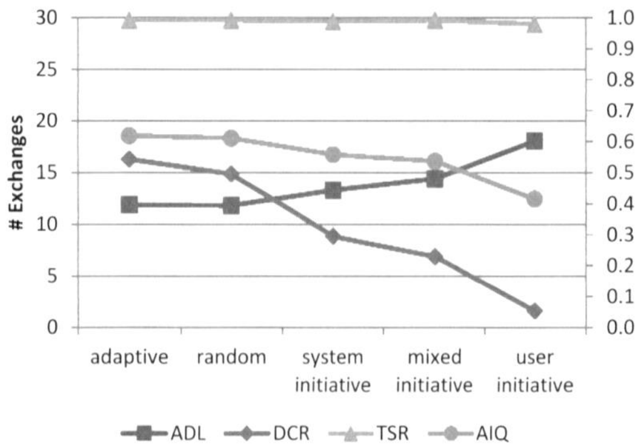

Figure 5: The average dialogue length (ADL), task success rate (TSR), the dialogue completion rate (DCR), and the average Interaction Quality (AIQ) for all for dialogue strategies. With decreasing DCR, also AIQ decreases and ADL increases. (AIQ values are normalized to the interval [0–1].)

value of the last exchange of each dialogue. Furthermore, this measure is also used to investigate if adapting the course of the dialogue to IQ also results in higher IQ values.

4.3 Experimental Results

Figure 4 shows the ratio of complete, incomplete, and omitted dialogues for each strategy with respect to the total 5,000 dialogues. As can be seen, about the same ratio of dialogues is omitted due to being too short. The DCR clearly varies more strongly for the five strategies.

The results for DCR, TSR, ADL, and AIQ are presented in Table 1 and Figure 5. TSR is almost the same for all strategies, meaning that, if a dialogue completes, the system almost always found the correct user goal. DCR, ADL and AIQ on the other hand vary strongly. They strongly correlate with a Pearson's correlation of $\rho = -0.953$ ($\alpha < 0.05$) for DCR and ADL, $\rho = 0.960$ ($\alpha < 0.01$) for DCR and AIQ, and $\rho = -.997$ ($\alpha < 0.01$) for ADL and AIQ. This shows that by improving IQ, being a subjective measure, an increase in objective measures may be expected.

Comparing the performance of the adaptive strategy to the three non-adaptive strategy clearly shows that the adaptive strategy performs significantly best for all metrics. With a DCR of of 54.27%, the performance is comparable to the rate achieved on the training data of LGUS (cf. (Lee and Eskenazi, 2012)). The non-adaptive strategies achieve a much lower DCR having the system initiative strategy as second best with only 29.48%. This performance goes together with shorter dialogues shown by the ADL. Furthermore, the results for DCR clearly show that the user initiative strategy is unusable. Thus, this strategy will not be analyzed any further.

Furthermore, it is of interest if better objective performance also results in better IQ values for the complete dialogue. This is especially important since it is imperative for the relevance of the Interaction Quality. Adapting to IQ to improve the dialogue must also result in an increase of the IQ value. This effect has been validated by these experiments. The adaptive strategy has a significant higher average IQ (AIQ) value calculated from the IQ value for the whole dialogues, i.e., the IQ value of the last system-user-exchange, than all other non-adaptive strategies.

The question remains if adapting to IQ is the actual reason for the improvement. Maybe, the user simulated with LGUS only "likes" diversified initiative prompts better which is represented by the random strategy. While this statement is true to some extent (see ADL), reasonably adapting to IQ further improves the system performance significantly as shown by DCR and AIQ.

5 Reward Modelling with Interaction Quality

The presented results clearly show that AIQ and DCR are correlated. As almost all completed di-

Strategy	DCR	TSR	ADL	AIQ
adaptive	54.27%	99.18%	11.86	3.47**
random	49.53%	99.22%	11.82**	3.44**
system initiative	29.48%	98.75%	13.30*	3.23
mixed initiative	22.91%	99.20%	14.40*	3.15**
user initiative	5.32%	97.92%	18.04	2.66

Table 1: The results of the experiments for the five strategies given by dialogue completion rate (DCR), task success rate (TSR), average dialogue length (ADL) and average Interaction Quality (AIQ) rating the complete interaction for all completed dialogues. All results for DCR and TSR are significantly different (chi-squared test). Significant differences in ADL (unpaired t-test) and AIQ (Mann-Whitney U test) with the respective column below are marked with ** for the level of $\alpha < 0.01$ and with * for $\alpha < 0.05$. All other comparisons between non-neighbors are significant with $\alpha < 0.01$

alogues were also successful, a correlation between AIQ and task success may also be assumed. In this section, we investigate if this correlation may be exploited for modelling the reward function for reinforcement learning approaches to dialogue management. This would be very beneficial, as for state-of-the-art reinforcement learning approaches to dialogue management, e.g., (Lemon and Pietquin, 2012; Young et al., 2013), a positive or negative reward is added at the end of each dialogue depending on the successful achievement of the task. However, to do this, usually, the true user goal has to be know. This is either possible by asking the user or by using a user simulator for training. Here, Gašić et al. have shown that optimizing the strategy with real user dialogues yields better strategies than using a user simulator. However, asking the user to provide whether they consider the dialogue to be successful is time consuming and interruptive thus only possible in artificial lab settings. If there was a metric which allowed to automatically detect successful, or, more generally, good dialogues, this metric would be very useful for the described situation yielding the opportunity to optimize on real dialogues without disrupting the users.

Therefore, the correlation of the final IQ value and task success is analyzed. Based on all strategies, the dialogues are evaluated regarding the success rate with respect to the final IQ value and the dialogue length. An example for dialogue lengths

DL	IQ	success	failure	# dialogues
9	1	0.0%	100.0%	487
	2	0.0%	100.0%	40
	3	37.2%	62.9%	253
	4	93.8%	6.3%	512
	5	0.0%	100.0%	2
10	1	0.0%	100.0%	452
	2	0.0%	100.0%	38
	3	42.4%	57.6%	172
	4	96.6%	3.5%	406
	5	0.0%	100.0%	3
11	1	0.0%	100.0%	405
	2	2.9%	97.1%	35
	3	47.8%	52.3%	178
	4	84.0%	16.0%	100
	5	-	-	0
12	1	0.3%	99.7%	329
	2	23.1%	76.9%	52
	3	78.5%	21.6%	297
	4	96.3%	3.7%	270
	5	0.0%	100.0%	1

Table 2: Example of the task success rate with respect to IQ and the dialogue length (DL). Disregarding rows with less then 15 dialogues, there is clearly a trend for higher task success rates if the IQ value increases as well.

of 9–12 is depicted in Table 2. To compute those, again, dialogues with less than five exchanges are excluded. Clearly, a trend can be identified for higher task success rates when having a high final IQ for all dialogue lengths[7].

Based on this finding, an IQ threshold may be defined which separates dialogues regarded as being successful and dialogues regarded as being not successful. For a threshold of four, for example, all dialogues with a final IQ of five and four may be regarded as successful while all other dialogues are regarded as failure. However, not all dialogues above the threshold are necessarily actually successful and not all dialogues below the threshold are necessarily actually unsuccessful. Hence, to find a good threshold, the precision—representing this relationship—is calculated for both success and failure dialogues for different thresholds. The results are depicted in Table 3.

The best overall threshold indicated by a maximum unweighted average precision[8] (UAP) is four achieving a precision of 0.863 for success and of 0.826 for failure. While a threshold of four is also

[7]Rows with less than 15 dialogues are disregarded as sufficient data is needed to compute reasonable task success rates.

[8]The arithmetic average over all class-wise precisions.

Success IQ ≥	Precision Success	Failure	UAP
5	0.448	0.669	0.559
4	0.863	0.826	0.845
3	0.652	0.888	0.770
2	0.646	0.995	0.820
1	0.331	-	0.166

Table 3: The precision of success and failure dialogues (along with the unweighted average precision (UAP)) when setting all dialogue with final IQ greater or equal a given IQ value to be successful and the remainder to be a failure.

Success IQ ≥	Recall Success	Failure	UAR
5	0.008	0.995	0.502
4	0.595	0.953	0.774
3	0.798	0.789	0.794
2	0.992	0.730	0.861
1	1.000	-	0.500

Table 4: The recall of success and failure dialogues (along with the unweighted average recall (UAR)) when setting all dialogue with final IQ greater or equal a given IQ value to be successful and the remainder to be a failure.

the best threshold for success, the highest precision for failure is a threshold of two, i.e., regarding all dialogues as being a failure with a final IQ of one. Hence, to further maximize UAP, two thresholds may be defined: four for success and two for failure. This results in an UAP of 0.929 not regarding all dialogues with a final IQ of two or three.

Defining a threshold based on precision yields the downside that some actually successful dialogues are regarded as failure and vice versa. In fact, defining a threshold of four results in a recall—representing the percentage of dialogues being regarded as successful out of all truly successful dialogues—of 0.595 as shown in Table 4. This means that more than 40% of all truely successful dialogues are regarded as failure which is not ideal. Additionally, a recall of 0.953 for failure means that less than 5% of all truely failing dialogues are regarded as success. However, using the two thresholds defined above results in better rates. Still, 4.7% of all failing dialogues are regared as success. However, only 0.8% of all successful dialogues are regarded as failure which is much better. Having two thresholds, though, results in the need for more training dialogues as all dialogues between the two thresholds are obmitted: only 64% of all dialogues are used for training resulting in the need for 56% more dialogues for training.

6 Conclusion and Future Work

The contribution of this work is two-fold: first, we analyzed the performance of an adaptive dialogue strategy adapting the dialogue initiative to Interaction Quality and answered the question if IQ and objective measures correlate in such a setting. By comparing five different strategies, we could show that the dialogue completion rate, the average dialogue length, and the average interaction quality strongly correlate. In addition, we could show that the adaptive strategy clearly outperforms all non-adaptive strategies as well as the random strategy. Hence, not only the grounding strategy but also the dialogue initiative is suitable for rule-based quality-adaptive dialogue.

Second, we performed a more detailed analysis of the correlation of task success and Interaction Quality showing that by defining IQ thresholds separating dialogues regarded as success and failure is a reasonable approach achieving an unweighted average precision of 0.929. This is of special interest for reinforcement learning where this could be used to automatically detect task success. However, not all dialogues could be used for training the dialogue strategy resulting in the need for 56% more dialogues. Moreover, the effects on the resulting strategy of regarding dialogues which are truly failing as successful (in the sense of keeping the user satisfied) is unclear and must be analyzed in a further study performing reinforcement learning with the proposed method.

For future work on quality-adaptive dialogue, the same adaptation techniques should be tested with real users. While user simulators offer a good means of evaluating dialogues easily, real users usually give new insight by showing unseen behavior. Furthermore, other adaptation mechanisms may be applied, e.g., in a statistical dialogue management setting (Ultes et al., 2011).

Acknowledgments

This work was supported by the Transregional Collaborative Research Centre SFB/TRR 62 “Companion-Technology for Cognitive Technical Systems” which is funded by the German Research Foundation (DFG). Additionally, we would like to thank Sungjin Lee and Maxine Eskenazi for providing access to the Let’s Go User Simulator.

References

Chih-Chung Chang and Chih-Jen Lin. 2011. LIBSVM: A library for support vector machines. *ACM Transactions on Intelligent Systems and Technology*, 2:27:1–27:27. Software available at `http://www.csie.ntu.edu.tw/~cjlin/libsvm`.

Douglas Crockford. 2006. RFC 4627 - The application/json Media Type for JavaScript Object Notation (JSON). Technical report, IETF, July.

Klaus-Peter Engelbrecht, Florian Gödde, Felix Hartard, Hamed Ketabdar, and Sebastian Möller. 2009. Modeling user satisfaction with hidden markov model. In *SIGDIAL '09: Proceedings of the SIGDIAL 2009 Conference*, pages 170–177, Morristown, NJ, USA. Association for Computational Linguistics.

Milica Gačić, Catherine Breslin, Matthew Henderson, Dongho Kim, Martin Szummer, Blaise Thomson, Pirros Tsiakoulis, and Steve J. Young. 2013. Online policy optimisation of bayesian spoken dialogue systems via human interaction. In *International Conference on Acoustics, Speech and Signal Processing (ICASSP)*, pages 8367–8371. IEEE.

Milan Gnjatović and Dietmar Rösner. 2008. Adaptive dialogue management in the nimitek prototype system. In *PIT '08: Proceedings of the 4th IEEE tutorial and research workshop on Perception and Interactive Technologies for Speech-Based Systems*, pages 14–25, Berlin, Heidelberg. Springer-Verlag.

Sunao Hara, Norihide Kitaoka, and Kazuya Takeda. 2010. Estimation method of user satisfaction using n-gram-based dialog history model for spoken dialog system. In Nicoletta Calzolari, Khalid Choukri, Bente Maegaard, Joseph Mariani, Jan Odijk, Stelios Piperidis, Mike Rosner, and Daniel Tapias, editors, *Proceedings of the Seventh conference on International Language Resources and Evaluation (LREC'10)*, Valletta, Malta, May. European Language Resources Association (ELRA).

Tobias Heinroth, Dan Denich, and Alexander Schmitt. 2010. Owlspeak - adaptive spoken dialogue within intelligent environments. In *IEEE PerCom Workshop Proceedings*, March. presented as part of SmartE Workshop.

Ryuichiro Higashinaka, Yasuhiro Minami, Kohji Dohsaka, and Toyomi Meguro. 2010. Issues in predicting user satisfaction transitions in dialogues: Individual differences, evaluation criteria, and prediction models. In Gary Lee, Joseph Mariani, Wolfgang Minker, and Satoshi Nakamura, editors, *Spoken Dialogue Systems for Ambient Environments*, volume 6392 of *Lecture Notes in Computer Science*, pages 48–60. Springer Berlin / Heidelberg. 10.1007/978-3-642-16202-2_5.

Srinivasan Janarthanam and Oliver Lemon. 2008. User simulations for online adaptation and knowledge-alignment in troubleshooting dialogue systems. *Semantics and Pragmatics of Dialogue (LONDIAL)*, page 45.

Sungjin Lee and Maxine Eskenazi. 2012. An unsupervised approach to user simulation: toward self-improving dialog systems. In *Proceedings of the 13th Annual Meeting of the Special Interest Group on Discourse and Dialogue*, pages 50–59. Association for Computational Linguistics, July.

Oliver Lemon and Olivier Pietquin. 2012. *Data-Driven Methods for Adaptive Spoken Dialogue Systems*. Springer New York.

Diane J. Litman and Shimei Pan. 2002. Designing and evaluating an adaptive spoken dialogue system. *User Modeling and User-Adapted Interaction*, 12(2-3):111–137.

Michael F. McTear. 2004. *Spoken Dialogue Technology: Towards the Conversational User Interface*. Springer, London.

Florian Nothdurft, Frank Honold, and Peter Kurzok. 2012. Using explanations for runtime dialogue adaptation. In *Proceedings of the 14th ACM International Conference on Multimodal Interaction*, pages 63–64. ACM, October.

M. Oshry, R. Auburn, P. Baggia, M. Bodell, D. Burke, D. Burnett, E. Candell, J. Carter, S. Mcglashan, A. Lee, B. Porter, and K. Rehor. 2007. Voice extensible markup language (voicexml) version 2.1. Technical report, W3C - Voice Browser Working Group, June.

Antoine Raux, Dan Bohus, Brian Langner, Alan W. Black, and Maxine Eskenazi. 2006. Doing research on a deployed spoken dialogue system: One year of let's go! experience. In *Proc. of the International Conference on Speech and Language Processing (ICSLP)*, September.

Verena Rieser and Oliver Lemon. 2008. Learning effective multimodal dialogue strategies from wizard-of-oz data: Bootstrapping and evaluation. In *ACL*, pages 638–646.

Alexander Schmitt and Stefan Ultes. 2015. Interaction quality: Assessing the quality of ongoing spoken dialog interaction by expertsand how it relates to user satisfaction. *Speech Communication*.

Alexander Schmitt, Benjamin Schatz, and Wolfgang Minker. 2011. Modeling and predicting quality in spoken human-computer interaction. In *Proceedings of the SIGDIAL 2011 Conference*, pages 173–184, Portland, Oregon, USA, June. Association for Computational Linguistics.

Alexander Schmitt, Stefan Ultes, and Wolfgang Minker. 2012. A parameterized and annotated spoken dialog corpus of the cmu let's go bus information system. In *International Conference on Language Resources and Evaluation (LREC)*, pages 3369–337, May.

Stefan Ultes and Wolfgang Minker. 2013. Interaction quality: A review. *Bulletin of Siberian State Aerospace University named after academician M.F. Reshetnev*, (4):153–156.

Stefan Ultes and Wolfgang Minker. 2014. Managing adaptive spoken dialogue for intelligent environments. *Journal of Ambient Intelligence and Smart Environments*, 6(5):523–539, August.

Stefan Ultes, Tobias Heinroth, Alexander Schmitt, and Wolfgang Minker. 2011. A theoretical framework for a user-centered spoken dialog manager. In *Proceedings of the Paralinguistic Information and its Integration in Spoken Dialogue Systems Workshop*, pages 241 – 246. Springer, September.

Stefan Ultes, Alexander Schmitt, and Wolfgang Minker. 2012. Towards quality-adaptive spoken dialogue management. In *NAACL-HLT Workshop on Future directions and needs in the Spoken Dialog Community: Tools and Data (SDCTD 2012)*, pages 49–52, Montréal, Canada, June. Association for Computational Linguistics.

Stefan Ultes, Alexander Schmitt, and Wolfgang Minker. 2013. On quality ratings for spoken dialogue systems – experts vs. users. In *Proceedings of the 2013 Conference of the North American Chapter of the Association for Computational Linguistics: Human Language Technologies*, pages 569–578. Association for Computational Linguistics, June.

Stefan Ultes, Hüseyin Dikme, and Wolfgang Minker. 2014a. Dialogue management for user-centered adaptive dialogue. In *Proceedings of the 5th International Workshop On Spoken Dialogue Systems (IWSDS)*, January.

Stefan Ultes, Hüseyin Dikme, and Wolfgang Minker. 2014b. First insight into quality-adaptive dialogue. In *International Conference on Language Resources and Evaluation (LREC)*, pages 246–251, May.

Vladimir N. Vapnik. 1995. *The nature of statistical learning theory*. Springer-Verlag New York, Inc., New York, NY, USA.

Marilyn Walker, Diane J. Litman, Candace A. Kamm, and Alicia Abella. 1997. Paradise: a framework for evaluating spoken dialogue agents. In *Proceedings of the eighth conference on European chapter of the Association for Computational Linguistics*, pages 271–280, Morristown, NJ, USA. Association for Computational Linguistics.

Marilyn Walker. 2000. An application of reinforcement learning to dialogue strategy selection in a spoken dialogue system for email. *Journal of Artificial Intelligence Research*, 12:387–416.

Steve J. Young, Milica Gačić, Blaise Thomson, and Jason D. Williams. 2013. Pomdp-based statistical spoken dialog systems: A review. *Proceedings of the IEEE*, 101(5):1160–1179.

Metaphor Detection in Discourse

Hyeju Jang, Seunghwan Moon, Yohan Jo, and Carolyn Penstein Rosé
Language Technologies Institute
Carnegie Mellon University
Pittsburgh, PA 15213, USA
{hyejuj, seungwhm, yohanj, cprose}@cs.cmu.edu

Abstract

Understanding contextual information is key to detecting metaphors in discourse. Most current work aims at detecting metaphors given a single sentence, thus focusing mostly on *local* contextual cues within a short text. In this paper, we present a novel approach that explicitly leverages *global context* of a discourse to detect metaphors. In addition, we show that syntactic information such as dependency structures can help better describe local contextual information, thus improving detection results when combined. We apply our methods on a newly annotated online discussion forum, and show that our approach outperforms the state-of-the-art baselines in previous literature.

1 Introduction

Detecting metaphors in text is an active line of research which has attracted attention in recent years. To date, most of the previous literature has looked at lexical semantic features such as selectional restriction violations (Martin, 1996; Shutova and Teufel, 2010; Shutova et al., 2010; Shutova et al., 2013; Huang, 2014) or contrast in lexical concreteness and abstractness (Turney et al., 2011; Broadwell et al., 2013; Tsvetkov et al., 2013). While these approaches have been shown to be successful in detecting metaphors given a single sentence, metaphor detection in discourse brings a new dimension to the task. Consider the following excerpt from an online *Breast Cancer* discussion forum as an example:

> *welcome, glad for the company .... just sad to see that there are so many of us. Here is a thought that I have been thinking since I was diagnosed. This disease should be called the "Hurry up and Wait" illness. Since the day I heard the dreaded words "you need to have a biopsy", I feel like I am on a speeding train. It rushes into every station where you have to make instant decisions, while this ominous clock is ticking. Wait for test results, wait for appointments, wait for healing.*

In the example above, it is difficult to identify *"rushes into every station"* as a metaphorical expression using the previous approaches, because it does not violate selectional restrictions or have any notable contrast in lexical concreteness and abstractness. The reason for this is clear: the action of *rushing into stations* itself makes perfect sense literally when it is viewed *locally* as an isolated phrase, while the contextual cues for this metaphor are embedded globally throughout the discourse (*e.g. diagonsed, disease, biopsy* are semantically contrasted with *train, rushes,* and *station*). This clearly demonstrates the need for a new set of computational tools to represent context beyond a single sentence, in order to better detect metaphorical expressions that have contextual connections outside the sentence in which they are used.

Context for metaphor detection. Metaphor is a semantic phenomenon that describes objects often with a view borrowed from a different domain. As such, it is natural that metaphors inherently break the lexical coherence of a sentence or a discourse. Klebanov et al. (2009), for example, showed in their study that words related to the topic of discussion are less likely to be metaphorical than other words in text, implying that contextual incoherence might serve as a cue for detecting metaphors. Based on this observation, the idea of leveraging textual context to detect metaphors has been recently proposed by some researchers (Broadwell et al., 2013; Sporleder and Li, 2009).

Proceedings of the SIGDIAL 2015 Conference, pages 384–392,
Prague, Czech Republic, 2-4 September 2015.

Our contributions. We extend the previous approaches for detecting metaphors by explicitly addressing the *global* discourse context, as well as by representing the *local* context of a sentence in a more robust way. Our contribution is thus twofold: first, we propose several textual descriptors that can capture global contextual shifts among a discourse, such as semantic word category distribution obtained from a frame-semantic parser, homogeneity in topic distributions, and lexical chains. Second, we show that global and local contextual information are complimentary in detecting metaphors, and that leveraging syntactic features is crucial in better describing lexico-semantic information in a local context. Our method achieves higher performance on a metaphor disambiguation task than state-of-the-art systems from prior work (Klebanov et al., 2014; Tsvetkov et al., 2013) on our newly created dataset from an online discussion forum.

The rest of the paper is organized as follows. Section 2 relates our work to prior work. Section 3 explains our method in detail, specifically in regards to how we use global context and local context for metaphor detection. Section 4 describes the *Breast Cancer* dataset annotated and used for our experiment. In Section 5, we present our experimental results and show the effectiveness of our method with the task of metaphor disambiguation. Section 6 analyzes the results and identifies potential areas of improvement, and we give our concluding remarks in Section 7.

2 Relation to Prior Work

The main approaches to computationally detecting metaphors can be categorized into work that considers the following three classes of features: selectional preferences, abstractness and concreteness, and lexical cohesion.

Selectional preferences relate to how semantically compatible predicates are with particular arguments. For example, the verb *drink* prefers *beer* as an object over *computer*. The idea behind using selectional preferences for metaphor detection is that metaphorical words tend to break selectional preferences. In the case of "*the clouds sailed across the sky*", for instance, *sailed* is determined to be metaphorically used because *clouds* as a subject violates its selectional restriction. The idea of using violation of selectional preferences as a cue for metaphors has been well studied in a variety of previous work (Martin, 1996; Shutova and Teufel, 2010; Shutova et al., 2010; Shutova et al., 2013; Huang, 2014) In general, this work can be further categorized into work that uses lexical resources and the work that uses corpus-based approaches to obtain selectional preferences

From the observations that metaphorical words (source domain) tend to use more concrete and imagination rich words than the target domain of metaphors, the **abstractness/concreteness** approaches computationally measure the degree of abstractness of words to detect metaphors. Take the following two phrases as examples that demonstrate this concept: *green idea* (metaphorical expression) and *green frog* (literal expression.) The former has a concrete word (*green*) modifying an abstract concept (*idea*), thus being more likely to be metaphorical. The idea of leveraging abstractness/concreteness in detecting metaphors has been proposed and studied by several groups of researchers (Turney et al., 2011; Broadwell et al., 2013; Tsvetkov et al., 2013; Assaf et al., 2013; Neuman et al., 2013). Note that most of this work uses datasets that comprise grammatically restricted sentences (*e.g.* ones with S+V+O or A+N structures) for their experiments, in order to test their hypothesis in a controlled way.

Another line of work considers **lexical coherence** of text as a cue for metaphor. The lexical coherence approach is motivated by the observation that metaphorical words are often semantically incoherent with context words. There have been several approaches proposed to compute lexical coherence. Broadwell et al. (2013), for instance, employed topic chaining to categorize metaphors, whereas Sporleder and Li (2009) have proposed to use lexical chains and semantic cohesion graphs to detect metaphors. Shutova and Sun (2013) and Shutova et al. (2013) have formulated the metaphor detection problem similar to outlier detection or anomaly detection tasks, and proposed to use topic signatures as lexical coherence features. Schulder and Hovy (2014) used TF-IDF to obtain domain term relevance, and applied this feature to detect metaphors.

Klebanov et al. (2014) propose to use various lexical features such as part-of-speech tags, concreteness ratings, and topic scores of target words to detect word-level metaphors in a running text. Our approach is different from theirs in that we explicitly gather global contextual information from discourse to detect metaphors and that we leverage the syntactic structures to better represent local contextual information.

3 Our Method

In this section, we describe our method to measure nonliteralness of an expression in context. Specifically, we describe how we use contextual information as features for metaphor classification in discourse.

We first define *lexical cohesion* before we introduce our motivation and method for utilizing global contexts as features for detecting metaphor. A text is said to be lexically cohesive when the words in the text describe a single coherent topic. Specifically, lexical cohesion occurs when words are semantically related directly to a common topic or indirectly to the topic via another word. Figure 1 illustrates the lexical cohesion among words shown as a graph.

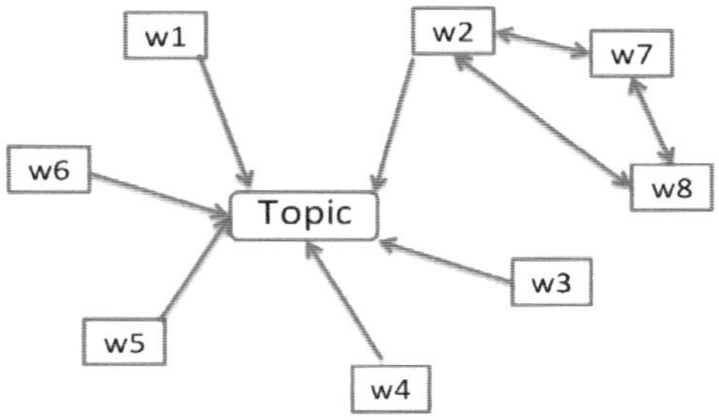

Figure 1: Graph representation depicting lexical cohesion among words in a given text. Edges represent lexical relatedness between a topic and a word or between words. For example, w_1 is directly related to the topic of discussion, whereas w_7 is only indirectly related to the topic through w_2.

The intuition for our main idea is that metaphorically-used words would often break lexical cohesion of text, while literal expressions would maintain a single connected graph of topically or semantically related words. Therefore, we identify that these incohesive words may serve as cues for nonliteral expressions. The following two examples illustrate the described phenomenon, both of which contain the same phrase *"break the ice"*.

> *... Meanwhile in Germany, the cold penetrated the vast interior of Cologne cathedral, where worshippers had to break the ice on holy water in the font. The death toll from the cold also increased ...*

> *... "Some of us may have have acted as critics at one point or another, but for the most part its just as filmgoers," he said. And, breaking the ice at a press conference, he praised his vice-president, French actress Catherine Deneuve ...*

The phrase *"break the ice"* in the first example is used with words such as *cold* and *water* which are semantically coherent with its literal meaning, whereas in the second example, the phrase is used with *press conference*, *praised*, and *vice-president*, which are far from the literal meaning of *break* and *ice*.

Note that this contextual information lies in different parts of a discourse, sometimes locally in the same sentence as the target word or globally throughout multiple surrounding sentences in a discourse. Given this observation, we categorize contextual information into two kinds depending on the scope of the context in text: *global* and *local*. Global contexts range over the whole document, whereas local contexts are limited to the sentence that contains the expression of interest. Section 3.1 explains how we represent global contexts. Section 3.2 describes the features we use for local contexts, and how we leverage syntactic information to make a more robust use of the semantic features in local context.

3.1 Global Contextual Features

We use the following features to represent global contexts of a given text.

Semantic Category: Lexico-semantic resources (*e.g.* `FrameNet`, `WordNet`) provide categorical information for much of the English lexicon. If a target word is used literally, the document may have a high proportion of words in the same semantic category. If the word is used metaphorically, the document may contain more words that share different semantic categories. To implement this intuition, we use `SEMAFOR` (Das et al., 2014) to assign each word to one of the categories provided by the `FrameNet 1.5` taxonomy (Baker et al., 1998). Then, we compute the relative proportion of the target word's category with regards to categories appearing in the document to measure the alignment of categories of the target word and the surrounding contexts. Formally, we define the value of the *global word category feature* as

$$\frac{\sum_{w \in d} \mathbb{1}(c_w = c_{tw})}{N_d},$$

where c_w is the category of word w, c_{tw} is the category of the target word, and N_d is the number of words in document d. $\mathbb{1}(.)$ is an indicator function that equals 1 when the expression inside is true and 0 otherwise.

We have also used WordNet[1]'s 44 lexnames in our preliminary experiment to obtain word categories. However, we have found that its coarse categorization of words (44 categories as opposed to FrameNet's 1204) led to poorer performance, thus we have used FrameNet here instead.

Topic Distribution: Our intuition for using topic distributions is that non-literal words tend to have a considerably different topic distribution from that of the surrounding document (global context). To implement this idea, we run a topic model to obtain a word-topic distribution (= P(topic|word)) and document-topic distribution (= P(topic|document)). We use Latent Dirichlet Allocation (LDA) (Blei et al., 2003) to find 100 topics from the entire corpus, and calculate the topic distribution per document and the topic distribution per word from the trained topic model. Specifically, we begin by training our model for 2,000 iterations on a large data set. Then, for the estimation on test documents we apply this model to our test data set for 100 iterations of Gibbs sampling.

The original LDA computes P(word|topic) instead of P(topic|word). In order to compute P(topic|word), the first 20 iterations out of 100 are used as a burn-in phase, and then we collect sample topic assignments for each word in every other iteration. This process results in a total of 40 topic assignments for a word in a document, and we use these topic assignments to estimate the topic distributions per word as in (Remus and Biemann, 2013). We used the GibbsC++ toolkit (Phan and Nguyen, 2007) with default parameters to train the model.

Finally, we use the cosine similarity between P(topic|document) and P(topic|word) as features that represent the global alignment of topics between the target word and the document.

Lexical Chain: We use *lexical chains* (Morris and Hirst, 1991) to obtain multiple sequences of semantically related words in a text. From the intuition that metaphorical words would not belong to dominant lexical chains of the given text, we use the lexical chain membership of a target word as a cue for its non-literalness. Because each discourse instance of our dataset tends to be short and thus does not produce many lexical chains, we use a binary feature of whether a target word belongs to the longest chain of the given text. In our implementation, we use the ELKB toolkit (Jarmasz and Szpakowicz, 2003) to detect lexical chains in text which is built on Roget's thesaurus (Roget, 1911). Note that a similar approach has been used by Sporleder and Li (2009) to grasp topical words in a text.

Context Tokens: In addition, we use unigram features to represent the global context. Specifically, we use binary features to indicate whether the context words appeared anywhere in a given discourse.

3.2 Local Contextual Features

The local contextual information within a sentence is limited because it often contains fewer words, but the information could be more direct and richer because it reflects the immediate context of an expression of interest. We represent local contextual information using the semantic features listed below, combined with grammatical dependencies to induce relational connections between a target word and its contextual information.

Semantic Category: We follow the same intuition as using semantic categories to represent global features (Section 3.1), and thus compare the target word's semantic category and that of other words in the same sentence to induce local contextual information. However, since a sentence often has only a small number of words, the proportion of the target word's category in one sentence depends too much on the sentence length. Therefore, we instead look at the words that have dependency relations with the target word, and create nominal features by pairing word categories of lexical items with their dependency relations. The paired dependency-word category features specifies *how* local contextual words are used in relation to the target word, thus providing richer information. We also specify the target word's category as a categorical feature, expecting that the interplay between the target word's category and other words' categories is indicative of the non-literalness of the

[1] https://wordnet.princeton.edu/man/lexnames.5WN.html

target word.

Semantic Relatedness: If the semantic relatedness between a target word and the context words is low, the target word is likely to be metaphorically used. From the observation that the words that are in grammatical relation to the target word are more informative than other words, we use the dependency relations of a target word to pick out the words to compute semantic relatedness with. To represent the semantic relatedness between two words, we compute the cosine similarity of their topic distributions.

We use the semantic relatedness information in two different ways. One way is to compute average semantic relatedness over the words that have dependency relations with a target word, and use it as a feature (AvgSR). The other is to use semantic relatedness of the words in grammatical relations to the target word as multiple features (DepSR).

We use the same techniques as in Section 3.1 to compute topic distribution using an LDA topic model.

Lexical Abstractness/Concreteness: People often use metaphors to convey a complex or abstract thought by borrowing a word or phrase having a concrete concept that is easy to grasp. With this intuition, Turney et al. (2011) showed that the word abstractness/concreteness measure is a useful clue for detecting metaphors.

To represent the concreteness of a word, we used Brysbaert's database of concreteness ratings for about 40,000 English words (Brysbaert et al., 2014). We use the mean ratings in the database as a numerical feature for the target word. In addition, we also use the concreteness ratings of the words in grammatical relations to the target word as local context features.

Grammatical Dependencies: We use the `stanford-corenlp` toolkit (Manning et al., 2014) to parse dependency relations of our data and apply grammatical dependencies as described above for each semantic feature. We use grammatical dependencies only between content words (*e.g.* words with syntactic categories of noun, verb, adjective, and adverb).

4 Data

We conduct experiments on data acquired from discussion forums for an online breast cancer support group. The data contains all the public posts, users, and profiles on the discussion boards from October 2001 to January 2011. The dataset consists of 1,562,459 messages and 90,242 registered members. 31,307 users have at least one post, and the average number of posts per user is 24.

We built an annotated dataset for our experiments as follows. We first picked seven metaphor candidates that appear either metaphorically or literally in the *Breast Cancer* corpus: *boat*, *candle*, *light*, *ride*, *road*, *spice*, and *train*. We then retrieved all the posts in the corpus that contain these candidate words, and annotated each post as to whether the candidate word in the post is used metaphorically. When the candidate word occurs more than once in a single post, all occurrences within a post were assumed to have the same usage (either metaphorical or literal).

Note that our annotation scheme is different from the VU Amsterdam metaphor-annotated dataset (Steen et al., 2010) or the essay data used in (Klebanov et al., 2014), where every word in the corpus is individually labeled as a metaphor or a literal word. Our approach of pre-defining a set of metaphor candidate words and annotating each post as opposed to every word has several practical and fundamental benefits. First, metaphors often have a wide spectrum of "literalness" depending on how frequently they are used in everyday text, and there is a continuing debate as to how to operationalize metaphor in a binary decision (Jang et al., 2014). In our work, we can circumvent this metaphor decision issue by annotating a set of metaphor candidate words that have a clear distinction between metaphorical and literal usages. Second, our annotation only for ambiguous words ensures to focus on how well a model distinguishes between metaphorical and literal usage of the same word.

We employed Amazon Mechanical Turk (MTurk) workers to annotate metaphor use for candidate words. A candidate word was highlighted in the full post it originated from. MTurkers were asked to copy and paste the sentence where a highlighted word is included to a given text box to make sure that MTurkers do not give a random answer. We gave a simple definition of metaphor from Wikipedia along with a few examples to instruct them. Then, they were asked whether the highlighted word is used metaphorically or literally. Five different MTurk workers annotated each candidate word, and they were paid $0.03 for annotating each word. For

candidate	#		%	
	N	L	N	L
boat*	54	281	16.12	83.88
candle*	4	18	18.18	81.82
light	503	179	73.75	26.25
ride	234	185	55.85	44.15
road	924	129	87.75	12.25
spice*	3	21	12.50	87.50
train	94	41	69.63	30.37
all	1816	854	68.01	31.99

Table 1: Metaphor use statistics of data used for MTurk (* indicates metaphor candidates for which the literal usage is more common than the nonliteral one, **N**: nonliteral use **L**: literal use).

annotation quality control, we requested that all workers have a United States location and have 98% or more successful submissions. We excluded annotations for which the first task of copy and paste failed. 18 out of 13,348 annotations were filtered out in this way.

To evaluate the reliability of the annotations by MTurkers, we calculated Fleiss's kappa (Fleiss, 1971), which is widely used to evaluate inter-annotators reliability. Using a value of 1 if the MTurker coded a word as a metaphorical use, and a value of 0 otherwise, we find kappa value of 0.81, suggesting strong inter-annotator agreement.

We split the data randomly into two subsets, one as a development set for observation and analysis, and the other as a cross-validation set for classification. The development set contains 800 instances, and the cross-validation set contains 1,870 instances. Table 1 shows the metaphor use statistics of the annotated data.

5 Evaluation

We evaluate our method on a metaphor disambiguation task detailed in Section 5.1. Section 5.2 lists the metrics we used for the evaluation on this test set. Section 5.3 describes the baselines we compare our method against on these metrics. We detail our classification settings in Section 5.4 and report our results in Section 5.5.

5.1 Task

The task for our experiment is metaphor disambiguation: given a candidate word, decide whether the word is used as a metaphor or as a literal word in a post. For example, *boat* in (1) is used metaphorically, whereas *boat* in (2) is used literally. The task is thus to classify each of the seven candidate metaphors defined in Section 4 into either a metaphor or a literal word.

(1) *Just diagnosed late November. Stage I and with good prognosis. ... Now I am having to consider a hysterectomy and am really scared and don't know what to do. I have no children and don't really think I want to. I really want to do what is best for me but it is so hard to know. Anyone else been in the same <u>boat</u> with the endometriosis?*

(2) *Good Morn Girls, It is 52 this morn. WOW! there is a bad storm rolling in at this time and tornado watches but those are pretty common. ... Hubby started his truck driving school today. We use to have ski <u>boats</u> so he and I could both drive a semi. Backing is the hardest part cause the trailer goes opposite of the direction you turn but once you get use to it, it's not hard. ...*

5.2 Evaluation Metrics

We report four evaluation metrics: accuracy, precision, recall, and F-score.

Accuracy: Accuracy is the percentage of correctly classified instances among all instances.

Precision: Precision is the percentage of correctly classified instances among instances assigned to a particular class (metaphor or literal) by the model.

Recall: Recall is the percentage of correctly classified instances among all nonliteral or literal instances. Precision and recall are recorded for both metaphorical and literal labels.

F-score: F-score is the harmonic mean of precision and recall.

5.3 Baselines

We compare our method to a context unigram model as well as two other baselines from recent work on metaphor detection: Klebanov et al. (2014), and Tsvetkov et al. (2013).

Context unigram model uses all the context words including the target word in a post as features.

Type	Model	A	P-M	R-M	P-L	R-L	F1
Baseline	Tsvetkov et al. (2013)	0.245	0.857	0.168	0.236	0.991	0.207
	Klebanov et al. (2014)	0.833	0.830	0.984	0.866	0.340	0.694
	U	0.836	0.867	0.929	0.697	0.535	0.751
Global	U+GWC	0.842	0.869	0.934	0.716	0.541	0.759
	U+GT*	0.843	0.873	0.931	0.711	0.557	0.763
	U+LC	0.839	0.866	0.934	0.709	0.530	0.753
	U+GWC+GT+LC*	0.845	0.871	0.936	0.724	0.546	0.762
Local	U+LWC	0.849	0.874	0.939	0.735	0.557	0.634
	U+SR(AvgSR)	0.852	0.873	0.965	0.563	0.243	0.628
	U+SR(DepSR)	0.858	0.880	0.943	0.756	0.580	0.783
	U+AC	0.853	0.880	0.936	0.735	0.582	0.778
	U+LWC+SR+AC*	0.862	0.885	0.942	0.759	0.598	0.791
Global+Local	ALL*	0.860	0.882	0.943	0.761	0.589	0.788
	ALL-LC*	0.863	0.886	0.941	0.759	0.605	0.793

Table 2: Performance on metaphor disambiguation evaluation. (**Models**) U: context unigram, GWC: global word category, GT: global topic dist., LC: lexical chain, LWC: local word category, SR: semantic relatedness, AC: abstractness/concreteness. (**Metrics**) A: accuracy, P-M: precision on metaphors, R-M: recall on metaphors, P-L: precision on literal words, R-L: recall on literal words, F1: Average F1 score over M/L., *: statistically significant improvement over baselines

Tsvetkov et al. (2013) use local contextual features (such as abstractness and imageability, supersenses, and vector space word representations), and targets for two syntactic constructions: subject-verb-object (`SVO`) and adjective-noun (`AN`) tuples. Note that the output of this system is a sentence level label rather than a word (*e.g.* they output a binary label that indicates whether the target sentence contains any metaphorical phrase). Thus, we take the output of their sentence level label on the sentence that contains our target word, and treat their output as a label for our target word disambiguation task. Although it is therefore not a fair comparison, we included this system as a baseline because this is a state-of-the-art system for metaphor detection tasks. In addition, we can make this comparison to contextualize results with regards to how a state-of-the-art non-discourse model (i.e. not using global context) will perform in more general discourse contexts.

Klebanov et al. (2014) use target word lexical features such as part-of-speech tags, concreteness rating, and topic score. Their approach does not use any contextual information as our method does. As a result, the same words are most likely to obtain the same features. Note that Klebanov et al. (2014) evaluated their approach for each content word in a given text, but in our paper we evaluate how their method performs on ambiguous words in particular.

5.4 Classification

We used the `LightSIDE` toolkit (Mayfield and Rosé, 2010) for extracting features and performing classification. For the machine learning algorithm, we used the logistic regression classifier provided by `LightSIDE` with L_1 regularization. We used basic unigram features extracted by `LightSIDE`, and performed 10-fold cross validation for the following experiments. Instances for each fold were randomly chosen.

5.5 Results

The classification results on the *Breast Cancer* corpus are shown in Tables 2 and in 3.

Note that both our global context features (*e.g.*U+GWC+GT+LC, U+GT) and local context features (*e.g.*U+LWC+SR+AC) perform significantly better than all of the baselines ($p < 0.05$). This indicates that our contextual features successfully capture additional information from discourse both locally and globally. In general, it can be seen that local features are more powerful indicators of metaphors than global features. Note also that Tsvetkov et al. (2013) performs poorly on this task, probably due to the reasons mentioned in Section 5.3. It is interesting to note that

Target word	A	P-M	R-M	P-L	R-L	F1
boat	0.843	0.886	0.935	0.500	0.351	0.843
light	0.831	0.857	0.920	0.738	0.594	0.773
ride	0.843	0.847	0.888	0.836	0.782	0.838
road	0.926	0.936	0.983	0.823	0.543	0.806
train	0.711	0.759	0.887	0.429	0.231	0.559

Table 3: Performance on metaphor disambiguation task per target word with the best setting ALL-LC. Note that the performance results on target words *candle* and *spice* are not reported because of their small number of instances.

Klebanov et al. (2014) performs poorly at recall on literal words. We conclude that our methods significantly outperform the baselines in detecting metaphors in discourse.

6 Discussion

The results of our methods on the metaphor disambiguation task are promising, indicating that both global features and local features can serve as strong indicators of metaphor.

Note that the combined global+local features did not show significant improvement over the local features on this task in Table 2. We had believed that local and global features (aside from unigram features) would provide synergistic predictions, however we found that the local features provided stronger predictions and drowned out the effect of the global features.

We identify the following possible sources of errors of our method: first of all, the low performance of lexican chain (LC) features is noticeable. This might be due to errors originating from the output of the `ELKB` toolkit which we employ to obtain lexical chains. More specifically, `ELKB` builds lexical chains using a standard thesaurus, which is extremely vulnerable to noisy text such as our online discussion forum (which contains typos, abbreviations, medical terms, etc.).

Secondly, the semantic relatedness scores obtained from LDA gives high scores to frequently co-occurring words, thus inevitably reducing effectiveness in disambiguating frequently used metaphors. While this is an issue inherent in any distributional semantics approach, we find that our LDA-based features do improve overall performance.

7 Conclusion

We summarize our contributions as follows: we identified that both global and local contextual features can serve as powerful indicators of metaphor, and proposed several methods to represent contextual features in discourse. We also extended previous literature that considers local contextual information by explicitly incorporating the syntactic information, such as dependency relations, into local contextual features, resulting in an improved performance. The performance was evaluated on our newly built *Breast Cancer* dataset, which provides examples of metaphors in a discourse setting. We showed that our method significantly outperforms the systems from recent literature on a metaphor disambiguation task in discourse. Our method can be easily applied to disambiguate all the content words in text once we have correspondingly labeled data.

Acknowledgments

This research was supported in part by NSF Grant IIS-1302522.

References

Dan Assaf, Yair Neuman, Yohai Cohen, Shlomo Argamon, Newton Howard, Mark Last, Ophir Frieder, and Moshe Koppel. 2013. Why dark thoughts aren't really dark: A novel algorithm for metaphor identification. In *Computational Intelligence, Cognitive Algorithms, Mind, and Brain (CCMB), 2013 IEEE Symposium on*, pages 60–65. IEEE.

Collin F Baker, Charles J Fillmore, and John B Lowe. 1998. The berkeley framenet project. In *Proceedings of the 17th international conference on Computational linguistics-Volume 1*, pages 86–90. Association for Computational Linguistics.

David M. Blei, Andrew Y. Ng, and Michael I. Jordan. 2003. Latent dirichlet allocation. *J. Mach. Learn. Res.*, 3:993–1022, March.

George Aaron Broadwell, Umit Boz, Ignacio Cases, Tomek Strzalkowski, Laurie Feldman, Sarah Taylor, Samira Shaikh, Ting Liu, Kit Cho, and Nick Webb.

2013. Using imageability and topic chaining to locate metaphors in linguistic corpora. In *Social Computing, Behavioral-Cultural Modeling and Prediction*, pages 102–110. Springer.

Marc Brysbaert, Amy Beth Warriner, and Victor Kuperman. 2014. Concreteness ratings for 40 thousand generally known english word lemmas. *Behavior research methods*, 46(3):904–911.

Dipanjan Das, Desai Chen, André FT Martins, Nathan Schneider, and Noah A Smith. 2014. Frame-semantic parsing. *Computational Linguistics*, 40(1):9–56.

Joseph L Fleiss. 1971. Measuring nominal scale agreement among many raters. *Psychological bulletin*, 76(5):378–382.

Ting-Hao Kenneth Huang. 2014. Social metaphor detection via topical analysis. In *Sixth International Joint Conference on Natural Language Processing*, page 14.

Hyeju Jang, Mario Piergallini, Miaomiao Wen, and Carolyn Penstein Rosé. 2014. Conversational metaphors in use: Exploring the contrast between technical and everyday notions of metaphor. *ACL 2014*, page 1.

Mario Jarmasz and Stan Szpakowicz. 2003. Not as easy as it seems: Automating the construction of lexical chains using rogets thesaurus. In *Advances in Artificial Intelligence*, pages 544–549. Springer.

Beata Beigman Klebanov, Eyal Beigman, and Daniel Diermeier. 2009. Discourse topics and metaphors. In *Proceedings of the Workshop on Computational Approaches to Linguistic Creativity*, pages 1–8. Association for Computational Linguistics.

Beata Beigman Klebanov, Chee Wee Leong, Michael Heilman, and Michael Flor. 2014. Different texts, same metaphors: Unigrams and beyond. *ACL 2014*, page 11.

Christopher D. Manning, Mihai Surdeanu, John Bauer, Jenny Finkel, Steven J. Bethard, and David McClosky. 2014. The Stanford CoreNLP natural language processing toolkit. In *Proceedings of 52nd Annual Meeting of the Association for Computational Linguistics: System Demonstrations*, pages 55–60.

James H Martin. 1996. Computational approaches to figurative language. *Metaphor and Symbol*, 11(1):85–100.

Elijah Mayfield and Carolyn Rosé. 2010. An interactive tool for supporting error analysis for text mining. In *Proceedings of the NAACL HLT 2010 Demonstration Session*, pages 25–28. Association for Computational Linguistics.

Jane Morris and Graeme Hirst. 1991. Lexical cohesion computed by thesaural relations as an indicator of the structure of text. *Comput. Linguist.*, 17(1):21–48, March.

Yair Neuman, Dan Assaf, Yohai Cohen, Mark Last, Shlomo Argamon, Newton Howard, and Ophir Frieder. 2013. Metaphor identification in large texts corpora. *PloS one*, 8(4):e62343.

Xuan-Hieu Phan and Cam-Tu Nguyen. 2007. Gibbslda++: Ac/c++ implementation of latent dirichlet allocation (lda).

Steffen Remus and Chris Biemann. 2013. Three knowledge-free methods for automatic lexical chain extraction. In *HLT-NAACL*, pages 989–999.

Peter Mark Roget. 1911. *Roget's Thesaurus of English Words and Phrases...* TY Crowell Company.

Marc Schulder and Eduard Hovy. 2014. Metaphor detection through term relevance. *ACL 2014*, page 18.

Ekaterina Shutova and Lin Sun. 2013. Unsupervised metaphor identification using hierarchical graph factorization clustering. In *HLT-NAACL*, pages 978–988.

Ekaterina Shutova and Simone Teufel. 2010. Metaphor corpus annotated for source-target domain mappings. In *LREC*.

Ekaterina Shutova, Lin Sun, and Anna Korhonen. 2010. Metaphor identification using verb and noun clustering. In *Proceedings of the 23rd International Conference on Computational Linguistics*, pages 1002–1010. Association for Computational Linguistics.

Ekaterina Shutova, Simone Teufel, and Anna Korhonen. 2013. Statistical metaphor processing. *Computational Linguistics*, 39(2):301–353.

Caroline Sporleder and Linlin Li. 2009. Unsupervised recognition of literal and non-literal use of idiomatic expressions. In *Proceedings of the 12th Conference of the European Chapter of the Association for Computational Linguistics*, pages 754–762. Association for Computational Linguistics.

Gerard J Steen, Aletta G Dorst, J Berenike Herrmann, Anna Kaal, Tina Krennmayr, and Trijntje Pasma. 2010. *A method for linguistic metaphor identification: From MIP to MIPVU*, volume 14. John Benjamins Publishing.

Yulia Tsvetkov, Elena Mukomel, and Anatole Gershman. 2013. Cross-lingual metaphor detection using common semantic features.

Peter D Turney, Yair Neuman, Dan Assaf, and Yohai Cohen. 2011. Literal and metaphorical sense identification through concrete and abstract context. In *Proceedings of the 2011 Conference on the Empirical Methods in Natural Language Processing*, pages 680–690.

User Adaptive Restoration for Incorrectly Segmented Utterances in Spoken Dialogue Systems

Kazunori Komatani†, Naoki Hotta‡, Satoshi Sato‡, Mikio Nakano¶

† The Institute of Scientific and Industrial Research (ISIR), Osaka University
Ibaraki, Osaka 567-0047, Japan
‡ Graduate School of Engineering, Nagoya University
Nagoya, Aichi 464-8603, Japan
¶ Honda Research Institute Japan Co., Ltd.
Wako, Saitama 351-0188, Japan
komatani@sanken.osaka-u.ac.jp

Abstract

Ideally, the users of spoken dialogue systems should be able to speak at their own tempo. The systems thus need to correctly interpret utterances from various users, even when these utterances contain disfluency. In response to this issue, we propose an approach based on a posteriori restoration for incorrectly segmented utterances. A crucial part of this approach is to classify whether restoration is required or not. We improve the accuracy by adapting the classifier to each user. We focus on the dialogue tempo of each user, which can be obtained during dialogues, and determine the correlation between each user's tempo and the appropriate thresholds for the classification. A linear regression function used to convert the tempos into thresholds is also derived. Experimental results showed that the proposed user adaptation for two classifiers, thresholding and decision tree, improved the classification accuracies by 3.0% and 7.4%, respectively, in ten-fold cross validation.

1 Introduction

To make spoken dialogue systems more user-friendly, users need to be able to speak at their own tempo. Even though not all users speak fluently, i.e., some speak slowly and with disfluency, conventional systems basically assume that a user says one utterance with no pause. Systems need to handle utterances by both novice users who speak slowly and experienced users who want the systems to reply quickly.

We propose a method for spoken dialogue systems to interpret user utterances adaptively in terms of utterance units. We adopt an approach based on our a posteriori restoration for incorrectly segmented utterances (Komatani et al., 2014). The proposed system responds quickly while also interpreting utterance fragments by concatenating them when a user speaks with disfluency or speaks slowly with pauses. Another approach for this issue is to adaptively change the parameters of voice activity detection (VAD) for each user during dialogues, but automatic speech recognition (ASR) engines with such adaptive control are uncommon, and implementing an online-adaptive VAD module is difficult. Our a posteriori restoration approach does not require changing ASR engines, and the system can restore interpretation of user utterances after ASR results are obtained.

Our a posteriori restoration approach needs to classify whether two utterance fragments close in time need to be interpreted together or not, i.e., whether these are two different utterances or a single utterance incorrectly segmented by VAD. If these need to be interpreted separately, the system normally responds to the two fragments on the basis of their ASR results. If they need to be interpreted together, the system immediately stops its response to the first fragment, concatenates the two segments, and then interprets it.

Misclassification causes erroneous system responses. If the system incorrectly classifies the restoration as not being required, its response often becomes erroneous because the original user utterance is interrupted in its middle. If the system classifies the restoration as being required even though it is actually not, the system takes an unnecessarily long time before it starts responding,

Proceedings of the SIGDIAL 2015 Conference, pages 393–401,
Prague, Czech Republic, 2-4 September 2015.

and its response tends to be erroneous because an unnecessary part is attached to the actual utterance.

We adapt the classification to each user and show through experiments that the adaptation improves classification accuracy. We focus on the tempo of each user and use it to adapt the classifier. Since the temporal interval between two utterance fragments is an important parameter in the classifier (Komatani et al., 2014), we adapt its threshold to user behaviors obtained during the dialogue.

2 Related Work

The aim of our restoration is to resolve a problem with utterance units. Spoken dialogue systems that do not consider the problem naively assume that the following three items are always in agreement:

1. Results of voice activity detection (VAD)
2. Units of dialogue acts (DAs)
3. Units of user turns

The second item is used to update dialogue states in the system and the third determines when the system starts responding.

These three do not agree, however, in cases of real user utterances. Since the first item is the input information, existing studies on the problem can be categorized into two: handling disagreements between 1 and 2 and between 1 and 3. The disagreement between 1 and 2 was tackled by (Nakano et al., 1999) and (Bell et al., 2001). The purpose of those studies was to incrementally understand fragmented utterances and determine whether each fragment forms a DA with another. The disagreement between 1 and 3 was tackled by (Sato et al., 2002), (Ferrer et al., 2003), and (Kitaoka et al., 2005), who determined the timing at which a system needs to start responding. Raux and Eskenazi also tackled this problem by changing the thresholds for silence duration in a VAD module (Raux and Eskenazi, 2008) and incorporating partial ASR results into their model (Raux and Eskenazi, 2009).

Our a posteriori restoration framework mainly considers the former disagreement by restoring fragmented ASR results. Unlike previous studies, such as (Nakano et al., 1999) and (Bell et al., 2001), which are based on syntactic parsing, our method assumes that the DA boundaries are a subset of the VAD boundaries. The latter disagreement is partially considered in our framework by classifying whether to respond to a fragmented utterance or not. Our problem setting relates in part to the one tackled by the above-mentioned studies, in which the system determines more precise timing to respond. Our approach can thus be used together with these studies to improve turn-taking (Kitaoka et al., 2005; Raux and Eskenazi, 2008; Raux and Eskenazi, 2009).

User-adaptive spoken dialogue systems can be categorized into two types: adaptation of the system's output and adaptation during input interpretation. Several previous studies have adapted the system output to users by changing behaviors such as the contents of the system utterances (Jokinen and Kanto, 2004) and dialogue management (Komatani et al., 2005), pause and gaze duration (Dohsaka et al., 2010), how to respond to a user (e.g., head nods or short vocalization like "uh-huh") (de Kok et al., 2013), etc. On the other hand, there have been only a few studies on adaptation during input interpretation. As one example, Paek and Chickering (2007) exploited the history of a user's commands and adapted the system's ASR language model to the user.

Our adaptation is concerned with both of the above types; its result changes turn-taking, i.e., whether the system responds to fragments or not, and input interpretation, i.e., in which unit the system interprets user utterances. As far as we know, this is the first user adaptation method proposed for the restoration of utterance units.

3 Posteriori Restoration for Incorrectly Segmented Utterances

We first explain how conventional systems respond to an incorrectly segmented utterance. Here, a user utterance is segmented into a pair of utterance fragments denoted as first and second fragments. Given such a pair, one type of conventional system that does not allow barge-ins keeps responding to the first fragment, ignoring the second fragment of the user utterance that follows. Another type of conventional system that allows barge-ins can terminate its response for the first fragment but responds on the basis of an ASR result for the second fragment only.

An outline of our a posteriori restoration process is shown in Fig. 1. When a pair of utterance fragments is close in time, this process is invoked at the timing when the second fragment starts. The process consists of two steps:

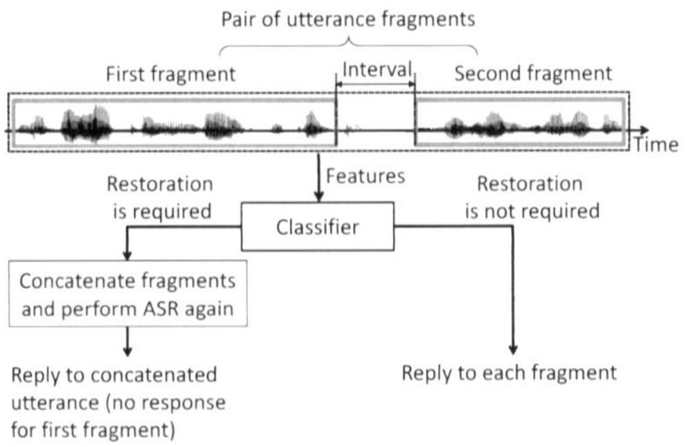

Figure 1: Overview of proposed restoration process.

1. Classify whether a pair of utterance fragments resulted from an incorrect segmentation or not, i.e., whether restoration is required or not.

2. Restore the utterance if it has been incorrectly segmented. The system also restores turn-taking, i.e., terminates its response to the first fragment and waits until the second fragment ends. The aim here is to avoid the system speaking during a user utterance.

If restoration is required, the system performs ASR again after concatenating the fragments to restore the ASR results, which may be erroneous due to incorrect segmentation. The system then responds on the basis of the ASR result for the concatenated fragments after the second fragment ends.

If restoration is not required, i.e., the fragments are deemed to be two utterances, the system responds normally; that is, it generates responses based on the ASR results for each fragment.

There is a trade-off between the occurrences of erroneous system responses caused by incorrect segmentation and response delay resulting from the restoration. Our approach gives weight to preventing the erroneous responses at the expense of a small delay of system responses. We endeavor to reduce damage stemming from the delay: by producing fillers such as "Well" to prevent unnatural silences (Komatani et al., 2014) and improving implementation to reduce the delay itself.

4 Obtaining Appropriate Thresholds from Dialogue Tempos

The threshold for the temporal interval between a pair of utterance fragments plays a dominant role

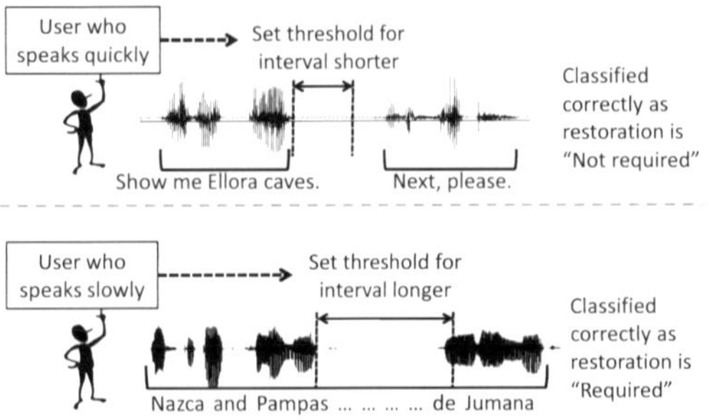

Figure 2: Examples of user-adapted restoration.

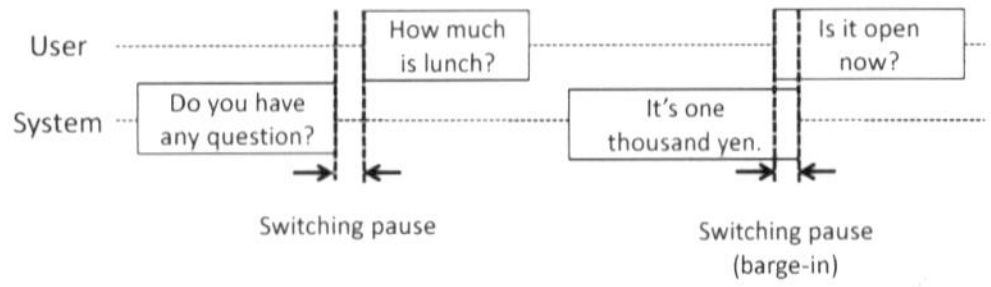

Figure 3: Examples of switching pauses.

in the classification of whether the pair is required to be restored. We assume that appropriate thresholds depend on the way each user speaks. Examples of how the thresholds need to change are given in Fig. 2.

It is assumed that brisk users speak with less disfluency and with shorter pauses. Thus, the threshold needs to be set shorter, which avoids unnecessary restoration and subsequent late responses. We should point out here that such users often repeat their utterances when the system's response is not quick enough because they think the system has not heard their utterance, and this causes utterance collision (Funakoshi et al., 2010).

In contrast, "slow" users often speak with long pauses during their utterances. In this case, the threshold needs to be set longer, which enables the system to restore utterances even when longer pauses exist in a single utterance.

4.1 Definition of Dialogue Tempo

We define dialogue tempo as a quantitative parameter showing how each user speaks. Specifically, it is defined as the average duration of switching pauses, which are times between when a system finishes speaking and a user starts speaking, as depicted in Fig. 3. We calculate this per user from the beginning of the dialogue. The duration of a switching pause becomes negative when the user barges in, i.e., the user starts speaking during a system utterance. Although speaking rate can also be used for defining the tempo, we here use the duration of switching pauses. Although the tempo is calculated for each dialogue here, it can be accumulated per user when a user ID can be obtained (e.g., mobile phones, in-car interfaces, etc.).

4.2 Appropriate Threshold for Interval

We set appropriate thresholds for each user to investigate the relationship of the threshold to the dialogue tempo. By "appropriate" here we mean that the threshold can classify whether the restoration is required or not with high accuracy. The restoration for a pair is classified as "required" if its interval is shorter than the threshold and "not required" otherwise.

Here, we set the threshold as a discriminant plane (point) of a support vector machine (SVM) whose only feature is the temporal interval between two utterance fragments. A reference label was manually given, i.e., whether the restoration is required or not. We used the SMO module in Weka (version 3.6.9) (Hall et al., 2009) as an SVM implementation. The parameters were set to its default values, e.g., its kernel function was polynomial. The SVM is able to set the discriminant plane that maximizes distances between classes. If a user's training data did not contain both positive and negative labels, we set fixed values for the threshold as exceptions: large enough (2.00 seconds) when all labels in training data were "restoration is not required" and small enough (0.00 seconds) when they were all "restoration is required".

4.3 Target Data

Our target data were collected by our system that introduces the world heritage sites (Nakano et al., 2011). In total, speech data of 35 participants were recorded. Each participant engaged in 8-minute dialogues four times. Participants were not given any special instructions prior to or during the dialogues.

We used data of only 26 of the 35 participants because nine participants did not have sufficient utterance pairs. Specifically, we used the data only of participants who had more than six utterance pairs whose temporal intervals were close in time (less than 2.00 seconds), with each fragment longer than 0.80 seconds. This was because our target is originally a single utterance, and we regard pairs whose intervals are greater than 2.00 seconds and which are very short as not such an utterance (Komatani et al., 2014).

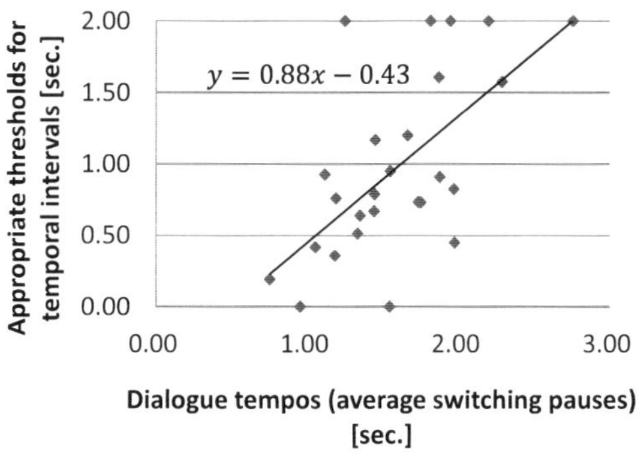

Figure 4: Correlations between appropriate thresholds and dialogue tempos per participant.

We obtained 3,099 utterances from the 26 participants. The data included 390 utterance pairs that satisfy the above conditions to possibly be a single utterance. We manually assigned the labels of whether the pair is a single utterance in accordance with the procedure in (Hotta et al., 2014). Since 240 pairs were originally single utterances and 150 pairs were not, the classification accuracy by the majority baseline was 61.5%.

4.4 Correlation between Dialogue Tempos and Appropriate Thresholds

We investigated the correlation between dialogue tempos and the appropriate thresholds for restoration for each of the 26 participants. All 3,099 utterances were used to obtain the dialogue tempos of each participant. We excluded outliers: specifically, utterances whose switching pauses are less than -3.5 seconds and more than 6 seconds were excluded, since such large values simply indicate that the participant was thinking deeply. These values were determined experimentally.

Figure 4 plots the correlation, where the x-axis denotes the dialogue tempos and the y-axis denotes the appropriate thresholds, both in seconds. The correlation coefficient was 0.63. The linear regression function is derived as

$$y = 0.88x - 0.43. \quad (1)$$

This function is used in the next section for obtaining appropriate thresholds from the dialogue tempos per participant.

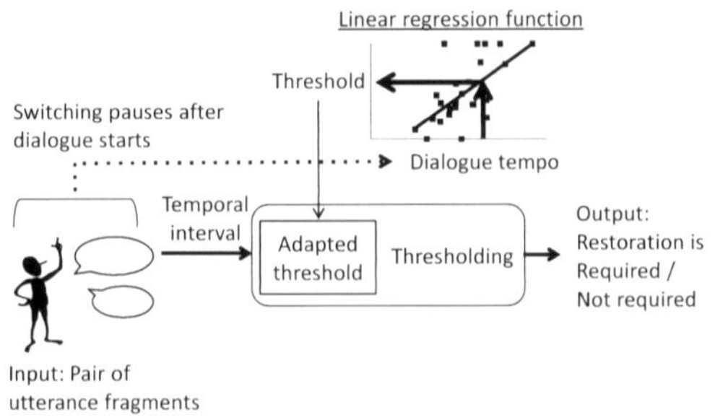

Figure 5: User-adapted classification in thresholding.

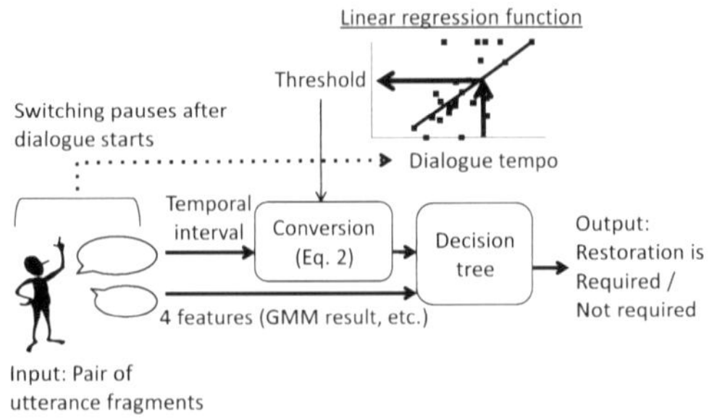

Figure 6: User-adapted classification in decision tree.

5 Adapting Classifiers for Restoration to Users

We investigate whether the correlation between dialogue tempos and appropriate thresholds is helpful or not. The correlation is used to derive the user-adaptive threshold from the user's dialogue tempo and thus to improve classification accuracy for whether restoration is required or not. First, the system obtains the appropriate thresholds for the temporal intervals from the user's dialogue tempos by using the linear regression function. It then adapts the classifier to each user. We examine user adaptation for two classification methods: thresholding and decision tree.

5.1 Thresholding

Thresholding is the simplest method for classification on the basis of the temporal interval between utterance fragments. We first examine the effectiveness of user adaptation with this method.

The process flow of thresholding with user adaptation is shown in Fig. 5. Its input is a pair of utterance fragments (and the temporal interval between them). The system calculates the user's dialogue tempo on the basis of switching pauses from when the dialogue starts and obtains a threshold value corresponding to the tempo by the linear regression function. The system then classifies whether the restoration is required or not by using the adapted threshold. The restoration for a pair is classified as "required" if its temporal interval is shorter than the adapted threshold and is "not required" otherwise.

5.2 Decision Tree

We also use a decision tree, which is a more complicated classifier than thresholding. We show that user adaptation is also effective in this case.

The process flow of the decision tree with user adaptation is depicted in Fig. 6. In addition to the temporal interval between a pair of utterance fragments, we use four features that were shown to be effective in our previous report (Hotta et al., 2014): an average confidence score of the first fragment, noise detection results by a Gaussian mixture model (GMM), F0 range of the first fragment, and maximum loudness in the first fragment.

The user adaptation is performed by converting the temporal interval only out of these five features. The interval is converted in both the training and classification phases in the decision tree learning. Instead of adapting the thresholds to each user, we convert its feature values. This is because, in the normal training phase of decision tree learning, a single decision tree having fixed thresholds across different users is obtained. Our approach is to relatively convert the feature values for the interval in accordance with each user, and thus enabling the system to classify adaptively to users with a constant threshold. Specifically, we use ratios between the threshold values of a target user and the average one of all users. The feature value is converted using Eq. (2), where we denote an original interval i by a user j as I_{ij} and its converted value as $\hat{I_{ij}}$:

$$\hat{I_{ij}} = I_{ij} \times \frac{T_0}{T_j}, \quad (2)$$

where T_j is a threshold value adapted to user j, which is obtained from the user's dialogue tempo and the linear regression function, and T_0 is a constant set to 0.519 seconds, which was the average interval of all users.

Our aim with this conversion is as follows. The correlation depicted in Fig. 4 shows that thresh-

Table 1: Deviation of parameters in linear regression function.

	a	b
Avg.	0.883	−0.431
Std. dev.	0.034	0.057

olds need to be smaller for users with quicker dialogue tempos. This conversion makes the feature values of the interval relatively larger for such users (having smaller T_j) by multiplying the ratio T_0/T_j. This is equivalent to setting a relatively smaller threshold even though fixed and common thresholds are used in decision tree learning.

6 Experimental Evaluation

We investigated whether the user adaptation contributes to improving the classification accuracy. We also experimentally checked the upper limit and convergence speed of the proposed adaptation by comparing the accuracy with its batch version, in which all utterance data from a target user is assumed to be always available.

6.1 Performance of User Adaptation

We investigated the classification accuracy for the two methods, thresholding and decision tree, as discussed in Section 5.

Experiments were conducted under two conditions: closed test and cross validation. In the closed tests, we used the same data in both adaptation and test phases, and under the cross-validation condition, we set each user as a unit.

Specifically, in thresholding, we extracted the data of one user from the data of all 26 participants, derived linear regression functions from the data of the 25 participants, and calculated the classification accuracy using the data of the one separated user. This process was repeated 26 times. During this cross validation, we investigated the deviations of the two parameters of the linear regression function $y = ax + b$, shown in Eq. (1). The results are listed in Table 1. The two parameter values, a and b, only changed slightly, and their averages were almost the same as the coefficients in Eq. (1), which were calculated using all data. This indicates that the linear regression function only depends only a little on the training sets and thus has more generality than the decision tree. This is because the number of parameters is small (only two).

As a result of this stability of the parameters, for simplicity of experimentation, we assumed that the linear regression function was known under the decision tree learning condition, that is, that the dialogue tempos of each user can be converted to the intervals, which are used in Eq. (2).

6.1.1 Thresholding Adapted to Users

Classification accuracies in thresholding are listed in the left column of Table 2. The condition "no adaptation" denotes the case where a constant threshold (0.822 seconds) was used to classify all data. This threshold was determined optimally for all data by an SVM (SMO in Weka) in the same manner as discussed in Section 4.2.

The results show that the user adaptation improved classification accuracies by 3.3 and 3.0 percentage points for the closed test and cross-validation conditions, respectively. We can also see that the accuracies of the closed test and cross-validation conditions were almost equivalent under both adaptation conditions ("no" and "online"). This suggests that no overfitting occurred in these cases and thus a similar performance will be obtained for unknown users. The number of parameters is small, which is why they are stable, as already shown in Table 1.

6.1.2 Decision Tree Learning Adapted to Users

Classification accuracies for decision tree learning are listed in the right column of Table 2. The condition "no adaptation" denotes normal decision tree learning, that is, no feature values were converted using Eq. (2). These results show that the user adaptation improved the accuracies by 2.1 and 7.4 percentage points for the closed test and cross-validation conditions, respectively. The difference in the cross-validation condition was statistically significant by the McNemar test ($p = 3.2 \times 10^{-4}$).

We can see that the accuracies of the cross-validation conditions were lower than those in the closed test. This is because a decision tree has many more parameters to be trained than thresholding, and thus the obtained trees were overfitted to the training data. This means that the accuracies under the closed test condition were unreasonably high. Note that the accuracy under the "no adaptation" condition in the cross validation was lower than that of the thresholding. This means that the complicated classifier makes the accuracy worse.

Table 2: Classification accuracies with/without adaptation.

	Thresholding		Decision tree	
	closed	cross validation	closed	cross validation
No adaptation	281/390 (72.1%)	281/390 (72.1%)	312/390 (80.0%)	271/390 (69.5%)
Online adaptation	294/390 (75.4%)	293/390 (75.1%)	320/390 (82.1%)	300/390 (76.9%)

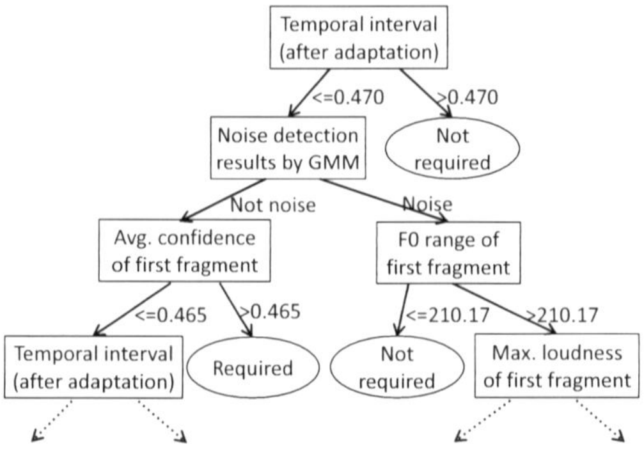

Figure 7: Obtained decision tree (depth < 4).

In contrast, when user adaptation was performed, the accuracy under the "online adaptation" condition in cross validation outperformed that of thresholding. This implies that user adaptation makes the features more general and essential, and thus overfitting was avoided even when the more complicated classifier (decision tree) was used.

Figure 7 shows the top part of the obtained decision tree, whose depth did not exceed four. The feature at the top was the temporal interval after the user adaptation. This fact also confirms that the feature was effective in the decision tree.

6.2 Comparison with Batch Adaptation

In all experiments discussed thus far, each user's dialogue tempo was calculated by using the duration of switching pauses from the beginning of the dialogue until the target utterance. We call this "online adaptation".

We also virtually calculated dialogue tempos by using the whole dialogue containing the target utterance. This condition, called "batch adaptation", virtually assumes that the dialogue data of a target user has been sufficiently obtained beforehand. It thus corresponds to a case where the target user's characteristics have already been obtained. We discuss its performance under this condition, since this can be regarded as an upper limit of user adaptation. Since performances of the batch adaptation were calculated as the closed tests, those of the online adaptation were calculated also as the closed tests.

Table 3: Classification accuracies by adaptation methods.

	Thresholding	Decision tree
No	281/390 (72.1%)	312/390 (80.0%)
Online	294/390 (75.4%)	320/390 (82.1%)
Batch	306/390 (78.5%)	331/390 (84.9%)

Table 3 shows the classification accuracies under the no adaptation and two adaptation conditions. Here, for simplicity of experiments under the decision tree condition, we assume that the shapes of decision trees used in the online adaptation were the same as the batch adaptation; the available number of switching pause durations to calculate dialogue tempos increased online. The results show that the accuracies of the batch adaptation were higher than online adaptation conditions by 3.1 and 2.8 percentage points for thresholding and decision tree, respectively. This implies that the classification performance is unstable in online adaptation when the number of available utterances of the target user is small.

6.3 Convergence Speed of Adaptation

We further investigated the convergence speed of the online adaptation. We conducted the following experiments only for thresholding because of the simplicity of implementation. It is natural that the classification accuracy of the online adaptation converges into that of batch adaptation when the number of a target user's available utterances increases, as batch adaptation assumes that all utterances are obtained beforehand. We plot the classification performance when the number of a target user's available utterance increased to analyze its convergence speed. Here, the performances were calculated as the closed tests, similarly with the previous section.

Figure 8 shows the number of correct classifica-

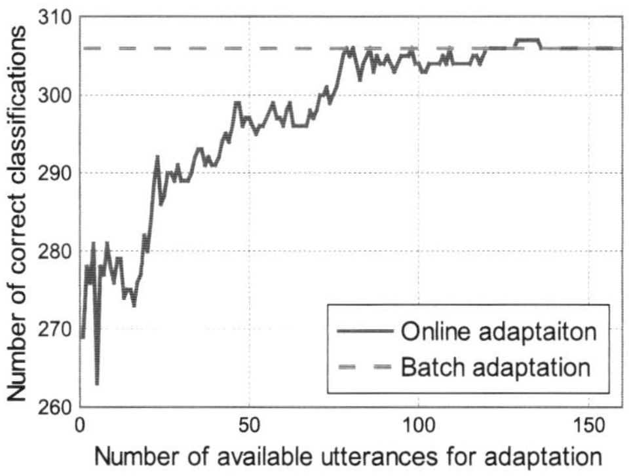

Figure 8: Convergence speed of adaptation (in thresholding)

tions when the number of available utterances for the online adaptation increased. Vertical and horizontal axes denote the number of correct classifications and available utterances for the adaptation, respectively. More specifically, the horizontal axis shows that the user's dialogue tempo was calculated by using data from the beginning of the dialogue to the x-th utterance. The dashed line at the upper part of the graph denotes the case of batch adaptation, i.e., $y = 306$, as listed in Table 3.

We can see that when the number of available utterances was small ($x < 10$), the number of correct classifications was significantly varied and also small (about 275). The correct classification results increased when the available utterances increased and became equivalent to that of batch adaptation after $x = 80$. This shows that the performance converged with about 80 utterances.

These results lead us to the following conclusions. First, when the number of available utterances is small, i.e., less than 10, it is better not to adapt the classifier because the performances were lower than under the "no adaptation" condition, whose number of correct classifications was 281, as shown in Table 3. Performance does not degrade if we adapt the classifier after about 10 utterances are obtained from the target user. Second, although it is unlikely that a one-shot user will make 80 utterances at once, it is possible to obtain such a number of utterances when user IDs are available and a user's utterances are obtained through several sessions. User IDs can be obtained when the system is used through personal terminals (e.g., cell phones) or by using techniques such as speaker identification.

7 Conclusion

We developed a user-adaptive method to classify whether restoration is required for incorrectly segmented utterances by focusing on each user's style of speaking. We empirically showed the correlation between dialogue tempo and appropriate thresholds for temporal intervals between utterance fragments, which are an important feature for the classification. We then investigated classification accuracies by adapting two classifiers: thresholding and decision tree. Results showed that the accuracies improved in both classifiers more than in the baselines using a constant threshold for all users.

Several issues remain as future work to improve the classification accuracy even more. First, we intend to exploit aspects other than the dialogue tempos based on switching pauses to represent each user's style of speaking, such as speaking rate and the frequency of self-repairs. Lexical or semantic features, which were used in previous studies such as (Nakano et al., 1999), can also be used together. Second, we want to adapt features other than the temporal interval between two utterance fragments used in this paper. For example, the maximum loudness of the first fragment can be adapted to each user. In addition, since some users have habitual intonation at the end of utterances, this can also be a target of adaptation. Third, the experiments in this paper were conducted using already recorded dialogue data between a human and a system. It is possible that the user behaviors in this data were influenced by the system performance when the data was collected. We therefore need to conduct another experiment where a system with the proposed method actually interacts with humans. Other metrics such as user satisfaction and completion time will be helpful to verify the performance. Finally, variations of speaking styles exist within the same user as well as across users when the system is used repeatedly (Komatani et al., 2009). This occurs especially when the user first starts using the system, i.e., novice users. We need much more data per user to analyze this, but it is possible that such a consideration can improve the classification accuracy.

Acknowledgments

This work was partly supported by the Casio Science Promotion Foundation.

References

Linda Bell, Johan Boye, and Joakim Gustafson. 2001. Real-time handling of fragmented utterances. In *Proc. NAACL Workshop on Adaption in Dialogue Systems*, pages 2–8.

Iwan de Kok, Dirk Heylen, and Louis-Philippe Morency. 2013. Speaker-adaptive multimodal prediction model for listener responses. In *Proc. International Conference on Multimodal Interaction (ICMI)*, pages 51–58.

Kohji Dohsaka, Atsushi Kanemoto, Ryuichiro Higashinaka, Yasuhiro Minami, and Eisaku Maeda. 2010. User-adaptive coordination of agent communicative behavior in spoken dialogue. In *Proc. Annual Meeting of the Special Interest Group on Discourse and Dialogue (SIGDIAL)*, pages 314–321.

Luciana Ferrer, Elizabeth Shriberg, and Andreas Stolcke. 2003. A prosody-based approach to end-of-utterance detection that does not require speech recognition. In *Proc. IEEE International Conference on Acoustics, Speech & Signal Processing (ICASSP)*, volume 1, pages 608–611.

Kotaro Funakoshi, Mikio Nakano, Kazuki Kobayashi, Takanori Komatsu, and Seiji Yamada. 2010. Non-humanlike spoken dialogue: A design perspective. In *Proc. Annual Meeting of the Special Interest Group on Discourse and Dialogue (SIGDIAL)*, pages 176–184.

Mark Hall, Eibe Frank, Geoffrey Holmes, Bernhard Pfahringer, Peter Reutemann, and Ian H. Witten. 2009. The WEKA data mining software: an update. *SIGKDD Explor. Newsl.*, 11:10–18, November.

Naoki Hotta, Kazunori Komatani, Satoshi Sato, and Mikio Nakano. 2014. Detecting incorrectly-segmented utterances for posteriori restoration of turn-taking and ASR results. In *Proc. Annual Conference of the International Speech Communication Association (INTERSPEECH)*, pages 313–317.

Kristiina Jokinen and Kari Kanto. 2004. User expertise modeling and adaptivity in a speech-based e-mail system. In *Proc. Annual Meeting of the Association for Computational Linguistics (ACL)*, pages 87–94.

Norihide Kitaoka, Masashi Takeuchi, Ryota Nishimura, and Seiichi Nakagawa. 2005. Response timing detection using prosodic and linguistic information for human-friendly spoken dialog systems. *Journal of The Japanese Society for Artificial Intellignece*, 20(3):220–228.

Kazunori Komatani, Shinichi Ueno, Tatsuya Kawahara, and Hiroshi G. Okuno. 2005. User modeling in spoken dialogue systems to generate flexible guidance. *User Modeling and User-Adapted Interaction*, 15(1):169–183.

Kazunori Komatani, Tatsuya Kawahara, and Hiroshi G. Okuno. 2009. A model of temporally changing user behaviors in a deployed spoken dialogue system. In *Proc. International Conference on User Modeling, Adaptation, and Personalization (UMAP)*, volume 5535 of *Lecture Notes in Computer Science*, pages 409–414. Springer.

Kazunori Komatani, Naoki Hotta, and Satoshi Sato. 2014. Restoring incorrectly segmented keywords and turn-taking caused by short pauses. In *Proc. International Workshop on Spoken Dialogue Systems (IWSDS)*, pages 27–38.

Mikio Nakano, Noboru Miyazaki, Jun ichi Hirasawa, Kohji Dohsaka, and Takeshi Kawabata. 1999. Understanding unsegmented user utterances in real-time spoken dialogue systems. In *Proc. Annual Meeting of the Association for Computational Linguistics (ACL)*, pages 200–207.

Mikio Nakano, Shun Sato, Kazunori Komatani, Kyoko Matsuyama, Kotaro Funakoshi, and Hiroshi G. Okuno. 2011. A two-stage domain selection framework for extensible multi-domain spoken dialogue systems. In *Proc. Annual Meeting of the Special Interest Group on Discourse and Dialogue (SIGDIAL)*, pages 18–29, June.

Tim Paek and David Maxwell Chickering. 2007. Improving command and control speech recognition on mobile devices: using predictive user models for language modeling. *User Modeling and User-Adapted Interaction*, 17(1-2):93–117.

Antoine Raux and Maxine Eskenazi. 2008. Optimizing Endpointing Thresholds using Dialogue Features in a Spoken Dialogue System. In *Proc. SIGdial Workshop on Discourse and Dialogue*, pages 1–10.

Antoine Raux and Maxine Eskenazi. 2009. A finite-state turn-taking model for spoken dialog systems. In *Proc. Human Language Technologies: The 2009 Annual Conference of the North American Chapter of the Association for Computational Linguistics (HLT NAACL)*, pages 629–637.

Ryo Sato, Ryuichiro Higashinaka, Masafumi Tamoto, Mikio Nakano, and Kiyoaki Aikawa. 2002. Learning decision trees to determine turn-taking by spoken dialogue systems. In *Proc. Int'l Conf. Spoken Language Processing (ICSLP)*, pages 861–864.

Incremental Coordination: Attention-Centric Speech Production in a Physically Situated Conversational Agent

Zhou Yu[1]
Carnegie Mellon University
5000 Forbes Avenue
Pittsburgh, PA
15213
zhouyu@cs.cmu.edu

Dan Bohus
Microsoft Research
One Microsoft Way
Redmond, WA
98052
dbohus@microsoft.com

Eric Horvitz
Microsoft Research
One Microsoft Way
Redmond, WA
98052
horvitz@microsoft.com

Abstract

Inspired by studies of human-human conversations, we present methods for incrementally coordinating speech production with listeners' visual foci of attention. We introduce a model that considers the demands and availability of listeners' attention at the onset and throughout the production of system utterances, and that incrementally coordinates speech synthesis with the listener's gaze. We present an implementation and deployment of the model in a physically situated dialog system and discuss lessons learned.

1 Introduction

Participants in a conversation coordinate with one another on producing turns, and often co-produce language by using verbal and non-verbal signals, including gaze, gestures, prosody and grammatical structures. Among these signals, patterns of attention play an important role.

Goodwin (1981) highlights a variety of coordination mechanisms that speakers use to achieve *mutual orientation* at the beginning and throughout turns, such as pausing, adding phrasal breaks, lengthening spoken units, and even changing the structure of the sentence on the fly to secure the listener's attention. His work suggests that, beyond a simple errors-in-production view, "disfluencies" help to coordinate on turns, and generally facilitate co-production among speakers and listeners. Goodwin (1981) presents sample snippets of conversations recorded in the wild, annotated to show when the gaze of a listener turns to meet the gaze of the speaker (marked with *) and when mutual gaze is maintained (marked with an underline). In the examples reproduced below from Goodwin's work, pauses and repeats are used to align grammatical sentences with a listener's gaze:

Anyway, Uh:, We went *t- I went ta bed

Restarts can be used as a means of aligning the timing of a full grammatical utterance with the start of the process by which gaze is moving towards the speaker (process indicated by the broken underline), as in the following:

She- she's reaching the p- she's at the *point I'm

While most work to date in spoken dialog systems has focused on the acoustic channel in physically situated multimodal systems, an opportunity arises to use vision to take the participants' attention into account when coordinating on the production of system utterances. We investigate this direction and introduce a model that incrementally coordinates language production and speech synthesis with the listeners' foci of attention. The model centers on computing whether the listener's attention matches a set of attentional demands for the utterance at hand. When attentional demands are not met, the model triggers a sequence of linguistic devices in an attempt to recover the listener's attention and to coordinate the system's speech with it. We introduce and demonstrate the promise of incremental coordination of language production with attention in situated systems.

Following a brief review of related work, we describe the proposed approach in more detail in Section 3. In Section 4, we discuss lessons learned

[1] Research conducted during an internship at Microsoft Research

Proceedings of the SIGDIAL 2015 Conference, pages 402–406,
Prague, Czech Republic, 2-4 September 2015.

from an in-the-wild deployment of this approach in a directions-giving robot.

2 Related work

The critical role of gaze in coordinating turns in dialog is well known and has been previously studied (*i.a.*, Duncan, 1972; Goodwin, 1981). Kendon (1967) found that speakers signal their wish to release the turn by gazing to the interlocutor. Vertegaal et al. (2003) found evidence that lack of eye contact decreases the efficiency of turn-taking in video conferencing.

Most previous work on incremental processing in dialog has focused on the acoustic channel, including efforts on recognizing, generating, and synthesizing language incrementally. For instance, Skantze and Hjalmarsson (2010) showed that an incremental generator using filled pauses and self-corrections achieved (in a wizard of Oz experiment) shorter response times and was perceived as more efficient than a non-incremental generator. Guhe and Schilder (2002) have also used incremental generation for self-corrections.

Situated and multiparty systems often incorporate attention and gaze in their models for turn taking and interaction planning (Traum and Rickel, 2002; Bohus and Horvitz, 2011). Sciutti et al. (2015) used gaze as an implicit signal for turn taking in a robotic teaching context. In an in-car navigation setting, incremental speech synthesis that accommodates user's cognitive load was shown to improve user experience but not users' performance on tasks (Kousidis, et al., 2015).

3 Model

Motivated by observations from human-human communication dynamics, we propose a model to coordinate speech production with the listeners' focus of attention in a physically situated dialog system. We believe that close coordination between language production and listeners' attention is important in creating more effective and natural interactions.

The proposed model subsumes three subcomponents. The first component defines *attentional demands* on each system output. For successful collaboration, certain utterances require the listener's focus of attention to be on the system or on task-relevant locations (*e.g.*, the direction the robot is pointing towards), while other utterances do not carry high attentional demands. The second component is an inference model that tracks the listener's focus of attention, *i.e.*, the *attentional supply*. The third component alters the system's speech production in an incremental manner to coordinate in stream with the listeners' attention. The component regulates production based on identifying when the attention supply does not match the demands.

In the following subsections, we discuss the model's components in more detail, and their implementation in the context of *Directions Robot*, a physically situated humanoid (Nao) robotic system that interacts with people and provides directions inside our building (Bohus, Saw and Horvitz, 2014). Figure 1 shows a sample dialog with the robot. The proposed coordination model can be adapted to other multimodal dialog systems with adjustments based on the task and the situational context.

3.1 Attentional demands

We consider two types of attentional demand. The first one, which we refer to as *onset demand*, encapsulates Goodwin's observation (1981) that participants in a conversation generally aim to achieve mutual orientation at the *beginnings* of turns. The model specifies that, at each system phrase onset, the listeners' attention must be on the system. In our implementation, we require that at least one of the addressees of the current utterance is attending. The system infers attention under uncertainty from visual scene analysis, and we express the attentional demand by means of a probability threshold. In the current implementation, this threshold was set to 0.6: the onset attentional demand is satisfied if the probability that at least one of the addressees is attending to the robot is greater than 0.6 when the system is launching a phrase.

In addition, a second type of attentional demand, denoted *production demand*, is defined at the level of the dialog act by the system developer. During certain system acts, for instance ones that

1 S:	Hi there!
2 S:	Do you need help finding something?
3 U:	Yes
4 S:	Where are you trying to get to?
5 U:	Room 4505
6 S:	To get to room 4505, • walk along that hallway, • turn left and keep on walking down the hallway. • Room 4505 will be the 1st room on your right.
7 S:	By the way, • would you guys mind swiping your badge on the reader below so I know who I've been interacting with?

Figure 1. Sample interaction with the Directions Robot.

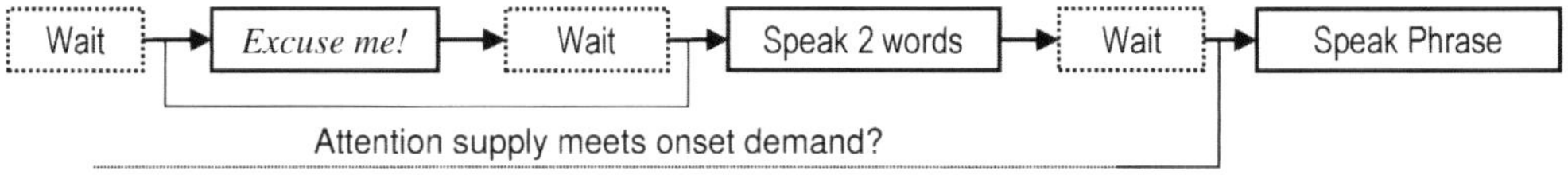

Figure 2. Actions taken to coordinate with attentional demands at phrase onset.

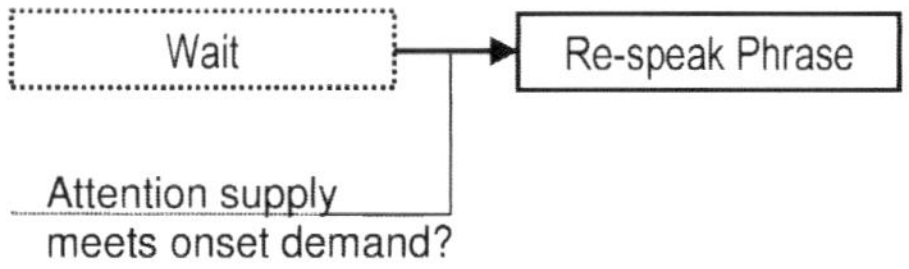

Figure 3. Actions taken to coordinate production with attentional demands.

carry important content or that are deemed as unexpected for the listeners, it is important for addressees to attend to the system or to certain task-relevant objects. The production demand defines where the listeners' attention is expected during the production of the system's utterances, *i.e.*, it defines a set of permitted targets. For instance, when the robot is giving directions in turn 6 from Figure 1, the production demand is set to *Robot* or *PointingDirections*—the locations that the robot points to via its gestures as it renders directions. Similarly, when the robot asks users to swipe their badge in turn 7, the production demand is set to *Robot* and *Badge* indicating that these are the appropriate targets of attention throughout that particular utterance. In contrast, other dialog acts, such as the robot asking *"Where are you trying to get to?"* in turn 4, are naturally expected at that point in the conversation, do not impose high cognitive demands, and can be conveyed without requiring attention on the robot throughout the utterance.

3.2 Attention supply

The Directions Robot is deployed in front of a bank of elevators. In this environment, the attention of engaged participants can shift between a variety of targets including the robot, other task-related attractors (*e.g.*, the direction that the robot is pointing, the sign next to the robot, the user's badge, and the badge reader), personal devices such as smartphones and notepads, and other people in the environment. To simplify, in the implementation we describe here, we model attention supply only over the three targets already mentioned above: *Robot*, *PointingDirection*, *Badge*, and we cluster all other attentional foci as *Elsewhere*.

The robot tracks the (geometric) direction of visual attention for each participant in the scene via a model constructed using supervised machine learning methods. The model leverages features from visual subsystems (*e.g.*, face detection and tracking, head-pose detection, etc.) and infers the probability that a participant's visual attention is directed to the robot, or to the left, right, up, down, or back of the scene. These probabilities are then combined via a heuristic rule that takes into account the dialog state and the robot's pointing to infer whether the participant's attention is on *Robot*, *PointingDirection*, *Badge*, or *Elsewhere*.

3.3 Coordinative policy

The third component in the proposed model, the *coordinative policy* controls the speech synthesis engine and deploys various mechanisms, such as pauses, restarts, interjections, to coordinate the system's speech with the listeners' attention.

Figure 2 shows a diagram of the currently implemented coordinative policy for onset attentional demand. If the listeners' attention does not meet the attentional demand at the beginning of a phrase, the system will perform a sequence of actions, starting with a wait (pause), followed by an attention drawing interjection such as "*Excuse me!*", followed by another wait action, followed by launching the phrase. If the onset attentional demand is still not satisfied the phrase is interrupted after 2 words, then another wait action is taken, followed finally by launching the entire phrase. The wait actions are chosen with a random duration between 1.5 and 2.5 seconds. The interjection is skipped if it was already produced once in this utterance, or if the preceding phrase or the remainder of the utterance contains only one word. As soon as the attention supply matches the onset demand, the system launches the phrase. If the demand is met during the interjection, the interjection will still be completed. In addition, the policy will not switch from a wait action to a verbal action if the system detects that the user is likely speaking.

We set both onset and production attentional demands on a per dialog act basis. The surface realization of a single dialog act can however involve multiple *phrases*, defined here as continuous speech units separated by a pause longer than 250 ms, as signaled by runtime events generated by the speech synthesis engine (• is used to demark phrases in the example from Figure 1.) The coordinative policy uses the attentional demand information specified on the dialog act, but operates at the phrase level. In other words, the onset demand is checked at the beginning of every phrase in the dialog act.

In addition to reasoning about onset attention, the proposed model also assesses if production demand is met at the end of phrases, *i.e.* if the accumulated attention throughout the phrase matched the production demand specified for the dialog act. If this is not the case, a wait is triggered (to re-acquire onset attention), and then the phrase is repeated. If the onset demand is met at any point during the wait, the system immediately repeats the phrase. The variability of the wait durations, coupled with variability in the attention estimates and the times when the specified onset or production attentional demand is met, leads to a variety of production behaviors in the robot.

4 Deployment and lessons learned

We implemented the model described above in the Directions Robot system and deployed it on three robots situated in front of the bank of elevators on floors 2, 3, and 4 of a four-story building. Appendix A contains an annotated demonstrative trace of the system's behaviors. Additional videos and snippets of interactions are available at: http://1drv.ms/1GQ1ori. While a comprehensive evaluation of the model is pending further improvements, we discuss below several lessons learned from observing natural interactions with the robots running the current implementation.

A first observation is that the usefulness and naturalness of the behaviors triggered by the robot hinges critically on the accuracy of the inferences about attention. When the model incorrectly concludes that the participants' attention is not on the robot (false-negative errors), the coordinative policy triggers unnecessary pauses, interjections and phrase repeats that can be disruptive and unnatural. The attention inference challenge includes the need to recognize both the participants' *visual* focus of attention (which in itself is a difficult task in the wild) and *cognitive* attention as being on task. Cognitive attention does not overlap with visual attention all the time. For example, at times participants would shift their visual attention away from the robot as they leaned in and cocked their ear to listen closely. Problems in inferring attention are compounded by lower-level vision and tracking problems.

Second, we believe that there is a need for better integration of the coordinative policy with current existing models for language generation, gesture production, multiparty turn-taking and engagement. Beyond the number of words in a phrase, the current policy does not leverage information about the contents of phrases that are about to be generated. This sometimes leads to unnatural sequences, such as "*Excuse me! By the way, would you mind [...]*" Another important question is how to automatically coordinate the robot's physical pointing gestures when repeating phrases or when phrases are interrupted. With respect to turn taking, problems detected in early experimentation led to an adjustment of the coordinative policy that we described earlier: the system does not move from a wait to a verbal action if it detects that the user is likely speaking. Beyond this simple rule, we believe that the floor dynamics in the turn-taking model need to take into account the system's discontinuous production, *e.g.*, take into account the fact that the pauses injected within utterances might be perceived by the participants as floor releases. Further tuning of the timings of the pauses, contingent on the dialog state and expectations about when the attention might return, as well as a tighter integration with the engagement model might be required. For instance, we observed cases where the robot's decision to pause to wait for a participant's attention to return from the direction that the robot was pointing (before continuing to the next phrase) was interpreted as the end of the utterance and the participant walked away before session completion.

Third, we find that the definition of attentional demands (both onset and production) need to be further refined (in some cases on a per-dialog state basis) and modeled at a finer level of granularity, down to the phrase level. In an utterance like "By the way, would you mind swiping your badge?", the "By the way" phrase is in fact an attention attractor, and itself does not require attentional demands and thus should be modeled separately.

5 Conclusion

We presented a model for incrementally coordinating language production with listeners' foci of attention in a multimodal dialog systems. An initial implementation and in-the-wild deployment of the proposed model has highlighted a number of areas for improvement. While further investigation and refinements are needed, the interactions collected highlight the potential and promise of the proposed approach for creating more natural and more effective interactions in physically situated settings.

Appendix A: Description of demonstrative sample trace (video at http://1drv.ms/1GQ1ori): At time t_1 the participant's (P_{11}) attention is on the robot and the robot begins giving directions. At the end of the first phrase (t_2), P_{11}'s attention has switched to the other participant as they discuss whether 4800 is really the room they're looking for. Overall the production attention supply (mean of instantaneous attention level over the duration of the phrase, shown in plot A) has exceeded production demand on the initial phrase, so the system deems that no repetition of the phrase is necessary. At the same time, instead of launching the next phrase, the system waits because onset attentional demand is not met. At t_3, onset demand is still not met. Thus, the system launches an interjection followed by launching the first two words at t_4. At t_5, P_{11}'s attention is still not on the robot (according to the inference model, displayed in plot B), and the robot pauses. At t_6, the onset attentional demand is met and the robot re-launches the phrase "go along that hallway". At the end of the phrase (t_7), both the production demand for this phrase and the onset demand for the next phrase are met. However the system has detected that P_{11} is speaking and, instead of launching the next phrase, it waits, allowing P_{11} to finish his contribution. Next, at t_8, the robot provides directions to the new room while P_{11} is attending.

References

Bohus, D., and Horvitz, E., 2011. Multiparty Turn Taking in Situated Dialog: Study, Lessons, and Directions, *In Proc. of SIGDial 2011*, Portland, OR.

Bohus, D., Saw, C.W., and Horvitz, E. 2014. Directions Robot: In-the-Wild Experiences and Lessons Learned. *In Proc. of AAMAS 2014*, Paris, France.

Duncan, S. 1972. Some Signals and Rules for Taking Speaking Turns in Conversation, *Journal of Personality and Social Psychology*, 23, 283-292.

Goodwin, C., 1981. *Conversational Organization: Interaction Between Speakers and Hearers*, New York: Academic Press.

Guhe, M., & Schilder, F. 2002. Incremental Generation of Self-corrections Using Underspecification. *Language and Computers*, 45(1), 118-132.

Kendon, A. 1967. Some Functions of Gaze Direction in Social Interaction. *Acta Psychologica* 26, 22–63

Kousidis, S., Kennington, C, Baumann,T., Buschmeer, H., Kopp, S., and Schlangen, D. 2014. A multimodal In-car Dialogue System that Tracks the Driver's Attention. *In Proc. of ICMI 2015*, Istanbual,Turkey.

Traum, D., and Rickel, J., 2002. Embodied Agents for Multi-party Dialogue in Immersive Virtual World, *In Proc. of AAMAS 2002*,Bologna, Italy.

Sciutti, A., Schillingmann, L., Palinko, O., Nagai, Y., and Sandini, G., 2015. A Gaze-contingent Dictating Robot to Study Turn-taking. *In Proceedings of HRI 2015*, Portland, OR, USA.

Skantze, G., and Hjalmarsson, A., 2010. Towards Incremental Speech Generation in Dialogue Systems, *In Proc. of SIGDial 2010*, Tokyo, Japan.

Vertegaal, R., Weevers, I., Sohn, C. and Cheung, C. 2003. GAZE-2: Conveying Eye Contact in Group Videoconferencing Using Eye-controlled Camera Direction. *In Proc. of CHI 2003*, Fort Lauderdale, FL.

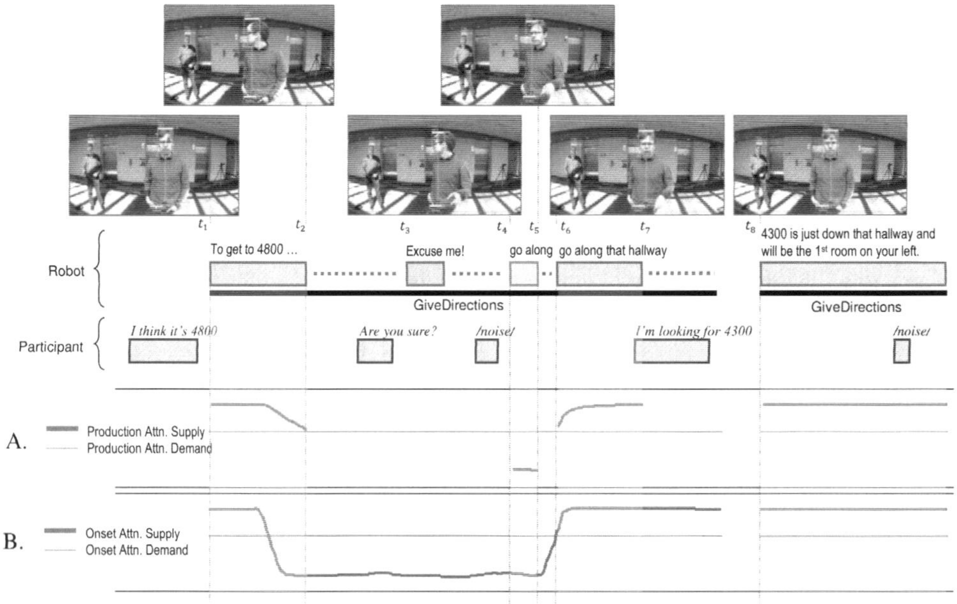

Hyper-parameter Optimisation of Gaussian Process Reinforcement Learning for Statistical Dialogue Management

Lu Chen[1], **Pei-Hao Su**[2] and **Milica Gašić**[2*]
[1]Key Lab. of Shanghai Education Commission for Intelligent Interaction and Cognitive Eng.
SpeechLab, Department of Computer Science and Engineering
Shanghai Jiao Tong University, Shanghai, China
[2] Department of Engineering, University of Cambridge, Cambridge, UK
chenlusz@sjtu.edu.cn, phs26@cam.ac.uk, mg436@eng.cam.ac.uk

Abstract

Gaussian processes reinforcement learning provides an appealing framework for training the dialogue policy as it takes into account correlations of the objective function given different dialogue belief states, which can significantly speed up the learning. These correlations are modelled by the *kernel function* which may depend on *hyper-parameters*. So far, for real-world dialogue systems the hyper-parameters have been hand-tuned, relying on the designer to adjust the correlations, or simple non-parametrised kernel functions have been used instead. Here, we examine different kernel structures and show that it is possible to optimise the hyper-parameters from data yielding improved performance of the resulting dialogue policy. We confirm this in a real user trial.

1 Introduction

Spoken dialogue systems enable human-computer interaction via speech. The dialogue management component has two aims: to maintain the dialogue *state* based on the current spoken language understanding input and the conversation history, and choose a response according to its dialogue *policy*. To provide robustness to the input errors, a number of statistical approaches are proposed to track a distribution over all dialogue states at every dialogue turn, called the *belief state* (Young et al., 2013; Thomson and Young, 2010; Williams et al., 2013; Henderson et al., 2014; Sun et al., 2014). The system response is then based on the belief state, rather than an inaccurate estimate of the most likely dialogue state.

The state-of-art statistical methods for policy learning are based on reinforcement learning (RL) (Young et al., 2013), which makes it possible to learn from interaction with the users. However, most RL methods take too many dialogues for policy training. In Gaussian process reinforcement learning (GPRL) the *kernel function* defines prior correlations of the objective function given different belief states, which can significantly speeds up the policy optimisation (Gašić and Young, 2014). Alternative methods include Kalman temporal difference (KTD) reinforcement learning (Pietquin et al., 2011). Typically, statistical approaches to dialogue management rely on the belief state space compression into a form of a *summary space*, where the policy learning can be tractably performed (Williams and Young, 2007; Pinault et al., 2009; Thomson and Young, 2010; Crook and Lemon, 2011). GPRL allows the learning to be performed directly on the full belief state. However, only non-parametrised kernel functions have been considered for this purpose (Gašić and Young, 2014).

Here we address the important problem of how to define the structure of the kernel function for a real-world dialogue task and learn the hyper-parameters from data for a policy that operates on the full belief state. Using only a small-size dataset for hyper-parameter optimisation, we show that the policy with the optimised kernel function outperforms both the policy with hand specified kernel parameters and the one with a standard non-parametrised kernel function. This is particularly beneficial for policy training with real users.

This paper is organised as follows. In section 2, we briefly review GP-Sarsa and the hyper-parameter optimisation. Section 3 introduces the kernel functions examined here. The experimental results are shown in section 4, followed by conclusions and future work directions in section 5.

Lu Chen was supported by the NICaiA project (the EU FP7 No. 247619). Pei-Hao Su is supported by Cambridge Trust and the Ministry of Education, Taiwan.

Proceedings of the SIGDIAL 2015 Conference, pages 407–411,
Prague, Czech Republic, 2-4 September 2015.

2 GP-Sarsa and hyper-parameter optimisation

The expected cumulative reward given belief state $\mathbf{b}$ and action a is defined by the Q-function as:

$$Q^\pi(\mathbf{b}, a) = E^\pi \left(\sum_{\tau=t+1}^{T} \gamma^{\tau-t-1} r_\tau | \mathbf{b}_t = \mathbf{b}, a_t = a \right),$$

where r_τ is the immediate reward at τ-th dialogue turn, T is the number of dialogue turns and $\gamma \in [0, 1]$ is a discount factor. GP-Sarsa is an online RL algorithm that models the Q-function as a Gaussian process (Engel et al., 2005). It makes the learning tractable by utilising the kernel span sparcification algorithm and constructing a set of representative belief state and action called the *dictionary*. The computational complexity of GP-Sarsa is $O(Tm^2)$ where m is the size of the dictionary and T is the number of turns of all interactions.

In the case of Gaussian process regression, the kernel function parameters can be estimated by *evidence maximisation* in such a way that they capture the correlations that occur in the data (Rasmussen and Williams, 2005). This approach has been extended for the case of GP-Sarsa, however its benefits have so far only been shown for a toy dialogue problem (Gašić et al., 2010).

Using a data corpus of belief state-action pairs and rewards, the hyper-parameters can be found by minimising the negative log marginal likelihood via a conjugate gradient method (Rasmussen and Nickisch, 2010) to find the optimal hyper-parameters. The computational complexity of the gradient calculation is $O(nT^3)$, where n is the number of hyper-parameters and T is the total number of dialogue turns in the corpus (see appendix A).

3 Kernel functions

In Gaussian process regression, the kernel function $k(\cdot, \cdot)$ must be positive definite (Rasmussen and Williams, 2005). The kernel functions have some interesting properties (Duvenaud et al., 2013). If k_1 and k_2 are kernels,

- $k_1 + k_2$ is kernel. Adding two kernels can be thought of as an OR-like operation, as the resulting kernel will have high value if either of the two base kernels have a high value.
- $k_1 \cdot k_2$ is kernel. Multiplying two kernels can be thought of as an AND-like operation, as the function value is only expected to be similar to some other function value if both kernels have a high value.

3.1 Standard kernel functions

There are many valid kernel functions (Rasmussen and Williams, 2005). The following three ones are the basic kernels used in our experiments.

- Gaussian kernel: $k(\mathbf{x}_i, \mathbf{x}_j) = p^2 \exp(-\frac{||\mathbf{x}_i - \mathbf{x}_j||_2^2}{2l^2})$, where p and l are the hyper-parameters. If the distance between $\mathbf{x}_i$ and $\mathbf{x}_j$ is more than the lengthscale l, the outputs are uncorrelated. The output variance p^2 determines the average distance of the function from its mean.
- Linear kernel: $k(\mathbf{x}_i, \mathbf{x}_j) = \langle \mathbf{x}_i, \mathbf{x}_j \rangle$
- δ-kernel: $k(\mathbf{x}_i, \mathbf{x}_j) = \delta(\mathbf{x}_i, \mathbf{x}_j)$, where the function values are correlated if and only if the inputs are the same.

3.2 Kernels for dialogue management

The kernel for two belief-action pairs is normally decomposed as the product of separate kernels over belief states and actions, $k_B(\cdot, \cdot)$ and $k_A(\cdot, \cdot)$.

The elements of the dialogue state are *concepts* that occur in the dialogue and are described by the underlying *ontology*. For instance, in a restaurant information domain, these usually include *goal-food*, *goal-area*, *history-food*, *history-area* and so on. The belief tracker maintains a probability distribution for each of them. We first define kernel function on each concept $k_{B_i}(\cdot, \cdot)$, then combine them to form the kernel function for the whole belief state $k_B(\cdot, \cdot)$, as illustrated in Figure 1.

The Gaussian kernel and the linear kernel were used as basic kernel functions for each concept in the belief state. In the case of Gaussian kernels, if they share the same hyper-parameters across different concepts, we refer to them as *concept independent*, otherwise, they are called *concept dependent*. While the linear kernel is used for problems involving distributions (Jebara et al., 2004), Gaussian kernel is a more natural choice here as the Q-function for belief states is a non-linear smooth function. Additionally, we investigated two integration methods: one is to sum up the kernels for all concepts, the *sum kernel*; another is to multiply kernels for all concepts, the *product kernel*.

The action kernel is defined on summary actions and given that the total number of summary actions is usually small, e.g. 20, the δ-kernel is chosen as the action kernel.

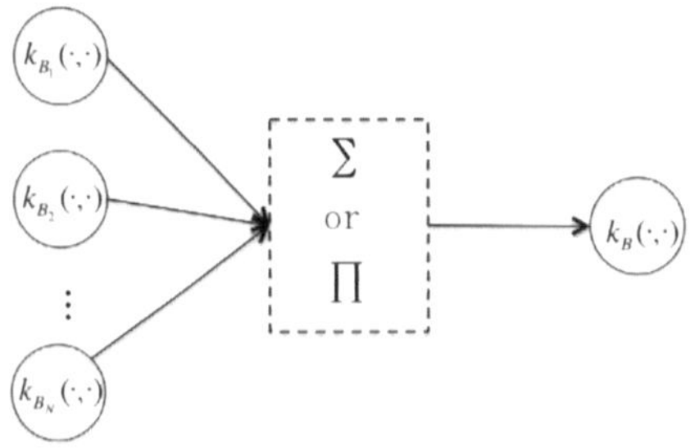

Figure 1: Kernel structure for belief state

Name	Kernel	Learnt	Combine	Concept dep.
GHSI	Gaussian	N	Sum	N
GLSI	Gaussian	Y	Sum	N
GLSD	Gaussian	Y	Sum	Y
LS	Linear	/	Sum	/
GHPI	Gaussian	N	Prod	N
GLPI	Gaussian	Y	Prod	N
GLPD	Gaussian	Y	Prod	Y
LP	Linear	/	Prod	/

Table 1: Summary of kernels

4 Experiments and results

The training data for hyper-parameter optimisation was generated using an agenda-based user simulator (Schatzmann et al., 2007). The dialogue policy training and evaluation is performed both on the user simulator and human users. The system operates on the TopTable dialogue domain which consists of about 150 restaurants in Cambridge, UK (TopTable, 2012). Each restaurant has 9 slots, e.g. food, area, phone, address and so on. The state decomposes into 21 concepts. Each concept takes from 4 to 150 values. Each value is given a belief in $[0, 1]$ by the BUDS state tracker (Thomson and Young, 2010). The summary action space consists of 20 summary actions.

4.1 Experimental procedure

The hyper-parameter are optimised as follows.

1. **Training data generation**: We used a random policy to generate simulated dialogues out of which a small number of *successful* dialogues were used as training data.[1]
2. **Interval estimation**: We estimated appropriate *intervals* for concept independent hyper-parameters according to the properties of Gaussian kernel as described in section 3.1. In our experiments, we only restricted the range of lengthscale l. For the sum Gaussian kernel, the belief state for each concept is a probability distribution, so the lengthscale l is in interval $(0, \sqrt{2}]$. For product Gaussian kernel, the product of Gaussian kernels is still a Gaussian kernel, therefore the lengthscale l should be less than the maximum distance between two whole belief states (5.29 in the TopTable domain).
3. **Concept independent hyper-parameter optimisation**: We sampled initial concept independent hyper-parameters from the estimated intervals and then minimised the negative log likelihood to find the concept independent optimised hyper-parameters. We repeated this N times, and the hyper-parameters with the overall smallest negative log likelihood was chosen as the final concept independent hyper-parameters.
4. **Concept dependent hyper-parameter optimisation**: We initialised them as concept independent hyper-parameters, then minimised the negative log likelihood to get the concept dependent optimised hyper-parameters.

[1]We used 73 dialogues for concept independent and 147 dialogues for concept dependent hyper-parameter optimisation, with respectively 505 and 1004 dialogue turns. We found that the smaller data set was not sufficient to capture correlations for the concept dependent kernels.

After the hyper-parameters are obtained, we trained and evaluated the policies with these optimised kernels. For comparison, the policies with hand-tuned Gaussian kernel hyper-parameters and linear kernel were also trained and evaluated.

4.2 The results on the user simulator

During training, intermediate policies were recorded at every 1000 dialogues. Each policy was then evaluated using 1000 dialogues when testing. The reward was calculated as 20 for a successful dialogue, deducted for the number of turns.

We compared four different sum and product kernels (Table 1) and the results are given in Figure 2. The results in Figure 2(a) show that the policies with optimised sum Gaussian kernels perform significantly better than the policy using hand-tuned hyper-parameters (GHSI) and the linear kernel (LS). Also, in the later learning stages, the policy with concept dependent kernel (GLSD) appears to have reached a better performance than the one with concept independent kernel (GLSI).

The policies using the product kernels follow similar trends, except that the concept dependent product kernel (GLPD) performs significantly bet-

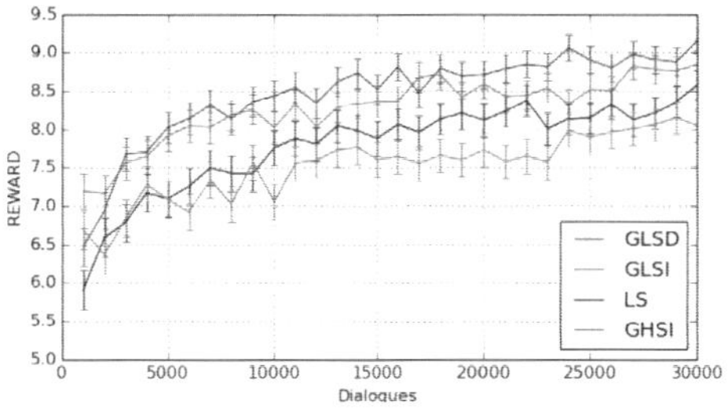

(a) Sum kernels.

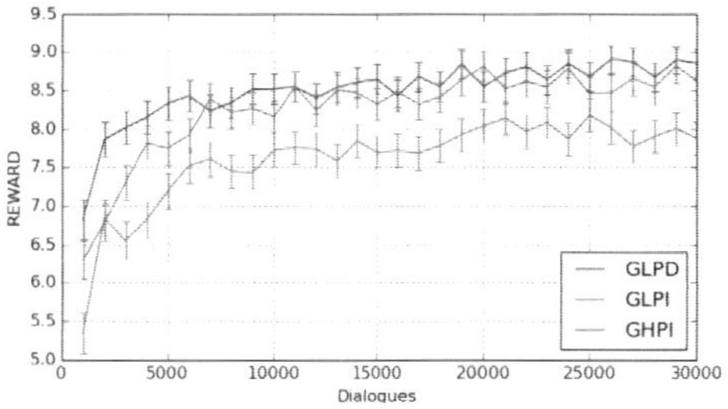

(b) Product kernels.

Figure 2: Comparison of policies with two kernels. Vertical bars denote standard errors. The average success rates for GHSI and GHPI are respectively 91.8% and 92.9% at the end of training.

ter than other kernels at the initial stages of training (Figure 2(b)).[2] The best performing product (GLPD) and sum (GLSD) kernel converge to similar performance, with the product kernel performing better in the early stages of training, at the expense of a larger dictionary.

4.3 Human experiments

In order to further evaluate the effect of the optimised kernels, policies were trained using crowdsourcing via the Amazon Mechanical Turk service in a set-up similar to (Jurčíček et al., 2011; Su et al., 2015). At the end of each dialogue, a recurrent neural network (RNN) model was used to predict the dialogue success used as the reinforcement feedback (Su et al., 2015).

The GLSD kernel and the GLPD kernel were selected for on-line policy training and compared to the LS kernel. Figure 3 shows the learning curve of the reward during training, demonstrating the advantage of Gaussian kernels over the simple linear kernel.

To confirm this result, all optimised policies were evaluated after 500 training dialogues. The results are given in Table 2. It can be seen that the policies with optimised kernels, especially the GLPD kernel, perform much better than the policy with linear kernel. [3]

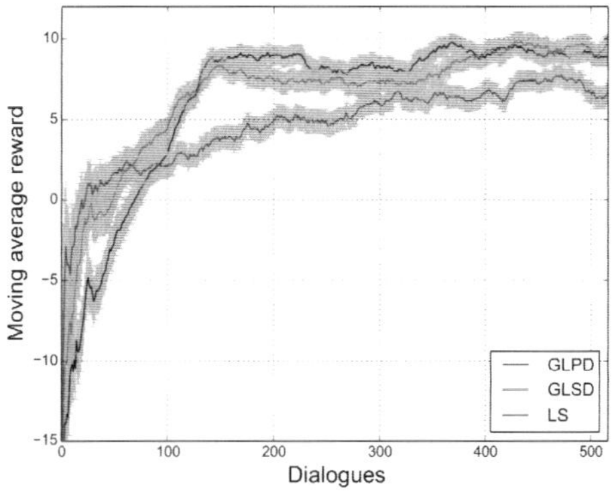

Figure 3: Learning curve of reward during on-line policy optimisation. For both plots, the moving average was calculated using a window of 100 dialogues. Yellow lines are standard errors.

Kernel	#Diags	Reward	Success(%)
LS	347	8.46 ± 0.57	77.2 ± 2.3
GLSD	336	9.56 ± 0.56	79.5 ± 2.2
GLPD	423	10.52 ± 0.47	82.3 ± 1.9

Table 2: Evaluation of policies with three kernels.

5 Conclusions and Future work

This paper has investigated the problem of kernel structure and hyper-parameter optimisation of Gaussian process reinforcement learning for statistical dialogue management. We have demonstrated that the optimised kernels yield significant improvements in the policy performance both when training with a simulated user and real users.

The work in this paper has focused on optimising the kernel function for the belief state space off-line. The future work will consider joint optimisation of the hyper-parameters and the policy. This will rely on finding a less computationally expensive method for hyper-parameter optimisation, also allowing more complex actions kernels to be investigated.

[2]The result of the product linear kernel (LP) is not reported due to poor performance. In the TopTable domain two belief states for *history* concepts are typically very different, so the linear kernel for these concepts is often close to 0. This results in a very small overall kernel value that leads to slow convergence.

[3]In (Gašić and Young, 2014), summary space-based policies were outperforming full-space policies because the summary space kernels could be regarded carefully hand-coded kernels on full-belief space and full-space kernels were not optimised.

References

Paul A Crook and Oliver Lemon. 2011. Lossless value directed compression of complex user goal states for statistical spoken dialogue systems. In *INTERSPEECH*, pages 1029–1032.

David Duvenaud, James Robert Lloyd, Roger Grosse, Joshua B. Tenenbaum, and Zoubin Ghahramani. 2013. Structure discovery in nonparametric regression through compositional kernel search. In *Proceedings of the 30th International Conference on Machine Learning*, pages 1166–1174.

Y Engel, S Mannor, and R Meir. 2005. Reinforcement learning with Gaussian processes. In *ICML '05: Proceedings of the 22nd international conference on Machine learning*, pages 201–208, New York, NY.

Milica Gašić and Steve Young. 2014. Gaussian processes for pomdp-based dialogue manager optimization. *IEEE/ACM Transactions on Audio, Speech, and Language Processing*, 22(1):28–40.

M Gašić, F Jurčíček, S Keizer, F Mairesse, J Schatzmann, B Thomson, K Yu, and S Young. 2010. Gaussian processes for fast policy optimisation of pomdp-based dialogue managers. In *Proceedings of SIGDIAL*.

Matthew Henderson, Blaise Thomson, and Steve Young. 2014. Word-based dialog state tracking with recurrent neural networks. In *Proceedings of 15th Annual Meeting of the Special Interest Group on Discourse and Dialogue*.

T Jebara, R Kondor, and A Howard. 2004. Probability product kernels. *J. Mach. Learn. Res.*, 5:819–844, December.

Filip Jurčíček, Simon Keizer, Milica Gašić, Franois Mairesse, Blaise Thomson, Kai Yu, and Steve Young. 2011. Real user evaluation of spoken dialogue systems using amazon mechanical turk. In *Proceedings of Interspeech*, pages 3061–3064.

Olivier Pietquin, Matthieu Geist, and Senthilkumar Chandramohan. 2011. Sample Efficient On-line Learning of Optimal Dialogue Policies with Kalman Temporal Differences. In *IJCAI 2011*, pages 1878–1883, Barcelona, Spain, July.

Florian Pinault, Fabrice Lefèvre, and Renato de Mori. 2009. Feature-based summary space for stochastic dialogue modeling with hierarchical semantic frames. In *INTERSPEECH*.

Carl Edward Rasmussen and Hannes Nickisch. 2010. Gaussian processes for machine learning (gpml) toolbox. *The Journal of Machine Learning Research*, 11:3011–3015.

Carl Edward Rasmussen and Christopher K. I. Williams. 2005. *Gaussian processes for machine learning*. MIT Press.

J Schatzmann, B Thomson, K Weilhammer, H Ye, and SJ Young. 2007. Agenda-Based User Simulation for Bootstrapping a POMDP Dialogue System. In *HLT/NAACL*, Rochester, NY.

Pei-Hao Su, David Vandyke, Milica Gašić, Dongho Kim, Nikola Mrksic, Tsung-Hsien Wen, and Steve Young. 2015. Learning from real users: Rating dialogue success with neural networks for reinforcement learning in spoken dialogue systems. *Submitted to Interspeech*.

Kai Sun, Lu Chen, Su Zhu, and Kai Yu. 2014. A generalized rule based tracker for dialogue state tracking. In *Proceedings of IEEE Spoken Language Technology Workshop (SLT)*.

Blaise Thomson and Steve Young. 2010. Bayesian update of dialogue state: A pomdp framework for spoken dialogue systems. *Computer Speech & Language*, 24(4):562–588.

TopTable. 2012. Toptable. `https://www.toptable.com`.

JD Williams and SJ Young. 2007. Scaling POMDPs for Spoken Dialog Management. *IEEE Transactions on Audio, Speech, and Language Processing*, 15(7):2116–2129.

Jason Williams, Antoine Raux, Deepak Ramachandran, and Alan Black. 2013. The dialog state tracking challenge. In *Proceedings of the SIGDIAL Conference*, pages 404–413.

Steve Young, Milica Gašić, Blaise Thomson, and Jason D Williams. 2013. Pomdp-based statistical spoken dialog systems: A review. *Proceedings of the IEEE*, 101(5):1160–1179.

A Marginal log likelihood for GPRL

Algorithm 1 Log likelihood and gradient

Require:

rewards $\mathbf{r}$, belief state-action pairs $\mathbf{B}$, Gram matrix: $\mathbf{K}(\boldsymbol{\theta})$, $\frac{\partial}{\partial\theta_j}(\mathbf{K}(\boldsymbol{\theta}) + \sigma^2\mathbf{I}), \Theta = \{\boldsymbol{\theta}, \sigma\}$, $\forall i, \mathbf{H}[i,i] = 1, \mathbf{H}[i,i+1] = -\gamma, \mathbf{H}[i,j] = 0, j \neq i, j \neq i+1$

Find $\boldsymbol{\alpha}$ so that $\mathbf{L}\mathbf{L}^\mathsf{T}\boldsymbol{\alpha} = \mathbf{r}$

$\mathcal{L}(\Theta) = \frac{1}{2}\mathbf{r}^\mathsf{T}\boldsymbol{\alpha} + \sum_{i=1}^{T} L_{ii} + \frac{T}{2}\log 2\pi$

Find $\mathbf{W}$ so that $\mathbf{L}\mathbf{L}^\mathsf{T}\mathbf{W} = \mathbf{I}$

For $j = 0$ to $dim(\Theta) - 1$ **do**

$$\mathbf{D}^j = \frac{\partial}{\partial\theta_j}(\mathbf{K}(\boldsymbol{\theta}) + \sigma^2\mathbf{I})$$

$$\frac{\partial}{\partial\theta_j}\mathcal{L} = -\frac{1}{2}\mathtt{tr}((\boldsymbol{\alpha}\boldsymbol{\alpha}^\mathsf{T} - \mathbf{W})\mathbf{H}\mathbf{D}^j\mathbf{H}^\mathsf{T})$$

end for

return $\mathcal{L}(\Theta)$, $\frac{\partial}{\partial\theta_j}\mathcal{L}(\Theta)$

Learning Domain-Independent Dialogue Policies via Ontology Parameterisation

Zhuoran Wang[1]*, Tsung-Hsien Wen[2], Pei-Hao Su[2], Yannis Stylianou[1]
[1]Toshiba Research Europe Ltd., Cambridge, UK
[2]Engineering Department, University of Cambridge, UK

Abstract

This paper introduces a novel approach to eliminate the domain dependence of dialogue state and action representations, such that dialogue policies trained based on the proposed representation can be transferred across different domains. The experimental results show that the policy optimised in a restaurant search domain using our domain-independent representations can be deployed to a laptop sale domain, achieving a task success rate very close (96.4% relative) to that of the policy optimised on in-domain dialogues.

1 Introduction

Statistical approaches to Spoken Dialogue Systems (SDS), particularly, Partially Observable Markov Decision Processes (POMDPs) (Young et al., 2013), have demonstrated great success in improving the robustness of dialogue policies to error-prone Automatic Speech Recognition (ASR). However, building statistical SDS (SSDS) for different application domains is time consuming. Traditionally, each component of such SSDS needs to be trained based on domain-specific data, which are not always easy to obtain. Moreover, in many cases, one will need a basic (e.g. rule-based) working SDS to be built before starting the data collection procedure, where developing the initial system for a new domain requires a significant amount of human expertise.

In this paper, we introduce a simple but effective approach to eliminate domain dependence of dialogue policies, by exploring the nature and commonness of the underlying tasks of SDS in different domains, and parameterising different slots defined in the domain ontologies into a common feature space according to their relations and potential contributions to the underlying tasks. After the parameterisation, the resulting policy can be applied to different domains that realise a same abstract task (see §3.3 for examples).

Existing works on domain-extension/transfer for SDS include domain-independent intermediate semantic extractors for Spoken Language Understanding (SLU) (Li et al., 2014), domain-general rules (Wang and Lemon, 2013; Sun et al., 2014) and delexicalised deep classifiers (Henderson et al., 2014; Mrkšić et al., 2015) for dialogue state tracking, and domain-extensible/transferable statistical dialogue policies (Lemon et al., 2006; Gašić et al., 2013; Gašić et al., 2015). When compared to the closely related methods by Gašić et al. and Lemon et al. that manually tie slots in different domains, our approach provides a more flexible way to parametrically measure the similarity between different domain ontologies and directly addresses the nature of the underlying tasks.

For the ease of access to the proposed technique (§3), we start from a brief review of POMDP-SDS in §2. Promising experimental results are achieved based on both simulated users and human subjects as shown in §4, followed by conclusions (§5).

2 POMDP-SDS: A Brief Overview

A POMDP is a powerful tool for modelling sequential decision making problems under uncertainty, by optimising the policy to maximise long-term cumulative rewards. Concretely. at each turn of a dialogue, a typical POMDP-SDS parses an observed ASR n-best list with confidence scores into semantic representations (again with associated confidence scores), and estimates a distribution over (unobservable) user goals, called a belief state. After this, the dialogue policy selects a semantic-level system action, which will be realised by Natural Language Generation (NLG) before synthesising the speech response to the user.

*ZW's present address is Baidu Inc., Beijing, China.

Proceedings of the SIGDIAL 2015 Conference, pages 412–416,
Prague, Czech Republic, 2-4 September 2015.

The semantic representations in SDS normally consist of two parts, a communication function (e.g. `inform`, `deny`, `confirm`, etc.) and (optionally) a list of slot-value pairs (e.g. `food=pizza`, `area=centre`, etc.). The prior knowledge defining the slot-values in a particular domain is called the domain ontology.

Dialogue policy optimisation can be solved via Reinforcement Learning (RL), where the aim is to estimate a quantity $Q(\mathbf{b}, \mathbf{a})$, for each $\mathbf{b}$ and $\mathbf{a}$, reflecting the expected cumulative rewards of the system executing action $\mathbf{a}$ at belief state $\mathbf{b}$, such that the optimal action $\mathbf{a}^*$ can be determined for a given $\mathbf{b}$ according to $\mathbf{a}^* = \arg\max_{\mathbf{a}} Q(\mathbf{b}, \mathbf{a})$. Due the exponentially large state-action space an SDS can incur, function approximation is necessary, where it is assumed that $Q(\mathbf{b}, \mathbf{a}) \approx f_\theta(\phi(\mathbf{b}, \mathbf{a}))$. Here θ denotes the model parameter to be learnt, and $\phi(\cdot)$ is a feature function that maps $(\mathbf{b}, \mathbf{a})$ to a feature vector. To compute $Q(\mathbf{b}, \mathbf{a})$, one can either use a low-dimensional summary belief (Williams and Young, 2005) or the full belief itself if kernel methods are applied (Gašić et al., 2012). But in both cases, the action $\mathbf{a}$ will be a summary action (see §3 for more details) to achieve tractable computations.

3 Domain-Independent Featurisation

For the convenience of further discussion, we firstly take a closer look at how summary actions can be derived from their corresponding master actions. Assume that according to its communication function, a system action $\mathbf{a}$ can take one of the following forms: $a()$ (e.g. `reqmore()`), $a(s)$ (e.g. `request(food)`), $a(s = v)$ (e.g. `confirm(area=north)`), $a(s = v_1, s = v_2)$ (e.g. `select(food=noodle, food=pizza)`), and $a(s_1 = v_1, \ldots, s_n = v_n)$ (e.g. `offer(name="Chop Chop", food=Chinese)`), where a stands for the communication function, s_* and v_* denote slots and values respectively. Usually it is unnecessary for the system to address a hypothesis less believable than the top hypothesis in the belief (or the top two hypotheses in the '`select`' case). Therefore, by abstracting the actual values, the system actions can be represented as $a\left(s = \mathbf{b}_s^{\text{top}}\right)$, $a\left(s = \mathbf{b}_s^{\text{top}}, s = \mathbf{b}_s^{\text{second}}\right)$ and $a\left(\mathbf{b}_{\text{joint}}^{\text{top}}\right)$, where $\mathbf{b}_s$ denotes the marginal belief with respect to slot s, $\mathbf{b}_{\text{joint}}$ stands for the joint belief, and $\mathbf{b}_*^{\text{top}}$ and $\mathbf{b}_*^{\text{second}}$ denote the top and second hypotheses of a given $\mathbf{b}_*$, respectively. After this, summary actions can be defined as a_s (for actions depending on s) and a (for those having no operands or only taking joint hypotheses as operands, i.e. independent of any particular slot). Furthermore, one can uniquely map such summary actions back to their master actions, by substituting the respective top (and second if necessary) hypotheses in the belief into the corresponding slots.

Based on the above definition, we can re-write the master action $\mathbf{a}$ as $\mathbf{a}_s$, where s denotes the slot that $\mathbf{a}$ depends on when summarised. Here, s is fully derived from $\mathbf{a}$ and can be null (when the summary action of $\mathbf{a}$ is just a). Recalling the RL problem, conventionally, ϕ can be expressed as $\phi(\mathbf{b}, \mathbf{a}_s) = \delta(a_s) \otimes \psi(\mathbf{b})$ where δ is the Kronecker delta, $\otimes$ is the tensor product, and generally speaking, $\psi(\cdot)$ featurises the belief state, which can yield a summary belief in particular cases.

3.1 "Focus-aware" belief summarisation

Without losing generality, one can assume that the communication functions a are domain-independent. However, since the slots s are domain-specific (defined by the ontology), both a_s and $\mathbf{b}$ will be domain-dependent.

Making $\psi(\mathbf{b})$ domain-independent can be trivial. A commonly used representation of $\mathbf{b}$ consists of a set of individual belief vectors, denoted as $\{\mathbf{b}_{\text{joint}}, \mathbf{b}_\circ\} \cup \{\mathbf{b}_s\}_{s \in S}$, where $\mathbf{b}_\circ$ stands for the section of $\mathbf{b}$ independent of any slots (e.g. the belief over communication methods, such as "by constraint", "by name", etc. (Thomson and Young, 2010)) and S stands for the set of informable (see Appendix A) slots defined in the domain ontology. One can construct a feature function $\psi(\mathbf{b}, s) = \psi_1(\mathbf{b}_{\text{joint}}) \oplus \psi_2(\mathbf{b}_\circ) \oplus \psi_3(\mathbf{b}_s)$ for a given s and let $\phi(\mathbf{b}, \mathbf{a}_s) = \delta(a_s) \otimes \psi(\mathbf{b}, s)$, where $\oplus$ stands for the operator to concatenate two vectors. (In other words, the belief summarisation here only focuses on the slot being addressed by the proposed action, regardless of the beliefs for the other slots.) As the mechanism in each ψ_* to featurise its operand $\mathbf{b}_*$ can be domain-independent (see §3.3 for an example), the resulting overall feature vector will be domain-general.

3.2 Ontology (slot) parameterisation

If we could further parameterise each slot s in a domain-general way (as $\varphi(s)$), and define

$$\phi(\mathbf{b}, \mathbf{a}_s) = \delta(a) \otimes [\varphi_a(s) \oplus \psi_a(\mathbf{b}, s)] \quad (1)$$

the domain dependence of the overall feature function ϕ will be eliminated[1]. Note here, to make the definition more general, we assume that the feature functions φ_a and ψ_a depend on a, such that a different featurisation can be applied for each a.

To achieve a meaningful parameterisation $\varphi_a(s)$, we need to investigate how each slot s is related to the completion of the underlying task. More concretely, for example, if the underlying task is to obtain user's constraint on each slot so that the system can conduct a database (DB) search to find suitable entities (e.g. venues, products, etc.), then the slot features should describe the potentiality of the slot to refine the search results (reduce the number of matching entities) if that slot is filled. For another example, if the task is to gather necessary (plus optional) information to execute a system command (e.g. setting a reminder or planning a route), where the number of values of each slot can be unbounded, then the slots features should indicate whether the slot is required or optional. In addition, the slots may have some specific characteristics causing people to address them differently in a dialogue. For example, when buying a laptop, more likely one would talk about the price first than the battery rating. Therefore, features describing the priority of each slot are also necessary to yield natural dialogues. We give a complete list of features in §3.3 for a working example, to demonstrate how two unrelated domains can share a common ontology parameterisation.

3.3 A working example

We use restaurant search and laptop sale as two example domains to explain the above idea. The underlying tasks of the both problems here can be regarded as DB search. Appendix A gives the detailed ontology definitions of the two domains.

Firstly, the following notations are introduced for the convenience of discussion. Let V_s denote the set of the values that a slot s can take, and $|\cdot|$ be the size of a set. Assume that $h = (s_1 = v_1 \wedge \ldots \wedge s_n = v_n)$ is a user goal hypothesis consisting a set of slot-value pairs. We use $\mathrm{DB}(h)$ to denote the set of the entities in the DB satisfying h. In addition, we define $\lfloor x \rfloor$ to be the largest integer less than and equal to x. After this, for each informable slot s defined in Table A.1, the following quantities are used for its parameterisation.

- **Number of values**
  - a continuous feature[2], $1/|V_s|$;
  - discrete features mapping $|V_s|$ into N $(= 6)$ bins, indexed by $\min\{\lfloor \log_2 |V_s| \rfloor, N\}$.
- **Importance**: two features describing, respectively, how likely a slot will and will not occur in a dialogue.
- **Priority**: three features denoting, respectively, how likely a slot will be the first, the second, and a later attribute to address in a dialogue.
- **Value distribution in the DB**: the entropy of the normalised histogram $(|\mathrm{DB}(s = v)|/|\mathrm{DB}|)_{v \in V_s}$.
- **Potential contribution to DB search**: given the current top user goal hypothesis h^* and a pre-defined threshold τ $(= 12)$
  - how likely filling s will reduce the number of matching DB records to below τ, i.e. $|\{v : v \in V_s, |\mathrm{DB}(h^* \wedge s = v)| \leq \tau\}| / |V_s|$;
  - how likely filling s will not reduce the number of matching DB records to below τ, i.e. $|\{v : v \in V_s, |\mathrm{DB}(h^* \wedge s = v)| > \tau\}| / |V_s|$;
  - how likely filling s will result in no matching records found in the DB, i.e. $|\{v : v \in V_s, \mathrm{DB}(h^* \wedge s = v) = \emptyset\}| / |V_s|$.

The importance and priority features used in this work are manually assigned binary values, but ideally, if one has some in-domain human dialogue examples (e.g. from Wizard-of-Oz experiments), such feature values can be derived from simple statistics on the corpus. In addition, we make the last set of features only applicable to those slots not observed in the top joint hypothesis.

The summary belief features used in this work are sketched as follows. For each informable slot s and each of its applicable action types a, $\psi_a(\mathbf{b}, s)$ extracts the probability of $\mathbf{b}_s^{\mathrm{top}}$, the entropy of $\mathbf{b}_s$, the probability difference between the top two marginal hypotheses (discretised into 5 bins with interval size 0.2) and the non-zero rate $(|\{v : v \in V_s, \mathbf{b}_s(v) > 0\}|/|V_s|)$. In addition, if the slot is requestable, the probability of it being requested

[1] An alternative featurisation can be $\phi(\mathbf{b}, \mathbf{a}_s) = \delta(a) \otimes \varphi_a(s) \otimes \psi_a(\mathbf{b}, s)$, but our preliminary experiments show that $\otimes$ results in similar but slightly worse policies. Therefore, we stick with $\oplus$ in this paper.

[2] The normalisation is to make this feature to have a similar value range to the others, for numerical stability purposes in Gaussian Process (GP) based policy learning (see §4).

System	Reward	Success (%)	#Turns
$\text{DIP}_{\text{in-domain}}$	12.5±0.3	98.3±1.2	7.2±0.3
$\text{DIP}_{\text{transferred}}$	12.2±0.4	97.8±0.9	7.4±0.3

Table 1: Policy evaluations in the laptop sale domain based on simulated dialogues.

System	#Dialogues	Success (%)	Score
$\text{DIP}_{\text{in-domain}}$	122	84.4	4.51
$\text{DIP}_{\text{transferred}}$	140	81.4	4.83

Table 2: Policy evaluations using human subjects.

by the user (Thomson and Young, 2010) is used as an extra feature. A similar featurisation procedure (except the "requested" probability) is applied to the joint belief as well, from which the obtained features are used for all communication functions. To capture the nature of the underlying task (DB search), we define two additional features for the joint belief, an indicator $[\![|\text{DB}(\mathbf{b}_{\text{joint}}^{\text{top}})| \leq \tau]\!]$ and a real-valued feature $|\text{DB}(\mathbf{b}_{\text{joint}}^{\text{top}})|/\tau$ if the former is false, where τ is the same pre-defined threshold used for slot parameterisation as introduced above. There are also a number of slot-independent features applied to all action types, including the belief over communication methods (Thomson and Young, 2010) and the marginal confidence scores of user dialogue act types in the current turn.

4 Experimental Results

In the following experiments, the proposed domain-independent parameterisation (DIP) method were integrated with a generic dialogue state tracker (Wang and Lemon, 2013) to yield an overall domain-independent dialogue manager. Firstly, we trained DIP dialogue policies in the restaurant search domain using GP-SARSA based on a state-of-the-art agenda-based user simulator[3] (Schatzmann et al., 2007), in comparison with the GP-SARSA learning process for the well-known BUDS system (Thomson and Young, 2010) (where full beliefs are used (Gašić and Young, 2014)), as shown in Figure 1. It can be found that the proposed method results in faster convergence and can even achieve slightly better performance than the conventional approach.

After this, we directly deployed the DIP poli-

[3]For all the experiments in this work, the confusion rate of the simulator was set to 15% and linear kernels were used for GP-SARSA.

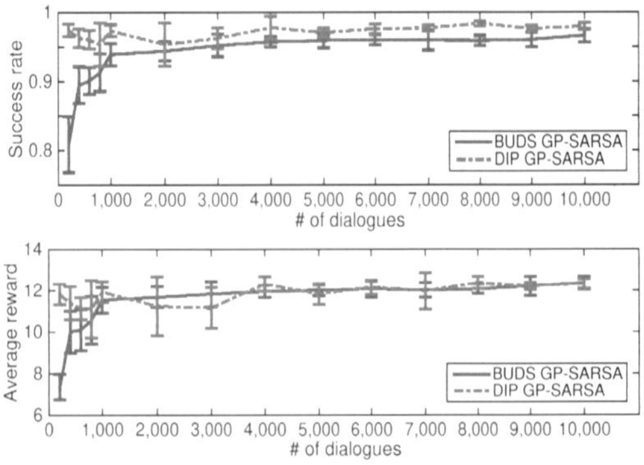

Figure 1: Training GP-SARSA policies for BUDS (full belief) and DIP in the restaurant search domain. Every point is averaged over 5 policies each evaluated on 1000 simulated dialogues, with the error bar being standard deviation.

cies trained in the restaurant search domain to the laptop sale domain, and compared its performance with an in-domain policy trained using the simulator (configured to the laptop sale domain). Table 1 shows that the performance of the transferred policy is almost identical to the in-domain policy.

Finally, we chose the best in-domain and transferred DIP policies and deployed them into end-to-end laptop sale SDSs, for human subject experiments based on MTurk. After each dialogue, the user was also asked to provide a subjective score for the naturalness of the interaction, ranging from 1 (very unnatural) to 6 (very natural). The results are summarised in Table 2, where the success rate difference (3%) between the in-domain policy and the transferred policy is statistically insignificant, and surprisingly, the users on average regard the transferred policy as slightly more natural than the in-domain policy.

5 Conclusion

This paper proposed a domain-independent ontology parameterision framework to enable domain-transfer of optimised dialogue policies. Experimental results show that when transferred to a new domain, dialogue policies trained based on the DIP representations can achieve very close performance to those policies optimised using in-domain dialogues. Bridging the (very small) performance gap here should also be simple, if one takes the transferred policy as the prior and conducts domain-adaptation similar to (Gašić et al., 2015). This will be addressed in our future work.

Acknowledgements

The authors would like to thank David Vandyke, Milica Gašić and Steve Young for providing the BUDS system and the simulator, as well as for their help in setting up the crowdsourcing experiments.

References

Milica Gašić and Steve Young. 2014. Gaussian processes for POMDP-based dialogue manager optimization. *IEEE/ACM Transactions on Audio, Speech and Language Processing*, 22(1):28–40.

Milica Gašić, Matthew Henderson, Blaise Thomson, Pirros Tsiakoulis, and Steve J. Young. 2012. Policy optimisation of POMDP-based dialogue systems without state space compression. In *SLT 2012*.

Milica Gašić, Catherine Breslin, Matthew Henderson, Dongho Kim, Martin Szummer, Blaise Thomson, Pirros Tsiakoulis, and Steve Young. 2013. POMDP-based dialogue manager adaptation to extended domains. In *SIGDIAL 2013*.

Milica Gašić, Dongho Kim, Pirros Tsiakoulis, and Steve Young. 2015. Distributed dialogue policies for multi-domain statistical dialogue management. In *ICASSP 2015*.

Matthew Henderson, Blaise Thomson, and Steve J. Young. 2014. Robust dialog state tracking using delexicalised recurrent neural networks and unsupervised adaptation. In *SLT 2014*.

Oliver Lemon, Kallirroi Georgila, and James Henderson. 2006. Evaluating effectiveness and portability of reinforcement learned dialogue strategies with real users: the TALK TownInfo evaluation. In *SLT 2006*.

Qi Li, Gökhan Tür, Dilek Hakkani-Tür, Xiang Li, Tim Paek, Asela Gunawardana, and Chris Quirk. 2014. Distributed open-domain conversational understanding framework with domain independent extractors. In *SLT 2014*.

Nikola Mrkšić, Diarmuid Ó Séaghdha, Blaise Thomson, Milica Gašić, David Vandyke Pei-Hao Su, Tsung-Hsien Wen, and Steve Young. 2015. Multi-domain dialog state tracking using recurrent neural networks. In *ACL-IJCNLP 2015*.

Jost Schatzmann, Blaise Thomson, Karl Weilhammer, Hui Ye, and Steve Young. 2007. Agenda-based user simulation for bootstrapping a POMDP dialogue system. In *HLT-NAACL 2007; Companion Volume, Short Papers*.

Kai Sun, Lu Chen, Su Zhu, and Kai Yu. 2014. A generalized rule based tracker for dialogue state tracking. In *SLT 2014*.

Blaise Thomson and Steve Young. 2010. Bayesian update of dialogue state: A POMDP framework for spoken dialogue systems. *Computer Speech and Language*, 24(4):562–588.

Zhuoran Wang and Oliver Lemon. 2013. A simple and generic belief tracking mechanism for the Dialog State Tracking Challenge: On the believability of observed information. In *SIGDIAL 2013*.

Jason D. Williams and Steve Young. 2005. Scaling up POMDPs for dialog management: The "Summary POMDP" method. In *ASRU 2005*.

Steve Young, Milica Gašić, Blaise Thomson, and Jason D. Williams. 2013. POMDP-based statistical spoken dialogue systems: a review. *Proceedings of the IEEE*, PP(99):1–20.

A Ontology Definitions for the Example Domains

	Slot	#Values	Info.	Rqst.
Restaurant	food	91	yes	yes
	area	5	yes	yes
	pricerange	3	yes	yes
	name	111	yes	yes
	phone	–	no	yes
	postcode	–	no	yes
	signature	–	no	yes
	description	–	no	yes
Laptop	family	5	yes	no
	purpose	2	yes	yes
	pricerange	3	yes	yes
	weightrange	3	yes	yes
	batteryrating	3	yes	yes
	driverange	3	yes	yes
	name	123	yes	no
	price	–	no	yes
	weight	–	no	yes
	hard drive	–	no	yes
	dimension	–	no	yes

Table A.1: Ontologies for the restaurant search and laptop sale domains. "Info." denotes informable slots, for which user can provide values; "Rqst." denotes requestable slots, for which user can ask for information.

Reward Shaping with Recurrent Neural Networks for Speeding up On-Line Policy Learning in Spoken Dialogue Systems

Pei-Hao Su, David Vandyke, Milica Gašić,
Nikola Mrkšić, Tsung-Hsien Wen and **Steve Young**
Department of Engineering, University of Cambridge, Cambridge, UK
{phs26, djv27, mg436, nm480, thw28, sjy}@cam.ac.uk

Abstract

Statistical spoken dialogue systems have the attractive property of being able to be optimised from data via interactions with real users. However in the reinforcement learning paradigm the dialogue manager (agent) often requires significant time to explore the state-action space to learn to behave in a desirable manner. This is a critical issue when the system is trained on-line with real users where learning costs are expensive. Reward shaping is one promising technique for addressing these concerns. Here we examine three recurrent neural network (RNN) approaches for providing reward shaping information in addition to the primary (task-orientated) environmental feedback. These RNNs are trained on returns from dialogues generated by a simulated user and attempt to diffuse the overall evaluation of the dialogue back down to the turn level to guide the agent towards good behaviour faster. In both simulated and real user scenarios these RNNs are shown to increase policy learning speed. Importantly, they do not require prior knowledge of the user's goal.

1 Introduction

Spoken dialogue systems (SDS) offer a natural way for people to interact with computers. With the ability to learn from data (interactions) statistical SDS can theoretically be created faster and with less man-hours than a comparable handcrafted rule based system. They have also been shown to perform better (Young et al., 2013). Central to this is the use of partially observable Markov decision processes (POMDP) to model dialogue, which inherently manage the uncertainty created by errors in speech recognition and semantic decoding (Williams and Young, 2007).

The dialogue manager is a core component of an SDS and largely determines the quality of interaction. Its behaviour is controlled by a *policy* which maps belief states to system actions (or distributions over sets of actions) and this policy is trained in a reinforcement learning framework (Sutton and Barto, 1999) where rewards are received from the environment, the most informative of which occurs only at the dialogues conclusion, indicating task success or failure.[1]

It is the sparseness of this environmental reward function which, by not providing any information at intermediate turns, requires exploration to traverse deeply many sub-optimal paths. This is a significant concern when training SDS on-line with real users where one wishes to minimise client exposure to sub-optimal system behaviour. In an effort to counter this problem, *reward shaping* (Ng et al., 1999) introduces domain knowledge to provide earlier informative feedback to the agent (additional to the environmental feedback) for the purpose of biasing exploration for discovering optimal behaviour quicker.[2] Reward shaping is briefly reviewed in Section 2.1.

In the context of SDS, Ferreira and Lefèvre (2015) have motivated the use of reward shaping via analogy to the 'social signals' naturally produced and interpreted throughout a human-human dialogue. This non-statistical reward shaping model used heuristic features for speeding up policy learning.

As an alternative, one may consider attempting to handcraft a finer grained environmental reward

[1] A uniform reward of -1 is common for all other, non-terminal turns, which promotes faster task completion.

[2] Learning algorithms are another central element in improving the speed of convergence during policy training. In particular the sample-efficiency of the learning algorithm can be the deciding factor in whether it can realistically be employed on-line. See e.g. the GP-SARSA (Gasic and Young, 2014) and Kalman temporal-difference (Daubigney et al., 2014) methods which bootstrap estimates of sparse value functions from minimal numbers of samples (dialogues).

Proceedings of the SIGDIAL 2015 Conference, pages 417–421,
Prague, Czech Republic, 2-4 September 2015.

function. For example, Asri et al. (2014) proposed diffusing expert ratings of dialogues to the state transition level to produce a richer reward function. Policy convergence may occur faster in this altered POMDP and dialogues generated by a task based simulated user may also alleviate the need for expert ratings. However, unlike reward shaping, modifying the environmental reward function also modifies the resulting optimal policy.

We recently proposed convolutional and recurrent neural network (RNN) approaches for determining dialogue success. This was used to provide a reinforcement signal for learning on-line from real users without requiring any prior knowledge of the user's task (Su et al., 2015). Here we extend the RNN approach by introducing new training constraints in order to combine the merits of the above three works: (1) diffusing dialogue level ratings down to the turn level to (2) add reward shaping information for faster policy learning, whilst (3) not requiring prior task knowledge which is simply unavailable on-line.

In Section 2 we briefly describe potential based reward shaping before introducing the RNNs we explore for producing reward shaping signals (basic RNN, long short-term memory (LSTM) and gated recurrent unit (GRU)). The features the RNNs use along with the training constraint and loss are also described. The experimental evaluation is then presented in Section 3. Firstly, the estimation accuracy of the RNNs is assessed. The benefit of using the RNN for reward shaping in both simulated and real user scenarios is then also demonstrated. Finally, conclusions are presented in Section 4.

2 RNNs for Reward Shaping

2.1 Reward Shaping

Reward shaping provides the system with an extra reward signal F in addition to environmental reward R, making the system learn from the composite signal $R + F$. The shaping reward F often encodes expert knowledge that complements the sparse signal R. Since the reward function defines the system's objective, changing it may result in a different task. When the task is modelled as a fully observable Markov decision process (MDP), Ng et al. (1999) defined formal requirements on the shaping reward as a difference of any potential function ϕ on consecutive states s and s' which preserves the optimality of policies. Based on this

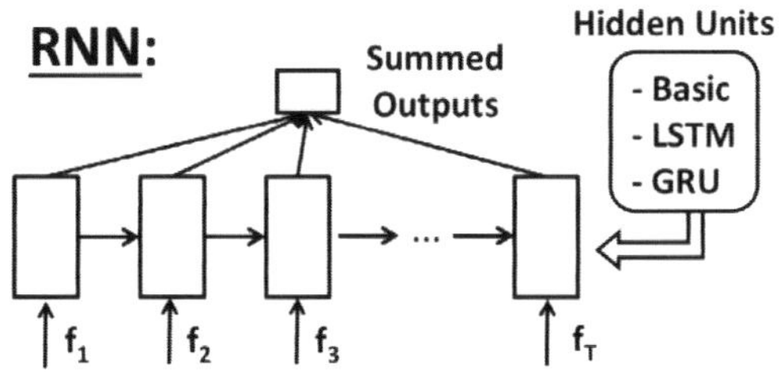

Figure 1: RNN with three types of hidden units: basic, LSTM and GRU. The feature vectors $\mathbf{f}_t$ extracted at turns $t = 1, \dots, T$ are labelled $\mathbf{f}_t$.

property, Eck et al. (2015) further extended it to POMDP by proof and empirical experiments:

$$F(b_t, a, b_{t+1}) = \gamma\phi(b_{t+1}) - \phi(b_t) \qquad (1)$$

where γ is the discount factor, b_t the belief state at turn t, and a the action leading b_t to b_{t+1}.

However determining an appropriate potential function for an SDS is non-trivial. Rather than hand-crafting the function with heuristic knowledge, we propose using an RNN to predict proper values as in the following.

2.2 Recurrent Neural Network Models

The RNN model is a subclass of neural network defined by the presence of feedback connections. The ability to succinctly retain history information makes it suitable for modelling sequential data. It has been successfully used for language modelling (Mikolov et al., 2011) and spoken language understanding (Mesnil et al., 2015).

However, Bengio et al. (1994) observed that basic RNNs suffer from vanishing/exploding gradient problems that limit their capability of modelling long context dependencies. To address this, long short-term memory (Hochreiter and Schmidhuber, 1997) and gated recurrent unit (Chung et al., 2014) RNNs have been proposed. In this paper, all three types of RNN (basic/LSTM/GRU) are compared.

2.3 Reward Shaping with RNN Prediction

The role of the RNN is to solve the regression problem of predicting the scalar return of each completed dialogue. At every turn t, input feature f_t are extracted from the belief/action pair and used to update the hidden layer h_t. From dialogues generated by a simulated user (Schatzmann and Young, 2009) supervised training pairs are created which consist of the turn level sequence of these feature vectors f_t along with the scalar dialogue return as scored by an objective measure of task completion. Whilst the RNN models are trained on dialogue level supervised targets, we hypothesise that their subsequent turn level predictions can guide policy exploration via acting as informative reward shaping potentials.

To encourage good turn level predictions, all three RNN variants are trained to predict the dialogue return not with the final output of the network, but with the constraint that their scalar outputs from each turn t should sum to predict the return for the whole dialogue. This is shown in Figure 1. A mean-square-error (MSE) loss is used (see Appendix A). The trained RNNs are then used directly as the reward shaping potential function ϕ, using the RNN scalar output at each turn.

The feature inputs f_t for all RNNs consisted of the following sections: the real-valued belief state vector formed by concatenating the distributions over user discourse act, method and goal variables (Thomson and Young, 2010), one-hot encodings of the user and summary system actions, and the normalised turn number. This feature vector was extracted at every turn (system + user exchange).

3 Experiments

3.1 Experimental Setup

In all experiments the Cambridge restaurant domain was used, which consists of approximately 150 venues each having 6 attributes (slots) of which 3 can be used by the system to constrain the search and the remaining 3 are informable properties once a database entity has been found.

The shared core components of the SDS in all experiments were a domain independent ASR, a confusion network (CNet) semantic input decoder (Henderson et al., 2012), the BUDS (Thomson and Young, 2010) belief state tracker that factorises the dialogue state using a dynamic Bayesian network and a template based natural language generator. All policies were trained by GP-SARSA (Gasic and Young, 2014) and the summary action space contains 20 actions. Per turn reward was set to -1 and final reward 20 for task success else 0.

With this ontology, the size of the full feature vector was 147. The turn number was expressed as a percentage of the maximum number of allowed turns, here 30. The one-hot user dialogue act encoding was formed by taking only the most likely user act estimated by the CNet decoder.

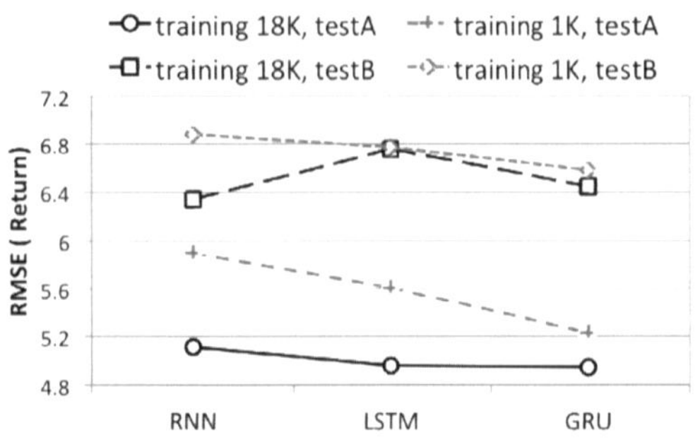

Figure 2: RMSE of return prediction by using RNN/LSTM/GRU, trained on 18K and 1K dialogues and tested on sets *testA* and *testB* (see text).

3.2 Neural Network Training

Here results of training the 3 RNNs on the simulated user dialogues are presented.[3] Two training sets were used consisting of 18K and 1K dialogues to verify the model robustness. In all cases a separate validation set consisting of 1K dialogues was used for controlling overfitting. Training and validation sets were approximately balanced regarding objective success/failure labels and collected at a 15% semantic error rate (SER). Prediction results are shown in Figure 2 on two test sets; *testA:* 1K dialogues, balanced regarding objective labels, at 15% SER and *testB:* containing 12K dialogues collected at SERs of 0, 15, 30 and 45 as the data occurred (*i.e.* with no balancing regarding labels).

Root-MSE (RMSE) results of predicting the dialogue return are depicted in Figure 2. The models with LSTM and GRU units achieved a slight improvement in most cases over the basic RNN. Notice that the model with GRU even reached comparable results when trained with 1K training data compared to 18K. The results from the 1K training set indicate that the model can be developed from limited data. This enables datasets to be created by human annotation, avoiding the need for a simulated user. The results on set *testB* also show that the models can perform well in situations with varying error rates as would be encountered in real operating environments. Note that the dataset could also be created from human's annotation which avoids the need for a simulated user. We next examine the RNN-based reward shaping for policy training with a simulated user.

[3] All RNNs were implemented using the Theano library (Bergstra et al., 2010). In all cases the hidden layer contained 100 units with a sigmoid non-linearity and used stochastic gradient descent (per dialogue) for training.

Figure 3: Policy training via simulated user with (GRU/HDC) and without (baseline) reward shaping. Standard errors are also shown.

Figure 4: Learning curves of reward with standard errors during on-line policy optimisation for the baseline (black) and proposed (green) systems.

3.3 Policy Learning with Simulated User

Since the aim of reward shaping is to enhance policy learning speed, we focus on the first 1000 training dialogues. Figure 2 shows that the GRU RNN attained slightly better performance than the other two RNN models, albeit with no statistical significance. Thus for clearer presentation of the policy training results we plot only the GRU results, using the model trained on 18K dialogues.

To show the effectiveness of using RNN with GRU for predicting reward shaping potentials, we compare it with the hand-crafted (HDC) method for reward shaping proposed by Ferreira and Lefèvre (2013) that requires prior knowledge of the user's task, and a baseline policy using only the environmental reward. Figure 3 shows the learning curve of the reward for the three systems. After every 50 training iterations each system was tested with 1000 dialogues and averaged over 10 policies. The simulated user's SER was set to 15%.

We see that reward shaping indeed provides the agent with more information, increasing the learning speed. Furthermore, our proposed RNN method further outperforms the hand-crafted system, whilst also being able to be applied on-line.

3.4 Policy Learning with Human Users

Based on the above results, the same GRU model was selected for training a policy on-line with humans. Two systems were trained with users recruited via Amazon Mechanical Turk: a baseline was trained with only the environmental reward, and another system was trained with an additional shaping reward predicted by the proposed GRU. Learning began from a random policy in all cases.

Figure 4 shows the on-line learning curve of the reward when training the systems with 400 dialogues. The moving average was calculated using a window of 100 dialogues and each result was averaged over three policies in order to reduce noise. It can be seen that by adding the RNN based shaping reward, the policy learnt quicker in the important initial phase of policy learning.

4 Conclusions

This paper has shown that RNN models can be trained to predict the dialogue return with a constraint such that subsequent turn level predictions act as good reward shaping signals that are effective for accelerating policy learning on-line with real users. As in many other applications, we found that gated RNNs such as LSTM and GRU perform a little better than basic RNNs.

In the work described here, the RNNs were trained using a simulated user and this simulator could have been used to bootstrap a policy for use with real users. However our supposition is that RNNs could be trained for reward prediction which are substantially domain independent and hence have wider applications via domain adaptation and extension (Gašić et al., 2015; Brys et al., 2015). Testing this supposition will be the subject of future work.

5 Acknowledgements

Pei-Hao Su is supported by Cambridge Trust and the Ministry of Education, Taiwan. David Vandyke and Tsung-Hsien Wen are supported by Toshiba Research Europe Ltd, Cambridge Research Lab.

References

Layla El Asri, Romain Laroche, and Olivier Pietquin. 2014. Task completion transfer learning for reward inference. In *Proc of MLIS*.

Yoshua Bengio, Patrice Simard, and Paolo Frasconi. 1994. Learning long-term dependencies with gradient descent is difficult. *Neural Networks, IEEE Transactions on*, 5(2):157–166.

James Bergstra, Olivier Breuleux, Frédéric Bastien, Pascal Lamblin, Razvan Pascanu, Guillaume Desjardins, Joseph Turian, David Warde-Farley, and Yoshua Bengio. 2010. Theano: a CPU and GPU math expression compiler. In *Proceedings of the Python for Scientific Computing Conference*.

Tim Brys, Anna Harutyunyan, Matthew E. Taylor, and Ann Nowé. 2015. Policy transfer using reward shaping. In *Proc of AAMAS*.

Junyoung Chung, Caglar Gulcehre, KyungHyun Cho, and Yoshua Bengio. 2014. Empirical evaluation of gated recurrent neural networks on sequence modeling. *arXiv preprint arXiv:1412.3555*.

Lucie Daubigney, Matthieu Geist, Senthilkumar Chandramohan, and Olivier Pietquin. 2014. A comprehensive reinforcement learning framework for dialogue management optimisation. *Journal of Selected Topics in Signal Processing*, 6(8).

Adam Eck, Leen-Kiat Soh, Sam Devlin, and Daniel Kudenko. 2015. Potential-based reward shaping for finite horizon online pomdp planning. *Autonomous Agents and Multi-Agent Systems*, pages 1–43.

Emmanuel Ferreira and Fabrice Lefèvre. 2013. Social signal and user adaptation in reinforcement learning-based dialogue management. In *Proc of MLIS*.

Emmanuel Ferreira and Fabrice Lefèvre. 2015. Reinforcement-learning based dialogue system for human-robot interactions with socially-inspired rewards. *Computer Speech & Language*, 34(1):256–274.

Milica Gasic and Stephanie Young. 2014. Gaussian processes for pomdp-based dialogue manager optimization. *TASLP*, 22(1):28–40.

Milica Gašić, Dongho Kim, Pirros Tsiakoulis, and Steve Young. 2015. Distributed dialogue policies for multi-domain statistical dialogue management. In *ICASSP*.

Matthew Henderson, Milica Gašić, Blaise Thomson, Pirros Tsiakoulis, Kai Yu, and Steve Young. 2012. Discriminative spoken language understanding using word confusion networks. In *IEEE SLT*.

Sepp Hochreiter and Jürgen Schmidhuber. 1997. Long short-term memory. *Neural computation*, 9(8):1735–1780.

Grégoire Mesnil, Yann Dauphin, Kaisheng Yao, Yoshua Bengio, Li Deng, Dilek Hakkani-Tur, Xiaodong He, Larry Heck, Gokhan Tur, Dong Yu, et al. 2015. Using recurrent neural networks for slot filling in spoken language understanding. *TASLP*, 23(3):530–539.

Tomas Mikolov, Stefan Kombrink, Lukas Burget, Jan H Cernocky, and Sanjeev Khudanpur. 2011. Extensions of recurrent neural network language model. In *ICASSP*.

Andrew Y. Ng, Daishi Harada, and Stuart Russell. 1999. Policy invariance under reward transformations: Theory and application to reward shaping. In *ICML*.

J. Schatzmann and S. Young. 2009. The hidden agenda user simulation model. *IEEE TALSP*, 17(4):733–747.

Pei-Hao Su, David Vandyke, Milica Gašić, Dongho Kim, Nikola Mrkšić, Tsung-Hsien Wen, and Steve Young. 2015. Learning from real users: Rating dialogue success with neural networks for reinforcement learning in spoken dialogue systems. In *Proc of Interspeech*.

Richard S. Sutton and Andrew G. Barto. 1999. *Reinforcement Learning: An Introduction*. MIT Press.

B. Thomson and S. Young. 2010. Bayesian update of dialogue state: A pomdp framework for spoken dialogue systems. *Computer Speech and Language*, 24:562–588.

Jason D. Williams and Steve Young. 2007. Partially observable Markov decision processes for spoken dialog systems. *Computer Speech and Language*, 21(2):393–422.

Steve Young, Milica Gašic, Blaise Thomson, and Jason Williams. 2013. Pomdp-based statistical spoken dialogue systems: a review. In *Proc of the IEEE*, volume 99, pages 1–20.

A Training Constraint/Loss Function

For all RNN models the following MSE loss function is used on a per-dialogue basis:

$$\text{MSE} = \left(R - \sum_{t=1}^{T} r_t \right)^2 \quad (2)$$

where the current dialogue has T turns, R is the return and training target, and r_t is the scalar prediction output by the RNN model at each turn.

Effects of Game on User Engagement with Spoken Dialogue System

Hayato Kobayashi **Kaori Tanio** **Manabu Sassano**
Yahoo Japan Corporation
9-7-1 Akasaka, Minato-ku, Tokyo 107-6211, Japan
{hakobaya, katanio, msassano}@yahoo-corp.jp

Abstract

In this study, we examine the effects of using a game for encouraging the use of a spoken dialogue system. As a case study, we developed a word-chain game, called *Shiritori* in Japanese, and released the game as a module in a Japanese Android/iOS app, *Onsei-Assist*, which is a Siri-like personal assistant based on a spoken dialogue technology. We analyzed the log after the release and confirmed that the game can increase the number of user utterances. Furthermore, we discovered a positive side effect, in which users who have played the game tend to begin using non-game modules. This suggests that just adding a game module to the system can improve user engagement with an assistant agent.

1 Introduction

Making users actively utter queries is important in a spoken dialogue system since they are generally not familiar with speaking to a system compared to typing on a keyboard. There have been several studies based on *gamification* for addressing this problem (Jurgens and Navigli, 2014; Gustafson et al., 2004; Hjalmarsson et al., 2007; Bell et al., 2005; Rayner et al., 2010; Rayner et al., 2012). Gamification is a concept of applying game design thinking to non-game applications, leveraging people's natural desires for socializing, learning, mastery, competition, achievement, and so on. However, it takes much time and effort to gamify a whole system, i.e., to consider how to design a game-like framework and combine new and current systems.

We therefore explore the possibilities of using of a game instead of gamifying a whole system. In other words, we address the question of whether a small module of an existing dialogue game can make users actively use the whole system. To this end, we developed a word-chain game as a case study and released the game as a module in the running Android/iOS app *Onsei-Assist* (Yahoo! JAPAN, 2015), which we describe later. We analyzed the log of user utterances after its release and confirmed that our results clearly answer this question positively.

The following are our main contributions.

- We analyzed vast amounts of dialogue data, i.e., more than tens of millions of user utterances cumulated via a running app of a spoken dialogue system.
- We discovered that just adding an existing game module to the system can have a positive impact on the non-game modules of the system from a case study of a word-chain game. This suggests that a game can help increase user engagement with an assistant agent.

The remainder of this paper is structured as follows. In Section 2, we introduce related studies on gamification for natural language processing systems. In Section 3, we briefly describe a spoken dialogue app, Onsei-Assist, whose log was used throughout our analysis. In Section 4, we explain how we developed a word-chain game module using a crowdsourcing service and in Section 5, we analyze the effects of using the game in Onsei-Assist. We conclude the paper in Section 6.

2 Related Work

We now briefly describe related studies on gamification for natural language processing systems, especially for spoken dialogue systems. When a gamified system is completely a game, the system is called a *game with a purpose (GWAP)*, or a *serious game*. Although a GWAP is sometimes differ-

Proceedings of the SIGDIAL 2015 Conference, pages 422–426,
Prague, Czech Republic, 2-4 September 2015.

entiated from gamification, we do not differentiate them for simplicity.

There have been many studies involving gamification for annotation tasks including anaphora resolution (Hladká et al., 2009; Poesio et al., 2013), paraphrasing (Chklovski and Gil, 2005), term associations (Artignan et al., 2009), and disambiguation (Seemakurty et al., 2010; Venhuizen et al., 2013). Recent studies (Vannella et al., 2014; Jurgens and Navigli, 2014) showed that designing linguistic annotation tasks as video games can produce high-quality annotations compared to text-based tasks.

There are several GWAPs based on spoken dialogue systems. DEAL is a game with a spoken language interface designed for second language learners (Hjalmarsson et al., 2007). In the NICE fairy-tale game system (Gustafson et al., 2004), users can interact with various animated characters in a 3D world. This game yields a spontaneous child-computer dialogue corpus in Swedish (Bell et al., 2005). CALL-SLT is an open-source speech-based translation game designed for learning and improving fluency, which supports French, English, Japanese, German, Greek, and Swedish (Rayner et al., 2010; Rayner et al., 2012).

However, each of these games or gamified systems was custom-made for a certain purpose, and to the best of our knowledge, we are the first to examine the effects of an existing dialogue game with an entertainment purpose, i.e., word-chain game, to a non-game system, especially in a spoken dialogue system.

3 Onsei-Assist

We used the log of a Japanese Android/iOS app of a spoken dialogue system, Onsei-Assist (Yahoo! JAPAN, 2015), throughout this analysis. Onsei-Assist is a Siri-like personal assistant developed by Yahoo Japan Corporation, where "Onsei" means "voice" in Japanese. It produced more than 20 million of utterances within a year of release on April 2012 via pre-installs to smartphones and downloads (more than one million) in GooglePlay.

Onsei-Assist was developed based on a client-server architecture, where the main system consists of four servers: a speech recognition server, meaning understanding server with natural language processing, response generation server, and speech synthesis server. The processing flow is as follows. A client, or smartphone, sends voice signals from a microphone to the speech recognition server and receives a recognition result of the user utterance in textual form; consequently, it sends the text to the meaning understanding server. This server differentiates the meaning of the utterance from the text and extracts information of variables such as named entities (e.g., Tokyo) and numerical expressions (e.g., 2014). It then generates a response pattern and sends it to the response generation server, which completes a response text by obtaining the required information via the API of several services. It also returns the response text with its prosody calculated by the speech synthesis server.

Onsei-Assist supports more than 20 services, each of which are launched by triggers based on natural sentences such as

- Route search ("From Osaka to Tokyo", "When does this train arrive?"),
- Weather information ("Today's weather", "Will it rain tomorrow?"),
- News ("News about the general election"),
- Web/image search ("Search for Tokyo Tower"),

and so on. In addition to such task-oriented dialogue modules, it can have a chat with users for general queries such as "How old are you?" and "Hello". Our system generates a response by choosing one from a pre-defined sentences based on a rule-based algorithm and learned model.

Table 1 shows examples of the log of user utterances, each of which is a tuple of five elements, i.e., (Time Stamp, User ID, Type, User Utterance, System Response). We obtained the log of more than 13 million utterances of 489 thousand users for our analysis.

4 Word-chain Game

First, we explain a word-chain game called *Shiritori* in Japanese. The principle of the word-chain game is to say a word based on rotation so that its head character is the same as the tail character of the previous word, e.g., (app**le**, **e**e**l**, **l**i**p**, **p**ine, ...). It is a well known speech dialogue game in Japan since a syllable is basically represented by a character of a Japanese syllabary, i.e., Hiragana. The concrete rule used in this analysis is that each player must say a word based on rotation satisfying the following four conditions:

Time Stamp	User ID	Type	User Utterance	System Response
2014-8-1 12:34	UserA	Weather	今日の天気 (Today's weather)	晴れです (It's sunny)
2014-8-2 22:22	UserB	Chat	こんにちは (Hello)	こんにちわ (Hello)
2014-8-3 23:00	UserC	Chat	ありがとう (Thank you)	いえいえ (Your welcome)

Table 1: Example of log of user utterances.

1. The head of the word must be the same as the tail of the previous word.
2. The word must be a noun.
3. The word must not be a word already said in the game.
4. The tail of the word must not end with "ん (n)".

Conditions 2 and 3 prevent the game from being too long, and condition 4 is set because there is no word whose head character is "ん (n)" in Japanese.

Next, we explain the development of a word-chain game module for Onsei-Assist. We used a crowdsourcing service for obtaining words that people would usually use in the game because we worried that unfamiliar words extracted from Wikipedia and dictionaries could seriously deteriorate user satisfaction from a practical standpoint.

The process of collecting words is as follows. We prepared 1,150 seed words from dozen of employees in our company by using a simple word-chain game program developed only for this purpose. We created a crowdsourcing task asking workers to answer an appropriate word for each seed word based on the above rule. We repeated the task three times. Table 2 lists the results of the task for each repeated stage. Since the crowdsourcing service we used does not allow us to add a rule-check mechanism, we checked whether the results followed the rule after the task finished. About 90% of the answers were correct. Finally we obtained a sufficient amount of words (6,148) with their frequencies. We extracted the top 20 words based on frequency for each of the 66 Japanese head characters in the extracted words. This prevented the game from being too difficult since the workers rarely answered with words whose tail character was rare in Japanese. For example, the dictionary has only two words for the character "ぴ (pi)". Therefore, users can easily win by aiming for such a tail character.

We developed a word-chain game module for Onsei-Assist using the above dictionary. Figure 1 shows two screen shots when playing the word-chain game module. In the module, the game starts by a user's trigger utterance such as "しりとり (Word-chain game)". The system replies with a response such as "いいですよ。りんご (OK. Ri-n-go)", and a user needs to say a word whose head character is "ご (go)" as the response. If the user says something that does not follow the rule, the system replies an error message such as "しりとりになっていません。(It's not a chained word)". The user can stop the game by using an ending word such as "ギブアップ (Give up)".

Stage	#Words	#Answers	#Errors
1	1,403	3,379	71
2	2,951	9,314	826
3	6,148	25,645	2,285

Table 2: Results of crowdsourcing task for obtaining possible words obeying word-chain game rule. #Words, #Answers, and #Errors represent number of distinct words, workers' answers, and errors due to breaking of rules, respectively.

Figure 1: Screen shots when playing word-chain game module. Right and left balloons in each screen shot represent user and system's utterances, respectively.

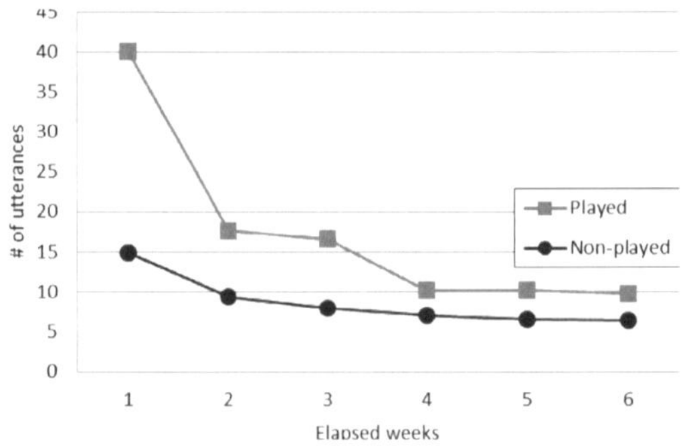

Figure 2: Average number of utterances over new users versus elapsed weeks. `Played` and `Non-played` represent users who had played and had not played the game on the first day, respectively.

5 Log Analysis

We conducted an analysis based on short- and long-term effects. For short-term effects, we define the reply rate of a system response R as the rate of the number of replies, which were uttered in a short period by users who received R, per the number of times R occurs in the log. The period was set to 20 minutes. We obtained a reply rate of more than 90% for every system response in the word-chain game. This is quite high, considering the fact that even a question-type system response "どうしました？ (What's happening?)" is about 80%. This implies that the game leverages users' natural desires for competition. In fact, the reply rates after a user won or failed (especially for saying a word already said) were 90.22% and 95.78%, respectively. This clearly indicates that users tend to retry to win after they failed.

For long-term effects, we averaged the number of utterances in a week over new users. Then we plotted it against elapsed weeks as shown in Figure 2, where `Played` and `Non-played` represent users who had played and had not played the game on the first day, respectively. We regard users who have not used the system over the last two months as new users to obtain sufficient data. The table clearly indicates that `Played` tended to use the system more frequently than `Non-played`. We also examined the difference between before and after game plays of active users. Table 3 shows the average number of utterances over game plays of active users in the week before and after each game. For extracting active users and obtaining a fair evaluation, we only considered game plays such that a user corresponding to each game play had used the system at least once and had not played the game for a week before game play. We found that game plays increased the average number of utterances by about 150% (from 24.60 to 43.61) despite the fact that we excluded utterances about the game. Note that these results are basically better than the results on new users in Figure 2 since we focused on active users. A possible reason is that users have become more familiar with this assistant agent through playing the game. Thus they began to use non-game modules more frequently.

	Before	After
(a) # of game plays	29,448	
(b) # of utterances	724,416	1,491,125
(c) # of game utterances	0	206,940
$((b) - (c))/(a)$	24.60	43.61

Table 3: Average number of utterances over game plays of active users week before and after each game play.

6 Conclusion

We examined the effects of using a game for encouraging the use of a spoken dialogue system. We developed a word-chain game, called *Shiritori* in Japanese, as a case study and released the game as a module in a running Android/iOS app, Onsei-Assist, based on a spoken dialogue technology. We analyzed the log after the release and confirmed that the game can increase the number of user utterances. Furthermore, we discovered a positive side effect, in which users who have played the game tend to begin using non-game modules. This implies that a game can help to improve user engagement with an assistant agent. In other words, it is important to consider adding an entertaining module, such as a game, when developing a spoken dialogue system, as well as a useful module such as a route search.

For future research, we will examine other games such as a word association and quiz games. Since a game can be regarded as a simplification of a complex mechanism for natural dialogues, we hope to obtain generalized knowledge for improving spoken dialogue systems, if we can clarify which game can effectively improve which module in such systems.

References

Guillaume Artignan, Mountaz Hascoët, and Mathieu Lafourcade. 2009. Multiscale Visual Analysis of Lexical Networks. In *Proceedings of the 13th International Conference on Information Visualisation (IV 2009)*, pages 685–690. IEEE Computer Society.

Linda Bell, Johan Boye, Joakim Gustafson, Mattias Heldner, Anders Lindström, and Mats Wirén. 2005. The swedish NICE corpus - spoken dialogues between children and embodied characters in a computer game scenario. In *INTERSPEECH 2005 - Eurospeech, 9th European Conference on Speech Communication and Technology*, pages 2765–2768. ISCA.

Tim Chklovski and Yolanda Gil. 2005. Improving the design of intelligent acquisition interfaces for collecting world knowledge from web contributors. In *Proceedings of the International Conference on Knowledge Capture*, pages 35–42. ACM.

Joakim Gustafson, Linda Bell, Johan Boye, Anders Lindström, and Mats Wirén. 2004. The NICE Fairy-tale Game System. In *Proceedings of the 5th SIGdial Workshop on Discourse and Dialogue (SIGDIAL 2004)*, pages 23–26. Association for Computational Linguistics.

Anna Hjalmarsson, Preben Wik, and Jenny Brusk. 2007. Dealing with DEAL: a dialogue system for conversation training. In *Proceedings of the 8th SIGdial Workshop on Discourse and Dialogue (SIGDIAL 2007)*, pages 132–135. Association for Computational Linguistics.

Barbora Hladká, Jiří Mírovský, and Pavel Schlesinger. 2009. Play the Language: Play Coreference. In *Proceedings of the Joint Conference of the Association for Computational Linguistics and International Joint Conference of the Asian Federation of Natural Language Processing (ACL-IJCNLP 2009)*, pages 209–212. Association for Computational Linguistics.

David Jurgens and Roberto Navigli. 2014. It's All Fun and Games until Someone Annotates: Video Games with a Purpose for Linguistic Annotation. *Transactions of the Association of Computational Linguistics*, 2(1):449–464.

Massimo Poesio, Jon Chamberlain, Udo Kruschwitz, Livio Robaldo, and Luca Ducceschi. 2013. Phrase detectives: Utilizing collective intelligence for internetscale language resource creation. *ACM Transactions on Interactive Intelligent Systems*, 3(1):3:1–3:44.

Emmanuel Rayner, Pierrette Bouillon, Nikolaos Tsourakis, Johanna Gerlach, Yukie Nakao, and Claudia Baur. 2010. A Multilingual CALL Game Based on Speech Translation. In *Proceedings of the Eighth International Conference on Language Resources and Evaluation (LREC 2010)*. European Language Resources Association (ELRA).

Manny Rayner, Pierrette Bouillon, and Johanna Gerlach. 2012. Evaluating Appropriateness Of System Responses In A Spoken CALL Game. In *Proceedings of the Eighth International Conference on Language Resources and Evaluation (LREC 2012)*, pages 2690–2694. European Language Resources Association (ELRA).

Nitin Seemakurty, Jonathan Chu, Luis von Ahn, and Anthony Tomasic. 2010. Word Sense Disambiguation via Human Computation. In *Proceedings of the ACM SIGKDD Workshop on Human Computation*, pages 60–63. ACM.

Daniele Vannella, David Jurgens, Daniele Scarfini, Domenico Toscani, and Roberto Navigli. 2014. Validating and Extending Semantic Knowledge Bases using Video Games with a Purpose. In *Proceedings of the 52nd Annual Meeting of the Association for Computational Linguistics (ACL 2014)*, pages 1294–1304. Association for Computational Linguistics.

Noortje Venhuizen, Valerio Basile, Kilian Evang, and Johan Bos. 2013. Gamification for Word Sense Labeling. In *Proceedings of the 10th International Conference on Computational Semantics (IWCS 2013)*, pages 397–403. Association for Computational Linguistics.

Yahoo! JAPAN. 2015. Onsei-Assist (in Japanese). `http://v-assist.yahoo.co.jp/`.

Evaluation of Crowdsourced User Input Data for Spoken Dialog Systems

Maria Schmidt, Markus Müller, Martin Wagner, Sebastian Stüker and Alex Waibel
Karlsruhe Institute of Technology
Karlsruhe, Germany
maria.schmidt@kit.edu

Hansjörg Hofmann and Steffen Werner
Daimler AG
Sindelfingen, Germany
hansjoerg.hofmann@daimler.com
steffen.s.werner@daimler.com

Abstract

Using the Internet for the collection of data is quite common these days. This process is called crowdsourcing and enables the collection of large amounts of data at reasonable costs. While being an inexpensive method, this data typically is of lower quality. Filtering data sets is therefore required. The occurring errors can be classified into different groups. There are technical issues and human errors. For speech recording, technical issues could be a noisy background. Human errors arise when the task is misunderstood. We employ several techniques for recognizing errors and eliminating faulty data sets in user input data for a Spoken Dialog System (SDS). Furthermore, we compare three different kinds of questionnaires (QNRs) for a given set of seven tasks. We analyze the characteristics of the resulting data sets and give a recommendation which type of QNR might be the most suitable one for a given purpose.

1 Introduction

Similar to research in other areas, Automatic Speech Recognition (ASR) systems and SDSs are facing the challenge how to get new training data, e. g., if there is the urge to cover new domains. Until several years ago, a common procedure was to record the required audio samples in an anechoic chamber and let experts (e. g., linguistics students) create the transcriptions. Although the data collected via this method is of high quality and can be used as a gold standard, researchers found that this approach is very time-consuming and results in quite little data related to the effort.

A few years ago, companies like Amazon Mechanical Turk started to offer so-called crowdsourcing approaches, which means that Human Intelligence Tasks (HITs) are performed by a group of non-experts. Furthermore, these tasks are open calls and are assigned to the different crowdsource workers. Especially in industrial contexts, crowdsourcing seems to be the means to choose because development cycles are short and much data for ASR or SDS development can be generated right as it is needed, although the data collected needs to be checked for quality (Snow et al., 2008).

Our work analyzes crowdsourced data collected by the company Clickworker (Eskenazi et al., 2013, ch. 9.3.4). The data consists of user input to an in-car SDS, where the crowdworkers had to input one German utterance for each of the seven tasks, after which they had to transcribe the utterance themselves. This procedure was conducted for three different types of QNRs: pictures, semantics, and text. We show the differences among these QNRs as well as an overall quality evaluation of the collected data. For this, we make use of Natural Language Processing (NLP) tools.

2 Related Work

2.1 Collection of Speech Data via Crowdsourcing

Crowdsourcing is a common part for collecting speech data nowadays. Eskénazi defines it as "a crowd as a group of non-experts who have answered an open call to perform a given task" (Eskenazi et al., 2013). Such a call will be advertised using special platforms on the Internet. Even though the participants are called "non-experts", they are skilled enough to perform these tasks. For collecting speech data, recording audio from a variety of different speakers helps to build better systems. Different speakers have different backgrounds. This is reflected in their speaking style and choice of words (Hofmann et al., 2012). These aspects are key for training a speaker-independent

Proceedings of the SIGDIAL 2015 Conference, pages 427–431,
Prague, Czech Republic, 2-4 September 2015.

system. The choice of participants should reflect the target audience of the system. Using untrained workers is also cheaper than to hire experts.

2.2 Using ASR to Improve the Quality

Using an ASR system is an integral part of the collection of annotated speech data. Such systems are being used to optimize the collection methods. (Williams et al., 2011) have shown how to process HITs for difficult speech data efficiently. One approach is to first create a transcription and let crowdworkers correct it. Since humans are optimistic about correcting errors (Audhkhasi et al., 2012), a two step approach was proposed in (Parent and Eskenazi, 2010): let the workers first rate the quality/correctness of transcriptions and perform the corrections in a separate step.

Another approach (van Dalen et al., 2015) deals with the combination of automatic and manual transcriptions. The errors produced are orthogonal: while humans tend to introduce spelling errors or skip words, automatic transcriptions feature wrong words, additional or even missing words. The usual approach for combining multiple transcriptions is ROVER (Fiscus, 1997) requiring an odd (typically three) amount of different transcriptions to be merged to break the tie. By the use of an ASR system, van Dalen et. al have shown that two manual transcriptions are sufficient to produce high quality.

3 Analysis of Crowdsourced User Input Data for Spoken Dialog Systems

In this section, we describe our approach to analyze the given corpus containing crowdsourced user input data for a goal-oriented in-car SDS.

3.1 The Corpus

The underlying German utterances for our analysis were collected by the German company Clickworker (http://www.clickworker.com/en). The participants were asked to invoke seven specific actions of an imaginary SDS deployed in a car. First, they got a task description, then they should record an audio of their input via a browser-based application on their own PC incl. microphone at home. After that the subjects were asked to transcribe their own utterance without hearing or seeing it again. In the following we describe the tasks 1, 4 and 5 exemplarily: In task 1, the imaginary user tells the system that he/she wants to listen to a certain radio station. Task 4 comprises the navigation to the address “Stieglitzweg 23, Berlin”. In task 5, the user should call Barack Obama on his cell phone. There were three different QNRs, each one asking for all seven tasks named above. The QNRs differed in the way how the tasks were presented to the subject: by means of pictures, text, or semantics (see Figure 1). In the pictures QNR, the participants were shown one or more pictures depicting the task they should perform. Without any written text, this type of task description does not imply the use of specific terms. For type text, the participants were presented a few lines describing the situation they are in and the actions they should perform. This form of textual representation of the objects is more influencing towards the use of specific terms. In the semantics QNR, the participants are influenced the most, as they get presented a few keywords. This does not favor the use of different words. Each participant answered all seven tasks, but was presented only one type of task description across them. Each type of QNR was assigned to approximately 1,080 users resulting in 22,680 utterances (34.7 hours) in total, i. e., roughly 7,560 per QNR. Most subjects were between 18 and 35 years old, a smaller number of subjects was up to 55 years old. 90% of the subjects were between 18 and 35 years old, 8% between 36 and 55. The smallest group was aged over 55 which resulted in 2% of the data. Our participants were 60% men and 40% women.

3.2 Evaluation of Self-Entered Transcripts

To be able to tell the overall quality of the underlying corpus, we had to analyze the self-entered transcripts, too. For this purpose, we developed an NLP analysis chain which contains a large part of preprocessing (i. e. mainly cleaning the text) apart from the actual analysis. Concerning preprocessing, we first applied a basic tokenizer to split the punctuation marks from the rest of the text. Second, we went over the transcripts with a spell checker called LanguageTool (https://www.languagetool.org/). For all misspelled words, we checked whether it equals one of the predefined, special keywords which should be entered for the current task (e. g., “Michael Jackson”, “Stieglitzweg”). If such a keyword was found, we processed the next word; if not, we checked which of the correct alternatives proposed by LanguageTool is most similar to one of the

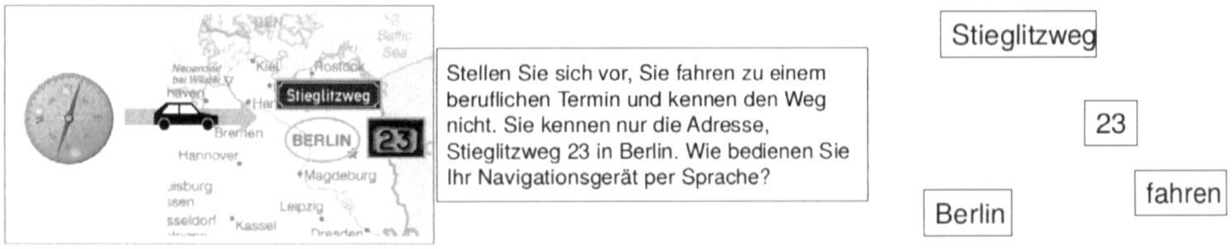

Figure 1: Instructions for task 4 in form of pictures, text and semantic entities

words on our "synonymously used words" list by using the Levenshtein distance. Third, after deciding which spelling is the most appropriate one for each word, we store the corrected utterances and use them for further analysis. The latter included Part-of-Speech (POS) Tagging with the TreeTagger (Schmid, 1994) to investigate, which and how many different POS patterns, i.e. types of sentence patterns, occur in the corpus and how the QNRs differ from each other on this level. Further, we investigated the most frequent words used in each task, and how many words in total are used in a specific task and in a specific QNR. With our analysis, we provide answers to the following questions: (a) How large is the linguistic variation in the data set (on sentence and word level)? (b) Which pros and cons do the presented QNRs have? (c) Which QNR is the right one for a certain purpose? We present the results in Section 4.2.

3.3 Evaluation of Self-Recorded Audio Data

To determine the usability of the recordings, we compared the length of the recordings and analyzed them using an ASR system. Generally, we assume that most recordings are done appropriately and that their quality resembles a normal distribution. We conducted our analysis using the Janus Recognition Toolkit (JRTk) (Woszczyna et al., 1994) which features the IBIS decoder (Soltau et al., 2001). For each task, a certain answer length is expected. This length may vary, but a significantly shorter or longer audio file indicates an error. Whether due to a technically false recording setup or a misunderstanding of the task description, in both cases the recording needs to be discarded. Even if the length is within a suitable range, the transcription of the audio might be wrong. To see if the transcription matches the spoken words, we use JRTk to perform a forced alignment. We use a GMM/HMM-based recognizer for German with 6,000 context-dependent quintphone states for aligning a phoneme sequence to the audio using forced Viterbi alignment. If there is a mismatch between audio and transcriptions, there will be phonemes covering unusual long or short parts of the audio.

4 Results & Discussion

4.1 Results of the Audio Data Analysis

We divided the recordings into 21 different sets as there are 3 different QNRs and 7 tasks each. Table 1 shows a detailed overview of the recording lengths for different tasks. While task 4 produces the longest recordings, the semantics QNR produces the shortest recordings.

Task	Pictures	Semantics	Text
1	5.21s	5.04s	5.04s
2	5.75s	5.65s	6.01s
3	4.97s	4.56s	5.01s
4	6.80s	6.44s	6.79s
5	5.45s	5.26s	5.39s
6	5.46s	5.51s	5.78s
7	5.37s	4.73s	5.21s

Table 1: *Average length of recordings.*

We also performed a forced Viterbi alignment: Figure 2 shows a histogram of the length of the longest phoneme per utterance used to indicate whether recording and transcription fit together. Since we do not have multiple transcriptions per utterance, we could not determine an optimal parameter set for identifying mismatched cases. But our preliminary results indicate that the longer the longest phoneme, the more likely a mismatch.

4.2 Results of the Transcript Analysis

Aiming at answering the questions posed in Section 3.2, we show the results of the transcript analysis in the following together with a short discussion. Tables 2 and 3 show the total number of utterances in the respective QNR data sets. The sec-

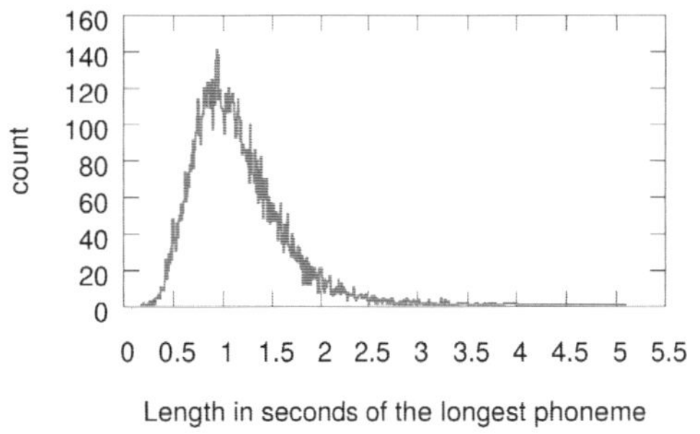

Figure 2: *Longest phoneme length per utterance.*

total number of utterances	7,546	
number of obligatory entities	5,420	72%
number of insufficient utterances	2,126	28%
number of asked for entities	3,033	40%
number of insufficient utterances	4,513	60%

Table 2: *Picture QNR with its dismissal rate.*

total number of utterances	7,581	
number of obligatory entities	6,947	92%
number of insufficient utterances	634	8%
number of asked for entities	6,126	81%
number of insufficient utterances	1,455	19%

Table 3: *Semantics QNR with its dismissal rate.*

# words used	pictures	semantics	text	avg.
Task 1	199	176	237	204
Task 2	216	206	256	226
Task 3	279	225	326	277
Task 4	327	260	309	299
Task 5	266	179	253	233
Task 6	297	188	264	250
Task 7	340	229	377	315
Average	275	209	289	258

Table 4: *Variance of used words across all QNRs.*

Task	Most frequent sentences
1	Ich möchte den Sender SWR3 hören
4	Navigiere [mich] zu[m] Stieglitzweg 23 in Berlin
5	Barack Obama [auf [dem]] Handy anrufen

Table 5: *Most common sentences for tasks 1, 4, 5.*

ond line of each table displays how many obligatory semantic entities were named, i.e. whether the two main content words (nouns in many tasks) were named, like "Sender, SWR3". The third line displays the number of insufficient utterances according to this criterion. Similarly, line four and five tell how many entities, which were actually asked for, i.e. all three (or four) items, were named and how many utterances were dismissed accordingly. As shown, the pictures QNR has to dismiss the most entities, while the semantics QNR dismisses the least. The values of the text QNR are in between the latter two QNRs. In total over all QNRs, we have dismissal rates of 17% and 37%.

Table 4 displays the variance of words used for all three QNRs and across tasks 1-7. It is valid for all tasks that the semantics QNR has the lowest number of different words. This is probably caused by displaying three exact semantic items, inevitably being the corresponding words. For tasks 1-3 and 7, the text QNR has the highest number of different words, while the pictures QNR leads the number of different words in tasks 4-6.

The analysis of the most frequent POS sequences per QNR showed that in the semantics QNR, most people used a polite modal construction "Ich möchte den Sender SWR hören" (PPER VMFIN ART NN NN VVINF). In the other QNRs "Radio SWR3" (NN NN) is the most common one among finite and infinite constructions.

Table 5 displays the most common sentence for each task. As you can see, there is a wide variety of linguistic patterns in each task.

5 Conclusion

We have presented various methods for evaluating the collected data set and that different types of QNRs lead to different styles in performing the tasks. With respect to the actual application scenario, the way in presenting the task to the participants has to be chosen in the correct manner.

The **semantics** QNR is precise by using three semantic items and is the best choice for generating exact phrases; it generates very few utterance dismissals. But at the same time it displays the words themselves. To avoid the mere usage of these, one approach for future studies would be to display the semantic items in English. Simultaneously, the QNR would be easily reusable for the generation of data from other languages.

The **pictures** QNR is optimal to generate a very high linguistic variance in the data. The downside of this approach is the high dismissal rate, if one aims at generating specific utterances.

The **text** QNR is a good compromise between the latter two QNRs. Looking at the data analyzed in this work, the text QNR has a lower priming effect on formulations than the semantics QNR.

References

Kartik Audhkhasi, Panayiotis G Georgiou, and Shrikanth S Narayanan. 2012. Analyzing quality of crowd-sourced speech transcriptions of noisy audio for acoustic model adaptation. In *Acoustics, Speech and Signal Processing (ICASSP), 2012 IEEE International Conference on*, pages 4137–4140. IEEE.

Maxine Eskenazi, Gina-Anne Levow, Helen Meng, Gabriel Parent, and David Suendermann. 2013. *Crowdsourcing for Speech Processing: Applications to Data Collection, Transcription and Assessment*. John Wiley & Sons.

Jonathan G Fiscus. 1997. A post-processing system to yield reduced word error rates: Recognizer output voting error reduction (rover). In *Automatic Speech Recognition and Understanding, 1997. Proceedings., 1997 IEEE Workshop on*, pages 347–354. IEEE.

Hansjörg Hofmann, Ute Ehrlich, André Berton, and Wolfgang Minker. 2012. Speech interaction with the internet–a user study. In *Intelligent Environments (IE), 2012 8th International Conference on*, pages 323–326. IEEE.

Gabriel Parent and Maxine Eskenazi. 2010. Toward better crowdsourced transcription: Transcription of a year of the let's go bus information system data. In *Spoken Language Technology Workshop (SLT), 2010 IEEE*, pages 312–317. IEEE.

Helmut Schmid. 1994. Probabilistic part-of-speech tagging using decision trees. In *Proceedings of the international conference on new methods in language processing*, volume 12, pages 44–49. Citeseer.

Rion Snow, Brendan O'Connor, Daniel Jurafsky, and Andrew Y Ng. 2008. Cheap and fast—but is it good?: evaluating non-expert annotations for natural language tasks. In *Proceedings of the conference on empirical methods in natural language processing*, pages 254–263. Association for Computational Linguistics.

Hagen Soltau, Florian Metze, Christian Fugen, and Alex Waibel. 2001. A one-pass decoder based on polymorphic linguistic context assignment. In *Automatic Speech Recognition and Understanding, 2001. ASRU'01. IEEE Workshop on*, pages 214–217. IEEE.

R van Dalen, K Knill, P Tsiakoulis, and M Gales. 2015. Improving multiple-crowd-sourced transcriptions using a speech recogniser. In *Proceedings of the International Conference on Acoustics, Speech and Signal Processing (ICASSP). Institute of Electrical and Electronics Engineers.*

Jason D Williams, I Dan Melamed, Tirso Alonso, Barbara Hollister, and Jay Wilpon. 2011. Crowdsourcing for difficult transcription of speech. In *Automatic Speech Recognition and Understanding (ASRU), 2011 IEEE Workshop on*, pages 535–540. IEEE.

Monika Woszczyna, N. Aoki-Waibel, Finn Dag Buø, Noah Coccaro, Keiko Horiguchi, Thomas Kemp, Alon Lavie, Arthur McNair, Thomas Polzin, Ivica Rogina, Carolyn Rose, Tanja Schultz, Bernhard Suhm, M. Tomita, and Alex Waibel. 1994. Janus 93: Towards spontaneous speech translation. In *International Conference on Acoustics, Speech, and Signal Processing 1994*, Adelaide, Australia.

A distributed cloud-based dialog system for conversational application development

Vikram Ramanarayanan[†], **David Suendermann-Oeft**[†], **Alexei V. Ivanov**[†] **& Keelan Evanini**[‡]
Educational Testing Service R&D
[†] 90 New Montgomery St, # 1500, San Francisco, CA
[‡] 600 Rosedale Road, Princeton, NJ
<vramanarayanan,suendermann-oeft,aivanou,kevanini>@ets.org

Abstract

We have previously presented HALEF–an open-source spoken dialog system–that supports telephonic interfaces and has a distributed architecture. In this paper, we extend this infrastructure to be cloud-based, and thus truly distributed and scalable. This cloud-based spoken dialog system can be accessed both via telephone interfaces as well as through web clients with WebRTC/HTML5 integration, allowing in-browser access to potentially multimodal dialog applications. We demonstrate the versatility of the system with two conversation applications in the educational domain.

1 The HALEF spoken dialog system

The HALEF (Help Assistant–Language-Enabled and Free) framework leverages different open-source components to form a spoken dialog system (SDS) framework that is modular and industry-standard-compliant: Asterisk, a SIP- (Session Initiation Protocol), WebRTC- (Web Real-Time Communication) and PSTN- (Public Switched Telephone Network) compatible telephony server (van Meggelen et al., 2009); JVoiceXML, an open-source voice browser that can process SIP traffic (Schnelle-Walka et al., 2013) via a voice browser interface called Zanzibar (Prylipko et al., 2011); Cairo, an MRCP (Media Resource Control Protocol) speech server, which allows the voice browser to initiate SIP or RTP (Real-time Transport Protocol) connections from/to the telephony server (Prylipko et al., 2011); the Kaldi (Povey et al., 2011) and Sphinx-4 (Lamere et al., 2003) automatic speech recognizers; Festival (Taylor et al., 1998) and Mary (Schröder and Trouvain, 2003)–text-to-speech synthesis engines; and an Apache Tomcat-based web server that can host dynamic VoiceXML (VXML) pages and serve media files such as grammars and audio files to the voice browser. HALEF includes support for popular grammar formats, including JSGF (Java Speech Grammar Format), SRGS (Speech Recognition Grammar Specification), ARPA (Advanced Research Projects Agency) and WFST (Weighted Finite State Transducers). Figure 1 schematically depicts the main components of the HALEF system. Note that unlike a typical SDS, which consists of sequentially-connected modules for speech recognition, language understanding, dialog management, language generation and speech synthesis, in HALEF some of these are grouped together forming independent blocks which are hosted on different virtual machines in a distributed architecture. In our particular case, each module is hosted on a separate server on the Amazon Elastic Compute Cloud (EC2)[1]. This migration to a cloud-based distributed computing environment allows us to scale up applications easily and economically. Further, added integration and compatibility with the WebRTC standard[2] allows us to access HALEF from within a web browser, thus allowing us to design and develop multimodal dialog interfaces (that potentially can include audio, video and text, among other modalities). For further details on the individual blocks as well as design choices, please refer to (Mehrez et al., 2013; Suendermann-Oeft et al., 2015). In this framework, one can serve different back-end applications as standalone web services on a separate server. Incorporating the appropriate start URL of the web service in the VXML input code that the voice browser interprets will then allow the voice browser to trigger the web application at the appropriate point in the callflow. The web services in our

[1] http://aws.amazon.com/ec2/
[2] http://www.w3.org/TR/webrtc/

Proceedings of the SIGDIAL 2015 Conference, pages 432–434,
Prague, Czech Republic, 2-4 September 2015. ©2015 Association for Computational Linguistics

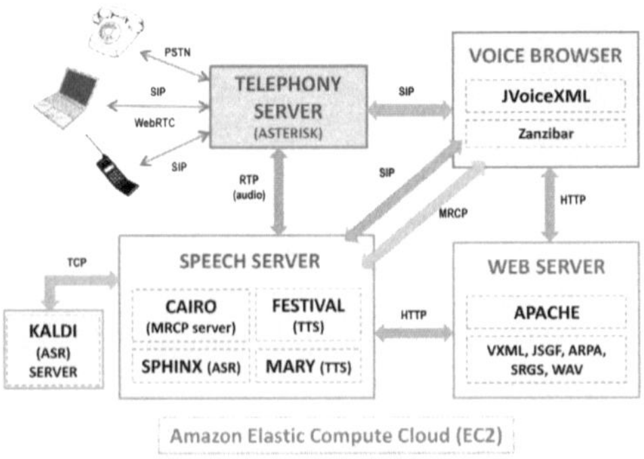

Figure 1: System architecture of the cloud-based HALEF spoken dialog system depicting the various modular open-source components.

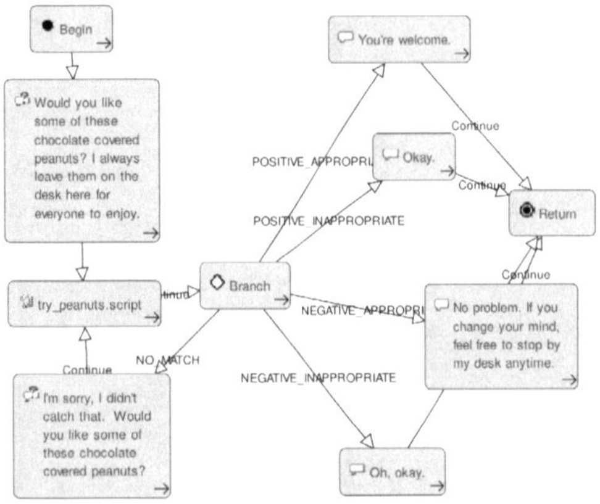

Figure 2: Example design of a workplace pragmatics-oriented application.

case typically take as input any valid HTTP-based GET or POST request and output a VXML page that the voice browser can process next. In the next section, we describe a software toolkit that can dynamically generate a sequence of VXML pages from a dialog flow specification.

We also developed a logging interface that helps users view log messages from the Tomcat server, speech server and voice browser in real time to facilitate debugging and understanding of how to improve the design of the item dialog flow. This web-based tool allows designers to observe in real time the output hypotheses generated by the speech recognition and natural language understanding modules at each dialog state, as well as hyperlinks to the grammars and speech audio files associated with that state. This allows even dialog flow designers with minimal spoken dialog experience to monitor and evaluate system performance while designing and deploying the application.

2 The OpenVXML dialog-authoring suite

Also integrated into the HALEF framework is OpenVXML (or Open Voice XML), an open-source software package[3] written in Java that allows designers to author dialog workflows using an easy-to-use graphical user interface, and is available as a plugin to the Eclipse Integrated Developer Environment[4]. OpenVXML allows designers to specify the dialog workflow as a flowchart, including details of specific grammar files to be used by the speech recognizer and text-to-speech prompts that need to be synthesized. In addition, they can insert "script" blocks of Javascript code into the workflow that can be used to perform simple processing steps, such as basic natural language understanding on the outputs of the speech recognition. The entire workflow can be exported to a Web Archive (or WAR) application, which can then be deployed on a web server running Apache Tomcat that serves Voice XML (or VXML) documents.

3 Applications

Figures 2 and 3 show example workflows of conversational items developed using OpenVXML. The caller dials into the system and then proceeds to answer a sequence of questions, which can be either be stored for later analysis (so no online recognition and natural language understanding is needed), or processed in the following manner. Depending the semantic class of the callers' answer to each question (as determined by the output of the speech recognizer and the natural language understanding module), they are redirected to the appropriate branch of the dialog tree and the conversation continues until all such questions are answered. Notice that in the case of this simple example we are using rule-based grammars and dialog tree structures, though the system can also natively support more sophisticated statistical modules.

4 Conclusions

We have presented a prototype conversation-based application that leverages the open-source

[3] `https://github.com/OpenMethods/OpenVXML`
[4] `www.eclipse.org`

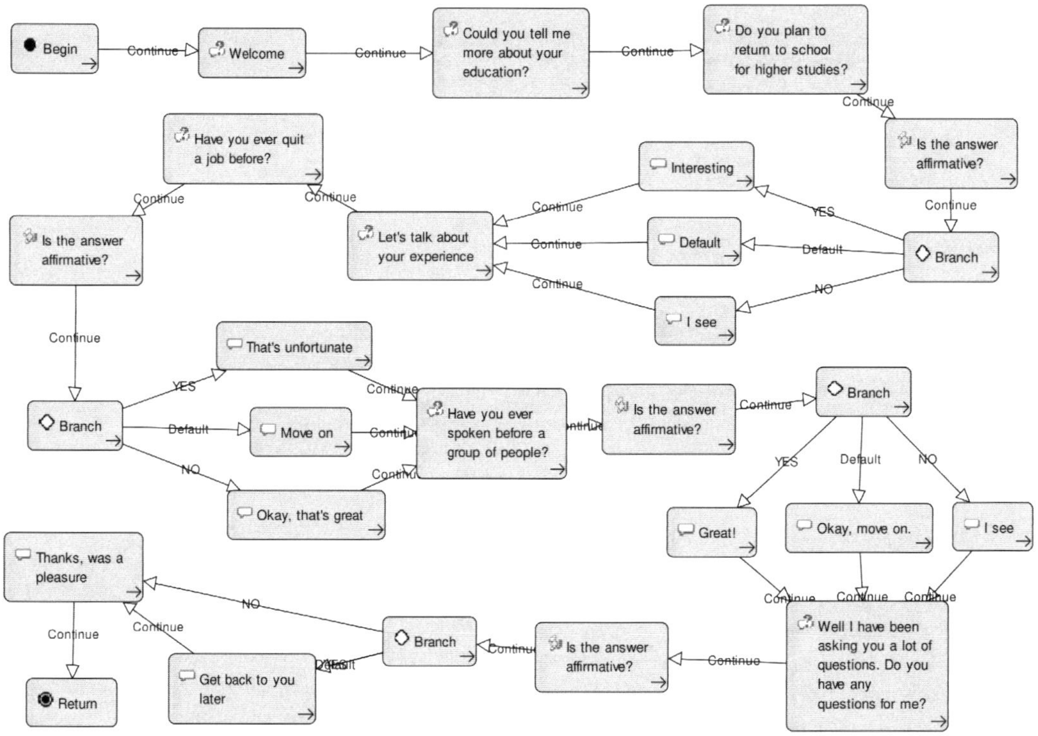

Figure 3: Example workflow design of a demo interview test application.

HALEF spoken dialog framework. HALEF can be accessed online at the following URL: `https://sourceforge.net/p/halef`. One can also call into HALEF for a demo of the interview item at the following US-based telephone number: `(206) 203-5276 (Extension:7749)`.

5 Acknowledgements

The authors would like to thank Lydia Rieck, Elizabeth Bredlau, Katie Vlasov, Eugene Tsuprun, Juliet Marlier, Phallis Vaughter, Nehal Sadek, and Veronika Laughlin for helpful input in designing the conversational items.

References

P. Lamere, P. Kwok, E. Gouvea, B. Raj, R. Singh, W. Walker, M. Warmuth, and P. Wolf. 2003. The CMU SPHINX-4 Speech Recognition System. In *Proc. of the ICASSP'03*, Hong Kong, China.

T. Mehrez, A. Abdelkawy, Y. Heikal, P. Lange, H. Nabil, and D. Suendermann-Oeft. 2013. Who Discovered the Electron Neutrino? A Telephony-Based Distributed Open-Source Standard-Compliant Spoken Dialog System for Question Answering. In *Proc. of the GSCL Workshop*, Darmstadt, Germany.

Daniel Povey, Arnab Ghoshal, Gilles Boulianne, Lukas Burget, Ondrej Glembek, Nagendra Goel, Mirko Hannemann, Petr Motlicek, Yanmin Qian, Petr Schwarz, Jan Silovsky, Georg Stemmer, and Karel Vesely. 2011. The Kaldi speech recognition toolkit. In *Proc. of the ASRU Workshop*, Hawaii, USA.

D. Prylipko, D. Schnelle-Walka, S. Lord, and A. Wendemuth. 2011. Zanzibar OpenIVR: An Open-Source Framework for Development of Spoken Dialog Systems. In *Proc. of the TSD Workshop*, Pilsen, Czech Republic.

D. Schnelle-Walka, S. Radomski, and M. Mühlhäuser. 2013. JVoiceXML as a Modality Component in the W3C Multimodal Architecture. *Journal on Multimodal User Interfaces*, 7:183–194.

Marc Schröder and Jürgen Trouvain. 2003. The German text-to-speech synthesis system MARY: A tool for research, development and teaching. *International Journal of Speech Technology*, 6(4):365–377.

David Suendermann-Oeft, Vikram Ramanarayanan, Moritz Teckenbrock, Felix Neutatz, and Dennis Schmidt. 2015. HALEF: an open-source standard-compliant telephony-based modular spoken dialog system–A review and an outlook. In *Proc. of the IWSDS Workshop 2015, Busan, South Korea*.

P. Taylor, A. Black, and R. Caley. 1998. The Architecture of the Festival Speech Synthesis System. In *Proc. of the ESCA Workshop on Speech Synthesis*, Jenolan Caves, Australia.

J. van Meggelen, J. Smith, and L. Madsen. 2009. *Asterisk: The Future of Telephony*. O'Reilly, Sebastopol, USA.

A TV Program Discovery Dialog System Using Recommendations

Deepak Ramachandran, Mark Fanty
Ronald Provine, Peter Z. Yeh, William Jarrold
Adwait Ratnaparkhi
Nuance Communications, Inc.
1198 E Arques Ave, Sunnvale CA, 94085

Benjamin Douglas
Google, Inc.
1600 Amphitheatre Pkwy
Mountain View, CA 94041

Abstract

We present an end-to-end conversational system for TV program discovery that uniquely combines advanced technologies for NLU, Dialog Management, Knowledge Graph Inference and Personalized Recommendations. It uses a semantically rich relational representation of dialog state and knowedge graph inference for queries. The recommender combines evidence for user preferences from multiple modalities such as dialog, user viewing history and activity logs. It is tightly integrated with the Dialog System, especially for explanations of recommendations. A demo of the system on a iPad will be shown.

1 Introduction

In this demonstration, we present a conversational prototype system that enables users to explore and discover suitable TV programming content. This prototype combines several state of the art techniques for Natural Language Processing, Linguistics, and Artifical Intelligence developed at Nuance Communications. It runs on an iPad touchscreen with support for multimodal inputs (voice and touch); engages in sustained conversations with questions, suggestions and explanations from the system; and uses live data feeds from cable providers and knowlege graphs.

Many features of the dialog system have been demonstrated in an earlier prototype (Ramachandran et al., 2014), including the use of trained Named Entity Recognition and Relation Extraction models for input processing, Belief Tracking and Dialog Management algorithms that use a relational (rather than slot-based) representation of dialog states, and expanded inferences for queries and explanations using the Freebase (Bollacker et al., 2008) knowledge graph.

User	football games this weekend
Sys	Football games this weekend. Would you like College Football or Classic College Football?
User	or next weekend
Sys	Football games this weekend or next weekend. Would you like Classic College Football, College Football, or Rose Bowl?
User	romantic movies tomorrow
Sys	Ok starting a new search. Romantic movies tomorrow. Would you like something with Sandra Bullock, Nicole Kidman, Kristen Stewart, or more suggestions?
User	I don't like sandra bullock.
Sys	Ok, I'll remember you don't like Sandra Bullock. How about something with Nicole Kidman, Kristen Stewart, Hugh Grant or more suggestions?
User	I want a movie about the gulf war
Sys	Ok starting a new search. Movies set during the Gulf war. Would you like Courage Under Fire, Jarhead, or The Finest Hour?
User	Explain the second one
Sys	Because you like action movies and have shown an interest in movies directed by Sam Mendes.
User	More explanation.
Sys	This film is an adaptation of the book "Jarhead: a Marine's Chronicle of the Gulf War and Other Battles", whose subject is the Gulf War.

Table 1: Example dialog with our system demonstrating the relational representation and state-tracking, expanded inference with freebase including explanations, and recommendations from the user profile.

In this version, we will additionally demonstrate the integration of the dialog system with a recommender engine that scores individual programs as being relevant to the user's interests. It takes input from both user behavior (viewing history and screen touches) and spoken indications of interest. Recommendations are presented along with explanations of the scores, greatly aiding transparency, a key desideratum for recommender systems (Tintarev and Masthoff, 2007).

2 Demo Overview

Our system is primarily designed to assist the user in finding a suitable TV program to watch. Its prime function is to understand the search constraints of the user and do a database lookup to retrieve and present the best results. However, to model the full complexity of a conversation it has a number of advanced features:

Proceedings of the SIGDIAL 2015 Conference, pages 435–437,
Prague, Czech Republic, 2-4 September 2015. ©2015 Association for Computational Linguistics

Figure 1: Screenshots of our IPad Conversational Prototype for two different users after the query "Movies playing this weekend". The first user is mainly interested in children's programs and the second one in action movies.

1. A *relational representation* of user intent which can represent boolean constraints (e.g. " a James Bond movie without Roger Moore") and fine shades of meaning (see Fig. 3).
2. A *stateful* dialog model that can interpret successive utterances in the context of the current conversation (e.g. combining search constraints) and track the shift of conversational focus from one topic to another.
3. Fully *mixed-initiative* dialog at every turn, with a dynamic refinement strategy using stastical techniques to find the best question to ask the user.
4. Potential for the user to ask for movies by a wide variety of subjects or related concepts e.g. "movies about the Civil War", "movies with vampires", activating a search on a knowledge graph for results.
5. A tightly integrated *recommender* system that maintains a user profile of preferences the user has shown for TV programs. The profile is updated based on both user activity and spoken preferences of the user. The user profile is used to re-rank the result of every search query the user makes.
6. The generation of *explanations* in natural language for the results of each search, to help the user understand the reasoning process of the backend inference and the recommender.

Table 1 shows a sample dialog exhibiting all the features above. Fig. 1 shows some screenshots from the GUI of our application.

3 System Overview

Our system uses a hub-and-spoke architecture (see Fig. 2) to organize the processing of each dialog turn. We review the major components briefly below, see (Ramachandran et al., 2014) for more details.

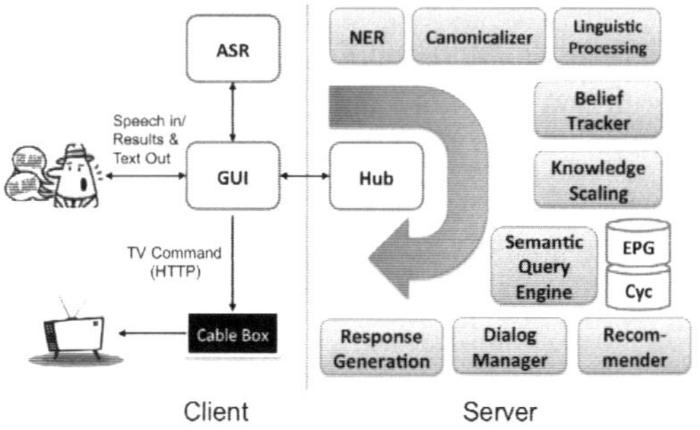

Figure 2: Architecture overview. The Hub invokes the spokes in a clockwise order.

3.1 NLU and State Tracking

In addition to a Named-Entity Recognizer for finding propositional concepts, we have a Relation Extraction component trained to produce a tree structure called a *REL-Tree* (analogous to a dependency tree, see Fig. 3) over entities from the NER.

For successive turns of the dialog, we use a *belief tracking* component that merges the REL-Tree for an input utterance with the dialog state, which is a stack of REL-Trees, each one representing a different topic of conversation. The merging algorithm is a rule-based rewriting system written in the language of tree-regular expressions.

3.2 Dialog Management, Backend and Knowledge Expansion

The Dialog Manager is a Nuance proprietary tool inspired by Ravenclaw (Bohus and Rudnicky, 2003). It maintains a *mixed-initiatve* paradigm at all times, with subdialog strategies for question answering, device control, and explanations.

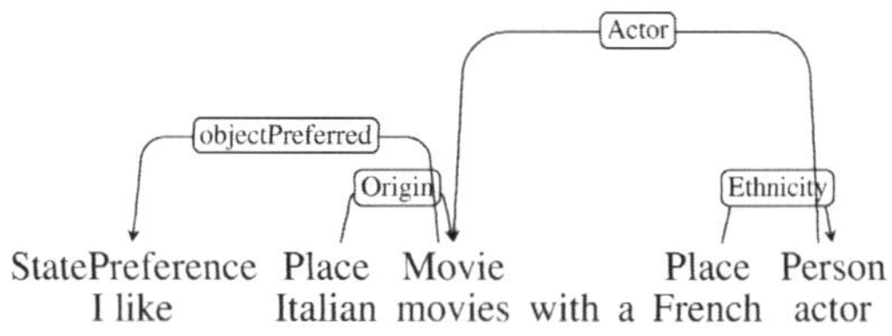

Figure 3: Example REL-Tree for the utterance "I like Italian movies with a French actor". Both "French" and "Italian" are labeled with the Entity type "Place" but their relations in the REL-Tree yield different meanings.

The Backend Service maps queries to either a structured database query in SQL or to a query on the Freebase knowledge graph (Bollacker et al., 2008) for more unstructured inferences (e.g. "movies about lawyers"). The resulting inference can be translated to a logically-motivated explanation of the results.

3.3 Recommendations

User preferences for each user are stored in a user profile database and the recommender engine uses the profile to score seach results by how relevant they are to each user.

3.3.1 Input of User Preferences

There are 2 ways the user's behavior affects his profile:

1. Logged interactions with the client such as clicks on icons indicating interests in particular programs/actors/genres etc, or a history of programs watched.
2. Speech from the user stating likes or dislikes of programs ("I like *Big Bang Theory*"), or attributes ("I don't like horror movies").

Each of these interaction types have a different weight in the recommender scoring algorithm (e.g. explicitly stating a liking for a particular movie has higher weight than a click in the UI). User utterances about preferences are modeled as a separate intent (REL-tree) and handled as a separate task in the DM. Subdialogs can be launched to elicit or resolve user preferences.

3.3.2 Recommendation Engine

Every program in the user's history is represented by a vector of features such as genre, actors, rating, and saliency-weighted words from the description, along with an associated affect (explicitly disliked, just viewed, explicitly liked). Candidate programs for recommendation are scored by a K-Nearest Neighbor algorithm; being near (cosine distance) multiple liked programs in feature space results in a high score. Individual features that are explicitly liked or disliked will further increase or decrease the score in a heuristic fashion, so a program with a good score, but with an actor the user dislikes, will have its score lowered. Instead of running the scoring algorithm dynamically on every query, the scores for all programs in the current 2-week window of the program schedule are computed offline for each user. The re-ranking of results from the backend is accomplished by doing a database join at query time. This reduces the latency of the retrieval down to real time.

3.3.3 Surfacing Recommendations

The scores generated by the recommender are used to re-rank the results of any search query performed by the user. Users with differing taste profiles can have dramatically different sets of results (see Fig. 1). This behavior can be controlled by the user, who can ask for re-ranking by different criteria.

Along with query results, the highly weighted components of the recommender scoring function for each program are passed to the DM which can use them to generate natural language explanations for the presented results on demand. The explanations can distinguish between instance-level preferences (e.g. "You like Big Bang Theory") and categorical preferences ("You like romantic comedies") and also between stated preferences ("You like [i.e. stated you like] bruce willis") vs those inferred from behavior ("You watched Die Hard", "You showed an interest [i.e. clicked in the UI] in Die Hard."). Detailed explanations like these improve the transparency of the system and have shown to dramatically improve usasbility and evaluation scores (Tintarev and Masthoff, 2007). These explanations are interleaved with those from the Freebase inference (Section 3.2).

4 Conclusion

In summary,our demo shows a tight integration of recommendation technology wih a dialog system and believe that our ability to understand preference statements and generate explanations for recommender results is novel.

References

D. Bohus and A. Rudnicky. 2003. Ravenclaw: Dialog management using hierarchical task decomposition and an expectation agenda. In *Eurospeech*.

K. Bollacker, C. Evans, P. Paritosh, T. Sturge, and J. Taylor. 2008. Freebase: a collaboratively created graph database for structuring human knowledge. In *SIGMOD*.

D. Ramachandran, P. Yeh, W. Jarrold, B. Douglas, A. Ratnaparkhi, R. Provine, J. Mendel, and A. Emfield. 2014. An end-to-end dialog system for tv program discovery. In *SLT*.

N. Tintarev and J. Masthoff. 2007. A survey of explanations in recommender systems. In *Data Engineering Workshop, 2007 IEEE 23rd International Conference on*, pages 801–810. IEEE.

Description of the PatientGenesys Dialogue System

Leonardo Campillos **Dhouha Bouamor** **Éric Bilinski** **Anne-Laure Ligozat**
Pierre Zweigenbaum **Sophie Rosset**
LIMSI - CNRS
Campus universitaire Bâtiment 508
Rue John von Neumann
91405 ORSAY cedex
firstname.lastname@limsi.fr

Abstract

This paper describes the work-in-progress prototype of a dialog system that simulates a virtual patient (VP) consultation. We report some challenges and difficulties that are found during its development, especially in managing the interaction and the vocabulary from the medical domain.

1 Introduction

Virtual Patients (VPs hereafter) are used in health care education. PatientGenesys is an interdisciplinary project that aims at developing a computer tool to provide continuing education to medical doctors. Trainer doctors will create new tailored clinical cases for the medical students to train consultation skills, in a 3D environment. At present, three prototype clinical cases have been created (anesthesiology, cardiology, and pneumopathy). This paper presents an overview of previous VP systems in Section 2 and describes the architecture of our system in Section 3; then, in Section 4, we put forward some conclusions. The system only supports French, but all examples are in English for the sake of understandability.

2 Previous work and motivation

VPs have been applied to several medical education tasks, ranging from history taking communication skills (Deladisma et al., 2007), dealing with mentally ill patients (Hubal et al., 2003; Kenny and Parsons, 2011) or training Pharmacy students (Park and Summons, 2013). We refer to (Cook et al., 2010) and (Kenny and Parsons, 2011) for a recent overview of VP systems. Although most systems are available for English, there are VPs for other languages (López Salazar et al., 2012). The PatientGenesys system is one of the few for the French-speaking community. However, some of the challenges we have found in designing a VP dialogue system may be raised regardless of users' language. The first difficulty concerns the lack of available corpora to train the system, which hinders using machine learning approaches. The second challenge concerns the variability of medical discourse. A concept may be referred to with different acronyms and jargon terms (e.g. *tonsillectomy* and *surgical removal of tonsils*) and lay terms from other registers (e.g. *tonsils operation*). The third one concerns the design of a core dialogue system that will be able to address dialogues of new clinical cases robustly. Future challenges will be raised when the system is to be adapted to other languages, mainly due to the ambiguities of medical terms in each language.

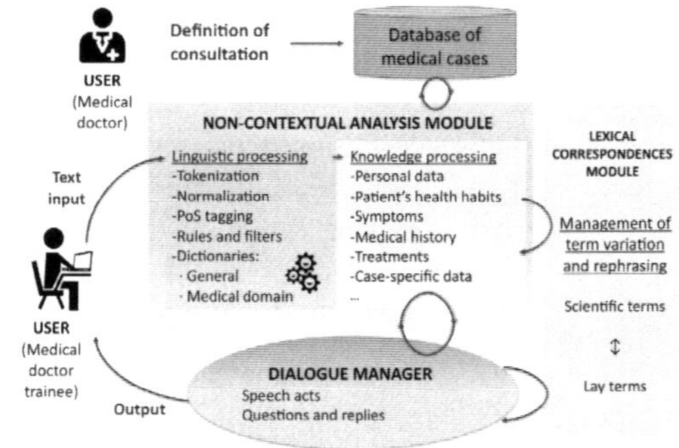

Figure 1: Overview of the PatientGenesys system

3 Architecture of the system

The system uses a user-initiative strategy (i.e. it will not ask questions). This is due to its pedagogical goals, which focus on training doctors in consultation skills. Input is text data, whereas output is spoken (text-to-speech, TTS). Four modules make up the system as shown in Figure 1: non-contextual analysis, lexical matching module, database of medical cases, and dialogue manager.

Proceedings of the SIGDIAL 2015 Conference, pages 438–440,
Prague, Czech Republic, 2-4 September 2015.

3.1 Database of medical cases

Knowledge on a medical case, provided by the instructor, defines patient state and knowledge. Frame-based structures organize the information in schemata. Cognitive frameworks already exist to model patient data and discourse (Patel et al., 1989). We use the YAML formalism (Ben-Kiki et al., 2005) to code information. General sections of patient data correspond to those proposed for VP data standards (Triola et al., 2007).

- Personal data: patient's name, family status, profession, height and weight.
- Lifestyle data: activities, diet habits, social behavior and addictions.
- Patient history data: family history, past diseases and treatments, allergies and surgeries.
- Symptoms data: type of symptom, anatomic place, onset time or duration, observations.
- Current treatments: International Nonproprietary Name, dose and method of administration, frequency and observations.

3.2 Non-contextual analysis module

Two main processes are involved in this stage: linguistic and knowledge processing. Linguistic processing consists of the following steps:

- Tokenization, normalization, downcasing, and Part-of-Speech (PoS) tagging with the French TreeTagger (Schmid, 1995).
- Spelling correction, to fix misspellings that may hinder text recognition.
- Linguistic annotation identifies verb tense, inflectional and derivative variants of terms referring to the same concept (e.g. *to operate* and *operation*), and other information, based on syntactic and semantic grammars written using wmatch, a word-based regular expression engine (Galibert, 2009). An example is the rule ANATOMY + *operation*, which tags the entity *tonsils operation* as a surgery.

Knowledge processing involves these steps:

- Entities are recognized using wmatch semantic rules and lists of medical terms. Vocabulary lists were drawn from the French component of the Unified Medical Language System (UMLS) (Bodenreider, 2004) and the VIDAL drug database.[1] Affixes are also applied: e.g. the suffix *-tomy* is used to detect surgical procedure entities (e.g. *appendectomy*). There are three broad types of named entities: general entities (e.g. date, frequency or age), domain-specific entities (e.g. drugs, symptoms), and discourse entities to classify speech acts (e.g. telling hello).
- Domain knowledge processing is used to enhance the understanding of input questions about patient illness. Medical knowledge comes from hierarchical relations extracted from the UMLS (e.g. *hypertension* IS_A *cardiovascular disease*).

3.3 Lexical matching module

The aims of this component are, first, to rephrase the technical descriptions found in the provided medical case into natural, patient-level language; and, second, to map the elements found in the question to those found in the medical case. This module relies upon different lists of medical vocabulary and concepts:

- Lists of medical term variants and UMLS concept unique identifiers (CUIs) are used to index each concept and map it to variants or acronyms. For example, C0020538 is the index for *HT* or *hypertension*. We also used the UMLF (Zweigenbaum et al., 2005).
- A non-UMLS list of medical terms, similar to the previous list, collects items that were not found in the UMLS.
- Lists of medical and lay terms map acronyms or technical terms (e.g. *ligamentoplasty*) to lay terms (e.g. *ligament repair*).

3.4 Dialogue manager module

The system uses a frame-based design in order to allow flexible interactions. The type of speech act and data contents of each turn are stored (e.g. *type: tell_past_disease*; *content: hypertension*). Information from the previous utterance is used to both repeat the previous turn and process anaphora and ellipsis. The domain model is based on each clinical case. Two types of anaphoric expressions are handled: co-reference and non-co-reference binding (respectively, *that* and *other* in Example 3.1).

[1] http://www.vidal.fr/

Example 3.1.
–Which symptoms do you have?
–I have pain in my abdomen.
–Have you ever had that before?
–No.
–And do you have any other symptoms?
–No.

Ellipsis is related to short questions—usually by using *wh-* words—immediately after the system has given a piece of information (Example 3.2).

Example 3.2.
–I had a tonsils operation.
–When?
–I had a tonsils operation in my childhood.

The following types of speech acts are covered:

- Greetings: e.g. telling hello/bye and related speech acts (*How are you?, It is a pleasure*).
- General conversational management acts: e.g. showing agreement, lack of understanding, asking for repetition, or giving thanks.
- General questions: e.g. quantity or frequency.
- Clinical interview questions: these can be divided into general clinical questions and case-specific questions, which are specific to the actual clinical case.

4 Conclusion

We presented the on-going development of the PatientGenesys dialogue system, which aims at creating VP simulations to train medical students. The project is raising challenges regarding the lack of training corpora, the design of a robust dialogue system, and the variability of the medical jargon.

5 Acknowledgments

This work was funded by the FUI Project PatientGenesys (F1310002-P).

References

Oren Ben-Kiki, Clark Evans, and Brian Ingerson. 2005. Yaml ain't markup language (yaml^{TM}) version 1.1. *yaml. org, Tech. Rep.*

O. Bodenreider. 2004. The unified medical language system (umls): integrating biomedical terminology. *Nucleic acids research*, 32(suppl 1):D267–D270.

D. A. Cook, P. J. Erwin, and M. M. Triola. 2010. Computerized virtual patients in health professions education: a systematic review and meta-analysis. *Academic Medicine*, 85(10):1589–1602.

A. M. Deladisma, M. Cohen, A. Stevens, P. Wagner, B. Lok, Th. Bernard, Ch. Oxendine, L. Schumacher, K. Johnsen, R. Dickerson, et al. 2007. Do medical students respond empathetically to a virtual patient? *The American Journal of Surgery*, 193(6):756–760.

D. A. Evans, M. R. Block, E. R. Steinberg, and A. M Penrose. 1986. Frames and heuristics in doctor-patient discourse. *Social science & medicine*, 22(10):1027–1034.

O. Galibert. 2009. *Approches et méthodologies pour la réponse automatique à des questions adaptées à un cadre intéractif en domaine ouvert.* Ph.D. thesis, Université Paris Sud.

R. C. Hubal, G. A. Frank, and C. I. Guinn. 2003. Lessons learned in modeling schizophrenic and depressed responsive virtual humans for training. In *Proceedings of the 8th International Conference on Intelligent User Interfaces*, IUI '03, pages 85–92, New York, NY, USA. ACM.

P Kenny and T Parsons. 2011. Embodied conversational virtual patients. *Conversational Agents and Natural Language Interaction: Techniques and Effective Practices. Information Science Reference*, pages 254–281.

V. López Salazar, E. M. Eisman Cabeza, J. L. Castro Peña, and J. M. Zurita López. 2012. A case based reasoning model for multilingual language generation in dialogues. *Expert Syst. Appl.*, 39(8):7330–7337, June.

M. Park and P. Summons. 2013. A computer-generated digital patient for oral interview training in pharmacy. *Advanced Science and Technology Letters*, pages 28:126–131.

V. L. Patel, D. A. Evans, and D. R. Kaufman. 1989. Cognitive framework for doctor-patient interaction. *Cognitive science in medicine: Biomedical modeling*, pages 253–308.

H. Schmid. 1995. Treetagger— a language independent part-of-speech tagger. *Institut für Maschinelle Sprachverarbeitung, Universität Stuttgart*, 43:28.

M. M. Triola, N. Campion, J. B. McGee, S. Albright, P. Greene, V. Smothers, and R. Ellaway. 2007. An XML standard for virtual patients: exchanging case-based simulations in medical education. In *AMIA Annu Symp Proc*, pages 741–745.

P. Zweigenbaum, R. H. Baud, A. Burgun, F. Namer, É. Jarrousse, N. Grabar, P. Ruch, F. Le Duff, J.-F. Forget, M. Douyère, and S. Darmoni. 2005. A unified medical lexicon for French. *International Journal of Medical Informatics*, 74(2–4):119–124, March.

The Cohort and Speechify Libraries for Rapid Construction of Speech Enabled Applications for Android

Tejaswi Kasturi, Haojian Jin, Aasish Pappu, Sungjin Lee
Beverly Harrison, Ramana Murthy, Amanda Stent
Yahoo Labs
{kasturit,haojian,aasishkp,junion,rmurthy,stent}@yahoo-inc.com

Abstract

Despite the prevalence of libraries that provide speech recognition and text-to-speech synthesis "in the cloud", it remains difficult for developers to create user-friendly, consistent spoken language interfaces to their mobile applications. In this paper, we present the Speechify / Cohort libraries for rapid speech enabling of Android applications. The Speechify library wraps several publicly available speech recognition and synthesis APIs, incorporates state-of-the-art voice activity detection and simple and flexible hybrid speech recognition, and allows developers to experiment with different modes of user interaction. The Cohort library, built on a stripped-down version of OpenDial, facilitates flexible interaction between and within "Speechified" mobile applications.

1 Introduction

There are now numerous libraries that provide access to cloud-based ASR and NLU for mobile applications, including offerings from Microsoft[1], AT&T[2] and Nuance[3]. However, speech does not yet live up to its promise on mobile devices. Partly, this is because developers who are not expert speech technologists may make suboptimal decisions regarding interaction management, choice of speech API, and consistency across apps. Also, individual speech-enabled apps are less user-friendly than an app *ecosystem* within which a user may move fluidly from GUI interaction to hands/eyes-free interaction and from one app to another as interest and attention demand. In this paper we present the Speechify/Cohort libraries for development of speech-enabled Android apps. Speechify enables rapid development of usable speech-enabled applications; Cohort allows the user of a suite of Speechified applications to be hands-free/eyes-free when they need it, to use the rich multimodality of the applications themselves when they want to, and to move naturally and fluidly within and between applications. The Speechify and Cohort libraries will be made available on github[4].

2 Speechify

The Speechify library is designed to solve the following problem: when an organization is speech enabling a suite of mobile applications, it is easy to end up with a poor user experience because of inconsistencies in implementing features like:

- choice of speech API - Speechify wraps several publicly available speech recognition and speech synthesis APIs, including the Google Android[5] and Pocketsphinx (Huggins-Daines et al., 2006) speech recognition engines and the Google Android and Ivona speech synthesizers.
- mode of user interaction - Speechify supports push-to-talk, wait-to-talk, and always-on speech recognition (see Section 2.1). In addition, it can detect when the user is moving and switch to speech interaction.
- hybrid speech recognition - Speechify includes a module for tunable hybrid embedded/cloud-based speech recognition, to permit the speed of embedded recognition for command and control, with the flexibility of cloud-based recognition for open-vocabulary input (see Section 2.2).

[1] https://www.projectoxford.ai/
[2] http://developer.att.com/sdks-plugins
[3] http://dragonmobile.nuancemobiledeveloper.com
[4] https://github.com/yahoo
[5] http://developer.android.com/reference/android/speech/

Proceedings of the SIGDIAL 2015 Conference, pages 441–443,
Prague, Czech Republic, 2-4 September 2015.

- voice activity detection and acoustic echo cancellation - Speechify includes a state-of-the-art voice activity detection/acoustic echo cancellation module, allowing more accurate speech input in noisy environments (see Section 2.3).

2.1 Interaction Management

Speechify is built for applications that may or may not require hands-free interaction, depending on the user's other activities. Therefore, Speechify supports three modes for interaction:

- push-to-talk - In this mode, when the user taps any non-interactive part of the application's display, a microphone icon is presented in a transparent overlay on the application, and the user may speak. We do not use a push-to-talk button because a user who is driving, running or walking may not have attention to spare to find a push-to-talk button.

- wait-to-talk - In this mode, when the application is not itself talking, a microphone icon is presented in a transparent overlay on the application to indicate that the application is listening. In this mode, the user cannot "barge in" on the system.

- always-on - In this mode, the application is always listening, even when it is itself talking. We use state-of-the-art voice activity detection and acoustic echo cancellation to minimize recognition errors in this mode (see Section 2.3).

Speechify supports one additional feature for interaction management: it incorporates movement detection, so that when the user starts moving it can switch to always-on mode.

In addition to providing the developer with flexibility to experiment with different modes for speech interaction, the microphone overlay and speech control menu provided by Speechify enable a consistent interface and interaction for the user across multiple "Speechified" applications.

2.2 Hybrid Recognition

Cloud-based speech recognition offers unparalleled ease of access to high-accuracy, large vocabulary speech recognition. However, even on fast networks the latency introduced by cloud-based recognition may negatively impact ease of use for speech-enabled applications. For many applications, the majority of speech input is aimed at command and control (requiring only a small, fixed vocabulary), while a minority requires a very large open vocabulary (especially for search). A hybrid recognition approach may offer a good trade-off of accuracy and speed.

Recognizer	WER	RTF
Google	18.16	0.67
PocketSphinx	38	0.15
Hybrid (threshold=47000)	16.45	0.57

Table 1: Hybrid recognition can give simultaneous improvements in recognition accuracy and recognition speed

There are three general approaches to hybrid recognition: a voted combination of multiple recognizers run in parallel (Fiscus, 1997); lattice rescoring of the outputs of multiple recognizers (Richardson et al., 1995; Mangu et al., 1999); or heuristic selection of recognition output. Only the third is currently an on-device option. Speechify supports tunable on-device heuristic selection between (a) the output of any wrapped cloud-based recognizer, and (b) the output of PocketSphinx, an embedded recognizer.

To assess the tradeoffs for hybrid recognition, we ran an experiment using the Google Android cloud-based recognizer and PocketSphinx. For PocketSphinx we used an off-the-shelf acoustic model trained on broadcast news speech, with a grammar based on the prompts recorded by the speakers. We used 38 prompts each recorded by 7 speakers (from both genders, and with a variety of accents) in a noisy environment, for a total of 266 utterances. The results in terms of word error rate (WER) and real time factor (RTF; processing time / utterance length) are shown in Table 1. We get a small decrease in real time factor, along with a useful increase in recognition accuracy, through the use of hybrid recognition.

2.3 Voice Activity Detection

In a noisy environment or when the phone is in speaker mode, background noise or system speech may cause high rates of recognition errors for speech-enabled mobile apps. Speechify includes a state-of-the-art, on-device module for voice activity detection and acoustic echo cancellation. The module uses a three-stage process: feature extrac-

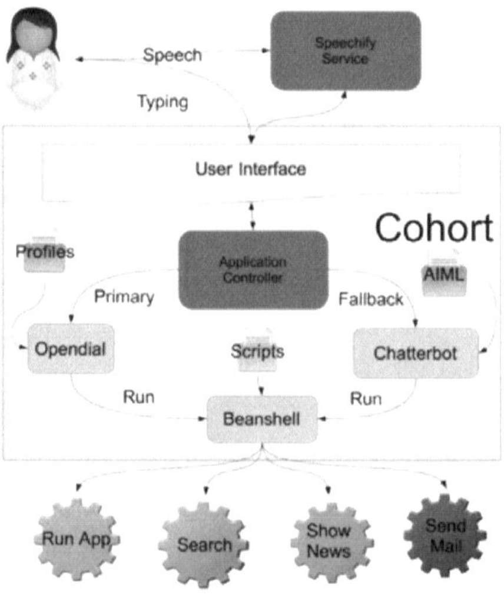

Figure 1: Cohort Architecture

tion, classification of short regions of voice activity, and smoothing. Only low-level acoustic features (such as MFCCs) are used. The classifier for both classification and smoothing is a lightweight random forest implementation. On the data from the recent IEEE AASP voice activity detection challenge (Giannoulis et al., 2013), our approach obtained very good F scores of 98.7% (balanced test data) and 97.6% (unbalanced test data).

3 Cohort

The Cohort library is a wrapper around a stripped-down version of OpenDial (Lison, 2013), and is designed to allow the user to navigate hands-free within and between Speechified applications. Cohort frees the application developer to think mainly about the functionality of the application itself, while Cohort deals with aspects related to speech interaction.

The architecture of Cohort and Speechify is presented in Figure 1. Participating apps must be Speechified, and must supply an application profile (as an OpenDial rule set). Cohort:

- automatically registers all participating apps on each user's phone
- passes control to each app as requested by the user through speech input
- handles contextual disambiguation of commands like "list" that apply to multiple apps, through the Opendial machinery
- supports basic speech commands like "pause" or "start" for all apps

The Cohort library also wraps a simple AIML-based chatbot, suitable for jokey conversations or backoff in case of errors. Cohort comes with a simple text input interface for debugging.

4 Demo

In general it takes less than 25 lines of code to Speechify an app, and about the same number of lines of OpenDial rules to subscribe an app to Cohort. We have "Speechified" and "Cohort-subscribed" three mobile applications: an email client, a news reader, and an Android "home page" app. We will demonstrate user interactions through and between these apps, and present the code necessary to make each app work in the Speechify/Cohort framework.

References

Jonathan G Fiscus. 1997. A post-processing system to yield reduced word error rates: Recognizer output voting error reduction (rover). In *Proceedings of ASRU*.

Dimitrios Giannoulis, Emmanouil Benetos, Dan Stowell, Mathias Rossignol, Mathieu Lagrange, and Mark D Plumbley. 2013. Detection and classification of acoustic scenes and events: an ieee aasp challenge. In *Proceedings of the IEEE Workshop on Applications of Signal Processing to Audio and Acoustics*.

David Huggins-Daines, Mohit Kumar, Arthur Chan, Alan W Black, Mosur Ravishankar, and Alex Rudnicky. 2006. Pocketsphinx: A free, real-time continuous speech recognition system for hand-held devices. In *Proceedings of ICASSP*.

Pierre Lison. 2013. Ph.D. thesis, University of Oslo.

Lidia Mangu, Eric Brill, and Andreas Stolcke. 1999. Finding consensus among words: lattice-based word error minimization. In *Proceedings of Eurospeech*.

Frederick Richardson, Mari Ostendorf, and JR Rohlicek. 1995. Lattice-based search strategies for large vocabulary speech recognition. In *Proceedings of ICASSP*.

Author Index

Association for Computational Linguistics
209 N. Eighth Street
Stroudsburg, Pennsylvania 18360

ISBN 978-1-5108-1156-0

CURRAN ASSOCIATES INC.
proceedings
.com

International Conference on Computer Applications in Shipbuilding (ICCAS 2022)

Yokohama, Japan
13 - 15 September 2022

The Royal Institution of
Naval Architects